THE VIETNAM WAR
AND INTERNATIONAL LAW

Volume 3

The Vietnam War and International Law:

The Widening Context

AMERICAN SOCIETY OF INTERNATIONAL LAW

EDITED BY

RICHARD A. FALK

Volume 3

Princeton University Press

Princeton, New Jersey

1972

Note of Acknowledgments

WE CONTINUE to be indebted to the many people who produced this volume. We thank the authors and their publishers for permission to reprint material. Detailed permissions appear in the back.

I would also like to thank the members of the Civil War Panel of the American Society of International Law for their continuing support of this editorial effort to facilitate the study of the legal aspects of the Vietnam War. Special thanks are again due Stephen M. Schwebel, the Executive Vice President for his active participation in the work of the Panel and for his central role in arranging publication.

Once again Princeton University Press has cooperated closely with the American Society of International Law. We are particularly grateful to Sanford Thatcher of the Press for supporting this project of the Panel and to Marjorie Putney for mastering for a third time the complex logistics of such a publishing enterprise.

I would thank my gifted research assistant, Claudia Cords, for helping with the assembly of these materials and countless other unimaginable details of preparation and my most excellent secretary, June Traube, for assorted favors and contributions to the final product. The work on this volume was rendered more pleasant and efficient by being carried on under the auspices of the Center of International Studies.

RICHARD A. FALK

Contents

II. WAR CRIMES

A. General Considerations

B. Judicial Applications

III. The Constitutional Debate on the Vietnam War

A. Matters of Executive Prerogative

B. Matters of Legislative Prerogative

C. Matters of Judicial Prerogative

THE VIETNAM WAR
AND INTERNATIONAL LAW

Volume 3

Introduction*

THE PANEL ON the Role of International Law in Civil Wars of the American Society of International Law has decided to sponsor the publication of a third volume in its series *The Vietnam War and International Law*. Its so doing reflects the judgment of the Panel that the continuation of the war has given rise to legal issues not adequately treated in the two earlier volumes. Our effort here, as before, has been to bring together the most significant legal writing on the subject and to provide, to the extent possible, a balanced presentation of opposing points of view.

Volume 3 concentrates on several legal dimensions of the war that have provoked a particularly large quantity of scholarly writing in the last two years: the invasion of Cambodia in May–June 1970 and the war crimes issue which captured major public attention after the disclosures of the Son My Massacre in November 1969.

In Part I the Cambodian Operation is dealt with by a series of authors. An initial article by Jean Lacouture predicts that the operation would have the effect of converting the Vietnam War into the Indochina War. The invasion of Laos in February 1971 for the purpose of disrupting North Vietnamese supply efforts along the Ho Chi Minh Trail and the persistent bombing of much of Indochina as a whole makes it clear that the combat theater has now been effectively, and perhaps irreversibly, expanded. The Cambodian Operation aroused public controversy and produced international law arguments in support of and in opposition to the Administration's action. We republish here a representative sampling of this debate which centered around the legal status of a claim to cross an international frontier so as to negate the consequences of adversary violations of neutral status; more specifically, was the American claim to cross into Cambodia and destroy North Vietnamese sanctuaries a proper application of the doctrine of collective self-defense?

The character of President Nixon's decision to place U.S. forces in Cambodia also generated Constitutional debate as to whether the President was acting within his authority as Commander-in-Chief. This debate, in part, concerns the extent to which the President is empowered by the Constitution to extend on his own initiative (that is, without prior Congressional authorization) the battlefield of an ongoing war to include an additional country. As of May 1970, it could

* This Introduction has been prepared by the Editor on behalf of the Panel as a whole.

also be argued that the broad mandate of the Gulf of Tonkin Resolution authorized the Cambodian Operation as it fell within the President's Mandate "to take all necessary measures to repel armed attack against the forces of the United States and to prevent further aggression." Such a line of argument is no longer available since Congress terminated the Gulf of Tonkin authorization as of July 10, 1970. Subsequent Congressional action, including the Cooper-Church Amendment, limited the President's authority to employ American ground troops in Indochina after the cutoff date of June 30, 1970, but left intact the authority to use air power and apparently even artillery firing across the border. These issues of Constitutional prerogative involve the interaction between domestic and international law, particularly by raising the question as to whether Congress has a role in joining with the President to assess American obligations under international law in circumstances where a controversial claim to act in collective self-defense is being put forward.

The disclosure that American military forces had taken part in a large-scale massacre of South Vietnamese civilians on March 18, 1968 in the village of Son My occasioned serious concern about whether the war itself and its principal battlefield tactics entailed the commission of war crimes. In the background of this inquiry are the criminal proceedings that were brought by the victorious powers in World War II against German and Japanese military and civilian leaders, especially the Nuremberg Judgment and the decision in the *Yamashita* case. Telford Taylor has given these concerns public prominence by measuring the battlefield tactics of the Vietnam War against the *Nuremberg/Yamashita* standards in a widely discussed book, *Nuremberg and Vietnam: An American Tragedy.*

In Part II we present a variety of perspectives, including that of General Taylor on the relation between allegations of war crimes in Vietnam and the international law on this subject that the United States Government did so much to develop. We also include a second set of selections that deal with whether what has been called "the Nuremberg argument" should be entertained on its merits by a domestic court in the United States. This discussion bears on such practical questions as to whether war resisters of various kinds should be able to rest their legal case on allegations as to the criminality of the war. In the background are also questions about whether domestic courts are suitable forums for the application of international law bearing on issues of war and peace.

In Part III we carry forward the debate in Volume 2 as to the distribution of functions among the coordinate branches of governments in the area of war and peace. Such a debate is relevant because its outcome may influence greatly the way in which international law is received in this area by a domestic society. For instance, without overstating the distinction between political and nonpolitical, it can be argued that upgrading of legislative and judicial roles tends to increase the prospects for a nonpolitical application of international law by removing somewhat the law-applying role from the policy-forming process. In any event, much scholarly discussion has concerned itself with the separation of powers doctrine as applied to the legal subject matter of the Vietnam War. The resolution of these issues will clearly determine the role of distinct branches of government in applying international law to controversies arising out of an ongoing war.

Part IV exists for the sake of a single article by Thomas M. Franck and Nigel S. Rodley that deals with the legal status of the insurgent regime (the Peoples' Revolutionary Government of South Vietnam) in the struggle for the control of South Vietnam. This article deals with an important international legal problem that goes beyond the facts of the Vietnamese struggle. The high incidence of civil warfare makes it useful to clarify the relevance of international law to the relationships of an insurgent regime with foreign countries and with the international community as a whole.

Part V concerns itself with some of the issues posed by a termination of the Vietnam War on some basis other than a clear-cut victory for one side. In this spirit, a perspective on negotiations remains useful, as does speculation about the idea of neutralization and proposals aimed at strengthening the role of the International Control Commission in postwar Indochina.

In Part VI we present three articles about Vietnam-type wars as world order problems, analysis about how to inhibit intervention in such conflicts, about how to moderate their impacts, and about how such conflicts do, in fact, end.

Finally, the appendices include documents of major historical interest that bear on the issues discussed in the text.

The Panel hopes to encourage further study of the relevance of international law to the ongoing war in Indochina. Such study may generate ideas about how to prevent and contain such conflicts, as well as strengthen world order values that emphasize, above all, the minimization of violence. In these regards this series of readings on the war in Vietnam complements the volume of case studies of civil war situations done under Panel auspices and published in 1971 by the Johns Hopkins University Press under the title *The International Law of Civil War* and the work-in-progress of the Panel being guided by John Norton Moore and Wolfgang Friedmann under the general title *Law and Civil War in the Modern World.*

Richard J. Barnet
Thomas Ehrlich
Richard A. Falk
Tom J. Farer
G. W. Haight
Eliot D. Hawkins
Brunson MacChesney

Myres S. McDougal
John Norton Moore
Stephen M. Schwebel
John R. Stevenson
Howard J. Taubenfeld
Burns H. Weston
Wolfgang Friedmann, *Chairman*

I. THE CAMBODIAN INCURSION OF 1970

A. The Expanded Zone of Combat

From the Vietnam War to an Indochina War

JEAN LACOUTURE

DURING the last week of April 1970 the Vietnam war
became the Second Indochina War. On April 24 and
25 representatives of the four movements of the Indochinese Left convened at a certain spot in south China to seal an
alliance that had been contracted many years before by three of
the movements—the North Vietnamese Lao Dong, the Pathet
Lao and the South Vietnamese National Liberation Front
(NLF)—and to which Prince Sihanouk, overthrown a month
earlier by the Cambodian Right, was now adhering in a con-
spicuously unconditional manner. The *Indochinese* revolutionary
front thus came into being.

Five days later, President Nixon announced the entry into
Cambodia of sizable American contingents backed up by South
Vietnamese units. This operation, dubbed "Total Victory," was
presented in Saigon as an attempt to wind up the war and be
done with it. In this manner a strategy was defined which confuses the idea of victory with that of extending the conflict outside Vietnam. In the light of the disclosures made two weeks
before by a subcommittee of the Senate Foreign Relations Committee regarding American participation in the fighting in Laos,
the conclusion is inescapable that on April 30, 1970, the United
States embarked on what is now the Second Indochina War.

Thus Richard Nixon became the first Republican President
to increase the responsibilities of the United States on that Asian
landmass into which Washington's best strategists have so often
insisted that no American army must ever plunge. And the
operation was launched under conditions that the worst enemies
of the United States might have hoped for. "We must have two
or three Vietnams!" Ernesto "Che" Guevara had trumpeted in
1967 in the name of the worldwide revolution. And there they
are, from Luang Prabang to Kep: two or three Vietnams, that
is to say, the whole of that territory of Indochina which French
colonization seems, in retrospect, to have put together to serve
as the framework for a revolutionary undertaking—a framework that is more open to Vietnamese energies than the restricted
territory of Vietnam alone.

The very word "Indochina" was created by colonization and for colonization; the Danish-born geographer Malte-Brun coined the term in 1852. In 1887, an Indochinese administration was set up, under the authority of a governor general presiding sometimes in Saigon and sometimes in Hanoi, composed of the following elements—the colony of Cochin China in the south; the protectorates of Annam in the east, which retained a cere-monial sovereign residing in Hué, and of Tonkin, in the north, where an "imperial delegate" resided; and the kingdoms of Cambodia and Laos in the west, whose monarchical systems were left intact by the colonizers. This arrangement was a strange combination of three Vietnamese countries strongly marked by Chinese influence and Confucian historical tradition and the little kingdoms of the Mekong, which belong, rather, with the cultural sphere of India and are wholly dominated by the strict-est form of Buddhism.

In concocting this amalgam of nations and civilizations, the French colonizers were, like their British rivals in Nigeria, at-tempting to set up the most economical kind of operation, one by which some of the colonized peoples are made to exploit the others. And to a large extent they succeeded. In Vietnam they managed to maintain a class of mandarins, which enabled them to develop an artful indirect kind of colonization. In Laos and Cambodia, a class made up of Vietnamese petty officials, small businessmen and artisans served as the motor of French coloniza-tion. In this way a relatively economical system of exploitation was established, and the three peoples to be dominated were, in appearance, lined up against one another.

In fact, the French colonizers overshot their objective; in spite of themselves they united, in a strange way, these three dif-ferent peoples, at very dissimilar levels of development, and in so doing imposed on them a single historical framework which the revolutionaries are now making use of for their own pur-poses. Of course, the Vietnamese intermediaries did inspire ill feeling and hatred of the kind which recently exploded in Cam-bodia. But this ill-will does not appear to be great enough to de-flect the three peoples from developing together on converging courses in the years to come.

II

This Indochinese concept, intimately bound up with history

and with colonial methods, was, indeed, very quickly seized upon by the revolutionaries, who retained the framework imposed by their enemy the better to struggle against him. This was what one of the founders of the Vietminh dubbed one day the strategy of "the glove turned inside out."

On February 3, 1930, in Hong Kong, the Vietnamese Communist Party was founded; Ho Chi Minh (then Nguyen Ai Quoc) immediately became its top leader. But six months later the leader called his comrades together in another conference in the course of which he gave the party a new name, rechristening it the Indochinese Communist Party (ICP). It was after consulting with the leaders of the Third International that the future president of the Democratic Republic of North Vietnam reached this decision, which in his eyes had the merit of giving the revolutionary effort he had just launched a more international character. It is worth noting, moreover, that the program which Nguyen Ai Quoc promulgated at that time included the following aims: (1) to overthrow imperialism, feudalism and the reactionary bourgeoisie in Vietnam, and (2) to achieve the complete independence of Indochina. Thus the first strategist of communism in this region restored a distinction consonant with the inequalities of the three countries in terms of development by calling for a *social* revolution in Vietnam and a *political* one in the peninsula as a whole.

It must be admitted that this Indochinese strategy was for a long time quite artificial, since the ICP remained for many years essentially Vietnamese. And it must be noted that when the Laotians and Cambodians truly embarked on revolutionary action they founded their own organizations—the Pathet Lao for the first and the Pracheachon for the second.

It was on an almost exclusively Vietnamese basis that Ho Chi Minh and his comrades launched the revolution in 1945. In the two neighboring countries the independence movement was sparked by very diverse forces: in Cambodia, they were, at first, two traditionally educated intellectuals, Hiem Chieu and Son Ngoc Minh, and in Laos a curious triumvirate of half-brother princes: the feudalist Petsarath, the liberal Souvanna Phouma and the Marxist Souphanouvong. Very quickly, moreover, the Vietnamese revolutionaries were to set up cells within the Laotian movement, while in Cambodia the local revolutionaries were to conserve a much greater degree of autonomy.

In 1951, six years after the outbreak of the colonial war against France, the three Indochinese movements concluded a Viet-Lao-Khmer alliance for the purpose of preparing to extend the fighting to the whole of the peninsula. Two years later, indeed, General Giap, pinned down by the French expeditionary corps in the key zones of the deltas of the Red River and the Mekong, suddenly decided to widen the theater of operations and entice his enemies onto new battlefields. In April 1953 he drew the French general staff toward Laos, encouraging them little by little to think that that was the terrain on which they could smash him. Between November 1953 and May 1954 came the creation, then the resistance, and finally the collapse of the entrenched camp of Dienbienphu. In broadening the First Indochina War, Giap faced the loss of everything. (This was a lesson which American strategists do not seem to have remembered; I shall have more to say on the subject.)

The Geneva Conference in 1954 was to bring the First Indochina War to an end. The Indochinese front was not, indeed, much in evidence at those councils: since the revolutionary parties had not had sufficient time to coördinate their efforts, Laos and Cambodia were represented there by governments whose only wish was to separate their problems from those of Vietnam and to draw a veil over the existence on their territories of groups that were more or less Marxist. But these groups were to grow bigger in the course of the ensuing years, and at the second Geneva Conference, the one devoted to Laos in the summer of 1962, the Indochinese theme was invoked much more often. The delegate from North Vietnam, Ung Van Khiem, hinted that a neutralization of the Indochinese region would be salutary. He specifically excluded the Democratic Republic of North Vietnam from this, but left the door open for the future.

This idea was taken up again in a much more precise and interesting form in various programs promulgated by the National Liberation Front of South Vietnam, founded in December 1960, which went on record as favoring an alliance of neutral nations comprised of Cambodia, Laos and South Vietnam. It seems astonishing today that observers at the time did not take greater note of the very great originality of this program and the audacity it took for those South Vietnamese underground fighters to place their future within a framework in which, at least for a time, Cambodia and Laos would be closer to them than North

Vietnam. Of course, for most of the American experts the NLF did not exist except as an echo of hypocritical orders dictated by Hanoi.

It was at the beginning of 1965, on the initiative of Prince Sihanouk, that Indochina emerged clearly as the major theme of all struggle against the American intervention and for political and economic reconstruction. On February 14, 1965, a "conference of Indochinese peoples" met in Phnom Penh. For Sihanouk this was most importantly an opportunity to have his country's frontiers guaranteed by the North Vietnamese and the NLF, whom he saw as the eventual victors and thus as his future neighbors. For Hanoi and the Front it was a chance to demonstrate the solidarity against imperialism of the revolution and neutralism, of the national masses and the national bourgeoisies, of the Vietnamese and their neighbors.

Geopolitical front, socio-economic alliance: at Phnom Penh were to be found all the factions opposed to American hegemony, from the intellectuals, mostly bourgeois and Catholic, of Tran Van Huu's "Committee for Peace and for the Renovation of South Vietnam" to the guerrilla fighters of the Pathet Lao and the bureaucrats of the Cambodian Sangkum. The major theme of the Phnom Penh meeting was the search for a formula for the neutralization of the whole of Indochina, the first step toward which might be an international conference like that of 1962, broadened to consider the future of the three countries. But the delegate from Hanoi, Hoang Quoc Viet, opposed this idea of Prince Sihanouk's: the bombardments of the North by the U.S. Air Force had just stiffened Hanoi's attitude still further. The Phnom Penh conference made no advance along the road to peace; but it confirmed and made manifest the "Indochinese" theme, and brought to light aspirations held in common by the most diverse delegations. It was, on this level, a success.

The American bombing of North Vietnam also contributed to the "materialization" of Indochina. It did this in three ways. First, the Vietnamese revolution, attacked at the very center of its strength, sought any and all means of hitting back, and all fronts thereafter became acceptable for striking a blow at the enemy. Secondly, this retaliation, with priority targets in South Vietnam, required a step-up in the transport of men and supplies from North to South by way of the Ho Chi Minh Trail, which goes through Laos for several hundred kilometers and through Cambodia for about a hundred. And finally, this aerial strategy gave an impetus to the increase of flights by American aircraft over the most diverse objectives—including, among others, frontiers; from this across a multiplicity of aerial incursions, in 1965 and 1966, which progressively nudged Cambodia into the war.

It was, however, in Laos that the greatest extension of the war outside the frontiers of Vietnam occurred. Since 1964—that is, since the actual dissociation of the neutralist coalition government formed in 1962, a sort of modus vivendi had been established, dividing the kingdom into two zones: in the west, seven provinces, from Luang Prabang to Savannaket, controlled (less and less) by the Vientiane government of Prince Souvanna Phouma, and to the east, from Sam Neua to the Cambodian frontier, five provinces controlled by the Pathet Lao and traversed by the Ho Chi Minh Trail. The double neutralization, both diplomatic and governmental, imposed by the 14 powers participating in the second Geneva Conference had thus given way to an actual partition.

After the halt of the bombings of North Vietnam in November 1968, however, the American bombers stepped up their raids on the Ho Chi Minh Trail linking North and South Vietnam across Laos and part of Cambodia. The frequency and amplitude of these bombings were described in a report of a Senate Foreign Relations subcommittee published in April 1970. Testifying before this subcommittee, Senator Stuart Symington declared that these raids had practically supplanted the raids over North Vietnam that had been halted, and revealed that the U.S. ambassador in Vientiane had the authority to order these bombings and specify where the bombs were to be dropped, which, according to the Senator from Missouri, made that diplomat virtually a "military proconsul." Directly challenged on this matter, former Ambassador Sullivan declared that since he had been replaced in Vientiane by his colleague Godley these bombing raids had doubled.

So Laos, where almost 40,000 North Vietnamese soldiers are permanently entrenched in a zone which covers almost half the country and against which the U.S. Air Force daily launches from 300 to 400 aerial strikes, has certainly been "in the war" for several years. But operations there took on a new dimension in February 1970, when the Pathet Lao, aided by its Vietnamese allies, overran the Plaine des Jarres, the strategic crossroads of the country, which the tacit partition of Laos had provisionally kept outside its sector. The strategic ascendancy of the communist forces was thus affirmed: it was becoming increasingly obvious that Prince Souphannouvong and his allies held the country in their hands, and that if they did not take either Vientiane or Luang Prabang it was in consequence of a political decision and not a strategic incapacity. (What is more, in spite of the redoubling of operations by the U. S. Air Force after the capture of the Plaine des Jarres, the Pathet Lao's military and political ascendancy grew still more, so that it was able, at the beginning of May, to take an important center in the south, Attopeu.)

But this strategic ascendancy has not been used (or not yet) by the leaders of the Pathet Lao in pursuit of "total victory." After his forces had seized the Plaine des Jarres, Souphanouvong sent his half-brother and rival Souvanna Phouma an offer to negotiate within the framework of the 1962 agreements, to the end of establishing a coalition government, restoring territorial unity and cutting short all foreign intervention. Obviously, the successes it had achieved in the course of the preceding months would enable the Pathet Lao to increase its demands and its share of power. But the situation of the Vientiane government was so bad that it accepted the principle of negotiation, with Washington's approval.

It will be up to future historians to find out whether or not this trend toward "appeasement" in Laos helped to set in motion the operation of March 1970 in Phnom Penh, and whether or not it was to prevent the initiation of a process which might have led to a generalized negotiation of Indochinese problems as a whole that the "ultras"—South Vietnamese, Cambodians, Thais (and perhaps, but not probably, Americans)—prepared and carried out the Phnom Penh coup d'état.

III

For it is, in any case, the Cambodian episode that has just given the war its true dimensions. We must inquire into the background of it, for the overlapping of strategic combinations and internal intrigue may throw light on the probable future evolution of Indochina as a whole. The affair began in the summer of 1966. Within a few weeks, the Sihanouk régime, which had managed until then to keep the kingdom out of the war and maintain a precarious balance at home between a feudal system adapted to the needs of a nascent capitalism and a progressive intelligentsia (very small in numbers but very active), found itself in a shaky condition at the very moment when the visit in August of General de Gaulle served to shore it up.

One may recall that General de Gaulle's speech at Phnom Penh caused a considerable stir. From then on, Sihanouk became the accomplice in what the entire anti-communist cause in Southeast Asia considered a most troublesome program. In their view, this outpost of Gaullist subversion had to go. In the end it was to be gotten rid of more easily than they imagined because Sihanouk's great ally in Paris was eliminated, and because his successors would turn out to be less attached to the policy General de Gaulle had defined in Phnom Penh.

But Sihanouk found himself on dangerous ground both internationally and at Phnom Penh. He had allowed his relations with Peking to degenerate, thus weakening himself in dealing with the Americans. At home, a few weeks after General de Gaulle's visit, general elections were held—elections which the Prince had wanted to be "freer" than such events had ever been before in Cambodia. The result was to bring a majority of influential landowners into the parliament. Khmer society became represented by those controlled by money and by feudal relationships. Sihanouk had wanted to pay tribute to democracy: instead, he placed the noose of feudalism around his neck.

In the next four years, his personal power was steadily eroded by private interests and those friendly to the Americans. At the same time, neutrality was encouraged and a start was made in establishing state control of the economy. In 1967, one of the leaders of the Left intelligentsia, Chau Seng, who under Sihanouk had held almost all the high offices except the ministries controlling the army and the police, warned the comrade-prince that intrigues were being brought to a boil by the chiefs of the former party of "national renovation," the traditional Right. The names of two of these had already been singled out: Prince Sirik Matak and General Lon Nol. Sihanouk had long been wary of the former and had sent him abroad from one embassy to another. But Lon Nol? He was a soldier, therefore disciplined; and since he was not even a prince, how could he possibly be ambitious enough to think of substituting himself for a descendant of the kings of Angkor?

From 1967 to 1969 Sihanouk, more and more responsive to pressures from the Right, seemed to be letting his relations with Peking become strained, allowing private interests to regain complete control over foreign commerce and banking, and launching a "red hunt" and an anti-Vietnamese campaign.

But why, in the fall of 1969, did Prince Sihanouk go so far as to entrust General Lon Nol with power three months before setting off on a long sojourn in France? Why did he thus entrust his régime to a man he had been warned against, and whose friendly relations with the West had long been known? This can be seen as an overestimation of his own charismatic power, which he believed to be so vast that he could wield it from afar. Or it can be seen as a sign of lassitude. Or it may be considered a Machiavellian trick. Like everyone else, Sihanouk was aware of the growth of the Vietnamese presence in his country. It is possible that in order to avoid having a direct confrontation with his associates, who were beginning to threaten his neutrality, he wanted to stand aside, leaving to General Lon Nol the chore of "cleaning out" Cambodia of the Vietnamese presence, to come back later with his hands clean and his country freer. This is only an hypothesis, but it cannot be completely discounted. One can be too subtle and be mistaken, not so much as to the objective as to the means used. Sihanouk underestimated either the ambition or the convictions of Lon Nol, and the influence of the general's friends in Saigon, if not in Washington.

Sihanouk, who was on the point of slipping into the Western camp, thus found himself abruptly recaptured by the party of revolution. This did not come about wholly by chance. With all his sudden changes of fortune and his diplomatic acrobatics, Norodom Sihanouk had fought almost constantly for over 15 years for peace and neutrality—a neutrality frankly oriented to the East and much more favorable to the interests of Peking and Hanoi than to those of the West. So it was not altogether surprising to find him at the opening of that curious conference of Indochinese revolutionaries which, as I said, was one of the two most obvious signs of the extension of the conflict, both ideologically and strategically, to the entire peninsula.

IV

The inspiration for the Indochinese conference which convened on April 24, 1970, in a little village in southern China about a hundred kilometers south of Canton came as in 1965 from Norodom Sihanouk. But it was no longer 1965. And it was no longer the colorful, laughing leader, the "star" of Phnom Penh loaded down with unshared powers, the ironic virtuoso of diplomatic tightrope-walking between East and West, who met with the "serious" revolutionary chieftains of Vietnam and Laos. This was now an exile struggling to throw his rivals out of Phnom Penh, a leader flung back by a Rightist coup into the arms of the very same *Khmers Rouges* he had been hunting down three months before. He was now a revolutionary, and as such all the more radical for having been recently converted.

It was in a barracks guarded by soldiers in coarse blue uniforms and surrounded by barbed wire emplacements, a barracks which the Chinese hosts entered only to find out whether the visitors needed anything, that the four groups of Indochinese leaders met for two days. The atmosphere of these sessions, one of the participants informed me, was "brotherly." The chosen language was French, which is spoken perfectly by the lawyer Nguyen Huu Tho, president of the NLF, by the engineer Souphanouvong, the leader of the Pathet Lao, by the militant Marxist Pham Van Dong (the son of a mandarin) and by Prince Sihanouk. It was, another witness said, a meeting of "old Indochina hands," a phrase that is all the more colorful for being the same one used by aging French ex-colonials when they get together in some dusty, sunny café in Marseilles or Nice for nostalgic chats about the good old days.

The greater part of the conference was given over to drafting the final communiqué, a mixture of threats to the United States and its "lackeys," optimistic proclamations of "final victory," and rather prudent or moderate reminders of the concluding texts of the Geneva conferences, denounced long since by Peking as null and void. An amusing (or significant) incident occurred at the last session. Prince Souphanouvong was in the chair: he called in turn upon his Cambodian and South Vietnamese colleagues to speak. He was preparing to wind up the proceedings himself when Pham Van Dong protested: "You've forgotten me!" "Our friend has anticipated the unification of Vietnam," Prince Sihanouk remarked, making everybody laugh except the delegate from the NLF.

The most interesting themes developed at that conference seem to have been three. First came the affirmation of a very firm

solidarity among the four movements—but a solidarity sufficiently flexible not to have led the chiefs of "red Indochina" (or
those who aspire to being such) into creating a common combat
structure. Second, there was the proclamation of the *original nature* of the different struggles and their diversity, from Hanoi to
Phnom Penh and from Saigon to Vientiane. Clearly, Pham Van
Dong and his delegation wanted to avoid the impression of being imperialists, or even excessively forceful federators. "They
were very diplomatic," a witness told me, thinking perhaps that
this diplomacy was not necessarily, in the long run, disinterested.
And third, there was the reminder of the *"neutralist"* themes
explicitly or implicitly formulated in the Geneva texts of 1954
and 1962, and in the political platforms of the NLF and the
Pathet Lao (not to mention, of course, the Sihanouk "line")—
theses which could be of use in later negotiations. So in proclaiming themselves certain of military victory the Indochinese
leaders were careful to leave out any form of political settlement.
Militant Indochina is, then, not just a war cry: it can also be a
program for peace.

V

In the meantime, the war is spreading and wreaking havoc.
What is most startling in President Nixon's decision of April 30
is its suicidal aspect. I am not speaking here about the consequences of this move for internal American politics, or about the
effects it will have on relations between Washington and Moscow. I do not even wish to comment on the obvious contradiction
between the two aspects of a strategy which claims that it will
rapidly reduce the number of men fighting in the Asian war
while it enlarges the field of battle. I prefer to confine myself to
a more specifically Indochinese aspect of the question.

There is, first of all, what might be called the gift that has been
made to General Giap. In all his steady stream of writings over
the last 10 years or so, Hanoi's commander-in-chief has never
ceased to assert that every extension of the field of battle serves
the revolutionary interests. This is so, he explains, for two reasons: (1) because it is to the advantage of the side with the
greater firepower and superior heavy equipment on the ground
to concentrate the fighting, while it is obviously in the interest
of the side with the greater mobility and lighter armament to
break up the fighting and seek to enlarge the combat zone; and

(2) because the revolutionaries basically count on the complicity
and support of the people, whereas a foreign force has to devote
a great deal of time and effort to winning over or controlling
by force the people among whom the fighting is going on.

For months, observers had been wondering whether Giap
would dare apply his own doctrine and himself extend the front
and the battle-zones outside the areas of Vietnam within which
he had been more or less held in check since the counterblow that
stopped the Tet offensive of February 1968. Now it is his enemies
who are spreading the fighting to all of Indochina, under conditions which, in Cambodia, are uniting the masses behind a pres-
tigious political chief who is entering the fray against these
enemies. Thus, the operation launched on April 30 seems to me
to be contributing to the revolutionary unification of the old
colonial Indochina.

Will such a united Indochina become the satellite of China?
Mao's speech of May 20 gave many observers the impression
that Peking was finally ripping off the mask and proclaiming
China's right to control the Indochinese area, much as the Soviet Union held Eastern Europe in thrall after World War II.
In my view, this interpretation is wrong. Of course the Chinese
leader took the opportunity the Cambodian operation afforded
him to attack in the harshest terms the American role of world
policeman, and to rejoice in seeing American power entrapped
in the Asian rice paddies. But it is noteworthy that his speech did
not mention any precise threat or specific action. His appeal was
to world revolution, for moral aid and approval, not a call for
military escalation. It was a song of triumph rather than a warlike gesture.

The evolution of the Indochina war is the fulfillment of
Peking's hopes. The character of the conflict more and more
clearly illustrates the validity of the warning of Lin Piao regarding the strategy of countryside versus cities, i.e. what is happening in Laos and Cambodia is as it was in Vietnam. The Chinese strategists do not predict complete victory. Revolution in
Indochina does not mean Chinese domination. But while a
united Indochina, more or less inspired by Hanoi, cannot oppose China, it can limit Chinese expansion. At present, Indochina is fighting under a Chinese banner but its aim is to survive under its own colors.

I. THE CAMBODIAN INCURSION OF 1970

B. International Law Aspects

United States Military Action in Cambodia:
Questions of International Law

JOHN R. STEVENSON[1]

I WELCOME the opportunity to present the administration's views on the questions of international law arising out of the current South Vietnamese and United States operations in Cambodia.[2]

I do not intend to review in any detail the legal justification of earlier actions by the United States in Viet-Nam. In 1966 the previous administration set forth at some length the legal justifications for our involvement in South Viet-Nam and our bombing of North Viet-Nam.[3]

In general, reliance was placed squarely upon the inherent right of individual and collective self-defense, recognized by article 51 of the U.N. Charter. This legal case involved the showing that North Viet-Nam had raised the level of its subversion and infiltration in South Viet-Nam to that of an "armed attack" in late 1964 when it first sent regular units of its armed forces into South Viet-Nam. The buildup of American forces in South Viet-Nam and the bombing of North Viet-Nam were justified as appropriate measures of collective self-defense against that armed attack.[4]

The legal case presented by the previous administration was vigorously attacked and defended by various scholars of the international legal community.[5] Many of the differences rested on disputed questions of fact which could not be proved conclusively. This administra-

---

1 Address made by the Legal Adviser of the State Department before the Hammarskjold Forum of the Association of the Bar of the City of New York at New York, N.Y., on May 28, 1970 (press release 166 dated May 30).

2 The views of the administration on the military and political issues have been expressed by the President and other officials. See, in particular, President Nixon's address of Apr. 30 (BULLETIN of May 18, 1970, p. 617) and his news conference of May 8 (BULLETIN of May 25, 1970, p. 641). [Author's footnote.]

3 For text of the Department's legal memorandum of Mar. 4, 1966, entitled "The Legality of United States Participation in the Defense of Viet-Nam," which was submitted to the Senate Committee on Foreign Relations on Mar. 8, 1966, see BULLETIN of Mar. 28, 1966, p. 474.

4 They were also justified on that basis in U.S. reports to the United Nations, pursuant to article 51. For texts of U.S. letters dated Feb. 7 and Feb. 27, 1965, to the President of the U.N. Security Council, see BULLETIN of Feb. 22, 1965, p. 240, and Mar. 22, 1965, p. 419. [Author's footnote.]

5 See the collection, in two volumes, *The Vietnam War and International Law*, edited by Richard A. Falk, sponsored by the American Society of International Law (Princeton University Press, 1968 and 1969). [Author's footnote.]

tion, however, has no desire to reargue those issues or the legality of those actions, which are now history. In January 1969, President Nixon inherited a situation in which one-half million American troops were engaged in combat in South Viet-Nam, helping the Republic of Viet-Nam to defend itself against a continuing armed attack by North Viet-Nam. Our efforts have been to extricate ourselves from this situation by negotiated settlement if possible or, if a settlement providing the South Vietnamese people the right of self-determination cannot be negotiated, then through the process of Vietnamization.[6] The current actions in Cambodia should be viewed as part of the President's effort to withdraw United States forces from combat in Southeast Asia.[7]

I appreciate this opportunity to discuss the questions of international law arising out of our actions in Cambodia. It is important for the Government of the United States to explain the legal basis for its actions, not merely to pay proper respect to the law but also because the precedent created by the use of armed forces in Cambodia by the United States can be affected significantly by our legal rationale.

I am sure you recall the choice that was made during the Cuban missile crisis in 1962 to base our "quarantine" of Cuba not on self-defense, since no "armed attack" had occurred, but on the special powers of the Organization of American States as a regional organization under chapter VIII of the U.N. Charter.[8]

Within a narrower scope, the arguments we make can affect the applicability of the Cambodian precedent to other situations in the future. I believe the United States has a strong interest in developing rules of international law that limit claimed rights to use armed force and encourage the peaceful resolution of disputes.

One way to have limited the effects of the Cambodian action would have been to obtain the advance, express request of the Government

[6] The President reviewed our efforts at negotiation and the progress of Vietnamization in his statement of Apr. 20 (BULLETIN of May 11, 1970, p. 601) and stated: ". . . our overriding objective is a political solution that reflects the will of the South Vietnamese people and allows them to determine their future without outside interference." [Author's footnote.]

[7] In his address of Apr. 30, announcing the use of force in Cambodia, President Nixon said: "We take this action not for the purpose of expanding the war into Cambodia, but for the purpose of ending the war in Viet-Nam and winning the just peace we all desire. We have made and we will continue to make every possible effort to end this war through negotiation at the conference table rather than through more fighting on the battlefield." [Author's footnote.]

[8] See Chayes, "Law and the Quarantine of Cuba," 41 *Foreign Affairs* (1963), p. 550. [Author's footnote.]

of Cambodia for our military actions on Cambodian territory. This might well have been possible.[9] However, had we done so, we would have compromised the neutrality of the Cambodian Government and moved much closer to a situation in which the United States was committing its armed forces to help Cambodia defend itself against the North Vietnamese attack. We did not wish to see Cambodia become a cobelligerent along with South Viet-Nam and the United States. We are convinced that the interests of the United States, the Republic of Viet-Nam, and Cambodia, and indeed the interests of all Asian countries, will best be served by the maintenance of Cambodian neutrality, even though that neutrality may be only partially respected by North Viet-Nam.

As the President has made clear, the purpose of our armed forces in Cambodia is not to help defend the Government of Cambodia, but rather to help defend South Viet-Nam and United States troops in South Viet-Nam from the continuing North Vietnamese armed attack.[10] This limited purpose is consistent with the Nixon doctrine, first set forth by the President at Guam on July 25, 1969,[11] that the nations

[9] On May 1 a Cambodian spokesman said that "the Cambodian Government as a neutral government cannot approve foreign intervention." However, on May 5, the Cambodian Government issued the following statement:

"In his message to the American people of April 30, 1970, President Nixon made known the important measures which he had taken to counter the military aggression of North Viet-Nam in Laos, Cambodia, and South Viet-Nam. One of these measures concerns the aid of the U.S. in the defense of the neutrality of Cambodia violated by the North Vietnamese.

"The Government of Salvation notes with satisfaction the President of the United States took into consideration in his decision the legitimate expressions of the Cambodian people, who only desire to live in peace within their territory, independent, and in strict neutrality. For this reason, the Government of Cambodia wishes to announce that it appreciates the views of President Nixon in his message of April 30 and expresses to him its gratitude.

"It is time now that the other friendly nations understand the extremely serious situation in which Cambodia finds itself and come to the assistance of the Cambodian people, who are victims of armed aggression. The Government of Salvation renews on this occasion its appeal for assistance made April 14, noting that it will accept from friendly countries all unconditional and diplomatic, military, and economic assistance."

Later statements have indicated even more clearly the Cambodian Government's approval of our actions. [Author's footnote.]

[10] This is to be distinguished from the furnishing of weapons and ammunition to Cambodia pursuant to the Foreign Assistance Act, 75 Stat. 424, 22 U.S.C. § 2161-2410, which is done to improve the ability of Cambodia to defend itself. [Author's footnote.]

[11] The President's statements were not for direct quotation. The President later restated the doctrine in his address to the Nation on Viet-Nam on Nov. 3, 1969 (BULLETIN of Nov. 24, 1969, p. 437), and in his foreign policy report to the Congress on Feb. 18 (BULLETIN of Mar. 9, 1970). [Author's footnote.]

of the region have the primary responsibility of providing the man-power for their defense.

The North Vietnamese have continued to press their attack against South Viet-Nam since 1964 and have made increasing use of Cambodian territory in the furtherance of that attack. They have used Cambodia as a sanctuary for moving and storing supplies, for training, regroupment, and rest of their troops, and as a center of their command and communications network. I assume that these facts are generally accepted, but it might be useful to give a few examples.

In the past 5 years 150,000 enemy troops have been infiltrated into South Viet-Nam through Cambodia. In 1969 alone, 60,000 of their military forces moved in from Cambodia. The trails inside Cambodia are used not only for the infiltration of troops but also for the movement of supplies. A significant quantity of the military supplies that support these forces came through Cambodian ports.

Since 1968 the enemy has been moving supplies through southern Cambodia to its forces in the Mekong Delta. Further, in the spring and summer of 1969, three to four regiments of regular North Vietnamese troops used Cambodian territory to infiltrate into the Mekong Delta. Up to that time, there had been no regular North Vietnamese combat units operating in this area.

As many as 40,000 North Vietnamese and Viet Cong troops were operating out of the Cambodian base areas against South Viet-Nam prior to April 30. As the war in South Viet-Nam intensified, Viet Cong and North Vietnamese troops have resorted more frequently to these sanctuaries and to attacking from them to avoid detection by or combat with United States and South Vietnamese forces.

During 1968 and 1969 the Cambodian bases adjacent to the South Vietnamese Provinces of Tay Ninh, Pleiku, and Kontum have served as staging areas for regimental-size Communist forces for at least three series of major engagements—the 1968 Tet offensive, the May 1968 offensive, and the post-Tet 1969 offensive.

Many of these North Vietnamese actions violate Cambodian neutrality. Flowing from the Fifth Hague Convention of 1907[12] are the generally accepted principles that a neutral may not allow belligerents to move troops or supplies across its territory, to maintain military installations on its territory, or to regroup forces on its territory. A neutral is obligated to take positive action to prevent such abuse of its

[12] Bevans, *Treaties and Other International Agreements of the United States of America, 1776-1949*, p. 654 (Department of State publication 8407 (1968). [Author's footnote.]

neutrality either by attempting to expel the belligerent forces or to intern them.

Both the previous Cambodian government under Prince Sihanouk and the present government headed by Lon Nol have made efforts to limit, if not prevent, these violations of Cambodia's rights as a neutral. While the Sihanouk government did not, in our judgment, do all that, under international law, it should have done, it unquestionably made some efforts. As a legal matter, it is clear that a neutral must take active measures commensurate with its power to protect its territory from abuse by a belligerent. It is likewise clear that a neutral's "duty of prevention is not absolute, but according to his power."[13] In any event, however, the control and restraint exercised by the previous Cambodian government was progressively eroded by constant North Vietnamese pressure. Prior to the ouster of Prince Sihanouk, regular supply of arms and munitions through the Port of Sihanoukville had become an established fact.

After the change of government on March 18, in which the United States was not involved in any respect, Cambodian police and other officials were driven out of many localities in the border area. When it became apparent to North Viet-Nam that the new Cambodian government was not willing to permit the same wide scope of misuse of its territory by North Vietnamese forces as the previous government, the decision was evidently taken to expel all Cambodian Government presence from the border areas and move militarily against the Cambodian army, with a view to linking up all the sanctuaries and the Port of Sihanoukville. This would have produced a unified and protected sanctuary from the Gulf of Siam along the entire border of South Viet-Nam to Laos, with virtually unrestricted movement and unlimited supply access. The threat posed by such a situation of renewed and increased attacks against United States and Vietnamese troops in South Viet-Nam is obvious. We also knew that enemy forces were instructed to emphasize attacks on U.S. forces and increase U.S. casualties.

That was the rapidly developing situation the President faced at the time of his April 30 decision to make limited military incursions into the sanctuaries in Cambodia, which had been militarily occupied by

[13] As the Harvard Research in International Law pointed out in its 1939 Draft Convention on Rights and Duties of Neutral States in Naval and Aerial War, "A neutral State is not an insurer of the fulfillment of its neutral duties. It is obligated merely to 'use the means at its disposal' to secure the fulfillment of its duties." 33 *American Journal of International Law* (1939), Suppl., p. 247. [Author's footnote.]

North Viet-Nam. It was impossible for the Cambodian Government to take action itself to prevent these violations of its neutral rights. Its efforts to do so had led to the expulsion of its forces. In these circumstances, the question arises of what are the rights of those who suffer from these violations of Cambodian neutrality.

It is the view of some scholars that when the traditional diplomatic remedy of a claim for compensation would not adequately compensate a belligerent injured by a neutral's failure to prevent illegal use of its territory by another belligerent, the injured belligerent has the right of self-help to prevent the hostile use of the neutral's territory to its prejudice.[14] Professor Castrén, the distinguished Finnish member of the International Law Commission, has stated that:[15]

> If, however, a neutral State has neither the desire nor the power to interfere and the situation is serious, other belligerents may resort to self-help.

The more conservative view is that a belligerent may take reasonable action against another belligerent violating the neutral's territory only when required to do so in self-defense.[16]

The United States Department of the Army Field Manual relating to the Law of Land Warfare states the following rule:[17]

[14] According to Greenspan, *The Modern Law of Land Warfare* (1959), p. 538: "Should a violation of neutral territory occur through the complaisance of the neutral state, or because of its inability, through weakness or otherwise to resist such violation, then a belligerent which is prejudiced by the violation is entitled to take measures to redress the situation, including, if necessary, attack on enemy forces in the neutral territory." [Author's footnote.]

[15] Castrén, *The Present Law of War and Neutrality* (Helsinki, 1954), p. 442. See also II Guggenheim, *Traité de Droit International Public* (Geneva, 1954), p. 346. [Author's footnote.]

[16] II Oppenheim, *International Law* (7th ed. 1952), p. 698. This is true whether or not the neutral has met its obligations to use the means at its disposal to oppose belligerent use of its territory. Stone, *Legal Controls of International Conflict* (1954), says (p. 401): "One clear principle is that, the right of self-preservation apart, an aggrieved State is clearly not entitled to violate the neutral's territorial integrity, simply because his enemy has done so. Diplomatic representations and claim are the proper course." A Columbia Law Review Note concludes: "Military action within neutral territory may be justified as a measure of self-defense or as an appropriate response to the failure of a neutral state to prevent the use of its territory by belligerent forces. . . . It is suggested . . . that international law should permit and encourage primary reliance on self-defense as a justification." Note, "International Law and Military Operations against Insurgents on Neutral Territory," 68 Col. L. Rev. 1127 (1968). See also *Corfu Channel Case*, ICJ Reports 1949, pp. 34-35 and 77. [Author's footnote.]

[17] FM 27-10 (July 1956) par. 520, p. 185. Similar provisions were contained in the U.S. Army *Rules of Land Warfare* of 1940 (par. 366) and in the *British Manual of Military Law*

Should the neutral State be unable, or fail for any reason, to prevent violations of its neutrality by the troops of one belligerent entering or passing through its territory, the other belligerent may be justified in attacking the enemy forces on this territory.

This rule can be traced to, among others, the decision of the Greco-German Mixed Arbitral Tribunal after the First World War, which had to deal with the German bombardment of Salonika in Greece. During the war the Allied forces had occupied Salonika despite Greece's neutrality, and the Germans responded with a bombardment. The tribunal stated that Allied occupation constituted a violation of the neutrality of Greece and that it was immaterial whether the Greek Government protested against that occupation or whether it expressly or tacitly consented to it. The tribunal then concluded that "in either case the occupation of Salonika was, as regards Germany, an illicit act which authorized her to take, even on Greek territory, any acts of war necessary for her defense."[18]

British naval vessels entered then neutral Norway's territorial waters in 1940 to liberate British prisoners on the *Altmark*, a German auxiliary vessel. A thorough analysis of that case by Professor Waldock led him to the conclusion that in some circumstances a breach of neutrality by one belligerent threatens the security of the other belligerent in such a way that nothing but the immediate cessation of the breach will suffice. Professor Waldock added:[19]

Accordingly, where material prejudice to a belligerent's interests will result from its continuance, the principle of self-preservation would appear fully to justify intervention in neutral waters.

As far back as the 18th century, Vattel had this to say:[20]

On the other hand, it is certain that if my neighbour offers a retreat to my enemies, when they have been defeated and are too weak to escape me, *and allows them time to recover and to watch*

(par. 655). See Greenspan, *The Modern Law of Land Warfare* (1959), p. 538, n. 23. [Author's footnote.]

18 Coenca Brothers v. The German State, 1927, translated in Briggs, *The Law of Nations: Cases, Documents and Notes* (1938), pp. 756-58.

19 Waldock, "The Release of the Altmark's Prisoners," 24 *British Year Book of International Law* (1947), p. 216, at 235-36. See also Tucker, *The Law of War and Neutrality at Sea* (Naval War College, International Law Studies, vol. XLX, 1955, p. 262). [Author's footnote.]

20 E. de Vattel, *Le Droit des Gens* (1758), translated by Charles Fenwick, vol. 3, bk. III, sec. 133, p. 277 (Carnegie Institution reprint 1916). [Author's footnote.]

for an opportunity of making a fresh attack upon my territory . . .
(this is) inconsistent with neutrality . . . he should . . . not allow them
to lie in wait to make a fresh attack upon me; *otherwise he warrants
me in pursuing them into his territory.* This is what happens when
Nations are not in a position to make their territory respected. It
soon becomes the seat of the war; armies march, camp, and fight in
it, as in a country open to all comers. [Emphasis added by author.]

The United States itself has sometimes in the past found it necessary
to take action on neutral territory in order to protect itself against
hostile operations. Professor Hyde cites many such instances, of which
I would note General Jackson's incursion into Spanish West Florida in
1818 in order to check attacks by Seminole Indians on United States
positions in Georgia; the action taken against adventurers occupying
Amelia Island in 1817, when Spain was unable to exercise control over
it; and the expedition against Francisco Villa in 1916, after his attacks
on American territory which Mexico had been unable to prevent.[21]

I have summarized these precedents and the views of scholars and
governments principally to show general recognition of the need to
provide a lawful and effective remedy to a belligerent harmed by its
enemy's violations of a neutral's rights. I would not suggest that those
incidents and statements by themselves provide an adequate basis for
analysis of the present state of the law. We all recognize that, whatever
the merits of these views prior to 1945, the adoption of the United
Nations Charter changed the situation by imposing new and important
limitations on the use of armed force.[22] However, they are surely
authority for the proposition that, assuming the charter's standards are
met, a belligerent may take action on a neutral's territory to prevent
violation by another belligerent of the neutral's neutrality which the
neutral cannot or will not prevent, provided such action is required in
self-defense.

In general, under the charter the use of armed force is prohibited
except as authorized by the United Nations or by a regional organization within the scope of its competence under chapter VIII of the charter or, where the Security Council has not acted, in individual or
collective self-defense against an armed attack. It is this latter basis on
which we rely for our actions against North Vietnamese armed forces
and bases in Cambodia.

[21] I. Hyde, *International Law* (2d ed., 1945), pp. 240-44. [Author's footnote.]
[22] In particular, article 2, par. 4, of the charter. [Author's footnote.]

Since 1965 we and the Republic of Viet-Nam have been engaged in collective measures of self-defense against an armed attack from North Viet-Nam. Increasingly since that time, the territory of Cambodia has been used by North Viet-Nam as a base of military operations to carry out that attack, and it long ago reached a level that would have justified our taking appropriate measures of self-defense on the territory of Cambodia. However, except for scattered instances of returning fire across the border, we refrained until April from taking such action in Cambodia. The right was available to us, but we refrained from exercising it in the hope that Cambodia would be able to impose greater restraints on enemy use of its territory.

However, in late April a new and more dangerous situation developed. It became apparent that North Viet-Nam was proceeding rapidly to remove all remaining restraints on its use of Cambodian territory to continue the armed attacks on South Viet-Nam and our armed forces there.

Prior to undertaking military action, the United States explored to the fullest other means of peaceful settlement.

We awaited the outcome of the Cambodian Government's efforts to negotiate with the North Vietnamese and the Viet Cong agreed limitations on the use by the latter of Cambodian territory—without success.

We have continually tried in the Paris talks to bring about serious negotiation of the issues involved in the war.

Soundings in the Security Council indicated very little interest in taking up the North Vietnamese violations of Cambodian territorial integrity and neutrality.

We welcomed the French proposal looking to the possibility of an international conference—although not publicly, for fear of discouraging Hanoi's participation. The Soviet Union, after initially indicating interest, backed away.

We were particularly pleased with the calling of the Djakarta conference of interested Asian states to deal with the Cambodian problem on a regional basis. The best long-run approach to East Asian security problems lies through cooperative actions such as this. In the short run, however, they cannot be expected to provide an adequate defense against the North Vietnamese military threat.

The United States has imposed severe limits on the activities of U.S. forces. They will remain in Cambodia only a limited time—not beyond June 30; in a limited area—not beyond 21 miles from the border; and with a limited purpose—to capture or destroy North Vietnamese supplies, to destroy base installations, and to disrupt communications. To the maximum extent possible, we have directed our forces at enemy base areas and have tried to avoid civilian population centers. We have limited our area of operations to that part of Cambodia from which Cambodian authority had been eliminated and which was occupied by the North Vietnamese.

The Cambodian Government and the Cambodian people are not the targets of our operations. During the period from 1967 to 1970 the Cambodian Government became increasingly outspoken in its opposition to the North Vietnamese occupation. In fact, Sihanouk's purpose in going to the Soviet Union and China when he was deposed was to solicit their help in persuading the North Vietnamese to get out of Cambodia. The Lon Nol government has expressed its understanding of our actions.

Our actions in Cambodia are appropriate measures of legitimate collective self-defense, and we have so reported to the United Nations, as required by article 51 of the United Nations Charter.[23]

[23] For text of a U.S. letter dated May 5 to the President of the U.N. Security Council, see BULLETIN of May 25, 1970, p. 652.

The Cambodian Operation
and International Law

RICHARD A. FALK

"I believe the United States has a strong interest in developing rules of international law that limit claimed rights to use armed force and encourage the peaceful resolution of disputes."
John R. Stevenson, Legal Adviser, "United States Military Actions in Cambodia: Questions of International Law," 62 *Department of State Bulletin* 765, 766 (1970).

". . . public, Congressional and international support also depends on a prompt and convincing demonstration of the legality of our actions; we cannot afford to wait until action is taken to start preparing our case."
William P. Rogers, Secretary of State, Memorandum dated June 13, 1970, reported in *New York Times*, June 24, 1970, p. 3.

The invasion of Cambodian territory by the armed forces of the United States and South Viet-Nam in the spring of 1970 raises serious questions of international law. The development of international law since the end of World War I exhibits a consistent effort to prohibit recourse to force by governments in international society. The Nuremberg Judgment called aggression against a foreign country "the supreme crime" against mankind. The United Nations Charter is built around the notion that the only occasions on which it is legal to use force are in response to an armed attack and as authorized by an organ of the United Nations. The Cambodian

* A shorter, less documented version of this article will eventually appear as a chapter in Laurence A. G. Moss and Jonathan Unger (eds.), Cambodia in the Expanded War, to be published by Simon and Schuster. The preparation of this article was greatly facilitated by the research and editorial assistance of Claudia Cords.

operation was obviously neither a response to a prior armed attack upon South Viet-Nam nor an action authorized or ratified by the United Nations.

In announcing the decision to the American public on April 30, 1970, President Nixon made no effort to justify the invasion under international law. Such a failure of explanation illustrates the extreme unilateralism that has been exhibited by the United States Government throughout the Viet-Nam War. This failure lends credence to the contention that the United States is conducting an imperial war of repression in Indochina and that it owes explanations for its policy, if at all, only to the American public and, even then, mainly to provide reassurance about the relevance of a challenged policy to the welfare of American troops. Perhaps the most remarkable passage in Mr. Nixon's April 30th address is the arrogant assertion that an American invasion of an Asian country is of no international concern:

> These actions [in Cambodia] are in no way directed at the security interests of any nation. Any government that chooses to use these actions as a pretext for harming relations with the United States will be doing so on its own responsibility and on its own initiative, and we will draw the appropriate conclusions.[1]

The United States Government had been on record over and over again in support of the position that when a border-crossing armed attack occurs, it is a matter of grave concern for the entire community of nations, and that it is a matter of collective determination whether or not a challenged action is disruptive of world order and its fundamental norms of prohibition.[2] What made Mr. Nixon's statement especially troublesome—and it

[1] Text of Address reprinted in 62 Department of State Bulletin 617 (1970). President Nixon's attitude toward international law as revealed in the Cambodian operation was foreshadowed in a significant passage in his book, Six Crises. In analyzing the 1960 campaign for the presidency Mr. Nixon acknowledges that Kennedy outmaneuvered him by advocating a hard line against Castro's Cuba. To differentiate his position from that of Kennedy and to shield the Bay of Pigs operation, then in a planning stage, from premature disclosure, Nixon felt obliged in 1960 to "go to the other extreme" and "attack the Kennedy proposal of such aid as wrong and irresponsible because it would violate our treaty commitments." Reflecting on his presentation, Nixon writes "that the position I had taken on Cuba hurt rather than helped me. The average voter is not interested in the technicalities of treaty obligations. He thinks, quite properly, that Castro is a menace, and he favors the candidate who wants to do something about it— something positive and dramatic and forceful—and not the one who takes the 'statesmanlike' and 'legalistic' view." Nixon, Six Crises 382, 384 (rev. ed., 1968). President Nixon's handling of the Cambodian invasion embodied the same scornful disregard for legal restraint, urging a bold course of action on the basis of sovereign prerogative that seemed designed to appeal to patriotic rather than to world-order impulses of the citizenry.

[2] One prominent example of the American attitude toward the Charter prohibition upon recourse to force was the initial statement by the U. S. delegate, Adlai Stevenson, in the Security Council debate occasioned by India's invasion of Goa on Dec. 18, 1961. Security Council, Official Records, 987th meeting, Dec. 18, 1961. Two portions of Ambassador Stevenson's statement are of particular relevance to the relationship between the Cambodian operation and the U.N. Charter, the fundamental legal document governing recourse to force in international affairs. The first, near the beginning of his presentation:

was not qualified or balanced by other statements—is the refusal to acknowledge the possible relevance of any external source of authority with respect to American claims to use force across an international boundary. The sovereign word is endorsed as the final word, and critical reactions by other countries are to be regarded, it would seem, as unwarranted and unacceptable interference in our affairs. Would the United States want the same rules of non-accountability to govern the behavior of China or the Soviet Union, or even small countries like Cuba or Israel? What if Cuba had attacked the exile base areas in Florida and Central America where planning was going forward for the Bay of Pigs operation that was to occur in April, 1961? Would the United States have indulged Cuban claims that such action was not directed at "security interests" of other nations? And not only security interests are at issue; more importantly, the concern is with the existence of minimum standards of international behavior applicable to all governments on a basis of mutuality. The United States made this very clear in 1956 when it refused to acquiesce in the limited invasion of Egyptian territory by its own allies. Such a refusal to overlook these actions at the height of the Cold War, during a period when the Soviet Union was so brutally intervening in Hungarian internal affairs, suggests how strongly the United States Government at one time supported a strict interpretation of U.N. Charter prohibitions on the use of force.

It is true that on May 5, 1970, Ambassador Charles Yost reported by letter to the President of the Security Council that the United States had acted in "collective self-defense" because of the intensification of North Vietnamese activity in Cambodian base areas.[3] It is also true that the Legal Adviser to the Secretary of State, John R. Stevenson, fully developed an international law argument in support of the Cambodian operation in an address delivered at the Hammarskjöld Forum of the Association of the Bar of the City of New York, which was subsequently published in the *Department of State Bulletin* as an official document.[4] But Mr. Stevenson spoke primarily to a domestic audience (and then not until May 28 and

"When acts of violence take place between nations in this dangerous world, no matter where they occur or for what cause, there is reason for alarm. The news from Goa tells of such acts of violence. It is alarming news, and, in our judgment, the Security Council has an urgent duty to act in the interests of international peace and security." (P. 66.)

Ambassador Stevenson made it clear that the Charter prohibition, aside from circumstances of self-defense, is not properly susceptible to self-serving interpretation:
"Let it be perfectly clear what is at stake here; it is the question of the use of armed force by one State against another and against its will, an act clearly forbidden by the Charter. We have opposed such action in the past by our closest friends as well as by others. We opposed it in Korea in 1950, in Suez and in Hungary in 1956 and in the the Congo in 1960." (P. 72.)

[3] U.N. Doc. S/9761, May 5, 1970; 62 Department of State Bulletin 652 (1970).

[4] John R. Stevenson, "United States Military Actions in Cambodia: Questions of International Law," 62 Department of State Bulletin 765 (1970) (hereinafter cited as Stevenson).

the publication date was not until June 22). Although his formulation constitutes the most authoritative legal argument put forth by the Administration, it hardly qualifies, because of its domestic setting and its timing, as compliance with the requirement that a government give an accounting to the world community of its decision to use military force in a foreign society. President Nixon's formulation has to be treated as the prime datum for assessing the merit of the Administration's contention that the invasion of Cambodia was consistent with the rules and standards of international law. Aggressors normally disguise their action by making claims of legal right. The Soviet Union claimed an invitation from the "legitimate" government as the basis for its action in Hungary in 1956 and again in Czechoslovakia in 1968, although in the latter case it relied more heavily upon an alleged right of collective intervention to maintain the integrity of the Socialist community.[5] It is always possible to put together a legal argument in support of any partisan position. The whole idea of legal order is based on the possibility of fair and reliable procedures to assess which of several competing legal arguments best fits the facts and governing legal rules. The purpose of this article is to demonstrate that the American invasion of Cambodia was a violation of international law, given the facts, the law, past practice, public policy, and the weight of expert opinion.

I. The Administration Argument

It seems necessary, first of all, to clarify to the extent possible the scope of the claim being asserted by the United States in relation to Cambodia. The shifting line of official explanation is ambiguous about the real objective. On April 30 President Nixon repeated several times in different formulations that the purpose of the invasion was to destroy North Vietnamese sanctuaries along the Cambodian border and thereby to protect American lives. In Mr. Nixon's words, "attacks are being launched this week to clean out major enemy sanctuaries on the Cambodia-Vietnam border." The timing of the attack was justified by reference to two separate circumstances:

(1) ". . . the enemy in the past 2 weeks has stepped up his guerrilla actions, and he is concentrating his main forces in these sanctuaries . . . where they are building up to launch massive attacks on our forces and those of South Viet-Nam."

(2) "North Viet-Nam in the last 2 weeks has stripped away all pretense of respecting the sovereignty or the neutrality of Cambodia. Thousands of their soldiers are invading the country from the sanctuaries; they are encircling the Capital Phnom Penh. . . . [I]f this enemy effort succeeds,

---

[5] The so-called Brezhnev doctrine rests on the subordination of individual Socialist countries to the interests of world Socialism as these interests are construed by "the camp of Socialism" as a whole. For some interpretation see Falk, "The Legitimacy of Zone II as a Structure of Domination", in Davis, East, and Rosenau (eds.), The Analysis of International Politics (forthcoming), and Firmage, "Summary and Interpretation" in Falk (ed.), The International Law of Civil War, to be published in 1971.

Cambodia would become a vast enemy staging area and a springboard for attacks on South Viet-Nam along 600 miles of frontier, a refuge where enemy troops could return from combat without fear of retaliation."

President Nixon seemed to suggest that the invasion was responsive to both of these occurrences, given the parallel American decision to provide the Lon Nol régime with arms assistance and to pay for Thai "volunteers." In essence, then, alleged North Vietnamese actions within Cambodia were given as the sole basis for initiating a military attack across the boundary. Mr. Nixon seemed to emphasize *future* danger rather than any *immediate* threat to the safety of American lives—"Unless we indulge in wishful thinking, the lives of Americans in Vietnam after our next withdrawal of 150,000 would be gravely threatened." And in the course of a news conference on the evening of May 8, Mr. Nixon made even clearer that the focus of his concern was the rather distant set of circumstances existing after the scheduled withdrawal of 150,000 American soldiers has been completed in April, 1971.[6]

The invasion claim was limited in mission, scope, and duration, although in *execution* villages were destroyed that were neither sanctuaries nor weapons depots, and vast quantities of rice belonging to Cambodian peasants were either confiscated or destroyed. The mission was confined to the destruction of sanctuaries which were supposed to have included, according to Mr. Nixon, "the headquarters for the entire Communist military operation in South Viet-Nam." The scope of the invasion, at least for American ground forces, was confined to a 21.7-mile strip of Cambodian territory along the border, and the invasion, again at least for American troops, was to be terminated by the end of June, 1970.[7] In reporting on the invasion, Mr. Nixon said on June 3 that

> The success of these operations to date has guaranteed that the June 30 deadline I set for withdrawal of all American forces from Cambodia will be met. . . . This includes all American air support, logistics, and military advisory personnel.

[6] Mr. Nixon was asked how he could have announced on April 20th that Vietnamization was going so well that 150,000 Americans could be withdrawn by the spring of 1971 and then on April 30th that the Cambodian operation was necessary to protect the Vietnamization program from disruption. The President's response included these two sentences: "I found that the action that the enemy had taken in Cambodia would leave 240,000 Americans who would be there a year from now without many combat troops to help defend them, would leave them in an untenable position. That is why I had to act." 62 Department of State Bulletin 642 (1970).

[7] The failure by the Government to disclose additional American activity in Cambodia makes it difficult to describe the claim with accuracy. Only on June 21, 1970, was it reported that American air strikes were regularly penetrating far beyond the announced 21.7-mile limit. These raids were initiated at the same time as the invasion, but have not been officially acknowledged or defended as yet. The report also indicated doubt as to whether the raids would end with the June 30th pull-out of American troops. The purpose of these raids is to prevent the North Vietnamese from establishing a new supply route into South Viet-Nam. New York Times, June 22, 1970, pp. 1, 20. It has become subsequently clear, of course, that the United States regularly provides close air support to Cambodian ground operations.

The only remaining American activity in Cambodia after July 1 will be air missions to interdict the movement of enemy troops and material where I find that is necessary to protect the lives and security of our men in South Viet-Nam.

Initially the main official response to the legal challenges directed at the President's decision consisted of an effort to show that the Cambodian operation was a valid exercise of Mr. Nixon's powers as Commander-in-Chief of the armed forces.[8] At his May 8th news conference, Mr. Nixon said: "As Commander in Chief, I alone am responsible for the lives of 425 or 430,000 Americans in Viet-Nam. That's what I've been thinking about and the decision that I made on Cambodia will save those lives." Such an assertion of responsibility—presumably a responsibility shared in common with all Heads of State—is hardly relevant to a discussion of the status of the invasion in international law. Surely, the lives of the North Vietnamese armed forces are deeply endangered by the use of air fields in Thailand, Guam, and Okinawa. The point here is that such an explanation is at best responsive to the line of criticism that has contended that the initiation of the Cambodian invasion by Presidential decision amounted to an act of Executive usurpation in violation of the United States Constitution.[9]

Subsequently, as has already been indicated, the Legal Adviser did indeed develop a full-dress international law argument consisting of the following main elements: (1) a contention of clear and present danger to American and South Vietnamese troops arising out of the expansion of sanctuary activity in Cambodia by North Viet-Nam and the National Liberation Front; (2) a limited claim by the United States to use force in Cambodia proportional and responsive to this danger; (3) a claim that the inability of the Cambodian Government to prevent its neutral territory from being used as a sanctuary for armed forces engaged in the Viet-Nam War amounts to an abrogation, in part, at least, of Cambodia's neutral status, and justifies belligerent action of limited self-help; (4) a claim that Cambodia has been primarily invaded by North Viet-Nam and is a victim of North Vietnamese aggression; (5) the absence of any formal complaint by the Cambodian Government concerning the invasion suggests that there has been no victim of aggression and hence no aggression; and (6) the contention that North Viet-Nam is guilty of aggression against South Viet-Nam and that the United States and South Viet-Nam are entitled to take whatever steps are necessary to assure the success of their action in collective self-defense.

The Legal Adviser's argument deserves the most careful consideration

[8] The validity of such executive authority has been largely supported even in the U.S. Senate, which affirmed by a vote of 79–5 the power of the President as Commander-in-Chief to take military action in Cambodia to protect the welfare of American troops in South Viet-Nam. The vote was taken in relation to an amendment offered to modify the Cooper-Church amendment. New York Times, June 23, 1970, pp. 1, 3.

[9] See W. D. Rogers, "The Constitutionality of the Cambodian Incursion," below ; New Yorker, May 16, 1970, pp. 31–33.

so far as an analysis of the facts, rules of law, and legal expectations is concerned.   As Mr. Stevenson himself says,

> It is important for the United States to explain the legal basis for its actions not merely to pay proper respect to the law but also because the precedent created by the use of armed forces in Cambodia by the United States can be affected significantly by our legal rationale.[10]

However, even if this line of argument is persuasive, which I do not believe it is, nevertheless the President's failure to reconcile a national decision to invade a foreign country with the rules of international law constitutes a major negative precedent that cannot be undone by any subsequent legal explanation.   There are, in essence, two separate precedents both of which, in my judgment, violate international law: (1) the manner in which the claim was put forward; and (2) the substance of the claim.   These are both serious world-order issues.   Issue (1) bears upon the rôle of international law as providing a basis for governments to communicate claims and counterclaims in situations of conflict, while issue (2) concerns the framework of restraint that should be operative in the conduct of international relations.   My argument is that the timing and location of Mr. Stevenson's legal presentation makes it virtually irrelevant to issue (1), but important to an assessment of issue (2).

II. Some Difficulties of Legal Analysis

There are several special factors complicating the analysis of the Cambodian operation:

(1) *The extent of United States responsibility for South Vietnamese actions in excess of limitations of space, time, and mission imposed by the United States Government.*   The underlying claim of the United States Government rests on a theory of collective self-defense.   From a legal point of view, it is the victim of attack, not its external ally, that defines the necessities of action in self-defense.   Of course, the realities of United States control do not change the legal situation, except to give evidence of the non-independence and illegitimacy of the Saigon régime.   With respect to the Cambodian operation, it does not seem legally acceptable to confine United States responsibility to the actions of its troops.   The undertaking is a joint one, and the American claim is derivative from the alleged South Vietnamese right of self-defense; furthermore, American advisers are operating in conjunction with the Saigon régime at every level of military and political operations.   Thieu and Ky have repeatedly stated their Cambodian objectives in broader terms than the United States, and South Vietnamese troops have penetrated Cambodian territory beyond the 21.7-mile limit.   In my judgment, the United States, from a legal perspective, is a co-venturer, responsible for the full extent of claim being made by the Saigon régime.   Indeed, Secretary of Defense Laird confirmed on June 23, 1970, that the armed forces of South Viet-Nam will have a free rein to act in Cambodia after the June 30th deadline, thereby

[10] Stevenson, p. 766.

making explicit American complicity with the wider and vaguer South Vietnamese invasion claim.[11]

When the United Kingdom, France, and Israel initiated the Suez War in 1956 as a joint venture, there was no effort to assess relative degrees of legal responsibility for the event. It seems reasonable, then, to resolve this initial complication by measuring United States responsibility by the full extent of the South Vietnamese claim and conduct in Cambodia.

(2) *The Cambodian operation represented only a battlefield decision to protect troops in the field and did not constitute an expansion of the United States rôle in Indochina.* The argument has been made by supporters of the Administration's decision that the Cambodian operation has only tactical significance in relation to the Viet-Nam War. In this spirit, the strike against the Cambodian sanctuaries is not different in legal character from the decision to attack and capture Hamburger Hill. Such matters of battlefield tactics may be criticized as ill-conceived or ill-executed, but they are not appropriately challenged on legal grounds.

This position is defective in a fundamental respect. If a battlefield tactic involves a separate issue of legality, then it is subject to legal scrutiny; sustained border-crossing by armies is always a separate legal event of first-order magnitude in international affairs. The main effort of modern international law is to moderate warfare, and this effort depends greatly on maintaining respect for boundaries. Besides, since July 1, 1970, the United States has engaged in a series of air strikes inside Cambodian territory that are designed to provide close support for troops of the Lon Nol régime.[12]

(3) *The failure of the United Nations to pass judgment.* The political organs of the United Nations system have been singularly ineffective throughout the long course of the Viet-Nam War. This ineffectiveness is a result of several factors. First, the United States possesses sufficient political influence within the Organization to prevent an adverse judgment against it. Second, the non-membership of China and North Viet-Nam in the Organization makes these governments opposed to any United Nations rôle; in their eyes, the United Nations, at least as presently constituted—with Formosa continuing to represent China in the Security Council—is itself an illegitimate actor and is in no position to act on behalf of the world community. Third, the United Nations has been totally ineffective whenever the two super-Powers were deeply and directly involved in a political conflict. Fourth, the Lon Nol Government has not complained to the United Nations about the invasion of its territory or the destruction of its villages either by United States and South Vietnamese forces or by North Vietnamese and NLF forces.

In these circumstances, it is impossible for the United Nations to play any positive rôle, even to the extent of interpreting the requirements of its

---

[11] For an extensive account, see New York Times, June 24, 1970, pp. 1, 7.

[12] See Sterba, "Cambodia: Fact and Fable of U.S. Air Missions," *ibid.*, Aug. 16, 1970, §4, p. 6.

own Charter.[13] The Secretary General, U Thant, has tried to undertake peace initiatives at various points during the long course of the war, but his efforts have been resented by the governments of both sides, particularly by the United States during the Johnson Administration.

Although the United Nations has been unable to act as an Organization, the Charter continues to provide governing legal standards for a case like this one. The Charter is itself *declaratory* of prior legal standards embodied in the Kellogg-Briand Pact of 1928 and provides the most authoritative guidelines for identifying the outer limits of permissible state behavior. And surely the United States Government has not yet claimed the discretion to act in violation of the Charter. Indeed, the Charter is a treaty that has been ratified with the advice and consent of the Senate, and is, according to the U. S. Constitution, part of "the supreme law of the land."

(4) *The failure of the Cambodian Government to condemn the invasion.* The Cambodian operation has an ambiguous character. The claim to eliminate the sanctuaries was explicitly linked by President Nixon in his April 30th speech with the struggle for political control of Cambodia. The United States, South Viet-Nam, and North Viet-Nam have intervened in this struggle in a variety of ways. The overthrow on March 18, 1970, of Prince Sihanouk as Head of State, and his subsequent efforts to organize a counter-movement to regain power, have been deeply destabilizing occurrences for Cambodia.[14] The Lon Nol régime almost immediately, and somewhat inexplicably, unleashed a campaign against ethnic Vietnamese who were living in Cambodia, resulting in several reported massacres, large-scale forced resettlement, and the creation of a large number of refugees.[15]

This régime was evidently unable to rule its population without strong external support. The campaign against ethnic Vietnamese, and the insistence that North Viet-Nam abandon its Cambodian base areas were part of a larger effort by a weak régime to create a political climate appropriate for foreign help.

Cambodia has now become the scene of increasing foreign intervention. The Thieu-Ky régime of South Viet-Nam, despite Lon Nol's anti-Vietnamese policies, is seeking to maintain Lon Nol in power. Thailand has mobilized forces along the Western boundary of Cambodia and is reported to have sent contingents of ethnic Khmers to Cambodia to fight on behalf of the Lon Nol régime. The United States tried to persuade Thailand to send 5,000 troops to Cambodia by agreeing to finance the entire military operation.[16]

---

[13] Mr. Stevenson came close to acknowledging that an American complaint before the invasion about North Vietnamese violations of Cambodian neutrality would not have resulted in a positive response: "Soundings in the Security Council indicated very little interest in taking up the North Vietnamese violations of Cambodian territorial integrity and neutrality." Stevenson, p. 770.

[14] For background see Leifer, Cambodia: The Search for Security (1967).

[15] New York Times, April 19, 1970, §1, p. 28, §4, p. 3.

[16] *Ibid.*, pp. 1, 9; April 26, 1970, p. 1; *Christian Science Monitor*, April 23, 1970, p. 2.

Under these circumstances it is difficult to accord any serious respect to the Lon Nol régime as a government of Cambodia. This régime does not seem able to represent the interests of its people. Its failure to protest the invasion, pillage, and occupation of its territory bears witness to its own illegitimacy, just as the willingness of the Saigon régime to enter into a friendship pact with a governing group that had so recently initiated ruthless anti-Vietnamese policies, exhibits its illegitimacy in relation to the Vietnamese people. These régimes are struggling at all costs to maintain power in the face of a highly unfavorable domestic balance of power. In this setting, their invitations to foreign governments to send in armies are of only slight legal consequence.[17] The failure of the Cambodian Government to protest the invasion of its territory by foreign forces does not, under these circumstances, amount to a valid legal authorization. Cambodia may be the victim of aggression even if its governing élite does not choose to regard it as such, especially if, as is the case, a counter-government exists that has protested the invasion. Unless such a position is taken, outside forces could intervene to place a régime in power and then use its invitation to validate its later plans of domination. There is a need to move beyond a pretense of legitimacy whenever a government demonstrates both its dependence on foreign sources of authority for its own existence and its willingness to jeopardize the independence of its country, the welfare of its people, and the inviolability of its territory on behalf of some foreign Power whose support is needed to keep the régime in control.

George McT. Kahin, an outstanding specialist on Asian affairs, pointed out the following defects of the argument that the decision to invade Cambodia did not provoke protest from the Lon Nol régime:

> It must be noted that Cambodia renounced the SEATO protocol providing protection for the former Indochina states. In point of fact, Sihanouk formally requested SEATO powers in May 1965 to amend Article IV to *exclude* Cambodia from SEATO's perimeter of intervention. His request was ignored but he was advised that the language of the treaty provided that intervention would not be undertaken without the request and consent of the Cambodian government.[18]

It is clearly evident that, whatever took place *subsequent* to the invasion, there is no evidence or even claim that the Cambodian Government re-

---

[17] The German reliance during the Nazi period upon Fifth-Column tactics to undermine the governing process in countries which were the targets of aggression should be recalled in the Cambodian context. A "Quisling" régime is one that operates in the name of a nation, but serves as agent of its dismemberment and destruction. Vidkun Quisling was the head of the Nationalist Party of Norway, a pro-Nazi group with no parliamentary representatives and little popular following. In April, 1940, when Hitler invaded Norway, Quisling welcomed the German occupation of Norway and eventually obtained dictatorial powers in Norway from the Germans. The Quisling experience is an extreme case, but it usefully illustrates the undesirability of accepting a constituted regime as automatically empowered to act as the legitimate government of a country.

[18] The Congressional Record, memorandum prepared by George McT. Kahin, "Cambodia: The Administration's Version and the Historical Record," pp. 57428–57431, at p. 57431.

quested or authorized the invasion, or participated in any way to define its limits.[19] In the post-invasion context, a weak, tottering régime could not be expected to protest an invasion of its territory by its principal "friend." Without American support, the Lon Nol régime would have no prospect whatsoever of maintaining power.

III. The Fundamental Legal Analysis: Aggression or Collective Self-Defense

Under modern international law an invasion of a foreign country that is not authorized by a competent international institution is either an act of aggression or an exercise of self-defense. Under most circumstances, states that initiate large-scale, overt violence across an international boundary have been identified as "the aggressor." It is almost impossible for the invading government to make out a persuasive case of self-defense. Possibly the only recent counter-example was the Israeli initiation of the June War in 1967 under conditions of evident and imminent provocation and danger.

In reporting the invasion to the Security Council, the United States seemed to rest its legal case on a claim of collective self-defense. This case was later developed into a serious legal argument in Mr. Stevenson's address at the Hammarskjöld Forum.[20] The obligations of international law can be divided into two categories: *substantive norms that restrain behavior of governments*, and *procedural norms applicable to situations of alleged violation of substantive norms*. In the area of war and peace, the procedural norms are as important as the substantive norms.

Substantive Norms. The United Nations Charter provides a convenient starting point for an analysis of the norms governing recourse to force in international affairs. Article 2 of the Charter has the following key paragraph:

[19] For Administration interpretation on this point see Stevenson, p. 766, especially note 9.

[20] There is a curious inconsistency in Mr. Stevenson's presentation. At the outset of his address he refers to the legal controversy over whether South Viet-Nam and the United States had a good legal basis for asserting a claim of collective self-defense, and contends that "Many of the differences rested on disputed questions of fact which could not be proved conclusively." He goes on to say that "this administration, however, has no desire to reargue those issues or the legality of those actions, which are now history." (P. 765.) But, then, throughout the address, he asserts the position of the prior Administration; for instance: "Since 1965 we and the Republic of Viet-Nam have been engaged in collective measures of self-defense against an armed attack from North Viet-Nam." (P. 770.) The Cambodian invasion is justified as a temporary extension of the underlying claim to be exercising rights of collective self-defense. By forswearing argument on whether a case for self-defense exists in Viet-Nam, Mr. Stevenson must be understood as saying either that it makes no difference or that, once troops are engaged in battle, then, whether their cause is legal or illegal, it is proper to carry out their mission. The extension of such reasoning to other settings exposes its absurdity. Should the burglar be exonerated merely because he has persisted? Or should the notion of burglary be abandoned once the burglar finds himself engaged in an encounter with the homeowner or the police?

(4) All Members shall refrain in their international relations from the threat or use of force against the territorial integrity or political independence of any state, or in any other manner inconsistent with the Purposes of the United Nations.

Article 51 qualifies this prohibition upon force by its limited authorization of self-defense:

Nothing in the present Charter shall impair the inherent right of . . . self-defense if an armed attack occurs against a Member of the United Nations, until the Security Council has taken the measures necessary to maintain international peace and security. . . .

The prohibition and the exception have not been defined, despite numerous international efforts, in any more specific way.

The Charter law is fairly clear: it is not permissible to use force against a foreign territory except in response to an armed attack.[21] This Charter conception expresses general international law, except that a literal reading of its language might be taken to prevent non-Members of the United Nations from claiming self-defense. North Viet-Nam and South Viet-Nam are not Members of the Organization, but this analysis will proceed on the assumption that any *state* is legally entitled to act in self-defense, whether or not a Member of the United Nations. Although there are some difficulties associated with treating South Viet-Nam as a *state,* given the language and proclaimed intentions of the Geneva Accords of 1954 to create a unified Viet-Nam no later than July, 1956, nevertheless, for purposes of this article, South Viet-Nam will be treated as a sovereign state entitled to exercise rights of self-defense.[22]

Especially, so far as the United States is concerned, the invasion of Cambodia rests on a claim of *collective* self-defense. Such a claim places a heavier burden of demonstration on the claimant, as its own territory and political independence are not at stake. Some experts even argue that under no circumstances can a state satisfy the requirements of self-defense merely by associating its action with a state that is acting in valid individual self-defense: *alliance relations* are not sufficient to vindicate the claim of the non-attacked state to participate in the exercise of rights of collective self-defense. The infringement of some more direct legal interest must serve as the basis of the claim to join in the defense of an attacked state.[23] The United States has no such distinct legal interest in relation to the defense of South Viet-Nam—neither regional, cultural, historical, nor even ideological—such as would justify its participation in the Cambodian invasion, even if South Viet-Nam could validly claim to be acting in self-defense. Dr. Bowett, who argues in favor of this restrictive view of col-

---

[21] For one persuasive analysis along these lines see Louis Henkin, "Force, Intervention, and Neutrality in Contemporary International Law," 1963 Proceedings, American Society of International Law 147–162.

[22] But see Vietnam and International Law, Legal Memorandum prepared by the Consultative Council of the Lawyers Committee on American Policy Towards Vietnam 34–41 (2nd rev. ed., 1967).

[23] D. W. Bowett, Self-Defence in International Law 206, 216–217 (1958).

lective self-defense, emphasizes the distinction between self-defense and the enforcement of international law:

> . . . our contention is simply that a state resorting to force not in defence of its own rights, but in the defence of another state, must justify its action as being in the nature of a sanction and not as self-defence, individual or collective. The aim is to redress the violation of international law, not to protect its own rights.[24]

Such a view takes seriously the idea of "self" embodied in the concept of self-defense. Bowett concludes that

> The requirements of the right of collective self-defence are two in number; firstly that each participating state has an individual right of self-defence, and secondly that there exists an agreement between the participating states to exercise their rights collectively.[25]

In the context of the Cambodian operation it is clear that the first requirement of collective self-defense has not been met. Since the Charter fails to authorize states to uphold international law as a separate justification for the use of force, then it seems clear that the United States could not, under any circumstances, associate itself with a South Vietnamese claim of self-defense unless the exercise of the right of self-defense were converted into a United Nations action, as happened, of course, in relation to the defense of South Korea in 1950.

Such a conception of self-defense has been criticized as unduly restrictive and unrealistic, given the evolution of collective security arrangements. For instance, Myres S. McDougal and Florentino P. Feliciano, in a major work on the modern international law of force, contend that collective self-defense can be validly claimed "whenever a number of traditional bodies-politic asserting certain common demands for security as well as common expectations that such security can be achieved only by larger cooperative efforts . . . present themselves to the rest of the general community as one unified group or collectivity for purposes of security and defense." [26] This broader conception of collective self-defense underlies the various regional security pacts that the United States organized during the Dulles era as part of its containment policy directed at what was conceived to be a monolithic Communist movement intent upon world conquest.[27] Under this broader view of collective self-defense, which is probably more descriptive of practice and is generally accepted as being compatible with modern international law, the United States would be entitled to join in the Cambodian operation *provided* the facts validated

[24] *Ibid.* 207.

[25] *Ibid.*; see also J. Stone, Legal Controls of International Conflict 245 (1954), especially the assertion that "under general international law, a State has no right of 'self-defence' in respect of an armed attack upon a third State."

[26] McDougal and Feliciano, Law and Minimum World Public Order 248 and, generally, 244–253 (1962).

[27] Stanley Hoffmann has recently written that "Professor McDougal's theory . . . will remain an astounding testimony to the grip of the Cold War on American thought and practice." "Henkin and Falk: Mild Reformist and Mild Revolutionary," 24 Journal of International Affairs 118–126, at 120 (1970).

the underlying claim by South Viet-Nam. Even McDougal and Feliciano place a *higher* burden of demonstration for claims of collective than for individual self-defense:

> . . . it may be appropriate to require a higher imminence of attack and more exacting evidence of compelling necessity for coercive response by the group as such than would be reasonably demanded if the responding participant were a single state.[28]

As it is, "the traditional requirements imposed upon resort to self-defense" are most exacting: ". . . a realistic expectation of instant, imminent military attack and carefully calculated proportionality in response."[29] There was nothing about the events in Cambodia that could qualify as establishing "a realistic expectation" of "instant, imminent military attack" such as could justify a claim of individual self-defense under these circumstances. Since it is more difficult to establish a claim of collective self-defense than individual self-defense, the demonstration that no basis for individual self-defense exists entails a rejection of the official United States argument.

Prior to May 1, 1970, the invasion date, there was no report of increased fighting along the border, and there were no indications of increased South Vietnamese or American casualties as a result of harassment from across the Cambodian border. Mr. Nixon never claimed more than that the expansion of the Cambodian base area might place American troops in great jeopardy by April, 1971 (or almost a year after the invasion). Such a contention overlooks the prospects for interim changes either by way of negotiated settlement or successful Vietnamization of the war. The Cambodian base areas were sanctuaries used to provide logistic support to the anti-régime side in the war to control South Viet-Nam.[30] In this sense, and to a far greater extent, the United States has relied upon external base areas in Japan, South Korea, Thailand, Okinawa, Guam, and elsewhere, to conduct its belligerent operations in South Viet-Nam. Would the United States regard a Soviet air strike against these base areas as a legitimate exercise of the right of collective self-defense by North Viet-Nam or by the Provisional Revolutionary Government of South Viet-Nam? Consideration of a hypothetical reciprocal claim helps to expose the unreasonableness of the United States position and the utter absurdity of the Administration contention that expanding the combat area across the Cambodian border is not a major escalation of the war. Note also that this same unreasonable-

[28] McDougal and Feliciano, *op. cit.* 251.

[29] *Ibid.* 67; the most widely relied-upon description of conditions appropriate for a claim of self-defense was given by Daniel Webster on April 24, 1841, in a diplomatic note to Canada. Mr. Webster, in his capacity as U.S. Secretary of State, wrote that there must be shown by the claimant government a "necessity of self-defence, instant, overwhelming, leaving no choice of means, and no moment for deliberation." 29 British and Foreign State Papers 1129, 1138 (1840–1841).

[30] A learned and instructive discussion of the status of sanctuaries in international law is present in Fried, "United States Military Intervention in Cambodia in the Light of International Law," paper presented to the International Conference of Lawyers on Vietnam, Laos, and Cambodia, Toronto, Canada (May 22–24, 1970) 7–25 (hereinafter cited as Fried).

ness pertains to the South Vietnamese claim of self-defense which is put forward in more extravagant terms, relating itself to the internal Cambodian struggle for control, to the treatment of Vietnamese inhabitants by the Cambodian regime, and to the presence of North Vietnamese military personnel in any part of Cambodia. Any objective reading of the facts amply demonstrates that there was no *instant necessity* that might lend legal support to the Cambodian operation as an exercise of the right of individual or collective self-defense.

There is, in addition, no relationship of proportionality between the claim to invade Cambodia and the alleged impact on the struggle taking place in South Viet-Nam. Indeed, it was the build-up of pressure by the Lon Nol régime to alter the long persisting *status quo* in the base areas that appeared to be the initial unsettling force. The Lon Nol régime insisted that the North Vietnamese cease to use these base areas altogether, and, as we have already mentioned, also brought provocative pressure to bear on Vietnamese residents living in Cambodia. Such tactics, presumably a dual consequence of the weakness and reactionary orientation of the régime and the strength of American pressure, were part of the effort by the Lon Nol régime to mobilize support in the building struggle against the forces supporting the deposed Prince Sihanouk, who has in recent months joined dynastic with revolutionary legitimacy, a potent political linkage in any developing country. Therefore, the main precipitating event seems to be the consequence of changes in the political situation in Cambodia, rather than any *imminent* threat to South Viet-Nam; these changes were supported, not resisted, by American action. The American claim to destroy base area camps within the 21.7-mile border strip had the predictable consequence of pushing North Vietnamese and NFL troops back toward the center of Cambodia, intensifying the struggle for political control of Cambodia, and utterly destroying any prospect for the resumption of the delicate, if stable, condition of relative neutrality that Cambodia had managed to maintain under Sihanouk's rule. Therefore, the Cambodian operation seemed ill-conceived in relation to the principal alleged danger, the collapse of a pro-Western régime in Phnom Penh and its replacement by a radical anti-Western régime.

Mr. Nixon's report to the nation on June 3, 1970, stated that "all of our major military objectives have been achieved" in the Cambodian operation.[31] These objectives were described on that occasion mainly in terms of the capture of war matériel. Reports from military officers in the field indicated that probably no more than half of the war matériel stored in the base areas was discovered and captured by the withdrawal date of June 30, 1970.[32] In that event, the alleged success of the operation would seem vir-

---

[31] 62 Department of State Bulletin 761 (1970). The legal status of the invasion is not, of course, determined by the military success or failure of the operation. However, the reasonableness of a limited claim of self-defense depends on the proportionality of means and ends, and an assessment of military success or failure may give some insight into whether the force used was proportional to the end sought.

[32] New York Times, June 9, 1970, pp. 1, 5. Vice President Agnew described American objectives in more grandiose (and possibly more criminal) terms in the following

tually unrelated to the level of future military activity in South Viet-Nam. There is no evidence that equipment shortages are likely to result for North Viet-Nam or the NLF if as much as one half or more of the war matériel captured will still remain in the Cambodian base areas. In addition, the North Vietnamese, especially during the heavy bombardment of North Viet-Nam between February, 1965, and October, 1968, demonstrated great resourcefulness in circumventing efforts to interdict their supply routes.

The element of proportionality seems absent from the claim of self-defense, whether the claim is considered from the angle of the United States or from the perspective of the Saigon régime. Indeed, the invasion seems to have aggravated the very conditions it was designed to cure. Even long-time supporters of American military action have criticized the invasion as lacking any rational relationship to its proclaimed goals.[33] Certainly, Mr. Nixon's assertion that the Cambodian operation would shorten the war seems without any foundation. The arena of violence has been widened, a new country has become a theater of military operations and its people a victim of invasion,[34] and, taken in conjunction with the stepped-up American military operations in Laos, an all-Indochina war has emerged in place of the Viet-Nam War. Such an enlargement of the arena of violence and an expansion of principal actors involved in combat appear greatly to complicate the search for a negotiated settlement, which remains the proclaimed end of United States policy.

The Cambodian operation is properly compared to the earlier American extension of the war to North Viet-Nam, and much of the legal analysis of self-defense claims in the earlier setting fits the Cambodian operation as well.[35] From the point of view of legal doctrine, the assertion of a claim of self-defense against Cambodia has even less merit than did the earlier

---

statement: "The purpose of the strikes into the sanctuaries is not to go into Cambodia but to take and reduce these supply depots, *the hospital complexes,* the command network, the communications, the weapons and munitions factories and maintenance facilities that are there." (Emphasis added.) Hospitals as a military objective of the invasion were mentioned a second time in Mr. Agnew's remarks. See transcript of CBS TV broadcast "Face the Nation," May 3, 1970, p. 3; the second reference is to be found on p. 6.

[33] See Letter to the Editor, New York Times, May 25, 1970, p. 32, signed by five men, including Bernard Brodie, Morton H. Halperin, and Thomas Schelling, who write of themselves and of the Cambodian operation as follows: "We, the undersigned, have spent our professional lives in the study of strategy and American foreign policy . . . the move into Cambodia simply does not make sense." See also Les Gelb and Morton H. Halperin, "Only a Timetable Can Extricate Nixon," Washington Post, May 24, 1970, pp. B1–B2.

[34] After the South Vietnamese armed forces captured the Cambodian city of Kompong Speu, extensive pillage took place. One of the Cambodian military officers on the scene, Major Soering Kimsea, reacted by saying that "the population now has more fear of the South Vietnamese than of the Vietcong. They took everything—furniture, radios, money. . . . What they didn't take, they broke. . . . Monks were robbed too." New York Times, June 23, 1970, p. 2.

[35] I have written a legal analysis of this earlier phase of the conflict. See 1 Falk, ed., The Vietnam War and International Law 362–400, 445–508 (1968); see Vols. I and II for main legal positions in relation to the war.

assertion against North Viet-Nam. To cross the Cambodian boundary with large armies and supporting air-force bombardments is to make a unilateral decision to attack the territory of a foreign country under circumstances where an armed attack on South Viet-Nam was neither imminent nor probable. The most that can be said is that political changes taking place in Cambodia were jeopardizing its neutrality from both sides. This kind of circumstance may involve competing claims of limited intervention, but it certainly does not support a claim of self-defense.

Such a conclusion must be understood in relation to the entire effort of international law to remove from national governments the discretion to initiate or expand warfare across boundaries on the basis of a calculation of national advantage. Central to this endeavor is the restriction of occasions upon which it is permissible to cross openly the boundary of a foreign country with armed force. The United States, until the Viet-Nam War, had played a central rôle in using international law to build slowly an external framework of restraint based on widely shared normative conceptions.[36] Although it is true that no agreed definitions of self-defense exist, there has been a general acknowledgment that the core meaning of self-defense relates to responses against either an *actual armed attack* or a credible impression of *imminent armed attack*.[37] The diplomatic practice of the United States Government lends support to this interpretation —the United States Government has condemned as aggression the attacks by North Korea on South Korea in 1950, by Israel on Egypt in 1956, and by Belgium on the Congo in 1960, in which instances there was considerable provocation by the target countries. Egypt, for instance, was being used as a base area for persistent and *officially sanctioned* attacks by paramilitary forces upon Israeli territory, with the scale and frequency of attacks mounting in the months before the invasion. Nevertheless, the United States interpreted the Suez operation as a violation of the Charter and of general international law. In other words, the mere use of foreign territory as a base area has not been previously claimed by the United States to constitute such a violation of rights as to validate a claim of self-defense.[38] Under these circumstances the assertion of such a claim is

[36] There has been a steady erosion of this rôle under the pressure of geo-political and ideological considerations. Among the instances where this pressure has been resolved at the expense of legal restraints are Guatemala (1954), Lebanon (1958), Bay of Pigs (1961), the Stanleyville operation (1964), Dominican Republic (1965), as well as a number of less visible interventions in the affairs of foreign countries through the activities of the CIA. See note 2 above.

[37] There are certain special circumstances of imminence, especially in relation to nuclear weapons, that make it unreasonable to limit the right of self-defense to the victim of the first act of violence. The Cuban missile crisis of 1962 and the Middle East War of 1967 are cases where it is plausible to argue that the "victim" state was also the one that struck first.

[38] The precedents relied upon by Mr. Stevenson to establish a basis for the invasion are not very convincing, as they consisted either of brief "incidents" or involved extensions of claims of "hot pursuit." Stevenson, pp. 768–769. The United States has, indeed, denied such precedents to other countries claiming the right to strike across boundaries against external base areas. Such strikes, because of their short duration,

itself an illegal act of aggression that may amount, if on a sufficient scale, to an armed attack upon Cambodia giving rise to a right of self-defense on the part of the state of Cambodia (even if this right is not claimed by the presently constituted regime).

In summary, then, the American contention that the Cambodia operation is a valid exercise of the right of collective self-defense seems without foundation in international law for reasons of *doctrine, diplomatic practice,* and *public policy.*

A Special Limited Claim. The American legal position has also been asserted in the form of a special limited claim to eliminate the base areas on Cambodian territory. This position has not been developed in a serious fashion by the United States Government. The Deputy Secretary of Defense, David Packard, did allude to this line of justification in the course of a virtually unreported speech given to the Rotary Club in Fort Worth, Texas. On that occasion Mr. Packard did say:

> Under international law we had every right to strike the enemy in areas put to such uses. The inability of Cambodia over a period of years to live up to its legal obligations as a neutral state freed us from the obligation to stay out of these areas. They were not under Cambodian control. They were not neutral.

Interestingly, Mr. Packard attributed the timing of the invasion to the changed political situation: "Our failure to disrupt the Cambodian bases earlier was dictated by political considerations which, as long as Prince Sihanouk remained in power, it was felt overrode military considerations." Mr. Packard went on to say: "With the downfall of Sihanouk, there was no longer any reason to believe that the action by South Vietnam or the United States in the occupied border areas would be objectionable to the government of Cambodia." [39] Note that Mr. Packard does not rest the case on any imminent threat to the security of American forces or on any building up of North Vietnamese capabilities. He did, in passing, mention the expansion of base area operations by "occupying enemy forces" as increasing "the potential danger faced by American forces." What is important here is that, in the context of arguing on behalf of the alternate theory of enforcing Cambodia's neutral duties, Mr. Packard undercuts any assertion that conditions of imminent attack created an emergency justifying recourse to self-defense.

On its own grounds, however, the claimed right to make a limited use of force to remedy the failure by Cambodia to uphold its neutral duties vis-à-vis North Viet-Nam faces formidable difficulties.[40] First of all, the South Vietnamese claim is clearly not limited to the enforcement of neutral

---

small magnitude, and generally light casualties represent a far less serious use of force than the Cambodian invasion.

[39] Address by David Packard, Department of Defense News Release, May 15, 1970, p. 5.

[40] See Note from Columbia Law Review, "International Law and Military Operations against Insurgents in Neutral Territory," reprinted in 2 Falk, ed., The Vietnam War and International Law 572–593.

duties; it takes precedence over the American definition of the mission and provides the primary legal measure of what is being claimed. Secondly, sustained uses of overt force against foreign territory by governments for purposes other than self-defense are not compatible with the language of the Charter or the practice of the United Nations.[41]   Thirdly, the United States has consistently condemned as illegal much more modest claims to use force against base areas across boundaries.

During the Algerian war of independence, French forces in 1957 attacked Sakret-Sidi-Yousseff, a town in Tunisia being used as a sanctuary and staging area by Algerian insurgents.   The United States rejected the French claim that it was permissible to destroy external base areas and supply depots on the Tunisian side of the Algerian border and expressed its public displeasure, even though France was an American ally at the time.   Similarly, Adlai Stevenson, as United States Representative in the Security Council, condemned in 1964 a British raid against Habir in Yemen, which was in reprisal for the use of the town as a base for operations against the British colonial occupation of the Protectorate of Aden.   Finally the United States has on numerous occasions joined in criticizing and censuring Israel for attacking external base areas.   The expansion of the theater of violent acts across a boundary by overt and official action has been consistently regarded as illegal under modern international law.

Mr. Packard's assertion that the Lon Nol government would probably not find an invasion objectionable is also a very fragile basis upon which to launch a large-scale invasion that caused the death and displacement of many Cambodians, subjected the country to civil war conditions, and has entailed widespread destruction of Cambodian villages, forests, and croplands.   No United States official even contends that Cambodia requested or even authorized the invasion, nor was there evident any attempt to secure consent in advance.[42]

Furthermore, contrary to Mr. Nixon's contention on April 30th that "American policy" since 1954 has been "to scrupulously respect the neutrality of the Cambodian people," the number of border-crossing and airspace violations has been extensive ever since the intensification of the Viet-Nam War in 1964.[43]   Prince Sihanouk complained frequently about American violations of Cambodian neutrality, prominently displayed in Phnom Penh captured American equipment, complained to the International

[41] For an analysis of the compatibility between special claims to use force and international law (including the U.N. Charter), see Falk, "The Beirut Raid and the International Law of Retaliation," 63 A.J.I.L. 415 (1969).   Note that the Beirut raid conducted by Israeli military units on Dec. 28, 1968, was far more limited in scope, duration, and effects than has been the Cambodian operation.   It seems questionable whether a use of armed forces on the scale of the Cambodian operation can be ever considered as a special claim falling outside of the Charter, but must be justified, if at all, as an exercise of the right of self-defense.   Cf. Stevenson, pp. 768–769.

[42] See text above,   and note 19.

[43] For summary of U. S. and South Vietnamese violations of Cambodian neutrality prior to April 30, 1970, see Kahin, note 18 above, p. 57429; cf. also Chomsky, "Cambodia," New York Review of Books 39–50, at 40 (June 4, 1970); Fried, Appendix 1, "Protests by Cambodia about Violations of its Territory," pp. 1–9.

Control Commission, and invited American citizens to visit Cambodia and inspect for themselves evidence of U. S. raids against border areas. These American incursions, although more disruptive for Cambodians than the North Vietnamese use of Cambodian territory as a sanctuary, did not draw Cambodia into the war, and were generally consistent with the maintenance of Cambodian peace and security and the confinement of the war to the territory of South Viet-Nam.

Furthermore, there seems to be something peculiarly perverse about widening the war at a time when the official claim is that American involvement is being diminished. Casualties have been far lower during the withdrawal process initiated by Nixon than at other times during the war. If these base areas could be tolerated for so many years—even when American objectives were being set forth in more ambitious terms—then what was the reason to assert suddenly a claim based on Cambodia's failure to uphold neutral duties? The only partially satisfactory explanation of the timing of the Cambodian operation has to do with the fear that the Lon Nol régime was on the verge of collapse.[44] Such explanation lacks much plausibility because the invasion has had the primary effect of pushing the régime closer to either foreign dependence or collapse and may encourage the virtual partition of the country between South Viet-Nam, North Viet-Nam, Laos, and Thailand. Such an outcome has nothing to do with the enforcement of neutral rights, or, for that matter, with self-defense.

As with the claim of self-defense, there is no support in doctrine, practice or policy to vindicate an American claim of the proportions of the Cambodian operation. In the past, the organs of the world community have consistently condemned *lesser* claims—single raids lasting a few hours —to attack or destroy external base areas relied upon by the insurgent side in an internal war. Here, the limits are not narrow—a 21.7-mile territorial belt and a period of two months, besides less restrictive time and space zones for air attacks.[45] Mr. Packard reports that even these limits were imposed on the operation by the President "because he wants the American people to understand that this is a temporary and limited operation." [46] What about respect for norms prohibiting border-crossing uses of force? What about the welfare and autonomy of the Cambodian people who are the most permanent victims of the claim? Again, we are left with an *imperial* impression, the President giving an *internal* account,

---

[44] For speculation on motivation see Schurmann, "Cambodia: Nixon's Trap," Nation 651–656 (June 1, 1970); Scott, "Cambodia: Why the Generals Won," New York Review of Books 28–34 (June 18, 1970).

[45] The air strikes have continued on a regular basis since the July 1 withdrawal deadline. President Nixon has made no effort to change his earlier pledge on this point. It also is clear that these air strikes are intended to influence the military struggle in Cambodia, as well as to interdict supplies and troops that might be used against Americans in South Viet-Nam. A new "credibility gap" has arisen as a result of the discrepancy between the actual bombing patterns in Cambodia and the official statements on the subject. A useful summary of this situation is to be found in a newspaper article by Sterba, note 12 above.

[46] Packard, *loc. cit.* 6.

without any sense of obligation to respect world standards. Such a peremptory claim to enforce neutral rights is the essence of unilateralism which it has been the overriding purpose of modern international law to discourage and moderate in the area of war and peace.

Procedural Norms. One of the most disturbing features of the American rôle in the Cambodian operation is the evidence that the U. S. Government has acted without any sense of respect for the rules and procedures of law and order on an international level. The minimum legal burden imposed on a Head of State is to provide a legal justification to the international community for undertaking action that raises fundamental issues of international law as manifestly as does the invasion of a foreign country.

Yet the American claim to undertake the Cambodian operation was made in peremptory form. American policy was put forward as an exhibition of sovereign discretion, moderated by some sense of limits, but not subject to review or challenge. In this spirit it is necessary to recall Mr. Nixon's assertion forewarning foreign governments that any effort to regard our invasion of Cambodia as a serious breach of international order—or as a flagrant violation of the Charter—would be entirely unacceptable to us. Even the outrageous invasion of Czechoslovakia in 1968 was accompanied by some Soviet effort to give an international accounting, admittedly a flimsy one. I am comparing the American assertions vis-à-vis Cambodia with a sub-legal standard of comparison by citing the Czech occupation, and not in any sense intimating that the Soviet contention was consistent with the obligations of international law just because there was some effort to provide an international justification for the action. The provision of an explanation in such a setting is a necessary, but hardly *sufficient* condition of legality.

The United States did make certain gestures of compliance with Charter norms after the Cambodian operation was under way. Ambassador Yost made a short report on behalf of the United States to the President of the Security Council on May 5, 1970, explaining that the Cambodian operation was an exercise of the right of collective-self-defense.[47] Administration officials have subsequently developed a variety of legal arguments in response to objections raised in the domestic arena. To put forward legal arguments is not, of course, to be confused with the over-all persuasiveness of a legal position which must depend on weighing an argument against the facts, norms, and policies at stake, as well as against

---

[47] U.N. Doc. S/9761, *loc. cit.* note 3 above. Ambassador Yost's legal position was developed as follows: "The measures of collective self-defense being taken by U. S. and South Vietnamese forces are restricted in extent, purpose and time. They are confined to the border areas over which the Cambodian Government has ceased to exercise any effective control and which has been completely occupied by North Vietnamese and Viet Cong forces. Their purpose is to destroy the stocks and communications equipment that are being used in aggression against the Republic of Viet-Nam. When that is accomplished, our forces and those of the Republic of Viet-Nam will promptly withdraw. These measures are limited and proportionate to the aggressive military operations of the North Vietnamese forces and the threat they pose."

arguments developed in support of contrary legal positions. For reasons already discussed, the United Nations cannot provide a suitable forum for legal appraisal in the Indochina context. In any event, the United States since the beginning of its involvement in the Viet-Nam War has displayed only a nominal willingness to operate within a Charter context.[48]

Beyond the obligation to justify recourse to international force to the Security Council is the obligation to seek a peaceful settlement of an international dispute. Articles 2(3) and 33 of the Charter express this obligation in clear form. The Cambodian operation is only the latest instance of a continuing American refusal to seek a peaceful settlement of the conflicts that exist in Indochina. It is not possible here to make a detailed analysis of the failure by the United States to respond to the NLF proposal of May, 1969, for a settlement of the Viet-Nam War, the American failure to offer any counter-proposal, and the failure to appoint a negotiator of prestige and stature from November, 1969, when Henry Cabot Lodge resigned, until June, 1970, when David Bruce was designated as his successor. The Thieu-Ky Government has never made a secret of its opposition to a negotiated end to the war; its presence in Paris is a result of American pressure. Indeed, President Nixon's initial appointment of Mr. Lodge, known as an ardent supporter of the Saigon régime, and his subsequent non-replacement of a chief delegate for more than seven months after Mr. Lodge's resignation seemed designed to *reassure* the Thieu-Ky group that the United States has no intention of encouraging serious negotiations in Paris, rather than to convince North Viet-Nam and the Provisional Revolutionary Government of South Viet-Nam that we are interested in serious negotiations.[49] Such an American posture is made even more cynical by the frequent reiteration to the American public of our eagerness for serious negotiations, and by the allegation that negotiations are being blocked by the stubborn refusal of the other side to discuss anything other than the terms of its "victory." The effort to convey contradictory messages to the Saigon régime and to the American public places an overwhelming burden upon the credibility and sincerity of our negotiating posture and represents a serious failure to carry out the procedural norms relating to peaceful settlement.

The Cambodian operation, then, illustrates a refusal on the part of the United States to comply with minimum procedural norms of international law:

(1) There has been no indication of any willingness to submit to community review the claim to attack a foreign state.

[48] For more detailed appraisals of the U.N. rôle in relation to the Viet-Nam War, see articles by Bloomfield and Gordon in 2 Falk, ed., The Vietnam War and International Law 281–357.

[49] For the text of the ten-point proposal setting that was supported by North Viet-Nam and the National Liberation Front and put forward in the Paris negotiations, see Kolko (ed.), Three Documents of the National Liberation Front 15–23 (1970). This proposal represents a serious basis for negotiations. It has never drawn either a response or a counter-proposal of comparable detail from the U. S.-South Vietnamese Delegations.

(2) There has been no official effort to reconcile the invasion with the requirements of international law beyond the nominal letter of report to the Security Council. This failure to provide an external explanation of recourse to force against a foreign country violates Charter norms, at least as these norms have been interpreted on past occasions by the United States in relation to foreign states.

(3) There has been a failure to comply with the legal duty to seek a peaceful solution to the conflicts taking place in Indochina.

(4) South Viet-Nam has also provided no accounting for its more extensive claims to occupy Cambodian territory, and the United States seems legally responsible to the full extent of these wider claims—claims which even its own legal arguments, developed since April 30th, have not tried to justify.

IV. Some Concluding World-Order Comments

The development of international law is very much a consequence of the effective assertion of claims by principal states. Such claims create legal precedents that can be relied upon on subsequent occasions by other states. The Cambodian operation, in this sense, represents both a violation of existing procedural and substantive rules of international law and a very unfortunate legislative claim for the future. It will now be possible for states to rely on the Cambodian operation in carrying out raids against external base areas or even when invading a foreign country allegedly being used as a sanctuary. It will no longer be possible for the United States Government to make credible objections to such claims. The consequences of such a precedent for the Middle East and southern Africa seem to be highly destabilizing.

In this case, the precedent was established without any effort to justify the claim from the point of view of international public policy. One of the important thresholds of restraint had involved respect for international boundaries, especially with regard to the initiation of full-scale armed attacks. International law has relied on second-order restraints to limit the combat area, even when the wider prohibition on recourse to violence has failed. The precedent set by the Cambodian operation seriously erodes this second-order restraint and appears to increase the discretion of national governments as to the permissible limits of force in international affairs.

Covert and sporadic uses of force across international boundaries have been part of the way in which a balance has been reached between the use of external sanctuaries by insurgent groups and the security of the target state. Peremptory strikes against these external base areas have been generally condemned, but the short duration of these claims and the direct response to provocative actions by groups operating from the target state have usually meant that such retaliatory force has not greatly nor indefinitely expanded the theater of combat operations. The Cambodian operation was a campaign that included at its height more than 74,000 men (31,000 Americans, 43,000 South Vietnamese), heavy air support, the occupation of a large area of foreign territory for a long period of time, and the prospect of future incursions by land and air.   As such, it widens considerably the prior understanding of the limits of retaliatory force. Such widening is of serious consequence for at least three reasons:

(1) There are many conflict situations in which one or both contending factions can claim the need to attack external base areas.

(2) The claim to destroy the external base areas of the insurgent will undoubtedly generate counter-claims to destroy the external base areas of incumbent factions.

(3) The unilateral character of a determination as to when it is appropriate to attack external base areas is very subjective, tends to be self-serving, and is difficult to appraise.

In essence, then, the Cambodian operation represents a step backward in the struggle to impose restraints on the use of force in the conduct of foreign relations.   In the specific setting of the Viet-Nam War, the Cambodian operation is a further extension of the United States' illegal involvement in Indochina.   It has widened the theater of combat, complicated the task of negotiating a settlement, brought additional governments into positions of active co-belligerency, and has been convincingly justified by neither a demonstration of military necessity nor a claim of legal prerogative.

The Cambodian operation is, perhaps, the most blatant violation of international law by the United States Government since World War II, but it represents only the most recent instance in a series of illegal uses of force to intervene in the internal affairs of a sovereign society.   Until Cambodia, the United States Government either disguised its interventions, as in Guatemala in 1954, or made a serious effort to justify them, as in relation to the Dominican intervention of 1965.   The Cambodian operation represents a peremptory claim to take military action; such action violates the letter and spirit of general international law and the Charter of the United Nations, and seems to vindicate the allegation that the United States is acting in Southeast Asia with imperial pretensions rather than as one among many states subject to a common framework of minimum restraint in its international conduct.

Within the present world setting, the United States is contributing to the deterioration of the quality of international order rather than to its improvement.   Such a rôle is particularly tragic at this juncture of world history, a crossroads in human destiny at which the converging dangers of population pressure, ecological decay, and the possibility of nuclear war create the first crisis of world order that threatens the survival of man as a species and the habitability of the planet.[50]   The prospects for creative response are vitally linked with the orientations toward issues of international order that prevail in the principal national centers of power and authority in the world.   Unless constructive changes are sought by national governments, there is no way to meet the threats posed, in part, by

[50] A depiction of this crisis and some proposals for overcoming it are the subject of my forthcoming book: This Endangered Planet: Prospects and Proposals for Human Survival, to be published in 1971 by Random House.

the present fragmented political organization of world society. One precondition for change is a greater reluctance by powerful governments to rely on military capabilities to promote their foreign policy goals. Recent actions by the Soviet Union and by the United States have displayed, above all, a return to the political consciousness associated with pre-World War I attitudes of sovereign prerogative and *raison d'état*, and a total abandonment of the serious search for a new system of world order responsive to the needs of our time, except to be prudent about provocative acts in a crisis situation in which the nuclear contingency appears relevant. It is in this sense that the Cambodian operation bears witness to the persistence of the war system and to the strength and vitality of the most destructive attitudes and forces active in our world.

There is, perhaps, some reason for encouragement in the report that the Secretary of State, William P. Rogers, circulated a memorandum addressed to the Assistant Secretary of State, dated June 13, 1970, in which the following language appears:

> When crises occur in any area of the world those in the department who are most directly involved should be careful to insure that the legal implications are not overlooked.[51]

Imagine, if such sentiments began to shape the choice of policy, as well as to influence the process of its rationalization!

[51] New York Times, June 24, 1970, p. 3.

Legal Dimensions of the Decision to Intercede in Cambodia

JOHN NORTON MOORE

In appraising national security decisions, such as the recent decision to send United States combat forces into the North Vietnamese and Viet Cong border sanctuaries in Cambodia, it is useful to focus on three interrelated questions. First, is the decision consistent with national and international law? Second, is the decision consistent with the national interest? And third, are there other alternatives which are likely to be more satisfactory in implementing the national interest? Each of these questions represents an important perspective for appraisal. Although the answer to the first question is important for answering the second and third questions, international lawyers should resist the temptation to regard an affirmative answer to the legal question as equivalent to proof that a decision is the best option for national action. Conversely, international lawyers should also avoid the temptation to regard personal doubts about the efficacy of a particular option as equivalent to proof of the illegality of the option. An international legal perspective is a critical input in national security decisions and should have a major rôle in defining the national interest and in introducing and delimiting options for national action.[1] On the other hand, efforts to overuse international law, whether by way of support or criticism of national action serve only to obscure the vital rôle that an international-legal perspective should play.

I. The International Law Issues

A. *A Brief Background of the Cambodian Conflict*

Cambodia emerged from the Geneva Conference of 1954, which ended the first Indochina War, as a fully autonomous state. Article 12 of the Final Declaration by the Conference provided that "each member of the Geneva Conference undertakes to respect the sovereignty, the independence, the unity and the territorial integrity. . . . [of Cambodia, Laos and Viet Nam], and to refrain from any interference in their internal affairs."[2]

---

[1] See Falk, "Law, Lawyers, and the Conduct of American Foreign Relations," 78 Yale Law J. 919 (1969); Moore, "The Control of Foreign Intervention in Internal Conflict," 9 Virginia J. Int. Law 205, 310–314 (1969).

[2] The Final Declaration, signed July 21, 1954; the Agreement on the Cessation of Hostilities in Cambodia, signed July 20, 1954; and the Declaration by the Royal Government of Cambodia of July 21, 1954, are reproduced in Further Documents relating to the discussion of Indo-China at the Geneva Conference, Misc. No. 20 (1954), Cmd. No. 9239, at 9, 11, 40 (1954). The Text of the Final Declaration is also reprinted in 60 A.J.I.L. 643 (1966). See, generally, R. Randle, "The Settlement for Cambodia," in Geneva 1954: The Settlement of the Indochinese War 482–503 (1969).

In addition, Articles 4, 13, and 21 of the Agreement on the Cessation of Hostilities in Cambodia, which was signed by the Vice Minister of National Defense of North Viet-Nam, made clear that foreign military forces were to be withdrawn from Cambodia.

At the Conference, the Chinese Premier, Chou En-lai, sought an agreement to prevent Cambodia from joining military alliances such as SEATO. Although there was general Conference agreement on the neutralization of Cambodia, the Cambodian Delegation successfully held out for an agreement permitting Cambodia to request foreign military assistance in the event its security was threatened.[3] Robert Randle's description of the Geneva negotiations is quite specific on this point.

> Sam Sary [a member of the Cambodian Delegation] said he would not sign the agreements because they limited the freedom of the Cambodian government to decide whether or not it would join an alliance; moreover, the agreements limited Cambodia's right to request military assistance from the United States or any other country. Limitations such as these, Sam Sary said, were unacceptable restrictions upon Cambodia's newly won independence. The Cambodian minister also expressed concern for the future of his country, which he said might become an object of Communist expansionism, and he wanted to reserve the right to ask the United States to establish bases on Cambodian territory.
>
> The great-power ministers argued with Sam Sary to no avail. The American diplomat assured him the SEATO pact, then being prepared, would give Cambodia some assurance against Communist aggression, but Sam Sary persisted. Mendès-France's midnight deadline passed; and shortly after 2 a.m. the Cambodian minister announced that he had seventeen other demands! Molotov thereupon announced that he would acquiesce in the first demand: Cambodia would be permitted to request foreign military assistance in the event its security was threatened.[4]

This understanding was embodied in a unilateral declaration by the Cambodian Delegation at Geneva which stated:

> The Royal Government of Cambodia is resolved never to take part in an aggressive policy and never to permit the territory of Cambodia to be utilized in the service of such a policy.
>
> The Royal Government of Cambodia will not join in any agreement with other States, if this agreement carries for Cambodia the obligation to enter into a military alliance not in conformity with the principles of the Charter of the United Nations, or, as long as its security is not threatened, the obligation to establish bases on Cambodian territory for the military forces of foreign Powers.
>
> The Royal Government of Cambodia is resolved to settle its international disputes by peaceful means, in such a manner as not to endanger peace, international security and justice.
>
> During the period which will elapse between the date of the cessation of hostilities in Viet-Nam and that of the final settlement of political problems in this country, the Royal Government of Cambodia

[3] R. Randle, *op. cit.* at 339–341, 486. See also M. Field, The Prevailing Wind: Witness in Indo-China 169–170 (1965).

[4] R. Randle, *op. cit.* at 340.

will not solicit foreign aid in war material, personnel or instructors except for the purpose of the effective defence of the territory.[5]

The second and fourth paragraphs of this declaration were incorporated in Article 7 of the Agreement on the Cessation of Hostilities in Cambodia. The declaration was also adverted to in Article 4 of the Final Declaration of the Conference, in which the Conference took note of Cambodia's declaration "not to request foreign aid, whether in war material, in personnel or in instructors, except for the purpose of the effective defence of . . . [its] territory . . . ," and in Article 5 of the Final Declaration in which the Conference took note of the Cambodian declaration:

> that . . . [it] will not join in any agreement with other States if . . . [the] agreement includes the obligation to participate in a military alliance not in conformity with the principles of the Charter of the United Nations . . . or, so long as . . . [its] security is not threatened, the obligation to establish bases on Cambodian . . . territory for the military forces of foreign Powers.

In short, the Conference provided that Cambodia was to remain neutral but would have the right to obtain the full range of foreign assistance when necessary for the effective defense of Cambodia. In the absence of such a threat to Cambodian security, foreign military bases were to be prohibited on Cambodian territory even if Cambodia consented to their presence.

After the Geneva Conference Prince Norodom Sihanouk moved rapidly to establish Cambodian neutrality. Though from time to time he was accused by both Communist and non-Communist states as being pro-Western or pro-Communist, the mercurial Prince seems to have been genuinely preoccupied throughout most of the interim years with preservation of Cambodian neutrality as the best way to preserve the existence of Cambodia.[6] In May, 1955, Sihanouk did enter into a military aid agreement with the United States, but the defensive nature of the agreement and the limited quantities of military supplies were unanimously declared by the International Commission for Supervision and Control in Cambodia as "not in excess of . . . [Cambodia's] effective defence requirements."[7] In November, 1957, Cambodia's neutral status was enacted into law by the National Assembly of Cambodia. The neutrality law stipulated that Cambodia was to be "a neutral country." Consistently with the earlier Geneva understanding, it also provided that in case of aggression Cambodia reserved the rights to: "(1) self-defence by arms; (2) call on the United Nations; and (3) call on a friendly country."[8] In its Sixth Interim Report the International Commission for Supervision and Control in Cambodia took note of this Cambodian law after stating that Cambodia "has continued

---

[5] Cited note 2 above.   [6] See M. Field, note 3 above, at 161–251.

[7] R. Randle, note 2 above, at 501. In its Sixth Interim Report the International Commission for Supervision and Control in Cambodia reiterated that "the imports of war materials by the Royal Government were not in excess of requirements for its effective defence." Cambodia No. 1 [1958], Cmnd. No. 526, at 8 (1958).

[8] See Sixth Interim Report, cited above, at 9. See also M. Field, note 3 above, at 232.

to fulfil most satisfactorily its responsibility under Articles 7 and 13(c) of the Geneva Agreement." [9]

During the early sixties Sihanouk began to take a progressively harsher line toward the United States, culminating in renunciation of American aid in 1963 and termination of diplomatic relations in 1965. Apparently, from 1965 until the recent Cambodian crisis, the United States has not provided Cambodia with significant military or economic assistance. In contrast, as the Viet-Nam War heated up, the Viet Cong and North Vietnamese military presence and influence in Cambodia grew progressively. By March and April of this year the *New York Times* reported estimates ranging from forty to fifty thousand Viet Cong and North Vietnamese troops in Cambodia.[10] It seems to be generally accepted that at least during the last several years sizeable Viet Cong and North Vietnamese forces have used Cambodian territory for infiltration into South Viet-Nam, for supply, command, communications and training functions in support of belligerent activities in South Viet-Nam, and as staging areas and sanctuaries for repeated attacks on targets in South Viet-Nam.[11]

Perhaps because he suspected a Communist victory in Indochina, during the last few years Sihanouk seemed increasingly reluctant to challenge the substantial North Vietnamese and Viet Cong forces operating on Cambodian territory. In February of this year, however, Cambodian forces began engaging North Vietnamese forces and by March domestic opposition to the sizeable Vietnamese forces in Cambodia led to a Cambodian demand that the North Vietnamese leave Cambodian territory.[12] At the same time,

[9] See Sixth Interim Report, note 7 above, at 9. Art. 13(c) of the Agreement on the Cessation of Hostilities in Cambodia provides that the International Supervisory Commission shall: "Supervise, at ports and airfields and along all the frontiers of Cambodia, the application of the Cambodian declaration concerning the introduction into Cambodia of military personnel and war materials on grounds of foreign assistance."

[10] New York Times, March 17, 1970, at 1, col. 8 (City ed.); April 4, 1970, at 3, col. 1 (City ed.); April 23, 1970, at 4, col. 4 (City ed.). See also the Staff Report, "Cambodia: May 1970" prepared for the Senate Committee on Foreign Relations, 91st Cong., 2d Sess. 6 (Comm. Print June 7, 1970), reprinted in 9 Int. Legal Materials 858, 864 (1970).

[11] According to John Stevenson, the Legal Adviser of the Department of State:

"In the past 5 years 150,000 enemy troops have been infiltrated into South Viet-Nam through Cambodia. In 1969 alone, 60,000 of their military forces moved in from Cambodia. The trails inside Cambodia are used not only for the infiltration of troops but also for the movement of supplies. A significant quantity of the military supplies that support these forces came through Cambodian ports. . . .

"During 1968 and 1969 the Cambodian bases adjacent to the South Vietnamese Provinces of Tay Ninh, Pleiku, and Kontum have served as staging areas for regimental-size Communist forces for at least three series of major engagements—the 1968 Tet offensive, the May 1968 offensive and the post-Tet 1969 offensive." Stevenson, "United States Military Actions in Cambodia: Questions of International Law," 62 Dept. of State Bulletin 765, 767 (1970); reprinted in 64 A.J.I.L. 933 and in 9 Int. Legal Materials 840, 846–847 (1970).

[12] See New York Times, March 16, 1970, at 1, col. 5 (City ed.); March 17, 1970, at 1, col. 8 (City ed.). "Cambodia had sent notes to the Vietcong and Hanoi Governments demanding that the troops leave by yesterday, but the deadline passed with no apparent exodus of troops." *Ibid.*

Prince Sihanouk traveled to Moscow and Peking, apparently to persuade the Soviets and Chinese to assist in removing the Vietnamese presence.[13] During his absence on March 18, Prime Minister Lon Nol and Deputy Prime Minister Sirik Matak formally deposed Prince Sihanouk as Chief of State.   The coup, if it can be accurately called that, was limited.   Since the summer of 1969 Lon Nol had been Prime Minister, a position he had also held once before in 1966–1967, and Sirik Matak, a cousin of Sihanouk's, had been First Deputy Prime Minister.   Apparently Sihanouk's personal power, which, according to Jean Lacouture, had been eroding since 1966,[14] had been slipping faster during the last year as a result of economic problems, more active political opposition, and the increased presence of North Vietnamese in Cambodia.   Perhaps as a reflection of this reduction in personal power, in the summer of 1969 Sihanouk requested Lon Nol to form a new government to replace that of Pen Nouth, who resigned after a long illness.   Lon Nol seems to have accepted only on the condition that he be named Prime Minister and empowered to appoint his own ministers and have them report to him instead of to Sihanouk.[15]   Apparently Sihanouk accepted Lon Nol's conditions.   Lon Nol was the overwhelming choice of a special session of Congress called by Sihanouk to name a new government, and he took office on August 12, 1969.[16]   During the next few months the Lon Nol government took a number of actions over the opposition of Sihanouk, including closing the Phnom Penh Casino and diverting taxes to the Government which had previously been paid to Sihanouk personally.[17]   After January 6, when Sihanouk left for France on vacation, Lon Nol and Sirik Matak were in control of the Cambodian Government.   According to an account by Robert Shaplen, Lon Nol and Sirik Matak sent word to Sihanouk in Paris that he could return as Chief of State "if he accepted what had already been implied as early as the previous summer and was now made explicit—that he would no longer run things single-handed in his old manner."[18]   When Sihanouk refused to receive the emissaries, the coup was formally approved by the Cambodian National Assembly.   On March 18 the Assembly unanimously voted to dismiss Sihanouk as Chief of State and named Cheng Heng, the head of the Assembly, as Acting Chief of State.[19]   On March 21, Cheng Heng was sworn in as Chief of State.   According to the *New York Times*, there was no evidence of foreknowledge of the Lon Nol takeover among

[13] See *ibid.*, March 16, 1970, at 11, col. 1 (City ed.).   Staff Report, note 10 above, at 1; 9 Int. Legal Materials at 860 (1970).

[14] J. Lacouture, "From the Vietnam War to an Indochina War," 48 Foreign Affairs 617, 624–625 (1970).

[15] See New York Times, March 19, 1970, at 16, cols. 8–9.

[16] *Ibid.*, col. 9.

[17] *Ibid.*; R. Shaplen, "Letter From Indo-China," The New Yorker, May 9, 1970, at 130, 135.   [18] R. Shaplen, *loc. cit.* at 136.

[19] *Ibid.*, at 139.   According to the Staff Report prepared for the Senate Committee on Foreign Relations: "On March 18, Sihanouk was removed as Chief of State by unanimous vote of the Cambodian Parliament."   Staff Report, note 10 above, at 2; *loc. cit.*, at 860.

senior United States officials.[20]   Robert Shaplen is even more explicit on this point.   He writes that "there is no evidence that the Americans participated in the coup or that they were even apprised of it until a few hours before it took place, although they were undoubtedly aware of what might happen and did nothing to try to prevent it." [21]   For the most part, the new government did not seem to have serious recognition problems, foreign governments simply assuming that the Lon Nol Government was the legitimate successor Government of Cambodia.   In fact, even Peking, North Viet-Nam and North Korea did not formally break diplomatic relations until as late as May 5.[22]

The more conservative Lon Nol Government continued to seek North Vietnamese and Viet Cong withdrawal and intensified the military effort to dislodge them from border sanctuaries.   There were also several small-scale cross-border operations conducted by the South Vietnamese forces against the border sanctuaries, some in collaboration with Cambodian forces.[23]   The North Vietnamese and Viet Cong reacted with military initiatives apparently directed at widening the sanctuaries, restoring supply routes to the Cambodian port of Sihanoukville, and threatening the viability of the new government.[24]   Throughout the month of April the daily accounts of the Cambodian fighting indicate a steadily deteriorating military situation.[25]   On April 20 Cambodia requested the use of units of ethnic Cambodians from Viet-Nam which had been associated with American-operated units in South Viet-Nam.[26]   Two days later Cambodia appealed to the United Nations Security Council for assistance from all countries

[20] New York Times, May 6, 1970, at 17, col. 6 (City ed.).

[21] R .Shaplen, note 17 above, at 139.

[22] See New York Times, May 7, 1970, at 1, col. 5.   North Viet-Nam and the Viet Cong, however, recalled their diplomats from Phnom Penh on March 25, 1970.   See New York Times, March 26, 1970, at 17, col. 1.

The Staff Report prepared for the Senate Committee on Foreign Relations points out that: "On May 5, Sihanouk announced in Peking the formation of a Royal Government of National Union.   It was recognized by Communist China the same day and by North Vietnam and the Provisional Revolutionary Government the following day."   Staff Report, note 10 above, at 4; 9 Int. Legal Materials at 862.   With respect to this government-in-exile, Robert Shaplen suggests that "Sihanouk is more a captive of Peking today than a spearhead of an independent government-in-exile. . . ."   R. Shaplen, note 17 above, at 135.   See also note 51 below.

[23] See Staff Report, note 10 above, at 1–4; 9 Int. Legal Materials at 859–862.

[24] The New York Times reported "an acceleration of the Communist invasion" following efforts by the new government "for negotiations on its demand for the withdrawal of Vietnamese Communist troops."   New York Times, May 7, 1970, at 16, col. 1 (City ed.).

[25] See, e.g., ibid., April 8, 1970, at 1, col. 8 (City ed.); April 9, 1970, at 1, col. 4 (City ed.); April 10, 1970, at 1, col. 4 (City ed.); April 13, 1970, at 1, col. 2 (City ed.); April 20, 1970, at 1, col. 8 (City ed.); April 21, 1970, at 1, col. 6 (City ed.); April 23, 1970, at 1, col. 8 (City ed.); April 25, 1970, at 3, col. 4 (City ed.); April 27, 1970, at 1, col. 8 (City ed.); April 27, 1970, at 5, col. 1 (City ed.).

[26] See New York Times, May 4, 1970, at 1, col. 6 (City ed.).   Apparently about 2,000 ethnic Cambodians arrived in Phnom Penh on May 1 and 2.   Ibid.

to help the new government fight "invading Vietcong and North Vietnamese forces." [27]   On April 23 the *New York Times* reported that:

> An atmosphere of heightening national emergency is overtaking Cambodia.
>
> The emergency atmosphere is due to evidence that the Cambodian Army is unable to turn back the Vietnamese Communist forces, who at one point are within 15 miles of the capital, and to the lack of response from any nation except Indonesia to Premier Lon Nol's appeal to all nations for arms aid. . . .[28]
>
> Military analysts said the 30,000-man Cambodian Army would be no match for the 40,000 to 50,000 North Vietnamese and Vietcong soldiers in Cambodia, if a determined assault were pressed by the Communist forces.[29]

On April 27, three days before the United States and South Viet-Nam interceded in Cambodia, the *New York Times* described the situation in Cambodia as "rapidly deteriorating." [30]

This brief account of the events leading up to the United States and South Vietnamese intercession in Cambodia on April 30 necessarily omits a number of important events, such as repeated United States protests against North Vietnamese and Viet Cong use of neutral Cambodian territory, Cambodian protests against sporadic allied incursions into Cambodian territory, Cambodian requests to the International Supervisory Commission for investigation of the activities of belligerents in both camps, the formation by Sihanouk of a Cambodian government-in-exile, and the apparent complicity of some Cambodian Army officers in the killing of substantial numbers of Vietnamese civilians living in Cambodia.[31]

B. *The Rights and Duties of Cambodia*

Cambodian obligations with respect to the war in Viet-Nam stem from at least four sources: the United Nations Charter, the Geneva Accords, the customary international law of non-intervention, and the customary international law of neutrality.

Cambodia is, of course, bound by Article 2(4) of the United Nations Charter which prohibits "the threat or use of force against the territorial integrity or political independence of any state. . . ." To the extent that the North Vietnamese use of force against South Viet-Nam violates Article 2(4) of the Charter,[32] Cambodia would also be prohibited from providing assistance to the North Vietnamese forces.

[27] See *ibid.*, April 23, 1970, at 4, col. 5 (City ed.).

[28] *Ibid.*, at 1, col. 8 (City ed.).   [29] *Ibid.*, at 4, col. 4 (City ed.).

[30] *Ibid.*, April 27, 1970, at 5, col. 1 (City ed.).

[31] See *ibid.*, April 11, 1970, at 1, col. 4 (City ed.); April 14, 1970, at 1, col. 5 (City ed.); April 18, 1970, at 1, col. 1 (City ed.); April 25, 1970, at 3, col. 1 (City ed.); but see *ibid.*, April 23, 1970, at 5, col. 3 (City ed.), announcing the formation by the Cambodian Government of a "Commission responsible for the safety of all foreigners. . . ."

[32] For a discussion of the legal issues raised in the Viet-Nam War and whether the North Vietnamese use of force against South Viet-Nam violates Art. 2(4) of the Charter, see 1 and 2 Falk (ed.), The Vietnam War and International Law (1968 and 1969).

Secondly, "as long as its security is not threatened" Cambodia is obligated by Article 7 of the Agreement on the Cessation of Hostilities in Cambodia not to permit the establishment of "bases on Cambodian territory for the military forces of foreign Powers." Moreover, arguably it is bound by Article 12 of the Final Declaration of the Conference "to refrain from any interference in . . . [the] internal affairs [of Viet Nam]." [33] North Vietnamese and Viet Cong bases in Cambodia used to prosecute the Viet-Nam War would seem to violate these provisions of the Geneva Accords, at least to the extent that Cambodia is able to prevent their establishment in Cambodia.

Thirdly, Cambodia is bound by the customary law of non-intervention. [34] The General Assembly Declaration of 1965 on Inadmissibility of Intervention is representative of many authoritative pronouncements:

> [N]o State shall organize, assist . . . or *tolerate* subversive, terrorist or armed activities directed towards the violent overthrow of the regime of another State. . . . (Emphasis added.) [35]

Thus, to the extent that it is politically and militarily feasible, Cambodia is under an obligation to prevent the use of its territory for Viet Cong armed attacks directed against the Saigon Government.

Finally, Cambodia is bound by the customary international law of neutrality, which according to most commentators survived the United Nations Charter. [36] Application of the customary law of neutrality would seem particularly appropriate in view of the neutralization of Cambodia by the Geneva Accords as well as by Cambodian internal law, and the repeated declarations of Cambodian and non-Cambodian spokesmen recognizing Cambodian neutrality. [37] The duties of a neutral include obligations to prevent belligerents from transporting troops or supplies across neutral territory and to prevent neutral territory from being used for base camps, munitions factories, supply depots, training facilities, communications networks, or staging areas for attack. Belligerent troops seeking asylum must be disarmed and interned for the duration of the conflict. [38] These obligations do not require neutrals to engage in impossible political or military efforts but only to employ "due diligence" or the "means at their

[33] But see R. Randle, note 2 above, at 414–415.

[34] For a general discussion of the customary law of non-intervention see Moore, note 1 above, at 242–246, 315–332.

[35] Res. 2131, U. N. General Assembly, 20th Sess., Official Records, Supp. 14, at 11–12 (U.N. Doc. A/6014) (1965); 60 A.J.I.L. 662 (1966).

[36] See G. Schwarzenberger, A Manual of International Law 218 (5th ed., 1967); J. Stone, Legal Controls of International Conflict 382 (1959). See also M. Greenspan, The Modern Law of Land Warfare 540 (1959); Note, "International Law and Military Operations against Insurgents in Neutral Territory," 68 Col. Law Rev. 1127, 1142–1146 (1968).

[37] See, *e.g.,* the declaration of the Royal Government of Cambodia of May 29, 1955, in R. Randle, note 2 above, at 489.

[38] See, generally, on the duties of a neutral state, E. Castrén, The Present Law of War and Neutrality 459, 470–488 (1954); 2 Oppenheim, International Law 687–726 (7th ed., Lauterpacht, 1952); M. McDougal and F. Feliciano, Law and Minimum World Public Order 436–469 (1961); G. Schwarzenberger, note 36 above, at 219–226.

disposal" to prevent belligerent violations.[39]   Though the Sihanouk Government seems sometimes to have co-operated with North Vietnamese and Viet Cong forces to the point of violating Cambodian neutrality, the extremely precarious military and political posture of Cambodia should be taken into account in assessing Sihanouk's actions.[40]   In any event, at least since February of this year, the Cambodian Government seemed to be genuinely engaged in attempting to prevent North Vietnamese and Viet Cong violations of Cambodian neutrality.

With respect to Cambodian rights to defend its political and territorial integrity, Cambodia would seem to have the option pursuant to both Article 51 of the United Nations Charter and the Geneva Accords to request foreign assistance in defense against an armed attack.   The sustained North Vietnamese and Viet Cong attacks on Cambodian forces during the last several months and the military occupation of sizeable areas of Cambodian territory from which Cambodian officials have been ousted certainly constitute an "armed attack" within the meaning of Article 51 of the Charter, and a "security threat" within the meaning of Article 7 of the Agreement on Cessation of Hostilities in Cambodia.   Cambodia may consequently lawfully request external assistance for its defense.

It should also be pointed out that Cambodia has an obligation under international law to protect ethnic Vietnamese residing in Cambodia.   A deliberate governmental policy aimed at killing ethnic Vietnamese civilians residing in Cambodia would violate the Conventon on the Prevention and Punishment of the Crime of Genocide, in force since 1951.[41]   There is some evidence that the deaths of Vietnamese civilians in Cambodia in April may have resulted from a Cambodian governmental policy, if not of commission at least of omission.[42]   Subsequent actions by which the Cambodian Government has moved more vigorously to protect Vietnamese refugees suggest that the principal impetus to the earlier killings may have been traditional Cambodian-Vietnamese antagonisms inflamed by the North Vietnamese and Viet Cong attacks and coupled with a lack of effective

[39] See E. Castrén, cited above, at 442; M. Greenspan, note 36 above, at 537–538; 3 Hyde, International Law Chiefly as Interpreted and Applied by the United States 2344 (1945); L. Oppenheim, cited above, at 757–758; J. Stone, note 36 above, at 391.   Greenspan says: "the practice of the two world wars appears to indicate that a small neutral state is not at fault for failure to offer resistance to the invasion of its territory, where such resistance would be hopeless." (P. 537.)

[40] One writer points out: "[I]t has been suggested by a student of Cambodian foreign policy that Prince Sihanouk believed that the continued independence of his state depended upon entering into a modus vivendi with the Chinese People's Republic and the Democratic Republic of Vietnam.   At present, Cambodia is threatened by a Communist inspired insurgency; the consequence probably would have been far worse for the Cambodian government had impartiality been maintained throughout the war in Vietnam." Note, note 36 above, at 1145.

[41] 78 U.N. Treaty Series 277 (1951).   See, generally, McDougal and Arens, "The Genocide Convention and the Constitution," 3 Vanderbilt Law Rev. 683 (1950).

[42] See the New York Times articles, note 31 above.

control over middle echelon Cambodian Army officers.[43] In any event, Cambodia has a continuing obligation for the protection of Vietnamese civilians in Cambodia.

C. The Lawfulness of North Vietnamese and Viet Cong Activities in Cambodia

Whether incident to operations in Viet-Nam or an internal conflict in Cambodia, North Vietnamese and Viet Cong military activities in Cambodia are unlawful.

If North Vietnamese and Viet Cong activities are sought to be justified as incidental to hostilities in South Viet-Nam, they violate both the Geneva Accords and the customary international law of neutrality, whether or not North Vietnamese claims of acting in defense in the Viet-Nam War are accepted. Thus, North Viet-Nam agreed, pursuant to Article 4 of the Cambodian Cease-fire Agreement and Article 12 of the Final Declaration, to withdraw her forces from Cambodia and to respect the sovereignty and territorial integrity of Cambodia. And pursuant to the customary law of neutrality, it is unlawful for a belligerent to violate neutral territory by using it for the transport of military forces or supplies, the establishment of staging areas for attack, or the establishment of training, command, communication, or supply facilities.[44] Such violations may amount to aggression against the neutral, giving rise to a corresponding right of defense. As McDougal and Feliciano put it:

> By violating a neutral state, an aggressor-belligerent may compound its offense and commit a new and separate act of aggression. In such situations, the permission of self-defense becomes available to the target neutral and the whole panoply of sanctioning measures contemplated in the United Nations Charter becomes relevant.[45]

Some scholars support a right of a belligerent state to take preventive action to forestall an impending occupation of a neutral state by enemy belligerents.[46] In view of Sihanouk's jealous guarding of Cambodian neutrality, his lack of even formal diplomatic relations with the United States or South Viet-Nam, and the total lack of factual basis for the claim,

[43] In late April the Cambodian Government announced the formation of a "Commission responsible for the safety of all foreigners. . . ." New York Times, April 23, 1970, at 5, col. 3 (City ed.).

[44] See, generally, on the duties of a belligerent toward neutral states, E. Castrén, note 38 above, at 440–442; M. Greenspan, note 36 above, at 534; C. C. Hyde, note 39 above, at 2336–2344; L. Oppenheim, note 38 above, at 690.

Since France ratified in 1910 the Hague Convention Respecting the Rights and Duties of Neutral Powers and Persons in Case of War on Land, 36 Stat. 2310, Treaty Series No. 540, 1 Bevans 654, North Viet-Nam might be bound as a successor state. See J. B. Scott (ed.), The Reports to the Hague Conferences of 1899 and 1907, at 898 (1917). In any event, the general obligations of neutrality stemming from the Hague Conventions seem firmly established as customary international law.

[45] M. McDougal and F. Feliciano, note 38 above, at 404.

[46] See M. Greenspan, note 36 above, at 539–540; L. Oppenheim, note 38 above, at 698. But see C. C. Hyde, note 39 above, at 2341.

any North Vietnamese claim to this effect would seem considerably more far-fetched than the German claim rejected by the Nuremberg Tribunal that the German invasion of Norway was justifiable preventive action.[47]

It may also be urged that the law of neutrality has been modified by the Charter to permit belligerents which are acting in self-defense to violate neutral territory when such action is necessary for effective defense. Even aside from the difficulty in characterizing North Vietnamese activities in South Viet-Nam and Cambodia as lawful defense, however, any such theory would work dangerously to expand the permissible areas of conflict. At least in the absence of an authoritative community determination pursuant to Chapter VII of the Charter, such a theory would add yet another technique of conflict expansion through self-serving claims subject to little factual verification. Community policies for minimization of conflict suggest that it is important to preserve the requirement of prior or immediate threat of belligerent use of neutral territory as at least a minimum prerequisite for lawful belligerent activities in neutral territory. Although the Charter may increase the customary law requirements for lawful belligerent activities on neutral territory, it seems doubtful that it should decrease those requirements. For these reasons, most scholars seem to have rejected arguments that the Charter has eliminated the law of neutrality applicable to belligerent activities on neutral territory.[48]

If North Vietnamese and Viet Cong military activities are sought to be justified as participation in an internal conflict in Cambodia, such activities would violate both the Geneva Accords and the customary international law of non-intervention, even if the internal conflict characterization were accepted. Pursuant to Article 12 of the Final Declaration of the Geneva Conference North Viet-Nam undertook "to respect . . . the territorial integrity . . . [of Cambodia] and to refrain from any interference in . . . [its] internal affairs." The majority view today seems to support a rule of customary law prohibiting external intervention in civil strife, absent some prior foreign intervention on behalf of insurgents.[49] This rule is reflected in the General Assembly Declaration of 1965 on Inadmissibility of Intervention which provides that: ". . . [N]o State shall . . . assist . . . armed activities directed towards the violent overthrow of the regime of another State, or interfere in civil strife in another State. . . ."[50] Thus, even if the claim were accepted that North Vietnamese and Viet Cong forces were assisting the Sihanouk government-in-exile at its invitation and that that government was the widely recognized government of Cambodia,[51]

[47] Nazi Conspiracy and Aggression, Opinion and Judgment 38 (1947).

[48] See authorities cited in note 36 above. One scholar writes: "The thesis that under the Pact and Charter the neutral state has a duty to assist the victim of aggression is tenable only if there exists a set of standards which members of an international tribunal can apply impartially, regardless of their ideological inclinations to determine which side has in fact struck the first blow." Note, note 36 above, at 1144.

[49] See Moore, note 1 above, at 316–320, 333–339.

[50] Res. 2131, note 35 above.

[51] A claim that the Sihanouk government-in-exile is a widely recognized government would seem far-fetched. According to the New York Times, even the Soviet Union issued a statement in which it "seemed . . . to indicate that it recognized the new

North Vietnamese and Viet Cong intervention in the internal strife between the Lon Nol and Sihanouk governments would be unlawful, absent prior external intervention on behalf of the Lon Nol Government. The reality seems to be, however, that the fighting in Cambodia is principally between Cambodians on the one hand and North Vietnamese-Viet Cong on the other. Even after four months of fighting, few Cambodians seem to be fighting with the North Vietnamese forces, and the situation seems more closely to resemble an external armed attack than intervention in an internal conflict. As such, North Vietnamese and Viet Cong military actions against the Lon Nol Government are a violation of Article 2(4) of the Charter.

It is also relevant in appraising the North Vietnamese-Viet Cong legal position in Cambodia that, far from pursuing peaceful settlement according to Article 33 of the Charter or reporting military measures to the Security Council pursuant to Article 51 of the Charter, they have consistently denied even the presence of any North Vietnamese or Viet Cong forces in Cambodia [52]—surely a monumental credibility gap!

D. *The Lawfulness of United States and South Vietnamese Activities in Cambodia*

United States and South Vietnamese activities in Cambodia reflect two major claims: (1) that military activities in Cambodia are lawful defensive measures incident to the defense of South Viet-Nam, and (2) that some such activities are lawful defensive measures incident to the defense of Cambodia. Some South Vietnamese activities in rescuing ethnic Vietnamese residing in Cambodia may, in view of the widespread killing of Vietnamese civilians by Cambodians, also justify humanitarian intervention.

1. Activities incident to the defense of South Viet-Nam

For at least two years North Vietnamese and Viet Cong military units have made major use of Cambodian border areas in support of their military operations in South Viet-Nam. According to Robert Shaplen:

> By mid-1969 . . . [Sihanouk] was forced to acknowledge that between forty and fifty thousand Communist troops were spread out over eight or nine Cambodian provinces, about half of the troops in the usually deserted northeastern border areas and the rest farther south, particularly in the mountainous region of the Elephant Range, just northeast of Sihanoukville and across from Vietnam's Mekong Delta.[53]

---

government [Lon Nol government] as legal—if not to the Soviet Union's liking." New York Times, April 25, 1970, at 4, col. 4 (City ed.). See also note 22 above.

[52] New York Times, March 17, 1970, at 14, col. 8 (City ed.).

[53] Shaplen, note 17 above, at 133–134. Shaplen continues: "[Sihanouk] . . . then denounced the Communist incursions and showed less hostility toward the Americans; in fact, he even called upon them to maintain "a presence in Southeast Asia" after the end of the Vietnam war. Secretly, he accepted American intelligence obtained in various ways . . . which enabled him to pinpoint Communist troops and installations, and he used this material in making diplomatic complaints to the Vietcong and to Hanoi. . . ." *Ibid.* at 134. In contrast to the forty to fifty thousand experienced North Vietnamese and Viet Cong troops in Cambodia, the Cambodian Army was inexperienced and poorly equipped and, at the beginning of serious clashes with North

The military activities of these troops in Cambodia have included transportation of combatants and supplies, construction of command, communication, training and supply facilities, and use of Cambodian territory for launching attacks on targets within South Viet-Nam. Such activities have been substantial and continued and are not mere isolated or sporadic occurrences. Prior to the United States and South Vietnamese intercession, the Government of Cambodia was unable effectively to prevent these North Vietnamese and Viet Cong activities in Cambodia. In fact, it is evident from *New York Times* accounts of Cambodian military efforts that, far from the use of the sanctuaries being hindered, the military situation throughout April was steadily deteriorating for the Cambodian Government.[54] By April 20 the Cambodian Army was fighting North Vietnamese within fifteen miles of Phnom Penh, the capital of Cambodia.[55] By the end of the month repeated Cambodian appeals to reconvene the International Supervisory Commission for Cambodia [56] and a Cambodian appeal to the Security Council had gone unanswered, and Peking, Hanoi and Moscow had rejected an Asian nation initiative for talks on preserving Cambodian neutrality.[57] The possibility of effective Cambodian control of North Vietnamese and Viet Cong use of Cambodian territory incident to activities in South Viet-Nam seemed by the end of April to be remote.

On April 30, large-scale United States and South Vietnamese military operations were begun in the border regions of Cambodia. The announced principal purpose of the operations was to clear out the North Vietnamese and Viet Cong border sanctuaries.[58] Although, according to the *Agénce France-Presse*, an initial statement from a Cambodian spokesman was to the effect that "I do not think the Cambodian Government as a neutral government can approve foreign intervention," [59] the over-all position of the Cambodian Government seems to have been one of tacit consent tinged with concern lest favoritism of one side lead to a loss of neutrality. Later statements of the Lon Nol Government have indicated at least non-opposition to the United States and South Vietnamese actions.[60] United States

---

Vietnamese troops, numbered only about 35,000. As such, the Cambodians seemed badly outmatched by the attacking forces. See Staff Report, note 10 above at 10, 9 Int. Legal Materials at 866.

[54] See the New York Times articles, note 25 above.

[55] New York Times, April 21, 1970, at 1, col. 6 (City ed.).

[56] See *ibid.*, March 22, 1970, at 16, col. 4; March 24, 1970, at 3, col. 2; March 26, 1970, at 17, col. 2; April 1, 1970, at 2, col. 4.

[57] See *ibid*, April 27, 1970, at 3, col. 5 (City ed.) (Peking and Hanoi); April 28, 1970, at 1, col. 8 (City ed.) (Moscow).

[58] See President Nixon's address to the Nation, 62 Dept. of State Bulletin 617 (1970).

[59] New York Times, May 1, 1970, at 3, col. 7.

[60] On May 5 the Cambodian Government issued the following statement:

"In his message to the American nation of 30 April, 1970, the President of the United States, Richard Nixon, made public important measures that he has taken to oppose the growing military aggression of North Vietnam on the territory of Laos, Cambodia and South Vietnam. One of these measures concerned aid of the United States of America in the defense of the neutrality of Cambodia, violated by the North Vietnamese.

"The Salvation Government notes with satisfaction that the President of the United States of America has taken into account in his decision the legitimate aspirations of

ground combat operations in Cambodia seem for the most part to have been limited to a self-imposed 21-mile depth along the Cambodian border. Ground combat operations even within this region were announced to be subject to an eight-week deadline for withdrawal of American troops from Cambodia. Consistent with the announced deadline, by July 1 American units had been withdrawn. South Vietnamese operations have been more sweeping and have not been limited by the same deadline.

The principal legal issue presented by these United States and South Vietnamese military operations in Cambodian border regions is the scope of defensive rights under the Charter against belligerent operations in neutral territory. It is well established in customary international law that a belligerent Power may take action to end serious violations of neutral territory by an opposing belligerent when the neutral Power is unable to prevent belligerent use of its territory and when the action is necessary and proportional to lawful defensive objectives.[61] Scholars endorsing this

the Cambodian people, which desires only to live in peace, in its territorial integrity, in its independence and in its strict neutrality. For that reason, the Government of Cambodia wishes to declare that it respects the sentiments of President Richard Nixon in his message of 30 April, 1970 and expresses its gratitude for them.

"It is high time now that other friendly nations understand the extremely grave situation in which Cambodia finds herself and come to the aid of the Cambodia people, victims of armed aggression. The Salvation Government renews on this occasion its appeal for help issued 14 April, 1970, and points out that it will accept all unconditional help from friendly countries in all forms (military, economic and diplomatic)." New York Times, May 5, 1970, at 16, col. 8.

The statement of John R. Stevenson, the Legal Adviser of the Department of State, contains a slightly different version of the declaration of the Cambodian Government of May 5. Perhaps the only difference worth noting is that the Department of State version contains the slightly stronger language "appreciates the views" rather than "respects the sentiments" of President Nixon. Stevenson also points out: "Later statements have indicated even more clearly the Cambodian Government's approval of our actions." See Stevenson, note 11 above, at 766, note 9; 64 A.J.I.L. 935; 9 Int. Legal Materials at 843–844, note 8 (1970).

On May 6 the High Command of the Cambodian Armed Forces released a communiqué that:

"[United States and South Vietnamese forces are] useful not only in fending off dangers for the American and South Vietnamese forces but also to drive these Vietcong and North Vietnamese aggressors from our territory.

"They are indispensable because these occupiers have solidly installed their military aud subversive organizations in the zones that they, the Vietcong and North Vietnamese, are seeking to widen as far as possible in view of their future actions." New York Times, May 6, 1970, at 18, col. 2.

Though, in general, Cambodian Government statements prior to the May 1 incursion indicate a request for military supplies rather than foreign troops, there was some ambiguity in the requests. Thus, on April 15, Lon Nol said:

"The Salvation Government has the duty to inform the nation that in view of the gravity of the present situation, it finds it necessary to accept all unconditional foreign aid, wherever it may come from, for the salvation of the nation." New York Times, April 15, 1970, at 1, col. 3.

[61] One example of this principle in state practice is the German bombardment of Salonika in neutral Greece during World War I after it had been occupied by the Allied Powers. The Greco-German Mixed Arbitral Tribunal held that the occupation of Salonika by the Allies "entitled Germany to take even on Greek soil any acts of war necessary for her defense." See Coenca Brothers v. German State, 7 Recueil des

view include, among others, McDougal and Feliciano,[62] Greenspan,[63] Hyde,[64] Castrén [65] and Lauterpacht.[66] For the most part, the customary

Décisions des Tribunaux Arbitraux Mixtes 683, 687 (1927), discussed in McDougal and Feliciano, note 38 above, at 407, note 49. Other examples are the seizure of the Italian ship, the *Anna Maria*, in the neutral Tunisian port of Sousse by Allied Forces during World War II after a series of warlike acts by German and Italian forces on Tunisian territory, and the British entry into neutral Norwegian territorial waters in 1940 to liberate British prisoners held on the *Altmark*, a German auxiliary vessel which had entered Norwegian territorial waters to evade capture by the Royal Navy.

Professor Waldock after a study of the *Altmark* incident concluded that:

"A breach of the rules of maritime neutrality in favour of one belligerent commonly threatens the security if not the existence of the other belligerent. The breach is thus seldom really capable of being remedied in full by subsequent payment of compensation. Nothing but the immediate cessation of the breach will suffice. Accordingly, where material prejudice to a belligerent's interests will result from its continuance, the principle of self-preservation would appear fully to justify intervention in neutral waters. The disposition in the past of some neutral opinion to condemn any such action out of hand was therefore not consistent with general principles and in any case flowed from a view of the superior merits of neutral status which no longer obtains. *The right of a belligerent to intervene in a proper case to enforce neutrality is now generally recognized. . . .*" (Emphasis added.) Waldock, "The Release of the *Altmark's* Prisoners," 24 Brit. Yr. Bk. Int. Law 216, 235–236 (1947).

For a discussion of the *Anna Maria* incident, see McDougal and Feliciano, note 38 above, at 407, note 49.

The United States has also entered foreign territory on a number of occasions to suppress continuing raids launched from the foreign territory against the United States. The principal examples are General Jackson's incursion into Spanish West Florida in 1818 to check raids by Spanish Indians into American territory after the failure of the Spanish authorities to check the raids, and the incursion by an American military force into Mexico to check cross-border raids by the Mexican bandit Francisco Villa which the Mexican authorities had allowed to continue. See 1 Hyde, International Law Chiefly as Interpreted and Applied by the United States 240–244 (2d rev. ed., 1945).

[62] Thus Professors McDougal and Feliciano point out: "where a nonparticipant is unable or unwilling to prevent one belligerent from carrying on hostile activities within neutral territory, or from utilizing such territory as a 'base of operations,' the opposing belligerent, seriously disadvantaged by neutral failure or weakness, becomes authorized to enter neutral territory and there to take the necessary measures to counter and stop the hostile activities." *Op. cit.*, note 38 above, at 568. See also *ibid.* at 76, 406–407.

[63] Similarly, Greenspan states: "Should a violation of neutral territory occur through the complaisance of the neutral state, or because of its inability, through weakness or otherwise, to resist such violation, then a belligerent which is prejudiced by the violation is entitled to take measures to redress the situation, including, if necessary, attack on enemy forces in the neutral territory." *Op. cit.*, note 36 above, at 538.

[64] Charles Cheney Hyde writes: "The obligation resting upon the belligerent with respect to the neutral is not of unlimited scope. Circumstances may arise when the belligerent is excused from disregarding the prohibition. If a neutral possesses neither the power nor disposition to check warlike activities within its own domain, the belligerent that in consequence is injured or threatened with immediate injury would appear to be free from the normal obligation to refrain from the commission of hostile acts therein." *Op. cit.* note 39 above, at 2337–2338. See also *ibid.* at 2338–2341.

[65] Professor Castrén says: "A belligerent may not violate the territorial integrity of a neutral State merely because the other belligerent side has done so. Nevertheless, the situation is different if the neutral State has not taken countermeasures, or if the enemy, in spite of the efforts of the neutral state, has succeeded in acquiring a

international law of neutrality seems as applicable after the United Nations Charter as before. In fact, the statements by McDougal-Feliciano, Greenspan, and Castrén referred to were all written after the Charter. Although the Charter introduces additional restrictions on the use of force, nothing in the Charter would seem to cut against the strong community policies for isolating and minimizing coercion that are served by the law of neutrality, at least in the absence of a Security Council decision to take measures under Chapter VII of the Charter. The Charter, however, does introduce restrictions on the use of force, which to the extent that they were not already subsumed under customary international law, seem additionally applicable to the appraisal of rights of defense against belligerent operations in neutral territory. Under a restrictive view of such rights under the Charter, the Charter requires that the use of force must be a defensive response to an armed attack and must be necessary and proportional to lawful defensive objectives.[67] As applied to rights of defense against belligerent operations in neutral territory, this would seem to require that the use of force against belligerent operations in neutral territory should be necessary and proportional to lawful defense objectives. Although the consent of the neutral state may be one factor in appraising the exercise of rights of defense against belligerent operations in neutral territory, it does not seem required either by the customary international law of neutrality or by the additional Charter requirements, provided other applicable criteria are met.

Necessity and proportionality are shorthand for community policies restricting coercion to situations where there is no reasonable alternative to the use of force for protection of fundamental values and restricting the responding use of force to that reasonably necessary for defense of the threatened values.[68] In the somewhat overly restrictive language of the famous *Caroline* case, there must be shown a "necessity of self defense, instant, overwhelming, leaving no choice of means and no moment for deliberation."[69] And as McDougal and Feliciano indicate, responding coercion must "be limited in intensity and magnitude to what is reasonably

---

permanent stronghold in its territory, in which case the other belligerent side is entitled to drive off the violator from there. A belligerent is further not bound to tolerate the *continual* passage of enemy military transports through neutral territory." *Op. cit.* note 38 above, at 462–463. See also p. 442.

[66] L. Oppenheim (Lauterpacht ed.), note 38 above, at 695, note 1, 698. Lauterpacht adopts the view that: "Normally, diplomatic representations and a claim for compensation are the proper remedy for any disregard of neutral duties of this nature. However, circumstances may arise in which subsequent redress by the neutral must, in *natura rerum*, be wholly inadequate and in which the aggrieved belligerent must, therefore, be held to be justified in resorting to self-help."

[67] Some scholars would urge a less restrictive interpretation not limiting the right of self-defense to that of Art. 51. See, *e.g.*, D. W. Bowett, Self-Defence in International Law 184–193 (1958); M. McDougal and F. Feliciano, note 38 above, at 233–241 (1961); J. Stone, Aggression and World Order 92–101 (1958).

[68] See M. McDougal and F. Feliciano, note 38 above, at 217–218, 229–244, 259.

[69] Mr. Webster to Mr. Fox, April 24, 1841, 29 British and Foreign State Papers 1129, 1138 (1840–1841).

necessary promptly to secure the permissible objectives of self-defense . . .
by compelling the opposing participant to terminate the condition which
necessitates responsive coercion." [70] As applied to the scope of defense
rights against belligerent operations in neutral territory, necessity and proportionality would also seem to subsume community policies for isolating
conflict by restricting permissible areas of belligerent operations as well as
community policies permitting the use of force reasonably necessary for
the defense of major values. As such, the level of belligerent activity on
neutral territory, the seriousness of the threat posed by that activity for
the protection of major values, the level of control of such activity by the
neutral state, and the scope of the responding coercion are all important
features in assessing the lawfulness of defensive rights against belligerent
operations in neutral territory.

The United States and South Vietnamese military operations aimed at
the North Vietnamese base complexes in Cambodian border areas complied
with these standards. The level of North Vietnamese and Viet Cong
activity on Cambodian territory was substantial and continuing. Activities
in Cambodia included elaborate base camps, repeated use of staging areas
for launching large-scale attacks on targets in South Viet-Nam, and a
major logistics and communications network. At the time of the intercession, the number of North Vietnamese and Viet Cong personnel operating in Cambodia may have been 40,000 or more. In short, the level of
belligerent activity in Cambodia was not occasional, low-level, or merely
threatened, as was alleged in the German invasion of Norway, but was an
existing major adjunct to North Vietnamese belligerent operations within
South Viet-Nam. The existence of such large-scale operations in neighboring Cambodian border regions, which in some areas were as close as 35 or
40 miles from Saigon, posed a continuing threat to the effective defense of
South Viet-Nam. Moreover, even though the security threat had existed
for some time, if North Vietnamese and Viet Cong forces succeeded in
military operations directed against the Cambodian Government—as in
late April it looked as if they might—it could be expected that the security
threat to South Viet-Nam would increase. As to the level of control of
the neutral state, Cambodian officials had for the most part been driven
out of the contested border areas, and by all accounts the Government
forces were sorely pressed to defend Phnom Penh and the provincial capitals, much less to take effective action against the sanctuaries. In this
context, the United States and South Vietnamese response seems of a
scope reasonably related to the prompt achievement of permissible defensive
objectives. The co-ordinated action was aimed at the North Vietnamese
and Viet Cong base areas and was not a punitive reprisal raid directed at
the host state, as has been true of some Israeli raids in reprisal against
guerrilla activities emanating from Jordanian and Lebanese territory.[71]

[70] M. McDougal and F. Feliciano, note 38 above, at 242.

[71] See, generally, Falk, "The Beirut Raid and the International Law of Retaliation,"
63 A.J.I.L. 415 (1969); Blum, "The Beirut Raid and the International Double Standard: A Reply to Professor Richard A. Falk," 64 ibid. 73 (1970). See also the ex-

At least United States forces placed a self-imposed 21-mile geographical limit on the invasion of Cambodian territory and an eight-week time limit for the withdrawal of combat units. It also seems relevant in appraising the action that Cambodia did not formally protest the presence of United States or South Vietnamese troops, as on April 22 it had protested the presence of North Vietnamese and Viet Cong troops. Although there were some Cambodian statements critical of the joint operation, on balance it seems to have received at least the tacit consent of the Cambodian Government. This tacit consent is another factor which makes the case stronger than that for Israeli action against guerrilla complexes in Jordan, Lebanon and Syria, or French action in the Algerian War against Tunisian frontier areas.

Military operations within Cambodia, as within South Viet-Nam, must be carried out in a manner that is consistent with the laws of war. In fact, they should be carried out with a sensitivity which goes beyond the present inadequate protection accorded noncombatants and prisoners of war in internal conflicts. Past military operations within Viet-Nam have demonstrated that this is not always the case and that the military has a better job to do both in implementing existing regulations and in evaluating their adequacy for internal conflicts.[72]

2. Activities incident to the defense of Cambodia

The level of North Vietnamese attacks on Cambodian military forces and the virtual occupation of large areas of Cambodian territory over Cambodian objection seem at least by late April to have constituted an armed attack on Cambodia justifying individual and collective defense under Article 51 of the Charter.[73] To meet this situation, on April 14 Cambodia

---

change of correspondence between Professor Julius Stone and Professor Falk, *ibid.* 161–163.

[72] See, generally, Moore, "The Control of Foreign Intervention in Internal Conflict," 9 Virginia J. Int. Law 205, 309–310 (1969); Rubin, "Legal Aspects of the My Lai Incident," 49 Oregon Law Rev. 260 (1970).

[73] It is firmly established that collective as well as individual defense is permitted pursuant to Art. 51 of the Charter. See, *e.g.*, Kelsen, The Law of the United Nations 791–805 (1950); McDougal and Feliciano, Law and Minimum World Public Order 244–253 (1961); Stone, Legal Controls of International Conflict 245 (1959). In fact, Art. 51 was drafted largely to reassure the Latin American delegates that collective defense pursuant to regional arrangements would not be disturbed. See, generally, Jessup, A Modern Law of Nations 165 (1948); McDougal and Feliciano, *op. cit.* above, at 235; Russell and Muther, A History of the United Nations Charter 688–712 (1958); Kunz "Individual and Collective Self-Defense in Article 51 of the Charter of the United Nations," 41 A.J.I.L. 872 (1947). The right of collective defense is also confirmed by a host of defense agreements representing a diversity of ideological groupings and including NATO, SEATO, the Rio Pact, the Warsaw Pact, and the Arab League.

One of the few scholars disagreeing with this almost universally accepted interpretation of Art. 51 has been Dr. Bowett. He argues that: "[T]he situation which the Charter envisages by the term is . . . a situation in which each participating state bases its participation in collective action on its own right of self-defence. It does not, therefore, generally extend the right of self-defence to any state which desires

made an appeal to the United States and other nations for arms and military supplies.[74]   On April 20 Cambodia further requested assistance in the form of ethnic Cambodian mercenaries fighting in South Viet-Nam, and on April 22 Cambodia complained to the Security Council seeking assistance from all countries in fighting North Vietnamese and Viet Cong forces. Subsequent to the joint United States-South Vietnamese intercession in Cambodia on April 30, the Cambodian Government negotiated military aid agreements with Thailand[75] and South Viet-Nam.[76]   The agreement with South Viet-Nam provides that South Vietnamese military forces "which had come with the agreement of the Cambodian Government to help Cambodian troops to drive out the Vietcong and North Vietnamese forces, will withdraw from Cambodia when their task is completed."   Although prior to the April 30th intercession Cambodia had not requested United States combat troops to assist in meeting the North Vietnamese and Viet Cong attack, at least not openly, the worsening military position of the Cambodian forces seemed to have been one motivating factor in the United States action against the border sanctuaries.   Thus, in his April 30th address to the nation President Nixon called attention to the North Vietnamese attacks on Cambodian forces and the Cambodian request to the United States and other nations for assistance.   The general United States de-emphasis of objectives concerning the defense of Cambodia seemed to result primarily from a desire to disturb the neutrality of Cambodia as little as possible by the action and to re-emphasize the Nixon doctrine that the United States would provide assistance but not American combat forces for the long-range defense of Cambodia.   In a statement on May 5 in which the Lon Nol Government at least tacitly accepted the United States action, Lon Nol seemed to take an intermediate view of the objectives of the United States action.   The statement referred to the action as "aid . . . in the defense of the neutrality of Cambodia violated by the North Vietnamese." It also said that "the Government of Cambodia wishes to declare that it respects the sentiments of President Nixon in his message of 30 April, 1970 and expresses its gratitude for them."[77]

In view of the magnitude of the North Vietnamese and Viet Cong attacks on Cambodian forces and the Cambodian acceptance of the April 30th intercession, it would seem that the United States and South Vietnamese military actions in Cambodia could also be characterized as lawful measures of collective defense of Cambodia.

---

to associate itself in the defence of a state acting in self-defence."   Self-Defence in International Law 216 (1958).   Not only does Bowett's interpretation conflict with the history of Art. 51, the almost universal acceptance of the claim in state practice, and the writings of most international law scholars, but it would seem poor policy as well.   See the discussion of his position in McDougal and Feliciano, *op. cit.* above, at 247–253.

[74] New York Times, April 23, 1970, at 1, col. 8, and 5, col. 3 (City ed.).

[75] See *ibid.*, June 2, 1970, at 1, col. 5 (City ed.); June 3, 1970, at 1, col. 5 (City ed.).

[76] See *ibid.*, May 28, 1970, at 1, col. 2 (City ed.).

[77] The full statement of May 5 is set out in note 60 above.

The minimal involvement of native Cambodians on the side of the North Vietnamese forces suggests that a characterization of the Cambodian conflict as "civil strife" is less appropriate than a characterization as "external armed attack." Even if the "civil strife" characterization were accepted, however, assistance to the Lon Nol Government to offset the prior massive foreign intervention on behalf of insurgent forces (the Sihanouk government-in-exile?) would, to the extent that the Lon Nol Government is the widely recognized Government of Cambodia, be lawful.

3. Activities incident to the rescue of ethnic Vietnamese in Cambodia

Because of the killings of ethnic Vietnamese civilians residing in Cambodia, some of the South Vietnamese military operations in Cambodia aimed at evacuating ethnic Vietnamese refugees may have constituted permissible humanitarian intervention. The justification for humanitarian intervention could only extend to operations principally concerned with evacuating refugees rather than those aimed at affecting authority structures in Cambodia. Since South Vietnamese military actions seem to be defensible on broader grounds, there seems little point in focusing on this possible claim other than to reassert that the killings of ethnic Vietnamese in Cambodia is another example of the need for an unambiguous right of humanitarian intervention.[78]

4. A closer look at context

When the United States and South Viet-Nam interceded in Cambodia on April 30, the factual basis seemed to be present for both the exercise of collective defense in defense of Cambodia and the exercise of defensive rights aimed at belligerent activities in a neutral state. Not surprisingly, objectives relating both to the defense of Cambodia and the destruction of North Vietnamese base areas in Cambodia seemed to have influenced the operation. In fact, Cambodian defense and the possibility of intensified belligerent activities directed against South Viet-Nam are so interrelated that it seems probable that the precarious military position of the Cambodian Government was a principal triggering event of the operation. Prior to the events of March, the Sihanouk Government had exercised some restraint on North Vietnamese and Viet Cong activities in Cambodia. The fall of Sihanouk followed by a North Vietnamese-Viet Cong armed attack on the Lon Nol Government threatened to lead to unrestrained North Vietnamese and Viet Cong belligerent use of Cambodian territory. This North Vietnamese armed attack on Cambodia, as well as North Vietnamese use of Cambodian territory as a base for belligerent operations, sets apart the Cambodian case as a much stronger case for action directed against belligerent operations in a third state than prior instances, such as the *Caroline* affair between Britain and the United States, French action against the Tunisian frontier village of Sakiet Sidi Youssef during the

[78] See, generally, Lillich, "Forcible Self-Help by States to Protect Human Rights," 53 Iowa Law Rev. 325 (1967); Moore, note 72 above, at 261–264.

Algerian War,[79] or even Israeli raids against guerrilla bases in Jordan, Lebanon and Syria (which should be distinguished from Israeli reprisal raids directed against the Jordanian and Lebanese Governments.)

Other distinctions between the Cambodian case and these or other instances of actions directed against belligerent operations in a third state may also be relevant to legal appraisal. Such distinctions include the presence or absence of consent of the host state, the lawfulness of the defensive effort (the anti-colonial context of the Algerian War makes the French effort suspect), the scope and intensity of belligerent activities in the host state, and the proportionality of the coercive response.[80] It is instructive in this regard to compare the Cambodian situation with that of the *Caroline* affair, which spawned the most frequently quoted test of necessity. The *Caroline* affair took place during the Canadian rebellion of 1838. As William Edward Hall describes it in his treatise:

> A body of insurgents collected to the number of several hundreds in American territory, and after obtaining small arms and twelve guns by force from American arsenals, seized an island at Niagara within the American frontier, from which shots were fired into Canada, and where preparations were made to cross into British territory by means of a steamer called the Caroline. To prevent the crossing from being effected, the Caroline was boarded by an English force while at her moorings within American waters, and was sent adrift down the falls of Niagara.[81]

British actions in the *Caroline* case were not in support of the defense of the United States against a major external armed attack, did not take place with the tacit consent of the United States Government, and were directed against sporadic actions of "several hundreds" of insurgents rather than the long-continued belligerent activities of as many as 40,000 combat troops of a foreign nation, all features present in the Cambodian case. Nevertheless, Professor Hall goes on to suggest that even the English

[79] See M. Clark, Algeria in Turmoil—The Rebellion: Its Causes, Its Effects, Its Future 363–366 (1960).

[80] The comparison suggested by Professor Richard A. Falk between the United States and South Vietnamese action against the North Vietnamese and Viet Cong base areas in Cambodia and a hypothetical Soviet air strike against U. S. base areas in Japan, South Korea, Thailand, Okinawa, and Guam is only superficially helpful. Among other differences, the governments of Japan, South Korea, Thailand, Okinawa and Guam have not requested assistance from the Soviet Union and would be unlikely to consent to Soviet air strikes on their territory; those host governments have not appealed to the U.N. Security Council for assistance in defense against an armed attack from U. S. forces; there are no treaty obligations prohibiting the United States and its host governments from establishing U. S. military bases on their territory; the United States utilizes the base areas with the consent of the host governments; and the strategic posture of the geographically remote U. S. base areas would make a Soviet air strike a far more provocative action than the Cambodian incursion. Perhaps more important, Professor Falk's seemingly neutral comparison disregards the basic Charter distinction between force used in extension of national values and force used in defense against an armed attack. There is no escape from the fundamental obligation to assess the lawfulness of the contending factions by this basic Charter principle.

[81] W. E. Hall, A Treatise on International Law 246 (2d ed., 1884).

response in the *Caroline* case met the "somewhat too emphatic language" of the *Caroline* test of necessity.[82] In assessing the lawfulness of all of these instances of action directed against belligerent activities emanating from the territory of a third state, a detailed examination of necessity and proportionality in context would seem the most reliable guide. The context of the Cambodian case, particularly the dual basis for the exercise of defensive rights in Cambodia, would seem a strong basis for lawfulness.[83]

5. Additional obligations under the United Nations Charter

Measures taken by Members in the exercise of defensive rights must, pursuant to Article 51, be "immediately reported to the Security Council. . . ." The Cambodian operation with South Viet-Nam was reported by the United States to the Security Council on May 5.[84] This report, at least in substance if not in speed, complied with the Charter requirement. The Charter does not require that defensive action taken pursuant to Article 51 first be submitted to the Security Council for approval.[85] Nevertheless, for a number of reasons, it would have seemed desirable to have raised the North Vietnamese and Viet Cong attacks on Cambodia in the Security Council. Perhaps the most important reason is that every time the Security Council is shunted aside and not encouraged to assume responsibility for dealing with a threat to the peace, the erosion of United Nations utility and authority continues. From a *realpolitik* perspective, it seems unlikely that in the Cold War context of the Cambodian situation the Security Council would have been able to take effective action to preserve the neutrality of Cambodia. But the Security Council might have been effectively used as a forum to expose the blatant North Vietnamese and Viet Cong

[82] *Ibid.* at 246–247. Professor Hyde also writes that the facts of the *Caroline* case "seem to have satisfied" the *Caroline* test of necessity. See 1 Hyde, note 61 above, at 239–240.

[83] For statements critical of the lawfulness of the Cambodian intercession, see Edwards, "The Cambodian Invasion Violates International Law," Cong. Rec. E4551 May 21, 1970); Brief of New York University Law Students, Cong. Rec. E4443 (May 19, 1970). The emphasis in the N.Y.U. law students' brief that North Vietnamese and Viet Cong activities did not constitute an "armed attack" within the meaning of Art. 51 of the U.N. Charter is wholly unpersuasive. Though fact selection is an inevitable task in appraising complex public order disputes, the mind boggles at a fact-selection process which virtually ignores the continuing North Vietnamese and Viet Cong attacks from the Cambodian sanctuaries on U. S. and South Vietnamese forces and the massive North Vietnamese and Viet Cong military attack on Cambodia.

[84] Letter from the U. S. Permanent Representative to the President of the Security Council, May 5, 1970. U.N. Doc. S/9781 (1970); 62 Dept. of State Bulletin 652 (1970); 64 A.J.I.L. 932; 9 Int. Legal Materials 838 (1970).

[85] See Bowett, Self-Defence in International Law 193, 195 (1958); Brierly, The Law of Nations 319, 320 (5th ed., 1955); Jessup, A Modern Law of Nations 164–165, 202 (1948); Kelsen, The Law of the United Nations 800, 804, 804, note 5 (1964); *idem,* "Collective Security under International Law," 49 Int. Legal Studies 61–62 (1956); "Collective Security and Collective Self-Defense under the Charter of the United Nations," 42 A.J.I.L. 783, 791–795 (1948); McDougal and F. Feliciano, Law and Minimum World Public Order 218–219 (1961); Stone, Legal Controls of International Conflict 244 (1954); Thomas and Thomas, Non-Intervention 171 (1956).

activities in Cambodia, much as it was used during the *Pueblo* crisis. The importance of such appeals to authority, both in terms of international and domestic audiences, should not be underestimated. Possible drawbacks from raising the Cambodian issue in the Security Council, such as the possibility of a challenge to the credentials of the Lon Nol Government, the possibility of forcing a more militant Soviet stand, or the possibility of forcing a confrontation on the Indochina War which would be detrimental to the United Nations are real, and may have been taken into account in the decision (or non-decision) not to go to the Security Council. In the context of events in Cambodia during April, however, it is questionable whether they outweigh the costs involved in not objecting in the Security Council to the stepped-up North Vietnamese-Viet Cong activities in Cambodia.

6. Obligations under the SEATO Treaty

It is probably fair to say that the initial understanding of the signatories to the Southeast Asia Collective Defense Treaty was that in the event of a request from the Cambodian Government for assistance to meet a North Vietnamese armed attack, each signatory would "act to meet the common danger in accordance with its constitutional processes." Article IV, paragraph 1, of the treaty provides:

> Each Party recognizes that aggression by means of armed attack in the treaty area against any of the Parties or against any State or territory which the Parties by unanimous agreement may hereafter designate, would endanger its own peace and safety, and agrees that it will in that event act to meet the common danger in accordance with its constitutional processes. Measures taken under this paragraph shall be immediately reported to the Security Council of the United Nations.[86]

By a Protocol to the SEATO Treaty concluded the same day, Cambodia was unanimously designated by the parties as a protocol state "for the purposes of Article IV of the Treaty." [87] Cambodia did not sign the SEATO Treaty or the Protocol, however, and under Sihanouk Cambodia sought to withdraw from SEATO protection as a protocol state.[88] The action of Sihanouk and the general political collapse of SEATO make it pointless to consider whether the United States and other signatories were "obligated" under the terms of Article IV of the SEATO Treaty to respond to a Cambodian request for assistance. Article IV, paragraph 3, of the treaty, however, may contain some lingering relevance for the Cambodian incursion. It provides:

> It is understood that no action on the territory of any State designated by unanimous agreement under paragraph 1 of this Article or on any

[86] Southeast Asia Collective Defense Treaty, signed at Manila, Sept. 8, 1954, 6 U. S. Treaties 81, T.I.A.S., No. 3170; 60 A.J.I.L. 646 (1966).

[87] Protocol to the Southeast Asia Collective Defense Treaty, signed at Manila, Sept. 8, 1954, *loc. cit.* above.

[88] See New York Times, April 30, 1965, at 2, col. 6.

territory so designated shall be taken except at the invitation or with the consent of the government concerned.

The purpose of paragraph 3 seemed to be to reassure the protocol states, none of which were signatories to the SEATO Treaty. that action pursuant to Article IV would not be taken against their will. Quite apart from the issue of whether the treaty has any continuing validity, it is unlikely that paragraph 3 was intended to alter the existing international law of neutral rights and duties, by which a belligerent Power may take action to end serious violations of neutral territory by an opposing belligerent when the neutral Power is unable to prevent belligerent use of its territory —whether or not the neutral consents to the action. Since the action against the sanctuaries was largely based on the international law of neutral rights and duties and did not invoke the collective defense provisions of the SEATO Treaty, paragraph 3 would seem to have only minimal relevance. In any event, the subsequent consent of the Cambodian Government makes the issue largely moot. The broad language of paragraph 3, however, is an additional reason suggesting that it would have been preferable to secure the unambiguous prior consent of the Cambodian Government to the United States and South Vietnamese actions.

II. THE CONSTITUTIONAL ISSUES

President Nixon's decision to intercede in Cambodia and Congressional reactions to it present two principal Constitutional issues. First, the Constitutional authority for the President's decision to intercede in Cambodia and, second, the Constitutional authority for a range of proposed Congressional restraints on military operations in Indochina. For the most part, discussion of these issues has been subject to a degree of confusion even greater than that attributable to the vagueness of the Constitutional structure or polemical argument about the Indochina War. A principal cause of the additional confusion seems to be the failure to focus on the full range of Constitutional issues in the use of the armed forces abroad. These principal issues include:

A. *The Initial Commitment of the Armed Forces to Combat Abroad*

1. What authority does the President have, acting on his own, to commit the armed forces to combat abroad?
2. When Congressional authorization is necessary, what form should it take?
3. What authority does Congress have to limit Presidential authority to commit the armed forces to combat abroad?

B. *The Conduct of Hostilities*

1. What authority does the President have, acting on his own, to make command decisions incident to the conduct of a Constitutionally authorized conflict?
2. What authority does Congress have to limit command options incident to the conduct of a Constitutionally authorized conflict?

C. *The Termination of Hostilities*

1. What authority does the President have, acting on his own, to terminate or negotiate an end to hostilities?
2. What authority does Congress have to require termination of hostilities?
3. When Congress terminates hostilities, what form should the termination take?

Elsewhere I have sought to shed modest light on each of these issues.[89] At practice require Congressional authorization of major initial commitments to combat abroad, and accord Congress the authority to terminate hostilities abroad. On the other hand, the President seems to have some independent authority initially to commit the armed forces to "minor" hostilities abroad. Though the parameters of this independent authority are unclear, Constitutional history and policy support a test of "the commitment of regular combat units to sustained hostilities" as the threshold for requiring Congressional authorization. The President also has unquestioned authority as Commander-in-Chief to make command decisions incident to the conduct of a Constitutionally authorized conflict and any Congressional authority to limit such command options is subject to a severe burden of Constitutional justification. Moreover, though Congressional authorization or termination of conflict does not require any particular formality such as a formal declaration of war, Congressional action should be based on careful analysis of the context giving rise to authorization or termination and should clearly advert to the scope of the authority granted or the Congressional intent to terminate hostilities. With this necessarily simplified overview of the Congressional and Presidential rôles,[90] resolution of the Constitutional issues surrounding the Cambodian incursion depends on characterization of those issues in the context of the full range of Con-

[89] See Moore, "The Constitution and the Use of the Armed Forces Abroad," Testimony before the Subcommittee on National Security Policy and Scientific Developments of the House Committee on Foreign Affairs, June 25, 1970; *idem*, "The National Executive and the Use of the Armed Forces Abroad," 21 Naval War College Review 28 (1969).

the risk of some oversimplification, in general, Constitutional structure and

[90] See, generally, on the merits of the war power controversy, Kurland, "The Impotence of Reticence," 1968 Duke Law J. 619; Moore, "The Constitution and the Use of the Armed Forces Abroad"; "The National Executive and the Use of the Armed Forces Abroad," *loc. cit.* above; Reveley, "Presidential War-Making: Constitutional Prerogative or Usurpation?" 55 Virginia Law Rev. 1243 (1969); Velvel, "The War in Viet Nam: Unconstitutional, Justiciable and Jurisdictionally Attackable," 16 Kansas Law Rev. 449 (1968); Francis D. Wormuth, "The Vietnam War: The President v. the Constitution" (An Occasional Paper of the Center for the Study of Democratic Institutions, 1968); Note, "Congress, The President, and the Power to Commit Forces to Combat," 81 Harvard Law Rev. 1771 (1968). See also the memoranda prepared by Yale law students and professors: "Indochina: The Constitutional Crisis," 116 Cong. Rec. (No. 76, May 13, 1970), and "Indochina: The Constitutional Crisis—Part II," 116 Cong. Rec. (No. 82, May 21, 1970); and the proceedings of the Symposium on "The Constitution and the Use of Military Force Abroad" held at the University of Virginia Feb. 28–March 1, 1969, reprinted in 10 Virginia Journal Int. Law 32 (1969).

stitutional issues and a more detailed look at the Constitutional authority on each relevant issue.

A. *The Constitutional Authority for the President's Decision to Intercede in Cambodia*

The Constitution provides that "the President shall be Commander-in-Chief of the Army and Navy of the United States. . . ." Hamilton wrote in *The Federalist* that this provision means that the President has "the supreme command and direction of the military and naval forces. . . ."[91] It seems never to have been questioned that this power includes broad authority to make strategic and tactical decisions incident to the conduct of a Constitutionally authorized conflict. Constitutional practice includes a range of Presidential command decisions unquestionably taken on Presidential authority. Examples include President Roosevelt's decision in World War II to give priority to the Atlantic rather than the Pacific theater, Roosevelt's decisions committing American forces to landings in French North Africa (at the time neutral territory), Italy, and the Pacific Islands, and President Truman's decision to use the atomic bomb against Japan.

The limited nature of the Cambodian action both geographically and temporally and its close relation to the Vietnamization effort in support of American withdrawal strongly suggest that the action is most appropriately characterized as a command decision incident to the conduct of the Viet-Nam War. For the most part the actions of United States military forces were directed against North Vietnamese and Viet Cong sanctuaries in Cambodian border regions rather than in direct support of the Cambodian Government. The cautious United States response to Cambodian Government requests for assistance during April also suggests that the action was aimed largely at what was perceived as an increased threat to the United States position in Viet-Nam, even though the increased threat was in large measure attributable to fear of the effects of a collapse of the Cambodian Government in the face of increased North Vietnamese attacks. The Sihanouk Government had exerted some restraint on North Vietnamese and Viet Cong belligerent activities in Cambodia and the Lon Nol Government was vigorously but precariously seeking to reassert the neutrality of Cambodia. Had the Cambodian Government fallen to one controlled by the North Vietnamese, it seemed likely that belligerent activities in Cambodia in support of the struggle in South Viet-Nam would increase, perhaps endangering the program of phased United States withdrawal which was a cornerstone of President Nixon's policy. There is reasonable basis for saying, then, that even a decision to commit United States forces in direct support of the Lon Nol Government would have been under the circumstances a command decision incident to the Viet-Nam War. In any event, the more limited decision to intercede against the border base areas seems most appropriately characterized as a command decision incident to the

[91] The Federalist, Number 69, at 463 (Heritage Press, 1945).

conduct of the Viet-Nam War. As such, there is little doubt that President Nixon was acting within his Constitutional authority as Commander-in-Chief.

Although the Cambodian incursion seems more accurately characterized as a decision concerning the conduct of hostilities incident to the Viet-Nam War rather than an initial commitment to new hostilities, the Southeast Asia Resolution lends substantial support to Presidential authority. The Southeast Asia Resolution, which is the principal Constitutional authorization for the Viet-Nam War, provides that:

> [Sec. 1. . . .] Congress approves and supports the determination of the President, as Commander in Chief, to take all necessary measures to repel any armed attack against the forces of the United States and to prevent further aggression. . . .
>
> Sec. 2. . . . the United States is, therefore, prepared, as the President determines, to take all necessary steps, including the use of armed force, to assist any member or protocol state of the Southeast Asia Collective Defense Treaty requesting assistance in defense of its freedom.[92]

In view of the continued use of Cambodian border sanctuaries in support of armed attacks launched against South Vietnamese and United States forces, the President would seem to have Congressional authorization under Section 1 of the Southeast Asia Resolution for limited actions directed against the sanctuaries. Apparently the sanctuaries have served as staging areas for the 1968 Tet offensive, the May, 1968, offensive and the post-Tet 1969 offensive, among others, and these continued armed attacks on United States forces would seem to qualify under Section 1 of the resolution. It should be emphasized that the issue is not merely one of anticipated attacks from the sanctuaries or a remote threat of attack but a continuing pattern of armed attack on United States and South Vietnamese forces substantially aided by the existence of the sanctuaries.

Since Cambodia, like Viet-Nam, is a protocol state of SEATO, the language of Section 2 of the resolution would, in the event of a request for assistance from Cambodia, also seem to authorize a Presidential decision to take military action necessary to the defense of Cambodia. There is some evidence from its legislative history that the resolution was understood at the time of its passage to include action in defense of Cambodia. Thus, in his address to Congress on August 5, 1964, requesting the Southeast Asia Resolution, President Johnson specifically asked for a resolution broad enough to "assist nations covered by the SEATO treaty." [93] In an exchange between Senators Cooper and Fulbright on the floor of the Senate during the discussion of the resolution it was said:

> Mr. Cooper. . . . Does the Senator consider that in enacting this resolution we are satisfying that requirement [the Constitutional processes requirement] of Article IV of the Southeast Asia Collective De-

[92] 78 Stat. 384 (Approved Aug. 10, 1964).

[93] President's Message to Congress, Aug. 5, 1964, in Background Information Relating to Southeast Asia and Vietnam, Senate Committee on Foreign Relations 122, at 124 (Rev. ed., Comm. Print, June 16, 1965).

fense Treaty? In other words, are we now giving the President advance authority to take whatever action he may deem necessary respecting South Vietnam and its defense, *or with respect to the defense of any other country included in the treaty?* [Emphasis added.]

Mr. Fulbright. I think that is correct.

Mr. Cooper. Then, looking ahead, if the President decided that it was necessary to use such force as could lead into war, we will give that authority by this resolution?

Mr. Fulbright. That is the way I would interpret it. If a situation later developed in which we thought the approval should be withdrawn, it could be withdrawn by concurrent resolution.[94]

Moreover, the resolution is entitled the "Southeast Asia Resolution," not the "Viet-Nam Resolution." As such, Section 2 of the resolution would seem to lend substantial authority to President Nixon's decisions to provide military support requested by the Cambodian Government, such as the military equipment or Khmer mercenary forces requested by the Cambodian Government in April. And though the action against the sanctuaries was apparently not requested in advance, subsequent Cambodian Government approval of the action and further Cambodian requests for assistance raise the possibility that this action may also be brought within the authority of Section 2 of the resolution.

The Southeast Asia Resolution has been criticized as hurriedly rushed through Congress and as predicated on an exaggerated attack on American destroyers in the Gulf of Tonkin.[95] Although the abbreviated debate preceding the passage of the resolution was a sorry exercise of Congressional responsibility, the resolution is nevertheless a valid exercise of the Congressional war power.[96] It is also relevant in considering Congressional involvement that an amendment introduced by Senator Wayne Morse in March, 1966, to repeal the resolution was tabled in the Senate by a vote of 92 to 5.[97] In fact, according to the *New York Times*, a resolution to reaffirm it would have easily passed.[98] Prior to the Cambodian decision a new effort to repeal the resolution had begun, but at the time of the action the resolution to repeal had cleared only the Senate Foreign Relations Committee.[99]

In summary, quite apart from whatever independent authority the

[94] 110 Cong. Rec. 18409–18410 (1964).

[95] See "The Gulf of Tonkin, The 1964 Incidents," Hearings before the Senate Committee on Foreign Relations, 90th Cong., 2d Sess. (Comm. Print, Feb. 20, 1968), and Part II, Supplementary Documents (Comm. Print, Dec. 16, 1968). There seems to be no doubt that the first attack on Aug. 2 occurred.

[96] For a review of the Congressional debates on the Southeast Asia Resolution and the Constitutional issues concerning authority for the Viet-Nam War, see Moore and Underwood, "The Lawfulness of United States Assistance to the Republic of Vietnam," 112 Cong. Rec. 14943, 14960–14967, 14983–14989 (daily ed., July 14, 1966).

[97] 112 Cong. Rec. 4226 (daily ed., March 1, 1966).

[98] New York Times, March 2, 1966, at 1, col. 8 (City ed.).

[99] See "Fulbright Panel Votes to Repeal Tonkin Measure," New York Times, April 11, 1970, at 1, col. 5 (City ed.).

President may have initially to commit the armed forces to combat abroad,[100] the President had Constitutional authority for the actions directed against the sanctuaries under his power as Commander-in-Chief to take command decisions incident to a conflict in progress and under Section 1 of the Southeast Asia Resolution to repel armed attacks against United States forces. Under Section 2 of the resolution and possibly under his power as Commander-in-Chief to take command decisions incident to a conflict, the President also had Constitutional authority to provide military assistance at the request of the Cambodian Government.

B. *The Constitutional Authority for Congressional Restraints on Military Operations in Indochina*

The decision to intercede in Cambodia has given rise to or accelerated a number of Congressional initiatives intended to confine belligerent operations to Viet-Nam or to require termination of the American combat presence after a particular date.[101]   These initiatives raise issues concerning the authority of Congress to terminate hostilities, the form of Congressional termination of hostilities, and the authority of Congress to limit Presidential command options incident to the conduct of a Constitutionally authorized conflict.

The Constitution does not specifically address the issue of Congressional authority to terminate hostilities. Moreover, apparently there is no instance in the Constitutional history of the United States in which Congress has terminated a war over the objection of the President. Nevertheless, it seems a fair inference from the power to declare war, the power to raise and maintain an Army and a Navy, and the power to authorize appropriations, as well as the absence of any evident Constitutional scheme for entrusting the power to terminate hostilities exclusively to the President, that Congress has authority to terminate hostilities abroad. Congress is also the most broadly based and democratically responsive branch of government, and unless there is a strong functional reason such as secrecy, speed, or decisiveness which would suggest entrusting the power exclusively to the President, which seems not to be the case, Congress probably ought

---

[100] The President has only limited power initially to commit the armed forces to combat abroad. Nevertheless that power probably includes the power to take at least limited action in defense against attacks made on U. S. military forces stationed abroad and the power to provide military assistance short of the commitment of regular combat units to sustained hostilities. Although the Cambodian incursion seems more appropriately characterized as a decision relating to the conduct of hostilities rather than initial commitment, even if it were an initial commitment decision, the President probably has independent Constitutional authority to take limited action to defend U. S. forces stationed in South Viet-Nam and to provide low-level military assistance to the Cambodian Government. See Moore, note 89 above.

[101] See, *e.g.*, the resolutions appended to the "Report on the Termination of the Southeast Asia Resolution," the Senate Foreign Relations Committee, Report No. 91-872 (Comm. Print, May 15, 1970); S. 3964 (introduced by Senators Dole and Javits on June 15, 1970); H. J. Res. 1151 (introduced by Representative Findley on March 26, 1970); H. R. 17598 (introduced by Representative Fascell).

to be able to terminate as well as commence hostilities.[102] The complete absence of instances in which Congress has terminated hostilities against the wishes of the President despite numerous highly unpopular conflicts, however, suggests that the exercise of a Congressional policy for termination of hostilities which conflicts with a Presidential policy should be adopted only with the greatest reluctance. The President is the chief representative of the Nation for negotiation of an end to hostilities, has an almost exclusive responsibility to make command decisions concerning the conduct of hostilities, and in many instances has better information concerning the over-all strategic situation than individual members of Congress. As such, Congress should be particularly cautious in undercutting a Presidential policy.

Should Congress choose to terminate hostilities, termination, like authorization, should clearly advert to the context and meaning of the Congressional action. Just as the Southeast Asia Resolution has been criticized as being hurried through Congress without adequate debate, so, too, Congressional action seeking to terminate hostilities in Indochina should be based on adequate debate and should be clearly understood as to meaning and scope. Congressional termination must also allow adequate protection of United States forces during withdrawal from hostilities, as fairly appraised under all the circumstances. Though termination would not seem to require any particular magic formula, it is unclear whether it would have to be in the form of a bill vetoable by the President or whether a concurrent resolution of Congress would be sufficient. The language of Section 3 of the Southeast Asia Resolution indicating that the resolution can be terminated "by concurrent resolution of the Congress' suggests that, at least with respect to the Indochina conflict, a concurrent resolution would be adequate.

The third issue presented by the Congressional initiatives surrounding the Cambodian crisis is the authority of Congress to limit Presidential command options incident to a war. The Constitution makes the President Commander-in-Chief. There is no parallel in the powers entrusted to Congress. Professors Egger and Harris in their study of *The President and Congress* conclude that this means that "the President has the . . . exclusive power . . . of exercising military command in time of peace and in time of war; this command power, moreover, involves as an absolute minimum, upon which the Congress is powerless to encroach, the direction of military forces in combat. . . ." [103] Corwin points out that "Congress has never adopted any legislation that would seriously cramp the style of a President attempting to break the resistance of an enemy or seeking

---

[102] See the "Legal Memorandum on the Constitutionality of the Amendment to End the War," prepared under the supervision of Professors Abram Chayes and Frank Michelman and introduced in the record of the Hearings before the Subcommittee on National Security Policy and Scientific Developments of the House Committee on Foreign Affairs, June 25, 1970.

[103] R. Egger and J. Harris, The President and Congress 35 (1963). See also 2 Watson, The Constitution 913–917 (1910).

to assure the safety of the national forces."[104]   In fact, Roland Young reports that during World War II "No method was worked out by which Congress as a whole was informed on the developments of the war, and, in the aggregate, members of Congress had no more intimate knowledge of how the war was going than the average reader of a metropolitan news-paper."[105]   In *Ex Parte Milligan*, a famous case arising out of the Civil War, Chief Justice Chase pointed out that Congressional authority did not extend to interference with command decisions.   According to the Chief Justice, Congressional authority

> necessarily extends to all legislation essential to the prosecution of war with vigor and success, except such as interferes with the com-mand of the forces and the conduct of campaigns.   That power and duty belong to the President as commander-in-chief.[106]

In addition to the textual grant of power to the President as Com-mander-in-Chief and the uninterrupted Constitutional practice supporting an exclusively Presidential command power, there are strong policy reasons inherent in the nature of Congress and the Presidency that support the exclusive nature of the Presidential power.   Tactical decisions incident to a conflict are frequently decisions in which speed, secrecy, superior sources of information and military expertise are at a premium.   In general the Presidency seems better suited to such decisions than Congress.[107]   To give one example, Roland Young reports that the one attempt at a secret session of the Senate during World War II resulted in a garbled version of the session being leaked to the press.[108]   More recently, the report on Cambodia prepared by the Staff of the Senate Foreign Relations Com-mittee dramatically details the difficulties encountered by an important Congressional committee in seeking to inform itself as to the conduct of the war.[109]   Perhaps for these reasons Hamilton wrote in *The Federalist*: "Of all the cases or concerns of government, the direction of war most

---

[104] E. M. Corwin, The President: Office and Powers 1787–1957, p. 259 (1957).

[105] R. Young, Congressional Politics in the Second World War 145 (1956).

[106] 71 U. S. (4 Wall.) 2 at 139 (1866) (Opinion of the Chief Justice and Justices Wayne, Swayne, and Miller).   See also Swain *v.* United States, 28 Ct. Cl. 173, 221 (1893), aff'd, Swain *v.* United States, 165 U. S. 553 (1897).

[107] Professor Watson points out that the provision making the President Com-mander-in-Chief may have resulted from the difficulties Washington experienced with the Continental Congress in the conduct of hostilities during the War for Independence. He writes: "[D]uring the Revolution Washington experienced great trouble and embar-rassment resulting from the failure of Congress to support him with firmness and dis-patch.   There was a want of directness in the management of affairs during that period which was attributable to the absence of centralized authority to command.   The mem-bers of the Convention knew this and probably thought they could prevent its recur-rence by making the President Commander-in-Chief of the Army and Navy."   D. Watson, note 103 above, at 912.

[108] R. Young, note 105 above, at 145.

[109] See the Staff Report, "Cambodia: May 1970," prepared for the Senate Com-mittee on Foreign Relations, 91st Cong., 2d Sess. (Comm. Print, June 7, 1970), re-printed in 9 Int. Legal Materials 858 (1970).

peculiarly demands those qualities which distinguish the exercise of power by a single hand." [110]

Despite the strong case for denying Congressional authority to limit Presidential command options incident to a Constitutionally authorized conflict, it seems unwise to take an absolutist position. That the reasons for exclusive Presidential authority are strong does not necessarily mean that all Congressional decisions limiting command options would be unconstitutional in an era of limited war. One example of a permissible limitation might be a Congressional prohibition on the use of internationally prohibited chemical or biological weapons. Though reasons suggesting Executive authority are still relevant to such decisions, the profound effects for international relations and the grave risk of escalation and unnecessary suffering suggest a strong Congressional competence in such decisions. In any event, the command of the armed forces during a Constitutionally authorized conflict is a core area of Presidential authority and apparently has never been limited by Congressional action. Congressional limitation of such command options would usually be most unwise and would in every case bear a heavy burden of Constitutional justification. That limitations on Presidential command authority are pursued indirectly by limitations on appropriations would not seem significantly to alter Congressional power. Appropriations measures, like any other Congressional measures, must conform to the limits of the Constitution.

Applying these Constitutional principles to the proposed legislation inspired by the Cambodian action, it would seem that Congress would have authority to terminate United States participation in hostilities in the Indochina War. Thus measures such as the McGovern-Hatfield Amendment,[111] which would prohibit the expenditure of military appropriations anywhere in Indochina after June 30, 1971, would seem to be Constitutional if at the time of enactment there were sufficient time allowed for a safe withdrawal of United States forces.[112] The wisdom of setting a deadline for unilateral withdrawal is another matter and one which seems highly dubious in view of the complete absence of historical precedent and the certainty of undercutting the Presidential negotiating position.

As to form of termination, the double vote by the Senate to repeal the Southeast Asia Resolution [113] is precisely the kind of ambiguous and unclear Congressional action which should be avoided. In fact, by a strange quirk of partisan Senatorial warfare it was unclear whether a vote to repeal the Southeast Asia Resolution was a vote to terminate Presidential authority

[110] The Federalist, Number 74, p. 497 (Heritage Press, 1945).

[111] An Amendment to the Defense Authorization Bill, H.R. 17123, 91st Cng., 2d Sess. (1970).

[112] See, generally, the "Legal Memorandum on the Constitutionality of the Amendment to End the War," note 102 above.

[113] See New York Times, June 25, 1970, at 1, col. 1; July 11, 1970, at 7, col. 4. The first vote to repeal was on June 24, 1970, and took the form of an amendment to the Foreign Military Sales Act, H. R. 15628, 91st Cong., 2d Sess. (1970). The second vote to repeal was on July 10, 1970, and took the form of a concurrent resolution, S. Con. Res. 64, S. Rept. 91–872, 91st Cong., 2d Sess. (1970).

or to affirm a Constitutional interpretation that the President would have Constitutional authority even if the Southeast Asia Resolution had never existed. Neither camp seems to have clearly adverted to whether the vote on repeal of the resolution was directed at revoking authority for future actions in Southeast Asia on the authority of the resolution or whether it was intended to be an exercise of the Congressional authority to terminate the Indochina War as of the date of repeal. In the absence of clear Congressional intent to terminate hostilities, the President would certainly be justified in interpreting any repeal to mean only the former. Again, the wisdom of repeal of the principal Constitutional authority for a major war while that war continues seems highly suspect. Repeal, of course, would also require action by the House of Representatives.

Perhaps the legislation most directly related to the Cambodian incursion is the Cooper-Church Amendment [114] which passed the Senate by a vote of 58 to 37 on June 30, 1970.[115] The Amendment provides that:

> In concert with the declared objectives of the President of the United States. . . . no funds authorized or appropriated pursuant to this act or any other law may be expended after July 1, 1970, for the purposes of—
>> (1) Retaining United States forces in Cambodia;
>> (2) Paying the compensation or allowances of, or otherwise supporting, directly or indirectly, any United States personnel in Cambodia who furnish military instruction to Cambodian forces or engage in any combat activity in support of Cambodian forces;
>> (3) Entering into or carrying out any contract or agreement to provide military instruction in Cambodia, or to provide persons to engage in any combat activity in support of Cambodian forces; or
>> (4) Conducting any combat activity in the air above Cambodia in direct support of Cambodian forces.
>
> Nothing contained in this section shall be deemed to impugn the constitutional power of the President as Commander in Chief, including the exercise of that constitutional power which may be necessary to protect the lives of United States armed forces wherever deployed. . . .[116]

The principal Constitutional issue in appraising the Cooper-Church Amendment is whether it should be characterized as within the Congressional authority to withdraw authorization for assistance to the Cambodian Government and termination of such assistance or whether it encroaches on the Presidential authority to take command decisions incident to the Viet-Nam War. To the extent that the Amendment prohibits actions directed against the sanctuaries in direct support of the military effort in Viet-Nam (the extent to which the Amendment would prohibit future actions directed against the sanctuaries is unclear), it would seem to be dealing with command options. On the other hand, if it only seeks to limit the United States involvement in Southeast Asia by proscribing military support of the Cambodian Government, a stronger case can be made that it is within the Congressional authority to terminate hostilities. Never-

[114] An Amendment to the Foreign Military Sales Act, cited above.
[115] New York Times, July 1, 1970, at 13, col. 1 (City ed.).
[116] Ibid., cols. 5–6.

theless, the interrelation between the survival of the Cambodian Government and the military effort in Viet-Nam lends some support to the proposition that even direct military assistance in support of the Cambodian Government is within the Commander-in-Chief's power. The ambiguity as to the conduct proscribed by the Cooper-Church Amendment, the difficulty in characterizing the Constitutional effect of the Amendment, and the uncertainty of the limits of Congressional authority to proscribe Presidential command options suggest that the Amendment is in a Constitutional twilight zone likely to precipitate a clash between Congress and the President and that resolution of the Constitutional issue will depend largely on the actions of each branch of government rather than any analytically discoverable *a priori* Constitutional hypothesis. With respect to form, since Congressional termination of hostilities, whether in whole or in part, should, like Congressional authorization, be carefully considered and debated on its own merits by both Houses of Congress, it seems a poor precedent that the Cooper-Church Amendment took the form of an amendment to the Foreign Military Sales Act, which will be linked with the broader bill rather than considered individually by the House as well as the Senate.[117]

C. *The Need for Congressional-Executive Co-operation on War-Peace Issues*

The uncertainty of the division of the war powers between Congress and the President suggests a need for co-operation rather than conflict. The Constitutional structure is inescapably one of interdependency. Though Congress has the major power over decisions to commit or withdraw forces from combat, the President can by design of foreign policy sometimes dictate the Congressional action. Moreover, Congress seems to be largely dependent on the methods to wage or to withdraw from conflict which the President chooses. And for his part, although the President has great power to commit the nation diplomatically and to control the course of Constitutionally authorized hostilities, Congress has the power of the purse and great power to mobilize public opinion against a course pursued by the President.

This interdependency suggests that the President should candidly inform Congress of developments affecting national security and that Congressional leaders should be consulted prior to major military decisions, even if they fall within the President's authority as Commander-in-Chief. Failure to inform Congressional leaders prior to the Cambodian intercession involved a high cost in the authority of the action and in Congressional disaffection from Presidential initiatives. Constitutional authority is not an adequate substitute for full co-operation with Congress.

The interdependency between Congress and the President also suggests that Congress should be sensitive to the need for co-operation with the President. Under the pressures of global defense needs and the continuing

[117] Spokesmen for the Senate have implied that, if the House wants the Foreign Military Sales Bill, it also will have to accept the Cooper-Church Amendment.

Cold War, Congress in this century may have relinquished too much of its Constitutional rôle in war-peace issues. Though it is a Constitutional option open to Congress, that body should be hesitant to cede blanket advance authority to the President in resolutions such as the 1955 Formosa Resolution, the 1957 Middle East Resolution and the 1964 Southeast Asia Resolution. Such resolutions run the dual risk of precluding meaningful Congressional participation when events change and of proving an unreliable basis for Congressional support when a President needs it. This is not to suggest that Congress should use only formal declarations of war, a suggestion which seems largely a red herring. Nor is it to suggest that, in authorizing the commitment of forces abroad, Congress should limit the needed flexibility of the President. But it is to suggest that Congress should exercise its power to commit American blood and resources to hostilities abroad with careful deliberation and awareness of context.

In its understandable interest in reassuming a greater rôle in war-peace decisions, Congress should not lose sight of the need to protect legitimate Presidential authority. In the wake of the Cambodian action there are a number of general bills in both Houses of Congress aimed at reasserting the Congressional rôle.[118] Most of those which seek to delimit Presidential authority in advance run the dual risk of unconstitutional encroachment on Presidential authority and of irrelevance as conditions change. The real need seems to be for more careful consideration of Congressional measures authorizing and terminating hostilities and for greater liaison between the President and Congress during the course of major hostilities. For example, a regular meeting at least once every sixty days between the President and key Congressional leaders during the course of major hostilities might assist in avoiding unnecessary friction between the two branches.[119] In the long run, a policy of co-operation rather than conflict seems better calculated to promote the national interest in the successful conduct and termination of hostilities abroad.

III. International Law and the Functioning of the National Security Process

In the last few years a great deal of attention has been focused on the rôle *actually* played by international law in national security decisions.[120]

[118] See S. 3964 (introduced by Senators Dole and Javits on June 15, 1970); H. J. Res. 1151 (introduced by Representative Findley on March 26, 1970); H. R. 17598 (introduced by Representative Fascell).

[119] Representative Paul Findley of Illinois has modified his original proposal defining in advance the authority of the President to use the armed forces abroad, and has instead proposed a requirement for a Presidential report when the armed forces are committed abroad and a regular meeting between the President and the Senate and House Foreign Relations Committees during the course of sustained hostilities. As modified, the proposal is a constructive step for increasing the co-operation between Congress and the President.

[120] See, *e.g.*, Scheinman and Wilkinson, International Law and Political Crisis (1968). The American Society of International Law currently has a Panel on the Rôle of International Law in Government Decision-Making in War-Peace Crises, which has a number of thoughtful studies in process.

The results are frequently discouraging. It is surprising, then, that so little attention has been devoted to the rôle that international law *ought* to play in such decisions and how the national security process might be better structured to take it into account more systematically. In a recent article in the *Virginia Journal of International Law* this writer has urged that an international legal perspective is an important perspective in national security decisions and that the present structure of the process is inadequate for reliably bringing such perspectives to the attention of national decision-makers.[121] The Cambodian decision dramatically illustrates the continuing high cost of failing to structure an international legal perspective into the national security process. Although the United States intercession in Cambodia was lawful, the ambiguity surrounding certain features of the operation (for example, the consent of the Cambodian Government) contributed unnecessarily to domestic and international misunderstanding of the action. There were at least two options which were likely to be persuasively presented by someone focused on an international legal perspective which might have strengthened the United States response. First, North Vietnamese and Viet Cong attacks on and from Cambodia might have been vigorously protested by the United States in the Security Council during March or April. The Cambodian complaint to the Security Council on April 22 would have seemed a particularly opportune time to press a complaint in the Security Council. The North Vietnamese belligerent use of neutral Cambodian territory and attacks on the Cambodian Government presented about as clear a case of impermissible action as is ever possible in complex world order disputes. To ignore the North Vietnamese actions when there was no longer room for doubt as to their armed attack on Cambodia was unnecessarily to undercut both the United Nations and the United States authority positions. Second, a prior understanding with Cambodia might have been obtained for public release at the time of the operation. In view of the consent requirement of Article IV, paragraph 3, of the SEATO Treaty, such an advance agreement would have seemed particularly advisable. Though concern has been expressed that such an agreement might have undercut the neutrality of Cambodia, it should have been possible to word it in such a way that neutrality was supported rather than compromised. Thus, Cambodia might have "recognized the right of the United States and South Viet-Nam to take defensive action against the unlawful belligerent activities of the North Vietnamese and Viet Cong forces on neutral Cambodian territory." The agreement might also have emphasized that under international law it is not a breach of neutrality for a neutral state to use force against unlawful belligerent activities on its territory,[122] that Cambodia had no intention of relinquishing its neutrality, and that the action was geographically and temporally limited. Though such

---

[121] Moore, note 72 above, at 310–314.

[122] See M. Greenspan The Modern Law of Land Warfare 536–537, 584 (1959). Similarly, lawful actions by one belligerent directed against violations of neutral territory by another belligerent do not constitute hostilities against the neutral. See 2 Oppenheim, International Law 685 (7th ed., Lauterpacht, 1952).

an advance agreement was not strictly required by international law, it would have both materially strengthened the United States position and the continuing neutrality of Cambodia. As a minor third point, the United States should have immediately reported its action to the Security Council instead of waiting five days. Finally, President Nixon's speech to the Nation on April 30 and other public pronouncements on Cambodia might have been more focused and carried greater impact had they emphasized the international legal right of a belligerent to take action to end serious continued violations of neutral territory by an opposing belligerent. These suggestions are not put forth as grand new solutions to the tensions which produced the Cambodian crisis but only to illustrate how an international legal perspective might have been sensitive to a range of issues and options which could have improved the United States response to the situation. Had the proposed Cambodian intercession been illegal, of course, then an international legal perspective might have been even more important in counseling restraint.[123]

The Constitutional debate surrounding the Cambodian situation also illustrates a need more systematically to structure a Constitutional-legal perspective into the foreign policy process. The rhetoric of both the Executive and the Congress was frequently overly broad, contributing to a potentially costly confusion. For example, President Nixon failed to make clear that the Southeast Asia Resolution was a principal Constitutional basis for the Viet-Nam War. Partly as a result of this failure clearly to support retention of the resolution, the Senate voted twice to repeal the resolution amid great confusion as to the meaning of the vote. And in its eagerness to reassert a stronger Congressional rôle, Congress sometimes seemed unrealistically to downgrade the independent authority of the President as Commander-in-Chief, as, for example, in the resolutions introduced in both Houses of Congress seeking narrowly to define in advance the limits of Presidential authority to commit the armed forces to combat abroad.

There is no real remedy to the lack of an international legal perspective significantly, however, and the writer is more than ever convinced of the in the national security process other than increasing the awareness of the importance of such a perspective. Institutional changes may help soundness of his earlier recommendation to upgrade the office of Legal Adviser of the Department of State to Under Secretary of State for International Legal Affairs and to make the new Under Secretary a permanent *ex officio* member of the National Security Council. Perhaps, in addition, the President should add to his staff an Assistant to the President for International Legal Affairs. It might also be helpful for the Senate Foreign Relations Committee and the House Foreign Affairs Committee to add similar positions to their staffs.[124]

---

[123] In the sense that non-compliance with international law subjects a state to all the sanctions of the global community, however imperfect those sanctions may be in particular instances, states do not have a genuine option whether or not to comply with international law.

[124] See Moore, note 72 above, at 310–314, 340–342.

CONCLUSION

Though the decision to intercede in Cambodia was lawful both under international law and the United States Constitution, the functioning of the national security process in the Cambodian crisis indicates a need for greater sensitivity to the legal dimensions of security decisions. Several options which could have been pursued, particularly referral to the United Nations Security Council and advance agreement with the Cambodian Government, do not seem to have been adequately considered. Similarly, failure to inform Congressional leaders of the pending decision may have unnecessarily weakened the authority of the action. For international lawyers, the principal lesson of the Cambodian crisis may be that they have failed to convince national decision-makers that an international legal perspective should be heard. If so, soul-searching among international lawyers might more sensibly give way to a concerted effort to ensure that others practice what the lawyers preach.

Commentaries

GEORGE H. ALDRICH
WOLFGANG FRIEDMANN
JOHN LAWRENCE HARGROVE

COMMENTS ON THE ARTICLES ON THE LEGALITY OF THE UNITED STATES ACTION IN CAMBODIA

George H. Aldrich *

I appreciate this opportunity to offer a few comments on points made in the preceding papers. Space does not permit any full statement of the legal basis for the action taken in Cambodia by the United States, and I will merely refer readers to the statements made by the Legal Adviser at the Hammarskjöld Forum on May 28, 1970.[1]

In the first place, I fail to understand Professor Falk's allegation that there had been no armed attack from Cambodia prior to the American and South Viet-Nam operations. The facts are generally accepted, I believe, that North Vietnamese and Viet Cong forces have used Cambodian territory for years in pursuit of their continuing armed attack against South Viet-Nam. They have used it as a base area, as a safe haven for the storage of supplies, and for the rest and regroupment of their troops, and as an area from which many armed attacks had been launched across the border. On many occasions our troops and those of South Viet-Nam have been fired on from across the border.

As for Professor Moore's criticism that the United States should have tried to obtain some statement of Cambodian consent prior to beginning operations in Cambodia, I think it fairly can be said that the United States Government considered that possibility. Such a statement of consent might very well have been obtainable, but the decision was taken not to seek it in order to avoid any consequent impairment of Cambodia's neutrality.

I note Mr. Rogers stated concern about the Constitutional argument that the President has the power to protect United States troops. Mr. Rogers seems to be saying that he sees no logical line that could be drawn to delimit such an assertion of power; if the President thought it necessary to use force in Cambodia, why could he not equally use it against Communist China or the Soviet Union, who were supplying arms and equipment to North Viet-Nam? It would be worth considering whether international law may not provide a line that would be relevant here for Constitutional purposes. In other words, the President's power under the Constitution to take action to protect our troops may be greater where the action is lawful under international law than where it is unlawful. In my opinion, whereas it was lawful to act against the sanctuaries in Cambodia, it would not be permissible under international law to take similar action

* Deputy Legal Adviser, Department of State. The views expressed are those of the author and do not represent the views of the U. S. Government.

[1] Printed in 62 Department of State Bulletin 765–770 (1970); reprinted in 64 A.J.I.L. 933 (1970).

against Communist China or the U.S.S.R., whose territory is not being used in a similar fashion in the course of an armed attack.

Wolfgang Friedmann *

If the intervention of the United States forces in the neutral state of Cambodia had been an isolated event, it would probably have aroused little legal criticism and moral indignation. At what point and within what limits a state may violate the neutrality of another state in order to respond to violations of neutrality by a third state with which the responding state is at war, is far from clear. But it is open to serious doubt whether the occupation of sanctuaries by North Vietnamese troops, which had existed and were known to the United States and had been acquiesced in for several years, constituted an imminent threat of attack. Little had occurred in recent months to alter this situation. Nevertheless, if the United States forces had operated from United States territory in order to destroy military installations across the border clearly directed against the United States, the situation could have been likened to the Cuban missile crisis of 1962. The United States response to the installation of Soviet missiles on Cuban territory on that occasion was of doubtful legality, because it interfered, to a limited extent, with the freedom of the seas in time of peace. But it was overwhelmingly accepted by United States and world opinion, because it was clearly felt to be a response to a deliberate provocation and potential threat to the United States by a major Power, and because it was moderate, limited, and clearly defensive in character.

The Cambodian action is basically different. In the first place, it is not an action taken in defense of United States territory or security. It was launched from South Viet-Nam in conjunction with South Vietnamese operations, and its justification clearly stands and falls with the legality of the United States posture in Viet-Nam. This is not the place to reopen the Viet-Nam debate. Suffice it to say that it is a minimum condition of the justification of the United States intervention in Cambodia that its intervention in Viet-Nam should be regarded as in conformity with Article 51 of the Charter, and as an act of defensive aid and response to a request for help from a government attacked from outside. I have repeatedly stated my reasons for rejecting this contention,[1] and for regarding the United States intervention in Viet-Nam as a deliberate violation of the Geneva Accords (with which the United States had undertaken not to interfere by the threat or use of force) and a determined attempt to prevent the unification of Viet-Nam under Communist control. The open refusal of the United States to consider the nation-wide elections provided in the Geneva Accords for 1956, coupled with the military and diplomatic support for the South Vietnamese régime, which the United States elevated into an independent state, are the most significant aspects of this action.

Second, the Cambodian intervention, extending the Vietnamese intervention which was a major exercise in the world-wide "containment" policy

* Columbia University School of Law.
[1] *E.g.*, in this JOURNAL, Vol. 61 (1967) at 776 ff.

of the United States, in disregard of international commitments, continues a pattern of United States action that has become increasingly apparent over the last fifteen years.[2] The ouster of the incumbent government of Guatemala in 1954, the Dominican intervention of 1965, the Vietnamese intervention, escalating from 1954 to the present day, and now the invasion of Cambodia, are assertions of imperial power, of "spheres of influence," which increasingly disregard the integrity, independence, and self-determination of smaller nations. It is therefore no accident that the United States did not seek the request of the Cambodian Government for its intervention, of which it was informed after the invasion was under way. Nor did the United States even attempt to justify its intervention legally until many weeks after the event. The Soviet Union has, of course, acted similarly on occasions: in Hungary in 1956, when it set up a government of its own choosing and then asked that government to request U.S.S.R. intervention; and even more blatantly in Czechoslovakia in 1968, when the U.S.S.R. intervened without a request from either government or any insurgents. But this country has now put itself on the same legal and moral plane. It has forfeited the claim, which in the earlier postwar phase it could assert with some justification, to be the champion of international order and the defender of the integrity of small nations.

Third, we should seek to relate the legality—and the morality, which in international law is a closely related perspective—of the United States action to the basic issues of world order. Professor Moore has, in his defense of the United States intervention in Viet-Nam,[3] been very eloquent on the need to refer the lawfulness of assistance "to genuine self-determination and the requirements of minimum world public order. . . ." In the present debate he has been noticeably reticent on these issues. Of course, North Viet-Nam has violated Cambodian neutrality. But the establishment of depots and units in sanctuaries near the South Vietnamese border did not interfere with the ordinary life of the people of Cambodia, who went about their business more or less in peace. It is the massive United States-Vietnamese invasion, with all the attendant aerial operations, that has set into motion a process—so painfully familiar from Viet-Nam—of destruction and devastation, the displacement of hundreds of thousands, and the probable ruin of a small country. And this is how the great majority of the world—friends as well as foes—sees it. The North Vietnamese assuredly are neither democrats nor pacifists. Having been thwarted in the attempt to gain control of Viet-Nam through the processes agreed upon at Geneva in 1954, they have from 1960 onwards increasingly resorted to force in order to attain their objectives. Yet it is the United States which has taken the major steps that have involved an ever widening part of the Southeast Asian Continent in war (international and civil), in devastation, and in the total disruption of the life of the people, whose

[2] For a recent confirmation of this interpretation, see Townsend Hooper, a former Under Secretary of the Air Force, "Legacy of the Cold War in Indo China," 48 Foreign Affairs 60–61 (July, 1970).

[3] See, *e.g.*, "The Lawfulness of Military Assistance to the Republic of Viet-Nam," 61 A.J.I.L. 1, 31 (1967).

only choice is between conflicting tyrannies. But of these contending forces, one is indigenous and only marginally dependent on foreign support. The other is essentially the creation of, and dependent on, a foreign Power, whose base is in another part of the world.

The Cambodian invasion marks a further escalation not only in the scale of the war but in the United States' disregard for the processes of international law. The Cambodian Government was not asked whether it wanted the occupation or not. It acquiesced after the event, and it is now quite clearly a client government of the United States and, even more ironically, after the withdrawal of the United States ground forces, dependent upon its ancient enemy, the South Vietnamese, who in turn depend upon United States help for their own survival and their military operations. That only a perfunctory report was made to the United Nations well after the event is hardly surprising. The major Powers, including the United States, have increasingly detached their international strategies and policies from the United Nations.

Those who hold international law in disdain and regard the present world situation as one in which the confrontation of the super-Powers in Orwellian fashion is inevitable may accept this state of affairs. But as international lawyers we can only record the United States intervention in Cambodia as a further deliberate step away from any attempt to put the use of force under some international control, and as a new move in the pursuit of imperial policies of confrontation.

John Lawrence Hargrove *

Professor Falk has argued that the incursion of United States land forces into Cambodia was not justifiable from the point of view of international law, and Professor Moore that it was. There is a sense in which both are wrong.

In defense of the action, a sufficiently plausible argument can be made for its international legality to save the Administration's case from being thrown out on the pleadings. (This is true if one gives the Administration the benefit of all the doubts on the facts, and takes as assumed the underlying legal premise regarding the conflict in South Viet-Nam itself: namely, that the Republic of Viet-Nam is an entity legally capable of coming under

* Director of Studies, American Society of International Law.

"armed attack" from the Democratic Republic of Viet-Nam, within the meaning of Article 51 of the United Nations Charter; I shall accept this premise *arguendo.*) There is nothing in the law of the Charter which necessarily excludes an exercise of the right of self-defense on the territory of a foreign state which is not itself the attacker, even without the valid consent of that state. Should, for example, Canada be militarily occupied by a Power hostile to the United States, and used as a base from which to sustain an attack against the American industrial Midwest, there is no basis for supposing that in all conceivable circumstances the Charter would restrict the use of defensive force by the United States to United States territory. The test would be whether there was an armed attack and thus a right of self-defense, and, if so, whether the action in question was necessary to put an end to the injury being inflicted by such attack and proportionate to it.

The same test applies to the Cambodian action. In that case there has been a systematic pattern of conduct, aimed at and resulting in armed violence on South Vietnamese territory, sustained by foreign military forces on Cambodian territory for years. It is unreasonable to assume that international law would provide no right of defense against such conduct under any circumstances, *i.e.,* would deny that it could ever amount to an armed attack. And when it does amount to an armed attack, the test of legitimate defense is not *where* defensive force is exercised but whether it is necessary and proportionate. On these last points the Administration's case can be endowed with a certain *prima facie* plausibility by reference to the fact that less radical measures had clearly proved inadequate, and by reference to the intended limits of time and geography to be placed on the incursion.[1]

The difficulty, however, is that being satisfied of this sort of *prima facie* legality is not sufficient to discharge a President's responsibility toward the law as he makes decisions about the international use of force. So far as international law is concerned, a President's duty is not just to be able to make out a case for legality which is not patently absurd, but to be willing to forgo actions which are in their sum effect injurious to the international legal order. He must therefore be concerned in advance with the full panoply of practical consequences which his action may have for the viability of law as a guide to conduct. However reasonable the United States' legal case may appear in the Oval Room, he must ask: Will it in fact be credited by other governments, and if so, with what deleterious effect on the evolution of the principles the United States has invoked? Or will they dismiss our action as simple lawlessness? Either way, will they in fact take our action as a means of justifying violence of their own in other circumstances even less defensible legally? Will our action further impair the ability of the United States to invoke legal restraints to reduce the level of violent conduct generally?

---

[1] It should be noted that the fact of Cambodian neutrality, whatever its other legal consequences, serves neither to enlarge nor diminish the scope of lawful force by or against any of the parties. The Charter, which exhaustively catalogues the kinds of permissible force, speaks only of self-defense (aside from force authorized by international organization decision), not of neutrality.

In the Cambodian case, it would have been reasonable to predict that the legal justification eventually put forward by the Administration, if noticed at all, would be largely discounted in the international community as contrivance if not pettifoggery. This is substantially because, on the Administration's own previously stated premises, the United States action just did not appear either necessary to put an end to the injury being inflicted by military movements from Cambodia into Viet-Nam, or proportionate to that injury. It looked instead like a massive military invasion undertaken ostensibly to deal with a long-standing situation which the world had previously been led to believe was sufficiently manageable as not to impede a program of fairly rapid withdrawal of United States ground combat forces from *Viet-Nam,* to say nothing of Cambodia. With the addition of the fact of a strong and obvious, but legally immaterial, extraneous inducement for the invasion (shoring up the Cambodian régime), and the fact that even many friendly governments have doubts about the international status of the Viet-Nam conflict itself, the task of devising a legal explanation which would be widely convincing internationally was recognizably foredoomed. Unfortunately, as if to make sure on this score, the Administration constructed a public record which pointedly indicated that the decision was taken and initially executed without consideration even of the existence of international legal restraints on using force against the territory of another, despite the workmanlike effort of State Department Legal Adviser Stevenson to repair the damage after the fact.

The sum practical effect has been a further enfeeblement of these restraints—an effect surpassed, among United States actions in recent years, probably only by our acquiescence in the indefinitely extended occupation of foreign territory by Israel as a means of compelling a favorable political settlement. So far as international law is concerned, it is likely that most of the world's international policy-makers would accept the proposition that the United States invaded Cambodia on a grand scale on nothing more, at best, than a legal technicality. There is little reason to hope that their memories will fail them when in the future they come to weigh their own decisions about the resort to violence.

We can learn from this experience something about the rôle of law and lawyers in the international conduct of states. In a national legal order, private persons want to know: Can the system be made to permit me to do what I want? How can I turn it to my purposes? Their lawyers are paid to produce the answers, and the system usually provides ways to tell, eventually, whether the answers were right or wrong. The public international legal order, however, is for many reasons a radically different affair. Here, such questions should be put (by governments to their lawyers) only as a first step, if at all; the fundamental and controlling legal question must always be: What will we be doing to the system itself? Here the proper concern of legal counselors is not so much with nice lawyers' arguments showing how to establish legality, as with the wise husbanding of the legal order.

United States Military Intervention in Cambodia in the Light of International Law

JOHN H. E. FRIED*

"You might say it's a case of the unwilling helping the ungrateful kill the unwanted."—An American Sergeant in Vietnam, to reporter, *New York Times*, February 18, 1971, p. 12

"This is the curse of evil deed:/ Bound as it is to sprout, to lead/ To ever further evil."—Friedrich von Schiller

BY ITS OWN logic, an adamant U.S. policy led within half a generation to an increasingly massive military buildup of South Vietnam; to veiled U.S. military intervention in South Vietnam; to open U.S. war in South and North Vietnam; to change of strategy toward gradual "Vietnamization"—and, by spring 1970, to the invasion of Cambodia. That attack, proclaimed as strictly "limited" both in duration (2 months) and area (certain small border regions) became a continuous U.S. war[1] engulfing much of Cambodia; and led by February 1971 to the U.S. invasion of Laos.[2]

The invasion of Cambodia, then, not only widened the Vietnam War into an All-Indochina War, with unforeseeable ultimate consequences; it was *designed* as an aspect of or condition for an indefinite continuation (in "Vietnamized" strategy) of a U.S. military intervention that has been illegal from the beginning. While the analysis that follows cannot overlook this, it will concentrate on the question of whether that invasion, seen by itself, violates rules of international behavior that are the

---

* This is a somewhat revised version (mid-February 1971) of a paper presented to the International Conference of Lawyers on Vietnam, Laos, and Cambodia. Toronto, May 22-24, 1970.

[1] Assiduously nurtured misconceptions threaten to corrode elementary notions of fact and law. Withdrawal of U.S. ground forces from Cambodia did of course *not* end the U.S. war there, as the U.S. has continued to advise, equip, train, and pay for the Saigon forces there, and to perform air combat and support operations there. If the invasion of Laos was a "South Vietnamese show" (because there the U.S. from the outset only bombed from the air) neither did the air bombing of Pearl Harbor in 1941 constitute an attack.

[2] "Underlying the decision [to attack Laos] also was the increased apprehension among American officials of what appeared to be a worsening situation in Cambodia. . ." (Alvin Shuster, in *New York Times*, Feb. 8, 1971, p. 14.)

"Laos would *not have been possible* had it not been for Cambodia." (President Nixon, at press conference, Feb. 17, 1971, *New York Times*, Feb. 18, 1971, p. 14.) (Unless indicated, italics are supplied, throughout.)

dam separating the world, including the U.S., from ever-greater disasters.

I. Basic Facts

(1) The 1954 Geneva Conference confirmed "the sovereignty, the independence, the unity, and the territorial integrity" not only of Vietnam (and Laos) but also of Cambodia: "In their relations with Cambodia, Laos, and Vietnam, each member of the Geneva Conference undertakes to respect [their] sovereignty, independence, unity and territorial integrity, and to refrain from any interference in their internal affairs."[3] Mr. Bedell Smith, the American delegate, formally declared: "The Government of the United States . . . takes note" of this and other provisions of the Declaration," and "will refrain from the threat or use of force to disturb them, in accordance with Art. 2 (sec. 4) of the Charter of the U.N. dealing with the obligation of Members to refrain from the threat or use of force."[4]

(2) Even if the U.S. had not given that pledge, it would still be bound not to use or threaten force against Cambodia, in view of its obligations under the U.N. Charter, the Kellogg-Briand Pact of 1928, and general principles of international law.

(3) Whereas the basic international obligations of, and toward, Cambodia are of course unaffected by Cambodia's political coloration, it should be noted that the Sihanouk regime was not Communist or pro-Communist. For example, it took some very drastic measures against the *Khmer Rouge*. In 1969, the staunchly anti-Communist U.S.-trained General Lon Nol who eventually overthrew the Sihanouk regime on March 18, 1970, was made Premier by the Prince himself.

On May 16, 1955, Cambodia signed a Military Aid Agreement with the U.S., against misgivings of the (Indian-Polish-Canadian) International Control Commission in Cambodia (I.C.C.),[5] and against formal protest by the Democratic Republic of Vietnam (North Vietnam).

In fall 1955, the I.C.C. reported that "a small (U.S.) Military Assistance Advisory Group, about thirty in number, headed by a U.S. Brig-

---

[3] Art. 12 of the Final Declaration of 21 July 1954, Cmnd. 9239.

[4] Cmnd. 9239.

[5] In view of "assurance" to the I.C.C. that Cambodia "will always and scrupulously respect the terms of the Geneva Agreement" and "will follow a policy of *neutrality*," the I.C.C. accepted the Military Aid Agreement, "although it may still be argued that some of [its] clauses in terms go beyond the limitations imposed by the Geneva Agreement." (*I.C.C. Third Interim Report*, for the period April 1 to July 28, 1955, Cmnd. 9597, Cambodia No. 3, 1955, pp. 5-6.)

adier General, has arrived in Cambodia. The Group is now busily assessing the defense needs of the country."[6] Soon afterwards, the Group achieved full strength. For years its military personnel traveled freely within Cambodia and were able to acquire military and intelligence data.

If eventually Cambodia terminated that military aid arrangement, it did so after it had for years unsuccessfully protested against violations of Cambodian territory by Saigon and U.S. forces.

If Prince Sihanouk—like many public figures of many countries—objected to the U.S. military intervention in Vietnam and pleaded to end it, this again did not show any anti-U.S. bias.[7] The Vietnam War created great problems for Cambodia; above all, Cambodia wished desperately not to be drawn into it. When Sihanouk, long before his country was invaded, protested against U.S. plans and pressures to do so, he protested against something which was public knowledge and which, after the "lid was taken off" was again widely confirmed in the U.S. press.

As a sign of its disapproval of U.S. policies toward Cambodia, Sihanouk severed diplomatic relations with the U.S. in 1965, but thereafter made various gestures to improve the strained relationship. For example, on 10 June 1968, Cambodia released without conditions two U.S. nationals captured three weeks earlier on a Philippine tugboat in Cambodian river waters, as a tribute to the memory of Senator Robert Kennedy;[8] the widow of President Kennedy was invited to, and visited, Cambodia as Sihanouk's guest; and he in turn visited President Johnson at the White House.

[6] *I.C.C. Interim Report*, for the period April 1 to Sept. 30, 1955, Section, "Entry of War Matériel into Cambodia," Cmnd. 967, p. 23.

[7] In summer 1965, soon after severing diplomatic relations with the U.S., he candidly stated his views: "The progressive escalation of the war (the American raids of terror on North Vietnam and the countermeasures that the Socialist world will inevitably take) might ruin attempts at compromise. . . . In perpetuating the war in South Vietnam, in supporting the Saigon leaders who are universally unpopular, known as her 'creatures,' the United States has forced the majority of the common people and the majority of the elite of South Vietnam into the arms of the Communists. . . . This is not the way to combat Communism. . . . This 'anti-Communist' war, by reason of the imperialist character that it forcibly assumes in the eyes of the masses, on the contrary, favors communism." He was looking forward to good relations with an America that "would no longer be, in our eyes, an imperialistic nation that seeks to impose her policy and her government upon us." (Interview with Robert Scheer, *Ramparts* [July 1965], reproduced in M. G. Raskin and Bernard B. Fall, eds., *The Viet-Nam Reader*, 1965, pp. 358-360.)

[8] Information to the U.N. Security Council of 11 June 1968 (S/8629), *Report of the Security Council, 16 July 1967—15 July 1968*, GAOR, 23rd Sess., Supp. 2 (A/7202), para. 806.

VIOLATION OF CAMBODIAN TERRITORY BY THE U.S. SIDE

Cambodia has since January 1956 frequently protested against violations of her neutral territory by Saigon forces, and subsequently for many years also by U.S. forces. These reports, providing details as to place, time, type of violation, such as "killings, ill-treatment, wounding, arrests and abductions of Cambodian citizens, theft and destruction of their property" (No. 553/DGP/X of 16 Sept. 1957), the number of victims, etc., were submitted to the International Control Commission for Cambodia; and in later years, i.e., to the Co-Chairmen of the Geneva Conference (e.g., 7 February 1964, alleging "incessant and murderous aggression against Cambodia," including aerial bombardment). For over half a decade, Cambodia also transmitted vehement complaints against such acts by U.S. and Saigon ground and air forces to the U.N. Security Council. There were 40 such protest notes during 1967, and 100 between January 1968 and mid-1969.[9]

The protests to the Security Council against "aggressive acts by U.S.-South Viet-Namese forces" continued, becoming increasingly urgent and claiming increasingly serious violations, until 27 March 1970. For example, the communication of 26 February 1970 (S/9668) concluded:

> The Royal Government of Cambodia has lodged a strong and indignant protest against these repeated violations of Cambodian airspace, followed by deliberate firing and spraying of defoliants on the peaceful and innocent inhabitants of the frontier regions and their dwellings, which have been committed by the U.S.-South Viet-Namese forces.[10] It has called upon the Government of the U.S.A. to take immediate steps to indemnify the victims, make reparations for damage caused, and put an end to such acts of aggression once and for all.

Over the years, the U.S. and Saigon insisted that their Vietnamese adversaries were using Cambodian border areas for military purposes; Cambodia strenuously, often desperately, denied these charges. Toward the end of 1967, such U.S. complaints reached a height, and a U.S. invasion seemed imminent. Mr. Chester Bowles went on a special mission to Phnom Penh. Prince Sihanouk insisted that the U.S. had not

---

[9] For additional data, see Appendix to this article.

[10] Regarding the effects of pre-invasion defoliation, see "Report on herbicidal damage by the United States in Southeastern Cambodia" based on on-the-spot investigation by U.S. experts A. H. Westing, E. W. Pfeiffer, J. Lavorel, and L. Matarasso, dated Phnom Penh, Dec. 31, 1969, in T. Whiteside, ed., *Defoliation*, 1970.

produced any evidence of such sanctuaries, in spite of the fact that "without our [Cambodia's] authorization, American planes have been traversing our [Cambodia's] skies *thousands of times* and taking photographs of our country in its length and breadth."[11]

At the conclusion of the talks, Sihanouk informed the press that Mr. Bowles, on behalf of "The United States has agreed that *if* it has information concerning Vietcong or North Vietnamese infiltration, it will transmit their information to the Cambodian Government. . . . Cambodia will then send her own troops or those of the [International Control] Commission to investigate and, if the information is verified, demand that the forces leave Cambodian territory."[12]

The record, then, contradicts the official U.S. position that ever since 1954 "American policy has been to scrupulously respect the neutrality of the Cambodian people," and that "for five years [since 1965 when the U.S. open war in Vietnam began] neither the United States nor South Vietnam has moved against these enemy sanctuaries because *we did not wish to violate the territory of a neutral nation.*"[13] The latter statement, incidentally, implies correctly that the invasion *did* "violate the territory of a neutral nation"; but it implies incorrectly that only a *"move"* (massive ground invasion *plus* air action, as staged in spring 1970) violates obligations toward neutrals, whereas the U.S. actions during the preceding years (bombings, strafings, and defoliation from the air of Cambodian border areas, artillery bombardments across the border, and smaller ground incursions) did *not* violate those obligations.

It appears from announcements by Sihanouk and press reports that

[11] *New York Times*, Jan. 6, 1968. In an interview with *Look* magazine, Sihanouk stated: "Oh, yes, we do have some Vietcong crossing into Cambodia, but further north, in unpopulated areas. They come over mostly to get food and never in large groups—not even up to company strength. We usually give them at least 24 hours to get out, as they often claim the Americans are lying in wait for them." (*Look* [April 2, 1968], 65.)

[12] Agence France Presse, datelined Phnom Penh, Jan. 10, 1968, *New York Times*, Jan. 11, 1968, p. 1. Immediately afterwards, controversy developed between Cambodia and the U.S. over whether or not the U.S. had really pledged not to invade Cambodia.

[13] President Nixon's TV address of April 30, 1970, *New York Times*, May 1, 1970, p. 2. Curiously, Mr. Nixon continued, to prove the scrupulous U.S. respect for Cambodian neutrality: "We have maintained a skeleton diplomatic mission of fewer than 15 in Cambodia's capital, and that only since last August" [1969], while during "the previous four years we did not have any diplomatic mission whatever in Cambodia [because Cambodia had severed diplomatic relations with the U.S.—see above] and for the past five years we have provided no military assistance whatever and no economic assistance to Cambodia." The implication is that actions violative of another country's neutrality can *only*, or *at all*, be committed through embassies or assistance programs.

in early 1970, the Cambodian Government obtained information that North Vietnamese and/or NLF forces were using Cambodian border areas. The Prince took off for Paris, Moscow, and Peking to solicit support for his demand that those troops leave. Prior to the coup against him, he issued warnings that "a great power" supported efforts, while he was abroad, to overthrow his regime. He was in Moscow when the coup occurred in Phnom Penh on March 18.

On March 30, the new regime transmitted Cambodia's first protest about violations of its territory by Vietcong and North Vietnamese troops to the U.N. Security Council. It complained, i.e., about the occupation by a force estimated at 3,000, of a village 7 kilometers inside the border. Between April 1 and May 1, 1970, Cambodia transmitted 13 ever-more vehement protests against numerous attacks and occupations by Vietcong and North Vietnamese forces inside Cambodia.[14] There are indications that Saigon forces invaded and bombed Cambodian territory very soon after Lon Nol's take-over on March 18. The *New York Times* reported[15] that there were "witnessed South Vietnamese air strikes on Communist positions in Cambodia on March 20 and 24, and ground incursions and air strikes by South Vietnamese forces on March 27 and 28." On May 2, the *Daily News* (New York) stated that "American and South Vietnamese forces were crossing the Cambodian border—*for the first time openly.*" This constituted the start of the *combined* U.S.-South Vietnamese "Operation Total Victory."

II. The "Sanctuary" Justification of the Invasion

In a manner reminiscent of the start of the attack by Axis Powers on certain countries in World War II, the invasion of Cambodia was started without notification of its government. Even Germany's invasion of neutral Belgium in 1914 was preceded by a German ultimatum. The absence of any reasoned formal warning or announcement alone casts grave doubts on the legality of the Cambodian invasion.

Insofar as justifications were given, they were not those previously adduced by the U.S. for its war in Vietnam. Unsatisfactory as those justifications had been, they were not available in this case. Cambodia is not under a SEATO "umbrella." No U.S. "commitment" could be alleged. And while the absence of any formal request from the *Saigon*

---

[14] S/9730, S/9734, S/9741, S/9743, S/9754, S/9759, S/9760, S/9762, S/9763, S/9769, S/9773, S/9776, S/9780.

[15] Despatch by Ralph Blumenthal, datelined Khanbin, South Vietnam, in *New York Times*, April 15, 1970, also referring to a *Cambodian* ammunition dump being guarded by South Vietnamese troops.

regime for U.S. "collective self-defense" assistance in Vietnam was revealed only years after the U.S. started its war in Vietnam in alleged compliance with that nonexistent request, the absence of any such request from the *Cambodian* government became immediately known.

WHAT IS A "SANCTUARY"?

A "sanctuary" is a sacred place of worship and, in a wider sense, a sacred place of refuge. Such sanctuaries played a considerable role in antiquity and the Middle Ages.

The term has been revived to denote with strong emotional disapproval, places that are, but in fairness *should not be*, beyond the U.S. military reach. Such use of the term, incidentally, stands the meaning on its head: a sanctuary must be respected exactly *because* it is a *holy* place; so that whoever invades it commits not only a crime but a sin.

In any case, the sanctuary argument implies that Cambodian border areas have been illegally and unfairly used by the opponent; that this abuse of neutral territory gave the opponent an unfair, unilateral advantage, and "immunity" not enjoyed by the U.S.; indeed, it was not infrequently implied that this allegedly unfair, illegal "immunity" enjoyed exclusively by the other side, cheated the U.S. of military success in Vietnam.

Precisely put, the argument means: (a) enemy forces, in *violation* of the law of neutrality, made use of Cambodian places; (b) the Sihanouk regime was unwilling or unable, and apparently the Lon Nol regime was also unable, to end this abuse; so that (c) the U.S. is justified to use self-help.

To clarify this, we must realize that the term "sanctuary" has been applied to *four types* of situations that actually and legally *differ* from each other: (1) places (jungle "caches," thatched huts, etc.) in which weapons, food, and medical supplies destined for the enemy can be stored; (2) places in which enemy soldiers can stay; (3) places from which enemy soldiers can reach (infiltrate into) combat areas; and (4) places to which enemy soldiers can withdraw from combat areas.

1. Depots of War Matériel: Depots of war matériel in neutral territory are not, in and of themselves, unlawful, for the following considerations:

International law does not prohibit belligerents from obtaining war matériel, and much less food and medical supplies, from neutral countries. On the contrary, the principal international treaty on neutrality, Hague Convention V of 1907, specifically permits private persons and firms of neutral countries to export war matériel to belligerents.[16] The U.S. has been adamant in asserting this right for American industry and business.[17] Altogether, the provision of strategic matériel from neutral countries to parties engaged in international or civil conflict is an accepted, albeit sometimes deplored, fact of the world scene, and considered legal. As random examples, various neutral countries export such goods to Israel and the United Arab Republic. Even assuming, then, that Cambodia provided war items to the adversaries of the U.S., this would not have been illegal for either the provider or the destinee.

Now, by normal interpretation under the principle of *a maiori ad*

[16] In 1907, it was "assume[d] that trading activities are in the hands of private enterprise." (Wolfgang Friedmann, *The Changing Character of International Law*, 1964, p. 364, quoted in *Digest of International Law*, M. N. Whiteman, ed. [State Dept. Publ. 8354], Vol. 11, 412.) The Convention forbade such exports by *governments* of neutral countries. However, "the possibility of maintaining this separation in practice has become very difficult. . ." (Tucker, quoted in Whiteman, p. 429.) Developments since then have contributed "to blur that distinction between the activities of individuals and of States. . ." (Castrén, Finland, *The Present Law of War and Neutrality*, Helsinki, 1954, p. 456, quoted in Whiteman, p. 431.) The distinction "underwent a gradual invalidation" (Skubiszewski, Poland) in M. Sørenson (Denmark), ed., *Manual of International Law*, 1968, pp. 891-892. For further views, see Whiteman, pp. 427-433.

The question is irrelevant in the Cambodian case. The U.S. has neither complained about the sale of war matériel by governments to the enemy, nor based its invasion of Cambodia on this ground.

Of great significance is, however, the fact that during World War II, the still neutral U.S. became by official government policy the "arsenal" for states at war with Hitler Germany. Secretary of War Stimson justified this by adopting the interpretation of the Kellogg Pact by the International Law Association (Budapest, 1934), namely, that a neutral "can decline to observe toward the State violating the [Kellogg] Pact the duties prescribed . . . for a neutral." (G. Hackworth, *Digest of International Law*, 1943, VII, 680-681; also quoting a similar statement of 2 Oct. 1941 by U.S. Supreme Court Justice Robert A. Jackson.)

For the text of the "celebrated Articles of Interpretation" of the Kellogg Pact, as Mr. Stimson called them, see, e.g., D. W. Bowett, *Self-Defense in International Law*, 1958, p. 160. Bowett also quotes Brierly, Lauterpacht, and Quincy Wright as backing the conclusions drawn by the I.L.A. Wright considered that violation of the Kellogg Pact gave neutrals not only the right "but possibly even a duty, to discriminate against the offending State." (Bowett, pp. 160-161.)

[17] For example, U.S. Secretary of War Robert Lansing stated: "It should be understood that generally speaking, a citizen of the U.S. can sell to a belligerent government or its agents any article of commerce which he pleases. He is not prohibited from doing this by any rule of international law." (Quoted by Gerhard von Glahn, *Law Among Nations*, 1965, pp. 632-633.) The rule has traditionally been applied also to arms sales to rebels. Glahn quotes approvingly a well-known British decision of 1817 to this effect. See, furthermore, Art. 7 of 1907 Hague Conventions V and XIII.

minus, if neither the neutral acts wrongly by providing, nor the belligerent by obtaining goods, then neither the neutral's permission or sufferance to *store* such goods, nor the belligerent's use of neutral territory for their storage, violates international law. Throughout these years, the U.S. has obtained and stored incomparably larger amounts of war matériel for use in Vietnam, in a number of neutral countries.

The U.S. maintains depots storing large quantities of war matériel at military bases or "sanctuaries" in various neutral countries of the world, whence they are routinely transported by aircraft and freighter to Vietnam. Hence, the U.S. cannot complain or use force for the mere reason that some Cambodian jungle caches contain some war matériel, or rice, or medical supplies, to be moved to Vietnamese combat zones on the backs of humans, or by bicycle, buffalo, or truck. Either such depots are illegal for all sides to the conflict, or legal for all sides.

Can it be objected that the U.S. in storing war matériel, for example, in West German or Japanese "sanctuaries" acts legally because those neutrals *agreed* to such storage—but that the Provisional Revolutionary Government of South Vietnam or the Democratic Republic of Vietnam forces acted illegally by storing such goods in Cambodian caches because Cambodia had *not* agreed to this? It is a paradox: by this argument, they and Cambodia would be beyond reproach if Cambodia did *not* interpret her neutral duties more scrupulously than do the pro-U.S. neutrals. The paradox must be admitted, but it works both ways. If the U.S. asserted that Cambodia agreed to or tacitly suffered those caches, then the U.S., in view of its own and its neutral friends' behavior had no case: the very *assertion* that Cambodia openly or impliedly consented, *prevented* the U.S. from claiming this consent to be illegal. The U.S. failed to ascertain that its own assertion was incorrect. Only after the U.S. would have ascertained that Cambodia did *not* expressly or tacitly agree to those caches could the U.S. have claimed the violation of Cambodia's neutrality by the enemy.

However, even in such case, the U.S. would have been obliged to seek other, nonforceful remedies. In view of its own vast use of neutral depots, it could not claim such extreme unfairness and disadvantage as to allow it to invade Cambodia to capture the caches.

Was the Cambodian port of Sihanoukville an illegal "sanctuary"? A major—perhaps the main—reason for the invasion was to capture Cambodia's only deep-water port, Sihanoukville, and thus interdict its use for unloading of war matériel arriving from overseas for North Vietnamese and NLF forces. We can disregard the fact that the invasion would have been illegal under the U.N. Charter and general international law even *if* such use of the port had been improper on the part of neutral Cambodia or those belligerents. It was *not* improper, for the reasons just discussed. Huge quantities of war matériel for U.S. use in Vietnam have rightfully and routinely been loaded and unloaded in neutral ports in different parts of the world (and various transit routes in those neutral countries been used to transport them to and from those ports). The U.S. had no right to deny the same operations, on a much smaller scale, to either neutral Cambodia or its own adversaries. Thus, insofar as the purpose of the invasion was the capture of the port, the illegality of the invasion is further underscored by the illegality of that aim.

2. *Use of Neutral Territory by Belligerent's Armed Forces*: Traditional international law forbids any belligerent to make use of neutral territory by his armed forces.[18] In particular, he is forbidden to move troops across such territory (Hague Convention V, Art. 2). Under an age-old custom, belligerent forces—individuals, groups, or entire formations—may however enter neutral territory, whether adjacent to the theater of war or not (unless the neutral in its discretion forbids it), whereupon the neutral is obliged to disarm and intern them (same Convention, Art. 11).

If belligerent forces may not move (by any means of transport) *across* neutral territory, they are logically also forbidden to use neutral territory as a stopover for their troops, or move them in and out, as and until needed for or capable of war duties, because in all such ways neutral territory would serve the belligerent's war effort.

When we consider the U.S. conduct throughout its belligerency in Vietnam, we find a settled policy to *use numerous neutral countries*, not only for obtaining, storing, transporting, etc. war matériel (see above) but also *for its armed forces*. For example, the U.S. has freely transported contingents of its land, air, and naval forces stationed in NATO and SEATO countries to Vietnam. At its discretion, the U.S. has *trained* its forces undisturbed on its far-flung bases within various neutral territories for combat in Vietnam. In some non-NATO and non-SEATO neutral countries, notably Japan, U.S. bases have also served for years as staging and waiting areas for U.S. forces destined or held in reserve for Vietnam duty. In Japan, as well as in NATO and SEATO

---

[18] See, e.g., Australian authority J. G. Starke, *An Introduction to International Law*, 5th edn., London, 1963, p. 440.

neutral countries, U.S. bases as well as local industry and facilities have been constantly used to repair and re-equip U.S. military aircraft, naval ships, etc. in furtherance of the U.S. war in Vietnam.

Furthermore, over the years, altogether hundreds of thousands of U.S. military personnel have been sent to neutral territories such as Taiwan, Japan, Hong Kong, and Singapore for *"rest and recreation."* Such furloughs are certainly to be welcomed and, if the neutral country agrees, legitimate. But after furlough, the men have with equal regularity left those neutrals to rejoin the armed forces; in an undetermined proportion of cases, the very purpose has been to strengthen them for resumed war assignments in Indochina. This has violated a basic rule of the international law of war, incorporated as treaty obligation into U.S. military law (United States Department of the Army Field Manual 27-10)[19]—namely, that belligerent forces received on neutral territory must not be allowed to leave but must be interned by the neutral power. This is undisputed; e.g., the British Manual, *The Law of War on Land*,[20] provides specifically: "671 . . . a neutral State which received belligerent troops on its territory must intern them . . . they are *not permitted to rest, refresh and re-equip* themselves and *then to rejoin* the armed forces of the belligerent State" (i.e., whether for war or any other assignment).

If, in short, neutral nations are being utilized almost on a scale of continents by the U.S., does the U.S. have the "clean hands" required to complain about, and use force, against the use of some Cambodian hideouts by the other side?

Nor can it be argued that, regardless of the vast quantitative and qualitative discrepancy, the U.S. is acting legally because all those pro-U.S. neutrals have *consented* to serve as "sanctuaries" for the U.S. The

---

19 FM 27-10 of 18 July 1956, *The Law of Land Warfare*, incorporates (para. 532) this provision of Art. 11 of Hague Convention V of 1907 (36 Stat. 2310; T.S. 540) and comments (para. 533): "A neutral [may] permit belligerent troops to enter its territory without violating its neutrality, but the troops *must be interned* . . . and appropriate measures must be taken to *prevent their leaving the neutral country.*" They are in general "to be treated as prisoners of war."

Art. 14 of Hague Convention V of 1907 (incorporated as para. 539 into FM 27-10) even demands that *"wounded or sick* belonging to the belligerent armies . . . brought . . . into neutral territory must be guarded by the neutral Power so as to ensure their *not taking part again in the operations of the war.*"

Art. 37 of the more elaborate Geneva "Wounded and Sick" Convention of 1949 (47 Stat. 2074; T. S. 847), incorporated as para. 540 into FM 27-10) reiterates this rule which is also undisputed international practice. (See e.g., *Canadian Forces' Manual on the Geneva Conventions of 1949*, CFP 122 of 17 June 1968, para. 1037, pp. 1-23.)

20 Quoted in Whiteman, *l.c.*, 368.

argument begs the question, namely, whether those neutrals *can* lawfully grant such consent. Doubtlessly, under traditional treaty and customary international law, they could not do so; they would grossly violate the duties of neutrals. Neutral Switzerland or Ireland would never have granted such sanctuaries to any Axis or Allied power during World War II.

Hence, there are only two alternative answers, and neither validates the U.S. attack on Cambodia. Either the use of neutral countries by the U.S. for its Vietnam War effort with their consent implies that the international rules *forbidding* this have been tacitly *abrogated*, so that such behavior is now proper; then, the use of Cambodian border areas with neutral Cambodia's consent would be equally proper. Or the wide use by the U.S. of neutral countries, and the latter's consent, are *illegal*, in which case the use by PRG and DRNV, although on a small scale, of neutral Cambodia, and the latter's consent would also be illegal; but the U.S. could under the principles of *tu quoque* and "clean hands" not complain, and much less use force.[21]

Under either construction, Cambodia could not be subjected to U.S. attack: if she licitly consented to the presence of enemy troops on her territory, she was blameless; if she illicitly consented, she still acted much less improperly than do the neutrals consenting to much larger use of their territory by the U.S.

3. Infiltration from Neutral Territory into Combat Areas: The same applies to the argument that enemy soldiers enjoyed the unfair advantage of being able to move from neutral Cambodia into South Vietnam. In this respect again the other side is accused of something that the U.S. has been doing ever since 1965 on a vastly larger scale.

Neither by military nor by legal logic can it be said that if PRG or DRNV forces move by primitive means from inside the Cambodian border into South Vietnam, this *is* infiltration from a neutral sanctuary;

---

[21] The American authority Hyde emphasized that a belligerent aggrieved by the negligence of the neutral to prevent use of its territory by the opponent may not even ask *indemnity* from the negligent neutral if the claimant himself had no "clean hands": "In case . . . a belligerent suffered harm through the *neglect* of a neutral to prevent the violation of its own territory by the opposing belligerent, the value of the claim to *reparation* might be weakened if, notwithstanding such neglect, the conduct of the aggrieved belligerent was the *proximate cause* of the acts committed by the enemy. The belligerent claimant *should show clean hands as a condition* to its exaction of indemnity." *International Law, Chiefly as Interpreted and Applied by the United States* (C. G. Hyde, rev. edn., 1965, III, 2345.)

whereas if U.S. ground troops move into South Vietnam by modern transport from, say, West Germany, or if U.S. aircraft that took off from Japan bomb South Vietnam, this is *not* infiltration from a neutral country. Both cases are identical, insofar as belligerent forces departed from neutral territory for war purposes. The rationale of the law of neutrality is that neutral territories should in principle not be used to influence the conduct or course of war between others. But the military difference, which is also legally pertinent, is that the American "infiltration" has been on a vastly larger scale, both in numbers of personnel "infiltrated" and in destructiveness of weapons.

It may be said that neutral Cambodia was obligated to prevent infiltration from her soil into South Vietnam *even though* the various neutral countries from which U.S. military personnel have moved there have, contrary to the same obligation, *not* prevented this. The arguments regarding the other aspects of "sanctuary" apply.

Furthermore, the neutral's obligation is limited by its own *bona fide* capacities, as discussed below. Here, the error in the argument that the ability to infiltrate from across the border gave the opponent so unfair and so formidable an advantage as to justify massive invasion of neutral Cambodia must be stressed. As observed in one of the latter's communiqués to the U.N. Security Council, the U.S. with one million troops at its disposal should be able to prevent such occasional intrusions. The opponent has not had the physical capacity to prevent the movement of U.S. personnel by aircraft or troop ships into South Vietnam.

Within the context of "unfair" military advantage, the crucial role of *Thailand* for the U.S. war in Indochina cannot be overlooked. With its vast U.S.-built military bases and facilities, Thailand has throughout served as "sanctuary" in every military sense—depot, arsenal, repair shop, training and staging area, takeoff and return point for daily air missions, and as a "rest and recreation" area. Thailand's support role has been so large (including contribution of troops) that it classifies as belligerent, not neutral, and therefore in a strictly legal sense does not count among American "neutral sanctuaries."[22] But with the other side incapable of starting war actions against her, she has tactically and strategically been not only an indispensable but unmolested sanctuary for the U.S. war—including the invasion of, and subsequent operations in, Cambodia.

---

[22] The fact that Thailand has been for years in a state of war does, of course, say nothing about the legality, or not, of its role.

4. "Sanctuary" Prevents "Hot Pursuit" of Enemy Forces: A last aspect of the "sanctuary" argument requires only brief mention (although at the turn of 1967 and 1968 it seemed to make a U.S. attack on Cambodia imminent), because it was not invoked when that attack did start in 1970—namely, that the U.S. has been improperly denied the right to pursue enemy troops withdrawing into neighboring Cambodia.

It suffices to remember that there has been an age-old undisputed right, sanctioned by international convention, for belligerent forces to seek refuge in neutral states, and for the latter to receive them.[23]

The notion that the opponent has the right to pursue into the neutral territory is untenable. At least since the end of the eighteenth century, the law of warfare has forbidden hot pursuit; even before that time it had constituted a violation of neutrality that rendered the invader liable to make amends to the neutral.[24]

The implication, then, that it is normal or just to pursue fleeing enemy troops into neutral territory in order to kill or to capture them there, is erroneous and misleads public opinion. For two hundred years, the term has been used exclusively in an altogether different connotation, namely, in maritime law, unrelated to war or neutrality: If a foreign ship violates some rules within another state's territorial waters, and then tries to escape to the open sea, certain ships of the littoral state may under specific conditions pursue it in order to arrest it and bring it back for proper action.[25] By definition, this can never cause harm to lives or property on neutral territory.[26]

THE FALLACY OF THE "SANCTUARY" ARGUMENT

To summarize: If the (figurative, not legal) term "sanctuary" conveys that it is illegal or improper for belligerents to maintain "caches" of war matériel or food or medicine in neutral territory, or to transport such goods through or obtain them from neutral countries, or the like, this notion is groundless. None of this violates international law or the practice of states, as evidenced, e.g., by the practice of the neutral U.S.

[23] The neutral is, thereupon, obligated to intern them. But, for the reasons discussed above, if Cambodia openly or tacitly admitted some fleeing NLF or DRNV soldiers and then failed to intern them, the U.S. had no right to punish her by massive invasion because (apart from the evident disproportion of the response) the U.S. has routinely moved its own military personnel into and out of neutral countries which have not interned them.

[24] Oppenheim-Lauterpacht, *International Law*, 7th edn., 1952, II, 627.

[25] Such "hot pursuit" was used by the U.S. during Prohibition. See, e.g., U.S.-British Convention for Prevention of Smuggling of Intoxicating Liquors, 43 Stat. 1761; T.S. 685 (1924).

[26] See International Convention on the High Seas, 1958; and, e.g., Myres S. McDougal and Associates, *Studies in World Public Order*, 1960, p. 811, n. 204, citing other authorities.

involving billions of dollars worth of war matériel for other nations' wars in World Wars I and II, and ever since then; this is also seen in the fact that, in turn, the U.S. has openly and constantly made wide use of such depots in various neutral countries of the world for its war in Indochina.

In contradistinction, the use by a belligerent of neutral territory for the training, staging, maintenance, or recreation of his forces is by traditional international law forbidden—as is "infiltration" of belligerent forces from and to neutral territory, to and from the war zone.

However—and this is of decisive importance—to do all this has been the constant practice of the U.S. during this war, with the approval of the neutral countries so used. The U.S. has been transporting its forces ("infiltration") into South Vietnam from various neutral countries in different parts of the world, not by oxcarts but by modern aircraft and transport ships; it has maintained and trained forces destined for Vietnam duty in such neutral countries, not in hidden jungles and under search by enemy aircraft, but unperturbed in up-to-date installations; it has been able to have its military personnel rest in hotels in neutral countries and not have them detained there but return to war duty.

Whether this most extraordinary phenomenon indicates a tacit *abolition* of the old rule must at least be left open. It must be strongly urged that the old rule (still prominently presented in the military manuals, including that of the U.S. Army) has *not* been abolished. Such construction is not only based on formal legalism—it cannot be said that a *custom* has emerged that would invalidate the contrary international treaty—but for persuasive substantive reasons: the tacit abolition of those eminently important provisions would erode the concept of neutrality, would make hostilities more sanguinary, and unfairly favor the belligerent state able to obtain more neutral "sanctuaries" than his opponent can.

The question of whether the permissiveness of the neutral countries concerned—from West Germany to Japan—toward this use of their territories has violated their own duties under the law of neutrality, must also be left open. However, if their permissions *are* illegal, then the illegal permissions *cannot make the use of their territories legal for the U.S.*

What counts most is that the large and powerful U.S. cannot apply one standard to itself and its neutral friends, and another to its small opponents and small Cambodia. What is *legal* for the U.S. must also be legal for the adversary. If, in turn, all this has been *illegal* for the

U.S. side—if, in other words, the U.S. and the permissive pro-U.S. neutrals have broken the law of neutrality on so large a scale, then the U.S. has no right to complain about the identical but much smaller illegality on the other side.

Cambodia Did Not Fail in Her Duty to Prevent Violations of Her Neutrality: It is true that the law as laid down in international treaties and quoted in military manuals requires neutrals not only *not to agree* to, but actively *to prevent* use of their territories by forces of foreign belligerents.

Legally, and by common sense and elementary fairness, it is impossible to posit that pro-U.S. neutrals have *not* been under this duty to prevent, but that Cambodia *has been* under such duty.

However, even if it were permissible to proceed from this odd assumption, we would find that Sihanouk's Cambodia did not fail in her duty. For, the duty is by the same traditional law limited to the neutrals' *capacity* to prevent violations of its neutrality; the Hague Convention XIII of 1907 (Art. 8 and Art. 23) states a principle long since undisputed, by stipulating that the neutral is "bound to exercise such surveillance as the *means at its disposal allow*."[27] The literature is unanimous on this matter of grave importance.[28] See, at random, Oppenheim-Lauterpacht's authority: "a neutral can be made responsi-

[27] Prior to 1907, it was sometimes asserted, especially by the United States, that a neutral country must use *"due diligence"* against violations of its neutrality. Some controversy developed about the exact meaning of "due diligence." Because the interpretation may determine the fate of an innocent state, the 1907 Hague Conference dropped the concept of "due diligence" and demanded from the neutrals, as the text in Convention XII, quoted above, shows, "the employment of the means *at their disposal*." Since then, the term "due diligence" is to be understood in this sense. (Oppenheim-Lauterpacht, *l.c.*, II, 758.) The treatise also points out that (a) had the United States' interpretation of due diligence "been generally accepted, *the most oppressive obligations* would have become incumbent upon neutrals"; (b) "no such general acceptance has taken place"; and (c) the concept of "due diligence" . . . *"can have no other meaning than . . . such diligence* as can be *reasonably expected* when *all the circumstances and conditions* of the case are taken into consideration." (*L.c.* 757-758.)

[28] See, e.g., in addition to Oppenheim-Lauterpacht: Hyde, *l.c.*, 2334, quoting Secretary of State Thomas Jefferson's view, 1795: "a neutral is not deemed to be guilty of delinquency for which it is chargeable with responsibility, when it employes the *means at its disposal* to prevent unlawful activities within its territory"; H. B. Jacobini, *International Law*, 1968, p. 345, quoting a case arising from the War of 1812; D. W. Bowett, *Self-Defense in International Law*, 1958, pp. 170-171, quoting Hyde, the award of the German-Portuguese arbitration tribunal, Hall, and other authorities; Rodick, *The Doctrine of Necessity in International Law*, 1928, p. 117: There is no "legal justification and excuse for a belligerent violation of neutral rights in a case where the neutral has not failed in any duty which it owes to the particular belligerent." (Quoted by Bowett, p. 168.)

ble only for such acts favouring or damaging a belligerent as he could by due diligence have prevented, and which *by culpable negligence* he failed to prevent. It is by no means obligatory for a neutral to prevent such acts under all circumstances and conditions. *This is in fact impossible. . . .*"[29]

Since Cambodia did not intentionally fail to protect her neutrality, the U.S. could not base military intervention in Cambodia on such failure.

Yet, can it be argued that all this is contradicted by the doctrine expounded in the U.S. Department of the Army Field Manual 27-10 (para. 520): "Should the neutral State be unable, or fail for any reason, to prevent violations of its neutrality by the troops of one belligerent entering or passing through its territory, the other belligerent *may* be justified in attacking the enemy forces on this territory." The answer is *no*. The statement is very subtle. It must be read with a magnifying glass; after all, the fate of entire countries may be at stake. It does *not* say that *every* entry into or passage through neutral territory by forces of a belligerent constitutes by itself a violation of neutrality. It says that *if* such forces violate the neutrality of a neutral state while entering or passing through it, the other belligerent *may* attack them there. The distinction is crucial. It permits the U.S. to claim that such entry or passage by U.S. forces is *not* a violation of neutrality. Otherwise, the U.S. Field Manual would declare (a) that U.S. troops entering, for example, Japanese or British territory while the U.S. is a belligerent in Indochina, violate Japan's or Britain's neutrality; and (b) if Japan or Britain "for any reason" (including treaty arrangements with the U.S.) fails to prevent this, the other side (or any of their allies) can lawfully attack U.S. forces in Japan or Britain.

The key word in this unilateral interpretation of international law by the U.S. Army[30] is "may" ("the other belligerent *may* be justified. . ."). When, under what circumstances, he *may* be justified is simply not spelled out in the Manual. Since neutral territory is in principle "inviolable," and unilateral use of force in principle forbidden (the Manual itself refers to "Crimes against Peace"),[31] this extreme

---

[29] *L.c.*, 757-758.

[30] Hence, as the Manual emphasizes at the outset (ch. 1, sec. 1, para. 1), such statements as para. 520, which reproduce neither statutory nor treaty provisions, "should not be considered binding upon courts and tribunals applying the law of war" but are, in the Manual's view, "of evidentiary value *insofar* as they bear upon questions of custom and practice."

[31] Paras. 498 and 500, in sec. II ("Crimes under International Law") of ch. 8.

form of self-help may—if at all compatible with the present world order—only be used as an extreme last resort. This means it must not be used as a sudden surprise (as in Cambodia) but after nonviolent forms for the redress of grievances had been fully tried by the aggrieved belligerent.[32] The U.S. has not sought, nor claimed to have tried, those other forms of redress of grievances.

Attack on the Lawless Opponent in Neutral Territory as Ultimate Resort for Self-Preservation: Modern history shows a single case of a counterinvasion of a neutral country in response to that neutral's invasion by the opponent. In 1914, large German armies swept into neutral Belgium, whence they were to sweep into France and crushingly defeat her (the notorious *Schlieffen* plan). In that situation of ultimate danger—but also, it must be noted, to honor their treaty obligations as guarantors of Belgium's neutrality so blatantly violated by Germany[33] —France and her ally Great Britain counterinvaded Belgium to battle the Germans there. It is for extreme situations of this sort, when the belligerent's very *self-preservation* is endangered by a lawless opponent, that an "ultimate resort" to force against that lawless opponent on the territory of the innocent neutral is considered permissible.[34] Apart from all other considerations refuting the legality of the

[32] See, e.g., Morris Greenspan, *The Modern Law of Land Warfare*, 1959, quoted in note 34 below.

[33] Britain's declaration of war against Germany was based on that ground.

[34] Regarding the "ultimate resort" doctrine, see the authorities quoted in Whiteman, *l.c.*, 190-193. The *Digest's* section "Belligerent Remedies for Breach of Neutrality" opens with this quotation from Greenspan, *The Modern Law of Land Warfare*, p. 584: "In general, the remedies for breach of neutrality, either by the neutral state or by a belligerent, consist in *protest* to the power concerned, *demand for compensation, retaliatory* action in the nature of reprisals and, in the *ultimate resort, declaration of war*. Since it is obvious that retaliatory action can easily develop into war, recourse should *first* be had to *peaceful* methods of resolving the dispute, such as those outlined in Article 33 of the United Nations Charter."

Julius Stone (*Legal Controls of International Conflict*, 1959, pp. 400-401) is quoted as stating, *i.a.*: "One clear principle is that, the *right of self-preservation apart*, an aggrieved State is *clearly not entitled* to violate the neutral's territorial integrity, simply because his enemy has done so." Stone is speaking of "self-help" actions against the enemy in neutral *waters*, where of course damage to the territory or persons of the neutral state is excluded.

A very strict limitation on the right to use force even in neutral waters is set by Tucker in a study prepared for the U.S. Naval College: "Despite . . . dearth of precedents it is the opinion of a number of publicists that if the neutral State is unable to enforce its rights against one belligerent making unlawful use of its waters the other belligerent may—as *an extreme measure*—resort to hostile action . . . in neutral waters. . . . It is still the opinion of perhaps the majority of writers that the *only exception* ought to be *self-preservation* —interpreted *in the most narrow sense*." (Robert Tucker, "The Law of War and Neutral-

U.S. attack on Cambodia, it would be absurd to claim, and it was not claimed, that U.S. self-preservation was at stake.

Precedent: *French Bombing Raid on an Algerian NLF "Sanctuary" in Tunisia, 1958*: Invasion, even if genuinely nonhostile, of a neutral country is so generally abhorred that precedents are lacking. However, post-1945 history chronicles one single air raid against a "sanctuary," namely, during the French-Algerian War. As an isolated event, it was *not* an invasion. It resembles any one of the numerous U.S. and Saigon *pre*-invasion attacks on Cambodian border areas. Also, in that war, France was not an intruder; she did fight for her territorial integrity.[35]

By early 1958, the French-Algerian War had lasted almost four years. The NLF received rather open support in neighboring Tunisia and Morocco—the two protectorates to which France had granted independence in 1956 "without a fight." But in Algeria, the French military "refused to accept a defeat like at Dien Bien Phu or a capitulation without defeat" as in Tunisia and Morocco. "The officers were convinced that only the Tunisian and Moroccan aid prevented the liquidation of the [Algerian] rebels."[36]

On February 8, 1958, 25 French aircraft bombed and machine-gunned for an hour the Tunisian village of Sakhiet Sidi Youssef, about 1½ kilometers from the Algerian border, killing 69 and injuring 130 persons, and wholly or partly destroying over 100 houses, 40 shops and several public buildings.[37] General Sagan, the commander in Algeria, stated that only military objectives such as buildings used as camps and command posts for the Algerian rebels were attacked. The De-

---

ity at Sea," U.S. Naval War College, *International Law Studies*, 1955 [1957], pp. 220, 221-223; quoted in Whiteman, *l.c.*, 193.)

The "dearth of precedents" is itself instructive: Tucker cites *one* attack each on an enemy ship in neutral waters in the Russian-Japanese war of 1905, in World War I, and in World War II; and one mine-sowing action (*ibid.*, p. 193). The single attack in neutral waters during World War II (the British stopped the German ship *Altmark* and, without damaging it, forcefully liberated British prisoners from it) is still debated among international lawyers.

[35] As Raymond Aron, not a French chauvinist, wrote: "Algeria is legally an integral part of the national territory, it is inhabited by a million French who have built up (*qui ont édifié*) Algeria and who cannot conceive to stay there as foreigners. If Algeria were to become independent (*devient un Etat*) France . . . would vow to itself the mediocre position of Spain (*la France sera . . . vouée à la médiocrité espagnole*)." (*Immuable et Changeante, De la IVᵉ à la Vᵉ République*, Paris, 1959, pp. 177-178.)

[36] *Ibid.*, p. 177.

[37] This summary is based on U.N. documents and the detailed well-documented recital in *Kiesinger's Contemporary Archives*, issue of May 31–June 7, 1958, pp. 18203-18207.

fense Minister invoked France's "right of legitimate self-defense against anti-aircraft forces installed on Tunisian territory"; the village was "a nest of rebels and murderers"; in the preceding 7 months, 30 French aircraft had been fired on in the Sakhiet area, and 2 forced down; in spite of French warnings of reprisals, early on February 8 still another French aircraft was hit from there. Premier Félix Gaillard declared in the National Assembly on February 11: ". . . Sakhiet was an active center of [Algerian] rebellion . . . NLF services and camps were installed side by side with those of the Tunisian troops . . . events confirmed the importance of the infiltration. . . . There is no international law which compels a State that is being attacked from its neighbor's territory to put up with it indefinitely. . ." After many months of restraint the aircraft "hit back [at] military objectives which represented a grave and permanent danger. . ."

Yet, the reaction to the French raid was distinctly negative; while the reaction to Tunisia's vehement responses were remarkably mild.

Tunisia's responses included unilateral abrogation of the extraterritorial status of Bizerte (then still a French naval prefecture); severe restrictions, such as cutting off of telephone communications, food supplies, and services, on French troops and warships (still in Tunisia under treaty rights) and request for their immediate evacuation; recall of Tunisia's ambassador from Paris; request that France close five of her seven consulates in Tunisia; expulsion of French residents from frontier areas; and a request to the U.N. Security Council to condemn "the deliberate act of aggression" at Sakhiet and to take measures "to end a situation which threatens Tunisia's security and international peace."

Criticism within France was expressed not only in the press and in the National Assembly, for example, by Robert Schuman, Jules Moch, and M. Pleven; before the Tunisian ambassador left Paris, ex-Premier Mendès-France, François Mauriac, and other prominent personalities demonstratively visited him to express their sympathy.

The U.S. immediately disassociated itself from the raid, and counseled against any further military actions of this sort. On February 9, Secretary of State Dulles informed the French ambassador in Washington of U.S. "concern." On February 10, a State Department statement described the U.S. Government as "profoundly disturbed." Grave disquiet was expressed by other governments, and offers of good offices extended by Britain, Italy, Lebanon, and, in personal letters to the French Premier and President Bourguiba, by President Eisenhower.

France and Tunisia accepted a joint Anglo-American mission of good offices even before the U.N. Security Council met on the Algerian complaint and the French countercomplaint[38] on February 18.

The course of the ensuing negotiations under the auspices of the U.S.-U.K. conciliation team again shows a radical difference from the U.S. attitudes in the Cambodian case. For example, the conciliators accepted Tunisia's rejection of French demands for a joint French-Tunisian control of the border and for establishment of a "no-man's-zone" along the borders inside Algeria. Bourguiba declared that he would continue to allow Algerians to enter Tunisia provided they would not disturb the French residents there. In fact, the only U.S.-U.K. proposition bearing on the sanctuary problem was that neutral observers would ensure against military airfields in southern Tunisia being used by the Algerian NLF. Their other main propositions—such as an accelerated timetable for the evacuation of all French forces, except those at Bizerte—veered significantly toward Tunisia's position. France specifically accepted these propositions as the basis for her direct negotiations with Tunisia.

Particularly instructive in view of official justifications of the U.S.-Saigon invasion of Cambodia (and Laos) was Foreign Minister Pineau's impassioned defense in the National Assembly on April 15, 1958, of his government's acceptance of a peaceful settlement[39] with Tunisia, against the accusations by right-wing deputies that this constituted an American dictate. Pineau's main arguments were: (a) Rejection of the Anglo-American good offices would "inevitably" have led to French military intervention in Tunisia "and practically to the reoccupation[40] of Tunisia, at least in part." (b) Indeed, by accepting the

---

[38] It asserted, *i.a.*, that the Algerian NLF general staff had been installed in Tunisia since July 1957, with the Tunisian Government's permission; and that Tunisian authorities permitted and sometimes facilitated the movements of NLF forces. "The counter-action of the French Air Force originated in the numerous provocations suffered by our troops."

The Security Council unanimously decided on February 18 to adjourn consideraiton pending the results of the U.S.-U.K. conciliation efforts. (S/INF/13/Ref. 1, p. 3.)

[39] There is also a parallel with regard to the U.S.-Saigon invasion of Laos: for weeks prior to its start in early February 1971, the press reported strenuous efforts by the opposing Laos factions to reach a compromise that would have prevented at least an invasion of their country.

[40] The use of the word "*re*-occupation" refers to the fact that Tunisia had become independent from France only two years earlier. At the time of the Sakhiet incident, France still had, under treaty rights, some 150,000 troops stationed in Tunisia. Pineau stated in the National Assembly on Feb. 14, 1958, that an estimated six to seven thousand Algerian rebels were operating on Tunisian territory, and that the Tunisian army was smaller than

good offices, France avoided the risk "of extending the conflict to the whole of North Africa." (c) France must not be provoked by the rebels into transforming the internal (French-Algerian) conflict into an international war, in which eventual intervention by other nations would become inevitable. (d) And "Firmness does not consist—as some people who claim a monopoly on patriotism maintain—in yielding to the temptation to extend the war . . . but in resisting this temptation. . . . We have been criticized for not giving our troops in Tunisia orders to march. Nothing would have been easier. The Government's orders have been quite the reverse . . . because we wished to . . . respect the independence of States to which we had agreed."[41]

Yet, the Gaillard government was defeated by the National Assembly on the issue, and fell. The commotion created by Sakhiet led to the revolt by "ultras" and dissatisfied army officers. Civil war was avoided by the return to power of Charles de Gaulle. He at once agreed with Tunisia to withdraw all French forces (except those at Bizerte) within four months. The agreement contained nothing about netural supervision of the former French military airfields.

Thereafter, the support by Tunisia, Morocco, and also Egypt for the Algerian cause increased. By September 1958, the Provisional Government of the Algerian Republic openly set up headquarters in Cairo and Tunis. Algerian NLF or ALN (Armée de Libération Nationale) troops were rather openly stationed in Tunisia and Morocco. Although the French-Algerian War lasted another four years after Sakhiet (the cease-fire agreement was signed on March 18, 1962), Sakhiet remained the only French air raid against an Algerian "sanctuary."

Since the French-Tunisian dispute was transferred from the U.N. Security Council to a conciliation effort and then settled between the parties, the Council had no occasion[42] to take a substantive stand on Tunisia's charge that France's one-hour raid on Sakhiet constituted "aggression," or on France's claim that (in current language) use of the Sakhiet "sanctuary" by the Algerians, in connivance with neutral Tunisia, was not legitimate under the U.N. Charter. But the international reaction to the raid; the attitude of the U.S.-U.K. conciliation team; the terms of the bilateral settlement; the subsequent concern of govern-

---

that. French military measures against the Algerians there, thus, might not have required an *invasion* by (additional) French forces into Tunisia.

[41] Quoted in translation from *Journal Officiel* in *Kiesinger's Contemporary Archives, l.c.*

[42] France and Tunisia advised the U.N. Security Council of the settlement on June 18, 1958. This obviated the need for further debate.

ments, including the U.S., inside and outside the U.N., to prevent the French-Algerian war from spreading; and, not least, France's subsequent four-year abstention from military measures against Algerian use of neutral soil—all this shows a high degree of consensual disapprobation of military measures against neutral "sanctuaries," and insistence on nonviolent methods of settlement.

That conclusion is strengthened by reference to the *Corfu Channel* doctrine of the International Court of Justice[43] and, for example, by the consistently strict position of the Security Council, with U.S., concurrence, against the use of force in the Arab-Israeli conflict, even in reply to provocations and wrongful actions conceded by the Council.

It is also indicative of the *opinio juris* that immediately after the start of the U.S. invasion of Cambodia, the negotiation and conference method was strongly urged not only, for example, by Secretary-General U Thant but by a special meeting of 11 pro-American Asian and Pacific governments. That meeting was supposed to decide on arms supplies to the Lon Nol regime. However, the delegates did not even consider this but instead insisted that the hostilities in Cambodia must *end*. Hence, they demanded a conference, or other negotiating method, as opposed to the military method.[44]

III. Further Justifications of the Attack

Apart from the "sanctuary" argument, the attack on Cambodia was accompanied by several "justifications," coupled with dark threats[45] which are disruptive of the basic tenets of world order.

1. The Attack Was Necessary to "Buy Time":[46] Never has an attack on a neutral country been justified by such an argument. The invasion of spring 1970 was being justified not by a then existing but by a potential future danger for the U.S. strategic *timetable*: if enemy forces would

---

[43] See, e.g., the view of McChesney (quoted in Whiteman, *l.c.*, p. 193) that the British action in 1940 against the *Altmark* (which did not even damage the German ship), as reply to the *Altmark's* violation of neutral Norwegian waters, "would now be illegal" in the light of the *Corfu Channel* doctrine and the U.N. Charter.

[44] See newspaper reports on the meeting of May 16 and 17, 1970, and Indonesian President Suharto's summary of its results, as reported in the *New York Times*, May 24, 1970 ("Suharto Fears a Widening of War in Indochina"), p. 30.

[45] For example: "I again warn the North Vietnamese that if they continue to escalate the fighting when the U.S. is withdrawing its forces, I shall . . . *take the action I consider necessary to defend the security* of our American men." (President Nixon's TV address, April 30, 1970, announcing the attack, *New York Times*, May 1, 1970, p. 2.)

[46] Statement by Secretary of Defense Laird (*New York Times*, May 3, 1970, p. 2.)

infiltrate from the Cambodian border areas in larger numbers by *April 1971*, the partial withdrawal of U.S. ground troops scheduled for that future date might be jeopardized. The argument was, furthermore, based on the very expectation that the attack of spring 1970 would fail: Its aim would *not* be achieved. The enemy will build new "sanctuaries." But this will take some time during which the fighting capacity of the Saigon forces will be so much improved that the April 1971 deadline will be kept.[47]

The invasion, then, will "buy time" for the continuing U.S. war, eventually to be fought under the "Vietnamization" strategy. That strategy will cast the U.S. forces into a role not only profoundly humiliating but blatantly illegal under international law: in order to help the U.S.-paid, U.S.-equipped Saigon forces to conquer South Vietnam and keep her conquered, U.S. air and naval forces will be at Saigon's beck and call to bomb, napalm, and defoliate ("logistic support").

Military experts have pointed at the military illogic of this plan.[48] But even if it were militarily "sound,"[49] it proclaims the following: any nation may invade another nation, in preparation for its changed military strategy in a war in a third country. Since the U.S. military intervention in Vietnam has been illegal in the first place, the doctrine actually reads: A nation that has illegally intervened in a foreign nation has the right to indefinitely continue that military intervention through change of strategy, for which purpose it has the right to attack other countries.

If, however, the U.S. interventions in Indochina are *not* considered

---

[47] Similarly on Feb. 17, 1971, President Nixon declared that "even if the *Laotian* operation had *not* been undertaken . . . the troops withdrawal program [for 1971] *could have gone ahead on schedule.*" The Laotian operation "concerned . . . *next* year [1972]." (*New York Times*, Feb. 18, 1971, p. 14.)

[48] President Johnson, in a message of Dec. 31, 1963 to Mr. Thieu's predecessor General Duong Van Minh, stated: "As the forces of your government become increasingly capable of dealing with this aggression, American military personnel in South Vietnam can be progressively withdrawn." (Committee on Foreign Relations, U.S. Senate, *Background Information Relating to S.E. Asia and Vietnam*, 4th rev. edn., 90th Cong., 2nd Sess., 1968, p. 133.)

[49] A report by staff members of the U.S. Senate Foreign Relations Committee on their visit to South Vietnam (Dec. 1969) states: "When Vietnamese military self-sufficiency is discussed by American officers [in South Vietnam] it is never put in a context of less than two to four years. In fact, planning in connection with Vietnamization seems vague. . . . There does not seem to be a fixed timetable. Construction work on American bases throughout the country appears to be continuing . . . the talk in Saigon among Vietnamese as well as Americans is in terms of keeping some 25,000 [U.S.] troops there for years." (*Vietnam: December 1969*, expurgated U.S. Senate Foreign Relations Committee Print, Feb. 2, 1970, p. 10.)

illegal, then, under this doctrine, any other nation, e.g. , the Soviet Union or China, is allowed to intervene in another country's civil war (analogous to the U.S. intervention in Vietnam), sow destruction there for years, and then start destroying adjacent countries as a prerequisite for its conditional change of combat strategy in the first country.

2. *The U.S. Cannot Allow Itself to Suffer the First Defeat in Its Proud History*: The doctrine of the need to avert defeat means that a state engaged in war (even if that war were *not* illegal) is entitled, nay, in honor *bound* to widen the war by *illegal* war action, rather than to extricate itself.

At Nuremberg, the defense tried to argue that Hitler Germany had been engaged in a "life and death" struggle: to stave off catastrophe, it could disregard legal restraints and take desperate measures. The International Nuremberg Tribunal, as well as the Nuremberg Tribunals composed exclusively of U.S. judges, of course rejected this "extreme emergency" (*Notstand*) doctrine. One of the U.S. tribunals answered it as follows:

> The contention that the rules and customs of war can be violated if either party is hard pressed in war must be rejected. . . . War is by definition a risky and basically unrational means of "settling" conflicts—why right-thinking people all over the world repudiate and abhor aggressive war. It is an essence of war that one or the other side must lose, and the experienced generals and statesmen knew this when they drafted the rules and customs of land warfare. In short, these rules and customs of warfare are designed specifically for all phases of war. They comprise the law for such emergency. To claim that they can be wantonly—and at the sole discretion of any one belligerent—disregarded when he considers his situation to be critical, means nothing more nor less than to abrogate the laws and customs of war entirely.[50]

[50] Judgment by U.S. Military Tribunal III, Nuremberg, Krupp Case, *Trials of War Criminals before the Nuremberg Military Tribunals. . .* , IX, 1347.

Similarly, Judgment by U.S. Military Tribunal V, Nuremberg, case against Field-Marshal von Leeb, et al., *Trials. . .* , XI, 541: "It has been the viewpoint of many German writers . . . that military necessity includes the right to do anything that contributes to the winning of a war. We content ourselves on this subject with stating that such a view would eliminate all humanity and decency and all law from the conduct of war and it is a contention which this Tribunal repudiates as contrary to the accepted usages of civilized nations."

In the case of Hitler Germany, at least the premise was correct: the Third Reich did face utter defeat. In the present case, even the premise is false. Since the avowed U.S. war aim is self-determination for the South Vietnamese and neutralization of South Vietnam, and the other side has always been ready to accept this (in fact has constantly demanded this), hostilities could end immediately on this basis. It would be no defeat for the U.S. The only obstacle is the incompatible U.S. determination to maintain the Thieu regime at the cost of indefinite further war. Would it be a victory for the U.S. to remain virtually the captive of that regime?[51] Would, as President Nixon implied, its replacement by a coalition government make the U.S. a "second-class Power"? The worth and pride of a nation is not measured by the frequency with which it imposes its will on smaller nations.

3. Had the U.S. Not Attacked Cambodia, U.S. "Credibility" Would Have Been "Lost": Generalized, this constitutes a novel definition, or different type, of the "just war"; State *A*—and hence any state—has the right (or, out of self-respect, perhaps the duty), if unable to achieve its war aim against State *B* (North Vietnam), to extend its war into State *C* (Cambodia)—or, as the subsequent invasion of Laos showed, also into still other states; this in order to forestall in undetermined outside countries a future psychological reaction (loss of "belief" in State *A*'s determination) considered undesirable by State *A*.

4. The War Is a Test of America's "Responsibilities of Power": On May 7, 1970, Ellsworth Bunker, U.S. Ambassador to Saigon, speaking at the U.S. Military Academy at West Point, defined the entire Vietnam War "as a test of America's commitment to 'the struggle for freedom' and the 'rule of law.' "[52] In the same address, he acknowledged what he called the war's "moral ambiguities" but dismissed them by referring to the "world policeman" doctrine: "But as the world's most powerful nation we cannot escape the responsibilities of power."[53] This doctrine is, indeed, largely dictating U.S. world policies. Yet no country, however powerful, is or can be delegated the role of the world's policeman. Any doctrine of hegemonic power implies two canons of

---

[51] "Thieu is determined to maintain himself in power . . . while many believe that Thieu has the support of no more than 20% of the people . . . it is felt that as long as he can count on American support . . . he will not . . . involve other non-Communist political elements in governing the country." (*Vietnam: December 1969, l.c.,* 12.)

[52] As reported in the *Daily News* (New York City), May 9, 1970, p. 8.

[53] *Ibid.*

behavior—one for the hegemonial nation and one for the other nations —and thus destroys the very fundaments of world order as built up over centuries. It also runs counter to the most elementary and realistic test of any rule of international behavior, namely, the requirement of *acceptance* by the rest of the world community. Furthermore, the "policeman" figure of speech actually conceals its full meaning. A policeman is under the rule of the law: he may *pursuant to rules not determined by himself, arrest* a suspect; but he may *not try,* and *much less execute,* the suspect. The role arrogated for the "most powerful nation" is that of policeman *plus* judge *plus* executioner (as photographs from Indochina vividly prove). In essence, the doctrine claims that a country is, in proportion to its power to destroy, above or exempt from the law, or entitled to lay down the law for others. It is a crude expression of the "might makes right" claim—which, because of its inevitable dialectic repercussions, is fraught with dangers for the would-be "world policeman."

IV. Other Considerations

1. U.S. Intervention in Cambodia Is a Part of the Illegal Intervention in Vietnam: A central aim of the present world order is to prevent armed hostilities. Hence, states are bound to seek to *end* as quickly as possible[54] any hostilities (even those exceptionally permissible) in which they may nevertheless be engaged. This, incidentally, has always been a moral if not legal obligation of states. The attack on Cambodia was, as mentioned before, designed toward precisely the opposite end, namely, to improve the chances for the *continuation* of the U.S. war (under the changed strategy of "Vietnamization"). Since the intervention in Vietnam has from its beginning been illegal, pursuant to the U.N. Charter, the 1954 Geneva Accords, the SEATO Treaty, the Kellogg Pact, and general international law,[55] the intervention in Cambodia, being an integral part of it, is also illegal. It compounds the original illegality because it further deteriorates the chances for peace in Indochina.

Throughout the Vietnam conflict, there has been a flickering ray of hope. All sides have considered the Geneva Accords of 1954 still

[54] This evident logic of the U.N. Charter has been expressed in numerous Security Council Resolutions wherein the Council, even within days or hours after occurrence of armed hostilities, demanded a cease-fire and withdrawal of forces, without pronouncing on the merits of the case.

[55] See, e.g., Fried, rapporteur, *Vietnam and International Law*, 1967.

valid.[56] The eventual settlement would have to confirm the independence, unity, territorial integrity, and neutrality of Vietnam and Cambodia. If, then, those agreements are merely *suspended*, all parties are, under the principle of good faith, obligated (in the language of the Vienna Convention on the Law of Treaties), to refrain from acts tending to render the *resumption* of the operation of the (Geneva) agreements impossible.[57]

By enabling the U.S.-trained, U.S.-equipped, U.S.-paid, and U.S.-advised forces of one of the two rival South Vietnam regimes to establish themselves in Cambodia (another "Vietnamization" unthinkable under the 1954 Geneva agreements), the U.S. rendered any eventual settlement, including the reestablishment of Cambodia's independence, much more difficult.

2. *Use of Illegal Methods of Warfare in Cambodia*: Since an attack on neutral territory against a misbehaving opponent is, if permitted at all, by definition exclusively directed against such opponent and not against the neutral country, the attacker must conduct his operation in a manner *least damaging* to the neutral country. He must also, of course, abide by the laws and customs of warfare toward the opponent. Published eyewitness reports indicate that some of the methods of warfare used in Cambodia by the U.S. and U.S.-advised Saigon forces have disregarded those rules. This also vitiates the attack because it indicates that the strategy for the attack included the commission of war crimes.[58]

[56] See, e.g., on the American side, U.S. draft resolution submitted by Ambassador Goldberg to the President of the U.N. Security Council on Jan. 31, 1966. It would have the Council note "that the provisions of the Geneva Accords of 1954 and 1962 *have not been implemented*," and the Council call "for . . . a conference looking toward the *application of the Geneva accords of 1954* and 1962." (U.S. Senate Committee on Foreign Relations, 90th Cong., 2nd Sess., *Background Information Relating to Southeast Asia and Vietnam*, 1968, p. 175.)

[57] The U.N. International Law Commission commented in 1966 that the respective draft article (Art. 68) "is intended to make clear that [during a treaty's suspension] the legal nexus between the parties established by the treaty remains *intact* and that it is only the *operation* of its provisions which is suspended." Regarding the obligation "to refrain from acts *calculated to render the operation of the treaty impossible* as soon as the ground or cause of suspension ceases, [the] Commission considered this obligation to be implicit in the very concept of 'suspension' and to be imposed on the parties by their [general] obligation . . . to perform the treaty *in good faith*." (Reproduced, e.g., in 8 *Indian Journal of International Law* 1 [Jan. 1968], 157.)

[58] For example, a correspondent accompanying "Task Force Shoemaker" into Cambodia reported on the third day of the campaign: "American ground troops who in Vietnam had

3. The Destructiveness of the U.S. Attack Violates the Principle of Proportionality: According to official construction, the U.S. has been using self-help in Cambodia against *outsiders'* (PRG and DRNV) abuse of Cambodian territory. Even if this were legal, the destructiveness of the operations has been all out of proportion to this end, and would therefore to this extent be illegal. This applies, *i.a.*, to the systematic leveling of cities and villages, the B-52 bombings (the largest, until then, of the Vietnam War), the bulldozing of the countryside, the confiscation of vast quantities of rice not identified as the opponents' military supplies—all of which were reported within the first two weeks of the campaign, and which therefore would be illegal even if any such action were theoretically permissible in a *war* against Cambodia.

4. Antagonism against Ethnic Vietnamese in Cambodia: The establishment of the Lon Nol regime was followed by the massacre and other persecutions of ethnically Vietnamese people in Cambodia. Mass expulsions took place under appalling conditions. Two explanations were given: that some of the victims were, or were suspected of being, Vietcong sympathizers; and that the Khmers are traditionally hostile to the ethnic Vietnamese living among them. Paradoxically, the invading Saigon troops participated in those acts against their own ethnic group.

Such atrocities constitute "War Crimes or Crimes against Humanity." There is an analogy in the Nazi arguments that Jews had to be exterminated because Jews were Communists or Communist sympathizers; and that in some German-occupied territories where anti-Semitism was endemic, local people participated in their slaughter. The U.S. Nuremberg Tribunal that dealt with these matters indignantly rejected such arguments. It called instigation to pogroms by

---

trouble separating friend from foe *among the civilian population* now have a whole new set of problems in *sorting out* the Cambodians."

The gravest questions of international law immediately arise: What criteria for "civilian foe" status had been established? How was thereupon the "sorting out" done? What happened to those "sorted out"? The report continues:

Villages are being burned. Thousands of civilians are fleeing for their lives. . . . The pattern of Vietnam is being repeated. The American troops are putting the torch to homes because they may be useful to the Communists. Livestock are shot for the same reason. Palls of smoke rose over the region yesterday. Clusters of houses smoldered. "I had orders to burn everything" said one young tank commander . . . U.S. air strikes were ordered on the town [of Memot] because North Vietnamese troops were reported there. "The whole place is blown away," said a helicopter pilot as he flew over it. (*New York Post*, May 4, 1970, p. 5 [AP].)

Nazi police units "a crime which, from a moral point of view, was perhaps even worse than their own directly committed murders. . . . To invade a foreign country, seize innocent inhabitants, and shoot them is a crime, the mere statement of which is its own condemnation. But to stir up passion, hate, violence and destruction among the people themselves, aims at breaking the moral backbone. . . ."[59]

It is not suggested here that the U.S. contributed to these illegalities; although, if U.S. forces in Cambodia (or anywhere else) capture persons entitled to prisoner of war status, and then hand them over to Saigon forces without previously ascertaining the latters' "willingness and ability" to treat them as prescribed in the 1949 Geneva Prisoners of War Convention, this violates one of the most important safeguards of that Convention.[60] Altogether, the strategy to enable Saigon forces to take highly destructive war actions in Cambodia and to establish themselves there, burdens the decision-makers with an additional responsibility: namely, that all this was likely (in view of the well-known antagonisms between Khmers and Vietnamese, and the well-known behavior pattern of Saigon troops even within South Vietnam) to exacerbate the ethnic tensions in Cambodia and cause more suffering to the population. Within the first month of the invasion, the Cambodian Army asked the U.S. to make the Saigon forces withdraw, as they "committed pillage, violation of women, arson, massacre of children and women. Now they do not want to leave our territory despite the complaints of our population."[61]

Certain longstanding U.S. war policies in South Vietnam have been based upon and exploited ethnic antagonisms, especially the use of Montagnard tribesmen against ethnic Vietnamese.[62] The same use has been made of ethnic Cambodians in South Vietnam. In May 1970, "our Cambodians" (as the *New York Daily News* called them) were transferred from South Vietnam to Cambodia for combat.

[59] Judgment of 8/9 April 1948 in U.S.A. *vs.* Oswald Pohl, et al. (*Einsatzgruppen Case*), *Trials. . .* , IV, 435

[60] Art. 12, incorporated as para. 88 in U.S. Army Field Manual 27-10.

[61] Statement by Cambodian Army Information Service, Phnom Penh, May 25, 1970, reported by Clayton Fritchey, *New York Post*, May 29, 1970, p. 27.

[62] The South Vietnam Liberation Front protested against the Saigon regime's exploitation of ethnic differences in its first program of 1960. See also Sec. 10 of their programmatic statement of 22 March 1966. (Reproduced in South Vietnam National Front for Liberation, *Documents*, Giai Phong Publishing House, Dec. 1968, pp. 16, 28, 75-76.)

V. Threat of War as Instrument of National Policy

Why has the U.S. been so obstinate about this war? One ominous answer is that Vietnam is to be understood as a warning. The U.S. policies in Indochina *serve notice* that the U.S. would act *similarly elsewhere* to prevent what the U.S. considers a threat of Communist take-over. How widely such threat is interpreted was evidenced by the U.S. military intervention in the Dominican Republic, the U.S. support for the establishment of the present dictatorship in Greece, and elsewhere.

The "warning" rationale is analyzed in a book intending to show that making others fear an American war is, and must remain, the "most powerful" instrument of U.S. foreign policy:

> . . . the roots of courage lie in understanding that *the opponent can have a war whenever he chooses* (italics in original). . . . He simply has to attack something he knows is *"ours"*: our own country, territories, or allies or related rights, that is, the *status quo*. The wish not to have other Vietnams is "most dangerous" and "most destructive. . . . The war in Vietnam represents one case . . . where our threat [to make war in order to maintain any *status quo* we consider "ours"] has been seriously questioned. Our struggle [in Vietnam] is one to maintain this threat. . . . The correct interpretation of our action in Vietnam is, therefore, that it shows what we can and will do *and do again* (italics in original) to defend our position."

After detailed elaboration, the book concludes: "our nation's most powerful foreign policy instrument [is] the American threat of war."[63]

This is merely one bold description of a policy diametrically opposite to the renunciation of war as an instrument of national policy (Kellogg Pact) and to the prohibition of the use or threat of force (U.N. Charter), which are cornerstones of the present world order.

The doctrine implies that the threat must be "credible." We must not

---

[63] James L. Payne, *The American Threat: The Fear of War as an Instrument of Foreign Policy*, 1970, pp. 155-158, 223.

After presenting Hitler's boldness as model ("Hitler's bold moves . . . against Austria and Czechoslovakia gave him a reputation for forcefulness and determination throughout Europe"), the author continues: "What we do about the aggression of one opponent offers *other enemies* an *indication of our determination to oppose them* . . . we dislike communism, and . . . *we oppose its extension because we do not like it and believe it is hostile to us*. . . . Our failure to respond would suggest that we are not so willing to oppose 'communist' (quotation marks in original) aggression in general." (Pp. 106-107.)

only threaten or use force against potential changes in "our *status quo*"; we must also show *determination to be victorious.*

The frustration of some U.S. military leaders must be understood in this light. When in 1965 the U.S. decided to enter the war openly with overwhelmingly destructive might, the planners expected that resistance would *have* to cease within days or, at the most, weeks. That this has not happened after over half a decade of enormous military effort by the most powerful nation against a small underdeveloped country seems to deny, as it were, the laws of physics. Hence the sequence of one more "last" effort, followed by still another "last effort," as the invasion of Cambodia was followed by that of Laos.

The frustration is understandable. The U.S. should, by the premises of its military strategy, have won in 1965. Why, then did it not?

It appears that the world has, indeed, reached a turning point. Vietnam has proven that even unparalleled application of the most up-to-date weapons (except nuclear weapons) does not prevail under certain circumstances over a small determined opponent.

The experience is not altogether new. In the 1920's, General Pétain was unable with his vastly superior forces to defeat the uprisings in North Africa. Germany had similar experiences in World War II, for example, in Yugoslavia.

We seem to face, then, a historic phenomenon, comparable in its repercussions to the defeat of the Hapsburgs' armored knights, in spite of their supposedly invincible superiority, by ill-clad, ill-armed Swiss peasants at the battle of Morgarten in 1315. That battle presaged the demise of feudalism in Europe. The all-important difference is that then the world did not live under the shadow of nuclear destruction.

APPENDIX: COMPLAINTS BY CAMBODIA ABOUT VIOLATIONS
OF HER NEUTRALITY, JANUARY 1956—APRIL 1970[1]

1. Complaints against South Vietnamese and Eventually U.S. Policies, January 1956—May 1965: The International Commission for Supervision and Control in Cambodia (I.C.C.) received Cambodia's first

[1] The data here given are not complete. For example, the Cambodian Government lodged numerous complaints with the International Control Commission in Phnom Penh after 31 Dec. 1958, but the Commission ceased publishing its own reports (which summarized or quoted previous complaints) as of 1 January 1959. See *Documents Relating to the British Involvement in the Indo-China Conflict, 1949-1965.* (Misc. No. 25, Dec. 1965, Cmnd. 2834, p. 257.)

complaints of violations of her sovereignty in January 1956. It reported, citing particulars, South Vietnamese attempts to occupy Cambodian territory as well as ambushes, wounding, kidnapping, and maltreatment of civilians in five Cambodian provinces since November 1955. The I.C.C. summarized these charges as follows: "(1) Use of force and trespassing by [South] Vietnamese soldiers on Cambodian territory. (2) Attempted occupation of islands off Cambodia by Vietnamese forces. . . . (3) Penetration into Cambodian territory by armed or unarmed Vietnamese citizens other than soldiers. . . . (4) Concentration of Vietnamese troops on the Vietnamese side of the border."[2]

Cambodia's first complaint to the I.C.C. was followed by others, charging increasingly severe and frequent South Vietnamese illegalities. Interestingly, each of the three I.C.C. reports for the period ending 31 December 1956, the year 1957, and the year 1958, respectively, states that the I.C.C.: "received *no* report from the Royal [Cambodian] Government of violations or threats of violations of Cambodian territory by forces of the Democratic Republic of Vietnam" (*North* Vietnam) but "several [namely, 7 between 1 Oct. 1955 and 31 Dec. 1956; 28 during 1957; and 32 during 1958] letters from the Royal Government informing it of the buildup of military forces and reinforcements of military installations in *South* Vietnam . . . along the Cambodian borders as well as of reported violations or threats of violations of Cambodian territory by *South* Vietnam."[3]

For example, in September 1957, the Cambodian Government: "forwarded to the Commission . . . a 'Statement of facts proving' . . . establishment of a large-scale [South Vietnamese] Military Post at Lon Giang in the Province of Tay-Ninh to lodge 60,000 new [South Vietnamese] recruits"; establishment of various other South Vietnamese military posts; "anchoring of 4 big warships . . . at about 3 km from the Cambodian frontier"; and an "inspection tour carried out by a representative of Ngo Dinh Diem and [a] U.S. Colonel in the area of Khanh Binh."[4]

Faced with this situation, Cambodia's National Assembly (Sangkum Congress) passed a law in November 1957, to which the I.C.C. at-

---

[2] *Fifth Interim Report of the International Commission . . . in Cambodia, for the period Oct. 1, 1955 to Dec. 31, 1956.* (Cmnd. 253 [Sept. 1957], p. 19.)

[3] *Fifth Interim Report. . .* , p. 19, App. G, pp. 35-38; *Sixth Interim Report . . . for the period Jan. 1, 1957 to Dec. 31, 1957.* (Cmnd. 526, pp. 6-8, App. B, pp. 14-32); *Seventh Interim Report . . . for the period Jan. 1, 1958 to Dec. 31, 1958* (Cmnd. 887, pp. 2-4, App. B, pp. 11-18.

[4] Letter No. 553/LGP/X, dated 16 Sept. 1957; *Sixth Interim Report. . .* , p. 16.

tached much importance. It stipulated that: "(a) The Kingdom of Cambodia is a neutral country. (b) It will abstain from all military or ideological alliance with [any] foreign country. . . . (c) It will not attack any foreign country. [However,] (d) in case of agression, the Kingdom reserves the right to (1) self-defense by arms; (2) call on the United Nations; (3) call on a friendly country."[5]

However, South Vietnam's policy continued. The I.C.C. report for 1958 (the last to be issued) quotes Cambodian protests against, i.a., South Vietnam's installing two additional big military bases, one of them "having an air field" in the border area; dispatch to the area of 1,050 parachutists; and again various raids into Cambodia, resulting in death, injuring and kidnapping of civilians, destruction and theft of property, etc.[6] By 1963, Cambodia severed diplomatic relations with Saigon. As American participation in those actions became more open, Cambodia also complained of them.

On February 7, 1964, Prince Sihanouk formally advised the Co-Chairmen of the Geneva Conference:

I have the misfortune to bring to your attention that regular forces of the Republic of Vietnam are continuing their *incessant and murderous aggressions* against Cambodia. The last example is the aerial bombardment of a peaceful Khmer [Cambodian] village. . . . This criminal and unjustifiable attack follows a long series of attacks which are as many infringements of the most legitimate rights of nations. Our frontier population live in anguish and demand effective protection.

Cambodia . . . urgently demands the reconvening of the Geneva Conference [or] the immediate establishment at the expense of the United States which is responsible for the South Vietnamese war and the military operations, of fixed International Control Commission points at sensitive (*névralgiques*) points on our frontiers; thus in order to make known the truth about the alleged movements of South Vietnamese rebels ["Vietcong"] in Khmer territory which serve as pretexts for these terrorist raids against our villages.[7]

Fifteen months later (May 5, 1965), the Prince stated in a message to the British Prime Minister: "that peaceful Cambodia is continually

5 *Sixth Interim Report. .* , p 9; see also pp. 42-43.

6 *Seventh Interim Report. . .* , pp. 11-18.

7 Cmnd. 2834, p. 244. See also Cambodian Government Communiqué, 18 Feb. 1964, pp. 247-248.

suffering aggression on land and from the air by the American and South Vietnamese Armed forces." He requested British "support for our demand for the cessation of the attacks by the United States and the Saigon and Bangkok Governments whose armed forces are massacring our civilian inhabitants, destroying our villages and violating our air space and territorial waters. . . . Cambodia cannot remain eternally passive in the face of these repeated aggressions and if no international means is swiftly taken to bring them to an end, she will be obliged to modify her neutral status and have recourse to assistance pacts with certain big friendly powers."[8]

2. *Complaints against South Vietnamese and U.S. Policies to the U.N. Security Council*: For years prior to the 1970 invasion, Cambodia also transmitted numerous complaints against South Vietnamese and U.S. policies toward her to the U.N. Security Council. Their complete recital would fill many pages. They are reproduced in Security Council documents, and summarized in the Year Books of the United Nations.

For example, the Year Book for 1965 states: "Between March and September 1965, the representative of Cambodia addressed a *further series* of communications to the President of the Security Council following upon those submitted during 1964 (see Y.U.N., 1964, pp. 139–45) . . . further alleg[ing] violations of Cambodian territory and air space by forces of the Republic of Viet-Nam and the United States. . . . No denials or countercharges were submitted in connexion with these charges."[9]

Among the complaints referred to is one of October 1965 alleging that Cambodian inhabitants were incited by loudspeakers from helicopters "to leave for South Viet-Nam in anticipation of an imminent attack on Cambodia" and that "three successive [U.S.-South Vietnamese] raids on three villages in the province of Svay Rieng . . . left seven dead and six seriously wounded, and resulted in heavy damage. This has been verified by the International Control Commission and by foreign military attachés."[10]

The Year Book for 1967 reports that:

There were *over 40 complaints* addressed to the Security Council in 1967 by Cambodia concerning violations of Cambodian territory, air

---

[8] *Ibid.*, p. 244.   [9] *Y.U.N., 1965*, p. 189.

[10] *Ibid.* The Cambodian representative also referred on other occasions to on-the-spot verifications of "attacks and violence," by I.C.C. personnel, foreign military and press attachés, and Cambodian and foreign correspondents. (See, e.g., *Y.U.N.*, 1967, p. 152.)

space and territorial waters by "U.S.-South Vietnamese forces". . . .
Cambodia stated that it had protested most strongly these acts of
aggression and provocation. . . .

As evidence . . . the Cambodian representative . . . supplied details on scores of incidents . . . [and] listed numerous resulting
deaths and injuries . . . as well as damage to dwellings, livestock and
other property.

The Cambodian representative also described a number of large-
scale penetrations by U.S.-South Viet-Namese forces, ranging from
100 to 200 soldiers, transported by up to 60 helicopters and supported by aircraft and artillery fire, which attacked villages and
guard posts with consequent casualties, sometimes burning or temporarily occupying Cambodian villages . . . [and alleged that] these
deliberate aggressive acts were part of a policy of intimidation
directed against Cambodia with the intention of forcing it to renounce its policy of strict neutrality and nonalignment.

. . . On 11 September, the Cambodian representative informed the
Security Council that on 15 July 1967 Cambodian Defence Forces
. . . had captured a South Viet-Namese soldier disguised as a Viet-
Cong. Under interrogation this captive had revealed that the task of
his company was to disguise its men as Viet-Cong and so smuggle
them into Khmer territory in order to identify strategic points and
seek evidence of the presence of Viet-Cong.

The sole aim of these acts in Cambodian territory, the Cambodian representative wrote to the Security Council "was to find pretexts for extending the war to Cambodia."[11]

During 1967, there was one countercharge against Cambodia. In a
letter of 28 April, the Permanent Observer of the Republic of [South]
Vietnam charged "that between May 1966 and March 1967 Cambodian
armed forces had violated Viet-Namese air space eight times and had
crossed the frontier 16 times, forcibly abducting Viet-Namese nationals, causing casualties and stealing cattle."[12]

[11] *Y.U.N.*, 1967, p. 152.
[12] By letter of 25 July 1967, the Permanent Observer of the Republic of Vietnam at the
U. N. finally replied to Cambodia's complaints lodged between June 1964 and March 1967:
"His Government had not thought it necessary to deny each time" the Cambodian charges
"which were often of a minor nature and attributable either to the imprecise character
of the common frontier or to deliberate acts of provocation by the Viet-Cong. All charges
had been investigated. His Government had recognized as valid complaints concerning five
incidents occurring between June 1964 and March 1967 and had agreed to pay damages

Cambodia's reply of 26 June 1967 to the Security Council rejected these accusations as "unfounded." They were "designed to mislead international opinion and to justify acts of aggression committed almost daily by the Saigon authorities and their American masters against the territorial integrity of Cambodia. . . ."

Between January 1968 and mid-1969, Cambodia submitted to the Security Council over 100 protests. Many referred, with indications of time, place, and damage, and often names of victims, to numerous incidents.[13]

The protests reported increasingly serious violations and became increasingly urgent. Thus, of the ten Cambodian protests dated between 31 December 1969 and 18 February 1970, three each reported "a series of aggressive acts by U.S.-South Viet-Namese forces" against seven Cambodian provinces (S/9586, S/9625, S/9653), two each against six (S/9605, S/9645) and one (S/9638) against four of those Cambodian provinces. Again, there were no U.S. or Saigon denials or counter-charges.

Between 25 February and 25 March 1970, six Cambodian protests followed, still complaining about "aggressive acts" by "U.S.-South Viet-Namese forces."[14]

3. First Protests of Lon Nol Regime against Vietcong and North Viet-namese Forces: The first complaint to the U.N. Security Council about Vietcong and North Vietnamese forces was dated 30 March 1970. It reported three events of 27 March: arrest of 2 Cambodian policemen (of whom one was "released a few moments later") by *"Viet-Cong and North Viet-Namese* forces" about 20 kilometers from the frontier; 3 Cambodians killed and 8 seriously wounded in an engagement with a "large" such unit about 3 kilometers from the frontier; and the occupation by an estimated 3,000 Vietcong and North Vietnamese of a village about 7 kilometers inside the frontier. This same complaint reported

---

to the victims. It has found completely baseless the other complaints lodged by the Cambodian Government, which had disregarded repeated protests against the use of Cambodian territory by the Viet-Cong and the North Viet-Namese as a base for aggression into the territory of the Republic of Viet-Nam." (*Ibid.*)

[13] These communications are summarized in *Report of the Security Council, 16 July 1967 —15 July 1968, l.c.*, para. 807, pp. 110-112; and *Report of the Security Council, 16 July 1968—15 July 1969*, GAOR, 24th Sess., Supp. 2 (A/7602), para. 799, pp. 102-104.

[14] The communications from the U.S. dated 9 March 1970 (S/9692), in reply to Cambodian protest against U.S. attacks on Dak Dam on 16-17 Nov. 1969, acknowledged some impropriety, offering apologies and indemnification to victims.

three events of 28 March: the advance forces of 2 large Vietcong and North Vietnamese columns were sighted, who had infiltrated into Cambodia the day before; another such unit, estimated 600 strong, was sighted about 10 kilometers inside Cambodia; and a Cambodian military post about 5 kilometers from the frontier was attacked by such elements. (S/9729.) The next day, Cambodia reported that on 31 March, an estimated "several thousand heavily armed" Vietcong and North Vietnamese units had forcibly entered the Snoul region, province of Kratie, and attacked a Cambodian detachment 8 kilometers inside Cambodia. (S/9730 and Add. 1 of 1 April 1970.)

On 3 April, the Cambodian Deputy Permanent Representative addressed two letters to the U.N. Security Council. The first (S/9733) complained about violations by "*U.S.-South Viet-Namese forces*" between 17 and 27 February 1970: namely, firing of rocket shells and artillery in different Cambodian localities, machine-gunning and rockets thrown from 6 helicopters flying in Cambodian airspace. The second letter stated the casualties (1 dead, 13 wounded, 3 missing) caused by the previously reported *Vietcong-North Vietnames*e attack in the Snoul region, and added that on 31 March, another attack 2 kilometers inside Cambodia by some 100 cost 2 armed villagers dead, 1 wounded, 19 missing.

Self-Defense and Cambodia:
A Critical Appraisal

JOHN C. BENDER

On April 30, 1970, Richard M. Nixon, President of the United States, announced that United States combat troops, in conjunction with the armed forces of South Vietnam, were participating in ground assaults in Cambodia in order to destroy sanctuaries on the Cambodian-South Vietnamese border that had been previously used by troops of both North Vietnam and the Viet Cong.[1] In a subsequent letter to the President of the Security Council, Charles W. Yost, the Permanent Representative of the United States to the United Nations, described these actions as "appropriate measures of collective self-defence . . . ."[2]

For a number of years, the existence of sanctuaries in Cambodia has been a matter of some concern with respect to their strategic and tactical significance to the conduct of hostilities in the Vietnam war. The military has reportedly asserted the importance of denying the use of these sanctuaries to the enemy;[3] the border between South Vietnam and Cambodia has been the scene of a number of incidents, which have occasioned protests from the Cambodian government;[4] and recommendations for invading the sanctuaries or "hot pursuit"[5] of enemy forces into Cambodia have been made on various occasions by, among others, Minister Thanat Khoman of Thailand,[6] President Nguyen Van Thieu of South Vietnam,[7] a special subcommittee of the House Armed Services Committee[8] and General William C. Westmoreland.[9] In the past the United States has refrained from committing itself to large-scale troop movements in Cambodia. However, various tactical policies involving more limited breaches of Cambodian territorial sovereignty have been approved in order to meet battlefield

---

[1] Address by President Richard M. Nixon, April 30, 1970, in N.Y. Times May 1, 1970, at 2, col. 1.

[2] U.N. Doc. S/9781, at 1 (1970) [hereinafter referred to as Yost Letter].

[3] See, e.g., N.Y. Times, Mar. 26, 1969, at 5, col. 3; id., Mar. 10, 1968, § 1, at 1, col. 8; id., Dec. 16, 1967, at 10, cols. 5, 6; id., Nov. 24, 1967, at 1, col. 2.

[4] See, e.g., id., Nov. 11, 1968, at 19, col. 4; id., Jan. 20, 1968, at 1, col. 6; id., Feb. 6, 1967, at 6, col. 6; id., Sept. 22, 1966, at 5, col. 5; id., Aug. 14, 1966, § 1, at 1, col. 6.

[5] The doctrine of "hot pursuit" in international law "refers to the right of a coastal state to pursue and apprehend the vessels of another state on the high seas when those ships have violated a law of the coastal state in its territorial waters." Note, International Law and Military Operations Against Insurgents in Neutral Territory, 68 Colum. L. Rev. 1127 (1968). Since the pursuit may not lawfully continue into the territorial waters of another state, there is no analogous doctrine of pursuit on land, where a breach of the territorial integrity of adjacent states would necessarily be involved. Id. See N. Poulantzas, The Right of Hot Pursuit in International Law 11-12 (1969).

[6] N.Y. Times, Oct. 8, 1967, § 1, at 15, col. 1.

[7] Id., Jan. 16, 1968, at 11, col. 1.

[8] Id., Dec. 14, 1967, at 4, col. 4.

[9] Id., Mar. 10, 1968, § 1, at 1, col. 8.

exigencies[10] and high-altitude bombing runs have been conducted over Cambodian territory that was thought to contain enemy sanctuaries.[11]

The recent actions in Cambodia represent a significant departure from past policies. The political significance of this departure is obvious, and was acknowledged by the President in his announcement and evidenced in the public and private demonstrations of support and opposition, both domestic and foreign, in the days and weeks that followed. Yet the actions announced by the President also had legal significance, in that self-defense is a doctrine of international law, recognized under both the rules of customary international law and the United Nations Charter. Too often, the claims of legality or illegality of state action in a particular context are made and viewed only as part of the polemics surrounding an incident whose success or failure is dependent upon political convenience and military and economic strength. To so judge the success of foreign policy is, however, to dangerously underestimate the precedential significance of state action, especially in an area where the precedents established serve to limit or expand the degree of discretion that is accepted as permissible in the use of force as an instrument of state policy.

This Article will attempt to critically review those aspects of recent United States actions in Cambodia that affect the claimed legality of those actions under the rules of international law relating to self-defense.

I

In international law, the doctrine of self-defense provides the state with a legal basis for actions taken in response to the illegal use of force by another state, in the absence of effective action by the international community.[12] When properly invoked, the doctrine will serve to excuse state actions involving both the unilateral use of force and a breach of the territorial integrity of another state that would otherwise be illegal under both rules of customary international law and the Charter of the United Nations.[13]

Self-defense in international law is, like its counterpart in municipal law,[14] an emergency measure and an exception to the regular processes of the legal order. As such, it is essentially preventive in nature, rather than retributive, and is therefore distinguishable from both sanctions and reprisals.[15]

The concept of collective self-defense expands the principle of self-

---

10 See discussion of "protective reaction" p. 137 infra.

11 N.Y. Times, May 9, 1969, at 1, col. 8.

12 2 L. Oppenheim, International Law § 52aa, at 156 (7th ed. H. Lauterpacht 1952).

13 Id. § 326, at 698.

14 For a summary of the characteristics of the doctrine of self-defense in the criminal codes of various nations, see Weightman, Self-Defense in International Law, 37 Va. L. Rev. 1095, 1097-98 (1951).

15 D. Bowett, Self-Defence in International Law 13-14, 19-21 (1958); Waldock, The Regulation of the Use of Force by Individual States in International Law, 81 Hague Recueil Des Cours 455, 464 (pt. 2, 1952).

defense beyond the perimeters of the basic concept of preventive action by the victim of an attack. Both in customary international law and under article 51 of the United Nations Charter, states other than the victim state may, in defense of the victim, respond with force to an attack.[16] The difficulty with such a concept is, however, that there appear to be no criteria in international law that limit the interstate relationships on which agreements for collective self-defense may be based. In effect, the only requirements that would distinguish an exercise of collective self-defense from an illegal "war of sanction" are that it be defensive, rather than retributive in character, and that the action taken actually be in response to the necessity of defense of one of the participating states and proportional to the need for such defense.[17]

In evaluating recent United States-South Vietnamese actions in Cambodia, it is therefore appropriate to consider the motives that prompted those actions, in order to determine whether they were in fact taken in response to a perceived necessity for the defense of South Vietnam. Obviously, it is not an easy task to determine the motives and hierarchy of considerations that determine the actions of states. But those motives and hierarchies do exist, and have in the past been subject to review. When the Nuremberg Tribunal considered Germany's plea of self-defense with respect to the occupation of Norway, the evidence submitted, and the consideration of the Tribunal, was directed to the question of "[h]ow widely the view was held in influential German circles that the Allies intended to occupy Norway . . . ."[18] Unknown to Germany, Allied plans for the occupation of the Norwegian coast actually existed at the time of the German invasion; however, the decisive consideration was whether or not Germany actually believed that an Allied occupation was imminent. The Tribunal's decision rejecting the plea of self-defense was based on a finding that the motive for the German occupation was not based on a belief in the necessity of self-defense. The Tribunal rejected the argument that Germany alone was able to determine whether the necessity for defensive action existed, with the observation that "whether action taken under the claim of self-defense was in fact aggressive or defensive must ultimately be sub-

---

[16] I. Brownlie, International Law and the Use of Force by States 330-31 (1963).

It has been argued that collective self-defense is not, strictly speaking, *self*-defense unless each of the states participating in the joint defensive effort have individually been threatened in a manner that would justify an exercise of individual self-defense. D. Bowett, supra note 15, at 205-07.

State practice does not, however, support the existence of such a distinction, in view of the proliferation of treaties providing for collective self-defense in the event of an attack by a third party on one of the treaty members. I. Brownlie, supra at 328-30. See also M. McDougal & F. Feliciano, Law and Minimum World Public Order 244-50 (1961).

[17] See I. Brownlie, supra note 16, 330-33. Brownlie defines a "war of sanction" as one whose object is "to extirpate the source of aggression and to impose measures intended to prevent further breaches of the peace by the aggressor state." Id. at 332. He maintains that such a war "has no place in the United Nations Charter except in so far as action may be authorized by a competent organ . . ." of the United Nations. Id.

[18] International Military Tribunal (Nuremberg), Judgment and Sentences, in 41 Am. J. Int'l L. 172, 205 (1947).

ject to investigation and adjudication if international law is ever to be enforced."[19]

In applying these considerations to the decision to initiate operations in Cambodia, it is necessary to question the extent to which the principal motive for the decision was concerned with an emergency defense of South Vietnam. An examination of President Nixon's speech of April 30 indicates a number of other considerations that were relevant to the decision to commit United States forces to operations in Cambodia. There, the President indicated that his decision would "guarantee the continued success of our withdrawal and Vietnamization program,"[20] that it was taken "for the purpose of ending the war in Vietnam,"[21] and that if resort were had only to diplomatic protest in this situation, the "credibility of the United States would be destroyed in every area of the world where only the power of the United States deters aggression."[22] However laudable these considerations might be in other contexts, they are not appropriate motives for the exercise of the right of collective self-defense with respect to South Vietnam.

Other factors surrounding the decision indicate that the action was not taken as an emergency defensive measure in response to some newly arisen threat. Instead, recent developments in Cambodia seem to have provided a political opportunity to extend ground actions into that country, in order to obtain a tactical advantage in the context of the ongoing hostilities in Vietnam.[23]

Although the United States has denied that its actions constitute military support of the Lon Nol Government,[24] and it seems clear that the Lon Nol Government was not given prior notice of the initiation on the ground operations,[25] reports of prior military cooperation between the Cambodian, United States and South Vietnamese armed forces[26] would at least indicate the possibility that the Lon Nol Government would be receptive

---

[19] Id. at 207.

[20] N.Y. Times, May 1, 1970, at 2, col. 1.

[21] Id., col. 5.

[22] Id.

[23] Secretary of Defense Melvin Laird has reportedly referred to the replacement of the Government of Prince Norodom Sihanouk by that of Premier Lon Nol as presenting a "political opportunity" or in the words of an anoymous White House source "diplomatic opening" for cleaning out the sanctuaries in Cambodia. See id., May 10, 1970, § 4, at 2, col. 6. Reports of the text of a recently released staff report of the Senate Foreign Relations Committee indicate that a similar assessment was widely shared among United States and South Vietnamese military officials in Saigon. See id., June 7, 1970, § 1, at 6, col. 1.

[24] Id., May 17, 1970, § 1, at 3, col. 6. In his April 30 speech, President Nixon stated that:

With other nations, we shall do our best to provide the small arms and other equipment which the Cambodian Army of 40,000 needs and can use for its defense.

But the aid we will provide will be limited for the purpose of enabling Cambodia to defend its neutrality and not for the purpose of making it an active belligerent on one side or the other.

Id., May 1, 1970, at 2, col. 3.

[25] Id., May 2, 1970, at 1, col. 5.

[26] See, e.g., id., Apr. 9, 1970, at 2, col. 4; id., Mar. 28, 1970, at 1, col. 8; id., Mar. 26, 1970, at 1, col. 6; id., Mar. 21, 1970, at 1, col. 1.

to obtaining direct military support from the armed forces of the United States and South Vietnam. Subsequent developments relating to the duration and extent of the joint United States-South Vietnamese operations[27] also raise serious questions as to whether these operations were ever regarded as limited emergency measures appropriate to an exercise of the right of collective self-defense of South Vietnam.

II

In evaluating the factual circumstances under which the doctrine of self-defense may be invoked, the classical statement of the doctrine to be considered is still that formulated by Daniel Webster, in connection with the case of the *Caroline*. There, an armed body of men, acting under the orders of a British officer, crossed from Canada into the United States and destroyed the Caroline, a ship that had been used by Canadian insurgents. During the course of diplomatic correspondence with the British, Webster asserted that if self-defense were to be an acceptable justification for the destruction of the Caroline, they would have to demonstrate a "necessity of self-defense, instant, overwhelming, leaving no choice of means, and no moment for deliberation."[28] Further, he stated that, in view of the infringement of United States territorial integrity, it would be necessary to show that the actions taken in self-defense involved "nothing unreasonable or excessive; since the act, justified by the necessity of self-defense, must be limited by that necessity, and kept clearly within it."[29] From this formulation, the two requirements that customary law makes prerequisite to a lawful assertion of the right of self-defense are necessity and proportionality.

Necessity. In applying the requirement of necessity, the need for defensive action must be seen to be "instant" in view of the imminence of the threat perceived. Thus, self-defense would not legally justify unilateral coercive actions on the basis of remote future contingencies.[30] This does not, however, mean that preemptive or anticipatory action is necessarily excluded from the scope of measures that may be regarded as a valid exercise of the right of self-defense.

The concept that self-defense permits anticipatory or preemptive action is usually justified on the grounds that appropriate defensive measures may require that an aggressor not be given the opportunity to deliver the first blow.[31] The concept is, however, open to certain objections. Since it gen-

---

27 See discussion of proportionality pp. 137-38 infra.

28 Letter from Daniel Webster to Mr. Fox, Apr. 24, 1841, in British Parliamentary Papers, vol. 61 (1843); British & Foreign State Papers, vol. 29, at 1129; quoted in Jennings, The Caroline and McLeod Cases, 32 Am. J. Int'l L. 82, 89 (1938).

29 Id.

30 Schwarzenberger, The Fundamental Principles of International Law, 87 Hague Recueil Des Cours 195, 333 (pt. 1 1955).

31 See, e.g., Waldock, supra note 15, at 498. However, the question of whether anticipatory action in self-defense is permitted under article 51 of the U.N. Charter has been the subject of much debate. The relevant portion of article 51 reads:
Nothing in the present Charter shall impair the inherent right of individual or collective self-defence *if an armed attack occurs* . . . . [emphasis added]

erally requires an evaluation by the putative victim of the intent of another state on the basis of circumstantial evidence, it obviously presents the opportunity for misjudgment, which could lead to serious breaches of international peace. By the requirements of necessity, standards are imposed on the process of evaluation of the alleged threat in an attempt to minimize extravagant claims. Though the claimed victim state will itself determine whether there is a necessity for anticipatory attack, the legality of its actions is provisional and subject to later review.[32] To the extent that an anticipatory attack will involve a breach of another state's right of territorial integrity, as opposed to an exercise of force which, for example, takes place on the high seas, the standards imposed on evaluating the necessity of the actions should be stringently applied.[33] If the territory involved is that of a neutral, the community interest in restricting the area of hostilities would seem to suggest that an even more demanding standard be required.

In applying these considerations to the joint United States-South Vietnamese operations in Cambodia, it is necessary to remember that, in his speech of April 30, President Nixon indicated that the actions taken were preemptive and designed to forestall the possibility of attacks on South Vietnam at a future date. The threat to South Vietnam was described as being based on increased enemy activity in Cambodia, during the course of which the enemy was "concentrating his main force in [the] sanctuaries . . ."[34] along the Cambodian-South Vietnamese border and "building up to launch massive attacks on our forces and those of South Vietnam."[35] At the same time, the enemy was "invading [Cambodia] from the sanctuaries . . . [and] encircling the capital, Pnompenh."[36]

The threat to South Vietnam and American forces in South Vietnam would materialize if enemy forces were able to expand their area of control to either include a band of land running the length of the Cambodian-South Vietnamese border or all of Cambodia. In either event, "it would mean that South Vietnam was completely outflanked and the forces of Americans . . . as well as South Vietnamese would be in an untenable military position."[37]

The time at which these enemy activities were expected to result in the

---

If "strictly construed," the provision would appear to make resort to individual or collective self-defense contingent upon the occurrence of a prior armed attack and there are distinguished authorities who hold that this is the proper interpretation. See, e.g., 2 L. Oppenheim, supra note 12, § 52aa, at 156; Kunz, Individual and Collective Self-Defense in article 51 of the Charter of the United Nations, 41 Am. J. Int'l L. 872, 878 (1947). For a fuller exposition of the arguments pro and con on this point see I. Brownlie, supra note 16, at 257-61; M. McDougal & F. Feliciano, supra note 16, at 232-41.

[32] See notes 18-19 supra and accompanying text; M. McDougal & F. Feliciano, supra note 16, at 218-20. But cf. Schwarzenberger, supra note 30, at 331-32.

[33] D. Bowett, supra note 15, at 20-21.

[34] N.Y. Times, May 1, 1970, at 2, col. 2.

[35] Id.

[36] Id.

[37] Id., col. 3.

actual feared attack on South Vietnam is not clear. The speech indicated that "hit and run" attacks had been staged from Cambodian sanctuaries for five years, but it specified that it was enemy activities from the sanctuaries within the preceding ten days that constituted the basis for preemptive action.[38] However, in both the speech and in the news conference of May 8, primary emphasis has been placed on the threat that would result when, by the spring of 1971, 150,000 American troops had been withdrawn from Vietnam pursuant to the "Vietnamization" program. In explaining the apparent contradiction between the actions announced on April 30, and the apparent satisfaction with the course of the Vietnamization program he had expressed in a speech ten days earlier, the President indicated "that the action that the enemy had taken in Cambodia [during the preceding ten days] would leave the 240,000 Americans who would be there [Vietnam] a year from now without many combat troops to help defend them [and] would leave them in an untenable position."[39] If a substantial threat caused by increased enemy activities was contingent upon American troop withdrawals that would not be completed for another year, it would seem difficult to conclude that the need for action was "instant," leaving "no moment for deliberation."

The availability of alternatives to a course of action involving the use of force is another aspect of the requirement of necessity. The alternatives to be considered in each case should obviously include those listed in article 33(1) of the United Nations Charter, as well as the possibility of action by the United Nations. Additionally, the importance of the principle of territorial integrity would seem to require that the possibility of defensive action on the territory of the victim state be considered an obligatory alternative to preemptive actions on the territory of another state.[40] Such a requirement has the obvious virtue of limiting the possibilities of serious disputes arising from a misapprehension of the hostile intent of another state, as well as minimizing the possibility of a state invoking the legal right of self-defense solely for reasons relating to political advantage. The argument is even more compelling in the case where preemptive action will occur on the territory of a neutral state.

This point is relevant to the joint operations in Cambodia, insofar as the mode and scope of past defensive actions on the part of the United

---

38 It should be noted that, at the time of the announcement of the Cambodian operations, there were reports indicating that enemy forces had, during the two weeks preceding the announcement, "disengaged from both South Vietnamese and American troops operating near the border of Cambodia and of Laos." Id., May 2, 1970, at 3, col. 6. The staff report of the Senate Foreign Relations Committee apparently indicates that after Prince Sihanouk had been deposed on March 18, 1970, enemy forces in the sanctuaries in Cambodia had initially gone into defensive positions and soon thereafter had begun to disperse westward into Cambodia. Id., June 7, 1970, § 1, at 6, col. 1.

39 Id., May 9, 1970, at 8, cols. 1, 2.

40 See I. Brownlie, supra note 16, at 367; Note, International Law and Military Operations Against Insurgents in Neutral Territory, 68 Colum. L. Rev. 1127, 1131 (1968).

States indicate an ability to effectively avoid operations that involve extensive troop movements in Cambodia. According to the Yost letter, "[f]or five years North Viet-Nam has maintained base areas in Cambodia . . . ."[41] During most of this time, prevailing policy seemed to have favored defensive actions within South Vietnam and avoidance, when possible, of infractions of the Cambodian-South Vietnam border.

However, on May 8, 1969, it was announced that B-52's had been used to bomb enemy sanctuaries in Cambodia for the first time[42] and the rubric "protective reaction" has been used to describe a policy that permitted either bombing or artillery fire in response to enemy fire from Cambodia, while apparently prohibiting the use of American ground forces in Cambodia. On March 28, 1970, it was announced that this concept had been broadened to permit ground forces to cross the Cambodian-South Vietnamese border in direct response to enemy attacks.[43] Despite this recent shift in tactics, "protective reaction" was still characterized as a defensive concept, which permitted the use of American troops in Cambodia in only a responsive, rather than preemptive, situation.

In terms of evaluating the possibility of alternative actions to the joint ground offensive in Cambodia announced by President Nixon on April 30, it is apparent that, at the level of hostilities encountered in the past, it was possible to effectively conduct defensive operations in South Vietnam against enemy troops using Cambodian sanctuaries. On that basis, only a substantial increase in the use of the sanctuaries should justify a change in tactics that violates the territorial integrity of a third, neutral state and exends the area of hostilities between United States-South Vietnamese and enemy forces.

Proportionality. The second requirement of self-defense, that of proportionality, limits the scope and intensity of responsive force to that which is necessary to secure the legally permissible objectives of self-defense and requires that there be some proportionate relationship between responsive force and the provocation.[44] Since the responsive force is only legally justified by necessity, it must remain within the scope of that necessity in order to retain its legality.

While a determination of the limits of a proportionate response is obviously difficult to make without an extensive review of information that is not in the public domain, it is nonetheless apparent from statements issued in connection with the Cambodian operations, that consideration was given to the extent of force that could be justified by the claimed necessities of the situation. Thus, the Yost letter states:

> The measures of collective self-defence being taken by the United States and South Viet-Namese forces are restricted in extent, purpose

---

41 Yost Letter, supra note 2, at 1.
42 N.Y. Times, May 9, 1969, at 1, col. 8.
43 Id., Mar. 29, 1970, § 1, at 1, col. 7.
44 Falk, International Law and the United States Role in the Vietnam War, 75 **Yale L.J.** 1122, 1144 (1966); M. McDougal & F. Feliciano, supra note 16, at 241-42.

and time. They are confined to the border areas over which the Cambodian Government has ceased to exercise any effective control and which has been completely occupied by North Viet-Namese and Viet Cong forces. Their purpose is to destroy the stocks and communications equipment that are being used in aggression against the Republic of Viet-Nam. When that purpose is accomplished, our forces and those of the Republic of Viet-Nam will promptly withdraw. These measures are limited and proportionate to the aggressive military operations of the North Viet-Namese forces and the threat they pose.[45]

Restrictions on American forces operating in Cambodia were thereafter made more specific. The President indicated that American troops would not proceed more than 30 to 35 km. into Cambodia, since this was the area under enemy control.[46] While it was announced that all American forces would be withdrawn from Cambodia by the end of June, the same deadline was not regarded as being applicable to the South Vietnamese. However, since American logistical support and air support were to be withdrawn from Cambodia with the rest of the American forces, it was assumed that South Vietnamese operations would be similarly terminated.[47]

So stated, the scope and magnitude of the Cambodian operations seem reasonably proportional to the claimed threat of increased guerilla activities from the sanctuaries along the Cambodian-South Vietnamese border. Actual operations in Cambodia have not, however, adhered to the standards originally established for them. South Vietnamese forces have expanded the scope of their operations beyond the perimeters of the areas initially deemed relevant to defensive operations,[48] and have stated that operations in Cambodia will continue beyond any immediately foreseeable deadline.[49] The United States has not objected to this extension of the scope of operations and had previously admitted the possibility that it would provide air cover for South-Vietnamese forces that remain in Cambodia.[50]

Neutrality. Cambodia's status as a neutral in the Vietnam war suggests, under customary rules of international law, one additional basis on which the United States-South Vietnamese actions in Cambodia might be considered.

Traditionally, state practice has supported the right of a belligerent state to take unilateral coercive action in the event that a neutral is either unwilling or unable to deny the use of its territory as a base of operations for an opposing belligerent.[51] In the traditional view, a neutral has the duty to maintain an attitude of impartiality towards all of the parties to a

45 Yost Letter, supra note 2, at 2.
46 N.Y. Times, May 6, 1970, at 17, cols. 3, 4.
47 Id., May 9, 1970, at 8, col. 2.
48 See id., May 25, 1970, at 1, col. 8.
49 Id., May 28, 1970, at 1, col. 3.
50 Id., May 26, 1970, at 7, col. 1. However in an address of June 3, 1970, President Nixon stated that "[t]he only remaining American activity in Cambodia after July 1 will be air missions to interdict the movement of enemy troops and material . . . ." Id., June 4, 1970, at 18, col. 6.
51 I. Brownlie, supra note 16, at 313-14; 2 L. Oppenheim, supra note 12, § 326, at 698.

conflict. Thus, in the event of a breach of the neutral's territorial integrity by one of the belligerents, the neutral state has not only a right to oppose such a breach, but also a duty to do so, since a failure would favor one belligerent over the other.[52]

Actions taken by a belligerent in the territory of a neutral state that has either been unwilling or unable to deny the use of its territory to an opposing belligerent as a base of operations have in the past been variously described as an application of the right of self-preservation, self-help or self-defense.[53] The question has thus been raised as to whether, under contemporary rules of international law, the exercise of this right need conform to the requirements of necessity and proportionality applicable to a legal exercise of the right of self-defense. The better argument would seem to require that it should.[54]

The requirements of the doctrine of self-defense represent a reasonable balancing of the community interest in limiting both the geographic area of active hostilities and the possibility of drawing previously uninvolved states into an active dispute, against the interest of an individual state in ensuring its security from illegal attack. This balance is reflected in the obligations imposed by the United Nations Charter, where self-defense is the only excuse provided for a state's departure from its duty to "refrain in . . . international relations from the threat or use of force . . . ."[55]

The United States has reported to the United Nations, pursuant to the provisions of article 51 of the Charter, that the operations in Cambodia are an exercise of the right of collective self-defense.[56] To now claim that those operations may be justified on grounds other than that of self-defense would at best be inconsistent; to attempt to assert that self-defense need not be based on the requirements of necessity and proportionality would be to establish a precedent destructive of requirements that have only too recently evolved to control the discretionary use of force by states.

---

[52] 2 L. Oppenheim, supra note 12, § 326, at 698.
[53] See I. Brownlie, supra note 16, at 309, 313.
[54] See id. at 315-16; cf. Note, supra note 5, at 1139.
[55] U.N. Charter art. 2, para. 4.
[56] See generally Yost Letter, supra note 2.

United States Recognition Policy and Cambodia

WILLIAM SPRAGUE BARNES

The recent change from the so-called neutralist Sihanouk Government to the anti-communist Lon Nol Government in Cambodia and the subsequent military action there raises once again questions of international law, recognition, maintenance of diplomatic relations and the effect that United States policy may have on the internal and external status of a new government. On the basis of a comparison of the present Cambodian situation with the long, stormy history of our relations with Latin American governments, this Article concludes that consultive, collective decision making is the most appropriate means of settling the issue of recognition and that the United States should therefore initiate procedures of consultation with the countries in Indochina and the fourteen nations that have actively indicated a concern over maintaining the neutrality of Cambodia.[1]

II. UNITED STATES POLICY ON RECOGNITION OF GOVERNMENTS

In the Senate hearings on the United States Recognition of Foreign Governments held in 1969,[2] the empirical axiom was stated that recognition of a foreign government does not imply that the United States necessarily approves of that government. The discussion did not clarify the converse proposition, namely, that nonrecognition does not imply disapproval; however, the converse position is probably valid since the withholding of recognition is a political act designed to raise doubts as to the stability of a new regime. As indicated by George H. Aldrich, then Acting Legal Advisor to the Department of State:

> Each case of recognition—or nonrecognition—involves its own set of factual and political circumstances and depends, in the final analysis, on the judgment of the executive branch. The decision whether to extend recognition is made after weighing a number of considerations relevant to the basic question of whether recognition or nonrecognition would better serve the foreign policy of the United States.[3]

During the testimony at the Senate hearings, the concept of recognition was not distinguished from the notion of maintaining or breaking diplomatic

---

[1] The fourteen nations were those represented at the International Conference on the Settlement of the Laotian Question, in Geneva, July 23, 1962. See discussion p. 122 infra. For a detailed discussion of the Conference see Czyzak & Salans, The International Conference on the Settlement of the Laotian Question and the Geneva Agreements of 1962, 57 Am. J. Int'l L. 300 (1963).

[2] Hearings on S. Res. 205 (U.S. Recognition of Foreign Governments) Before the Senate Comm. on Foreign Relations, 91st Cong., 1st Sess. (1969) [hereinafter cited as Hearings].

[3] Id. at 9.

relations.[4] Nor is this distinction pertinent. Dean Adrian S. Fisher, former Legal Advisor, testified that

> [a]s a matter of international law, using that often misused term in a general sense of nations' understanding of what is proper, neither the recognition of an entity as a state, the recognition of a regime as a government or the establishment of diplomatic relations with a new government, not one of the three of these acts necessarily involves approval of the form, ideology, or policy of the government.[5]

In an effort to define United States policy, two recurring inquiries seemed to surface as the basis for United States recognition policy: first, what is the likelihood that the new government would retain control of the territory and population;[6] and second, are United States interests on the whole helped or hurt by the decision to recognize?[7] The first, especially if it includes the capacity to engage in foreign relations, is one of three broadly recognized international legal requirements applicable to the recognition of states: an independent government, a defined territory, and effective control.[8] The

---

[4] See T. Chen & L. Green, The International Law of Recognition 99 (1951) [hereinafter cited as Chen & Green]:

Since continuity of States is not interrupted by a change in government, the recognition of governments must be considered as an entirely different matter from the recognition of States. Cases often arise, however, in which this distinction is not altogether self-evident. It is sometimes difficult to say whether a given case belongs to the category of a change in the personality of the State or a change of Government. The difficulty may arise in such cases as civil war, temporary anarchy, or some other drastic change in the body politic. The existence of a civil war invests the revolting community with a certain amount of authority, not dissimilar to State sovereignty. Writers on international law are not agreed whether two separate international personalities have thereby been created. If the struggle is one aiming at secession, then it might turn out that the change is one of statehood, as well as of government.

See also 2 M. Whiteman, Digest of International Law 29 (1963):

Recognition of a government indicates a willingness on the part of the recognizing state to carry on diplomatic relations with that government. Technically speaking, however, it is possible for a government to be recognized and for the actual establishment of a diplomatic mission to be delayed or postponed, or not maintained, for one reason or another. Thus, it is possible for recognition to take place as the result of high officers of two governments signing a treaty calling for the carrying on of relations between the two governments or states, and the matter of arranging diplomatic intercourse may not take place simultaneously with the signing of the treaty. Further, high-ranking diplomatic officers may be recalled, upon request or otherwise, and not replaced for long periods of time, without cessation of recognition by either country.

The Restatement (Second) of Foreign Relations Law of the United States § 98 (1965) reaches a similar understanding in distinguishing diplomatic relations from recognition:

(1) Recognition does not require the initiation or resumption of diplomatic relations between the government of the recognizing state and the recognized government.
(2) The breaking of diplomatic relations does not withdraw or otherwise affect previous recognition of a state or its government.

[5] Hearings 18.

[6] Id. at 9, 10.

[7] Id. at 12. For example, the recognition of Castro's Government coming a few days after his takeover from Batista was justified on the grounds that recognition would help United States' interests there. On the other hand, recognition was withheld from the Maximillian Empire in Mexico during the United States Civil War. This was done because Mexican relations with France were such that to recognize the new Mexican Government would have been to recognize France's right to intervene in the Civil War.

[8] See generally H. Lauterpacht, Recognition in International Law §§ 10-12, at 26-30 (1947). Professor Lauterpacht considers these requirements to be "definitive and exhaustive." He further contends that

second inquiry, involving United States interests, is purely political.

In the history of inter-American relations, however, there developed additional stringent requirements for recognition. Along with the ability to retain control, the government must secure the general acquiescence of its people and display an ability and willingness to discharge its international and treaty obligations.[9] Whether the two additional criteria—that is, popular acquiescence and willingness to fulfill international obligations—are to be construed as part of international law, ordering the expectations of nations and not merely a matter of United States policy, is a question that is worth considering within the context of the current situation in Cambodia and the other Indochinese nations.

---

[t]hey have nothing to do with the degree of civilization of the new State, with the legitimacy of its origin, with its religion, or with its political system. Once considerations of that nature are introduced as a condition of recognition, the clear path of law is abandoned and the door wide open to arbitrariness . . . .

Id. § 13, at 31 (footnotes omitted).

[9] Consider 2 M. Whiteman, supra note 4, at 73:

(1) whether the government is in *de facto* control of the territory and in possession of the machinery of the State;

(2) whether it is administering the government with the assent or consent of the people, without substantial resistance to its authority, *i.e.*, whether there is public acquiescence in the authority of the government; and

(3) whether the new government has indicated its willingness to comply with its international obligations under treaties and international law.

Other factors increasingly borne in mind, as appropriate, for example, are the existence or nonexistence of evidence of foreign intervention in the establishment of the new regime; the political orientation of the government and its leaders; evidence of intention to observe democratic principles, particularly the holding of elections; the attitude of the new government toward private investment and economic improvement. Importantly, also, the interest of peoples, as distinguished from governments, is of concern. These, and other criteria, depending upon the international situation at the time, have been considered, with varying weight.

See also Restatement (Second) of Foreign Relations Law of the United States §§ 101, 103 (1965) concerning the minimum requirements for recognition of a revolutionary regime. Section 101 applies the standards of control of territory and population, or a "reasonable promise" of doing so. Section 103 adds an additional requirement:

Before recognizing a revolutionary regime as the government of a state, the United States requires satisfactory indications that the regime is willing to carry out the obligations of the state under international law and applicable international agreements.

An example of the application of this additional criteria of recognition is the United States' renewal of diplomatic relations with Panama. On that occasion Dean Acheson stated:

The United States today is renewing diplomatic relations with Panama. . . .

The decision of this government to take this action was reached after an exchange of views with the other American Republics. It followed upon receipt of assurances that the government of Arnulfo Arias accepts and will fulfill the international obligations of Panama and upon determination that it is actually in control of the machinery of government and the national territory of Panama and is generally accepted by the populace.

21 Dep't State Bull. 990 (1949). See also M. Ball, The OAS in Transition 498-502 (1969); C. Ronning, Law and Politics in Inter-American Diplomacy 6-32 (1963); W. Neumann, Recognition of Governments in the Americas (Foundation Affairs Pamphlet No. 3, 1947); Dozer, Recognition in Contemporary Inter-American Relations, 8 J. Inter-Am. Studies 318 (1966); Fenwick, The Recognition of *De Facto* Governments: Is There a Basis for Inter-American Collective Action?, 58 Am. J. Int'l L. 109 (1964).

III. United States Recognition Policy in Indochina

A. *Historical Foundations*

In order to apply the recognition experience of the United States, as developed in its relations with Latin America, to the situation in Indochina, some background information on Southeast Asia is necessary. One of the first official acts in the chronology of events in United States-Southeast Asian relations was the statement of February 7, 1950, issued by the Department of State, according diplomatic recognition to the governments of the semi-independent states within the French Union: Vietnam, Laos, and Cambodia.[10]

In the statement, one paragraph seems to link this act of recognition to United States political goals, and the subsequent history of Indochina has borne out the interventionist tone of this document.

> It is anticipated that the full implementation of these basic agreements and of supplementary accords which have been negotiated and are awaiting ratification will promote political stability and the growth of effective democratic institutions in Indochina. This Government is considering what steps it may take at this time to further these objectives and to assure, in collaboration with other like-minded nations, that this development shall not be hindered by internal dissension fostered from abroad.[11]

Prior to this United States action, the British granted recognition to the Chinese People's Republic. In an attempt to counterbalance the Chinese threat, the United States promised recognition to the Bao Dai regime in Vietnam.[12] Ho Chi Minh then secured Chinese recognition of his guerilla movement as the only government that was representative of unanimity amongst the Vietnamese people.[13] At the same time India refused to recognize any new governments in Indochina until they had demonstrated their ability to maintain full control of their territory and secure support from their people.[14]

After the United States recognition of Bao Dai, most of the western nations followed suit, while the Sino-Soviet bloc stood firmly behind Ho Chi Minh.

When Sihanouk took over the leadership of Cambodia, he professed a policy of total independence from France, and at the same time established a posture of neutrality, partially to appeal to India, Burma, Korea, Indonesia, and the Philippines. These nations were, at that time, uniting to resolve the issue of recognition for the Indochinese states.[15] Sihanouk, however, continued to participate in agreements with the French, involving military aid and a central Indochina bank.[16] During 1952 Cambodia continued to press the French Government for increased steps toward total inde-

---

10 22 Dep't State Bull. 291 (1950).
11 Id. at 292.
12 N.Y. Times, Jan. 7, 1950, at 4, col. 8.
13 Id., Jan. 20, 1950, at 4, col. 3; id., Jan. 21, 1950, at 5, col. 1.
14 Id., Feb. 2, 1950, at 6, col. 3; id., Apr. 29, 1950, at 3, col. 5.
15 Id., June 21, 1950, at 20, col. 7.
16 Id., Dec. 17, 1951, at 5, col. 4.

pendence, and as a result, Sihanouk was granted broader powers. In 1953, after Ho Chi Minh announced plans to weld Laos and Cambodia into an Indochinese state,[17] Sihanouk pledged that his army would fight to the last man to stop the spread of Communism in Cambodia. However, as a price for this resolve, he demanded complete independence for his country.[18]

In June of 1951 Sihanouk made his first trip into exile, a device he has used repeatedly to gain international concessions. He crossed the border into Thailand to dramatize the Cambodian desire for independence and in the hope that the Thai Government would plead his cause before the United Nations. His reception was cool, however, and a week later he returned to Cambodia.[19] Sihanouk subsequently refused all negotiations with the French until 1954, by which time Cambodia had adopted a neutralist stance, embarked on its own foreign policy, maintained an anti-Communist position and courted direct relations with the United States.

When Robert McClintock was named the first resident Ambassador to Cambodia in October 1954[20] a new era in United States-Cambodian relations seemed imminent. Sihanouk, however, abdicated a few months later, ostensibly to work for constitutional reforms, but in fact to set up a popular socialist party, which won eighty-nine of the ninety-one seats in the next national elections. In addition, he aligned Cambodia with the community of neutral nations.[21] While he was thus engaged, the United States signed a military aid pact with the Cambodian Government.[22] When final independence was declared, Sihanouk was at the height of his popularity, maintaining strict neutrality, rejecting military alliance and the presence of foreign troops or bases in Cambodia.

Cambodia continued to refuse to have formal diplomatic relations with either North Vietnam, South Vietnam or Laos, and was unwilling to become a member of the Southeast Asia Treaty Organization for fear it would violate her position of neutrality. At the end of March 1956, after engaging in another resignation ploy, Sihanouk managed to gain recognition by the Soviet Union and economic aid from China, and to maintain continued competition for his favor from the United States.[23]

While Laos and South Vietnam were struggling to maintain a semblance of order in the face of civil war and insurgency, Cambodia was quietly establishing full diplomatic relations with Egypt and announcing formal diplomatic recognition of the Chinese People's Republic.[24]

The first invasion of Cambodia by South Vietnamese troops was alleged

---

[17] Id., Apr. 14, 1953, at 4, col. 3.

[18] Id., Apr. 23, 1953, at 4, col. 4; id., May 5, 1953, at 5, col. 4.

[19] Id., June 15, 1953, at 1, col. 2; id., June 17, 1953, at 3, col. 5; id., June 21, 1953, at 1, col. 8.

[20] 31 Dep't State Bull. 615 (1954).

[21] N.Y. Times, Mar. 3, 1955, at 1, col. 5; id., Mar. 11, 1955, at 5, col. 1; id., Apr. 7, 1955, at 10, col. 1; id., Sept. 13, 1955, at 10, col. 3.

[22] Id., May 17, 1955, at 2, col. 3.

[23] Id., Mar. 31, 1956, at 3, col. 6; id., May 18, 1956, at 3, col. 3; id., May 10, 1956, at 2, col. 5; id., Dec. 2, 1956, at 15, col. 1.

[24] Id., Apr. 2, 1958, at 11, col. 1 (Cambodia recognized CPR on July 18, 1958).

to have occurred in June, 1958, at which time Sihanouk requested the United States to intervene.[25] On May 3, 1960, Cambodia repulsed a second border crossing by the South Vietnamese.[26] After being installed as chief of state in 1960, Sihanouk urged the United States to revise its military aid policy, and in conjunction with the Sino-Soviet bloc, to guarantee Cambodia and Laos as a neutralized buffer zone to establish peace in Southeast Asia.[27]

In 1960 world attention focused on Laos. As in the case of Cambodia in 1970, an annoyingly neutralist leader, Souvanna Phouma, was ignored by the United States. However, when he was overthrown by a conservative General Phouma Nosavan, and an anti-communist government was proclaimed by Boun Oum,[28] the United States quickly recognized it, while Ho Chi Minh continued to support Souvanna Phouma. Subsequent events in Laos proved that the United States had made a mistake in 1960 by ignoring the neutralist and opposition elements. India still recognized the Souvanna Phouma regime as the legitimate government of Laos while Britain and France favored the coalition government, which finally emerged with Souvanna Phouma firmly back in control by 1962.[29] In that year, when the fourteen-nation conference was called, the Kennedy Administration, concerned with the crisis in Laos, pursued a policy designed to ensure that all concerned powers would declare officially their intent to respect Cambodian neutrality.[30] Nevertheless, French and United States military aid, including troops, were maintained, leading to tensions in relations between the United States and Cambodia by the end of 1963. Cambodia threatened to break off diplomatic relations if the United States persisted in ignoring the aggressive incursions across the border by South Vietnamese troops, and finally did so in May 1965.[31] Australia assumed responsibility for the protection of United States interests there.[32] Even though Sihanouk was anxious to maintain consular relations,[33] and subsequently invited better relations, the United States turned its full attention to the war in Vietnam, offering evidence of North Vietnamese use of Cambodian territory as a justification for the continuing total rupture of relations. This rupture of diplomatic relations was hastened by the intransigence of the United States

---

25 Id., June 26, 1958, at 1, col. 8.

26 Senate Comm. on Foreign Relations, Background Information Relating to Southeast Asia and Vietnam, 90th Cong., 2d Sess. 6 (4th rev. ed. 1968) [hereinafter cited as Background Report].

27 President de Gaulle, in Feb., 1964, proposed a variation of Sihanouk's proposal recommending the neutralization of the former French possession in cooperation with Communist China. He said that it is impossible to assure the future of the area without the participation of the Government in Peking. The United States characteristically rejected the French proposal, calling it "naive and misguided." N.Y. Times, Feb. 1, 1964, at 1, col. 8.

28 Background Report, supra note 26, at 7.

29 Id. at 10.

30 N.Y. Times, July 3, 1962, at 1, col. 7.

31 Id., May 4, 1965, at 1, col. 5.

32 52 Dep't State Bull. 1000 (1965).

33 Id. at 853.

in refusing to participate in the proposal, renewed by Russia, calling for an international conference to guarantee Cambodian neutrality. During 1967, the deterioration of United States-Cambodian relations continued; Sihanouk announced that diplomatic relations had been established with North Vietnam and that both Hanoi and the Vietcong had recognized the frontiers of Cambodia.[34] On the other hand, Sihanouk accused pro-Peking leftists of subversive activity[35] and denied that communists were allowed to move supplies through his territory into South Vietnam.

As early as December of 1967, it was reported that the United States was considering support of a South Vietnamese pursuit of Vietcong into the Cambodian territory that had been used by the North Vietnamese as a sanctuary. Sihanouk's reply warned aganist South Vietnamese forces crossing the border, but said that he would not stop United States troops from entering certain sections in pursuit of communist forces. This triggered a series of United States-Cambodian exchanges, which led to improved relations. On January 1, 1968, President Johnson remarked that he was "quite encouraged" by Sihanouk's offer to permit United States troops to pursue communist forces across the Cambodian border.[36] Three days later the White House announced the commencement of United States-Cambodian talks.[37] As a result of these talks Prince Sihanouk announced that his Government and the United States had agreed on ways to prevent the war from spilling over into Cambodia.[38] The next day, however, the Washington Post reported that officials in Washington had stated no desire to employ hot pursuit and would not resort to it if the Cambodian sanctuary problem were resolved.[39] On January 12,

> [f]ollowing five days of talks in Cambodia, Ambassador Bowles and Prince Sihanouk [issued] a joint communique stating that Bowles had "renewed American assurances of respect for Cambodian sovereignty, neutrality, and territorial integrity" and had expressed the hope that "effective functioning of the International Control Commission" would avert violations of Cambodia's territory and neutrality by forces operating in Vietnam. Bowles emphasized that the United States "has no desire or intention to violate" Cambodian territory and that it will "do everything possible to avoid acts of aggression against Cambodia as well as incidents and accidents which may cause losses and damage to the inhabitants of Cambodia."[40]

At the same time as the issuance of the joint communique,

> Assistant Secretary of State Bundy [said] in Washington that if a Communist force using Cambodia "creates circumstances where the right of self-defense is involved, we will have to weigh our action very

---

34 Background Report, supra note 26, at 42.
35 Id. at 45.
36 Id. at 54.
37 Id.
38 Id. at 54-55.
39 Id. at 55.
40 Id.

carefully." He further declared that the ultimate test for the Cambodian problem lies in whether the International Control Commission will supervise Cambodia's neutrality effectively.[41]

On January 13,

> Cambodia [made] public a note to the International Control Commission, asking it to ascertain, verify, and report Vietnam war incidents that occur in Cambodia and investigate and report "all foreign infiltration" into the country.[42]

The difference in posture between Bowles and Bundy may seem slight and subtle at first glance. There is, however, an implied threat of invasion expressed by Bundy if the "sanctuary problem" is not resolved. This threat is all the more serious because it was addressed to a government with which the United States had no diplomatic relations, and contradicted the American assurances of respecting Cambodia's territorial integrity.

Sihanouk was obviously intimidated; he subsequently threatened to resign in favor of Lon Nol unless China and other foreign powers called off the growing Communist guerilla activity in Cambodia. Despite the fact that Cambodia conceded that North Vietnam and the Vietcong were using Cambodian provinces for attacks against South Vietnam, during 1968 and well into 1969 the United States refused to deal with the Sihanouk regime as the legitimate government of Cambodia. Apparently the resumption of diplomatic relations in July of 1969 by the Nixon Administration was intended to mollify the situation so as to permit the United States to have on-the-spot reports on developments there. When during his visit to Moscow[43] Sihanouk was ousted by Lon Nol, the United States was quick to establish relations on a temporary basis "with the government which [had] been selected by the Parliament, and the United States [intended to] continue to deal with that government as long as it [appeared] to be the government of the nation."[44]

B. *Analysis*

As we study the effect that United States recognition policy has had on our subsequent relations with those nations that were not consistently recognized, we shall see how unilateral decisions, made without consulting the neighbors of the country in question, tended to backfire and place the United States in a difficult diplomatic posture. In view of the number of times that Sihanouk resigned and was then reinstated as chief of state in Cambodia, it should not be too difficult to predict the ultimate result of the present exile. Sihanouk has shown himself to be not only exceptionally popular and clever in his ability to read the events around him, but also extremely flexible. His return to power after this latest coup would in all likelihood surprise no one.

---

[41] Id.
[42] Id.
[43] N.Y. Times, Mar. 14, 1970, at 11, col. 5.
[44] 62 Dep't State Bull. 437 (1970).

In view of the present status of neighboring countries, continued recognition of Sihanouk's Government-in-exile as the legitimate Cambodian regime would seem appropriate. The World War II experience of continued relations with exiled governments[45] and the twenty-year continuity of the Sihanouk regime in Cambodia would support the position that the United States could well have refused to recognize the new Government until satisfied that other governments in the area had definitely agreed to withdraw from diplomatic relations with the Sihanouk Government.[46]

IV. COMPARATIVE LATIN AMERICAN POLICIES

The present Cambodian situation seems to be one of de facto recognition, somewhat in accordance with the United States position on recognition of de facto governments expressed at the First Meeting of the Inter-American Council of Jurists at Rio de Janeiro in 1950.[47]

In reviewing the Latin American experience, one must not overlook the initial delay in recognition of the newly independent South American republics by many European states. As Lauterpacht points out in his authoritative text on the subject, British and United States practice has consistently acknowledged a legal duty to recognize the existence of states, and both have adhered to principles of international law in the recognition of governments.[48] However, the United States has not been so insistent in holding back on full and final recognition until the new government has been constitutionally installed. Of course, a government may adopt a new constitution, rig an election, and claim popular support. Lauterpacht suggests that such a vote be accompanied by internationally supervised guarantees of electoral freedom.[49]

It is not proper to refer to a decision for recognition as being de facto because the decision is usually expressed as a formal act of sovereign competence referring to the particular government that is characterized as being in de facto control of the territory of the state. Fenwick suggests that there should be a longer delay between provisional and formal recognition, which he erroneously characterizes as between de facto and de jure recognition. During this period a special meeting of the regional or global international organizations could be called to consider the existence of the traditional

---

45 For a description of the United States and British diplomatic relations with the exiled governments during World War II see Oppenheimer, Governments and Authorities in Exile, 36 Am. J. Int'l L. 568 (1942).

46 The New York Times reported that the State Department did not consider the recognition of Cambodia affected by the coup. N.Y. Times, Mar. 20, 1970, at 14, col. 4.

47 2 M. Whiteman, supra note 4, at 8-9.

48 H. Lauterpacht, supra note 8, § 7, at 12-22. For a fuller discussion of the principle of subsequent legitimation by the people (Jefferson's "will of the nation substantially declared") see id. §§ 43-47, at 115-40.

49 "There is no reason why, once collective recognition based on the principle of consent of the governed has become a rule of international law, the international organization of States should not develop organs and procedures for achieving that object." Id. § 47, at 138.

conditions of recognition. A collective decision in respect to these conditions would be more effective than the present practices.[50]

A similar procedure was implemented in 1923 in Central America. In order to delay the decision until the new government, which may have come to power by a revolution or *coup d'etat*, had been constitutionally approved, the five Central American states agreed that they would not recognize any such government, "so long as the freely elected representatives of the people thereof have not constitutionally reorganized the country."[51] The United States felt a moral obligation to apply this principle so far as Central America was concerned, until it was denounced by these same nations in 1934. Thus, the policy was officially no longer followed by the United States after Hull's instructions with respect to Honduras in 1936.[52] Conditional or limited recognition has been used extensively in the Western Hemisphere. The United States, under Woodrow Wilson, refused recognition to Mexico until it committed itself to submit all American claims growing out of disturbances there to an international commission.[53]

The World War II situation led to a unique requirement for recognition with respect to governments instituted by force within the Western Hemisphere. The Emergency Advisory Committee for Political Defense of the Continent recommended to the American governments that they not recognize such governments for the duration of the conflict without consulting amongst themselves to determine whether the new government would agree to comply with its inter-American defense obligations.[54] An exchange of information as to the circumstances of the take-over was also recommended, and these recommendations were in fact applied to a change of government in Bolivia in 1944.[55] Efforts to suggest that the overthrow of legitimately established governments constitutes a threat to the peace and that therefore these governments should not be recognized have met with considerable opposition. Most recently, developments in the Western Hemisphere seem to be moving in the direction of the so-called Estrada Doctrine.[56]

Two contrasting viewpoints on recognition were described by Ambassador

---

50 Fenwick, supra note 9, at 112.

51 See 2 M. Whiteman, supra note 4, at 7-8, 84-85.

52 Id.

53 In 1943, Franklin D. Roosevelt extended limited recognition to the French Committee of National Liberation, which was in exile in London.

54 Fenwick, supra note 9, at 109.

55 2 M. Whiteman, supra note 4, at 257-60.

56 An attempt to reconcile the doctrines of Jefferson, Tobar and Estrada was made in Resolution XXXV of Bogotá Conference of 1948. The Guani Doctrine grew out of the situation during World War II and called for consultation before recognition in order to determine whether the new government complied with continental defense undertakings. For a discussion of the Jefferson and Tobar Doctrines see 2 M. Whiteman, supra note 4, at 68-69, 84-89.

One way to establish sound criteria for recognition policy is to elaborate conditions for admission of members to international organizations. In 1962, Guatemala proposed some requirements, the most important of which includes a republican form of government, a national congress composed of popularly elected nationals, and no extra continental bases or forces on its territory.

Armour in his report of the United States Delegation to the Bogota Conference in 1948.[57] One view would make diplomatic relations contingent on the observance of certain principles and practices. The other viewpoint calls for a continuity of diplomatic relations, even when changes in government were brought about by revolutions. This is the essence of the declaration made by Don Genaro Estrada of Mexico in 1930.[58] No grants of recognition are to be made, because such a practice is insulting, implying that judgment may be made based on the internal affairs of nations.[59] It should be noted that "automatic recognition" does not preclude a state from withholding or withdrawing diplomatic representatives; but Mexican practice goes further. For example, Mexico refused to recognize Franco and expressly recognized the Republican Government-in-exile in August 1945. Mexico has also withheld recognition under the above-mentioned hemisphere consultation procedure and has even made recognition conditional on the willingness of a government to offer certain guarantees.[60] We not only encounter contradictions to the Estrada Doctrine in Mexican practice, but we also find that it is difficult to maintain in a number of situations. For example, in December 1963, the Johnson Administration finally recognized the junta that had overthrown the constitutionally elected government in the Dominican Republic,[61] and announced that the United States was changing its policy to one more in line with the Estrada Doctrine. A few weeks later, when the Goulart Government fell in Brazil, the United States "automatically" extended recognition to the successor regime.[62] However, the obvious implication of this previously announced policy would have been the possibility of extending recognition to a less friendly change. As seemed imminent in the early stages of the rebellion in Santo Dominigo, the new recognition policy might result in seeming approval of the rebel government. Although the

---

57 18 Dep't State Bull. 714, 714-15 (1948).

58 See H. Lauterpacht, supra note 8, § 51, at 156-57; Chen & Green, supra note 4, at 128; 2 M. Whiteman, supra note 4, at 85 quotes the text of the declaration of Señor Don Genaro Estrada, which reads in part:

[T]he Mexican Government is issuing no declarations in the sense of grants of recognition, since that nation considers that such a course is an insulting practice and one which, in addition to the fact that it offends the sovereignty of other nations, implies that judgment of some sort may be passed upon the internal affairs of those nations by other governments, inasmuch as the latter assume, in effect, an attitude of criticism, when they decide, favorably or unfavorably, as to the legal qualifications of foreign régimes.

59 The doctrine has met severe criticism from a practical point of view. As an example, consider the dilemma faced by a recognizing government in a situation where there is a revolution in progress in a formally recognized state. The necessity of making a choice between possible governments would be an act of recognition. For this reason, as noted by Chen and Green, the Estrada doctrine does not differ greatly from de facto recognition. See Chen & Green, supra note 4, at 128; H. Lauterpacht, supra note 8, § 51, at 156-57.

60 See C. Sepúlveda, La Teoría y la Práctica del Reconocimiento de Gobiernos 60-61 (1954).

61 49 Dep't State Bull. 997 (1963).

62 The official United States position was that the change in government in Brazil occurred by constitutional means and therefore recognition was not a question. See Secretary Rusk's statement in his press conference of April 3, 1964, as printed in 50 Dep't State Bull. 608, 610 (1964).

timing was off, the Organization of American States did call for a cease-fire and the establishment of an international neutral zone in which American troops might serve as a buffer between the factions in the Dominican crisis.[63] Had the United States been more flexible in its interpretations of the Estrada Doctrine, it might have withheld action of any kind, especially direct military intervention, until the other member states of the OAS had been consulted. There is an analogy between the situation in April-May 1965 in the Dominican Republic and the Cambodian situation in April-May 1970. Both involved interventions that could have been avoided had the United States adopted a more collective, consultative type of recognition policy. There is some evidence that the United States policy with respect to recent changes of government in Latin America has developed in this direction. In fact, the approach of President Johnson provided for a reasonable delay in deciding on recognition until other concerned states had an opportunity to express their reaction to the change. This approach was used in the military take-over from the elected Government of Peru in 1968[64] and most recently in the ousting of General Ongania in Argentina.

Some mention should be made of the Hallstein Doctrine under which West Germany takes measures, including breaking diplomatic relations, against the states that recognize East Germany as a separate state. Of course, this doctrine applies to recognition of a part of a divided state as a means of securing the right of West Germany to represent an entire Germany in international affairs to the exclusion of any other German government. Grave doubts are being expressed concerning the success of the Hallstein Doctrine in achieving its objectives.[65]

Within the Western Hemisphere, a similar doctrine, the Betancourt Doctrine, has been developed by Venezuela. Under that doctrine recognition is denied to any government that comes to power by the forcible overthrow of a constitutional government.[66] For several years, Venezuela refused to continue diplomatic relations with the Castelo Branco Government of Brazil, but finally gave in on the issue in 1968 when Costa e Silva replaced him. Betancourt took the lead in proposing that the American states agree to consult together when unconstitutional changes occur.

Perhaps the ideal doctrine was expressed by Thomas C. Mann at Notre Dame Commencement in 1964:

[I]n each case where a government is overthrown by force there should be a careful, dispassionate assessment of each situation in the light of all

[63] Nanda, The United States' Action in the 1965 Dominican Crisis: Impact on World Order—Part I, 43 Denver L. Center J. 439, 440 & n.5 (1966).

[64] Secretary Rusk announced at a press conference on Oct. 10, 1968, that the United States was consulting with other nations of the hemisphere on the recognition of the new Peruvian Government. He said that "we want to, as far as we are concerned, move in whatever way the hemisphere as a whole is inclined to move." 59 Dep't State Bull. 480, 481 (1968). Subsequently the United States recognized the new government based on its consultations. Id. at 497.

[65] B. Bot, Non-Recognition and Treaty Relations 41-44 (1968).

[66] See Dozer, supra note 9, at 325-26.

the surrounding facts and circumstances so that decisions concerning recognition, trade, aid, and other related matters can be made which are consistent with our ideals, with international law, and with our overall national interests. In making this assessment, regard should also be paid to the fact that not only is each American Republic different from all others but that each *de facto* government is likewise different in its aims, its motives, its policies, and in the kinds of problems it faces. [I]f, as a result of this appraisal, a decision is made not to recognize a regime—and this may well be the case in the future as it has been in the past—then it should be made clear that nonrecognition is based squarely on a failure on the part of another government to abide by the established rules of international conduct.

[W]hen the decision is made to recognize a regime, it should be clear that there is no basis under international law for equating recognition with United States approval of the internal political policies and practices of another government. Resolution XXXV of the Ninth Inter-American Conference of American States makes this point very clear. It declares:

> That the establishment or maintenance of diplomatic relations with a government does not imply any judgment upon the domestic policy of that government.

[W]e should continue our established practice of consulting with other American Republics whenever a question of recognition arises.[67]

In summarizing the vicissitudes of recognition policy in the Western Hemisphere from Jefferson to Johnson, one is struck by the recurring conflict between the desire to eliminate the threat of nonrecognition as a means of influencing the internal affairs of states and the persistence of consultation and subsequent nonrecognition as a means of discouraging unconstitutional regimes. Wilson introduced the doctrine of legitimacy in such a context as to draw the charge of intervention, whereas a similar doctrine applied to the Sihanouk Government-in-exile would have precluded the kind of intervention that is now occurring in Cambodia. The lesson to be drawn from the Latin American experience is that the governments of a particular region should consult prior to recognition.

---

[67] 50 Dep't State Bull. 995, 998-99 (1964).

I. THE CAMBODIAN INCURSION OF 1970

C. Constitutional Aspects

The Constitutional Issues—
Administration Position

WILLIAM H. REHNQUIST

I am pleased to avail myself of the opportunity of discussing the legal basis for the President's recent action in ordering American Armed Forces to attack Communist sanctuaries inside the border of Cambodia. So much of the discussion surrounding these recent events has been emotional that I think the Association of the Bar performs a genuine public service in encouraging reasoned debate of the very real issues involved.

I wish in these remarks to develop answers to several questions which I believe lie at the root of the matter under discussion. After having explored these questions in their historical context, I will make an effort to apply to the Cambodian incursion what seem to me to be the lessons of both history and constitutional law.

First, may the United States lawfully engage in armed hostilities with a foreign power in the absence of a congressional declaration of war? I believe that the only supportable answer to this question is "yes" in the light of our history and of our Constitution.

Second, is the constitutional designation of the President as Commander-in-Chief of the Armed Forces a grant of substantive authority, which gives him something more then just a seat of honor in a reviewing stand? Again, I believe that this question must be answered in the affirmative.

Third, what are the limits of the President's power as Commander-in-Chief, when that power is unsupported by congressional authorization or ratification of his acts? One would have to be bold indeed to assert a confident answer to this question. But I submit to you that one need not approach anything like the outer limits of the President's power, as defined by judicial decision and historical practice, in order to conclude that it supports the action that President Nixon took in Cambodia.

Before turning to a more detailed discussion of these three questions, let me advert briefly to the provisions of the Constitution itself with respect to the war power and to the debates of the Framers on this subject. Article I, section 8 provides that Congress shall have the power "to declare war." Article II, section 2 designates the President as Commander-in-Chief of the Armed Forces.

This textual allocation of authority readily suggests that a division of the nation's war power between the President and Congress was intended. An examination of the proceedings of the Constitutional Convention as found in the Madison notes confirms that suggestion.[1] The Framers did not intend to precisely delimit the boundary between the power of the executive branch and that of the legislative branch any more than they did in any of the other broad areas they considered. While rejecting the traditional power of kings to commit unwilling nations to war, they at the same time recognized the need for quick executive response to rapidly developing international situations.

It is interesting to note that the question before the Convention on Friday, August 17, 1787, was a motion to approve the language of the draft as it then read conferring upon Congress the power "to make war," rather than "to declare war."[2] During the debate, Charles Pinckney urged that the warmaking power be confined to the Senate alone, while Pierce Butler asked that the power be vested in the President. James Madison and Elbridge Gerry then jointly moved to substitute the word "declare" for the word "make," thus in their words "leaving to the Executive the power to repel sudden attacks." Rufus King supported the substitution of the word "declare," urging that the word "make" might be understood to mean to "conduct war," which he believed to be an executive function.

After this brief debate with only New Hampshire dissenting, it was agreed that the grant to Congress should be of the power to "declare" war. Pinckney's motion to strike out the whole clause, and thereby presumably leave the way open to vest the entire warmaking power in the Executive, was then defeated by a voice vote.[3]

The Framers here, as elsewhere in the Constitution, painted with a broad brush, and it has been left to nearly two hundred years of interpretation by each of the three coordinate branches of the National Government to define with somewhat more precision the line separating that which the President may do alone from that which he may do only with the assent of Congress.

It has been recognized from the earliest days of the Republic by the President, by Congress, and by the Supreme Court, that the United States may lawfully engage in armed hostilities with a foreign power without a congressional declaration of war. Our

---

[1] J. Madison, Notes of Debates in the Federal Convention of 1787, at 475-77 (Ohio Univ. Press ed. 1966).

[2] Id.

[3] Id.

history is replete with instances of "undeclared wars," from the war with France in 1798 through 1800, to the Vietnamese war. The Fifth Congress passed a law contained in the first book of the *Statutes at Large,* authorizing President Adams to "instruct the commanders of the public armed vessels which are, or which shall be employed in the service of the United States, to subdue, seize and take any armed French vessel, which shall be found within the jurisdictional limits of the United States, or elsewhere, on the high seas."[4] Now this is clearly an act of war, engaging American ships in armed hostilities, and yet Congress authorized it without feeling at all obligated to declare war on France.

The President proceeded to carry out congressional instructions, and such naval seizures were not uncommon during the period of the undeclared war with France. The Supreme Court, in a case arising out of this undeclared war, recognized the differences between what it called "solemn" war, which required a declaration by Congress, and "imperfect" war, which did not.[5]

Other examples abound of congressional authorization for armed military action without Congress having declared war. This does not answer the question, obviously, as to what the President may do without congressional authorization. The fact that the United States can engage in armed hostilities without congressional declaration of war does not mean that it can do so without congressional authorization. But it focuses on substance rather than form, and I think history simply will not admit any other conclusion than that a declaration of war by Congress is not necessary to legitimize the engagement of American Armed Forces in conflict.

What power does the designation of the President as Commander-in-Chief confer upon him? This type of question is one that for obvious reasons has not been the subject of a lot of judicial precedents so one has to pick his way among historical actions and among occasional observations by Supreme Court Justices in order to get some idea of what was intended. Chief Justice Marshall, writing for the Court in *Little v. Barreme,*[6] in 1804 spoke of the power of the President to order the seizure of a ship on the high seas in a situation where Congress has not specified the procedure:

> It is by no means clear, that the President of the United States, whose high duty it is to "take care that the laws be faith-

---

4 Act of July 9, 1798, ch. 67, 1 Stat. 578.
5 Bas v. Tingy, 4 U.S. (4 Dall.) 36, 39-40 (1800).
6 6 U.S. (2 Cranch) 170 (1804).

fully executed," and who is commander-in-chief of the armies and navies of the United States, might not, without any special authority for that purpose, in the then existing state of things, have empowered the officers commanding the armed vessels of the United States, to seize and send into port for adjudication, American vessels which were forfeited, by being engaged in this illicit commerce.[7]

Justice Grier, speaking for the Supreme Court in its famous decision in the *Prize Cases*,[8] likewise viewed the President's designation as Commander-in-Chief as being a substantive source of authority on which he might rely:

> Whether the President in fulfilling his duties, as Commander-in-chief, in suppressing an insurrection, has met with such armed hostile resistance, and a civil war of such alarming proportions as will compel him to accord to them the character of belligerents, is a question to be decided *by him,* and this Court must be governed by the decisions and acts of the political department of the Government to which this power was entrusted. "He must determine what degree of force the crisis demands."[9]

Lest it be thought that Chief Justice Marshall and Justice Grier are not relevant to the twentieth century, Justice Jackson, concurring in *Youngstown Sheet & Tube Co. v. Sawyer*,[10] expressed a similar thought:

> We should not use this occasion to circumscribe, much less to contract, the lawful role of the President as Commander in Chief. I should indulge the widest latitude of interpretation to sustain his exclusive function to command the instruments of national force, at least when turned against the outside world for the security of our society.[11]

Presidents throughout the history of our country have exercised this power as Commander-in-Chief as if it did confer upon them substantive authority. They have deployed American Armed Forces outside of the United States. They have sent American Armed Forces into conflict with foreign powers on their own initiative. Presidents have likewise exercised the widest sort of authority in conducting armed conflicts already authorized by Congress.

These are actually, I believe, three separate facets of the President's power as Commander-in-Chief. They are the power to commit American Armed Forces to conflict where it hasn't

---

[7] Id. at 176.
[8] 67 U.S. (2 Black) 635 (1862).
[9] Id. at 670.
[10] 343 U.S. 579, 643 (1952).
[11] Id. at 645.

previously existed, the power to deploy American Armed Forces throughout the world, frequently in a way which might invite retribution from unfriendly powers, and the power to determine how a war that's already in progress will be conducted.

Congress has on some of these occasions acquiesced in the President's action without formal ratification; on others it has ratified the President's action; and on still others it has taken no action at all. On several of the occasions, individual members of Congress, and, at the close of the Mexican War, one House of Congress on a preliminary vote, have protested executive use of the Armed Forces. While a particular course of executive conduct to which there was no opportunity for the legislative branch to effectively object cannot conclusively establish a constitutional precedent in the same manner as it would be established by an authoritative judicial decision, a long continued practice on the part of the Executive, acquiesced in by the Congress, is itself some evidence of the existence of constitutional authority to support such a practice. As stated by Justice Frankfurter in his concurring opinion in the *Youngstown Steel* case:

> The Constitution is a framework for government. Therefore the way the framework has consistently operated fairly establishes that it has operated according to its true nature. Deeply embedded traditional ways of conducting government cannot supplant the Constitution or legislation, but they give meaning to the words of the text or supply them.[12]

The historical examples have been marshalled in numerous recent studies of the President's power, and I will but summarize some of them briefly. President Jefferson, in 1801, sent a small squadron of American naval vessels into the Mediterranean to protect United States commerce against the Barbary pirates. He was of the view that for these ships to take offensive, as opposed to defensive, action, congressional action would be necessary.

In 1845 President Polk ordered military forces to the coast of Mexico and to the western frontier of Texas in order to prevent any interference by Mexico with the proposed annexation of Texas to the United States. Following annexation, Polk ordered General Zachary Taylor to march from the Nueces River which Mexico claimed as the southern border of Texas, to the Rio Grande River, which Texas claimed as her southern boundary, and beyond. While so engaged, Taylor's forces encountered Mexican troops, and hostilities between the two nations commenced on April 25, 1846.[13]

---

[12] Id. at 610.

[13] 1 S. Morison & H. Commager, The Growth of the American Republic 591-93 (4th ed. 1950).

There had been no prior authorization by Congress for Taylor's march south of the Nueces. Justice Grier, in his opinion in the *Prize Cases*, commented on the fact, stating: "The battles of Palo Alto and Resaca de la Palma had been fought before the passage of the Act of Congress of May 13, 1846, which recognized *'a state of war as existing by the act of the Republic of Mexico.'* "[14]

In 1854 President Pierce approved the action of the naval officer who bombarded Greytown, Nicaragua, in retaliation against a revolutionary government that refused to make reparations for damage and violence to United States citizens. This action was upheld by Judge Samuel Nelson, then a judge in the Southern District of New York and later a Justice of the Supreme Court of the United States, in *Durand v. Hollis*.[15] In his opinion in that case, Judge Nelson said:

> The question whether it was the duty of the president to interpose for the protection of the citizens at Greytown against an irresponsible and marauding community that had established itself there, was a public political question, in which the government, as well as the citizens whose interests were involved, was concerned, *and which belonged to the executive to determine*; and his decision is final and conclusive, and justified the defendant in the execution of his orders given through the secretary of the navy.[16]

In April 1861 President Lincoln called for 75,000 volunteers to suppress the rebellion by the Southern States,[17] and proclaimed a blockade of the Confederacy.[18] These actions were taken prior to their later ratification by Congress in July 1861.[19] The Supreme Court upheld the validity of the President's action in proclaiming a blockade in the *Prize Cases*.[20]

In 1900 President McKinley sent an expedition of 5000 United States troops as a component of an international force during the Boxer Rebellion in China.[21] While Congress recognized the existence of the conflict by providing for combat pay,[22] it neither declared war nor formally ratified the President's action.

Similar incidents in Central America took place under the administrations of Presidents Theodore Roosevelt,[23] Taft[24] and

---

[14] 67 U.S. (2 Black) at 668.
[15] 8 F. Cas. 111 (No. 4186) (C.C.S.D.N.Y. 1860).
[16] Id. at 112 (emphasis added).
[17] Morison & Commager, supra note 13, at 649.
[18] Id. at 668-69.
[19] Id at 669.
[20] 67 U.S. (2 Black) 635 (1862).
[21] J. Rhodes, The McKinley & Roosevelt Administrations 127 (1922).
[22] Id.
[23] Morison & Commager, supra note 13, at 403-04.
[24] M. Rodriguez, Central America 119 (1965).

Wilson.[25] Naval or armed forces were sent to Panama,[26] Nicaragua,[27] and twice to Mexico[28] in the first two decades of the twentieth century. On none of these occasions was there prior congressional authorization.

Prior to the Vietnam conflict, the most recent example of Presidential combat use of American forces without congressional declaration of war was President Truman's intervention in the Korean conflict. In many senses, this is undoubtedly the high water mark of executive exercise of the power of Commander-in-Chief to commit American forces to hostilities.

Following the invasion of South Korea by the North Koreans in June 1950 and a request for aid by the United Nations Security Council, President Truman ordered air and sea forces to give South Korean troops cover and support and ordered the Seventh Fleet to guard Formosa.[29] Ultimately 250,000 troops were engaged in the Korean War which lasted for more than three years.

President Truman relied upon the United Nations Charter as a basis for his action, as well as his power as Commander-in-Chief. The fact that his actions were authorized by the United Nations Charter, however, does not reduce the value of the incident as a precedent for executive action in committing United States Armed Forces to extensive hostilities without a formal declaration of war by Congress. The United Nations Charter was ratified by the Senate and has the status of a treaty, but it does not by virtue of this fact override any consitutional provision.[30] If a congressional declaration of war would be required in other circumstances to commit United States forces to hostilities to the extent and nature of those undertaken in Korea, the ratification of the United Nations Charter would not obviate a like requirement in the case of the Korean conflict.

Presidents have likewise used their authority as Commander-in-Chief to deploy United States forces throughout the world. Critics of President Wilson claimed that his action in arming American merchant vessels in early 1917 precipitated our entry into the First World War. Similarly, President Roosevelt's critics have asserted that various actions he took to aid the Allies in the year 1941 played a part in our involvement in the Second World

---

25 Morison & Commager, supra note 13, at 442-43.
26 Id. at 403-04.
27 Id. at 438-39.
28 Id. at 442-43.
29 R. Morris, Great Presidential Decisions 400 (1965).
30 See Reid v. Covert, 351 U.S. 487 (1956); Geofroy v. Riggs, 133 U.S. 258 (1890).

War. Whatever substance there may be to these criticisms, these Presidential actions stand as the constructions placed by these two Presidents on their power as Commander-in-Chief of the Armed Forces.

The third facet of the power of Commander-in-Chief is the right and obligation to determine how hostilities, once lawfully begun, shall be conducted. This aspect of the President's power is one which is freely conceded by even those students who read the Commander-in-Chief provision least expansively. Indeed, it has seldom, if ever, been seriously challenged. Chief Justice Chase, concurring in *Ex parte Milligan*,[31] said:

> Congress has the power not only to raise and support and govern armies but to declare war. It has, therefore, the power to provide by law for carrying on war. This power necessarily extends to all legislation essential to the prosecution of war with vigor and success, *except such as interferes with the command of the forces and the conduct of campaigns. That power and duty belongs to the President as commander-in-chief.*[32]

And if we look back at several of our armed engagements in the past, whether declared wars or otherwise, this type of decision has been freely and frequently engaged in by the Commander-in-Chief. In the First World War, for example, it was necessary to make the tactical decision whether the United States troops in France would fight as a separate command under a United States general or whether United States divisions should be incorporated in existing groups or armies commanded by French or British generals. President Wilson and his military advisors decided that United States forces would fight as a separate command.

In the Second World War similar military decisions on a global scale were required—decisions that partook as much of political strategy as they did of military strategy. For example, should the United States concentrate its military and material resources on either the Atlantic or Pacific fronts to the exclusion of the other, or should it pursue the war on both fronts simultaneously? Where should the reconquest of Allied territories in Europe and Africa begin? What should be the goal of the Allied powers? It will readily be recalled by many of us that decisions such as these were reached by the Allied commanders and chief executive officers of the Allied nations without any formal congressional participation. The series of conferences attended by President Roosevelt and President Truman ultimately established

---

[31] 71 U.S. (4 Wall.) 2 (1866).
[32] Id. at 139 (emphasis added).

the Allied goals in fighting the Second World War, including the demand for unconditional surrender on the part of the Axis nations.

Similar strategic and tactical decisions were involved in the undeclared Korean War. Decisions such as whether the United States forces should pursue Korean forces into North Korea and as to whether United States Air Force planes should pursue Communist planes north of the Yalu River into China were made by the President as Commander-in-Chief without formal congressional participation.

While these examples help outline the contours of the President's power as Commander-in-Chief in the absence of congressional authorization, they do not, of course, mark a sharp boundary. It is abundantly clear, however, that Congress can by authorizing Presidential action remove any doubt as to its constitutional validity. Thus, when the Gulf of Tonkin Resolution was enacted,[33] Congress noted that whatever the limits of the President's authority in acting alone might be, whenever the Congress and the President act together "there can be no doubt" of his constitutional authority.[34]

Congress may, of course, authorize Presidential action by declaration of war, but its authorization may also take other forms. From the example of the Fifth Congress' delegation to President Adams of the power to stop French vessels on the high seas,[35] through the legislative acts authorizing President Eisenhower to use troops in Lebanon[36] and in Formosa[37] and authorizing President Kennedy to use Armed Forces in connection with the Cuban missile crisis,[38] to the Gulf of Tonkin Resolution in 1964,[39] both Congress and the President have made it clear that it is the substance of congressional authorization, and not the form which that authorization takes, which determines the extent to which Congress has exercised its portion of the war power.

It has been suggested that there may be a question of unlawful delegation of powers here, and that Congress is not free to give a blank check to the President. Whatever may be the answer to that abstract question in the domestic field, I think it is

---

[33] Act of Aug. 10, 1964, Pub. L. No. 88-408, 78 Stat. 384. See Documentary Supplement infra.

[34] H.R. Rep. No. 1708, 88th Cong., 2d Sess. 4 (1965).

[35] See text accompanying note 4 supra.

[36] Act of Mar. 9, 1957, Pub. L. No. 85-7, 71 Stat. 5.

[37] Act of Jan. 29, 1955, Pub. L. No. 84-4, 69 Stat. 5.

[38] Act of Oct. 3, 1962, Pub. L. No. 87-733, 75 Stat. 697.

[39] Act of Aug. 10, 1964, Pub. L. No. 88-408, 78 Stat. 384. See Documentary Supplement infra.

plain from *United States v. Curtiss-Wright Export Corp.*,[40] which was decided only a year after *Schechter Poultry Corp. v. United States*,[41] that the principle of unlawful delegation of powers does not apply in the field of external affairs. The Supreme Court in *Curtiss-Wright* made this clear:

> Whether, if the Joint Resolution had related solely to internal affairs it would be open to the challenge that it constituted an unlawful delegation of legislative power to the Executive, we find it unnecessary to determine. The whole aim of the resolution is to affect a situation entirely external to the United States, and falling within the category of foreign affairs.
>
> . . . .
>
> It results that the investment of the federal government with the powers of external sovereignty did not depend upon the affirmative grants of the Constitution. The powers to declare and wage war, to conclude peace, to make treaties, to maintain diplomatic relations with other sovereignties, if they had never been mentioned in the Constitution, would have vested in the federal government as necessary concomitants of nationality.[42]

The situation confronting President Nixon in Viet Nam in 1970 must be evaluated against almost two centuries of historical construction of the constitutional division of the war power between the President and Congress. It must also be evaluated against the events which had occurred in the preceding six years. In August 1964 at the request of President Johnson following an attack on American naval vessels in the Gulf of Tonkin, Congress passed the so-called Gulf of Tonkin Resolution. That resolution approved and supported the determination of the President "to take all necessary measures to repel any armed attack against the forces of the United States and to prevent further aggression." It also provided that the United States is "prepared as the President determines, to take all necessary steps, including the use of armed force, to assist any member or protocol state of the Southeast Asia Collective Defense Treaty requesting assistance in defense of its freedom."[43]

While the legislative history surrounding the Gulf of Tonkin Resolution may be cited for a number of varying interpretations of exactly what Congress was authorizing, it cannot be fairly disputed that substantial military operations in support of the

---

[40] 299 U.S. 304 (1936).

[41] 295 U.S. 495 (1935). In that case the Supreme Court had declared that Congress was not permitted to abdicate or to delegate to the President its domestic economic powers under the Constitution. Id. at 529.

[42] 299 U.S. at 315, 318.

[43] Act of Aug. 10, 1964, Pub. L. No. 88-408, 78 Stat. 384. See Documentary Supplement infra.

South Vietnamese were thereby authorized. Steadily increasing numbers of United States Armed Forces were sent into the Vietnamese combat during the years following the passage of the Gulf of Tonkin Resolution. United States Air Force planes bombed not only South Viet Nam, but North Viet Nam. When President Nixon took office in January 1969, he found nearly half a million combat and supporting troops engaged in the field in Viet Nam. His predecessor, acting under the authorization of the Gulf of Tonkin Resolution, had placed these troops in the field, and I for one have no serious doubt that Congress and the President together had exercised their shared war power to lawfully bring about this situation.

President Nixon continued to maintain United States troops in the field in South Viet Nam in pursuance of his policy to seek a negotiated peace which will protect the right of the South Vietnamese people to self-determination. He has begun troop withdrawals, but hostile engagements with the enemy continue. The President feels, and I believe rightfully, that he has an obligation as Commander-in-Chief to take what steps he deems necessary to assure the safety of American Armed Forces in the field. On the basis of the information avaliable to him, he concluded that the continuing build-up of North Vietnamese troops in sanctuaries across the Cambodian border posed an increasing threat both to the safety of American forces and to the ultimate success of the Vietnamization program. He also determined that, from a tactical point of view, combined American-South Vietnamese strikes at these sanctuaries had a very substantial likelihood of success. He, therefore, ordered them to be made.

The President's determination to authorize incursion into these Cambodian border areas is precisely the sort of tactical decision traditionally confided to the Commander-in-Chief in the conduct of armed conflict. From the time of the drafting of the Constitution it has been clear that the Commander-in-Chief has authority to take prompt action to protect American lives in situations involving hostilities. Faced with a substantial troop commitment to such hostilities made by the previous Chief Executive, and approved by successive Congresses, President Nixon had an obligation as Commander-in-Chief of the Armed Forces to take what steps he deemed necessary to assure their safety in the field. A decision to cross the Cambodian border, with at least the tacit consent of the Cambodian Government, in order to destroy sanctuaries being utilized by North Vietnamese in violation of Cambodia's neutrality, is wholly consistent with that obligation. It is a decision made during the course of an armed conflict already commenced as to how that conflict will be conducted, rather than a determination that some new and previously unauthorized military venture will be taken.

By crossing the Cambodian border to attack sanctuaries used by the enemy, the United States has in no sense gone to "war" with Cambodia. United States forces are fighting with or in support of Cambodian troops, and not against them. Whatever protest may have been uttered by the Cambodian Government was obviously the most perfunctory, formal sort of declaration. The Cambodian incursion has not resulted in a previously uncommitted nation joining the ranks of our enemies, but instead has enabled us to more effectively deter enemy aggression heretofore conducted from the Cambodian sanctuaries.

Since even those authorities least inclined to a broad construction of the executive power concede that the Commander-in-Chief provision does confer substantive authority over the manner in which hostilities are conducted, the President's decision to invade and destroy the border sanctuaries in Cambodia was clearly authorized under even a narrow reading of his power as Commander-in-Chief.

The Constitutionality of the Cambodian Incursion

WILLIAM D. ROGERS

I

Rarely, if ever, has the relationship between the President's authority as Commander-in-Chief and Congress's power to declare war been thrown into such sharp relief as by the Cambodian incursion. The issue is quite simple: Was the President within his power under Article II, Section 2, of the Constitution in ordering United States ground troops into Cambodia on April 30, 1970? [1] The Constitutional question stands alone, in this instance freed of the other issues which tended to divert debate over United States involvement in South Viet-Nam and recent presidential actions elsewhere.

The initial commitment of ground forces to Viet-Nam was defended in major part by reference to the SEATO Treaty.[2] The argument was then that the United States had undertaken a commitment in SEATO to meet a common danger in the event of an armed attack against a member or a protocol state. The Senate, in consenting to the ratification of the treaty, it was said, had made a formal determination that a Communist armed attack on South Viet-Nam endangered the United States. All else was for the Executive. The President was thus forearmed with the power and responsibility to determine whether such an armed attack had occurred and how the United States should thereupon execute its solemn treaty obligations to respond, even if no other party to the treaty requested us to do so. Whatever one may say about the force of this argument—and there is a good deal to be said [3]—the Cambodian incursion has not been

---

* Of the District of Columbia Bar.

[1] This is an issue different from that of the Constitutionality of the Cooper-Church Amendment, H.R. 15628, 91st Cong., 2d Sess. (1970), or the McGovern-Hatfield Amendment, H.R. 17123, 91st Cong., 2d Sess. (1970). The former restricts the use of appropriated funds in Cambodia after June 30, 1970; it therefore neither judges the Constitutionality of the incursion nor purports to restrict the President in the exercise of his authority as Commander-in-Chief in the future. In this fashion, Cooper-Church avoided the Constitutional conflict. McGovern-Hatfield is also an assertion of the Congress's power over the purse. It would force a withdrawal—absent a declaration of war—from Indochina by June 30, 1971. Like Cooper-Church, it does not seek to judge the Constitutionality of either the initial commitment of force to Viet-Nam or the April 30 incursion into Cambodia.

[2] Southeast Asia Collective Defense Treaty, Sept. 8, 1954, 6 U.S. Treaties 81, T.I.A.S., No. 3170; 60 A.J.I.L. 646 (1966). See U. S. Dept. of State, The Legality of United States Participation in the Defense of Viet-Nam, Part IV, B, 54 Dept. of State Bulletin 474 (March 4, 1966), 60 A.J.I.L. 565 (1966); reprinted in 1 The Vietnam War and International Law 583 et seq. (R. Falk ed., 1968) (hereinafter cited as Memorandum).

[3] See Wormuth, "The Vietnam War: the President versus the Constitution," in 2 The Vietnam War and International Law 711, 767–780 (R. Falk ed., 1969).

explained by the SEATO Treaty for the purpose of determining the scope of the President's and the Congress's war powers.

Cambodia is of course a "protocol" state, and thus declared to be within the scope of the treaty by its parties. But the President's explanation of the reasons for his action foreclosed any reliance on SEATO in this instance. The challenge he was meeting was not, he said, an armed attack against Cambodia. The challenge was the sanctuaries along the border containing headquarters, storage, and regroupment facilities which threatened the allied armed forces in South Viet-Nam. To have relied upon SEATO would not have squared with this statement of purpose. A SEATO justification would have meant that the incursion was for the purpose of defending the Government of Cambodia, and the Administration has taken great pains to deny that this was its purpose.[4] In short, the justification for the incursion is not to be found in SEATO, and the Administration does not rely on SEATO.

Nor was the justification to be found in the Tonkin Gulf Resolution[5] (although Tonkin Gulf sheds some interesting light on the domestic legal question, as to which more hereafter). Again, the question in the Cambodia case is simpler than it was in the case of our original Indochinese involvement. As to South Viet-Nam, the Administration contended that the President was justified by the Gulf of Tonkin Congressional authority to take "all necessary measures . . . to prevent further aggression." The 1966 State Department Memorandum put the matter thus:

> [T]he legality of United States participation in the defense of South Viet-Nam does not rest only on the constitutional power of the President under article II. . . . In addition, the Congress has acted in unmistakable fashion [by the Gulf of Tonkin Resolution] to approve and authorize United States actions in Viet-Nam.[6]

The effect of the Gulf of Tonkin authorization, it was then said, was that of an exercise of the Article I Constitutional functions; it remained only for the President to determine what measures were necessary under the resolution, "including the use of armed force," to defend freedom in Southeast Asia. Similar contentions have been advanced with respect to the delegations implied in the Cuba, Formosa and Middle East resolutions.[7]

---

[4] In this respect, see the Legal Adviser's statement at the Hammarskjöld Forum of the Association of the Bar of the City of New York on May 28, 1970, 62 Dept. of State Bulletin 765 (1970). It makes no mention of SEATO. Instead, Mr. Stevenson said:
"As the President has made clear, the purpose of our armed forces in Cambodia is not to help defend the Government of Cambodia, but rather to help defend South Viet Nam and the United States troops in South Viet Nam from the continuing North Vietnamese armed attack." (Footnote omitted.)

[5] Public Law 88-408, Aug. 10, 1964, 78 Stat. 384.

[6] Memorandum, cited note 2 above, Part IV, C.

[7] Respectively, S. J. Res. of Oct. 3, 1962, 76 Stat. 697; Ch. 4, Public Law No. 4 (H. J. Res. 159), approved Jan. 29, 1959, 69 Stat. 7, and H. J. Res. of March 9, 1957, 71 Stat. 5. See 2 Falk, note 3 above, at 790; Moore, "The National Executive and the Use of the Armed Forces Abroad," in 2 The Vietnam War and International Law 808, 817 (R. Falk ed., 1969).

Both the Middle East and the Cuban resolutions were cited as underpinning the Executive power to deploy United States armed forces in potentially explosive situations, in the one case in the 1958 landing in Beirut,[8] in the second, in connection with the United States quarantine of Cuba in the 1962 missile crisis.[9]

But the Gulf of Tonkin Resolution did not support the Constitutionality of the incursion into Cambodia. Section 1, which relates to the attack on United States surface vessels which triggered the resolution, authorizes the President to take measures "to repel any armed attack." But armed attack from these sanctuaries was not asserted as the reason for the incursion.

Section 2 states in declarative terms that the nation is prepared to use, "as the President determines," "all necessary steps, including the use of armed force" in aid of a SEATO member or protocol state "requesting assistance in defense of its freedom. . . ." Cambodia did not request the assistance of United States forces. It did ask for arms, but the Administration has not claimed that the request for arms constituted the kind of request that the President, under the resolution, should meet with several divisions of United States ground troops. Thus, whatever one may say about the intent and legislative history of the Gulf of Tonkin resolution— and again there is something to say [10]—it is clear that the resolution did not support the incursion into Cambodia in this instance. And the resolution has, of course, since been repealed.[11]

In short, two of the three pillars to the South Viet-Nam Constitutional argument were not available for Cambodia. The Cambodia incursion balanced on one. It was a shaky balance.

II

The single point on which the President's power was said to rest in this instance is his power as Commander-in-Chief. A fair summary of what was said by the President on April 30 and on June 3, by Secretary Rogers in his *CBS* interview on May 3, [12] and by Mr. Stevenson in his Hammarskjöld Forum statement, is this: The Viet Cong and North Vietnamese had

[8] As to the Constitutional effect of the Middle East resolution, Secretary Dulles had this to say at his news conference of May 20, 1958, a few days before the landing at Beirut:

"All I say is that, when the Congress by an overwhelming vote declares that the independence and integrity of a certain country is vital to the peace and national interest of the United States, that is certainly a meaningful declaration, and it places upon the President a greater responsibility to protect, in that area, the peace and interests of the United States than would have been the case had there not been such a declaration." Doc. 316, 1958 American Foreign Policy, Current Documents 938–939 (May 20, 1958).

[9] Presidential Proclamation No. 3504, Oct. 23, 1962, 27 Fed. Reg. 10,401; 57 A.J.I.L. 512 (1963).

[10] See Wormuth, note 3 above, at 780–799; Velvel, "The War in Viet Nam: Unconstitutional, Justiciable, and Jurisdictionally Attackable," in 2 The Vietnam War and International Law 651, 674–681 (R. Falk ed., 1969).

[11] 116 Cong. Rec. S 9670 (June 24, 1970).

[12] 62 Dept. of State Bulletin 646 (May 25, 1970).

established "privileged sanctuaries" across the Vietnamese border in Cambodia, which were being used for supply, training, regroupment, test and recreation, communications, and headquarters in the war in South Viet-Nam. These sanctuary areas were a threat to the allied forces in South Viet-Nam, particularly during the period of reducing the United States armed presence in South Viet-Nam. So, to eliminate the threat to United States and allied forces and to insure observance of the timetable of withdrawal, the United States attacked the sanctuaries.

The attack was large. Upwards of 50,000 men were involved, together with heavy bombing and artillery fire. The incursion was to be for sixty days, with even longer-term air bombardment for "interdiction" and for support to Cambodian and Vietnamese ground forces. And the incursion was made without notice to, or consultation with, the Congress, to say nothing of the Cambodian authorities. The President acted on his own.

Was he within his authority as Commander-in-Chief in ordering the attack? The Constitution speaks in maddening generalities. With Congress is lodged the responsibility to "declare" war, to raise and support the armies with two-year appropriations and to take other measures of national war power.[13] The President is to be Commander-in-Chief of such armies as the Congress determines to raise and support,[14] presumably in such wars as the Congress may declare and for other purposes as well, although the Constitution is silent as to what these purposes beyond declared wars may be. And, to return full circle, the Congress is to make all "necessary and proper" laws for the execution of "all . . . powers vested by this Constitution in the Government of the United States, or in any Department or Officer thereof." [15]

The experience in England would suggest that the Founders brought to the debate in Philadelphia a determination to insure civilian command of the armed forces and to permit the Congress, as the heir to Parliament, a voice in the determination to resort to armed conflict. And the contemporary practice of the Founders after Independence, through the French Naval War in 1798, the War of the Barbary Pirates, and the War of 1812 reflects no little concern with the limits to Executive authority.[16]

In his report to Congress of December 8, 1801, for example, Jefferson referred to the spectacular victory of the schooner *Enterprise* over an armed cruiser from Tripoli during the War of the Barbary Pirates. The American vessel was acting under strict orders not to attack, only to protect commerce from attack. Jefferson reported laconically that:

> Unauthorized by the Constitution, without the sanction of Congress, to go beyond the line of defense, the [enemy] vessel, being disabled from committing further hostilities, was liberated with its crew. The Legislature will doubtless consider whether, by authorizing measures of offense also, they will place our force on an equal footing with that of its adversaries. I communicate all material information on this subject, that in the exercise of this important function confided by the

---

[13] U. S. Constitution, Art. I, § 8, cl. 10, 11, 12, 13, and 14.
[14] *Ibid.*, Art. II, § 2, cl. 1.   [15] *Ibid.*, Art. I, § 8, cl. 18.
[16] See, generally, Wormuth, note 3 above at 718–726.

Constitution to the Legislature exclusively their judgment may form itself on a knowledge and consideration of every circumstance of weight.[17]

Hamilton took a stronger position. The President, he argued, should fight "Till the Congress should assemble and declare war. . . ."[18] The difference between the two is of no moment for present purposes. Both counseled a resort to the Congress, the one beforehand, the other as soon after the fact as possible.

The record since, however, is both rich and ambiguous. Scholars have attempted to count the number of instances in which United States armed forces have been deployed abroad.[19] The Department of State prefers the figure of 125 such instances.[20]

A wide number of these were ones in which the President alone had sent United States forces into foreign lands. In a number of instances, the President was reacting as Commander-in-Chief against a sudden and severe attack on the United States or its territories, people or armed forces. These cases may be set to one side. The Founders were clear that self-defense and response to armed attack on the United States were well within the unilateral power and responsibility of the President as Commander-in-Chief, at least "Till the Congress should assemble and declare war. . . ." To throw the full military might of the United States back at an aggressor was not to usurp the Congressional power to declare war. As Hamilton made clear, in that instance war was declared, not by the United States, but by the attacker.[21] So, as in the case of Pearl Harbor, the President may and must respond, and even move over to the attack, although he also may profitably request Congress to ratify his action at the earliest moment by a formal declaration of war, as Roosevelt did on December 8, 1941.

The great bulk of the rest of the cases, not involving sudden attack, have been fairly inconsequential in terms of the security, blood and treasure of the United States. Hostilities have been infrequent; most instances of unilateral Presidential deployment abroad did not involve war or the risk of war, whatever the Constitutional term may mean, and are certainly not precedents for Cambodia. The examples are varied, but they fall into recurring patterns. Force has often been employed abroad— sometimes under orders from Washington, sometimes on the initiative, usually wise, occasionally foolish, of the local commander—in quasi-police actions. The Army and the Navy have pursued outlaws, smugglers, pirates and Indians into foreign territory. In other cases the military has been

---

[17] *Ibid.* at 724. [18] *Ibid.* at 725.

[19] G. Rogers, World Policing and the Constitution 92–123 (1945) (lists 149 instances of the use of U. S. forces abroad); M. Offutt, The Protection of Citizens Abroad by the Armed Forces of the United States 1 (1928) (estimates that "United States [forces] have been landed on foreign soil . . . on more than one hundred occasions during the past hundred and fifteen years."); J. Clark, Right to Protect Citizens in Foreign Countries by Landing Forces (Rev. ed., 1912) (appendix lists forty-one instances of landing United States forces).

[20] Memorandum, p. 597. [21] See Wormuth, note 3 above, at 725.

deployed, usually in small parties, most notoriously and consistently in China, to protect American lives or property when local civil government has broken down.

Occasionally, United States forces have landed for this purpose in the midst of a local revolution or political change, and their presence has had a greater effect than the mere protection of the United States citizens who happen to be resident there, most recently, for example, in the Dominican Republic. And finally the armed forces have been deployed for frankly national security purposes to occupy areas of particular strategic interest to the United States preclusively, typically in the Caribbean during the days of coal-burning navies, usually without effective opposition and always under a claimed right of intervention which the United States has since solemnly forsworn in O.A.S. treaties and the United Nations Charter.

A hundred-odd such miscellaneous instances, together with Korea and Viet-Nam, constitute the record of unilateral Executive dispatch of United States troops to foreign soil in the past. Many commentators and most Executive spokesmen have read into that record a descending curve of Congressional responsibility, and a rapidly rising line of Presidential authority. It is even suggested that the one has canceled the other out and that the Congressional war-declaring responsibility, and whatever duties are inherent in the Constitutional command that Congress review its military appropriations every two years, are eighteenth-century curiosities of no practical relevance to the harsh realities of today.

This is too dour and too simple a reading of history. First, the curve of experience is not smooth. Korea was followed by Lebanon, and in the latter instance Dulles, who apparently had learned something from Acheson's troubles, at least made passing obeisance to Congress by requesting the Middle East resolution. Furthermore, if the cases are carefully examined, it will be seen that even those presidents whom history has called strong have displayed a rather more refined sense of the overlapping nature of the war power than some commentators have lately made out. In the paradigm example of the use of the powers of Commander-in-Chief, Lincoln called for 75,000 volunteers in April. But he asked for legislative ratification when Congress came back into session.[22] The record of experience does not show that there are no outer limits to the President's power, only that those limits are in some sectors unclear; and that there is no practical way yet devised for putting those limits to the conventional judicial tests.

The Cambodian incursion, however, goes beyond the past experience. There is no precedent for it—no precedent in either the sudden attack cases, or in the instances of hot pursuit of pirates or bandits, or in the landings to protect United States interests in the face of the disarray of local governments, or in the Latin American interventions.

Nor is there any precedent for Cambodia in the Korean War. Korea

[22] He received ratification in the Act of Aug. 6, 1861, Ch. 63, § 3, 12 Stat. 326 (confirming all acts, proclamations, and orders of the President, after the 4th of March, 1861).

is said to be the high-water mark of unilateral Executive warmaking by those who would defend Cambodia. Why did the Executive not seek Congressional ratification of President Truman's decision to resist the attack from the north with American ground troops? Why did he not seek a declaration of war? The matter was considered. Acheson advances two reasons for avoiding the parliamentary path. The first was that Congressional hearings would have opened "the possibility of endless criticism . . . hardly . . . calculated to support the shaken morale of the troops or the unity that, for the moment, prevailed at home." The second was that Truman proposed to pass on the Presidency "unimpaired by the slightest loss of power or prestige." [23]

The list has the ring of the universal about it. These, doubtless, are the reasons why in any instance parliamentary consideration of war has its drawbacks. It is interesting to note that in that case the Republican Senate leader, Robert Taft, attacked President Truman for acting in defiance of the Constitutional scheme. On June 18, 1950, Taft rose to contend that the Senate might at least have approved a joint resolution authorizing intervention and that, in the absence of authority of that sort, the President's unilateral action was of doubtful Constitutionality. [24]

But, even assuming the President was within his Constitutional authority in the Korean instance, Korea is not a convincing precedent for Cambodia. As stated, the Cambodian incursion is based squarely on the President's powers as Commander-in-Chief. It finds no support in either treaty or Congressional resolution. In Korea, on the other hand, the United Nations Charter and the far-reaching concept of collective self-defense against armed attack gave international validity as well as a Constitutional cachet to the President's action. There was no flavor of local grievance or internal revolution. The action was taken in response to a clear case of an armed attack constituting a "breach of the peace." The Security Council so branded it, and recommended that all U.N. Members render assistance to the Republic of Korea. Here was a clear case of the expression of the conscience of the community of nations, acting through the United Nations, whose Charter, condemning aggression and authorizing collective self-defense on the substantive side, arming the Security Council with certain procedural powers, had received the most solemn Senatorial ratification.

No such justification was available in the Cambodia case.

III

It is also interesting to compare Cambodia once again to the Viet-Nam action itself. By the very standards and rationale which the Executive set forth to explain South Viet-Nam, Cambodia fares badly.

[23] D. Acheson, Present at the Creation 415 (1969).

[24] "If the incident [a complete usurpation by the President of authority to use the Armed Forces of this country] is permitted to go by without protest, at least from this body [the Senate], we would have finally terminated for all time the right of Congress to declare war, which is granted to Congress alone by the Constitution of the United States." 96 Cong. Rec. 9323 (1950).

Whatever may now be said of the Administration's argument at the time the Gulf of Tonkin resolution was brought to the Congress and of its later significance and meaning, in point of fact the Administration did request that resolution and the Congress did pass it. Under Secretary of State Katzenbach called it—presumably together with the SEATO Treaty—the "functional equivalent" of a Congressional declaration of war.[25] The fact that the Administration thought the resolution desirable and appropriate in the earlier instance may say something about Cambodia.

The question becomes even more pointed because the Tonkin Gulf resolution was triggered by a sudden actual attack on United States Naval units. Its enactment was said to be urgent. The Cambodian incursion is explained, not by actual attacks from the sanctuaries, but by the desire to destroy war matériel stored there.

The Gulf of Tonkin resolution casts another light on the Cambodian incursion as well: Whatever the resolution may be interpreted to say, there are certain actions it excludes by omission. The crucial Section 2 sets forth that the United States is prepared to use armed force to assist any protocol state "requesting assistance in defense of its freedom." Cambodia had not requested United States Armed Forces. The resolution does not say that the United States is prepared to use force in any case which the President, on his own, deems to be threatening, whether or not the threatened state requests assistance. Congress did not go—and presumably would not have gone—that far. The Cambodian incursion, then, is not only not authorized by the resolution; it may be in conflict with its intent.

Finally, the failure to involve Congress in the Cambodian incursion brushed aside contemporary understandings and assurances given at the time of the Gulf of Tonkin resolution and failed to comport with the Executive's notions of shared power and responsibility which underlay our original commitment in strength to Viet-Nam itself. As Secretary of State Rusk said at the time:

> Therefore, as the southeast Asia situation develops, and if it develops, in ways which we cannot now anticipate, of course there will be close and continuous consultation between the President and the leaders of the Congress.[26]

IV

In short, the President's action as Commander-in-Chief in Cambodia would not appear to be supported by the historical record of unilateral Executive dispatch of troops abroad. It is not supported by the Korean

[25] Hearings on S. Res. 151 relating to United States Commitments to Foreign Powers before the Committee on Foreign Relations, 90th Cong., 1st Sess., at 82 (1967). Furthermore, the Gulf of Tonkin debates were studded with assurances that the resolution was not intended to justify a widening of the war. And, indeed, the geographic boundaries of the ground war were not expanded until Cambodia. 2 The Vietnam War and International Law 678–681 (R. Falk ed., 1969).

[26] Southeast Asia Resolution, Joint Hearing before the Committee on Foreign Relations and the Committee on Armed Services of the United States Senate, 88th Cong., 2d Sess. 3.

precedent. And it is not supported by Viet-Nam. The President's action here must be weighed on new scales.

The new scales constructed for Cambodia are the scales of purported military necessity. Cambodia, it is said, was a valid exercise of the President's duties because, by attacking across the border into neutral territory, he could save American lives and shorten the war in Viet-Nam. Cambodia was a tactical decision, like all the other tactical decisions made by field commanders. And it was made to protect United States troops.

At first blush, a more appealing argument for the prerogatives of a Commander-in-Chief is hard to imagine. The central principle of military command is the conservation of one's forces. Without troops, nothing is possible. But the doctrine of troop protection raises serious questions in these circumstances:

1. In the first place, the doctrine—that the President by himself may launch an attack if its avowed purpose is preclusive defense of his and his nation's ally's forces—appears to be a new one. Research has disclosed no instance in the past in which a President has purported to defend a major military effort across a national boundary into another nation, and a neutral at that, on the ground that the attack was necessary to defend United States troops.

It is possible to imagine narrow instances in which such a justification of a preclusive self-defense might be entirely convincing. For example, in this case, if the incursion had been limited to squads or platoons, and if it had been explicitly directed at enemy forces fresh from attack in South Viet-Nam, then something might be said for unilateral Presidential action.

But even then, the new doctrine should be restricted to the narrowest possible terms. The President's authority to launch an offensive against another country's territory to protect United States forces ought to be confined to those cases where, to borrow an international principle, there is a palpable "necessity of self-defence, instant, overwhelming, leaving no choice of means, and no moment for deliberation." [27] And, even in circumstances of undeniable immediate necessity, the Executive license should expire within the shortest possible time. The President's authority should extend for only so long as may be necessary to place the matter before the Congress and to allow the Congress an opportunity to resolve it.

For the new doctrine of unilateral Executive power, if not confined, implies some awesome possibilities. What is necessary to protect the armed forces is, of course, a peculiarly military determination, and it is therefore awkward for any deliberative body of civilians to make such a determination. On the other hand, to protect troops *anything* may be justified as a matter of pure logic—bombing across the Yalu in the Korean War, for example; or, in the present case, resumed bombing or even a land invasion across the DMZ into North Viet-Nam; an incursion into Laos, to cut the Ho Chi Minh trail or interdict a North Vietnamese movement into

[27] Mr. Webster, Secretary of State, to Mr. Fox, British Minister to the United States, April 24, 1841, 29 British and Foreign State Papers 1129, 1138 (1840–1841).

the Plaine de Jarres; an attack into Northern Thailand; or an atomic challenge to the supply lines in China or Russia. All could be said to be necessary because, as the President said on April 30, "The lives of American men are involved." In each case, one could argue that a pre-emptive attack would snuff out the challenge, shorten the hostilities, and enhance "the possibility of winning a just peace in Vietnam and the Pacific. . . ."

In fact, the justification for all first strikes comes down to defense of one's warmaking capability. The doctrine can go far. It should be confined to its narrowest possible Constitutional limits, for it could otherwise constitute a rationalization for anything a President chooses. The Constitution does not go that far, nor does the experience under the Constitution.

2. Furthermore, although tactics were important, it is hard to think that the Cambodian incursion was purely a tactical field decision. Its purpose and effect were neither so limited nor so innocent of larger consequences. It was not a quick reaction to an immediate tactical threat to United States troops—not the hot pursuit of raiding Indians. It was a new war, or at least such a change in the basic quality and character of the old that, if the Constitutional term means anything, Congressional responsibility should for that reason have been engaged under Article I.

For purposes of Constitutional analysis, the character of a deployment of United States forces abroad must be determined by all its circumstances, not merely by its proclaimed purpose. In this case, the sanctuaries had evidently been there for some years. It seems clear that there have been substantial quantities of weapons, ammunition, and communications equipment in Cambodia for a long time. This was no sudden military build-up. The events which triggered the incursion were the coup in Phnom Penh, the change in government, and the ouster of Sihanouk—political events, in short, rather than military ones.

Furthermore, there is a strong case for the proposition that this was "war," however one may construe the Constitutional term. It was not just a protective reaction, because it was an integral part of a far larger political-military picture. The incursion of United States ground troops into the sanctuaries was in sequence, and staged to co-ordinate with broader events: longer-term South Vietnamese operations in Cambodia, American air and logistical support for both Cambodian and South Vietnamese military operations, growing Thai involvement, and a continuing possibility of re-invasion by United States forces if matters did not go well. One purpose and effect of the President's decision may have been protection of United States ground forces, but there was much more. The United States move was one element in a new pattern of violent change in Cambodia itself.

This pattern, of which the United States is a part, has momentous potentialities. It could stimulate the development of something quite new in Southeast Asian hostilities: a defensive linking of South Viet-Nam and Thailand to shore up or perhaps replace or supplant the shaky Lon Nol government in a new anti-Communist alliance. If there is in the making a multinational Southeast Asian anti-Communist front, "consisting of Cambodia, Thailand, Laos and South Vietnam," as Ky has proposed, then it is hard to see how one can separate our actions in Cambodia from that new coalition.

But it is not necessary to go so far in order to suggest that the effect of the Cambodian incursion is far broader than the protection of United States troops. The United States is in South Viet-Nam as an act of collective self-defense with the Government of South Viet-Nam. We are associated with Saigon. South Viet-Nam has now thrown large numbers of troops into the hazard of events in Cambodia.[28] South Viet-Nam is at war in Cambodia. Its purpose is broader than the protection of United States or South Vietnamese troops. It is defending the Phnom Penh Government. Its ability to meet this new commitment will have large consequences for the United States' withdrawal. The self-defense of our ally rationalizes our presence in Indochina in the first place. Our ally is engaged in war in Cambodia. Is that fact irrelevant in the Constitutional analysis? Can it yet be said that in the eyes of domestic law our purposes are more limited and our actions more innocent?

One would think not. Cambodia may be explained on one level as a move to protect United States troops. But the events which set the incursion in motion were political. And the purposes and effect of the United States act are matters of grand strategy affecting the entire Southeast Asia balance. In matters so freighted with significance, the Commander-in-Chief should look to other counsels than his own. This was war. It is the Congress' responsibility to declare it so.[29]

V

Ultimately, to explain the dispatch of impressive United States ground forces into Cambodia as just another tactical field decision is to expand the scope of the President's unilateral authority by a quantum jump. The new doctrine suggests that his command authority embraces the use of force in the territory of another nation which he may consider appropriate for the protection of the military might of the United States. In a stroke, this makes the war-declaring power a prerogative of the Presidency.

Such an escalation of the Presidency's powers is not only inconsistent with the intent of the Founders; it is also bad policy and bad politics.

Executive monopolization of the war power would mean that the President and the President alone would bear the terrifying responsibility of determining whether to reply to supposed threats to our interests. No matter how long the period for deliberation, no matter how far removed the threat, no matter how minuscule, it would be the President whose prestige would be challenged and whose political fate would be at issue. The President belongs to one party; the Congress, several. Thus, to remit the

[28] New York Times, June 19, 1970, at p. 7, col. 1 (City ed.).

[29] We may leave to one side the techniques by which Congress could act. It would seem, in any event, that there are a variety of ways, in addition to more formalistic war declarations, by which Congress could exercise its Article I, Section 8, war powers. The point is not form, but the substance of shared responsibility.

war-peace issue to the Executive exclusively is to make the war-peace decision a partisan issue. The politicization of the Korean conflict and the impact of Viet-Nam on President Johnson are the consequences. It is too much to sacrifice the Presidency on the altar of war.

Furthermore, the warmaking decision must be shared because it is in the Congress that decisions are openly made and it is the Congress which is representative, particularly through the biennial elections in the House of Representatives. War is the most fateful of national decisions. To embark on it ought to be peculiarly a responsibility of the national Congress.

It is often said that the eighteenth century could allow itself the luxury of Congressional declarations of war but that the pace of events today does not tolerate deliberation. To the contrary; a century and a half ago Congress and the courts might well have indulged a patriotic President and his subordinate captains who, acting in hot pursuit or anger, gave chase to pirates, bombed towns in Nicaragua, or called for 75,000 volunteers. They had no alternative. But that was a time when the procedures of government took time. The convening of Congress could be a matter of weeks. The dispatch of a formal declaration of war to our embassies and consular posts around the world might require a month.

Not so now. Emergencies can be made known to the President within moments. Congressmen may be brought to Washington by air in hours. There is less reason now for Executive monopolization, not more. The emergencies which truly demand a reaction so immediate as to make Congressional involvement intolerable are fewer. (Atomic attack may be the only real item on such a list.)

In cases of real emergency, the President must act, of course. But he should, while acting, move also to invoke Congress' responsibility as speedily as possible. Debate may take time. The President surely may continue to discharge his emergency responsibilities until the parliamentary issue is resolved. But he should not preclude Congress' involvement or seek to turn his emergency duty into a right to make war at his discretion anywhere in the world.

The question is one of accommodation, of the sharing of responsibility, of consultation and imaginative joint lawmaking by the Congress and President when opportunity provides, as it certainly did in the case of Cambodia. Justice Jackson put the matter tidily in *Youngstown Sheet and Tube Co.* v. *Sawyer:*

> [I] have no illusion that any decision by this Court can keep power in the hands of Congress. . . . [P]ower to legislate for emergencies belongs in the hands of Congress. . . .
> . . . With all its defects, delays and inconveniences, men have discovered no technique for long preserving free government except that the Executive be under the law, and that the law be made by parliamentary deliberations.[30]

[30] 343 U. S. 579, 654–655 (1952).

Commentary

ROBERT H. BORK

The Cambodian incursion and its aftermath do raise important Constitutional questions, but they do not seem to me the questions posed by some of the other panelists. I think there is no reason to doubt that President Nixon had ample Constitutional authority to order the attack upon the sanctuaries in Cambodia seized by North Vietnamese and Viet Cong forces. That authority arises both from the inherent powers of the Presidency and from Congressional authorization. The real question in this situation is whether Congress has the Constitutional authority to limit the President's discretion with respect to this attack. Any detailed intervention by Congress in the conduct of the Vietnamese conflict constitutes a trespass upon powers the Constitution reposes exclusively in the President.

The application of Constitutional principles necessarily depends upon circumstances, and when President Nixon took office he faced two unavoidable facts that bear upon the Constitutional propriety of his subsequent actions. The first fact was the presence of United States troops engaged in combat in Viet-Nam. The President's responsibility for their safety invokes his great powers as Commander-in-Chief of our armed forces under Article II, Section 2, of the Constitution. The second fact was the engagement in Viet-Nam of our national interests. The President's ability to carry out his general policy of phased withdrawal as the South Vietnamese took over the war—a policy Congress has not in any way repudiated—will affect in many ways, both direct and indirect, the position of the United States in world affairs. The necessity for judgment and choice in carrying out that policy effectively invokes the President's powers as Chief Executive with primary responsibility for the conduct of foreign affairs.

These inherent powers of the President are themselves sufficient to support his order to attack the Cambodian sanctuaries seized by the enemy. It is completely clear that the President has complete and exclusive power to order tactical moves in an existing conflict, and it seems to me equally clear that the Cambodian incursion was a tactical maneuver and nothing more. The circumstances demonstrate that. The United States was conducting, with Congress's approval, armed hostilities in Viet-Nam, the enemy had extended the combat zone by seizing Cambodian territory and using it as a base for attacks upon American and South Vietnamese troops within South Viet-Nam, the Cambodian Government was unable to eject the North Vietnamese and Viet Cong who thus misused Cambodian territory, and the Government of Cambodia welcomed the American and South Vietnamese attack to clear out the enemy bases in Cambodia. The President's order did not begin a war with Cambodia or with anyone else. The decision to attack the sanctuaries was thus as clearly a tactical decision as is a directive to attack specified enemy bases within South Viet-Nam itself.

An attempt has been made to counter this argument by claiming that its logical extension places the entire war power in the hands of the President, that he could, for example, cite the need to defend the safety of American troops in Viet-Nam as justification for an order to bomb supply depots in China. This is a familiar but unsound form of argument. Its premise is that no principle can be accepted if it can be extrapolated to an undesirable result. That would be true only in those relatively rare cases in human affairs where only one principle or consideration is in play. That is not the case here. The Constitutional division of the war power between the President and the Congress creates a spectrum in which those decisions that approach the tactical and managerial are for the President, while the major questions of war or peace are, in the last analysis, confined to the Congress. The example posed—the decision to bomb Chinese depots —is at one extreme of the spectrum, since it would involve the decision to initiate a major war, while the actual case before us, attacks made with the full approval of the Cambodian Government upon bases being used by the enemy in an existing conflict, is at the opposite end of the spectrum. The counter-example offered thus actually emphasizes the tactical nature of the President's decision.

In addition to the inherent powers of the President, there was Congressional authorization for the course he took. The most obvious authorization was in the Tonkin Gulf Resolution. We have heard an attempt to distinguish that document away, but Section 1 expressly authorizes the President "to take all necessary measures to repel any armed attack against the forces of the United States *and* to prevent further aggression." (Emphasis added.) Both branches of that authorization cover the Cambodian incursion. Our forces were under armed attack mounted from and based upon the Cambodian sanctuaries, and the stated purpose of President Nixon's action was to repel that attack and to prevent further aggression. Lest there be any doubt of the intended breadth of the Tonkin Gulf Resolution, it should be recalled that Senator Fulbright, who led in its adoption, said at that time that the resolution was tantamount to a declaration of war. In a war the Commander-in-Chief certainly has the power, at an absolute minimum, to order troops across a border to attack an enemy operating from there, particularly when the move is welcomed by the government whose border is crossed.

It is perfectly clear that a President may conduct armed hostilities without a formal declaration of war by Congress and that Congress may authorize such action without such a declaration. Congress's power "to declare war" does not, even semantically, exclude such a course, and the Constitution has been interpreted in this fashion repeatedly throughout our history. The Korean War is the most recent major precedent, and there President Truman went much further than President Nixon, for he committed our troops to a new war without prior Congressional approval. The suggestion that Korea is not a precedent because President Truman acted with the sanction of the United Nations is without merit. The United Nations cannot give an American President any warmaking power not entrusted to him by our Constitution. Moreover, the approval of the United Nations was obtained only because the Soviet Union happened to be boycotting the Security Council at the time, and the President's Constitutional powers can hardly be said to ebb and flow with the veto of the Soviet Union in the Security Council.

I arrive, therefore, at the conclusion that President Nixon had full Constitutional power to order the Cambodian incursion, and that Congress cannot, with Constitutional propriety, undertake to control the details of that incursion. This conclusion in no way detracts from Congress's war powers, for that body retains control of the issue of war or peace. It can end our armed involvement in Southeast Asia and it can forbid entry into new wars to defend governments there. But it ought not try to exercise Executive discretion in the carrying out of a general policy it approves.

II. WAR CRIMES

A. General Considerations

The Nuremberg Principles

WILLIAM V. O'BRIEN

ONE of the principal arguments for selective conscientious objection asserts that aggressive war, war crimes, and crimes against humanity are violations both of international and U.S. municipal law. When it appears to an American citizen that his nation is guilty of such crimes in a particular war, he clearly has a moral right, it is argued, and ought to have a legal right, to refuse participation in such criminal activity. I will attempt to assess the validity and relevance of this approach. In so doing I will treat of the following subjects:

(1) The content of the so-called "Nuremberg principles";

(2) The status of these Nuremberg principles in public international law and in the municipal law of the United States;

(3) The degree of relevance of each of the Nuremberg principles to the issue of selective conscientious objection;

(4) The practical issues of defining "participation" in crimes violative of the Nuremberg principles and of the individual's capacity, responsibility, and legal right to make judgments about their interpretation and application to particular wars in which his country is engaged. In this last section I will also evaluate the present status of the laws of war.

The Legal Base for and the Content of the "Nuremberg Principles"

The London Charter annexed to the London Agreement of August 8, 1945, adhered to by the U.S., U.K., France, and the

Soviet Union, as well as nineteen other of the wartime "United Nations,"[1] established the Nuremberg International Military Tribunal to try the so-called "major" German war criminals. The legal foundation for the trial was two-fold:

(1) As belligerents the "United Nations" had the right to try captured enemies for violations of the international law of war.

(2) As conquerors exercising supreme authority in Germany, the victorious Allies in the war in the West had the right to try German nationals and others who would have been under the jurisdiction of the deposed German state.

The Nuremberg International Military Tribunal was established for major war criminals "whose offenses have no particular geographical location."[2] In addition to this tribunal, virtually all of the victorious allies established their own tribunals to try the so-called lesser war criminals either on the grounds that their alleged crimes had occurred within the territorial jurisdiction of the tribunal, now re-established by virtue of the defeat of the Axis powers, or because the individuals charged with war crimes were apprehended within their occupation zones. Thus the United States conducted a series of "Nuremberg trials" of individuals falling into the latter category and it was these trials that inspired the film *Judgment at Nuremberg*. These trials are reported in well-written and carefully edited reports published by the United States government. Overviews of the total number and nature of trials of the lesser war criminals may be obtained by consulting the United Nations War Crimes Commission *Reports* and by Appleman's *Military Tribunals and International Crime.*[3] For the dedicated scholar, a careful perusal of the *International Law Reports,* which covers many of the national tribunal trials of war criminals would be worthwhile.[4]

There are really four major substantive offenses defined by the London Charter and applied by the judgment of the International Military Tribunal. There are, in addition, two overlapping principles prescribed by the London Charter and applied by the Tribunal which are relevant to the issue of selective conscientious objection. Article 6 of the London Charter gives the Tribunal power "to try and punish persons [the major war criminals], acting in the interests of the European Axis countries, whether as individuals or as members of organizations," for the following crimes:

"(a) *Crimes against the peace:* Namely, planning, preparation, initiation, or waging of a war of aggression, or a war in violation of international treaties, agreements, or assurances, or participation in a common plan or conspiracy for the accomplishment of any of the foregoing.

"(b) *War crimes:* Namely, violations of the laws or customs of war. Such violations shall include, but not be limited to, murder, ill-treatment or deportation to slave labor or for any other purpose of civilian population of or in occupied territory, murder or ill-treatment of prisoners of war or persons on the seas, killing of hostages, plunder of public or private property, wanton destruction of cities, towns or villages, or devastation not justified by military necessity.

"(c) *Crimes against humanity:* Namely, murder, extermination, enslavement, deportation, and other inhumane acts committed against any civilian population, before or during the war, or persecutions on political, racial, or religious grounds in execution of or in connection with any crime within the jurisdiction of the Tribunal, whether or not in violation of the domestic law of the country where perpetrated."[5]

To these three categories of crimes—crimes against the peace, war crimes, and crimes against humanity—was added a somewhat ambiguous and controversial fourth count, (d), *conspiracy to commit any or all of the three categories of crimes, viz.:* "Leaders, organizers, instigators, and accomplices participating in the formulation or execution of a common plan or conspiracy to commit any of the foregoing crimes are responsible for all acts performed by any persons in execution of such plan."[6]

It is essential to distinguish between these categories of crimes. The second category, war crimes, was not a new one, although proceedings under this rubric on such a large scale were unprecedented. The novel aspect of the Nuremberg trial of the major war criminals and the real source of the charges of "Victor's Justice" and *ex post facto* condemnations was, on the one hand, the new concept of crimes against the peace, i.e., of illegal aggressive war, and, on the other hand, of individual liability for such crimes. For under older international law concepts such alleged crimes would have been considered "acts of state" for which there should only be corporative or community responsibility and punishment.

The question at Nuremberg, which is still controverted, was whether so-called aggressive war had been legally outlawed by the time of the Nazi invasions. Today there is no question but that unilateral first recourse to armed force is *prima facie* aggression. Today we have also established that, circumstances permitting (and they seldom do), individuals may be tried for complicity in wars of aggression, just as they have long been subject to trial for violations of the laws and customs of war.[7]

The third count, crimes against humanity, is of interest because of its recognition of higher law standards and their relation to an incomplete and developing positive international law. In practice, however, crimes against humanity were usually merged with the category of war crimes, e.g., the new and dreadful concept of genocide, a crime against humanity, also involves gross violations of the traditional law of belligerent occupation.[8]

In order to narrow down our discussion to the real legal and moral issues that are relevant to the selective conscientious objector, I would like first to dispose of three of the "Nuremberg principles" which, I contend, are not of central interest for this discussion, and then to turn to a more detailed examination of the two overlapping principles regarding the defenses of superior orders and of acts of state. The three Nuremberg principles which I consider relatively unimportant to the debate over selective conscientious objection—but which are raised in discussion on this subject—are the following:

(1) The concept of crimes against the peace, or aggressive war;

(2) The concept of genocide as a crime against humanity;

(3) The concept of conspiracy to commit any of the three categories of crimes.

Irrelevant Issues

As regards crimes against the peace ("planning, preparation, initiation, or waging of a war of aggression, or war in violation of international treaties, agreements, or assurances, or participation in a common plan or conspiracy for the accomplishment of any of the foregoing") we must emphasize that the characterization of a war as an illegal aggression does not brand every single participant on the aggressor's side as a "criminal." The contention that all participants in an aggressor's military forces were in principle criminals who might then be granted various excuses was put forth at Nuremberg by the French prosecutor, M. de Menthon. The Court implicitly rejected this approach and it was explicitly rejected by American Nuremberg tribunals.[9] However, either the logic or the propaganda potential or both of this approach has been used by Communist belligerents, notably by the North Koreans and Chinese Communists in the Korean War. All U.N. prisoners of war were declared aggressors and criminals in principle. Extension of normal legal rights to them was portrayed as a generous but legally unnecessary gesture.[10] But the proper view is that the illegal character of a war does not taint all members of the aggressor's armed forces with criminality under international law.

Consequently, I think that for the conscientious objector the real relevance of crimes against the peace lies not in the danger of his being made a war criminal simply by serving in the armed forces of an illegal belligerent but that such crimes reinforce his contention that in positive international law—as well as in individual moral judgments—there are such things as aggressive, illegal wars which ought not to be supported. But the issue of participation, not as a top decision-maker but as an ordinary soldier, in what is believed to be an aggressive, illegal war, is one of individual morality, not of international law.

Concerning genocide: Article I of the Convention on the Prevention and Punishment of the Crime of Genocide approved by the U.N. General Assembly on December 9, 1948, and entered into force on January 12, 1951, states that, "The Contracting Parties confirm that genocide, whether committed in time of peace or in time of war, is a crime under international law which they undertake to prevent and to punish."[11]

Under Article IV of the Convention, "persons committing genocide . . . shall be punished whether they are constitutionally responsible rulers, public officials, or private individuals."[12] Article V obligates contracting parties "to enact, in accordance with their respective Constitutions, the necessary legislation to give effect to the provisions" of the Convention.[13] Under Article VI, "persons charged with genocide . . . shall be tried by a competent tribunal of the State in the territory of which the act was committed, or by such international penal tribunal as may have jurisdiction with respect to those Contracting Parties which shall have accepted its jurisdiction."[14] It should be pointed out that *no* international criminal tribunal exists and none is likely to come into being in the present divided world. Hence the Genocide Convention is essentially dependent for enforcement on individual states which obtain custody over alleged violators of the Convention. Moreover, Article VII asserts that genocide shall not be considered as a political crime for the purpose of avoiding extradition in accordance with laws and treaties in force.[15] (Normally, extradition, i.e., transfer of a fugitive from justice from one sovereign jurisdiction to another, is limited to persons charged with acts which are criminal in both jurisdictions, and does not apply to political refugees.)

The concept of genocide in international law was the most important product of the debates and decisions about "crimes against humanity" that occurred in international and national war crimes proceedings, in the U.N., and in diplomatic and general political discussions following World War II. The term itself was coined by Raphael Lemkin[16] and it has a very definite historic meaning. Quite simply, genocide is what the Nazis and their allies did to the Jews and, to a lesser extent, to the Poles and other occupied peoples, and to such supposedly inferior groups as the gypsies. Genocide involves the systematic destruction of a group of human beings, to use the language of Article II of the Convention, "as such." Such destruction is not based on any argument of military necessity; it applies both in peace and war.

I emphasize the historic meaning of and normative rationale underlying the concept of genocide because the term has been widely, loosely, and most irresponsibly tossed around in the debates over the war in Vietnam which, above all else, occasions our present concern with selective conscientious objection. The term has been used by respected critics of the war as well as by enemy propagandists. Such usage is invalid in terms of law and mischievous in terms of informed public debate and international intercourse.

Killing many people (including noncombatants on a large scale), destroying vast areas of property, perpetuating a war which wears down the material and moral fiber of a nation—all these may be "war crimes" because of the means employed or because of violations of the principle of legitimate military necessity which requires proportionality between admissible political-military ends and the means employed to achieve them, or because of disproportionality between the probable good likely to emerge from a war and the demonstrable and projected evils resulting from it. But all these questions concern the justice of recourse to force in the first place, the reasonableness of continuance of the war in the second place, and the legality and proportionality of the means employed in the third place. In any event, they are questions of "war," not "genocide." In my opinion, however, the present indiscriminate use of the term by critics of U.S. defense and foreign policies is invalid and irrelevant to the SCO issue.

The charge of conspiracy to commit any of the three major categories of war crimes is perhaps the most irrelevant of the Nuremberg principles insofar as selective conscientious objection is concerned. First, it was developed to deal with an aggressive totalitarian state dominated by one man and his omnipotent party and all-powerful, repressive government. Despite all of the wild analogies that have been made between the Nazi society and the much advertised "Military-Industrial" complex, there is simply no way of establishing a plausible "conspiracy" theory with respect to contemporary American society.

Second, the concept of "conspiracy" at Nuremberg was an Anglo-American contribution which the French and Russians apparently either never entirely understood or cared about.

Third, and most important as concerns our subject, the selective conscientious objection problem obviously does not involve Secretaries Rusk or McNamara or Clifford or Generals Wheeler or Westmoreland. Nobody has to volunteer to serve in the government at such a level as to render him guilty of conspiracy in the Nuremberg sense, unless one wishes to argue that the Secretaries of Health, Education and Welfare or Housing and Urban Development are as much to blame for the war in Vietnam and SAC's contingency plans for nuclear deterrence as if they were adjacent to the Pentagon war room. I will return to this theme in my closing observations about "participation" in unjust wars.

The foregoing subjects are comparatively irrelevant to our problem but because they have been raised they had to be considered before they were dismissed.

Relevant Issues

Now let us turn to the real problems raised by the Nuremberg principles for the issues of selective conscientious objection. They are three-fold:

(1) The denial of the fighting man's recourse to superior orders and act of state as legitimate defenses.

(2) The existence of a body of international law governing the conduct of war, much of which is clearly part of the municipal law of the United States, and much of which is notoriously violated in modern wars.

(3) The possibility that an American fighting man may be captured and tried as a war criminal under rules which the United States took the lead in establishing and promulgating; or, alternatively, that he may be tried by a U.S. Court Martial for violations of U.S. and international law.

The Denial of the Defenses of Superior Orders and of Act of State: As we have observed, in contrast to the charge of crimes against the peace, which was a new, controversial, post-1918 concept, the concept of war crimes (violations against the law of war for which a belligerent could punish a captured enemy) was not new. What was new at the Nuremberg Trial of Major War Criminals and the lesser trials that followed was the prosecution of large numbers of individuals for such violations. On the whole, in previous wars sanctions for the law of war had taken one of two forms:

(1) reprisals;

(2) reparations imposed upon the defeated state by the victor.

The classic view in international law tended to be that in the execution of its chosen policies a state's armed forces engaged the corporative international legal responsibility of the state rather than the individual persons executing the policies. If punishment was justified and possible it should be directed against the state *qua* state rather than toward individuals, statesmen, commanders and troops. The efforts of the Allies of 1918 to change this attitude were almost entirely unsuccessful. Indeed, it is interesting to recall that the U.S. delegation to the Versailles Conference opposed the other Allies on the issue of individual responsibility—under international law—for alleged war crimes, basing their objections on classical international law doctrine.[17] Defense counsels at all the Nuremberg war crime trials laid heavy stress on the traditional concept that only the state as an international person is legally responsible for its acts and that, therefore, war crimes proceedings should be limited to cases of individual misbehavior, e.g., pillage, rape, voluntary acts of cruelty and destruction. They did not get very far.

In the first place, the Tribunal was bound by the London Charter of August 8, 1945, and the Charter explicitly ruled out the defenses of act of state or superior orders as a *complete* defense for alleged war crimes. This is one of the disturbing features of the Nuremberg precedent. One is impelled to wonder what would have happened if the judges, in their own minds, had

come to a different decision. Could they have violated the rules
of the London Charter on the grounds that their own reading of
international law was different? In any event, the Tribunal appears to have honestly concluded that law and justice vindicated
the Charter's handling of the questions and, as we will show, the
precedent was established. Whether it was entirely fair at the
time is not relevant to the issue of selective conscientious objection. The precedent is there, it has come to be widely accepted
in international law, and it must be taken into consideration in
judging the issues of selective conscientious objection.

In summary, then, the Nuremberg principles most relevant to
this issue in the debate on selective conscientious objection are:

(1) There are violations of the international law of war, i.e.,
the so-called *jus in bello* governing the conduct of war, for
which individuals may be tried either before international tribunals when such come into existence, or before the national military tribunals of foreign powers which capture an individual
serviceman in war or obtain jurisdiction over him in some other
manner.

(2) The prevailing view in international law, based upon the
Nuremberg precedents, is that neither an act of state nor the
plea of superior orders is a complete defense for such violations,
but that a fair court, following the Nuremberg precedent, would
make a judgment as to the degree of "moral choice" which the
accused actually had when, under orders, he perpetrated the illegal acts of which he is accused.

*The Status of the Nuremberg Principles in Contemporary Inter-
national Law and in U.S. Municipal Law:* To assess the current
legal status of the Nuremberg principles we must first say a
word about the relation between public international law and
the municipal (i.e., domestic) law of the United States. Under
Article VI of the Constitution, treaties are the law of the land
and have an effect equal to legislative enactments, executive decrees within the President's competence, and judicial decisions.
If there is a disparity between a treaty provision and a legisla-

tive or other valid provision of U.S. law, the later in date prevails if the provisions cannot be reconciled. The presumption is that conflict between treaty provisions and legislation is not intended and the courts will attempt to find a construction which will avoid ruling for one provision over another. If a treaty provision is overridden by legislation and/or the judicial or executive branches, U.S. law has changed but U.S. obligations under international law have not, and the other parties to the broken treaty have a right to secure remedies under international law.[18]

Executive agreements are made by the executive without the advice and consent of the Senate as in the case of treaties. Nevertheless, the courts have ruled that executive agreements are just as binding in domestic law as are treaties and the same rules of interpretation apply to them in the event of an apparent conflict with domestic law as obtain in the case of treaties.[19] The London Charter of August 8, 1945, was an executive agreement. It laid down legal principles to guide U.S. and Allied prosecutors and judges in dealing with enemy war criminals. It did not, of course, deal with possible U.S. or other United Nations war criminals, but I would hope that it would be unthinkable for any U.S. government to take the position that the legal principles prescribed for accused enemy war criminals ought not to be taken as guidelines for the conduct of U.S. forces. The United States was in the war crimes prosecution business on a very large scale in the immediate postwar years. Moreover, the United States took the lead in obtaining support from the various organs of the United Nations, particularly the General Assembly, for the Nuremberg principles which we have summarized.

It would be clear from even the briefest summary of consideration of the Nuremberg principles within U.N. organs—even before turning to other relevant sources of international law— that the state of the law does not turn on such questions as "victor's justice" and *"ex post facto"* judgments. The Nuremberg principles are widely, if not universally, accepted as binding norms of international law. The United States took *the* leading role in producing this state of affairs, so the principles are certainly binding on the United States.

But the issue of the relevance of international state practice, amounting to customary international law, should be touched briefly. In the landmark case, *The Paquete Habana, The Lola,* the Supreme Court of the United States said:

> International law is part of our law, and must be ascertained and administered by the courts of justice of appropriate jurisdiction, as often as questions of right depending upon it are duly determined for their determination. For this purpose, where there is no treaty, and no controlling executive or legislative act or judicial decision, resort must be had to the customs and usages of civilized nations; and, as evidence of these, to the works of jurists and commentators, who by years of labor, research, and experience have made themselves peculiarly well acquainted with the subjects of which they treat. . . .[20]

The force of this statement on the relation of U.S. municipal law to international law may have, in some subject areas, been diminished by the U.S. Supreme Court's decision in the Sabbatino Case.[21] But the position of the *Paquete Habana* decision on the binding quality of customary rules of international law in the realm of the law of war remains relevant and binding to the SCO issue.

The United States has repeatedly gone on record as an adherent to the Nuremberg principles. The most central is the U.S. Army's Field Manual 27–10, *The Law of Land Warfare,*[22] which summarizes and interprets the general principles of the law of war, the conventional law of the Hague and Geneva conventions, and other sources of the law of war. FM 27–10 and its Navy counterpart, Robert W. Tucker's *The Law of War and Neutrality at Sea,* appear to be consonant with the position taken in my study with respect to war crimes, and the defense of superior orders.

In an even more concrete fashion, the U.S. government has recently demonstrated its respect for the Nuremberg principles in two highly controversial cases. In the court martial proceedings against Captain Howard B. Levy at Fort Jackson, South Carolina, concerning Levy's anti-Vietnam war, anti–Green Beret statements and agitation, trial officer (judge) Colonel Earl V. Brown ruled on May 17, 1967, that (in the words of Washington *Post* reporter Nicholas von Hoffman), "if the defense can prove that the United States is committing war crimes in Vietnam as a matter of policy he will acquit the young Army doctor of willfully disobeying an order to train Special Forces medical aides."[23] The burden thereby placed on counsel for the defense proved insuperable and on May 25, 1967, Colonel Brown ruled that:

> While there have been perhaps instances of needless brutality in this struggle in Vietnam about which the accused may have learned through conversations or publications, my conclusion is that there is no evidence that would render this order illegal on the grounds that these men would have become engaged in war crimes or some way prostitute their medical training by employing it in crimes against humanity. . . .[24]

There have, moreover, been court martial trials of U.S. military personnel charged with violations of the laws of war. One of the most recent was the trial in South Vietnam of S/Sgt. Walter Griffen, who was convicted in July, 1967, of unpremeditated murder in the killing of a Vietnamese prisoner although he testified that he had acted on the orders of his commanding officers.

U.S. municipal law, then, has recognized those Nuremberg principles most relevant to the SCO problem, namely, individual criminal liability before international or domestic tribunals for violation of the conventional law of war, of which there is a substantial body, and of the customary international law of war. The U.S. also recognizes the illegality of crimes against humanity, including genocide. U.S. law also rejects almost completely the plea of superior orders as a complete defense but follows the general line of the Nuremberg precedent and the general practice of states as reflected in discussion and resolutions of the organs of the United Nations and in national war crimes legislation and proceedings in holding out the possibility that superior orders may be considered, on a case-by-case basis, as a mitigating circumstance warranting diminishment of and possibly exemption from punishment, for acts which constitute war crimes.

But the record is mixed. While U.S. military tribunals have

heard arguments and evidence relative to alleged violations of the Nuremberg principles and the laws of war by U.S. forces, the federal courts thus far seem to have considered these principles irrelevant to cases of refusal of military service based specifically on the grounds that the U.S. involvement in Vietnam violates the Nuremberg principles generally and, specifically, the Treaty of London of August 8, 1945, as well as other treaties on war to which the United States is a party. In *U.S. v. David Henry Mitchell III*, the U.S. Court of Appeals (2nd Circuit) upheld a District Court's conviction of the defendant for willful failure to report for induction into the Armed Forces.[25] Mitchell "made no claim to be a conscientious objector but sought to produce evidence to show that the war in Vietnam was being conducted in violation of various treaties . . . and that the Selective Service system was being operated as an adjunct of this military effort."[26]

Upholding the District Court's ruling that evidence in support of these contentions was "immaterial," Judge Medina said that, "Regardless of the proof that appellant might present to demonstrate the correlation between the Selective Service and our nation's efforts in Vietnam, as a matter of law the congressional power 'to raise and support armies' and 'to provide and maintain a navy' is a matter quite distinct from the use which the Executive makes of those who have been found qualified and who have been inducted into the Armed Forces. Whatever action the President may order, or the Congress sanction, cannot impair this constitutional power of the Congress."[27]

The Supreme Court denied certiorari without comment, except for a dissent by Justice Douglas. In his dissent, Douglas specifically cites Article 6 (a) of the London Treaty concerning the crime of aggressive war and individual responsibility for participation in this crime. Douglas also quotes the language of Article 8 of the Treaty regarding superior orders.[28] Douglas claimed that the Mitchell case raised five major questions which ought to be considered in the light of the London Treaty which, whatever its constitutionality or fairness in 1945, "purports to lay down a standard of future conduct for all the signatories."[29]

Justice Douglas concluded his dissent by disavowing any opinion on the merits. But he favored certiorari by the Supreme Court, saying, "We have here a recurring question in present-day Selective Service cases."[30] On November 6, 1967, the Supreme Court once more denied certiorari in a case touching in part on the Nuremberg principles. In this case three privates, already in service, sought to bar the Department of Defense and the Army from sending them to take part in "the illegal and immoral Vietnam conflict."[31] This time Justice Potter Stewart joined Douglas in dissenting and urging that the issues raised by the appeal be dealt with by the Court.

This latter case is not clearly based on the Nuremberg principles. It turns mainly on the U.S. constitutional law question of the existence of a state of war. For our purposes the case is of significance because of the support given Douglas by Stewart and the modest prospect that there might be a trend toward reversal, or at least serious reconsideration of, the Court's position that the issues in both cases are political and military and, hence, not within the jurisdiction of the federal courts.

It should be added that although the main point in the most relevant case, *U.S. v. Mitchell*, as discussed in Medina's opinion and Douglas's dissent to the Supreme Court's denial of certiorari, is the legality under municipal and international law of the U.S. involvement in the Vietnamese conflict, Mitchell also charged war crimes and crimes against humanity. But it seems at present unlikely that the federal courts will judge on the merits *either* of allegations that the U.S. is guilty of crimes against the peace or of war crimes and crimes against humanity. This is so not only because of the present attitude of the Supreme Court and other federal courts, but because of the whole history of judicial reluctance to interfere with the Executive's exercise of the war powers, or even with the intricate relations between the Executive and the Legislative branches in determining when war exists and what war powers may be properly exercised by the Executive without explicit Legislative authorization.[32]

The Practical Likelihood That an Individual Soldier May Be Placed in Circumstances Obliging Him in One Way or Another to Commit and Be Tried for War Crimes: This remains the core of our inquiry. I will address this subject in two ways. First, I will summarize the record of the principal war crimes proceedings and report on what happened to ordinary soldiers accused of war crimes after the Second World War. Second, I will discuss in a purely speculative way the subject of "participation" in aggressive wars and wars in which war crimes are allegedly committed.

The 15-volume series edited by the United Nations War Crimes Commission summarizes in its first 14 volumes 89 war crimes cases tried before national tribunals against individuals who had allegedly violated international law and were physically within the territorial jurisdiction of the tribunal and/or individuals who were accused of violations of the law of the forum. In many instances there were numerous defendants, all tried in the same proceedings. The cases therein reported do not begin to reach the total number of such cases, some of which continue, as in the Federal Republic of Germany, to this day. But the series does cover quite well the best known of the so-called lesser war crimes proceedings, i.e., all of those other than the Nuremberg International Military Tribunal's decision and its Tokyo counterpart. I have searched through these fifteen volumes to find specific cases relevant to the issues of selective conscientious objection on the grounds of justifiable fear of trial as a war criminal. It must be said that the results of this inquiry yielded little that is of relevance to the problem of selective conscientious objection. (Note that the "United Nations" commission was an organ of the wartime alliance, not of the U.N. founded at San Francisco in 1945.)

If one begins with Chapter VII of Volume 15 of the series, "Defence Pleas," the prospects for finding arguments relevant to the issues of selective conscientious objection seem promising. After having noted that the Nuremberg International Military Tribunal, following the London Charter, had ruled out "superior orders" as a complete defense but permitted its consideration as a mitigating circumstance, the U.N. War Crimes Commission goes on to analyze the practice of the national tribunals whose decisions were summarized in the preceding 14 volumes. It is noted that three pleas were advanced very frequently, often overlapped, and were sometimes confused. These were:

(1) the plea of superior orders;

(2) the plea of duress;

(3) the plea of "necessity."[33]

These three pleas are then described and considered by the United Nations War Crimes Commission as they applied in various trials.

The pleas of superior orders and duress overlapped and they were in fact taken into account in mitigation of punishment. I will summarize some cases on these issues but at this point I will dispose of the third plea mentioned by the U.N. War Crimes Commission: "necessity," or "military necessity." The principal cases in which military necessity is discussed have to do with very high military commanders, not ordinary enlisted men or even junior officers. They are not, therefore, very relevant to the problem of selective conscientious objection. Whatever the moral dilemmas of generals and the intricacies of the concept of total command responsibility set forth in the case considered, our concern is for the "common man" who, out of moral or other scruples, demands the right to refuse military service in a particular war. Therefore I intend to pass over the otherwise interesting and complex plea of military necessity for violation of the normal laws of war.[34]

This brings us to the further and most basic point which emerges from the citations accompanying the general analyses of the pleas of superior orders and duress. Most of the precedent-making cases involved either or both of the following categories of defendants:

(1) High level commanders or governmental officials;

(2) Persons, at whatever level, who served—presumably by choice—in élite organizations or in particular kinds of operations which, whatever their last-minute scruples, predictably put them in positions wherein their commission of the criminal acts of which they were accused was foreseeable and likely. Out of all the 89 cases reported in the fifteen-volume U.N. War Crimes Law Reports only ten appear to bear directly on the problem of

comparatively minor persons, whether commissioned or enlisted personnel, being ordered to commit war crimes, and, of those ten, six concern German SS units. No doubt an intensive study of the national tribunal cases reported in the *Annual Digest of Public International Law Cases* and the *International Law Reports* would produce more cases of war crimes proceedings against involuntary war criminals. But certainly a survey of the U.N. War Crimes Commission's reports produces little that is of direct relevance to the issues of selective conscientious objection.

Practical Issues

In order to come down to the practical SCO issues of allegedly illegal wars, war crimes, and criminal participation in either or both, I propose to break this section down into three subjects:

(1) The judgment that one's nation is engaged in a war contrary to binding rules of international law;

(2) The judgment that, regardless of the legal permissibility of one's nation's recourse to force, illegal means are known to be in use to the point that the individual citizen has a right to disassociate himself from a war characterized by substantial recourse to such means;

(3) The judgment that *any* "participation" in a war which is illegal either in terms of the decision to have recourse to force as an instrument of foreign policy and/or the decision to use certain allegedly illegal means places the individual citizen in jeopardy of punishment under the Nuremberg principles and that, therefore, SCO has a valid basis in the Nuremberg precedents.

Judging the Legal Permissibility of Recourse to Armed Force by One's Nation: The state of the law with respect to recourse to armed force in international relations is simple and clear, but subject in practice to violent disagreements over facts and justifications. Today, all states are prohibited from first recourse to armed force as an instrument of foreign policy by virtue of the

U.N. Charter, particularly Article II (4).[35] The only legally permissible bases for recourse to armed force are participation in a U.N. enforcement action under Chapter VII of the Charter or individual and collective self-defense under Article 51 of the same chapter, a natural right which, I would contend, is not granted but merely reiterated by the Charter.[36] Thus it would be as illegal for the U.S. to launch an offensive to "liberate" Cuba from Communist rule as it would be for the Soviet Union to attack West Germany to liberate it from the rule of capitalist-militarist-*revanchist* cliques.

The practical problem, particularly since the Korean War and the establishment of the awful but seemingly effective world order of the nuclear balance of terror, is that international conflict seldom takes a clear-cut, aggressor-defender, invader-resister form. The most common form of modern international conflict is a deadly and complex combination of genuine domestic insurgency and substantial, often essential, support by so-called indirect aggression.

Whereas the rule of thumb in the League of Nations period was that the party which had failed to exhaust the peaceful remedies of the League and of general international law and organization and which had had first recourse to open armed force was the aggressor, the present state of international conflict makes judgments about the legal permissibility of war much more difficult. If for example, we were to eliminate, from the debate over the Vietnamese conflict all those who abhor war in principle on the one hand and all those who reject loss of American lives and treasure without the prospect of "victory" in the "national interest" on the other, we would probably come down to a debate over the facts and implications of the conflict, as to which party or parties did, in a meaningful, legally significant sense, start an international conflict engendering rights of collective self-defense on the other side. I think that it is demonstrable from the disagreements of highly informed statesmen, legislators, scholars, public figures, and concerned citizens that, simply in terms of one's own conscience, this is an extremely difficult decision to make.

Now, if one is then to go on to the legal—as distinct from the moral, political, strategic, or other—judgment about selective conscientious objection to a war on the grounds that it violates the U.N. *régime* restricting recourse to force, the Nuremberg principle condemning aggressive wars, and general contemporary international law, I would have to say that it is relevant to the high-level decision-maker and, perhaps, to high-level military commanders. Scruples about the legality of a war might lead, first, to dissent within the decision-making process and, second, to resignation. But, in terms of international law, this problem is not, in my judgment, very relevant to the plight of the ordinary draftee or even to a junior officer. As has been explained, the law of Nuremberg, and of most of the trials of the lesser war criminals, holds that mere service in the armed forces of a nation which is subsequently found by some authoritative international body or court to have engaged in aggression is—in itself and without the commission of war crimes and crimes against humanity—not a crime under international law.

Prescinding from the possibility of unfair trials of "aggressors" or threats thereof by a detaining power, which would not be considered legitimate by an unbiased third party, fear of punishment as a war criminal for mere participation in the armed forces of an aggressor state is not justified in the light of contemporary international law doctrine and practice.[37] I conclude, then, that the issue of participation in "crimes against the peace" is not the central issue insofar as SCO based on the Nuremberg precedent is concerned.

I will not undertake in this paper to deal with the questions of U.S. constitutional law concerning the existence of "war" and the legality of the Executive's commitment of the nation to armed conflict without a clear-cut declaration of war by the Congress.[38] Selective conscientious objection on such grounds would, I think, provide a stronger case for the objector than reliance primarily on the Nuremberg principle prohibiting aggressive war. Were I counseling such an objector, I would advise him to bring in the Nuremberg principle regarding crimes against the peace as a secondary, in a sense "background" argument, in support of the primary argument based on U.S. constitutional law rather than on international law.

Judging the Means Used in Warfare: In relating the Nuremberg principles to selective conscientious objection, the heart of the matter I believe concerns the possible commission of war crimes and crimes against humanity, either under direct order or out of tactical or individual necessity. In considering this issue I will also raise an additional category which I will describe as "operational necessity." In so doing I hope to meet Professor Paul Ramsey's call for a survey of the relevant laws of war.

If we limit ourselves to international law as a basis for SCO, the problem of judging the means of warfare becomes complicated. Three categories must be considered:

(1) the problem of judging persistent violations of conventional international law (i.e., treaty law, the "law on the books") which violations also run counter to the general practice of states;

(2) the problem of judging persistent violations of the laws of war which appear to be so frequently violated in the practice of states as to render questionable their continued validity and relevance, even if such laws are affirmed in treaties and appear to be the "law on the books";

(3) the problem of judging means of warfare which have been the object of moral, humanitarian, and even utilitarian condemnation or criticism but which are not legally impermissible under existing positive international law, and are at best controversial. Unfortunately, from the legal point of view, this third category includes most of the decisive—and much criticized—means of modern warfare.

The first two categories are highly relevant to the subject of selective conscientious objection, particularly if the "law on the books," the conventional law of war, is binding under the domestic law of the objector's state, as is the case in the United States with respect to every major international convention on the laws of war, except the Geneva Protocol on Chemical-Biological Warfare of 1925 and the Genocide Convention. The third category is the most difficult. When dealing with it one cannot argue that one wishes to avoid violation of clearly established international law and, presumably, of the law of one's own country through the process of incorporation of international law into domestic or, as it is called by international lawyers, "municipal law."[39] One must argue on moral or other grounds about what the law *should be,* not what it is, and such arguments are beyond the scope of this paper.

With these distinctions in mind, I will examine three categories of offenses against the laws of war and humanity:

(1) violations of the law protecting prisoners of war;

(2) violations of the law governing the means of war;

(3) violations of the law protecting civilian populations in war areas.

All three categories overlap. However, this is the breakdown which the principal controlling international agreements adopted. Thus, the second category will deal, *inter alia,* with the limitations on the means of combat arising out of consideration for their effect on noncombatants, whereas the third category will deal with post-combat situations of belligerent occupation or, as is increasingly the case, ambiguous situations where the conventional forces of a belligerent are theoretically in a situation of belligerent occupation but in which indigenous and other resistance elements continue a sub-conventional conflict.

Prisoners of war have the following basic rights:

(1) The right to lay down their arms, surrender, and acquire the status of prisoner of war.[40] This right is reiterated in all of the Geneva Conventions of 1949 even for irregular forces in "armed conflict not of an international character," for soldiers who are *hors de combat,* having "laid down their arms."[41]

(2) The right to "humane treatment," as provided for in a number of treaties culminating in the Geneva Convention Relative to the Treatment of Prisoners of War of August 12, 1949.[42] In terms of the Nuremberg precedent, "murder or ill treatment of prisoners of war," is a "war crime."[43] We will not discuss the detailed rules of the POW *régime.*[44] For the purposes of this paper it is sufficient to mention several provisions of international law which have in fact often been violated and which are fre-

quently raised in criticisms of belligerent behavior in contemporary conflicts.

Common Article 3 of the four Geneva Conventions states in part:

> To this end [that POW's be treated humanely] the following acts are and shall remain prohibited at any time and in any place whatsoever with respect to the above-mentioned persons:
>
> (a) violence of life and person, in particular murder of all kinds, mutilation, cruel treatment and torture;
>
> (b) taking of hostages;
>
> (c) outrages upon personal dignity; in particular, humiliating and degrading treatment;
>
> (d) the passing of sentence and the carrying out of executions without previous judgment pronounced by a regularly constituted court affording all the judicial guarantees which are recognized as indispensable by civilized peoples.[45]

Article 13 of the Geneva Convention Relative to the Treatment of Prisoners of War of 1949 provides:

> Prisoners of war must at all times be humanely treated. Any unlawful act or omission by the Detaining Power causing death or seriously endangering the health of a prisoner of war in its custody is prohibited, and will be regarded as a serious breach of the present convention. . . .
>
> Likewise, prisoners of war must at all times be protected, particularly against acts of violence or intimidation and against insults and public curiosity.
>
> Measures of reprisal against prisoners of war are prohibited.[46]

Anyone who reads newspapers and news magazines, or who watches television, has read about and seen innumerable examples of violations of these rules. A typical catalogue of them is offered by Eric Norden in "American Atrocities in Vietnam" in *Liberation,* an anti-war periodical.[47] Although this is an adversary critique the sources are, for the most part, objective and the charges are, on their face, probably accurate. Likewise, *Vietnam and International Law,* a publication of the Lawyers Committee on American Policy Towards Vietnam—composed of highly respected lawyers and scholars—asserts that:

Numerous reports and photographs published in the American world press indicate violations of international rules of warfare regarding, for example, the mistreatment of prisoners of war. . . .[48]

I take it that no knowledgeable person denies that these charges have considerable objective validity and that, in terms of international legal responsibility, the United States must answer for violations of the POW *régime* committed by U.S. military personnel and, to a lesser extent, by allies under the direction of or in the proximity of U.S. military personnel. I further assume that the fact, also widely acknowledged, that atrocities have been threatened or committed by the Vietcong and North Vietnamese troops against those who are POW's under international law standards, would *not* justify violation of the 1949 conventions and of the customary and conventional law on the subject that developed prior to 1949.

In short, I assume that it is "given" in the war in Vietnam (and in most foreseeable international conflicts including so-called U.N. "police actions" or "peace-keeping" operations wherein combat breaks out)[49] that violations of the international law *régime* of POW's have occurred and will continue to occur. It is at this point that we are obliged to return to the difficult but inescapable distinction between violations of treaty law which are unusual and those which are fairly common in the practice of states. First, it is a simple historical fact that, in modern times, most combatants desiring to surrender were given quarter and POW status; most of them did survive and, ultimately, return to their homes, although there have been millions —out of hundreds of millions—who were denied the rights of surrender, POW status, and protection. But the kinds of violations of POW rights described in Norden's article, and referred to by the Lawyers Committee are quite familiar—lamentably—to war veterans and to military historians. In *every* war there are innumerable instances of denial of quarter. This may result from a risky tactical situation, from outrage against recent enemy atrocities, or simply from frustration and grief over heavy losses recently suffered. Moreover, all armies include vicious and depraved individuals who murder and mistreat POW's.

But, on the whole, it seems highly unlikely that a reluctant participant in a war will be obliged to deny quarter. The exception would be the case of a desperate tactical situation where an individual or an entire unit might be ordered to deny quarter and to kill wounded or unwounded prisoners. Generally speaking, such an order ought to be disobeyed. A moralist would presumably have problems with the extreme case of duress. A lawyer could only say that denial of quarter, for any reason, is legally impermissible and that necessity or duress or superior orders would be no defense but ought to be considered in the category of possible mitigating circumstances. But if we try to link the likelihood of confronting such orders and situations with the issue of SCO on the grounds of the Nuremberg principles, it seems to me we are again stretching rather far to justify SCO. Nevertheless, this is a real issue and should be discussed further as the debate over SCO continues.

The issue of torture is much more central, critical, and intractable. The moral, legal, and practical dilemmas of this subject can hardly be exaggerated. The facts are well known. Most modern wars involve a high degree of sub-conventional, guerrilla warfare. The identity of enemy combatants and terrorists is sometimes almost impossible to establish by normal, legal, intelligence techniques. Fruitful interrogation of captured enemy troops and of persons in civilian clothes suspected of belligerent activities becomes the key to success in the conflict. All of the positive counter-insurgency methods of nation-building and gaining the allegiance of the population are frustrated if the enemy is sufficiently powerful, patient, and ruthless. Enlightened counter-insurgency measures have often failed in the face of guerrilla warfare and terror. If, as Norden and others claim, the United States is fighting in Vietnam the "dirtiest" war in its history, it is not surprising. The theory and practice of wars of "national liberation" are very dirty, by Western and international law standards, and are expressly designed, among other things, to *force* the counter-insurgent forces into "dirty" behavior in self-defense.[50]

But if selective conscientious objection to "particular" wars turns in considerable measure on repugnance to the practice of torture, then SCO will be *very* selective indeed. The selective CO will have to be exempted from virtually all contemporary conflicts, particularly those—which are the most likely—involving guerrilla warfare and terrorism in underdeveloped areas. It seems almost unnecessary to make the point that actual involuntary participation in torture is rather unlikely. Seemingly, in all armies and police forces, there are people who are willing to do the dirty work of torture, for various reasons, some of them very evil. In any case, there is no avoiding the dilemma. Torture of POW's is clearly prohibited by international law. It is practiced almost universally in modern conflicts. The relevance of the Nuremberg precedent would seem to be limited to the case of widespread, indiscriminate, systematic, often pointless and sadistic torture.

I doubt, but cannot prove, that the United States and its allies in the Vietnamese conflict have come so close to such a monstrous system of torture as to warrant SCO on the basis of the Nuremberg and other international law prescriptions regarding the protection of POW's. However, I readily grant that the existence of such practices might well produce conscientious objection, either selective or general. But, as I have indicated, I have a feeling that the more defensible position would be general objection to *all* modern wars, for it will seldom be the case that a modern war will be conducted without recourse to some kind of torture as a standard operating procedure in the interrogation of POW's and civilians suspected of belligerent sympathies or activities.

There are a number of ways of approaching the subject of the law governing the conduct of hostilities. Some authorities and decision-makers operate on the assumption, explicit or implicit, that, in the final analysis, there are no legal restrictions on "military necessity" as defined by the responsible commander or government official.[51] This attitude is clearly rejected by the Hague Conventions on Land Warfare of 1899 and 1907, by the four Geneva Conventions of 1949 mentioned above,[52] and by numerous earlier conventions that were supplemented or replaced by the 1949 conventions[53] and by the Nuremberg principles relative to war crimes and crimes against humanity. Such an attitude has been expressly condemned by every U.S. military field manual on the law of war since 1863.[54] In terms of our discussion, the only relevant question, then, for an American who respects international law and the treaty commitments of the United States, which are the supreme law of the land under Article VI of the Constitution, is, "What is the content of the international law of war with respect to the conduct of hostilities?"

The answer is difficult. Respected authorities have held that everything is permitted in combat which is not clearly prohibited.[55] As will be demonstrated, few of the principal means of modern warfare are regulated by binding international agreements. The practice of contemporary belligerents is notoriously permissive. The content of the law governing hostilities, the *jus in bello*—the law *in* war—is therefore determined, in the eyes of legal authorities, largely on the basis of their own understanding of international law, the manner in which it is made, and the proper techniques of interpreting and applying it. At present, then, the content of the *jus in bello* depends a great deal on the extent to which basic *principles* governing the conduct of hostilities are accepted. These principles may be divided into two categories: (1) negative prohibitions, i.e., principles stating what ought not to be done in war; (2) positive guidelines, principles stating what may be done, i.e., which measures a belligerent has a legal right to take. It should be noted that one of the most difficult problems involved in discussing this area is that it is often controverted, first, whether a prescription is a general principle or an ironclad rule, and, second, whether a principle or a more specific rule which was once widely accepted has survived long and widespread violations.

The most widely discussed prohibitions are the following:

(1) the prohibition against the intentional killing, or otherwise injuring, or attacking the rights, of noncombatants;

(2) the related prohibition against attacks on "non-military" targets;

(3) the likewise related prohibitions against "blind," or "indiscriminate" means of warfare which, by their very nature,

cause indiscriminate injury in populated areas or which "take out" very large populated areas in which, by any standard, significant numbers of noncombatants are known to be present;

(4) the prohibition, under the so-called "St. Petersburg principle" of the use of weapons which cause "superfluous suffering";

(5) the prohibition against "the use in war of asphyxiating, poisonous or other gases, and of all analogous liquids, materials or devices," as well as "the use of bacteriological methods of warfare"; [56]

(6) the prohibition, to use the language of the London Charter of 1945, of "wanton destruction of cities, towns, or villages, or devastation not justified by military necessity." [57]

It is important to point out that principle or rule 6 is distinct from rules one to three. It is derived from Article 23 (g) of the Hague Rules of Land Warfare and, in the practice of the Nuremberg International Military Tribunal and the other war crimes tribunals, applied primarily to the action of *ground forces*, not to aerial attacks. The most frequent charge under this category was indiscriminate recourse to inhumane "scorched earth" policies or retaliatory destruction of whole villages or areas, mainly by ground forces. The importance of this distinction and of the comparative status in international law of the various principles and/or rules will become evident shortly. [58]

There was a time when principles (or rules—authorities differ) were widely held to be binding under customary international law, although they were never explicitly agreed to in a convention of the stature of the Hague Conventions on Land Warfare of 1899 and 1907. [59] The fact is that these first three principles, as positive law, did not survive World War I. What I have called "operational necessity" rendered them impossible of observance. The weapons, the means of transportation and communication, the size of the forces, the difficulty of defining "noncombatant" and "non-military target" in a "total war," as well as the fanatical character of contemporary conflict, all resulted in such widespread violations of the first three principles that they ceased to create valid expectations of observance. Any statesman or military commander relying upon them as standards of behavior by an enemy ought rightly to be deposed and placed in a mental institution.

This does not mean that might—or technical facts—make right. It may mean that modern war is intrinsically immoral, as more and more people have come to believe. But in terms of the universal practice of belligerents of every type the first three principles represent, at best, goals, guidelines, preferred rules of the game to be observed if possible, but not legally binding prescriptions.[60] By the end of World War II the most distinguished authorities were reduced to stating that international law prohibits direct, intentional attack on persons and targets that have no conceivable military significance, an ambiguous and essentially irrelevant prohibition.[61]

Before proceeding to prohibitions four to six, which are to be taken more seriously in terms of binding international law, I would like to turn to the second category of general principles, a category which can be summed up in the concept of *proportion* between ends and means and which I have characterized as the principle of "legitimate military necessity."[62] Many authorities would frame this principle in the negative and make it a prohibition of disproportionate means. Following the tradition of the original U.S. Army field manual and the logic of the concept of the right of self-defense, I prefer to formulate the principle in the following, positive fashion:

> Military necessity consists in all measures immediately indispensable and proportionate to a legitimate military end, provided that they are not prohibited by the laws of war or the natural law, when taken on the decision of a responsible commander subject to judicial review.[63]

The latter part of that definition was strongly influenced by the vast accumulations of war crimes proceedings following World War II. Since the Korean and other conflicts revealed that the conditions of "victory" requisite to conducting war crimes trials were seldom present and since hopes for international criminal tribunals have so far proved vain, I have broadened my concept of review to mean review by a commander's superiors, by his allies, and by unbiased third-party opinion.[64]

No matter what one thinks about wars such as that in Vietnam, it seems to me quite clear that they are more limited than they might otherwise be because of the moderating influence of domestic criticism, enlightened policies of self-restraint by responsible statesmen and commanders, the attitudes of co-belligerents and political allies, and by "world opinion," which, whatever its content, dynamics, and objectivity, patently exists as a major factor in international politics to which all participants in the world arena pay a great deal of attention.

It is my belief that the interaction of policies and claims regarding their legal permissibility in the area of regulation of combat practices produces customary international law. The efforts of responsible statesmen and commanders to give content to the concept of legitimate military necessity may well produce prohibitions, or at least legal presumptions, against attacks involving the killing of large numbers of noncombatants or of whole populated areas. Indeed, I believe an argument can be made that there are emerging a number of tacit "rules of the game" as between the nuclear powers, the most important of which may be a prohibition of *first* recourse to nuclear weapons in *any* form.[65] I would further argue that this rule applies to so-called "counter-city" attacks on population centers with conventional means and that the "city-busting" air-raids of World War II are now viewed in retrospect with remorse and with a feeling that they were not justified in terms of military utility much less in terms of normative standards.

Still, the fact is that there was, during World War II, no adequate, binding international law prohibiting such raids. Ironically, although many *ground* commanders were tried and convicted as perpetrators of war crimes for "wanton" destruction (usually in extremely desperate strategic or tactical situations where the destruction was carried out in the interests of survival) there appear to have been no convictions of *Luftwaffe* or other enemy officers or their superiors for illegal air-raids.[66] It remained for a Japanese court, in a totally domestic litigation, to rule that the U.S. atomic attacks on Hiroshima and Nagasaki were contrary to international law.[67]

Judging Any *Participation in "Illegal" War:* In any event, this discussion recalls our earlier problem of relating SCO to the Nuremberg principles, war crimes trials, and international law. If an individual believes that the development of ever-more effective and terrible weapons and their intrinsic incompatability with the first three principles protecting noncombatants and population centers makes all modern war immoral, then he is a CO, not an SCO. If he believes that serving in the same armed force with troops who mount counter-city air attacks—or, as we have discussed, torture prisoners—is contrary to his conscience, he is really a CO, not an SCO. As concerns modern weapons systems, willingness to employ them and the abandonment of moral scruples appear to change in proportion to their availability and the exigencies of foreign and defense policy, as both the Egyptians and Indians, for example, have amply demonstrated. If, on the other hand, the issue is true apprehension that military service may require close collaboration with those who order and execute policies violative of the former immunity of noncombatants and non-military targets from direct, intentional attack, I would reiterate my earlier argument that one can avoid service in the Air Force, one need not become an officer or even a noncom. This still leaves us, however, with the man who faces the draft and possible combat service in which he may very well be required to employ means violative of prohibitions four to six. We shall now examine these issues which are very close to the heart of SCO.

The fourth prohibition of classical international law relevant to our inquiry is that prohibiting the use of weapons which cause "superfluous suffering" and render death "inevitable." The legal basis for this principle, endorsed by the Declaration of St. Petersburg of 1868[68] and Article 23 (e) of the Hague regulations of 1899 and 1907 Respecting the Laws and Customs of War on Land which provides:

> . . . it is especially forbidden—. . .
> e. To employ arms, projectiles, or material calculated to cause unnecessary suffering.[69]

The principal contemporary authorities on the law of war have emphasized the vague and subjective character of this principle.[70]

The main weapon discussed in current SCO debates is napalm, protest against which is almost the symbol of anti-war criticism of the Vietnam conflict.[71] In the light of this controversy it is instructive to consult the instructions of the U.S. Army's FM 27–10. Regarding "Employment of Arms Causing Unnecessary Injury," it is said:

> . . . [Hague Regulations, art. 23 (3)]
>
> b. *Interpretation.* What weapons cause "unnecessary injury" can only be determined in light of the practice of States in refraining from the use of a given weapon because it is believed to have that effect. The prohibition certainly does not extend to the use of explosives contained in artillery, projectiles, mines, rockets, or hand grenades. Usage has, however, established the illegality of lances with barbed heads, irregular-shaped bullets, and projectiles filled with glass, the use of any substance on bullets that would tend unnecessarily to inflame a wound inflicted by them, and the scoring of the surface or the filing off of the ends of the hard cases of bullets.[72]

Turning to "Weapons Employing Fire," the Army's Manual maintains:

> The use of weapons which employ fire, such as tracer ammunition, flame-throwers, napalm and other incendiary agents, against targets requiring their use is not violative of international law. They should not, however, be employed in such a way as to cause unnecessary suffering to individuals.[73]

It is known that napalm was used by Israeli forces in the Middle East war initiated June 5, 1967.[74] It is believed that a survey of the world's armed forces would demonstrate that virtually all of them have used or are prepared to use napalm or other "weapons employing fire" (e.g., flame-throwers) if such means are available to them. If this belief is correct, by the reasonable standards of the U.S. Army's Field Manual 27–10, such means, terrible as they may seem, are *not* considered "superfluous" in the practice of states. On the contrary, they are considered necessary and not generally disproportionate to the ends for which they are normally used. Of course, if used indiscriminately or cruelly they would violate the basic principle of legitimate military necessity, just as indiscriminate use of firearms, artillery, or any other means of warfare would become legally impermissible if that principle were violated.

Unless there is a more definite and conspicuous abstention from the use of napalm, and other weapons employing fire, by belligerents and by armed forces in training throughout the world, it would seem that objection to military service based in part on the prospect that it will involve complicity in the use of such weapons ought to be based, not on SCO and on regard for the Nuremberg principles, but on CO on the grounds that modern war exceeds all normative limits. This is not to dismiss the very real moral and human arguments and explanations for a revulsion against the use of napalm and similar means of war but, again, we are talking about international law, not morality or humanitarian impulses.

Much more serious, in terms of international law, are the proscriptions against "the use in war of asphyxiating, poisonous or other gases, and of all analogous liquids, materials or devices," as well as "the use of bacteriological methods of warfare." In view of the broad scope of this study it will be necessary to compress the alternative analyses of these rules into rather clear-cut formulations of issues which doubtless do violence to a highly complex and controversial subject. But the following would seem to be the issues and the main alternative positions regarding so-called "CB" warfare (chemical-biological, taken from the formulation "ABC" warfare, i.e., atomic-biological-chemical):

(1) A very sweeping prohibition of the use in war of "asphyxiating, poisonous or other gases, and of all analogous liquids, materials or devices," as well as of "the use of bacteriological methods of warfare" is binding as conventional international law on all adherents to the Geneva Protocol of June 17, 1925. The United States and Japan are the only major powers which are not adherents to the Protocol.[75] *Question* (1): Does such a widespread, formal, and long-standing prohibition carry such weight

as to engender obligations under international law for non-adherents?

(2) Upon analysis it appears that the prohibition of the Geneva Protocol of 1925 is really only against the *first* use of the proscribed means and that retaliation in kind against their first use would be permitted. It is also known that all serious military establishments are prepared to use CB warfare and train with a view to defense against CB warfare.[76] *Question* (2): Do these legal and practical limitations on the broad prohibitions of the Geneva Protocol lessen its importance, particularly as regards non-adherents?

(3) The practice of states since 1925 has seen virtually *no* use of CB warfare.[77] *Question* (3): Has the practice of states, by such a lengthy abstention from CB means, some of which became standard in World War I, produced a rule of *customary* international law, justifying expectations by statesmen, military commanders, and civilian populations that CB warfare will not be used, at least not in any circumstances other than as retaliation for similar or equally impermissible means?

(4) If there is a customary international law rule against the use, or at least the first use, of CB warfare, a question is raised as to the application of that rule with regard to a state, such as the United States, which is not a party to any conventional limitation on CB means. Yet, as we have noted, "international law is part of our law," according to the Supreme Court.[78] *Question* (4): Is the U.S. bound by a rule of customary international law not to use CB means, or to use them only as lawful reprisals after their first use by an enemy; and is this international legal obligation, if it exists, enforceable as a matter of municipal law and, therefore, relevant to the defense of a SCO that his nation is utilizing illegal means in the Vietnam war?

(5) On the other hand, it is argued that non-lethal gases are used almost universally to maintain internal order and that defoliants and crop-destroyers such as are being used in Vietnam are essentially domestic farm products. *Question* (5): Regardless of the status of lethal gases and controversial forms of biological warfare, is there not a valid exception to any alleged rule, name-

ly, that non-lethal gases and other materials permitted within the domestic public orders of the world should not be included in any general prohibition against CB warfare?

Before attempting to answer these five questions, one basic point should be made. The underlying issue (perhaps we should make it issue 6) is whether there is a definable category of "CB" means which are legally impermissible and whether use of *any* means within that category, no matter how reasonable in the abstract, is legally impermissible. In other words, does recourse to CB warfare in any form represent the crossing of a normative and practical threshold which has not hitherto been crossed, except by belligerents whose behavior was generally condemned? I would argue that, whatever the difficulties of defining CB warfare, there *is* a prohibited category of means, that these means were not in fact used by the major belligerents in World War II or the Korean War, and that the legal presumption is against their legal permissibility, no matter how "humane" or "proportionate" they might be.[79]

If this perspective be valid, one must say that the use, for the first time, of non-lethal gases "in war" by the U.S. in Vietnam represents a crossing of a legal threshold which, at best, is dangerous, and at worst may be illegal and highly dangerous to the hard-earned little corpus of law which governs this subject. In the light of this conclusion, I would answer the five questions posed as follows:

With respect to the first two questions,

(1) The Geneva Protocol of 1925 is a vulnerable document which is subject to a number of criticisms and abuses which need not concern us here. Alone, it would not bind a non-adherent such as the United States. It is also questionable whether it should prejudice all weapons developments after 1925 regardless of other considerations.

(2) However, concerning the third question, which seems to be central, it seems quite clear that, say, by the end of the Korean War, if not by the end of World War II, there was a rule of customary international law prohibiting CB means. The combination of *intent*, expressed in the Protocol of 1925, and *practice*,

in the form of general abstention from the use of CB, even in major wars, has produced, I believe, an international law rule prohibiting the use of such means.

(3) Accordingly, the legal presumption is *against* the U.S. policies regarding non-lethal gas in Vietnam, the more so since such means were previously available to the U.S. and other belligerents and were, in fact, not used. The use of defoliants is a very marginal case which could go either way. The use of crop-destroyers probably falls within the general prohibition of CB means.

In the interests of brevity, it may be concluded that all of the U.S. policies in Vietnam involving possible violation of the ban on CB means are at best controversial and at least some of the means being used are probably not legally permissible. If this statement offends those who find these means innocuous if not positively humane as compared to means which are more destructive and which are not specifically regulated by international law, one can only say that the imperfect law of war which has developed must be taken as it is, not as it ought to be either in terms of higher values on the one hand or military necessity on the other. Since this paper is concerned with international law, not morality or public opinion, I can only state that, whereas the use of napalm for example is accepted, not specifically prohibited, and therefore not assimilable into the general rule of customary international law prohibiting CB means (even though it might have been and might be in the future), the use of any means, no matter how mild, which can reasonably be included in the forbidden category of CB warfare, is legally impermissible and will remain so unless the practice of states countenances exceptions.

The draftee infantryman may very well be obliged to use tear- and nausea-gas grenades and dispensers that are technically illegal under international law. A draftee might very well get involved in preparations for delivery by air of non-lethal gases as well as defoliants and crop-destroyers, in large quantities, perhaps in a rather indiscriminate fashion. He may thereby become, technically, a war criminal or an accomplice to acts that a war crimes or other tribunal might deem to be contrary to international law. Just how important this prospect would loom in the total calculation by the individual as to the propriety of his serving in a particular war where such means were known to be in use must be left to the reader's judgment.

Finally, there is the international law proscription against "wanton destruction of cities, towns, or villages, or devastation not justified by military necessity." There is no question whatever about the validity and binding force of this rule in conventional international law, particularly in the Hague Conventions of 1899 and 1907, and it is one of the principal specific rules that make up the content of "war crimes" as defined at Nuremberg.[80] There is, further, no doubt that members of the armed forces at all levels, from high commanders to privates, may be held legally accountable for violation of this rule. It is, therefore, perhaps the most relevant of all those which we have considered in connection with the Nuremberg basis for SCO.

Moreover, participation in measures of wanton destruction—burning, dynamiting, bulldozing, and otherwise destroying a population center or area of a countryside—is just as likely to be the lot of a serviceman in a combat zone as any other "detail." Naturally, the principal responsibility for controversial acts of destruction falls upon the commander. In many cases the ordinary serviceman will have little or no way of knowing whether the destructive acts in which he is engaged are legitimate or not. Some destruction is clearly permitted by military necessity, i.e., clearing a field of fire, or destroying dangerous cover which the enemy could use to approach one's lines. On the other hand, retaliatory destruction of whole villages because of guerrilla activity in the area is, generally speaking, considered to exceed legitimate military necessity. War crimes tribunals have given mixed, but, on the whole, lenient treatment to commanders and forces employing "scorched earth policies" as a means of delaying pursuit by a superior enemy. The latter category of cases involves a considerable balancing of prudential judgments, even in retrospect, for which the ordinary soldier ought not to be held too closely accountable.[81]

Anyone who has an ordinary familiarity with recent conflicts in the Third World is aware that there is a comparatively high incidence of the kinds of destruction by ground troops which we have just termed generally unjustified by legitimate military necessity. Since guerrillas and regular forces using guerrilla tactics often blend into the indigenous society and utilize the population for all manner of vital functions and resources, the temptation is great for counter-insurgency forces to destroy entirely insurgent-held villages or even whole areas. The *rationale* may range from eliminating a source of persistent sniper fire to a systematic denial of food and shelter to the insurgents and their allies, willing or unwilling. We lack sufficient authority, I think, from the vast reports of war crimes trials and commentaries thereon after World War II adequately to judge this modern phenomenon of war. The problem was dealt with after World War II but it was always secondary to the basic problems of conventional military behavior Now so-called sub-conventional war, or conventional war in a basically guerrilla warfare context, has become the central form of contemporary armed conflict and the definition of means of destruction "justified by military necessity" is extremely difficult. I can only conclude that there is a very real problem here that needs more clarification in positive international law on the one hand and more imagination and restraint on the part of belligerents on the other.

As to the individual who includes this important part of the Nuremberg concept of war crimes in his objections to a particular war and his arguments for SCO, it seems to me that we are back to the point made in discussing involvement in controversial behavior toward POW's and hostages. If the individual wants even general assurance that military service will not involve him in the war crime of wanton destruction unjustified by military necessity, in the kinds of wars which are presently being fought and which can be anticipated, I am inclined to think that it would make more sense to claim CO rather than SCO.

The international law relative to the protection of civilian persons in time of war (to use the language of the Geneva Convention of 1949) is summarized in Articles 42–56 of the 1907 Hague Convention on the Laws and Customs of War on Land and on the provisions of the 1949 Geneva Convention. There is, then, a very substantial body of conventional law on this subject; more than on any other part of the law of war except that dealing with prisoners of war. There is, moreover, an enormous body of case law, international and national, arising out of World War II which deals with this subject. Accordingly, one might expect that it would furnish us with a great number of issues relevant to SCO based on the Nuremberg principles. In my opinion, however, this is not the case.

The reason, I think, for the comparative sparseness of provisions concerning the protection of civilians in war areas relevant to our inquiry is as follows: The law as codified in 1907 and again in 1949 is focused almost exclusively, with the exception of Article 3 of the 1949 Convention previously discussed, on international, i.e., *interstate* wars, not on civil wars or on mixed civil-international wars. The basic concept underlying both conventions is that of sovereign responsibility. When a territorial sovereign is displaced from part of its domain by an enemy invader, the (sovereign) invader assumes, so the traditional law runs, a temporary but significant responsibility under international law to act somewhat as a sovereign with respect to the civilian population and resources of the area under belligerent occupation.[82]

Everything in the traditional law flows from this concept of replacement of sovereign responsibility. The belligerent occupant is granted rights commensurate with the military necessities of continuing hostilities. There is a price, however, which the civilian population in the occupied areas must pay for this protection and assistance. The traditional law required that, when the regular forces of the territorial sovereign were displaced, the civilians should obey the orders of the belligerent occupant so long as they were consonant with international law. In a very real sense, the occupied population was *hors de combat,* much in the same manner as prisoners of war. The occupant's legal obligations rested on the assumption that most of the occupied population would, as far as possible, not contribute significantly to the continuation of the war effort by their own state or its allies.[83] The Second World War showed beyond doubt that this assumption is not valid in most modern war situations. One of the most conspicuous features of that war was the activity of resistance movements within occupied territories. Resistance activity ranged from spontaneous revolt to organized guerrilla operations by troops either left behind or infiltrated into occupied areas, or both. It is remarkable, and unfortunate for those who confront contemporary conflicts, that these developments were not adequately considered at Geneva when the 1949 Convention on this subject was drafted.

In the post-Korean conflict period, when conventional war directly involving any of the great powers became unlikely, the typical war has been a combination of a civil war and interventionary indirect aggression and counter-intervention involving, overtly or covertly, forces of foreign powers. It is obvious that these changes imply factual and doctrinal dilemmas which render unhelpful, if not irrelevant, international law rules based on past assumptions about war and its principal actors. Thus, if a joint U.S.–South Vietnamese–Korean force overruns and holds an area that was formerly a Vietcong stronghold and has more recently been jointly defended by the Vietcong and elements of the army of North Vietnam, the number of possible legal arguments as to legal title to and responsibility for the territory and the status of the occupants is too great to encumber these pages. Under these circumstances, the most sensible and humane approach to the law protecting civilian populations in war areas is to play down arguments about legal title and legitimacy and look to the practical needs of the civilian victims of war.

This involves, on the positive side, all and reasonable measures to maintain order, provide the basic necessities of life, and to protect the population from involvement in hostilities. In terms of limitations on the occupants of areas formerly held by an enemy—whether insurgents, alleged foreign "aggressors," or whatever—it would seem that the basic requirements of the traditional international law should serve as guides, if not as binding rules of conduct according to the conventional international law "on the books." Of these rules, only the most relevant and controversial will be mentioned here.

In the light of contemporary experience with mixed civil-international counter-insurgency conflicts it would seem that these limitations, accepted in treaties to which the U.S. and most powers are parties, fall into three categories: (1) rules which ought to be observed regardless of the demands of military or political utility and convenience and which are not unreasonable even in terms of such utility; (2) rules which are so frequently and widely violated as to cast doubt as to their binding character and practicality; (3) rules which fall in a gray area between the first two categories.

Unfortunately, it appears to me, there are not many rules that fall in the first category. Pillage, for instance, is prohibited. It is not only unjust and illegal, it is contrary to true military and political utility, *particularly* in counter-insurgency wars. At this point, I am afraid, we exhaust the first category of rules which are clearly binding and which are reasonable, even from the standpoint of the belligerent occupant.

When we contemplate the other basic rules of conventional international law limiting belligerent occupants we are dealing with subjects which are difficult and controversial. Certainly this is the case with many in the second category, for example, the rule prohibiting the occupant from forcing the inhabitants of an occupied area to furnish information about the army of the other belligerent. As observed in our discussion of prisoners of war, interrogation, and torture, information about the enemy is by all odds the most important element both in insurgency and counterinsurgency operations, particularly in underdeveloped countries with difficult terrain.

A number of rules seem to belong to the third category of controverted and unclear provisions of the existing conventional law. For example, the rule protecting the occupied society from radical and purportedly permanent changes in social, economic, and political institutions has been dated since at least 1917.[84] Western "democratic," Communist, Fascist, and other occupying powers have undertaken immediate fundamental changes in territories under their control. On the other hand, it may be argued that *real* change in institutions is difficult in counter-insurgency conflicts where the fortunes of war ebb and flow and that the *appearance* of change often may be all that a temporary occupant can achieve. Accordingly, the practical importance of this rule is probably quite variable and at times marginal. Observance of the rule requiring due process of law in the passing of sentences and carrying out of executions is also subject to a number of qualifications and probably to be considered in the third, gray area.

I have deliberately left one rule to be considered separately. It is the rule that the "taking of hostages" is prohibited. I will conclude this survey of the law regulating hostilities with some comments on this rule because, first, it raises important and difficult issues in modern war and, second, it could be highly relevant to the service of an individual in a typical modern conflict and, therefore, to the issues of SCO.

If we were to review the other basic rules limiting occupation forces, I think that it would be apparent that, with the possible exception of the rule about forcing the inhabitants to give information, it is rather unlikely that the ordinary soldier, or even junior officer, would be forced to break them in a way for which he would be responsible under the laws of war.

The rule prohibiting the taking of hostages, however, does reach down to any and all troops in an occupied area. It concerns the seizure of members of the population in an occupied area, often persons of power and prestige, and holding them for the purpose of threatening and/or actually carrying out their execution both as a deterrent to and punishment for acts hostile to the occupying power.

Three things should be said about the "taking of hostages." *First,* the prohibition of the Geneva Convention of 1949 is aimed ultimately at the *execution* of hostages even though the sole verb in the rule is "taking." Unless hostages are occasionally executed in the course of a conflict the taking of hostages would be no more than an injustice and inconvenience rather than a major war crime. *Second,* international law was not clear on this subject until the 1949 Convention. There is no prohibition of the practice in the Hague Convention of 1907. We have a significant history of recourse to this sanction of occupation rights by belligerents in modern history. Moreover, the most elaborate judicial treatment of the subject, the U.S. military tribunal's decision in the "Hostage Case," condoned the taking and execution of hostages in extreme situations where all law and order and all respect for the legitimate exercise of occupation powers had disappeared.[85] *Third,* to confuse the picture further, the history of contemporary military occupations leaves unanswered the question whether, on the whole, the taking and execution of hostages is an effective means of deterring and punishing opposition to an occupying power or whether it is rather a source of spiraling reprisals and counter-reprisals which incite the population and encourage resistance.

Rather than speculate on the various forms of participation in the taking and execution of hostages which might prove the lot of an individual soldier, I would prefer to leave the subject in this unsettled and ambiguous state as a final example of the practice and legal complications involved in determining: (1) the content and validity of the Nuremberg principles and the law of war; (2) the responsibility under municipal and international law for participation in acts regulated by these principles and rules of law. In this case, it would be easy for the individual SCO and his lawyer to look up the Geneva Convention of 1949 Relative to the Protection of Civilian Persons in Time of War and read the clear language of Article 3 prohibiting the taking of hostages and the related language of the same article requiring due process of law before sentencing and carrying out sentences of members of an occupied area, even in armed conflicts "not of an international character" (thus, *a fortiori* in armed conflicts of a mixed civil-international character).

To the best of my knowledge, taking and executing hostages in the manner of World War II practice by Germans, for example, has *not* been charged against the United States and its allies in the Vietnamese conflict. Very possibly the U.S. experts in counter-insurgency have learned the lessons ignored by the Germans in World War II and have decided not to try to win "The Other War" for the loyalty of the indigenous population by threats and reprisals against hostages. But desperate circumstances, such as an intense campaign by the enemy based in large measure on the taking and threatened execution of hostages, might well drive the South Vietnamese, the United States, and other allies to contemplate retaliation in kind. If this were to occur—or if it could be shown that something like a hostage policy has already been employed in Vietnam—an additional legal argument could be raised for SCO based on the Nuremberg principles and the international law of war.

Conclusions

If this analysis seems inordinately inconclusive for a comparatively detailed treatment of the subject of SCO and the Nuremberg principles, the author will deem his effort successful. For the purpose of this study has been neither to encourage nor discourage SCO generally or SCO on the basis of regard for international law as interpreted and applied by the United States. It has been concerned with penetrating facile rhetoric and purported statements of law on all sides of the controversy to demonstrate the limits, possibilities, and ambiguities of appeals to international law as a basis for SCO.

On the basis of this study the following conclusions appear to be warranted:

(1) The claim that a war is illegal under international law and that, therefore, any participant in such an illegal war risks treatment as a war criminal is not a good basis for SCO, either under international or United States law.

(2) Objections to allegedly illegal military, political, and other policies not directly involving the individual soldier are not very relevant to claims for SCO since they fall within the legal responsibility of high-level decision-makers who have voluntarily assumed their positions and participated in the making of these policies.

(3) The really relevant portion of the Nuremberg principles and of the law of war, insofar as the SCO in or out of the armed forces is concerned, is eminently that of "war crimes and crimes against humanity," i.e., the law governing the conduct of hostilities and belligerent occupation. Although there is a substantial body of conventional law on these subjects, each rule must be carefully considered in order to determine its meaning, its present validity in the light of the practice of states, and its practical feasibility in the mixed civil-international conflicts, mainly in the difficult

terrain of underdeveloped countries, before serious consideration should be accorded claims that it is violated and further claims that these violations justify refusal to participate in the war with respect to which the violations are alleged.

(4) There appears to be such a widespread tendency to violate some of the most definite laws of war—e.g., concerning denial of quarter; torture to obtain vital information; extremely broad interpretations of "military necessity" as justification for widespread destruction of inhabited towns and whole areas; and, possibly, reprisals against rebellious civilian populations such as the taking and execution of hostages—as to create a troublesome gap between the "law on the books" in international conventions and the usage of belligerents. This gap vastly complicates the task of the SCO whose principal objection to a particular war is its illegal conduct.

(5) Many of the most controversial methods of war, e.g., napalm, are not explicitly regulated by the law of war except by the broad principles of legitimate military necessity and proportionality. Hence SCO based on objections to means must be primarily moral and humanitarian rather than legal.

(6) Virtually all of the objections based on the Nuremberg principles and the law of war generally tend to apply across the board to most recent and foreseeable wars, thus raising the question whether the more persuasive claim might not be for CO on the grounds that all modern warfare exceeds permissible legal and moral limits, rather than that a *particular* war exceeds those limits.

However, I must say that the foregoing conclusions are reached with reluctance and a feeling that something is very definitely wrong with the present relationship between U.S. municipal law and international law. For, notwithstanding the many difficulties which I have mentioned, a dilemma remains for any American who takes seriously international law and official U.S. pronouncements supporting it. There is something wrong with a system which acknowledges the binding effect of international law, particularly conventional law, but which, apparently, manages to exclude most of this law from cases involving individual citizens who claim the right to invoke it as the basis for SCO. If the federal courts will not rule on "crimes against the peace" on the grounds that the claim involves "political questions," this is perhaps regrettable but understandable. But for the federal courts to refuse, as they apparently have, to consider international law "part of our law," and to apply it—particularly when it is formulated in treaties to which the U.S. is a party—directly in cases involving individual charges that United States policy concerning conduct of a particular war is illegal under both international and domestic U.S. law, is to leave a situation which would seem to require a restatement of the U.S. position on international law.

With respect to the law of war, international law is part of the law of the United States, *if* the Executive and/or the Legislative branches waive the preeminence which they have and which the Judiciary has accepted. In other words, the courts apparently are relatively powerless to protect individual SCO's from forced participation in violations of the law of war ordered and/or acquiesced in by the Executive and the Congress.

Yet it is axiomatic that the municipal laws of a state and the peculiarities of its internal constitutional processes do not release it from its responsibilities and obligations under international law. Nor, under the Nuremberg precedent, do the pleas of "act of state" or "superior orders" absolve the individual from responsibility for acts violative of international law. It would seem that the federal Judiciary will have to confront the issues raised by those who claim SCO on the basis of Nuremberg and international law, or else add another chapter to the record of judicial retreat before the determined advances of the Executive in the pursuit of its broad powers to conduct foreign relations and national security affairs. If this is to be the case, perhaps a somewhat more charitable note might be taken with respect to those defeated enemies of World War II who, also, were often caught up in the domestic laws, practices, and personal dilemmas of wartime and who were treated as war criminals.

NOTES

[1] U.S. Department of State, *Trial of War Criminals*, 13; Department of State Publication No. 2420 (1945), 39 AM. Jl. Intl. Law Supp. 257 (1945).

The other wartime "United Nations" which adhered to the London Agreement in conformity with Article 5 thereof were: Greece, Denmark, Yugoslavia, the Netherlands, Czechoslovakia, Poland, Belgium, Ethiopia, Australia, Honduras, Norway, Panama, Luxembourg, Haiti, New Zealand, India, Venezuela, Uruguay, and Paraguay.

See the United Nations War Crimes Commission, *The United Nations War Crimes Commission and the Development of the Laws of War* (London: Published for the United Nations War Crimes Commission by His Majesty's Stationery Office, 1948), p. 457, for the text of the Agreement of August 8, 1945, to which the London Charter was annexed. (Hereinafter cited as *UN War Crimes Commission.*)

The most convenient source document is Office of United States Chief of Counsel for Prosecution of Axis Criminality, *Nazi Conspiracy and Aggression, Opinion and Judgment* (Washington: U.S. Government Printing Office, 1947). Portions of the *Judgment* quoted on pp. 1–4 summarize the basic provisions of the Charter. For convenience this source, hereinafter cited as *Nuremberg Judgment*, will be cited and quoted as the principal primary source on the trial of the major war criminals before the Nuremberg International Military Tribunal.

The basic source document for the Nuremberg trials of major war criminals is Nuremberg International Military Tribunal, *Trial of the Major War Criminals Before the International Military Tribunal*, Nuremberg, 14 November, 1945–1 October, 1946 (published at Nuremberg, Germany, 1948), 42 volumes. The Judgment of the Tribunal appears in Vol. XXII, pp. 411–589. (This source will be cited hereinafter as NIMT, *Trial of Major War Criminals.*)

[2] *Nuremberg Judgment*, p. 1.

[3] *U.N. War Crimes Commission, op. cit.;* John Alan Appleman, *Military Tribunals and International Crimes* (Indianapolis: Bobbs-Merrill, 1954).

The Nuremberg Trials held by the United States are extremely well reported in a carefully edited series, *Trials of War Criminals Before the Nuremberg Military Tribunals Under Control Council Law No. 10*, at

Nuremberg, October, 1946–April, 1949 (Washington: U.S. Government Printing Office, 1951), 15 volumes. (Hereinafter cited as *U.S. Trials of War Criminals—Nuremberg.*)

These trials are also covered in part in an invaluable series of reports and analyses of virtually all international and national war crimes proceedings of note by the United Nations War Crimes Commission, *Law Reports of Trials of War Criminals* (London: Published for the United Nations War Crimes Commission by His Majesty's Stationery Office, 1947), 15 volumes. Volume 15 contains an analytical summary of all of the principal charges, issues, and defenses and the law on each as it emerged from the practice of the tribunals.

[4] See Hersch Lauterpacht, ed., *Annual Digest and Reports of Public International Law Cases* (London: Butterworth), for the years 1945–1949; the same and succeeding editors under the title *International Law Reports*, since the 1950 edition.

[5] *Nuremberg Judgment*, pp. 3, 4.

[6] *Ibid.*, p. 4.

[7] See Herbert W. Briggs, ed., *The Law of Nations, Cases, Documents and Notes*, 2nd ed. (New York: Appleton-Century-Crofts, 1952), pp. 96–98 and authorities cited therein; William W. Bishop, Jr., *International Law, Cases and Materials*, 2nd edition (Boston/Toronto: Little Brown, 1962), pp. 266, 267. The basic provisions of the U.N. Charter prohibiting first recourse to force as an instrument of foreign policy are found in the Preamble, in the Purposes set forth in Article 1, and most definitely in Article 2, paragraph 4, which states: "All Members shall refrain in their international relations from the threat or use of force against the territorial integrity or political independence of any state, or in any other manner inconsistent with the Purposes of the United Nations." Sanctions in support of this rule are provided for in Chapter VII of the Charter and Chapter XVII.

[8] In the Judgment of the Nuremberg International Military Tribunal only Streicher and von Schirach were found guilty of crimes against humanity but not of war crimes. Admirals Doenitz and Raeder were the only defendants found guilty of war crimes but not of crimes against humanity. The following were found guilty of what were characterized as "war crimes and crimes against humanity": Goering, Hess, von Ribbentrop, Keitel, Kaltenbrunner, Rosenberg, Frank, Frick, Funk, Sauckel, Jodl, Speer, Fritzsche, and Bormann. See *Nuremberg Judgment*, pp. 108–166. Seys-Inquart was, in effect, found guilty of "war crimes and crimes against humanity " See *Nuremberg Judgment*, pp. 54–55.

A typical linking of the two counts is demonstrated by two of the best-known of the U.S. war crimes proceedings at Nuremberg. In U.S. v. von Leeb *et al* ("The High Command Case"), Count One was "Crimes Against the Peace," Count Four was "Common Plan of Conspiracy." Count Two was "War Crimes and Crimes Against Humanity: Crimes Against Enemy Belligerents and Prisoners of War." Count Three was "War Crimes and Crimes Against Humanity: Crimes Against Civilians." *U.S. Trials of War Criminals—Nuremberg,* Vol. X, "The High Command Case," pp. 13–48.

Likewise, in U.S. v. List *et al,* "The Hostage Case," all four counts charged "War crimes and crimes against humanity" of various kinds. *Ibid.,* Vol. XI, pp. 765–776.

9 I have analyzed the International Military Tribunal's handling of this approach in "Military Necessity in International Law" 1 *World Polity* 109, 142–147 (Institute of World Polity, *World Polity, A Yearbook of Studies in International Law and Organization:* Utrecht/Antwerp: Spectrum Publishers, 1957) wherein the relevant passages of M. de Menthon's position are quoted, the silence of the International Military Tribunal on this position interpreted, and the rejection of this approach by the U.S. Military Tribunals at Nuremberg in the "High Command" and "Hostages" cases noted, with appropriate quotations. Relevant commentaries are cited therein. For the relevant passages of the "High Command Case," U.S. v. von Leeb *et al,* see *U.S. Trials of War Criminals,* Vol. XI, pp. 485–491: "The Hostage Case," U.S. v. List, *Ibid.,* pp. 1246–1248; see also the account of the latter disposition of this question in U.N. War Crimes Commission, *Law Reports of Trials of War Criminals, op. cit.,* in the commentary on the Hostage case entitled, "The Irrelevance to the Present Discussion of Illegality of Aggressive War," Vol. VIII, pp. 59, 60. M. de Menthon's presentation may be found in NIMT, *Trial of the Major War Criminals Before the International Military Tribunal, op. cit.,* Vol. V, pp. 368–391. In an article criticizing de Menthon's approach Paul de la Pradelle notes that it was abandoned by the French prosecutor Dubost in his final statement and that the Tribunal did not discuss it in the Judgment. See his article, "Le Proces des grands criminels de guerre et le developement du droit international," extrait de la *Nouvelle Revue de droit international privé* (Paris: Les Editions Internationales, 1947), pp. 15, 16.

10 This attitude has been examined by Martin O. Milrod in his unpublished M.A. dissertation of June, 1959, at Georgetown University, "Prisoners of War in Korea: The Impact of Communist Practice Upon International Law." At the time of the Korean War neither North Korea nor the Chinese People's Republic were parties to the several

Geneva conventions of 1949 relative to treatment of prisoners of war and other wartime problems. Milrod observes that:

> The USSR and its "bloc" (there perhaps was a "bloc" in those days) entered a reservation to Article 85 of the Convention, which relates to war criminals. Extending what was originally a French proposal, they adopted at Geneva the following approach: "Some delegations maintained that those who transgress the laws of war forfeit their benefits by placing themselves outside of the law. Prisoners condemned under the regulations established at Nuremberg did not come under international law, it was argued, but should be treated as common law criminals." See Angenor Krafft, "The Present Position of the Red Cross Geneva Conventions," 37 *Grotius Society Transactions* 131 (1951), p. 138. Quoted in Milrod, *op. cit.*, p. 136. Milrod cites the de Menthon arguments at Nuremberg, *Ibid.*

The communist belligerents further manipulated the Nuremberg principles by sweeping interpretations of the concept of war crimes and crimes against humanity, in addition to crimes against the peace, so that the basic protection of U.N. POW's was placed in question. See Dept. of State, *General Foreign Policy Series 34*, Conventions of 12 August, 1949 (Pub. No. 3938) (Washington: U.S. Government Printing Office, 1950); also reproduced in Dept. of the Army *Pamphlet No. 20–150* (Washington: U.S. Government Printing Office, 1950) p. 252; as cited in Milrod, *op. cit.*, p. 137.

11 For the text of the Genocide Convention see Res. No. 260 (III) A, U.N. Gen. Ass. Off. Rec., 3rd Sess. (I), Resolutions, p. 174; U.N. Doc. No. A/810; U.S. Dept. of State Publ. No. 3416 (1949); 45 *American Journal of International Law* Supplement 6 (1951). The source quoted here is Bishop, *International Law, op. cit.*, p. 476.

12 *Idem.*

13 *Idem.*

14 *Idem.*

15 *Idem.*

16 Raphael Lemkin, *Axis Rule in Occupied Europe* (Washington: Carnegie Endowment for International Peace, Division of International Law, 1944). Raphael Lemkin, "Genocide as a Crime Under International Law," 41 *American Journal of International Law* 145 (1947).

17 See Commission of Responsibilities, Conference of Paris, *Violations of the Laws and Customs of War*, Reports of Majority and Dissenting Reports of American and Japanese Members of the Commission of Responsibilities, Conference of Paris, 1919 (Carnegie Endowment for International Peace, Division of International Law, Pamphlet No. 32; Published for the Endowment; Oxford: At the Clarendon Press, 1919),

Annex II, Memorandum respecting Reservations by the United States of America, pp. 58–79; *U.N. War Crimes Commission,* pp. 39, 40.

[18] The two landmark Supreme Court decisions are Whitney v. Robertson, 124 U.S. 190 (1888); Cook v. U.S., 288 U.S. 102 (1933).

[19] See U.S. v. Belmont, 301 U.S. 324 (1937); U.S. v. Pink, 315 U.S. 203 (1942).

[20] 175 U.S. 677 (1900) as quoted in Bishop, *International Law, op. cit.,* p. 27.

[21] See Banco Nacional de Cuba v. Sabbatino, 376 U.S. 398 (1964); Lyman M. Tondel, Jr., ed., *The Aftermath of Sabbatino,* Background Papers and Proceedings of the Seventh Hammarskjold Forum, Richard A. Falk, Author of the Working Paper (Published for the Association of the Bar of the City of New York by Oceana Publications, Dobbs Ferry, N.Y., 1965); Ulf Goebel, *Challenge and Response* (Portland, Oregon: University of Portland Press, 1964).

[22] Department of the Army, July, 1956, FM 27–10, Department of the Army Field Manual 27–10, *The Law of Land Warfare* (Washington: U.S. Government Printing Office, 1956).

[23] Nicholas von Hoffman, "Nuremberg Defense Allowed in Levy Trial," Washington *Post,* May 18, 1967.

[24] Colonel Brown was quoted in Nicholas von Hoffman's story, "Levy Is Dealt Trial Setback," Washington *Post,* May 26, 1967.

[25] U.S. v. Mitchell, 369 F. 2nd 323 (1966).

[26] *Ibid.,* p. 324.

[27] *Ibid.*

[28] 386 S 972, 87 S. Ct. 1162 (1966).

[29] *Idem.,* p. 153

[30] *Idem.,* p. 154

[31] 88 S. Ct. 282 (1967). Dissents by Stewart and Douglas at 282–285. See Fred P. Graham, "Stewart Bids Court Weigh Legality of U.S. War Role," *The New York Times,* November 7, 1967, pp. 1, 15.

[32] Edward S. Corwin, *Total War and the Constitution* (New York: Knopf, 1951); Clinton Rossiter, *The Supreme Court and the Commander-in-Chief* (Ithaca, New York: Cornell University Press, 1951).

[33] U.N. War Crimes Comission, *Law Reports of Trials of War Criminals, op. cit.,* Vol. XV, p. 156.

[34] See William V. O'Brien, "The Meaning of 'Military Necessity' in International Law," 1 *World Polity* 109–176 (1957); William V. O'Brien, "Legitimate Military Necessity in Nuclear War," 2 *World Polity* 35–120.

[35] "All Members shall refrain in their international relations from the threat or use of force against the territorial integrity or political independence of any state, or in any other manner inconsistent with the Purposes of the United Nations." Art. II, paragraph 4 of the U.N. Charter.

[36] See J. L. Brierly, *The Law of Nations*, Sir Humphrey Waldock, ed. (6th ed.; New York/Oxford: Oxford University Press, 1963), pp. 416–421.

[37] See *supra*, p. 159 and note 9.

[38] See *supra*, p. 159.

[39] See D. P. O'Connell, *International Law*, 2 vols (London: Stevens; Dobbs Ferry, N.Y., 1965), Vol. I, pp. 37–88 on the question generally; pp. 67–71 on U.S. law and practice.

[40] Article 23 of Hague Convention IV of 1907 Respecting the Laws and Customs of War provides:

"In addition to the prohibitions provided by special Conventions, it is especially forbidden—

". . . c. To kill or wound an enemy who, having laid down his arms, or having no longer means of defense, has surrendered at discretion.

"d. To declare that no quarter will be given; . . ." DAP 27–1, p. 12.

[41] Common Article III of the Geneva Conventions of August 12, 1949, for the Amelioration of the Condition of Wounded and Sick in Armed Forces in the Field, for Amelioration of the Condition of the Wounded, Sick and Shipwrecked Members of Armed Forces at Sea, Relative to the Treatment of Prisoners of War, and Relative to the Protection of Civilian Persons in Time of War, provides:

In the case of armed conflict not of an international character occurring in the territory of one of the High Contracting Parties, each Party to the conflict shall be bound to apply, as a minimum, the following provisions:

(1) Persons taking no active part in the hostilities, including members of armed forces who have laid down their arms and those placed *hors de combat* by sickness, wounds, detention, or any other cause, shall in all circumstances be treated humanely, without any adverse distinction founded on race, colour, religion or faith, sex, birth, or wealth, or any other similar criteria. . . . *(Ibid.,* pp. 24–25, 49, 67–68, 135–136.)

[42] See *Ibid.*, pp. 67–134.

[43] *Nuremberg Judgment*, p. 4.

[44] See DAP 27–1, *op. cit.*, pp. 67–134; FM 27–10, Chapter 3, pp. 25–82.

[45] See the texts of the four conventions, *Ibid.*, pp. 24–25, 48–49, 67–68, 135–136.

[46] *Ibid.*, pp. 72–73.

[47] Eric Norden, "American Atrocities in Vietnam," *Liberation* (February, 1966), pp. 14–27.

[48] The Lawyers Committee on American Policy Towards Vietnam, *Vietnam and International Law* (Flanders, N.J.: O'Hare Books, 1967), p. 62.

[49] William V. O'Brien, "The Prospects for International Peacekeeping," James E. Dougherty and J. F. Lehman, Jr., eds., *Arms Control for the Late Sixties* (Princeton: Von Nostrand, 1967), pp. 213–230.

[50] Norden, *op. cit.* pp. 116, 119–20.

[51] See O'Brien, *The Meaning of Military Necessity, op. cit.* (see n. 73, p. 25) and authorities cited therein.

[52] See Hague Convention IV, Respecting the Laws and Customs of War on Land, of 18 October, 1907, in DAP 27–1, Preamble, pp. 5–6, and, in particular, Articles 22 and 23, pp. 12–13.

[53] See *supra*, pp. 206–207.

[54] FM 27–10, pp. 3–4.

[55] See H. Lauterpacht, "The Problem of the Revision of the Law of War," 29 *British Yearbook of International Law* 361 (1952).

[56] Protocol Prohibiting the Use in War of Asphyxiating, Poisonous or Other Gases, and of Bacteriological Methods of Warfare, June 17, 1925, 3 Hudson, *International Legislation* 1670–72 (1931). (Hereinafter cited as *Geneva Gas Protocol, 1925*.)

[57] *Nuremberg Judgment*, p. 4.

[58] See *infra*, p. 167.

[59] See William V. O'Brien, "Legitimate Military Necessity in Nuclear War," 2 *World Polity* 35, 83–86 and authorities cited therein (1960).

[60] *Ibid.*, pp. 85–86.

[61] See Myres S. McDougal and Florentino P. Feliciano, *Law and Minimum World Public Order* (New Haven & London: Yale University Press, 1961), pp. 71–80. They quote Lauterpacht's statement from the Article cited *supra*, n. 126, that:

> . . . It is clear that admission of a right to resort to the creation of terror among the civilian population as being a legitimate object *per se* would inevitably mean the actual and formal end of the law of war. For that reason, so long as the assumption is allowed to subsist that there is a law of war, the prohibition of the weapons of terror now incidental to lawful operations must be regarded as an absolute rule of law. (*Op. cit.*, pp. 364–365.)

[62] O'Brien, *Legitimate Military Necessity in Nuclear War, op. cit.*, pp. 35, 43–57.

[63] William V. O'Brien, "The Meaning of 'Military Necessity' in International Law," 1 *World Polity*, pp. 109, 138 ff.

[64] O'Brien, *Legitimate Military Necessity in Nuclear War, op. cit.*, pp. 63–65.

[65] I develop this line of thinking in William V. O'Brien, *Nuclear War, Deterrence and Morality* (Westminster, Md.: Newman Press, 1967), pp. 77–80.

[66] See U.N. War Crimes Commission, *Law Reports of Trials of War Criminals,* XV, 110.

[67] Richard A. Falk, "The Shimata Case: A Legal Appraisal of the Atomic Attack on Hiroshima and Nagasaki," *American Journal of International Law.* Vol 59, pp. 789–793. This article discusses a decision of the District Court of Tokyo. See *Japanese Annual of International Law* for 1964, pp. 212–52; digested in *American Journal of International Law,* Vol. 58, p. 1016, 1964.

[68] The Netherlands Government. *Documents Relating to the Program of the First Hague Conference.* (New York: Oxford University Press for the Carnegie Endowment for International Peace, 1921), p. 25.

[69] DAP 27–1, p. 12.

[70] M. W. Royse, *Aerial Bombardment* (New York: Vinal, 1928). McDougal and Feliciano, *Law and Minimum World Public Order, op. cit.,* pp. 615–618 and authorities cited therein.

[71] Clergy and Laymen Concerned about Vietnam, *In the Name of America* (New York, 1968), pp. 269–270.

[72] FM 27–10, art. 34, p. 18.

[73] *Ibid.,* art. 36, p. 18.

[74] See, for example, Randolph S. Churchill and Winston S. Churchill, *The Six Day War* (Boston: Houghton Mifflin, 1967), pp. 171, 173, and 182.

[75] Protocol Prohibiting the Use in War of Asphyxiating, Poisonous or Other Gases, and of Bacteriological Methods of Warfare, Manley O. Hudson, *International Legislation* (Washington/New York, Carnegie Endowment for International Peace, 1931–1950), Vol. III, pp. 1670–1672 (1931).

[76] William V. O'Brien, "Biological/Chemical Warfare and the International Law of War," 51 *Georgetown Law Journal* (1962), pp. 28–32.

[77] *Ibid.,* pp. 32–37, 56–57 and authorities cited therein.

[78] See *supra,* p. 173.

[79] O'Brien, "Biological/Chemical Warfare and the International Law of War," *op. cit.,* pp. 57, 63.

[80] See *supra,* p. 176.

[81] See United Nations War Crimes Commission, *Law Reports of War Criminals, op. cit.,* Vol. XV, pp. 175–176, for a summary of war crimes law on this subject. The best-known and most-cited cases are the "High Command" and "Hostage" cases tried before the U.S. Military Tribunal at Nuremberg. See *U.S. Trials of War Criminals—Nuremberg, op.*

cit., Vol. XI. The Judgments and relevant passages are to be found on pp. 462, 541, 609 for the "Hostage Case" 1230, 1232–1233, 1253–1254, and especially, the comments on the German scorched-earth tactics in their retreat from Finnmark, Norway, in 1944, 1295–1297 153.

82 Ernst H. Feilchenfeld, *The International Economic Law of Belligerent Occupation* (Washington: Carnegie Endowment for International Peace, 1942), pp. 10–11.

83 Julius Stone, *Legal Controls of International Conflict,* 1st ed (New York: Rinehart, 1954), pp. 723–732.

84 Feilchenfeld, *International Economic Law of Belligerent Occupation, op. cit.*, pp. 17–29.

85 *U.S. Trials of War Criminals—Nuremberg, op. cit.*, Vol. XI, pp. 1209–1222, and in the Judgment, pp. 1230, 1232, 1244–1253.

The Hostage Case

(excerpts)

If attacks upon troops and military installations occur regardless of the foregoing precautionary measures and the perpetrators cannot be apprehended, hostages may be taken from the population to deter similar acts in the future provided it can be shown that the population generally is a party to the offense, either actively or passively. Nationality or geographic proximity may under certain circumstances afford a basis for hostage selection, depending upon the circumstances of the situation. This arbitrary basis of selection may be deplored but it cannot be condemned as a violation of international law, but there must be some connection between the population from whom the hostages are taken and the crime committed. If the act was committed by isolated persons or bands from distant localities without the knowledge or approval of the population or public authorities, and which, therefore, neither the authorities nor the population could have prevented, the basis for the taking of hostages, or the shooting of hostages already taken, does not exist.

It is essential to a lawful taking of hostages under customary law that proclamation be made, giving the names and addresses of hostages taken, notifying the population that upon the recurrence of stated acts of war treason the hostages will be shot. The number of hostages shot must not exceed in severity the offenses the shooting is designed to deter. Unless the foregoing requirements are met, the shooting of hostages is in contravention of international law and is a war crime in itself. Whether such fundamental requirements have been met is a question determinable by court martial proceedings. A military commander may not arbitrarily determine such facts. An order of a military commander for the killing of hostages must be based upon the finding of a competent court martial that necessary conditions exist and all preliminary steps have been taken which are essential to the issuance of a valid order. The taking of the lives of innocent persons arrested as hostages is a very serious step. The right to kill hostages may be lawfully exercised only after a meticulous compliance with the foregoing safeguards against vindictive or whimsical orders of military commanders.

We are also concerned with the subject of reprisals and the detention of members of the civilian population for the purpose of using them as the victims of subsequent reprisal measures. The most common reason for holding them is for the general purpose of securing the good behavior and obedience of the civil population in occupied territory. The taking of reprisals against the civilian population by killing members thereof in retaliation for hostile acts against the armed forces or military operations of the occupant seems to have been originated by Germany in modern times. It has been invoked by Germany in the Franco-Prussian War, World War I, and in World War II. No other nation has resorted to the killing of members of the civilian population to secure peace and order insofar as our investigation has revealed. The evidence offered in this case on that point will be considered later in the opinion. While American, British, and French manuals for armies in the field seem to permit the taking of such reprisals as a last resort, the provisions do not appear to have been given effect. The American manual provides in part—[1]

"The offending forces or populations generally may lawfully be subjected to appropriate reprisals. Hostages taken and held for the declared purpose of insuring against unlawful acts by the enemy forces or people may be punished or put to death if the unlawful acts are nevertheless committed."

The British field manual provides in part—[2]

"Although collective punishment of the population is forbidden for the acts of individuals for which it cannot be regarded as collectively responsible, it may be necessary to resort to reprisals against a locality or community, for same act committed by its inhabitants, or members who cannot be identified."

In two major wars within the last 30 years, Germany has made extensive use of the practice of killing innocent members of the population as a deterrent to attacks upon its troops and acts of sabotage against installations essential to its military operations. The right to so do has been recognized by many nations including the United States, Great Britain, France, and the Soviet Union. There has been complete failure on the part of the nations of the world to limit or mitigate the practice by conventional rule. This requires us to apply customary law.

---

[1] Rules of Land Warfare, U. S. Army, Field Manual 27–10, *op. cit. supra*, par 358d, p. 89–90.
[2] British Manual of Military Law, par. 458.

That international agreement is badly needed in this field is self-evident.

International law is prohibitive law and no conventional prohibitions have been invoked to outlaw this barbarous practice. The extent to which the practice has been employed by the Germans exceeds the most elementary notions of humanity and justice. They invoke the plea of military necessity, a term which they confuse with convenience and strategical interests. Where legality and expediency have coincided, no fault can be found insofar as international law is concerned. But where legality of action is absent, the shooting of innocent members of the population as a measure of reprisal is not only criminal but it has the effect of destroying the basic relationship between the occupant and the population. Such a condition can progressively degenerate into a reign of terror. Unlawful reprisals may bring on counter reprisals and create an endless cycle productive of chaos and crime. To prevent a distortion of the right into a barbarous method of repression, international law provides a protective mantle against the abuse of the right.

Generally, it can be said that the taking of reprisal prisoners, as well as the taking of hostages, for the purpose of controlling the population involves a previous proclamation that if a certain type of act is committed, a certain number of reprisal prisoners will be shot if the perpetrators cannot be found. If the perpetrators are apprehended, there is no right to kill either hostages or reprisal prisoners.

As in the case of the taking of hostages, reprisal prisoners may not be shot unless it can be shown that the population as a whole is a party to the offense, either actively or passively. In other words, members of the population of one community cannot properly be shot in reprisal for an act against the occupation forces committed at some other place. To permit such a practice would conflict with the basic theory that sustains the practice in that there would be no deterrent effect upon the community where the offense was committed. Neither may the shooting of innocent members of the population as a reprisal measure exceed in severity the unlawful acts it is designed to correct. Excessive reprisals are in themselves criminal and guilt attaches to the persons responsible for their commission.

It is a fundamental rule of justice that the lives of persons may not be arbitrarily taken. A fair trial before a judicial body affords the surest protection against arbitrary, vindictive, or whimsical application of the right to shoot human beings in reprisal. It is a rule of international law, based on these fundamental concepts of justice and the rights of individuals, that the lives of persons may not be taken in reprisal in the absence of a judicial finding that the necessary conditions exist and the essential steps have been taken to give validity to such action. The possibility is great, of course, that such judicial proceedings may become ritualistic and superficial when conducted in wartime but it appears to be the best available safeguard against cruelty and injustice. Judicial responsibility ordinarily restrains impetuous action and permits principles of justice and right to assert their humanitarian qualities. We have no hesitancy in holding that the killing of members of the population in reprisal without judicial sanction is itself unlawful. The only exception to this rule is where it appears that the necessity for the reprisal requires immediate reprisal action to accomplish the desired purpose and which would be otherwise defeated by the invocation of judicial inquiry. Unless the necessity for immediate action is affirmatively shown, the execution of hostages or reprisal prisoners without a judicial hearing is unlawful. The judicial proceeding not only affords a measure of protection to innocent members of the population, but it offers, if fairly and impartially conducted, a measure of protection to the military commander, charged with making the final decision.

It cannot be denied that the shooting of hostages or reprisal prisoners may under certain circumstances be justified as a last resort in procuring peace and tranquility in occupied territory and has the effect of strengthening the position of a law abiding occupant. The fact that the practice has been tortured beyond recognition by illegal and inhuman application cannot justify its prohibition by judicial fiat.

Military necessity has been invoked by the defendants as justifying the killing of innocent members of the population and the destruction of villages and towns in the occupied territory. Military necessity permits a belligerent, subject to the laws of war, to apply any amount and kind of force to compel the complete submission of the enemy with the least possible expenditure of time, life, and money. In general, it sanctions measures by an occupant necessary to protect the safety of his forces and to facilitate the success of his operations. It permits the destruction of life of armed enemies and other persons whose destruction is incidentally unavoidable by the armed conflicts of the war; it allows the capturing of armed enemies and others of peculiar danger, but it does not permit the killing of innocent inhabitants for purposes of revenge or the satisfaction of a lust to kill. The destruction of property to be lawful must be imperatively demanded by the necessities of war. Destruction as an end in itself is a violation of international law. There must be some reasonable connection between the destruction of property and the overcoming of the enemy forces. It is lawful to destroy railways, lines of communication, or any other property that might be utilized by the enemy. Private homes and churches even may be destroyed if necessary for military operations. It does not admit the wanton devastation of a district or the willful infliction of suffering upon its inhabitants for the sake of suffering alone.

The issues in the present case raise grave questions of international law. Military men the world over debate both the law and the policy involved in the prosecution for war crimes of the high ranking commanders of defeated armies. This is partially brought about by the possibility of future wars and the further possibility that the victors of the present may be the vanquished of the future. This only serves to impress the Tribunal with the absolute necessity of affording the defendants a fair and impartial trial under the rules of international law as they were at the time the alleged offenses were committed. Unless this be done, the hand of injustice may fall upon those who so vindictively contend for more far reaching pronouncements, sustained by precedents which we would hereby establish.

Strict discipline is necessary in the organization of an army, and it becomes hard for many to believe that a violation of the orders of a superior may bring about criminal liability. Love of country and adherence to duty intervene .to palliate unlawful conduct. The passage of time and the thankfulness for a return to peaceful pursuits tend to lessen the demand that war criminals answer for their crimes. In addition thereto, there is a general feeling that excesses occur in all armies, no matter how well disciplined, and that military trials are held to convict the war criminals of the vanquished while those of the victor are cleansed by victory. Unless civilization is to give way to barbarism in the conduct of war, crime must be punished. If international law as it applies to a given case is hopelessly inadequate, such inadequacy should be pointed out. If customary international law has become outmoded, it should be so stated. If conventional international law sets forth an unjust rule, its enforcement will secure its correction. If all war criminals are not brought to the bar of justice under present procedures, such procedures should be made more inclusive and more effective. If the laws of war are to have any beneficent effect, they must be enforced.

The evidence in this case recites a record of killing and destruction seldom exceeded in modern history. Thousands of innocent inhabitants lost their lives by means of a firing squad or hangman's noose, people who had the same inherent desire to live as do these defendants. Wherever the German armed forces were

found, there also were the SS (Die Schutzstaffeln der National-
sozialistischen Deutschen Arbeiterpartei), the SD (Der Sicher-
heitsdienst des Reichsfuehrer SS), the Gestapo (Die Geheime
Staatspolizei), the SA (Die Sturmabteilungen der Nationalsozial-
istischen Deutschen Arbeiterpartei), the administrators of Goering's Four Year Plan, and the Einsatzstab Rosenberg, all participating in the administration of the occupied territories in varying
degrees.   Mass shootings of the innocent population, deporta-
tions for slave labor, and the indiscriminate destruction of public
and private property, not only in Yugoslavia and Greece but in
many other countries as well, lend credit to the assertion that
terrorism and intimidation was the accepted solution to any and
all opposition to the German will.   It is clear, also, that this had
become a general practice and a major weapon of warfare by the
German Wehrmacht.   The German attitude seems to be reflected
in the introduction to the German War Book, as translated by
J. H. Morgan [John Murray, London, 1915] on pages 53–55
wherein it is stated:

> "If therefore, in the following work the expression 'the law
> of war' is used, it must be understood that by it is meant not
> a *lex scripta* introduced by international agreements, but only
> a reciprocity of mutual agreement; a limitation of arbitrary
> behaviour, which custom and conventionality, human friendli-
> ness and a calculating egotism have erected, but for the observ-
> ance of which there exists no express sanction, but only 'the
> fear of reprisals' decides.   * * *   Moreover the officer is a
> child of his time.   He is subject to the intellectual tendencies
> which influence his own nation; the more educated he is the
> more will this be the case.   The danger that, in this way, he
> will arrive at false views about the essential character of war
> must not be lost sight of.   The danger can only be met by a
> thorough study of war itself.   By steeping himself in military
> history an officer will be able to guard himself against excessive
> humanitarian notions, it will teach him that certain severities
> are indispensable to war, nay more, that the only true humanity
> very often lies in a ruthless application of them.   It will also
> teach him how the rules of belligerent intercourse in war have
> developed, how in the course of time they have solidified into
> general usages of war, and finally it will teach him whether the
> governing usages of war are justified or not, whether they are
> to be modified or whether they are to be observed."

It is apparent from the evidence of these defendants that they
considered military necessity, a matter to be determined by them,
a complete justification of their acts.   We do not concur in the

view that the rules of warfare are anything less than they purport to be. Military necessity or expediency do not justify a violation of positive rules. International law is prohibitive law. Articles 46, 47, and 50 of the Hague Regulations of 1907 make no such exceptions to its enforcement. The rights of the innocent population therein set forth must be respected even if military necessity or expediency decree otherwise. We have hereinbefore pointed out that it is the duty of the commanding general in occupied territory to maintain peace and order, punish crime, and protect lives and property. This duty extends not only to the inhabitants of the occupied territory but to his own troops and auxiliaries as well. The commanding general of occupied territory, having executive authority as well as military command, will not be heard to say that a unit taking unlawful orders from someone other than himself was responsible for the crime and that he is thereby absolved from responsibility. It is here claimed, for example, that certain SS units under the direct command of Heinrich Himmler committed certain of the atrocities herein charged without the knowledge, consent, or approval of these defendants. But this cannot be a defense for the commanding general of occupied territory. The duty and responsibility for maintaining peace and order, and the prevention of crime rests upon the commanding general. He cannot ignore obvious facts and plead ignorance as a defense. The fact is that the reports of subordinate units almost without exception advised these defendants of the policy of terrorism and intimidation being carried out by units in the field. They requisitioned food supplies in excess of their local need and caused it to be shipped to Germany in direct violation of the laws of war. Innocent people were lodged in collection and concentration camps where they were mistreated to the everlasting shame of the German nation. Innocent inhabitants were forcibly taken to Germany and other points for use as slave labor. Jews, gypsies, and other racial groups were the victims of systematized murder or deportation for slave labor for no other reason than their race or religion, which is in violation of the express conventional rules of the Hague Regulations of 1907. The German theory that fear of reprisal is the only deterrent in the enforcement of the laws of war cannot be accepted here. That reprisals may be indulged to compel an enemy nation to comply with the rules of war must be conceded.

The High Command Case
(excerpts)

"Article 1

"The laws, rights, and duties of war apply not only to armies, but also to militia and volunteer corps fulfilling the following conditions:

"1. To be commanded by a person responsible for his subordinates;

"2. To have a fixed distinctive emblem recognizable at a distance;

"3. To carry arms openly; and

"4. To conduct their operations in accordance with the laws and customs of war.

"In countries where militia or volunteer corps constitute the army, or form part of it, they are included under the denomination 'army'."

This Article defines what constitutes a lawful belligerent. Orders to the effect that Red Army soldiers who did not turn themselves over to the German authorities would suffer penalty of being treated as guerrillas, and similar orders, and the execution of Red Army soldiers thereunder, are in contravention of the rights of lawful belligerents and contrary to international law.

It has been stated in this case that American occupational commanders issued similar orders. This Tribunal is not here to try Allied occupational commanders but it should be pointed out that subsequent to the unconditional surrender of Germany, she has had no lawful belligerents in the field.

Judge Harding at this point will continue with the reading of the judgment.

RESPONSIBILITY OF COMMANDERS
OF
OCCUPIED TERRITORIES

JUDGE HARDING: The defense in this case as to the field commanders on trial has been partially based on the contention that while criminal acts may have occurred within the territories under their jurisdiction, that these criminal acts were committed by agencies of the state with which they were not connected and over whom they exercised no supervision or control. It is conceded that many of these defendants were endowed with executive power but it is asserted that the executive power of field commanders did not extend to the activities of certain economic and police agencies which operated within their areas; that the activities of these agencies constituted limitations upon their exercise of executive power.

In this connection it must be recognized that the responsibility of commanders of occupied territories is not unlimited. It is fixed according to the customs of war, international agreements, fundamental principles of humanity, and the authority of the commander which has been delegated to him by his own government. As pointed out heretofore, his criminal responsibility is personal. The act or neglect to act must be voluntary and criminal. The term "voluntary" does not exclude pressures or compulsions even to the extent of superior orders. That the choice was a difficult one does not alter either its voluntary nature or its criminality. From an international standpoint, criminality may arise by reason that the act is forbidden by international agreements or is inherently criminal and contrary to accepted principles of humanity as recognized and accepted by civilized nations. In the case of violations of international agreements, the criminality arises from violation of the agreement itself—in other cases, by the inherent nature of the act.

War is human violence at its utmost. Under its impact excesses of individuals are not unknown in any army. The measure of such individual excesses is the measure of the people who compose the army and the standard of discipline of the army to which they belong. The German Army was, in general, a disciplined army. The tragedy of the German Wehrmacht and these defendants is that the crimes charged against them stem primarily from its highest military leadership and the leadership of the Third Reich itself.

Military subordination is a comprenhensive but not conclusive factor in fixing criminal responsibility. The authority, both administrative and military, of a commander and his criminal responsibility are related but by no means coextensive. Modern war such as the last war entails a large measure of decentralization. A high commander cannot keep completely informed of the details of military operations of subordinates and most assuredly not of every administrative measure. He has the right to assume that details entrusted to responsible subordinates will be legally executed. The President of the United States is Commander in Chief of its military forces. Criminal acts committed by those forces cannot in themselves be charged to him on the theory of subordination. The same is true of other high commanders in the chain of command. Criminality does not attach to every individual in this chain of command from that fact alone. There must be a personal dereliction. That can occur only where the act is directly traceable to him or where his failure to properly supervise his subordinates constitutes criminal negligence on his part. In the latter case it must be a personal neglect amounting to a wanton, immoral disregard of the action of his subordinates amounting to acquiescence. Any other interpretation of international law would go far beyond the basic principles of criminal law as known to civilized nations.

Concerning the responsibility of a field commander for crimes committed within the area of his command, particularly as against the civilian population, it is urged by the prosecution that under the Hague Convention, a military commander of an occupied territory is *per se* responsible within the area of his occupation, regardless of orders, regulations, and the laws of his superiors limiting his authority and regardless of the fact that the crimes committed therein were due to the action of the state or superior military authorities which he did not initiate or in which he did not participate. In this respect, however, it must be borne in mind that a military commander, whether it be of an occupied territory or otherwise, is subject both to the orders of his military superiors and the state itself as to his jurisdiction and functions. He is their agent and instrument for certain purposes in a position from which they can remove him at will.

In this connection the Yamashita case has been cited. While not a decision binding upon this Tribunal, it is entitled to great respect because of the high court which rendered it. It is not, however, entirely applicable to the facts in this case for the reason that the authority of Yamashita in the field of his operations did not appear to have been restricted by either his military superiors or the state, and the crimes committed were by troops under his command, whereas in the case of the occupational commanders in these proceedings, the crimes charged were mainly committed at the instance of higher military and Reich authorities.

It is the opinion of this Tribunal that a state can, as to certain matters, under international law limit the exercise of sovereign powers by a military commander in an occupied area, but we are also of the opinion that under international law and accepted usages of civilized nations that he has certain responsibilities which he cannot set aside or ignore by reason of activities of his own state within his area. He is the instrument by which the occupancy exists. It is his army which holds the area in subjection. It is his might which keeps an occupied territory from reoccupancy by the armies of the nation to which it inherently belongs. It cannot be said that he exercises the power by which a civilian population is subject to his invading army while at the same time the state which he represents may come into the area which he holds and subject the population to murder of its citizens and to other inhuman treatment. The situation is somewhat analogous to the accepted principle of international law that the army which captures the soldiers of its adversary has certain fixed responsibilities as to their care and treatment.

We are of the opinion, however, as above pointed out in other aspects of this case, that the occupying commander must have knowledge of these offenses and acquiesce or participate or criminally neglect to interfere in their commission and that the offenses committed must be patently criminal. But regardless of whether or not under international law such responsibility is fixed upon him, under the particular facts in this case, responsibility of the commanders in question rests upon other factors. In this respect we quote certain provisions of the handbook for the general staff in wartime, pertinent to executive power [*NOKW–1878, Pros. Ex. 42*]:

"5. The exercising of executive power by military commanders is governed by No. 20–24 of Army Manual 90 (of the army in the field).

"6. If a zone of operation is determined, the Commander in Chief of the Army and the commanders in chief of the armies receive at the declaration of a state of defense or at the declaration of a state of war authority for exercising executive power in this territory, without further order (pars. 2 and 9 of the Reich Defense Law).

"In other cases, the Fuehrer and Supreme Commander of the Wehrmacht can transfer such authority for exercising executive power to the Commander in Chief of the Army and the commanders in chief of the armies.

"7. The executive power comprises the entire state power including the right of issuing laws without prejudice to the independence of jurisdiction. Those persons invested with executive power can decree local orders affecting the territory in which authority for exercising has been turned over to them or transferred to them, set up special courts, and issue instructions to the authorities and offices competent in the territory named, with the exception of the Supreme Reich Authorities, the Supreme Prussian Provincial Authorities, and the Reichsleitung of the NSDAP.

"8. The Supreme Reich Authorities, Supreme Prussian Provincial Authorities, and the Reichsleitung of the NSDAP can decree orders for the territory into which executive power has been transferred, only by agreement with the persons invested with executive power. Their right of issuing instructions to the authorities and offices subordinated to them remains intact. Nevertheless the right of issuing instruction by the person invested with executive authority takes precedence.

"9. Authority for exercising executive power is incumbent only on the persons invested. It can be transferred further only in as much as an authorization is ordered thereto actually or legally.

"Accordingly persons invested with executive power are authorized to entrust subordinated offices with the execution of individual missions.

"10. The laws, decrees, etc., which are valid at the transfer of the executive power retain their validity so long as the person invested with executive power encounters no contrary order.

"11. The Commander in Chief of the Army regulates the exercising of executive power through the commanders in chief of the armies.

"The revision of questions which occur in the exercising of executive power does not fall into the realm of work of the army judges. The civilian commissioner with the High Command of the Army is assigned for that purpose to the Commander in Chief of the Army; the chiefs of the civil administration, to the commanders in chief of the armies. Persons invested with executive power are authorized however, to call in the army judges assigned to them as counselors, especially in the decreeing of legal orders of penal law content."

It is therefore apparent that executive power under German law is the exercise of sovereign powers within an occupied area conferred upon a military commander by the state. The defense has undertaken to minimize to a large extent this wide authority but in view of the above document, it does not appear to be the mere shadow of authority contended. In fact, these provisions fix upon an occupying commander certain responsibilities as to the preservation of law and order within his area.

The contention of defendants that the economic agencies were excluded from their exercise of executive power is disproved by various documents which will hereafter be cited in considering the guilt or innocence of defendants on trial. And regardless of that fact, the proof in this case also establishes a voluntary cooperation of defendants on trial with these economic agencies in the furtherance of their illegal activities.

The defense contends that the activities of the Einsatzgruppen of the Security Police and SD were beyond their sphere of authority as occupational commanders because the state had authorized the illegal activities of these police units and so limited the executive power of the occupational commanders. However, the occupational commanders in this case were bearers of executive power and, one and all, have denied receipt of any orders showing, or knowledge of, a state-authorized program providing for the illegal activities of the Einsatzgruppen.

One of the functions of an occupational commander endowed with executive power was to maintain order and protect the civilian population against illegal acts. In the absence of any official directives limiting his executive powers as to these illegal acts within his area, he had the right and duty to take action for their suppression. Certainly he is not in a position to contend that these activities were taken from his field of executive power by his superiors when he knew of no such action on their part.

The sole question then as to such defendants in this case is whether or not they knew of the criminal activities of the Einsatzgruppen of the Security Police and SD and neglected to suppress them.

It has been urged that all of the defendants in this case must have had knowledge of the illegal activities of the Einsatzgruppen. It has been argued that because of the extent of their murder program in the occupational areas and by reason of the communications available to the high commanders, and the fact that they were in command of these areas, they must necessarily have known of this program. The record in this case shows that some 90,000 so-called undesirable elements were liquidated by Einsatzgruppe D, largely within the area of the 11th Army. It also shows that some 40,000 Jewish women and children were liquidated in Riga which at that time was in the Commissariat Ostland, immediately to the rear of the Army Group North. The Einsatzgruppen and their subordinate units were organized to carry out this program within the operational areas of the army.

It is true that extermination of such a large number of people must necessarily have come to the attention of many individuals, and, also, it is established that soldiers in certain areas participated in some of these executions.

In many respects a high commander in the German Army was removed from information as to facts which may have been known to troops subordinate to him. In the first place, these troops were in many instances far removed from his headquarters. In addition the common soldiers and junior officers do not have extensive contacts with the high commanders and staff officers.

Another factor must also be taken into consideration in connection with the activities of the Einsatzgruppen. This is the dual nature of its functions. On the one hand, it was charged with the criminal liquidation of certain elements; on the other hand it exercised legitimate police activities in connection with the security of the rear communications of the armies, in which capacity it operated largely against guerrillas.

Another factor was the effort made to keep the criminal activities of these police units from the Wehrmacht. In the early stages of the war many of their mass executions, as is shown by the record, occurred under the guise of pogroms instigated by the SIPO and SD but actually carried out by local inhabitants. Racial hatreds and pogroms have been known in Europe for centuries. Pogroms occurred at the time of the Crusades and have recurred in the history of Europe, even in our time. It is established that pogroms were used by Einsatzgruppe A which operated in the area of the Army Group North and in the Commissariat Ostland, as a vehicle for their criminal activities. At times it is shown such pogroms were participated in by local militia which necessarily owed its existence to the German Army.

Another source of information was reports submitted by Einsatzgruppen to army headquarters, but it is noted that such reports concerned mainly activities within their legal sphere of combating partisans and the maintenance of security. However, such reports showed the execution of Jews, gypsies, and others as specific classifications of those liquidated. Reports of the mass murders carried out by these police units, however, were submitted through their own channels to the RSHA in Berlin and were not submitted to army headquarters or through such headquarters.

An army commander has two reliable and extensive official sources of information (1) superior orders, (2) reports of subordinate units.

It is true that no superior orders transmitted to the defendant field commanders show the mass murder program of the Third Reich have been introduced in evidence with the exception of the Commissar Order in which the executing agency was not the SD but the army itself.

Official reports of subordinate units normally furnish a vast amount of information. Reports of individual instances of illegal acts may however not be submitted to higher headquarters if for no other reason than that the suppression of such acts is the province of the subordinate and their occurrence might be a subject for criticism. Also the staff of high operational commands engaged in extensive combat operations is much less likely to bring such matters to the attention of the commander than the staff of a lower command.

Other factors to be considered as to the knowledge of criminal acts of the SIPO and SD by defendants is the time, the localities, the combat situation, the extent of the activities, and the nature of the command.

This, in brief, summarizes the main factors considered and the sources of knowledge appraised in determining the criminal responsibility of the defendants in this case in connection with activities of the Einsatzgruppen of the SIPO and SD. From this discussion it is apparent we can draw no general presumption as to their knowledge in this matter and must necessarily go to the evidence pertaining to the various defendants to make a determination of this question.

And it is further pointed out that to establish the guilt of a defendant from connection with acts of the SIPO and SD by acquiescence, not only must knowledge be established, but the time of such knowledge must be established.

When we discuss the evidence against the various defendants, we shall treat with greater detail the evidence relating to the activities of the Einsatzgruppen in the commands of the various defendants, and to what extent, if any, such activities were known to and acquiesced in or supported by them.

HITLER AND THE WEHRMACHT

The defense has asserted that there was considerable opposition to Hitler's plans and orders by the higher military leadership. General Franz Halder, who was chief of the German general staff from 1938 to 1942, testified that Hitler's plans to invade the Sudetenland caused the formation of a plot for a coup to overthrow Hitler, but that this plot was abandoned because of the Munich Pact. Be this as it may, the success of Hitler at Munich increased his prestige with all circles of the German people, including the higher military leadership.

In 1939, Hitler advised certain of the high military leaders of his decision to attack France by violating the neutrality of the Low Countries. On 11 October 1939, von Leeb wrote his Commander in Chief, von Brauchitsch, inclosing a memorandum prepared by him advising against this course of action. In it he argues that the invasion would develop into a long drawn-out trench warfare, and he continued [*von Leeb 39a, von Leeb Defense Ex. 39*]:

"* * * Besides, we will not be in a position to rally allies to our cause. Even now, Italy is sitting on the fence, and Russia has accomplished everything it had aimed at by virtue of our victories, and by this has again become a predominant and directly decisive factor as far as Central Europe is concerned. Furthermore, Russia's attitude remains uncertain in view of

The Matter of Yamashita

(excerpts)

IN THE MATTER OF THE APPLICATION OF GENERAL TOMOYUKI YAMASHITA. (No. 61, Miscellaneous)

GENERAL TOMOYUKI YAMASHITA,
Petitioner,

v.

LIEUTENANT GENERAL WILHELM D. STYER,
Commanding General, United States Army Forces,
Western Pacific (No. 672.)

... Mr. Chief Justice Stone delivered the opinion of the Court.

No. 61 Miscellaneous is an application for leave to file a petition for writs of habeas corpus and prohibition in this Court. No. 672 is a petition for certiorari to review an order of the Supreme Court of the Commonwealth of the Philippines (28 USCA § 349, 8 FCA title 28, § 349), denying petitioner's application to that court for writs of habeas corpus and prohibition. As both applications raise substantially like questions, and because of the importance and novelty of some of those presented, we set the two applications down for oral argument as one case.

From the petitions and supporting papers it appears that prior to September 3, 1945, petitioner was the Commanding General of the Fourteenth Army Group of the Imperial Japanese Army in the Philippine Islands. On that date he surrendered to and became a prisoner of war of the United States Army Forces in Baguio, Philippine Islands. On September 25th, by order of respondent, Lieutenant General Wilhelm D. Styer, Commanding General of the United States Army Forces, Western Pacific, which command embraces the Philippine Islands, petitioner was served with a charge prepared by the Judge Advocate General's Department of the Army, purporting to charge petitioner with a violation of the law of war. On October 8, 1945, petitioner, after pleading not guilty to the charge, was held for trial before a military commission of five Army officers appointed by order of General Styer. The order appointed six Army officers, all lawyers, as defense counsel. Throughout the proceedings which followed, including those before this Court, defense counsel have demonstrated their professional skill and resourcefulness and their proper zeal for the defense with which they were charged. . . .

The charge. Neither Congressional action nor the military orders constituting the commission authorized it to place petitioner on trial unless the charge preferred against him is of a violation of the law of war. The charge, so far as now relevant, is that petitioner, between October 9, 1944 and September 2, 1945, in the Philippine Islands, "while commander of armed forces of Japan at war with the United States of America and its allies, unlawfully disregarded and failed to discharge his duty as commander to control the operations of the members of his command, permitting them to commit brutal atrocities and other high crimes against people of the United States and of its allies and dependencies, particularly the Philippines; and he . . . thereby violated the laws of war."

Bills of particulars, filed by the prosecution by order of the commission, allege a series of acts, one hundred and twenty-three in number, committed by members of the forces under petitioner's command during the period mentioned. The first item specifies the execution of "a deliberate plan and purpose to massacre and exterminate a large part of the civilian population of Batangas Province, and to devastate and destroy public, private and religious property therein, as a result of which more than 25,000 men, women and children, all unarmed noncombatant civilians, were brutally mistreated and killed, without cause or trial, and entire settlements were devastated and destroyed wantonly and without military necessity." Other items specify acts of violence, cruelty, and homicide inflicted upon the civilian population and prisoners of war, acts of wholesale pillage and the wanton destruction of religious monuments.

It is not denied that such acts directed against the civilian population of an occupied country and against prisoners of war are recognized in international law as violations of the law of war. Articles 4, 28, 46, and 47, Annex to Fourth Hague Convention, 1907, 36 Stat 2277, 2296, 2303, 2306, 2307. But it is urged that the charge does not allege that petitioner has either committed or directed the commission of such acts, and consequently that no violation is charged as against him. But this overlooks the fact that the gist of the charge is an unlawful breach of duty by petitioner as an army commander to control the operations of the members of his command by "permitting them to commit" the extensive and widespread atrocities specified. The question then is whether the law of war imposes on an army commander a duty to take such appropriate measures as are within his power to control the troops under his command for the prevention of the specified acts which are violations of the law of war and which are likely to attend the occupation of hostile territory by an uncontrolled soldiery, and whether he may be charged with personal responsibility for his failure to take such measures when violations result. That this was the precise issue to be tried was made clear by the statement of the prosecution at the opening of the trial.

It is evident that the conduct of military operations by troops whose excesses are unrestrained by the orders or efforts of their commander would almost certainly result in violations which it is the purpose of the law of war to prevent. Its purpose to protect civilian populations and prisoners of war from brutality would largely be defeated if the commander of an invading army could with impunity neglect to take *reasonable measures for* their protection. Hence the law of war presupposes that its violation is to be avoided through the control of the operation of war by commanders who are to some extent responsible for their subordinates.

This is recognized by the Annex to Fourth Hague Convention of 1907, respecting the laws and customs of war on land. Article 1 lays down as a condition which an armed force must fulfill in order to be accorded the rights of lawful belligerents, that it must be "commanded by a person responsible for his subordinates." 36 Stat 2295. Similarly Article 19 of the Tenth Hague Convention, relating to bombardment by naval vessels, provides that commanders in chief of the belligerent vessels "must see that the above Articles are properly carried out," 36 Stat 2389. And Article 26 of the Geneva Red Cross Convention of 1929, 47 Stat 2074, 2092, for the amelioration of the condition of the wounded and sick in armies in the field, makes it "the duty of the commanders-in-chief of the belligerent armies to provide for the details of execution of the foregoing articles, [of the convention] as well as for the unforeseen cases." And, finally, Article 43 of the Annex of the Fourth Hague Convention, 36 Stat 2306, requires that the commander of a force occupying enemy territory, as was petitioner, "shall take all the measures in his power to restore, and ensure, as far as possible, public order and safety, while respecting, unless absolutely prevented, the laws in force in the country."

These provisions plainly imposed on petitioner, who at the time specified was military governor of the Philippines, as well as commander of the Japanese forces, an affirmative duty to take such measures as were within his power and appropriate in the circumstances to protect prisoners of war and the civilian population. This duty of a commanding officer has heretofore been recognized, and its breach penalized by our own military tribunals.[3] A like principle has been applied so as to impose liability on the United States in international arbitrations. Case of Jennaud, 3 Moore, International Arbitrations, 3000; Case of "The Zafiro," 5 Hackworth, Digest of International Law, 707.

We do not make the laws of war but we respect them so far as they do not conflict with the commands of Congress or the Constitution. There is no contention that the present charge, thus read, is without the support of evidence, or that the commission held petitioner responsible for failing to take measures which were beyond his control or inappropriate for a commanding officer to take in the circumstances.[4] We do not here appraise the evidence on which petitioner was convicted. We do not consider what measures, if any, petitioner took to prevent the commission, by the troops under his command, of the plain violations of the law of war detailed in the bill of particulars, or whether such measures as he may have taken were appropriate and sufficient to discharge the duty imposed upon him. These are questions within the peculiar competence of the military officers composing the commission and were for it to decide. See Smith v. Whitney, 116 US 167, 178, 29 L ed 601, 604, 6 S Ct 570. It is plain that the charge on which petitioner was tried charged him with a breach of his duty to control the operations of the members of his command, by permitting

[3] Failure of an officer to take measures to prevent murder of an inhabitant of an occupied country committed in his presence. Gen. Orders No. 221, Hq. Div. of the Philippines, August 17, 1901. And in Gen. Orders No. 264, Hq. Div. of the Philippines, September 9, 1901, it was held that an officer could not be found guilty for failure to prevent a murder unless it appeared that the accused had "the power to prevent" it.

[4] In its findings the commission took account of the difficulties "faced by the accused, with respect not only to the swift and overpowering advance of American forces, but also to errors of his predecessors, weakness in organization, equipment, supply . . . , training, communication, discipline and morale of his troops," and "the tactical situation, the character, training and capacity of staff officers and subordinate commanders, as well as the traits of character . . . of his troops." It nonetheless found that petitioner had not taken such measures to control his troops as were "required by the circumstances." We do not weigh the evidence. We merely hold that the charge sufficiently states a violation against the law of war, and that the commission, upon the facts found, could properly find petitioner guilty of such a violation.

them to commit the specified atrocities. This was enough to require the commission to hear evidence tending to establish the culpable failure of petitioner to perform the duty imposed on him by the law of war and to pass upon its sufficiency to establish guilt.

Obviously charges of violations of law of war triable before a military tribunal need not be stated with the precision of a common law indictment. Cf. Collins v. McDonald, supra (258 US 420, 66 L ed 696, 42 S Ct 326). But we conclude that the allegations of the charge, tested by any reasonable standard, adequately allege a violation of the law of war and that the commission had authority to try and decide the issue which it raised. Cf. Dealy v. United States, 152 US 539, 38 L ed 545, 14 S Ct 680; Williamson v. United States, 207 US 425, 447, 52 L ed 278, 290, 28 S Ct 163; Glasser v. United States, 315 US 60, 66, 86 L ed 680, 697, 62 S Ct 457, and cases cited.

. . . Mr. Justice Murphy, dissenting.

The significance of the issue facing the Court today cannot be over-emphasized. An American military commission has been established to try a fallen military commander of a conquered nation for an alleged war crime. The authority for such action grows out of the exercise of the power conferred upon Congress by Article 1, § 8, cl 10 of the Constitution to "define and punish . . . Offenses against the Law of Nations . . ." The grave issue raised by this case is whether a military commission so established and so authorized may disregard the procedural rights of an accused person as guaranteed by the Constitution, especially by the due process clause of the Fifth Amendment.

The answer is plain. The Fifth Amendment guarantee of due process of law applies to "any person" who is accused of a crime by the Federal Government or any of its agencies. No exception is made as to those who are accused of war crimes or as to those who possess the status of an enemy belligerent. Indeed, such an exception would be contrary to the whole philosophy of human rights which makes the Constitution the great living document that it is. The immutable rights of the individual, including those secured by the due process clause of the Fifth Amendment, belong not alone to the members of those nations that excel on the battlefield or that subscribe to the democratic ideology. They belong to every person in the world, victor or vanquished, whatever may be his race, color or beliefs. They rise above any status of belligerency or outlawry. They survive any popular passion or frenzy of the moment. No court or legislature or executive, not even the mightiest army in the world, can ever destroy them. Such is the universal and indestructible nature of the rights which the due process clause of the Fifth Amendment recognizes and protects when life or liberty is threatened by virtue of the authority of the United States.

The existence of these rights, unfortunately, is not always respected. They are often trampled under by those who are motivated by hatred, aggression or fear. But in this nation individual rights are recognized and protected, at least in regard to governmental action. They cannot be ignored by any branch of the Government, even the military, except under the most extreme and urgent circumstances.

The failure of the military commission to obey the dictates of the due process requirements of the Fifth Amendment is apparent in this case. The petitioner was the commander of an army totally destroyed by the superior power of this nation. While under heavy and destructive attack by our forces, his troops committed many brutal atrocities and other high crimes. Hostilities ceased and he voluntarily surrendered. At that point he was entitled, as an individual protected by the due process clause of the Fifth Amendment, to be treated fairly and justly according to the accepted rules of law and procedure. He was also entitled to a fair trial as to any alleged crimes and to be free from charges of legally unrecognized crimes that would serve only to permit his accusers to satisfy their desires for revenge.

A military commission was appointed to try the petitioner for an alleged war crime. The trial was ordered to be held in territory over which the United States has complete sovereignty. No military necessity or other emergency demanded the suspension of the safeguards of due process. Yet petitioner was rushed to trial under an improper charge, given insufficient time to prepare an adequate defense, deprived of the benefits of some of the most elementary rules of evidence and summarily sentenced to be hanged. In all this needless and unseemly haste there was no serious attempt to charge or to prove that he committed a recognized violation of the laws of war. He was not charged with personally participating in the acts of atrocity or with ordering or condoning their commission. Not even knowledge of these crimes was attributed to him. It was simply alleged that he unlawfully disregarded and failed to discharge his duty as commander to control the operations of the members of his command, permitting them to commit the acts of atrocity. The recorded annals of warfare and the established principles of international law afford not the slightest precedent for such a charge. This indictment in effect permitted the military commission to make the crime whatever it willed, dependent upon its biased view as to petitioner's duties and his disregard thereof, a practice reminiscent of that pursued in certain less respected nations in recent years.

In my opinion, such a procedure is unworthy of the traditions of our people or of the immense sacrifices that they have made to advance the common ideals of mankind. The high feelings of the moment doubtless will be satisfied. But in the sober after glow will come the realization of the boundless and dangerous implications of the procedure sanctioned today. No one in a position of command in an army, from sergeant to general, can escape those implications. Indeed, the fate of some future President of the United States and his chiefs of staff and military advisers may well have been sealed by this decision. But even more significant will be the hatred and ill-will growing out of the application of this unprecedented procedure. That has been the inevitable effect of every method of punishment disregarding the element of personal culpability. The effect in this instance, unfortunately, will be magnified infinitely for here we are dealing with the rights of man on an international level. To subject an enemy belligerent to an unfair trial, to charge him with an unrecognized crime, or to vent on him our retributive emotions only antagonizes the enemy nation and hinders the reconciliation necessary to a peaceful world.

That there were brutal atrocities inflicted upon the helpless Filipino people, to whom tyranny is no stranger, by Japanese armed forces under the petitioner's command is undeniable. Starvation, execution or massacre without trial, torture, rape, murder and wanton destruction of property were foremost among the outright violations of the laws of war and of the conscience of a civilized world. That just punishment should be meted out to all those responsible for criminal acts of this nature is also beyond dispute. But these factors do not answer the problem in this case. They do not justify the abandonment of our devotion to justice in dealing with a fallen enemy commander. To conclude otherwise is to admit that the enemy has lost the battle but has destroyed our ideals.

War breeds atrocities. From the earliest conflicts of recorded history to the global struggles of modern times inhumanities, lust and pillage have been the inevitable by-products of man's resort to force and arms. Unfortunately, such despicable acts have a dangerous tendency to call forth primitive impulses of vengeance and retaliation among the victimized peoples. The satisfaction of such impulses in turn breeds resentment and fresh tension. Thus does the spiral of cruelty and hatred grow.

If we are ever to develop an orderly international community based upon a recognition of human dignity it is of the utmost importance that the necessary punishment of those guilty of atrocities be as free as possible from the ugly stigma of revenge and vindictiveness. Justice must be tempered by compassion rather than by vengeance. In this, the first case involving this momentous problem ever to reach this Court, our responsibility is both lofty and difficult. We must insist, within the confines of our proper jurisdiction, that the highest standards of justice be applied in this trial of an enemy commander conducted under the authority of the United States. Otherwise stark retribution will be free to masquerade in a cloak of false legalism. And the hatred and cynicism engendered by that retribution will supplant the great ideals to which this nation is dedicated.

This Court fortunately has taken the first and most important step toward insuring the supremacy of law and justice in the treatment of an enemy belligerent accused of violating the laws of war. Jurisdiction properly has been asserted to inquire "into the cause of restraint of liberty" of such a person. 28 USCA § 452, 8 FCA title 28, § 452. Thus the obnoxious doctrine asserted by the Government in this case, to the effect that restraints of liberty resulting from military trials of war criminals are political matters completely outside the arena of judicial review, has been rejected fully and unquestionably. This does not mean, of course, that the foreign affairs and policies of the nation are proper subjects of judicial inquiry. But when the liberty of any person is restrained by reason of the authority of the United States the writ of habeas corpus is available to test the legality of that restraint, even though direct court review of the restraint is prohibited. The conclusive presumption must be made, in this country at least, that illegal restraints are unauthorized and unjustified by any foreign policy of the Government and that commonly accepted juridical standards are to be recognized and enforced. On that basis judicial inquiry into these matters may proceed within its proper sphere.

The determination of the extent of review of war trials calls for judicial statesmanship of the highest order. The ultimate nature and scope of the writ of habeas corpus are within the discretion of the judiciary unless validly circumscribed by Congress. Here we are confronted with a use of the writ under circumstances novel in the history of the Court. For my own part, I do not feel that we should be confined by the traditional lines of review drawn in connection with the use of the writ by ordinary criminals who have direct access to the judiciary in the first instance. Those held by the military lack any such access; consequently the judicial review available by habeas corpus must be wider than usual in order that proper standards of justice may be enforceable.

But for the purposes of this case I accept the scope of review recognized by the Court at this time. As I understand it, the following issues in connection with war criminal trials are reviewable through the use of the writ of habeas corpus: (1) whether the military commission was lawfully created and had authority to try and to convict the accused of a war crime; (2) whether the charge against the accused stated a violation of the laws of war; (3) whether the commission, in admitting certain evidence, violated any law or military command defining the commission's authority in that respect; and (4) whether the commission lacked jurisdiction because of a failure to give advance notice to the protecting power as required by treaty or convention.

The Court, in my judgment, demonstrates conclusively that the military commission was lawfully created in this instance and that petitioner could not object to its power to try him for a recognized war crime. Without pausing here to discuss the third and fourth issues, however, I find it impossible to agree that the charge against the petitioner stated a recognized violation of the laws of war.

It is important, in the first place, to appreciate the background of events preceding this trial. From October 9, 1944, to September 2, 1945, the petitioner was the Commanding General of the 14th Army Group of the Imperial Japanese Army, with headquarters in the Philippines. The reconquest of the Philippines by the armed forces of the United States began approximately at the time when the petitioner assumed this command. Combined with a great and decisive sea battle, an invasion was made on the island of Leyte on October 20, 1944. "In the six days of the great naval action the Japanese position in the Philippines had become extremely critical. Most of the serviceable elements of the Japanese Navy had been committed to the battle with disastrous results. The strike had miscarried, and General MacArthur's land wedge was firmly implanted in the vulnerable flank of the enemy. . . . There were 260,000 Japanese troops scattered over the Philippines but most of them might as well have been on the other side of the world so far as the enemy's ability to shift them to meet the American thrusts was concerned. If General MacArthur succeeded in establishing himself in the Visayas where he could stage, exploit, and spread under cover of overwhelming naval and air superiority, nothing could prevent him from overrunning the Philippines." Biennial Report of the Chief of Staff of the United States Army, July 1, 1943, to June 30, 1945, to the Secretary of War, p 74.

By the end of 1944 the island of Leyte was largely in American hands. And on January 9, 1945, the island of Luzon was invaded. "Yamashita's inability to cope with General MacArthur's swift moves, his desired reaction to the deception measures, the guerrillas, and General Kenney's aircraft combined to place the Japanese in an impossible situation. The enemy was forced into a piecemeal commitment of his troops." Id. p 78. It was at this time and place that most of the alleged atrocities took place. Organized resistance around Manila ceased on February 23. Repeated land and air assaults pulverized the enemy and within a few months there was little left of petitioner's command except a few remnants which had gathered for a last stand among the precipitous mountains.

As the military commission here noted, "The Defense established the difficulties faced by the Accused with respect not only to the swift and overpowering advance of American forces, but also to the errors of his predecessors, weaknesses in organization, equipment, supply with especial reference to food and gasoline, training, communication, discipline and morale of his troops. It was alleged that the sudden assignment of Naval and Air Forces to his tactical command presented almost insurmountable difficulties. This situation was followed, the Defense contended, by failure to obey his orders to withdraw troops from Manila, and the subsequent massacre of unarmed civilians, particularly by Naval forces. Prior to the Luzon Campaign, Naval forces had reported to a separate ministry in the Japanese Government and Naval Commanders may not have been receptive or experienced in this instance with respect to a joint land operation under a single commander who was designated from the Army Service."

The day of final reckoning for the enemy arrived in August 1945. On September 3, the petitioner surrendered to the United States Army at Baguio, Luzon. He immediately became a prisoner of war and was interned in prison in conformity with the rules of international law. On September 25, approximately three weeks after surrendering, he was served with the charge in issue in this case. Upon service of the charge he was removed from the status of a prisoner of war and placed in confinement as an accused war criminal. Arraignment followed on October 8 before a military commission specially appointed for the case. Petitioner pleaded not guilty. He was also served on that day with a bill of particulars alleging 64 crimes by troops under his command. A supplemental bill alleging 59 more crimes by his troops was filed on October 29, the same day that the trial began. No continuance was allowed for preparation of a defense as to the supplemental bill. The trial continued uninterrupted until December 5, 1945. On December 7 petitioner was found guilty as charged and was sentenced to be hanged.

The petitioner was accused of having "unlawfully disregarded and failed to discharge his duty as commander to control the operations of the members of his command, permitting them to commit brutal atrocities and other high crimes." The bills of particular further alleged that specific acts of atrocity were committed by "members of the armed forces of Japan under the command of the accused." Nowhere was it alleged that the petitioner personally committed any of the atrocities, or that he ordered their commission, or that he had any knowledge of the commission thereof by members of his command.

The findings of the military commission bear out this absence of any direct personal charge against the petitioner. The commission merely found that atrocities and other high crimes "have been committed by members of the Japanese armed forces under your command . . . that they were not sporadic in nature but in many cases were methodically supervised by Japanese officers and noncommissioned officers . . . that during the period in question you failed to provide effective control of your troops as was required by the circumstances."

In other words, read against the background of military events in the Philippines subsequent to October 9, 1944, these charges amount to this: "We, the victorious American forces, have done everything possible to destroy and disorganize your lines of communication, your effective control of your personnel, your ability to wage war. In those respects we have succeeded. We have defeated and crushed your forces. And now we charge and condemn you for having been inefficient in maintaining control of your troops during the period when we were so effectively besieging and eliminating your forces and blocking your ability to maintain effective control. Many terrible atrocities were committed by your disorganized troops. Because these atrocities were so widespread we will not bother to charge or prove that you committed, ordered or condoned any of them. We will assume that they must have resulted from your inefficiency and negligence as a commander. In short, we charge you with the crime of inefficiency in controlling your troops. We will judge the discharge of your duties by the disorganization which we ourselves created in large part. Our standards of judgment are whatever we wish to make them."

Nothing in all history or in international law, at least as far as I am aware, justifies such a charge against a fallen commander of a defeated force. To use the very inefficiency and disorganization created by the victorious forces as the primary basis for condemning officers of the defeated armies bears no resemblance to justice or to military reality.

International law makes no attempt to define the duties of a commander of an army under constant and overwhelming assault; nor does it impose liability under such circumstances for failure to meet the ordinary responsibilities of command. The omission is understandable. Duties, as well as ability to control troops, vary according to the nature and intensity of the particular battle. To find an unlawful deviation from duty under battle conditions requires difficult and speculative calculations. Such calculations become highly untrustworthy when they are made by the victor in relation to the actions of a vanquished commander. Objective and realistic norms of conduct are then extremely unlikely to be used in forming a judgment as to deviations from duty. The probability that vengeance will form the major part of the victor's judgment is an unfortunate but inescapable fact. So great is that probability that international law refuses to recognize such a judgment as a basis for a war crime, however fair the judgment may be in a particular instance. It is this consideration that undermines the charge against the petitioner in this case. The indictment permits, indeed compels, the military commission of a victorious nation to sit in judgment upon the military strategy and actions of the defeated enemy and to use its conclusions to determine the criminal liability of an enemy commander. Life and liberty are made to depend upon the biased will of the victor rather than upon objective standards of conduct.

The Court's reliance upon vague and indefinite references in certain of the Hague Conventions and the Geneva Red Cross Convention is misplaced. Thus the statement in Article 1 of the Annex to Hague Convention No. IV of October 18, 1907, 36 Stat 2277, 2295, to the effect that the laws, rights and duties of war apply to military and volunteer corps only if they are "commanded by a person responsible for his subordinates," has no bearing upon the problem in this case. Even if it has, the clause "responsible for his subordinates" fails to state to whom the responsibility is owed or to indicate the type of responsibility contemplated. The phrase has received differing interpretations by authorities on international law. In Oppenheim, International Law (6th ed. rev. by Lauterpacht, 1940, vol. 2, p. 204, fn. 3) it is stated that "The meaning of the word 'responsible' . . . is not clear. It probably means 'responsible to some higher authority,' whether the person is appointed from above or elected from below; . . ." Another authority has stated that the word "responsible" in this particular context means "presumably to a higher authority," or "possibly it merely means one who controls his subordinates and who therefore can be called to account for their acts." Wheaton, International Law (7th edn. by Keith, 1944, p. 172, fn. 30). Still another authority, Westlake, International Law (1907, Part II, p. 61), states that "probably the responsibility intended is nothing more than a capacity of exercising effective control." Finally, Edmonds and Oppenheim, Land Warfare (1912, p. 19, ¶ 22) state that it is enough "if the commander of the corps is regularly or temporarily commissioned as an officer or is a person of position and authority. . . ." It seems apparent beyond dispute that the word "responsible" was not used in this particular Hague Convention to hold the commander of a defeated army to any high standard of efficiency when he is under destructive attack; nor was it used to impute to him any criminal responsibility for war crimes committed by troops under his command under such circumstances.

The provisions of the other conventions referred to by the Court are on their face equally devoid of relevance or significance to the situation here in issue. Neither Article 19 of Hague Convention No. X, 36 Stat 2371, 2389, nor Article 26 of the Geneva Red Cross Convention of 1929, 47 Stat 2074, 2092, refers to circumstances where the troops of a commander commit atrocities while under heavily adverse battle conditions. Reference is also made to the requirement of Article 43 of the Annex to Hague Convention No. IV, 36 Stat 2295, 2306, that the commander of a force occupying enemy territory "shall take all the measures in his power to restore, and ensure, as far as possible, public order and safety, while respecting, unless absolutely prevented, the laws in force in the country." But the petitioner was more than a commander of a force occupying enemy territory. He was the leader of an army under constant and devastating attacks by a superior re-invading force. This provision is silent as to the responsibilities of a commander under such conditions as that.

Even the laws of war heretofore recognized by this nation fail to impute responsibility to a fallen commander for excesses committed by his disorganized troops while under attack. Paragraph 347 of the

War Department publication, Basic Field Manual, Rules of Land Warfare, FM 27-10 (1940), states the principal offenses under the laws of war recognized by the United States. This includes all of the atrocities which the Japanese troops were alleged to have committed in this instance. Originally this paragraph concluded with the statement that "The commanders ordering the commission of such acts, or under whose authority they are committed by their troops, may be punished by the belligerent into whose hands they may fall." The meaning of the phrase "under whose authority they are committed" was not clear. On November 15, 1944, however, this sentence was deleted and a new paragraph was added relating to the personal liability of those who violate the laws of war. Change 1, FM 27-10. The new paragraph 345.1 states that "Individuals and organizations who violate the accepted laws and customs of war may be punished therefor. However, the fact that the acts complained of were done pursuant to order of a superior or government sanction may be taken into consideration in determining culpability, either by way of defense or in mitigation of punishment. The person giving such orders may also be punished." From this the conclusion seems inescapable that the United States recognizes individual criminal responsibility for violations of the laws of war only as to those who commit the offenses or who order or direct their commission. Such was not the allegation here. Cf. Article 67 of the Articles of War, 10 USC § 1539, 11 FCA title 10, § 1539.

There are numerous instances, especially with reference to the Philippine Insurrection in 1900 and 1901, where commanding officers were found to have violated the laws of war by specifically ordering members of their command to commit atrocities and other war crimes. Francisco Frani, GO 143, Dec. 13, 1900, Hq Div Phil; Eugenio Fernandez and Juan Soriano, GO 28, Feb. 6, 1901, Hq Div Phil; Ciriaco Cabungal, GO 188, July 22, 1901, Hq Div Phil; Natalio Valencia, GO 221, Aug. 17, 1901, Hq Div Phil; Aniceta Angeles, GO 246, Sept. 2, 1901, Hq Div Phil; Francisco Braganza, GO 291, Sept. 26, 1901, Hq Div Phil; Lorenzo Andaya, GO 328, Oct. 25, 1901, Hq Div Phil. And in other cases officers have been held liable where they knew that a crime was to be committed, had the power to prevent it and failed to exercise that power. Pedro Abad Santos, GO 130, June 19, 1901, Hq Div Phil. Cf. Pedro A. Cruz, GO 264, Sept. 9, 1901, Hq Div Phil. In no recorded instance, however, has the mere inability to control troops under fire or attack by superior forces been made the basis of a charge of violating the laws of war.

The Government claims that the principle that commanders in the field are bound to control their troops has been applied so as to impose liability on the United States in international arbitrations. Case of Jeannaud (1880), 3 Moore, International Arbitrations (1898) 3000; Case of "The Zafiro" (1910), 5 Hackworth, Digest of International Law (1943) 707. The difference between arbitrating property rights and charging an individual with a crime against the laws of war is too obvious to require elaboration. But even more significant is the fact that even these arbitration cases fail to establish any principle of liability where troops are under constant assault and demoralizing influences by attacking forces. The same observation applies to the common law and statutory doctrine, referred to by the Government, that one who is under a legal duty to take protective or preventive action is guilty of criminal homicide if he wilfully or negligently omits to act and death is proximately caused. State v. Harrison, 107 NJL 213, 152 A 867; State v. Irvine, 126 La 434, 52 So 567; Holmes, Common Law, p. 278. No one denies that inaction or negligence may give rise to liability, civil or criminal. But it is quite another thing to say that the inability to control troops under highly competitive and disastrous battle conditions renders one guilty of a war crime in the absence of personal culpability. Had there been some element of knowledge or direct connection with the atrocities, the problem would be entirely different. Moreover, it must be remembered that we are not dealing here with an ordinary tort or criminal action; precedents in those fields are of little if any value. Rather we are concerned with a proceeding involving an international crime, the treatment of which may have untold effects upon the future peace of the world. That fact must be kept uppermost in our search for precedent.

The only conclusion I can draw is that the charge made against the petitioner is clearly without precedent in international law or in the annals of recorded military history. This is not to say that enemy commanders may escape punishment for clear and unlawful failures to prevent atrocities. But that punishment should be based upon charges fairly drawn in light of established rules of international law and recognized concepts of justice.

But the charge in this case, as previously noted, was speedily drawn and filed but three weeks after the petitioner surrendered. The trial proceeded with great dispatch without allowing the defense time to prepare an adequate case. Petitioner's rights under the due process clause of the Fifth Amendment were grossly and openly violated without any justification. All of this was done without any thorough investigation and prosecution of those immediately responsible for the atrocities, out of which might have come some proof or indication of personal culpability on petitioner's part. Instead the loose charge was made that great numbers of atrocities had been committed and that petitioner was the commanding officer; hence he must have been guilty of disregard of duty. Under that charge the commission was free to establish whatever standard of duty on petitioner's part that it desired. By this flexible method a victorious nation may convict and execute any or all leaders of a vanquished foe, depending upon the prevailing degree of vengeance and the absence of any objective judicial review.

At a time like this when emotions are understandably high it is difficult to adopt a dispassionate attitude toward a case of this nature. Yet now is precisely the time when that attitude is most essential. While peoples in other lands may not share our beliefs as to due process and the dignity of the individual, we are not free to give effect to our emotions in reckless disregard of the rights of others. We live under the Constitution, which is the embodiment of all the high hopes and aspirations of the new world. And it is applicable in both war and peace. We must act accordingly. Indeed, an uncurbed spirit of revenge and retribution, masked in formal legal procedure for purposes of dealing with a fallen enemy commander, can do more lasting harm than all of the atrocities giving rise to that spirit. The people's faith in the fairness and objectiveness of the law can be seriously undercut by that spirit. The fires of nationalism can be further kindled. And the hearts of all mankind can be embittered and filled with hatred, leaving forlorn and impoverished the noble ideal of malice toward none and charity to all. These are the reasons that lead me to dissent in these terms.

Mr. Justice Rutledge, dissenting.

Not with ease does one find his views at odds with the Court's in a matter of this character and gravity. Only the most deeply felt convictions could force one to differ. That reason alone leads me to do so now, against strong considerations for withholding dissent.

More is at stake than General Yamashita's fate. There could be no possible sympathy for him if he is guilty of the atrocities for which his death is sought. But there can be and should be justice administered according to law. In this stage of war's aftermath it is too early for Lincoln's great spirit, best lighted in the Second Inaugural, to have wide hold for the treatment of foes. It is not too early, it is never too early, for the nation steadfastly to follow its great constitutional traditions, none older or more universally protective against unbridled power than due process of law in the trial and punishment of men, that is, of all men, whether citizens, aliens, alien enemies or enemy belligerents. It can become too late.

This long-held attachment marks the great divide between our enemies and ourselves. Theirs was a philosophy of universal force. Ours is one of universal law, albeit imperfectly made flesh of our system and so dwelling among us. Every departure weakens the tradition, whether it touches the high or the low, the powerful or the weak, the triumphant or the conquered. If we need not or cannot be magnanimous, we can keep our own law on the plane from which it has not descended hitherto and to which the defeated foes' never rose. . . .

Targets in War:
Legal Considerations

GERALD J. ADLER

Since the Second World War, the United States has followed a policy of limited war. This theory has governed American conduct in controlled conflicts with smaller nations and guerrilla forces. The use of strategic and tactical air power has resulted, on occasion, in grim reports of injuries to civilians. What factors dictate the selection of a target and the amount of force to be used against it? Are these legal questions? If so, are there legal answers? Professor Adler examines the legal and military concepts which have governed this activity to date and attempts to formulate criteria for rational justification or condemnation of selected military operations.

I. THRESHOLD INQUIRY

There was a time in the not too distant past when the laws of war were fruitful grist for the mill of the international lawyer's pen. Such is not the case today. Indeed, it may be that there is nothing left of those laws. Or perhaps all that remains are the rules of belligerent occupation and the purely humanitarian concepts reflected in Red Cross-sponsored conventions. If, however, there does remain a vestige of what may be called combatant laws of war, it may well be that even that vestige should not be endowed with the term "law." This may be especially true in an age in which war is supposed to have lost its glamour and aggressive war, its legality.

Continued validity of a legal framework for the conduct of war is an issue most often reached in discussions about the weapons of war and the targets against which they are employed. If legal discussion is to be useful and normative, however, reasonable expectations of adherence to

The author is a retired flying officer of the Regular Air Force and wishes to acknowledge both his perspective and his own authority for otherwise unsupported statements in this article.

the norms must be considered lest continued talk about a law of war distorts the very concept of law. Strategy and international political realities are necessary ingredients which have too often been ignored in the framing of norms by lawyers. Perhaps it is for this reason that the laws of war are in such disarray.

In an attempt to put the international law of combatant warfare into order, or alternatively to conclude that there is no such legal concept, the principles which are supposedly applicable must be examined. This examination must determine whether evolved principles are valid today, and whether those with more power than academic lawyers are likely to accept the normative aspects of these principles. There may yet come a time when, as in the words of a popular ditty, "We ain't gonna study war no more," but, in the meantime, this attempt is made to perform a legal service for those who are in a position to achieve a durable peace, albeit by military means.

A.   Is There Really a Combatant Law of War?

The term, war, is frequently used without definition. Rectification of that omission may not be such a simple task. For the purpose of this article, war is not merely a legal relationship obtained only by certain formalities; nor is it completely unbridled violence. For a start, a definition generally sufficient for present purposes follows:

> When differences between States reach a point at which both parties resort to force, or one of them does acts of violence which the other chooses to look upon as a breach of the peace, the relation of war is set up, in which the combatants may use regulated violence against each other, until one of the two has been brought to accept such terms as his enemy is willing to grant.[1]

This article will, at this time, agree with the emphasis on force and regulated violence without questioning the source of the regulation. Without accepting the requirement for victory implicit in the above definition, the factual state of affairs emphasized is the portion of major concern. The political concept of aggression and aggressive war is not relevant to the existence of a state of war. Nor are the legal consequences which traditionally flow from the existence of a state of war relevant here.

Because it is so difficult to draw the line between force which is war and force which is not war, "the words 'force and violence' should be substituted for the word 'war.'"[2] In order to be consistent, however, with those who have written on the subject over the centuries, the word "war"

---

1.   J. HALL, INTERNATIONAL LAW 63 (4th ed.), in Jelf, *What is "War"? And What is "Aggressive War"?*, 19 GROTIUS SOC'Y TRANSACTIONS 103, 104 (1933).

2.   The suggestion was made in the League of Nations by the representative of Salvador in discussing hostilities between China and Japan. Eagleton, *The Attempt To Define War*, INT'L CONCILIATION 237, 280. *See id.* at 273, 285, 286 for similar suggestions to eliminate the word from the vocabulary of international affairs.

will be employed but shall be understood to mean force and violence.

Because, in a legal sense, it may be difficult to separate domestic from international violence, especially in a civil war context, and because conceptually the problems, principles, and solutions are often the same, "war" is not limited to "international force and violence." Nor is "regulated force and violence" used because such a definition begs the question. It may be regulated by an external standard, or it may merely be regulated by internal effectiveness.[3]

The problem with the law of force and violence, or the law and rules of war, is that only isolated applications have been developed. There has been no developed body of connected, coherent legal principles.[4]

> Springing originally from limitations upon a right (*i.e.*, the right to use violence), which in its extreme form constitutes a denial of all other rights, and developed through the action of practical and sentimental considerations, the law of war cannot be expected to show a substructure of large principles, like those which underlie the law governing the relations of peace . . . . It is, as a matter of fact, made up of a number of usages which in the main are somewhat arbitrary, which are not always very consistent with one another, and which do not therefore very readily lend themselves to general statements.[5]

Recognition of the truth in this statement is important. Arbitrary, inconsistent rules, however, will do more than preclude general statements or discovery of a substructure of large principles. If general principles are not discoverable within the rules, the rules will be ignored when new methods and weapons are developed.[6] A normative legal structure will be an impossibility. It may not take much in the way of principles, but until they are discovered or developed they cannot serve. Whether they lie on the borderline between law and morality,[7] or law and politics, or law and effectiveness, or elsewhere is not important. If they are not to be found, the subject is not law.

1. *Chivalry—A Vestigial Restriction*—At the time when laws were categorized in accordance with the performers, there existed a special

---

3. A United States Air Force Academy lecturer, for example, questioning "the right proportions of violence" in Vietnam, said that "[w]ar, to be effective, must be measured violence." Lecture by Prof. Peter Paret in AIR FORCE AND SPACE DIGEST, Dec. 1966, at 46.

4. J. RISLEY, THE LAW OF WAR 106 (1897). Although this observation was made in 1897, it remains true.

5. *Id.* at 106, 107 (quoting Hall).

6. *Cf.* Comment, 22 N.Y.U. INTRA. L. REV. 136, 147 (1967).

7. *See, e.g.*, Manisty, *The Navy and International Law*, 19 GROTIUS SOC'Y TRANSACTIONS 155, 193-194 (1933) (quoting Fischer Williams):

> As to the conduct of warlike operations, let it be enough to suggest that if there be less attempt to regulate in detail the conduct of war, the general requirements will remain that war must be carried on in such a way as to avoid as far as possible human suffering and destruction not conducive to victory, though it may be that this requirement will be recognised to be on the border line between law and morality.

law of arms based on canon and civil law, the law of chivalry. This was a law designed for the knights, that certain privileged class with the hereditary occupation of fighting.[8] This law of arms, which was developed in the late Middle Ages as knights fulfilled their pledged duty to protect the rights of persons, was merely designed to protect the rights of individual soldiers. Because there was no intention to regulate the conduct of troops of warring nations, chivalry lost most of its significance as a world of states developed.[9]

But chivalry in its most general sense did not die completely. Rather it seems to have been transformed into a concept of generosity in war. Given the indispensable factor of justice on the side of the belligerent, the idea evolved that while justice permitted the use of armies, machines, firearms, and other implements of war of which the enemy was not possessed, generosity forebade such use; war was carried on like a duel.[10] Generosity and the rectitude of the duel were so incorporated into the principles of international law that evil practices contrary to those principles were seen as " 'not war' in the same sense in which we are accustomed to speak of things which are 'not cricket.' "[11] Thus the poisoning of wells by the Germans in South-West Africa in 1915 was a "cowardly method of injuring an enemy, to which no soldier should stoop."[12]

Left over from the Middle Ages, the concept of chivalry was used in attempts to bar new weapons as unworthy of brave men. In a byplay reminiscent of the duel, the Germans in World War I complained that the British were not playing the game when they used bullets that would flatten on impact against aircraft; the British in turn deemed explosive bul-

---

8. *See generally* M. KEEN, THE LAWS OF WAR IN THE LATE MIDDLE AGES 15-19 (1965). Differing in substance from the law of chivalry was the *jus militare,* the law of the soldier, and the *jus armorum,* the entire body of chivalrous rules plus the customary rules observed by the professional soldier. *Id.* at 17.

9. *See id.* at 245-46.

10. Justice in war is indispensable but generosity is altogether a voluntary act. That leaves us at liberty to destroy an enemy by every possible means; this grants to him every thing that we would wish to be granted to ourselves in the like case; and thus war is carried on as a duel . . . .

C. VAN BYNKERSHOEK, A TREATISE ON THE LAW OF WAR 3 (Du Ponceau transl. 1810).

11. Jelf. *supra* note 1, at 106. The British Manual of Military Law formalized the idea that conventional rules of war are restricted by fairness and mutual respect without dishonorable means, expedients, or conduct, by "dictates of religion, morality, civilization and chivalry." J. GARNER, INTERNATIONAL LAW AND THE WORLD WAR 7-8 (1920); M. GREENSPAN, THE MODERN LAW OF LAND WARFARE 316 (1961). *But cf.* the comments made by the head of the International Rabbinical Assembly in calling for the abolition of the Geneva Convention because war is "not a 'game to be played by gentlemanly rules' ":

When we make rules for conducting a war . . . we pretend that knights in armor are still jousting with lances. We talk as if it is a football game that is being played and that civilians are merely spectators and that it is not "cricket" for spectators to be hurt.

Rabbi Eli A. Bohnen, in N.Y. Times, May 29, 1967, at 2, col. 4.

12. J. SPAIGHT, AIR POWER AND WAR RIGHTS 290 (3d ed. 1947).

lets used by German flyers "ungentlemenly missiles."[13] Such weapons denigrated the courage of the armed elite of the air, the modern descendant of medieval knights. Today there is a reflection of the same phenomenon in the subjective feeling among fliers that the fighter pilot who downs an enemy with a heat-seeking missile has not achieved the feat of his predecessor armed with machine gun or cannon. There is probably a vestige in the sanctuary given the parachuting flier and coordinate permission to fire only upon parachutists on hostile missions.[14]

It may that "[t]he function of international law is not to spend half its time as a despised and ineffective referee at a peculiarly bloody form of gladiatorial contest—a contest, indeed, in which the distinction between spectators and gladiators has worn very thin."[15] If, however, these remnants of chivalry appear anachronistic to those who have thought about controlling the conduct of war, the reason probably lies in the level of conduct sought to be obtained by the rules. Normally international rules of war are concerned with "only the bare minimum of moral obligations that nations and individuals must accept even in time of war."[16] The vestiges of chivalry seek to maximize ethical conduct. A profound jurisprudential gulf separates attempts to maintain minimum order from those which would raise ethical standards. If a certain standard is already accepted, however, and the results of maintaining that standard are more beneficial than harmful to all actors, there seems to be little reason for actively seeking to eliminate the anachronism.

2. *The Ultimate Restraint on War*—The natural law school teaches that mankind is obliged "to abstain from that which is productive of harm to one another, and to do what is productive of mutual good."[17] Working from this grand principle early natural lawyers developed a law of war which achieved stature among those states which recognized a binding law of nations.[18] But when the law of nations relates to war, its binding force is understandably subject to modification under the stress of vital national objectives or even national survival. The pre-World War I German *Kriegsraison*, for example, affirmed the observance of international law only when it was in accordance with the objects of war. If the military situation required it, the military commander could ignore the laws of

---

13. C. FENWICK, INTERNATIONAL LAW 667 (4th ed. 1965); M. McDOUGAL & F. FELICIANO, LAW AND MINIMUM WORLD PUBLIC ORDER 522 (1961) [hereinafter cited as McDOUGAL & FELICIANO]; J. SPAIGHT, *supra* note 12, at 207, 210.

14. *Cf.* U.S. DEP'T OF THE ARMY, FM 27-10, THE LAW OF LAND WARFARE 10 (1956). This sanctuary for the flier is especially strange when he may not only be armed but may well be rescued to fly hostile missions another day.

15. Manisty, *supra* note 7, at 162.

16. CLERGY AND LAYMEN CONCERNED ABOUT VIETNAM, IN THE NAME OF AMERICA 1 (1968).

17. T. RUTHERFORTH, INSTITUTES OF NATURAL LAW 483 (2d Am. ed. 1832).

18. *See, e.g.,* Du Ponceau, *Preface to* C. VAN BYNKERSHOEK, *supra* note 10, at vi.

war. This was a code of military convenience, not of law.[19]

If law is to be a restraining force on military means, society must in some way judge the merits of the applicable law. Having adjudged a violation of the law, the collective body of concerned but neutral states theoretically will act to preclude further violation.[20] But the theory will not work unless neutral states are also directly concerned. Fear for their own safety if they become involved or simple unconcern will give rise to "impunity in fact,"[21] a state of affairs which we will recognize in many past wartime situations. The bitter truth was voiced after World War I: "One lesson from the experience of the War is that we should not bind ourselves to observe any rules in war unless those who sign with us undertake to uphold them by force if need be against an enemy who breaks them."[22]

What then of moral constraint as the ultimate defense? Absent regular institutions to enforce the law of war, it is tempting to think in terms of moral consensus. Richard Falk does so in speaking of the conduct of the Vietnam War:

> [T]he sense of moral outrage widely shared by people and governments is itself relevant to the identification of rules of international law. Such shared attitudes identify the limits of acceptable behavior and possess or come to possess the quality of law . . . . Attributing this moral agency to international law is especially necessary in view of the absence of legislative procedures available to bring a new law into being and administrative procedures to interpret existing law in light of changed circumstances.[23]

Professor Falk envisions action by individuals, governments, and the organized international community to protect a state which falls victim to a violator of the laws of war. If morality is to be the ultimate restraint, however, we must first find the moral consensus. If a consensus can be found, perhaps it can be applied to the details of this study.

3. *Humane Warfare—A Contradiction in Terms?*—"War inevitably is a course of killings, assaults, deprivations of liberty, and destruction of property"[24] but it need not necessarily be the unrestrained strategy and

---

19. *See* C. Fenwick, *supra* note 13, at 655; J. Garner, *supra* note 11, at 5; M. Greenspan, *supra* note 11, at 314. The doctrine was reflected in the submarine warfare of World War I in violation of treaty and German law. *See* J. Garner, *supra* note 11, at 524.

20. *Cf.* J. Hall, The Law of Naval Warfare vi. (2d ed. rev. 1921); J. Risley, *supra* note 4, at 126.

21. This term for unpunished law violation was given by Rutherforth in contrast to an "impunity of right" established by positive law. T. Rutherforth, *supra* note 17, at 526.

22. Manisty, *supra* note 7, at 193.

23. Falk, *International Law and the Conduct of the Vietnam War*, in Clergy And Laymen Concerned About Vietnam, *supra* note 16 at 22, 25.

24. The Trial of German Major War Criminals, Proceedings of the Int'l Military Tribunal at Nuremberg 80 (1946) (argument of Jackson, chief of American prosecution).

tactics which found expression in the Pufendorf argument of 1672 that influenced the German view of prohibited weapons.[25] The argument was that humanity has a place so long as there is no hindrance to the speedy attainment of the object of war; therefore, all means are permitted except those which are positively condemnable because they cause unnecessary suffering.

Starting with the proposition that "when hostilities are to be waged against another nation, no one can expect that we shall compliment our enemies and wish them well"[26] it is possible to arrive at the unrestrained sheer savagery so typical of the religious wars of the 15th and 16th centuries. The popular passions which led to such violence found their 19th century counterpart with the democratic conscript army and the fanaticizing of national patriotism.[27] Von Clausewitz tells us that this is the natural state of affairs:

> [T]o introduce into the philosophy of War itself a principle of moderation would be an absurdity . . . .
> Let us not hear of Generals who conquer without bloodshed. If a bloody slaughter is a horrible sight, then that is a ground for paying more respect to War, but not for making the sword we wear blunter and blunter by degrees from feelings of humanity, until some one steps in with one that is sharp and lops off the arm from our body.[28]

With such an outlook it would not be possible to mitigate the savagery or even regulate the violence of war. Those who followed von Clausewitz in Germany, however, recognized the essential progress represented by international conventions relating to the treatment of wounded, sick, and captured soldiers.[29] This is not to say that the sword would be blunted. The soldier's sense of honor, justice, and self-interest, however, was extended to those no longer in the fight. International law had taken the existing institution of war and sought to regulate it with a view toward making war more humane. The principle which was generating the attempted regulation, however, "that the smallest amount of injury, consistent with self-defense and the sad necessity of wars, is to be inflicted"[30] was broader than that which the Germans had accepted with respect to those *hors de combat*. The proffered principle could in fact limit the force used in war. The next question is whether force has indeed been limited

---

25. See J. GARNER, *supra* note 11, at 279-80; M. GREENSPAN, *supra* note 11, at 316. See *generally* P. CORBETT, LAW AND SOCIETY IN THE RELATIONS OF STATES 24-25 (1951).

26. C. VAN BYNKERSHOEK, *supra* note 10, at 18.

27. See H. NICKERSON, CAN WE LIMIT WAR? 98, 113 (1933); J. RISLEY, *supra* note 4, at 73.

28. 1 C. VON CLAUSEWITZ, ON WAR 3, 288 (Graham transl. 1966).

29. See P. BORDWELL, THE LAW OF WAR BETWEEN BELLIGERENTS 115 (1908).

30. T. WOOLSEY, INTRODUCTION TO THE STUDY OF INTERNATIONAL LAW 210, 211 (6th ed. rev. 1908), *cited in* J. BAKER & H. CROCKER, THE LAWS OF LAND WARFARE 137 (U.S. Gov't Printing Office, 1918).

by the rules. If it has, there is at least some hope for a legal resolution of the subject.

4. *Limits on Force?*—The first systematic code of war, that of the Saracens, was based on the Koran and was supplemented by decisions of Mohammed and his followers.[31] Based partially on precepts of kindness and chivalry, the code forbade incendiary projectiles, cutting of trees, interception of water supplies, and the poisoning of wells or water courses. By the Middle Ages the laws of war, without burdensome distinctions between public and private international law, had four recognizable parts: The law of arms for conduct against enemies, military law for internal discipline, property law for the spoils of war, and peerage law for armorial disputes.[32] It is interesting to note that the law of arms, the only one of any concern to this undertaking, was developing at a time when even the heroes of chivalry butchered both enemy garrisons and civilian inhabitants. Death or slavery was the rule rather than the exception well into the Middle Ages. By the end of the 17th century, however, matters had progressed far enough so that a declaration of no quarter was seen as barbarous and intolerable.[33]

A major step forward in systematizing the rules of warfare was the 1863 Instructions for the Government of Armies of the United States in the Field[34] which conformed with existing usages of war and modified them in accordance with the requirements of the Civil War. The decade following saw some forward movement in the form of an 1864 Geneva Convention with additional articles in 1868, the St. Petersburg Declaration of 1868, and the Brussels Conference of 1874. The latter conferences will be discussed further, but in passing it is noteworthy that the result of the Geneva Convention, which was based neither on experience nor military requirements, was a hostilely-received patchwork. The St. Petersburg and Brussels meetings, on the other hand, which were largely the work of military men, had far better receptions.[35] In quick order, an 1875 meeting of the Institute of International Law recommended that governments instruct their armies in the rules of international law; a manual was issued by the Institute in 1880; the general plan of the Brussels Conference was

31. P. Bordwell, *supra* note 29, at 12.

32. M. Keen, *supra* note 8, at 239. Keen identifies the law of arms as the forerunner of conventional international law.

33. *See* J. Risley, *supra* note 4, at 124. The concept of permissible unrestrained warfare persisted in the cruel logic of Van Bynkershoek's 1737 treatise on war (*see* note 10 *supra*) but the trend was in the other direction. *Cf.* P. Bordwell, *supra* note 29, at 48.

34. General Orders, No. 100 (better known as Lieber's Code after the Columbia Univ. law professor who prepared them). *See* P. Bordwell, *supra* note 29, at 73-74.

35. *Compare* P. Bordwell, *supra* note 29, at 175 *with id.* at 112 *and* J. Garner, *supra* note 11, at 15. The probable lesson is that the military should at least understand the arguments behind rules of international law so that those rules which are impractical and likely to fail will not be adopted or if adopted may be changed. *Cf.* Manisty, *supra* note 7, at 160.

adopted by the Spanish-Portuguese-Latin American Military Congress at Madrid in 1892; and the First Peace Conference at The Hague in 1899 produced the Laws and Customs of War on Land.[36]

The Hague milestone was tested in the South African and Russo-Japanese Wars and found not appreciably deficient at the time of the Second Peace Conference in 1907. This was an era when the rules by which war was conducted were of great concern, at least to the writers. One, for example, was able to say in 1908 that the "rules are scarcely less certain and are probably less often violated than the rules of private law which are enforced by the courts . . . ."[37] To agree that the rules are not often violated may not, however, mean much. The preamble to the Hague Convention impliedly recognized that certain circumstances may lead to disregard of established rules which after all were only "inspired by the desire to diminish the evils of war, as far as military requirements permit."[38] The question is how extreme a military necessity is required to allow a bending or breaking of the rules.

The greatest test of this question came from the German military who viewed civilian jurists and academic writers as "impractical theorists and overzealous humanitarians."[39] All except Germany seemed to agree that necessity was not an excuse unless conformity would actually imperil the existence of the violating belligerent. The German view that mere convenience, utility, or strategical interest was enough to warrant violation was seen as "condemned by both the spirit and the letter of The Hague Conventions."[40] But true to the philosophy that "[w]hen the most ruthless methods are considered best calculated to lead us to victory, and a swift victory . . . then they must be employed," the Germans in World War I burned towns and massacred inhabitants, used civilians as protective screens for their soldiers, poisoned wells, bombarded undefended towns, and destroyed churches all in direct violation of various convention provisions.[41] Commenting on such acts, a noted authority pointed to correspondence between belligerents and neutrals to refute the impression that international law was not relevant in that war; he wrote that Germany's attempt

> with obvious misgivings on political grounds . . . to snatch victory from coming disaster by a deliberate crime against inter-

---

36. *See* P. BORDWELL, *supra* note 29, at 113; J. MOORE, INTERNATIONAL LAW AND SOME CURRENT ILLUSIONS 298 (1924). The understanding just prior to the Hague Conference which probably was understood by the participants was that the laws and customs must prevail except when both combatants were savage tribes. *Cf.* J. RISLEY, *supra* note 4, at 72.

37. P. BORDWELL, *supra* note 29, at 1.

38. Convention respecting the Laws and Customs of War on Land, preamble (1899). *See* P. BORDWELL, *supra* note 29, at 186; J. GARNER, *supra* note 11, at 10-11.

39. GARNER, *The German War Code*, 16 U. ILL. BULL. No. 49, at 6 (1918).

40. *Id.* at 11.

41. *Id.* at 10, 14.

national law . . . [failed] so signally that a repetition is improbable; for the conditions of success, geographical, tactical and
political, were more favourable than they are ever likely to be
again.[42]

Perhaps that was the expectation, but succeeding years and conflicts
have seen violations of almost every one of the rules of war. Natural law
tells us that it matters not that written laws may be broken because unwritten laws of perpetual validity will remain and the violation of rules
does not result in a positive law of nations authorizing the violation.[43]
The truth is that all wars will subvert accepted beliefs; that "when men
are struggling with arms in their hands for mastery, violations of law are
bound to occur because the means of securing the observance of law are
reduced to a minimum."[44] This does not mean that the law with its underlying principles ceases to exist.

In a manual for British army officers written prior to World War I,
three such principles were seen to be the foundations for the laws and
usages of war: 1) "the complete submission of the enemy at the earliest
possible moment with the least possible expenditure of men and money";
2) "humanity, which says that all such kinds and degrees of violence as
are not necessary for the purpose of war are not permitted to a belligerent";
3) "chivalry, which demands a certain amount of fairness in offence and
defense, and a certain mutual respect between the opposing forces."[45]
This paper shall study these principles and this hypothesis:

The more precise and detailed . . . a code is, and the further it
extends beyond the laying down of general principles by attempting to apply them to specific cases in advance, the more likely it
is to break down in practice. The principles, like those of war itself,
remain the same but their application varies in every war.[46]

B.   Should There Be a Law of War Today?

In a world in which aggressive war is outlawed, and only a limited
right of self-defense is supposed to exist, some would deem it improper
to speak of the laws of war without risking legitimation of the very idea
of war. From ancient times, until recently, war has been a basically legal
institution understood to be in accordance with divine authority and
natural reason.[47] As late as the turn of this century the proclamation that
"[w]ar is an element of the world's order established by God" may not

---

42.   J. HALL, supra note 20, at *v-vi.
43.   E.g., H. GROTIUS, THE LAW OF WAR AND PEACE xii (1646 ed. F. Kelsey
transl. 1925) [hereinafter cited as GROTIUS]; T. RUTHERFORTH, supra note 17, at 526.
44.   J. MOORE, supra note 36, at vii.
45.   E. EDMONDS & L. OPPENHEIM, LAND WARFARE 13 (1912).
46.   J. HALL, supra note 20, at 60.
47.   For war's status in the late Middle Ages, see M. KEEN, supra note 8, at 8-12.

have been surprising to an international community which at The Hague conferences accepted war as a legal procedure.[48]

An abrupt turn was taken with the 1928 Kellogg-Briand Pact, the Pact of Paris, which condemned "recourse to war for the solution of international controversies and renounce[d] it as an instrument of national policy . . . ."[49] Thus in 1933 it could hopefully be said that, at least for the signatories, "[w]ar is the antithesis of law, . . . that law and war are incompatible . . . [and] that . . . war would disappear—from the realm of law at any rate."[50] With such hopes, proposals to amend the laws of war were set aside as international lawyers and others sought to abolish war altogether.[51] Their failure would not surprise the natural lawyer for whom

> an injury will justify men in making use of force, both before and after it is committed . . . before it is committed in order to guard against it . . . after it is committed, in order, either to recover what is lost by it, or to hinder him, who has done it from doing the like again. Now, the use of force is war: and, consequently the law of nature, since it allows the use of force for any of these purposes, allows of war.[52]

Unless alternative means of preventing and repairing such injuries are found, a renunciation of war would appear as meaningless to an exponent of natural law as it did to the British Air Marshal who said: "The truth is that it is [aggressive] war itself that is wrong and immoral . . . for it must be right to defend one's country and oneself against attack."[53] The problem is apparent: "Wars are never aggressive but always defensive on the part of those who are responsible for waging them. Wars are never defensive but always aggressive on the part of those against whom they are

---

48. P. BORDWELL, supra note 29, at 114. (Quotation attributed to Count von Moltke). But see J. DYMOND, WAR 77 (West, Newman ed. 1915) for the proposition, written in 1823, that the general character and duties of Christianity are wholly incongruous with war. See also C. FENWICK, supra note 13, at 23.

49. General Treaty for the Renunciation of War, Jan. 17, 1929, art. I, 46 Stat. 2343 (eff. July 24, 1929).

50. Eagleton, supra note 2, at 237-38. The illegality of war in an international context that affirmed rights of states, was seen earlier by Hans Kelsen except when war was used as a sanction. Id. at 238-39 & n.2.

51. Cf. C. FENWICK, supra note 13, at 658; MANISTY, supra note 7, at 175.

52. T. RUTHERFORTH, supra note 17, at 237. Succinctly the natural lawyer saw three legitimate causes of war: defense, recovery of belongings, and punishment. Scott, Introduction to GROTIUS xxxvi. The comparison should be made with the international lawyer who also found three justifiable causes of war: 1) to secure what belongs to us; 2) to provide for future safety by reparation for injuries; 3) to protect selves and property from threatened injury. H. HALLECK, ELEMENTS OF INTERNATIONAL LAW AND LAWS OF WAR 145-47 (Lippincott ed. 1878).

53. Saundby, The Ethics of Bombing, AIR FORCE AND SPACE DIGEST, June 1967, at 48, 53. A similar thought was expressed by Livy: "War is just for those for whom it is necessary, and arms are blameless for those who have no hope left save in arms." GROTIUS *406.

waged."[54] Even when alternative means in the form of international organizations are provided, it may not be possible "to prevent war upon a
question in which each side regards the maintenance of its point of view
as vital to its welfare . . . ."[55]

It may well be that the fundamental concept of sovereign states precludes the absence of war. Mortimer Adler writing in 1944 said:

> War between nations is not a breach of the peace, because so
> long as there are sovereign nations there can be no peace between
> them but only a temporary cessation of hostilities that should be
> called an armed truce, not a condition of peace . . . .
> The fallacy of supposing that international law and inter-
> national courts and all the other pretensions of international arbi-
> tration can effectively set up and preserve a condition of peace
> among sovereign nations is allied to the fallacy of supposing that
> natural law is sufficient for the government of men . . . .
> [P]eace will not be made at the end of this war. What will
> be made will be another truce, perhaps on a larger scale and with
> more deceptive talk than ever before about covenants and world
> courts, but a truce nevertheless, and not a peace . . . . That means
> another war at a not too distant future.[56]

Although the conclusion that international law cannot presently stop
wars may give more reason for this study, no approval of belligerency is
given thereby. When accepting the current limits of international law, it
is agreed that "[t]he 'outbreak' of a war is a metajuristic phenomenon,
an event outside the range and control of the law."[57] The conduct of a
war, however, may be within the law's range and control. Hugo Grotius'
great 17th-century treatise on the law of war, for example, was itself
"a reasoned protest against war"; yet he wrote of a law controlling the
actions of belligerents, a law complete with principles applicable to new
problems.[58] Recognizing that "[a]ll things are uncertain the moment
men depart from law," he and his followers sought to ameliorate the evils
of an institution which they could not destroy.[59]

This was an amelioration and regulation of war not recognized by
the Napoleonic theory put into words by General von Clausewitz. Together
they viewed war's object as the bringing to terms of a hostile nation,
which in the case of a war between Great Powers required total and
absolute overthrow of the enemy. The side which moderated or humanized

---

54. A. PONSONBY, WARS & TREATIES 1815-1914, 10 (1918). Can this be the
reason that Grotius allowed that a war declared by public authority might be just on
both sides? Cf. Nussbaum, *Just War—A Legal Concept?*, 42 MICH. L. REV. 453, 464
(1943).

55. J. HALL, *supra* note 20, at vi.

56. M. Adler, War *and the Rule of Law*, in WAR AND THE LAW 189, 194, 198
(Puttkammer ed. 1944).

57. Nussbaum, *supra* note 54, at 477.

58. *See* Scott, *supra* note 52, at xxviii-xxix.

59. GROTIUS *xi; J. MOORE, *supra* note 36, at 37.

the struggle would suffer probable defeat.[60]

Nevertheless, moderation was to become the expressed will of the nations of the world whenever they gathered to discuss the problem. The Grotian attempts were echoed three hundred years later at The Hague: "Seeing that, while seeking means to preserve peace and prevent armed conflicts between nations, it is likewise necessary to bear in mind the case where the appeal to arms has been brought about by events which their care was unable to avert" the nations drafted Regulations respecting the Laws and Customs of War on Land.[61] The propriety of regulating war was later questioned when the 1932 Geneva Conference sought to prohibit certain ways of conducting war; for had not the world abolished war in the Kellogg-Briand Pact?[62] The doubts were once again put aside in favor of regulation.

> Our civilization is frequently accused of immaturity because it has not been able to abolish war. But it seems unlikely that severe conflicts of interest between states and alliances will soon disappear, and, for some, conflicts and armed action may be the only method of resolution. It is not war that is an indication of our immaturity, but the manner in which too often wars have been fought.[63]

This writer is saying that because wars will continue in a world with extremely limited international authority and sanctions, efforts to responsibly regulate and measure the violence of war ought not be condemned. International lawyers have long sought to limit the ravages and reform the practices of war. But if the law which is deduced or developed cannot be observed because it speaks in a legal vacuum, not only will the reputation and authority of international law vanish, but the eruption of an unnatural cork may well be the end of all institutions.

C. *The Necessity-Humanity Continuum*

1. *Humane Laws in War*—"One cannot make war in a sentimental fashion. The more pitiless the conduct of the war, the more humane it is in reality for it will run its course all the sooner."[64] This theory, voiced by German theorists since the days of von Clausewitz, is attractive to many non-German thinkers as well. The idea of taking certain military actions in order to shorten wars and save lives, especially the lives of friendly troops,

---

60. *Cf.* H. NICKERSON, *supra* note 27, at 43, 131; 1 C. VON CLAUSEWITZ, *supra* note 28, at 2; Saundby, *supra* note 53, at 49. For a proposition not far removed from von Clausewitz at his most limited see T. LAWRENCE, PRINCIPLES OF INTERNATIONAL LAW (5th ed. 1913), in J. BAKER & H. CROCKER, *supra* note 30, at 117: The object of warlike operations is "to destroy enemy resistance and induce terms as soon as possible."

61. Hague Convention No. IV, Annex, preamble, Oct. 18, 1907.

62. *Cf.* H. NICKERSON, *supra* note 27, at 188.

63. Paret, *supra* note 3.

64. Garner, *supra* note 39, at 9 (quoting General von Hindenburg).

repeats itself throughout the history of war. One of the most obvious examples of such thinking was the justification for the atomic bombings of Japan. If the theory is valid, although "[i]t is certainly noble to practice the duties of humanity, clemency, piety, and other magnanimous virtues in the midst of war,"[65] it will often be contrary to good strategy to do so. More important for this study, war-shortening, life-saving tactics become per se legal regardless of incidental injury.

Yet from the days when Homer offset his accounts of savagery with Greco-Roman humanity and Grotius promulgated a concept of moderation in accordance with moral and religious justice as a matter of right and duty, moderation, humanity, and clemency have been crystallized and applied by the great martial jurists.[66] Despite current doubts voiced about attempts to moderate war,[67] objective academicians, realistic humanitarians, and partisan military leaders have come to test the limits of permissible military actions in remarkably similar ways. The fundamental tenet of the test is the necessity-humanity continuum. The phrasing by a British military theoretician probably represents the current consensus:

> The test is whether the action in question genuinely furthers the aim and main strategic concept of the war . . . . It goes without saying, however, that all practical steps, short of prejudicing the success of the operation, should be taken to minimize the risk to civilians.[68]

Although one might quarrel with the limited nature of this statement of the test, it would be useful to examine the route taken to reach even this level of consensus.

2. *Legacy of Early Conventions*—The view held by Grotius and his followers in the natural law school was that in war those things which are necessary to attain the end in view are permissible; however, beyond the illegitimacy of useless injury there were no precise limitations on the use of force.[69] The paramount Grotian thesis was that "a belligerent should injure his enemy not because of the mere injury to the enemy, but because of the advantage to himself, and that means not leading to such advantage must be condemned. To state such a principle is to obtain its acceptance

---

65. C. Van Bynkershoek, *supra* note 10, at 19.
66. *Cf.* P. Bordwell, *supra* note 29, at 3, 8; Grotius at *513, *519-20; H. Halleck, *supra* note 52, at 213.
67. *See, e.g.,* Bohnen, *supra* note 11: "to talk about 'humane warfare is to mock God.'"; G. Griffin, An Operational Necessity (1967): "He points out the hopelessness of trying to apply humane laws to the inhumane lawlessness of war" (Book Review, Time, Aug. 25, 1967, at 82).
68. Saundby, *supra* note 53, at 53 (author is Air Marshal, R.A.F. (Ret.)).
69. *See* J. Baker & H. Crocker, *supra* note 60, at 114; Grotius *424; T. Rutherforth, *supra* note 17, at 521.

. . . ."[70] Thus all means necessary to achieve a given objective of war were legitimate.

By the end of the 19th century the principle of minimizing permissible destruction had been more formally engrafted onto the prohibition of useless, wanton destruction. The principle combined efficacy, humanity, and proportionality so as "to obtain justice as speedily as possible at the least possible cost of suffering and loss to the enemy, or to neutrals, as the result of belligerent operations."[71] This was the century which had witnessed the first great humanitarian convention at Geneva, that of 1864, the landmark international attempt to reduce the horrors of war. Although this Geneva convention, like most subsequent ones at Geneva, was not concerned with combatant laws of war, the 1868 Declaration of St. Petersburg was very much concerned with them. Believing that

> the progress of civilization should have the effect of alleviating as much as possible the calamities of war; [t]hat the only legitimate objects which states should endeavor to accomplish during war is to weaken the military force of the enemy; [t]hat for this purpose it is sufficient to disable the greatest possible number of men; [and] [t]hat this object would be exceeded by the employment of arms which uselessly aggravate the suffering of disabled men, or render their death inevitable . . .

those assembled declared the use of such arms contrary to humanity.[72] The spirit of those moderating years continued at the 1874 Brussels Conference where the delegates demonstrated their belief that while not losing sight of military necessity, they "had imbibed the humane spirit of the age and that they had a full appreciation of the power for good or evil which they held in their hands."[73] The spirit was to culminate in The Hague Peace Conferences of 1899 and 1907.

Although military necessity was a primary consideration in The Hague Conventions, it was implicitly limited to the use of only that degree of force which is required to attain a given objective. A general statement applicable to the subject of our inquiry was that "[t]he right of belligerents to adopt means of injuring the enemy is not unlimited."[74] The most apparent

---

70. P. BORDWELL, *supra* note 29, at 2. *But cf.* J. RISLEY, *supra* note 4, at 115, citing Grotius, Wolff, and Vattel for the conclusion that wanton infliction of pain and distress was a "lawful 'independent means of attack.'" Risley attributes to the 17th and 18th centuries the prohibition of disproportionate or wanton suffering except when incident to some strategical object.

71. J. RISLEY, *supra* note 4, at 73.

72. *See* P. BORDWELL, *supra* note 29, at 278. Bordwell points out that the understood contemporary emphasis in the second quoted clause was on "to weaken" rather than on "military," an emphasis lost on some later commentators. *Cf. id.* at 279. For text of declaration, see A. HIGGINS, THE HAGUE PEACE CONFERENCES 5-7 (1909).

73. A. HIGGINS, *supra* note 72, at 111.

74. Annex to Hague Convention No. IV, Respecting the Laws and Customs of War on Land, Regulations, art. 22, 36 Stat. 2295, T.S. No. 539 (Oct. 18, 1907) [hereinafter cited as Hague Regulations].

purpose of these early conventions was the attempt to establish an equilibrium between the standards of civilization and the necessities of war. Here was early recognition that "international law respecting war is not formed only by humane feelings, but it has as its basis both military necessity and efficiency and humane feelings, and is formed by weighing these two factors."[75]

Comments since the St. Petersburg Declaration, the first formal agreement restricting weapons use, have ranged from the feeling that it may go too far toward the humanity end of the continuum for most of the world, to the logical conclusion that if a threat would be sufficient, no violence is permissible.[76] But The Hague Regulations continued the spirit of St. Petersburg and forbade the employment of "arms, projectiles, or material of a nature to cause superfluous injury."[77] Carried forward a half-century into the 1949 Geneva Conventions the thesis remains valid: When the object of an attack is no longer an effective base of enemy power, humanity makes further violence impermissible.[78]

The concept of military necessity may be particularized only into permission for that destruction which is necessary, relevant, and proportional, in accordance with the situation, and only to bring about the submission of the enemy.[79] Because the concept was taken into account when the rules of war were framed, necessity is no defense for forbidden acts.[80] This must be the case lest commanders be led to use the concept of military necessity as justification for violations of international laws and usages as well as the treaty obligations of their own state. Almost any action would become justifiable if military necessity knew no law and the only objective was to make a situation so untenable for an enemy that he must sue for peace.[81] Aside from the problems of retaliation and reprisal, however, "the whole purpose and *raison d'être* of the laws of warfare is to lay down rules of conduct, of which in the opinion of civilisation no intentional breach can be justified under any circumstances . . . ."[82]

Because the prohibitive effect of the rules is so strong it becomes of

---

75. Shimoda v. Japan, 355 Hanrei Jiho 17 (Tokyo Dist. Ct. 1963), in 1 R. FALK & S. MENDLOVITZ, THE STRATEGY OF WORLD ORDER 314, at 342 (1966). *See also* U.S. DEP'T OF THE ARMY, *supra* note 14, ¶ 3:
    The law of war places limits on the exercise of a belligerent's power . . . and requires that belligerents refrain from employing any kind or degree of violence which is not actually necessary for military purposes and that they conduct hostilities with regard to the principles of humanity and chivalry.
76. *Compare* J. GARNER, *supra* note 11, at 282 *with* M. GREENSPAN, *supra* note 11, at 315.
77. Hague Regulations, art. 23(e).
78. *See* McDOUGAL & FELICIANO, *supra* note 13, at 79.
79. *See* C. FENWICK, *supra* note 13, at 654; McDOUGAL & FELICIANO 72.
80. *See* U.S. DEP'T OF THE ARMY, *supra* note 14, ¶ 3; M. GREENSPAN, *supra* note 11, at 314; J. HALL, *supra* note 20, at 9.
81. *Cf.* T. BARCLAY, LAW AND USAGE OF WAR 79 (1914).
82. J. HALL, *supra* note 20, at 9.

the utmost importance for those concerned with fostering obedience to law that the rules be not unreasonably restrictive:

> Only such modes of fighting should be prohibited as would meet with the overwhelming disapproval of civilisation, or whose use could contribute nothing, or practically nothing, to the success of the campaign . . . . If the prohibitions contained in the rules are governed by these principles, there remains no room for the doctrine of "necessity knows no law."[83]

The merit of this approach and of those principles in applying the concededly vague necessity-humanity criterion to the international law of weaponry will be tested further.

3. *Proportionality.*—For Grotius, on the strategic level, a fight not designed to obtain a right or to end a war was to be avoided; on the tactical level devastation was impermissible if the enemy could get subsistence from other sources or if the object of potential destruction was of no value to the enemy's war-making capacity.[84] For Professor Myres McDougal, the Grotian thesis maintains its validity; target selection, for example, is regulated by balancing military necessity and the minimum destruction of values, and by omitting as targets those elements of enemy power which are either not substantial or are already ineffective.[85]

Although it is said that devastation for purely military purposes is legitimate, the relationship between destruction and military value must be proportional.[86] McDougal would permit that violence which is indispensably necessary but prohibit that which is needless and results in a superfluity of harm measured by a gross imbalance of the military result and injury inflicted.[87] Thus there may be no gross disparity between the area destroyed and the area of the military installation, between the importance of a target and the zone of disparity.[88]

From the point when it was recognized "that extirpatory methods were as impracticable and wasteful as they were brutal and brutalizing"[89] international law has long condemned more than merely wanton acts. The act which is grossly disproportionate to the object to be attained stands equally condemned.[90] Proportionality thus represents a movable fulcrum

---

83. *Id.* at 8-9. Hall saw the slaughter of prisoners, for example, as meeting with civilization's overwhelming disapproval while explosive and poisonous bullets as well as bombardment for terror contributed only unnecessary suffering.
84. *See* GROTIUS, *supra* note 52, at *524, *533.
85. *See* McDOUGAL & FELICIANO 573.
86. *Compare* C. FENWICK, *supra* note 13, at 680-81 *with* McDOUGAL & FELICIANO 524.
87. McDOUGAL & FELICIANO 528, 616.
88. *Id.* at 650, 652.
89. J. MOORE, *supra* note 36, at 13.
90. *See* W. HALL, INTERNATIONAL LAW 551, 552 (4th ed. 1895).

on which the necessity-humanity scale may be balanced.[91] It is in effect
a compromise between two extremes, either of which carried to its logical
conclusion could, like most other legal rules, have destroyed the other.[92]

4. *Measured Violence or Limited Warfare*—In traditional German
theory, military necessity was available to bend or break a rule whenever
an object of war could not be attained by adhering to the law.[93] The idea
of so conditioning observance of the law would mean the end of the laws
of war altogether. The tautology which permits violence in accordance with
legitimate objectives of that violence haunts the problem.

Necessity can release all limits if the only question one asks is "What
is the bag?"[94] Those who believe that this is all we need ask would agree
with General Douglas MacArthur's conclusion that "the concept that when
you use force, you can limit that force" is a new concept in military operations, a "concept of appeasement."[95] They would agree with the analyst
of the Middle East War of 1967 who found proof in the Israeli victory
"that political restraints, applied in the turmoil of battle, can only increase
cost and diminish effectiveness."[96]

If military restraint is novel, if political restraint is unwise, then legal
restraint comes into question. It cannot be assumed that war has ever
been without limits or that military actions operate in a political vacuum.
On the other hand, there have indeed been strong political and legal
restraints on the use of military force in war. These restraints will probably
continue. The factors which determine the problem of target selection
are typical of these restraints.

II. TARGET SELECTION

A. *Noncombatants*

In the laws of war and in the emotions of what is usually called the
"civilized world community," the distinction between the soldier and the

---

91.   The mobility of the fulcrum is aided by conditional prohibitions in accordance
with circumstances and conditions. Thus, although the Hague regulations relating to
the employment of poison or poisoned weapons were absolute, those relating to the
destruction of property were merely conditional. *Compare* Hague Regulations art. 23(a)
with arts. 23(g), 27. *See also* U.S. DEP'T OF THE ARMY, *supra* note 14, ¶ 56. The
Geneva Conventions carry forth both types of prohibitions. *Cf.* M. GREENSPAN, *supra*
note 11, at 314-15.
92.   *Cf.* J. MOORE, *supra* note 36, at 32.
93.   *See* P. BORDWELL, *supra* note 29, at 5. Bordwell suggests that it would have
been better for the Germans to await an extraordinary occasion and plead justification
for law violation rather than to announce the principle in advance thus sanctioning
the principle almost as a law itself. *Id.*
94.   *Cf.* J. GARNER, *supra* note 11, at 283; MCDOUGAL & FELICIANO 616; M. ROYSE,
AERIAL BOMBARDMENT AND THE INTERNATIONAL REGULATION OF WARFARE 136 (1928).
For the proposition that World War II was the fulfillment of the overwhelming importance of that question *see* C. FENWICK, *supra* note 13, at 659.
95.   This was Gen. MacArthur's thesis after he was relieved of his Korean command. TIME, Oct. 6, 1967, at 31.
96.   Witze, *Kiss in the Desert*, AIR FORCE AND SPACE DIGEST, July 1967, at 8.

civilian is a creature of the late Middle Ages. Yet early in that period a remarkable anomaly in the noncombatant's status was apparent in the treatment afforded civilians in overrun areas and that given to soldiers taken prisoner, especially to those who had been wounded. Civilians were treated as enemies and suffered miseries far worse than the soldiers, for whom humane treatment was the rule.[97] The soldier's self-interest in such humanity is evident. Before that self-interest is dismissed as extralegal, however, it should be noted that such a reason for restraint may well be a most important factor in the laws of war.

As the feudal system merged into a monarchical order of states in Europe, the distinction between the combatant and the relatively immune noncombatant became clearer. The quarrels and territorial struggles among a variegated set of titled rulers were not of major concern to a civilian population seeking only to avoid trouble and carry on as normal. The union-like rules of professional soldiering, designed to make the trade more tolerable were not at all concerned with the civilian. With the exception of religious wars, unarmed and nonresisting civilians were irrelevant to the fight and thus only occasionally subject to ill treatment.[98] By the end of the 17th century, the plunder and devastation of an enemy's country and people, so common to the Tartars, the ancient world, and the early Middle Ages were seen as out of tune with the spirit of the age. Unnecessary barbarity was thought to have "no effect beyond throwing the nation back many stages in all that relates to peaceful arts and civilisation."[99] Thus war in both its means and ends was, for a while at least, confined to the military.

The French Revolution and the rise of Napoleon did much to upset the idea that war was only the soldier's affair. The passion of the religious wars was seen once more when thirty million citizens of the French state became a nation in arms. Their Grand Armée, without regard for the rules of the professional soldier, not only presented extreme danger for the adversary but also threatened the distinction between soldier and civilian. The reaction to Napoleon came in the form of large conscript armies which were raised in other continental European states. War had become as von Clausewitz put it, a "great *affair of State.*"[100]

But insulated from this strategic metamorphosis on the continent were the military theorists of Britain and the United States. Protected by sea power and distance, the notion continued "that war was exclusively the business of the armed forces, who were paid to fight and risk their lives, while civilians were noncombatants who had a right to be left

---

97. *See generally* M. KEEN, *supra* note 8, at 191-95, 243.
98. *Cf.* J. DYMOND, *supra* note 48, at 72; H. HALLECK, *supra* note 52, at 190; Saundby, *supra* note 53, at 48-49.
99. 3 VON CLAUSEWITZ, *supra* note 28, at 98-99.
100. *Id.* at 103; *see* Saundby, *supra* note 53, at 49.

unmolested to go about their lawful occasions."[101] As late as 1912, just before German airships and airplanes would shake comfortable British theory, British army officers were instructed without reference to the Napoleonic *levée en masse* and the subsequent century of practice and theory on the continent. Instead they were told that one of the purposes of the laws of war was to ensure that an individual must definitely choose to belong to either the armed forces or the peaceful population.[102]

Even after World War I and the telling sea blockade of Germany by Britain, John Bassett Moore would term the distinction between combatant and noncombatant the vital and fundamental principle of the modern law of war.[103] The distinction is still verbalized. The International Committee of the Red Cross puts it this way in one context: "[C]ivilian populations must 'in no circumstance be subject to aerial attack.' "[104] The validity of such assertions and theories must be tested.

Under the Grotian-enunciated law of nature the right to kill and injure extended beyond those bearing arms to enemy subjects anywhere and to all others in enemy territory because injury could be feared from all such persons.[105] Similarly, during the Middle Ages, war to the death had been sanctioned by rules in which the conquered could be slain or enslaved.[106] Despite too many similar instances in the history of more recent wars, today's positive sanctions concerning target selection do indeed "include a mental perspective of common humanity which encompasses the enemy civilians as well as those of the same nationality as the decision-maker."[107] To the extent that this mental perspective and common humanity is not shared, there will be aberrations. In general, however, the perspective will be common while applications of relative values will differ. In any case the values have changed so markedly that a law of nature could not today be enunciated in accordance with the Grotian view.

Early exceptions to the harsh natural law were made in Christian public wars for those who served the general interest and who were irrelevant to war, as well as for those who were required to preserve reasonable social relations. Thus, churchmen, pilgrims, hermits, oxherds,

---

101.   Saundby, *supra* note 53, at 50. The reference there is only to the pre-World War I view. Air Marshal Saundby continues: "Their part in the war, they believed, should be limited to waving good-bye to the troops, paying extra taxes, knitting cardigans, mittens, and balaclava helmets, and submitting to a few minor inconveniences." *Id.*

102.   E. EDMONDS & L. OPPENHEIM, *supra* note 45, at 18.

103.   J. MOORE, *supra* note 36, at viii, 4-5.

104.   N.Y. Times, Feb. 10, 1968, at 14, col. 5.

105.   Included within the permission were infants, women, old men, captives, and hostages. GROTIUS *458-61. Among authorities Grotius used were the Bible (Psalms): "[H]e will be happy who dashes the infants of the Babylonians against a rock"; and Homer: "Nor will he cruel fate escape, who still lies hidden in his mother's womb." *Id.* at *459, *466 n.2.

106.   M. KEEN, *supra* note 8, at 104.

107.   See Mallison, *The Laws of War and the Juridical Control of Weapons of Mass Destruction in General and Limited Wars,* 36 GEO. WASH. L. REV. 308, 336 (1967).

husbandmen, plowmen, merchants, and students were immune and given safe-conduct passes.[108] The attempt to specify those classes not to be harmed in war and international disputes continued after the American Revolution. Benjamin Franklin and his successors sought unsuccessfully to assure the nonmolestation of peaceful merchants, fishermen, and artisans by treaty.[109] Although they were not able to enshrine the principle in the 1856 Declaration of Paris, a noted post-Civil War author was able to say that an immunity was granted to the aged, ill, women, children, ministers, "men of science and letters, to professional men, artists, merchants, mechanics, agriculturists, [and] laborers" unless they resisted, took arms, or participated in hostile acts.[110]

It is not surprising that these wide exemptions would fall victim to the passions of war.[111] It need not follow, however, that the civilian population ought to be viewed as a means to a given end. For instance, the German war code rejected as contrary to the principles of war "the pretensions of the professors of international law" that the noncombatant population should be preserved as much as possible. Thus noncombatants in a besieged area would not be allowed to leave because their presence and consumption of food would hasten surrender.[112] One can ignore the inhumanity of a concept which refuses civilians the right of innocent egress and accept the German theoretical result without accepting the rationale. Rather than supporting the civilian involvement because of the military advantage in doing so, historically it is true that within the zone of land, sea, and air combat, military operations have long prevailed over civilian immunity.[113] When General Sherman said in the American Civil War that "we are . . . fighting . . . a hostile people, and must make old and young, rich and poor, feel the hard hand of war, as well as their organized armies"[114] he was speaking of people within the zone of combat, although his statement can certainly be read as being not too far removed from the harsh German code. In purely military terms, it is wasteful to attack civilians or civilian targets which do not have direct military value.

---

108. *See* M. KEEN, *supra* note 8, at 189-90, 197.
109. *See* P. BORDWELL, *supra* note 29, at 69-71.
110. H. HALLECK, *supra* note 52, at 190-91; *see* GROTIUS *520-22.
111. For examples of the discrepancies between wars and treaties and the resulting cruelties to civilians *see* A. PONSONBY, *supra* note 54 (Greek War, 1821-1828; Austro-Hungarian War, 1848-1849; Indian Mutiny, 1857-1858; Brazilian War, 1864-1870; Egyptian War, 1882).
112. Garner, *supra* note 39, at 27.
113. *See* McDOUGAL & FELICIANO 607; M. ROYSE, *supra* note 94, at 227; *cf.* art. 24(4), Draft Rules of Air Warfare, in Shimoda v. Japan, *supra* note 75, at 339 (permits bombardment of places in the neighborhood of land forces provided there exists a reasonable presumption that the military concentration is sufficiently important to justify such bombardment, having regard to the danger thus caused to the civilian population).
114. C. FENWICK, *supra* note 13, at 681. Neither Sherman nor his contemporary, Gen. Sheridan, sought to directly target hostile civilians but rather sought to reduce them to poverty and privation as a means to bring "prayers for peace more surely and quickly." *See* P. BORDWELL, *supra* note 29, at 79.

But when military operations take place in and around a civilian-occupied hamlet, for example, it is no longer accurate to speak of a strike directed at the hamlet as one directed at a civilian target. The problem with the German theory lies in its treatment of human beings as a means rather than an end, thus ignoring a Kantian categorical imperative which finds general respect in the law of war.[115]

Exemptions for civilians, even when desired, are severely strained in a guerrilla war against part-time or nonuniformed soldiers. At one time, if a combatant were not recognizable as a soldier by the unaided eye at rifle-shot distance, he might not have been given the soldier's privileged status of prisoner of war.[116] The twilight zone of legal permissibility in guerrilla-type activity extends beyond the requirement for bright uniforms and has caused commentators to condemn such activities despite their effectiveness.[117] For instance, the Brussels Conference of 1874 deadlocked on the relative legitimacy of guerrillas with removable badges, irregulars with external irremovable badges, and the *levée en masse*.[118] In any case, the varying privileges accorded the nonmilitary combatant began to disappear with the French *francs-tireurs* in the Franco-Prussian War and continued to decline during the Boer War but have not completely disappeared.[119] Even today there is major difficulty fitting the full-time Viet Cong into the letter of the 1949 Geneva Prisoner of War Convention and differentiating him from the civilian who is not allowed to remain neutral. The laws of war become blurred indeed, "when the enemy soldier, clad in black pajamas and a coolie hat, wraps his weapon in oil cloth, buries it in a rice paddy during the day, and becomes a soldier only at night."[120] When civilians, forced or not, perform military tasks, are issued weapons for use against attacking aircraft, and are formed into work groups to repair roads, bridges, and other transportation facilities destroyed or

---

115. *Cf.* Fulbright, *We Must Not Fight Fire With Fire*, N.Y. Times, Apr. 23, 1967, § 6 (Magazine), at 27, col. 1. Illustrative of a tactic violating the imperative was the German blitzkrieg of World War II, justified as a method of interfering with enemy troops and thus facilitating conquest. *Cf.* C. FENWICK, *supra* note 13, at 681. *But see* the Rickenbacker statement, regarding the North Vietnamese, TIME, Nov. 3, 1967, at 15: "You're not fighting human beings over there . . . . You're just fighting two-legged animals. The people are just slaves."

116. *See* P. BORDWELL, *supra* note 29, at 90.

117. *See, e.g., id.* at 92.

118. The Russian attempt to confine the codified usages of war to regular belligerents was opposed because of the effect of such action on national defense and the duty of citizens toward their country. *See generally id.* at 104-05; J. RISLEY, *supra* note 4, at 109-10.

119. Organized resistance units qualify as military entitled to prisoner of war status under the Third 1949 Geneva Convention if they are commanded by a responsible leader, have a fixed distinctive sign recognizable at a distance, carry arms openly, and conduct their operations in accordance with the laws and customs of war. These are essentially the same requirements as those promulgated at the 1874 Brussels Conference.

120. Publication of Military Assistance Command in Vietnam, in Denno, *The Fate of American POWs in Vietnam*, AIR FORCE AND SPACE DIGEST, Feb. 1968, at 40, 41.

damaged by bombing efforts, the military men on the other side will apply to them the same rules which are generally associated with military objectives.[121] Even if the presence of noncombatants will bring a reassessment of the legitimacy of striking a particular military target, it is unrealistic to believe that the presence of active noncombatants will or even should be considered.

There was belief at one time that standing well-disciplined armies and the distinction between soldier and privileged civilian was steadily making the methods of warfare less cruel and more humane.[122] As war becomes more totalitarian, however, civilians become less innocuous and the distinction disappears.[123] The Hague Conventions required warning civilians of bombardment if military exigencies permitted; the Draft Air Rules had no reference to warning except as other laws of war applied—there were generally no warnings in the world wars and only sporadic warnings in Korea.[124] Perhaps civilian immunity rested on the early inability to attack civilians. When they came within range, as in naval bombardment, the immunity was relaxed.[125] A simple condemnation of civilian targeting becomes unworkable when factory workers and peasants bear arms and tin buckets are as likely to be carrying fuel for trucks as water for children.[126]

The military-civilian distinction still exists if there can be such a thing as noninvolvement in the war.[127] The maker of machines of war is more dangerous than a soldier; the worker in the railways, docks, and all installations is not immune. The real problem is the marked change in civilian support of a war effort from the time of growing food and forging weapons.[128] This is not to say that because "all people who belong to a belligerent are more or less combatant . . . there arises the necessity to destroy the whole people and all the property of the enemy . . . ."[129] The world has yet to see such total war. The distinction has become blurred indeed, but it has not disappeared. Facts will determine its proper place and legitimacy will follow. Rather than attempting to substitute for a rule the supposed reason of that rule, and logically pursuing that reason, in order to eliminate the distinction, one is left with a rule of reason lying somewhere between passing the ammunition and mere moral or political support.

---

121. *See* Address by Maj. Gen. Gilbert L. Myers (U.S.A.F., Ret.), Air Force Ass'n Symposium, Mar. 17, 1967, in AIR FORCE AND SPACE DIGEST, May 1967, at 74, 78.

122. *See, e.g.,* 2 L. OPPENHEIM, INTERNATIONAL LAW 78 (2d ed. 1912).

123. C. FENWICK, *supra* note 13, at 657. The United States Army has been accused of obliterating the distinction. *See* N.Y. Times, July 3, 1970, at 5, col. 1 (defense argument in Mylai prosecution).

124. M. GREENSPAN, *supra* note 11, at 338-40.

125. McDOUGAL & FELICIANO, *supra* note 13, at 580-81.

126. *Cf.* N.Y. Times, Dec. 3, 1967, at 2, col. 4 (dispatch after visit to North Vietnam).

127. *See generally* J. SPAIGHT, *supra* note 12, at 45-47.

128. *See* McDOUGAL & FELICIANO 581-82.

129. Shimoda v. Japan, *supra* note 75, at 341-42.

A rule of reason is not unheard of in the legal profession. Nor is it unreasonable to expect reasonable interpretation and action based thereon.

B. *Traditional Military Targets*

The celebrated remark of General Curtis LeMay that an opponent should be bombed back into the Stone Age did not represent a novel strategy. Indeed it was said by Grotius and his disciples that the law of nations permitted destruction of all classes of property, not only fortifications and harbors, but cities, men, ships, crops, and even sacred buildings because of the mere possibility of conversion to war use.[130] The permission for widespread destruction, received early modification in the doctrines of necessity[131] and utility[132] and in the beginnings of an imperfect or limited war concept.[133] When General Sherman burned much of Atlanta he defended it on military logistics grounds.[134] The German war code permitting virtually all means was justified on the grounds of seeking early termination to wars.[135] Additional unlimited destruction is condemned in the interest of humanity; "war-stricken peoples should not be reduced to a condition of barbarism or savagery, but should, on the contrary, be enabled to resume the normal processes of peaceful life as soon as possible."[136] Whatever the reason, the Grotius-LeMay doctrines of unlimited destruction are not acceptable. Potential targets must be identified as having military value or value in terms of the objectives of the war. Both means and targets are limited. In today's technological world, human and computerized operations analysis will select them. Economists, mathematicians, and military men combine to determine which targets mean the most to an enemy war effort, which are to be attacked, in what order, and at what rate.[137] It is difficult to conceive of targeting going so far down the necessity ladder so as to legitimize reduction to the Stone Age.

Targets that are capable of being used for military purposes are generally conceded to be legitimate military targets.[138] The line between pos-

---

130. *See* GROTIUS *468-69; C. VAN BYNKERSHOEK, *supra* note 10, at 26.
131. *See* T. RUTHERFORTH, *supra* note 17, at 525: "If this is necessary to be done, in order to bring about the just ends of war, it lawfully may be done; but not otherwise."
132. *Cf.* P. BORDWELL, *supra* note 29, at 8: Although armies were slaughtered on both sides by the ancient Hindus, husbandmen, crops, trees, and plants were spared.
133. *Cf.* H. HALLECK, *supra* note 52, at 156: As in the hostilities authorized by the United States against France in 1798, only certain places, persons, or things are involved.
134. *See* P. BORDWELL, *supra* note 29, at 77.
135. *See id.* at 115.
136. J. MOORE, *supra* note 36, at 5.
137. *See generally* Schriever, *Systems Analysis,* AIR FORCE AND SPACE DIGEST, May 1968, at 57.
138. *See, e.g.,* art. 2 of the Hague Convention relating to bombardment by naval forces which permitted attacks on dry docks, repair plants, and stores of coal and fuel. J. HALL, *supra* note 20, at 79. The same is true of targeting railways, lines of communication, and bridges. *Cf.* Garner, *supra* note 39, at 27.

sible and probable military use is one for the operations analyst in terms of cost effectiveness and for the lawyers in terms of proportionality. Furthermore it may not be correct to assert that because railways, for example, are capable of military use, railway stations are legitimate targets.[139] The effective use of available power is inevitably tied to such questions. In a contemporary context, if military structures, boats, bridges, and means of transportation are legitimate military targets it may not be effective to target huts, sampans, bamboo foot bridges, and pack animals.[140] But it is legal. It may be effective to strike thermal power plants and chemical plants as a general proposition, but if the chief product of the chemical plant is fertilizer it is neither effective nor legal.[141] Because bridges made of bamboo are legitimate military targets, is it legitimate to bomb schools where bamboo handicraft is taught?[142] Assuming proper intelligence and identification it may be most effective to do so. If the soldier, his gun, the ammunition dump, the driver and the truck transporting the ammunition from the dump are military targets, so are the weapons and their means of transport at all stages of preparation. If the factories and the men who make the weapons are legitimate targets, are not the industrial areas and services supplying the factory permissibly targetable? It would seem so.[143] Then why is it not also legal to strike the chemical plant producing fertilizer, thus reducing the food supply available for the factory worker? The answer would appear to be that it is not legal because it is only marginally effective. The results of reducing the food supply will almost certainly be felt by others before the factory worker, if he will ever feel it; the results are not proportional to the injury inflicted.

The problem of drawing the line of impermissibility did not exist at the time when the laws of war relating to targets began to take shape. An understanding of the evolution of the historic concepts of fortified and defended places is, however, important in appreciating the reason for much of the confusion existing today in legal arguments concerning targets.

Great ritual surrounded the fortress, its seige, and its surrender in the Middle Ages, a time when land conquest was meaningless without conquest of the fort or castle.[144] As cannon and artillery fire became more effective and could converge on small fortified points, fortified areas were enlarged

139. Although all participants at the Washington Conference agreed that railway stations were military targets, the question is asked whether the relationship of a station to effective use of a railway line is so much greater than "a Cook's tourist agency or a railway ticket office in any part of a city or town" so as to legitimate its status as a military target. J. MOORE, *supra* note 36, at 199.

140. *Cf.* letter from a U.S. Air Force pilot in Vietnam partially reprinted in CLERGY AND LAYMEN CONCERNED ABOUT VIETNAM, *supra* note 16, at 212.

141. *Cf.* N.Y. Times, Mar. 24, 1968, at 8, col. 1. This assumes the illegitimacy of targeting food supplies. *But cf.* text at and following note 212 *infra*.

142. *Cf.* N.Y. Times, Apr. 17, 1968, at 3, col. 1.

143. For this reasoning see Saundby, *supra* note 53, at 53.

144. *See generally* M. KEEN, *supra* note 8, at 120-31.

to the size of small towns.[145] When a garrison was quartered within a town, the town was deemed fortified, and the homes of noncombatants became fair game lest immunity of the townspeople and of their homes would strengthen the ability of the military to survive.[146] Since there was no advantage to be gained from attacking civilian centers, it was reasonable for the code developed at the Brussels Congress of 1874 to permit sieges of "fortified places" but deny legitimacy to bombardment of "open, and undefended" towns and villages.[147]

The 1907 Hague Regulations for Land Warfare changed from a fortified to a defended-place concept and prohibited "attack or bombardment, by whatever means, of towns, villages, dwellings or buildings which are undefended . . . ."[148] Traditionally, an open town was one which could be entered without opposition, so that by analogy any place behind enemy lines was subject to attack.[149] Whether this was the reason for dropping the "open" concept is unclear, but the increased range of artillery probably had an effect on an extended defended-area concept.[150] In theory (and by World War I in practice), it was clear that a town need not actually be fortified or defended to become a permissible target; the presence of mines and a harbor, a combat force in occupation or transit, the provisioning of enemy troops, open resistance, or the presence of war material, depots, and public buildings was enough to effectively make the place constructively defended.[151]

Since a constructively defended place is a patent fiction, it might have been preferable to recognize the validity of the German concept that the only valid criterion is the value which the place possesses for the enemy in the existing situation.[152] There was legal movement in this direction when the Commission of Jurists to Consider and Report Upon the Revision of the Rules of Warfare drafted rules for aerial warfare. The defended-town test was dropped in favor of one which was concerned with the nature of the objective and the use which an enemy was currently making of the potential target.[153] Because the attempt to draft binding rules was abortive, conventional international law still speaks in the confused termi-

---

145. *See* McDougal & Feliciano 606; H. Nickerson, *supra* note 27, at 89.
146. *Cf.* J. Risley, *supra* note 4, at 116-17.
147. *See* McDougal & Feliciano 605; M. Royse, *supra* note 94, at 155.
148. Hague Regulations art. 25.
149. *See* M. Greenspan, *supra* note 11, at 332; Garner, *supra* note 39, at 27.
150. See McDougal & Feliciano 606.
151. *Cf.* J. Baker & H. Crocker, *supra* note 30, at 202; P. Bordwell, *supra* note 29, at 286; M. Greenspan, *supra* note 11, at 337; J. Hall, *supra* note 20, at 79; M. Royse, *supra* note 94, at 158. *But cf.* E. Edmonds & L. Oppenheim, *supra* note 45, at 34 for the technically correct thesis that the mere presence of supplies of value to an enemy, railways, communications, and bridges would not warrant bombardment of an undefended town. Other means would then be required to strike or neutralize the legitimate military targets.
152. German War Book 108, in J. Baker & H. Crocker, *supra* note 30, at 203.
153. *See generally* Comm'n of Jurists to Consider and Report Upon the Revision of the Rules of Warfare, General Report, Part II, Rules of Aerial Warfare (1924).

nology of defended and undefended places.[154] The purely fictional "constructive defended place" is an outgrowth of the permission to destroy military objectives in an undefended place when an army could not or did not want to occupy the place.[155] The Hague naval regulations echoed the permission and went further by permitting a commander to destroy a defended place entirely presumably because he could not occupy, get close enough, or take temporary possession of the place to destroy purely military objectives.[156] The naval permissions were too broad to legitimately meet a test which focuses on military objectives. The air rules, with the same problems of inability to occupy, spotlighted the objective but were militarily unrealistic in doing so. A functional legal approach to targeting probably can be spelled out only in terms of military necessity and proportionality. Lawyers and triers of fact who have long dealt with such terms as "reasonable," who have long balanced conflicting concepts, should not be bothered by judgments based on rules, the applicability of which can only be determined in a given factual setting. Failure to think in this way has too often caused failure of the rules of warfare. It is the real reason why the draft air rules were abortive. This need not be the case in the future as customary international law determines the legitimacy of military action. It need not be the case in future attempts at codification.

One of the more interesting examples of the progression of international legal codification and of attempts to interrelate necessity and proportionality in a targeting situation is in the restrictions concerned with religious, cultural, and medical institutions. Grotius had concluded that because sacred places are public and may be converted to war use they were not immunized from attack by the law of nations.[157] Yet when, during the War of 1812, public buildings were burned in Washington, widespread condemnation was heard.[158] The key to the condemnation was in the lack of even a purported military justification for the burning. This was implicitly recognized in the 1874 draft declaration of the Brussels Conference which called for sparing, whenever possible, public buildings not used for military purposes.[159] By the time of the 1907 Hague Conference, although public and private buildings within defended places could be attacked, a requirement was imposed to spare, whenever possible, buildings

154. *Cf.* Shimoda v. Japan, *supra* note 75, at 338-41.
155. *Cf.* M. ROYSE, *supra* note 94, at 163.
156. *See* The Hague Convention (IX) Respecting the Bombardment of Naval Forces in Time of War (1907); J. HALL, *supra* note 20, at 80; McDOUGAL & FELICIANO 607.
157. GROTIUS, *supra* note 52, at *468, *534. However, if the attacker was of the same belief as the attacked, *i.e.,* if they both believed in the same god despite differences in ritual, attack was illegal. Attacks by Jews upon the idols of Gentiles and by the Romans on the temple in Jerusalem were therefore legitimate. But the permission was restricted to a common respect for the dead, or in Grotian terms, a law of burials introduced by the law of nations. *Id.* at *469-70, *534.
158. P. BORDWELL, *supra* note 29, at 62-63.
159. Arts. 15-17. *See* J. RISLEY, *supra* note 4, at 117.

dedicated to public worship, art, science, or charity, in addition to historic places and hospitals, so long as they were not being used at the time for military purposes.[160] A duty to mark those places was imposed; but long-range artillery and night-flying aircraft would soon make most marking meaningless. Perhaps because artillery would be blind to such places in the vicinity of legitimate targets, the 1923 air rules contain the protection but remove the duty of marking in favor of optional lighting of such places or an optional cleared zone and notification of location.[161] The 1935 Pan-American International Treaty regarding Protection of Articles and Scientific Institutions and Historic Monuments contains the same general protection with the common caveat removing the protection when used for military purposes.[162]

The 1949 Geneva Convention took the approach of the Draft Air Rules, in providing for zones in accordance with agreements. Hospitals were to be situated as far as possible out of the way of combat areas.[163] Hospital zones and localities were to be free of attack and hospitals were to be made visible by day or night.[164] Problems presented by the absence of preagreed zones and radar bombing were not adequately met. The latest word in the area is the 1954 Hague Convention for Protection of Cultural Property in the Event of Armed Conflict: Cultural property is immune, except when military necessity prevents such immunity.[165] The necessity relates to actual use of the property, physical or tactical conditions of attack, and the capabilities and limitations of ordinance—a realistic approach to this anomalous targeting situation, an anomaly which would be removed by proper balancing of militarily necessary targeting with minimum incidental damage to nonmilitary targets. Such an approach would legitimize, for instance, the destruction of Monte Cassino in World War II and The Citadel at Hue in the Vietnam War, unless alternative means were available to neutralize military use of such institutions.

This varying standard for the institutions under discussion is also useful in judging targeting when concealment and dispersion measures are employed. Just as a nonpurposeful strike on a hospital located in a combat area is neither illegal nor criminal, communities in the area of retaliatory forces concealed and protected by hard cover will be hit, not as primary

---

160. Art. 26 of the Hague land regulations required notification before attack; art. 27 (and its companion art. 5 of the naval regulations) set forth this variable standard during warfare; and art. 56 provided for prosecution for wilful destruction during combat or after surrender. See P. BORDWELL, supra note 29, at 287-90; E. EDMONDS & L. OPPENHEIM, supra note 45, at 34-37, 94.

161. See T. BARCLAY, supra note 81, at 111; Comm'n of Jurists to Consider and Report Upon the Revision of the Rules of Warfare, supra note 153, at 28.

162. See U.S. DEP'T OF THE ARMY, supra note 14, at 57; M. GREENSPAN, supra note 11, at 343.

163. See U.S. DEP'T OF THE ARMY, supra note 14, at 257; M. GREENSPAN at 341-42.

164. M. GREENSPAN at 342, 347.

165. McDOUGAL & FELICIANO 605.

targets, but because it is not militarily feasible to insure direct hits on a military target even assuming knowledge of its exact location. If the approximate location is known and the best hardware is used, it is not an illegal indiscriminate attack when some nonmilitary targets are also struck. When factories are concealed in jungles, oil and gasolines dumps are hidden, and supplies are placed in populated areas, the fault lies with the side which so located the military target. There is no duty for one side to notify the enemy of the precise geographic coordinates of military resources; on the other hand, there is no duty for the opposing forces to withhold attack.[166] The question at all times is one of balancing military advantage with incidental damage. If the military target is important enough, attack is legal. If a prosecution for the action is forthcoming it should be directed at he who placed the military target in a populated area. Given a situation of continuing force and violence, the legal community must be sophisticated enough to impose realistic standards and constraints.

C. *Incidental Damage*

The concept of permissible incidental damage is an old one. Early naturalists concerned with just and unjust wars recognized that when a nation was punished in accordance with the law of nations, innocent members of the punished nation would suffer. But since this only resulted from their accidental connection with that nation, it was not an individual punishment impermissibly imposed by the law of nations. Although waging a just war, there was no right to kill innocent subjects not responsible for the unjust war which was being opposed. There were three exceptions: When necessary for defense; when the opponent intended not to spare lives (itself an unjust act releasing all the fury of the law of nature by the victim nation); and when not purposeful.[167] The first exception presents a problem of determining just what distinguishes the defensive from the offensive.[168] The second exception would balance legitimacy of response against the means of warfare chosen by the initiators of that warfare. Thus deliberate killing of innocent persons, as carried out by guerrilla terrorists, would open the door wide to all methods of warfare and types of weapons. The difficulty here is that other restraints will and

---

166. *But cf.* LIFE, Apr. 12, 1968, at 39 for reconnaissance photographs identifying fuel oil, trucks, and other war supplies supposedly immune from United States attack because of the location in populated areas of North Vietnam. Aside from the question of the legitimacy of bombing North Vietnam, no rule of customary or conventional international law prohibits attacking populated areas when military targets are located therein. The Department of Defense ruled, nevertheless, that stockpiled material could not be struck until moved from the cities. Sharp, *We Could Have Won in Vietnam Long Ago*, READER'S DIGEST, May 1969, at 118, 122 (author former Commander-in-Chief, Pacific).
167. *See* GROTIUS *421; T. RUTHERFORTH, *supra* note 17, at 519.
168. *See* text at note 54 *supra*.

should operate to prevent unlimited warfare.[169] The third exception is seen over and over in the laws of war. It must, therefore, be determined whether a legitimate attack with incidental damage to nonmilitary elements loses its original legitimacy.

If inevitably and almost invariably nonmilitary casualties will occur in striking a military target, it may be that alternative means of seeking an objective should be required. Such a requirement has not appeared, however, in the accepted laws of war. A more common modern approach is seen in the same Hague rules for naval warfare which have been characterized as being overly permissive;[170] the naval commander is cautioned to take care to do as little damage as possible to nonmilitary objectives. Even minor cautionary admonitions were not apparently characteristic of an earlier day. More common were broad approvals given to naval and land commanders who recognized danger to noncombatants in a projected course of action. Thus a pirate ship could be bombarded although it was known to contain women, children, and other innocent persons; in a seige, killing of noncombatants was a chance of war legally excusable under natural law theory.[171] It was different, however, if there was an opportunity to obtain the lawful purposes of war without endangering noncombatants.[172] At that point such killings became illegal. This express stamp of illegality for failure to pursue an alternative means towards an objective has been lost to the formal laws of war for some two centuries.

Such illegality may perhaps have been implied in the Hague land regulations which forbade destruction of an enemy's property unless "imperatively demanded by the necessities of war."[173] More usual, however, has been the distinction drawn between deliberate and accidental killing of innocent persons, without regard to alternatives. If noncombatants are killed during bombardment "a regrettable incident has taken place, but no violation of the laws of war has been committed."[174] Although indiscriminate bombardment is not permitted under such a standard, incidental nonmilitary damage is not illegal.[175] Saturation bombing, which will certainly hit nonmilitary targets, is by definition not indiscriminate because the target is confined to a particular area and the purpose is to destroy the military objectives; all other destruction is thus incidental and, if

---

169. These include treaties, world opinion, reprisal, and retaliation.

170. *See* text at note 156 *supra.*

171. *See* GROTIUS *°425; T. RUTHERFORTH, supra* note 17, at 522.

172. T. RUTHERFORTH, *supra* note 17, at 522.

173. Art. 23(g). The same implication was apparently present in the undefended place concept of the same regulation which expressly forbade attack on such places despite the presence of military targets. The constructive defended place, however, eliminated any implicit requirement to use other means of neutralizing military elements in an undefended place. *Compare* E. EDMONDS & L. OPPENHEIM, *supra* note 45, at 34 *with* text at notes 148, 151 *supra.*

174. T. LAWRENCE, *supra* note 60, at 417, in J. BAKER & H. CROCKER, supra note 30, at 206.

175. *Cf.* Shimoda v. Japan, *supra* note 75, at 340; M. GREENSPAN, *supra* note 11, at 337 (citing British Manual of Military Law).

not disproportionate, is legal.

When Grotius was attempting to temper his harsh natural law theories with his own apparent softer sensibilities, he posited a "law of love" springing from a duty imposed by religion, morality, mercy, and humanity which proscribed the foreseeable taking of life, especially when only property was at stake.[176] Scruples against the taking of life happily still remain in the conduct of wars fought by civilized nations, that is, by those nations whose people have been exposed to the Christian ethic and whose leaders recognize the merit in some restraints on warfare. Thus at the outbreak of World War II, the Royal Air Force was not allowed to attack German warships in docks or at quay sides, lest civilian casualties be caused[177] and in Vietnam there is clear evidence that despite the presence of military arms, trucks, and supplies, populated areas are not bombed.[178]

A legal assessment of such forebearance, in addition to the question of proportionality, should consider the possibility of alternative means for striking military objectives located in and near populated areas. Translating this into the international law of war, a requirement would be imposed for the use of direct fire weapons such as tanks, cannon, and other forms of mobile artillery when possible and effective, which, as opposed to bombs, are far more discriminating. In the broader context of all warfare, the International Committee of the Red Cross has in fact moved in a direction of such a requirement in draft rules which seek to minimize ancillary destruction by making the person responsible for ordering an attack select the means of attack which involves the least danger for the civilian population.[179] If adopted, this is a step forward from the military lifesaving theory most strongly expressed by the Germans but implicitly adopted by many other combatant nations:

> In the repression of infamy, human lives cannot be spared, and if isolated houses, flourishing villages and even entire towns are annihilated, that is regrettable but it must not excite ill-timed sentimentality. All this must not in our eyes weigh as much as the life of a single one of our brave soldiers.[180]

So it was that in a town called Ben Tre in South Vietnam in 1968, when the Viet Cong had nearly the whole town under their control, the South Vietnamese defenders were pinned down in their barracks, and both the United States advisory compound and the provincial tactical operations center were in danger of being overrun, 45 percent of the town was

---

176. *See* GROTIUS *477, *519.

177. Saundby, *supra* note 53, at 53.

178. *See* photographs in LIFE, Apr. 12, 1968, at 39. Another reason for non-bombardment may, of course, be the possibility of disproportionate civilian casualties relative to the target's military value, a legal factor previously discussed.

179. *See* Mallison, *supra* note 107, at 337 (citing art. 8(a) of the 1956 draft rules).

180. Garner, *supra* note 39, at 9 (quoting Gen. von Bissing).

destroyed, over 500 civilians were killed, and an unnamed American major said: "It became necessary to destroy the town to save it."[181] If the situation repeated itself artillery and air strikes would again be used against Ben Tre; heavy bombs, aircraft rockets, naval gunfire, napalm, and all the usually destructive ground weapons from howitzers to tank guns will continue to be used in battles for all the cities.[182] There are lessons and many questions for the international law of war in the ruins and death certificates of these towns. Given tactics of an enemy which involve innocent people, cannot a technologically sophisticated world do better than sheer destructive firepower? If it is important to win the hearts and minds of people, does it make sense to blow up cities in order to defend them? The questions are not new. Two thousand years ago Livy asked: "What sort of a policy is it, to destroy the things the possession of which is at stake, and to leave for himself nothing except the war?"[183] And hearken to Grotius:

> Seeking to win your country you destroy it;
> To make it yours, you wish to make it nothing;
> Your cause is harmed by this, with hostile arms
> You burn the land, lay low the ripened crops,
> And terror spread.
> Through all the fields. No one so wastes his own
> What you bid ruin with fire, with sword to reap,
> You hold to be another's.[184]

If it is not another's, there must be a better way. If it is another's, the questions must be rephrased. What about an enemy's nonmilitary institutions; are they legitimate targets?

D.   An Enemy's Economy

There is extant a nation-in-arms theory which plays havoc with a conventional target selection process. The theory is not a new one. By the time of the Middle Ages, immunities for certain classes of noncombatants, for example, were dead letters for those members of the class who gave aid and countenance to their sovereign in time of war.[185] Later the goods of the people were made liable for the misdeeds of their rulers

---

181. See N.Y. Times, Feb. 14, 1968, at 61, col. 5; id., Mar. 15, 1968, at 3, col. 2; TIME, Feb. 16, 1968, at 34.

182. Cf. N.Y. Times, Mar. 15, 1968, at 3, col. 2; Wicker, In the Nation, id., Feb. 20, 1968.

183. See GROTIUS *532. Compare the comment on the policy of Washington and Saigon to rely on firepower to defend the cities: "With that they can destroy South Vietnam, but they can never save it from Communism, or anything else." Wicker, supra note 182.

184. GROTIUS *532.

185. Compare text at note 108 supra with M. KEEN, supra note 8, at 190.

under principles of convenience and suretyship; wars of peoples versus peoples were enshrined as legitimate by the Grotian law of nations.[186] By 1737, Van Bynkershoek could say that "[w]e make war because we think that our enemy, by the injury that he has done us, has merited the destruction of himself and of all his adherents"; and Vattel in 1758 would term the subjects of the enemy state individually enemies.[187]

Eventually a split developed between Anglo-American theory holding to the Grotius-Vattel theory and continental jurists, like Rousseau, who viewed war as "a relation between states in which individuals are enemies only accidentally, not as men or even as citizens, but simply as soldiers."[188] This latter view, developed about the turn of the 19th century, has been proclaimed as inconsistent with practice and logic.[189] Yet the 1863 Instructions for the Government of Armies of the United States in the Field, while declaring "[t]he citizen or native of a hostile country is thus an enemy, as one of the constituents of the hostile state or nation, and as such is subjected to the hardships of the war," acknowledged "the distinction between the private individual belonging to a hostile country, and the hostile country itself, with its men in arms . . . . [T]he unarmed citizen is to be spared in person, property and honor as much as the exigencies of war will admit."[190] Although the theoretical construct differed from that put forth by Rousseau, practice ought not have been far apart. Simply put, Rousseau posited a relation of enmity in two instances only: Between two states at war with one another and between each state "and those subjects of the other whom for the purpose of the war it may be necessary to affect by acts of force, and so far only as it is necessary so to affect them . . . ."[191]

The difficulty was that some theoreticians and strategists were not willing to accept the apparent bridge presented by tempering terms seeking to spare the nonmilitary enemy except as absolutely necessary. At the turn of the 20th century, one writer, for example, found the Rousseau idea improper in a day when wars had been transformed from contests between princes into national struggles in which the people themselves are

---

186. See GROTIUS *443-44, *447. Support for such wars was found in the form of early declarations of war: "I declare and make war upon the peoples of the ancient Latins and upon the men of the ancient Latins"; "Let him be an enemy, and also those who are within his defences." Id. at *444.

187. C. VAN BYNKERSHOEK, supra note 10, at 2; see C. FENWICK, supra note 13, at 657.

188. Turlington, Treatment of Enemy Private Property in the United States Before the World War, 22 A.J.I.L. 270 (1928); H. BRIGGS, THE LAW OF NATIONS 1013 (2d ed. 1952).

189. C. FENWICK, supra note 13, at 656.

190. General Orders, No. 100 (Lieber's Code) arts. 21, 22, in H. BRIGGS, supra note 188, at 1014.

191. See 2 J. WESTLAKE, INTERNATIONAL LAW 38 (1907), in P. BORDWELL, supra note 29, at 5.

parties.[192] Another, finding that a state apart from individuals does not exist, termed the Rousseau doctrine an "objectionable fiction" which would lead to wholesale slaughters between armies and fleets deprived of any other weapon.[193] Some support in practice for these theses could have been drawn from more than a hundred years of wartime experience. Great Britain, during the American Revolution, had put forth the rule that "when, in war, one is not able to destroy the adverse party or to lead him to reason without reducing his country to distress, it is permitted to carry distress into his country . . . ."[194] From the French Revolution, von Clausewitz drew the lesson that when war becomes an affair of a people, every one of whom regards himself as a citizen of the state, conventional restrictions on warfare cannot exist.[195] Even Chancellor Kent can be cited for the proposition that with a declaration of war, the whole nation has declared war, and the subjects of one nation are the enemies of the other.[196]

Even assuming the validity of all of these objections to Rousseau's theory and further assuming that all members of an enemy nation may be treated as enemies, one cannot target the enemy populace without distinction because, as we have seen, the only use of force that is lawful, is that which is necessary. Furthermore, the social contract binding members of a society and to the corporate body cannot, in the abstract and lacking military necessity and proportionality, be treated as sufficient to warrant the use of force against the members of that society or even against the society itself.[197] The social contract, the consequent duties to assist and obey despite individual reservations, and the legal hostility of non-combatant enemy nationals do not excuse nonlenient treatment of those of the enemy who do not engage in hostile acts.[198]

But what does one say about sea blockade, an apparently legal and internationally recognized method of sea warfare, which seeks to starve an enemy nation into submission. Especially, one must wonder how a blockade can be justified as legal when, because the armed forces and essential workers must be fed and clothed, those who suffer most are women, children, the infirm, and the aged. Why, when the British blockade of Germany in World War I caused the death of far more civilians than died in all air attacks on Britain in both world wars, were the crews of

---

192. P. BORDWELL, *supra* note 29, at 4. Bordwell was bothered that General Sherman's march to the sea, which was designed to bring war home to the Georgians, would have been outlawed by the Rousseau theory unless it had a direct military purpose. *Id.*

193. J. RISLEY, *supra* note 4, at 74, 76. Risley foresaw, for instance, an inability to cripple an enemy's commerce. *Id.* at 76.

194. *See* P. BORDWELL, *supra* note 29, at 50.

195. *See* 3 C. VON CLAUSEWITZ, *supra* note 28, at 100-03.

196. *See* J. RISLEY, *supra* note 4, at 75.

197. *Cf.* T. RUTHERFORTH, *supra* note 17, at 518, 521.

198. *See* T. BARCLAY, *supra* note 81, at 20; H. HALLECK, *supra* note 52, at 160, 172; *cf.* C. FENWICK, *supra* note 13, at 657.

German zeppelins in that first war castigated as baby-killers?[199] Why did the Franco-German War of 1870 sanction by usage the bombardment of houses during a siege in order to induce surrender?[200] Why indeed, when such attempts to induce surrender are not only cruel and unnecessary, but more often than not are unsuccessful? Why stamp sea blockade as legal by custom when it is only questionably necessary, the harm to noncombatants is out of all proportion to the military results achieved, and the political results are counter-productive?

There are some who would say that when a whole nation is organized for war the only true noncombatants are those who are physically unable to contribute anything to the national resources. If such were the case, as John Basset Moore observed, one would have reverted "to conditions abhorrent to every man who cares for law, or for those elementary considerations of humanity the observance of which law is intended to assure."[201] Such a reversion would mean that since armies move on their bellies, "the most dangerous fighter is the tiller of the soil" a concept directly contrary to the law of even the harsh Middle Ages when the producer of foodstuffs was off-limits as a target.[202] To permit such an extension of a technical state of enmity, on the theory that the founders of international law did not realize that all national activities and resources contribute to the ability to wage war, would be a delusion. On the contrary, besides seeing "that extirpatory methods were as impracticable and wasteful as they were brutal and brutalizing, . . . they were [and are] the spokesmen of a loftier conception of the destiny and rights of man and of a more humane spirit."[203] It is neither necessary nor wise for international law to surrender the world to a different, grotesquely logical view. Which nonmilitary institutions are permissible targets under a concept which recognizes the contribution of an enemy people to the war effort but at the same time is limited by the necessity-proportionality-humanity spectrum?

Certainly, as Grotius said, a lack of money and crops may cause a war to diminish as much as abundance causes it to flourish.[204] But there is no right to weaken the resources of an enemy unless it is necessary to the ends of war to do so. Devastation which brings the end to war in the shortest time may in fact hinder attainment of reconciliation and the achievement of a lasting peace, presumably a goal of any war. It may be that in theory the Germans were correct in 1890 when they promoted the targeting of an enemy's resources, his finances, railroads, provisions, and prestige.[205] Naval strategists could certainly approve such targeting. Rec-

---

199. *See* Saundby, *supra* note 53, at 50.
200. *See* W. HALL, *supra* note 90, at 556, 557, in J. BAKER & H. CROCKER, *supra* note 30, at 199.
201. J. MOORE, *supra* note 36, at x.
202. *Compare id.* at xi *with* text at notes 108-10 *supra*.
203. J. MOORE, *supra* note 36, at 13.
204. GROTIUS *531.
205. *See* J. GARNER, *supra* note 11, at 280.

ognizing that it was necessary to force submission without intimidation or ill-treatment of the civilian population, sea blockade and capture at sea were designed to strangle the whole industrial life of an enemy.[206] If this sort of slow strangulation is less inhuman than other alternatives, it would, under our previously posited criteria, be legal.

Using somewhat different criteria, Churchill, when faced with the evils that gas chambers posed for humanity, proclaimed that the British goal of breaking the German economy and scientific power was less evil;[207] the result was target-area bombing. German industry was in a small area, especially in the Ruhr Valley, heavily defended, concealed, and camouflaged. The bombs fell generally in the location of the objectives: Armament and associated factories in the widest sense, oil production, and transportation. There was no real attempt to separate military targets from more general targets. In a nation geared for war, with military factories interspersed and unidentifiable, such targeting and bombing cannot be called illegal. This appraisal is entirely apart from the relative evils of Nazi practices. Appraisals of a quantum of evil to justify a given strategy are too subjective and emotive to be the basis for definitive legal criteria. Military relevance and target placement are, however, viable criteria.

Generally. the economy will become an incidental victim of war regardless of purposeful targeting. One need only look at Vietnam. High prices, declining tax receipts, rising government expenditures, fearful businessmen, and transportation problems plague South Vietnam. Most of this is probably incidental to military action. In North Vietnam, of the economic component, only the electric power system, steel industry, and portions of the transportation system were deemed key targets for aerial attack. These can probably be classified as military targets. But the result when the North was being bombed was a marked decrease in exports and increase in imports, port congestion, and generally such serious burdens on the economy and transportation that feeding and supplying both the civilian population and the armed forces were becoming problems. In addition, the production of cement, coal, fertilizer, chemicals, and paper were drastically reduced by direct air strikes. The effect on food and supplies should probably be called incidental to military operations and not an illegitimately achieved result. Striking factories with nonmilitary products is legal if the economy is a permissible target. Under customary international law it is. Whether it is a necessary, proportional, and cost-effective target is an entirely separate question.

---

206. See J. Hall, supra note 20, at 47-48. This is not the same sort of blockade intended to starve an enemy nation, although if passage of food supplies were not permitted, the result would be the same.
207. See J. Spaight, supra note 12, at 47; see generally M. Greenspan, supra note 11, at 335-39.

E. *An Enemy's Means of Sustenance*

Targeting the means of sustenance of any enemy presents some of the same problems. Assuming the economy itself to be either a marginal or nonnecessary, disproportional and noncost-effective target, legitimacy will hinge on the identification of pure or at least less marginal military targets. The dilemma in pursuit of such an identification is apparent in the permission given by the United States to its troops "to destroy . . . crops intended solely for consumption by the armed forces (if that fact can be determined)."[208] This qualified permission is an old one in the laws of war. Destruction of the forage and provisions of an enemy force, and even of standing crops when directly related to belligerent operations, have long been approved, but vines and fruit trees, for example, have always been impermissible targets.[209] The evident principle of nondestruction, that is, of food and crops not intended for the armed forces and of the ability of the land to provide food in the future, should be treated against past and present practice.

Deliberate crop destruction in South Vietnam is a convenient jumping-off place for such a test. While only a small part of the American defoliation program and generally confined to isolated areas away from thickly populated areas, rice crops are destroyed when they are significant sources of food difficult for the Viet Cong to replace and when elements loyal to the Republic of Vietnam are unable to move in for the harvest.[210] Granted that it is permissible to destroy a belligerent's morale and induce his surrender by making him hungry and even threatening his starvation by cutting off the supply of food and water,[211] the sad truth is that the civilian is the more usual victim of attempts to use starvation as a weapon against troops while little damage is done to the military. If utilitarianism is to be a criterion in legal limits on warfare, which is suggested by legal tests of necessity and proportionality and by military considerations of cost-effectiveness, targeting of food crops on the possibility or even probability of use by combatants is illegal. Certainty and immediacy of use would be required.

This conclusion is reinforced by the history of the treatment of food

---

208. U.S. DEP'T OF THE ARMY, *supra* note 14, ¶ 37. The words omitted referred to "chemical or bacterial agents harmless to man" but the principle is broader than the agency of destruction.

209. *See* H. HALLECK, *supra* note 52, at 212; J. RISLEY, *supra* note 4, at 116; T. RUTHERFORTH, *supra* note 17, at 525.

210. *See* Pond, Christian Science Monitor, Nov. 29, 1967, in CLERGY AND LAYMEN CONCERNED ABOUT VIETNAM, *supra* note 16, at 295. Another factor mentioned was the diversion of guerrilla manpower "from shooting to toting rice." *Id.*

211. *Cf.* H. WHEATON, ELEMENTS OF INTERNATIONAL LAW 428 n.166 (8th ed. Dana 1866), in J. BAKER & H. CROCKER, *supra* note 30, at 137. *See also* N.Y. Times, Aug. 11, 1966, in CLERGY AND LAYMEN CONCERNED ABOUT VIETNAM, *supra* note 14, at 301 for one account of American strategy regarding food of enemy troops.

as contraband for purposes of blockade.[212] It was in 1793 that Great Britain stopped vessels bound for France with grain, flour, or meal because of "the unusual mode of war employed by the enemy himself, in having armed almost the whole laboring class of the French nation . . . ."[213] In the United States, Thomas Jefferson and Benjamin Franklin sought to immunize those who live in peace, despite a nation being in arms, by declaring these basics for food production not contraband. The unsuccessful American attempt was made despite the realization that foodstuffs imported into a belligerent country could be immediately consumed by the military. It was not until 1900 that Lord Robert Salisbury, the prime minister and foreign minister of England, indicated that foodstuffs should be deemed contraband only if it could be shown that they were actually destined for military forces, not merely capable of such use, despite the "fancied belligerent right to seize whatever might possibly be useful to the enemy for purposes of war."[214]

But when the Salisbury compromise rule was put into multipartite legal form in the 1909 Declaration of London concerning the Laws of Naval War, foodstuffs, because susceptible of use in war, emerged as conditional contraband.[215] Because the condition was not determinable in a meaningful way, the British blockade of Germany from 1914 to 1918 resulted, as was perhaps intended, in mass starvation.[216] The British justification of such action was over a century old. Once again as in the action against Napoleon, it was the nation-in-arms theory: "The reason for drawing a distinction between foodstuffs intended for the civilian population and those for the armed forces . . . disappears . . . [i]n any country in which there exists such tremendous organizations for war . . . ."[217] The theory and the strategy of starvation, however, will not stand the test of legality: During the 1870-1871 siege of Paris, the garrison held while children died by the thousands; during the World War I blockade, the armies of the Central Powers operated unimpeded while deficiency diseases and starvation multiplied among German and Austrian children; and while Leningrad held in 1941-1942, deaths from starvation rose to 9,000 per day, mainly among the children and elderly.[218] The Biafran

---

212. See N.Y. Times, Feb. 15, 1970, § 4, at 13, col. 1 for this historical argument by Jean Mayer, prof. of nutrition at Harvard Univ. and Chmn., White House Conference on Food, Nutrition, and Health.

213. J. Moore, supra note 36, at 29. See generally id. at 29-32. See also J. Risley, supra note 4, at 280-302 (fearing starvation of British, arguments for repudiating 1856 Declaration of Paris). For American attempts to widen the immunities surrounding the Declaration of Paris, which put a stamp of approval on food as contraband, see text at notes 109-10.

214. J. Moore, supra note 36, at 31.

215. Art. 24. T. Barclay, supra note 81, at 202.

216. See H. Nickerson, supra note 27, at 122; cf. text at note 199 supra.

217. British Note of Feb. 10, 1915, to the United States in H. Briggs supra note 188, at 1014.

218. Mayer & Sidel, Crop Destruction in South Vietnam, 83 The Christian Century 823 (1966).

tragedy is a repeat of the same story; arms, not starvation, won for Nigeria.

The historical parallels enable us to give a legal response to contemporary proposals to attack the dike system of the Red River in North Vietnam so as to flood the rice fields and hamper internal distribution of vitally needed food. It is said that "[a]ttack or even the threat of attack on these water systems could measure the war's duration in months instead of years"; though many drown or die of starvation, "we could do what we always do—move on and feed the people and help to rebuild." This is supposedly valid since the enemy has not hesitated to destroy Allied food supplies.[219] Although certainly some dikes must have been hit and attacks on roads and other military targets have disrupted the production and distribution of food, there is a great gulf of legitimacy between incidental damage while striking in a proportional manner at a militarily necessary target and a purposeful strike at the means of feeding the nation.[220] Purposeful destruction of crops and intentional interference with a nation's food supply, historically ineffective, inhumane, and disproportional must be held to be presumptively impermissible.

F. *The Enemy Government and Its Loyalty Structure*

The governmental processes of an enemy, that is, the force behind belligerent operations, arguably should be subject to destruction. Assuming the seat of government to be centered at a given place, why, for example, ought not the Capitol or the Kremlin be targetable, always assuming the end to be gained is not disproportionate to incidental damage and destruction. Yet early immunities, deriving from the need to restrict force to those elements of an enemy which are necessary for continued resistance, were granted to the sovereign, his family and members of the civil government.[221] Immunity for the governmental processes, at least when only tangential to the purposes of armed action, may still be with us. The governmental structure of North Vietnam, for example, was excluded as a military target.[222] The emperor's palace in Japan was never targeted in World War II. But if a war room were operable from the basement of the White House, the reason for striking the headquarters of any military command would apply to the White House as well. This does not mean that the person of the President is important. It is not. It is true, of course,

---

219. For respective statements see Robinson, *Washington Report*, Feb. 19, 1968, in AIR FORCE AND SPACE DIGEST, Apr. 1968, at 57; PARADE, Nov. 3, 1968, at 2 (quoting Sen. Goldwater); N.Y. Times, Mar. 14, 1968, at 87, cols. 2-3 (Howard K. Smith, television commentator).

220. *Compare* N.Y. Times, May 6, 1967 at 3, col. 1 (Pentagon denial of deliberate targeting) *with id.* Dec. 3, 1967, at 2, col. 4 and May 14, 1968, at 18, col. 5 (recognizing incidental effect).

221. *See* J. BAKER & H. CROCKER, *supra* note 30, at 114.

222. *See* Hawkins, *An Approach to Issues of International Law Raised by United States Actions in Vietnam*, AM. SOC'Y OF INT'L LAW, THE VIETNAM WAR AND INTERNATIONAL LAW 163, 192 n.124 (quoting Sec'y of State Dean Rusk).

that if the President and many in the chain of succession could be removed from the active scene, the contingent military action plans for such an eventuality could eventually run downhill into disarray. On the other hand, if military reaction were swift and certain, or even swift and uncertain, there is some advantage to not eliminating what may be the only restraint in the system. Legitimacy for striking the heart of government is not a strictly legal matter. If the leaders of a nation can be put on trial for criminal action, one cannot condemn targeting them. In a wartime situation the political and military realities and reactions will take precedence.

Targeting the loyalty of the people to governmental authority must be judged by other criteria. There was a time when the law of war accepted rape and death without quarter as just for the inhabitants of a town which refused to surrender at siege, the theory being that the threat of such a possibility would induce the leaders to surrender.[223] It often did not work, perhaps because obedience to a demand for surrender was treasonable. The question is whether things have changed now, so as to make illegitimate, practices which are of doubtful efficacy and which seem so opposed to reason and morality. Two well-known international lawyers who prepared a manual for British army officers earlier this century, handling this question without facing the emotive practices of rape and murder, thought not: "On the contrary, destruction of private and public buildings by bombardment has always been, and still is, considered lawful, as it is one of the means to impress upon the local authorities the advisability of surrender."[224]

It was the development of modern weaponry and improved artillery that made the theory of intimidation underlying statements such as this attainable; bombardment for a psychological reason, the undermining of the nation's morale, had become respectable. Although at first generally condemned, the German *Kriegsbraugh im Landkriege* of 1902 proclaimed as legitimate the destruction of the spiritual power of the enemy through destruction of private property, terrorization of inhabitants, and bombardment without notice.[225] Demoralization by aerial bombing was accepted in World War I but the equipment was not yet good enough to be effective.[226]

By the end of the Second World War, however, morale had become by practice a permissible target. In such targeting, the stress is put on the fear of death or of death for a worthless or lost cause.[227] The area bombing of World War II was used to attack the collective will to fight, perhaps even more so than it was used to hit military and industrial complexes. Although the Casablanca Conference of 1943 declared the primary purpose

223.   *See generally* M. KEEN, *supra* note 8, at 120-24.
224.   E. EDMONDS & L. OPPENHEIM, *supra* note 45, at 34.
225.   *See* J. GARNER, *supra* note 11, at 4.
226.   M. ROYSE, *supra* note 94, at 192.
227.   McDOUGAL & FELICIANO, *supra* note 13, at 613.

of the air war against Germany to be "the progressive destruction and dislocation of the German military, industrial, and economic system, and the undermining of the morale of the German people to a point where their capacity for *armed* resistance is fatally weakened,"[228] there are indications of a broader purpose. The United States Strategic Bombing Survey points out that 23.7 percent of the tonnage dropped on Europe in urban raids was dispensed at night, over large cities, bringing destruction over large areas rather than to specific plants or installations. The survey then adds that this tonnage was "intended primarily to destroy morale, particularly that of the *industrial* worker."[229] The picture of the Allied philosophy is completed by noting that the preponderant purpose of the B-29 fire raids on Japan was to "secure the heaviest possible morale and shock effect by widespread attack upon the Japanese civilian population."[230]

It may be that striking at morale is merely another form of permissible psychological warfare differing only in degree from luring enemy soldiers to desertion by radio broadcasts or seeking information through rewards to children. The trouble is that while targeting morale aims at a political result, a loss of morale may not affect politics but may in fact have the reverse effect of causing more support for the government until the point is reached when only survival matters. At that point, it no longer remains possible to influence a government. If there is something wrong with the concept it probably lies in its failure to meet the requirements of the necessity-humanity continuum. Furthermore, it is not possible to separate the quasi-combatant from a genuine civilian for morale purposes.[231] If it is permissible to violently attack the morale of war workers, it may be that the best way to do so is to kill his family, who are genuine civilians. On the other hand, once deprived of his family and with nothing to lose, will he in fact work even harder against his enemy and make conquest more difficult?

The truth that moderation in war will deprive an enemy of a great weapon, despair, has been recognized for centuries.[232] When the victim loses all he possesses, he becomes an apostle of revenge and a new energy is put into the struggle. If frightfulness and terror are not to boomerang, an overwhelming, instantaneous success must result. Were this not so, if the will could be broken by terror attacks on nonmilitary elements of the nation, if rapid capitulation by the decision makers would follow, one could argue that such strategy is more merciful than a longer war.

---

228. *See id.* at 654.
229. *Id.*
230. *Id.*
231. *See generally id.* at 657-59.
232. *See* GROTIUS *535-36. Grotius cites Livy's account of the capture of Rome by the Gauls during which the Gauls decided not to burn all the houses down in order that what remained might serve as a pledge to break the morale of the Roman people. He compares this with the avarice of Hannibal which alienated all without military advantage.

However, not only is this not provable, it is probable that wars are lengthened and made more inhumane by brutalizing tactics.[233] The definitive proclamation between the world wars that "air raids conducted merely for the purpose of spreading panic and undermining the morale of the civil population have no sanction in international law"[234] is supportable not only in morality and humanity, but in military history and realism. Even after World War II, with all of its terror, the same support is present for contemporary international lawyers who decry as illegal extreme cruelty to noncombatants.[235] The impermissible line is reached in terror bombing of the civilian community with the aim of pressuring the political elite to accept the attacker's political demands. It is impermissible because it is inhumane and ineffective. Beyond that, the absolute rule of law, the irreducible principle of restraint, prohibits intentional terrorization or destruction of the civilian populace. The civilian population per se cannot become a legitimate objective of attack in war because such attack is almost certainly counterproductive; at best, the presumption of illegality, except perhaps in retaliation, is so strong as to be virtually irrebuttable.

III. Judgment

"War inevitably is a course of killing, assaults, deprivations of liberty, and destruction of property," but only "violations of the laws or customs of war" are war crimes.[236] What is a war crime? More specifically, which tactics of war are criminal? The focus is criminal because it has been so declared. Violations of the laws or customs of war are of too grave a nature to be characterized as tortious, or otherwise unacceptable, with resort to civil proceedings or the channels of diplomacy. Having characterized the problem as criminal, the potential criminal actors must be identified. Normally only certain segments of the military are potential criminals in crimes against peace and crimes against humanity, but here the focus is on the usual function of the military—combat.[237] Every member of

---

233. See P. Bordwell, supra note 29, at 94; H. Nickerson, supra note 27, at 149-50. But cf. the statement attributed to Sir Winston Churchill: "The man who wants to win has to be as ruthless as the man he wants to beat." N.Y. Times, May 2, 1968, at 58, col. 1. Thus were night terror bomb raids against Germany approved. There is no convincing evidence, however, that such raids shortened the war.

234. J. Hall, supra note 20, at 80. But cf. note 233 supra.

235. Cf. e.g., M. Greenspan, supra note 11, at 316; McDougal & Feliciano 79-80; Lauterpacht, The Problem of Revision of the Law of War, 29 Brit. Y.B. Int'l. L. 378-79 (1952).

236. Compare The Trial of German Major War Criminals, Proceedings of the Int'l Military Tribunal at Nuremberg 80-81 (1946) (argument of Jackson, chief of American prosecution) with Agreement for the Prosecution and Punishment of the Major War Criminals of the European Axis art. 6(b), Aug. 8, 1945, 82 U.N.T.S. 279.

237. Cf. U.S. Dep't of the Army, supra note 14, ¶ 498. This section recognizes the Nuremberg concept of individual responsibility for all the categories of crimes but points out the usual concern of the military with "war crimes." But see E. Edmonds & L. Oppenheim, supra note 45, at 95 (traditional superior orders defense).

the military is a potential criminal.

Whether because of lack of honor, morality, ignorance, zeal, or otherwise, there had been for years a general feeling, based on the history of warfare, that the burden placed on individual soldiers by the laws of war was theoretically proper but often impracticable.[238] To question the efficacy of holding an individual responsible for his acts does not, however, mean that those higher in the echelons of command would not be held to a higher degree of adherence. On the contrary, especially in those situations in which a high-ranking officer might have to act in an emergency and without orders, a duty to act in accordance with the doctrines governing his country, presumably including the laws of war, was imposed.[239] Similarly any member of the military with actual discretion, such as a pilot or a bombardier diverting because of a tactical situation to a target of opportunity, should be held to the same high degree of adherence.[240] This distinction between those with discretion and those without, is a natural development from the historical distinction between those responsible for war and those who follow, between those who command and those who obey.[241]

Allotting discretion to a military commander does not mean, of course, that his judgment may be arbitrary and unfettered. On the contrary, criminal evaluation of his conduct presupposes that he will be governed by principles of law, including those which appeal to conscience and inherent humanity.[242] Enshrining the principles into written con-

---

238. *Compare* M. KEEN, *supra* note 8, at 217 *with* J. DYMOND, *supra* note 48, at 18 *and* E. EDMONDS & L. OPPENHEIM, *supra* note 45, at 25. *See also* comment: "War . . . is nothing less than a temporary repeal of all the principles of virtue." J. DYMOND at 18 (quoting Robert Hall).

239. *Cf.* Manisty, *supra* note 7, at 156 (naval commander must act "in the spirit and manner his superior would desire").

240. Such an individual with an obviously illegal, briefed target and opportunity to purposely miss the target, should also be held responsible for his actions if he chooses to strike it. *But cf.* the hypothetical problem addressed to a chaplain by "a pilot or bombardier who tells him that he has been ordered to drop bombs in an area where he knows that women and children as well as civilians will be killed." N.Y. Times, Mar. 24, 1968, at 59, col. 3. The target obviously is not illegal, as we have seen, merely because of civilian casualties.

241. *Cf.* J. DYMOND, *supra* note 48, at 23; GROTIUS *516. *See also* these comments written in 1823 about the duties of a soldier: "His obedience is that of an animal which is moved by a goad or a bit without judgment of its own; and his bravery is that of a mastiff that fights whatever mastiff others put before it"; members of the French Republican "army were expressly prohibited from deliberating on any subjects whatever"; "A soldier must obey, how criminal soever the command, and how criminal soever he knows it to be"; but "It is at all times the duty of an Englishman steadfastly to decline obeying any orders of his superior which his conscience should tell him were in any degree impious or unjust." J. DYMOND at 20-23. For the *mens rea* requirement and the defense of superior orders see Adler, *Resistance to Law: National vs. International Standards*, 5 HOUS. L. REV. 619, 640-41 (1968).

242. *See* Garner, *supra* note 39, at 5 n.2 for the proposition that in cases not covered by the Hague regulations, military commanders "should remain under the protection and rule of the principles of the law of nations as they result from the usages established among civilized peoples, from the laws of humanity and the dictates of the public conscience." In a war against savages when the law of nations did not apply, the commander's discretion was tempered by the rules of justice and humanity applicable to the case. *See* E. EDMONDS & L. OPPENHEIM, *supra* note 45, at 14.

ventions is not necessary. Indeed those opponents of putting the laws of war into writing because military commanders ought to be "restricted only by traditions, usages, and customs, the exact meaning and application of which could be interpreted to meet the particular necessities of the moment"[243] have misconceived international law, ignoring the ability to evaluate actions as legitimate or not in accordance with standards set up by customary international law.[244] Certainly some freedom of action and judgment must be granted to a military commander, but recognizing that all military commanders are not humane, that subjective and objective reasonableness will often differ, and that military necessity can release all limits, written and unwritten restraints are imposed, disregard of which should bring both dishonor and punishment.[245]

The point is that as the rules are developed and applied to combat situations, care must be taken to recognize that in hazardous or technically complex operations, automatic response to commands, allowing virtually no room for interpretation, may be an absolute necessity. The military will and must demand that individual questioning of strategy and tactics be subordinated to quick reaction and disciplined routine. Officers, loyal to a system, will regard loyalty and obedience to authority as the highest of military virtues. This does not, however, imply unquestioning obedience to irresponsible authority. It does mean that in a discretionary situation with alternative courses of action available, those with the choice must be allowed to act in accordance with their general directions, but they must also be aware of their legally defined duties and responsibilities under a realistic international law of war.[246]

Violation of defined duties did not always bring criminal responsibility. There was a time, in the era of knights, when the most effective sanctions besides the fear of reprisals were dishonor and public reprobation, exercised under a universal jurisdiction to try offenders.[247] Those years in which personal combat was common saw little if any criminal condemnation for combatant actions. As weaponry moved, however, from the very personal dagger and battleaxe, through the lance, javelin, and sling, to impersonal muskets, cannon, and other firearms, the law tried to move in a different

---

243. *See* Garner, *supra* note 39, at 7 (referring to pre-World War I Germany).
244. *Cf.* Garner, *supra* note 242. *See also* GREAT GENERAL STAFF OF THE GERMAN ARMY, THE USAGES OF WAR ON LAND 84 (Morgan transl. 1915), in J. BAKER & H. CROCKER, *supra* note 30, at 119: "[W]ide limits are set in the subjective freedom and arbitrary judgment of the Commanding Officer; the precepts of civilization, freedom and honor, the traditions prevalent in the army, and the general usages of war, will have to guard his decision."
245. *Cf.* T. LAWRENCE, *supra* note 60, in J. BAKER & H. CROCKER, *supra* note 30, at 201.
246. *Cf.* T. WINTRINGHAM, NEW WAYS OF WAR 71-72 (1940); Simons, *The Liberal Challenge in the Military Profession*, AIR U.Q. REV., July-Aug. 1966, in AIR FORCE & SPACE DIGEST, Feb. 1967, at 48, 49. *See also* remarks of James Calvert, R. Adm., U.S.N., LIFE, Nov. 22, 1968, at 60.
247. *See generally* M. KEEN, *supra* note 8, at 20-22, 52, 58-59, 244. Universal criminal jurisdiction may have long existed for rape. *Cf.* GROTIUS *464.

direction. Certain weapons were outlawed and the users were branded criminals; a very personal brand. The greater destructive power of weapons, plus their relative lack of certainty and ability to discriminate, has made such movement understandable. Yet the more impersonal and technologically complete the war becomes, the less likely it is that personal condemnation will befall the human military trigger. He who puts civilians in overrun areas to the sword or who machine-guns the survivors of a submarine attack, will be criminally condemned. But the scientist who builds nondiscriminating terror weapons and the aircrews who drop bombs indiscriminately on nonmilitary targets will probably escape condemnation.[248] When there are alternative courses of action available, ought this be so?

Certainly, after Nuremberg, we are well past the age of the public war in which all acts were permissible because there was no party to judge the justice of the case or the limits of self-defense.[249] Whether it was just war, public war, the law of nations, or the agreement of mankind that gave impunity, is of no moment today. The concept of criminal responsibility for violation of the rules of war is here.[250] If the rules are to effectively sanction wartime conduct, they must be reasonable, realistic, and directed at those responsible for decision-making and at those implementers of policy with knowledge, discretion, and alternative courses of action. Judgment should turn upon these criteria when individual combatants are brought to trial. The law of combatant warfare exists. Application of the law to the facts of a given situation should come without difficulty for our legal system.

Indeed recent well-known incidents relating to United States forces in Vietnam indicate that the law of combatant warfare is sufficiently well-defined to bring both vocal abhorrence and individual punishment.[251] If unnecessary, premeditated, or wanton murder within the zone of combat can bring about a judgment of criminality, there seems to be no reason in principle why the law of combatant warfare cannot equally be utilized for both restraint and judgment when violence goes beyond the individual soldier and harmless noncombatant.

---

248. *See* Krutch, *Epitaph for an Age*, N.Y. Times, July 30, 1967, § 6 (Magazine), at 10, 48; TIME, Aug. 25, 1967, at 12.

249. *See generally* GROTIUS *456-57; H. HALLECK, *supra* note 52, at 154; C. VAN BYNKERSHOEK, *supra* note 10, at 3.

250. *See, e.g.,* art. III of the treaty of the Washington Conference: "[A]ny person in the service of any Power who shall violate any of those rules, whether or not such person is under orders of a governmental superior, shall be deemed to have violated the laws of war and shall be liable to trial and punishment." Manisty, *supra* note 7, at 177-78. Nonratification by France kept the treaty from formal effect.

251. For successful application, albeit with a light sentence imposed, *see* the case of Lt. Duffy, N.Y. Times, Mar. 29, 1970, at 1, col. 4. For the comments of Gen. Taylor, Nuremberg counsel, on the Mylai "massacre" *see id.*, Jan. 10, 1970, at 30, col. 3 (generally affirming application). *See also id.*, June 22, 1970, at 1, col. 4 (conviction in another Vietnam incident).

History has defined the law regarding target selection. The necessity-humanity continuum with the proportionality fulcrum is the measure of legitimacy, whether in the context of soldier or civilian, an enemy's economy or his means of sustenance, his governmental structure or the morale of his people. The problem is not in the standard. Rather it is in the will to restrain and the will to punish.

Certainly a nation at war is loath to punish its own. Certainly it is difficult to compel restraint in a situation of continuing death and violence. Nevertheless, the law has always recognized that not all killings are murder. Justifiable or excusable killings are tragic. War is tragic. But war and murder are not synonymous. Whether murder comes from the action of a bullet, a shell, a bomb, a tactical concept, a strategic plan, or a general philosophy, it remains murder. Murder of a child, a town, or a people need not happen. A combatant nation must be prepared to prevent murder from occurring in war or be prepared, individually and collectively, to be judged.

Son My:
War Crimes and Individual Responsibility[1]

RICHARD A. FALK

No voice has been more passionate and persuasive in its call for a renewal of the laws of war than that of Josef Kunz. Especially in the period since the end of World War II Professor Kunz wrote against the prevailing tendency to regard the idea of law-in-war as little more than a relic from the pre-nuclear age.[2] The Vietnam War has emphasized, although the Korean War, the three Middle Eastern wars, and the many lesser wars throughout the world since 1945 should have made it plain, that the development of nuclear weapons did not mark the end of so-called conventional warfare, nor assure us that there would be either peace or catastrophe in world society. The massacre at Son My was, I suppose, the most macabre possible demonstration that the law of war remains relevant, and that its effective enforcement would mitigate the horrifying experience of warfare for a society torn apart by struggling armies.

But there is a danger of misunderstanding. The most minimal reading of customary rules of international law prohibit the acts that took place at Son My, and yet they happened. Rules of international law do not assure conforming conduct unless the military and civilian leadership of the armed forces gives these rules active and genuine respect and unless the official tactics of the war are themselves sensitive to the basic principles of limitation on warfare embodied in the rules of customary and treaty international law.

Thus, new rules more responsive to the actualities of contemporary warfare would offer no assurance of their respect. An entire political climate of support for such rules must be brought into being. In working, then, for the reform and revitalization of the laws of war—the

---

[1] The spelling Son My follows the Vietnamese practice. As Richard Hammer has pointed out, Son My (and not Song My or Songmy) is what appears "On all Vietnamese maps, in all Vietnamese writings," Richard Hammer, *One Morning After: The Tragedy at Son My*, New York, Coward, McCann, 1970, p. xiii. In an earlier version I used the mistaken spelling in my title "Songmy: War Crimes and Individual Responsibility," *Trans-Action* (Jan. 1970), 33-40; republished, in somewhat modified form, under the title "War Crimes: The Circle of Responsibility," *The Nation* (Jan. 26, 1970), 77-82.

[2] Josef Kunz, *The Changing Law of Nations*, Columbus, Ohio State University Press, 1968, pp. 831-868.

essence of Professor Kunz' eloquent plea—it is essential to work for a new political climate, as well as to urge the adoption of new rules and procedures for interpretation and enforcement.[3] The Vietnam War has amply demonstrated how easily modern man and the modern state— with all its claim of civility[4]—can relapse into barbarism in the course of pursuing belligerent objectives in a distant land where neither national territory nor national security is tangibly at stake.

I. Son My in Context

The dramatic disclosure of the Son My massacre produced a flurry of public concern over the commission of war crimes in Vietnam by American military personnel. Such a concern is certainly appropriate, but insufficient if limited to inquiry and prosecution of the individual servicemen involved in the monstrous events that apparently took the lives of upwards of 400 civilians in the Mylai No. 4 hamlet of Son My village on March 16, 1968.[5] The Son My massacre itself raises a serious basis for inquiry into the military and civilian command structure that was in charge of battlefield behavior at the time.

The evidence now available suggests that the armed forces have made efforts throughout the Vietnam War to suppress, rather than investigate and punish, the commission of war crimes by American personnel. The evidence also suggests a failure to protest or prevent the manifest and systematic commission of war crimes by the armed forces of the Saigon regime in South Vietnam.[6]

[3] Concern with rules, procedures, and institutions alone can lead to banal forms of legalism; it is essential to be concerned also about the politics of a legal order so that ideas of justice do not collide with the actualities of the law. In a somewhat different setting I have explored these issues in Falk, "Law, Lawyers, and the Conduct of American Foreign Relations," 78 *Yale Law Journal* 919 (1970). See Section V below for specific proposals along these lines.

[4] Future students of the American scene will be struck, no doubt, by the fervent appeals for civility at home while the war rages on in Vietnam. One such prominent appeal, of late, has come from Chief Justice Warren E. Burger, who in addressing the American Bar Association, contended that "unseemly, outrageous episodes" in courtrooms were undermining public confidence in the judicial process. The Chief Justice did not note that one of the reasons for these episodes is that antiwar defendants have not been allowed by courts to make their arguments about the illegality and criminality of the war and of war policies. For an account of Mr. Chief Justice Burger's speech see *New York Times*, Aug. 9, 1970, pp. 1, 34.

[5] For principal accounts see Hammer, cited note 1; Seymour M. Hersh, *My Lai 4: A Report on the Massacre and Its Aftermath*, New York, Random House, 1970; see also *The Son My Mass Slaying*, South Viet Nam, Giai Phong Editions, 1969 (pamphlet); Noam Chomsky, "After Pinkville," *New York Review of Books* (Jan. 1, 1970), 3-14.

[6] This point is made by Alfred P. Rubin, "Legal Aspects of the My Lai Incident," 49 *Oregon Law Review* 260, 267-68 (1970). (Reprinted in this volume.)

The scope of proper inquiry is even broader than the prior paragraph suggests. The official policies developed for the pursuit of belligerent objectives in Vietnam appear to violate the same basic and minimum constraints on the conduct of war as were violated at Son My. B-52 pattern raids against undefended villages and populated areas, "free bomb zones," forcible removal of civilian populations, defoliation and crop destruction, and "search and destroy" missions have been sanctioned as official tactical policies of the United States government. Each of these tactical policies appears to violate the international laws of war binding upon the United States by international treaties ratified by the U.S. government with the advice and consent of the Senate. The overall conduct of the war in Vietnam by the U.S. armed forces involves a refusal to differentiate between combatants and noncombatants and between military and nonmilitary targets. Detailed presentation of the acts of war in relation to the laws of war is available in a volume bearing the title *In the Name of America* published under the auspices of the Clergy and Laymen Concerned about Vietnam, in January 1968, or several months before the Son My massacre took place.[7] Ample evidence of war crimes has been presented to the public and to its officials for some time without producing an official reaction or rectifying action. A comparable description of the acts of war that were involved in the bombardment of North Vietnam by American planes and naval vessels between February 1965 and October 1968 appears in a book by John Gerassi.[8]

The broad point, then, is that the United States government has officially endorsed a series of battlefield activities that appear to constitute war crimes. It would, therefore, be misleading to isolate the awful happening at Son My from the overall conduct of the war. It is certainly

[7] *In the Name of America*, Clergy and Laymen Concerned About Vietnam, Turnpike Press, Annandale, Virginia, 1968. An introduction to the volume by such distinguished religious leaders as Rev. Martin Luther King, Rev. William Sloan Coffin, John Bennett, and Rev. Richard Fernandez was totally ignored by the media and thus the volume made no impact outside already sensitized antiwar groups. Other early publications—pre-Son My—on the war crimes aspects of the war include John Duffett, ed., *Against the Crime of Silence: Proceedings of the Russell International War Crimes Tribunal*, Flanders, N.J., O'Hare Publications, 1968; Frank Harvey, *Air War—Vietnam*, New York, Bantam, 1967; and see "Kill Anything that Moves," an essay review of the Harvey book in Philip Slater, *The Pursuit of Loneliness: American Culture at the Breaking Point*, Boston, Beacon Press, 1970, pp. 29-52; and another sensitive reaction to Harvey's book—Robert Crichton, "Our Air War," *New York Review of Books* (Jan. 4, 1968), 3-5; Eric Norden, "American Atrocities in Vietnam," *Liberation* (Feb. 1966), 1-19 (reprint).

[8] See John Gerassi, *North Vietnam: A Documentary*, Indianapolis, Ind., Bobbs-Merrill, 1968.

true that the perpetrators of the massacre at Son My are, if the allegations prove correct, guilty of the commission of war crimes, but it is also true that their responsibility is mitigated to the extent that they were executing superior orders or were even carrying out the general line of official policy that established a moral climate in which the welfare of Vietnamese civilians is totally disregarded.[9]

II. Personal Responsibility: Some Basic Propositions

The U.S. prosecutor at Nuremberg, Robert Jackson, emphasized that war crimes are war crimes no matter which country is guilty of them.[10] The United States more than any other sovereign state took the lead in the movement to generalize the principles underlying the Nuremberg Judgment that was delivered against German war criminals after the end of World War II.[11]

At the initiative of the United States, in 1945 the General Assembly of the United Nations unanimously affirmed "the principles of international law recognized by the Charter of the Nuremberg Tribunal" in Resolution 95 (I). This Resolution was an official action of governments. At the direction of the membership of the United Nations, the International Law Commission, an expert body containing international law experts from all of the principal legal systems in the world, formulated the Principles of Nuremberg in 1950.[12]

[9] One of the most revealing inquiries in this regard accompanied the prosecution and defense of Lt. James B. Duffy who was accused of killing a Vietnamese prisoner under his control. The court-martial proceedings, especially several witnesses for the defense, made it evident that "the body count philosophy" was the proximate cause of Sgt. Duffy's action even though there was no specific superior order given to kill "enemy" prisoners. For an account of the Duffy trial and some accompanying documents see "Tan Am Base Vietnam—Feb. 12—1000 Hrs.," *Scanlan's* (April 1970), 1-11. See *New York Times*, March 28, 1970, pp. 1, 13; April 5, 1970, p. 6.

[10] Indeed, this was a principal theme in the Opening Statement of Robert H. Jackson at Nuremberg. See Jackson, *The Case Against the Nazi War Criminals*, New York, Knopf, 1946, pp. 8-11, 70-78, 86-91.

[11] For documentary record see *Report of Robert H. Jackson to the International Conference on Military Trials, London 1945*, Dept. of State Publ. 3080, released Feb. 1949. For a fully researched inquiry into prevailing attitudes toward Nuremberg see William J. Bosch, *Judgment on Nuremberg: American Attitudes Toward the Major German War-Crimes Trials*, Chapel Hill, North Carolina University Press, 1970.

[12] For official text see GAOR, 5th Sess., Supp. No. 12 (A/1316), p. 11. The seven Principles are as follows:

Principle I: Any person who commits an act which constitutes a crime under international law is responsible therefor and liable to punishment.

Principle II: The fact that internal law does not impose a penalty for an act which constitutes a crime under international law does not relieve the person

These Principles offer the most complete set of guidelines currently available on the legal relationship between personal responsibility and war crimes.[13]

Neither the Nuremberg Judgment nor the Nuremberg Principles fixes definite boundaries on personal responsibility. These boundaries will have to be drawn in the future as the circumstances of alleged violations of international law are tested by competent domestic and international tribunals. However, Principle IV makes it clear that superior orders are no defense in a prosecution for war crimes, provided the individual accused of criminal behavior had a moral choice available to him.[14]

who committed the act from responsibility under international law.

Principle III: The fact that a person who committed an act which constitutes a crime under international law acted as Head of State or responsible government official does not relieve him from responsibility under international law.

Principle IV: The fact that a person acted pursuant to order of his Government or of a superior does not relieve him from responsibility under international law, provided a moral choice was in fact possible for him.

Principle V: Any person charged with a crime under international law has the right to a fair trial on the facts and law.

Principle VI: The crimes hereinafter set out are punishable as crimes under international law:

    a. *Crimes against peace*: (i) Planning, preparation, initiation or waging of a war of aggression or a war in violation of international treaties, agreements or assurances; (ii) Participation in a common plan or conspiracy for the accomplishment of any of the acts mentioned under (i).

    b. *War crimes*: Violations of the laws or customs of war which include, but are not limited to, murder, ill-treatment or deportation to slave-labour or for any other purpose of civilian population of or in occupied territory, murder or ill-treatment of prisoners of war or persons on the seas, killing of hostages, plunder of public or private property, wanton destruction of cities, towns, or villages, or devastation not justified by military necessity.

    c. *Crimes against humanity*: Murder, extermination, enslavement, deportation and other inhuman acts done against any civilian population, or persecutions on political, racial or religious grounds, when such acts are done or such persecutions are carried on in execution of or in connexion with any crime against peace or any war crime.

Principle VII: Complicity in the commission of a crime against humanity as set forth in Principle VI is a crime under international law.

13 For a cautious, but helpful analysis, see William V. O'Brien, "The Nuremberg Principles," in James Finn, ed., *A Conflict of Loyalties*, New York, Pegasus, 1968, pp. 140-194. (Reprinted in this volume.)

14 One of the most significant repudiations of the superior orders defense is contained in

The Supreme Court upheld in *The Matter of Yamashita* a sentence of death against General Yamashita imposed at the end of World War II for acts committed by troops under his command.[15] The determination of responsibility rested upon the obligation of General Yamashita for the maintenance of discipline by troops under his command, which discipline included the enforcement of the prohibition against the commission of war crimes. Thus General Yamashita was convicted even though he had no specific knowledge of the alleged war crimes, which mainly involved forbidden acts of violence against the civilian population of the Philippines in the closing days of World War II. Commentators have criticized the conviction of General Yamashita because it was difficult to maintain discipline under the conditions of defeat during which the war crimes were committed, but the imposition of responsibility sets a precedent for holding principal military and political officials responsible for acts committed under their command, especially when no diligent effort was made to inquire, punish, and prevent repetition.[16] *The Matter of Yamashita* has an extraordinary relevance to the failure of the U.S. military command to secure adherence to minimum rules of international law by troops serving under their command. The following sentences from the majority opinion of Chief Justice Stone in *The Matter of Yamashita* have a particular bearing:

> It is evident that the conduct of military operations by troops whose excesses are unrestrained by the orders or efforts of their commands would almost certainly result in violations which it is the purpose of the law of war to prevent. Its purpose to protect civilian populations and prisoners of war from brutality would largely be defeated if the commands of an invading army could with impunity neglect to take reasonable measures for their protection. Hence the law of war presupposes that its violation is to be avoided through the control of the operations of war by commanders who are to some extent responsible for their subordinates.[17]

U.S. v Wilhelm List, et al. (The Hostage Case), reprinted in *Trials of War Criminals Before the Nuremberg Military Tribunals*, Washington, D.C., U.S. Government Printing Office, 1950, XI, 757-1319.

[15] For a full account and critical interpretation of General Yamashita's conviction and execution written by a member of the prosecution staff see A. Frank Reel *The Case of General Yamashita*, Chicago, University of Chicago Press, 1949.

[16] See Reel's recent reassessment of his earlier analysis in A. Frank Reel, "Must We Hang Nixon Too?," *The Progressive* (March 1970), 26-29.

[17] 327 U.S. 1, 5 (1945).

The Field Manual of the Department of the Army, FM 27-10, adequately develops the principles of responsibility governing members of the armed forces. §3 (b) makes it clear that "the law of war is binding not only upon States as such but also upon individuals and, in particular, the members of their armed forces." The entire manual is based upon the acceptance by the United States of the obligation to conduct warfare in accordance with the international law of war. The substantive content of international law is contained in a series of international treaties that have been properly ratified by the United States. These include 12 Hague and Geneva Conventions.

These international treaties are listed in the Field Manual and are, in any event, part of "the supreme law of the land" by virtue of Article VI of the U.S. Constitution. Customary rules of international law governing warfare are also made explicitly applicable to the obligation of American servicemen in the Manuals issued to the armed forces. The extent of legal obligation is established by very broad norms of customary international law, especially the prohibition upon inflicting unnecessary suffering and destruction as measured by the criterion of military necessity. A competent tribunal would have to apply this general norm—certainly no more general, however, than basic Constitutional norms involving "due process," "equal protection," and "privileges and immunities." It is important to realize that not every violation of law needs to be discovered in a treaty rule although where a treaty rule applies to a specific issue—such as the identification of prohibited targets—then it takes precedence over more abstract norms of customary international law.

It has sometimes been maintained that the laws of war do not apply to a civil war, which is a war within a state and thus outside the scope of international law. Some observers have argued that the Vietnam War represents a civil war between factions contending for political control of South Vietnam. Such an argument may accurately portray the principal basis of the conflict, but surely the extension of the combat theater to include North Vietnam, Laos, Thailand, Cambodia, and Okinawa removes any doubt about the international character of the war from a military and legal point of view.[18] Nevertheless, even assuming for the sake of analysis that the war should be treated as a

18 Also the international character of the conflict has underlay protests against the treatment of American prisoners of war held in North Vietnam. For legal discussion of this issue see my debate with Professor John Norton Moore, reprinted in Falk, ed., *The Vietnam War and International Law*, Princeton, Princeton University Press, 1968, Vol. 1, 362-508, esp. pp. 362-373, 403-438, 470-490.

civil war, the laws of war are applicable to a limited extent, an extent great enough to cover the events at Son My and the commission of many other alleged war crimes in Vietnam. §11 of the Field Manual recites Article 3 common to all four Geneva Conventions on the Law of War (1949) and establishes a minimum set of obligations for civil war situations:

> In the case of armed conflict not of an international character occurring in the territory of one of the High Contracting Parties, each Party to the conflict shall be bound to apply, as a minimum, the following provisions:
>
> (1) Persons taking no active part in the hostilities, including members of armed forces who have laid down their arms and those placed *hors de combat* by sickness, wounds, detention or any other cause, shall in all circumstances be treated humanely, without any adverse distinction founded on race, colour, religion or faith, sex, birth or wealth, or any other similar criteria.
>
> To this end, the following acts are and shall remain prohibited at any time and in any place whatsoever with respect to the above-mentioned persons:
>
> (a) violence to life and person, in particular murder of all kinds, mutilation, cruel treatment and torture;
> (b) taking of hostages;
> (c) outrages upon personal dignity, in particular, humiliating and degrading treatment;
> (d) the passing of sentences and the carrying out of executions without previous judgment pronounced by a regularly constituted court, affording all the judicial guarantees which are recognized as indispensable by civilized peoples.
>
> (2) The wounded and sick shall be collected and cared for. An impartial humanitarian body, such as the International Committee of the Red Cross, may offer its services to the Parties to the conflict.
>
> The Parties to the conflict would further endeavor to bring into force, by means of special agreements, all or part of the other provisions of the present Convention.[19]

[19] Geneva Convention for the Amelioration of the Condition of the Wounded and Sick in Armed Forces in the Field, Aug. 12, 1949 [1955] 3 U.S.T. 3114, T.I.A.S. No. 3362, 75 U.N.T.S. 31; Geneva Convention for the Amelioration of the Condition of Wounded, Sick

Such a limited applicability of the laws of war to the Vietnam War flies in the face of the official American contention that South Vietnam is a sovereign state that has been attacked by a foreign state, North Vietnam. This standard American contention, repeated in President Nixon's speech of November 3, 1969, would suggest that the United States government is obliged to treat the Vietnam conflict as a war of international character to which the entire law of war applies.

Several provisions of the Army Field Manual clearly establish the obligation of the United States to apprehend and punish the commission of war crimes.[20]

These provisions make it amply clear that war crimes are to be prosecuted and punished and that responsibility is acknowledged to extend far beyond the level of the individuals who performed the physical acts that inflicted harm. In fact, the effectiveness of the law of war depends, above all else, on holding those in command and in policy-making positions responsible for the behavior of the rank-and-file soldiers on the field of battle. The reports of neuropsychiatrists, trained in combat therapy, have suggested that unrestrained behavior by troops is an expression almost always of tacit authorization, at least, on the part of commanding officers; a form of authorization that conveys to the rank-and-file soldier the absence of any prospect of punishment for the outrageous behavior.[21] It would thus be a deception to punish the triggermen at Son My without also looking further up the chain of command to identify the truer locus of responsibility.[22]

---

and Shipwrecked Members of Armed Forces at Sea, Aug. 12, 1949, [1955] 3 U.S.T. 3217, T.I.A.S. No. 3363, 75 U.N.T.S. 85; Geneva Convention Relative to the Treatment of Prisoners of War, Aug. 12, 1949, [1955] 3 U.S.T. 3316. T.I.A.S. No. 3364, 75 U.N.T.S. 135; Geneva Convention Relative to the Protection of Civilian Persons in Time of War, Aug. 12, 1949, [1955] 3 U.S.T. 3516, T.I.A.S. No. 3365, 75 U.N.T.S. 287. For some consideration of the application of the laws of war to a Vietnam-type conflict see Falk, id., Vol. 2, 361-571.

20 The Law of Land Warfare, Department of the Army Field Manual, FM 27-10, July 1956, §§506-511, pp. 181-183.

21 See Edward M. Opton, Jr., and Robert Duckles, "Mental Gymnastics on Mylai," The New Republic (Feb. 21, 1970), 14-16.

22 It might also be a deception to punish the civilian and military leaders as war criminals, the opposite kind of deception from that which results from punishing the men on the battlefield. By punishing the leaders, the public is able to distance itself from events which it largely acquiesced in at the time of their occurrence. The enterprise of criminal punishment has not yet demonstrated that the punishment of criminals reduces the prospects for crime even in domestic society, much less in international society. At the same time, the identification of crime is essential for the establishment of limits on permissible behavior and to encourage the formation of clear lines of moral consciousness that might condition and guide future leaders and their followers.

III. Comments on the Son My Massacre

The events took place on March 16, 1968. The Secretary of Defense admitted knowledge of these events eight months before their public disclosure. The disclosure resulted from the publication in the *Cleveland Plain Dealer* in November 1969 of a photograph of the massacre taken by Ronald Haeberle. The lapse of time, the existence of photographs, the report of the helicopter pilot, the large number of American personnel (approximately 80 men of Company C, First Battalion, 20th Infantry Division) involved in the incident, creates a deep suspicion that news of the massacre was suppressed at various levels of command and that its disclosure was delayed at the highest levels of military and civilian government. The numerous other reports of atrocities connected with the war have also not been generally investigated or punished with seriousness. In fact, other evidence of atrocities has been ignored or deliberately suppressed by military authorities at all levels of the U.S. command structure.

The massacre at Son My exhibits a bestiality toward the sanctity of civilian lives that exceeds earlier atrocities that took place at Lidice or Guernica. At Lidice, Czechoslovakia, on June 10, 1942, the male population of the town was shot, women were taken off to concentration camps, and the children sent off to schools and families.[23] At Son My women and children were not spared. At Guernica bombs were dropped on an undefended Spanish village, terrorizing and killing the inhabitants, a scene made universal by Picasso's mural commemorating the horrifying events. Such military tactics are daily employed by American forces in Vietnam. At Son My civilians were systematically chosen; they were the intended victims of the act, not the uncertain, random victims of an air attack.

The Son My massacre is the culmination of the policies of counterinsurgency warfare in South Vietnam. It is not, however, an isolated atrocity, as many other occurrences in South Vietnam have revealed a brutal disregard of Vietnamese civilians and have disclosed little or no effort by military commanders to punish and prevent this behavior. In addition, the Son My massacre is consistent with the overall effort of "denying" the National Liberation Front its base of support among the civilian population of Vietnam, whether by the assassination of

---

[23] For an account of the Lidice massacre see Jakob Bedrnik Hutak, *With Blood and with Iron; the Lidice Story*, London, Hale, 1957. It is true that Son My was not an occurrence that was ordered by the United States military command in Vietnam in any explicit fashion.

civilians alleged to be NLF cadres (from December 1967 to December 1968 several thousand civilians were killed in the Phoenix Operation), by fire-bomb zone attacks against villages in NLF-held territory, defoliation and crop destruction, and by search-and-destroy missions that involved the destruction of the homes and villages of many thousand Vietnamese civilians. It is estimated by the U.S. Senate Subcommittee on Refugees, chaired by Senator Edward Kennedy, that over 300,000 South Vietnamese civilians have been killed since the beginning of the war, mainly by U.S. air strikes and artillery. Such a figure represents a number six times as great as American war dead, and suggests the indiscriminate use of weapons against the very people that the U.S. government contends it is fighting the war to protect.[24]

The massacre at Son My stands out as a landmark atrocity in the history of warfare, and its occurrence represents a moral challenge to American society. This challenge was summarized by Mrs. Anthony Meadlow, the mother of David Paul Meadlow, one of the soldiers at Son My, in a simple sentence: "I sent them a good boy, and they made him a murderer."[25] Another characteristic statement about the general character of the war was attributed to an army staff sergeant: "We are at war with the ten-year-old children. It may not be humanitarian, but that's what it's like."[26]

IV. Personal Responsibility in Light of Son My

The massacre at Son My raises two broad sets of issues about personal responsibility for the commission of war crimes:

The legal scope of personal responsibility for a specific act or pattern of belligerent conduct

The extralegal scope of personal responsibility of citizens in relation to war crimes and to varying degrees of participation in an illegal war

1) The War Criminal: Scope of Responsibility: We have already suggested that evidence exists that many official battlefield policies relied upon by the United States in Vietnam amount to war crimes.

---

[24] For a full presentation of United States war crimes in Vietnam see Edward S. Herman, "Atrocities in Vietnam: Myths and Realities" (mimeographed), a slightly fictionalized report of one war crime reveals the overall moral depravity of the American conduct in Vietnam. Daniel Lang, *Casualties of War*, New York, McGraw-Hill, 1969.

[25] *New York Times*, Nov. 30, 1969, Sec. 4, p. 1.

[26] *New York Times*, Dec. 1, 1969, p. 12.

These official policies should be investigated in light of the legal obligations of the United States and if found to be "illegal," then these policies should be ceased forthwith and those responsible for the policy and its execution should be removed and barred from positions of leadership.[27] These remarks definitely apply to the following war policies, and very likely to others: 1) the Phoenix Program; 2) aerial and naval bombardment of undefended villages; 3) destruction of crops and forests; 4) "search-and-destroy" missions; 5) "harassment and interdiction" fire; 6) forcible removal of civilian population; 7) reliance on a variety of weapons prohibited by treaty. In addition, allegations of all war atrocities should be investigated and reported upon.[28] These atrocities—committed in defiance of declared official policy—should be punished. Responsibility should be imposed upon those who inflicted the harm, upon those who gave direct orders, and upon those who were in a position of command entrusted with overall battlefield decorum and with the prompt detection and punishment of war crimes committed within the scope of their authority.

Finally, political leaders who authorized illegal battlefield practices and policies, or who had knowledge of these practices and policies and failed to act are similarly responsible for the commission of war crimes. The following paragraphs from the Majority Judgment of the Tokyo War Crimes Tribunal are relevant:

> A member of a Cabinet which collectively, as one of the principal organs of the Government, is responsible for the care of prisoners is not absolved from responsibility if, having knowledge of the commission of the crimes in the sense already discussed, and omitting or failing to secure the taking of measures to prevent the commission of such crimes in the future, he elects to continue as a member of the Cabinet. This is the position even though the Department of which he has the charge is not directly concerned with the care of prisoners. A Cabinet member may resign. If he has knowledge of ill-treatment of prisoners, is powerless to prevent future ill-treatment, but elects to remain in the Cabinet thereby continuing to participate in its collective responsibility for protection of prisoners

---

[27] The purpose of such action would be to confirm the limits of official discretion and to assert criteria for responsible leadership. Punishment would not be an objective.

[28] Modest efforts along these lines have been undertaken by a group of courageous young Americans who have been working with returning veterans of the Vietnam War: National Committee for a Citizens' Commission of Inquiry on U.S. War Crimes in Vietnam.

he willingly assumes responsibility for any ill-treatment in the future.

Army or Navy commanders can, by order, secure proper treatment and prevent ill-treatment of prisoners. So can Ministers of War and of the Navy. If crimes are committed against prisoners under their control, of the likely occurrence of which they had, or should have had knowledge in advance, they are responsible for those crimes. If, for example, it be shown that within the units under his command conventional war crimes have been committed of which he knew or should have known, a commander who takes no adequate steps to prevent the occurrence of such crimes in the future will be responsible for such future crimes.[29]

The United States government was directly associated with the development of a broad conception of criminal responsibility for the leadership of a state during war. A leader must take affirmative acts to prevent war crimes or dissociate himself from the government. If he fails to do one or the other, then by the very act of remaining in a government of a state guilty of war crimes, he becomes a war criminal.[30]

Finally, as both the Nuremberg and the Tokyo Judgments emphasize, a government official is a war criminal if he has participated in the initiation or execution of an illegal war of aggression. There are considerable grounds for regarding the United States involvement in the Vietnam War—wholly apart from the conduct of the war—as involving the violation of the United Nations Charter and other treaty obligations of the United States.[31] If U.S. participation in the war is found illegal, then the policy-makers responsible for the war during its various stages are theoretically subject to prosecution as alleged war criminals.

29 See Louis B. Sohn, ed., *Cases on United Nations Law*, Brooklyn, N.Y., Foundation Press, 1956, quoted in excerpt from Judgment of the International Military Tribunal for the Far East, Nov. 4-12, 1948, pp. 898-967, at p. 909.

30 For various perspectives on the scope and extent of criminal responsibility in relation to the Vietnam War see George Wald, "Corporate Responsibility for War Crimes," *New York Review of Books* (July 2, 1970), 4-6; Townsend Hoopes, "The Nuremberg Suggestion," *Washington Monthly* (Jan. 1970), 18-21; James Reston, Jr., "Is Nuremberg Coming Back to Haunt Us?" *Saturday Review* (July 18, 1970), 14-17, 61.

31 For succinct argument along these lines see Quincy Wright, "Legal Aspects of the Viet-Nam Situation," in Falk, *Vietnam*, Vol. 1, 271-291; a more extended legal analysis reaching these conclusions has been prepared by the Consultative Council of the Lawyers Committee on American Policy Towards Vietnam, published under the title *Vietnam and International Law*, John H. E. Fried, rapporteur, Flanders, N.J., O'Hare, 2nd rev. edn., 1968.

2) Responsibility as a Citizen: The idea of prosecuting war criminals involves using international law as a sword against violators in the military and civilian hierarchy of government. But the Nuremberg Principles imply a broader human responsibility to oppose an illegal war and illegal methods of warfare. There is nothing to suggest that the ordinary citizen, whether within or outside the armed forces, is potentially guilty of a war crime merely as a consequence of such a status. But there are grounds to maintain that anyone who believes or has reason to believe that a war is being waged in violation of minimal canons of law and morality has an obligation of conscience to resist participation in and support of that war effort by every means at his disposal. In this respect, the Nuremberg Principles provide guidelines for citizens' conscience and a shield that can and should be used in the domestic legal system to interpose obligations under international law between the government and the society. Such a doctrine of interposition has been asserted in a large number of selective service cases by individuals refusing to enter the armed forces. This assertion has already enjoyed a limited success.[32]

The issue of personal conscience is raised for everyone in the United States. It is raised more directly for anyone called upon to serve in the armed forces. It is raised in a special way for parents of minor children who are conscripted into the armed forces. It is raised for all taxpayers whose payments are used to support the cost of the war effort. It is raised for all citizens who in various ways endorse the war policies of the government. The circle of responsibility is drawn around all who have or should have knowledge of the illegal and immoral character of the war. The Son My massacre put every American on notice as to the character of the war.

And the circle of responsibility does not end at the border. Foreign governments and their populations are pledged by the Charter of the United Nations to oppose aggression and to take steps to punish the commission of war crimes. The cause of peace is indivisible, and all those governments and people concerned with Charter obligations have a legal and moral duty to oppose the continuation of the American involvement in Vietnam and to support the effort to identify, pro-

---

[32] *United States v Sisson* 297 F Supp. 902 (1969). For some insight into the reasoning of war resisters see Norma Sue Woodside, *Up Against the War*, New York, Tower Publications, 1970; Willard Gaylin, *In the Service of their Country/War Resisters in Prison*, New York, Viking, 1970; see also Philip Berrigan, *Prison Journals of a Priest Revolutionary*, New York, Holt, Rinehart and Winston, 1970.

hibit and punish the commission of war crimes. The conscience of the entire world community is implicated by inaction, as well as by more explicit forms of support for U.S. policy.

V. Some Standard Objections

Several objections to the position that I have taken are frequently made. The purpose of this section is to consider these objections briefly.

All War Is Hell: This objection emphasizes that war is the basic evil and that the effort to prohibit certain acts of conduct is futile (all prohibitions yield to military necessity) or, worse yet, deceptive (fostering the belief that war can somehow be reconciled with the dictates of conscience, provided only that the rules of the game are upheld). There is an undeniable element of validity in both grounds of this objection, but in my view, there is a far larger element of misapprehension and nihilism present. First of all, the minimum objective of the laws of war is to deter military behavior that causes death, suffering, and destruction, but which is not related to the rational pursuit of belligerent objectives—that is, which is not consistent with a reasonable interpretation of military necessity. The events at Son My appear to be of such a character as to work *against* rather than *for* the military objectives of the American involvement in Vietnam. In any event, the safeguarding of noncombatants, of prisoners of war, of sacred cultural and religious sites, of the sick and wounded, and the prohibition of certain weapons and tactics of warfare has had the effect of sparing a certain finite number of people—especially the aged, the infirm, and the young —from the full horror of warfare in which plunder, pillage, and wanton destruction were regarded as unavoidable aspects of warfare. The modern history of international law, beginning with the work of Grotius in the early seventeenth century, proceeded from the perception that it is desirable and possible to reduce the suffering associated with war even if it is impossible to eliminate the institution of war itself from the experience of mankind. Recent warfare in Vietnam, Korea, Nigeria, and the Congo suggest the importance of strengthening, rather than abandoning, the long tradition of the law of war.

The Crimes of the Other Side: A second principal objection to the position in my text is that it is not even-handed, that it imposes responsibility for war crimes on one side and ignores (or worse, overlooks) the war crimes of the other side. In this view, the National Liberation Front and North Vietnam are guilty of a variety of atrocities including systematic recourse to wanton terror against the civilian population of South Vietnam. My response to this contention is partly a logical one, namely, that the commission of war crimes by the other side is irrelevant (or at least must be shown to be relevant) to the commission of war crimes by the United States in Vietnam. In this vein, I find no connection whatsoever between allegations of "enemy" war crimes and the American reliance on concentrated firepower, napalm, B-52 raids, and chemical poisons; in both instances, the principal victims are Vietnamese civilians. Furthermore, the high technology military machine used by the United States inflicts the great proportion of civilian casualties and results in the destruction of most villages. Such a comparison of effects is a natural consequence of a 500:1 edge in relative firepower and expresses the character of a war between a high technology political system and a low technology political system. Finally, my best information suggests that the alleged atrocities attributed to the other side have either been exaggerated or have involved recourse to discriminating tactics of violence such as satisfy the military necessity test in this kind of military struggle for political control (for instance, the selective assassination of village officials loyal to the Saigon regime).

Laws of War Are Obsolete in Counterinsurgency Situations: The objection here is that in counterinsurgency warfare of the Vietnam variety the traditional bases of the laws of war are undermined. There are no discernible lines of battle, no military targets, no uniforms by which to differentiate "the guerrilla fighter" from the rest of the population. A successful insurgency, it is true, works to blur, and eventually to eliminate the distinction between the insurgent and the general civilian population. How can the incumbent fight against such an enemy without using tactics that suspend deference to the civilian population or to nonmilitary targets. Furthermore, in primitive country, there are very few military targets. Reliance on airpower as a continuing weapon leads to destroying anything that stands or moves in territory where the insurgent holds sway. Ideas of "free bomb zones," search-and-destroy missions, and incidents such as took place at Son My are the logical sequel of such a doctrine of counterinsurgency warfare. At such a point, the continuation of the war by relying on modern weapons does take on a genocidal character.

In a more technical vein, to the extent that The Hague and Geneva treaty rules are obsolete, then it is appropriate without awaiting new treaties, to attempt new applications of the basic customary rules at stake: the avoidance of unnecessary suffering and destruction; the maintenance of the distinction between civilian and military targets and personnel, at least to the extent possible; and the avoidance altogether of the inherently cruel.

Some may say that war crimes have been committed by both sides in Vietnam and, therefore, prosecution should be even-handed, and that North Vietnam and the Provisional Revolutionary Government of South Vietnam should be called upon to prosecute their officials guilty of war crimes. Such a contention needs to be understood, however, in the overall context of the war, especially in relation to the identification of which side is the victim of aggression and which side is the aggressor. More narrowly, the allegation of war crimes by the other side does not operate as a legal defense against a war crimes indictment. This question was clearly litigated and decided at Nuremberg.

Others have argued that there can be no war crimes in Vietnam because war has never been "declared" by the U.S. government. The failure to declare war under these circumstances raises a substantial constitutional question, but it has no bearing upon the rights and duties of the United States under international law. A declaration of war is a matter of internal law, but the existence of combat circumstances is a condition of war that brings into play the full range of obligations under international law governing the conduct of a war.

VI. Proposals

The evidence suggests that the current condition of the laws of warfare is inadequate for several principal reasons:

1. The rules were evolved long ago under conditions that seem remote from the nature of modern warfare.
2. Such remoteness in time and tactics tends to obscure the persisting relevance of underlying policies—the prohibition of cruel and unnecessary suffering not clearly related to the legitimate pursuit of belligerent objectives.

Hence, the rules need to be restated and the climate for their effective implementation needs to be created. Technicians need to prepare new draft treaties and statesmen have to be persuaded to sign and adhere.

The widespread revulsion with the persistence of war creates the basis for such constructive developments.

I would propose three concrete steps at the present time:

(1) A Second Series of Hague Conferences to agree upon a new code of warfare. Such conferences should be regarded as political occasions (as contrasted to the 1949 series of meetings of experts in Geneva) on which a new moral and legal consensus is formed such as emerged, quite unexpectedly, from The Hague Conferences of 1899 and 1907. It would be difficult, of course, to reach agreement on many matters, partly for reasons of ideology, partly for reasons of technology and military doctrine, but it would clearly be worth the effort. The process of proposing, discussing, and responding would heighten the awareness of government officials and would help revive a clearer appreciation of the basic policies to be served by the laws of war. This appreciation would, I think, without being too optimistic or naive, be likely to influence the decision processes of governments during a period of war and would make the international community more likely to repudiate departures from these policies.

(2) A National Board of Legal Experts appointed, perhaps by a legal society such as the American Bar Association, to undertake an inquiry into the extent to which the laws of war were violated during the course of the Vietnam War.[33] Such a Board should be empowered to subpoena military and civilian officials and to hear testimony from soldiers and from civilian complainants. The purpose of the inquiry would be to facilitate a process of moral and legal clarification about the manner in which the Vietnam War was waged. The Board could be entrusted with the capacity to recommend the preparation of criminal indictments against any individual whom it had reason—after a due process inquiry—to believe committed war crimes, but such an authority is probably not desirable. First of all, it would be impractical to discharge such a mandate given the likely numbers of individuals who might become implicated. Second, there is no clear evidence that criminal punishment deters crime or rehabilitates the criminal. Third, the Vietnam War depended for support on so many aspects of societal cooperation that it seems to be "scapegoating" whether one selects the

---

[33] This suggestion closely resembles the recommendation of Leonard B. Boudin in a paper given at the 1970 Annual Meeting of the American Bar Association in St. Louis under the title "Nuremberg and the Indochinese War" (mimeographed draft dated August 12, 1970).

triggermen or the prominent leaders; in the one case, the leadership attempts to isolate itself from the crime, whereas in the other, the populace attempts to relinquish its own responsibility. The National Board should issue a report containing its findings and recommendations. The objective should be educational in the broad sense of raising the national level of consciousness about the issue of war crimes.

(3) A National Proclamation of Amnesty: Part of the process of moral clarification should involve amnesty for those who refused to participate in a war deemed unjust. The criminality of the official policies accounted for much of the opposition to the war, and it seems almost a continuation of those war policies to punish as criminals those who refused to take part. Indeed, the use of criminal law and of prison to punish war resisters has eroded respect for law in general and has created in the minds of many young Americans a dangerous tension between legality and legitimacy. It will be difficult to relax this tension without a grant of amnesty for those in jail or exile because of war resistance.

VII. Conclusion

This article has examined some of the wider implications of the Son My disclosures. These disclosures suggest the existence of a far wider net of responsibility than is implicit in the criminal prosecution of the perpetrators of the massacre. These individuals—many of whom have been described as men of good character and spotless records—were caught up in a brutalizing climate of warfare in which disregard for the lives and welfare of the Vietnamese civilian population was the essence of fighting the war. Their acts were merely an extreme enactment of official policy. In repudiating official policy it is necessary to move beyond ideas of crime and punishment. The need is for self-education and for a moral and legal renewal, epitomized by a new code of laws and by a belated realization that war resistance was behavior in the nation's service. By proceeding along these lines it may be possible to gain something even from the massacre at Son My.

Legal Aspects of the
My Lai Incident

ALFRED P. RUBIN

THE LATIN MAXIM that the law is silent in time of conflict has never had application to international law. There is, in fact, a large body of international law today which purports to regulate the conduct of conflict. Recognizing that international conflict almost by definition involves hurting people, a major part of the international law relating to conflict is devoted to fixing rules that are intended to minimize the hurt that is inflicted on the helpless in conflict situations. When considering this body of law, it is irrelevant that the conflict itself may be "illegal" or "unjustifiable"; the rules to limit the hurt to the helpless apply to all parties to a conflict regardless of its origin.

There are two great sources for the body of substantive rules that apply in situations of conflict. The first is the law expressly accepted by the state whose conduct is being measured in the form of a commitment to other states: Convention, Treaty, Protocol, etc. The second is the body of general international law evidenced by the actions of states, justifications, declarations, diplomatic correspondence, etc., indicating an underlying conviction that a certain course of behavior is permitted or not as a matter of obligation to another state or states. One problem is that this second body of law is difficult to distinguish from international morality, just as in primitive societies and informal associations it is difficult to distinguish between that which is forbidden by law and that which is merely "not done." In the delicate area of conflict, which involves questions of national security and honor, much work has been done to translate arguable rules of conduct into express commitments which are binding because of the form in which they are made. This reduces the area for quarrel over the distinction between moral and legal obligations by making into express legal obligations all the rules states have been able to agree to abide by. There is, of course, a vast residuum of practices underlying the express commitments of states, and the silence or ambiguity of the express formulation agreed on does not necessarily imply an absence of binding rule of law.

To illustrate the working (and not working) of the law of war, a detailed analysis of the international law applicable to a single incident, viewed as narrowly as possible in order to better focus the discussion, seems useful. A particularly shocking incident was reported to have occurred when American servicemen under normal military discipline were accused of being involved in shooting to death a group of South Vietnamese women, children, and old men at My Lai in South Vietnam. The incident is reported to have occurred in March of 1968. The victims appear to all have been nationals of South Vietnam. The Americans were operating in South Vietnam with the permission of the government of South Vietnam, but not of North Vietnam which also claims authority over the territory and the allegiance of the victims.

THE 1949 GENEVA CONVENTIONS

The United States and the competing governments of North and South Vietnam are each party to the four Conventions concluded under the auspices of the International Red Cross at Geneva on August 12, 1949. Two of those Conventions, one dealing with the situation of civilians and the other with prisoners of war, are directly pertinent to the legal analysis of the case.[1] Both Conventions are applicable to circumstances:

...of declared war or of any other armed conflict which may arise between two or more of the High Contracting Parties, even if the state of war is not recognized by one of them.[2]

By inference, then, this seems to say that at least one of the parties must recognize the existence of a war in order for these conventions to apply. Since no party to the conflict now going on in South Vietnam seems to have formally recognized a state of war to exist, there is some question as to whether the provisions of the Conventions apply at all to this conflict. To the extent that the substantive rules of the Conventions merely reflect or codify rules of general international law, however, those rules would apply regardless of difficulties concerning the formal application of the Conventions. We shall return to this point later.

Both Conventions apply expressly, but not in all their terms, to cases of "armed conflict not of an international character occurring in the territory of one of the High Contracting Parties."[3] It is certainly possible that both North Vietnam and South Vietnam regard this part of the Conventions as applying to the My Lai incident. If this part of the

---

[1] T.I.A.S. No. 3365; 75 U.N.T.S. 287, and T.I.A.S. No. 3364; 75 U.N.T.S. 135.
[2] Article 2 in both Conventions.
[3] Article 3 in both Conventions.

Conventions does apply, then the following substantive rules, laid down in the Conventions in identical words, would also apply:

... Persons taking no active part in the hostilities, including members of armed forces who have laid down their arms and those placed *hors de combat* by ... detention, or any other cause, shall in all circumstances be treated humanely ...

To this end, the following acts are and shall remain prohibited at any time and in any place whatsoever with respect to the above-mentioned persons:

(a)   violence to life and person, in particular, murder ...

(b)   the passing of sentences and the carrying out of executions without previous judgment pronounced by a regularly constituted court ...

Had the My Lai incident involved South Vietnamese soldiers slaughtering South Vietnamese persons placed *hors de combat* by detention or any other cause, and assuming the "conflict not of an international character" to be within the purview of the Geneva Conventions, it could be argued clearly that a breach of the Conventions had occurred, and the next step would have been to see what rules of international law apply in the case of such breaches. However, the case is not so simple.

The United States has, for its own purposes, insisted that the conflict in South Vietnam does partake of international character.[4] Indeed, since American servicemen captured by the enemy in Southeast Asia are entitled to prisoner of war treatment only if the Prisoner of War Convention applied in its other terms to the situation in Vietnam, at least to those phases of the conflict involving American military units fighting against non-American participants in the struggle, and since in fact American military personnel in South Vietnam act directly as officials of the United States and do not derive their authority from any delegation of state authority from the Government of South Vietnam, it is difficult to see how any part of the conflict pitting American servicemen against non-Americans can be regarded by the United States as a "conflict not of an international character."[5] Therefore, to understand the legal obligations which must be felt by the United States to arise out of the My Lai incident, it must be assumed that the simple formula requiring merely humane treatment for persons placed *hors de combat* is not directly applicable.

The Prisoner of War Convention provides for a system of safeguards for persons belonging to one of a listed series of categories who have fallen into the hands of the enemy. The categories include mem-

---

[4] Meeker, *The Legality of U.S. Participation in the Defense of Viet Nam*, DEP'T OF STATE BULL. Mar. 28, 1966.

[5] This is not to say that South Vietnam must look at the conflict in the same way. The conflict can be regarded as "not of an international character" insofar as all participants in any single episode have the same nationality or are acting for (or against) a single state. It is only when a second state is involved that a different view must be taken, even if the second state is helping the first to defend itself.

bers of regular armed forces and other traditional groups clearly inappropriate to the women, children, and old men of My Lai. But the irreducible minimum for entitlement to prisoner of war status is that the persons "carry arms openly and respect the laws and customs of war."[6] The inhabitants of My Lai, on the other hand, are alleged to have concealed their weapons and are supposed to have violated some of the laws and customs of war. Thus, while they would seem generally to fit the class of persons the Prisoner of War Convention was designed to protect, the Convention rejects them as unfit for its safeguards. It rejects them even if it were assumed that all were part of organized Viet Cong outfits or had taken up arms spontaneously to resist invading forces "without having had time to form themselves into regular trained units."[7] Article 5 of the Convention requires prisoner of war status for captives in conflict under the Convention in cases of doubt "until such time as their status has been determined by a competent tribunal." But it seems arguable that there was never any sufficient quantum of "doubt" about the people of My Lai to bring them within the purview of this provision.

The Civilians Convention applies to protect persons "who, ... in any manner whatsoever, find themselves, in case of a conflict ... in the hands of a Party to the conflict ... of which they are not nationals."[8] Even in the case of spies and saboteurs, persons protected by the Convention are entitled to be "treated with humanity."[9] A difficulty here is that Article 4 of the Civilians Convention provides that persons "protected by," that is, within the general purview of the Prisoner of War Convention "shall not be considered as protected persons within the meaning of the present Convention." It is not clear that persons like the residents of My Lai, who would be "protected by" the Prisoner of War Convention were it not for their participation in violations of the rules of war such as carrying concealed arms, etc., can be considered outside the Prisoner of War Convention. Would not the inhabitants of My Lai, therefore, be more logically regarded as persons "protected by" the Prisoner of War Convention who have forfeited their substantive rights by their own illegal actions?

On the other hand, that approach, while logical, leads to an anomaly. If, as pointed out before, the Conventions protect from inhumane treatment those who violate the laws of war in a conflict *not* of an international character, as they do, then should they not *a fortiori* protect to at

---

[6] Article 4, especially subparagraphs 4(2)(c) and (d) and 4(6) of 1949 Prisoner of War Convention (T.I.A.S. No. 3364; 74 U.N.T.S. 135).

[7] In view of the duration of the conflict, the latter of these categories seems particularly inappropriate.

[8] Article 4, of 1949 Civilians Convention (T.I.A.S. No. 3365; 75 U.N.T.S. 287).

[9] *Id.*, Article 5.

least the same extent the same individuals acting in a conflict of an international character? *I.e.*, if a state may not treat inhumanely its own nationals in any conflict circumstances, should a foreign state be able legally to indulge in inhumane treatment of the same people doing the same things in the same conflict? International law has traditionally spoken more loudly to protect people from the oppression of second states than from the oppression of their own state.[10] While the United States might, then, seek technical legal grounds to avoid classifying the My Lai incident as having involved a breach of either convention, in a public appearance on December 9, 1969, the President of the United States condemned the killing, thereby indicating the United States will not follow such a course.

It will, therefore, be assumed *arguendo* that the substantive terms of the Civilians Convention apply to the inhabitants of My Lai to protect them from the United States.

INTERNATIONAL OBLIGATIONS AND AMERICAN PERFORMANCE

The substantive protection to which persons are entitled who fall within the terms of the Civilians Convention are many. For present purposes it seems necessary merely to point out that if the allegations concerning the slaughter of the entire population of My Lai are correct, there has been a clear violation of Articles 32 and 33 of the Convention. Those Articles prohibit the High Contracting Parties from "taking any measure of such a character as to cause physical suffering or extermination of protected persons in their hands" and punishing any protected person for any offense not personally committed by the person punished. Collective penalties and reprisals are also specifically forbidden.

Assuming the Convention to have been breached by American military personnel acting in their official capacities in the territory of South Vietnam, it does not follow that the United States as an international person has violated its obligations under the Civilians Convention. The Convention does not require the High Contracting Parties to have absolute, iron control over the behavior of every member of their armed forces. Even in time of peace, no one expects a country's criminal law

---

10 Article 4 of the Civilians Convention also excepts "nationals of a co-belligerent state...while the state of which they are nationals has normal diplomatic representation in the state in whose hands they are." The Thieu Government in South Vietnam has had normal diplomatic representation in the United States at all pertinent times. If that representation can be called normal diplomatic representation of the state of South Vietnam there would be the same anomaly: The government of South Vietnam would be restricted by Article 3 of the Convention to "humane" treatment of its rebel nationals while the United States would seem to be free to maltreat them as long as the Thieu Government did not object.

to prevent the occurrence of criminal behavior by individuals; the expectation is only to deter that behavior by the threat of punishment and perhaps to attempt to rehabilitate the accused criminal after he has been through certain legal forms of trial and conviction.

All four Geneva Conventions of 1949 seek to deter what are called "grave breaches" in two basic ways: first, to require the High Contracting Parties to educate their officials as to the standards of behavior that must be observed in situations within the purview of the Conventions; and second, to punish those individuals actually involved in committing "grave breaches." To see how the rules of law apply to incidents like that alleged to have occurred at My Lai, let us turn to the text of the Civilians Convention and to United States practice under that Convention, bearing in mind that all four Conventions contain identical substantive language.

Article 144 of the Civilians Convention says:

The High Contracting Parties undertake in time of peace, as in time of war, to disseminate the text of the present Convention as widely as possible in their respective countries, and in particular to include the study thereof in their programmes of military and, if possible, civil instruction so that the principles thereof may become known to the entire population.

Furthermore, any civilian, military, police or other authorities who in time of war assume responsibilities in respect of protected persons must possess the text of each Convention and be specially instructed as to their provisions.

The American Department of Defense has in fact undertaken a fairly elaborate program at least to inform persons subject to its control, that is American military personnel, of the existence of the Conventions and the gist of their most important provisions. Indeed, it seems likely that the United States is doing far more at this time with regard to disseminating information about the Conventions than any other country.[11] It must be recognized, however, that no program of education can be effective; a point of diminishing attention and boredom, if not contempt, is soon reached in lecturing about the complex to the uninterested. It must be remembered that servicemen are interested in their own survival and rights far more than in the survival and rights of those who have been trying to kill them. Furthermore, in the stress of combat and near-combat situations the relatively abstract commands of the Conventions are not likely to bear much relation to reality in the mind of a serviceman who is not by capacity, interest, or training attuned to the niceties of the law. In expecting education to be effective

---

[11] A rundown of American efforts in this regard has been published in 1964 PROCEEDINGS OF THE AMERICAN SOCIETY OF INTERNATIONAL LAW 89.

in this area, the framers of the Conventions may have been over-optimistic; certainly increased hours of instruction are not likely to result in increased concern about the Conventions in any way pertinent to the problems raised by the My Lai incident.

As to distributing the text of the Conventions, the United States does not seem to have lived up to its apparent obligations. Surely not every American serviceman into whose custody a person protected by one of the Conventions might fall has a copy of the text. This is a lapse that might be easily remedied. But, again, it would be unrealistic to expect the wider dissemination of the texts of the Geneva Conventions to have much practical effect. Even if junior officers in the field had copies, would they have the time or will to peruse them in circumstances similar to those at My Lai? How many would have the technical education to read the texts with understanding? If a soldier thought he perceived a discrepancy between an order he received and something he might find in one of the Conventions would he be likely to be influenced by the Convention's text to run the risk involved in disobeying an order (see below)? Despite the peremptory language of Article 144 of the Civilians Convention, it would seem very unlikely that any state would be willing to disseminate the text of the Conventions to its men in the field merely for fear that doing so would result in bringing into question (thus delaying the carrying out of) apparently inconsistent orders which at a staff level have been determined to be consistent with the Conventions. It is very doubtful that any High Contracting Party has complied with its literal undertakings in this regard.[12] Thus it is possible to argue, aside from the futility of the commitment, that the literal commitment is greater than the obligation actually felt by the High Contracting Parties to disseminate the texts of the Geneva Conventions of 1949. Accordingly, it may be doubted that failure to abide by the precise terms of the Conventions requiring dissemination of the texts to the lowest official level represents a violation of its international obligations by the United States. No state can levy such an accusation without being subject to the cry, *Tu quoque*. In other words, the real obligation seems to be less than the express obligation.

It would seem, thus, that such failures of the United States as may seem to exist with regard to obligations to educate its officials as to the existence and meaning of the Geneva Conventions of 1949 are either venial, of no practical effect, or legally not failures at all.

Let us turn now to the obligations with regard to "grave breaches" after they occur. Article 147 of the Civilians Convention, and its counterparts in the other Conventions, defines "grave breaches" to include

---

[12] *Cf.* Draper, *The Geneva Conventions of 1949*, RECUEIL DES COURS 59, 151-153 (1965).

"willful killing" of a person protected by the Convention as well as other acts less clearly pertinent to the My Lai situation.

Article 146 of the Civilians Convention provides:

The High Contracting Parties undertake to enact any legislation necessary to provide effective penal sanctions for persons committing, or ordering to be committed, any of the grave breaches of the present Convention defined in the following Article.

Article 146 also provides that the High Contracting Parties must "search for persons alleged to have committed or to have ordered to be committed such grave breaches, and to bring such persons, regardless of their nationality, before its own courts," or, in some cases, hand them over for trial to some other High Contracting Party.

Leaving aside, for a moment, the vital issue of jurisdiction, the United States has provided for "effective penal sanctions" in the case of "willful killing." Under the constitutional provision giving the Congress the power to "make rules for the government and regulation of the land and naval forces"[13] the Congress has enacted a Uniform Code of Military Justice.[14] Under the Code, it is murder to kill a human being "without justification or excuse" when one has a premeditated design to kill. More likely pertinent to the My Lai facts as reported is the provision defining "voluntary manslaughter" to include a killing committed "unlawfully," "in the heat of sudden passion caused by adequate provocation." The penalty for voluntary manslaughter is entirely at the discretion of a court martial with no expressed upper limit.

To the extent that this rather awkward language can be made to fit the My Lai facts, a prima facie case exists, but it is still not clear that the United States has discharged its international obligation to make grave breaches of the Convention subject to effective penalties. There is the possible defense of superior orders.

The Uniform Code of Military Justice grapples with the problem of superior orders. Article 90 of the Code provides:

Any person who is subject to this chapter who willfully disobeys a lawful command of his superior commissioned officer shall be punished, and if the offense is committed in time of war, by death or such other punishment as a court martial shall direct.

In time of peace, the court martial may direct any punishment other than death, including life imprisonment. Even if the order were given by someone other than a commissioned officer, the spectre of punishment would remain. Article 91 provides that any enlisted member who willfully disobeys the lawful order of a noncommissioned officer or petty officer shall be punished as court martial may direct. Moreover,

---

[13] U.S. Const. art. 1, §8, cl. 14.
[14] 10 U.S.C. §§801-940 (1964).

any person subject to the Code who violates or fails to obey any lawful *general order* or regulation shall be punished as a court martial may direct under Article 92. It would seem, therefore, that even if the order given were not specific or were misunderstood, he who is subject to the Code and who fails to carry out his understanding of that general order may be subject to punishment.

These three provisions of the Code, Articles 90, 91, and 92, cannot, however, legally be used to compel a man to murder. In all three cases, the injunction to obey an order is restricted to the case of a *lawful* command or *lawful* order. An order to commit a crime would not be lawful. Therein lies the great dilemma of military justice. How is the enlisted man or the officer in the heat of danger to make a judgment that an order given him is unlawful? If, acting on the assumption the order is unlawful, he refuses to obey it, and sitting back in the quiet of Headquarters, a Headquarters that may indeed have issued the order in question, a group of officers decide that the order, though perhaps questionable, was lawful after all, the person subject to the Code failing to react to the order may find himself in prison for a very long time. Further, enforcement of the criminal law including the law codified in the Uniform Code of Military Justice is not by tribunal alone. Enforcement of the law is frequently by group pressure. The man who refuses to obey an order which his friends are carrying out finds himself in an intolerable position in a combat situation, perhaps subject even to being shot by his companions or his superior officer, obviously without legal recourse, merely for questioning an order.

These problems are well known, and the instances of the victors in a war applying a harsher measure, a more rigid standard of judgment, to the vanquished than it applies to its own personnel in time of war have been often documented, particularly in the Nuremberg tribunals. An example often commented upon was the conviction of the Nazi Admirals Doenitz and Raeder after World War II of the war crimes involved in ordering unrestricted submarine warfare under circumstances in which American and British naval authorities had themselves ordered similar unrestricted submarine warfare.[15] To my knowledge, none of the American or British commanders giving the illegal orders was ever brought before a tribunal. The illegal orders were certainly obeyed.

The Geneva Conventions of 1949 attempted to take account of this unfortunate, and apparently unavoidable, dilemma by providing that the obligations of states to punish breaches of the Conventions be extended only to *grave* breaches of each Convention, it being the thought that any actions as serious as willfully killing civilians would be ob-

---

[15] 10 M. WHITEMAN, DIGEST OF INTERNATIONAL LAW 660-666 (1968).

viously immoral, and any orders to commit such acts obviously illegal to the actors. It seems clear now that the framers of the Convention were again over-optimistic. It may be concluded, then, that the United States has provided effective penal sanctions for the grave breach involved in willfully killing civilians (at least where military personnel are involved), but that the likelihood of those "effective penal sanctions" being effective to deter the crime when committed because of a misunderstanding of superior orders is small. The difficulty here seems to lie in the nature of armed conflict and the traditional discipline required by all military forces. The Conventions' answer to those real problems is to ignore them. Perhaps there is no alternative.

Nonetheless, as to American military personnel, the mechanism to prosecute grave breaches at least exists. Whether the United States has lived up to its other prosecutory obligations under the convention, however, is at least doubtful. With regard to grave breaches alleged to have been committed in South Vietnam by persons who are not American nationals or members of the armed forces of the United States, there appears to be no American legislation in effect to implement the obligation contained in Article 146 of the Civilians Convention. That obligation is

... to bring such persons, *regardless of their nationality,* before its own courts [or] ... hand such persons over for trial to another High Contracting Party concerned, provided such High Contracting Party has made out a *prima facie* case (emphasis added).

The fact that South Vietnam may also be violating its obligations in this respect seems irrelevant. This failure on the part of South Vietnam cannot be interpreted as evidence that the obligations of the Geneva Conventions are more apparent than real. Unlike the position with regard to the dissemination of texts and information, some countries, including the United States, have taken the obligation to punish their own nationals very seriously in some cases (although perhaps for reasons of internal military discipline rather than international obligation), and a few even have enacted legislation to permit the full prosecution of foreign nationals for war crimes committed on foreign soil precisely as required by the Conventions.[16] Furthermore, the provisions for individual responsibility for war are the heart of the Conventions' enforcement system and not, as in the case of the dissemination provisions, a kind of futile gesture.

Since instances of South Vietnamese nationals committing grave breaches of the Civilians Convention are notorious—indeed, one instance appeared live on American television during the Tet Offensive—

---

[16] *E.g.,* British legislation: The Geneva Conventions Act, 5 & 6 Eliz. 2, ch. 52 (1957).

and many allegations complete with names and dates have appeared in the American press, the failure of the United States to live up to its commitment to prosecute seems clear. The political reasons for that failure are obvious, but the failure remains.

Although political reasons may explain the failure of the United States to prosecute South Vietnamese nationals, no equivalent justification exists where an American national is involved. Certain practical difficulties might arise in some cases such as the difficulty of procuring witnesses or of setting a proper place for trial (the United States could hardly establish a U. S. District Court in Vietnam, and less formal courts are likely to run into constitutional due process objections). Nonetheless, there is no reason why the United States should not supply at least some mechanisms for the cases in which these difficulties can be overcome.

Let us see whether the United States has in fact fulfilled its obligation under the Conventions to the extent of being able at least to attempt to try all American nationals involved in grave breaches. Although none of the men involved in the My Lai incident was a civilian at the time the incident was committed, some have since returned to civilian life. In *Toth v. Quarles*,[17] the United States Supreme Court held that an American discharged from the military service could not be tried by military court martial any longer. What court, then, can be used to try Americans accused of serious crimes committed abroad, but who are not subject to courts martial?

The laws of the United States, do provide for the punishment by federal, nonmilitary courts of persons in some cases who are accused of committing murder or manslaughter overseas.[18] In these provisions, murder is defined as the unlawful killing of a human being with malice aforethought. Manslaughter is the unlawful killing of a human being without malice, and includes killing in the commission of an unlawful act not amounting to a felony, or in the commission in an unlawful manner or without due caution and circumspection, of a lawful act which might produce death. The killings perpetrated in My Lai by Americans might be criminal by these definitions contained in the *United States Code*. Those provisions apply to all Americans even if they were subject to the Uniform Code of Military Justice at the time the offenses were committed. But the power of American tribunals to punish these offenses is limited to those cases involving offenses committed within the "special maritime and territorial jurisdiction of the United States." The special maritime and territorial jurisdiction of the United States as used in the Code includes the high seas and some

---

[17] 350 U.S. 11 (1955).
[18] U.S.C. §§1111-1112 (1964).

other waters, and "Any lands reserved or acquired for the use of the United States and under the exclusive or concurrent jurisdiction thereof, or any place purchased or otherwise acquired by the United States . . . "[19] It may be doubted that any part of South Vietnam outside of specific military base compounds can be considered lands reserved or acquired for the use of the United States. Certainly the land on which My Lai was located is not such land.

It seems clear, therefore, that at least since the decision in *Toth v. Quarles* (1955) the United States has been unable legally to bring to trial by court martial or in federal nonmilitary court Americans not in the military service who have committed grave breaches of the 1949 Geneva Conventions while outside the maritime and territorial jurisdiction of the United States. Thus it would appear that the United States has not yet carried out its obligations under the 1949 Geneva Conventions insofar as these Conventions would apply to those persons.[20]

CONCLUSION

It would seem that the United States is generally discharging its international obligations with regard to atrocities such as are alleged to have been committed by American military personnel in South Vietnam. The United States also seems to be generally discharging its obligations under the Geneva Conventions of 1949 to educate its people with regard to those Conventions. On the other hand, the United States seems to have ignored its obligations to search out and bring before its own courts persons accused of committing grave breaches of the Conventions who are not directly subject to the jurisdiction of American courts martial. While the failure to disseminate the texts of the Conventions, if a violation of a literal commitment, is none the less not a violation that has significant consequences, the failure to conform to the scheme of the Conventions with regard to searching out and punishing war criminals, those accused of grave breaches, goes to the heart of the Conventions' enforcement system. If the United States cannot even punish all Americans who can be proved to have taken part in a grave breach of a Convention, then it is difficult to see

[19] 18 U.S.C. §7 (3) (1964).
[20] There is a possibility of a "military commission" being established to try accused war criminals. Although there is no direct statutory authority for establishing military commissions, they have been set up ad hoc by the United States in some cases and held constitutionally permissible. *See* 10 U.S.C. 821 (1959); Madsen v. Kinsella, 343 U.S. 341 (1952). Military commissions have been used to try aliens for acts committed abroad (*In re* Yamashita, 327 U.S. 1 [1946]), and in time of war in the United States (*Ex parte* Quiriu, 317 U.S. 1 [1942]). There is no record of any military commission having been set up by the United States with regard to events in the Korean or Vietnam wars.

how American respect for the principles of the Conventions can be alleged convincingly. This situation exists regardless of the apparent failures of other states to provide better for the discharge of their obligations under the 1949 Geneva Conventions and the underlying general international law.

Legal Aspects of the My Lai Incident—
A Response to Professor Rubin

JORDAN J. PAUST*

IN HIS ARTICLE[1] Professor Rubin states a very real problem concerning the use of the 1949 Geneva Civilian Convention[2] for the prosecution of persons accused of having committed war crimes at My Lai when he says that Article 4 of the Civilian Convention might be technically construed by some to free the United States to maltreat nationals of South Vietnam.

It is the purpose of this article to provide a broader understanding of the legal questions involved concerning the protection of the alleged My Lai victims under the 1949 Geneva Civilian Convention. The main thesis proposed is that nationals of South Vietnam are protected under Part II of the Civilian Convention regardless of the determination concerning protected status under Article 4 of that Convention.[3] To reach that conclusion we must first determine that Article 2 of the Civilian Convention applies—a conclusion also relevant to the problem of prisoners of war in the Vietnamese conflict.

Articles 2 and 3

Our first inquiry should concern the applicability of Article 2 of the Civilian Convention for it is the jurisdictional article or the article which defines the situation that must exist before any of the protective

* The opinions expressed herein are those of the author and not necessarily those of the Judge Advocate General's School, the U.S. Army, or any other governmental agency.

1 Alfred P. Rubin, "Legal Aspects of the Mai Lai Incident," 49 *Oregon Law Review* 260, 264 n. 10 (1970). (Reprinted in this volume.)

2 *Geneva Convention Relative to the Protection of Civilian Persons in Time of War* (1949), 6 U.S.T. 3516 (1955). (Hereafter referred to as the Civilian Convention.)

3 The reader should note that the Civilian Convention contains four parts. Part I (Articles 1-12) is entitled "General Provisions"; Part II (Articles 13-26) is entitled "General Protection of Populations Against Certain Consequences of War"; Part III (Articles 27-141) is entitled "Status and Treatment of Protected Persons"; and Part IV (Articles 142-159) is entitled "Execution of the Convention." The protections found in Part II are not as extensive as those found in Part III, and persons protected under these different parts of the Convention are not always the same under Part II as under Part III. For example, Article 4 defines the "protected persons" entitled to the protections of Part III, but Part II contains its own groupings of persons entitled to protection.

provisions of the general convention apply.[4] It generally states that the Convention shall apply when there is: (1) a declared war between two or more High Contracting Parties, (2) any other armed conflict between two or more High Contracting Parties even if a state of war is not recognized by one of them, or (3) a partial or total occupation of the territory of a High Contracting Party even if the said occupation meets with no armed resistance.[5]

Article 3 defines an entirely different situation since it involves a case of "armed conflict not of an international character,"[6] and Article 2

[4] In other words, if Article 2 does not apply then only the limited protections found in Article 3 of Part I could be applicable to a conflict. If Article 2 does apply, then there is a possibility that Parts II, III, and IV of the Convention will also be applicable. Articles 2 and 3 are actually the jurisdictional articles for two different "conventions"—one convention composed of Article 2 and the other composed of Article 3 alone.

[5] Article 2 reads as follows:

In addition to the provisions which shall be implemented in peacetime, the present Convention shall apply to all cases of declared war or of any other armed conflict which may arise between two or more of the High Contracting Parties, even if the state of war is not recognized by one of them.

The Convention shall also apply to all cases of partial or total occupation of the territory of a High Contracting Party, even if the said occupation meets with no armed resistance.

Although one of the Powers in conflict may not be a party to the present Convention, the Powers who are parties thereto shall remain bound by it in their mutual relations. They shall furthermore be bound by the Convention in relation to the said Power, if the latter accepts and applies the provisions thereof.

[6] Article 3 reads as follows:

In the case of armed conflict not of an international character occurring in the territory of one of the High Contracting Parties, each Party to the conflict shall be bound to apply, as a minimum, the following provisions:

(1) Persons taking no active part in the hostilities, including members of armed forces who have laid down their arms and those placed *hors de combat* by sickness, wounds, detention, or any other cause, shall in all circumstances be treated humanely, without any adverse distinction founded on race, colour, religion or faith, sex, birth or wealth, or any other similar criteria.

To this end, the following acts are and shall remain prohibited at any time and in any place whatsover with respect to the above-mentioned persons:
(a) violence to life and person, in particular murder of all kinds, mutilation, cruel treatment and torture;
(b) taking of hostages;
(c) outrages upon personal dignity, in particular humiliating and degrading treatment;
(d) the passing of sentences and the carrying out of executions without previous judgment pronounced by a regularly constituted court, affording all the judicial guarantees which are recognized as indispensable by civilized peoples.
(2) The wounded and sick shall be collected and cared for.

An impartial humanitarian body, such as the International Committee of the Red Cross, may offer its services to the Parties to the conflict.

obviously involves a situation in which two or more High Contracting Parties are involved in an armed conflict, or at least in which one High Contracting Party and one recognized belligerent are involved in an armed conflict or an occupation of the territory of a High Contracting Party. It is sufficient for our purpose to state that under the generally accepted view it is not the way a country looks at the cause of the war, the legality or morality of the actions of its adversary in conducting the hostilities, or even the nature of the political relationship of one adversary to another that is important if in fact two or more High Contracting Parties are involved in actual armed hostilities. If two or more High Contracting Parties are involved, then Article 3 would not apply at all under the leading view since the conflict is international in nature and Article 3 "applies to non-international conflicts only,"[7] or to "internal" armed conflict.

Under the leading view, the Vietnamese conflict would not constitute a "non-international" conflict regardless of the validity of any arguments that the struggle between the NLF (Vietcong) and the government of South Vietnam is in the nature of a "civil war." The conflict cannot be divided up among the parties according to the nature of the involvement of one against the other; it is one armed conflict. The conflict is of one type as far as application of the Geneva Conventions is concerned even if it could be analyzed some other way for other legal purposes: in an examination of the question of intervention or the question of whether or not the NLF or anyone in South Vietnam is bound by the laws of Vietnam. The conflict has seen the direct involve-

---

The Parties to the conflict should further endeavor to bring into force, by means of special agreements, all or part of the other provisions of the present Convention.

The application of the preceding provisions shall not affect the legal status of the Parties to the conflict.

[7] J. Pictet, *Commentary, Geneva Conventions Relative to the Protection of Civilian Persons in Time of War*, 1958, IV, 34. (Hereafter referred to as Pictet.)

Note that a question might be raised as to whether the two or more High Contracting Parties must be involved against each other (thus a conflict "between" two or more parties) or merely involved on the same side against some third party so as to make the conflict an "international" conflict and not a "non-international" conflict (so that as opposed to Article 3, Article 2 applies by default). At least in the Vietnamese conflict the war exists "between" two or more High Contracting Parties, but this question of Convention interpretation and applicability continues for future problems. Consider the involvement of only two countries where country *X* aids country *Y* in putting down an insurgent group within country *Y*. Does a conflict exist "between" *X* and *Y*? Is it an "international" conflict nevertheless? Disagreement continues. See, Carnegie Endowment for International Peace, *Report of the Conference on Contemporary Problems of the Law of Armed Conflicts* (Geneva, 15-20 September 1969), 1971, pp. 52-53.

ment in armed hostilities of the United States, South Vietnam, North Vietnam,[8] South Korea, Thailand, Australia, New Zealand, and the Philippines. This multiple involvement of two or more High Contracting Parties to the Convention is sufficient for the nonapplication of Article 3 under the leading view. The only other possibility of an application of Article 3 would concern an Alice-in-Wonderland conclusion that South Vietnam and the NLF are involved in a separate armed conflict in which the forces of the United States, South Korea, Thailand, Australia, New Zealand, the Philippines, and North Vietnam do not participate at all.[9]

But our question concerns the application of Part II of the Civilian Convention and it is not necessary to prove that Article 3 does not apply. It is only necessary to show that Article 2 does apply. As far as the author is aware, there has been no formal declaration of war by any of the parties to the conflict. There may have been a "partial occupation" of the territory of South Vietnam by the forces of North Vietnam but traditionally this would depend on the intention of the North Vietnamese forces to hold the territory and whether or not the territory is in their effective control.[10] The strongest basis for arguing that Article 2 applies among the situations outlined above seems to concern the language that the Convention shall apply if "any other armed conflict" occurs between two or more High Contracting Parties, even if the state of war is not recognized by one of them. It does not seem that anyone is foolish enough to argue that an armed conflict does not exist in Vietnam—the remaining inquiry will thus be whether or not someone has to recognize that conflict as being a "state of war."

First of all it is important to note that the Article specifically mentions a declaration of war. Apparently the language "any other armed conflict" involves something else and would not require a declaration of war and possibly not even war. That "something else" could apparently be the recognition of the existence of a state of war (something

---

[8] Regular army units from North Vietnam have operated in the South with the result that there are now around 8,000 North Vietnamese prisoners held in the South. See *infra*, footnote 16.

[9] The application of this Alice approach (or actually that of Humpty Dumpty since in his view words mean anything that he wants them to mean) would concern an argument that South Vietnam need only apply Article 3 protections to the NLF since some conflict not of an international nature exists alongside and independent of the international conflict to which Article 2 applies.

[10] See, e.g., L. Oppenheim, *International Law* (7th edn., Lauterpacht, 1952), II, 434-436; U.S. Army, Pamphlet No. 27-161-2, II *International Law*, 1962, p. 159.

less than formal declaration) or even the mere factual existence of an armed conflict without any recognition of a state of war. It would depend upon one's reading of the language "even if the state of war is not recognized by one of them." Alternative interpretations are possible, but it is the purpose here to suggest that Professor Rubin's view which would require that one party recognize that a state of war exists[11] is not the generally accepted view nor does it seem correct in light of the history of the Convention and its purpose.

The weight of authority is that it is the factual existence of an armed conflict which is important and not the recognition of a state of war. Pictet states that there is "no need for a formal declaration of war, or for the recognition of the existence of a state of war. . . . The occurrence of *de facto* hostilities is sufficient."[12]

The background of the Convention is important in pointing to the meaning of the phrase. A. Esgain and W. Solf have stated: "This article resolved doubt as to the applicability of the convention to armed conflicts which are not considered by one or all of the belligerents as constituting a state of war."[13] And Draper has stated:

[11] Rubin, *supra* note 1 at 261. Note that Professor Rubin seems to go further in requiring "formal" recognition (a term not used in the Convention) as opposed to mere recognition (formal recognition sounds like declaration).

[12] Pictet, *supra*, note 7 at 20-21. See Oppenheim, *International Law*, II, 369 n. 6 stating: "The intention was probably to say by 'one or both of them.' This, it appears, is the correct interpretation of the Convention. Hostilities may occur between States in circumstances in which the belligerents on both sides attach importance to avoiding a formal state of war between them." And see also Carnegie Endowment for International Peace, *Report of the Conference on Contemporary Problems of the Law of Armed Conflicts* (Geneva, 15-20 September 1969), 1971, p. 49 n. 22, stating that the phrase "must be interpreted as meaning that the Conventions apply even if *none* of the parties has recognized a state of war."

[13] A. Esgain and W. Solf, "The 1949 Geneva Convention Relative to the Treatment of Prisoners of War: Its Principles, Innovations, and Deficiencies," 41 *North Carolina Law Review* 537, 545 (1963). Note that Article 2 is common to all four of the 1949 Geneva Conventions.

The application of Article 2 of the Civilian Convention to the Vietnamese conflict also means that Article 2 of the 1949 Geneva Convention Relative to the Treatment of Prisoners of War, 6 U.S.T. 3318 (1955), applies to that conflict. This defeats one of Hanoi's chief arguments for the non-applicability of the Geneva Conventions and for the denial without reason of the protections of that Convention to prisoners of war held by North Vietnam. It seems incredible that someone would argue for inhumane treatment of persons taken out of the fighting even if some law was not applicable to bind conduct. If for the oriental mind the ideal government is by moral principles (*Li*), the written law (*Fa*) is a necessary evil used only when moral principles and group responsibility have failed, and the good man does not get into legal disputes which are contrary to

The earlier Geneva Conventions were considered to apply only in a case of war, either validly declared or recognized by either belligerent as amounting to a state of war in International Law. Thus, in a case where both contestants denied a state of war, the earlier Conventions were not legally applicable . . . certain states were fully aware of certain advantages that flowed from a refusal to treat the conflict as a war. It is that type of situation which is covered by the words "or of any other armed conflict. . . ." In the light of the experience of the Second World War and of the compelling humanitarian motives underlying the preparation of these Conventions it was inevitable that the protection of war victims could not be left to the hazardous and debatable determination of the existence of a legal state of war. The phrase "armed conflict" was devised as the solution of this difficulty.[14]

Article 2 was adopted at the Diplomatic Conference on the proposal of the International Committee of the Red Cross without debate, but concerning discussion of another article at least one reference was made which seems to support Pictet's view and that of Draper concerning the background of the article. Mr. Castberg of Norway stated: "It was a step forward in international law to say explicitly that, even

---

human values, then it is even more incredible that an oriental mind would make legal arguments contrary to the human values expressed by almost all nations of the world in the 1949 Geneva Conventions (and these values are not merely through the "eyes of the deer").

For a look at the traditional oriental mind plus the new egocentric Communist view toward laws (a view necessary for any international lawyer to understand if he is concerned with the regulation of public conduct and social response), see S. Leng, *Justice in Communist China*, 1967.

[14] G. Draper, *The Red Cross Conventions*, 1958, pp. 10-11, citing: "Report on the work of the Conference of Government Experts for the study of the Conventions for the Protection of War Victims (Geneva, April 14-26, 1947), Geneva 1947, p. 8" for the origin of the phrase and its intent to overcome the need for a recognition of a legal state of war.

Professor Rubin apparently feels that the drafters could have been even more explicit. It may be noted here that a failure to declare war does not obviate the need to follow the general law of war. (U.S. Army, Field Manual No. 27-10, *Law of Land Warfare*, paras. 8 and 9, 1956.) It would be surprising to find an implied intention of the drafters of the Geneva Conventions which (contrary to the rule for the general law of war) holds that the Convention law does not apply if no recognition exists by a party to the conflict. Indeed it seems that the drafters intended to avoid such difficulties and provide protections for the victims of armed conflicts which cannot be consented away by states directly by mutual consent (see Articles 7 and 8), or by unilateral declaration (see Articles 148 and 158), or indirectly by a mutual refusal to recognize that an armed conflict in fact exists.

if war was not recognized, the rules concerning the conduct of war should be applied."[15]

It is the author's opinion that Article 2 does not require recognition of the existence of a state of war, but even if we accept the restrictive interpretation postulated in Professor Rubin's article it would seem sufficient here to point out that the United States seems to have recognized the existence of an international armed conflict and a "state" of war, even though that recognition has not been extremely formal. Numerous statements have been made referring to the "war" in Southeast Asia[16] or the "armed conflict between the parties to the convention,"[17] and United States federal courts have stated that a war in fact exists in Southeast Asia for certain purposes.[18] Furthermore, North Vietnam in a response to an International Committee of the Red Cross request referred to the Vietnamese conflict as an "undeclared war of aggression" and stated that the United States and Saigon were "undertaking a war."[19] A Joint Manila Communiqué of 24 October 1966 also exists in which the government of South Vietnam along with the United States, South Korea, Thailand, Australia, New Zealand, and the

[15] II B *Final Record of the Diplomatic Conference of Geneva of 1949*, 1949, p. 11. (Hereafter referred to as II B *Final Record.*)

[16] See, e.g., L. Meeker, "The Legality of United States Participation in the Defense of Viet-Nam," *Department of State Bulletin*, 54 (March 28, 1966), 474, 475. This source is also valuable to show direct North Vietnamese involvement in the war at least since 1964. Today there are around 8,000 North Vietnamese prisoners held in the South. *Department of State Bulletin*, 63 (December 21, 1970), 737, 738. The United States recently sent a letter to the Security Council of the United Nations which outlines North Vietnamese involvement in Cambodia, and in that message the April 30, 1970 address of President Nixon was quoted and he referred to the conflict as the "war in Viet-Nam." U.N. Doc. S/9781, May 5, 1970; *Department of State Bulletin*, 62 (1970), 652. The reader should also note that Meeker's "article" was not merely an article but a Memorandum of Law from the Office of the Legal Adviser, Department of State, and in Part I, Section G it is stated, "a formal declaration of war would not place any obligations on either side in the conflict by which that side would not be bound in any event."

[17] Department of State, *Vietnam Information Notes*, Nos. 2, 9 (August 1967).

[18] See *Berk v. Laird*, 317 F. Supp. 715 (E.D.N.Y. 1970). The court quotes President Johnson's State of the Union message of January 10, 1967 at 725 where he referred to the "limited war" in South Vietnam.

See also *United States v. Averette*, 19 U.S.C.M.A. 363, 365 (1970) where the United States Court of Military Appeals stated that though no formal declaration of war has occurred (and perhaps some Constitutional protections are lost upon declaration by Congress), "we emphasize our awareness that the fighting in Vietnam qualifies as a war as that word is generally used and understood."

[19] Letter of August 31, 1965 from North Vietnamese Minister of Foreign Affairs to the ICRC. See *International Review of the Red Cross*, 5 (1965), 527, 636.

Philippines have recognized the applicability of the 1949 Geneva Conventions to the conflict. That recognition would necessarily concern recognition of the existence of an international armed conflict and that Article 2 applies, since the protections of the Conventions were declared to be applicable and not Article 3 alone. It seems that the state of war has been recognized by at least two parties though no formal declaration of war has yet occurred. Article 2 of the Civilian Convention would then be applicable even under Professor Rubin's strict view.

Article 4

The real difficulty centers around the words found in Article 4 of the Civilian Convention. This article would be applicable if Article 2 applies and would define "protected persons" under the general Convention (i.e., persons entitled to the general protections found in Part III). The problem language states that: "nationals of a co-belligerent state, shall not be regarded as protected persons while the state of which they are nationals has normal diplomatic representation in the state in whose hands they are."[20] Some have found this language more than a difficulty and have abandoned all hope of arguing for any protection for the nationals of South Vietnam under the Civilian Convention relative to the United States as a power to the conflict.[21] Professor

[20] 6 U.S.T. 3520 (1955). The entire article is set forth below:

Persons protected by the Convention are those who, at a given moment and in any manner whatsoever, find themselves, in case of a conflict or occupation, in the hands of a Party to the conflict or Occupying Power of which they are not nationals.

Nationals of a State which is not bound by the Convention are not protected by it. Nationals of a neutral State who find themselves in the territory of a belligerent State, and nationals of a co-belligerent State, shall not be regarded as protected persons while the State of which they are nationals has normal diplomatic representation in the State in whose hands they are.

The provisions of Part II are, however, wider in application, as defined in Article 13.

Persons protected by the Geneva Convention for the Amelioration of the Condition of the Wounded and Sick in Armed Forces in the Field of August 12, 1949, or by the Geneva Convention for the Amelioration of the Condition of Wounded, Sick and Shipwrecked Members of Armed Forces at Sea of August 12, 1949, or by the Geneva Convention relative to the Treatment of Prisoners of War of August 12, 1949, shall not be considered as protected persons within the meaning of the present Convention.

[21] Note, "Jurisdictional Problems Related to the Prosecution of Former Servicemen for Violations of the Law of War" 56 *Virginia Law Review* 947, 948-50 (1970); and D. Shaneyfelt, "War Crimes and the Jurisdiction Maze," 4 *International Lawyer* (A.B.A) 924, 925 (1970). The reader may note that the present author also disagrees with a conclusion of the above articles concerning jurisdiction in Paust, "After My Lai: The Case for War Crime Jurisdiction Over Civilians in Federal District Courts," 50 *Texas Law Review* 4 (1971) and concludes that jurisdiction exists in the Federal courts.

Rubin took another approach—he made an assumption that the civilians who are nationals of South Vietnam enjoy the protections of the Civilian Convention.[22] Actually it seems that neither approach is necessary since an argument can be made for the application of at least part of the Civilian Convention to the nationals of South Vietnam (even assuming that South Vietnamese are not protected persons within the meaning of Article 4 and that South Vietnam is a separate, independent State).

At least one author[23] has argued for complete application of the protections of the Civilian Convention,[24] and has done so on the following grounds:

> As the condition of "normal diplomatic representation" indicates, the nationals of a co-belligerent state are excluded from the Convention's protection because it is assumed that normal diplomatic protection is sufficient to prevent or to stop violations on the part of the power under whose authority they find themselves. This *ratio-legis* is inapplicable in the case of South Vietnam. South Vietnamese in the contested regions are not protected by the Saigon Government against possible excesses by American forces in the pursuit of *pacification* activities.

This attack based on an assumed lack of effective diplomatic protection for some of the civilians of South Vietnam is interesting but, at a minimum, would seem to require more direct proof. Furthermore, the argument is based on the assumption that it is the individual and not the State which is to be represented. This is contrary to the plain language of Article 4 which only requires that the State have normal diplomatic representation. What the author seems to be arguing is that the purpose or essence of the exception from protection is lacking and, therefore, the protection should be reinstated. Pictet in his Commentary on the Conventions[25] admits that it was assumed that co-belligerents do not need protection; but he also indicates that effective

[22] Rubin, *supra*, note 1 at 264.

[23] Henri Meyrowitz, "The Law of War in the Vietnamese Conflict," in *The Vietnam War and International Law*, 1969, Vol. 2, 516, 545 n. 55. (Edited by Richard A. Falk for the American Society of International Law.)

[24] By "complete" protections the author means that all protections are applicable (Parts II and III). Complete protections (including those of Part III) are only possible if the person in question is a "protected person" under Article 4 since Part III only applies to a "protected person" as defined by Article 4.

[25] Pictet, *supra*, note 7 at 49.

individual representation is not the test for "normal diplomatic representation," but representation such as "that which functions in peace time comprising at least one diplomatic representative accredited to a Ministry of Foreign Affairs."[26] Pictet states that the definition of the drafters is not adequate and would further require that replies to the representative be "satisfactory" and that the "representations" made "will be followed by results." Pictet's suggestions also leave us with a vague standard, but they seem short of Meyrowitz's proposed test of effective individual representation. None of these seem to provide a concrete platform for the formulation of basic protections for the victims of war. In the desire to gain humane treatment, some have been content to rest on the shaky platform in Article 4; for if the provisions of Article 4 are met, then the protections of Part III of the Convention would apply. The prize of protections for the usual victims of war would then be great, for Part III of the Convention contains 114 articles that concern the status and treatment of persons protected under Article 4. Perhaps the most important provisions of Part III would be Articles 27, 32, and 33.[27]

[26] *Id.* (citing II A *Final Record*, p. 814).
[27] The Articles read as follows:

Article 27

Protected persons are entitled, in all circumstances, to respect for their persons, their honour, their family rights, their religious convictions and practices, and their manners and customs. They shall at all times be humanely treated, and shall be protected especially against all acts of violence or threats thereof and against insults and public curiosity.

Women shall be especially protected against any attack on their honour, in particular against rape, enforced prostitution, or any form of indecent assault.

Without prejudice to the provisions relating to their state of health, age and sex, all protected persons shall be treated with the same consideration by the Party to the conflict in whose power they are, without any adverse distinction based, in particular, on race, religion or political opinion.

However, the Parties to the conflict may take such measures of control and security in regard to protected persons as may be necessary as a result of the war.

Article 32

The High Contracting Parties specifically agree that each of them is prohibited from taking any measure of such a character as to cause the physical suffering or extermination of protected persons in their hands. This prohibition applies not only to murder, torture, corporal punishment, mutilation and medical or scientific experiments not necessitated by the medical treatment of a protected person, but also to any other measures of brutality whether applied by civilian or military agents.

Article 33

No protected person may be punished for an offence he or she has not personally committed. Collective penalties and likewise all measures of intimidation or of terrorism are prohibited.

Pillage is prohibited.

Reprisals against protected persons and their property are prohibited.

Part II of the Convention

A more solid platform for the protection of populations engaged in an international armed conflict seems to be found in Part II of the 1949 Civilian Convention. Indeed, Article 4 directs the reader to Part II of the Convention and clearly states that these provisions are "wider in application" than the application of Article 4 itself. Actually, Article 4 is a definitional article in that it defines a specific class of persons (protected persons) that shall receive the protections listed in Part III concerning the treatment of protected persons. Part II, however, concerns more people than those specifically labeled as "persons protected" in Article 4. "It covers the whole population of the Parties to the Conflict, both in occupied territory and in the actual territory of those Parties. . . . It could have formed a special Convention on its own."[28] Thus Part II can apply even though Article 4 and Part III may not.

Article 13 of Part II itself declares: "The provisions of Part II cover the whole of the populations of the countries in conflict, without any adverse distinction based, in particular, on race, nationality, religion or political opinion, and are intended to alleviate the sufferings caused by war."[29] Pictet states that Part II is intended to provide the civilian population with general protection (more general than Part III in intention), and "to shield certain categories of the population who, by definition, take no part in the fighting: children, women, old people, the wounded and the sick."[30] Furthermore, he states:

> . . . the provisions in Part II are as general and extensive in scope as possible: Article 13, independently of the rest of the Convention, defines the field of application of Part II, by specifying that it covers the whole of the populations of the countries in conflict. The provisions in Part II therefore apply not only to protected persons, i.e. to enemy or other aliens and to neutrals, as defined in Article 4 but also to the belligerents' own nationals . . . the mere fact of a person residing in a territory belonging to or occupied by a party to the conflict, is sufficient to make Part II of the Convention applicable to him.[31]

This means that nationals of South Vietnam are accorded the protections of Part II of the Civilian Convention since they are a population of an ally engaged in an international conflict and no adverse distinction is allowed on the basis of nationality or political opinion.

Pictet's comments are supported by a statement of Mr. Pilloud

---

28 Pictet *supra*, note 7 at 50.   29 6 U.S.T. 3526-3528 (1955).
30 Pictet, *supra*, note 7 at 118.   31 *Id.*, at 118-119.

(International Committee of the Red Cross) at the 1949 Diplomatic Conference of Geneva that Part II embraces the entire population of countries at war while the article defining "persons protected" referred mainly to those of the enemy nationality;[32] and also by a Report of Committee III of the 1949 Diplomatic Conference at Geneva that Part II: "applies to the whole of the populations of countries in conflict; they thus concern not only the relations between a given State and its own nationals . . . duties to its own nationals."[33] Pictet's comments are also supported by an unofficial statement found in a United States Army pamphlet that Part II "goes beyond Article 4" and is: "applicable to the whole of the population of countries in conflict: [it] thus concerns not only the relations between a given state and aliens, but also the relations between a given state and its own nationals."[34] Furthermore, the practice of the United States has been to declare that all protections of the 1949 Geneva Conventions apply in Vietnam.[35]

Perhaps the most interesting and difficult question concerns the scope of any protections accorded to the whole of the population of South Vietnam under Part II. A close look at Part II reveals that not

[32] II A *Final Record*, p. 626.

[33] *Id.*, at 816. It may be noted here that an interesting possibility exists for a civil suit by a person protected under Part II against his own government for a breach of an Article in Part II since a duty exists for a government to protect its own nationals when it is engaged in an international conflict and this seems to apply in home territory and abroad. The problem is that the individual would have to show that this treaty creates an individual right of action (probably not contemplated by the drafters and not now existent as a general right under international law). See Pictet, *supra*, note 7 at 603 declaring that Article 148 does not grant an individual or direct action for damages against the State in whose service the person committing the breach was working. He bases this conclusion on the fact that in 1958 only States could bring claims against another State and that these would form part, in general, of what are called "war reparations." Of course this does not mean that international law forbids the suit by an individual against his own State for not living up to its treaty commitments, there are also no cases known to the author (it would apparently depend upon municipal law or the express grant of a right to sue in some international convention such as the European Convention on Human Rights of 1950). At least a possible basis for prosecution exists for a government against its own national, even though the violation occurred against its own nationals on home territory and the war was somewhere else. The author admits that these are remote possibilities, but they are nevertheless interesting.

[34] U.S. Army, Pamphlet No. 27-161-2, II *International Law*, 1962, pp. 130-131; U.S. Army Field Manual No. 27-10, *The Law of Land Warfare*, 1956, p. 101.

[35] MACV *Directive* 20-5, *Inspections and Investigations*, paras. 5 (b) and 6 (a) (1) (March 16, 1968); and MACV *Directive* 190-6, *Military Police*, ICRC Inspections of Detainee/Prisoner of War Facilities, para. 4 (a) (January 8, 1969). These are the most recent examples of commander directives. See also 62 *American Journal of International Law* 765 (1968) for related MACV Directives.

many of the articles concern specific protections of civilians. Article 24 concerns children under fifteen who are orphaned or separated from their families as a result of the conflict (an article which may cover some of the alleged killings at My Lai); Article 25 concerns family correspondence; and most of the other articles concern civilian hospitals and other things that the parties may endeavor to protect.

The one article important in our inquiry seems to be Article 16 of the Civilian Convention. It states:

> The wounded and sick, as well as the infirm, and expectant mothers, shall be the object of particular protection and respect.

> As far as military considerations allow, each Party to the conflict shall facilitate the steps taken to search for the killed and wounded, to assist the shipwrecked and other persons exposed to grave danger, and to protect them against pillage and ill-treatment.[36]

By plain language, Article 16 accords protected status to anyone who is wounded, sick, infirm, or an expectant mother. There is no limitation on this protected status. Thus, if anyone at My Lai was wounded, sick, infirm, or an expectant mother, that person(s) was entitled to particular protection and respect under Part II of the Civilian Convention.

The next paragraph of Article 16 states that each belligerent, as far as military considerations allow, shall facilitate steps to search for and assist "persons exposed to grave danger" and to protect them against ill-treatment. Thus, if anyone at My Lai was a person "exposed to grave danger" he would have been entitled to protection against ill-treatment and entitled to assistance as far as military considerations at the time allowed. The Army pamphlet refers to these persons as "helpless persons";[37] they are apparently those who at the moment in question are no longer fighting or are out of combat (whether or not they had engaged in combat operations before and even though they are not protected under the Prisoner of War Convention).[38] The question

---

[36] *Supra*, note 2, 6 U.S.T. 3528 (1955).

[37] U.S. Army, Pamphlet No. 27-161-2, II *International Law*, 1962, p. 131. See IV Harbridge House, *Prisoner of War Study*, Progress Meeting 1, 3, D, Aug. 12-14, 1968 (prepared for the Department of the Army) stating that Article 16 relates to "killed and wounded and *other persons who need protection*." (emphasis added)

[38] This distinction may be found in the language "as far as military considerations allow," since military necessity allows the engagement and killing of persons if they are still fighting; but it should never be forgotten that war does not justify murder. Protection is accorded once they are captured and in control. See Article 4 of the Civilian Convention, *supra*, and Pictet, *supra*, note 7 at 118. And see IV Harbridge House, *Prisoner of War*

of who exposed the people to grave danger is nowhere discussed and does not seem a factor in determining whether a person is protected under Article 16 (i.e., it is sufficient that the people be exposed to grave danger). Similarly, it does not seem to matter who wounds an individual, for the moment a member of the population is wounded he is in a protected status under Article 16.[39]

The meaning of the word "wounded" or "sick" is not stated in the Convention, but it is to be interpreted by common sense and good faith.[40] The phrase "other persons exposed to grave danger" should be similarly interpreted since it "covers any civilians who while not being either wounded or shipwrecked are exposed to some grave danger as a result of military operations. A particular case which the Conference had in mind was civilians trapped in air-raid shelters."[41] Furthermore, a general interpretation of the language "other persons exposed to grave danger" that includes anyone in serious danger would be more consistent with current international legal developments which seek to protect and spare from attack as far as possible any member of a civilian population during an armed conflict as long as the civilian is not directly engaged in armed hostilities.[42]

Thus, the possible grouping of persons entitled to protection under Part II of the Civilian Convention would include any member of the population who is: (1) exposed to grave danger, (2) wounded, (3) sick, (4) infirm, (5) an expectant mother, (6) shipwrecked, (7) a child under the age of fifteen who is an orphan or has been separated from his family as a result of the war, and (8) a member of a hospital staff protected under Article 20 of the Civilian Convention.

Study, Progress Meeting 1, 2, D, Aug. 12-14, 1968 (prepared for the Department of the Army) using language "other *noncombatants* exposed to grave danger." (emphasis added)

[39] One might also continue the reasoning to the category "expectant mother" and conclude that it does not matter how she got that way.

[40] Pictet, *supra*, note 7 at 134. This would be in conformity with the general principle that treaties be interpreted in good faith expressed as *pacta sunt servada*.

[41] *Id.*, at 136. We might add here that this looks very close to a situation where civilians are trapped in their own homes.

[42] See Resolution XXVIII of the XXth International Conference of the Red Cross at Vienna in 1965, cited at *International Review of the Red Cross* 75 (1967), 305, which was unanimously affirmed by the United Nations General Assembly in 1968, G. A. Res. 2444, 23 U.N. GAOR, Supp. 18, at 50, U.N. Doc. A/7218 (1969). The ICRC Resolution generally condemns indiscriminate warfare, prohibits attacks upon the civilian population, and requires that a distinction be made at all times between those taking part in hostilities and civilians generally. And see Resolution XIX of the XXIst International Conference of the Red Cross at Istanbul in 1969 (the Istanbul Declaration). See also, J. Pictet, *The Principles of International Humanitarian Law*, Geneva, 1966, pp. 51-52, regarding his stated principles of protection and the "ratione personae" restriction.

It would not seem hard to argue that many of the people at My Lai were in fact "exposed to grave danger," assuming that the statements appearing in the newspapers are correct.[43] One would argue then that as certain persons were exposed to grave or serious danger they became entitled to protection and assistance under Article 16 of the 1949 Geneva Civilian Convention, and that a failure to protect them or to refrain from attacking them would violate Article 16.

It should be noted that Pictet states that the word "respect" means "to spare, not to attack," and the word "protect" means "to come to someone's defence, to give help and support," also that these words: "make it unlawful to kill, ill-treat or in any way injure an unarmed enemy, while at the same time they impose an obligation to come to his aid and give him any care of which he stands in need."[44] Apparently the obligation is an affirmative one and not merely an obligation to refrain from certain conduct. In other words, an obligation is imposed on each party to the conflict to affirmatively protect certain people by coming to their aid, giving them proper care or assistance, coming to their defense, and protecting them affirmatively from pillage or illtreatment (not merely refraining from attacking these people). If this is correct, then the failure to seek to restrain others from attacking civilians exposed to grave danger would also violate the duty to grant aid and protection to those civilians under Article 16.[45] A violation of Article 16 would thus stand regardless of the outcome of related and more difficult issues of law involving questions of complicity in the commission of a war crime or responsibility for the acts of subordinates.[46]

[43] See e.g., Seymour M. Hersh, "My Lai 4: A Report on the Massacre and Its Aftermath," *Harper's Magazine* (May 1970), 53.

[44] Pictet, *supra*, note 7 at 134.

[45] How far one must go to seek to restrain others is a difficult question. At the Diplomatic Conference the delegate from France considered that it was the duty of the State to protect by violence the group of persons threatened in a case where one group threatens to exterminate another. See II B *Final Record*, p. 13.

[46] An example of one of these separate legal issues is whether X would be guilty of aiding and abetting Y in the commission of a war crime when X stands by smiling while Y kills a two-year-old child in Y's control; or whether X would be guilty of a war crime in the same situation because of his further responsibility as commander (or perhaps agent of the State) for acts of his subordinates if X happened to be the unit or local area commander. The reader should note here that Article 16 imposes a duty on the *party* to the conflict, and is apparently silent as to individual responsibility. It may well be that individuals cannot be prosecuted for a violation of Article 16 as such, but can be prosecuted for the commission of a "grave breach" (see *infra*) or a war crime which is linked to the legal protection afforded certain people under Article 16. In other words, Article 16 creates protected status for certain people and it is unlawful to violate that protected status (or a violation of Article 16 would concern an unlawful act). The unlawful act can

War Crimes and Grave Breaches

The unofficial position of the United States is that any violation of the law of war is a war crime.[47] Thus, a violation of Article 16 of the Civilian Convention (itself a part of the law of war) would be a war crime.[48] A further inquiry would concern whether or not a violation of Article 16 (in Part II of the Convention) would constitute a "grave breach," as opposed to an ordinary breach or an ordinary war crime, of the Civilian Convention under Article 147 which provides:

> Grave breaches to which the preceding Article relates shall be those involving any of the following acts, if committed against persons or property protected by the present Convention: wilful killing, torture or inhuman treatment, including biological experiments, wilfully causing great suffering or serious injury to body or health, unlawful deportation or transfer or unlawful confinement of a protected person, compelling a protected person to serve in the forces of a hostile Power, or wilfully depriving a protected person of the rights of fair and regular trial prescribed in the present Convention, taking of hostages and extensive destruction and appropriation of property, not justified by military necessity and carried out unlawfully and wantonly.[49]

This is an important consideration because, unlike the case of an ordinary breach, under Article 146 of the Geneva Civilian Convention every signatory to the treaty must enact legislation necessary to provide effective penal sanctions against grave breaches of the Convention, and must search for anyone who has committed a grave breach or who has ordered the commission of a grave breach. Furthermore,

---

be prosecuted either as a general war crime or a "grave breach" of the Convention (i.e., Article 16 does not itself make the individual responsible, but a violation is an unlawful act for which the individual can be held responsible due to the "grave breach" section or the general law of war). See Paust, "My Lai and Vietnam: Norms, Myths, and Leader Responsibility" (forthcoming).

47 U.S. Army, Field Manual No. 27-10, *The Law of Land Warfare*, 1956, p. 178. It is doubtful, however, that all violations would be treated as crimes of the same gravity or require the same penal sanctions. Furthermore, some laws of war may not impose individual responsibility, or may not impose it directly, but may only create State responsibility.

48 *Accord*. Oppenheim, *International Law*, II 567 n2.

49 *Supra*, note 2, 6 U.S.T. 3618 (1955). Note that absolutely no exception is made for the killing of enemy sympathizers or persons who had engaged in hostile activity at some prior time. Once a person is captured and in control, the killing would be murder and a "grave breach."

every signatory must bring such violators of the treaty before its own national courts or extradite them to a signatory which makes out a *prima facie* case against them.[50] There is no exception to the duty to search for violators; there is no exception to the duty to prosecute or extradite.[51] These obligations, consented to by almost every nation in the world, make the question of whether a grave breach has been committed a very important question, since the gravity of the offense itself and the concomitant obligations of nations make these types of war crimes far different from the normal.[52]

The language of Article 147 provides no real problem concerning the nature of the activity involved (i.e., killing, torture, inhumane treatment generally, depriving a suspected enemy combatant, etc. of a fair and regular trial, or the illegal destruction of property not justified by some imperative military need), but the problem seems to center on the language: "if committed against persons or property protected by the present Convention." Does this limit Article 147 to include only grave breaches against persons protected under Article 4 (as Pictet

---

[50] Article 146 reads as follows:

The High Contracting Parties undertake to enact any legislation necessary to provide effective penal sanctions for persons committing, or ordering to be committed, any of the grave breaches of the present Convention defined in the following Article.

Each High Contracting Party shall be under the obligation to search for persons alleged to have committed, or to have ordered to be committed, such grave breaches, and shall bring such persons, regardless of their nationality, before its own courts. It may also, if it prefers, and in accordance with the provisions of its own legislation, hand such persons over for trial to another High Contracting Party concerned, provided such High Contracting Party has made out a *prima facie* case.

Each High Contracting Party shall take measures necessary for the suppression of all acts contrary to the provisions of the present Convention other than the grave breaches defined in the following Article.

In all circumstances, the accused persons shall benefit by safeguards of proper trial and defence, which shall not be less favourable than those provided by Article 105 and those following of the Geneva Convention relative to the Treatment of Prisoners of War of August 12, 1949.

[51] For example, no power to grant immunity from prosecution is stated, and it is doubtful whether the granting of immunity can be consistent with the duty to prosecute all grave breaches. Of course, the granting of immunity by one sovereign, even if effective politically, does not affect the power of another nation. A granting of immunity might well be a violation of the treaty and the Supreme Law of the Land in the United States, just as much as a refusal to prosecute for some other reason.

[52] It is doubtful whether such an absolute obligation to prosecute or extradite as exists concerning grave breaches may be found in the general law of war for other violations. For example, see Article 146, *supra*, note 50, which states that concerning ordinary breaches the parties to the conflict shall take all measures necessary for their suppression. It does not affirmatively state that such offenses must be prosecuted and it certainly imposes no duty to extradite the offender.

would seem to imply),[53] or does Article 147 include grave breaches against anyone protected anywhere in the Convention?

One can argue that the language "persons . . . protected" in Article 147 is to be interpreted in the technical sense under Article 4, or that it is meant here in the general sense—anyone who is protected anywhere "by the present Convention." The more general interpretation of the language "persons protected" would also conform with the idea that Article 147 seeks to list the more serious breaches of the Convention in a separate article. It does not attempt to classify persons, but attempts to summarize "grave" breaches according to the gravity of the conduct more than according to the political nature of the victim. No matter how the Article 147 question is resolved, a violation of Article 16 would still be a violation of the law of war and a prosecution can be based on that alone.

THE NATURE OF GRAVE BREACH ENFORCEMENT

Why was the term "grave breaches" used in the Conventions instead of "crimes" or "war crimes"? The Diplomatic Conference did not attempt to create a code of international penal law and for that reason the word "crime" was intentionally not used. Instead of the creation of international penal law the Conference undertook to enumerate certain acts as "grave breaches" which would become "crimes" in the traditional sense once they were adopted by a domestic legal system as part of its national penal law.[54] It was this domestic system of enforcement that the Delegates preferred in view of the inherent difficulties in creating an international penal code when an international criminal court and enforcement system could not effectively exist. Furthermore, the important question of the drafting of a penal code for war crimes was being considered by the United Nations International Law Commission at this time.[55]

---

[53] Pictet, *supra*, note 7 at 597. It should be noted that if Pictet is willing to include within the ambit of Article 147 the protections of property found in Part II of the Convention (namely Articles 18, 21, and 22) why wouldn't he be as willing to include within Article 147 the protections of human beings found within the same part of the Convention? It is the author's opinion that if "property protected by the present Convention" means property protected anywhere within the Convention, then the same interpretation should apply to human beings (the assumption being one which free men cherish—that human protections are at least as important as those of property). The implication from Draper, *supra*, note 14, is that the protected status under Part II is relevant to the "grave breaches" article. Does the specific reference to Part II in Article 4 itself help?

[54] See II B *Final Record*, pp. 85-87, 114-117.

[55] Pictet, *supra*, note 7 at 588; II B *Final Record*, p. 117.

The Delegates, however, recognized that the individual responsibility of the author of a breach of the Convention could be prosecutable as a violation of international law. The Delegates of the United States and the Netherlands objected to the use of the word "war crimes" as proposed by the Delegate of the Soviet Union since "the term 'war crimes' was under consideration by the International Law Commission of the United Nations, and that a war crime was a breach or violation of the laws of war, so that the word 'breach' or 'violation' was preferable in view of the objections raised to the use of the expression 'war crime.' "[56] This view had been previously stated by the Delegate of the Netherlands and his prior statement seems to express the final intent of the Delegates that a violation of the Convention was also a violation of the international law of war and that individual acts were thus covered by the law of war without the necessity of using the term "war crimes" or "crimes." He stated that: " '*War crimes*' were breaches of the provisions in the laws of war and *were thus covered* by the word '*breach.*' The latter word could, however, be replaced by the word '*violation.*' " (emphasis added)[57]

The Delegates, then, seem to have contemplated two enforcement possibilities for individual violations of the "grave breach" provisions; one under the international law of war and the other under the domestic law of each nation-signatory. Unless domestic law merely adopts international law by way of implementation for enforcement purposes, there would be a distinction concerning the nature of the law for enforcement of grave breaches of the Geneva Conventions, and this distinction might become important in certain countries concerning the nature of the forum to be adopted for the prosecution of the illegal conduct. A particular domestic forum might prosecute only violations of international law, only violations of domestic law, or both. For example, in the United States courts-martial may prosecute a "grave breach" as a violation of domestic law (the Uniform Code of Military Justice)[58] or of international law in combination with the domestic implementing legislation.[59] A military commission would prosecute the offense as one in violation of international law as implemented by domestic law,[60] and so might the federal district courts.[61] The number

---

[56] II B *Final Record*, p. 117.

[57] II B *Final Record*, p. 87.   [58] 10 U.S.C. §§ 801-940 (1968).

[59] 10 U.S.C. § 818 (1968). A violation of the law of war under Section 818.

[60] 10 U.S.C. §§ 818 and 821 (1968). See articles *supra*, note 27.

[61] Paust, "After My Lai: The Case for War Crime Jurisdiction Over Civilians in Federal District Courts," *supra*, note 21.

of forum possibilities in countries throughout the world is perhaps itself a sad commentary on the state of international law enforcement
and points to the dominance of tribal attitudes as opposed to those of
mankind.

As a final statement it is hoped that this article provides more than
an assumption that some of the South Vietnamese nationals are protected by the 1949 Geneva Civilian Convention, or a feeling that they
ought to be protected, and that this short comment will be accepted by
the reader as a further addition to the collection of thought in Professor Rubin's interesting article.

Nuremberg and Vietnam:
Who Is Responsible for War Crimes?

TELFORD TAYLOR*

OPINION OR "reaction" samplings taken shortly after the first views of the Son My incidents revealed that nearly two-thirds of those interviewed denied feeling any shock. Some observers found this lack of public indignation or shame, as well as some of the comments recorded by the samplers, more upsetting than the killings themselves.

It is neither surprising nor particularly disturbing, however, that many of those interviewed refused to believe that anything untoward had occurred. "I can't believe an American serviceman would purposely shoot any civilian," declared Alabama's George Wallace. "Any atrocities in this war were caused by the Communists." Others described the reports as "a prefabricated story by a bunch of losers," or labeled them incredible because "it's contrary to everything I've learned about America." These outright rejections of undisputed information are a familiar defense mechanism, activated in order to ward off the shock which would accompany acceptance.

There was also a widespread disposition to discount the Son My stories on the ground that "incidents such as this are bound to happen in a war." So, too, are murders and robberies "bound to happen" in our streets, and they are likely to happen much more often if we cease to regard them as reprehensible. In fact, Son My was unusual, both in its scale and the candor with which the operation was carried on, with Army photographers on the scene and commanders in helicopters circling overhead. Those who resorted to this "sloughing-off" justification are, nonetheless, correct in assuming that unjustifiable killings of prisoners and civilians on a smaller scale are bound to and indeed do happen in a war, and what they overlook is that in the United States Army, when detected they have generally not gone unpunished. During the Second World War many American soldiers were court-martialed and severely punished for killing or assaulting civilians in violation of local law or the laws of war. The fact that we are now fighting in

---

* The author, who was chief prosecutor at the Nuremberg trials, raises the issue that if there is criminal guilt in the Son My episode, "it doesn't lie most heavily on the shoulders of those who, at least up to now, are being brought to trial."

Asia instead of Europe is hardly a worthy basis for suspending their application.

A Lurking Thought

Nevertheless, there is one respect in which the public reactions, insofar as those interviewed were slow to denounce the troops who did the shooting at Son My, is sound. The thought is rarely articulated, and yet may well be lurking in the back of the mind, that if there is criminal guilt in this episode, it does not lie most heavily on the shoulders of those who, at least up to now, are being brought to trial. There may also be grounds for doubt that Army court-martial proceedings at Fort McPherson, Fort Benning, or some other Army post are the most suitable forum in which to test the issues that Son My raises. These questions, taken in reverse order, are the substance of this article.

In the long wake of the Son My disclosures, about a dozen soldiers—a company and a platoon commander, noncoms and privates—faced criminal charges for their parts in the incident. Defense lawyers made motions and brought a number of legal actions, in Army channels and in the federal courts, to delay or prevent the court-martial proceedings. The situation was further complicated because a number of the soldiers involved at Son My had been discharged from service before the Army took official cognizance of the killings, and there was a question whether these men might be brought to trial at all, as the Supreme Court has held that ex-servicemen cannot be court-martialed for offenses committed while in service.

ONE POINT that was much pressed by defense counsel and others was the extraordinary amount and intensity of the publicity that followed the Son My disclosures, and its possibly prejudicial effect on the trial proceedings. This, of course, is a general problem in the administration of justice which has been the subject of wide concern in recent years, and especially since the Warren Commission's comments on the conduct of police and press at the time of President Kennedy's assassination. Under the rubric of "fair trial and free press," the problem has stimulated a flood of books and articles, and I confess having myself contributed to the glut. Bar and press associations have waged a war of words over the proper balance between the needs of justice and what the journalists call the public's "right to know." The Supreme Court underlined the gravity of the matter in 1966, by overturning the murder conviction of Dr. Samuel H. Sheppard, on the ground that his notorious trial in 1954 had been unfair "because of the trial judge's failure to protect Sheppard sufficiently from the massive, pervasive and prejudicial publicity that attended his prosecution."

There is no gainsaying the seriousness of this problem in the case of the Son My defendants, for the television and newspaper publicity was indeed glaring and often accusatory. Most of it would not have been tolerated under the much more rigorous standards observed in Britain, where pretrial publicity can be and often is the basis for criminal contempt penalties against the offending news organs.

But it has never been, and should not now be, the rule that publicity furnishes the basis for not proceeding against an accused individual at all—in effect, for granting him immunity from prosecution because of the publicity that has surrounded his case. After all, Jack Ruby was tried for murder after millions of television viewers had watched him pump a bullet into Lee Oswald's stomach, and while this would have made it very difficult for Ruby to deny that he fired the fatal shot, no one seriously suggested that he must therefore escape justice entirely. There is simply no way that sensational crimes can be kept out of the press, especially when most of the publicity precedes the apprehension or accusation of those eventually charged.

A MUCH more doubtful question is whether an Army general court-martial is an appropriate judicial forum for the trial of the Son My cases. On the face of things the charges are simple enough—that Lieutenant X or Corporal Y killed or assaulted one or more human beings —but, as has been seen, the simplicity is deceptive, and searching issues of fact and law start from the cases at every turn.

If matters follow the customary course, the courts-martial will be "convened" by the commanding general of the post or military area within which the trial is to be held. This means that the commander will designate the members of the court, who function essentially like a jury, except that they not only determine guilt or innocence, but also fix the sentence if the defendant is found guilty. The members will be subordinates of the commander, will probably not be lawyers, and, since none of those as yet charged with responsibility for Son My are of high rank, the members of the court need not be. Presiding over the proceedings will be a military judge, responsible not to the commander but to the Army judge advocate general in Washington. The judge will wear a black robe, so that his rank will not be visible though everyone will know what it is, and he will instruct the court on such legal issues as may arise. The court's judgment is subject to review as of right in a Court of Military Review responsible to the judge advocate general, and may then be reviewed by the civilian Court of Military Appeals, if that body thinks the case important enough to warrant its attention.

Consider the issues that are likely to confront a court-martial in the Son My cases, bearing in mind that the defendants are represented by counsel, several of whom are not only able but also very prominent in legal circles. In its strictest form, "superior orders" as a defense depends on whether or not the defendant knew the order to be unlawful. Of course, it will first have to be determined what orders were in fact given to the troops entering Son My, but let us assume that the soldiers could reasonably have thought that they were being told or encouraged to kill the inhabitants. What did "unlawful" mean to them? According to their own accounts, two or three of the soldiers *did* regard the goings-on as unlawful and took no part. But what standard of "lawfulness" were they and the others instructed or trained to apply? What sort of indoctrination had they had not only from manuals or training sessions, but from observation of what was going on around them in Vietnam?

What Is an "Order"?

These questions lead to another very basic one: what, for present purposes, is an "order"? Everyone who has done military service knows that there are occasions when the rule-book does not fit the circumstances; no one is expected to follow it, and may even get into serious trouble if he does. The departure from the rules may be a matter of unspoken but accepted practice and it would, for example, be quite unnecessary for an officer to tell his men in so many words to take no prisoners if, by prior experience and the temper of the moment, the men sense that this is how things are going to be today.

The ultimate question of "guilt" in the trials of the Son My troops is how far what they did departed from general American military practice in Vietnam as they had witnessed it. This may not be germane to the question of legality under the Geneva Conventions or the Articles of War. But the defense of superior orders has its true base not in technicality but in equity, and is properly invoked by the low-ranking soldier in mitigation of punishment for conduct, even though unlawful, that is not too far removed from the behavior authorized or encouraged by his superiors in the force in which he serves.

Now, the searching feature of the situation is that this defense cannot be put forward or tested without, in substance, putting American military practice in Vietnam on trial. Who, other than the defendants and their counsel, is prepared to do that? One may well wonder whether either a judge advocate officer sitting as military judge or a "jury" of officers appointed by a post commandant,[1] is likely to have much enthusiasm for such a proceeding, the evidentiary ramifications and politico-military implications of which are painfully obvious.

The shortcomings of court-martial procedure in cases of this type were sharply revealed earlier this year in the case of Lieutenant James Duffy, who was charged with the murder of an unarmed Vietnamese civilian prisoner in 1969. The gist of the charge was that Duffy had ordered or allowed one of his sergeants to shoot the prisoner. Duffy put forth, in miniature, the same sort of defense that may be expected, in gross, in the Son My courts-martial. He did not claim that his superior officer had ordered him to kill the Vietnamese prisoner. He and his supporting witnesses testified rather that their commanders laid emphasis on the desirability of a "high body count"; that one of their superiors had been "angry" on a prior occasion when prisoners were taken; that the practice had developed of not taking prisoners in order to increase the body count.

Was this defense factually credible? The court-martial gave no meaningful answer. The military judge instructed the court that the rules of land warfare applied to the war in Vietnam, and that the question was whether Duffy thought he was obeying an order "that a man of ordinary sense and understanding would know to be illegal." The court thereupon convicted Duffy of premeditated murder, but on being informed that this crime carries a mandatory life sentence, revoked the verdict and convicted him of involuntary manslaughter. The president of the court, Col. Robert W. Shelton, was reported to have made some reference to "the ramifications to the Army" of Duffy's defense. According to the account in the *New York Times*:

Several military lawyers attending the court-martial as spectators said privately that a full acquittal of Lieutenant Duffy would have

[1] A defendant who is an enlisted man is entitled to demand that enlisted men be included in the court, but the demand is rarely made in practice because the commanders are inclined to appoint discipline-minded top sergeants.

been damaging to the Army. The Army, they said, already was under heavy pressure because of the publicity about the alleged Son My massacre and other suspected war crimes.

"But the court didn't want to make Duffy suffer that badly to get the Army off the hook," said one young law officer. "To a lot of us it looks like another example of the M.G.R.—the mere gook rule—being applied," he asserted.

He explained that the expression had been adopted facetiously by some Army legal officers who believed that military courts were lenient to Americans who killed Vietnamese civilians, because the Vietnamese were regarded as somehow second-class human beings or "mere gooks."

What is one to make of all this? "Involuntary manslaughter" denotes an unintentional negligent killing, and is a singularly inappropriate label for the conduct on which Duffy's conviction was based. To reverse the famous Gilbertian line, the crime was made to fit the punishment.

If ever a case cried out for an explanatory opinion, it was this one, but opinions are not part of court-martial practice. If the court had thought Duffy's defense to be fabricated, it is hard to see why the murder conviction was revoked, since the willful killing of an unarmed, helpless prisoner abundantly supports it. If there was in fact no such body count practice as Duffy and his witnesses described, could Duffy nevertheless have believed that it existed? That is unlikely, and the inference seems inescapable that the members of the court believed the body count testimony, at least in part, and gave it decisive effect in mitigation. But who was responsible for the body count practice, and how widespread is it?

This last is the question that no ordinary court-martial will want to answer, and one over which many in high authority may wish to draw a veil. And since it is also the question that most deeply affects the integrity of the Army, it is the one that most needs answering. An ordinary court-martial is not a body of sufficient stature or independence to grapple with such far-ranging and ominous matters. It may wish to convict so that the Army will not "look bad," and cloak its actual reasons in silence. It is too easily swayed by what Colonel Shelton called "ramifications to the Army," and unable to articulate the legal or moral significance of what it does.

Both in fairness to the defendants and in response to the public need, accordingly, there is much to be said for trying the Son My cases before a special military commission, to which able civilian judges and lawyers, outside the military chain of command, might be appointed. As has been seen, the defense of superior orders does not eliminate criminal responsibility but rather shifts it upward, and that is the direction in which an ordinary court-martial will be least anxious to look.

The Duffy case was not the first in which the defense was based on the assertion that war crimes in Vietnam are not isolated atrocities, but are a manifestation of command policy. In 1967, Dr. Howard B. Levy, then a captain in the Army medical service, was court-martialed on charges that included disobedience to orders in that he refused to give medical training to "aidmen" of the Special Forces, better known as "Green Berets." At his trial, Levy justified his refusal on the ground that American troops in Vietnam were committing war crimes, and that he therefore should not train troops about to be sent there. Surprisingly, the military judge allowed him to offer evidence in support of his contention, but on short notice his lawyers were unable to satisfy the judge that there was a criminal "pattern of practice" in Vietnam. In any event, the argument was fraught with difficulties; nothing decided at Nuremberg or elsewhere suggests that a soldier is entitled to disobey an intrinsically legal order at Fort Jackson because other soldiers, halfway round the world, are given illegal orders. Such a theory would equally justify the cook in refusing to feed the aidmen.

But Dr. Levy had another argument, which was not sharply articulated until later—that the order to train the aidmen was itself illegal and in violation of medical ethics. According to the evidence he submitted to the court, Green Beret aidmen engaged in combat. They were "soldiers first and aidmen second." Furthermore, it was their purpose to use medicine as a political lever, and Green Beret publicity described the "use of medicine as a weapon."

UNDER THE laws of war, doctors, nurses and medical corpsmen are military personnel, but they are noncombatants, like chaplains. They are expected to treat enemy wounded, carry special medical identity cards and are entitled to wear or display the Red Cross and be immune from deliberate enemy attack. The Geneva conventions and the Army rules of land warfare draw a clear separation between combat troops and noncombat medical personnel, and condemn misuse of medical noncombat status or of the Red Cross emblem.

Accordingly, there was at least some basis for argument that Dr.

Levy was being unlawfully ordered to train the aidmen in unlawful activities. Furthermore, the dispensation of medicines by unqualified persons, or on a politically selective basis or as a bribe, raises serious questions of medical ethics as well as bare legality.

Nevertheless, Levy's contention failed, and he served a prison term at Leavenworth. The case is important for present purposes because of the military judge's ruling that evidence in support of criminal command practice was to be admitted—a ruling that was sure to be cited in support of comparable offers of proof in the Son My proceedings. It is an ironic touch that Dr. Levy submitted the evidence to justify disobedience to orders, whereas the Son My defendants would offer it to establish that they were obeying orders.[2]

While the Army legal services were interrogating, clearing, and charging the soldiers involved at Son My, the incident was under investigation by two other bodies. One of these is a special subcommittee of the House Armed Services Committee, officially entitled the "My Lai Incident Subcommittee," composed of four Congressmen and chaired by R. Edward Hébert of Louisiana. The other was an inquiry initiated by the secretary of the Army and the Army chief of staff, and conducted by Lieut. Gen. William R. Peers, into the reasons why high-level review of the Son My killings had been so long delayed.

The Hébert subcommittee issued its report on July 14, 1970, in which it declared that what happened at Son My "was so wrong and so foreign to the normal character and action of our military forces as to immediately raise a question as to the legal sanity at the time of these men involved." More significant were the subcommittee's conclusions that the "My Lai matter was covered up within the American Division and by the district and province advisory teams," and that the Army had been most uncooperative: "The manner in which most of the American Division officers, in both command and staff capacities, testified before the subcommittee suggests an extreme reluctance on their part to discuss the allegation and its justification with any real specificity." An angry Chairman Hébert declared that "the committee was hampered by the Department of the Army in every conceivable way."

General Peers submitted his report on March 14, 1970, but only portions of it have been made public, for the stated and apparently suffi-

---

[2] In June 1970, Daniel A. Switkes, a captain in the Army medical service, brought suit in the New York federal court asking that the Army be enjoined from sending him to Indochina, basing his case in part on the contention that he was "entitled not to be forced to become an accomplice to war crimes."

cient reason that release of the restricted parts might "prejudice the rights of defendants in current and potential criminal proceedings." He concluded "that there were serious deficiencies in the actions taken by officials in the Americal Division, the 11th Brigade, and Task Force Barker, after the incident at Son My," in that those officials did not "take appropriate action to investigate or report." On this basis he recommended that charges of "dereliction of duty and failure to obey regulations," and in some cases of "false swearing," be brought against 14 officers, ranging in rank from captain to major general.

The matter was then transferred to the jurisdiction of Lieut. Gen. Mathew O. Seaman, commander of the First Army at Fort Meade in Maryland, who shortly announced dismissal, for lack of evidence, of the charges against seven of the officers.[3] The seven remaining under charges included the commanders, at the time of Son My, of the Americal Division and the 11th Brigade, to which Task Force Barker was subordinated.

Why was the Son My incident "covered up" by the Army? The published portions of the Peers report do not reach that question. What has been released is, however, of great interest in that it describes the history and training of the units and headquarters involved at Son My, and mentions and quotes from a number of the tactical and other directives that are supposed to govern the conduct of military operations in Vietnam.

On their face, as regards the laws of war, the directives are virtually impeccable. United States forces observe the Geneva conventions, and all military personnel are to be adequately indoctrinated in their provisions. All troops arriving in Vietnam are to receive "information cards," covering treatment of "The Enemy in Your Hands," and stressing "humanitarian treatment and respect for the Vietnamese people." The "Rules of Engagement" issued by the American commander in Vietnam, then Gen. William Westmoreland, instructed the troops to "use your fire power with care and discrimination, particularly in populated areas." Another directive stipulated that firepower should be so used as to avoid "incidents involving friendly forces, noncombatants, and damage to civilian property." Directly pertinent to Son My was the directive on minimization of civilian casualties, which called for protection of the inhabitant "whether at any one time he lives in a V.C. or G.V.N. [Government of Vietnam] controlled hamlet,"

---

[3] One of the officers cleared by General Seaman had invoked the privilege against self-incrimination while testifying before the Hébert subcommittee.

since whether it is the one or the other may well depend "to a large extent upon factors and forces beyond his control." The instructions issued by the headquarters of the 11th Brigade were generally in line with these directives.

BUT, of course, the question remains whether the picture painted by these directives bears any resemblance to the face of war in Vietnam, and on this score, once again, the Peers report as published is silent. Of what use is an hour or two of lectures on the Geneva Conventions if the soldier sent into combat sees them flouted on every side? How "real" do the instructions to the ground troops appear in the light of the lieutenant's testimony at the Duffy trial, of the "mere gook" rule described by the Army lawyers, or of the Army major's remark after the destruction of Ben Tre, with heavy loss of civilian life: "It was necessary to destroy the town to save it"?

Despite the careful wording of the orders and the optimistic releases from the Pentagon about "pacification," virtually all observers report death, destruction and troop attitudes that indicate that the restraint called for by the orders is not exercised. Shortly after the Son My disclosures, four sergeants in Vietnam wrote a letter expressing hearty approval: "You know this is a V.C. village, they are the enemy, they are a part of the enemy's war apparatus. Our job is to destroy the enemy, so kill them . . . I want to come home alive, if I must kill old men, women or children to make myself a little safer, I'll do it without hesitation." One may indeed sympathize with the desire to "come home alive," but if that aim now requires the slaughter of all the Vietnamese who might be sympathetic to the Viet Cong, then all our talk of "pacification," to say nothing of the Hague Conventions, is the sheerest hypocrisy, and we had better acknowledge at once that we are prepared to do what we hanged and imprisoned Japanese and German generals for doing.

The letter of the four sergeants, of course, does not embody Army policy, but it is indicative of troop attitudes that the Army has allowed to develop and, alas, in many cases to prevail. The attitudes themselves are a natural product of the surroundings and nature of the war. The Viet Cong do infiltrate and dominate the villages, and depend on the rural population for both support and concealment, and many of the villagers cooperate with them, whether out of fear or favor. After a few air strikes and "zippo raids" the villagers have less reason than before to like Americans, and so distrust soon turns to hate, as Richard Hammer has so compellingly explained in *One Morning in the War*:

Pretty soon you get to hate all these people. You get to fear them, too. They're all out for your ass one way or another, out to take you for everything you've got. You don't know which ones are your enemies and which ones are your friends. So you begin to think that they're all your enemies. And that all of them are something not quite human, some kind of lower order of creature. You give them names to depersonalize them, to categorize them as you've become convinced they ought to be categorized. They become dinks and slopes and slants and gooks, and you begin to say, and believe, "The only good dink is a dead dink." You echo the comments of your buddies that, "One million of them ain't worth one of us. We should blow up all those slant-eyed bastards."

Other witnesses tell much the same story: retired Marine Colonels James A. Donovan and William R. Corson; Dr. Robert Jay Lifton of Yale; Dr. Gordon Livingston, a graduate of West Point and Johns Hopkins who served as a major in Vietnam. "No one has any feelings for the Vietnamese," a Texas private told journalist Jonathan Schell. "The trouble is no one sees the Vietnamese as people. They're not people. Therefore it doesn't matter what you do to them." These attitudes are often aggravated by atrocious conduct of the Viet Cong; Son My pales into numerical insignificance beside the massacre of thousands in Hue during the Tet offensive, when the Viet Cong also overran Quang Ngai and raced through the hospital shooting doctors, nurses, and bed-ridden patients. "One tends not to want to be too compassionate in dealing with an enemy like that," a soldier told William Beecher of the *New York Times*.

If these observers are not to be trusted, there remains the record of what has happened. Perhaps the Department of Defense has accurate totals of South Vietnamese civilians killed, maimed and made homeless by the war, but probably much of this misery has remained untabu-lated and is known only to the victims. Early in 1968, the late Senator Robert Kennedy stated that our population transfers, village destruc-tion, and defoliation had created two million refugees, in a country of sixteen million people. A year later Professor Gabriel Kolko of Buffalo put the figure at 3,153,000, apparently based on evidence given in hearings conducted by the Senate Judiciary Committee. The American Friends Service Committee estimates that some 150,000 civilians have been killed *annually* by combat operations. The Saigon Government reported 26,000 civilians killed and 74,000 wounded during 1967 in the regions it controlled. To be sure, some of these were killed by the Viet

Cong, but the disparity of firepower as between the two sides, and American monopoly in the air, make it a certainty that we are responsible for the greater part of the civilian casualties.

A Massacre Now

Whether these figures are double or half the actuality is not of much legal or moral significance. As Colonel Donovan reminds us, those "who talk about the massacre of South Vietnamese that may happen at some future date if our troops leave the battlefield are apparently oblivious to the fact that a massacre of the Vietnamese people has been going on for five years, and much of the bloodshed has resulted from U.S. firepower."

The Army leadership can hardly have been blind to the probable consequences to civilians of a massive employment of American troops in Vietnam to engage in counterinsurgency operations. Indeed, General Peers called attention in his report to the dangers to noncombatants from "frequent employment of massive firepower" and from "the intermingling of the nonuniformed foe and the populace," and declared that: "Early in the conflict, these factors and many others associated with this unique war caused great concern at the highest levels for the protection of noncombatants and the minimization of casualties to those persons not directly involved." But how did this concern manifest itself, other than in the bland language of the various directives and "rules of engagement"?

We may pass until later the question whether heavy firepower should have been used at all. Assuming that decision to have been made, there is no gainsaying the difficulties that the American command faced in achieving a "minimization" of civilian casualties and maintaining a humane and considerate attitude among the troops. "There are no agreed 'rules of land warfare' between antagonists . . . when one . . . is a regular force . . . and the other includes old men, women, and children, as well as guerrilla troops," writes Col. William Corson. "And it is doubtful such rules can even be written. However, lacking such rules, if the United States is to avoid the moral and legal dilemmas associated with brutality in warfare, not only the U.S. fighting man, but the entire American society must have a thorough knowledge of the end the United States has in view. . . ."

NEITHER the "fighting man" nor "American society" has had any such understanding, and what is far worse, neither has our political and military leadership, for such an understanding would have revealed the unsuitability of zippo raids and free-fire zones as measures to "pacify" the countryside. Still, assuming that firepower is envisaged as playing a major role in counterinsurgency warfare, then it is plain that certain accompanying measures are urgently required to "minimize" the inevitably destructive consequences.

Before embarking on a counterinsurgency war in Indochina, for example, some of the staff planners might well have cast a glance across the South China Sea to the Philippines, where we fought a counterinsurgency campaign 70 years ago.

> Damn, damn, damn the Filipinos,
> Civilize them with a Krag

sang the soldiers in 1900, as they hunted Emilio Aguinaldo's irregulars, and today's soldier songs in Vietnam, as reported by Jonathan Schell, are redolent of the same sort of "humor."[4] When East and West meet in such unpleasant circumstances, racial slurs and scorns are inevitable, and probably "slope" and "dink" would have become standard Army vocabulary under the best of conditions.

Given the circumstances and purposes of the war, however, it should have been a matter of the highest priority to insure, by indoctrination and subsequent policing, that the troops should treat the Vietnamese as human beings with lives worth preserving. Unfortunately, feelings of racial superiority are not confined to enlisted men, and it is highly probable that many officers have a "mere gook rule" in the back of their minds when they order an air strike or mark out a free-fire zone. In any event, it is all too clear that the Army's attitude and performance in this area have been woefully inadequate.

American military and economic missions had been in Indochina since the end of the Second World War, and by the time President Johnson took office there were already some 15,000 military personnel in South Vietnam. It is difficult, therefore, to attribute the blunders that accompanied the massive build-up to lack of information. We knew the size, density of population and terrain of the country, and it

---

[4] The "Filipino" song was sung to the Civil War tune "Tramp, Tramp, Tramp, the Boys are Marching." The Krag Jorgensen rifle was the standard infantry weapon at the turn of the century. One of the Schell reported lyrics:

Bomb the schools and churches,
Bomb the rice fields, too,
Show the children in the courtyards
What napalm can do.

must have been apparent that however good the aim and intention, the bullets, bombs, and shells were going to hit a lot of buildings and people that were simply unfortunate enough to be there. Once the population transfers and search-and-destroy missions became standard practice, the prospect of heavy civilian casualties, and masses of refugees, became a certainty. Bad enough that was, but far worse the failure to provide sufficient housing and hospitals to relieve the suffering we caused, and soon the point was reached where large operations were designed so as not to "generate" refugees for lack of a place to put them.

Maddening Difficulties

I have stressed, and I believe rightly, the maddening difficulties and dangers that troops and commanders alike—soldiers at all levels— faced in the conditions, some of our own making, that have developed in South Vietnam as our commitment deepened. For the lower ranks, these circumstances must count powerfully in mitigation of their culpability. But in these confused, complex, and shifting circumstances, the responsibility of the higher officers for training, doctrine and practice is all the greater.

During the Second World War, the German Army in occupied Europe faced conditions that, in some countries, were not totally dissimilar to those prevailing in Vietnam, and had a like mission of "pacification." There, too, villages were destroyed and the inhabitants killed, and after the war a number of field marshals and generals implicated in the actions were brought to trial at Nuremberg in the so-called "High Command Case." In summing up at the close of the trial, the prosecution dealt with this same issue of comparative responsibility as between the troops and their leaders:

Somewhere, there is unmitigated responsibility for these atrocities. Is it to be borne by the troops? Is it to be borne primarily by the hundreds of subordinates who played a minor role in this pattern of crime? We think it is clear that that is not where the deepest responsibility lies. Men in the mass, particularly when organized and disciplined in armies, must be expected to yield to prestige, authority, the power of example, and soldiers are bound to be powerfully influenced by the examples set by their commanders. That is why . . . the only way in which the behavior of the German troops in the recent war can be made comprehensible as the behavior of human beings is by a full exposure of the criminal doctrines and orders which were pressed on them from above by these defendants and others. Who could the German Army look to, other than von Leeb and the senior field marshals, to safeguard its standards of conduct and prevent their disintegration? If a decision is to be rendered here which may perhaps help to prevent the repetition of such events, it is important above all else that responsibility be fixed where it truly belongs. Mitigation should be reserved for those upon whom superior orders are pressed down, and who lack the means to influence general standards of behavior. It is not, we submit, available to the commander who participates in bringing the criminal pressures to bear, and whose responsibility it is to insure the preservation of honorable military traditions.

When General Peers submitted his report charging several high-ranking officers with dereliction of duty in covering up Son My, the press reported sharp controversy in military circles on whether the airing of dirty linen would be "good" or "bad" for the Army as an institution. Of course, both Son My and the cover-up were indicative of serious weaknesses, but once Son My had happened, its exposure was not merely "good" but essential to the integrity of the Army's leadership. What officer with any respect or sense for the values of the military profession could serve with pride in an organization where serious crime in the lower ranks is buried in the files on orders from above? The burying is itself an offense, known to the law as "misprision of felony," and Son My could not have been permanently covered up without infecting the higher reaches of the Army leadership with criminality.

THE TROUBLE now is that the uncovering is not being carried nearly far enough. General Peers was directed to investigate only what happened *after* Son My—specifically "the adequacy of . . . investigations or inquiries and subsequent reviews and reports within the chain of command," and "whether any suppression or withholding of information by persons involved in the incident had taken place." But so far as is publicly known, *the Army has undertaken no general investigation of the killings themselves, to determine the level of responsibility for the conditions that gave rise to Son My or the many similar though smaller incidents.*

Now the Son My court-martial proceedings carry the prospect of inquiry into those ominous problems—into body counts, and zippo raids, and free-fire zones, and "mere gook rules." The motive force will be the defendants' effort to shake off culpability either by showing that what they did was not "wrong," however unlawful, or that if wrong, others more highly placed were primarily responsible. Such an inquiry is unlikely to be either complete or dispassionate.

"Regardless of the outcome of . . . the My Lai courts-martial and other legal actions," Col. William Corson has written, "the point remains that American judgment as to the effective prosecution of the war was faulty from beginning to end and that the atrocities, alleged or otherwise, are a result of failure of judgment, not criminal behavior." Col. Corson overlooks, I fear, that negligent homicide is generally a crime of bad judgment rather than evil intent. Perhaps he is right in the strictly causal sense that if there had been no failure of judgment, the occasion for criminal conduct would not have arisen. The Germans in occupied Europe made gross errors of judgment which no doubt created the conditions in which the slaughter of the inhabitants of Klissura occurred, but that did not make the killings any the less criminal.

Try L.B.J.?

Still, there is a real question how far the criminal process is appropriate as a scale in which to weigh the responsibility of those in high authority for the crimes committed in Vietnam. The pages of *The Washington Monthly* and the New York *Village Voice* have recently been the vehicle for a running debate on the subject between Townsend Hoopes, former undersecretary of the Air Force and author of an interesting account of top-level policy formulation from 1965 to 1969, and two newspaper reporters, Geoffrey Cowan and Judith Coburn. The reporters thought that if Justice Jackson's promise at Nuremberg were to be kept, President Johnson and his associates ought to be brought before a like bar of justice; Mr. Hoopes's reaction to this, not unnaturally, was one of dismay. The antagonists never squarely locked horns, so that not even the most dispassionate judge could award the laurels of victory to either side. Mr. Hoopes's defense, nonetheless, was something less than satisfying, for the burden of it was that American leaders are intrinsically "good" men. "Lyndon Johnson, though disturbingly volatile, was not in his worst moments an evil man in the Hitlerian sense," Mr. Hoopes declared, while "his principal advisers were, almost uniformly, those considered to be among the ablest, the best, the most humane and liberal men that could be found for public trust."

THAT IS what trial lawyers call "character testimony." Whatever its value in a fraud or perjury case, it is not very relevant to a determination whether certain proven conduct is criminal, and whether the defendant was implicated. How much the president and his close advisers in the White House, Pentagon and Foggy Bottom knew about the volume and cause of civilian casualties in Vietnam, and the physical devastation of the countryside, is speculative. Something was known, for the late John McNaughton (then assistant secretary of defense) returned from the White House one day in 1967 with the message that "We seem to be proceeding on the assumption that the way to eradicate the Viet Cong is to destroy all the village structures, defoliate all the jungles, and then cover the entire surface of South Vietnam with asphalt."

Whatever the limits and standards of culpability for civilians in Washington, the proximity and immediate authority of the military commanders ties the burden of responsibility much more tightly to their shoulders. The divisional and other commands in Quang Ngai Province, within which Son My is situated and where civilian casualties and physical destruction have been especially heavy, were subordinated to the Third Marine Amphibious Force, commanded by Lieut. Gen. Robert E. Cushman, who in turn was directly responsible to the top Army headqarters in Vietnam, the Military Assistance Command Vietnam (MACV). At the time of Son My, Gen. William Westmoreland headed MACV, with Gen. Creighton Abrams as his deputy and Lieut. Gen. William R. Rossen in charge of a headquarters of MACV in northern South Vietnam. From MACV, the chain of command runs through the commander-in-chief Pacific (Adm. Ulysses Grant Sharp Jr.) to the Chiefs of Staff in Washington.

It is on these officers that command responsibility for the conduct of operations has lain. From Gen. Westmoreland down they were more or less constantly in Vietnam, and splendidly equipped with helicopters and other aircraft which gave them a degree of mobility unprecedented in earlier wars, and consequently endowed them with every opportunity to keep the course of the fighting and its consequences under close and constant observation. Communications were generally rapid and efficient, so that the flow of information and orders was unimpeded.

THESE circumstances are in sharp contrast to those that confronted General Yamashita in 1944 and 1945, with his forces reeling back in disarray before the oncoming American military powerhouse. For failure to control his troops so as to prevent the atrocities they committed, Brig. Gens. Egbert F. Bullene and Morris Handwerk and Maj. Gens. James A. Lester, Leo Donovan and Russel B. Reynolds found him guilty of violating the laws of war and sentenced him to death by hanging. The sentence was first confirmed by the area commander, Lieut. Gen. William D. Styer, and then by Gen. Douglas MacArthur, as commander-in-chief, United States Army Forces in the Pacific. In his statement on the confirmation, Gen. MacArthur said of Yamashita:

> It is not easy for me to pass penal judgment upon a defeated adversary in a major military campaign. I have reviewed the proceedings in vain search for some mitigating circumstance on his behalf. I can find none. Rarely has so cruel and wanton a record been spread to public gaze. Revolting as this may be in itself, it pales before the sinister and far-reaching implication thereby attached to the profession of arms. . . . This officer, of proven field merit, entrusted with high command involving authority adequate to responsibility, has failed this irrevocable standard; has failed his duty to his troops, to his country, to his enemy, to mankind; has failed utterly his soldier faith. The transgressions resulting therefrom as revealed by the trial are a blot upon the military profession, a stain upon civilization and constitute a memory of shame and dishonor that can never be forgotten . . .
>
> I approve the findings and sentence of the Commission and direct the commanding general, Army Forces in the Western Pacific, to execute the judgment upon the defendant, stripped of uniform, decorations and other appurtenances signifying membership in the military profession.

Whether or not individuals are held to criminal account is perhaps not the most important question posed by the Vietnam War today. But the Son My courts-martial are shaping the question for us, and they can not be fairly determined without full inquiry into the higher responsibilities. Little as the leaders of the Army seem to realize it, this is the only road to the Army's salvation, for its moral health will not be recovered until its leaders are willing to scrutinize their behavior by the same standards that their revered predecessors applied to Tomayuki Yamashita 25 years ago.

II: WAR CRIMES

B. Judicial Applications

The Nuremberg Trials and
Conscientious Objection to War:
Justiciability under
United States Municipal Law

BENJAMIN FORMAN

INTRODUCTION

Conscientious objection to military service may be broadly characterized as a challenge to the selective service laws on moral [1] or legal [2] grounds, or as objection on moral or legal grounds to participation in a particular war. This paper addresses itself to the latter type of conscientious objection, and, more specifically, to the issue whether, under the municipal law of the United States, an individual who alleges that his participation in a specific war would be contrary to the international law principles and rules established at the Nuremberg Trials [3] may litigate that question in support of a claim of right to conscientious objector status. It does not

* The views expressed are the private views of the author and do not necessarily carry official sanction of any Department or Agency of the United States Government.

[1] "Moral" is used herein in the broadest sense of personal moral code, religious belief, and sociological and philosophical views and in contrast to "legal."

[2] *Cf.* United States v. Nugent, 346 U. S. 1, rehearing denied, 346 U. S. 853.

[3] The term "Nuremberg" is used generically in this paper to include the trials in Japan by the International Military Tribunal for the Far East. For citations to the pertinent source materials on these trials, see 11 Whiteman's Digest of International Law 890, 930, 936, 944, 970, 997, in particular, and Ch. XXXV, *passim*.

deal with the question whether compulsory military service can be required if a particular war is alleged to be unconstitutional because Congress has not declared war, or is alleged to be otherwise illegal on non-Nuremberg grounds.[4]

So defined, the issue might hypothetically be raised for judicial consideration in a variety of ways. Thus, on Nuremberg grounds: (1) a male falling within the purview of section 3 of the Military Selective Service Act of 1967 [5] might refuse to submit to registration; (2) a registrant might refuse to report for induction or might refuse to be sworn in after reporting for induction; (3) after having been inducted, a serviceman might refuse to carry out normal military duties unrelated geographically or functionally to combatant service; (4) a member of the armed forces might refuse to perform military duties functionally, but not geographically, related to the combatant services of others, *e.g.*, might refuse to train other servicemen for combat operations; (5) a member of the armed forces might refuse to obey orders assigning him to the zone of combat operations or desert upon the receipt of such orders; (6) a member of the armed forces in the zone of combat operations might refuse to perform any combatant duties or desert; (7) a member of the armed forces in the zone of combat operations might refuse to obey a specific combat order, carry out a specific combat mission, or serve in a particular military unit; (8) finally, the issue might be raised by civilians charged with knowingly counseling, aiding or abetting others to violate the Military Selective Service Act of 1967, or of conspiring to do so.

In the context of these hypothetical cases, the Nuremberg problem may be examined as a series of sub-issues. What principles and rules were established by the Nuremberg Trials? Were these principles and rules valid only for those trials or are they now part of the general corpus of international law? To what extent are they part of the municipal law of the United States? To what extent are they justiciable, *i.e.*, are they political questions; are they ripe for adjudication in these hypothetical cases; does the individual concerned have standing to invoke the applicability of particular principles and rules? Is the individual's belief that a particular war is illegal on Nuremberg grounds relevant to the question of criminal intent to violate applicable United States statutes?

THE NUREMBERG NORMS

The crimes established by the Charter of the International Military Tribunal [6] fall into the following categories: [7] (1) crimes against peace; (2) war crimes; (3) crimes against humanity; (4) membership in a criminal group or organization.

---

[4] *Cf.* United States *v.* Mitchell, 246 F. Supp. 874, 897 (D.C. Conn.); United States *v.* Sisson, Criminal No. 68-237-W, D.C. Mass., April 1, 1969; United States *v.* Sisson, 294 F. Supp. 511 (D.C. Mass., 1968).

[5] 50 U.S.C. App. 453.

[6] Exec. Agreement Series, No. 472, 59 Stat. 1546–1552; 39 A.J.I.L. Supp. 258 (1945).

[7] In this respect, the relevant articles of the Charter are 6, 9, 10, and 11.

As interpreted and applied by the International Military Tribunal and by the United States Tribunals in the "subsequent proceedings" at Nuremberg pursuant to Control Council Law No. 10, the principles and rules relevant to this paper which were enforced at Nuremberg may be summarized thus:

Crimes against peace.—Aggressive war has been a crime under international law at least since the Pact of Paris (Kellogg-Briand) of 1928.[8] Individuals who plan, prepare, initiate or wage aggressive war are subject to punishment regardless of their official positions. However, knowledge of aggressive intentions and participation in the planning and initiation of aggressive war is not sufficient to make participation in the war criminal, even by high-ranking military officers, unless the possessor of such knowledge, after he acquires it, is in a position to shape or influence the policy that brings about its initiation or its continuance after initiation, either by furthering or by hindering or preventing it. No military man in the field can be regarded as guilty of the crime against peace merely because he carried out military operations.

War crimes.—The crimes enumerated in Article 6(b) of the Charter were recognized as war crimes under international law prior to the Charter. They were covered by Articles 46, 50, 52, and 56 of the Hague Convention of 1907, and Articles 2, 3, 4, 46, and 51 of the Geneva Convention of 1929. Violations of these provisions constitute crimes for which guilty individuals are punishable. Although the Hague Convention by its terms is applicable only if all the belligerents are parties to the convention, the rules laid down in the convention were by 1939 recognized by all civilized nations as being declaratory of the laws and customs of war. A superior may be held responsible for war crimes committed by his subordinates if the acts in question were committed pursuant to his orders or if he has actual knowledge, or should have knowledge, that his subordinates are about to commit or have committed a war crime and he fails to take the steps necessary to insure compliance with the law of war or to punish violators thereof. "Superior orders" is not a defense unless the accused did not know and could not reasonably have been expected to know that the act ordered was unlawful; it may, however, be considered in mitigation of punishment when not a defense.

Crimes against humanity.—Within the meaning of the Charter: (i) those traditional war crimes committed in occupied areas that were so vast in scale as to require the participation of the state are crimes against humanity; (ii) inhumane acts committed by the state against its own civilians prior to the outbreak of war are not crimes against humanity; (iii) inhumane acts committed by the state against its own civilians in execution of, or in connection with, aggressive war do constitute crimes against humanity. The fact that domestic law does not impose a penalty for an act which is a crime against humanity does not relieve the person who committed the act from responsibility under international law.

[8] 46 Stat. 2343; 22 A.J.I.L. Supp. 171 (1928).

Membership in a criminal group.—A criminal organization is analogous to a criminal conspiracy in that the essence of both is co-operation for criminal purposes. It must be formed or used in connection with the commission of crimes denounced by the Charter.[9] Membership in such a group is not sufficient to subject an individual to punishment. The crime of membership excludes persons who had no knowledge of the criminal purposes or acts of the organization and excludes those drafted into membership, unless they were personally implicated in the commission of criminal acts.[10]

Were these norms valid only as to the individuals indicted at the Nuremberg Trials? The answer is clearly no. As indicated above, crimes against peace and the war crimes enumerated in Section 6(b) of the Charter were adjudged to be existing crimes under international law prior to the Charter. The current status of aggression as an international crime has since been reinforced by the United Nations Charter. Insofar as the Section 6(b) war crimes are concerned, the Hague Convention of 1907 is still in force, and the relevant provisions of the Geneva Conventions of 1929 have been re-enacted in the Geneva Conventions of 1949. Similarly, insofar as crimes against humanity are concerned, those crimes which involve inhumane acts in occupied territories unquestionably fall within the ambit of traditional war crimes and could be dealt with as such in lieu of being denominated crimes against humanity; those crimes which involve inhumane acts by a state against its own nationals are now, as recognized by the Genocide Convention, subsumed under the rubric of genocide and are not limited to the commission of the proscribed acts during war or in execution of aggressive war. Also relevant in this connection is the affirmation by the General Assembly of the United Nations of the principles of international law recognized by the Nuremberg Charter and the Judgment of the Tribunal.[11]

UNITED STATES DOMESTIC LAW

To what extent are the Nuremberg norms part of the municipal law of the United States? In the context of litigation in the courts of the United States, this question must be examined in the light of the following tenets of United States law. As the Supreme Court has held,

> International law is a part of our law and as such is the law of all States of the Union, but it is a part of our law for the application of its own principles, and these are concerned with international rights

[9] The Tribunal found the Leadership Corps of the Nazi Party, the Gestapo, and the S.S. to be criminal organizations. The S.A. was not found criminal. The Reich Cabinet and the General Staff and High Command were found not to be "organizations."

[10] Thus, persons employed by the Gestapo for purely clerical, stenographic, janitorial or similar unofficial tasks were not held criminal on this score.

[11] Res. 95(I), Dec. 11, 1946. For a discussion of the effect of General Assembly resolutions, see Falk, "On the Quasi-Legislative Competence of the General Assembly," 60 A.J.I.L. 782 (1966).

and duties and not with domestic rights and duties. (*Skiriotes* v. *Florida*, 313 U. S. 69–72–73.)

Thus, a statute which is subsequent in time and inconsistent with a treaty renders the treaty null from the municipal law point of view, even though the international law obligations of the United States remain unaffected.[12] Further, under the Constitution,[13] there is no common law of crimes against the law of nations in the United States,[14] and no treaty is self-executing with respect to enacting our criminal law.

In sum, from an international criminal law point of view, therefore, it would appear that the Nuremberg norms are part of our municipal law and may be enforced by our courts, at least by military commissions,[15] against enemy personnel.[16] Insofar as acts committed in the United States by American nationals are concerned, however, they may be enforced only to the extent that provision has been made therefor in our criminal laws.

With respect to war crimes of the kind enumerated in Article 6(b) of the Charter, adequate provision is made in the Uniform Code of Military Justice for persons subject to the military law of the United States, regardless of the locus of the offense, and, to some extent, in Federal or State criminal laws for persons not so subject.[17] The story is different with respect to crimes against peace and crimes against humanity. No statute of the United States provides that planning, initiating or waging aggressive war is a criminal offense. Similarly, except for those international crimes against humanity which may be otherwise prosecuted on different charges as a traditional war crime or as a traditional municipal law crime (such as homicide or peonage), no statute of the United States proscribes as such the offense of a crime against humanity.

JUSTICIABILITY OF THE NUREMBERG NORMS

Granted that the Nuremberg norms are binding on the United States in its international relations, and that, to the extent noted above, these norms are part of the municipal law of the United States, what relevance do they have to the outcome of the hypothetical cases postulated earlier in this paper? Stated another way, do these norms afford a defense to the individual concerned in a trial for violating the selective service laws, the Uniform Code of Military Justice, or other applicable statute?

Ad limine, it should be observed that the Military Selective Service Act of 1967 allows exemption from military service on grounds of conscientious objection only to those "who, by reason of religious training

[12] Reid *v.* Covert, 354 U. S. 1, 18; 51 A.J.I.L. 783 (1957).

[13] Art. I, Sec. 8, Cl. 10.

[14] See, *e.g.*, 18 U.S.C. 1651, 1653, *re* piracy.

[15] *Cf.* Arts. 21 and 18 of U.C.M.J. (10 U.S.C. 821 and 818); Madsen *v.* Kinsella, 343 U. S. 341, 346–355, 46 A.J.I.L. 556 (1952).

[16] *Cf.* Ex parte Quirin, 317 U. S. 1; 37 A.J.I.L. 152 (1943); Army Field Manual FM 27-10, pp. 178–183 (July, 1956).

[17] See Levie, "Penal Sanctions for Maltreatment of Prisoners of War," 56 A.J.I.L. 433 (1962).

and belief, [are] conscientiously opposed to participation in war in any form.''[18]   As a statutory matter, therefore, one who is opposed to military service only in a particular war, as distinguished from ''war in any form,'' is not entitled to exemption.[19]   Accordingly, since our courts are bound to follow this statute regardless of its compatibility with international law, this ground is itself sufficient to make the Nuremberg issue irrelevant in disposing of hypothetical cases (1), (2), and (8).

Another fundamental obstacle confronting these individuals, insofar as they seek to justify their actions on the ground that a particular war is illegal because it is an aggressive war, is the doctrine that political questions are not justiciable.   Admittedly, not every case or controversy which touches foreign relations lies beyond judicial competence.   However, those questions which involve the exercise of a discretion constitutionally committed to the Executive or the Congress are political questions.[20]   Clearly, the decision to conduct military operations against hostile forces is a matter vested by the Constitution exclusively in the Congress and the President.[21]   Indeed, since as a municipal law matter, no treaty outlawing aggressive war can derogate from the constitutional powers of the Congress and the President to wage war,[22] and since no United States statute provides that planning, initiating, or waging aggressive war is a crime, even were the Executive Branch and the Congress to embark knowingly on an admitted aggressive war, that decision would belong in the domain of political power and not be subject to judicial intervention.

A related doctrine which appears applicable here is that of a judicial abstention grounded upon the exercise of judicial discretion.   Assuming that the question of aggressive war is not a political question, the facts that (i) no definition of aggression has been agreed to by the United Nations, (ii) different standards for defining aggression have been proposed by nations with divergent interests and social ideologies, and that (iii) the political effect of a municipal adjudication of the issue would have sensitive implications for our relations with third countries, strongly argue for judicial abstention.[23]   Those of you who are familiar with the *Sabbatino* opinion will realize that I am paraphrasing the court there.

Assuming, *arguendo,* that these bars to justiciability may be overcome, is the legality of a particular war an issue which is ripe for adjudication in hypothetical cases (1), (2), (3) and (8)?

[18] Sec. 6(j) (50 U.S.C. App. 456(j)); see United States v. Seeger, 380 U. S. 163.

[19] United States v. Kurki, 255 F. Supp. 161 (D.C. Wis.), certiorari denied, 390 U. S. 926.

[20] Baker v. Carr, 369 U. S. 186, 217.

[21] Cf. Luftig v. McNamara, 373 F. 2d 664, 665–666 (C.A.D.C.), certiorari denied, sub. nom., Mora v. McNamara, 389 U. S. 934. In this connection, it is not without significance that, in the international sphere, competence to determine the question of aggression is vested by the United Nations Charter in a political body, the Security Council.

[22] ''This Court has regularly and uniformly recognized the supremacy of the Constitution over a treaty.'' Reid v. Covert, loc. cit. above, at 17.

[23] Cf. Banco Nacional de Cuba v. Sabbatino, 376 U. S. 398; 58 A.J.I.L. 779 (1964).

With respect to hypothetical case (1), the registration requirement is separable from the remaining provisions of the Selective Service Act and is valid and enforceable regardless of the validity *vel non* of the other provisions on Nuremberg or other grounds.[24]

With respect to cases (2), (3) and (8), the Nuremberg issue is equally premature. It is entirely a matter of conjecture whether the service assignments of the individuals concerned would involve them in direct participation in the particular war.[25] Nor can Nuremberg be made an issue on the theory that the selective service system is operated as an adjunct of the military effort in the zone of combat operations. The Congressional power to raise and support armies and to provide and maintain a navy is a matter quite distinct from the use which the Executive makes, or the Congress sanctions, of those found qualified and inducted into service.[26] To contend otherwise is to contend that, if the United States is engaging in conduct contrary to international law, it has lost the right to enforce any duty upon its citizens which can be deemed in any manner to enable it to engage in such conduct. On this thesis, not only would the selective service laws be unenforceable but so would our tax and other laws. As pointed out earlier, however, international law does not in this respect have primacy over our municipal law.

Further, it seems clear that the individuals concerned in hypothetical cases (1), (2), (3), (4), (5), (6), and (8) do not have standing to raise any Nuremberg issue. To have standing, the party seeking relief must have "a personal stake in the outcome of the controversy."[27] In this context, that personal stake must be a showing that they would subject themselves to criminal liability by participation in the particular war.

No Nuremberg norm makes it criminal to be a soldier or, as such, to carry on belligerent activities injurious to others in accordance with the laws and customs of war, even though the war be an aggressive war. The crime against peace can be committed only by those in a position to shape or influence the policy that initiates or continues it. So viewed, there can be no doubt that the individuals concerned in none of the hypothetical cases have standing to litigate the issue of aggressive war.

As to war crimes and crimes against humanity, liability is similarly individual. The individual must himself commit the substantive offense or conspire to do so. For conspiracy to exist, there must be at least the degree of criminal intent necessary for the substantive offense itself,

[24] *Cf.* Richter *v.* United States, 181 F. 2d 591, certiorari denied, 340 U. S. 892. Moreover, a registrant must exhaust his administrative remedies before he can offer his claim of conscientious objection as a defense to a prosecution for refusal to be inducted.

[25] *Cf.* United States *v.* Bolton, 192 F. 2d 805 (C.A. 2).

[26] *Cf.* United States *v.* Mitchell, 369 F. 2d 323, 324 (C.A. 2), certiorari denied, 386 U. S. 972.

[27] *Cf.* Flast *v.* Cohen, 88 S. Ct. 1942, 1953.

plus informed and interested co-operation, stimulation, and instigation.[28] Further, membership in the regular armed forces of a state does not, under Nuremberg, constitute membership in a criminal organization. Accordingly, the allegation that others may be committing war crimes or crimes against humanity is inadequate to confer standing in any of the hypothetical cases.

Turning now to hypothetical case (7), the standing of that individual to litigate the Nuremberg issue with respect to war crimes and crimes against humanity is self-evident. Article 92 of the Uniform Code of Military Justice [29] requires those subject to the Code to obey only those orders which are "lawful," and the Nuremberg rule that obedience to superior orders is not a defense is recognized in our military law.[30] Hence an individual who refuses to obey a specific combat order or to carry out a specific combat mission on the ground that the action ordered is contrary to the laws and customs of war not only has standing to raise that defense but cannot be punished for violation of orders if that contention be proven. With respect to refusal to serve in a particular military unit on the ground that it is a criminal organization, however, the matter of standing is less certain. Even assuming that the individual has adequate reason to believe that the unit in question is criminal under Nuremberg, or, indeed, could prove it to be so in a trial, it does not follow that this issue is justiciable as to him. Under Nuremberg, membership alone is not sufficient to attach individual liability and the crime of membership excludes those drafted into membership who are not personally implicated in the commission of criminal acts.

The last sub-issue to be considered is whether the illegality of a particular war on Nuremberg grounds is justiciable if only to establish that the conduct of these hypothetical individuals in refusing to participate in the war lacked criminal intent. Any such contention mistakenly confuses motive with motivation.[31] "One who is a martyr to a principle . . . does not prove by his martyrdom that he has kept within the law." [32]

---

[28] Cf. Ingram v. United States, 360 U. S. 672, 678; Direct Sales Co. v. United States, 319 U. S. 703, 713.   [29] 10 U.S.C. 892.

[30] Department of the Army Field Manual FM 27-10, pp. 182–183 (July, 1956); Manual for Courts-Martial United States, 1968, par. 216d.

[31] Cf. United States v. Berrigan, 283 F. Supp. 336 (D. Md.); 63 A.J.I.L. 147 (1969).

[32] Hamilton v. Regents, 293 U. S. 245, 268 (Cardozo, J., concurring).

War Crimes and Vietnam:
The "Nuremberg Defense" and the
Military Service Resister*

ANTHONY A. D'AMATO

HARVEY L. GOULD

LARRY D. WOODS

The case of Captain Howard B. Levy—the Green Beret "Medic"
Case[1]—at first seemed like hundreds of similar cases involving American servicemen being prosecuted for resistance to military orders involving Vietnam. Captain Levy had refused an order to teach derma-
tology to Special Forces (Green Beret) medics in the United States who
were preparing for service in Vietnam, on the ground that his teaching
would be "prostituted" by the Green Berets who in his opinion would
commit war crimes once they arrived in Vietnam. The law officer for
the military court, surprisingly, and on his own initiative, thereupon
called for a private session in which he would hear evidence on the
"Nuremberg defense"—the charge that the Green Berets were committing war crimes in Vietnam and that the government cannot constitu-

---

* Messrs. Gould and Woods assisted in the research for this article under Professor D'Amato's supervision in the Senior Research Program at Northwestern
University.

1. Levy v. Resor, 17 U.S.C.M.A. 135, 37 C.M.R. 399 (1967); N.Y. Times,
May 18, 1967, at 2, col. 3 (ruling to hear evidence of war crimes); Note, 9 HARV.
INT'L L.J. 169 (1968). Levy's case is in its first civilian review stage, in the Middle
District of Pennsylvania. N.Y. Times, April 20, 1969, at 32, col. 1. Levy finished all
but nine days of his two-year military sentence at Fort Leavenworth when Justice
William O. Douglas ordered him freed on 1000 dollars bail in August, 1969.

tionally place a soldier against his will in substantial jeopardy of becoming implicated in such crimes. This decision by the law officer lifted Levy's case out of the ordinary and gave it historical significance. After hearing the evidence, the law officer ruled that none of it was admissible in open court. The net effect was to suggest to the public that an American military court was willing to be open minded about the introduction of a war-crimes allegation but that such a defense in fact had no intrinsic merit.

A closer look at the law officer's ruling reveals otherwise. The law officer held the proffered evidence inadmissible not on the merits but because it was strictly irrelevant to Captain Levy's own circumstances. Although there was testimony in the private session that Green Berets were engaging in criminal activity in Vietnam that violated international laws of warfare, there was no evidence that the *medics* among the Green Beret troops were themselves engaged in war crimes or that their medical *training* was being prostituted by being utilized in criminal activity.[2] While narrowly conceived, this ruling is reasonable inasmuch as Captain Levy was not himself in danger of serving in Vietnam as a member of the Green Berets, and his particular medical expertise, taught in this country, could only serve to ameliorate whatever wartime crimes they might commit. Thus the Levy case may have been the weakest possible situation to introduce a "Nuremberg defense." On the other hand, the case does stand for the important precedent that a war-crimes defense is available, in relevant circumstances, to in-service resisters.

Much has been published in recent years concerning aspects of the legality of the American involvement in Vietnam,[3] creating confusion and an understandable readership reaction that any attempt to discuss "law" and Vietnam is either frustrating or phony.[4] Most writers have discussed these issues in terms abstracted from probable justiciability, calling the entire war effort illegal because it is a war of aggression in violation of the United Nations Charter or an undeclared war in violation of the United States Constitution.[5] Surely no judge would

---

2. N.Y. Times, May 26, 1967, at 5, col. 2.

3. *See generally* the essays collected in THE VIETNAM WAR AND INTERNATIONAL LAW (R. Falk ed. 1968).

4. *Compare* Andonian, *Law and Vietnam*, 54 A.B.A.J. 457 (1968) *with* D'Amato, *Vietnam and Public International Law*, 2 VANDERBILT INT'L L.J. 100 (1969).

5. *See, e.g.*, Lawyer's Committee on American Policy Toward Vietnam, *American Policy Vis-A-Vis Vietnam, in Light of our Constitution, The United Nations Charter, The 1954 Geneva Accords, and the Southeast Asia Collective Defense Treaty*, Memorandum of Law, 112 CONG. REC. 2666 (1966); Wright, *Legal Aspects of the Viet-Nam Situation*, 60 AM. J. INT'L L. 750 (1966). For a more realistic and highly creative view, see Falk, *International Law and the United States Role in the Viet Nam War*, 75 YALE L.J. 1122 (1966).

have the temerity to invalidate the entire war effort on such con-
clusory grounds as these.[6] However, if we move out of metaphysics
and into the narrow question of whether some *methods* of conducting
war are illegal, the area of inquiry is arguably justiciable and susceptible
of adversary legal argumentation. In this age of blind progress, when
man has reached the potential of summary destructability of the whole
human race by thermonuclear weapons, virulent germ warfare, nerve
gas, or the somewhat slower processes of environmental pollution, it is
possible that some American judges may be ready to review the judgments of military leaders on matters they say are related to national
security. A military decision to use chemical and gas weapons in Vietnam, for example, might in an appropriate case be examined by an
American court in light of the international laws of warfare relating to
such weaponry and the possible shortsightedness of such deployment
as a precedent that some day may really imperil American security.

It is with such considerations in mind that we propose to discuss
first the concept of "war crimes" as articulated at Nuremberg and elsewhere, and to consider the legal applicability of this body of international
law in domestic American courts. Following that, in the second part of
our essay, we present the kinds of evidence needed to substantiate claims
of the commission of war crimes. We then consider possible defenses
to allegations of war crimes, and close with a discussion of the justiciability of war crimes questions in American courts in possible service-re-
sister cases.

I

APPLICABILITY OF THE LAWS OF WARFARE TO AMERICAN LAW

A most authoritative capsule statement of the content of war crimes
under international law is that found in the Charter of the International
Military Tribunal at Nuremberg[7] and affirmed by a unanimous resolution of the General Assembly of the United Nations:[8]

> War crimes [are] violations of the laws or customs of war [which]
> include, but [are] not limited to, murder, ill-treatment or deporta-
> tion to slave-labour or for any other purpose of civilian population
> of or in occupied territory, murder or ill-treatment of prisoners of
> war or persons on the seas, killing of hostages, plunder of public or

---

6. It is true that Justices Douglas and Stewart did dissent from the denial of
certiorari in Mora v. McNamara, 389 U.S. 934 (1967), a case in which many of the
"larger issues" of the Vietnamese war were posited. However, their (minority) position
on certiorari is no indication of how they would vote on the merits.

7. 1 Trial Maj. War Crim. 11, (art. 6(b)) (Int'l Mil. Trib. 1947); 59 Stat.
1547 (1945).

8. G.A. Res. 95(I) U.N. Doc. A/236 at 1144 (1946).

private property, wanton destruction of cities, towns, or villages, or devastation not justified by military necessity.

More specific formulations of the laws of war are found in international treaties. The United States is a party to twelve conventions pertinent to land warfare[9] which typically contain very detailed provisions.[10] Despite the particularity of these conventions, courts dealing with war-crimes cases have not adopted an overly technical approach but rather have looked to substantial violations that contradict the underlying humane purpose of these laws. In *In Re Yamashita*,[11] for example, a 1946 case involving the conviction of a Japanese commander for failure to restrain his troops from committing war crimes against civilians, the United States Supreme Court placed decisive weight on the "purpose of the law of war" to "protect civilian populations and prisoners of war from brutality."

The laws of warfare are part of American law, enforceable in American courts, not only because the United States is party to most of the major multilateral conventions on the conduct of military hostilities but also because the laws of warfare are incorporated in international customary law, which under the Constitution is part of American law.[12] This international customary law, in turn, derives much of its content from major international conventions.[13] Thus, while the United States is not a party to the Geneva Protocol of 1925 on Poisonous Gases and Bacteriological Warfare,[14] for example, the substance of this convention has nevertheless passed into the customary laws of warfare and is in that manner binding on the United States.[15]

---

9. See the listing in U.S. DEP'T OF THE ARMY, THE LAW OF LAND WARFARE § 5 (Field Manual No. 27-10, 1963) [hereinafter cited as FIELD MANUAL].

10. *E.g.*, Geneva Convention Relative to the Treatment of Prisoners of War, Aug. 12, 1949, [1955] 3 U.S.T. 3316, T.I.A.S. No. 3364, 75 U.N.T.S. 135, containing 143 articles and 5 annexes.

11. 327 U.S. 1, 15 (1946).

12. The Paquete Habana, 175 U.S. 677, 700 (1900).

13. For a statement of this theory, see D'Amato, *Treaties as a Source of General Rules of International Law*, 3 HARV. INT'L L.J. 1 (1962); D'Amato, The Concept of Custom in International Law 138-217 (doctoral dissertation in Columbia University Library 1968) (analysis of treaties at Nuremberg trials).

14. Protocol Prohibiting the Use in War of Asphyxiating, Poisonous, or Other Gases, and of Bacteriological Methods of Warfare, of June 17, 1925, 94 L.N.T.S. 65; 3 M. HUDSON, INTERNATIONAL LEGISLATION 1670 (1931).

15. *See* D'Amato, *supra* note 13; North Sea Continental Shelf Cases, [1969] I.C.J. 4, 42-43. Whether the multilateral conventions generate rules of customary international law or whether they exist in parallel with customary rules to the same effect, the Nuremberg Tribunal held that provisions in the Hague Conventions of 1907 and the Geneva Conventions of 1929 were applicable to Germany not directly but because they were "regarded as being declaratory of the laws and customs of war," 1 Trial Maj. War Crim. 255 (Int'l Mil. Trib. 1947), and held the Hague Conventions of 1907 applicable to World War II despite the formal exclusion in those conventions

Although the United States is subject to the laws of warfare, any given conflict has to be examined specifically to determine the applicability of the various international conventions and to determine whether it is in fact a "war" for legal purposes. The Geneva Conventions of 1949,[16] which constitute an important source for much of the laws of land warfare to be examined later in this essay, were ratified by the United States,[17] the Soviet Union,[18] Communist China,[19] and both North[20] and South Vietnam.[21] It would be most difficult for the United States to argue that the Geneva Conventions of 1949 do not apply vis-a-vis the National Liberation Front which is not a party, inasmuch as the United States has consistently characterized the NLF as a political arm of Hanoi in the South. Indeed the United States would probably resist any attempt by the NLF to ratify the Convention, on the ground that the NLF is not an independent political state or entity. In any event, the United States has never denied nor contested the applicability of the international law of warfare to the American military engagements in Vietnam. In a 1966 memorandum on Vietnam the Department of State said that

> a formal declaration of war would not place any obligations on either side in the conflict by which that side would not be bound in any event. The rules of international law concerning the conduct of hostilities in an international armed conflict apply regardless of any declaration of war.[22]

In 1965 President Johnson directed Secretary Rusk to inform the international committee of the Red Cross that the United States was abiding

---

of wars which involved non-parties (Russia was not a party). *See also id.* at 334 (applicable to Czechoslovakia though it was not a party). Even more remarkable was the extensive use of the 1929 Geneva Convention on Prisoners of War, to which Germany itself was not a party; *see* United States v. von Leeb, 11 Trials of War Criminals Before the Nuremberg Military Tribunals 462, 535-38 (1950); *see also* Tanabe Koshiro Case, 11 L. Rep. Trials War Crim. 1, 4 (U.N. War Crimes Comm'n 1947) (applying the Convention to Japan, also a non-party).

    16. In addition to the Prisoners of War Convention, *supra* note 10, these are: Geneva Convention for the Amelioration of the Condition of the Wounded and Sick in Armed Forces in the Field, Aug. 12, 1949, [1955] 3 U.S.T. 3114, T.I.A.S. No. 3362, 75 U.N.T.S. 31; Geneva Convention for the Amelioration of the Condition of Wounded, Sick and Shipwrecked Members of Armed Forces at Sea, Aug. 12, 1949, [1955] 3 U.S.T. 3217, T.I.A.S. No. 3363, 75 U.N.T.S. 85; Geneva Convention Relative to the Protection of Civilian Persons in Time of War, Aug. 12, 1949, [1955] 3 U.S.T. 3516, T.I.A.S. No. 3365, 75 U.N.T.S. 287.

    17. 213 U.N.T.S. 378-84 (1955).

    18. 191 U.N.T.S. 365-68 (1954).

    19. 260 U.N.T.S. 438-45 (1956).

    20. 275 U.N.T.S. 335-42 (1957).

    21. 181 U.N.T.S. 349-52 (1953).

    22. U.S. Dep't of State, *The Legality of United States Participation in the Defense of Viet-Nam*, 112 CONG. REC. 5506 (1966) (art. I (G)).

by the "humanitarian principles" of the 1949 Geneva convention and that it expected "other parties" in the Vietnamese war to do the same.[23] The N.L.F. "presence" at the Paris Peace talks removes any final doubt that it has achieved belligerent status and thus is entitled to the benefits, and burdens, of the laws of war.[24] Finally, the laws of war continually apply to both sides in a conflict irrespective of whether one side has committed or is committing frequent violations of these laws.[25]

The international laws of warfare apply to military combat situations however characterized by the parties. The Geneva Conventions of 1949 specifically state their applicability to "all cases of declared war or of any other armed conflict . . . even if the state of war is not recognized by one of [the Parties]."[26] Nor is a declaration of war needed; the United States Army *Field Manual* holds:

> As the customary law of war applies to cases of international armed conflict and to the forcible occupation of enemy territory generally as well as to declared war in its strict sense, a declaration of war is not an essential condition of the application of this body of law. Similarly, treaties relating to "war" may become operative notwithstanding the absence of a formal declaration of war.[27]

Insofar as it may become necessary to procure a judicial determination that war, or even armed conflict, exists in Vietnam, American courts have historically displayed a common sense approach to determining whether a state of war or armed conflict was occurring or had occurred in foreign lands.[28]

---

23. New York Times, Aug. 14, 1965, at 1, col. 3.

24. Address by Farer and Petrowski, "The Nuremberg Trials and Objection to Military Service in Vietnam," before the American Society of International Law, Washington, D.C., April 25, 1969 (to be published in 1969 PROC. AM. SOC'Y INT'L L.).

25. *See* R. WOETZEL, THE NUREMBERG TRIALS IN INTERNATIONAL LAW 120-21 (1960). Similarly it is no bar to the trial of war criminals that equally guilty nationals of the victorious state might escape punishment. M. GREENSPAN, THE MODERN LAW OF LAND WARFARE 421 (1959).

26. This is stated in Article 2, common to all four conventions, *supra* notes 10 & 16.

27. FIELD MANUAL *supra* note 9, at para. 9.

28. In Bas v. Tingy, 4 U.S. (4 Dall.) 37, 39 (1800), the Supreme Court found that the United States was at war with France despite the absence of a declaration of war, referring to the facts of "bloodshed, depredation and confiscation" in conflicts between vessels of the two nations. The Court of Military Appeals held for various purposes that the United States was "at war" during the Korean conflict, United States v. Ayres, 4 U.S.M.C.A. 220, 15 C.M.R. 232 (1954), United States v. Bancroft, 3 U.S.M.C.A. 3, 11 C.M.R. 3 (1953), and held in 1968 that the United States was "at war" in Vietnam for the purpose of suspending the two-year statute of limitations on prosecuting military offenders who had gone absent without leave, United States v. Anderson, 17 U.S.C.M.A. 588, 38 C.M.R. 386 (1968). For similar decisions interpreting the existence of a state of war during the Korean conflict for the purpose of

Once it is agreed that the laws of warfare apply to the United States generally and in the Vietnamese war in particular, a more vexing problem concerning the applicability of the international law of war crimes to American courts remains—the image that many jurists have of the Nuremberg judgments as representing the application of *ex post facto* law to the Nazi defendants after the Second World War. Of course, even if the Nuremberg tribunal had articulated laws of war for the first time the Nuremberg precedents nevertheless stand for all combat situations since then. It is worthy of note that on December 11, 1946, the United States joined in a unanimous General Assembly resolution affirming "the principles of international law recognized by the Charter of the Nuremberg tribunal and the judgment of the tribunal."[29] Despite these arguments, however, American courts might be reluctant to invoke a precedent that itself was tainted by a retroactive application of criminal law. Thus it is important here to analyze the Nuremberg judgments closely to see if this jurisprudential objection is well founded.

Analysis of the September 30, 1946 verdict and sentencing of the major Nazi war criminals at Nuremberg indicates that the Allied prosecutors may have done themselves a disservice in their zeal to introduce the new crimes of "crimes against peace" and "crimes against humanity." Ultimately, the tribunals handed down what were principally convictions of traditional "war crimes," crimes which had been invoked after the first world war[30] and which were so generally regarded as an established part of international law that no significant objection to their inclusion was made at Nuremberg. The twenty two defendants were indicted variously on four counts: (1) Conspiracy to wage wars of aggression; (2) initiating or waging wars of aggression ("crimes against peace"); (3) war crimes; and (4) crimes against humanity. The final sentencing can be summarized as follows:[31]

---

construing insurance claims, see Carious v. New York Life Ins. Co., 124 F. Supp. 388 (S.D. Ill. 1954); Weissman v. Metropolitan Life Ins. Co., 112 F. Supp. 420 (S.D. Cal. 1953). In United States v. Bancroft, *supra*, 11 C.M.R. at 5, the court suggested the following factors as indicative of a state of war: (1) Movement to and the presence of large numbers of military personnel on battlefields; (2) number of casualties involved; (3) sacrifices required; (4) number of recruits who must be drafted; (5) national emergency legislation; (6) number and types of executive orders promulgated to deal in some way with the hostilities; (7) amount of money being expended for the express purpose of maintaining the armed forces in the theater of operations. Certainly these same factors would overwhemingly indicate a state of war in Vietnam.

29. G.A. Res. 95(I) U.N. Doc. A/64/Add. 1 at 188 (1947).

30. For an historical account of earlier trials, *see* R. WOETZEL, *supra* note 25, at 172-89.

31. Table derived from data in 1 Trial Maj. War Crim. 279-366 (Int'l Mil. Trib. 1947).

Defendant	Counts				Sentence
	(1)	(2)	(3)	(4)	
Goering	1	1	1	1	D
Hess	1	1	0	0	C
von Ribbentrop	1	1	1	1	D
Keitel	1	1	1	1	D
Kaltenbrunner	0		1	1	D
Rosenberg	1	1	1	1	D
Frank	0		1	1	D
Frick	0	1	1	1	D
Streicher	0			1	D
Funk	0	1	1	1	C
Schacht	0	0			Acquitted
Doenitz	0	1	1		A
Raeder	1	1	1		C
von Schirach	0			1	B
Sauckel	0	0	1	1	D
Jodl	1	1	1	1	D
von Papen	0	0			Acquitted
Seyss-Inquart	0	1	1	1	D
Speer	0	0	1	1	B
von Neurath	1	1	1	1	B
Fritzsche	0		0	0	Acquitted
Bormann	0		1	1	D (in absentia)
Total Indictments	22	16	18	18	
Total Convictions	8	12	16	16	

Key

0	=	Indicted but not convicted
1	=	Indicted and convicted
A	=	Ten years imprisonment
B	=	Fifteen to twenty years imprisonment
C	=	Life imprisonment
D	=	Death by hanging

The table reveals the following configurations:

All defendants except Hess[32] who were convicted of the innovative crime of waging aggressive warfare (under counts 1 or 2) were *also* convicted of the traditional "war crimes" indictment (count 3). Hess,

---

32. The Tribunal did not find evidence sufficiently connecting Hess with the commission of war crimes, but did note that there was "evidence showing the participation of the Party Chancellery, under Hess, in the distribution of orders connected with the commission of War Crimes; that Hess may have had knowledge of, even if he did not participate in, the crimes that were being committed in the East, and proposed laws discriminating against Jews and Poles; and that he signed decrees forcing certain groups of Poles to accept German citizenship." 1 Trial Maj. War Crim. 284 (Int'l Mil. Trib. 1947).

the sole exception of twelve, did not receive the death penalty.

Every defendant, except Streicher and von Schirach, who was convicted of the "crime against humanity" (count 4) was also convicted of the traditional "war crimes" count.

This interdependence of counts 3 and 4 is bolstered by the way the final verdicts were read in open court on October 1, 1946. For each defendant except Streicher and von Schirach, counts 3 and 4 were considered together under the paragraph heading "War Crimes and Crimes against Humanity." This followed the way the evidence was presented at trial as well as the pattern of article 6 of the Charter of the International Military Tribunal.[33] For the rubric "crimes against humanity" was explicitly considered in article 6, and by the tribunal itself during its proceedings, as comprehending the most heinous of the war crimes in addition to innovatively making criminal the murder or maltreatment of the German government's own citizens (such as Jews, Jehovah's Witnesses, Freemasons, and political opponents of the Nazi regime).[34] Content analysis of the tribunal's verdicts, furthermore, shows that except for Streicher and von Schirach each defendant convicted under count 4 could be said to have been convicted under an aggravated-war-crimes charge amounting to a "crime against humanity." With respect to four of these defendants—Keitel, Sauchel, Jodl, and Speer—there is no mention in the verdict of crimes against German citizens and thus their conviction under court 4 was solely an aggravated version of the traditiional war crimes indictment.

Thus, despite criticism of the Nuremberg trials relating to the major war criminals on *nulle poena sine lege* grounds, the overwhelming component of the verdicts was the traditional "war crimes" charge. In this essay, therefore, the Nuremberg precedents are referred to solely as establishing the international law of "war crimes," and not the more dubious and propagandistic "crimes against peace" and "crimes against humanity" which unfortunately have served to weaken the popular image of the validity of the Nuremberg proceedings.

A second source of possible judicial reluctance to accept or give much weight to a war-crimes defense in American civilian or military courts is a feeling, usually not articulated, that the international law of war crimes is not "real" law but rather the embodiment of an abstract idealism out of touch with such brutal facts as are revealed in the Vietnamese war. War is, in other words, an all-out struggle, and there is no room for judicial intervention in its processes even granting that after the war is over a Nuremberg-type trial might be held. The reply

---

33. Text in 1 Trial Maj. War Crim. at 10-16 (Int'l Mil. Trib. 1947).

34. *See* R. WOETZEL, *supra* note 25, at 177.

that American courts must apply this law insofar as it is reflected in treaties to which the United States is a party is itself an ineffective rejoinder inasmuch as judicial attitude plays a significant role not only in the ultimate disposition of cases but also in the preliminary decision whether to hear argument. The controversies in many branches of the law dealing with "standing" and "political questions" attest to the delicacy of judicial attitude as a factor in determining whether to hear certain types of arguments. Thus, it may be more effective to argue that the concept of war crimes in international law reflects an extremely realistic philosophy of law, warfare, and social control, which serves the best interests of the United States.

To begin with, the laws of warfare implicitly acknowledge, and realistically discount, the question of the legality of commencement of military hostilities. Although resort to the "threat or use of force" is illegal in international relations under the United Nations Charter,[35] even a state which starts a flagrant war of aggression is entitled to the benefit of the laws of warfare and must accept its burdens.[36] At Nuremberg, the allied tribunals rejected the argument of several prosecutors that everything the German and Japanese militarists did during the war was criminal because the war itself was an act of aggression.[37] Second, the laws of warfare, like the whole of international law, express the reciprocal self-interest of the governments that conceived them and support them. It may not be overly cynical to point out that the many provisions relating to the treatment of prisoners of war that are listed in the United States Army *Field Manual* may operate to defuse incipient resistance on the part of soldiers by assuring them, at least on paper, that if captured by the enemy they will be given prisoner-of-war-treatment. Similarly, rules designed to protect civilians in part may have operated to give governments greater freedom of action in mobilizing civilians to support and pay for standing armies and armaments. A government thus may have been willing to pay the price of a limitation of legal methods of warfare to obtain greater access to war-making ability. To the extent that this may have been one of the many motives involved, we should not fail to extract the price of compliance from governments that are involved in warfare. Third, by helping to preserve lives of captured soldiers and the infrastructure of the

---

35. U.N. CHARTER art. 2, para. 4.

36. *E.g.*, Trial of Willy Zuehlke, 14 L. Rep. Trials War Crim. 139, 144 (U.N. War Crimes Comm'n, Neth. Spec. Ct. Cassation 1948); Trial of Wilhelm List, 8 L. Rep. Trials War Crim. 34, 59 (U.N. War Crimes Comm'n, U.S. Mil. Trib. 1948); Trial of Josef Alstoetter, 6 L. Rep. Trials War Crim. 1, 52 (U.N. War Crimes Comm'n, U.S. Mil. Trib. 1947).

37. *See* M. McDOUGAL & F. FELICIANO, LAW AND MINIMUM WORLD PUBLIC ORDER 531-34 (1961) [hereinafter cited as McDOUGAL & FELICIANO].

civilian economy of both sides, the laws of warfare help not only to restore peace but also to justify the battle.[38] Finally the laws of warfare provide a legal means of removing from the scene leading enemy commanders via post-war military criminal tribunals, thus facilitating post-war governance of the losing side.

But can they really be "laws" when it is notorious that they are frequently flouted and violated during wartime? Nearly any promulgated law of general applicability that is consistent on its face[39] exerts some pressure toward compliance with its terms. Imagine the simplest of laws—a "stop sign" at a street intersection in a town in which every driver goes through the intersection without bringing his vehicle to a complete stop. Does this habit of disobedience mean that the stop sign is not really a law? Of course, it may be argued pedantically that it is a law because it *might* be enforced some day. More important, however, it may be observed that the drivers in this imaginary town slow down and proceed with caution when approaching the corner with the stop sign, even though they do not comply with its terms. If so, the sign influences human behavior. Indeed, its main purpose—to prevent traffic accidents at that corner—may be completely fulfilled despite the total lack of literal compliance.

In wartime, some soldiers and commanders may disobey the laws of warfare listed in their field manuals; but some may do so only in special circumstances, and others may refrain from doing so altogether. A soldier who disobeys is gambling that his side will eventually win so that the enemy will not try him for war crimes, that he will not be captured by the enemy during the war and identified as a war criminal, and that his own side, though winning, will not court-martial him.[40] In addition, he must consider that his own side might suffer from his acts by virtue of reciprocal disobedience of the laws of warfare by the adversaries. In World War II pressures such as these caused considerable compliance with the laws of war even by German commanders in the darkest days of their battle.[41] Moreover, the consider-

---

38. This may have special significance to the United States, since it bases its entire intervention in the Vietnamese war on the ground of resisting an *illegal* takeover of South Vietnam by Communist forces. In particular, when atrocities by the Communist side were cited in defense of the American massacre of over 100 Vietnamese civilians in the village of Songmy, a British member of Parliament replied, "I thought the Americans were in this war to show that they had a different standard of morality from the Communists." Lewis, *Atrocity Charge Stirring British*, N.Y. Times, Nov. 22, 1969, at 3, cols. 1, 4.

39. *See generally* L. FULLER, THE MORALITY OF LAW (1964).

40. *Cf.* Levie, *Penal Sanctions for Maltreatment of Prisoners of War*, 56 AM. J. INT'L L. 433 (1962).

41. *See* McDOUGAL & FELICIANO, *supra* note 37, at 54-55.

able resistance of German generals evidently forced Hitler to put into writing such orders as that of October 18, 1942, commanding the execution of captured British commandoes in Africa.[42] Reports from Vietnam suggest that American military officers take considerable pains to avoid any *overt* departure from the laws respecting treatment of prisoners.[43] What violations a field commander will not commit openly or in the absence of written orders from a superior effectively reduces the number of instances that he will have occasion to contravene the laws of warfare. Thus the laws of warfare, like all laws, at least operate to make the prescribed conduct more difficult than if there were no law at all.

It is perhaps a failure to look upon the laws of warfare as embodying pressures toward behavioral conformity, coupled with an overreaching attempt to appear realistic, that lead Professor McDougal to articulate a doctrine of the laws of war that tends to relativize them out of existence. Yet his "policy-oriented jurisprudence"[44] on the laws of

42. For text and commentary, *see* VON KNIERIEM, THE NUREMBERG TRIALS 428-39 (1959). Similarly, on June 6, 1941, Hitler issued his Commissars Order, providing that any Soviet political commissars who were captured were to be shot immediately. Von Knieriem writes, *id.* at 425, that the "Nuremberg Tribunals who judged the German generals have acknowledged to a large extent that the generals did everything within their powers to prevent the Commissars Order from being implemented."

43. For example, Sergeant Donald W. Duncan, former Special Forces "Green Beret" in Vietnam, and holder of two Bronze Stars, Legion of Merit, Vietnamese Silver Star, Army Air Medal, Combat Infantry Badge, Master Parachutist, and other decorations, testified before the Russell Tribunal in Copenhagen that during a mission in the An Lao valley in 1965 his team of eight men captured four Viet Cong prisoners. Radioing back to base, Duncan was informed to "get rid of them." Pretending not to understand this order, he effected helicopter transport for the prisoners, and when he got back to base was faced with an angry commander who made it plain that the prisoners should have been murdered. It would have been "standard practice" to kill the prisoners in such a situation, Duncan said, although the captain—for fear of radio monitoring and subsequent legal ramifications—would not say directly over the radio to "kill the prisoners." AGAINST THE CRIME OF SILENCE: PROCEEDINGS OF THE RUSSELL INTERNATIONAL WAR CRIMES TRIBUNAL 473-74 (Duffett ed. 1968) [hereinafter cited as RUSSELL TRIBUNAL]. In his book, Duncan recounts an American instruction class for the Green Berets in "Counter-Measures to Hostile Interrogation" in which the techniques of hostile interrogation are presented in great detail but not any counter-measures, of which the instructor says there are none. A sergeant asks the instructor whether the only reason for teaching the class is for training in the *use* of the methods of interrogation (involving torture such as lowering of a prisoner's testicles into a jeweler's vise, mutilation, etc.). The instructor replies: "We can't tell you that, Sergeant Harrison. The Mothers of America wouldn't approve. Furthermore, we will deny that any such thing is taught or intended." D. DUNCAN, THE NEW LEGIONS 123-25 (Pocket Books ed. 1968). In his testimony before the Russell Tribunal, Duncan states that this dialogue is a word for word quote. RUSSELL TRIBUNAL, *supra*, at 463.

44. D'Amato, Book Review, 75 HARV. L. REV. 458 (1961).

war cannot be bypassed as it is by far the most comprehensive and important statement to be offered in this field in recent times.[45]

Professor McDougal views the laws of warfare, and international law generally, as guides to alternative policies for decisionmakers. "Legal rules," he once wrote, "exhaust their effective power when they guide a decisionmaker to relevant factors and indicate presumptive weightings."[46] When a military commander chooses to follow a policy coincident with the requirements of the laws of warfare, he does so not because of any prescriptive element of "oughtness" in the law itself but because he deems the law appropriate and in the common interest.[47] In Professor McDougal's system, what is reasonable to the decision-maker is legal.[48]

In search of some standards of reasonableness, Professor Mc-Dougal articulates broader generalizations which account for specific laws. For the laws of warfare, he combines two admittedly "complementary" generalizations—military necessity and the minimum destruction of values[49]—into the single "fundamental policy" of the "minimizing of unnecessary destruction of values."[50] Obviously this formula gives great latitude to the military commander on the spot. Anything he chooses to do, by virtue of the fact that he has decided to do it despite its costs, can be rationalized as an application of the principle of minimizing unnecessary destruction. Nor does Professor McDougal stop with the military commander. He writes that we must refer to the political purposes of the belligerent since these general political objectives affect and determine the legality of the more specific military applications of the formula.[51] But already the Vietnam war seems to undermine the usefulness of this approach. For the American political

---

45. *See* McDougal & Feliciano, *supra* note 37, at 1-96, 520-731.

46. M. McDougal, Studies in World Public Order 887 n.109 (1960).

47. McDougal & Feliciano, *supra* note 37, at 52.

48. "For all types of controversies the one test that is invariably applied by decision-makers is that simple and ubiquitous, but indispensable, standard of what, considering all relevant policies and all variables in context, is *reasonable* as between the parties." M. McDougal, *supra* note 46, at 778.

49. McDougal & Feliciano, *supra* note 37, at 521.

50. *Id.* at 72; *see id.* at 530.

51. It is not easy to see how military objectives could be evaluated as legitimate or nonlegitimate save in terms of their relation to some broader political purpose postulated as legitimate. To put the point comprehensively, it is most difficult rationally to appraise the necessity of a particular exercise of violence without relating it to a wider context of which it is a part—a context which includes a series of objectives, each of a higher or lower order of generality, with the more general affecting and determining the more specific.

Id. at 526.

objectives in Vietnam have undergone numerous ambiguous changes,[52] the most recent objective being a withdrawl from Vietnam consistent with the security of loyal South Vietnamese citizens to whom the United States had promised that it would never withdraw until the war was won by the American-Saigon coalition. Indeed, the notion of a clear military objective, which apparently seems to be an important aspect of Professor McDougal's view of the laws of warfare, may have vanished after 1945. The limited wars fought since then in the shadow of potential nuclear conflagration have made it almost impossible to articulate any consistent strategy of political-military "victory."[53]

Just as the concept of military necessity grows to global breadth if we adopt a subjective standard and generalize to the political level, so too Professor McDougal's formula of minimizing unnecessary destruction could justify any military action the more it is divorced from specific rules regulating the conduct of hostilities. If we postulate as legitimate the Allied demand upon Japan in 1945 of unconditional surrender, then the atomic bombings of Hiroshima and Nagasaki would appear to have been reasonable steps toward that goal.[54] On the other hand, by rejecting vague generalizations and subjective standards of reasonableness, a court might appraise the atomic bombing—particularly the *second* "demonstration" bombing of Nagasaki—in terms closely analogous to traditional prohibitions of blind aerial bombardment of undefended non-military population centers.[55] At Nuremberg, Professor McDougal's view of the laws of warfare, may have vanished conviction since it would have been nearly impossible to prove the requisite criminal intent if a defendant's state of mind had been an element in judging whether his underlying act was reasonable or was criminal. Rather, the Nuremberg judgments are replete with citations of multilateral conventions particularizing the international laws of war.

---

52. *See, e.g.*, THE REALITIES OF VIETNAM (Beal & D'Amato eds. 1968); E. GRUENING & H. BEASER, VIETNAM FOLLY (1968).

53. An example is President Truman's removal of General MacArthur during the Korean War when MacArthur wanted to bomb the airfields in mainland China that were the bases of Chinese aircraft fighting within Korea.

54. *See* 1 H. TRUMAN, MEMOIRS 419-20 (1955); Falk, *The Shimoda Case: A Legal Appraisal of the Atomic Attacks Upon Hiroshima and Nagasaki*, 59 AM. J. INT'L L. 759, 765 (1965) (*semble*) (position of the Japanese government).

55. This is what the district court of Tokyo did in the *Shimoda Case*, reported in Falk, *supra* note 54. Of course, there could be no specific legal prohibitions against the use of nuclear weapons when they had not yet been invented, but the court concluded that the atomic bombing of Hiroshima and Nagasaki violated the international laws of war by analogizing the effects of the bombing (radiation poisoning even after eighteen years) to prohibitions against the use of chemical-biological weapons, and by citing the Hague regulations restricting bombing of undefended cities to military objectives. *Cf.* D'Amato, *Legal Aspects of the French Nuclear Tests*, 61 AM. J. INT'L L. 66, 73-77 (1967).

Claims made by various defendants that their actions were dictated by military necessity or were reasonable in light of military or political objectives were met with strict citations by the prosecutors and the tribunals of the laws of warfare and an unwillingness on the part of the court to second-guess the defendants' phenomenological perspectives.[56]

Professor McDougal's reasonableness test, balancing the complementary prescriptions of military necessity and minimum destruction of values, is not unlike attempts to rewrite the American Bill of Rights into a simple balancing test between freedom of individual action and the public interest in national security.[57] A moment's reflection will demonstrate that this is precisely the evaluation that public prosecutors make before deciding to prosecute cases involving the exercise of speech or religion, and their decision probably reflects the majority opinion of the public. The Bill of Rights, however, is anti-majoritarian; it safeguards "unreasonable" speech, religion, assembly, and privacy. Similarly, although the laws of warfare must seem at times to be highly unreasonable to military commanders or political leaders, they fulfill the function of drawling lines between permissible and impermissible conduct in a way which would be impossible for such generalized notions as military necessity or minimum destruction of values.

II

EVIDENCE OF WAR CRIMES

In the first part of this Article we have attempted to show that the body of international laws relating to war crimes is applicable to soldiers in United States forces and to these soldiers in the Vietnamese war. American courts may nevertheless be reluctant to entertain a Nuremberg defense because they fear that the restrictive rules of evidence and the nature of the evidence itself will render the defense impractical and inconclusory. Consequently, in this part we discuss the special rules of evidence that are used in war crimes trials and then marshal the available relevant evidence, sufficient to meet the standards of proof at Nuremberg, that American forces commit war crimes in Vietnam.

A. Admissible Evidence

American courts are familiar with highly technical and restrictive rules of evidence, which are nonetheless workable because courts most

---

56. *See generally* R. WOETZEL, *supra* note 25, at 96-189.
57. *Cf.* Justice Frankfurter's majority opinion in Communist Party of America v. Subversive Activities Control Bd., 367 U.S. 1 (1961).

of the time deal with cases arising out of events physically proximate to the court. The accessibility of witnesses, documents, photographs, and even sites, allows the luxury of complex verification and authentication procedures. But where the facts offered for proof in a case involve alleged war crimes committed in a foreign combat zone, the usual luxuries of evidentiary verification must be modified.[58] Not only is the locus of the evidence in a foreign country, but also other branches of the government, particularly the executive and military, may be expected to resist judicial probing into as sensitive a subject as war crimes.[59] Our purpose in this section is to show that there is indeed ample precedent for judicial relaxation of the technical rules of evidence in war-crimes cases, particularly for the type of cases relying on Nuremberg defenses envisaged in the present essay.

The Nuremberg Charter explicitly exempted the tribunal from "technical rules of evidence."[60] It also permitted the tribunal to take judicial notice of "official government documents,"[61] and the tribunal broadly interpreted this permission to allow judicial notice of any and all evidence collected and presented by any Allied power.[62] A great mass of documentary material was introduced at the trials: orders and directives purportedly signed by the defendants themselves, copies of speeches, diaries, record books, photographs, motion pictures, depositions, popular books and excerpts therefrom, personal affidavits, investigating commission reports, and quotations from speeches, letters and statements of famous men.[63] The prosecution introduced affidavits of expert witnesses at many points in the trials, and the evidence was

---

58. *Cf.*, *e.g.*, CAL. CODE CIV. PRO. § 117g (West Supp. 1968) (small-claims court procedures, purpose of such courts would be frustrated by expense of rigid adherence to evidentiary rules).

59. For example, Stanley R. Resor, Secretary of the Army, dismissed the murder charges against several Green Beret soldiers who were in the process of being court martialled for the murder of a South Vietnamese agent on the ground that the Central Intelligence Agency refused to supply witnesses for the trial. Frankel, *Beret Case Raises Many Issues*, N.Y. Times, Oct. 1, 1969, at 3, col. 4.

60. 1 Trials Maj. War Crim. 15 (art. 19) (Int'l Mil. Trib. 1947).

61. *Id.* (art. 21).

62. *See* J. APPLEMAN, MILITARY TRIBUNALS AND INTERNATIONAL CRIMES 101-03 (1954).

63. *E.g.*, 9 Trials Maj. War Crim. 674-84 (Int'l Mil. Trib. 1947) (correspondence of Neville Henderson and Lord Halifax), 12 Trial Maj. War Crim. 166 (Int'l Mil. Trib. 1947) (Gunther, *Inside Europe*), 9 Trials Maj. War Crim. 472 (Int'l Mil. Trib. 1947) (Dahlerus, *Last Attempt*), 12 Trials Maj. War Crim. 305-44 (Int'l Mil. Trib. 1947) (Luther, *The Jews and their Lies*), 14 Trials Maj. War Crim. 368 (Int'l Mil. Trib. 1947) (Ford, *The International Jew*), 11 Trials Maj. War Crim. 436 (Int'l Mil. Trib. 1947) (works of Neville Henderson and Sumner Welles), 4 Trials Maj. War Crim. 519-27 (Int'l Mil. Trib. 1947) (Hilter, *Mein Kampf*), 2 Trials Maj. War Crim. 357 (Int'l Mil. Trib. 1947) (Ambassador Dodd's *Diary*).

allowed.[64] The judges at many points stated that they would assign probative weight to the evidence in accordance with the manner in which it was authenticated,[65] and many of the exchanges between counsel and judges concerned the question of probative value.[66]

The various national trials of lesser war criminals following Nuremberg made even more explicit the evidentiary latitude afforded courts in war-crimes cases. A British Royal Warrant of 14 June 1945 relaxed evidentiary rules for British military courts for trials involving alleged violations of the laws and usages of war, specifically allowing the court to "take into consideration any oral statement or any document appearing on the face of it to be authentic," allowing hearsay evidence if the witness were "unable . . . to attend without undue delay" or if a document could not be produced "without undue delay," and admitting "any document purporting to have been signed or issued officially by any member of any Allied or enemy force."[67] The British trials conducted under this warrant made clear what may be a fundamentally important factor in all war crimes trials—that although one or two affidavits or documents might not be authentic, nevertheless if the overwhelming preponderance of the evidence points to the commission of war crimes it would be unjust *not* to admit all purportedly authentic evidence, and leave it to the judges to determine its value.[68] Because of the difficulty of getting unimpeachable evidence of facts

---

64. *E.g.*, 14 Trials Maj. War Crim. 283-86 (Int'l Mil. Trib. 1947).

65. *See* Ferencz, *Nurenberg Trial Procedure and the Rights of the Accused*, 39 J. Crim. L.C. & P.S. 144, 148-49 (1948); von Knieriem, *supra* note 42, at 161-64.

66. *E.g.*, 7 Trials Maj. War Crim. 243, 250-52, 264-66 (Int'l Mil. Trib. 1947) (certification of documents), 8 Trials Maj. War Crim. 285 (Int'l Mil. Trib. 1947) (identification), 12 Trials Maj. War Crim. 165 (Int'l Mil. Trib. 1947) (unsolicited letter refused admission), 15 Trials Maj. War Crim. 87-88 (Int'l Mil. Trib. 1947) (uncertified affidavit), 5 Trials Maj. War Crim. 106 (Int'l Mil. Trib. 1947) (prejudiced witness), 5 Trials Maj. War Crim. 366 (Int'l Mil. Trib. 1947) (irrelevancy), 14 Trials Maj. War Crim. 556-58 (Int'l Mil. Trib. 1947) (impeachment of witness), 9 Trials Maj. War Crim. 610, 615-17 (Int'l Mil. Trib. 1947) (documents not genuine), 15 Trials Maj. War Crim. 531-33 (Int'l Mil. Trib. 1947) (inaccurate translation), 11 Trials Maj. War Crim. 375-78 (Int'l Mil. Trib. 1947) (unofficial document inadmissible). At one point Sir David Maxwell-Fyfe argued that Article 19 of the Charter, freeing the court from technical rules of evidence, "is an important matter in the view of the Prosecution and, therefore, we have to argue against its being whittled down." 14 Trials Maj. War Crim. 240 (Int'l Mil. Trib. 1947).

67. 2 L. Rep. Trials War Crim. 126, 131 (U.N. War Crimes Comm'n 1947) (Regulation 8(i)). Exactly the same wording is found in the "Mediterranean Regulations" binding United States Military Commissions (military courts having jurisdiction in the Mediterranean); text in 3 L. Rep. Trials War Crim. 110 (U.N. War Crimes Comm'n 1947). For citations to similar provisions in Australian and Canadian law, see 2 L. Rep. Trials War Crim. 126 (U.N. War Crimes Comm'n 1947).

68. 1 L. Rep. Trials War Crim. 85 (U.N. War Crimes Comm'n 1947); 2 L. Rep. Trials War Crim. 131-38 (U.N. War Crimes Comm'n 1947); M. Greenspan, *supra* note 25, at 510.

that occur during the vast disruption of war, this approach best fulfills the purpose of judicial inquiry in such cases.[69]

In light of the nearly complete United States control over the trials of alleged Japanese war criminals, Japanese proceedings provide the best precedents for American courts in war-crimes cases. The major Japanese defendants were tried by the International Military Tribunal for the Far East, a court established, chartered, and approved by General Douglas MacArthur, who as Supreme Allied Commander for postwar Japan also appointed the judges. Its charter provided that the Tokyo tribunal "shall not be bound by technical rules of evidence," and in particular may admit as evidence:

1) A document, regardless of its security classification and without proof of its issuance or signature, which appears to the Tribunal to have been signed or issued by any officer, department, agency or member of the armed forces of any government.

2) A report which appears to the Tribunal to have been signed or issued by the International Red Cross or a member thereof, or by a doctor of medicine or any medical personnel, or by an investigator or intelligence officer, or by any other person who appears to the Tribunal to have personal knowledge of the matters contained in the report.

3) An affidavit, deposition or other signed statement.

4) A diary, letter or other document, including sworn or unsworn statements which appear to the Tribunal to contain information relating to the charge.

5) A copy of a document or other secondary evidence of its contents, if the original is not immediately available.[70]

General MacArthur also set up the United States Military Commission for Manila which tried General Yamashita for permitting his men to commit war crimes and massacre civilians, a case important because of the fact that it reached the United States Supreme Court. At the trial, numerous affidavits, depositions, letters, documents, and newspaper articles, admitted over the objections of the defense,[71] formed the basis for General Yamashita's conviction.[72] Yet the Supreme Court held

---

69. More attention to the purpose of evidentiary rules is resulting in parallel liberalization of the hearsay rule in American and British courts involving domestic cases. *See, e.g.,* Dallas County v. Commercial Union Assurance Co., 286 F.2d 388 (5th Cir. 1961); G. WILLIAMS, THE PROOF OF GUILT 147 (1955). The proposed Rules of Evidence for the United States District Courts and Magistrates contains the draft rule that "A statement is not excluded by the hearsay rule if its nature and the special circumstances under which it was made offer strong assurances of accuracy and the declarant is unavailable as a witness." Rule 8-04(a), 46 F.R.D. 161, 377 (1969).

70. INT'L MIL. TRIB. FOR THE FAR EAST, CHARTER art. 13.

71. 4 L. Rep. Trials War Crim. 78-81 (U.N. War Crimes Comm'n 1947).

72. *In re* Yamashita, 327 U.S. 1, 52-56 (1946) (dissenting opinion of Rutledge, J.).

that there was no denial of due process.[73]   Both *In re Yamashita* and the charter of the Tokyo tribunal therefore stand as important precedents in American law for the relaxation of strict rules of evidence in cases involving allegations of war crimes.

It must be noted, for present purposes, that the existing evidentiary precedents are all from cases in which individual defendants were charged with the commission of war crimes.   The present essay, however, does not concern such cases.   Rather, it concerns cases which involve the question of whether a serviceman may resist assignment to Vietnam, or to a specific combat zone or division in Vietnam, on the grounds that other persons in Vietnam are committing war crimes or that there is a pattern of violation of the laws of war in a combat zone to which the resister may be sent.   The permissibility of relaxing evidentiary standards in such a case, however, follows a fortiori from the precedents just examined.   A court should allow such a serviceman at least as much latitude as prosecutors receive in war-crimes cases where the burden is on the prosecutors to prove beyond a reasonable doubt the commission of war crimes.

B.   Required and Available Evidence

The purpose of this subsection on the legally required and factually available evidence of war crimes in Vietnam is not to prove facts or to make judgments better left to courts, but to outline the kinds and availability of evidence, and the legal arguments necessary to support a reasonable allegation by an American service resister that American forces commit war crimes in Vietnam.   We shall here present examples of the kinds of evidence that would be relevant to the substantive law of war crimes that should satisfy the Nuremberg criteria of sufficiency and admissibility.

We make no attempt here to cover all the possible violations of the laws of warfare in the complex Vietnam war.   For example, we shall not deal with the issues of defoliation and crop destruction *per se*, forced dislocation of refugees in South Vietnam, pillage, conditions in prisoner-of-war camps, or the care and medical treatment of civilian war victims.[74]   The murder of civilians, such as the American massacre of the villagers of Songmy on March 16, 1968, is so obviously a capital violation of the laws of war as to need no extended comment here.[75]

---

73.   *See id.* at 18-23.

74.   *See, e.g.*, Note, *The Geneva Convention and the Treatment of Prisoners of War in Vietnam*, 80 HARV. L. REV. 851 (1967); Meyrowitz, *Le droit de la guerre dans le conflit Vietnamien*, 13 ANNUAIRE FRANÇAIS DE DROIT INTERNATIONAL 153 (1967).

75.   N.Y. Times, Nov. 23, 1969, § 4, at 2, col. 4.   Though the matter is clear

Instead we shall concentrate on three basic and illustrative categories that are crucial to Vietnam and that also may be extrapolated to other possible future situations: murder or torture of prisoners of war, aerial bombardment of non-military targets, and the use of prohibited weapons of warfare. For each of these we shall attempt to summarize the relevant international law, with particular reference to the Nuremberg precedents, and indicate the kinds of substantive evidence available with respect to its violation in Vietnam.

Considerable use will be made in this subsection of testimony given before the Bertrand Russell International War Crimes Tribunal whose hearings were held in Copenhagen and Stockholm in 1967 and whose findings and principal evidence were recorded in a book published in 1968.[76] Although this was an unofficial "tribunal,"[77] the proceedings were at least as formal as many of the commissions and meetings which produced affidavits, depositions, and written testimony that were admitted in the various post-World War II war crimes trials. Additionally there is evidence of consistency of the witnesses' testimony at the Russell proceedings and in books, newspapers, and before American courts.[78] Most importantly, the great detail and close questioning by members of the panel at Copenhagen and Stockholm of the many witnesses' testimony give that testimony high credibility value, for at Nuremberg and Tokyo, it will be recalled, the tribunals placed decisive weight on the intrinsic credibility of testimony. Finally, the factual correlation between the substance of testimony produced at the Russell proceedings and evidence of others reported elsewhere (newspapers, books, etc.) lends credibility to the whole.

1. Prisoners of War

a. The Law

Although there is variety and complexity in the laws of war con-

---

from a legal point of view, the gravity of the massacre, in which over 100 and perhaps as many as 500 old men, women, and children were shot down in cold blood by American troops, should not be minimized. The lack of immediate reaction from the Saigon government suggests that such incidents may not be rare. An unnamed New York Times correspondent attributes the lack of urgency in investigating the incident to "a diminished capacity for moral outrage on the part of a population that has endured a quarter-century of fighting in which neither side has made much distinction between combatants and civilians." N.Y. Times, Nov. 21, 1969, at 18, col. 7. *See* R. Falk, *Songmy: War Crimes and Individual Responsibility*, 7 TRANSACTION 33 (1970).

    76. RUSSELL TRIBUNAL, *supra* note 43.

    77. *See* D'Amato, Book Review, 57 CALIF. L. REV. 1033 (1969).

    78. *E.g.*, United States v. Mitchell, 369 F.2d 323 (2d Cir.), *cert. denied*, 386 U.S. 972 (1966); Testimony of Donald Duncan (see note 43 *supra*), in RUSSELL TRIBUNAL, *supra* note 43, at 457-513; D. DUNCAN, *supra* note 43, at 123-27; N.Y. Times, May 25, 1967, at 2, col. 4 (testimony of Moore and Duncan at Capt. Levy's trial).

cerning the standards of incarceration and treatment of prisoners of war,[79] it is perfectly clear that murder or torture of such persons is a war crime.[80] According to the Nuremberg precedents,[81] captors may not shoot prisoners even though they are in a combat zone, require a guard, consume supplies, slow up troop movements, and appear certain to be set free by their own forces in an imminent invasion. The Hague Conventions of 1907 require that prisoners be humanely treated,[82] and the Geneva Convention of 1949 prohibits "causing death or seriously endangering the health of a prisoner of war."[83] In particular it stipulates that "no physical or mental torture, nor any other form of coercion, may be inflicted on prisoners of war to secure from them information of any kind whatever."[84] Both combatants and non-combatants are entitled to prisoner-of-war status.[85] Although captured civilians do not share all the rights of prisoners of war, they have the same right against killing or torture.[86] While the law is less certain with respect to partisan guerrillas, the grounds for uncertainty do not seem applicable in Vietnam,[87] and in any event any captured person has the right to a fair

---

79. See, e.g., Petrowski, *Law and the Conduct of the Vietnam War*, in 2 THE VIETNAM WAR AND INTERNATIONAL LAW 439, 507-15 (Falk ed. 1969).

80. See McDOUGAL & FELICIANO, *supra* note 37, at 576 and cases therein cited. A prisoner of war may be executed for an offense committed during captivity, but only after a fair judicial trial. *Id.* See also M. GREENSPAN, *supra* note 25, at 131-42.

81. See Thiele Case, 3 L. Rep. Trials War Crim. 56-59 (U.N. War Crimes Comm'n, U.S. Mil. Comm'n, Germany 1945); M. GREENSPAN, *supra* note 25, at 103.

82. Arts. 4, 23, Annex to Convention IV Respecting the Laws and Customs of War on Land, in THE HAGUE CONVENTIONS AND DECLARATIONS OF 1899 AND 1907, at 100, 108, 116 (Scott ed. 1915); see In re Yamashita, 327 U.S. 1, 14 (1946).

83. Art. 13, Geneva Prisoners of War Convention, *supra* note 10.

84. *Id.* art. 17. See also Trial of Yoshio Makizawa, 15 L. Rep. Trials War Crim. 101 n.4 (U.N. War Crimes Comm'n, U.S. Mil. Comm'n, Shanghai 1946). Mere interrogation of POW's is not unlawful—Killinger Case, 3 L. Rep. Trial War Crim. 67, 68 (U.N. War Crimes Comm'n, Brit. Mil. Ct., Wuppertal, Germany 1945). The prohibition against physical or mental torture may sound quaint in this age of violence, but as Professor Chomsky has said: "I suppose this is the first time in history that a nation has so openly and publicly exhibited its own war crimes. Perhaps this shows how well our free institutions function. Or does it simply show how immune we have become to suffering? Probably the latter." N. CHOMSKY, AMERICAN POWER AND THE NEW MANDARINS 10 (1969).

85. Art. 3, Hague Convention of 1907, *supra* note 82; art. 4, Geneva Prisoners of War Convention, *supra* note 10.

86. Art. 27, Geneva Civilian Persons Convention, *supra* note 16. Article 33 of this convention prohibits reprisals against these civilian persons.

87. The Bauer Case held that guerrillas and irregular troops have the status of belligerents. 8 L. Rep. Trials War Crim. 15 (U.N. War Crimes Comm'n, Permanent Mil. Trib. Dijon 1945). But in the Hostages Case, 8 L. Rep. Trials War Crim. 34, 58 (U.N. War Crimes Comm'n, U.S. Mil. Trib. 1948), the execution of captured partisans (Greece and Yugoslavia) by an occupying power in complete command of the territory was not held to be a war crime, the court stating that "[this] rule is based on the theory that the forces of two states are no longer in the field and that a con-

judicial determination of his status before maltreatment or execution.[88] It follows that a captured person cannot be tortured for the purpose of determining his status. All four Geneva conventions of 1949 provide that all persons "taking no active part in the hostilities, including members of armed forces who have laid down their arms," shall be protected at all times and places against "violence to life and person, in particular murder of all kinds, mutilation, cruel treatment and torture."[89]

The foregoing standards obviously apply to the treatment of persons captured in Vietnam by American soldiers. The question remains whether murder or torture of prisoners by South Vietnamese troops engages American responsibility. First, article 12 of the 1949 Geneva Prisoners of War Convention sets forth the duties of American soldiers who turn over prisoners to South Vietnamese soldiers:

> Prisoners of war may only be transferred by the Detaining Power to a Power which is a party to the Convention and after the Detaining Power has satisfied itself of the willingness and ability of such transferee Power to apply the Convention. . . .

> Nevertheless, if that Power fails to carry out the provisions of the Convention in any important respect, the Power by whom the prisoners of war were transferred shall, upon being notified by the Protecting Power, take effective measures to correct the situation or shall request the return of the prisoners of war. Such requests must be complied with.[90]

Various war-crimes courts have held that knowingly releasing prisoners to someone else who will murder them is a war crime.[91] Second, active

---

tention between organised armed forces no longer exists." In any event, the Nuremberg trials uniformly held that summary execution of guerrillas was a war crime; guerrillas were in all cases entitled to a judicial determination of their status. McDOUGAL & FELICIANO, *supra* note 37, at 550 & n.77 (citing cases).

88. Geneva Civilian Persons Convention, *supra* note 16, arts. 3 & 5. *See also* McDOUGAL & FELICIANO, *supra* note 37, at 550.

89. Art. 3, Geneva Conventions of 1949, *supra* note 16.

90. Prisoners of War Convention, note 10 *supra*. The phrase "any important respect" in article 12 clearly includes murder or torture of POW's; *see id.* art. 130 ("grave breaches . . . involve wilful killing, torture, or inhuman treatment"). If the transferee Power murders the prisoners, obviously the last clause of article 12 providing for their return is futile; article 12 would thus have to be construed as requiring the transferring Power, at the very least, not to make any more such transfers. The Soviet Union and other associated powers have entered reservations that hold the transferring Power responsible for the deeds of the accepting Power. M. GREENSPAN, *supra* note 25, at 102.

91. Rauer Case, 4 L. Rep. Trials War Crim. 113, 115-17 (U.N. War Crimes Comm'n, Brit. Mil. Ct., Wuppertal, Germany 1946); Essen Lynching Case, 1 L. Rep. Trials War Crim. 88 (U.N. War Crimes Comm'n, Brit. Mil. Ct., Essen, Germany 1945); Jaluit Atoll Case, 1 L. Rep. Trials War Crim. 71 (U.N. War Crimes Comm'n, U.S. Mil. Comm'n, Marshall Islands 1945).

complicity by American troops in the torture or murder of prisoners, even if the actual physical acts are carried out by South Vietnamese soldiers and "interrogators," would be a direct violation of the laws of war by the Americans.[92] Third, it may at least be argued that to the extent that the Saigon government has been under the effective control of, if not owing its very existence to, the United States, the latter is responsible for the war crimes of the South Vietnamese.[93] Finally, the Supreme Court's reasoning in *In re Yamashita* obligates American officers and soldiers to take "reasonable" and "appropriate" measures to prevent violations of the law of war "which are likely to attend the occupation of hostile territory by an uncontrolled soldiery."[94] Whatever the precise relationship between American and South Vietnamese forces, if there is "to some extent"[95] authority of the former over the latter, *In re Yamashita* imposes a positive obligation to take steps to stop the commission of war crimes by the South Vietnamese.[96]

b. The Evidence

Four former experienced American combat soldiers at the Russell proceedings offered direct evidence of the murder of prisoners by Americans.[97] They gave detailed accounts of the behead-

---

92. *E.g.*, Rauer Case, 4 L. Rep. Trials War Crim. 113 (U.N. War Crimes Comm'n, Brit. Mil. Ct., Wuppertal, Germany 1946); Schosser Trial, 3 L. Rep. Trials War Crim. 65 (U.N. War Crimes Comm'n, U.S. Mil. Comm'n, Dachau 1945). "Being concerned in the killing" is given a wide definition in the Schonfeld Trial, 11 L. Rep. Trials War Crim. 64, 68-73 (U.N. War Crimes Comm'n, Brit. Mil. Ct., Essen 1946).

93. See Wright, *Legal Aspects of the Viet-Nam Situation*, 60 AM. J. INT'L L. 750 (1966); E. GRUENING & H. BEASER, VIETNAM FOLLY 352-69 (1968); V. HARTKE, THE AMERICAN CRISIS IN VIETNAM 24-28 (1968).

94. *In re* Yamashita, 327 U.S. 1, 15 (1946). The Court was careful to point out, in the face of considerable evidence that General Yamashita had extremely limited control of the chaotic situation in the Philippines and had highly circumscribed authority both de jure and de facto, that "the law of war presupposes that its violation is to be avoided through the control of the operations of war by commanders who are to some extent responsible for their subordinates." *Id.* The degree of the General's control over the situation is spelled out in Yamashita Trial, 4 L. Rep. Trials War Crim. 1, 21-29 (U.N. War Crimes Comm'n, U.S. Mil. Comm'n, Manila 1946).

95. *In re* Yamashita, 327 U.S. 1, 15 (1946).

96. Justice Murphy, dissenting in *In re* Yamashita, 327 U.S. 1, 26, 39 (1946), would have been satisfied of Yamashita's guilt if there had been any evidence of "some element of knowledge or direct connection with the atrocities." *See also id.* at 41, 50 (Rutledge, J., dissenting).

97. David Kenneth Tuck was a former Specialist Fourth Class with the 25th Infantry Division in Vietnam from January 1966 to February 1967. RUSSELL TRIBUNAL, *supra* note 43, at 403. Carl Campbell was a former marine Private First Class in Delta Company, 1st Battalion, 7th Marine Regiment. *Id.* at 514. James Jones fought in the infantry in Vietnam from February 1965 to May 1966. *Id.* at 516.

ing[98] and shooting[99] of wounded prisoners, and the murder of prisoners by pushing them out of helicopters.[100]   They characterized these actions as "everyday thing[s],"[101] "expected" combat behavior,[102] the result of orders given in basic training[103] or instruction in special classes,[104] and "standard operating policy."[105]   The soldiers responsible told their superiors that the prisoners were killed while attempting to escape.[106]   Later, on September 29, 1969, a former Green Beret soldier stated on a television interview on WPIX-TV in New York City that he personally shot a prisoner while in South Vietnam and witnessed other shootings.[107]   Evidence from sources other than former soldiers is available to substantiate these charges,[108] though it has less credibility value than direct testimony.

Another former American soldier, Peter Martinsen, who served as interrogator with the 541st Military Intelligence Detachment in Vietnam

---

For the credentials of Donald Duncan, former Special Forces "Green Beret" in Vietnam, see note 43 *supra*.

98.   RUSSELL TRIBUNAL, *supra* note 43, at 404 (beheading by machete).

99.   *Id.* at 419, 474-75.   Tuck testified that the "only" prisoners captured in the jungle would be the "wounded." *Id.* at 423.

100.   *Id.* at 405, 516.

101.   *Id.* at 405 (Tuck).

102.   *Id.* at 424 (Tuck).

103.   *Id.* at 515 (Campbell).

104.   *Id.* at 474 (Duncan, who *taught* some of these classes); see D. DUNCAN, *supra* note 43, at 126.

105.   RUSSELL TRIBUNAL, *supra* note 43, at 406, 411 (Tuck).

106.   *Id.* at 406 (Tuck).   A Gestapo order issued in 1944 instructed various regional Gestapo headquarters that certain prisoners of war were to be shot and "the reason for the shooting will be given as 'shot whilst trying to escape' or 'shot whilst resisting' so that nothing can be proved at a future date." The Stalag Luft III Case, 11 L. Rep. Trials War Crim. 31, 33 (U.N. War Crimes Comm'n, Brit. Mil. Ct., Hamburg 1947).

107.   N.Y. Times, Oct. 1, 1969, at 3, col. 1.

108.   *See* M. McCARTHY, VIETNAM 14 (1967); *United States v. Griffen*, Washington Post, July 27, 1967, § A, at 27, col. 2; Touhy, *A Big "Dirty Little War,"* New York Times, Nov. 28, 1965, § 6, at 43, quoted in CLERGY AND LAYMEN CONCERNED ABOUT VIETNAM, IN THE NAME OF AMERICA 80, 81, 85 (1968) [hereinafter cited as NAME OF AMERICA]; Langguth, *Brutality is Rising on Both Sides in South Vietnam*, N.Y. Times, July 7, 1965, at 7, col. 1, quoted in NAME OF AMERICA, *supra* at 71 (American soldier tells friends of pushing prisoner out of helicopter).
      Photographs of a Viet Cong prisoner of war being dropped to his death from a U.S. Army helicopter were published on page one of the Chicago Sun-Times, Nov. 29, 1969.   The photographer, who took the pictures from a nearby escort helicopter, described the incident on the backs of the photographs.   He wrote, "The Picture isnt too Pretty—but the whole Episode had Good Results as the other 2 'charlie's' told us Everything we wanted to know." *Id.* at 16, col. 3.   In a letter accompanying the photos, the photographer explained that three prisoners were taken up into the helicopter for interrogation, and after the first one was dumped the other two told their captors what they wanted to know.   The photographer also said, "Let's hear it for fear." *Id.* at 16, cols. 1-2.

from September 1966 to June 1967,[109] described to the Russell tribunal his own beating of a prisoner[110] and stated that he subsequently released the prisoner to an American lieutenant[111] who wired a field-telephone generator to the prisoner's genitals and administered electric shocks.[112] The field-telephone method, which has been confirmed by other accounts in books and newspapers as a distinctly American contribution to the history of torture,[113] was according to Martinsen used on women as well as men,[114] and involved "hundreds of [American] interrogators" who participated in the torture of captured Vietnamese prisoners of war.[115]

There is substantial, undenied evidence of South Vietnamese torture and murder of prisoners of war. Methods of torture include mutilation,[116] disembowlment,[117] near-drowning,[118] bamboo slivers under fingernails,[119] smothering with wet towels,[120] dragging the prisoner behind a moving vehicle,[121] pouring water with hot pepper into the nose,[122] wire-cage confinement,[123] and rice-paddy strangulation.[124] After torture, the captors usually execute the prisoner.[125] Peter Hamill, correspondent for the New York Post, wrote in 1966 that there are no huge prisoner-of-war camps springing up in South Vietnam as there were during the second World War; prisoners are "usually executed."[126] A New York Times correspondent similarly observed in 1969 "the rela-

---

109. RUSSELL TRIBUNAL, *supra* note 43, at 425-26. Martinsen received the Vietnam Service Medal, Vietnam Expeditionary Medal, Army Commendation Medal, Good Conduct Medal, and National Defense Medal.

110. *Id.* at 427.

111. *Id.*

112. *Id.*

113. *See, e.g.*, NAME OF AMERICA, *supra* note 108, at 80, 81, 85.

114. RUSSELL TRIBUNAL, *supra* note 43, at 456.

115. *Id.* at 439.

116. N.Y. Herald Tribune, April 25, 1965, quoted in NAME OF AMERICA, *supra* note 108, at 80-81 (cutting off of fingers, ears, fingernails or sexual organs of prisoners).

117. D. DUNCAN, *supra* note 43, at 131-32; RUSSELL TRIBUNAL 471-72, 476-77.

118. Shown on television in a film documentary prepared by the Canadian Broadcasting System. NAME OF AMERICA, *supra* note 108, at 86.

119. Tuohy, *supra* note 108.

120. NAME OF AMERICA, *supra* note 108, at 83.

121. K. KNOEBL, VICTOR CHARLIE 115 (1967) (the victim usually dies from this torture).

122. Sheehan, *Vietnam: The Unofficial Brutality*, N.Y. Times, Sept. 30, 1965, at 4, col. 4, quoted in NAME OF AMERICA, *supra* note 108, at 81.

123. B. FALL, LAST REFLECTIONS ON A WAR 232 (1967) (the cage is an iron frame covered with barbed wire; if the prisoner moves out of a crouch his body is "punctured all over").

124. K. KNOEBL, *supra* note 121, at 113.

125. Testimony of Senator Young (Ohio), 112 CONG. REC. 16395 (1966).

126. NAME OF AMERICA, *supra* note 108, at 66-67.

tively low number of prisoners claimed by either side."[127]   He reported
that "South Korean and South Vietnamese soldiers have a particularly
widespread reputation for killing prisoners; Americans less so."[128]

Apart from the general political argument suggested earlier[129] that
the United States might be responsible for everything done by the
Saigon regime, what is the actual American involvement in these
South Vietnamese actions? First, there is considerable evidence that
prisoners captured by American soldiers are "handed over" to the South
Vietnamese for torture and execution.[130] As this does not discharge
American responsibility,[131] perhaps the reason for the practice is that
stated by a former "Green Berets" sergeant:

> [L]et your [South Vietnamese] counterpart do it. . . . The idea
> being that, since you are an American, it could be resented—your
> torturing or killing these people. In other words, you don't want
> the charge of prejudice or racism thrown at you.[132]

Second, there is testimony that much of the torture is done under the
direction[133] or supervision[134] of American soldiers, that in some cases
Americans are in complete control,[135] and that some of the methods of
torturing were taught to the South Vietnamese by Americans.[136] Finally, there is much evidence indicating that American soldiers are often
witnesses to these acts,[137] and that either through choice or circum-

---

127. Kamm, *Songmy 2: The Toll of Frustration and Fury*, N.Y. Times, Nov.
23, 1969, § 4, at 2, col. 6.

128. *Id.* at cols. 6-7.

129. See text accompanying note 93, *supra.*

130. Testimony of Senator Young, *supra* note 125; Sheehan, *supra* note 122,
quoted in NAME OF AMERICA, *supra* note 108, at 78-79; Bighart, *Green Berets Called
Tolerant of Brutality in South Vietnam*, N.Y. Times, May 25, 1967, at 2, col. 4
(testimony at trial of Capt. Levy that American policy is to turn all prisoners over to
South Vietnamese).

131. See notes 90-96 *supra* and accompanying text.

132. RUSSELL TRIBUNAL, *supra* note 43, at 473; *see* D. DUNCAN, *supra* note 43, at
125.

133. RUSSELL TRIBUNAL, *supra* note 43, at 404 (Tuck's testimony). Duncan testified that the Vietnamese interpreter does much of the actual torture, *id.* at 495, and that
he is hired by the Special Forces ("Green Berets") directly (not through a Saigon
agency), and is paid, clothed, and supported by the Americans. During his service,
however, he is exempt from military duty in the army of the Republic of Vietnam.
Id. at 494-95.

134. *Id.* at 516 (Jones' deposition, stating that Vietnamese torturers worked under
supervision of American officers who gave the instructions).

135. *Id.* at 471-72 (Duncan's testimony) (money, supplies, communications all
furnished by Americans).

136. *Id.* at 518 (deposition of John Hartwell Moore, former U.S. Army PFC, in
Vietnam from December 1963 to May 1964). The field-telephone generator torture
and the killing of prisoners by pushing them out of helicopters are undoubtedly
American-inspired.

137. *E.g.*, M. BROWNE, THE NEW FACE OF WAR 116 (1968); NAME OF AMERICA,

stances, they do nothing about it.[138]

2. Bombardment of Non-Military Targets

a. The Law

The involvement of the United States in acts of aerial bombardment is beyond question as the United States has been in sole command of the airplanes enjoying virtually uncontested flights over Vietnam. Though much of the following evidentiary examples concern North Vietnam, where the bombing substantially ended in March, 1968, the issue as to North Vietnam is far from moot as there are hundreds of men now in prison or threatened with imprisonment who refused to serve in Vietnam prior to 1968.[139] Moreover, it is important to examine carefully the issue of aerial bombardment because the United States, perhaps in part as a result of its vast inventory of planes and bombs, may again resort to bombing in North Vietnam,[140] Laos,[141] or elsewhere, and of course because the bombing continues in South Vietnam.

Under the traditional approach to the war-crimes concept, no legal issue is presented with respect to the bombing of genuinely strategic military targets such as factories, ammunition depots, oil refineries, airports, and—particularly in the Vietnam context—roads, bridges, viaducts, railroad tracks, trucks, trains, tunnels, and any other transporta-

---

supra note 108, at 83, 85; RUSSELL TRIBUNAL, *supra* note 43, at 439; NEWSWEEK, Sept. 13, 1965, quoted in NAME OF AMERICA, *supra* note 108, at 85; D. DUNCAN, *supra* note 43, at 131-32.

138. N.Y. Times, May 25, 1967, at 2. col. 4 (testimony of Robbin Moore, author of *The Green Berets*) ("If he [the American soldier] tried to stop it [the torture] he would be relieved, and his career would suffer.") In 1965 the Department of State disclosed that it was conducting discussions with the Saigon government "in an effort to curb what is reported to be the frequent use of torture by South Vietnamese troops to extract information." Garrison, *U.S. Tries To Curb Vietnam Torture*, N.Y. Times, July 28, 1965, at 2, col. 4, quoted in NAME OF AMERICA, *supra* note 108, at 67. It is worthy of note that mere knowledge of war crimes may be a factor in assessing guilt of a defendant even though he is on trial for completely different war crimes in a different area. The judgment against Admiral Doenitz at Nuremberg specifically mentioned the fact that Doenitz had knowledge that large numbers of citizens of occupied countries were confined in German concentration camps, even though this area was totally outside Doenitz' jurisdiction and actions. 1 Trial Maj. War Crim. 314 (Int'l Mil. Trib. 1947).

139. Farer & Petrowski, *supra* note 24; Chomsky, *Reflections on a Political Trial*, 11 N.Y. REV. OF BOOKS 23, 30 (1968).

140. Senator Tower (Texas) recently stated that the United States should resume bombing of North Vietnam. N.Y. Times, Oct. 2, 1969, at 18, col. 1.

141. American aerial bombardment in Laos, primarily along the Ho Chi Minh trail, seems to have increased in intensity after March 1968 when President Johnson ordered a substantial halt to the bombing of North Vietnam. N.Y. Times, April 1, 1968, at 1, col. 5.

tion facilities.[142]   Furthermore, we assume that accidental and incidental damage to non-military and non-strategic targets is not a war crime.[143]

Quite different is deliberate—or more precisely non-accidental—bombing of targets having no military or strategic value. Some such targets are specifically banned under the traditional international laws of warfare. The Geneva conventions of 1949 prohibit any attack against hospitals or mobile medical units whether they have as patients wounded soldiers[144] or civilians.[145]   The 1907 Hague Regulations do not contain as blanket a prohibition, but cast a wider net:

> In sieges and bombardments all necessary steps must be taken to spare, as far as possible, buildings dedicated to religion, art, science, or charitable purposes, historic monuments, hospitals, and places where the sick and wounded are collected, provided they are not being used at the time for military purposes.[146]

The Charter of the International Military Tribunal at Nuremberg,[147] includes in its definition of war crimes the "murder, ill-treatment . . . of civilian population of or in occupied territory" and the "wanton destruction of cities, towns, or villages."[148]   In the *Shimoda Case*,[149] the District Court of Tokyo in a long and reasoned judgment found the aerial target prohibitions of non-military objectives to include "schools, churches, temples, shrines, hospitals, and private houses."[150] Not included in this list, but assimilable under the category of "wanton destruction," are dikes the opening or bombing of which would flood and ruin vast areas. Professor Kolko has reported the Allied warnings of 1945 to Seyss-Inquart, the German High Commissioner in Holland, warning him to stop the opening of dikes, which openings had resulted in mass hardship and destruction.[151]   General Eisenhower wrote on April 23, 1945, to German Commander Blaskowitz, a subordinate of Seyss-Inquart, to cease opening the dikes immediately, and if he fails

---

142. Traditional, necessary methods of warfare of course do not contravene the laws of war.

143. According to M. GREENSPAN, *supra* note 25, at 486-87, accident that is not due to culpable negligence is a defense to a war-crimes charge.

144. Art. 19, Geneva Convention on Wounded and Sick, *supra* note 16.

145. Art. 18, Geneva Convention on Civilian Persons, *supra* note 16.

146. Art. 27, Annex to Hague Convention IV, *supra* note 82.

147. See text accompanying note 8 for full quotation.

148. Also, see art. 46 of Annex to Hague Convention IV, *supra* note 82: "family honor and rights, the lives of persons and private property, as well as religious convictions and practice must be respected."

149. Falk, *The Shimoda Case: A Legal Appraisal of the Atomic Attacks Upon Hiroshima and Nagasaki*, 59 AM. J. INT'L L. 759 (1965).

150. *Id.* at 773.

151. RUSSELL TRIBUNAL, *supra* note 43, at 224.

"he and each responsible member of his command" will be considered by Eisenhower "as violators of the laws of war who must face the certain consequences of their acts."[152] In Churchill's memoirs it is stated that Seyss-Inquart agreed to stop further flooding.[153] In the Nuremberg judgment against Seyss-Inquart there is no mention of the dikes incident, thus indicating the tribunal's satisfaction with his immediate capitulation to the Eisenhower demand.[154] It is clear that had Seyss-Inquart not agreed on this point, the most important charge against him would have been his opening of the Holland dikes. Since Seyss-Inquart was sentenced to death by hanging for other war crimes, we may conclude that the opening of dikes was so clearly a war crime—in Eisenhower's view if not in Seyss-Inquart's as well—that it was never totally committed. Even in total war, some acts may be so clearly criminal that they are not done and post-war criminal proceedings therefore will have no occasion to charge a defendant for such a crime and establish a substantive precedent that it is illegal.

One might look at the list of prohibited targets—schools, churches, hospitals, private homes, dikes—and conclude simply that all targets that are not military objectives are illegitimate targets. Such a generalization was attempted in the Hague Rules of Air Warfare of 1923, a careful document that according to Greenspan "has strong persuasive authority" but nevertheless is not binding since it was not ratified by any state.[155] The Hague Rules allowed aerial bombardment "only when directed at a military objective," while prohibiting terror bombing[156] and the bombardment of cities, towns, villages, dwellings or buildings not in the immediate neighborhood of land forces or military objectives.[157] The apparent acceptability of this neat generalization was shattered, however, by the German attacks on "enemy morale" during World War II and the British response in kind as a consequence of "the enemy's adoption of a campaign of unrestricted air warfare."[158] On the other hand, even the Allied air raids and the German V-rocket bombardments of the Second World War were not specifically directed to non-military targets but rather constituted a "blind" bombardment of cities having important military targets, many of which were con-

---

152. H. Coles & A. Weinberg, Civil Affairs: Soldiers Become Governors 830-31 (1964).

153. W. Churchill, Triumph and Tragedy 469 (1953).

154. 1 Trial Maj. War Crim. 327-30 (Int'l Mil. Trib. 1947).

155. M. Greenspan, supra note 25, at 352.

156. Hague Rules of Air Warfare of 1923 art. 22, reprinted in M. Greenspan, supra note 25, at 654.

157. Id. art. 24, reprinted in M. Greenspan, supra note 25, at 655.

158. British Directive of October 29, 1942, in McDougal & Feliciano, supra note 37, at 653.

cealed. Despite this conduct by some parties to the Second World War, and despite the difficulty of articulating a workable rule restricting terrorist aerial bombing, there is authority for a prohibition of "blind" bombardment.[159] Even Professor McDougal would circumscribe "strategic bombing" to effect the "minimization of unnecessary discrepancies between the dimensions of assigned target areas and those of the specific material establishments within such areas which are determined to be military objectives."[160] He agrees with the late Judge Lauterpacht that unless there is some limitation deliberate terror bombing "comes too close to rendering pointless all legal limitations on the exercise of violence."[161] Regardless of the ultimate resolution of this question it can be said, at the very least, that if war crimes exist at all they include the deliberate seeking out and bombing of specific schools, hospitals, dikes, churches, and private residences removed from "military targets." Such a conclusion does not challenge directly the notions of strategic bombing or terror bombing, but rather places the emphasis on the deliberate selection of traditionally proscribed non-military targets.

b. The Evidence

The tonnage of bombs dropped into Vietnam, an agricultural country slightly larger in size than New York State, has exceeded the total tonnage of all the Allied bombing in the European and Asian theatres in World War II, including the atomic bombs. Have all these bombs fallen upon military objectives? Harrison Salisbury, a *New York Times* correspondent distinguished for accuracy and ideological neutrality, visited North Vietnam at the end of 1966 and surveyed the wreckage, looking in particular for evidence of military installations. He concluded, "When you totaled all the 'military objectives' in North Vietnam, they didn't total much."[162] Let us first consider North Vietnam, looking at the American bombing partly through Salisbury's eyes.

---

159. *The Shimoda Case,* Falk, *supra* note 54, at 776, takes issue with the alleged legality of "blind" bombardment.

160. McDOUGAL & FELICIANO, *supra* note 37, at 657.

161. *Id.* The deliberate American shooting of over 100 Vietnamese civilians at Mylai 4 hamlet, Sonymy village, on March 16, 1968, has led to a general court-martial and criminal investigations handled at the highest American levels. Statement of Stanley R. Resor, Secretary of the Army, N.Y. Times, Nov. 27, 1969, at 18, cols. 5-8. But as James Reston has pointed out, "The B-52's hit villages like this all the time in the 'free zone,' killing anybody in the area. Ditto the artillery guns. The only difference in the attack of Company C [in Songmy] was that they saw the human beings in the village and killed them with their M-16's anyway, and then told their story on TV." N.Y. Times, Nov. 26, 1969, at 44, cols. 5-6. Clearly there ought to be no legal distinction between a face-to-face massacre of unarmed, unresisting civilians and a deliberate aerial bombardment of such people.

162. H. SALISBURY, BEHIND THE LINES—HANOI 103 (1967).

Salisbury visited the remains of the Polish Friendship School in Hanoi, which was bombed and wrecked in two raids over ten days apart,[163] and then visited the victims of this bombing—children who had severe hemorrhages from bomb fragments.[164] Four Russell tribunal commissions of inquiry composed of doctors, lawyers, and scientists from many countries, visited throughout North Vietnam and compiled statistical and photographical evidence.[165] They reported that up to the end of 1966, American aircraft had attacked the following types and numbers of schools: 301 schools of the second degree, 24 schools of the third degree, 29 kindergarten schools, ten primary schools, 20 technical and professional secondary schools, three universities, two primary seminaries, and one advanced seminary.[166] When the second commission of inquiry was in North Vietnam on January 20, 1967, a plane attacked the classroom of the Tan Thanh school in the province of Ninh Binh with an air-to-ground missile, killing two teachers, 17 children (six to eight years old), and wounding seven others.[167] In an underdeveloped country where villages are largely composed of huts made of bamboo and straw, a school may present an attractive target since it "is one of the few modern buildings, and therefore perfectly visible from the air."[168]

A Japanese commission of inquiry reported to the Russell tribunal that the internationally known Hansen's disease hospital at Quynh Lap, the Quang Binh provincial hospital, and the Ha Tinh provincial hospital were targets of bombing missions 39 times, 13 times, and 17 times respectively.[169] A French surgeon reported that he visited the Viet Tri Hospital which was bombed on August 11 and 14, 1966, and again bombed on January 18, 1967, with explosive and fragmentation bombs.[170] This same hospital was visited independently by a correspondent for *Life Magazine*, who described the fragmentation bombs used as cluster-bomb units—bursting cannisters that scatter explosive balls which in turn spray steel pellets coated with napalm over a wide area.[171] Mary McCarthy, who visited Hanoi, reported of "ghost hospitals" and described the wreck of Hoa Binh Hospital.[172] The Russell

---

163. *Id*. at 131.
164. *Id*. at 133.
165. Each of the commissions was subject to bombing attacks in the course of their visits. RUSSELL TRIBUNAL, *supra* note 43, at 149.
166. *Id*. at 312i.
167. *Id*. at 153.
168. *Id*. (Dr. Abraham Behar, Assistant at the Faculty of Medicine of Paris).
169. *Id*. at 162.
170. *Id*. at 175.
171. Lockwood, *Recollections of Four Weeks with the Enemy*, LIFE, April 7, 1967, at 44.
172. M. McCARTHY, HANOI 61 (1968).

tribunal commissions reported that American aircraft had bombed and strafed 12 province hospitals, seven specialized hospitals, 22 district hospitals, 29 village infirmary-maternity homes, and ten others—a total of 9,072 hospital beds—between 1965 and 1967.[173]

Mary McCarthy,[174] Harrison Salisbury,[175] and the Russell tribunal commissions,[176] have all reported and described the bombing of the famous Vietnamese leprosarium at Quyuh Lap. Although this health center is known throughout the world of medicine and science, is marked by the red cross, and has given fame to the small town of Quyuh Lap where it is the only notable structure, it was the target of 39 separate bombing missions.[177] Mary McCarthy reports seeing photographs of the "pandemonic scenes as doctors and attendants sought to carry lepers to safety on their backs and on stretchers."[178] She reports the North Vietnamese statistics of 160 demolished secluded buildings which had housed more than 2,000 lepers.[179] The Americans used all types of bombs and strafed with machineguns the flee ing lepers.[180] The North Vietnamese Ministry of Public Health made repeated statements after the early attacks, calling attention to the nature of the destruction and attempting in vain to dissuade the United States attacks.[181] Three bombing and strafing missions also completely destroyed the Thanh Hoa tuberculosis sanatorium, the second most important sanatorium in North Vietnam.[182] It covered two and a half hectares, contained 30 buildings, and was well-marked with many large Red Cross flags.[183]

The second Russell tribunal commission of inquiry submitted documents and photographs on the bombing destruction of ten churches in North Vietnam.[184] According to Vietnamese sources, Americans destroyed more than 80 churches and more than 30 pagodas from the air since 1965.[185] Visiting Hanoi, Salisbury found that "the churches whose towers rose above the landscape had suffered repeated dam-

173. RUSSELL TRIBUNAL, *supra* note 43, at 312g.
174. M. McCARTHY, *supra* note 172, at 28.
175. H. SALISBURY, *supra* note 162, at 134.
176. RUSSELL TRIBUNAL, *supra* note 43, at 180-84, 150-51.
177. *Id.* at 181, 312h.
178. M. McCARTHY, *supra* note 172, at 28.
179. *Id.* She adds: "I apoligize for using North Vietnamese statistics, but the Americans have not supplied any."
180. RUSSELL TRIBUNAL, *supra* note 43, at 181.
181. *Id.* at 150.
182. *Id.* at 203-05.
183. *Id.*
184. *Id.* at 154.
185. *Id.*

age."[186]   He inspected the St. Francis Xavier Cathedral, "bombed into a shattered hulk on April 24, 1966."[187]

North Vietnam is a land of dikes and dams. A member of the second commission of inquiry reported to the Russell tribunal that he was in Nam Dinh when it was bombed on December 31, 1966, and that contrary to the American report that the railroad junction in that city had been hit, "not a single bomb hit the railroad junction;" rather, "they all struck the dam which protects the city from floods of the Black River."[188]   Harrison Salisbury reports that the whole city of Nan Dinh is six to fourteen feet below water level during the rainy season, and that its dikes showed evidence of large craters and filled-in portions indicating bombing attacks.[189]   He found similar evidence of repeated bombing of the dikes and water-control works in the Phat Diem region.[190]   At the Russell hearings it was reported that Americans twice bombed the dike at Traly, in Thai Binh province.[191]   Americans also bombed the dike in Quang Binh province several times, destroying 1,500 hectares of paddy fields.[192]   The second Japanese investigation team reported that 100 bombs fell on the dike along the Thuond River, including attacks during repairs.[193]   Japanese investigation teams provided many other examples at the Russell hearings.[194]   A reporter for the *Christian Science Monitor* published an eyewitness account of almost daily attacks on dikes along the Red River delta area where "no military targets are visible."[195]

After March, 1968, the bombing of North Vietnam was limited to the narrow southern panhandle of that country; nevertheless, actual bombing missions were increased.[196]   At the same time, as Lawrence Petrowski observes, far fewer American planes were shot down, indicating the likelihood that the bombing was directed at civilian targets in

---

186. H. SALISBURY, *supra* note 162, at 122.
187. *Id.*
188. RUSSELL TRIBUNAL, *supra* note 43, at 148.
189. H. SALISBURY, *supra* note 162, at 101.
190. *Id.* at 123. *Cf.* Quarterly Review Staff, *The Attack on the Irrigation Dams in North Korea*, 6 AIR UNIV. Q. 40 (1953).
191. RUSSELL TRIBUNAL, *supra* note 43, at 229.
192. *Id.*
193. *Id.*
194. *Id.* at 229-35.
195. N. CHOMSKY, *supra* note 84, at 15.
196. Comparative mission totals were:

	1967	1968
April	2,925	3,412
May	3,237	3,593
June	3,607	3,792
July (3 weeks)	3,819	2,723

N.Y. Post, July 23, 1968, quoted in Petrowski, *Law and the Conduct of the Vietnam War*, in 2 THE VIETNAM WAR AND INTERNATIONAL LAW 439, 490 (R. Falk ed. 1969).

the heavily populated areas.[197]   A retired Air Force captain familiar
with operations in Vietnam explained to Petrowski that the normal procedure was to allow low echelon personnel to assign targets to airborne
squadrons which were unable to hit primary objectives or had ordnance
left over from their first strike.[198]   "Often, all area targets, even the
most questionable targets like fishing villages, rice paddies, or clusters
of huts with seemingly normal activity around them, had been hit several times, even scores of times."[199]

As for South Vietnam itself, a predominantly rural country outside
of Saigon, newspapers frequently report the bombing of villages—sometimes mistaken bombing of "friendly" villages,[200] often bombing of villages in which there are mostly women and children and few if any
Viet Cong,[201] and usually heavy bombing of villages in areas that have
been declared to be "free-fire zones."[202]   Two journalists who flew
daily with the American forward air control have reported:

> In August, 1967, during Operation Benton, the "pacification" camps
> became so full that Army units in the field were ordered not to
> "generate" any more refugees. . . [N]ow peasants were not warned
> before an airstrike was called in on their village. They were killed
> in their villages because there was no room for them in the swamped
> pacification camps. The usual warnings by helicopter loudspeaker
> or air dropped leaflets were stopped. . . . . Village after village was
> destroyed from the air as a matter of *de facto* policy. Airstrikes on
> civilians became a matter of routine. It was under these circum-
> stances of official acquiescence to the destruction of the countryside
> and its people that the massacre of Songmy occurred.[203]

Other reports have indicated the deliberate bombing in South Vietnam
of sampans, often carrying only fleeing women and children,[204] as well

---

197. Petrowski, *supra* note 196, at 490.

198. *Id.* at 491 n.144.

199. *Id.*

200. N.Y. Times, Oct. 31, 1965, quoted in NAME OF AMERICA, *supra* note 108, at
222.

201. B. FALL, *supra* note 123, at 228-30. Senator Hartke refers to a UNESCO
study estimating that in the rural villages about 70 percent of the population are
children. V. HARTKE, *supra* note 93, at 124.

202. Editorial, N.Y. Times, Nov. 22, 1969, at 36, col. 2.

203. Orville Schell and Jonathan Schell, Letter to the N.Y. Times, Nov. 26, 1969,
at 44, col. 5. Joseph P. Lyford, president of the Fund for Peace, has requested that
the United States Senate investigate the reported massacre of South Vietnamese civilians
in the town of Lang Vei on March 2, 1967. The incident was the result of an apparently intentional and deliberate attack by two Air Force F-4 Phantom jets using
antipersonnel bombs and machine guns. *Lang Vei Massacre*, THE NEW DIMENSION,
Jan. 1970, at 2.

204. B. FALL, *supra* note 123, at 228-29; M. BROWNE, *supra* note 137, at 165-66.

as hospitals[205] and schools.[206]

Official American response to the evidence of bombing of non-military targets has either been to deny the allegations[207]—an expectable response since to admit them would be to involve the highest levels of command in criminal guilt—or to claim that the bombing of such targets was "accidental."[208] Some observers accept the Pentagon's position that the bombing is restricted to military objectives and that there is a sincere intent to avoid civilian casualties.[209] These observers add that "without access to classified information and to the pilots' briefing rooms, it would be rather fatuous to enter into the factual side of the bombing debate."[210] To the contrary, it would be a bold departure from the Nuremberg precedents to make the issue of guilt turn on briefing sessions and classified information. Whatever such sources might or might not reveal about motivation, it is the resulting conduct that counts. The major Nazi war criminals convicted of conspiracy to wage wars of aggression were found guilty at Nuremberg on the basis of their presence at meetings and their positions of responsibility; their intent was inferred from the subsequent patterns of conduct. The Belsen trial specifically established the rule that a systematic course of conduct sufficed to prove intent.[211]

Although evidence is concededly limited, there are in addition several factors which indicate that the American bombing of non-military targets in Vietnam is not accidental. In the first place, repeated bombing missions against the same target, such as the 39 separate missions that bombed the leper colony and sanatorium at Quyuh Lap, belie the explanation that the bombing was accidental,[212] particularly inasmuch as the

---

205. B. FALL. *supra* note 123, at 232; NAME OF AMERICA, *supra* note 108, at 412-13.

206. RUSSELL TRIBUNAL, *supra* note 43, at 559-60.

207. Stanley R. Resor, Secretary of the Army, stated to the Senate Armed Services Committee that "what apparently occurred at Mylai [the massacre of the villagers of Songmy] is wholly unrepresentative of the manner in which our forces conduct military operations in Vietnam." N.Y. Times, Nov. 27, 1969, at 18, col. 7. Harrison Salisbury observed: "I could begin to see quite clearly that there was a vast gap between the reality of the air war, as seen from the ground in Hanoi, and the bland, vague American communiques with their reiterated assumptions that our bombs were falling precisely upon 'military objectives' and accomplishing our military purposes with some kind of surgical precision which for the first time in the history of war was crippling the enemy without hurting civilians or damaging civilian life." H. SALISBURY, *supra* note 162, at 69.

208. Sheehan, *Washington Concedes Bombs Hit Civilian Areas in North Vietnam*, N.Y. Times, Dec. 27, 1966, at 1, col. 4; H. SALISBURY, *supra* note 162, at 126.

209. R. HULL & J. NOVOGROD, LAW AND VIETNAM 166 (1968).

210. *Id.*

211. The Belsen Trial, 2 L. Rep. Trials War Crim. 1 (U.N. War Crimes Comm'n, Brit. Mil. Ct., Luncburg 1945).

212. *See, e.g.,* M. McCARTHY, *supra* note 162, at 28.

United States has used reconnaissance flights extensively.[213]   Second, the military has repeatedly claimed that its bombing is extremely accurate,[214] a position which is certainly credible in light of American technology.   Third, psychological motivations probably influence bomber pilots to sometimes attack dramatic non-military targets:

> A bomb dropped into a leafy jungle produces no visible result. . . .
> A hit on a big hydroelectric dam is another matter.   There is a huge explosion visible from anywhere above.   The dam can be seen to fall.   The waters can be seen to pour out through the breach and drown out huge areas of farm land, and villages, in its path.   The pilot who takes out a hydroelectric dam gets back home with a feeling of accomplishment.   Novels are written and films are made of such exploits.[215]

Fourth, and most important, there is massive evidence of the use in Vietnam of antipersonnel bombs,[216] which have an insignificant effect upon fixed military or economic installations but are effective against personnel in dense population centers.[217]   These bombs are often equip-

---

213.   RUSSELL TRIBUNAL, *supra* note 43, at 306.

214.   *See* H. SALISBURY, *supra* note 207.

215.   Joseph Harsch, distinguished correspondent for the *Christian Science Monitor*, quoted in N. CHOMSKY, *supra* note 84, at 14.   Similarly an article in *Flying* describes a lucky young pilot who can napalm a village and then engage in strafing runs over the fleeing citizens.   NAME OF AMERICA, *supra* note 108, at 205.

216.   Prokosch, *Conventional Killers*, THE NEW REPUBLIC, Nov. 1, 1969.   The "pineapple" bomb contains steel pellets in a hollow cylinder which are propelled by the explosion upon impact with the ground in a sun-burst pattern.   RUSSELL TRIBUNAL, *supra* note 43, at 249-50.   Sergeant Duncan reported in *Ramparts* that the Department of Defense placed contracts for the manufacture of 14.8 billion steel pellets for use in anti-personnel bombs.   *Id.* at 167 n.2.   The "mother bomb" is a casing which holds 640 "guava" bomblets; it explodes at an altitude of about one kilometer flinging the guava bomblets over an area of one by one-half kilometers.   Upon impact, the gauva bomblet explodes, discharging 300 steel balls 5.56 mm in diameter.   *Id.* at 250.   *See also* the carefully documented evidence and eyewitness accounts of J.B. Neilands, Professor of Biochemistry at Berkeley, *id.* at 269-73.   The damage to people can be intense and painful, according to Dr. Masahiro Hashimoto's testimony at the Russell hearings.   The small steel balls can cause complicated fractures of thigh-bones and other large bones, they can trace complex paths through internal organs (often fatally), and they cannot be left in the body because their alloy make-up is incompatible with human tissues and body fluids.   RUSSELL TRIBUNAL, *supra* note 43, at 262-63.   Another type of bomb used extensively in North and South Vietnam, is the napalm or jellied gasoline bomb.   *Id.* at 186.   This material burns with an extremely high temperature—enough to weld body and bone tissue together—and also generates carbon monoxide which is fatal to humans in the vicinity of the bomb drop.   *Id.*

217.   Duncan reported that the steel balls cannot pierce cement and can only penetrate earthern or sand bag military revetments to a depth of two or three inches.   Duncan, *And Blessed Be the Fruit*, RAMPARTS, May, 1967.   *See also* M. McCARTHY, *supra* note 172, at 102-03; NAME OF AMERICA, *supra* note 108, at 270-81; RUSSELL TRIBUNAL, *supra* note 43, at 135, 156, 162-66, 251-61.   Dr. Jean Vigier, Director of Research at the French National Center for Scientific Research and former officer-in-charge of armaments inspection of the French Army, testified at the Russell hearings

ped with delayed-action fuses, the very notion of which is incompatible with an intent to strike against military targets in the traditional sense.[218] These four factors lead inevitably to the conclusion that the bombing of non-military targets cannot persuasively be described as accidental.

3. Chemical Warfare[219]

a. The Law.

The Geneva Protocol of 1925 states that the "use in war of asphyxiating, poisonous or other gases, and of all analogous liquids, materials, or devices, has been justly condemned by the general opinion of the civilized world," and prohibits among the parties the use of such weapons.[220] By virtue of the number of parties to this treaty[221] as well as the expressions of adherence to its underlying principles by non-parties such as the United States,[222] the Protocol has created customary international law binding upon all countries.[223] The practice of states subsequent to 1925 has generally confirmed the status of the principles of the Protocol in customary international law.[224] Except for the widely condemned use of gas by Italy against Ethiopia in 1935-36

---

that the antipersonnel bombs will not harm fixed military or economic installations, but are effective against personnel in dense population centers. RUSSELL TRIBUNAL, *supra* note 43, at 253-54.

218. Farer & Petrowski, *supra* note 24.

219. Germ warfare, and radiological weapons, are often discussed in the same context as chemical warfare. Since the present essay is shaped by the availability of evidence pertaining to the Vietnam war, these other kinds of weaponry are not discussed here. Nor is any position taken as to the legality per se of the use of antipersonnel bombs, though it may be noted that, apart from questionable analogies to the use of "dum-dum" bullets proscribed in early conventions, antipersonnel bombs have been used in many wars against enemy soldiers without ever forming the basis for post-war criminal proceedings. *See generally* E. McCARTHY, THE ULTIMATE FOLLY (1969). *See also* Meyrowitz, *Les Armes Psychochimiques et le Droit International,* 1964 ANNUAIRE FRANCAIS 81.

220. Protocol Prohibiting the Use in War of Asphyxiating, Poisonous, or Other Gases, and of Bacteriological Methods of Warfare, of June 17, 1925, in 3 M. HUDSON, INTERNATIONAL LEGISLATION 1670 (1931); 90 L.N.T.S. 65.

221. Some 80 states have ratified including the major powers except for Japan and the United States. N.Y. Times, Nov. 26, 1969, at 16, col. 5.

222. According to President Nixon, "The United States has long supported the principles and objectives of this protocol." N.Y. Times, Nov. 26, 1969, at 16, col. 2.

223. See D'Amato, *supra* note 13.

224. See notes 13, 15 *supra*. The Nuremberg Tribunal stated the principle of the applicability, despite its terms, to Germany of the 1907 Hague Convention in noting that "by 1939 these rules laid down in the convention were recognised by all civilised nations, and were regarded as being declaratory of the laws and customs of war . . . ." 1 Trial Maj. War Crim. 254 (Int'l Mil. Trib. 1947). *See also* United States v. Ohlendorf, 4 Trial Maj. War Crim. 459-60 (Int'l Mil. Trib. 1950); United States v. Greifelt, 5 Trial Maj. War Crim. 153 (Int'l Mil. Trib. 1950); United States v. Von List, 11 Trial Maj. War Crim. 1240 (Int'l Mil. Trib. 1950).

and some small gas attacks by Japan against Chinese forces between 1937 and 1943,[225] the belligerents did not use gas in the otherwise "total" Second World War.[226] On June 8, 1943, President Roosevelt declared that the United States would not use gas unless enemy forces first used it, adding that "use of such weapons has been outlawed by the general opinion of civilized mankind."[227] President Nixon recently reaffirmed this statement in calling upon the United States Senate to ratify the Geneva Protocol.[228]

In contrast to its application to the treatment of prisioners of war and bombardment of non-military targets, the Geneva Protocol gives rise to problems of legal interpretation in the Vietnam context. It is not clear whether defoliants, napalm, "tear gas," and "riot-control" gas are the types of "gas" outlawed by the laws of war. A respectable argument can be made that the only practical legal distinction is that between gas and no-gas,[229] and thus the use of gas of any kind is illegal.[230] Minimally, however, the Geneva Protocol of 1925 and sub-

---

225. See McDougal & Feliciano, *supra* note 37, at 633-34 for a documented account. *See also* O'Brien, *Biological Chemical Warfare and the International Law of War*, 51 Geo. L.J. 1 (1962).

226. See the discussion of the total war concept in Falk, *supra* note 54, at 783, 788-93.

227. 8 Dep't State Bull. 507 (1943). The argument that abstention from gas warfare in World War II was due solely to fear of retaliation by the other side, and not because of an international legal prohibition, can never be proved. But even if it were true, the fear of reciprocal noncompliance plays an important part in many if not most of the rules of international law. *See* D'Amato, *International Law—Content and Function: A Review*, 11 J. Conflict Resolution 504 (1967).

228. President Nixon stated that the United States "reaffirms its oft-repeated renunciation of the first use of lethal chemical weapons." N.Y. Times, Nov. 26, 1969, at 16, col. 1. Continuing worldwide approval of the objectives of the Geneva Protocol is demonstrated by the passage of a United Nations General Assembly resolution on December 5, 1966, joined by ninety states including the United States, that invited "all states to strictly conform to the principles and objectives" of the Protocol and "condemned any act contrary to these objectives." G.A. Res. 2162, 21 U.N. GAOR A/Res/2162 (XXI) (1966). It is clear that one of the main reasons for the durability of the Geneva Protocol is the clear line between use and non-use of gas. This factor in itself constitutes a partial refutation of those who would contextualize and relativize the laws of war out of existence. For a critique of the contextual approach see Falk, *supra* note 54 at 788-93. Professor Schelling has articulated the relevant physical-psychological factors: "Gas only on military personnel; gas used only by defending forces; gas only when carried by projectile; no gas without warning— a variety of limits is conceivable. . . . But there is a simplicity to 'no gas' that makes it uniquely a focus for agreement when each side can only conjecture at what alternative rules the other side would propose . . . ." T. Schelling, Arms and Influence 131 (1966). Has the distinction been shattered by the use of "tear gas" and "riot-control gas" in Vietnam?

229. *See* T. Schelling, *supra* note 228.

230. In an authoritative text on international law it is stated that "some gases are not so deadly or so cruel as others, but the dangers of recognizing any categories of permitted gases and thus sanctioning the manufacture of the necessary equipment for

sequent practice reflects a revulsion against the *kinds* and *uses* of gases employed in the first world war. Placing the Protocol in its 1925 context does not limit its proscriptions only to the use of gases used in the first world war; to do so would be to circumscribe absurdly the broad legislative goals of the nations that drew up and signed the Protocol. Clearly they were aware of new technology which would result in weapons analogous to, but not the same as, mustard, chlorine, and related gases. The Protocol specifically outlawed the use of "asphyxiating, poisonous or other gases, and . . . all analogous liquids, materials or devices."[231] However, it is reasonable to assume that the "gases and analogous liquids" the signatories contemplated were those that could and did result in fatalities or near-fatalities. Excluded might be a hypothetical psychochemical gas which rendered its victims temporarily tranquil with no side or aftereffects. Under this interpretation, which is less extensive than one reading the Protocol as banning all gases, the question becomes an evidentiary and factual one—whether the gases, liquids or sprays used by the United States in Vietnam are lethal and hence illegal.[232]

b. The Evidence.

The evidence suggests that the various toxic gases and liquids used by the United States in Vietnam are lethal and thus come under the proscriptions of customary international law and the Geneva Protocol. Although the *names* of such gases—"tear gas" and "riot-control gas"—suggest only temporary debilitation, in fact their effect depends upon their degree of saturation in the air and upon the victim's physical

---

using them are obvious and great, so that, it is submitted, the society of States has adopted the right policy in endeavoring to extirpate this mode of warfare *in toto*." 2 OPPENHEIM, INTERNATIONAL LAW; A TREATISE 343 n.2 (H. Lauterpacht ed., 8th ed. 1955). In fact, tear gas was used in World War I, and the Geneva Protocol may have been framed with the question of tear gas in mind. See Meselson, *Behind the Nixon Policy for Chemical and Biological Warfare*, 26 BULL. ATOMIC SCI. 23, 31 (1970).

231. See note 220 *supra*.

232. President Nixon has acknowledged the existence of "our chemical warfare program" while reiterating the American renunciation of the first use of "lethal" chemical weapons. N.Y. Times, Nov. 26, 1969, at 16, col. 1. The sole question becomes whether the United States has used "lethal" chemical weaponry. This question should not be confused with the rationalization sometimes given that eye-irritating and nausea-inducing gases are more "humane" than bombs, shooting, and hand-grenades, and therefore are legal. *See, e.g.*, TIME, April 2, 1965, at 20, quoted in NAME OF AMERICA, *supra* note 108, at 119. For *any* type of weapon, including atomic bombs, can be rationalized as being more "humane" than ordinary bombs and shooting because they end the war quicker and thus save lives. Such a rationale, obviously, would wipe out all the laws of warfare, since both sides would naturally think that doing the most brutal and hitherto illegal acts would bring the enemy to its knees faster and hence be humane.

characteristics.[233]   According to Dr. David Hilding of the Yale Medical School, the eye-irritation and nausea-inducing gases which the United States admits it uses in Vietnam[234] "probably produce the designed effect in a few persons of the proper weight, height, and general condition, but the dosage for others will be wrong."[235]   Babies will "writhe in horrible cramps" until their strength "is unequal to the stress and they turn black and blue and die."[236]   One of the "riot-control" gases— DM (adamsite), used alone or more frequently in combination with CN (tear gas)[237]—was described by a Canadian doctor working in Vietnam as having about a ten percent mortality rate in adults and a 90 percent mortality rate in children.[238]   These figures may be compared with the ten percent mortality rate that has been ascribed to the gases used in World War I in 1915.[239]   (CS, an extra-strength tear gas that induces choking as well as tears, has substantially replaced use of these two gases.)

A primary use of these gases in Vietnam has been to flush persons out of the intricate tunnels and shelters constructed by the Viet Cong and civilians hiding from the shells, bombs, and napalm used above ground.[240]   In this manner, very high concentrations of the gas build up in the enclosures.   In January 1966, in a well-documented incident, an Australian soldier trapped in a tunnel was killed by tear gas even though he was wearing a gas mask.[241]   There was medical testimony at the Russell hearings that the gas concentration in tunnels and hideouts is mortal.[242]   Professor M.F. Kahn of the Faculty of Medicine of Paris

---

233. S. HERSH, CHEMICAL AND BIOLOGICAL WARFARE 156-57 (1969).

234. *Id.* at 142-54; Frankel, *U.S. Reveals Use of Nonlethal Gas Against Vietcong*, N.Y. Times, March 23, 1965, at 1, col. 8; V. HARTKE, *supra* note 93, at 127-28. *See generally* E. McCARTHY, THE ULTIMATE FOLLY (1969).

235. Hilding, Letter to the N.Y. Times, written on March 26, 1965 (cited in RUSSELL TRIBUNAL, *supra* note 43, at 344-45).

236. *Id.* A New York Times editorial stated that these gases "can be fatal to the very young, the very old and those ill with heart and lung ailments." N.Y. Times, March 24, 1965, at 42, col. 1 quoted in RUSSELL TRIBUNAL, *supra* note 43, at 344. Doctors Sidel and Goldwyn wrote in 277 NEW ENGLAND J. MED. (1967) that "Chemical and biological weapons are notoriously uneven in their dispersal and therefore in the amount absorbed by each recipient; to ensure that every person receives an incapacitating dose, some will have to receive an overdose. Furthermore, the young, the elderly and the infirm will be the particularly susceptible victims."

237. S. HERSH, *supra* note 233, at 52.

238. *Id.* at 157 (letter of Dr. Alje Vennema of Burlington, Ontario).

239. A. PRENTISS, CHEMICALS IN WAR (1937).

240. CBW: CHEMICAL AND BIOLOGICAL WARFARE 91 (Rose ed. 1969) [hereinafter cited as CBW]. The gas is injected into the tunnels by a high-velocity wind machine nicknamed "Mighty Mite." *Id.*

241. N.Y. Times, Jan. 13, 1966, at 3, col. 1; V. HARTKE, *supra* note 93, at 128; RUSSELL TRIBUNAL, *supra* note 43, at 344.

242. RUSSELL TRIBUNAL, *supra* note 43, at 532-33 (Dr. Erich Wulff).

has reported of hundreds of civilian deaths resulting from the use of "tear gas" and "riot-control gas" in the tunnels and shelters of South Vietnam.[243] But even open-air use can be lethal; it was reported to the Russell tribunal that American use of gas against the village of Vinh Quang in South Vietnam on September 5, 1965, resulted in 35 deaths, nearly all women and children.[244] Although the Departments of State and Defense have claimed that tear gas and riot-control gas was used in Vietnam solely as a humanitarian weapon to separate the Viet Cong from innocent civilians in villages where the civilians were used as shields,[245] it has been reported that the American command in Saigon told the Pentagon in the spring of 1969 "that tear gas had rarely been used to save civilian lives."[246] The greatest amount of CS had been used against enemy camps, bunkers and caves.[247] It has been further reported that gas attacks are used as a prelude to fragmentation bombs in order to force the enemy out into the open.[248] Because the gases used by the United States in Vietnam are lethal in some concentrations, and because they have been used in the manner which the Geneva Protocol was designed to prevent, such gases appear to be used in violation of the laws of war.

The United States also freely admits that it uses defoliant and herbicide sprays extensively in South Vietnam and that their use will not be curtailed as a result of President Nixon's statement reaffirming the renunciation of the first use of lethal or incapacitating chemicals.[249] Although not technically "gases," these spray chemicals ejected in mist or cloud-like form are covered by the language of the Geneva Protocol which applies to "gases, and . . . all analogous liquids, materials or devices."[250] The defoliant and herbicide sprays have been condemned by some writers as directed against the civilian population's food supply.[251] We take no position here on the legality of such a

---

243. CBW, *supra* note 240, at 93-96.

244. RUSSELL TRIBUNAL, *supra* note 43, at 341. *See also id.* at 330 (testimony of Dr. Dehar); *cf.* Mennonite Central Comm. Newsletter, Nov. 10, 1967 (death of boy from overdose of gas).

245. S. HERSH, *supra* note 233, at 142-51.

246. Smith, *U.S. Command in Saigon Rejects Pentagon View that Use of Tear Gas Reduces Civilian Casualties*, N.Y. Times, Sept. 29, 1969, at 11, col. 1.

247. *Id.* at col. 4.

248. N.Y. Times, Feb. 22, 1966, at 1, col. 5; Hersh, *supra* note 233, at 152-53.

249. N.Y. Times, Nov. 26, 1969, at 16, col. 7; V. HARTKE, *supra* note 93, at 126-27.

250. Protocol cited *supra* note 220. On a hot day these sprays can revolatize into gases. *See* Christian Science Monitor, Nov. 25, 1967, at 16, col. 4 quoted in NAME OF AMERICA, *supra* note 108, at 294-95. There is a report that gas masks have been used against the spray. NAME OF AMERICA, *supra* note 108, at 120.

251. *See, e.g.*, Meyrowitz, *The Law of War in the Vietnamese Conflict*, in 2

use,[252] but rather suggest that the direct effects of spraying can be lethal to some victims depending upon concentration and personal characteristics. The most common sprays[253] contain arsenic and calcium cyanamide,[254] which are virulent poisons.[255] It was reported to the Russell tribunal that a spraying of Cocong, Ben Tre Province, in June, 1966, caused toxic symptoms in 5,000 villagers; 900 developed high fevers with violent purging and loose bowels, and some died.[256] Moreover, the eating of sprayed foods can be lethal, particularly to children who may not heed the warnings of the NLF not to eat sprayed fruits.[257]

Napalm[258] and supernapalm,[259] used extensively by the United States in Vietnam,[260] might arguably be considered "analogous liquids, materials or devices" within the prohibitions of the Geneva Protocol.[261] This argument, however, is open to the objection that, as a liquid, napalm was not contemplated in the Geneva Protocol which addressed itself primarily to gases. A different approach might be to recognize

---

THE VIETNAM WAR AND INTERNATIONAL LAW, *supra* note 3, at 516, 558; Hersh, *supra* note 233, at 125-26.

252. There would appear, however, to be at least an inconsistency in the American position that it is intervening in South Vietnam to save the villagers from unwanted Viet Cong domination and the policy of destroying the food supply of both Viet Cong and villagers.

253. These include 2,4D and 2,4,5-T. *See* S. HERSH, *supra* note 233, at 131.

254. The basic formulae vary with the region, climate, and target plant, but nearly all include arsenic and cyanide compounds. CBW, *supra* note 240, at 67; RUSSELL TRIBUNAL, *supra* note 43, at 367; NAME OF AMERICA, *supra* note 108, at 288. The amount of 2,4D used in Vietnam has almost exhausted the domestic supply; the military is demanding four times the total annual production, which in 1965 alone was 77 million pounds. CBW, *supra* note 240, at 66.

255. CBW, *supra* note 240, at 89-90; RUSSELL TRIBUNAL, *supra* note 43, at 372.

256. RUSSELL TRIBUNAL, *supra* note 43, at 368.

257. CBW, *supra* note 240, at 90. "Miss Thuy-Ba, M.D., chief of the medical staff of a provincial NLF hospital, described to us a lethal case she observed. A five-year-old boy was brought to the hospital after he had eaten contaminated fruit. He had severe abdominal pain, vomiting, then diarrhea with blood in his stools, followed by collapse and death." *Id.*

258. Jellied gasoline. The type developed for use in Vietnam also contains polystyrene, which makes the napalm adhere to the flesh as it burns. S. HERSH, *supra* note 233, at 54; NAME OF AMERICA, *supra* note 108, at 269-71.

259. Napalm with 30 percent white phosphorus added. The phosphorus increases combustibility and in addition penetrates deeply into the skin, causing liver and kidney poisoning which in most cases is fatal. CBW, *supra* note 240, at 88.

260. S. HERSH, *supra* note 233, at 53-55; RUSSELL TRIBUNAL, *supra* note 43, at 374-75.

261. Protocol cited *supra* note 220. *Contra*, Brownlie, *Legal Aspects of CBW*, in CBW, *supra* note 240, at 141, 150. The intense heat generated by burning napalm—2000°F. to 3600°F. (RUSSELL TRIBUNAL, *supra* note 43, at 375)—arguably may bring the substance within the alleged legal ban against weapons causing "unnecessary harm" *See* Brownlie, *supra*, at 150; Petrowski, *supra* note 196, at 503. However, the standards, if any, as to what constitutes "unnecessary" suffering are vague and subjective.

that napalm emits large quantities of carbon monoxide when it burns, a deadly asphyxiating gas that is at least equally effective in terms of the number of victims killed or injured as the direct burning by napalm itself.[262] Indeed, the carbon monoxide gas spreads over a wider area than the burning napalm.[263] Thus, as a lethal-gas-producing "device" —to use the term of the Geneva Protocol—napalm may come within the prohibition of the laws of war even though its most obvious and dramatic effect is combustion.

In this part of the paper we have discussed the rules of evidence for proof of war crimes, the evidence legally required for such proof, and examples of the available evidence. In the following two sections we discuss government defenses to war-crimes allegations and whether the service resister will be able to fashion a suit that will be held procedurally and substantively justiciable.

III

DEFENSES TO WAR-CRIME ALLEGATIONS

The international law of war crimes contains several general so-called "defenses" that might be raised to counteract claims that war crimes are being or have been committed in Vietnam. In this section we shall consider briefly those defenses that might be relevant to a service resister's claim that American soldiers abroad are committing war crimes. We shall consider the concepts of reprisals and *tu quoque*, military necessity, obedience to superior orders, ignorance of the law, and duress.

A. Reprisals and Tu Quoque

In defense of a war crimes accusation, a belligerent sometimes claims the right of reprisal. It argues that since the other side commits war crimes, it may do so in return, as a punishment, or to deter the other side from doing so again.[264] It sometimes also raises a defense of *tu quoque*: as both sides are committing the alleged violation, it is not a

---

262. RUSSELL TRIBUNAL, *supra* note 43, at 376-77 (testimony of Gilbert Dreyfus, Professor of Biochemistry at the University of Paris Medical School).

263. Carbon monoxide is toxic at the one per cent atmospheric saturation level. *Id.* at 377. It gives rise to hallucinations, motor disturbances, and paralysis which prevent walking and all desire to escape. *Id.* By thus preventing the victim from escaping from the fire, it greatly increases the lethality of napalm. CBW, *supra* note 240, at 88.

264. MCDOUGAL & FELICIANO, *supra* note 37, at 679. The emphasis on deterrence as well as punishment can justify an act of somewhat greater gravity in specific reprisal for a prior illegal act by the other side. *See also Naulilaa Incident*, in BRIGGS, THE LAW OF NATIONS 951-53 (2d ed. 1952).

war crime after all.[265]   Although there is considerable controversy as to the meaning and breadth of these defenses,[266] it is minimally clear that if they are valid defenses at all, they relate only to acts committed by both sides that are similar, proportional, usually geographically contiguous, and, in the case of reprisals, acts done in specific retaliation for a prior illegal act by the other side.[267]   Absent these limitations, any war crime would immediately lead to a complete abandonment of all legal restraints on war activities of both sides, by virtue of war crimes of escalating gravity by each side in turn.   The various Nuremberg trials considering these defenses have accordingly interpreted strictly the requirements of similarity and proportionality.[268]

The Nuremberg tribunal rarely heard the defense of reprisals for war-crimes violations, not—as one commentator has implied—because the Allies did not commit such crimes,[269] but rather because the Allies probably decided not to prosecute defendants who might have had legitimate reprisal or *tu quoque* defenses to avoid the embarrassment that such revelations would cause.   Notably absent were prosecutions of Axis bomber-pilots, perhaps because the Allies themselves engaged in area bombing.   But then the doctrine of *tu quoque* cannot be summarily dismissed as it has been by some writers[270] who say that no criminal can defend himself on the basis that others are not being prosecuted for a similar crime.   In fact, in the judgment for Admiral Doenitz, the Nuremberg tribunal stated that Doenitz violated the laws of maritime war relating to the rescue of shipwrecked survivors, but that "in view of" a statement of Admiral Nimitz that the United States engaged in unrestricted submarine warfare in the Pacific Ocean the tribunal in sentencing would not assess this particular violation of Doenitz.[271]

In any event, the concepts of legitimate reprisals and *tu quoque* appear inapposite when applied to the Vietnamese war.   There is no evidence that either the North Vietnamese or the Viet Cong have engaged in the use of gas or chemical warfare.   Despite some terror bombing activities in which they have been engaged, notably around Saigon, they have not engaged in bombing remotely proportional to the American bombing of non-military targets in North and South Viet-

---

265. McDougal & Feliciano, *supra* note 37, at 679-82.
266. *See* Levie, *Maltreatment of Prisoners of War in Vietnam*, in 2 The Vietnam War and International Law, *supra* note 3, at 361, 392-96.
267. McDougal & Feliciano, *supra* note 37, at 679-86.
268. *See* 15 L. Rep. Trials War Crim. 177-82 (U.N. War Crimes Comm'n, 1947); United States v. List, 11 Trials Maj. War Crim. 1250 (Int'l Mil. Trib. 1948); United States v. von Leeb, 11 Trials Maj. War Crim. 528 (Int'l Mil. Trib. 1948).
269. Brand, *Digest of Laws and Cases*, in 15 L. Rep. Trials War Crim. 1, 177 (U.N. War Crimes Comm'n 1947).
270. *E.g.*, R. Woetzel, *supra* note 25, at 120.
271. 1 Trials Maj. War Crim. 313 (Int'l Mil. Trib. 1947).

nam. As for prisoners of war, it has not been publicly alleged that captured American soldiers have been tortured or murdered.[272] But even if they were, the 1949 Geneva Prisoners of War Convention flatly prohibits reprisals against prisoners of war,[273] echoing the 1929 Geneva Convention that was upheld by a United States Military Commission in the *Dostler Case* of 1945.[274]

B.   Military Necessity

Another possible defense is military necessity.[275] It is true that the United States Military Tribunal at Nuremberg held in the *Hostages Case*[276] that "military necessity or expediency do not justify a violation of positive rules [*i.e.*, the laws of war]"—although, as the tribunal pointed out,[277] this generalization does not apply when the particular conventional law of war itself contains a military-necessity exception.[278] The law on necessity might be changing to allow a defense of military necessity to a prohibited war crime when the immediate *survival* of the actor—as opposed to a military *advantage*[279]—is at stake.[280] To the

---

272. The late Bernard Fall wrote: "From all the accounts I received from Intelligence in Viet-Nam, there is no evidence of torture of American prisoners by the Viet Cong, and released United States prisoners have confirmed this." B. FALL, *supra* note 123, at 233. Levie, *supra* note 266, has made much of the fact that captured American pilots have been paraded through the crowd-lined streets of Hanoi, in violation of the Geneva Convention on Prisoners of war. *Id.* at 380. But this does not amount to physical torture or murder, and indeed in contrast to the inevitable lynchings of downed Allied pilots in Axis-held countries during World War II, *e.g.* 1 Trials Maj. War Crim. 292 (Int'l Mil. Trib. 1947), Essen Lynching Case, 1 L. Rep. Trials War Crim. 88 (U.N. War Crimes Comm'n, Brit. Mil. Ct., Essen 1945), North Vietnamese restraint seems remarkable. *See* Fallaci, *Two American POW's*, LOOK July 15, 1969 at 30, 32 ("The people of the village . . . could have killed me if they wanted to. In a way, I deserved it. I had destroyed their village . . . ."), *See also* RUSSELL TRIBUNAL, *supra* note 43, at 558; H. SALISBURY, *supra* note 162, at 139.
273. Art. 13, Geneva Prisoners of War Convention, *supra* note 10.
274. Dostler Case, 1 L. Rep. Trials War Crim. 22, 31 (U.N. War Crimes Comm'n, U.S. Mil. Comm'n, Rome 1945).
275. "Military necessity" is not used here in Professor McDougal's sense of one of the two fundamental complementary policies underlying the laws of warfare, see text accompanying note 49 *supra*, but rather in the narrower, more traditional meaning of a defense plea by an individual accused of violating a particular rule of warfare.
276. 8 L. Rep. Trials War Crim. 34, 66 (U.N. War Crimes Comm'n, U.S. Mil. Trib., Nuremberg 1948). *See also* Milch Trial, 7 L. Rep. Trials War Crim. 27, 44 (U.N. War Crimes Comm'n, U.S. Mil. Trib., Nuremberg 1947) (Musmanno, J., concurring).
277. Hostages Case, 8 L. Rep. Trials War Crim. 34, 69 (U.N. War Crimes Comm'n, U.S. Mil. Trib., Nuremberg 1948) (*quoting* art. 23(g) of the Annex to Hague Convention IV of 1907, cited *supra* note 82).
278. *E.g.*, art. 6(b) of the Nuremberg Charter, quoted in text *supra* note 7 (on the devastation of enemy property); art. 23(g) of Hague Convention IV, Annex, 1907, cited *supra* note 82 (on the destruction or seizure of enemy property).
279. *Cf.* J. STONE, LEGAL CONTROLS OF INTERNATIONAL CONFLICT 252 n.25 (1959).
280. Even this possible exception would be denied under traditional precedents; see text accompanying note 81 *supra*.

extent that this modification is in effect, it would be applicable in Vietnam, if at all, only to the killing of prisoners by American soldiers in combat zones. The United States certainly could not raise necessity as a defense to aerial bombardment, gas warfare, or the torturing or killing of prisoners of war by Americans or South Vietnamese troops. As for the killing of prisoners in combat zones, the exigencies of the immediate situation—the lack of a reasonable alternative, the inability to transport the prisoners out of the zone by helicopter, the danger to the captors of leaving wounded and disarmed prisoners alone in the jungle, for example—would have to be proved in justification.[281] Consequently, it is not at all clear that military necessity is a plausible defense in this type of situation.

C.   Superior Orders

The defense of obedience to superior orders is relevant to the service resister's suit because the United States may argue that soldiers in Vietnam and the resister himself when he is in Vietnam can not be guilty of war crimes if they are following orders. But this position simply misstates the law. If superor orders were a complete defense to the soldier who actually carries out an order to commit a war crime, then only the top commanders, in infinite regress, would ever be guilty of a war crime, and as Professor McDougal wryly observes, the elite would then claim the act-of-state doctrine to absolve themselves.[282] At the Nuremberg trials nearly every defendant claimed that he was acting under the express orders of Hitler and/or Himmler. Hardly a single war-crime conviction would have been possible if the defense of superior orders had been allowed. Yet in fact there were many convictions for war crimes involving all ranks of officers and soldiers as well as civilians.[283] The public little realizes how many war-crimes trials took place; the United States alone conducted 950 cases, trying 3,095 defendants of whom 2,647 were convicted.[284]

Although a soldier is trained to follow orders, he acts at his own peril if he obeys an order to commit a war crime. The Nuremberg Charter specifically provided that

---

281. This may be difficult to prove. It was testified at the Russell hearings that prisoners do not hinder American infantry from moving on since the infantry travels by helicopter anyway. RUSSELL TRIBUNAL, *supra* note 43, at 424.

282. McDOUGAL & FELICIANO, *supra* note 37, at 691.

283. *See, e.g.*, Belsen Trial, 2 L. Rep. Trials War Crim. 1 (U.N. War Crimes Comm'n, Brit. Mil. Ct., Luneburg 1945) (staff members of concentration camps).

284. J. APPLEMAN, MILITARY TRIBUNALS AND INTERNATIONAL CRIMES 267 (1954). In addition to the American military commissions, the following countries had their own military commissions trying war criminals: Australia, France, the Netherlands, Poland, Norway, Canada, China, Greece. Separate from, and in addition to these, were the Nuremberg and Tokyo Tribunals.

The fact that the defendant acted pursuant to order of his Government or of a superior shall not free him from responsibility, but may be considered in mitigation of punishment if the Tribunal determine that justice so requires.[285]

The judgments of the tribunal held that this provision correctly stated the international law on the subject.[286]   The charters and regulations of the Tokyo tribunal and of the various national military tribunals of the Allied powers included similar provisions.[287]   In *Levy v. Resor*,[288] the Army law officer allowed Levy to raise a war-crimes defense to the charge of willful disobedience of a superior order, thus recognizing that superior orders do not protect a soldier against personal jeopardy for a war-crimes conviction.   In brief, superior orders cannot be pleaded in exculpation but only in mitigation of a sentence,[289] and thus the service resister faced with such an argument in an American court can justifiably contend that he has no defense of superior orders.

D.   Ignorance of the Law

Although "ignorance of the law" is generally not allowed as a defense to criminal prosecutions, courts trying war crimes have been more liberal, recognizing that the pressure of military discipline makes it unreasonable to expect a soldier to adopt a questioning attitude to the legality of all his orders.   Such courts have used as standards of guilt actual knowledge or reason to know that the orders are unlawful.[290] Knowledge may be inferred in cases where the orders are manifestly or obviously unlawful—for example, orders to kill or torture prisoners of war.[291]   On the other hand, a soldier may have a defense of ignorance of the law on the legality of the use of napalm, since this is a difficult legal question even for scholars.   Notwithstanding these general principles, the present essay concerns a service resister who is claiming that he does not want to be put into a position where he may receive orders to commit war crimes in Vietnam.   Clearly he is not in ignorance of the law.   To him, even if not to the average soldier, there would be

---

285.   Art. 8, in 1 Trials Maj. War Crim. 12 (Int'l Mil. Trib. 1947).

286.   1 Trials Maj. War Crim. 224 (Int'l Mil. Trib. 1947).

287.   J. DINSTEIN, THE DEFENSE OF "OBEDIENCE TO SUPERIOR ORDERS" IN INTERNATIONAL LAW 156-64 (1965).

288.   See Note, 9 HARV. INT'L L.J. 169 (1968); FIELD MANUAL, *supra* note 9, at 182-83 (superior orders not a defense).

289.   Hostages Case, 8 L. Rep. Trials War Crim. 34, 74 (U.N. War Crimes Comm'n, U.S. Mil. Trib., Nuremberg 1948).   An extremely well documented summary of the rejection, in the national trials of war criminals after World War II, of the plea of superor orders as a reason for an a priori discharge of the defendants from criminal responsibility is given in J. DINSTEIN, *supra* note 287, at 194-95.

290.   Hostages Case, 8 L. Rep. Trials War Crim. 34, 50 (U.N. War Crimes Comm'n, U.S. Mil. Trib., Nuremberg 1948).

291.   McDOUGAL & FELICIANO, *supra* note 37, at 691-92 (citing cases).

criminal responsibility for carrying out such orders.

E. Duress

It is important to consider the viewpoints both of the average soldier in Vietnam and of the service resister with respect to the defense of duress. Duress, or the deprivation of any voluntary alternative to commission of an illegal act, is of course a defense to criminal prosecution under any legal system. War-crimes tribunals, however, have commonly required a high degree of compulsion for exemption from liability.[292] In the Krupp trial,[293] the United States Military Tribunal held that only the avoidance of a threatened serious and irreparable evil not disproportionately less grave than the act itself would support such a defense. Lacking the degree of compulsion required for exemption, the accused may plead duress in mitigation of his punishment.[294]

Like the doctrine of superior orders, the defense of duress obviously cannot apply in infinite regress so that only the commander-in-chief of the armies can be held guilty of a war crime. Thus, from the standpoint of the argument that war crimes are being committed in Vietnam, the defense of duress—though possibly applicable in some individual cases—cannot be used to excuse the commission of so many crimes. Although it is true that the United States Army may, upon considering duress, choose to prosecute some but not all of the soldiers and officers who are present at the time of the commission of war crimes,[295] it is clear that a crime was committed irrespective of whom the Army chooses to prosecute.

When we take the perspective of the service resister who argues that he himself may be placed in jeopardy of committing a war crime if sent to a combat zone in Vietnam where such crimes have been and are being committed, the analysis perforce becomes more complex. Considered in the abstract, the argument can be made that a service resister cannot legitimately maintain that assignment to Vietnam will place him in jeopardy of committing a war crime because he will know what acts are war crimes and can simply refrain from doing them. If he cannot refrain, because of duress, then it follows that he cannot be held criminally liable for his acts. However compelling in theory, such an argument is not convincing in the real-world context of military combat. In the first place, a soldier who gives in to the threat of summary court-

---

292. *Id.* at 693.

293. The Krupp Trial, 10 L. Rep. Trials War Crim. 69, 149 (U.N. War Crimes Comm'n, U.S. Mil. Trib., Nuremberg 1948). In this trial, all defendants except one were convicted.

294. The Flick Trial, 9 L. Rep. Trial War Crim. 1, 18-21 (U.N. War Crimes Comm'n, U.S. Mil. Trib., Nuremberg 1947).

295. N.Y. Times, Nov. 22, 1969, at 1, col. 2.

martial and execution by his commanding officer if he does not execute a prisoner of war, may later find, when prosecuted for his act, that he is unable to convince the court that he was under duress. His commanding officer may deny the allegation, other witnesses may not be available, and the court may look with general skepticism upon the defense of duress on the ground that a single commander of a platoon cannot physically coerce every man in his unit simultaneously to commit illegal acts. Second, if an American soldier who has committed a war crime is caught and tried by the *enemy* during the war, he may find it especially hard to prove to the court that he acted under duress. Third, a service resister may know in advance that a certain act would constitute a crime against the laws of war, but he may also believe that once placed in a military company where his fellow soldiers are committing such acts he will not or may not have the courage and fortitude necessary to refrain from such acts himself. A group psychology seems to animate combat units, making it unrealistic for a court in advance to proclaim that each soldier retains his individual will power at all times.[296] When the facts of the American massacre of the civilian inhabitants of Mylai hamlet in Songmy village in Vietnam became public, Mike Wallace interviewed veteran Paul Meadlo on the Columbia Broadcasting System:

> Q. It's hard for a good many Americans to understand that young, capable, American boys could line up old men, women and children and babies and shoot them down in cold blood. How do you explain that?
>
> A. I don't know.
>
> . . .
>
> Q. Why did you do it?
>
> A. Why did I do it? Because I felt like I was ordered to do it, and it seemed like that, at the time I felt like I was doing the right thing, because like I said I lost buddies. I lost a damn good buddy, Bobby Wilson, and it was on my conscience. So after I done it, I felt good, but later on that day, it was gettin' to me.[297]

At Songmy, the American troops had encountered little if any hostile fire, found virtually no enemy soldiers, and suffered only one casualty, apparently a self-inflicted wound.[298] Yet squad leader Sergeant Charles West told a *Life Magazine* reporter that

> The yanigans were doing most of the shooting. I call them yanigans because they were running around doing unnecessary shooting. In

---

296. *See* Shils & Janowitz, *Cohesion and Disintegration in the Wehrmacht in World War II*, 12 PUB. OPIN. Q. 280, 281 (1948); *cf.* D'Amato, *Psychological Constructs in Foreign Policy Prediction*, 11 J. CONFLICT RESOLUTION 294 (1967).

297. Transcript in N.Y. Times, Nov. 25, 1969, at 16, cols. 6, 8. Meadlo admitted killing "ten or fifteen" men, women, and children during the massacre. *Id.* at col. 3.

298. LIFE, Dec. 5, 1969, at 36.

a lot of cases they weren't even shooting at anything. Some were shooting at the hootches that were already burning, even though there couldn't possibly be anything alive in there. The guys were hollering about "slants." It wasn't just the young guys, older guys were shooting too. They might have been wild for a while, but I don't think they went crazy. If an individual goes crazy, you can't reason with him. Once everything was secured, everything did cease. If these men had been crazy, they would have gone on killing people.[299]

Both Paul Meadlo's and Charles West's descriptions give an impression of individual soldiers being swept up in the activities of the platoon, of a kind of group combat behavior for which it would be unrealistic to apply normal concepts of duress, intentionality, or individual self-control. Fourth, even though a soldier may successfully refrain from engaging in the commission of a war crime, if the other soldiers in his unit are violating the laws of warfare he may find himself accused of being an accomplice in the crime. Indeed there is some risk, particularly if he is tried by an enemy war-crimes court, that the court will infer that he took an active hand in the group criminal behavior. Fifth, a soldier may find that he is forced to participate in the commission of a war crime under the very real threat that if he does not participate he will be assigned to a combat post where there is a virtual certainty of being killed by the enemy.[300] Even assuming that the soldier could prove the existence of such a threat to a court, the court probably would not accept the threat as amounting to duress on the ground that the potential assignment to the hazardous combat post would in itself be within the legal discretion of the commander. Finally, it is difficult to be certain about what constitutes an "order" in a combat situation such that a soldier could afterwards clearly allege that he did what he was explicitly told to do under the threat of an immediate explicit penalty. Statements of participants in the Songmy massacre indicate the vagueness of the alleged orders to kill the civilian villagers.[301]

With all these considerations in mind, it is unreasonable to place faith on the possible defense of duress as fully protecting a soldier who

---

299. *Id.* at 43.

300. Former U.S. Infantry Specialist Fourth Class David Tuck testified at the Russell tribunal that American soldiers who disobey orders in Vietnam are sent "further out with the artillery outfit that had just been hard hit" in hopes that they will get killed. RUSSELL TRIBUNAL, *supra* note 43, at 421.

301. Ex-Sergeant Charles West told a *Life* reporter that Captain Medina related to his company that "the order was to destroy My Lai and everything in it." But then later West said, "Captain Medina didn't give an order to go in and kill women or children." LIFE, Dec. 5, 1969, at 39. Although these statements logically could both be true, their juxtaposition indicates the kind of confusion that may normally exist in the mind of each soldier. Moreover, each member of a squadron may have a different impression of what the order was. Ex-Private Meadlo said that "I felt I was ordered to do it." Quoted in text accompanying note 297 *supra*.

is placed into a war zone where war crimes are being committed by his fellow soldiers. Consequently, putting aside the questions of justiciability discussed in the following and final part of this Article, American courts ought to permit in-service and even draft resisters to raise offensively or as an affirmative defense the charge that they may be forced to commit war crimes in Vietnam.

IV

JUSTICIABILITY IN AMERICAN COURTS

Up to now for purposes of brevity we have referred in this essay to the service resister refusing orders to report for combat duty in Vietnam on the basis of his possible or probable implication in the commission of war crimes. Let us now view the complainant along a spectrum of possible fact situations.[302] An American soldier who refuses to obey an order to torture a prisoner of war would face no difficulties in defending himself before a court-martial. Clearly he would have a valid "Nuremberg defense" based on the argument that the international law of war crimes on this matter is part of American law,[303] that his military obligation is only to obey "lawful" orders,[304] that the order given him is unlawful, and that the so-called defense of superior orders is not available to him.[305] He would face no serious procedural hurdles nor any questions of justiciability.

To discuss the difficulties which aggrieved parties differently situated would have to meet, let us consider the case of a soldier trained in this country in the techniques of torturing prisoners of war and awaiting receipt of combat orders to report for duty in Vietnam as a member of a "Special Forces" interrogation unit.[306] He asks a federal court for

---

302. A range of possible cases may include: A civilian invoking the Nuremberg principles as an affirmative defense to justify his refusal of induction into the armed forces. *Cf.* United States v. Holmes, 387 F.2d 781 (7th Cir. 1967), *cert. denied,* 391 U.S. 936 (1968); Mitchell v. United States, 369 F.2d 323 (2d Cir. 1966), *cert. denied,* 386 U.S. 972 (1967). A civilian invoking Nuremberg as a defense against prosecution for counseling draft-evasion. *Cf.* United States v. Spock, 416 F.2d 165 (1st Cir. 1969). As a defense to prosecution for destroying draft records. *Cf.* United States v. Berrigan, 283 F. Supp. 336 (D. Md. 1968). As a defense in a court-martial prosecution for refusing to obey an order to report to Vietnam. *Cf.* United States v. Johnson, 18 U.S.C.M.A. 246, 38 C.M.R. 44 (1967). A civil action for injunction by a soldier seeking to avoid training other soldiers for actions that will involve war crimes. *Cf.* Noyd v. McNamara, 378 F.2d 538 (10th Cir.), *cert. denied,* 389 U.S. 1022 (1967). A soldier refusing combat orders based on a Nuremberg defense. *Cf.* Luftig v. McNamara, 373 F.2d 665 (D.C. Cir.), *cert. denied sub nom.* Mora v. McNamara, 389 U.S. 934 (1967).
303. See text accompanying notes 12-28 *supra.*
304. UNIFORM CODE OF MILITARY JUSTICE art. 92, 10 U.S.C. § 892 (1964).
305. FIELD MANUAL, *supra* note 9, at 182-83; text accompanying notes 282-89 *supra.*
306. See note 44 *supra.*

an injunction against the Secretary of Defense to stop the expected orders. First, he must state a possible claim. His claim would be that of a constitutional deprivation of due process of law under the fifth amendment on the ground that he would be placed in a combat situation where there is a significant probability that he will be implicated in the commission of a war crime. As will be recalled from the discussion of this point in the last section of this essay, the claimant may allege that if he is only obeying orders he will still be responsible, and even if he obeys such orders under duress he nevertheless will have to prove such duress as an affirmative defense, and will entail serious risk of being held responsible for the criminal delict in an American court or in a court of the enemy state. In addition, he can claim that it would be a violation of due process to be placed in a position where he may be forced to commit an immoral act even on the assumption that the fact of such coercion would absolve him from actual criminal liability. Even if he is not eventually tried by a court as a war criminal, he still would have committed the crime. The primary delict, to paraphrase *Marbury v. Madison*,[307] exists even though a court is unavailable to enforce it.

After stating a claim, the claimant would have to and should be able to meet certain procedural hurdles. He would have to allege and argue that a possible war-crimes conviction would deprive him of life, liberty, or reputation measurable at over the jurisdictional amount of 10,000 dollars.[308] He would also have to overcome the defense of sovereign immunity.[309] And he would have to convince the court not to dismiss his case on the ground that he must first exhaust his military remedies.[310] Finally, after overcoming these initial procedural hurdles, he would have to satisfy the court that he has standing, that the issue is ripe, and that the issues raised are justiciable.

A. Standing and Ripeness

The in-service resister and even the draft refuser have a very personal stake in the controversy because, for the reasons discussed in the

---

307. 5 U.S. (1 Cranch) 137 (1803).

308. 28 U.S.C § 1331(a) (1964). A correct phrasing of the "matter in controversy" should suffice for purposes of this statute. *See* Velvel, *The War in Viet Nam: Unconstitutional, Justiciable, and Jurisdictionally Attackable,* 16 KAN. L. REV. 449, 495-96 (1968). *See also* Giles v. Harris, 189 U.S. 475 (1903) (deprivation of federal rights by state officers); Note, *Draft Reclassification for Political Demonstrations—Jurisdictional Amount in Suits Against Federal Officers,* 53 CORNELL L. REV. 916 (1968).

309. Velvel, *supra* note 308, at 497-98.

310. He should argue that the interest in securing the proper resolution of these federal issues should outweigh the policy of ordinarily not interfering with the military. See Wolff v. Selective Service Local Bd. No. 16, 372 F.2d 817 (2d Cir. 1967); Hammond v. Lenfest, 398 F.2d 705 (2d Cir.), *rev'd per curiam on rehearing,* 398 **F.2d 718 (1968).**

previous section, they may be placed in jeopardy of becoming implicated in the commission of a war crime. Consequently, they should be able easily to meet the requirement of standing. The more difficult problem arises with respect to the issue of ripeness.

The draft resister is far from the combat situation in which he may be implicated in a war crime; the in-service resister is closer; and of course the soldier within that combat zone who refuses an order to commit a war crime is there, and has no "ripeness" problem at all. Where the claimant stands on the spectrum from potential draftee to combat soldier is of course a basic factor in a court's willingness to consider his case sufficiently ripe for adjudication. But even more important in deciding the issue of ripeness in a Nuremberg defense case is the court's willingness to recognize—in light of the realities of the American military situation—the difficulty of raising the claim as a serviceman in Vietnam. Clearly there is some degree of probability that even a potential draftee will wind up in a Vietnam combat zone.[311] Moreover, the probability is outside the claimant's own control, and hence the lack of ripeness that was indicated in the leading case of *United Public Workers of America v. Mitchell* is not present here.[312] Similarly, with respect to potential *enlistees*, it has been reported that promises of training assignments to applicants considering whether to enlist are routinely broken.[313] In a regimented military situation where the exigencies of training can preclude for long periods of time any contact with the world outside the training base, or where an order to report immediately to an airplane leaving for Vietnam can come without warning at any time, a soldier or even potential draftee must take advantage of any opportunity that arises to press his case. He may have only one good chance left. Courts should at least be willing to recognize that the claim presented may be the only physically possible opportunity for the claimant to have a judicial hearing on his allegations of deprivation of due process. In such a situation, the claimant's case is as "ripe" as it will ever be and the court should consider his case.

---

311. *See* United States v. Bolton, 192 F.2d 805 (2d Cir. 1951).

312. 330 U.S. 75 (1947). The Court wrote: "We can only speculate as to the kinds of political activity the *appellants desire* to engage in . . . ." (emphasis added).

313. *E.g.*, none of the fourteen defendants involved in the Presidio mutiny trial in San Francisco received the assignment he had expected. Private Roy Pulley was assured by his recruiter that he would be trained in fixed-wing aircraft maintenance, but wound up being trained as a helicopter machine-gunner. Barnes, *The Presidio "Mutiny"*, 161 NEW REPUBLIC, July 5, 1969, at 21, 22. Perhaps this sort of fraud in the inducement is militarily advantageous from the military's point of view in that embittered, calloused, disillusioned soldiers make better killers on the battlefield. If so, the practice should not come as a surprise.

B.   Political Question

Implicit to some extent in the previous discussion has been the question whether the issue the claimant raises is of the type that a federal court feels competent to adjudicate.   The Supreme Court has attempted to draw a line between the suitability of the plaintiff and the suitability of the issues, a line which at least is roughly workable for purposes of categorization.[314]   The only example of issue-adjudicability for cases originating in federal courts is the much-discussed doctrine of "political questions."

Courts have refused to adjudicate some cases involving Vietnam issues on the ground that they raise political questions.   The appellate court for the District of Columbia affirmed a dismissal of Robert Luftig's request for an injunction against the Secretary of Defense on the primary ground that his complaint that the American military effort in Vietnam was entirely illegal presented "political questions."[315]   The Supreme Court denied certiorari under the case name *Mora v. McNamara*, but Justices Douglas and Stewart filed substantial dissenting opinions.[316] A basic distinction between the *Mora* case and the situation envisaged in the present essay is that *Mora* involved the allocation of powers between President and Congress in engaging the United States in a war, whereas the present situation involves a result that neither Congress nor the President, jointly or severally, may authorize—depriving a citizen of due process of law.   In the *Steel Seizure Case*, despite the drama of a highly "political" issue, the doctrine of political questions did not bar the Supreme Court from stopping the President from doing what he had no legal power to do.[317]   In the situation envisaged in the present essay, the claim is that no branch of the government may constitutionally place the claimant in a position where there is a non-frivolous likelihood that he will be forced to participate or become implicated in criminal acts.

Even in cases where there have been adequate grounds for conceding plenary power to the legislative or executive branches, a substantial showing of impact upon the valued personal interests of the claimant has been enough to dissuade federal courts from invoking the doctrine of political questions.[318]   In support of this judicial tendency

---

314.   *See* Flast v. Cohen, 391 U.S. 83 (1968); Schwartz & McCormack, *The Justiciability of Legal Objections to the American Military Effort in Vietnam*, 46 TEX. L. REV. 1033 (1968).

315.   Luftig v. McNamara, 373 F.2d 664 (D.C. Cir. 1967), *aff'g* 252 F. Supp. 819 (D.D.C. 1966).

316.   389 U.S. 934 (1967).

317.   Youngstown Sheet & Tube Co. v. Sawyer, 343 U.S. 579 (1952).   *See Ex parte* Quirin, 317 U.S. 1, 25 (1942); Little v. Barreme (The Flying Fish), 6 U.S. (2 Cranch) 170 (1804).

318.   *See, e.g.,* Afroyim v. Rusk, 387 U.S. 253 (1967); Kennedy v. Mendoza-

an argument could be made that, since the possible future criminality of the claimant is involved, it would be a violation of due process of law for a court to exclude—by invocation of such a doctrine as "political questions"—the most highly relevant issues invoked by the claimant.[319]

Apart from the question of the allocation of powers among the three branches of the federal government, the doctrine of "political questions" as expressed in *Baker v. Carr* refers to the element of "judicially discoverable and manageable standards" for resolving a controversy.[320] In a basic sense the entire present essay has addressed itself to the problem of justiciability raised by this language in *Baker v. Carr*. We have attempted to show clear legal standards of the international law of war and the availability of evidence (appropriate to this *type* of case, as demonstrated in the many "Nuremberg" trials) that would make the controversy manageable by an American court. Consequently, the claims raised in a "Nuremberg defense" should be held justiciable in American courts.

CONCLUSION

In this Article we have attempted to establish first that the international laws of warfare are part of American law, and have argued that these laws, when taken as prohibitions of specific methods of waging war, are a practical and effective means of controlling unnecessary suffering and destruction. Second, we have analyzed these laws as they apply to treatment of prisoners of war, aerial bombardment of non-military targets, and chemical and biological warfare, and have marshalled a portion of the available evidence that American forces commit war crimes in Vietnam. Third, we have discussed the defenses of *tu quoque*, reprisal, military necessity, superior orders, ignorance of the law, and duress, and have concluded that a service resister can state a valid claim that his service in Vietnam may place him in substantial danger of being responsible for commission of war crimes. Finally, we have maintained that in-service and possibly draft resisters raising a "Nuremberg defense" have standing, and raise questions which are both ripe and justiciable.

Martinez, 372 U.S. 144 (1963); Greene v. McElroy, 360 U.S. 474 (1959); Reid v. Covert, 354 U.S. 1 (1957); Korematsu v. United States, 323 U.S. 214 (1944); United States *ex rel.* French v. Weeks, 259 U.S. 326 (1922).

319. If the claimant is a defendant in a criminal case (*e.g.*, refusing to obey induction or combat orders), he would clearly be deprived of due process if a court excluded the basic issues relevant to his defense on the doctrine of "political questions." *See* United States v. Sisson, 297 F. Supp. 902 (D. Mass. 1969) (Wyzanski, J.).

320. 369 U.S. 186, 217 (1962); *see* Scharpf, *Judicial Review and the Political Question: A Functional Analysis*, 75 YALE L.J. 517, 567-73 (1966).

By framing these issues in narrow, justiciable terms, we have attempted to show that American legal institutions can find a way to be responsive to matters which go to the heart of the American commitment to the rule of law in world affairs.

Conscience and Anarchy:
The Prosecution of War Resisters

JOSEPH L. SAX

The Justice Department . . . would be derelict in duty if it did not bring charges against these men—and all others—who openly violated a federal statute. To do less would be to condone anarchy.

Editorial, *New York Times*, January 8, 1968

THE recent indictments returned against Benjamin Spock and four others for conspiring to counsel and abet draft resistance are only the most prominent of a number of cases in which conscientious refusal to comply with the laws relating to military service are coming before the courts. Nearly a thousand men were sent to prison in 1967 for violation of the Selective Service laws, many of them for following the dictates of their consciences, and the numbers of prosecutions are rising at a rapid rate. Though many legal arguments have been put to the courts, almost none have prevailed except where the defendant has been able to show some technical violation of administrative procedures on the part of the Selective Service System. Arguments directed to the legality of the Vietnam war, as well as those based upon an asserted exercise of the right of free speech or a claim of conscientious objection to a particular war, are faring very badly in the courts.

Thus we are going to be increasingly confronted with a

claimed right to violate the law and escape conviction, a claim which may be made in form of an appeal to a criminal jury to nullify the law despite the contrary instructions of a judge, and thereby to repudiate both an unjust application of the law and an unjust governmental policy. At this prospect the editorial writers have already recoiled in horror. The way of civil disobedience is the way of anarchy, they solemnly intone, and millions nod their agreement. The virtues of unbending obedience to the law have not always seemed quite so obvious to Americans. The principle was not so clear in 1850, for example, when the Congress of the United States duly enacted a statute making it a crime punishable by fine and imprisonment to rescue or assist in the escape of a fugitive slave, for there was then "no lack of volunteers to help those [runaway slaves] who sought freedom . . . among them lawyers, doctors, and ministers."

In those days, it was not merely college leftists or radicals who spoke the language of resistance. Senator Salmon P. Chase chaired a meeting in Highland County, Ohio, which resolved that "disobedience to the enactment [of the Fugitive Slave Law] is obedience to God." The Common Council of Chicago adopted a resolution denouncing the Act and forbidding city policemen to render any assistance in its enforcement. Similar scenes were enacted throughout Ohio, Indiana, Michigan, and Illinois. William W. Patton, pastor of the Congregational Church in Hartford, Connecticut, preached a sermon in 1850 which was typical of what was being said in pulpits throughout the North:

Who is not proud of being an American; of dwelling in a land where men are bought and sold like swine in the pens, and where the Christian who ventures to aid the fugitive from bondage is fined a thousand dollars and imprisoned six months?
We owe no allegiance to such a law, and whoever else may regard it, we shall treat it as a nullity as far as possible.

Nor was public outrage at the law limited to rhetorical opposition. While courts and officials were friendly to the claims of slave owners, who had the law behind them, public feeling against the Fugitive Slave Laws ran deep. In Boston, when a runaway slave was seized and brought before the court, a crowd "collected and rescued the prisoner . . . and hurried him through the square . . . they went off toward Cambridge, the crowd driving along with them and cheering as they went." In Syracuse, a number of prominent citizens participated in the rescue of a fugitive slave; "Eighteen citizens were indicted, [but] such was the sentiment of the community that prosecutions were unavailing." This was the typical response in Northern cities, and one may wonder how many of our contemporaries would have stood ready to commit those civil disobedients to jail, or to say of them, as it has been so casually said of Doctor Spock and his fellow defendants, "they have no right to expect to be exemplary martyrs without suffering some degree of martyrdom. No cross, no crown."

Indeed those who find the argument for civil disobedience so at odds with the principles of civilized society might ask themselves how they would vote as jurymen in a typical mercy killing prosecution, where the tormented defendant ends the life of a wife or child whose continued suffering he can no longer endure. Similarly, those who believe that we must convict to preserve "a government of law rather than of men" might usefully remind themselves that it is men and not law that determines whether prosecutions will be initiated against persons such as Doctor Spock; and, one must add, the decision makers are not exactly disinterested men at that.

Moreover, one wonders how many of those who deplore civil disobedience have forgotten that one of the most important controversies in Anglo-American legal history was fought over the right of a defendant to argue that he was morally entitled to an acquittal, though every judge in the nation would find him guilty. During the eighteenth century in England, the government made liberal use of two crimes against its political opponents—treason and seditious libel. Though there was considerable popular sentiment opposed to prosecutions aimed at repressing conscientious dissent and protest, the government was undaunted, and the judiciary upheld laws prohibiting a wide variety of anti-government conduct.

Lawyers for the defendants in such cases argued that the public, speaking through a jury, was not bound to enforce the law as laid down by the judges, but should make an independent conscientious decision whether the defendant's conduct should be treated as a crime. The issue came to a head in 1783 with the prosecution of William Davies Shipley, the Dean of St. Asaph, for seditious libel. Shipley, "one of a great many respectable gentlemen, who, impressed with the dangers impending over the public credit of the nation exhausted by a long war," published a pamphlet which, it was charged, was designed to promote rebellion.

Shipley was represented by one of the most distinguished and eloquent members of the English bar, Thomas Erskine, who sought to put the question of justification to the jury, and to urge them of their right to nullify a judge's rulings if they believed that in justice the defendant was entitled to an acquittal. But Mr. Justice Buller, the presiding magistrate, adamantly refused to adopt this view and instructed the jury that they had nothing to do with the case except to find whether the defendant in fact published the pamphlet, and that it was for the court to decide upon the criminality of his conduct:

the question for you to decide is, Whether he is or is not guilty of publishing this pamphlet? . . . there is no contradiction as to the publication; and if you are satisfied with this in point of fact, it is my duty to tell you in point of law you are bound to find the defendant guilty.

Though the judge was firm in his ruling, he nonetheless permitted Erskine to argue to the jury that "they therefore call upon you to pronounce that guilt, which they forbid you to examine into. . . . Thus without inquiry into the only circumstance which can constitute guilt, and without meaning to find the defendant guilty, you may be seduced into a judgment which your consciences may revolt at, and your speech to the world deny. . . . I shall not agree that you are therefore bound to find the defendant guilty unless you think so likewise."

The significance of the role given to the jury was soon demonstrated, for the verdict they returned in the Dean of St. Asaph's case was the unconventional one, "guilty *only* of publishing." This led to an extraordinary interchange between Justice Buller, Erskine, and the jury. The judge told the jury that such a verdict was not correct, but that they must generally decide whether they found the defendant guilty. But this the jury refused to do, apparently responding to Erskine's plea that a simple guilty verdict would represent a determination of criminality, which the judge had told them they were not entitled to make. At the same time, the jury made clear it was not willing wholly to thwart the judge's direction, and, after some pressure from the bench, acquiesced in the recording of a verdict of "guilty of publishing, but whether a libel or not the jury do not find."

Ultimately, Shipley was released upon the technical ground that the indictment against him was defective, but the question raised in his case promoted a controversy which raged for nearly a decade thereafter, until it was resolved, in accordance with the principle for which Erskine had argued, by the enactment of Fox's Libel Law in 1792. The extensive debates in Parliament over the bill demonstrated quite clearly that the issue was whether the defendant was entitled to appeal to the jury for acquittal upon a principle which no formal lawmaker—legislature or judge—would accept, and thereby to recognize the propriety of what we would call civil disobedience. Thus in the debate in the House of Commons, one member, speaking in support of the bill, referred to the famous case of the Seven Bishops, where the Court had left the question of criminality to the jury, recalling that "two of the judges made no difficulty in declaring that the petition which they presented was a libel; but the jury acquitted them. Such was the excellence of our constitution, which provided a check against the influence of bad judges, in bad times."

Of course the issue was not formally put in terms of the jury's right to nullify the law. Lawyers argued the more technical issue whether the alleged seditious nature of the publication was a question of law or of fact, or (that marvellous invention of attorneys) a mixed question of law and fact. Thus the problem was often put as merely the traditional question of proper allocation of functions between the judge and the jury, rather than as a debate over the jury's right to nullify the law. And as a technical lawyer's question, the controversy could be viewed in that limited sense. But seen in its overall historical and political perspective, it is clear that a much bigger principle was at stake —whether the jury could be told that it had a right to refuse to enforce the law of seditious libel. That underlying issue was expressly laid bare in the debates by members like Earls Camden and Stanhope who referred to "the right of the jury to take both the law and the fact in their own hands" so that "juries might go according to their consciences in the law." It was the purpose of the bill to recognize the legitimacy of such conduct, they indicated, for though "some juries were found resolute enough to disregard the instruction, and find a verdict for the defendant, others were overawed by the presence and perhaps the menaces of a magistrate robed, learned and dignified, and found a verdict against their consciences."

The enactment of Fox's Libel Law was an explicit acceptance of those views; and its consequence, as Lord John Russell made explicit some years later in his *History of the English Government and Constitution,* was to permit

the verdicts of juries to check the execution of a cruel or oppressive law, and in the end to repeal or modify the law itself. . . . Thus, not only are juries in fact the real judges in England, but they possess a power no judge would venture to exercise, namely, that of refusing to put the law in force. . . . It has been the cause of amending many bad laws which judges would have administered with exact severity, and defended with professional bigotry.

A similar development took place in America. In the trial of John Peter Zenger for seditious libel in 1735, the role of the jury was much controverted, and counsel argued "the right of the jury to find such a verdict as they in their conscience do think is agreeable to the evidence." And in referring to the case of the Seven Bishops, counsel said, "How unhappy might it have been for all of us at this day if that jury . . . had left it to the Court to judge whether the Petition of the Bishops was or was not a libel? No, they took it upon them, to their immortal honor to determine both law and fact . . . and therefore found them Not Guilty." The jury then brought in a verdict of not guilty, "Upon which," according to Zenger, "there were three huzzas in the Hall, which was crowded with people, and the next day I was discharged from my imprisonment."

It was not only counsel for defendants who advocated the right of jury nullification, but the founders of the nation themselves. For example, in 1771 John Adams said of the juror that "it is not only his right, but his duty . . . to find the verdict according to his own best understanding, judgment, and conscience, though in direct opposition to the direction of the court." And Alexander Hamilton said in 1804 that the jury in a criminal case is duty bound to acquit, despite the instruction of the judge, "if exercising their judgment with discretion and honesty they have a clear conviction that the charge of the court is wrong." Until 1835 the federal courts in America time and again specifically instructed juries that they were the judges both of the law and the fact in a criminal case, and were not bound by the opinion of the court.

This history is useful because it reveals an intermediate position between the usual philosophical poles of debate over civil disobedience. For it neither adopts the view that every man shall be the ultimate judge of his own conduct, nor does it hold that a conviction is required in every prosecution where the defendant has violated a law that judges say is valid. Rather it indicates the ability of a viable legal system to accommodate itself to those situations in which violation of the law should be viewed as justifiable. Upon reflection it should be clear that such a notion meets some very important needs in a legal system.

For example, it is a much admired tenet of judicial theory that not every unjust law is necessarily unconstitutional. No doubt that is a sound principle of judicial administration; but it does not tell us what *is* to be done about unfair and unjust prosecutions.

In the ordinary case, we have relied upon the good sense of

prosecutors to refrain from pursuing those causes where rigorous enforcement of the law might produce unjust results. Of course there are many such cases—as where a thwarted girl friend charges statutory rape, or a domestic quarrel gets out of hand and one spouse assaults the other. In such situations the disparity between law and justice is generally resolved by a decision not to prosecute. Our substantial reliance on such restraint to keep the criminal system working with reasonable equity has made us forget something that our legal forebears knew very well—that there is a class of cases in which the government cannot be relied upon to exercise ordinary restraint: those cases in which the men in power at a particular time are themselves the "victims" of the crime. It is no accident that the historical development I described earlier arose in the context of so-called crimes against the state, such as seditious libel and treason. Indeed, this very point was raised during the parliamentary debates on Fox's Libel Law, where the right of the jury to take the law into its own hands was said to be needed precisely because seditious libel cases involved "censures upon public men and the acts of government" and there was therefore a special danger of "political craft and oppression . . . perverting justice." Nor is it an accident that in our own time the cases in which the disparity between law and justice is most sharply illuminated are those in which the defendant's real crime is his challenge to the traditional authority of governmental officials—such as harassing prosecutions against civil rights workers in the South.

Another traditional protection for defendants is also likely to be absent in prosecutions for political offenses. This is the frequent willingness of a court to stretch its interpretations to prevent an undesirable result, a practice which has led to the proposition that "hard cases make bad law." However inclined a court might be in ordinary cases to interpret the law generously for a defendant's benefit, that inclination cannot but be very sharply reduced when a policy to which the government is deeply committed is at stake. It is, after all, not very likely that a court, in the midst of a war, will declare that war illegal.

We are inclined to look upon contemporary courts as a solid

bastion of civil liberties, but it is well to remember that judicial enunciation and application of libertarian doctrines have often come considerably after the heat of political passion has died down. It took a good many years for the Supreme Court to turn away from the excessive preoccupation with subversion which characterized the McCarthy period; the liberalism of the 'sixties was of little aid to the victims of the 'fifties. Similarly, development of the First Amendment's free speech provision came too late for those who were prosecuted during the fear-filled days of the First World War period; the stirring judicial language we remember today came from cases in which the Court in fact upheld the convictions. Nor did the judiciary stop the uprooting of Japanese-American citizens in World War Two, or the sedition prosecutions of a century and a half earlier. We are perhaps too much moved by the glamor which surrounds the Court's boldness in the civil rights area, which, while commendable, did not take place in a context of intense hostility from the other branches of the federal government; the problem of the political prosecution did not have to be faced.

One can certainly sympathize with a court which is reluctant to enter any such fray; indeed we even have a technical term that helps courts avoid such decisions—the "political question" doctrine. However much one appreciates the situation of a court, the fact remains that the defendant in such a case is likely to find himself at a considerable disadvantage.

Still another difficulty with looking to the judiciary for full adequacy of justice is created by the legal doctrine that courts should decide cases only on the precise record before them. This, too, is an appropriate general rule of judicial adminstration, but one which can present serious problems in a politically motivated prosecution. For example, in the case of the harassing prosecution against the civil rights worker for trespass or loitering, the facts relating to the precise issue before the court may be perfectly neutral; but the surrounding context may indicate a pattern of intense effort by local officials to find such persons committing minor violations of a kind which are practically unavoidable. Thus, in such a situation, the general context may indicate a use of the law by local officials to thwart efforts to bring those very officials to task for their derelictions.

To be sure, juries are to some extent responsive to considerations of context even under the present system and do grant acquittals against the law, as Kalven and Zeisel have shown in their recent study of jury behavior. The examples of jury revolt which they found, however, were largely in cases where the stakes were rather trivial and the statutes themselves were not highly regarded by the public, such as game laws, gambling, or moonshining; or where the defendant makes a particularly sympathetic impression. In general, though, they find the jury's power of nullification little used, and the explanation they give for this restraint is precisely responsive to the observations being made here. They say that "perhaps one of the reasons the jury exercises its very real power so sparingly is because it is officially told it has none." The issue is whether there is a need to expand the criminal defendant's opportunity to make a broader appeal to the community's sense of justice in those cases where at present both juries and the larger public which they represent feel obliged to follow the judge's instruction and convict.

Were this additional right of appeal recognized, no one can say how much impact it would have on the criminal process. The reference made earlier in this article to the colloquy between jury, judge, and counsel in the Dean of St. Asaph's case (examples of which can be found in other seditious libel prosecutions of that period) suggests that the jury is significantly affected by the extent to which they believe they are, or are not, free to disregard judicial views of the law and to implement their own sense of justice. Kalven and Zeisel agree that a jury's behavior is affected by its view of the authority it has, though they note the difficulty of demonstrating that proposition.

Obviously no change in legal rules would be likely to be of much avail to the harassed civil rights worker in the South, where public passions are very strong, or in the case of a law such as Prohibition, which was almost universally condemned and disregarded by the public. But a willingness to acknowledge the appropriateness of nullifying prosecutorial overreaching may very well have an impact on the government's readiness to prosecute in situations such as that of Vietnam war resisters, where public opinion is widely divergent.

Moreover, it is important to recognize that the comments made here are not directed simply to the question of jury behavior in individual cases. What is really at stake is the general public attitude toward vigorous dissent of a kind which goes beyond the limits of judicially acceptable protest. The readiness of the general public to accept the notion that such protestors have a right to argue, and to have accepted, the justness of their conduct, is a critical indicator of society's view about the relation between the government and the people; it measures the ability to perceive a difference between the citizen's obligation to the demands of the individuals who hold public office at a particular time, and to the principles upon which his nation was founded. Those two concepts may not often be at odds; but a willingness to recognize that they may be, and that vigorous forms of protest may be appropriate to bring them back into alignment, is an important measure of the underlying political philosophy of a society. That distinction was openly recognized and debated in England at a time and in circumstances to which we now look back as representative of a great moment in the development of individual liberty. The current prosecutions against war resisters pose a similar challenge to us.

To be sure, a philosophy which authorizes acquittal in the case of an unjust prosecution may operate to produce the same result when popular passions are misdirected and it is the government which stands on the side of justice; the reference to prosecutions against civil rights workers necessarily brings to mind the converse situation, where Southern juries have used the power of nullification to acquit persons guilty of crimes against civil rights advocates. It is well to remember, though, that such acquittals occurred under the present law, where juries were exercising their naked power, rather than any right to acquit. Unless we are to return to the seventeenth-century practice of penalizing juries which bring in erroneous verdicts, there is no legal means to prevent unjust acquittals where overwhelming popular passion prevails, and the preceding comments are not going to affect that phenomenon in any event.

The relevant question, therefore, is whether a change in the concept of the jury function is likely to lead to a significant increase in the number of unjust acquittals. History is certainly against the notion. There is no evidence of any such result when the right of jury nullification was recognized either in England or the United States. It was widely observed that the enactment of Fox's Libel Act in 1792, which was the culminating victory of those who wanted to enlarge the jury's function, did not impede the government in obtaining criminal convictions. And fifteen years after the passage of the Act, it was reported in the parliamentary debates that "notwithstanding it had been declared by magistrates of the greatest learning that the establishment of such a system would produce infinite confusion and disorder . . . the functions of judges and juries have been executed within their respective limits . . . to the advancement of justice and to the dignity of its administration."

Certainly there is little reason to believe that juries would be long inclined to let persons walk the streets whose freedom genuinely jeopardized the community. Even from Southern juries, for all their passionate feeling on the race question, convictions are beginning to be obtained more frequently. Since there has been no change in the legal status of the jury role, they are no doubt responding, in varying degrees, to a fear that violence and vigilantism were getting out of hand, to the adverse economic impact on their community of the image of lawlessness, to a genuine moderation of racial attitudes, and to an increasing sense that the federal government was serious in its desire to obtain convictions, and was not simply going through the motions. These are substantive considerations of a rather high order, and it is difficult to believe that as they mount in the direction of encouraging deserved convictions, a change in the legal rules is going to outweigh them.

This is perhaps an indirect way of noting that the fear of unjust acquittals is directed almost exclusively to conduct which is violent and seriously antisocial by its very nature, whereas the conduct at stake in the political prosecutions which are at issue here is generally directed to acts that are rather trivial (such as trespass); or are largely symbolic in their nature, and usually at the periphery of free speech; or urge passive resistance as a means to press for changes in the law. Thus, the self-interest of the community in convicting those who engage in violent acts is inevitably strong, and the risks of unjust acquittals in such situations is both lesser and of less concern to the maintenance of the social order than is the risk to be apprehended from authorizing the just acquittal.

In this sense, it is probably not even appropriate to view the issue as whether we should recognize the justness of permitting the law to be violated; rather, it is whether the legal system ought to expand somewhat to recognize a broader spectrum of rights through which citizens can protest against allegedly unjust laws, rights which go beyond the conventional confines of free speech. The legal system should stand ready to accommodate some degree of advocacy of passive resistance (to the draft, for example) as an appropriate means for testing public feeling about the administration of that law, or about the underlying policies that call that law into play. It is by no means likely, as many seem to assume, that a society which permits such conduct will collapse. Indeed, such fears on the part of English lawmakers and judges in the eighteenth century about the potential effects of seditious utterances, which they held as firmly as do our contemporary critics of resistance tactics, have been proved erroneous.

It is time for us to come to terms with our own contemporary version of the seditious libel problem, and recognize, as our forebears did, that it will sometimes be necessary to protest an unjust law by violating it and putting the question of justification to one's fellow citizens. It was not at all obvious to them, as it apparently is to many of our contemporaries, that one had all the protection one might need in petitioning the legislature to repeal a law, or asking a judge to make a ruling of invalidity.

They thought resistance and nullification were tools that would sometimes have to be used to persuade a captious government that it was misguided. Our fellow citizens who think a resistance movement is the resort only of anarchists ought to listen to Theophilus Parsons, speaking to the Massachusetts Constitutional Convention in 1788:

Let him be considered as a criminal by the general government, yet only his fellow-citizens can convict him; they are his jury, and if they pronounce him innocent, not all the powers of Congress can hurt him; and innocent they certainly will pronounce him, if the supposed law he resisted was an act of usurpation.

Those who think resisters are tearing at the fabric of the society might wish to consider the possibility that a society is best able to survive if it permits a means for taking an issue back to the public over the heads of public officialdom; when it recognizes that a government may have so implicated itself in a wretched policy that it needs to be extricated by popular repudiation in a forum more immediately available—and less politically compromised—than the ballot box.

Nuremberg Law and U.S. Courts

BEVERLY WOODWARD

The Court: You see the case, Mr. Mitchell, as far as the law is concerned, is a relatively simple case. . . .
Defendant Mitchell: I do not agree that the issues of my defense are clearcut and simple. I think they involve many things—Nuremberg trials, international law, conventions on war crimes and torture and genocide, et cetera. . . .
Mr. Owens [prosecutor]: . . . . I think we could get far afield if we are allowed to introduce various philosophies, etc. that are not pertinent to the case.

—From *Transcript of Proceedings, U.S. vs. David Henry Mitchell, III.*
U.S. District Court, District of Connecticut, Sept. 8, 13-15, 1965.

IT HAS BEEN over three years since the young draft resister, David Henry Mitchell, III, launched his effort to persuade our courts to enforce the principles of international law proclaimed at Nuremberg. Unfortunately, that effort has not been a particularly successful one. Nor have the subsequent legal battles, initiated by others who believe American action in Vietnam to be in violation of international law, had much greater success. True, in the cases of Captain Howard Levy and of the Fort Hood Three, American courts did take some steps toward confronting the extremely important questions first raised by Mitchell. We now know that not every judge in the land (when faced with a case of noncooperation with the military) will brush aside a defense based on the Nuremberg Charter and judgment with the label of "irrelevant." But we have yet to see anything like a "full-scale" Nuremberg defense presented to and weighed by either a civilian or a military court. Nor is this surprising. The obstacles, both political and legal, to such a "self-judgment" of the nation seem to many insurmountable. In fact, one can conclude without contradiction that the issues raised by Mitchell were altogether "relevant" to his defense and yet not justiciable in our courts or for that matter in any existing court. Such a conclusion is admittedly not very satisfying. One is not inclined

to let the matter rest there; for it indicates that our constitutional system is, for the time being at least, incapable of coming to grips with the central problems of our time.

Before reaching conclusions, let me state the problem. Although the cases of David Mitchell, Captain Levy, and the Fort Hood Three are quite familiar in some circles, it is probably true that the details of these cases are not widely known. What, then, did these men contend and how did our courts respond to their contentions? And what links these three cases together?

The second question can be answered with one word: Nuremberg. At the end of World War II the United States and its allies (calling themselves the United Nations) made an agreement to try the "major war criminals of the European Axis countries." Though numerous observers considered the Nuremberg trials nothing better than examples of the vengeance that the victor will wreak upon the vanquished, supporters of the trials held quite different views. In their eyes the trials were an effort to establish firmly certain principles of international law which had been proclaimed or implied in declarations and treaties made between the two world wars, but which until that time had not been enforced. The major principle to be established was that the initiation and the waging of an aggressive war constituted crimes under international law, and that these were crimes for which individuals could be held accountable. As America's representative Mr. Justice Jackson said at the time:

> Repeatedly, nations have united in abstract declarations that the launching of an aggressive war is illegal. They have condemned it by treaty. But now we have the concrete application of these abstractions. . . . [And he declared further that] if certain acts in violations of treaties are crimes, they are crimes whether the United States does them or whether Germany does them, and we are not prepared to lay down a rule of criminal conduct against others which we would not be willing to have invoked against us.

The cases of David Mitchell, Captain Levy, and the Fort Hood Three, then, involved three attempts to test the force of Justice Jackson's declaration. They all were attempts to show that the United States' actions in Vietnam render it guilty of one or more of the three categories of crimes enumerated by the Charter of the Nuremberg tribunal: crimes against peace, war crimes, and crimes against humanity. In each case the contention was proffered as a defense against a charge of having refused to obey some order: Mitchell had refused to report for induction, Captain Levy had refused to train medics in the United States Special Forces, and the three Army privates known as the Fort Hood Three had refused to board a plane bound for Vietnam. (The last case is complicated because it involves both a suit and a court-martial. The three men were ordered to board the plane shortly after having brought a suit against the Army to prevent it from shipping them to Vietnam; the Army's action thus resulted in their being court-martialed before their suit could be heard.)

As might be imagined, such contentions did not receive a friendly hearing in our courts. In fact, it was only Captain Levy who was allowed to present evidence to support his position (and that evidence was later held to be insufficient to prove his claims).[1] In the case of the court-martial of the Fort Hood Three the Army law officer ruled out of order the argument that the war in Vietnam is illegal with the statement: "I rule that it is a matter of law, that the war in Vietnam is legal, and I forbid you to argue that it isn't." Mitchell was also not allowed to present evidence supporting his contentions as to the nature of the war. Instead, he was told that such evidence was "immaterial and irrelevant" as a defense to the charge brought against him. In a self-justifying statement issued after Mitchell's first trial, the judge expressed himself on this matter rather strongly. He said:

> Leaving aside the sickening spectacle of a 22-year-old citizen of the United States seizing the sanctuary of a nation dedicated to freedom of speech to assert such tommyrot and leaving aside the transparency of his motives for doing so, the decisive point is that such political or philosophical views, even if sincerely entertained, are utterly irrelevant as a defense to the charge of willful refusal to report for induction in the armed forces of the United States. . . .

Nevertheless, Mitchell and the Fort Hood Three (Dennis Mora, David Samas, and James Johnson) were given some support when their cases reached the Supreme Court. Although the Court refused to review these cases, the decisions were not unanimous. In

---

[1] Captain Levy (unlike the defendants in the other cases mentioned here) charged the government not with crimes against peace or crimes against humanity, but with war crimes. Of the three categories of crimes enumerated in the Nuremberg Charter, this category was the most firmly established in international law. Moreover, there exists in national military law the necessary "machinery" for prosecuting individual military men who are believed to have committed a war crime. This may account in part for the fact that Captain Levy was permitted to raise the "war crimes" issue. However, his accusation was not that certain individuals were guilty of committing war crimes, but that the government was supporting the commission of war crimes *as a matter of policy*. Clearly the political obstacles to holding that such a charge is correct are much greater than in the case involving the individual military man.

Mitchell's case Mr. Justice Douglas dissented, and when the suit instituted by the Fort Hood Three reached the Supreme Court Mr. Justice Stewart added his dissent to that of Justice Douglas. In the Mitchell case Mr. Justice Douglas presented a list of five questions which he contended the Court was called upon to answer in spite of their "extremely sensitive and delicate" nature. These questions were:

(1) whether the Treaty of London [which includes the Charter of the Nuremberg tribunal] is a treaty within the meaning of Art. VI, cl. 2 [of our constitution]; (2) whether the question as to the waging of an aggressive "war" is in the context of this criminal prosecution a justiciable question; (3) whether the Vietnam episode is a "war" in the sense of the Treaty; (4) whether petitioner has standing to raise the question; (5) whether, if he has, it may be tendered as a defense in this criminal case or in amelioration of punishment.

[In addition Justice Douglas stated] There is a considerable body of opinion that our actions in Vietnam constitute the waging of an aggressive "war," . . . . Even those who think that the Nuremberg judgments were unconstitutional by our guarantee relating to *ex post facto* laws would have to take a different view of the Treaty of London that purports to lay down a standard of future conduct for all the signatories.

When Mr. Justice Stewart dissented from the refusal to hear the case of the Fort Hood Three, he said: "There exist in this case questions of great magnitude. Some are akin to those referred to by Mr. Justice Douglas in Mitchell *v.* United States. . ." (Then he went on to mention certain other questions in the case, questions relating to the constitutionality of an undeclared war.) In sum, both justices agreed that the question of the war's status under international law, and particularly with reference to the principles enunciated and enforced at Nuremberg, was a question of the first importance for the judiciary.

But even though this question and others related to it are without doubt of the first importance, it is questionable whether the judiciary can at present come to grips with them in any kind of satisfactory way. Some of the principal difficulties involved are discussed below.

THE CENTRAL CONTENTION of the defendants in the cases I am discussing was that they would be guilty of complicity in crime if they obeyed the particular order that had been issued to each of them. But that contention had an obverse side. At the same time they asserted that the orders issued to them were *invalid*, principally on the grounds that it is a violation of due process to compel any individual to commit an illegal act.[2] Theirs were therefore cases of what I have elsewhere labeled "civil challenge." That is, they all had violated some command on the grounds that the command was without validity and they had done so with the hope of being vindicated in the courts and thereby influencing public policy. If they had won their cases, the effect would have been considerable. Mitchell, for example, sought nothing less than to bring the war in Vietnam to an end by having the draft declared invalid when used as an instrument in the prosecution of that war

Already the problems begin to manifest themselves. They are both of a technical and a political nature. First, the political problems: Can the judiciary which has neither the power of "the sword or the purse" effectively bring a war to an end? Can it even exert an

---

[2] In addition, some defendants, such as Mitchell, have argued that even though a given command does not create complicity in crime, it may still be invalid if it results from or supports action which is in violation of the Constitution and/or of international law.

Professor Roger Fisher of the Harvard Law School has suggested to me that it is plausible to argue that a command or law is invalid if it places the individual in the position of committing an illegal act, whether he obeys the law or command or whether he disobeys it. This, in effect, was the position taken by the defendants in the cases being discussed.

effective impact on the way in which an ongoing war is conducted? What would be the actual result of a ruling by the Supreme Court favorable to the defendant in a case such as one of these? Would the Executive acquiesce to a ruling which crippled its powers to wage a particular war or would we have chaos and a breakdown of civil order?

It is difficult to answer such questions before the event. They do, however, make understandable the efforts of our courts, and particularly the Supreme Court, to avoid making the experiment. The Court has recently suffered a barrage of abuse for actions and judgments that were considerably less adventurous. Not that action by the Court is impossible. But I do wish to indicate that no matter how compelling a case might be made that the United States is involved in an aggressive and illegal war, the Court might hesitate a long moment before making such a ruling.

The technical problems have to do with definitions. To ascertain the existence of complicity in a crime, one must be able to define the crime and to define what constitutes complicity in it. In this case that means having criteria for determining the existence of the three kinds of crime enumerated in the Nuremberg Charter and having criteria for identifying complicity in such crimes. But such criteria are lacking. Mitchell, for example, argued that since the armed forces are engaged in at least one illegal enterprise (whatever their other activities may be), he would be guilty of complicity were he even to submit to induction. His critics, on the other hand, argue that no ordinary soldier was tried at Nuremberg. Individual responsibility was meant to apply only to the leaders, not to run-of-the-mill draftees (let alone to draftees who didn't even fight in the war).

Yet Mitchell could reply:

That's what they did at that trial. How do I know what they will do at the next one? Let's look at the statement of the "Nuremberg Principles,"[3] as formulated by the International Law Commission of the United Nations. They state that "complicity in a crime against peace . . . is a crime under international law," and they include in their definition of a crime against peace the "waging of a war of aggression. . . ." I don't see them saying anywhere that only those in the highest positions are capable of "waging a war of aggression."[4]

Mitchell's assertion that he might be guilty of complicity if he accepted induction into the Army was complemented by his assertion that the order to report for induction was invalid. It was invalid, he argued in part, because the draft is at present an essential instrument in the prosecution of an illegal war. The United States Court of Appeals for the Second Circuit, which made the final ruling in Mitchell's case, replied to this argument by stating that "whatever action the President may order, or the Congress sanction," cannot impair the constitutional power of Congress to raise and support armed forces.

The Court's ruling, though, seems altogether too sweeping. Do the judges really mean *whatever* action the President may order? Or would they concede that the "Nuremberg Principles" support the *legal* correctness of the position of the young man who refused to go into Hitler's army (apart from the assumed moral correctness of his position)? If so, then is it correct to say that the President may order the armed forces to commit *any action whatsoever* without impairing Congress's constitutional power to draft an army? Was not Mitchell correct when he said, " 'Providing for the common defense' is not a license for crime. . . ," implying that a power which is used in that way must perhaps be revoked?

---

[3] The "Nuremberg Principles" were formulated by the International Law Commission at the request of the United Nations General Assembly. They are considered by many commentators to be highly authoritative guides with regard to the international legal obligations of the individual.

[4] A draft resister might also argue, and Mitchell did, that he should not be compelled to contribute to an illegal enterprise whether or not he might be held guilty of complicity for doing so.

Of course, it is possible that the United States is not involved in an aggressive war and it is possible that even if it is, that fact would not be sufficient grounds for invalidating the draft. But that does not eliminate the theoretical problems that Mitchell has raised.[5] *If* American actions in Vietnam are aggressive and illegal, then there must be some orders which are invalid (either because they result from or support unconstitutional action or because they create complicity). And there must be some who are accomplices.

Perhaps the Fort Hood Three were right in drawing the line at the point when they were ordered to go to Vietnam. Or perhaps it is at some later point of involvement that one becomes an accomplice. In any case the courts have failed so far to provide any kind of satisfactory criteria, and so have the jurists who formulated the "Nuremberg Principles."

Efforts to provide authoritative definitions of the crimes enumerated in the Nuremberg Charter have fared no better than efforts to define complicity in those crimes. Those who have followed the proceedings of the United Nations are well aware that there is no agreement concerning the meaning of the term "aggression." It is less well known, yet equally true, that the terms "war crimes" and "crimes against humanity" also have been given widely varying interpretations. It is apparent that only a few scholars wish to define these terms as precisely as possible. Those who are politically active prefer to use them—and abuse them—for polemical purposes.

In fact, if we think about it for a moment it becomes evident that the difficulties I have been calling technical are in reality largely political. Definitions of political crimes have to be politically acceptable definitions. Unfortunately, existing political realities militate against the acceptance of common definitions just as much as they do against the application of such definitions. These realities have probably not been given sufficient attention by those who view Nuremberg law as valid and enforceable international law. But to make that clear requires that we consider the situation in which the Nuremberg trials came to be and the presuppositions of those who most strongly supported the trials.

HOWEVER JUSTIFIED the Nuremberg trials may have been, they undoubtedly constituted an unprecedented step in modern legal history. This unprecedentedness of the trials was the main source of the many objections raised against them, objections to which I have alluded earlier. Although it was true that, between the wars, there had been many solemn declarations condemning the resort to war and the Kellogg-Briand Pact was supposed to have "outlawed" war, nevertheless the notion of individual accountability for launching or waging an aggressive war had certainly never before been clearly formulated. Nor had certain of the crimes listed in the Charter of the tribunal been recognized or clearly defined before that time. For these reasons the defendants and many others declared that those tried were the victims of *ex post facto* legislation. But others argued that when men commit deeds which are without precedent yet at the same time horrendous and clearly criminal in nature, then special procedures are required if justice is to be done. That provided a justification for the punishment of those involved in the crime of genocide, but not for the punishment of those responsible for initiating a war of aggression, since wars of aggression had often occurred in the past. Here the justification was formulated in terms of the necessities of the future. Many argued that war itself had become a crime against

---

[5] In a recent dissent—written for the case of *O'Brien v. U.S.* (88 S. Ct. 1673)—Mr. Justice Douglas questioned whether the constitutionality of conscription is in all cases beyond question. He specifically questioned the constitutionality of the draft in the absence of a declaration of war by Congress. What Mitchell contended was that the draft might also be unconstitutional when used to help fight a war of aggression.

mankind. To some extent this had been recognized even before World War II and the advent of nuclear weapons. But now it was clearly essential that the renunciation of aggression become a serious thing. Therefore, individual responsibility for the initiation and conduct of aggressive war must be firmly declared and established. On this basis, then, the Nuremberg trials took place. It was, as Conrad Lynn declared in a brief written for Mitchell, "an important moment in legality's desperate attempt to keep abreast of morality."

Many writers stressed, though, that Nuremberg could only be justified by the future. Only if the victors and enforcers of justice at Nuremberg showed themselves ready to submit to the same principles which they had proclaimed, only if an international criminal jurisdiction were created would Nuremberg show itself to have been a worthwhile precedent. No one was more insistent that the Nuremberg trials should have this *general* significance and should mark the beginning of a fundamentally different international order than Mr. Justice Jackson, who was largely responsible for the wording of the Charter and the establishment of the International Military Tribunal and who later acted as Chief American Prosecutor at the trials.[6]

But the hopes of Justice Jackson and other supporters of Nuremberg have yet to be fulfilled. There exists no International Criminal Court, and each of the powers which sat in judgment at the International Military Tribunal has since been involved in actions which might be considered aggressive—the Soviet Union in Eastern Europe, France in Indochina, Britain at the Suez Canal, the United States in Vietnam. Whenever one of these powers' so-called vital interests has been involved, considerations of international law have not restrained it. The inability of the international community to agree on a definition of aggression is an important symptom of this situation. Only too often one nation's aggression turns out to be another nation's "legitimate self-defense" or "legitimate support of self-defense."

Yet if we consider the fact that the nation-state remained the dominant political reality after World War II, and if we consider at the same time some of the implications of the "Nuremberg Principles," then this outcome will seem almost inevitable. For if read carefully, these principles can only be viewed as "subversive" of the authority of the nation-state. Consider Principles II, III, and IV as formulated by the International Law Commission:

II—The fact that internal law does not impose a penalty for an act which constitutes a crime under international law does not relieve the person who committed the act from responsibility under international law.

III—The fact that a person who committed an act which constitutes a crime under international law acted as Head of State or responsible government official does not relieve him from responsibility under international law.

IV—The fact that a person acted pursuant to order of his Government or of a superior does not relieve him from responsibility under international law, provided a moral choice was in fact possible to him.

These principles in effect assert the supremacy of international law over national law.[7] Consequently, the failure of national authorities to take the steps necessary to

---

[6] At the time of the signing of the agreement to try the European war criminals, Justice Jackson stated: "The definitions under which we will try the Germans are *general* definitions. They impose liability upon war-making statesmen of *all* countries alike. . . . If we can cultivate in the world the idea that aggressive war-making is the way to the prisoner's dock rather than the way to honors, we will have accomplished something toward making the peace more secure." (Emphasis added.)

[7] This point was made explicit in the judgment of the International Military Tribunal when it declared that "the very essence of the Charter is that individuals have international duties which transcend the national obligations of obedience imposed by the individual state."

render these principles effective is hardly astonishing.

Nevertheless, in the United States there has been some governmental recognition of these principles, probably mainly as a result of the key role played by this country in bringing about the Nuremberg trials. Section 511 of the current *Army Field Manual* (No. 27–10) states that "the fact that domestic law does not impose a penalty for an act which constitutes a crime under international law does not relieve the person who committed the act from responsibility under international law." As can easily be seen, this is an almost exact repetition of Principle II as framed by the International Law Commission. That individuals have duties under international law has also been affirmed by the Supreme Court, notably in *Ex parte Quirin,* which was cited in the Nuremberg judgment. But it is necessary to remark that this case involved enemy saboteurs, not citizens of our own country. And while it is all very well to state that individuals have responsibilities under international law, that cannot be considered enough as long as the supremacy of international law over national law in cases of conflict is not explicitly established.

This supremacy certainly cannot be said to be established in the United States. The Constitution states, as Mitchell stressed, that treaties are part of the law of the land (Article VI), but it is now an accepted judicial doctrine that Congress may annul a treaty by later legislation, even without action by other parties to the treaty. And in *Reid v. Covert* the Supreme Court declared: "This Court has regularly and uniformly recognized the supremacy of the Constitution over a treaty . . . [since to do otherwise] would permit amendment of that document in a manner not sanctioned by Article V." (In a moment I shall point out the difficulty that is hereby created in the case of the Treaty of London.) As for customary international law, it is not evident that it stands on any higher footing. In the often quoted case of the

Paquete Habana the Supreme Court stated:

International law is part of our law, and must be ascertained and administered by the courts of justice of appropriate jurisdiction, as often as questions of right depending upon it are duly presented for their determination. For this purpose, where there is no treaty, *and no controlling executive or legislative act or judicial decision,* resort must be had to the customs and usages of civilized nations. . . .[8] (Emphasis supplied.)

This statement hardly seems to confer any more authority on custom or usage than that granted by Chief Justice Marshall in 1814 when he asserted in *Brown v. United States:*

This argument [that it might require an act of the legislature to justify the condemnation of property which according to modern international usage ought not to be confiscated] must assume for its basis the position that modern usage constitutes a rule which acts directly upon the thing itself by its own force, and not through the sovereign power. This power is not allowed. This usage is a guide which the sovereign follows or abandons at his will.

In view of the seemingly subservient status of customary international law and of treaties, it seems possible that the United States was not really "free" to enter into Nuremberg, in spite of Justice Jackson's no doubt sincere declaration that this country would feel itself bound by the same laws it was applying to the Germans. For the Nuremberg Charter appears to supersede all national constitutions insofar as it rules out the defenses of "act of state" and of "superior orders." To adhere to Nuremberg might involve disobeying constitutionally valid orders

---

[8] Brierly in *The Law of Nations* quotes from the decision in the case of *Over the Top* (5 Federal Reporter, 838): "International practice is law only in so far as we adopt it, and like all common or statute law it bends to the will of Congress." He goes on to remark that "there is, however, a presumption that neither Parliament nor Congress will intend to violate international law. . . ." That presumption, however, is likely to be ill-founded at times.

unless a constitutional amendment made it clear that Nuremberg Law was to take precedence in cases of conflict and that only Nuremberg Law would be valid in such cases. But no such amendment has been passed.[9]

T HE SHAKY STATUS of international law in our domestic legal system is not the only source of the difficulties involved in making Nuremberg law effective.[10] Even if our courts were clearly required to give international law precedence, there would still remain the problem of insuring the enforcement of judicial decrees based on international law. For example, in order to protect a David Mitchell or the Fort Hood Three or Captain Levy against the injury caused by the illegal actions of the United States government, it would be necessary for the Supreme Court to have the capacity to restrain the other branches of our government in matters that are considered vital. This can be a hazardous undertaking for the Court. As Hamilton stated in *The Federalist,* the judiciary "must ultimately depend upon the aid of the executive arm . . . for the efficacy of its judgments."

When it is the executive arm itself which

has gone beyond the law, the Court finds itself in an awkward position. This is particularly true when the delict involved is as large-scale an affair as a war. Either the Court can officially shut its eyes and ignore the illegalities that are occurring, a course which may eventually undermine its authority, or it can attempt to intervene and risk provoking a severe internal crisis and perhaps a more rapid loss of its authority. This may truly be said to be a Scylla-and-Charybdis situation for the Court and yet one that is seemingly unavoidable.

A further problem is created for the Court by the fact that its rulings, if heeded and enforced, can affect directly only the government of which it forms a part. A war may involve breaches of international law by both sides, yet a national court has a rather limited capacity to affect the total context in which the illegalities perpetrated by its own side are occurring. National courts are likely to view this fact as adding to the risks of judicial intervention.

A final problem concerns the wording of the Charter and the "Principles" themselves. Both these documents manifest a crucial structural defect: these documents clearly state that individuals have duties under international law, but at the same time fail to create corresponding rights for the protection of the individual who is trying to carry out these duties. In the Shimoda case, initiated by the victims of the atomic attacks on Hiroshima and Nagasaki, the District Court of Tokyo stated in its decision: "It is still proper to understand that individuals are not the subject of rights in international law, unless it is concretely recognized by treaties. . . ." Unfortunately, the Treaty of London (which, as I have stated, included the Charter of the International Military Tribunal) did not proclaim the existence of such individual rights, let alone establish a procedure whereby the individual could assert these rights and receive effective protection if they were being infringed upon. Nor has this defect

---

[9] A remark by the law officer in the trial of Captain Levy indicated his uncertainty as to what exactly the relation is between Nuremberg law and American domestic law: "Well, as you must realize, this question is pretty much wide open. But it seemed to me from my reading of the instructions to the judges in Nuremberg that, since obedience to a superior was not a defense if the order required the commission of crimes against humanity—although those instructions did not so provide—it would seem to me that an ordinary extrapolation of that rule would in domestic law provide a defense although I have no precedent." The problem concerns just what sort of "extrapolation" should be allowed.

[10] There is only one national constitution which clearly grants superior status to international law as it affects individuals; not surprisingly that is the constitution of West Germany. It provides that "general rules of international law shall form part of federal law" and that such rules "shall take precedence over the laws and create rights and duties directly for the inhabitants of the federal territory."

since been corrected. Nuremberg law, therefore, may by its very terms claim to supersede our Constitution and all national constitutions; yet it provides no internationally guaranteed rights for the protection of individuals against orders of their national government that run counter to the declared international obligations of the individual.[11]

It can be seen, then, that great difficulties surround the enforcement of Nuremberg law. Indeed, this discussion of the obstacles has hardly been exhaustive; but it need not be in order to make my point. It should be clear that as things stand, Nuremberg law must be applied through the medium of the nation-state and that this is a medium likely to prove both recalcitrant and ineffective.

There remains, however, the question of the significance of this conclusion. Does it really matter that Nuremberg has thus far proven to be an ineffective precedent? Perhaps the whole enterprise was unrealistic in the first place. Perhaps "legality's desperate attempt to keep abreast of morality" cannot possibly succeed under contemporary conditions.

Naturally, the individuals who have tried to make a legal case against the war in Vietnam do not want to accept such judgments as correct. It is all very well for theorists and philosophers to show, even to "prove," that morality, legality, and politics have little in common with one another—for the intellect generally finds pleasure in making distinctions. The results are quite different, however, for the individual whose life is a life of action and who seeks to act with coherence and integrity. Even if he recognizes that the law has certain necessary limitations as

[11] This lack may not nullify the obligations proclaimed at Nuremberg and in the "Principles," but it does put in question their binding quality. As Wolfgang Friedmann has stated: "An international law of the individual must surely comprise both rights and duties."

an enforcer and creator of morality, he will resist the notion that the law must necessarily be an enforcer and creator of gross immorality. If the law cannot help him to be good, at least it should not compel him to do evil—and penalize him when he resists.

It can be granted, of course, that the law may sometimes run athwart certain versions of God's commands. Theologically defined notions of the good may not conform to notions of the good as defined politically. But it is not this conflict which is crucial at present to the conscientious individual. What troubles him is that the laws of the world, that is, the laws arising from the nation-state "security" system, seem, when considered in their totality, actually to work against some of man's primary political needs. Rather than creating stability and providing a framework within which there would be at least some hope of harmonious living-together, these laws seem almost to guarantee chaos and destruction.

American resisters, therefore, believe that it is necessary to challenge our government. It is a government which is wont to speak in moral terms and to justify its actions in moral terms. It is, in a word, a self-righteous government. To be sure, the resisters themselves have been accused of speaking in self-righteous and pious terms; but their language is perhaps a natural and inevitable reflection of the kind of language they have heard for so long. In any case, the resisters do not wish to abdicate the moral-political debate. They do not advocate the divorce of morality and politics or of morality and legality. Instead, they challenge the government to allow that debate to take place in a meaningful way within our existing legal and political institutions. If that is not possible, and they strongly suspect that it is not, then they insist that it is their right to try to create new institutions and new standards of legitimacy.

III. THE CONSTITUTIONAL DEBATE ON THE VIETNAM WAR

A. Matters of Executive Prerogative

The President, the People, and the Power to Make War

ERIC F. GOLDMAN

THE CONSTITUTION of the United States declares in the plainest possible English: "The Congress shall have Power . . . To declare War." Yet in the last twenty years Americans have fought two major wars—in Korea and in Vietnam—without a congressional declaration of war. Apart from the question of who has the right to send the armed forces into serious combat action, Vietnam has been a glaring instance of momentous foreign policy carried out with only the most cursory control by Congress.

Naturally, many Americans opposed to the Vietnam war are crying outrage. Many others, for or against the war or somewhere in between, ask a worried question: What has happened to the traditional constitutional procedure whereby the President leads in international affairs but Congress has a potent check on him when the decision involves life and death for the nation's young men and sweeping consequences for the whole country? Is there no way to bring foreign policy back under greater popular control, by restoring the congressional role or through some other technique?

On the surface, the questions have clear-cut answers, most of which revolve around the contention that particular recent Presidents simply have refused to play by the constitutional rules. Yet in actuality the answers are entangled in complex considerations of just what the Founding Fathers did and did not write into the Constitution, how their decisions have been put into practice over two centuries, and whether the circumstances of warmaking have not changed so much that some of the basic old rules simply do not apply.

The wise and hardheaded men who assembled in 1787 to write a constitution for the United States were members of a generation that had just fought a bitter war against the British executive, King George III. They were sick of battles and their devastation and intensely concerned to circumscribe any decision for war. A gangling freshman congressman from Illinois, denouncing the Mexican-American War a half century later, stated the mood of most of the Founding Fathers as accurately as any historian can. Representative Abraham Lincoln wrote in 1848 that the Constitutional Convention gave the warmaking power

to Congress because "kings had always been involving and impoverish-
ing their people in wars, pretending generally, if not always, that the
good of the people was the object. This, our Convention understood
to be the most oppressive of all kingly oppressions; and they resolved
to so frame the Constitution that *no one man* should hold the power of
bringing this oppression upon us." (The italics are Lincoln's.)

So the Congress, not the President, was to decide war or peace. But
the Founding Fathers lived in an era filled with violence between
countries that was not formal war. The new nation would be at a sharp
disadvantage if, in the event of depredations against its commerce or
maraudings on its land, its armed forces were immobilized until congressmen could gather from thirteen states in their horse-drawn vehicles. The Founding Fathers made one man who was on the scene, the
President, Commander in Chief of the Army and Navy. The wording
of the first draft of the Constitution gave Congress the exclusive power
to "make" war. On the floor of the convention, "make" was changed to
"declare," assigning the President the right to use the Army and Navy
in order to meet specific emergencies while retaining for the House
and Senate the power to decide full-scale war.

The Constitution has often been called a bundle of compromises,
and so it was—not least between those who wanted a strong and those
who wanted a weak Chief Executive. The Founding Fathers may have
made the President the Commander in Chief, but they gave Congress
the power of the purse in determining the size and nature of the armed
forces. Until late in the convention, the right to make treaties was
vested in the Senate alone. But there were obvious advantages in having one man initiate treaties, receive foreign ambassadors, name and
instruct American ambassadors. The Chief Executive would do these
things, although he was to appoint ambassadors only with the approval
of a Senate majority and make treaties with the "Advice and Consent"
of two thirds of the Senate.

In foreign affairs, as in all areas, the Founding Fathers were notably
spare in laying down specific dictates and in the language that they
used to write the provisions. Yet they said enough to make it clear that
they envisaged a foreign policy system in which the President would
lead, but in collaboration with Congress, especially the Senate, and in
which the Chief Executive would be subject to continuing scrutiny and
formidable restraints whenever his activities touched that most serious
aspect of foreign affairs, general war.

On August 22, 1789, President George Washington, sound Constitutionalist that he was, appeared with his Secretary of War in the Senate chamber to "advise" with the senators on a treaty with the southern Indians and to seek their "consent." The reading of the document began. The wasp-tempered Senator William Maclay, from the back country of Pennsylvania, was annoyed because the passing carriages made it difficult for him to hear the words; he and other senators, in the process of forming an agrarian political opposition to President Washington, were ready to be annoyed at anything that came from this administration with its "monarchical" tendencies. The President wanted an immediate vote, but the Maclay group called for time to study the documents connected with the treaty. George Washington, according to Maclay, "started up in a violent fret." Had he not brought along the Secretary of War precisely to answer any questions that might arise? President Washington calmed down, the delay was granted, the treaty was ratified. But Maclay wrote in his diary, "The President wishes to tread on the necks of the Senate. . . . This will not do with Americans." As for George Washington, he is said to have let it be known that "he would be damned if he ever went there again." He did not go there again for advice on a treaty, and neither did any other President.

The clash over this minor document was a preview of the coming years, when the collaboration between the Chief Executive and the Congress, in the case of treaties or other aspects of international affairs, proved prickly and at times violent. Inevitably, Presidents tended to feel that they had superior information and were acting only after mature consideration of the matter; congressmen were interfering out of impulse, ignorance, politics, or a yen to encroach on White House prerogatives. Inevitably, congressmen, considering themselves sound in judgment and closer to the popular will, tended to believe that Chief Executives were trying, as Senator Maclay had declared, to create situations in which "advices and consents [would be] ravished, in a degree, from us."

Before many decades it also became clear that while Congress might have the war power, a determined Chief Executive could put the House and the Senate in a position where they had little alternative except to vote war. The Democratic President elected in 1844, the unsmiling, tenacious James K. Polk, believed it was manifest destiny for America to expand. Texas had been formally annexed, but Mexico still considered it a rebellious province, and border disputes continued; California lay a luscious plum ready for the plucking from Mexico.

President Polk kept trying to maneuver Mexico into acceptance of his ambitions, while he built a fervid public opinion behind expansionism. Finally the President ordered General Zachary Taylor into territory claimed by Mexico, and Mexican troops attacked American cavalry, killing or wounding sixteen.

On Sunday, May 10, 1846, President Polk went to church but, as he put it, "regretted" that he had to spend the rest of the Sabbath on a quite different matter—working out a war bill and a strategy for Congress. The measure provided an appropriation of ten million dollars and the calling up of fifty thousand volunteers. The disciplined Democratic majority in the House of Representatives limited debate to two hours, and only in the last minutes did the Polk leaders present a preamble to the bill that was a declaration of war. The House and the Senate included a strong anti-war faction. But now all members were in the position where they either voted for the whole measure or— with a good deal of public opinion near hysteria—voted against money and troops for General Taylor's forces. The House approved, 174-14; the Senate, 40-2.

Those dogged fourteen Noes in the House included ex-President John Quincy Adams; and Representative Abraham Lincoln, just arrived in Washington, would soon begin his sharpshooting against the war. Major intellectuals joined in the assault. Henry Thoreau spent a night in the Concord lockup for refusing to pay his poll tax in protest, and when his aunt paid the money, much to his annoyance, he went back to Walden Pond and wrote his famous essay "Civil Disobedience." The agitation went on, but within five months American troops were swinging along the plaza of Mexico City, gazing in awe and in triumph at the great baroque cathedral and the pink walls of the Halls of Montezuma, asserting by their mud-spattered presence that President Polk was about to achieve in abundance the territorial acquisitions he sought.

Half a century later the obverse of the coin was showing. Of all wars the United States has fought, none has come to be considered more pointless and reprehensible than the Spanish-American War, and that venture was the doing of Congress, driven on by public opinion. During the 1890's a rebellion in the Spanish colony of Cuba, brutally combatted by the Madrid government, caught up a mounting jingo sentiment in the United States. Before long the principal opponents of armed intervention were the American businessmen owning property in Cuba, who wanted things settled without dislocating their economic arrangements, and the two Presidents of the era, Grover Cleveland and William McKinley.

When Congress roared through a resolution recognizing the "belligerency" of the Cuban rebels, President Cleveland denounced the move as an intrusion on the powers of the Chief Executive and privately remarked that if Congress declared war, he as Commander in Chief would refuse to mobilize the Army. President McKinley tried, too; he undertook negotiations with Madrid to bring better treatment of the rebels. But the popular uproar, stoked by tabloid papers, kept increasing. William McKinley's face grew haggard from the pills he was taking trying to get to sleep; once he sat on a big crimson brocade lounge in the White House and burst into tears as he spoke of the way Congress was forcing the country into war. Finally, the President capitulated. He planned to run for re-election; besides, he was scarcely deaf to voices like that of the senator who thundered to Assistant Secretary of State William R. Day, "Day, by —, don't your President know where the war-declaring power is lodged? Tell him by —, that if he doesn't do something, Congress will exercise the power." President McKinley sat working on a war message as the Spanish government conceded major American demands—a concession made before the message actually reached the House and the Senate—and he added poignantly that he hoped Congress would give the Spanish terms "just and careful attention."

A war of territorial seizure maneuvered through by a determined President, an ugly war forced by public opinion and Congress, six wars or significant uses of the armed forces in a little more than a hundred years, more and more instances of acrid White House-Congress clashes in foreign affairs—during the late eighteenth and nineteenth centuries the constitutional system was hardly functioning with glowing results in international matters. Yet the wars or quasi-wars did not pile up long casualty lists; they did not slash through everyday living. The most disruptive conflict, the Civil War, was removed by its very nature from the usual questions of constitutional responsibility. Whatever the underlying reality, even the Mexican-American War was fought under an authorization overwhelmingly granted by Congress. If the wars created savage debates, they spread little bitter feeling that questions of life and death were too far removed from grass-roots control.

President Theodore Roosevelt has often been called "the first modern President," and he was that in many ways. In international affairs the world was taking on its twentieth-century form of great powers jockeying for global position, vast economic stakes overseas, and armed forces designed to strike swiftly. These trends inevitably centered more foreign policy power in the hands of the American President, who was far more able than the cumbersome Congress to operate in this kind of arena. The rambunctious Teddy Roosevelt, no man to turn away from power, responded by driving deep into the American system the doctrine that the Chief Executive is—to use his phrase— "the steward" of the nation, endowed under the Constitution with vast "inherent powers" to act in behalf of what he considers the good of the country.

ACTION accompanied doctrine. Did T.R. deem it to be in the national interest for the United States to have a canal across Central America so that the Navy could be moved quickly from one ocean to another, and was the Colombian government proving balky? In 1903 T.R. saw to it that Panamanian rebels set up an independent state covering the desired canal zone, and the new nation, to no one's surprise, gave him what he wanted. ("I took the Canal Zone," said President Theodore Roosevelt, "and let Congress debate.") Did T.R. arrive at the conclusion during the Russo-Japanese War of 1904-05 that the security of the United States was best served by a Japanese victory? In entire secrecy he informed Tokyo that, if needed, America would act as an ally, which could have proved a commitment for war. Did the triumphant Japanese then seem a bit too cocky? In 1907 T.R. ordered the entire American fleet on a razzle-dazzle trip around the world, loosing all kinds of diplomatic reverberations. Congressional opponents stirred, particularly those from eastern regions fearing the lack of naval protection, and they talked of denying the appropriation for the fleet movement. Very well, T.R. replied. He had enough money to send the ships to the Pacific Coast, and they could stay there.

It was all very much Teddy Roosevelt, and more than a little rococo. Yet this first modern President was also anticipating in a serious way the modern presidential trend. Stirred on by changed conditions, he was moving through that broad arch erected by the Founding Fathers —between, on the one side, the clear power of the Chief Executive to lead in foreign affairs and to command the armed forces and, on the other side, the powers of Congress to do certain specific things.

As the twentieth century progressed and the enmeshments of the world grew tighter and more troublesome, Presidents probed still more vigorously the limits of the arch. This development was not only implicit in the circumstances; it was furthered by the difference between the vantage of the Chief Executive and the Congress. The President felt full blast the forces of modernity, which came crashing daily into his office. As the leader of the whole nation, he was heavily influenced by considerations of collective security, the moral position of the United States before international opinion, and the problems that tied in with the stability of the country's economy. Of course members of Congress knew these same concerns, but they were also subject to local, more inward-looking pressures. The House and the Senate continued to include strong blocs which represented the decades-old view that the business of America is America and which resented the persistent intrusion of the world. The abrasion between the two ends of Pennsylvania Avenue in matters of foreign policy sharpened. More and more, Presidents viewed Congress as the adversary and thought in terms of skirting around it or, if necessary, ignoring it.

This occurred at critical points on the road toward American participation in both World Wars I and II. During the European phase of World War I, Germany climaxed three years of friction with the United States by announcing unrestricted submarine warfare. President Wilson had long been troubled by considerations of the moral position of the United States with respect to the conflict, and the feeling of his responsibility to assert American rights on the high seas; now he could not overlook the fact that hundreds of ships, fearful of submarines, were clinging to port and great supplies of wheat and cotton were piling up, threatening to dislocate the nation's economic life. In February, 1917, President Wilson asked Congress for authority to arm merchantmen, an act that could scarcely fail to lead to war. The debate was stormy, and in the upper house eleven senators filibustered the measure to death. Thereupon the President announced that "a little group of willful men had rendered the great government of the United States helpless and contemptible" and ordered the merchantmen armed anyhow. War was declared in April.

After the eruption of the second European war in 1939 President Franklin Roosevelt was convinced that for the good of the United States it belonged at the side of the antifascist powers. Yet he faced tremendous anti-intervention sentiment, so amply reflected in Congress that as late as the summer of 1941, a year after the fall of France, the House extended the draft law by exactly one vote. Under the circumstances, F.D.R. undertook an extraordinary series of executive actions, which sought to hem in Japan economically and to help the nations fighting Nazi Germany. Weeks before Pearl Harbor these moves included an order that in effect meant convoying—despite a congressional ban on convoying—and an order to the Army Air Forces and the Navy to shoot first at German and Italian vessels found in the western Atlantic, which amounted to *de facto* warfare.

By the time America was fighting in World War II, it was manifest that President Roosevelt had made war and was continuing to conduct foreign policy with only a defensive concern for congressional opinion. Plenty of angry comment was made about this, yet still the warmaking power did not become a major national issue. In the case of both World Wars I and II, a semblance of congressional authority was preserved by the ultimate declarations of war voted by the House and Senate. Of more significance, the two wars were generally accepted by the public; they were led by widely popular Chief Executives; and if they brought serious problems to the society, they did not seem to tear it apart.

In June 1950, President Harry Truman was visiting his Missouri home when he learned of the invasion of South Korea by North Korea. Flying back to Washington, he mulled over the news. This was plain aggression, the President told himself; aggression unchecked during the 1930's had led to World War II; he was not going to be party to another such tragedy. The next morning the reports were grim: South Korea appeared about to collapse. That night Harry Truman ordered American armed forces into the Korean fighting. Then the United Nations Security Council, on motion of the United States representative, "recommended" assistance to South Korea, and the President summoned congressional leaders, as he put it, "so that I might inform them on the events and decisions of the past few days." The Korean War was under way, grinding on for more than three years, costing the nation 33,629 battle deaths and 103,284 wounded. At no time did President Truman ask congressional authority for the war.

BEHIND this White House attitude were all the reasons that had been accumulating for decades. But other and profoundly important elements had also entered into the relationship between the Chief Executive and Congress in the conduct of foreign affairs. The simple fact was that the traditional concept of a President leading in foreign policy and then, if necessary, going to Congress for a declaration of war had become obsolete. Historically, war meant that a nation, using whatever weapons seemed feasible, attempted to conquer another country or to beat it into submission. In an era of Cold War, and after the development of nuclear weapons, armed conflicts were taking a different form. Small Communist nations, unofficially backed by large ones, were probing remote areas. The United States was replying not by war in the conventional sense but by what was being called "limited war"— limited in the use of weapons because nuclear power was ruled out and limited in objective, which was not to crush the enemy but to stop him from spreading Communism and to discourage similar efforts in the future.

All the while, the relationship of war to the home front was altering. By the 1950's the United States was so complex a society and Washington so overweening a force that a declaration of war had immense impact. This was partly psychological, but it also involved fundamental workaday facts. Over the decades, by laws and even more by precedents, a declaration of war had come to confer on the President sweeping powers over the entire national life, particularly in the sensitive area of economic affairs. Fighting a limited war, President Truman wanted to limit its home effects, and the opposition to them which could be so easily aroused.

So PRESIDENT Harry Truman went on fighting the Korean War on the authority of President Harry Truman. At times he spoke of the "authorization" or "summons" resulting from the action of the U.N. Security Council; the references were not taken too seriously. The war took calamitous turns. It exacerbated American social problems that were already serious. The very idea of "limited war"—"fighting a war with one hand tied behind you," as people said—ground on the nerves of a nation accustomed to striding in for the knockout. Public opinion, which at first strongly favored the Korean intervention, swung against it and to an extent that had not occurred during any previous conflict; by 1951 the Gallup poll reported a majority believing that the whole intervention was a mistake and favoring prompt withdrawal. Opposition leaders in Congress now were storming against "Truman's War," that "unconstitutional" war; and this time the attacks were building a feeling that something was definitely wrong with the warmaking procedures of the United States.

After the Korean War, and as part of the mounting American concern over Communist expansionism, the United States stepped up negotiations with other nations for regional defense pacts. These agreements were impeccably constitutional; they were treaties, negotiated by the executive branch, then debated in the Senate and approved by a two-thirds vote. Yet they contained clauses that could be construed to give Presidents further leverage in foreign affairs. A typical pact was SEATO, negotiated in 1954 by the Eisenhower Secretary of State, John Foster Dulles. It bound the United States, in the event of "armed aggression" by a Communist nation in Southeast Asia, to "act to meet the common danger in accordance with its constitutional processes" and, in the case of other types of threats in the area, to "consult" on the measures to be adopted—whatever a President might take all that to mean, in whatever specific circumstances he found himself.

Simultaneously, an old procedure—a joint House-Senate congressional resolution concerning international affairs—was gathering fresh meaning. After the lambasting President Truman took during the Korean War, Presidents who contemplated moves that might result in war or quasi-war sought some form of mandate from the House and the Senate. They also wanted to gather bipartisan support behind their action or projected action and behind their general policy, and—of great importance in their minds—they sought to present a united front to warn off Communist or Communist-allied nations from adventurous plans.

The joint resolutions came in rapid succession: in 1955, when President Eisenhower thought he might use armed forces to protect Formosa from Red China; in 1957, when he was considering intervening in the Middle East to prevent strategic areas from falling under Soviet control; and in 1962, when President Kennedy was maneuvering to isolate Castro's Cuba. The joint resolutions varied in a number of ways. But they were alike in their general pattern of giving congressional approval to a specific action or contemplated action of the Chief Executive and to his broadly stated policy for a particular troubled area of the world.

During the presidential campaign of 1964, the celebrated shots were fired in the Gulf of Tonkin by North Vietnamese gunboats against an American destroyer. A heated debate has broken out concerning just how honest President Lyndon Johnson was in reporting the total episode to the public and concerning the larger circumstances surrounding it. The relevant facts here are that the President believed that he should, by retaliating, discourage the North Vietnamese from any such further attacks; that as a politician running for office, he wanted to underline that he was as anti-Communist as his opponent, Barry Goldwater; that the South Vietnamese situation was disintegrating and he did not know what he might want to do about it in the coming months; that he was acutely aware of what had happened to his friend Harry Truman; and that he did not overlook the potentialities of the new type of regional pacts and joint resolutions.

President Johnson ordered a harsh retaliatory bombing of North Vietnamese patrol-boat bases. Then he summoned congressional leaders and told them he thought a joint resolution, like the Formosa and Middle East and Cuban resolutions, should be put through Congress swiftly. The document reached the House and Senate the next morning. It approved the bombing; spoke of America's "obligations" under SEATO to defend South Vietnam; declared that the United States was "prepared, as the President determines, to take all necessary steps, including the use of armed force," to assist any SEATO nation "in defense of its freedom"; and provided that the resolution remain in force until the Chief Executive declared it no longer necessary or the Congress repealed it by majority votes.

The House devoted most of its time to speeches approving the retaliatory bombing of the previous evening, and Representative Henry S. Reuss, from Milwaukee, said all that could be said on that subject. He was reminded, Reuss observed, of the story about the bartender who called the saloon owner on the intercom and asked, "Is Casey good for a drink?"

"Has he had it?"

"He has."

"He is."

The Senate spent more time on the general authorization granted by the resolution. Members rose to ask, Didn't the language mean that the Congress was empowering the President to take any steps he deemed wise, including waging war, in Southeast Asia? Senator J. William Fulbright, the floor leader for the resolution, and a number of other senators replied that President Johnson had stated that it was his policy not to use combat forces in Southeast Asia; the resolution simply backed this policy; it had to be broad and to be approved quickly to show the North Vietnamese how much the American people, without regard to party, were against armed Communist expansion in Southeast Asia. How many congressmen wanted to vote No on such a proposition, especially three months before an election? The debate on the Tonkin Resolution in the House took just forty minutes, and the tally was 416-0. The Senate, after only eight hours of discussion, approved 88-2.

As PRESIDENT Johnson went on escalating the Vietnam war, he brandished freely the foreign policy powers of the White House, including making executive agreements—some secret—that went well beyond the Truman moves and entangled the United States and Asian countries in ways the full purport of which is still not known. More than the Korean War, Vietnam distorted American society at a time when it was still less able to stand further dislocation. And as a large part of public opinion and of Congress turned against the involvement, the cries once again went up, against "Johnson's war," that "unconstitutional horror." But this time there was a difference.

Lyndon Johnson used to carry the difference around with him on a piece of paper crumpled in his pocket. When the subject of his authority for the war came up, he would pull out the slip containing the Tonkin Resolution and read from it. The two Eisenhower joint resolutions and the Kennedy one had concerned crises that went away, or at least seemed to; the problem treated in the Tonkin Resolution turned into a major war, and L.B.J. exploited the document fully, privately and publicly. On one private occasion, he took it out and read emphatically the resolution's reference to American "obligations" under SEATO. With still more stress, hand clapping on knee, he repeated the phrases that the United States was "prepared, *as the President determines*, to take *all* necessary steps." Lyndon Johnson demanded to know, Did Congress limit its authorization in *any* way? Embittered by the opposition to the war and the personal attacks on him, he continued in a deliberately provocative allusion to nuclear bombs, which he had no intention of using: Did Congress limit at all even *what kind* of weapons he could use? The President put the paper away. Besides, he added, if they have changed their minds, why don't they just vote, as the resolution says, to repeal it?

Lyndon Johnson knew perfectly well that few congressmen would dare face their constituents if, by such a vote for repeal, they undercut a President and a Commander in Chief in the middle of a grave war which he had entered with the insistence that it was vital to American security and world peace. The new regional pacts and even more the joint resolutions—inaugurated with the best of intentions to meet contemporary circumstances—had given the Chief Executive still more war power, and done it in a manner that came close to caricaturing the intent of the Founding Fathers. For they were nothing less than a means by which Congress, with all the whereases of constitutional procedure, duly voted itself into impotence.

In 1967 President Johnson's Under Secretary of State, Nicholas deB. Katzenbach, appeared before the Senate Foreign Relations Committee. His remarks, reflecting the L.B.J. mood, came close to saying that the Chief Executive has the right to do anything he considers best in international matters without regard to Congress. Midway in the testimony a committee member, Senator Eugene J. McCarthy, got up and walked out muttering, "There is only one thing to do—take it to the country." This reaction was a factor in projecting McCarthy into his anti-war presidential candidacy. It was a reaction that was being felt throughout the country—combining discontent with the war and what it was doing to the nation with the charge that President Johnson was manipulating and bulldozing the American people through a war they did not want to fight.

Inevitably, a flood of proposals have come, some for amendments to the Constitution, others for congressional action.* Almost all seek to return to Congress—and thus, presumably, closer to "the people"— greater participation in foreign affairs, with the usual assumption that the Congress would be less likely to venture into unwise wars than the President. The most serious of these moves has been a resolution proposed by Senator Fulbright and adopted by the Senate in 1969, which went at one major aspect of the problem through the concept of a "national commitment." It was "the sense of the Senate," the resolution declared, that the United States can make a commitment to a foreign nation only through a specific document agreed upon by both the legislative and executive branches.

But serious doubts are provoked by any of these proposals. The nub of the situation is the power of the Chief Executive as Commander in Chief and those general or "inherent powers" that have come to cluster about the office of the Presidency. Is there really a way to restrict the powers of the Commander in Chief without possibly doing more harm than good in an era when one man's swiftly pressing the button may be necessary for some degree of national survival, or his prompt decision to use non-nuclear armed forces could be essential to achieving a

* This article was written in early 1970 and therefore includes no treatment of the numerous developments since that time concerning war powers and related matters. However, the author feels that nothing which has happened affects his essential points.

purpose generally agreed upon by the country? Do the words exist that could inhibit "inherent powers" without simultaneously harassing the President, or blocking him, in taking actions that are widely considered necessary? Is this not particularly true in a period when his office is the one instrumentality that can make decisive moves in behalf of the national interest, whether that interest be expressed in domestic or foreign affairs—in orders to armed forces to strike abroad or to enforce federal laws at home, to affect importantly the deployment of economic and social resources inside the country or eight thousand miles away, or to assert at home or abroad the nation's bedrock values? Yet if the proposals do not cut back on any of these essentials, how effectively do they close off the routes by which Presidents have moved independently to war?

THE Fulbright resolution concerning "national commitments," for example, might discourage certain kinds of the global wheeler-dealing of a Theodore Roosevelt or a Lyndon Johnson. But the resolution is merely an expression of senatorial opinion; it puts no effective check on a Chief Executive acting as Commander in Chief or wielding "inherent powers." Neither T.R. nor L.B.J. would have considered the basic moves of their foreign policies subject to the resolution, and almost certainly it would not have prevented American entrance into, say, the Vietnam war.

Apart from the difficulty of controlling the President by new language, there is a still more troublesome question—whether, in fact, the Congress and "the people" are less likely than a Chief Executive to get the country into an unwise war. There is not only the glaring instance of the Spanish-American War; other examples, most notably the War of 1812, give pause. Then a rampant faction in Congress—a group with dreams of conquering Canada, who brought the phrase "war hawks" into the American language—helped mightily in pushing the United States into a conflict that was a credit neither to the good sense nor the conscience of the nation. Similarly, in the early, frightened Cold War days, President Truman was worried, and justly so, about a considerable congressional bloc that was restless to take on Russia.

Yet whatever must be said about the dangers or difficulties of restricting the presidential power to make war, the fact remains that something is decidedly wrong with the process as it has emerged full-blown in the 1960's. It *is* a travesty of democracy to have so vital a decision so completely in the hands of one man. As Benjamin Franklin observed during the Constitutional Convention, the nation can never be sure "what sort" of human being will end up in the White House; some might be overly ambitious or "fond of war." The country can also never be certain—no matter how able and peace-minded the Chief Executive—that he will not be led into an unfortunate decision by his dogmas or his limitations. Lyndon Johnson, to use a striking instance, was a Chief Executive of high abilities in a number of respects; he had a strong personal urge to be a peace President and well-seasoned political reasons for avoiding the travail of war. Yet he escalated the Vietnam intervention relentlessly, lashed ahead by old-style certitudes and an inadequate understanding of the forces at work in Asia.

Ideally, what is needed is the creation in modern terms of a system something like the one envisaged by the Founding Fathers, in which the President would have his powers as Commander in Chief and would lead in foreign policy while being guided and checked to some degree by Congress. Toward that end, no good purpose is served by continuing the practice of congressional joint resolutions in international affairs. Either the resolution must say so little that it does not significantly present a bipartisan front to the enemy, or it must be so sweeping that it hands the Chief Executive a blank check.

Beyond this negative suggestion there are all those difficulties in conceiving of a single congressional move that would better the situation. Probably improvement will have to come not by the beguiling expedient of one action but by slower and more complex changes within the existing relationship. For this purpose it is essential to note that in every instance when the United States has gone through all the prescribed constitutional forms, with the President recommending war and the Congress "declaring" it, the House and the Senate have never really "declared war." Five consecutive times, from the War of 1812 through World War II, what Congress actually did was to recognize an existing state of war, allegedly caused by other nations. This was not simply the result of the natural desire to make the enemy appear the cause of the fighting. More importantly, it reflected the facts that by the time Congress considered a declaration of war, a long train of actions had made combat involvement inevitable or next to inevitable and that, in most instances, the actions had been taken by the White House.

The problem of increasing the participation of Congress in foreign policy therefore involves less the matter of a declaration of war than a continuing role for the legislative branch in the decisions that lead to large-scale military intervention. Thinking along these lines, it is useless to assume that the built-in tension between the White House and the Hill can be removed. Yet changes could be made that would increase the degree of genuine collaboration.

ALL MODERN Presidents have called in congressmen to "consult" concerning major foreign policy moves. The vital point is the nature of the "consulting." Is it a session in which the Chief Executive really listens to his guests, or is it one in which he is simply informing them of what he proposes to do or has done or, asking their advice, receives it merely with a politeness calculated to grease relations with the Hill? The presidential attitude takes shape from many things, but in no minor degree from the type of men with whom he is talking. And outstanding congressmen can not only influence Presidents; they can rouse opinion in their own chambers and in the nation as a whole, which is certain to have its effects in the White House.

In his *Memoirs* President Truman touched upon the kind of congressional leaders with whom he was dealing during the Korean War. At times bitingly, he indicated how little he thought of the ability of a number of them to rise above narrow-gauged partisanship, of their knowledgeability in world affairs, even of their willingness to observe discretion when the Chief Executive revealed to them information that was necessary for understanding but seriously affected national security.

Truman, a former senator, knew his Congress only too well. For years students of American government have been pointing to the deplorable effects of the seniority system in Congress, and nowhere has it operated more lamentably than in placing men on that critical body for international matters, the Senate Committee on Foreign Relations. In the early twentieth century, when the White House was enormously aggrandizing its power over foreign policy, a number of the senators who were the chairmen or the ranking minority figures on the committee were close to the clownish in their inappropriateness. Since the advent of nuclear weapons, which brought the gravest of issues before the committee, the chairman and first minority senator have at times been able, informed, and dedicated. Yet to run down the list of the number-one and number-two figures since 1945, not to speak of the total makeup of the body, is to come upon some men whose lack of qualifications is staggering.

The problem is not simply one of bringing to the Foreign Relations Committee senators who will command, and justly command, the ear of the President and the country. There is the further consideration of whether they will insist upon equipping themselves with the kind of staff that permits them to operate with knowledge and force. One of the basic reasons for the overweening supremacy of the White House in international affairs has been its machinery for accumulating facts and its capacity to withhold or distort information and to project its interpretations of events. There is no reason why a Congress that took seriously its role, and was backed by the public in its assertiveness, could not establish information machinery that would enable it to fight the battle of Pennsylvania Avenue on more equal terms.

The potential of such congressional action has been strikingly demonstrated in recent years. During the Vietman debate in the L.B.J. days, the Senate Foreign Relations Committee, headed by the sharp-minded J. William Fulbright and more or less adequately staffed, began to operate like a countervailing power in international matters. Lyndon Johnson may have come to detest William Fulbright, but he read carefully every word the senator said. The committee launched hearings that were a prime factor in building congressional and public opinion against the war and in ultimately changing Johnson policies. Fulbright has apologized for the "perfunctory" attention his committee gave to the Tonkin Resolution in the early days, and the remark is of more than personal significance. It is an open question whether the United States would have ended up fighting in Vietnam if the Senate Foreign Relations Committee had been vigilant, continuously informed, and articulate during the years from 1954 when the essential shape of affairs in Southeast Asia was developing.

The slow and intricate process of building a realistic base for congressional participation in international affairs—will the American people press for it? A natural aftermath of war is the urge to forget about its horrors, including the way that the country got into them. Yet Vietnam has been a shock to millions and to groups containing many influential figures, and certainly the foreseeable trend of events will keep ever present the possibility of large-scale United States combat involvement. Perhaps the present high feelings about Vietnam will carry over sufficiently to create a congressional stance that will give the American people some degree of responsible surveillance over the disposition abroad of their lives, their fortunes, and their sacred honor.

The Power of the Executive
to Use Military Forces Abroad

QUINCY WRIGHT

The problem of executive and congressional relations in foreign affairs—and especially in military affairs—has become more acute with the changed attitudes toward war which have followed World War I. The change in attitude is a consequence of the shrinking of the world which increased the probability of serious international conflict, the development of weapons of extraordinary destructiveness, the challenge to democracy with the rise of totalitarian ideologies and the more active involvement of the United States in international affairs. The danger to both democracy and security of uncontrolled military action by the President has been recognized and procedures for meeting it have moved in two directions—increased international control and increased national control.

The United States took the initiative after World War I in proposing the League of Nations to control war, and after Senate rejection of the Covenant it proposed in the widely ratified Kellogg-Briand Pact of 1929 the legal outlawry of war and obligatory settlement of international disputes and conflicts by peaceful means. With the failure of this legal approach to prevent serious hostilities in Manchuria and Ethiopia and in World War II, the United States again took the initiative in an effort to sanction that law by the Nuremburg Charter establishing individual liability for crimes against peace, humanity, and the law of war, and by the United Nations Charter providing sanctions against aggressive war. It was felt that the reconciliation of democracy with an efficient foreign policy requiring concentration of the foreign relations and war powers in the Executive had to be effected by creating a less dangerous and more law-governed world in which the deliberate processes of democracy could function without danger to national security. This was President Wilson's meaning in declaring that "the world must be made safe for democracy" and by President Kennedy's statement, in recognition of the need for "peaceful coexistence" of states with different social and economic systems, that "the world must be made safe for diversity."

The "cold war" began with Soviet efforts to increase the area of communism by subversion, threat, and force inconsistent with Charter obligations and the United States response of attempting to contain or even roll back communism by actions equally inconsistent with Charter obligations. This situation, coupled with the Charter requirement for great power unanimity to initiate sanctions, created discouragement with the international approach to the problem. United Nations action in the Korean situation during the temporary absence of Soviet representation in the Security Council was the major effort to implement collective security. President Truman, motivated by the desires to contain communism and to implement the Charter purpose to prevent aggression, took the initiative. He assumed that even without congressional support he had adequate constitutional authority to contribute United States forces to this effort in accord with Charter obligations and Security Council resolutions. The Korean effort was successful in accomplishing its initial purpose of driving the North Korean aggressors back to the armistice line in three months, but, unfortunately, the objective was enlarged to eliminate communism in North Korea and to unite all of Korea under the South Korean government as called for by a United Nations Resolution of 1947. This led to the entry of China which felt itself threatened by the march of American forces to its boundaries, to prolongation of hostilities for three years, to extensive United States casualties, to much criticism of President Truman for his independent action in committing United States forces, to the relief of General MacArthur who had advised the movement into North Korea, and to considerable disenchantment with collective security.[1]

Although before Korea the United Nations had had a measure of success in maintaining its principles in the Indonesian, Palestine, Kashmir, and Greek frontier situations, and after Korea in the Suez invasions of 1956 and the Cyprus and the Congo situations, it has been unable to establish peace in the Middle East since the Seven Days war or in Kashmir, Southeast Asia, Korea or Central Europe.[2] In spite of this, governments and large areas of opinion continue to assert that in the long run the United Nations idea, perhaps implemented by more effective sanctioning arrangements including an international police force, is the only ultimate solution of the problem of reconciling the efficient conduct of foreign policy with democracy in national constitutions, especially in that of the United States with its checks and balances.

Attention in the United States has, however, shifted to the second alternative, that of more effective control of the executive use of force by national law originated in Congress and interpreted by the courts. President Eisenhower obtained congressional support for his military assistance to the Taiwan government in the Straits of Formosa in 1955 and his intervention in Lebanon in 1958, as did President Johnson for his reprisals in the Gulf of Tonkin in 1964 which was deemed adequate to cover the later extension of intervention in Vietnam. On the other

---

1. Wright, *Collective Security in the Light of the Korean Experience*, 1951 PROC. AM. SOC'Y. INT'L. L. 165.
2. Wright, *Peace Keeping Operations of the U. N.*, 7 INTERNATIONAL STUDIES: JOURNAL OF THE INDIAN SCHOOL OF INTERNATIONAL STUDIES 169 (1965).

hand, the interventions in Guatemala in 1954 by the Eisenhower Administration, in Cuba in 1961 by the Kennedy Administration and in the Dominican Republic in 1964 by the Johnson Administration were carried on without formal Congressional support although efforts were made to gain support from the Organization of American States in the latter interventions. In none of these interventions did the United Nations give the United States any support, thus sharply differentiating them from the Korean action, the permissibility of which under international law and the Charter could hardly be questioned. The United States attempted to rationalize these interventions on grounds of collective self-defense permissible under the Charter, but this effort was viewed with skepticism in United Nations circles and by many jurists foreign and domestic.[3]

The effort to control the Executive by national procedures has taken the forms of (1) clear definition of the circumstances under which the President must obtain explicit Congressional support for the use of armed force, (2) elimination of the President's capacity to make military commitments without formal treaty consented to by the Senate or formal agreement supported by Congressional resolutions, (3) Congressional action to deter or terminate presidential military action not approved by Congress, and, (4) establishment of the jurisdiction of courts to judge the legality of the initiation and conduct of military action.

(1) The effort to draw a legal line limiting presidential use of force has faced the question: Is the use of armed force short of war presumed to be an executive or a legislative function? The controversy began with the making of the Constitution when the power of Congress to "make" war was changed to the power to "declare" war apparently in order to permit the President to take immediate defensive action. The controversy has not ended. Advocates of congressional control insist that democratic principles require control of military action by the organ of government which most closely reflects public opinion, and that the Constitution vests the power to use military force in Congress by giving it exclusive power to declare war, to provide for calling forth the militia, and to maintain an army and navy. An act of 1878 made it unlawful and a penal offense to "employ any part of the army of the United States as a *possee comitatus* or otherwise, for the purpose of executing the laws, except in such cases and under such circumstances as such employment of said forces may be expressly authorized by the Constitution or by act of Congress." [4] Extreme supporters of this

---

3. *See* Wright, *Legal Aspects of the Vietnam Situation*, 60 Am. J. Int'l. L. 750 (1966); Wright, *The Cuban Quarantine*, 57 Am. J. Int'l. L. 546 (1963); Wright, *Intervention and Cuba in 1961*, 1961 Proc. Am. Soc'y. Int'l. L. 2; Wright *Legal Aspects of the U-2 Incident*, 54 Am. J. Int'l. L. 836 (1960); Wright, *Subversive Intervention*, 54 Am. J. Int'l. L. 521 (1960); Wright, *U. S. Intervention in the Lebanon*, 53 Am. J. Int'l. L. 112 (1959).   ·

4. Act of June 18, 1878, ch. 263, § 15, 20 Stat. 152; Q. Wright, Control of American Foreign Relations 192 (1922) [hereinafter cited as Control].

position insist that Congress cannot delegate its war power and must act in the light of the particular circumstances before the armed forces can be used. Draftees in the Vietnam hostilities have not been able to persuade the Courts that they need not serve unless Congress declares war, but the Massachusetts act of 1970 declaring that its citizens need not serve in an undeclared war may bring the issue to the Supreme Court.[4a]

Advocates of presidental power, on the other hand, cite political theorists such as Locke and Montesquieu on the necessarily executive character of the conduct of foreign relations, including military action. They note that under the Constitution, the President is Commander-in-Chief of the armed forces in time of peace and war; that the necessities of unity, speed, secrecy, and authority can only be met by presidential action; and that, in fact, as early as 1794 Congress implemented its constitutional authority to provide for calling forth the militia to execute the laws of the Union, suppress insurrection, and repel invasion by authorizing the President to make such a call not only for the militia but also for the army and navy.[5] They point out that the congressional act of 1878 recognized power to use armed force in circumstances authorized by the Constitution or by act of Congress and that these exceptions constitute a complete authority of the President to use force short of formal war.

The Supreme Court has held that it belongs to the President himself to determine the exigencies in which a call for the militia under the congressional act of 1792 is justifiable,[6] and the same principle would seem to apply to uses of the regular forces if, as was assumed in the Constitutional Convention, as Commander-in-Chief he uses them for necessary defense of the territory and probably other purposes such as protection of citizens abroad. President Fillmore, like all other presidents except Buchanan, insisted that the Constitution itself granted the President power to utilize the regular armed forces, even though power to call forth the militia depended upon congressional delegation. "Probably", he added, "no legislation could add to or diminish the power thus given but by increasing or diminishing or abolishing altogether the army and navy." [7] The Supreme Court, as well as long practice, has sustained this position in the *Neagle, Debs* and other cases.[8] A House of Representatives report in 1956 [9] listed chrono-

---

4a. Acts of Mass., ch. 174, April 2, 1970.
5. Act of May 2, 1792, ch. 28, 1 STAT. 264; Act of Feb. 28, 1795, ch. 36, 1 STAT. 424; *See also* Act of Jan. 21, 1903, ch. 196, 32 STAT. 775.
6. Martin v. Mott, 25 U.S. (12 Wheat.) 19 (1827); CONTROL *supra*, note 4, at 309.
7. RICHARDSON, MESSAGES OF THE PRESIDENTS 105 (1897); CONTROL *supra*, note 4, at 192.
8. In re Neagle, 135 U.S. 1 (1890); In re Debs, 158 U. S. 564 (1895); CONTROL *supra*, note 4, at 193, 305. *See also* Durand v. Hollins, 4 Blatch. 451, Fed. Cas. No. 4156 (1860) supporting the President's authorization of the bombardment of Greytown, Nicaragua to protect American Citizens.
9. THE POWER OF THE PRESIDENT AS COMMANDER-IN-CHIEF OF THE ARMY AND NAVY OF THE U.S., H. R. Doc. 443, 84th Cong., 2d Sess. (1956).

logically 50 instances from 1789 to 1955 of presidential use of armed forces abroad and in United States territory, indicating that such uses were generally based on Presidential power as Commander-in-Chief and that explicit congressional support was considered necessary only by President Buchanan,[10] though Presidents Wilson and Eisenhower considered it generally desirable. While the Court has found some domestic uses of armed force unconstitutional, such as the Truman action in the steel strike in 1952, it supported uses of force abroad with the exception of the application of prize law in time of war and the seizure of alien vessels at sea in time of peace. It held that the seizure of a French private vessel in 1804 by order of President Jefferson went beyond congressional authorization.[11] This report also lists 61 juristic and official opinions on the subject from 1935 to 1955, the majority of which support a broad construction of the president's power as Commander-in-Chief.

A study for the Senate Committee on Foreign Relations in 1951 stated that "Since the Constitution was adopted there have been at least 125 incidents in which the President without congressional authorization has ordered armed forces to take action or maintain positions abroad." [12]

The President's power to initiate military action seems to be clearly established in constitutional law by practice, judicial opinion, and the text of the Constitution and legislation; but is there a line separating such circumstances from the exclusive congressional power to declare war? The Supreme Court has distinguished between war in the material sense and war in the legal sense,[13] the former referring to actual hostilities of considerable magnitude and the latter to the legal situation existing during a period of time, determined by the intent rather than the action of states, in which the belligerents are juridically equal, and the rights and duties of all states, whether belligerent or neutral, are different from those in time of peace.[14] The broadest conception of presidential power to use armed force assumes that this power extends to such uses of any magnitude, so long as it does not constitute war in the legal sense, which can be initiated for the United States only by congressional action manifesting its intent to establish a "state of war." The courts have, however, held that the President may *recognize* that action by rebels or by a foreign country against the United States manifest an *animus belligerandi* and create a

---

10. *Id.*
11. Little v. Barreme, 6 U.S. (2 Cranch) 170 (1804); *See also* note 28 *infra.*
12. SENATE COMM. ON FOR. REL., 82 CONG., 2d SESS., POWERS OF THE PRESIDENT TO SEND THE U.S. ARMED FORCES OUTSIDE THE UNITED STATES (Comm. Print 1951).
13. The Three Friends, 166 U. S. 1 (1897); this follows Justice Nelson's dissenting opinion in The Prize Cases, 67 U. S. (2 Black 635) 690 (1863).
14. Q. WRIGHT, A STUDY OF WAR 8 (1965).

legal state of war. Justice Nelson, dissenting in the Prize cases dealing with the Civil War, held that only Congress could put the United States in a situation of legal war whether by declaration or recognition and before it acted hostilities could be only war in the material sense. The majority opinion, however, held that President Lincoln was competent to recognize that Confederate action had initiated a "state of war." This permitted him to exercise war powers such as declaring a war blockade of the Confederacy months before Congress had in any way recognized the situation.[15] Similarly, President McKinley authorized a war blockade of Cuba and Puerto Rico without congressional authority, although a few days later Congress declared that war with Spain existed and had existed before this blockade proclamation by action of the Spanish government. President Polk's authorization of military action on the Mexican frontier—which resulted in two battles—induced him to inform Congress that war existed by the action of Mexico, a suggestion which Congress accepted in declaring war on Mexico. President Wilson informed Congress in April, 1917, that the actions of Germany in sinking American ships at sea constituted war against the United States and Congress declared that war had been thrust upon the United States by action of Germany. President Roosevelt's statement to Congress after Pearl Harbor was similar. It is clear that the President's recognition power can, in fact, initiate a state of legal war for the United States without congressional action and most American wars have started in this way, ostensibly by action of the enemy, thus virtually nullifying the theoretically exclusive power of Congress to declare war.

The United States has been in a legal state of war since the Constitution went into effect only six times (1812, 1846, 1861, 1898, 1917 and 1941) and in all cases the President recognized that war existed before Congress acted, though in all but the Civil War the date of the beginning of the war was determined by Congress. Other military incidents, only two of which were authorized by Congress, were of sufficient magnitude to be called war in the material sense (1798, 1801, 1816, 1899, 1900, 1914, 1950 and 1965). The President has initiated 170 lesser military actions abroad, generally without explicit congressional authority.[16]

It has been suggested that the actual or probable magnitude of hostilities should be the test of presidential action under his power as Commander-in-Chief. This means that the President should get explicit congressional support if the circumstances suggest that the use of force is likely to escalate into a situation which could be called war in the material sense. In an effort to make such a test less vague, Professor John N. Moore suggests that congressional approval should

---

15. The Prize Cases, 67 U.S. (2 Black) 635 (1863).
16. Q. WRIGHT, A STUDY OF WAR 636, 650, 1545 (1964); *See also* C. Berdahl, *War Powers of the Executive of the United States* in 9 U. of ILL. STUDIES IN THE SOCIAL SCIENCES (1920).

be obtained if regular combat units are to be used but that independent presidential action should be permissible for uses of naval and marine forces in naval or landing operations where substantial casualties and commitment of resources is not to be expected.[17] This test can, perhaps, better be stated that the President should obtain congressional support in advance for military action which will probably require congressional action, as by appropriations, before it is completed. All tests based on magnitude, however, involve prediction of future magnitude. A small operation beginning with only military advisors or small landing forces may escalate, requiring large force and Congressional appropriations, as in the Viet Nam situation.

Another type of test depends upon the purpose for which force is used, permitting independent presidential action to enforce the laws, to suppress insurrection, or to repel invasion as provided in the congressional act of 1794 pursuant to the constitutional clause concerning the militia, but requiring congressional support if the purpose is political such as military pressure in aid of diplomacy, territorial acquistion, or intervention to influence the policy or ideology of a foreign government. The use of force for such political purposes seems to be prohibited by contemporary international law as set forth in the Kellogg-Briand Pact, the Nuremburg Charter, and the United Nations Charter. Consequently, this test would require congressional support only if the purpose of hostility is in violation of international law. Such an idea is suggested by several Supreme Court opinions holding that the executive in conducting war or engaging in lesser military activity must act on the presumption that the United States intends to observe international law unless Congress makes explicit authorizations to the contrary.[18]

However, the meaning of these three permissible uses of force is not free from controversy. Does enforcement of law refer to treaties and international law as well as acts of Congress? Does suppression of insurrection refer only to insurrection in the United States or can it cover assistance requested by foreign governments to suppress insurrections in their territories? Does repelling invasion permit only action within the territory of the United States and pursuit over the boundary as stated by Attorney General Wickersham in his references to uses of the militia,[19] or does it include action on the high seas or abroad to frustrate an armed attack upon the United States or an ally as suggested by the United Nations Charter? Does it permit action to repel an immediately anticipated attack as implied by Secretary Webster's opinion in the Caroline incident of 1840[20] or even preemp-

---

17. Moore, *The National Executive and the Use of Force Abroad,* 21 NAVAL WAR COLLEGE REV. 32 (1969).
18. Miller v. United States, 78 U. S. (11 Wall.) 268 (1871); Mitchell v. Harmony, 54 U. S. (13 How.) 115 (1852); Flemming v. Page, 50 U. S. (9 How.) 603 (1850); CONTROL *supra,* note 4, at 169.
19. 29 OF. ATT'Y. GEN. 322 (1912); CONTROL, *supra* note 4, at 300.
20. CONTROL *supra* note 4, at 206.

tive action to prevent or deter a more remote danger of attack? These problems might be solved by decision of international organs applying international law but unilateral judgment by the President would often be unconvincing to many jurists, foreign and domestic, and many congressmen.

(2) The problem of commitments to use armed force in the future by excutive agreement has been highly controversial from the 1790's to the present time. The commitments for collective defense which the executive may have made with Spain as a *quid pro quo* for the acquisition of bases were criticized by Congress in 1969.[21] Such commitments have actually been made by authority of the President alone, but their meaning has not always been clear and they have been vigorously criticized, especially those made with Caribbean countries by Theodore Roosevelt, with European countries by Franklin Roosevelt, and with Southeast Asian countries by Lyndon Johnson. Majority opinion probably holds that since their implementation is likely to require Congressional action, they should be made only by treaty assented to by the Senate or by executive agreements formally authorized by Congress. Executive agreements not so authorized doubtless may be used to clarify treaty or congressionally supported commitments.[22] The United Nations Charter, which is a treaty, undoubtedly commits the United States to use armed force if called for by a decision of the Security Council in pursuance of its responsibilities under Chapter 7 of the Charter, though it is controversial whether this is true when the explicit agreement called for by Article 43 of the Charter has not been made. The Congressional Act of 1945 authorized participation in United Nations sanctions only after Congress had approved such an agreement. Apparently Congress intended to prevent the President from making explicit agreements in pursuance of the general Charter commitment. There is also controversy on Charter provisions distinguishing decisions from recommendations of the Security Council. President Truman authorized the use of forces in Korea in June 1950 and this was clearly permissible under the Charter but probably not obligatory because of the lack of prior agreement and the recommendatory character of the Security Council's resolution. In view of these circumstances it was argued by Senator Taft and others that the President should have obtained explicit congressional authorization. Practice would indicate, however, that the President's powers as Commander-in-Chief permit him to use force short of war in pursuance of a treaty to which the United States is a party.[23]

---

21. The Washington Post, Feb. 25, 1969, at A 17, col. 1; *id.*, Feb. 26, 1969, at A 5, col. 1.
22. CONTROL, *supra* note 4, at 234; Wright, *The U. S. and International Agreements*, 38 AM. J. INT'L. L. 682 (1944); W. MCCLURE, INTERNATIONAL EXECUTIVE AGREEMENTS 363 (1941).
23. Wright, *Constitutional Procedures in the U. S. for Carrying Out Obligations for Military Sanctions*, 38 AM. J. INT'L L. 682 (1944).

(3) Apart from the influence which legal standards and understandings might have in influencing the President's exercise of discretion in using armed forces abroad, what practical courses might Congress embark upon to control presidential action? The most important is refusal to appropriate funds for enterprises of which it disapproves. If faced by the *fait accompli* of United States soldiers fighting abroad, Congress is, however, under strong pressure to make the appropriation called for, as demonstrated in the Vietnam situation. Even those senators, like Fulbright, who opposed the operation regularly voted appropriations.

Congressional resolutions stating a policy calling for a withdrawal of forces or negotiation may have influence although it has been held by presidents, as well as by the Supreme Court, that they are not obligatory because in the field of foreign policy the Constitution has reposed authority in the President.[24] Congress may repeal existing resolutions authorizing the use of armed force, such as those dealing with Formosa (1951), the Middle East (1957), and the Gulf of Tonkin (1965). The President however, may consider that he is competent to act in the circumstances without the resolution.

Congressional hearings and congressional debates may inform and influence public opinion which may in turn bring pressure upon the President—especially if an election is pending. The final resort is impeachment of the President, feasible only if supported by strong public opinion.

These possibilities of congressional control or influence have all been discussed and some of them utilized in the Vietnam situation. They undoubtedly contributed to President Johnson's decision to stop bombing in North Vietnam, to initiate negotiations, and to withdraw from contention for the nomination in 1968. The capabilities of Congress indicate the advisability of close cooperation between the President and Congress in making important decisions even if the President has the constitutional authority to act alone.[25]

(4) The possibility of judicial control to limit presidential use of force has been much discussed, especially in connection with the draft during Vietnam hostilities. Judicial action to protect private property against military encroachment has proved feasible. The Supreme Court held that Jefferson's authorization to seize a French private vessel on the high seas in 1804 was contrary to congressional authorization and illegal,[26] and it also held that President Truman's use of armed force to end the steel strike by seizing the mills in 1952 was illegal.[27] Courts have also regularly decided on the legality under international law of

---

24. CONTROL, *supra* note 4, at 279.
25. On Constitutional understandings urging cooperation between President and Congress, *see* CONTROL, *supra* note 4, at 346-371.
26. *See* note 11, *supra*.
27. Youngstown Co. v. Sawyer, 343 U. S. 579 (1952).

seizures of alien ships in time of peace and as prizes in time of war.[28] In presidential action utilizing armed forces in retaliation for injuries to U.S. citizens abroad or to quell riots or rebellions in United States territory, as in the Dorr rebellion of 1842 and the Pullman strike of 1894, the courts have assumed jurisdiction but have usually sustained the president's action on the ground that the necessity to use force is a political question and the courts must accept the President's judgment.[29]

Courts-martial may judge the propriety of acts of members of the United States armed forces under the Articles of War, and Military Commissions may judge the behavior of prisoners of war and civilians in occupied territory in accordance with the law of war. Such decisions of military tribunals may be appealed to the regular U.S. Courts. Military tribunals have dealt with the refusal of drafted soldiers to carry out orders for military action claimed to be contrary to the law of war, such as maltreating enemy prisoners of war or civilians, but they have insisted on the duty to obey superior orders, have declined to find the action in clear violation of international law and have, in any case, refused to allow draft exemptions on the ground that illegal action is habitual in a particular theater of war.[30]

Courts also apply the United States draft act recognizing the exemption of conscientious objectors to all war. This ground of exemption has been extended in recent decisions from religious to philosophical objections to all war if an individual regards these objections as binding on his conscience; [31] but the courts have refused to entertain pleas of conscientious objection to service in particular hostilities on the ground that they are illegal under international law, the United Nations Charter, other treaties, or that they are unconstitutional because not declared by Congress. The courts have held that these questions are political and the decision belongs to the political organs of the government, especially the President, and they must follow the political judgment under the principle of separation of powers.[32]

---

28. The Paquete *Habana*, 175 U. S. 677 (1900); Murray v. Schooner *Charming Betsy*, 6 U. S. (2 Cranch.) 64 (1804); CONTROL, *supra* note 4, at 171-172.
29. In re Debs, 158 U. S. 564 (1895); Luther v. Borden, 48 U. S. (7 How.) 1 (1849); Martin v. Matt, 25 U. S. (12 Wheat.) 19 (1827); Perrin v. United States, 4 Ct. Cl. 543 (1868).
30. In the court martial of Captain Howard Levy (unreported) it was stated that the obligation to observe superior orders might also be taken into account, thus relieving the soldier of guilt in performing acts which he believes contrary to the law of war. The Nuremberg Charter permitted superior orders as a ground for mitigating punishment for war crimes if the individual had no freedom of choice. Wright, *The Law of the Nuremberg Trial*, 41 AM. J. INT'L L. 38, 55, 71 (1947).
31. U.S. v. Seeger, 380 U.S. 163 (1965).
32. The Supreme Court refused to review lower court decisions convicting draftees or officers who refused military service because of conscientious objection to service in the Vietnam War on moral grounds, Noyd v. U.S., 378 F.2d 538, *cert. denied,*

The Nuremberg Charter and the United Nations Charter distinguish between legal hostilities in individual or collective self-defense or in sanctioning operations authorized by the United Nations, and illegal or aggressive hostilities prohibited by these instruments. This distinction was insisted upon by American counsel in the Nuremburg trials and in other war crimes trials. These tribunals and the U.S. Supreme Court enforced it against enemy persons, but the doctrine of political questions has made it impossible to enforce this distinction to judge the legality of military actions of the United States government in United States courts. Efforts to obtain a declaratory judgment that particular hostilities are illegal or that taxes need not be paid when the receipts will be used in preparation for illegal hostilities have failed on the ground that the issue is political.[33]

It has been suggested that this distinction might be applied by the International Court of Justice even though the effort of the United Nations to establish an International Criminal Court with jurisdiction over individuals alleged to have committed offenses against the law of nations has failed to date.[34] The United States is a party to the optional clause of the World Court Statute and another state, such as Sweden, also party to the optional clause, might initiate an action against the United States on the ground that an intervention such as that in Vietnam is contrary to Charter obligations, general observance of which is essential to the security of the applicant state, and that each member of the United Nations has a legal interest in observance of Charter obligations by all members. The United States could hardly utilize its domestic jurisdiction reservation on such an application calling for interpretation of treaty obligations, though the court might refuse to give judgment on the ground of insufficient legal interest by the applicant, as it did in the Southwest Africa case.[35] There is also

---

389 U. S. 1022 (1967); or on the ground that its initiation or conduct violated international law and that voluntary participation would constitute a war crime, Holmes v. U. S. 387 F.2d 781, *cert. denied,* 391 U. S. 936 (1968); Spiro v. U. S. 384 F.2d 159, *cert. denied,* 390 U. S. 956 (1968); Hart v. U. S. 382 F.2d 1020, *cert. denied,* 391 U. S. 952 (1968). Justice Douglas dissented in all of these cases, Justice Black in the *Spiro* case, and Justice Stewart in the *Holmes* case. *See also* Heisler, *Problems of Raising the Defense of International Law (in Draft Cases),* 25 NAT'L LAWYERS' GUILD PRACTITIONER 96 (1966); Faulkner, *International Law and the Military Draft,* in AGAINST THE CRIME OF SILENCE: PROCEEDINGS OF THE BERTRAND RUSSELL INT'L WAR CRIMES TRIBUNAL 91 (J. Duffett ed. 1968).

33. Velva v. Johnson, 287 F. Supp. 846 (1968); Farmer v. Rountree, 252 F.2d 490 (6th Cir. 1958), *cert. denied,* 357 U. S. 906 (1958), *petition for rehearing denied,* 358 U. S. 858 (1958), *aff'g* 149 F. Supp. 327 (M.D. Tenn. 1956).

34. Wright, *Proposal for an International Criminal Court,* 46 AM. J. INT'L. L. 60 (1952).

35. Southwest Africa Case, [1966] I.C.J. 6; 61 AM. J. INT'L. L. 117 (1967); Article 63 of the Statute of the I.C.J. seems to recognize the legal interest of each party to a multilateral treaty in its observance by all of the parties. The United States, in its reservation to the optional clause, assumed that it could prevent a judgment on the interpretation of a multilateral treaty to which it was a party in a litigation between other parties.

the possibility of a request for an Advisory Opinion on this issue by the United Nations General Assembly; this opinion would not be subject to United States veto as would be a Security Council request. If the International Court assumed jurisdiction on such an issue the possibility of application to it in case of dubious uses of armed forces abroad by the President might modify the position of the United States courts in holding that the issue is political. They might give a judgment on such matters to avoid the possibility of an international judgment against the United States; furthermore the development of a series of precedents in the World Court clarifying the distinction between legal and illegal uses of force would tend to remove the issue from the political realm.

The feasibility of giving a larger measure of judicial control whether by national or international tribunals over the initiation and conduct of hostilities, as contemplated in the war crime trials, probably depends on the termination of the cold war, an increased sentiment of internationalism everywhere, and a general strengthening of institutions for maintaining international law and the principles of the United Nations Charter.

I conclude that the Constitution and practice under it have given the President, as Commander-in-Chief and conductor of foreign policy, legal authority to send the armed forces abroad; to recognize foreign states, governments, belligerency, and aggression against the United States or a foreign state; to conduct foreign policy in a way to invite foreign hostilities; and even to make commitments which may require the future use of force. By the exercise of these powers he may nullify the theoretically exclusive power of Congress to declare war. His discretion is limited only by his constitutional duty to respect private rights, especially those of property, and the Constitutional understandings that he ought not to exercise these powers without Congressional support if such exercise is likely to lead to major hostilities requiring new appropriations, to violation of international law tending to induce foreign reprisals, or to national obligations to use armed force in future contingencies. Congressional powers to refuse appropriations, to impeach, to recommend, and to influence public opinion and elections, are inadequate to prevent a presidential *fait accompli* in the military field even though opposed by large sections of Congress and the public and widely believed at home and abroad to be violations of international law.

Under the conditions of a jungle world in which national power is a major factor in maintaining national security, public manifestations of conflict between the President and Congress may assist an actual or potential enemy to jeopardize national security in time of crisis. Continuous cooperation between the two branches of the government is therefore desirable,[36] but the exigencies of the world situation may require a decision with speed, secrecy, and authority inconsistent with

---

36. CONTROL, *supra* note 4, at 346-356.

the deliberation involved in Congressional action. Furthermore, Congress and the public are likely to be ill informed of the situation, ignorant of international law, and more belligerent than the President, as they were in the Spanish Crisis of 1898.[37] Presidents, therefore, though aware in recent years of the need to placate Congress and the public, have often exercised their powers in this field independently, utilizing the advice of military and civilian advisers and the secret service, thus reducing the effective influence of Congress and public opinion in a way inconsistent with the principles of democracy.[38]

Presidential independence in the conduct of foreign and military affairs, although said to be necessary for national security, may in fact be dangerous if uncontrolled by international law. Experience in the 20th century has indicated that national security cannot be obtained by isolation from world politics, by balancing military power, or by maintenance of dominant military power. Neither nationalism, interventionism, nor imperialism can provide permanent security in the contemporary world in which technological distances between nations are shrinking more rapidly than moral distances and offensive power is increasing more rapidly than defensive power. With the steady advance of science and technology, the means for sudden, destructive attack from a distance has increased more rapidly than means for defense or deterrence, and with the lagging development of universal cultural and ideological understanding, the causes of conflict have increased more rapidly than the will for peaceful adjustment.[39] Internationalism, which recognizes that nations with distinctive cultures exist but that none can be secure unless all are secure, has been given legal substance in the agreements of statesmen designed to supersede the rule of national power above law by the rule of international law above national power.[40] The Hague Conventions, the League of Na-

---

37. W. Millis, THE MARTIAL SPIRIT (1931); J. McCamy, THE ADMINISTRATION OF AMERICAN FOREIGN AFFAIRS 311, 336, 353 (1950). Machiavelli and Woodrow Wilson, for different reasons, thought democracies were more likely to observe international law. See CONTROL, supra note 4, at 236.
38. Elihu Root believed that the requirements of democracy and sound foreign policy could be reconciled only by increasing the role of international law and educating the public on the subject. Root, The Effect of Democracy on International Law in 1917 PROC. OF THE AM. SOC. OF INT'L LAW Law 2, 7-8; CONTROL, supra note 4, at 370.
39. Q. WRIGHT, A STUDY OF WAR 1278, 1284, 1519 (1964); Wright, THE ROLE OF INTERNATIONAL LAW IN THE ELIMINATION OF WAR 137 (1961).
40. Chief Justice Warren recognized the need to subordinate national sovereignty to International Law in an address at a conference sponsored by the Center for the Study of Democratic Institutions inspired by Pope John XXIII's encyclical, "Peace on Earth." "World Peace through law," said Chief Justice Warren, "should be our preoccupation." Louis Henken in a report to the New York Council on Foreign Relations concluded, "In regard to the law against force, there is no longer any doubt about its validity, its desirability, its necessity." How NATIONS BEHAVE: LAW AND FOREIGN POLICY (1968) Arthur Larson and Wilfred Jenks have brought to-

tions Covenant, the Kellogg-Briand Pact, the Nuremburg Charter, and the United Nations Charter have progressively developed international law to "outlaw" war in the traditional sense which implied the equal right of sovereign states to initiate a "state of war," and to utilize armed force to realize their policies during a state of war. With war in this sense outlawed, international law permits states to use force in international relations only for individual or collective self-defense against armed attack or in support of sanctioning action authorized by the United Nations. Force may not be used as an instrument of national policy or for the settlement of international disputes.[41] Under this "new international law," conflict between Presidential power under the Constitution and national obligations under international law is more probable and more dangerous than in the past.[42] National security in the present world requires a subordination of constitutional power to international law, but, though the Supreme Court has held that international law is applicable by national courts,[43] the constitutional theory of separation of powers has denied the competence of the judiciary to decide on "political questions" said to include Presidential decisions in the realm of foreign and military policy.[44] With this doctrine, only in limited fields such as seizures of private property and problems dealt with by prize courts and military commissions has the judiciary been able to limit presidential discretion by international law. These situations concern private rights protected by constitutional guarantees as well as by rules of international law. They concern the conduct rather than the initiation of hostilities and are not usually of political importance. But courts have often refused to interfere with Presidential or congressional decisions concerned with foreign and military affairs claimed to encroach upon civil liberties.[45]

---

gether reports from fifteen nations of the world, indicating that, with the possible exception of certain communist countries, national legal systems recognize that national sovereignty is limited by law and that these legal systems have enough in common to establish international law as a synthesis of all of them. SOVEREIGNTY WITHIN THE LAW at 461 (1965). THE UNITED STATES ARMY FIELD MANUAL ON THE LAW ON LAND WARFARE (1956) accepts the Nuremberg Charter's definition of war crimes, including the "Crime against Peace," and states, "Any person whether a member of the armed forces or a civilian who commits an act which constitutes a crime under international law is responsible therefor and liable to punishment. *Id.* at 178.

41. Wright, A STUDY OF WAR 891, 1532 (1964); Wright, THE ROLE OF INTERNATIONAL LAW IN THE ELIMINATION OF WAR 59-65 (1961) *See also* Root, *The Effect of Democracy on International Law* in 1917 PROC. OF THE AM. SOC. OF INT'L LAW 2.

42. CONTROL *supra* note 4, at 4-9.

43. The Paquete *Habana,* 175 U. S. 677 (1900).

44. Wright, *International Law in its Relation to Constitutional Law,* 17 AM. J. INT'L L. 234 (1917); CONTROL *supra* note 4, at 124, 172; Wallace McClure believes the constitution permits a broader application of international law by the courts. MC-CLURE, WORLD LEGAL ORDER: POSSIBLE CONTRIBUTIONS BY THE PEOPLE OF THE U. S. (1960).

45. CONTROL, *supra* note 4 at 83, 94; Selective Service Draft Cases, 245 U. S. 366 (1918). With Justice Douglas dissenting, the Supreme Court declined to apply the free-

Increased competence of the International Court of Justice to pronounce on the legality of the initiation of military action under contemporary international law might so clarify the law in this field that Congress would be willing to consider the issue legal rather than political and extend the jurisdiction of national courts to judge presidential action in the field in order to avoid national liability before the International Court. The constitutional understanding requiring the President to observe international law might then become a rule of constitutional law. In this way the world rule of law might be promoted, national security enhanced, and the opportunity offered for democratic processes to influence important diplomatic and military decisions. This condition, however, awaits an increase in world-mindedness among peoples and governments and an increased effectiveness of international institutions.

---

dom of speech guarantee of the Constitution to protect words and acts considered criminal incitement to draft evasion under the Selective Service Act. United States v. O'Brien, 391 U. S. 367 (1968). Judge Hubert, however, in the Federal District Court of Chicago considered that the citizens of Libertyville, Ill., a suburb of Chicago, were entitled to present arguments that the stationing of an ABM system in their vicinity would violate human rights guarantees. "There must be some point," he said, "where executive insanity can be stopped." The Washington Post, Mar. 5, 1969, at A 2, col. 4; id., Mar. 6, 1969, at A 20, col. 1.

Presidential War-Making:
Constitutional Prerogative or Usurpation?

W. TAYLOR REVELEY, III

AMONG the principal rites of an unpopular war is the inquisition: the investigation of those men and institutions responsible for the decision to fight. Often the inquisition seeks only scapegoats.[1] But occasionally it is less concerned with fixing blame than with avoiding future evil. Much of the current inquiry into the scope of the President's constitutional authority to commit American troops to foreign conflict partakes more of the redemptive than the punitive.[2] Reasoned consideration of the question, however, is difficult for at least three reasons. The problem is many-faceted; the relevant context, in both its precedential and policy elements, unusually rich; and passions on the matter notably high. Thus, there is danger of a simplistic analysis based upon only a few of the pertinent factors, supported by selected bits of precedent and policy, and given direction by a visceral reaction to Vietnam. Karl Llewellyn's injunction that the reader should till an author "for his wheat, sorting out his chaff"[3] is singularly appropriate regarding treatments of this aspect of presidential power. What follows is an attempt to delineate the bounds of the problem—an attempt undertaken with an awareness of the inherent opportunities for error.

---

[1] Some of the present assaults on the military seem to be in this vein. *See, e.g.,* Finney, *Questions over Military: Bombardment on What It Is Doing and Why,* N.Y. Times, May 25, 1969, § 4, at 1, cols. 2-6; *The Military-Industrial Complex,* NEWSWEEK, June 9, 1969, at 74-87. *See generally Military: Servant or Master of Policy,* TIME, April 11, 1969, at 20-26.

[2] Among the better treatments of the question are F. WORMUTH, THE VIETNAM WAR: THE PRESIDENT VERSUS THE CONSTITUTION (April 1968) (Occasional Paper: Center for the Study of Democratic Institutions) [hereinafter cited as WORMUTH]; Kurland, *The Impotence of Reticence,* 1968 DUKE L.J. 619; Moore, *The National Executive and the Use of the Armed Forces Abroad,* 21 NAVAL WAR COLLEGE REV. 28 (Jan. 1969); Schwartz & McCormack, *The Justiciability of Legal Objections to the American Military Effort in Vietnam,* 46 TEXAS L. REV. 1033 (1968); Velvel, *The War in Viet Nam: Unconstitutional, Justiciable, and Jurisdictionally Attackable,* 16 KAN. L. REV. 449 (1968); *President's War Powers—I & II,* C.Q. GUIDE TO CURRENT AM. GOV'T 63, 67 (Spring 1968); Note, *Congress, the President and the Power to Commit Forces to Combat,* 81 HARV. L. REV. 1771 (1968).

[3] K. LLEWELLYN, THE BRAMBLE BUSH 10 (1960).

POLITICAL OR JUDICIAL RESOLUTION OF THE ISSUE?

In theory, both the judicial and the political processes are available to set the limits on presidential use of force abroad. As a rule, the judicial and political processes differ notably in their mode of decision-making. Courts generally reach the result dictated, or at least suggested, by pre-existing law. Thus, judges emphasize precedent over policy and strive for an impartial decision, rather than for one that recognizes the relative power of the interests concerned. Political interaction, on the other hand, usually alters the legal status quo to meet the changing needs and demands of the community. Thus, policy is emphasized over precedent, and the decision is shaped by the relative power of the participants.

These distinctions, however, lose much of their force in the context of constitutional limits on presidential power. Unlike cases involving statutory or even common law, constitutional questions leave courts far freer to make basic community decisions, not only because the judiciary is free of any actual or potential legislative ukase but also because it is interpreting an unusually ambiguous and evolutionary document.[4] In the sensitive area of presidential power, the judiciary's instinct for self-preservation and its desire to hand down effective judgments necessitate that some account be taken of the relative strength of the opposing interests. The contextual features which increase the judiciary's room for maneuver have the converse effect upon the political decision-maker. His ability to alter the legal status quo is reduced when the norms in question are of constitutional stature. Thus, he must give far more attention to existing doctrine than usual, and he is pushed close to the role of the impartial applier of the law.

Though it is important to recognize that the judicial and political processes would not be dissimilar in their approach to the limits on presidential use of force abroad, significant differences remain. A judicial resolution would be more focused and clear-cut than a political one, but also more inflexible. It would be more concerned with the dictates of doctrine and less with the balance of power, and it would run a greater risk of being ignored or subverted than a political decision.[5] While judicial involvement in the question at hand has been vigorously urged,[6] the immediate prospect of such involvement is dim.[7] Accord-

---

[4] See text at notes 22-23 *infra*.

[5] See note 104 *infra*.

[6] *See, e.g.,* Schwartz, *supra* note 2; Velvel, *supra* note 2, at 479-503(e). *But see* Moore, *supra* note 2, at 35-36; Note, 81 HARV. L. REV., *supra* note 2, at 1794.

ingly, to the extent that the issue is resolved, its resolution will come through the interaction of the President, Congress and the electorate—a method often used to settle fundamental constitutional questions.[8]

THE ISSUE MORE FULLY DEFINED

The issue is best framed in terms of the constitutional limits on presidential power to pursue a foreign policy which may easily lead to armed conflict, rather than simply in terms of executive power to commit troops to foreign combat.[9] Resort to arms is rarely the first step in

---

[7] Though given ample opportunity to resolve the constitutionality of American participation in the Vietnam War, federal courts have consistently declined to consider the matter, primarily because they view it as a political question. *See, e.g.,* Mora v. McNamara, 387 F.2d 862 (D.C. Cir.), *cert. denied,* 389 U.S. 934 (1967); Luftig v. McNamara, 373 F.2d 664 (D.C. Cir), *cert. denied,* 387 U.S. 945 (1967); United States v. Mitchell, 369 F.2d 323 (2d Cir. 1966), *cert. denied,* 386 U.S. 972 (1967); Velvel v. Johnson, 287 F. Supp. 846 (D. Kan. 1968); Schwartz, *supra* note 2, at 1051 n.61.

[8] *See* G. SCHUBERT, JR., THE PRESIDENCY IN THE COURTS 347-48 (1957).

[9] It is well to note in passing the existence of a second level of legal restraints. Under international law, the United States, and possibly the President as an individual, are forbidden to use military force unilaterally except in self-defense, and are enjoined, whenever arms are employed, to follow the laws of war. The primary international stricture against the use of force by states to resolve their disputes is U.N. CHARTER art. 2, para. 4: "All Members shall refrain in their international relations from the threat or use of force against the territorial integrity or political independence of any state, or in any manner inconsistent with the Purposes of the United Nations." Article 2(4), however, is subject to the proviso stated in article 51: "Nothing in the present Charter shall impair the inherent right of individual or collective self-defense if an armed attack occurs against a Member of the United Nations, until the Security Council has taken measures necessary to maintain international peace and security." As there is no general consensus on the precise scope of the article 51 exception, the ban in article 2(4) on the use of force has proved less expansive than might have been expected.

The laws of warfare have been codified in several multilateral treaties, especially the Hague Conventions of 1907, *e.g.,* Peaceful Settlement of Disputes, Oct. 18, 1907, 36 Stat. 2199, T.S. No. 536; Laws and Customs of War on Land, Oct. 18, 1907, 36 Stat. 2277, T.S. No. 539; Naval War, Oct. 18, 1907, 36 Stat. 2396, T.S. No. 544; and the Geneva Prisoner of War Convention, Aug. 12, 1949, 6 U.S.T. 3316, T.I.A.S. No. 3364.

The potential liability of the President, should he be guilty of waging an illegal war under international law, or of conducting in an illegal manner a struggle otherwise justified, stems from the precedent set by the Nuremberg and Tokyo War Crimes proceedings, in which individuals were held responsible for their participation in military operations deemed beyond the law. The tribunals' actions were affirmed unanimously by the United Nations General Assembly in its 1946 adoption of the principles of the Nuremberg Charter, G.A. Res. 95, U.N. Doc. A /64/ Add. 1, at 188 (1946). Barring the conquest of the United States, the President runs no risk of actual trial for violation of the Nuremberg principles, but they are likely to affect his conduct. Were he widely believed to be a war criminal, his political effectiveness would plummet,

the conduct of any American foreign policy. Armed force is generally used only *in extremis* to salvage a policy which more pacific modalities could not preserve and advance. Thus, the decision to use the military is usually taken under circumstances which make its dispatch hard to resist; pressures for commitment, both domestic and foreign, will exist which could have been avoided or mitigated had a different foreign policy been pursued.[10] Though there is not a one-for-one correlation, it is generally true that to limit presidential war-making, it is first necessary to limit presidential policy-making.[11]

both at home and abroad. And, perhaps more fundamentally, his own personal commitment to the law usually dictates adherence to these principles, at least as he understands them. *See* Falk, *International Law and the United States Role in Viet Nam: A Response to Professor Moore*, 76 YALE L.J. 1095, 1100-01 n.12 (1967); Schwartz, *supra* note 2, at 1033-35.

Arguably these international provisions bear on domestic constitutional law. At one extreme, the possibility exists that presidential war-making in violation of international law is per se unconstitutional. *See* Falk, *International Law and the United States Role in the Viet Nam War*, 75 YALE L.J. 1122, 1155 (1966). *But see* Falk, *International Law and the United States Role in Viet Nam: A Response to Professor Moore*, 76 YALE L.J. 1095, 1150-51 (1967). A middle reading of the relationship would place a breach of international law among the factors suggesting unconstitutionality. At the other pole is an analysis which finds no necessary link between domestic and international law. The prevailing American authority supports the second extreme, holding that the constitutionality of presidential use of force abroad is strictly a matter for domestic law. *See* Moore, *International Law and the United States Role in Viet Nam: A Reply*, 76 YALE L.J. 1051, 1092-93 (1967). Thus, a war illegal under international doctrine may nonetheless be quite constitutional.

[10] To remain in power, a President and his congressional supporters can ill afford to admit that they have fruitlessly pursued a costly foreign policy. Thus, once objectives are proclaimed and sought, their realization becomes important for the political survival of their proponents, irrespective of whether the goals in question have continuing merit. Similarly, to maintain the credibility of American commitments to contain communism, it has been felt essential to honor pledges to support other noncommunist governments, regardless of the inherent importance of the country being assisted. With reference to John F. Kennedy's decision to deepen American involvement in Vietnam, it has been authoritatively stated that

> he believed that a weakening in our basic resolve to help in Southeast Asia would tend to encourage separate Soviet pressures in other areas. . . .
>
> [T]his concern specifically related to Khrushchev's aggressive designs on Berlin . . . . President Kennedy clearly did believe that failure to keep the high degree of commitment we had in Viet-Nam . . . had a bearing on the validity of our commitments elsewhere.

Bundy, *The Path to Viet-Nam: A Lesson in Involvement*, 57 DEP'T STATE BULL. 275, 280 (1967). See note 20 *infra*.

[11] Recognition of the relationship between the President's control of foreign policy and his capacity to use the military abroad is not a recent phenomenon. It was clearly noted by Charles A. Beard, writing of times far more placid than the present:

> [The President] may do many things that vitally affect the foreign relations of the country. He may dismiss an ambassador or public minister of a foreign

Presidential war-making, as an actuality or feared potentiality, has been an issue throughout our history. The controversy has been fueled by the unpopularity of most of our wars,[12] by a deep-rooted fear with us since the framing of the Constitution that the President is grasping to himself all decision-making power,[13] and by the nature of the Constitution itself. The document is notably vague concerning the allocation of authority between the President and Congress over American foreign relations. Each is granted a line of powers which, in isolation, could support a claim to final authority. Edward S. Corwin has spoken of these grants as "logical incompatibles" and indicated, in words now hallowed and hackneyed by frequent invocation, that "the

---

power for political as well as personal reasons, and, if on the former ground, he might embroil the country in war. His power to receive any foreign representative authorizes him to recognize the independence of a new state, perhaps in rebellion against its former legitimate sovereign, and thus he might incur the risk of war [for example, Mr. Roosevelt's recognition of the republic of Panama in revolt against Columbia]. He may order a fleet or ship to a foreign port under circumstances that may provoke serious difficulty; the ill-fated battleship Maine was sent to the harbor of Havana by President McKinley at a time when it was regarded by many Spaniards, though not officially, as an unfriendly act. . . . As commander-in-chief of the army he might move troops to such a position on the borders of a neighboring state as to bring about an armed conflict. A notable instance of such an action occurred in the case of the opening of the Mexican War, when President Polk ordered out troops into the disputed territory, and, on their being attacked by the Mexicans, declared that war existed by act of Mexico. Again, in his message to Congress the President may outline a foreign policy so hostile to another nation as to precipitate diplomatic difficulties, if not more serious results. This occurred in the case of the Venezuelan controversy, when President Cleveland recommended to Congress demands which Great Britain could hardly regard as anything but unfriendly.
C. BEARD, AMERICAN GOVERNMENT AND POLITICS 196-97 (3d ed. 1920) (footnote omitted); *accord*, Morgenthau, *The American Tradition in Foreign Policy*, in FOREIGN POLICY IN WORLD POLITICS 246 (3d ed. 1967 R. Macridis). The Morgenthau theory is even more expansive than Beard's: "[The Executive] can narrow the freedom of choice which constitutionally lies with Congress to such an extent as to eliminate it for all practical purposes." *Id*. at 264.

[12] With the exception of the two World Wars, all substantial military efforts of the United States have been bitterly condemned by various elements of the population. *See* Fleming, *Other Days—Other Vietnams*, THIS WEEK, Dec. 31, 1967, at 4-7.

[13] Arthur Schlesinger has noted:
There has been nothing more continuous throughout American history than commentary on the supposed tendency of the presidency to absorb all the powers of the American system. The theory . . . of the President as the great moloch generating its own divinity and about to swallow all power can be reproduced at every stage in our history, beginning with those who . . . complained against the presidency of General Washington.
A. SCHLESINGER, JR. & A. DE GRAZIA, CONGRESS AND THE PRESIDENCY: THEIR ROLE IN MODERN TIMES 91 (1967); *see* M. CUNLIFFE & EDITORS OF AMERICAN HERITAGE, THE AMERICAN HERITAGE HISTORY OF THE PRESIDENCY 170-83 (1968).

Constitution, considered only for its affirmative grants of powers capable of affecting the issue, is an invitation to struggle for the privilege of directing American foreign policy." [14] Beyond its complementary grants of powers, the Constitution encourages confusion and struggle by the highly abstract terms in which it states many important powers. "The Congress shall have Power . . . [t]o declare War" [15] and "[t]he executive Power shall be vested in a President of the United States of America," [16] for example, leave much to further definition. Finally, the document, partly because of its complementary and abstract nature, frequently fails to indicate where the ultimate authority lies on many questions, such as the peacetime stationing of American troops abroad.

Although the scope of presidential power to involve the country in war is not a new issue, it has become a matter of increasing importance since 1945. With the exception of two World Wars and the Cold War, armed force has generally played a very insignificant role in American diplomacy outside the Western Hemisphere. Even during the years immediately following Independence, when American security was believed to depend largely on the policies of European powers, no effort was made to influence those policies by the dispatch of United States forces to participate in European conflicts. Until the twentieth century, three factors in particular—geography, the state of military technology and a viable European balance of power—enabled the United States to regard foreign relations very casually. [17] American security

---

[14] E. CORWIN, THE PRESIDENT: OFFICE AND POWERS 1787-1957, at 171 (4th rev. ed. 1957). The fact that complementary powers were granted the President and Congress was not overlooked by the Framers. "Madison emphasized at some length in 1796 that 'if taken literally, and without limit' these passages from the Constitution 'must necessarily clash with each other,'" and that "there are no 'separate orbits' in which the various powers can move and no 'separate objects' on which they can operate without 'interfering with or touching each other.'" M. McDOUGAL & ASSOCIATES, STUDIES IN WORLD PUBLIC ORDER 451, 453 (1960); see A. SCHLESINGER, supra note 13, at 1-5, 19-20.

[15] U.S. CONST. art. I, § 8.

[16] Id. art. II, § 1.

[17] Woodrow Wilson's full awakening, though it preceded that of most of his countrymen, took place only after he assumed the presidency. A passage from A. LINK, WILSON THE DIPLOMATIST (1957), captures the lack of concern with foreign affairs typical of late nineteenth century America:

> In his first book, *Congressional Government*, an inquiry into the practical functioning of the federal government published in 1885, Wilson made only a passing reference to foreign affairs, and that in connection with the Senate's treaty-making power. Four years later Wilson published *The State*, an excellent pioneer text in comparative government. Out of a total of more than one hundred pages devoted to the development of law and legal institutions, he gave a page and a half to international law. In his analysis of the administrative

was not deemed to depend upon that of distant states; there were no wide-ranging defense commitments. Moreover, even had a President desired to use armed force abroad on more than a piddling scale, he would have been pressed to muster sufficient troops. For much of their history, the Army and Navy could aptly be described as "tiny, obscure bodies,"[18] with no draft laws in existence to swell their ranks and no federal income tax available to fund a large military establishment.

Under these circumstances, the armed efforts which were made tended to be modest in their use of men and resources; they were rarely directed against other established states; few were regarded as vital to our national defense; and thus most could have been easily abandoned or repudiated. Even if Presidents had believed that American interests required extensive use of force abroad, and had they possessed the capacity to act on their beliefs, the resulting danger would have had finite limits. Geography, military technology and the prevailing balance of power would have kept the ensuing conflicts within survivable bounds.

Conditions today, however, are radically different. The revolution in military technology has ended our geographic immunity,[19] leading,

structures of modern governments, he described the machinery of the foreign relations of the British Empire in five words, but devoted twenty-six pages to local government in England; and he gave thirteen times as much space to the work of the Interior Department as to the Department of State in the American government. Finally, in his summary chapters on the functions and objects of government, he put foreign relations at the bottom of his list of what he called the "constituent functions" and then went on to elaborate the functions and objects of government without even mentioning the conduct of external affairs! *Id.* at 5-6 (footnotes omitted).

Wilson began to show more interest in foreign affairs during the 1890's and early 1900's, concluding that the war with Spain had once again raised foreign questions to the fore in American politics, as well as greatly enhanced the power of the President. *Id.* at 6-9. Yet, ironically, he still failed to give serious attention to world developments prior to coming to the White House. Link concludes that "Wilson did not concern himself seriously with affairs abroad during the period from 1901 to 1913 both because he was not interested and because he did not think that they were important enough to warrant any diversion from the mainstream of his thought." *Id.* at 11.

[18] AMERICAN HERITAGE, *supra* note 13, at 190. In 1789 American armed forces on active duty totaled 718 men. By 1812 they had grown to over 12,000 but, with the exception of the Civil War years, never significantly exceeded 50,000 until their sudden increase to 200,000 during the Spanish-American War. After World War I, their number ranged between 250,000 and 300,000 for twenty years. Since 1950, however, there have been approximately 3,000,000 men under arms at all times. Note, 81 HARV. L. REV., *supra* note 2, at 1791 n.106. To conduct the Vietnam War, the number has swelled to almost 3,500,000. BUREAU OF THE CENSUS, U.S. DEP'T OF COMMERCE, STATISTICAL ABSTRACT OF THE UNITED STATES 255 (90th ed. 1969).

[19] The interdependence of Americans with other peoples is not due merely to ad-

first, to a belief that American security is intimately tied to that of many other countries and, second, to pledges that we will defend other nations.[20] Evolution in the balance of world power has left the United States as one of the two great superstates in a bipolar system which abhors the shift of territory from one bloc to another. And the revolution in American military capacity has provided the President with a potent, flexible means of intervention abroad on a moment's notice— a capacity which cold war Presidents have used freely in attempting to prevent a loss of territory to communism. Such initiation of force, even when clearly authorized by the Executive alone, was broadly supported until Vietnam, on the assumption that dissent might undermine American security.[21] Furthermore, the existence of nuclear weapons permits no assurance that all conflicts will remain within survivable limits. In sum, there has been reason for each cold war President to feel compelled to use force abroad, few restraints on his ability to act quickly and unilaterally, and strong popular feeling that his actions—whatever their nature—must be supported, although there has been little certainty about their ultimate consequences. Under these circumstances, the scope of presidential power to commit troops abroad becomes a matter of great import—far greater than ever before.

THE RELATIONSHIP OF THE CONSTITUTION TO THE ISSUE

What possible relevance can the Constitution, a product of the late

vances in military technology and concern for our security. Revolutionary advances in the exchange of ideas, information, goods and services have left no realistic alternative to participation in global affairs. *See* McDougal, Lasswell & Reisman, *Theories about International Law: Prologue to a Configurative Jurisprudence,* 8 VA. J. INT'L L. 188, 189-94 (1968).

[20] At present the United States has defense agreements with 48 foreign countries, and maintains approximately 400 major military installations abroad, stationing approximately 900,000 troops in foreign fields, other than Viet Nam. TIME, April 11, 1969, at 26. To maintain the credibility of commitments to defend such vital areas as Western Europe, with nuclear weapons if necessary, Washington has often felt compelled to protect friendly regimes in nations of little intrinsic significance. Fear has also existed that the loss of one such state could easily lead to the general collapse of others similarly situated. *See, e.g.,* Bundy, *supra* note 10, at 280-81.

[21] Once the President has committed troops to combat, he can generally rally support even from those opposed to his policies, by demanding that they back the boys in the field—or presumably face political oblivion. As President Johnson delicately suggested in his message to Congress of May 4, 1965, requesting additional appropriations for Vietnam: "To deny and to delay this means to deny and delay the fullest support of the American people and the American Congress to those brave men who are risking their lives for freedom in Vietnam." 111 CONG. REC. 9284 (1965); *see* C. ROSSITER, THE AMERICAN PRESIDENCY 51-52 (2d ed. 1960).

eighteenth century, have to an issue whose dimensions have changed radically even within the last twenty-five years? It seems that there are at least two major misapprehensions about the document. At one extreme is the assumption that it provides a wholly ascertainable, eternal set of dictates. Proponents of this position find much plain meaning in the constitutional language and read any ambiguous or incomplete provisions in light of the intent of the Framers.[22] To depart from this intent, formal amendment is deemed necessary. Adherents of strict construction also tend to assume that once the rules—that which is written in the document—are known, the whole of constitutional law has been grasped.

At the other extreme is the assumption that the document is simply a hollow shell, given content by the practice of the moment. Proponents of this position find virtually no plain meaning in the relevant provisions, and, even when meaning appears, give it little or no weight if contemporary practice is contrary. The intent of the Framers fares no better. Thus, the mere existence of current practice is proof of its constitutionality. Adherents of this view tend to assume that once the actual practice of the moment—the basic power machinations—are known, the whole of constitutional law has been grasped.

The problems with the position of the strict constructionists will be examined first. Plain meaning is an illusory goal in the interpretation of a document, such as the Constitution, which governs the continuing conduct of an immensely complex process in language notable for its abstraction, complementarity and frequent failure to speak to vital issues. Such a document must receive much of its meaning from sources other than its wording. Moreover, since it was designed to remain perpetually viable, the intent of the Framers, when available, binds subsequent interpreters far less than does the intent of the drafters of the typical contract or statute.

In determining the meaning of any constitutional provision, the ultimate criterion must be the long-term best interests of the country. If the Constitution is to remain functional, its interpretation has to move

---

22 [T]he mechanical, filiopietistic theory, purports to regard the words of the Constitution as timeless absolutes. The sole problem of an interpreter . . . is to find what meaning the words had in terms of the idiosyncratic purposes of the Framers in the light of the conditions and events of their day. It is assumed that this meaning can be discovered and can and must be applied without loss or change, to the problems of the present day, by completely different people under completely different conditions.

M. McDOUGAL, *supra* note 14, at 444 (footnote omitted).

in pace with our changing needs and values.[23] Encouraged by the Constitution's linguistic flexibility, and by the difficulty of its formal amendment process,[24] alteration by usage has proved to be the principal means of modifying our fundamental law.[25] The constitutional provisions governing the conduct of foreign affairs have been duly affected by this evolutionary[26] process.

Strict constructionists thus fail to recognize the extent to which the document's language must be supplemented before it becomes meaningful; they do not realize that the supplementation must ultimately

---

[23] [I]t is utterly fantastic to suppose that a document framed 150 years ago "to start a governmental experiment for an agricultural, sectional, seaboard folk of some three millions" could be interpreted today . . . in terms of the "true meaning" of its original Framers for the purpose of controlling the "government of a nation, a hundred and thirty millions strong, whose population and advanced industrial civilization have spread across a continent." Each generation of citizens must in a very real sense interpret the words of the Framers to create its own constitution. The more conscious the interpreters are that this is what they are doing the more likely it is that their interpretations will embody the best long-term interests of the nation. In truth, our very survival as a nation has been made possible only because the ultimate interpreters of the Constitution—presidents and congressional leaders, as well as judges—have repeatedly transcended the restrictive interpretations of their predecessors.

Id. at 446-47 (footnotes omitted).

[24] McDougal suggests that the American people in their frequent alteration of the Constitution by informal adaptation

have also been motivated by a wise realization of the inevitable transiency of political arrangements. The ultimate advantage of usage over formal textual alteration as a method of constitutional change is that, while it preserves the formal symmetry of the document, it reduces the danger of freezing the structures of government within the mold dictated by the expediencies or political philosophy of any given era. A formal amendment may be outmoded shortly after it is adopted, but usage permits continual adjustment to the necessities of national existence.

Id. at 545.

In constitutions in which the language is more detailed and its formal amendment less difficult, change by usage is the exception. *See* Note, *State Constitutional Change: The Constitutional Convention*, 54 VA. L. REV. 995, 998-1000 (1968).

[25] In innumerable respects, the division of functions between the different branches of the government and the scope of federal authority, as clearly contemplated by the Framers, have been altered by usage and prescription, without resort to formal textual amendment. "For every time that the Constitution has been amended," as Justice Byrnes has pointed out, "it has been changed ten times by custom or by judicial construction." This process of constitutional evolution has by no means been restricted to the numerous phases of government which the draftsmen deliberately left ambiguous or unsettled; in many instances the very words and phrases of the written Constitution have been given operational meanings remote from the intentions of their original penmen.

M. McDOUGAL, *supra* note 14, at 542 (footnotes omitted). For numerous instances of alteration by usage, see *id.* at 442-75, 540-60.

[26] For a summary of some of the more important changes, such as the end of the Senate's role as a coordinate director of treaty negotiations and preemption by the President of the power of recognition, see *id.* at 557-60.

be in terms of the best interests of the country and not simply in the lock-step of the Framers' intent; and they will not accept that upon occasion even the clear intent of the Drafters must be abandoned without the process of formal amendment, if the Constitution is to minister successfully to needs created by changing times. Their rigidity leads as well to one final misapprehension: that to know the rule is necessarily to know the law. An understanding of what is written in the Constitution, even assuming a viable interpretation of the language, simply provides information regarding peoples' expectations about the type of conduct that is constitutional. If acts forbidden by a reasonable reading of the rules continue to be performed, it is highly unrealistic to regard the rules as complete statements of the law. To constitute "the law" the course of conduct dictated by the rules must be the one followed in actual practice.[27]

Strict constructionists are equalled in their error by those at the opposite pole who automatically bestow the mantle of constitutionality on whatever happens to be the practice of the moment. Although the document must receive much of its meaning from sources other than its language and its interpretation must evolve to meet the differing needs of differing times, it is not simply a hollow shell whose principles are ever in flux. The goal of constitutional interpretation, as indicated, should be a reading that serves the long-term best interests of the country. In realizing that goal, serious attention should be paid the intent of the Framers for at least two basic reasons. First, the Founding Fathers may have ordained a practice which still has validity. If their design is workable, it should be respected, particularly when the constitu-

---

[27]   In any particular community it is possible to observe among its constituent social processes a process of effective power, *i.e.*, decisions of community-wide impact are in fact made and put into controlling effect. . . . [T]hese effective power decisions . . . [are] of two different kinds. Some . . . are taken from simple expediency, or sheer naked power, and enforced by severe deprivation or high indulgences, whether the community members like them or not. Other decisions, however, are taken in accordance with community expectations about how such decisions should be taken: they are taken by established decision-makers, in recognized structures of authority, related to community expectations of common interest, and supported by enough effective power to be put into effect in consequential degree.
        It is these latter decisions, those taken in accordance with community expectations and enforced by organized community coercion, which are . . . most appropriately called "law." In this conception law is, thus, a process of decision in which authority and control are conjoined. Without authority, decision is but arbitrary coercion, naked power; without control, it is often illusion. McDougal, *Jurisprudence for a Free Society*, 1 GA. L. REV. 1, 4 (1966); *accord*, Moore, *Prolegomenon to the Jurisprudence of Myres McDougal and Harold Lasswell*, 54 VA. L. REV. 662, 666 (1968).

tional language, read in light of the intent of the Drafters, seems to be clear. A better way of doing the job might be devised, but the design of the Framers should be honored lest its disregard undermine public confidence in the rule of law. The general public tends to take a strict view when confronted with clear language and intent,[28] unless they feel that the applicable provision is blatantly detrimental to their interests.

Accordingly, when conspicuous government officials disobey or appear to disobey the rules in their conduct of public affairs, the general public's respect for prevailing norms suffers.[29] The government, one of whose major objectives must be the creation and maintenance of a rule of law, simply cannot ignore or seem to ignore the norms applicable to its proceedings without undermining the entire system. Thus, if it appears that the President is flouting the Constitution in his use of American troops abroad, an effect on lesser mortals will be unavoidable.[30] If the document seems to be irrelevant to him, more

[28] Direct support for this proposition would be comforting, since it figures in this Article's subsequent analysis. Unfortunately, the only authority offered here is personal opinion. It seems that most people feel that the rule of law necessitates undeviating adherence to the intent of the law-giver, until the language in which he embodied his intent is physically changed in accordance with formal processes of revision. Nothing less will suffice to assure these people that our society is governed according to law, and not pursuant to the whim of public officials. Thus, pending formal amendment of the language of the Framers, most people believe that their intent ought to remain binding. Cf. P. MISHKIN & C. MORRIS, ON LAW IN COURTS 78-81, 258-67 (1965) (the crisis of confidence engendered by judicial overruling of well-established doctrines).

[29] Since it would be virtually impossible to obtain the requisite level of obedience by coercion, the stability of our legal system depends largely upon voluntary obedience to the law. Thus, most people do not base their acceptance of laws primarily on fear that disobedience will result in apprehension and punishment. See H. HART, THE CONCEPT OF LAW 79-88 (1961). On the contrary, public support for the legal system is motivated by a variety of other factors—habit, desire to conform, belief that a given law embodies a moral command or that it serves individual self-interest, awareness that the legal system depends on acceptance of its norms, and assurance that other people and institutions are obeying the rules applicable to them. Should it appear that some elements of society disregard the law, then the willingness of their fellows to honor norms they find to be inconvenient or ill-advised will be notably lessened.

[30] Edward H. Levi recently noted:

> Our most pressing failure relates to our attitude toward the legal system. Civil disobedience and indifference to law have become sufficiently widespread to reflect and raise essentially naive questions as to the function of law in a modern society. It is paradoxical that the civil rights movement which in the almost immediate past built upon law, and depended so much on the morality of acquiescence, should now, to some extent, be the vehicle for the destruction of this acquiescence. *The undeclared Viet Nam war has further emphasized the morality of illegal acts . . . .*

Levi, *Unrest and the Universities,* U. CHI. MAGAZINE, Jan./Feb. 1969, at 25 (emphasis added).

humble rules will be regarded with equal disdain by many of his fellow citizens.[31]

Thus, absent necessity to abandon old constitutional patterns, the contemporary interpreter would do better to follow them, reshaping and extending them to meet the needs of the times.[32] Though the Framers may not have conceived of the conditions to which one of their provisions now applies, if its underlying principle remains tenable, the principle should be carefully and skillfully preserved. For example, if it seems clear that the Framers intended Congress to have a meaningful voice in decisions regarding the use of American troops abroad, then every effort should be made to give life to that guiding principle, using procedures attuned to contemporary needs.[33]

Those who view the Constitution as a hollow shell, accordingly, overlook the framework which the document does frequently provide, and they fail to accord its language and the Framers' intent the weight they are due if the long-term best interests of the country are to be served. The Shellists' emphasis on the practice of the moment also leads them to a final misapprehension: that to know what is actually done is necessarily to know the law. Practice, unless it is in accord with the rules, is simply the exercise of naked power, not law.

Americans have traditionally been concerned with constitutional rules. They want governmental power to be exercised in the prescribed manner. Much of the controversy surrounding the Vietnam War concerns not simply the merits of the conflict but also the constitutionality of the United States involvement. When practice is deemed to fall outside the rules, efforts will be made to bring it back within. Accordingly, immediate past precedent may or may not be upheld; its existence is not conclusive of its legality.

In this regard, it is well to remember that most government officials—including the President—voluntarily try to stay within the bounds of the constitutional provisions applicable to them.[34] Peoples' expectations

[31] The President could, of course, argue that he is attempting to amend the Constitution by usage, but the subtleties of such an argument would probably be lost on the general public. See note 28 *supra*.

[32] Moreover, adherance to established constitutional patterns may often increase the actor's political power and prestige. See note 180 *infra*.

[33] *Cf.* L. FULLER, THE MORALITY OF LAW 84-85 (1964).

[34] See note 74 *infra* and accompanying text. A useful analogy can be drawn between presidential adherence to constitutional law in matters such as the use of force abroad and nations in their obedience to customary international law. As a rule, both appreciate the need to support the prevailing norms, and thus voluntarily accept them. Rarely would either, if accused of illegal activity, fail to deny the charge vociferously, adducing legal argument to justify the action. But since the precise demands of con-

regarding the nature of the rules strongly influence the type of action actually taken, just as practice, in turn, shapes expectations. Constitutional law, thus, is found where community understanding of the type of conduct required by the rules and what actually happens are largely synonymous.[35]

One effective way to approach the constitutional question at hand is to study separately its practice and rule aspects, bringing them together after the features of each have been determined. Thus, an attempt needs to be made to learn the extent to which the President has unilaterally decided to commit American troops to foreign combat, irrespective of rule-based expectations regarding the constitutionality of his action. Once aware of what has in fact been the practice, there must be an attempt to determine what type of presidential conduct people have believed to be constitutional. If practice is then found to diverge significantly from the rules, the two courses must be reconciled in terms of the best interests of the country. Should practice be long-established and responsive to the needs of the times, the constitutional rules should evolve to meet it. Should practice, however, have needlessly and recently abandoned principles set out in the language of the document or evidenced by the Framers' intent, and embodied in continuing expectations, it should be altered to accord with the rules. A thorough examination of the nature just suggested would require several volumes.[36] For the purposes of this Article, it will suffice to trace

---

stitutional and international rules are often vague, and since there is little chance of clarification by judicial or legislative action (formal amendment in the case of the Constitution), both the President and nations have latitude in interpreting the relevant provisions. Each tends to define, fill in and alter the legal contours by a process of claim and concession. If presidential assertions of authority are acknowledged and acquiesced in by Congress, the electorate, and, should they choose to comment, the courts, the Executive assumes the power as his constitutional due. Even presidential claims rejected by one or more of these groups remain as potential sources of law, especially if the President has given them more than verbal substance. Nations proceed by a similar process of claim and concession. Finally, both the President and states are likely to ignore well-established rules when confronted with crisis. *See* M. Kaplan & N. Katzenbach, *Law in the International Community*, in 2 THE STRATEGY OF WORLD ORDER 34, 35-37 (R. Falk & S. Mendlovitz eds. 1966).

[35] See note 27 *supra* and accompanying text.

[36] All instances in which American troops were employed abroad would have to be examined to pinpoint the effective decision-makers. Expectations would have to be sought from a wide range of sources—"pre-1787 negotiations, subsequent practice by all branches of the government, statutory interpretations, judicial decisions and opinions, and the vast literature of expressions, formal and informal, about preferred public order." McDougal, *supra* note 27, at 18. And an intensive investigation would be required to identify the long-term best interests of the country and their policy implications.

briefly the allocation of power between the Executive and Congress since 1789, considering both the factors contributing to the present high state of presidential control and the existing restraints upon it. One constitutional rule, the congressional power to declare war, will be treated in detail, while other relevant provisions will receive more cursory attention. Finally, an attempt will be made to view practice and rules together in light of the long-term best interests of the United States, outlining what seem to be the present constitutional limits upon the President.

The Balance Between President and Congress: Practice

Historical Background

At the risk of gross over-simplification, three historical stages may be identified in the President's progress toward virtually complete control over the commitment of American troops abroad. The first ran from independence until the end of the nineteenth century and was a time of genuine collaboration between the President and Congress, and of executive deference to legislative will regarding the initiation of foreign conflicts. Numerous figures are bruited about as representing the number of times during the course of American history that the President has unilaterally employed force abroad. One total frequently cited lists 125, the great bulk occurring in the nineteenth century.[37] Their existence, it is often said, establishes that presidential war-making is no twentieth century *parvenu*.[38]

---

[37] Senate Comm. on Foreign Relations, 82d Cong., 1st Sess., Powers of the President to Send Armed Forces Outside the United States (Comm. Print 1951). The report states in part: "Since the Constitution was adopted there have been at least 125 incidents in which the President, without congressional authorization, . . . has ordered the Armed Forces to take action or maintain positions abroad." *Id.* at 2. For a similar finding, see J. Rogers, World Policing and the Constitution (1945), which describes 100 uses of American troops abroad between 1789 and 1945, and concludes that most of them were ordered unilaterally by the Executive. Since the publication of both these studies, there have been numerous additional instances of presidential use of force abroad, some of major impact.

[38] The State Department, in its defense of the Vietnam War, has stated:

Since the Constitution was adopted there have been at least 125 instances in which the President has ordered the armed forces to take action or maintain positions abroad without obtaining prior congressional authorization, starting with the "undeclared war" with France (1798-1800). For example, President Truman ordered 250,000 troops to Korea during the Korean war of the early 1950's. President Eisenhower dispatched 14,000 troops to Lebanon in 1958.

The Constitution leaves to the President the judgment to determine whether the circumstances of a particular armed attack are so urgent and the potential

As precedent for Vietnam, however, the majority of the nineteenth century uses of force do not survive close scrutiny. Most were minor undertakings, designed to protect American citizens or property, or to revenge a slight to national honor, and most involved no combat, or even its likelihood, with the forces of another state.[39] To use force abroad on a notable scale, the President of necessity would have had to request Congress to augment the standing Army and Navy.[40] Executives of this era, in any event, were generally reluctant to undertake military efforts abroad without congressional approval. Accordingly, there are instances during this period of presidential refusals to act because Congress had not been consulted or because it had withheld approval, and there are many occasions of executive action pursuant to meaningful congressional authorization.[41]

Some of the instances grouped within the 125 presidential uses of force are erroneously included, chiefly the Naval War with France of 1798-1800 and the Barbary Wars of 1801-05 and 1815, which were

consequences so threatening to the security of the United States that he should act without formally consulting the Congress.

Meeker, *The Legality of United States Participation in the Defense of Viet-Nam*, 54 DEP'T STATE BULL. 474, 484-85 (1966).

[39] For a description of the instances involved, see J. ROGERS, *supra* note 37, at 53, 56-67, 93-112; WORMUTH at 21-26. For a discussion of these events, see E. CORWIN, TOTAL WAR AND THE CONSTITUTION 144-50 (1947); R. LEOPOLD, THE GROWTH OF AMERICAN FOREIGN POLICY 96-98 (1962) [hereinafter cited as LEOPOLD]; Note, 81 HARV. L. REV., *supra* note 2, at 1787-89.

[40] The Executive's power to deploy American forces as their Commander-in-Chief posed few problems. During virtually all of the 19th century the President

moved military units at will and without protest; in so doing, he rarely exposed himself to the charge of provoking another nation to fire the first shot. Through his secretary of the navy he assigned permanent cruising squadrons to the Mediterranean in 1815, the Pacific in 1821, the Caribbean in 1822, the South Atlantic in 1826, the Far East in 1835, and the African coast in 1842. The purpose of these squadrons was to show the flag, protect shipping, and encourage commerce. No contingents were regularly stationed on foreign soil, either to garrison an overseas base or to honor a diplomatic commitment.

LEOPOLD at 99. Presidential deployment of armed forces did, however, impinge upon congressional power to declare war in Polk's dispatch of General Taylor into territory claimed by Mexico and in McKinley's dispatch of the *Maine* to Havana. Moreover, usurpation was threatened in Grant's abortive attempt to annex Santo Domingo and in Harrison's 1891 dispatch of a cruiser to seize Chilean ships that had violated American neutrality laws. *See id.* at 99-102, 117.

[41] See the instances cited in LEOPOLD at 97-98; WORMUTH at 6-20.

From 1836 to 1898, except for the administrations of Polk, Lincoln, and Cleveland, Capitol Hill tended to provide the initiative for the development of foreign policy. When, for example, the executive advocated expansionist policies—Pierce in Cuba, Seward in Alaska, Grant in Santo Domingo—he instantly encountered violent congressional opposition.

A. SCHLESINGER, *supra* note 13, at 24.

conducted with specific congressional approval.[42] When presidential orders to American naval commanders exceeded the congressional mandate during the 1798-1800 hostilities, the Supreme Court in *Little v. Barreme*[43] ordered damages paid to the owner of a ship seized pursuant to executive instruction. It is unlikely, however, that President Adams was attempting by his conflicting orders to expand his war powers at the expense of Congress, since he had previously divested himself of his role as Commander-in-Chief and, with Senate approval, conferred it upon George Washington. President Thomas Jefferson was almost as self-effacing; before receiving congressional approval of the First Barbary War, he refused to permit American naval commanders to do more than disarm and release enemy ships guilty of attacks on United States vessels.

The era in question included three formally declared wars.[44] The decision to enter the War of 1812 was made by Congress after extended debate. Madison made no recommendation in favor of hostilities, though he did marshal a "telling case against England" in his message to Congress of June 1, 1812. The primary impetus to battle, however, seems to have come from a group of "War Hawks" in the legislature.[45] Similarly, McKinley was pushed into war with Spain in 1898 by con-

---

[42] With respect to the Naval War: "President Adams took absolutely no independent action. Congress passed a series of acts which amounted, so the Supreme Court said, to a declaration of imperfect war; and Adams complied with these statutes." WORMUTH at 6; *accord*, LEOPOLD at 95. The acts were quite detailed regarding the nature of the hostilities authorized. *See* WORMUTH at 6-9; LEOPOLD at 95.

Though Jefferson unilaterally dispatched a naval squadron to the Mediterranean to protect American shipping from attack by Tripoli, he refused to permit offensive action until so authorized by Congress—much to Alexander Hamilton's outrage. See note 148 *infra*. Accordingly, an act was passed authorizing the President "fully to equip, officer, man and employ such of the armed vessels of the United States" as he found necessary to protect American commerce; to instruct the commanders of these ships to "subdue, seize, and make prize all vessels, goods, and effects, belonging to Bey of Tripoli, or to his subjects;" to commission privateers, and to take whatever "other acts of precaution or hostility as the state of war will justify." WORMUTH at 9-10; *see* LEOPOLD at 95-96.

When Algiers in 1815 attacked American shipping, President Madison obtained authorization to use force similar to that given in 1802 against Tripoli. WORMUTH at 10. Significantly, Congress refused the President's request for a formal declaration of war, granting him instead simply approval for limited hostilities. LEOPOLD at 96.

[43] 6 U.S. (2 Cranch) 169 (1804). See the discussion of *Little* in WORMUTH at 8-9.

[44] The greatest conflict of the period, the War Between the States, did not involve the use of force against foreign countries, though it gave rise to expectations about presidential power which have application in the foreign context. See notes 146, 158 *infra*.

[45] *See* LEOPOLD at 62-64, 94; A. SCHLESINGER, *supra* note 13, at 23.

gressional and popular fervor, though he himself inadvertently stoked their passion by sending the *Maine* to Havana. Full congressional authorization was given before the initiation of hostilities.[46] Congress was, on the other hand, presented with a presidential *fait accompli* in 1846. Polk provoked the Mexicans into a conflict which the legislators felt compelled to approve, particularly in light of the colored version of the facts presented by the President.[47] But within two years, the House of Representatives censured Polk for his part in the initiation of the conflict.[48]

The second of the three stages mentioned previously began at the turn of the century and continued into World War II. Close collaboration between the Executive and Congress became the exception, as did presidential deference to congressional views on the use of force abroad. The legislators, nonetheless, remained a strong force in the shaping of foreign policies. Their influence, unfortunately, was often negative, obstructing the efforts of Presidents who saw a need to use American power to defend nascent security interests abroad. American military capacity had grown to the point, however, that the Executives had notable capacity for maneuver without prior congressional action.

During the first two decades of the twentieth century, Congress generally chose to watch quietly as the President unilaterally intervened in the Western Hemisphere, presumably because majority sentiment favored militant American hegemony over this area.[49] Presidents

---

[46] Congress first passed a joint resolution authorizing the President to use armed force if necessary to insure Cuban independence and Spanish withdrawal from the island and then followed with a formal declaration of war when Spain recalled its ambassador from Washington and showed no sign of leaving Cuba. *See* LEOPOLD at 117, 169-79.

[47] Until the last decade of the 19th century "[o]nly in the case of Texas and the Mexican War did the executive encroach upon the legislature's constitutional prerogative" by the manner in which he deployed American forces. LEOPOLD at 99. Leopold concludes that Polk "remains the sole president in history who, by needlessly deploying the armed forces, provoked an attack by a potential enemy." *Id*. at 101. But he also notes that virtually no protest was voiced in Congress during the first three months of General Taylor's advance into disputed territory and argues that "the silent acquiescence by the legislature destroys some of the complaint that the executive had usurped its war-making powers." *Id*.

[48] By an 85-81 vote the House ruled that the war had been "unnecessarily and unconstitutionally begun by the President of the United States." CONG. GLOBE, 30th Cong., 1st Sess. 95 (1848). See WORMUTH at 11.

[49] It was in November, 1903, in connection with the revolution in Panama, that a President of the United States first succeeded in exercising the war-making power without the consent of Congress. The purpose for which such power was

enjoyed similar freedom in the Far East[50] although they exercised it less robustly. The first wholly unauthorized executive war-making, nonetheless, took place in China during the Boxer Rebellion at the turn of the century.[51]

During most of the 1920's and 1930's American force abroad was used sparingly, in part because of a more relaxed approach to the difficulties of the Latin states and in part as a result of a strong popular desire to

---

exerted on this occasion was so popular a one that it was acquiesced in, with only slight objections, by both Congress and the public, and a most dangerous precedent for the future was thus created.

Putney, *Executive Assumption of the War Making Power*, 7 Nat'l Univ. L. Rev. 1, 34 (May 1927).

Roosevelt, in fact, would have preferred congressional involvement in his disregard of Columbian sensibilities, but events overtook him. *See* Leopold at 231. Though Putney seems inaccurate in stating that Roosevelt's activities in Panama marked the first instance of unauthorized presidential war-making, see note 51 *infra* and accompanying text, it did signal the beginning of significant military intervention in Latin states, generally pursuant to unilateral presidential command. *See* H. Cline, The United States and Mexico 155-62, 174-83 (rev. ed. 1965); Leopold at 251, 316-21; Putney, *supra* at 33-41; Note, 81 Harv. L. Rev., *supra* note 2, at 1789-90.

50 Before the Spanish-American War the expansionist spirit had been confined mainly to navalists and their intellectual camp-followers. The conquest of the Philippines, however, opened the eyes of the American business man in the Far Eastern markets. With the acquisition of the Philippines our line of defense was thrust into the vicinity of China and Japan. Does this seem a strange lunge for a republic which vaunted its isolationism? If so, it can be explained by saying that our isolationist barricade had only one wall. We shut only our eastern door, for Americans marched out of their house in other directions. United States history is replete with exploits, successful and abortive, against the territories of our southern, western and northern neighbors. Isolationism accelerated rather than inhibited continental expansionism, for, in the beginning, we wanted to drive Europe out of North America. This impulse created a restlessness that drove Americans westward to San Francisco and in due course beyond the Golden Gate to Honolulu and Manila.

S. Adler, The Isolationist Impulse: Its Twentieth Century Reaction 19-20 (1957); *accord*, American Heritage, *supra* note 13, at 282.

51 McKinley committed several thousand American troops to the international army which suppressed the Chinese nationalists and rescued western nationals trapped in Peking. The President was accused of usurping congressional power to declare war by a few democrats, but "since the legislature had adjourned before the crisis broke and since neither party desired a special session in an election year, these complaints produced no results." Leopold at 117. For more detail, see *id.* at 215-18; J. Rogers, *supra* note 37, at 58-62.

To an extent, McKinley is vulnerable to a charge of unilateral war-making in his suppression of the Aguinaldo-led attempt to win independence for the Philippines during the years 1899-1902. According to Rogers, *id.* at 112, 126,000 United States troops were employed in putting down the movement. The decision to insist that Spain surrender all of the Philippines to the United States was made by the President alone, and Senate approval of the treaty of peace with Spain did not constitute a clear endorsement of American control of the islands. For discussion, see Leopold at 150-52, 180-88, 212.

avoid involvement in the struggles of the world's other great powers[52] —the pristine American psyche had been gravely offended by the tawdry aftermath of World War I. The mood of the country showed itself vividly when Japanese bombers deliberately sent an American gunboat, the *Panay*, to the bottom of the Yangtze River on December 12, 1937. Quite unlike the popular reaction to attacks on the *Maine* and on destroyers in the Tonkin Gulf, the *Panay* incident gave immediate and tremendous impetus to a congressional attempt to amend the Constitution to subject war decisions to popular referendum, except in case of invasion.[53]

Congressional devotion to neutrality and to nonintervention in the affairs of other states, especially those in Europe, made intelligent use of American influence difficult during and after the First World War. Wilson's troubles in bringing American power to bear against Germany, however, were minor compared to those experienced by Roosevelt under far more desperate circumstances.[54] Both Presidents, but especially Roosevelt, were forced to resort to deception and flagrant disregard of Congress in military deployment decisions because they were unable to rally congressional backing for action essential to national security.[55]

---

[52] Leopold states that Congress had few complaints about presidential use of force abroad during most of the interwar years. The placidity can be explained,

> partly by the peace which the United States enjoyed during this interlude and partly by the modification of its protectorate policy in the Caribbean. The republic did not fight any wars, declared or undeclared, and there was a marked reduction in the sort of police action that had been frequent before 1921. Nor did the deployment of ships and men lead to congressional charges of presidential warmongering, as was the case after 1939. On one point the legislators continued to agitate. At every session, amendments to the Constitution were proposed to alter the war-making clauses. The most frequent were designed to halt profiteering, to bar using conscripts outside the continental United States, to require that a declaration of war pass each house by a three-fourths vote rather than a simple majority, and to hold a popular referendum, except in cases of invasion, before a congressional decision to go to war could take effect.

LEOPOLD at 416-17.

[53] *See id.* at 416-17, 534.

[54] The Neutrality Acts of 1935, 1936 and 1937 made no distinction between an aggressor and his victim; under the acts, Americans, especially the President, were to avoid any dealings which might involve the United States in another war. These laws, and the congressional and popular attitudes which they represented, placed a disastrous limitation on Roosevelt's attempt to use American power and influence to head off the impending crisis. See the accounts in S. ADLER, *supra* note 50, at 239-73; LEOPOLD at 504-09, 526-28, 531, 537-42, 557-65.

[55] Among his major unilateral steps, Roosevelt in 1940 exchanged fifty destroyers for British bases in the Western Atlantic; in 1941 he occupied Greenland and Iceland, ordered the Navy to convoy ships carrying lend-lease supplies to Britain, and on

The trauma of the Second World War and of the Cold War led to a third stage in which Congress—in penance for its policies during the twenties and thirties and fearful lest its interference harm national security[56]—left direction of foreign affairs largely to the President, with the exception of a period of uproar during the early fifties.[57] As a rule, the legislators have presented no obstacles when the President wished to use force abroad, or to pursue policies likely to lead to its necessity. The Cold War has enjoyed bipartisan backing, both when the Executive acted wholly without congressional consent[58] and when he had authorization of sorts.[59] The decisions to employ arms off For-

September 11 of that year declared, in effect, that henceforth the United States would wage an air and sea war against the Axis in the Atlantic. See the accounts in E. CORWIN, *supra* note 39, at 22-34; LEOPOLD at 559-80; J. ROGERS, *supra* note 37, at 122-23.

After Germany's resumption of unrestricted submarine warfare, Woodrow Wilson in 1917 armed American merchantmen and instructed them to fire on sight. The President had sought congressional approval but had been thwarted by a Senate filibuster. He proceeded nonetheless, though he later admitted that his course was "practically certain" to lead to United States involvement in war. Message to Congress, Apr. 2, 1917. 55 CONG. REC. 102 (1917).

[56] One disquieting feature of the cold war was that perpetual crisis inhibited discussion. Criticism of the administration was apt to be interpreted as evidence of disloyalty; it was condemned as bringing aid and comfort to the enemy. The psychology of actual war—that of being either for or against one side—was applied to a situation that continued year after year. AMERICAN HERITAGE, *supra* note 13, at 287.

[57] A "Great Debate" over Truman's authority to send troops to Korea and Western Europe raged for three months in early 1951, culminating in a Senate resolution calling for congressional authorization before the dispatch of further troops to fulfill NATO commitments. The attempt under Senator John Bricker's aegis to limit the scope of treaties and the use of executive agreements—to reassert a strong congressional influence in the shaping of foreign policy—came to naught in 1954, after Eisenhower made clear his unalterable opposition. *See* LEOPOLD at 660-61, 716-17. The hysteria bred by Senator Joseph McCarthy, playing upon frustrations and fears engendered by developments in China, Eastern Europe and Korea, came close to rendering Truman incapable of conducting an effective foreign policy during the latter years of his presidency.

[58] The Korean War, for example, was entered with no prior congressional authorization, and never received even *ex post facto* blessing, perhaps because it was not an unpopular conflict at its inception. LEOPOLD at 683, notes that Truman's initial commitment of naval and air forces was met with "some grumbling in the Senate about the war-making power," but that "[t]he House broke into applause on hearing the news." Senator Taft questioned the President's right to initiate the use of American forces without congressional approval, but, according to Leopold, "he blamed the method, not the move, and said he would have voted for armed intervention if that issue had been presented." *Id.*

[59] Eisenhower was authorized in January 1955 to use force if necessary to defend Formosa and its outlying islands, and in March 1957 to block communist aggression in the Middle East. A joint congressional resolution adopted in October 1962 authorized President Kennedy to use force if necessary to prevent the spread of communism from

mosa, in Korea, Lebanon, Cuba, the Dominican Republic and Vietnam were essentially the President's, as were the policies that led Washington to feel that force was essential.

Nonetheless, Congress has played an indispensable role in postwar foreign affairs. Without congressional willingness to back their policies, Presidents could have done little. Moreover, well aware that Congress could at any time hamstring their initiative by refusing requisite legislation or appropriations, Presidents have consistently conferred with congressional leaders when shaping policy and have sought their advice —or at least informed them before the fact—when deciding to employ force abroad. The point, however, is that despite its latent power, Congress has had little part in shaping American foreign policy over the last quarter century, particularly where questions of the use of force are concerned. Foreign aid may have been subjected to an annual bloodletting but not the President's capacity to commit and maintain troops abroad.

It is possible that a fourth stage is now developing in public and congressional restiveness over Vietnam. Whether a new era will come to fruition or die with the end of the present conflict remains to be

---

Cuba or the development there of an externally supported military capability dangerous to the security of the United States. And President Johnson received in August 1964 a joint resolution providing in part that "the United States is . . . prepared, as the President determines, to take all necessary steps, including the use of armed force, to assist any member or protocol state of the Southeast Asia Collective Defense Treaty requesting assistance in defense of its freedom." Vietnam Joint Resolution, 78 Stat. 384 (1964).

When force was used in Lebanon, in the Atlantic off Cuba during the Missile Crisis and in Vietnam, however, it was unclear to what extent the respective Executives based their action upon prior congressional approval and to what extent upon claims of inherent presidential power. It seems likely that the three Presidents would have acted as they did, even without the resolutions. Eisenhower, in fact, did not claim to be acting pursuant to the Middle East Resolution when he intervened in Lebanon in July 1958, presumably because Congress had authorized force only when the attack came from a communist state. Johnson relied more heavily on the Gulf of Tonkin resolution, since in terms of its language it certainly authorized the war he waged. See the discussion in LEOPOLD at 792-96; Note, 81 HARV. L. REV., *supra* note 2, at 1792-93.

The executive interpretation of the Gulf of Tonkin Resolution has been bitterly contested as a misreading of congressional intent. *E.g.*, Velvel, *supra* note 2, at 472-79. The fact that this controversy could arise, however, points to a fundamental characteristic of recent congressional participation in decisions regarding the use of force. With the Gulf of Tonkin Resolution as perhaps the most egregious example, the acts in question have tended to be blank checks, leaving so much to presidential discretion as to vitiate their impact as anything other than demonstrations of national unity in time of crisis. See the discusssion in WORMUTH at 43-53; Pusey, *The President and the Power To Make War*, THE ATLANTIC MONTHLY, July, 1969, at 65; Note, 81 HARV. L. REV., *supra* note 2, at 1802-05.

seen. Should it come to fruition, it is difficult to determine whether it will be a return to nineteenth century collaboration or early twentieth century obstruction. Much will depend on Congress' ability to act decisively and quickly and on the nature of its decisions. And much will rest not only on the willingness of the President to involve Congress in the making of foreign policy but also upon congressional insistence that he do so.

The Factors Contributing to Presidential Ascendancy

To talk of causation is always hazardous business. It seems, however, that the growth of presidential power over foreign relations[60] has resulted largely from factors which can be grouped into three broad categories: historical developments; institutional aspects of the presidency which have made it more responsive to these developments than Congress; and finally, the greater willingness of many Presidents, than many Congresses, to exercise their constitutional powers to the fullest—and perhaps beyond. Among the relevant historical forces, the most important three are the ever-increasing pace, complexity and hazards of human life.[61] To meet the heightened pace of contemporary events, a premium has been placed on rapid, decisive decision-making. To deal with the complexity of the times, government by experts—men with access to relevant facts and with the capacity to fashion appropriate policies—has increasingly become the norm.[62] To survive the recurrent crises, there is emphasis on leadership which is always ready to respond and which can act flexibly and, if necessary, secretly. Moreover, there is continual concern that government be able to implement effectively whatever policies it adopts.

The presidency enjoys certain institutional advantages which make it a natural focus for governmental power, especially during times of rapid change, complexity and crisis. These advantages stem largely from the fact that the President, unlike Congress, is one rather than many. As a single man, always on the job, he is able to move secretly

---

[60] Executive control over domestic affairs has also increased, but presidential dominance in this area is notably less complete than in external matters. *See* Schlesinger, *The Limits and Excesses of Presidential Power*, SATURDAY REV., May 3, 1969, at 18-19.

[61] The increased pace, complexity and hazards have resulted from the demographic, technological and ideological explosion of the past hundred years. These factors have also produced a burgeoning interaction and interdependence among the peoples of the world. See note 19 *supra*.

[62] *See* Bracher, *Problems of Parliamentary Democracy in Europe*, 93 DAEDALUS 179, 183-85 (Winter 1964).

when the need arises, and to combine rapid, decisive action, with the flexibility in policy demanded by quickly changing developments. His singularity and continuity also facilitate long-range planning. Because he is at the center of an unsurpassed information network and because he is assisted by countless experts,[63] the possibility exists that his decisions will take into account the complexity of the problems faced. As the Chief Executive, he has more leverage in implementing his decisions that any other organ of government. These institutional advantages, though important in domestic affairs, are unusually significant in the conduct of foreign relations where unity, continuity, the ability to move swiftly and secretly, and access to up-to-date information are more often of the essence.[64]

A second historical development fundamental to the rise of the presidency has been the growing ability of the government to communicate directly with the governed. Beginning with an upsurge in newspaper circulation in the late 1800's and continuing with radio, motion pictures and now television, the capacity of decision-makers to go directly to the electorate has greatly increased, providing a tremendous opportunity to mold public opinion. Heightened ability to communicate directly with the people has redounded largely in favor of the President. As a single rather than a collective decision-maker, he provides an easy target for the public and the media to follow. As the country's chief initiator and implementor, rather than its leading deliberator and legislator, he provides a more exciting and thus newsworthy target. As the country's master of ceremony and the head of its first family, he commands attention. Walter Bagehot, in his celebrated treatment of the English constitution, adopted a phrase, "intelligible government," which describes contemporary presidential government perhaps better than it did the constitutional monarchy of Victoria. Bagehot argued that the great virtue of a monarchy, as opposed to a republic, was that it provided the people with a government which they could understand—one which acted, or so they thought, with a single royal will and provided a ruling family to whom

---

[63] For a discussion of the establishment, elements and functions of the Executive Office of the President, see C. ROSSITER, *supra* note 21, at 127-34.

[64] See THE FEDERALIST No. 64, at 273-74 (C. Beard ed. 1948) (J. Jay); *id.* No. 75, at 319-20 (A. Hamilton). It has been frequently stated, by de Tocqueville and Woodrow Wilson among others, that the power of the executive grows in relation to a nation's involvement in foreign affairs. *See* AMERICAN HERITAGE, *supra* note 13, at 265; C. ROSSITER, *supra* note 21, at 85-86.

they could relate.[65] The President provides intelligible government par excellence, and, unlike Victoria, he rules as well as reigns. Aware of their newsworthiness, Presidents seek to use it to further their ends.[66] The presidential press conference, special address and grand tour have provided effective tools for winning public support for executive policies,[67] especially those dealing with foreign affairs.[68]

---

[65]   The best reason why Monarchy is a strong government is, that it is an intelligible government. The mass of mankind understand it, and they hardly anywhere in the world understand any other. It is often said that men are ruled by their imaginations; but it would be truer to say they are governed by the weakness of their imaginations. The nature of a constitution, the action of an assembly, the play of parties, the unseen formation of a guiding opinion, are complex facts, difficult to know, and easy to mistake. But the action of a single will, the fiat of a single mind, are easy ideas: anybody can make them out, and no one can ever forget them.
W. Bagehot, The English Constitution 30 (World's Classics ed. 1949). Bagehot admitted that there exist an "inquiring few" for whom "intelligible government" is less important, because they can handle the "complex laws and notions" of constitutional rule. *Id.* Presumably, the "inquiring few" constitute a significant portion of the present American electorate.

[66] Theodore Roosevelt was the first President to appreciate fully and capitalize upon the Executive's appeal to the media. For an account of Roosevelt's use of the press, see American Heritage, *supra* note 13, at 266-67.

[67] *See* C. Rossiter, *supra* note 21, at 33, 114-18. A French commentator has observed:
    [I]n the realm of information, the political system of the United States has a real institution unforeseen in the Constitution: the presidential press conference. The importance of the press conference as a test of the American Chief Executive has often been noted. It should be emphasized that the institution of the press conference makes the press the representative of public opinion and gives to the press the role of intermediary between the citizens and their government which classic theory reserved to the legislature. It is characteristic that American senators and representatives often put their questions to the President by getting friendly or sympathetic reporters to ask certain questions at a presidential press conference.
Grosser, *The Evolution of European Parliaments*, 93 Daedalus 153, 159 (Winter 1964).

[68] The foreign tour focuses attention on the President and, if successful, enhances his political stature, thereby promoting his policies. Inherent in most foreign relations pronouncements of the Executive, particularly those dealing with the use of force, is an opportunity to "shield and enhance his authority by wrapping the flag around himself, invoking patriotism, and national unity, and claiming life-and-death crisis." Schlesinger, *supra* note 60, at 18. John Kennedy's dramatic address to the nation on October 22, 1962, certainly ranks among the most effective uses of the media to rally support for a presidential decision to use force abroad.
    Far more than in domestic affairs, contemporary Presidents seem willing to argue their foreign policies directly before the people. Grosser, *supra* note 67, at 159, comments:
    [T]he American presidential system, with the separation of powers, virtual direct election of the President and his nonparticipation in congressional debates, facilitates . . . recourse to a means of disseminating information that bypasses the legislature; but the situation is a phenomenon of modern civilization and not of institutional machinery. "The President from time to time shall report to the Congress on the State of the Union." The Founding Fathers certainly did not

A third force enhancing the position of the Executive has been the democratization of politics,[69] primarily a result of the way in which our political parties developed. While the party system has made increasingly democratic the process of electing the President, and given him a natural role as the external leader of Congress, it has done little to facilitate decisive action by the legislators and has left them exposed to the play of special interests.[70] The President rather than Congress has come to be seen as the symbol of national unity, as the chief guardian of the national interest, and as the most democratic organ of government.[71] Consequently, the capture of the presidency has become the primal objective of American politics.

It was not unnatural that the focus of party politics became the quest for the presidency, particularly in view of its notable power and the Presidents' unusual capacity to provide the heroes and folklore needed to cement party followers and the country into a cohesive whole.[72] Nor was democratization of the presidential nomination and election processes an abnormal development, since the President, institutionally, is the sole politician with a national constituency. This reality was appreciated and exploited first by Andrew Jackson, but received perhaps its classic statement from James K. Polk in his final annual message to Congress:

> If it be said that the Representatives in the popular branch of Congress are chosen directly by the people, it is answered, the people

intend this to mean only the annual message to Congress. In the Cuban crisis of October, 1962, a statement to Congress would have corresponded to the text of the Constitution, rather than a televised talk to the nation.

[69] See C. ROSSITER, supra note 21, at 88-89.

[70] See C. ROSSITER, PARTIES AND POLITICS IN AMERICA 17-24, 60-61, 62 (1960).

[71] E. CORWIN, supra note 14, at 307, states in resume:

In short, the Constitution reflects the struggle between two conceptions of executive power: that it ought always to be subordinate to the supreme legislative power, and that it ought to be, within generous limits, autonomous and self-directing; or, in other terms, the idea that the people are re-presented in the Legislature versus the idea that they are embodied in the Executive. Nor has this struggle ever entirely ceased, although on the whole it is the latter theory that has prospered. . . . "Taken by and large, the history of the presidency has been a history of aggrandizement."

[72] According to C. ROSSITER, supra note 21, at 107, the great Executives are

more than eminent characters and strong Presidents. They were and are luminous symbols in our history. We, too, the enlightened Americans, feel the need of myth and mystery in national life . . . . And who fashioned the myth? Who are the most satisfying of our folk heroes? With whom is associated a wonderful web of slogans and shrines and heroics? The answer, plainly, is the six Presidents I have pointed to most proudly.

For a discussion of the folklore of the Presidency, see AMERICAN HERITAGE, supra note 13, at 197-208.

elect the President. If both Houses represent the States and the people, so does the President. The President represents in the executive department the whole people of the United States, as each member of the legislative department represents portions of them.[73]

A fourth factor might best be termed good fortune—the frequent election of charismatic, far-sighted men to serve as President during times of great need. It is probably true that without crisis, it is difficult for a man to perform mighty acts. The converse—that given an emergency the incumbent Chief Executive will necessarily rise to meet it—does not hold. Some Presidents, so confronted, have been restrained by their concept of the presidency[74] and some by their ineptitude.

---

[73] *Quoted in* AMERICAN HERITAGE, *supra* note 13, at 94. A 1966 statement by Lyndon Johnson seems to go beyond Polk. The President declared that "[t]here are many, many who can recommend, advise, and sometimes a few of them consent. But there is only one that has been chosen by the American people to decide." Schlesinger, *supra* note 60, at 17.

[74] Presidents, like most other members of the American body politic, voluntarily obey its rules. Accordingly, their concept of the limits of their constitutional powers has a great bearing on the action which they are willing to take. It seems that presidential opinion has ranged widely, from the modest views of Buchanan to the brash interpretations of Franklin Roosevelt. Taft stated the basic tenet of the former in these words: "The true view of the executive functions . . . is, as I conceive it, that the President can exercise no power which cannot be fairly and reasonably traced to some specific grant of power or justly implied and included within such express grant as proper and necessary." *Quoted in* E. CORWIN, *supra* note 14, at 153. Buchanan adhered rigidly to his concept of the limits of his powers, going so far as to reject an 1860 Virginia proposal for a conference of states and, pending its conclusion, an agreement between the Secessionists and the President to abstain from violence. Buchanan strongly favored the plan but refused to act, stating:

> Congress, and Congress alone, under the war-making power, can exercise the discretion of agreeing to abstain "from any and all acts calculated to produce a collision of arms" between this and any other government. It would therefore be a usurpation for the Executive to attempt to restrain their hands by an agreement in regard to matters over which he has no constitutional control.

Quoted in WORMUTH at 12.

At the other extreme, Franklin Roosevelt believed that he possessed constitutional power to act even in direct opposition to existing law, if an emergency so warranted. E. CORWIN, *supra* note 14, at 251. His position resembled the executive "prerogative" formulated by John Locke "as the 'power to act according to discretion for the public good, without the prescription of law and sometimes even against it.'" *Quoted in id.* at 8. Roosevelt's activities leading to United States involvement in hostilities with Germany in the Atlantic were of dubious legality, if not clearly contrary to law upon occasion. *See* E. CORWIN, *supra* note 39, at 22-29. His September 7, 1942, dictate to Congress ordering the repeal of a certain provision of the Emergency Price Control Act was clearly in accord with the Lockian prerogative. *See* E. CORWIN, *supra* note 14, at 250-52.

Midway between Buchanan's and Franklin Roosevelt's reading of their constitutional

More Presidents than not, however, have provided the requisite leadership, with a corresponding increase in the power and prestige of the office.[75]

Finally, there is a momentum to the President's burgeoning influence. With each new function that the Executive has assumed, with each crisis that he has met, with each corresponding rise in his prestige, in popular expectations, in presidential folklore and myth, the office has become more potent. The President's varied powers feed upon one another to produce an aggregate stronger than the sum of his individual responsibilities.[76]

Presidential control over governmental affairs has been matched by a decline in congressional influence. Although Congress remains a powerful body, far more so than the legislature of any other sizable nation, the times in which it was able to dominate public affairs have passed. The existence of two co-equal houses militated against its ever being able to assert complete supremacy, thereby relegating the Executive to a ceremonial role. Unlike the institutional characteristics of

---

authority stands the "Stewardship Theory," described by Theodore Roosevelt in these terms:

> My view was that every executive officer . . . was a steward of the people . . . . My belief was that it was not only his right but his duty to do anything that the needs of the Nation demanded unless such action was forbidden by the Constitution or by the laws. . . . In other words, I acted for the public welfare . . . whenever and in whatever manner was necessary, unless prevented by direct constitutional or legislative prohibition.

Quoted in id. at 153. Few today would deny that the President has at least this much authority. *See id.* at 147-58. *See generally* A. SCHLESINGER, *supra* note 13, at 5-13.

[75] See the discussion in C. ROSSITER, *supra* note 21, at 89-114, 145-78. Arthur Schlesinger aptly notes that most advances in presidential power have engendered a counter-reaction, so that presidential aggrandizement has by no means been an uninterrupted progress forward. A. SCHLESINGER, *supra* note 13, at 15.

[76] As Clinton Rossiter lyrically noted, during an era when executive aggrandizement was viewed with greater tranquility than today:

> The Presidency . . . is a wonderful stew whose unique flavor cannot be accounted for simply by making a list of its ingredients. It is a whole greater than and different from the sum of its parts, an office whose power and prestige are something more than the arithmetical total of all its functions. The President is not one kind of official during one part of the day, another kind during another part—administrator in the morning, legislator at lunch, king in the afternoon, commander before dinner, and politician at odd moments that come his weary way. He is all these things all the time, and any one of his functions feeds upon and into all the others.

C. ROSSITER, *supra* note 21, at 41. Rossiter breaks down the various functions presently in the Executive's preserve as follows: (1) five responsibilities clearly stemming from his constitutional duties: Chief of State, Chief Executive, Commander-in-Chief, Chief Diplomat, Chief Legislator, and (2) five additional functions that have evolved over time: Chief of Party, Voice of the People, Protector of the Peace, Manager of Prosperity, and World Leader. For a discussion of each, see *id.* at 16-41.

the presidency, those of Congress have not attracted power during times of rapid change, complexity and recurrent crisis. The multitudes who make up the two houses of Congress, their constitutional task of deliberation and authorization, the decision-making process necessitated when many men are engaged in a legislative endeavor, and the diversity of the legislators' constituencies inevitably make Congress a more ponderous, public and indecisive decision-maker than the President, and one, it seems, in need of external guidance.[77]

Much of Congress' present eclipse, however, stems not from such inexorable factors, but rather from its own unwillingness to reform.[78] Unlike many Presidents, who have made a studied effort to adopt procedures which would enable them to wield power effectively, Congress has generally been reluctant to part with old ways, even at the cost of diminishing influence. Congressional decision-making procedures could be steamlined, its access to information and expert advice could be appreciably heightened, and its attention could be focused more on national problems and less on local and personal matters. Moreover, its regrettable public image could be improved by skillful use of the media. Latent congressional power to investigate, to set policy and to supervise exists should Congress choose to exercise it.[79] Beyond its inaction and image, the eclipse of Congress in this century can be attributed to its proclivity, when it does act, to make decisions unresponsive to the needs of the times.[80] Thus, a reversal of congressional fortunes will require not only a capacity to act but also the ability to make sound decisions.

Restraints on the Exercise of Presidential Power

Powerful as he has become, the President remains bound by numerous restraints. Fundamental limits on his action result from his own beliefs and from his own leadership ability. As noted earlier, the Presi-

---

[77] Rossiter goes further to suggest that even when Congress does act effectively, the result frequently is to increase the power of the President, since the implementation of congressional policy must often be left to him. *Id.* at 87-88.

[78] *See* Kurland, *supra* note 2, *passim.* Kurland argues that the ultimate responsibility for congressional decline lies with the people and not the legislators, since the electorate is concerned far more with ends than means; thus the voters exert little or no pressure on Congress to see to its own institutional well-being, so long as presidential policies are popular. *Id.* at 635. Credence is given this argument by the sudden embarrassment of those elements in the academic community who found presidential prerogative quite satisfying until Vietnam. *See* Schlesinger, *supra* note 60, at 17.

[79] *See* notes 165-77 *infra* and accompanying text.

[80] *See* Schlesinger, *supra* note 60, at 19.

dent generally acts within the law not so much because he fears the consequences of disobedience as because he voluntarily supports the system of which it is a part. Admittedly, when the question is the extent of his constitutional powers to respond to what he views as a threat to the country, an activist Chief Executive may find an unusually broad grant of authority.[81] But even if the President decides that a given course of action would be legal, it will fail miserably if he is unable to persuade[82] those whose assistance is essential to gain support for it, for there are very few matters of consequence which can be wholly accomplished by presidential dictate. Though it is unlikely, for example, that his order to dispatch troops to a foreign conflict would be disobeyed, his power to keep the troops in the field for a sustained period rests on his ability to convince the country of the wisdom of his policies. Even should the Executive win initial support for his action, if it proves ill-advised his freedom to pursue the policy will be short-lived.

Beyond these internal restraints lie a series of external limits. The President must be careful at all times to honor the bounds set by prevailing standards of "private liberty and public morality."[83] Clinton Rossiter aptly states that "[i]f [the President] knows anything of history or politics or administration, he knows that he can do great things only within 'the common range of expectation,' that is to say, in ways that honor or at least do not outrage the accepted dictates of constitutionalism, democracy, personal liberty, and Christian morality."[84] Lyndon Johnson's Vietnam debacle can be traced in good part to the offense the war caused various elements in the country on these scores. Arguably, again in the wake of Mr. Johnson's experience, it seems that a contemporary Chief Executive must take almost equal care not to offend the public sense of taste and style. To overstep any of these bounds risks a loss of public support, which, once gone, is difficult

---

[81] See the discussion of Franklin Roosevelt in note 74 *supra*.

[82] *See* R. NEUSTADT, PRESIDENTIAL POWER, THE POLITICS OF LEADERSHIP (1960).

> The President of the United States has an extraordinary range of formal powers, of authority in statute law and in the Constitution. Here is testimony that despite his "powers" he does not obtain results by giving orders—or not, at any rate, merely by giving orders. He also has extraordinary status, *ex officio*, according to the customs of our government and politics. Here is testimony that despite his status he does not get action without argument. Presidential *power* is the power to persuade.

Id. at 23.

[83] C. ROSSITER, *supra* note 21, at 46.

[84] *Id.* at 70.

to recover. An undercurrent of suspicion and even hatred of the President as a potential despot runs throughout American history;[85] an administration which brings it to the surface for whatever reason sacrifices much of its future effectiveness.

Other centers of power—both by what they do and what they might do—greatly restrain presidential action. Three competing institutions are particularly important: the federal bureaucracy, Congress and the judiciary. To implement his policies, the President must have the cooperation of the civil and military personnel who actually operate the governmental machinery. Since most of the bureaucracy falls within the presidential chain of command, obtaining their obedience ought to be among his less pressing problems. Such, however, is not the case. While the move toward rule by experts has increased presidential power at the expense of congressional, it has done even more to enlarge and strengthen the "permanent government."[86] Each incoming Executive, for example, inherits a mass of departments, agencies and committees, all committed to the expert conduct of foreign affairs. He directly appoints only the high command of most of these entities, and often has trouble controlling even his personal appointees. Feuds within the executive hierarchy and deliberate refusal by high officials to implement presidential policies are not unknown.[87]

The President's difficulties with his own people are minor beside the problems he faces in persuading the permanent officials to cooperate. Most were in place before his administration took office and most will survive it. They may passively oppose presidential policy by exhibiting great reluctance to alter existing procedures and programs,[88] or they may actively seek to determine national policy by pressing forward their own plans. Since Eisenhower's famed warning against the military-industrial complex, there has been increasing fear that this element of

---

[85] All strong Presidents, no matter how grateful posterity might be, have awakened the strange undercurrent of hatred, the persistent fear that the Founding Fathers had bequeathed a potential elective monarchy to the United States. The Kennedys were frequently referred to as a royal family, sometimes with affectionate mockery, more often with malice and suspicion. The latest example of the literature of antipresidential fantasy, Barbara Garson's pastiche *MacBird*, is bound by the same queer compulsion. Portraying Lyndon Johnson as the Macbeth-like assassin of Kennedy, it is a drama of monarchy and usurpation. . . . [I]t reveals obsessions akin to those of . . . bizarre bygone items . . . . AMERICAN HERITAGE, *supra* note 13, at 182.

[86] The term comes from A. SCHLESINGER, *supra* note 13, at 16.

[87] *See, e.g.,* Morgenthau, *supra* note 11, at 265-67.

[88] *See, e.g.,* C. ROSSITER, *supra* note 21, at 59-62; A. SCHLESINGER, *supra* note 13, at 16-17, 94-97.

the permanent government may be shaping basic national policies.[89] Even when the relevant parts of the bureaucracy attempt to implement presidential programs, they often fail for a variety of reasons, including, in some cases, incompetence. The diplomatic-military apparatus in Vietnam, for example, had only limited success in its good faith effort to realize Johnson's objectives.

Difficult as the bureaucracy may be, a greater limit upon presidential power is Congress.[90] In Richard Neustadt's words, we have "a government of separated institutions *sharing* powers." [91] Thus, virtually all presidential programs and ventures require implementing legislation and funding. Unlike parliamentary executives, the President has no ultimate weapons, such as dissolution or excommunication from party ranks, with which to beat reluctant legislators into submission. As a result, an abiding concern of the Executive and his assistants is the likely reaction of Congress to their proposals and actions.[92]

Legislators have a number of tools with which to restrain the President. Through legislation, they can restrict his options, hamstring his policies and, to an extent, even take the policy initiative from him.[93] It has been suggested that Congress is presently attempting to control the Executive by qualified legislation more than in the past,[94] and the movement headed by Senator Fulbright, if successful, would certainly

---

[89] It is not wholly accurate to describe the military-industrial complex as a part of the permanent government, for, broadly defined, it includes groups with no official or unofficial ties to the state.

> It is a vast, amorphous conglomeration that goes far beyond the Pentagon and the large manufacturers of weapons. It includes legislators who benefit politically from job-generating military activity in their constituencies, workers in defense plants, the unions to which they belong, university scientists and research organizations that receive Pentagon grants. It even extends to the stores where payrolls are spent, and the landlords, grocers and car salesmen who cater to customers from military bases.

The Military: Servant or Master of Policy, TIME, April 11, 1969, at 23. See *id.* at 20-26; *The Military-Industrial Complex*, NEWSWEEK, June 9, 1969, at 74-87; AMERICAN HERITAGE, *supra* note 13, at 287-88.

[90] *See* C. ROSSITER, *supra* note 21, at 49-56.

[91] R. NEUSTADT, *supra* note 82, at 42.

[92] [A]s I saw the executive branch in action, [i]t was haunted by a fear and at times an exaggerated fear of congressional reaction. The notion that the executive goes his blind and arrogant way, saying damn the torpedoes, full speed ahead, is just not true. I would say a truer notion is that the executive branch cowers day and night over the fear and sometimes quite an exaggerated and irrational fear of what the congressional response is going to be to the things it does.

A. SCHLESINGER, *supra* note 13, at 171; *accord, e.g.,* Morgenthau, *supra* note 11, at 267.

[93] *See* Morgenthau, *supra* note 11, at 263-64.

[94] A. SCHLESINGER, *supra* note 13, at 17. *But see* Kurland, *supra* note 2, at 629-31.

reduce presidential freedom in foreign affairs.[95] Through the power of the purse, the legislators can similarly limit the President. Although control of the purse has been virtually a nonpower in the hands of cold war Congresses when funds were sought for the military, present reluctance to embark on major defense spending and criticism of the military establishment[96] suggest that appropriations may emerge anew as a limiting factor. A few voices have even been heard to suggest that funds supporting troops in the field be cut—traditionally, an unthinkable position.[97]

The power of congressional committees to investigate and oversee, as the 1967 Fulbright hearings indicate, provides a means of sparking national debate, molding opinion and thereby influencing presidential action. Activity within Congress can frequently focus outside political pressure and bring it to bear on the Chief Executive. Similarly, legislators can work the political process privately as well, communicating quietly with the President to persuade him that his ideas are ill-advised or subject to great potential opposition. Congress can also work in tandem with rebellious elements in the bureaucracy to thwart presidential initiatives. Remote though the possibility is, the President must remain aware of the congressional capacity to impeach him or to censure his conduct by resolution—a fate that befell Polk at the hands of a House disturbed by his role in initiating the Mexican War.[98] The President is also continually hemmed in by the play of the political system—by sniping from members of the opposition party and by the demands and feelings of members of his own party.[99]

---

[95] On June 25, 1969, the Senate by a vote of 70-16 adopted the following resolution, a modified version of the one Senator Fulbright had introduced almost two years earlier:

> Resolved, That (1) a national commitment for the purpose of this resolution means the use of the armed forces of the United States on foreign territory, or a promise to assist a foreign country, government, or people by the use of the armed forces or financial resources of the United States, either immediately or upon the happening of certain events, and (2) it is the sense of the Senate that a national commitment by the United States results only from affirmative action taken by the executive and legislative branches of the United States Government by means of a treaty, statute, or concurrent resolution of both Houses of Congress specifically providing for such commitment.

S. Res. 85, 91st Cong., 1st Sess., 115 Cong. Rec. S7153 (daily ed. June 25, 1969). For a further discussion of Congress and national commitments, see 48 Cong. Dig. 193-224 (1969).

[96] See note 1 supra.

[97] See note 21 supra.

[98] See note 48 supra and accompanying text.

[99] C. Rossiter, supra note 21, at 62-64.

Finally, the Senate is constitutionally empowered to advise and consent to presidential treaties and appointments and has devised the power to delay and negate by filibuster. These senatorial prerogatives, coupled with the power of Congress over the legislation and appropriations necessary to implement the President's foreign policies, constitute the primary restraints on his action.

To date, the courts have served more to enlarge the presidential prerogative over foreign affairs than to restrain it.[100] The one opinion directly treating the scope of presidential power to use force abroad—an 1860 decision dealing with an 1854 reprisal against a small, stateless town in Central America[101]—took a broad view of the President's constitutional powers. Although given ample opportunity to speak in the Vietnam context, federal courts have uniformly refused to consider whether the conflict is unconstitutional for lack of congressional

---

[100] See, e.g., United States v. Curtiss-Wright Export Corp., 299 U.S. 304 (1936); The Prize Cases, 67 U.S. (2 Black) 635 (1863); Myers v. United States, 272 U.S. 52, 116-18 (1926) (dictum); In re Neagle, 135 U.S. 1, 63-68 (1890) (dictum); C. ROSSITER, supra note 21, at 56-59; C. ROSSITER, THE SUPREME COURT AND THE COMMANDER IN CHIEF passim (1951).

[101] Durand v. Hollins, 8 F. Cas. 111 (No. 4186) (C.C.S.D.N.Y. 1860). The court stated in part:

> As the executive head of the nation, the president is made the only legitimate organ of the general government, to open and carry on correspondence or negotiations with foreign nations, in matters concerning the interests of the country or of its citizens. It is to him, also, the citizens abroad must look for protection of person and of property, and for the faithful execution of the laws existing and intended for their protection. For this purpose, the whole executive power of the country is placed in his hands, under the constitution, and the laws passed in pursuance thereof; and different departments of government have been organized, through which this power may be most conveniently executed whether by negotiation or by force—a department of state and a department of the navy.
> Now, as it respects the interposition of the executive abroad, for the protection of the lives or property of the citizen, the duty must, of necessity, rest in the discretion of the president. Acts of lawless violence . . . cannot be anticipated . . . and the protection, to be effectual or of any avail, may, not unfrequently, require the most prompt and decided action. Under our system of government, the citizen abroad is as much entitled to protection as the citizen at home.

Id. at 112.

Although Captain Hollins burned the town in question long after the alleged attack on United States interests, the opinion speaks, not of a reprisal, but of a rescue situation, and grants the President broad powers to respond quickly to save threatened citizens and their property. WORMUTH at 22-24, 31-32, argues that the destruction of the town was strongly condemned by contemporary public and congressional opinion, and suggests that the Durand decision was an attempt by the judge, "a partisan Democrat, . . . to vindicate the action of a Democratic President." Id. at 32.

authorization.[102] The possibility remains, nonetheless, that an activist court, convinced of the unconstitutionality of presidential action, could order the Executive to desist. President Truman's immediate acceptance of the Supreme Court's ruling in the *Steel Seizure* case[103] suggests that a judicial command affecting the use of force abroad would be obeyed by the executive branch[104]—although perhaps not without great political cost to the Court and great stress upon our constitutional system.

---

[102] See note 7 *supra*.

[103] Youngstown Sheet & Tube Co. v. Sawyer, 343 U.S. 579 (1952).

[104] To a significant extent, it is possible to equate a decision such as *Youngstown*, which ordered the return to private management of domestic steel companies seized by executive command, with a hypothetical judicial decision ordering the President to withdraw troops from a conflict to which he has unilaterally committed them, unless he obtains immediate congressional authorization for their use. Both decisions affect American participation in foreign conflict. President Truman, for example, seized the steel mills restored in *Youngstown* because

> [a]ll the members of the Cabinet agreed . . . that it would be harmful to the country and injurious to our campaign in Korea if our steel mills were allowed to close down. We were then not only trying to keep our forces in Korea, as well as elsewhere, fully equipped, but we had allies to whom we had promised arms and munitions, and whose determination to resist Communism might depend on our ability to supply them the weapons they so badly needed.

H. TRUMAN, MEMOIRS, *quoted in* A. WESTIN, THE ANATOMY OF A CONSTITUTIONAL LAW CASE 9 (1958). The hypothetical decision, should Congress approve the President's action, would have only the psychological effect inherent in a judicial declaration that the war had been unconstitutionally waged in the past. Should Congress refuse authorization and the President withdraw the troops, the decision would be instrumental in reversing presidential war policy.

Although the decisions typified by *Youngstown* and the hypothetical both have strong foreign policy overtones, presidential obedience to the former is more assured. First, a *Youngstown* decision will generally enjoy greater domestic political support. Executive action the direct effects of which are felt primarily within this country will usually generate more political opposition than action whose principal effects are felt abroad. Thus, seizure of the steel industry is riskier for the President than waging war in Asia. Moreover, executive action which affects the well-established rights of powerful individuals in this country is more likely to spark political backlash than action that impinges upon the more inchoate rights of less powerful persons. Since Congress is unlikely to bring an action against the President for infringement of its right to participate in war decisions, the plaintiff in the hypothetical case would probably be a serviceman seeking to avoid participation in the conflict. See note 7 *supra*. Unlike the property rights at issue in *Youngstown*, a draftee or reservist's right to avoid involvement in an unauthorized war is not an interest that our legal system has traditionally recognized as worthy of protection. Further, the draftee's political power is miniscule compared to that of the steel magnate. Only when a series of draft cases has evoked significant moral and political condemnation do they begin to have a potential effect akin to *Youngstown*.

Second, presidential disregard of a court order is more difficult when compliance requires action solely within the United States and the reversal of a course of action whose substance has consisted largely of official proclamations. The steel mills, for

The ultimate restraint upon the President, however, does not come from his own beliefs and abilities or from competing centers of power, but rather from the activities of the electorate, which continually expresses its views in various manifestations of public opinion, and periodically in federal elections.[105] A President will fall from grace when his policies fail to meet popular needs and demands or when they involve him in activity which is widely viewed as illegitimate, because it transgresses popular conceptions of legality or morality.[106] An unpopular President and his supporters will ultimately be turned out of office, but before their dismissal, executive policies and personnel will have come back under attack from other centers of power, emboldened by the President's diminished popular standing.[107] Attacks from these centers will, in turn, further reduce popular confidence in the administration. The President will find it increasingly difficult to govern, even in areas distantly divorced from those in which his actions have offended the public.[108] Once lost, the mandate of heaven is difficult to regain.

---

example, could be returned to private ownership by an executive order rescinding the earlier seizure decree. It would be far easier for the President, as Commander-in-Chief, to disregard or subvert an order to bring home hundreds of thousands of troops from a distant country.

It is probable, however, that a President confronted with the hypothetical decision would seek congressional approval and, should it not be forthcoming, would like most other Americans, voluntarily obey the rules of our society, including the one which places final authority on constitutional questions in the hands of the Supreme Court. Thus, unless the President felt that the security of the country was utterly dependent upon prosecution of the war, he would be most unlikely to defy the Court. Moreover, even if the President were inclined to disregard its command, he would be restrained by knowledge that defiance could result in a constitutional crisis of disastrous consequences both for the legitimacy of his administration and the stability of the country.

[105] Since the success of American foreign policy frequently depends on the actions of other states and their peoples, executive use of force abroad is subject to their opinions and leadership selections, as well as to those of the American electorate.

[106] See notes 83-85 *supra* and accompanying text.

[107] These centers, of course, can act before public sentiment turns against the executive policies in question, and may be instrumental in effecting the shift. The Fulbright hearings, for example, led rather than followed public opinion. A. Schlesinger, *supra* note 13, at 106, does not believe that "there can be any question that the Senate Foreign Relations Committee opened up a national debate where one had really not existed before. The educational job performed by the senators on Vietnam has been quite extraordinary."

[108] The Presidency is "an unwieldy vessel which can navigate only when it has built up a head of steam and is proceeding at a brisk speed. When the pressure is dissipated and the speed drops, the craft is at the mercy of the elements . . . ." American Heritage, *supra* note 13, at 275.

In sum, during the last several decades the allocation of power between the President and Congress over the control of foreign relations
has been heavily weighted in favor of the Executive. His hegemony
has resulted from the interplay of a number of factors, most of them
a result of the presidency's institutional advantages in meeting contemporary challenges and opportunities. Nevertheless, executive control
over foreign policy is hardly without its limits, both actual and potential.

THE BALANCE BETWEEN PRESIDENT AND CONGRESS: RULES

The Constitution

With the foregoing overview of practice, it will be helpful now to
consider expectations—people's rule-based beliefs concerning the constitutional scope of the President's authority—irrespective of the actualities of his conduct. The appropriate place at which to begin such an
investigation is with the language of the relevant constitutional provisions which appear in articles I and II. They may be divided into four
categories: grants dealing with foreign affairs as a whole; those concerning specifically the military aspects of foreign affairs; grants of
inherent, nonenumerated powers; and provisions providing the President and Congress, respectively, with weapons with which to coerce
one another.

In the first category, the President is modestly endowed, at least in
terms of formal, stated grants of power. Generally, he holds the executive power of the Government[109] and has the authority to request
the executive departments to report to him,[110] as well as the power to
nominate men to fill principal offices.[111] He is enjoined to see that federal
law is faithfully executed and to inform Congress periodically of the state
of the nation[112] and is authorized to present Congress with legislative
recommendations.[113] More specifically, the President is empowered to
make treaties and diplomatic appointments with the approval of the
Senate,[114] and he is commanded to receive foreign diplomats.[115]

---

109 U.S. CONST. art. II, § 1.

110 *Id.* § 2.

111 *Id.*

112 *Id.* § 3.

113 *Id.*

114   [The President] . . . shall have Power, by and with the Advice and Consent of
the Senate, to make Treaties, provided two thirds of the Senators present concur;
and he shall nominate, and by and with the Advice and Consent of the Senate,
shall appoint Ambassadors, other public Ministers and Consuls, . . . and all

Congress has more extensive powers in this category. Generally, the legislators hold all the legislative power of the Government,[116] including the power over appropriations, the House having the privilege of initiating all money bills.[117] More specifically, Congress as a whole controls a wide range of matters with notable transnational impact, especially in an increasingly interrelated, interdependent world.[118] Policies regarding such matters as foreign commerce often fuel international conflict. The Senate, in effect a third branch of government in foreign affairs, has the power to give or withhold consent on treaties and appointments.[119]

In the second, specifically military category, presidential grants again lag behind their congressional counterparts. The Executive is simply named Commander-in-Chief, and given the power to commission officers.[120] His appointment prerogative mentioned previously also comes into play in the military sphere. Congress, on the other hand, has a battery of responsibilities, including, *inter alia*, the power to raise and support the armed forces and the power to declare war.[121]

---

other Officers of the United States, whose Appointments are not herein otherwise provided for, and which shall be established by Law . . . .
Id. § 2.

[115] "[H]e shall receive Ambassadors and other public Ministers . . . ." *Id.* § 3.

[116] *Id.* art. I, §§ 1, 8.

[117] *Id.* § 7.

[118] The Congress shall have Power to lay and collect Taxes, Duties, Imposts and Excises, to pay the Debts . . .
To borrow Money on the credit of the United States;
To regulate Commerce with foreign Nations . . .
To establish an uniform Rule of Naturalization . . .
To coin Money, regulate the Value thereof, and of foreign Coin, and fix the Standard of Weights and Measures . . .
To establish Post Offices . . .
To promote the Progress of Science and useful Arts, by securing for limited Times to Authors and Inventors the exclusive Right to their respective Writings and Discoveries . . .
To define and punish Piracies and Felonies committed on the high Seas, and Offenses against the Law of Nations . . . .
Id. § 8.

[119] See note 114 *supra*.

[120] U.S. CONST. art. II, §§ 2, 3.

[121] The Congress shall have Power To . . . provide for the common Defence . . .
To declare War, grant Letters of Marque and Reprisal, and make Rules concerning Captures on Land and Water;
To raise and support Armies . . .
To provide and maintain a Navy;
To make rules for the Government and Regulation of the land and Naval Forces;
To provide for organizing, arming, and disciplining, the Militia, and for gov-

In the third category, inherent powers, the President comes into his own. Whereas article II, section 1 vests in him "the executive Power," article I, section 1 vests in Congress only those "legislative Powers *herein granted.*" Moreover, while the legislative article is quite tightly drawn, the executive article, in Corwin's words, "is the most loosely drawn chapter of the Constitution." [122] Thus, the President can make a strong case that, as the holder of the executive power, he possesses residual authority to go beyond his enumerated powers to take whatever steps he deems necessary for the country's security. Congress, to the contrary, confronts a linguistic hurdle. Arguably, however, "herein granted" is not an insurmountable barrier where foreign policy is involved. [123]

In the final, coercive category, Congress regains its textual edge. The President can seek to bend the legislators to his will through the threat of veto and special session, [124] but Congress can virtually destroy him. Impeachment and censure remain remote possibilities, but hostile use or nonuse of legislative power is an ever present mode of persuasion.

Such is the relevant constitutional language. It strongly suggests that both the President and Congress are to have a role in decisions regarding foreign policy, especially those concerned with the use of force. But, as suggested earlier, [125] the language provides minimal guidance in most concete situations; the grants are complementary and abstract, and occasionally fail altogether to speak to contemporary problems.

Intent of the Framers

Like their language the intent of the Framers is somewhat ambiguous.

---

erning such Part of them as may be employed in the Service of the United States . . .

To exercise . . . Authority over all Places purchased . . . for the Erection of Forts, Magazines, Arsenals, Dock-Yards, and needful Buildings . . . .
Id. art. I, § 8.

[122] E. CORWIN, *supra* note 14, at 3.

[W]hereas "legislative power" and "judicial power" today denote fairly definable *functions* of government as well as fairly constant *methods* for their discharge, "executive power" is still indefinite as to *function* and retains, particularly when it is exercised by a single individual, much of its original plasticity as to *method*. It is consequently the power of government that is the most spontaneously responsive to emergency conditions; conditions, that is, which have not attained enough of stability or recurrency to admit of their being dealt with according to rule.
Id.

[123] *See* United States v. Curtiss-Wright Export Corp., 299 U.S. 304, 318 (1936); M. MCDOUGAL, *supra* note 14, at 496-503; *cf. id.* at 492-96.

[124] U.S. CONST. art. I, § 7; *id.* art. II, § 3.

[125] See notes 14-16 *supra* and accompanying text.

The relevant provisions were written only after long discussion and much compromise—processes certain to breed confusion about the exact nature of the end product. As is the case where many views are advanced, and where the drafters do not know from past experience what demands reality will make upon their rules, much that the Framers adopted was left either vague or unsaid, to be filled in by practice.

The Constitution's foreign affairs provisions were drafted against a background of legislative control of external matters in America,[126] and of executive domination in Britain.[127] The Framers wished to alter the American practice to profit from executive speed, efficiency and relative isolation from mass opinion,[128] without incurring the disadvantages of an unchecked British monarch. Thus, speed and efficiency, on the one hand, and restraint upon executive prerogative, on the other, appear to have been the basic objectives of the Drafters. Accordingly, they created an Executive independent from Congress,[129] who was

---

[126] Prior to the installation of the Constitution on March 4, 1789, the direction of foreign policy was in the hands of a unicameral legislature which functioned through a Committee of Secret Correspondence (1775-7), a Committee for Foreign Affairs (1777-81), and the Department of Foreign Affairs (1781-9). The last was under a secretary who was responsible to the Congress. LEOPOLD at 67 n.1.

[127] Madison stated in 1793 that "'[t]he power of making treaties and the power of declaring war are *royal prerogatives* in the *British government*, and are accordingly treated as *executive prerogatives* by British commentators. . . .'" *Quoted in* E. CORWIN, THE PRESIDENT'S CONTROL OF FOREIGN RELATIONS 21 (1917); *see* James Wilson's comment, I THE RECORDS OF THE FEDERAL CONVENTION OF 1787, at 65-66 (M. Farrand rev. ed. 1937) [hereinafter cited as RECORDS], and Hamilton's Analysis in THE FEDERALIST No. 69, at 295 (C. Beard ed. 1948) (A. Hamilton).

[128] The Framers seem to have been seriously concerned about the "temporary errors and delusions" of the people, their "passing popular whims" and "public passions." *See* THE FEDERALIST No. 49, at 220 (C. Beard ed. 1948) (J. Madison); *id.* No. 63, at 268 (J. Madison); *id.* No. 71, at 303 (A. Hamilton). Thus, they sought a check on mass opinion in a strong President, *id.* No. 71, at 303 (A. Hamilton), and in the Senate's "temperate and respectable body of citizens," *id.* No. 63, at 268 (J. Madison). *See also id.* No. 62, at 263-64 (J. Madison).

[129] The creation of an Executive, wholly outside the legislative sphere, was by no means a foregone conclusion when the Framers first met. C. ROSSITER, *supra* note 21, at 76-79, suggests that among the crucial decisions taken in favor of a strong Executive were that the office would be separate from the legislature; that it would be held by one man, who would have a source of election outside Congress, and a fixed term subject only to impeachment; that he would be eligible for reelection; that he would be granted his own constitutional powers, and not be saddled with a council whose approval he would have to obtain for various actions; and that he could not be a member of either house of Congress during his presidency. For further discussion, see *id.* at 74-81, 87; AMERICAN HERITAGE, *supra* note 13, at 12-24; E. CORWIN, *supra* note 14, at 3-16; A. SCHLESINGER, *supra* note 13, at 6-7.

perhaps at his strongest in external matters. Simultaneously, they placed in both Houses of Congress and in the Senate alone powers designed to prevent unilateral control of foreign relations by the President.[130]

Of the various grants of power to both the President and Congress, the one most central to the present question is the congressional power to declare war. If there are constitutional limits on presidential authority to use the military abroad *sua sponte*, this provision provides them more than any other.[131] "The Congress shall have Power to . . . declare War . . . " could mean any of a number of things, ranging from a relatively meaningless authority to recognize an existing state of large-scale conflict[132] to the authority to make virtually all decisions regarding the use of force by the United States.

It seems reasonably clear from proposals made and rejected at the Constitutional Convention, from debates there, subsequent statements by

---

[130] The Framers intended that the Senate share in the actual execution of certain aspects of our foreign relations. *See* E. CORWIN, *supra* note 127, at 84-88; THE FEDERALIST No. 64, at 272-74 (C. Beard ed. 1948) (J. Jay); M. McDOUGAL, *supra* note 14, at 436-37, 557-59. But in the interests of practicality, the implementation of foreign policy came quickly to rest almost exclusively with the Executive. The legislators retained, however, a strong voice in shaping the policies to be implemented, especially regarding the use of force abroad. *See* notes 37-48 *supra* and accompanying text.

[131] The Framers also viewed congressional control over the raising and support of the military as a primal check on presidential use of force, whether at home or abroad. *See, e.g.,* THE FEDERALIST No. 26, at 106-07 (C. Beard ed. 1948) (A. Hamilton); *id.* No. 41, at 177 (J. Madison). But with the establishment of a large standing military capacity, the assumption of world-wide defense commitments and a prevailing belief that presidential use of troops abroad requires bipartisan support in the interests of national security, the power of the purse has become relatively meaningless. *See* note 21 *supra* and accompanying text. In the wake of the disquiet induced by Vietnam, it is possible that Congress will once again use its control of appropriations as a check on the Executive, *see* text at notes 96, 97 *supra,* although it is unlikely that the President will ever be deprived of the mobile task forces which enable him to intervene abroad on short notice. To use its power over the purse to restrain such action, Congress would have to demonstrate willingness to refuse funds to carry on an intervention once begun, or to fund it only at the cost of other programs the President favors.

[132] Such recognition may have some effect. A formal declaration of this nature would effectuate certain legal results with potentially profound consequences. Treaties would be canceled; trading, contracts and debts with the enemy would be suspended; vast emergency powers would be authorized domestically; and legal relations between neutral states and the belligerents would be altered. But though there may have been a time when these changes in legal status were uniquely the result of the issuance of a formal declaration, this is clearly no longer true today. Countries have long engaged in undeclared hostilities which in terms of the effort involved, the impact on citizens, and the effect on domestic and international legal relations are often indistinguishable from a formally declared war.
Note, 81 HARV. L. REV., *supra* note 2, at 1772 (footnotes omitted).

the Framers and from practice in early years that the Drafters intended decisions regarding the *initiation* of force abroad to be made not by the President alone,[133] not by the Senate alone,[134] nor by the President and the Senate,[135] but by the entire Congress subject to the signature or veto of the President. The Framers recognized the potentially momentous consequences of foreign conflict and wished to check its unilateral initiation by any single individual or group.[136] Madison expressed this concern early in the Constitutional Convention: "A rupture with other powers is among the greatest of national calamities. It ought therefore to be effectually provided that no part of a nation shall have it in its power to bring them [wars] on the whole." [137] Foreign conflicts, since they involve the entire nation, are to be begun only after both legislative houses and the Executive have been heard, even at the cost of some delay in reaching a decision.[138]

---

[133] Mr. Butler, apparently the only proponent of his view, favored "vesting the power in the President, who will have all the requisite qualities [*e.g.*, dispatch, continuity, unity of office] and will not make war but when the Nation will support it." II RECORDS 318.

[134]   Mr. Pinkney opposed the vesting of this power in the Legislature. Its proceedings were too slow. It wd. meet but once a year. The Hs. of Reps. would be too numerous for such deliberations. The Senate would be the best depository, being more acquainted with foreign affairs, and most capable of proper resolutions. If the States are equally represented in Senate, so as to give no advantage to large States, the power will notwithstanding be safe, as the small have their all at stake in such cases as well as the large States. It would be singular for one—authority to make war, and another peace.

Id. (footnotes omitted).

[135] Hamilton presented a plan in which the Executive was "to make war or peace, with the advice of the senate . . . ." I RECORDS 300.

[136] See note 138 *infra*.

[137] I RECORDS 316. Madison was speaking to the possibility that individual states through their "violations of the law of nations & of Treaties" might bring foreign war upon the country as a whole. *Id.* The unfortunate consequences of war were alluded to by others among the Framers. Mr. Elseworth, for example, argued that "[i]t shd. be more easy to get out of war, than into it." II RECORDS 319. And Mr. Mason was "for clogging rather than facilitating war . . . ." *Id.*

[138] Objections were made to legislative involvement on this ground. See the comments of Messrs. Butler and Pinkney, II *id.* at 318. But the approach of Mr. Mason proved more persuasive; he stated that he was "agst. giving the power of war to the Executive, because not [safely] to be trusted with it; or to the Senate, because not so constructed as to be entitled to it." *Id.* at 319.

Fear existed that if the President were given the right to wage war unilaterally, he might unwisely engage the country in ruinous conflict or use the existence of war to raise military forces with which to seize control of the country. Moreover, the Executive, like the Senate, was not directly elected, and thus lacked the moral authority to commit the entire country to so potentially devastating a course. The House of Representatives possessed the legitimacy given by direct election, but, due to its close ties to the general public, was suspected of flighty judgment. Accordingly, the

The discussion to this point has been of Congress' power to *initiate* the use of force abroad—to take the country from a state of peace to one of war. When, however, war is thrust upon the United States by another power, the Framers apparently intended that there be unilateral presidential response if temporal exigencies do not permit an initial resort to Congress.[139] Under such circumstances, there is no longer a need for check and deliberation; all reasonable men would agree that the survival of the nation is worth fighting for; speedy and effective defense measures are the constitutional objectives given a direct attack upon the country.[140] Congressional involvement comes at a later point; as soon as feasible, the legislators are to be given an opportunity to ratify past presidential actions and authorize future conduct.[141]

Although the Framers did not delineate what constitutes a thrust of conflict upon the United States, it appears that any direct, physical assault upon American territory will suffice.[142] Moreover, if a blow

---

Representatives' passions were to be controlled by involving the Senate and President in war decisions. Involvement of the Senate, moreover, would ensure that force could not be initiated abroad unless a majority of the states agreed. In short, an attempt was made to devise a scheme in which war would be entered upon only after measured deliberation, thus avoiding involvement in conflicts where the costs, upon reflection, appeared to outweigh the gains, or where the primary "gains" would be executive aggrandizement or the satiation of popular passion. These checks were intended to insure that the fighting would be supported by most Americans, thus avoiding disastrous internecine struggle within the country over war policy.

[139] The Framers initially intended to grant Congress the power "to make" war, as opposed to declaring it. In due course, however, "Mr. M[adison] and Mr. Gerry moved to insert '*declare*,' striking out '*make*' war; leaving to the Executive the power to repel sudden attacks." The motion passed, though it had failed upon an earlier vote. *Id.* at 318-19, 313. What precisely those who voted in favor of the change intended is difficult to say in light of existing information, but it does seem clear that the amendment was not even remotely designed to empower the Executive to initiate hostilities. *See* WORMUTH at 3-4; Note, 81 HARV. L. REV., *supra* note 2, at 1773 n.16. Compare a provision temporarily inserted by the Committee of Style, which stated that "[n]o State, without the consent of the Legislature of the United States shall . . . engage in any war, unless it shall be actually invaded by enemies, or the danger of invasion shall be so imminent, as not to admit of a delay, until the Legislature of the United States can be consulted." II RECORDS 577.

[140] Arguably, under such circumstances constitutional procedures are superceded by an inherent right of the country, as a sovereign state, to protect its territorial integrity against foreign attack. Since the President is generally the citizen most able to galvanize a defensive reaction, he acts. Language in United States v. Curtiss-Wright Export Corp., 299 U.S. 304, 316-18 (1936), lends a measure of judicial support to this contention. *See also* M. McDOUGAL, *supra* note 14, at 496-503; L. SMITH, AMERICAN DEMOCRACY AND MILITARY POWER 291-92 (1951); Note, 81 HARV. L. REV., *supra* note 2, at 1778.

[141] See notes 41-42, 46-47 *supra* and accompanying text.

[142] "Polk's action set a precedent for also viewing as 'war' the invasion of disputed

is clearly imminent, the Executive need not wait for it to fall. Arguably, the change in world conditions since 1789—the end of our geographical immunity, the revolution in military technology and the new balance of power[143]—permits unilateral executive reaction to a sudden attack on a foreign state deemed essential to our security. Accordingly, a declaration of war by a foreign power of only paper force would not justify unilateral presidential response,[144] but the launching of nuclear weapons aimed at American cities would, even before the missiles reached their targets.[145] Perhaps a sudden assault upon Canada or West Germany would similarly justify immediate executive action.

The President obviously must be the one who determines when a thrust is in progress which justifies his unilateral response.[146] His judgment, however, may be repudiated when the matter is later placed before Congress.[147] Such repudiation, in the face of genuine enemy attack, is most unlikely; virtually all citizens will agree that the survival of the country is worth the price of conflict, and Congress will generally be far more prone to attack a President who fails to defend the nation, than one who responds vigorously.

Defense of the country, however, is not synonymous with offensive action against the attacker, though admittedly there is no clear line

---

territory claimed under a treaty of annexation." Note, 81 HARV. L. REV., *supra* note 2, at 1781.

[143] See notes 19-20 *supra* and accompanying text.

[144] For Franklin Roosevelt's response to declarations of war against the United States by Bulgaria, Hungary and Rumania at the outset of American involvement in World War II, see Note, 81 HARV. L. REV., *supra* note 2, at 1781.

[145] The sudden and provocative establishment of offensive weapons by an unfriendly state on the territory of an ally located near the United States might justify immediate preventive action by the President—for example, John Kennedy's response to the Cuban Missile Crisis in 1962.

[146] Absent such presidential discretion, the "sudden attack" exception to the necessity for prior congressional approval of hostilities would become meaningless. The exception assumes that the country is presented with an accomplished fact and with the need to respond before Congress could reasonably be expected to act. Mr. Justice Grier stated in 1863 that

> If a war be made by invasion of a foreign nation, the President is not only authorized but bound to resist force by force. He does not initiate the war, but is bound to accept the challenge without waiting for any special legislative authority. . . .
>
>   . . . .
>
> This greatest of civil wars was not gradually developed . . . . [I]t nevertheless sprung forth suddenly . . . . The President was bound to meet it in the shape it presented itself, without waiting for Congress to baptize it with a name; and no name given to it by him or them could change the fact.

The Prize Cases, 67 U.S. (2 Black) 635, 668-69 (1863).

[147] See note 48 *supra*.

between the offensive and the defensive. Under the Framers' rationale, rapid response should give way to check and deliberation once the country is secure from the prospect of immediate physical assault.[148] The nature of the Executive's defensive measures will depend upon the nature of the thrust, but at no time should his response be disproportionate to the assault. Should he be responding to a nuclear attack, presumably there would be little or no distinction between defensive and offensive action—the exchange would likely be terminal for both parties. But should enemy submarines shell coastal cities with conventional ordinance, the President need only clear the coasts of enemy ships; the launching of SAC and invasion of the enemy homeland ought to await congressional authorization. In sum, the Executive does not receive full war-time powers simply because another state has directly assaulted American territory.

While the President under the Framers' rationale can always respond to sudden attacks upon United States territory, and arguably upon the

---

[148] President Jefferson refused to take offensive measures during the First Barbary War until Congress approved them. See note 42 *supra* and accompanying text. Faced with a declaration of war by Tripoli and its attacks on American ships, he stated in his message to Congress of December 8, 1801, that "[u]nauthorized by the Constitution, without the sanction of Congress, to go beyond the line of defense, the vessel [a Tripolitan cruiser which had attacked a United States schooner], being disabled from committing further hostilities was liberated with its crew. The Legislature will doubtless consider whether, by authorizing measures of offense also, they will place our force on an equal footing with that of its adversaries." *Quoted in* E. CORWIN, *supra* note 127, at 132. Alexander Hamilton replied heatedly that "it is the peculiar and exclusive province of Congress, *when the nation is at peace* to change that state into a state of war; . . . in other words, it belongs to Congress *to go to War*. But when a foreign national declares, or openly and avowedly makes war upon the United States, they are then by the very fact already *at war*, and an declaration on the part of Congress is nugatory; it is at least unnecessary." *Quoted in id.* at 134.

One writer understands Hamilton's position to have been that "[a]s long as the United States is not the initial aggressor, the President's actions will remain 'defensive' requiring no further congressional action to enable him to continue to wage the war thrust on the country." Note, 81 HARV. L. REV., *supra* note 2, at 1779-80 (footnote omitted). In other words, once the Executive has beaten off an enemy assault, he then has discretion to take offensive measures. If this was Hamilton's position, it seems to be at odds with that of the Framers; they intended the process of check and deliberation to precede decisions to use force except when force was used to repel sudden attacks.

When the whole of Hamilton's reply is considered, however, his primary complaint appears to have been with Jefferson's bizarre understanding of what constitutes defensive action. *See* E. CORWIN, *supra* note 127, at 133-35. On this score, the merits are clearly against the President's release of an enemy ship and crew captured in the process of attacking an American vessel. While the Framers did not intend the Executive to take aggressive action on his own initiative, it is not at all plausible that they intended his defensive action to be so potentially self-defeating.

territory of states absolutely vital to our security, the Drafters did not intend unilateral presidential response to threats to American interests or citizens abroad, except under the most modest circumstances. As the constitutional provision granting Congress control over letters of marque and reprisal suggests,[149] the Framers intended "war" to be a broad concept. Judging by early practice, it appears that war in the constitutional sense was deemed to arise when the United States decided to settle a dispute with another state by the use of military force. The Naval War with France, from 1798-1800, involved neither appreciable force nor complete rupture of relations between the combatants; it did, however, require and receive congressional authorization.

Congress must be given an opportunity to say whether it finds the potential gains from the use of force worth the potential losses. The latter may be twofold.[150] First, there are the physical and economic costs, and the diminished legal rights produced by war. Their extent depends upon the scale of the fighting, the enemy's strength, his location and the harm to be inflicted on him. In any use of force today, unlike the nineteenth century, it is difficult to predict the ultimate price. What

---

[149] WORMUTH at 6, states:

> Even before the adoption of the Constitution, American law recognized that it was possible to wage war at different levels. In 1782 the Federal Court of Appeals, the prize court established under the Articles of Confederation, observed: The writers upon the law of nations, speaking of the different kinds of war, distinguish them into perfect and imperfect: A perfect war is that which destroys the national peace and tranquility, and lays the foundation of every possible act of hostility. The imperfect war is that which does not entirely destroy the public tranquility, but interrupts it only in some particulars, as in the case of reprisals.
> The framers of the Constitution accepted this conception and assigned the power to initiate both perfect and imperfect war to Congress, which was "To declare war, grant letters of marque and reprisal, and makes rules concerning captures on land and water."

(footnote omitted).

[150] Note, 81 HARV. L. REV., *supra* note 2, at 1775, defines war in the constitutional sense as having a "quantitative" and a "qualitative" aspect:

> There are two possible reasons for requiring [approval of hostilities] from the body most directly representative of popular sentiment. The first is that such a decision involves a risk of great economic and physical sacrifice not to be incurred without such approval. The second is that even in cases where no significant physical effort is likely to be required . . . . the very act of using force against a foreign sovereign entails moral and legal consequences sufficiently significant to require an expression of popular approval. . . . The first argues for a definition phrased in quantitative terms, which would require congressional action prior to engaging in "major" hostilities above a certain level of intensity. The second would result in a more comprehensive, qualitative definition which would forbid any use of force against a foreign sovereign without prior congressional approval.

(footnote omitted).

is initially intended to be a minor effort, perhaps involving only a bloodless show of force, can easily grow into a major war, even a nuclear one. Moreover, the world is today so interrelated and interdependent in economic, ideological and security matters that any use of force is likely to have repercussions which cannot be reliably charted in advance.

Second, there are the political and moral costs and the potential legal sanctions entailed in using force against another state. Since World War I there has been a steady move toward the complete outlawing of the use of force by international disputants, except in self-defense. Heightened respect for national independence and self-determination had led to the prohibition of one state's intervention in another's affairs and to emphasis on collective control over armed enforcement of international law—with an accompanying distaste for unilateral police action. Thus, many armed activities which would have been acceptable under nineteenth century standards of legality and morality are unacceptable today.[151] Accordingly, even if a contemporary use of force to protect American interests involved little fighting, it might be costly in terms of its violation of international political sensibilities, law and morality.[152] Whether the cost is justifiable is a decision in which Congress should have a voice.

Congressional authorization need not be by formal declaration of war: "[N]either in the language of the Constitution, the intent of the framers, the available historical and judicial precedents nor the purposes behind the clause" is there a requirement for such formality,[153] particularly under present circumstances when most wars are deliberately limited in scope and purpose.[154] A joint resolution, signed

---

[151] The landing of military units in backward states to protect American property or citizens, though common in the nineteenth century, would be acceptable today—if at all—only in situations in which public order has wholly collapsed, with great resulting danger to United States citizens; American property would have to suffer unaided. Similarly, armed reprisals against states delinquent in their adherence to international law, though common in the 1800's, are precluded today in favor of peaceful means of dispute resolution. See note 9 *supra*.

[152] So Senator William Fulbright characterized the 1965 American use of force in the Dominican Republic. 111 CONG. REC. 28374-79 (1965).

[153] Note, 81 HARV. L. REV., *supra* note 2, at 1802.

[154] Although formal declarations of war are effective devices for rallying support on the home front, empowering the Government to take all necessary emergency measures and serving notice on the enemy and all the world that our goal is conquest, [t]here are . . . numerous policy arguments why the formal declaration of war is undesirable under present circumstances. Arguments made include increased danger of misunderstanding of limited objectives, diplomatic embarrassment in

by the President, is the most tenable method of authorizing the use of force today.[155] To be meaningful, the resolution should be passed only after Congress is aware of the basic elements of the situation, and has had reasonable time to consider their implications. The resolution should not, as a rule, be a blank check leaving the place, purpose and duration of hostilities to the President's sole discretion. To be realistic, however, the resolution must leave the Executive wide discretion to respond to changing circumstances. If the legislators wish to delegate full responsibility to the President, it appears that such action would be within the constitutional pale so long as Congress delegates with full awareness of the authority granted.[156]

Since the Constitution was ratified, there have been countless manifestations of expectations that decisions to initiate the use of military force abroad must meaningfully involve the legislators. Presidents prior to 1900 generally held such expectations themselves and acted accordingly, and twentieth century Executives prior to the Cold War frequently gave the concept verbal support, though their conduct often belied their words.[157] Many members of Congress, particularly in

recognition of nonrecognized . . . opponents, inhibition of settlement possibilities, the danger of widening the war, and unnecessarily increasing a President's domestic authority. Although each of these arguments has . . . merit, probably the most compelling reason for not using a formal declaration . . . is that there is no reason to do so. As former Secretary of Defense McNamara has pointed out "[T]here has not been a formal declaration of war—anywhere in the world—since World War II."

Moore, *supra* note 2, at 33 (footnote omitted).

[155] Senate approval of a treaty would not suffice, as that would exclude the House from the decision-making process. An executive agreement, approved by the entire Congress and specifically described as authorization to use force, should be acceptable. Similarly, legislation to increase the size of the armed forces or to appropriate additional money to sustain a use of force might be regarded as authorization *if* legislative intent to that effect is made abundantly clear. Absent such clarity, simple legislation ought not to be regarded as implied approval, since it may have been adopted for reasons other than to ratify a presidential *fait accompli*. See note 21 *supra* and accompanying text. Nothing can be assumed from a congressional failure to act. The burden is not upon Congress to make its views clear or be deemed to have acquiesced, but rather upon the President to obtain legislative approval before he acts. *See* E. CORWIN, *supra* note 39, at 152-53; WORMUTH at 33; Velvel, *supra* note 2, at 455-56, 465-68; Note, 81 HARV. L. REV., *supra* note 2, at 1798-1803.

[156] The extent to which Congress may constitutionally delegate its war power to the President has been a matter of some controversy in the past. In the wake of United States v. Curtiss-Wright Export Corp., 299 U.S. 304 (1936), however, it seems unlikely that strict anti-delegation rules apply in the foreign context. *See* Moore, *supra* note 2, at 34. *But see* WORMUTH at 43-58.

[157] *See* E. CORWIN, *supra* note 14, at 201-02. See the collection of presidential statements in Putney, *supra* note 49, at 6-30.

the Senate, and much of the general public retain a view that the Constitution requires congressional involvement in decisions to initiate conflict abroad.

Constitutional argument in favor of the present high state of presidential prerogative has, as a rule, not frontally attacked these expectations. Rather, doctrinal justification for presidential practice, when offered, has tended to ignore the constitutional grants to Congress[158] and to read expansively the complementary provisions applicable to the Executive. The broad interpretation has been dictated, it is said, by the demands of national security. Accordingly, the President's powers have been rolled into one ill-defined, mutually supportive bundle and used to justify presidential authority to do virtually "anything, anywhere, that can be done with an army or navy." [159]

---

[158] A notable exception has been the expansive reading of the "sudden attack" exception. One writer argues that in the event of a direct attack, the President need not obtain prior congressional approval, even though he has sufficient time to do so. Significantly, however, in instances cited for support—First Barbary, Mexican and Civil Wars—authorization was sought and received concurrently with or immediately after the President's action. Note, 81 HARV. L. REV., *supra* note 2, at 1779-81, 1783, 1784 n.69. With regard to the place of the attack, a good case can be made that under present conditions, the enemy activity need not directly affect United States territory, if it poses a threat to American territorial integrity. *Compare id.* at 1782-85, *with* Mathews, *The Constitutional Power of the President to Conclude International Agreements*, 64 YALE L.J. 345, 359-65 (1955). Finally, regarding the nature of the presidential response, it has been argued, particularly in the wake of the Prize Cases, 67 U.S. (2 Black) 635 (1863), that the President possesses full power to conduct the hostilities as he sees fit, once war is thrust upon the United States. Under this view it becomes important to determine when an enemy assault constitutes "war," lest presidential powers be unleashed too readily. *See* Note, 81 HARV. L. REV., *supra*, at 1778-82. But as contended earlier, see note 148 *supra* and accompanying text, it does not appear that the President receives unilateral authority to do more than stifle an enemy attack. If such is the case, there is no need to haggle over when an attack is and when it is not war," since the President never enjoys unilateral authority to escalate the conflict.

[159] Youngstown Sheet & Tube Co. v. Sawyer, 343 U.S. 579, 641-42 (1952) (Jackson, J., concurring); *see* Velvel, *supra* note 2, at 453-72.
The President as the enforcer of the law is deemed to have constitutional authority to implement treaties, international law and the basic foreign policy objectives of the United States. *See, e.g.,* E. CORWIN, *supra* note 14, at 194-204; E. CORWIN, *supra* note 127, at 142-63; M. MCDOUGAL, *supra* note 14, at 487; 3 W. WILLOUGHBY, THE CONSTITUTIONAL LAW OF THE UNITED STATES 1567 (2d ed. 1929); Banks, *Steel, Sawyer, and the Executive Power*, 14 U. PITT. L. REV. 467, 506-16 (1953); Mathews, *supra* note 158, at 360-61, 363-65, 366-69; Note, 81 HARV. L. REV., *supra* note 2, at 1776-77, 1787-94. The President's constitutional role as the country's foremost diplomat has been read to include control over both the conduct and the shaping of our foreign relations. *See, e.g.,* the discussion in AMERICAN HERITAGE, *supra* note 13, at 276-78; E. CORWIN, *supra* note 14, at 170-226; E. CORWIN, *supra* note 127, at 1-32; M. MCDOUGAL, *supra* note 14, at 435-41, 487-92, 557-60; C. ROSSITER, *supra* note 21, at 90-91; Foley, *Some Aspects of*

The Present Constitutional Balance Between President and Congress

Constitutional law is most certain when peoples' expectations about the nature of constitutional behavior are actually realized in the conduct of public affairs[160]—when the constitutional rules governing the President's use of force abroad are given effect. Without such realization in practice, rule-based expectations about the scope of presidential authority are quixotic; without adherence to the rules, the Executive's practice is simply the illegitimate exercise of power. As suggested,[161] the ultimate goal of constitutional interpretation is constitutional law —both rule and practice—which serves the long-term best interests of the country. Thus, it is ill-advised to promote constitutional rules whose implementation would not meet contemporary needs, just as it is ill-advised to promote practices which needlessly flout the rules.

The previous discussion has demonstrated that practice with regard to the use of American troops abroad has been varied. Certainly, however, presidential action immediately before the two World Wars and during the last twenty-five years provides precedent for plenary executive control. The factors which have seemed to necessitate this practice, and its existence over a significant period of time, have naturally broadened expectations about the scope of the President's authority. It is doubtful, however, that most people now believe that

---

the Constitutional Powers of the President, 27 A.B.A.J. 485, 487-88 (1941); Mathews, *supra* note 158, at 362-63, 366, 369-70; Morgenthau, *supra* note 11, at 264-65; Note, 81 Harv. L. Rev., *supra* note 2, at 1777-78. As Commander-in-Chief, the Executive has constitutional authority to do whatever he feels necessary for the defense of the country. *See, e.g.,* the analysis in E. Corwin, *supra* note 14, at 227-62; M. McDougal, *supra* note 14, at 485-87; C. Rossiter, *supra* note 21, at 24-25; W. Willoughby, *supra,* at 1567-68; Foley, *supra,* at 485-87; Jones, *The President, Congress, and Foreign Relations,* 29 Calif. L. Rev. 565, 575-83 (1941); Mathews, *supra* note 158, at 352-65. The fact that he holds the executive power has been treated as confirmation of his plenary authority over foreign affairs; if his enumerated powers are found wanting in constitutional weight, his inherent authority as Chief Executive is thought to flesh them out as required. *See, e.g.,* E. Corwin, *supra* note 14, at 3-16, 147-58; M. McDougal, *supra* note 14, at 487-92; C. Rossiter, *supra* note 21, at 36, 78-79, 147, 259; C. Rossiter, *supra* note 100, at 65-77; J. Smith & C. Cotter, Powers Of The President During Crises 4-13, 125-46 (1960); W. Willoughby, *supra,* at 1567-68; Banks, *supra,* at 499-502, 516-22; Corwin, *The Steel Seizure Case: A Judicial Brick without Straw,* 53 Colum. L. Rev. 53 (1953); Foley, *supra,* at 485, 488-90; Gibson, *The President's Inherent Emergency Powers,* 12 Fed. B.J. 107 (1951); Jones, *supra* at 565-67, 575-83; Mathews, *supra* note 158, at 381-85; Note, 81 Harv. L. Rev., *supra* note 2, at 1775-76, 1792-94.

160 See notes 27, 29-31 *supra* and accompanying text.

161 See note 23 *supra* and accompanying text.

the President is entitled to initiate foreign wars *sua sponte*. The general public takes a relatively blackletter view of the Constitution,[162] and unless there is pressing need for its amendment, popular understanding of the rule of law dictates adherence to provisions whose language and initial intent seem clear. The power vested in Congress to declare war is a primal instance of such a provision. Even the strongest supporters of presidential prerogative would likely prefer to have congressional approval of American involvement in foreign war—if only they were confident that Congress would vote wisely. Accordingly, it is important to determine whether the present degree of presidential control over the use of force abroad is essential to long-term national interests, and is therefore the constitutional order that must prevail irrespective of countervailing expectations.

The primary argument for sanctification of present practice centers on past congressional inability to cope with questions of foreign policy, particularly those concerned with the use of force.[163] Fault can be found with the congressional decision-making process; it is too uninformed and inexpert, too indecisive and inflexible, overly public, almost always too slow and sometimes out-of-session when crises arise. There is also grave doubt as to the wisdom of the policies that would be generated even by a smoothly functioning legislative decisional process, particularly in light of the disastrous congressional approach to foreign affairs between World Wars.

The factors behind the contemporary strength of the presidency, noted above,[164] are relevant to the question whether Congress might regain some of its lost influence over foreign affairs without harm to national security. Thus, inquiry must determine the extent to which the present balance of power has resulted from the tendency of both Congress and the Executive to follow the path of least resistance, carried along by the interplay of their institutional characteristics and certain historical forces, and whether it exists because national security requires presidential hegemony. The more the latter is the case, the more any rules requiring meaningful congressional participation in decisions to use force abroad should be discarded. Conversely, the more

---

[162] See notes 28-31 *supra* and accompanying text. Opposition to presidential policies in Vietnam has undoubtedly played a part in rekindling expectations that Congress is constitutionally entitled to a meaningful voice in American decisions to go to war. See note 78 *supra*.

[163] See notes 77-80 *supra* and accompanying text.

[164] See note 80 *supra* and accompanying text.

presidential practice appears needlessly to have diverged from the rules, the greater the need for strenuous effort to bring it back into line.

At the outset, it must be readily admitted that no easy distinctions can be made between the path of least resistance and the security interests of the nation. Once any practice has developed in a reasonably efficient manner, any change will involve the costs of establishing new patterns and will risk the creation of a less viable order. The latter possibility is of particular concern in the present context.

Of the historical forces contributing to the existing allocation of power between the President and Congress, none has been more important than the increased pace, complexity and danger of the times. The President, who singly holds his office, who has unsurpassed access to information and experts, and who is always on the job, has been more able to meet current demands than has Congress, with its many men in office, inferior access to information and experts, and frequent inability to assemble its members quickly. It has been suggested that for these reasons Congress is inherently incapable of participating effectively in decisions regarding the use of troops abroad.

Such is not necessarily the case. To the extent that Congress' problem is its indecisive, inflexible, slow and noncontinuous decision-making process, improvement is possible. Legislators need to decide to act and to do so with reasonable dispatch. They need to restructure procedures such as the seniority system which now serve to clog debate and decision. When speed is of the essence,[165] the President can respond and then place the issue before Congress. It is questionable, however, that great speed is required in most decisions regarding the use of force. With the possible exceptions of Korea and the Cuban Missile Crisis, its necessity during the last twenty-five years has been exaggerated. Even in the Korean situation, congressional authorization could have been obtained since Congress was in session and the legislators are capable of rapid action when confronted with an act such as the North Korean invasion. In the Cuban situation, the President's reluctance to involve Congress appears to have been a fear of exposing the nature of the American response before it could be sprung full-blown on the unsuspecting Soviets, rather than a lack of time.

To the extent that Congress' problem stems from its inability to operate secretly, a defect precluding access to certain information and participation in highly sensitive decisions, existing procedures for exec-

---

[165] See note 140 *supra* and accompanying text and note 158 *supra*.

utive session could be further developed. The inclusion of legislators in selected secret decisions, on the assumption that national secrets would not be divulged, is not without precedent.[166] If secrets were in fact divulged, the practice could be abandoned. In situations such as the Cuban Missile Crisis, where it is felt that initial planning must take place while maintaining an outward appearance of normality, the President can either involve congressional leaders in the decision under a procedure previously established by Congress, or simply make the decision unilaterally and present it to Congress for approval after the need for secrecy had passed.

Cuban Missile Crises are rare. The secrecy argument usually arises in the context of classified information. Even were such data not available to the legislators, it is questionable that their ability to make basic foreign policy decisions would be materially impaired. Information is frequently deemed secret by the executive branch for reasons other than its inherent nature, and it has been suggested that ninety-five percent of the data needed to make an informed decision on most foreign policy issues can be found in *The New York Times*.[167]

Similarly, it is debatable that experts must make the basic decisions regarding the initiation of hostilities. The determination that military action is in our national interests requires the setting of priorities in light of existing values. It is largely a political decision, and thus arguably less susceptible to resolution by diplomatic and military experts than by politicians, although experts and relevant information are important to insure that the political decision-maker sees and understands the various alternatives and their probable consequences. Information and expertise are already available in the military and foreign relations committees of both houses. Cooperation of the executive branch would also be required, particularly regarding access to classified data. Once adequately buttressed by information and experts, Congress would be better prepared to make rapid, wise decisions and to avoid inundation and intimidation by the torrent of data and expert opinions flowing from the executive branch.

---

[166] See Note, 81 Harv. L. Rev., *supra* note 2, at 1797 n.143.

[167] As one who has had the opportunity to read . . . [top secret] cables at various times in my life, I can testify that 95 per cent of the information essential for intelligent judgement is available to any careful reader of *The New York Times*. . . . Secrecy in diplomatic communication is mostly required to protect negotiating strategies, techniques of intelligence collection, details of weaponary, and gossip about personalities. . . . The myth of inside information has always been used to prevent democratic control of foreign policy . . . .
Schlesinger, *supra* note 60, at 61-62.

A second historical force behind the power of the President has been the development of communication devices which permit direct contact between government officials and the electorate, and which the Chief Executive, as the most active, intelligible branch of government, has been able to exploit in an unsurpassed manner. Though Congress will never be able to compete with the President in manipulating the media to mold public opinion, it could greatly improve its present efforts. Whereas the President assiduously sees to his public image, Congress rarely employs professional image cultivators and seldom works to appear concerned and competent to deal with national problems.[168] Accordingly, the legislators' collective image tends to be one of a parochial and inefficient group, unduly concerned with trivia and self-interest, an image which could be dispelled in part by the use of professional public relations techniques and, more basically, by a willingness to grapple effectively with the country's problems.

Committee hearings are one area in which the legislators could use the media to greatest advantage, as the 1967 Fulbright proceedings indicate. But before committee efforts can have their maximum political and educational effect, they must be purged of the witchhunt aura imparted by past abuses. Responsible and civilized conduct of all committee proceedings would go far toward this end.[169]

A third force behind presidential aggrandizement has been the democratization of politics in this country, rewarding the branch of government which seemed most representative of all the people and thus most concerned with the welfare of the nation. It may be argued that since the President represents all the people, he is entitled to rule by plebiscite, appealing directly to the public for support, and regarding the legislature as a necessary evil. But such a view is compelling only if Congress is in fact an undemocratic body—as it was when malapportioned districts, excessive obeisance to the seniority system and undue devotion to local, special and personal interests were at their peak.[170] Reapportionment, a move toward younger leadership and a

---

[168] See Kurland, *supra* note 2, at 635.

[169] See *id*. at 633.

[170] Congress was possibly at its lowest ebb as a representative body of the national interest at the turn of the century. *See* AMERICAN HERITAGE, *supra* note 13, at 270-71. The Editors of *American Heritage* conclude that, over the long term,

> [i]f decisive leadership had been lacking in the White House, the United States might have become another sort of country, and an inferior one, pervaded by the spirit of what Emerson termed "village littleness." This is the spirit that infuses many of the activities (or inactivities) of Congress at its narrowest. It

growing concern with national problems preclude a dismissal of Congress on these grounds today.[171] Individual congressmen will always be somewhat more parochial than the President, as is appropriate for men who are the representatives of a part rather than the whole of the national electorate.

A corollary of the plebiscite view holds that the President alone possesses the willpower to make the hard decisions required for a practical foreign policy,[172] and that he alone is capable of persuading a reluctant electorate to support them. Congress, out of both a prediliction for

is expressed in such legislative slogans as To get along, go along (go along, that is, with the rest) and Vote your district first. *Id.* at 372.

[171] Since all states, regardless of their population, have two representatives in the Senate, presumably it can be argued that the upper house *institutionally* will always be less representative than the President. *See* Morgenthau, *supra* note 11, at 268. It is doubtful, however, that Senators from small states are necessarily less responsive to national sentiment than their colleagues from large states.

[172] Dependence upon the President for an intelligent approach to the world is necessitated, it is said, by the failings of untutored public opinion. The point is worth developing in some detail, as it accounts for much of the fear of involving the people, via their representatives in Congress, too extensively in foreign policy decision-making. Morgenthau, *supra* note 11, at 261, argues that

> there exists an inevitable incompatibility between the requirements of good foreign policy and the preferences of a democratically controlled public opinion. As de Tocqueville wrote with special reference to the United States, "Foreign politics demand scarcely any of the qualities which are peculiar to a democracy; they require, on the contrary, the perfect use of almost all those in which it is deficient . . . [A] democracy can only with great difficulties regulate the details of an important undertaking, perservere in a fixed design, and work out its execution in spite of serious obstacles. It cannot combine its measures with secrecy or wait their consequences with patience." The history of foreign policy conducted under democratic conditions illustrates the truth of these observations.

W. LIPPMANN, ESSAYS IN THE PUBLIC PHILOSOPHY 19-20 (1955), elaborates upon this theme:

> Experience since 1917 indicates that in matters of war and peace the popular answer in the democracies is likely to be No. . . . The rule to which there are few exceptions—the acceptance of the Marshall Plan is one of them—is that at critical junctures, when the stakes are high, the prevailing mass opinion will impose what amounts to a veto upon changing the course on which the government is at the time proceeding. Prepare for war in time of peace? No. It is bad to raise taxes, to unbalance the budget, to take men away from their schools or their jobs, to provoke the enemy. Intervene in a developing conflict? No. Avoid the risk of war. Withdraw from the area of conflict? No. The adversary must not be appeased. Reduce your claims on the area? No. Righteousness cannot be compromised. Negotiate a compromise peace as soon as the opportunity presents itself? No. The aggressor must be punished. Remain armed to enforce the dictated settlement? No. The war is over.
>
> The unhappy truth is that the prevailing public opinion has been destructively wrong at the critical junctures.

See also, e.g., J. SPANIER, AMERICAN FOREIGN POLICY SINCE WORLD WAR II 216, 256-57 (rev. ed. 1960).

the status quo and a fear of offending constituents, is said not to represent the true spirit of the nation, and to pose a negative force which the President must overcome.[173] Though admittedly the Executive is often more willing to make hard decisions than Congress, there is strong reason to believe that on most occasions the President could persuade the legislators, as well as the electorate, to support wise policies. During the Cold War Congress has shown itself quite receptive to presidential leadership in foreign affairs. Moreover, to eliminate Congress as a participant in the shaping of foreign policy removes the country's first line of defense against an Executive who is incapable of making sound decisions.

Yet another variant of the foregoing view treats Congress with more respect. The legislators are not dismissed as undemocratic or spineless; rather their opinions, like those of the people at large, are said to rest within the presidential bosom. Of all men, the President is deemed the best informed concerning popular and congressional opinion.[174] Thus, when he acts, he does so with an awareness of what Congress would very probably have done had it been given the opportunity. But the extent to which this happy state obtains, of course, depends upon the President—upon the caliber of his intelligence-gathering machinery, upon the degree of his receptiveness to views other than his own, upon his ability to understand information at his disposal. And much depends upon the extent to which the President is willing to bow to what he understands to be the will of Congress and the country; even certain knowledge of congressional opinion provides far less a check on a determined President than would the necessity of seeking formal congressional approval.

A fourth factor in the rise of the presidency has been the election of many men who have worked to enlarge the scope of their powers and

---

[173] See Morgenthau, *supra* note 11, at 267-68. See note 170 *supra*.

[174] A. SCHLESINGER, *supra* note 13, at 187-88, states:

I would say that any President incorporates, in a sense, a deep awareness of the probable congressional reactions. I think one of the great myths of the presidency is that the President is the most lonely man in the world. The fact is that no one sees more people or is exposed to a wider range of opinion or has imaginatively to expose himself to a wider hypothetical range of opinion than the President . . . . He is not the loneliest man in the world. He knows more, he is aware of more and he is aware of more possibilities and more probable reactions and objections than anyone else. And the President knows that he has to incorporate in himself a sense of all this if what he does is going to be accepted. So the fact that this is technically a decision of his own doesn't mean that in practice that these considerations of what other people feel or the Congress feels or the country feels are excluded from his processes in making that decision.

responsibilities. It is at this point that serious doubts arise as to the capacity of Congress to reverse the trend toward executive domination of foreign affairs. Though the legislators still have the power to force even a reluctant President to consult Congress about the employment of force abroad,[175] a majority of them may well choose not to assert it. Much of the leadership would oppose for reasons of personal power the changes in the decision-making process that would be required. Some legislators at any time will approve of the President's policies and be unwilling to think in institutional terms.[176] Some perhaps would fear that realistic procedures for congressional involvement in such crucial decisions could not be fashioned. Some will always prefer to avoid having to make such politically explosive decisions, and virtually all would be hard pressed to find the time to make the effort to reestablish and then sustain a congressional voice in foreign policy decisions. The tendency, accordingly, will be to make a few noises about executive usurpation without really disturbing the status quo.[177]

Should Congress not have the will to reassert itself, the fifth factor behind the President's rise, momentum, will continue to inure solely to his advantage. But should the legislators prove themselves capable of acting, and acting wisely, momentum may serve them also. Successful congressional involvement in one decision regarding the use of force would lead to greater opportunities for future participation as public and presidential confidence in Congress grew, as well as the legislators' confidence in themselves.

In sum, the President's control over decisions to use force abroad is a perfectly natural and explicable development, but it is not one inexorably necessitated by national self-interest. This is not to say that the President should surrender his power over the day-to-day conduct of foreign relations or relinquish his role as a forceful external leader. It is to say that Congress is capable of having a voice in shaping foreign policies and a decisive voice on whether the United States will

---

[175] See text at notes 90-99 *supra*.

[176] There are certain institutional interests which put the Congress as a whole against the presidency. But I think, that despite this, many people in Congress believe in and support the program of the President if he is of their party.
A. SCHLESINGER, *supra* note 13, at 162. See Kurland's conclusion that Americans are extremely result-oriented at note 78 *supra*.

[177] For example, the "Great Debate" over the President's authority to send troops to Korea and Western Europe, which raged for three months in early 1951 under the impetus of Senator Robert A. Taft, ultimately came to naught. See note 57 *supra*.

initiate the use of force abroad.[178] To have this influence, Congress would have to alter its institutional framework, but not radically. The primary transformation would have to be in willpower. Lacking to date has been both the will to make the structural changes essential to a systematic, informed voice in foreign affairs, and the will to use existing powers[179] to persuade an unconvinced President to seek meaningful congressional approval before initiating foreign conflict.[180]

Congressional participation in these decisions would not guarantee more peaceful foreign policies, though it should not lead to more conflict. It is difficult for Congress to fight a war through a reluctant President. Nor would congressional involvement ensure wise policies, as the legislators' myopia during the twenties and thirties indicates. Should Congress take stands that the President found in error on vital

---

[178] W. LIPPMANN, *supra* note 172, at 30, suggests the executive-legislative relationship that should prevail:

> The executive is the active power in the state, the asking and the proposing power. The representative assembly is the consenting power, the petitioning, the approving and the criticizing, the accepting and the refusing power. The two powers are necessary if there is to be order and freedom. But each must be true to its own nature, each limiting and complementing the other. The government must be able to govern and the citizens must be represented in order that they shall not be oppressed. The health of the system depends upon the relationship of the two powers. If either absorbs or destroys the functions of the other power, the constitution is deranged.

[179] It has been suggested that Congress, like the malapportioned plaintiffs in Baker v. Carr, 369 U.S. 186 (1962), can do very little to help themselves. Schwartz, *supra* note 2, at 1047, states:

> It is claimed that the action that is under attack has circumvented the very political process that the framers of the Constitution intended as a check on the President's power to commit American forces to combat. Thus, unless it is established through the courts that Congress has an indispensable role to play, the political branch can never perform its intended function.
>
> This situation, then, is much like the one in *Baker v. Carr*. There the decision in allocating power within the state was, as perhaps is the decision to commit troops to combat, political in the profoundest sense. But it became clear that despite the wide range of reasonable choice that might be open to state legislatures, apportionment was not being carried out under any rational standard but rather was being used simply to perpetuate the existing power structure. It thus became necessary for the Court to impose rationality in order to restore the very integrity of the political process.

It seems, however, that the situations of the *Baker* plaintiffs and Congress are significantly different. No amount of will power on the part of the former could have effected reapportionment of legislatures controlled by men from overrepresented districts. Congress, on the other hand, is perfectly capable *itself* of pressing the President into cooperation, *if* it chooses to do so.

[180] Since few Presidents are unaware that they are strongest when supported by Congress, and hamstrung when opposed, they are likely to bow with notable grace to congressional insistence on a role in shaping foreign policy—so long as the relationship remains that described by Lippmann, *supra* note 178, and so long as the legislators make their decisions in terms of their understanding of the national interest.

matters, however, he would probably do as Woodrow Wilson and Franklin Roosevelt did. No branch of government will ever find its powers respected if it insists on taking positions that do not respond to contemporary realities.

Congressional participation would have one clear benefit. It would add legitimacy to the use of American troops abroad. The Constitution as popularly understood would be heeded, with substantial gains for the rule of law.[181] Moreover, a congressionally authorized conflict would receive greater public backing than would presidentially authorized hostilities. Such political support is crucial in modern limited wars, which are more easily lost in domestic politics than on foreign battlefields. Of course, it is also possible that congressional involvement in the decision-making could lead to wiser policies; the mere process of articulating and debating goals and strategies might lead all concerned to a fuller understanding of the interests and alternatives at stake. It bears reiteration that the articulation and debate, if it is to be meaningful, must begin with the shaping of the policies that lead to the need to consider the use of force, and not with the actual determination whether to fight.

Unilateral Executive War Powers in Outline

Even with meaningful congressional participation in foreign affairs decision-making, it seems that independent executive power over the use of force would remain in at least five areas.

First. The President would doubtless continue to be the primary initiating force in American foreign relations.[182] He would structure our policies and present them to Congress for its advice and consent. In most instances, Congress would very likely accept and follow his guidance. He would retain his control over the recognition of states and governments and over the conduct and maintenance of diplomatic intercourse—each potentially important to questions of war and peace. Even when working under a meaningful congressional war resolution— one specifying the time, place and purpose of the use of force—his powers as Commander-in-Chief over strategy, tactics and weapons, and his control over negotiations with the enemy, allies and other states would have great impact upon the nature of the conflict.

Second. The President could respond unilaterally to direct, physical

---

[181] See notes 29-31 *supra* and accompanying text.
[182] See note 178 *supra* and accompanying text.

assaults upon the territory of the United States or its possessions. The blow need not have actually fallen before he initiates defensive measures, if the attack appears to be imminent and inevitable. The presidential response, however, should be proportionate to the assault, sufficient only to repel the attackers and to ensure that they lack the immediate capacity to strike again. Before proceeding beyond such defensive measures, the President should seek the authorization of Congress.[183] Though no reasonable congressman would oppose defense of American territorial integrity, once an attack is repelled many legislators might wish to limit in some manner the means taken to resolve the hostilities so commenced.

Third. American citizens or military units under sudden attack abroad can, of course, defend themselves to the best of their ability. When the attack takes place in international territory, air or sea, the situation becomes closely analogous to an assault on American territory, and the President could take all steps necessary to stifle the attack. He might, for example, have resisted with all available force recent North Korean attacks on American reconnaisance units.

But when the attack occurs within the territory of another state, he should use force to defend the beseiged only if his action is unlikely to risk the initiation of substantial hostilities, and only if it does not involve battle with the troops of the state in question, as opposed to battle with individuals not under its control.[184] The joint 1965 effort by the United States and Belgium to rescue whites trapped by rebellious elements in the Congo seems to have been a prime instance of constitutional rescue action by the President. An attempt to recover the *Pueblo* and its crew, once they were forced into port, however, would have risked renewal of the Korean War and almost surely would have involved a pitched battle with North Korean forces; thus, the venture would have required congressional authorization. Military reprisals

---

[183] For example, in the event of conventional shelling of coastal cities by foreign submarines, the President could clear coastal waters of enemy ships. An attack on the enemy homeland, however, should await congressional approval.

[184] When such individuals become disciplined insurgents who control appreciable territory, rather than a mob or ill-organized rebels, they should be treated as the forces of a *de facto* state for purposes of judging the appropriateness of presidential action against them. Moreover, special considerations become applicable when forces under the control of one country oppose United States presence in a third country. If such forces are irregular, and escalation of the conflict is unlikely, presidential action may be permissible. On the other hand, where intervention is likely to lead to increased hostilities, congressional involvement is mandatory.

against another state to avenge its attacks upon American citizens or troops should always have prior congressional approval.

Should the President conclude that an immediate response is essential, he could act and simultaneously go to Congress with his recommendations. Presumably the President could make the strongest case for immediate response when he is able to act effectively while the attack is yet in progress; upon its completion, there would generally be less cause for haste.[185] Similarly, should the President determine that secrecy is essential to a successful response, he could delay his submission of the matter to Congress.

Fourth. The President could respond unilaterally to attacks on American security interests abroad if he concludes that no delay can be brooked or if he feels that absolute secrecy in the initial planning and execution of the American response is essential. He must, however, inform Congress as soon as feasible, seeking ratification for the steps taken and authorization for future action. During the Korean invasion, arguably there was cause for unilateral presidential response in the interests of speed, and during the Cuban Missile Crisis in the interests of secrecy. Vietnam at no point required unilateral executive action on these grounds. Attacks on American destroyers in the Tonkin Gulf fell within category three above. As noted there, the President could take all necessary measures to repel the assaults, but he could not use them to justify his initiation of further hostilities.

Fifth. The President could deploy American forces, intelligence missions, military aid and advisers, although he should attempt in good faith to prevent their use in an offensive or provocative manner without congressional blessing. The prewar activities of Presidents Wilson and Roosevelt clearly violated this canon, but particularly in Roosevelt's case it is difficult to fault his action, considering the low ebb of congressional wisdom. It is well to reiterate a point made earlier: Neither Congress, nor for that matter the President, will find that

---

[185] Delay until congressional authorization might preclude action until the attack had been consummated and the need for defensive measures mooted. Moreover, the attacking state is less likely to regard as provocative steps taken to repel its assault, as opposed to the initiation of force against it in a rescue attempt or retaliatory raid. It seems, for example, that the United States could have recaptured the *Pueblo* even after it entered North Korean territorial waters, en route to captivity, with less risk of leading the attackers to take additional, unrelated military action (for example, invasion of South Korea) than would have been the case had Washington, at some later date, staged reprisal raids or attempted to rescue the ship and its crew.

their constitutional powers remain intact if their policies are dangerously ill-advised.

As in Vietnam, the commitment of military advisers can grow to
something far more than originally envisioned, particularly when the
government aided is battling indigenous insurgents who have external
backing. At some point during the American buildup, specific congressional authorization for the use of force should be sought. Perhaps the
logical moment would be before the introduction of regular American
units for probable combat use.[186]

CONCLUSION

To recapitulate, the goal here has been a brief development of
factors bearing on the scope of the President's constitutional authority
to commit American forces to foreign conflict. If realistic limits are
to be placed on his use of the military abroad, it seems necessary to
lessen presidential hegemony over the shaping of foreign policies which
lead to the need to use armed forces, as well as over actual military
deployment. The extent of the President's constitutional prerogative
in these areas, however, is not easily ascertained.

As a matter of practice, presidential control has moved unevenly
along a continuum, ranging from collaboration with and deference to
Congress in the early years of the Republic, to the presidential *faits
accomplis* of the Cold War. But even today there remain both internal
and external restraints on the President's use of the military abroad.
Not the least of the latter are the powers of Congress, both exercised
and latent.

Popular expectations regarding the constitutional uses to which the
Executive may put the military have not kept pace with his actual
practice. There continue to exist expectations, rooted in the language
of the Constitution and in the intent of the Framers, that Congress
must have a meaningful voice in decisions to initiate hostilities abroad.
A conflict therefore exists between expectations and practice. Some
shift in one or the other, or both, is necessary if constitutional law is
to obtain. The resolution should be one that results in that pattern of
expectations, realized in practice, which best serves the long-term interests of the country.

To this end, it appears that change should occur largely in the practice of the last twenty-five years. The present high state of presi-

---

[186] *See* Moore, *supra* note 2, at 32.

dential prerogative has evolved naturally out of a set of historical and institutional factors which enabled the President to respond to contemporary pressures more easily than Congress. If Congress has the will, however, it too can meet the demands of modern foreign policy decision-making. While certain changes in institutional structure will be necessary, the critical factor will be the development of a congressional willingness to act quickly and wisely on vital issues and to use its existing powers to make its influence felt.

It is sometimes suggested that claims of undue presidential aggrandizement are pointless, since restraints exist which can hamstring executive policies. Thus, it is said, leave all to the political process: If the President is a usurper, he will be struck down in good time. The reality ignored, however, is that peoples' conduct is very much influenced by what they believe they have an obligation to do. In so sensitive an area as national security, the natural tendency will be to leave matters as they stand, since the existing order is, after all, tenable, if not clearly constitutional. Accordingly, unless Congress believes that it has a constitutional duty to make its voice felt in these decisions, unless the President believes that he has a constitutional duty to seek and honor congressional views on a systematic basis, and, ultimately, unless the electorate insists on such a relationship between the two branches, presidential hegemony will continue undisturbed, save in those rare instances when executive policies result in lengthy, costly and seemingly fruitless struggles.

Comments on the National
Commitments Resolution

COMMITTEE ON FOREIGN RELATIONS

Senate Resolution 85 is an ill-advised way in which to seek to achieve some sort of balance in foreign policy matters between the executive and legislative branches. It could even jeopardize the fixing of ultimate responsibility in foreign policy decisions.

The issue is not a new one, however. It is as old as the history of the American Republic. Its currency derives from the war in Vietnam, but its roots go back to the founding of our country.

In fact, the American ship of state was launched in 1776 upon waves of discontent with executive authority. The Thirteen Colonies, therefore, embarked upon their new course without a chief executive. Only after the near debacle of colonial independence was the need for strong, centralized control of the National Government openly recognized. Nowhere was the necessity for executive power more clearly in evidence than in the realm of foreign relations.

As a Member of Congress in 1799, John Marshall noted that "the President is the sole organ of the Nation in its external relations and its sole representative with foreign nations * * *"

Nonetheless, there was lodged in the hearts and souls of the leaders of the New Government an ingrained distrust of the powers of the President. This has continued down to the present day.

The issue of executive power in foreign policy has tended to rear its head during the administrations of strong Presidents and to languish through inattention during the administrations of weak Presidents. And without exception the trend toward a stronger and stronger executive role in foreign policy has coincided with the rising preeminence of the United States in world politics during the 20th century. Presidents Theodore Roosevelt, Taft, and Wilson expanded that role materially. But the most significant changes have occurred since the beginning of World War II. Under President Franklin Roosevelt the use of executive agreements experienced a sharp increase. In particular his commitments to the transfer of destroyers for bases, the extension of the Monroe Doctrine principle to Iceland and Greenland, and the "shoot on sight" edict to American naval forces in the Atlantic are often cited as serious encroachments by the Executive Office on the assumed foreign policy "partnership" between the President and the Congress.

Concomitant with the incidents preceding American involvement in World War II was the sudden emergence of the United States as the most powerful nation in the world, largely as a result of that conflict. As a great power, American actions cause reverberations all around the globe and must, therefore, be carefully weighed and delicately executed. Not infrequently they must be carried out swiftly.

*Report of the Foreign Relations Committee on S. Res. 85, Apr. 16, 1969, pp. 39–44.

The decisionmaking process may be reduced by events to a matter of a single day, or even hours. On more than one occasion the time allotted by crisis incidents to those who must make the decisions has been less than the time it would take to assemble a quorum of the Congress.

Possibly an even greater factor which presses for increasing the power of the President in making foreign policy in recent decades has been the advent of the nuclear age. We live in a time when 15 minutes could spell the differene between life and death for millions of people— possibly even for life itself on earth. In the past 25 years there have been times when the only sure thing that could be said about the next 24 hours was that no one really knew if we would live through them.

More than ever, consequently, the authority to make decisions and take action supporting them must be located in one place. From the rather meager beginnings of our constitutional system when Congress shared more directly with the President some of the policy processes, we have now come to an age when the pressure of time and the multiplicity of other issues scarcely allow the Congress more than a passing glance at some of the most important decisions in the history of mankind.

It is imperative, therefore, that in determining a judgment on Senate Resolution 85 we recast the role of the Congress—and more particularly of the Senate—in foreign affairs against the backdrop of the nuclear age. Whether the division of responsibility between the President and the Senate can follow the lines of other years is a question central to the present dispute. Whether Senate Resolution 85 goes to the heart of that dispute, moreover, is also open to serious doubts. The implications of its intent, furthermore, may raise more questions than its enactment could resolve.

It is the purpose of this minority report, therefore, to explain why Senate Resolution 85 should not be adopted by the Senate of the United States.

SENATE RESOLUTION 85 WOULD ONLY CONFUSE

The scope of the resolution is ambiguous and thus lends itself to misinterpretation and misunderstanding. It would seem to be impossible to pin down the substance of such an attempted codification. Confusion arises from the explanation of intent by the sponsors of the resolution. Its sponsors say specifically that Senate Resolution 85 would not be legally binding upon the President in the conduct of foreign relations. Also, it should go without saying that a sense-of-the-Senate resolution could not change the constitutional responsibilities of the President.

According to the proposed resolution, in creating a national commitment of the United States to a foreign power, such action must be affirmative by both the executive and the Congress. The resolution further specifies that this "affirmative" action would have to be taken "through means of a treaty, convention, or other legislative instrumentality specifically intended to give effect to such a commitment." It is easy to understand how the sense of the Senate would be achieved without serious complications in such routine procedures as statutes, advice and consent to treaties, Senate resolutions, and joint resolutions. This already takes place in an orderly and undisputed manner.

What happens, however, when the President proceeds in making commitments by Executive order which flow automatically from the authority contained in a prior treaty or in furtherance of a policy stated in an earlier joint resolution of the Congress? Do these subsequent steps likewise require additional affirmative action by the Senate? Like the ripples flowing outward from a falling pebble's impact on the water of a quiet pond, so it must be obvious this could become a farcical process when carried on into infinity.

SENATE RESOLUTION 85 THREATENS CONSTITUTIONAL POWERS OF THE PRESIDENT

It would appear to invade areas of responsibility reserved under the Constitution for the President alone. Two areas of executive responsibility will illustrate the point:

One, the President alone under the Constitution has authority to recognize foreign governments and to enter into commitments which implement that recognition. In the conduct of the foreign relations of the United States, the President necessarily must have the power to make many commitments to foreign governments.

Two, as Commander in Chief of the Armed Forces of the United States, the President has the sole responsibility over them either within our country or outside it. Reasonable men may well disagree as to the conditions under which he should do so. The President has the constitutional power to send U.S. military forces abroad when he deems it to be in the national interest.

Because Senate Resolution 85 implies that the President and the Congress together would be the exclusive means by which the Government of the United States in the future could enter into commitments with a foreign power, it runs counter to constitutional intent.

The sponsors of Senate Resolution 85 have gone to great pains to assure us that they have no intentions of tampering with the constitutional powers of the President. Yet, the majority report on Senate Resolution 85 is replete with references to and charges against a "constitutional imbalance" which, it is asserted, has resulted from power grabs by a succession of Chief Executives. Whatever the intent of the sponsors, the mere language of the resolution calls to the forefront current constitutional misgivings loaded with serious implications.

It is difficult to believe that the press, or students of constitutional principles for that matter, would permit Senate Resolution 85 to go by unnoticed. Or that friend, foe, and especially the Chief Executive would take such an ambitious thrust by means of a Senate resolution to mean so little as its sponsors almost apologetically claim to intend it to mean.

MISCHIEFMAKING AT BEST

At best, Senate Resolution 85 has only the capabilities of mischiefmaking with the responsibilities of the President of the United States in foreign affairs, particularly in times like the present. In a world of 130-odd sovereign nations, some of the more powerful of which are monolithic in structure and capable of quick decisionmaking, the need for a President of the United States to act with dispatch has already arisen. It will surely recur again and again. Presidential decisionmaking in foreign policy provides a quality of leadership superior to the alternatives available under our system.

SENATE RESOLUTION 85 COULD DANGEROUSLY HOBBLE THE PRESIDENT

Does it strengthen the security of our country or serve the national interest to hobble the executive branch in times of crisis? The answer must be no. Mindful as we all are of the risk involved in increasing executive power in the field of foreign affairs, there would appear to be no reasonable alternative to assuming those risks save at the price of confusion, delay, and even inaction through some series of yet unspecified procedures implied in the commitments resolution.

Much as one may hesitate to repose such frightening authority in the executive branch alone, it is necessary to acknowledge that the alternative of joint dialog with the Congress in those particular circumstances would more likely obfuscate rather than clarify the issues. To have to revert to Senate debate and discussion at a time like that would be cumbersome at the very least and disastrous to the national interest in the extreme.

It serves to point up what has happened to the foreign policymaking process in a time of instant communications. The machinery of policy decisions assembled nearly two centuries ago simply has not been able to keep pace with the changing requirements of present-day realities.

SENATE RESOLUTION 85 SMACKS OF NEOISOLATIONISM

At a time when the world is getting smaller and when the problems among nations are becoming more complex, it ill behooves the leader of the free world to move away from its share of responsibility in coping with international crises. Yet, Senate Resolution 85 would have the effect of doing just that. Its point is not unrelated to the Ludlow amendment of the 1930's, which would have prevented a declaration of war by the Congress and President without first going to the people through a national referendum. As the Ludlow proposal would have diffused national responsibility in relation to the Congress, so the national commitments resolution would water down the responsibility which reposes with the President.

It is conceivable, should this resolution be enacted, that some President at some time would be required to plunge into a military crisis—say of the dimensions of Lebanon or Laos—in which he reached the conclusion that it was in the national interest to commit a limited number of troops in quick order. Such a decision in the wake of passage of Senate Resolution 85 would instantly become clouded with an aura of illegitimacy. The public doubts which would quickly surface in that circumstance could only impair the efforts of the President of the United States to act with dispatch and to conclude successfully the commitment. The implications of Senate Resolution 85 are heavily laden with overtones of neoisolationism.

If the democratic process is to be salvaged, we must be prepared to move toward more clean-cut presidential authority in foreign policy.

SENATE RESOLUTION 85 WRONG WAY TO STRENTHEN THE ROLE OF THE SENATE

Senate Resolution 85 is not the way to redress the balance of power in the making of foreign policy. Yet, its appealing intent is to try to do just that. It fails in that purpose by not binding the President and by flying in the face of the increasing need to repose the responsibility for critical decisionmaking in a place where it can be exercised quickly in time of crisis and with an opportunity to pin it down in fixing the responsibility for it. Neither of these latter two requirements could be met by simultaneous Senate affirmative action.

What would have been the complications had the above procedures been required at the time of the Lebanon crisis of 1958, or the Laotian crisis in 1962, both of which resulted in the landing of marines for a short but successful show of force?

Or for that matter, what would the sponsors of Senate Resolution 85 have had the Senate do differently in regard to the Tonkin Gulf resolution of August 1964? On that occasion that was Senate debate and a vote with only two nays. However that action may now be construed by some Vietnam critics in hindsight, it does nothing to enhance either the role of—or confidence in—the Senate to assert that the Members were "duped" by bad or insufficient intelligence.

In fact, Senate Resolution 85 could further weaken the Senate's role in foreign policy. The mere fact of the resolution seems to be a case of "special pleading" in itself. What it implies is that, for whatever reasons, the Senate has dropped the ball; or, as the sponsors of the resolution would prefer, had it stolen from them. (Imagine the impact on the prestige of my pro-football team whose only excuse for losing the game was that the other team had stolen the ball.) The very intent of the resolution demeans the role of the Senate in foreign policy of begging for such a role.

What's more, regardless of the intent of its sponsors, Senate Resolution 85 is already being interpreted from the outside as (a) an attack on the preceding administration for its policies in Vietnam, (b) a warning to this and future administrators in the same area, and (c) an apology for the unsuccessful efforts of the Senate in thwarting previous policy "mistakes."

Whether these allegations are true or false is irrelevant. Their real point is that, without achieving its intent of redressing the balance of power in foreign policy, Senate Resolution 85 introduces mischievous elements, inspires misinterpretations, and demeans both the high office of the President of the United States and the responsible role of the U.S. Senate in foreign policy.

The reporting of Senate Resolution 85 at this time in itself casts some small shadow over the proceedings of the committee. The Foreign Relations Committee has only recently authorized an extensive subcommittee study of our national commitments (the ad hoc committee chaired by Senator Symington for U.S. Security Agreements and Commitments Abroad). At the outset of those studies it would be difficult to predetermine what the subcommittee will discover during its investigations. Would not the Foreign Relations Committee be acting in better grace to suspend a national commitments resolution until after the in-depth study is completed?

TO STRENGTHEN ITS ROLE THE SENATE NEEDS DEEDS NOT WORDS

Is there, then, a meaningful role for the U.S. Senate in the shaping of foreign policy? The answer, of course, is yes. If the Senate is to succeed in achieving this new role, it, too, must update its procedures in the foreign relations field as well as upgrade its sense of responsibility by focusing more and more on larger and larger questions. The Senate could afford to address itself well in advance of crises to the broad outlines and directions of American policy. This becomes far more constructive as well as influential than in responding principally to crisis situations after the fact.

The Senate's role in foreign policy of the future can best be achieved by deeds rather than by words—and least of all by the sense-of-the-Senate resolution.

The role of the Senate Foreign Relations Committee in the policy process is whatever it decides it to be. Thus, the committee can hide behind the shelter of a resolution, or it can stand on its deeds.

In fact, it would seem to be more important that the committee and the Senate involve itself with the decision elements implicit in an ABM system as the current International Organization and Disarmament Affairs Subcommittee has been undertaking (the Gore group); or the question of policy toward mainland China; or to reexamine our foreign policy assumptions and commitments in many of the critical areas of the world, as the Subcommittee for U.S. Security Agreements and Commitments Abroad (Symington group) is now doing.

In the final analysis, then, the Senate through the Foreign Relations Committee should preserve its role in national policymaking by deeds and actions rather than by lamenting its role in a sense-of-the-Senate resolution.

THE NATIONAL COMMITMENTS RESOLUTION ONE YEAR LATER

(Statement by J. W. Fulbright, June 1970)

Last year by a vote of 70 to 16, the Senate adopted the National Commitments Resolution expressing the sense of the Senate that "a national commitment by the United States results only from affirmative action taken by the Executive and Legislative Branches of the U.S. Government by means of a treaty, statute, or concurrent resolution of both Houses of Congress specifically providing for such commitment." By its action of April 1970 in initiating hostilities within the territory of Cambodia without the consent or even the prior knowledge of Congress or any of its committees, the Executive Branch has shown disregard not only for the National Commitments Resolution but for the constitutional principles in which that Resolution is rooted.

Even before the invasion of Cambodia the Nixon Administration had shown its disregard for the National Commitments Resolution. In its comments of March 12, 1970, on the original Mathias proposal calling for repeal of the Formosa, Cuba, Middle East and Tonkin Resolutions, the Department of State declined either to support or oppose repeal, asserting that "* * * the Administration is not depending on any of these resolutions as legal or constitutional authority for its present conduct of foreign relations, or its contingency plans." More specifically, as to the war in Indochina, the State Department asserted that "* * * this Administration has not relied on or referred to the Tonkin Gulf Resolution of August 10, 1964, as support for its Vietnam policy."

Since the Executive Branch explicitly disavows the Tokin Resolution and the other resolutions as authorizations for its policy, a question remains as to where, in its view, the Executive does get its authority to conduct war. The apparent answer is that, despite the adoption of the National Commitments Resolution by an overwhelming vote of the Senate, the Administration still adheres to the position it took shortly after coming into office. In its comments of March 10, 1969, on the then pending National Commitments Resolution, the Department of State made the following assertion:

As Commander-in-Chief, the President has the sole authority to command our Armed Forces, whether they are within or outside the United States. And, although reasonable men may differ as to the circumstances in which he should do so, the President has the constitutional power to send U.S. military forces abroad without specific Congressional approval.

On the basis both of its statements and its actions, it seems evident that the present Administration, like a number of its predecessors, is basing its claim to war powers on either a greatly inflated concept of the President's authority as Commander-in-Chief, or on some vague doctrine of inherent powers of the Presidency, or both. Another possibility is that the matter simply has not been given much thought.

The Executive is conducting a constitutionally unauthorized, Presidential war in Indochina. The commitment without the consent or knowledge of Congress of American soldiers to fight in Cambodia—a country which has formally renounced the offer of protection extended to it as a protocol state under the SEATO Treaty, and to which, therefore, we are under no binding obligation whatever—evidences a conviction by the Executive that it is at liberty to ignore the National Commitments Resolution and to take over both the war and treaty powers of the Congress when Congressional authority in these areas becomes inconvenient. It is noteworthy that Secretary Rogers met with the Foreign Relations Committee in closed session on April 27, three days before the invasion of Cambodia was announced, ostensibly to "consult" the Committee on policy with respect to Cambodia, but failed to give the Committee any indication of the pending military operation, much less to seek the Committee's advice. It is also noteworthy that, in his address to the nation of April 30 explaining his decision to send American troops into Cambodia, the President did not think it necessary to explain what he believed to be the legal ground on which he was acting, other than to refer to his powers as Commander-in-Chief of the Armed Forces.

The fact that this attitude distinguishes the present Administration in no important way from several of its predecessors makes the matter even more disturbing. It is clear now beyond doubt that the National Commitments Resolution has had no effect on the Executive's attitude or behavior and that hereafter, in order to discharge its responsibilities in the field of foreign policy, the Congress shall have to resort to measures more binding than a sense-of-the-Senate resolution.

III. THE CONSTITUTIONAL DEBATE ON THE VIETNAM WAR

B. Matters of Legislative Prerogative

Congress and Foreign Policy†

NICHOLAS DeB. KATZENBACH

Neither the President of the United States nor any of his principal officials charged with foreign policy responsibilites doubts the involvement or power of Congress in foreign affairs. Visible evidence of that power can be found throughout the statute books in laws authorizing and funding foreign diplomatic and military activities, regulating foreign commerce, providing economic and military assistance to foreign nations, and ratifying treaty obligations. Members of Congress devote considerable time and attention to these formal assertions of the Congressional role and far greater amount of time and energy is spent by them, and by the Executive Branch, in informal consultation. Top officials of State and Defense spend substantial amounts of their time, at least as much as their colleagues in other departments, on Congressional relations and securing legislation on foreign aid occupies most of the time of the AID Administrator. There is genuine respect for the power of Congress — though not always for the views of its members.

Congress does not see the problem in the same light. There is considerable concern currently being expressed over the loss of Congressional influence. In a recent report the Senate Foreign Relations Committee said:

> Our country has come far toward the concentration in its national executive of unchecked power over foreign relations, particularly over the disposition and use of the armed forces. So far has this process advanced that, in the committee's view, it is no longer accurate to characterize our government, in matters of foreign relations, as one of separated powers checked and balanced against each other. The Executive has acquired virtual supremacy over the making as well as the conduct of the foreign relations of the United States.

---

†Irvine Lecture Delivered at The Cornell Law School on May 9, 1969.

The principal cause of the constitutional imbalance has been the circumstance of American involvement and responsibility in a violent and unstable world. Since its entry into World War II the United States has been deeply, and to a great extent involuntarily, involved in a series of crises which have revolutionized and are continuing to revolutionize the world of the 20th century. There is no end in sight to these global commotions; there is no end in sight to deep American involvement in them.[1]

This particular statement was, of course, touched off by dissatisfaction with Vietnam in particular and uneasiness about the extent of our foreign involvement generally. It was, therefore, a part of the crisis of confidence that affects the conduct of foreign affairs today. There is no consensus within the Congress or within the committee as to what changes should be made in our policy or even in its method of determination. Institutional loyalty is reflected in agreement by congressmen that Congress should play a greater role, but there is little real agreement on what that role should be.

The President needs the support of Congress for his foreign policy. He needs it because Congress, through its elected members, is probably his most important means of getting public support within the United States. He needs Congressional support because the United States cannot speak or act effectively with foreign countries if domestic division casts doubt upon what it says or does. He needs it because Congress can, and sometimes does, cripple and frustrate a particular foreign policy through legislative restrictions or refusal to appropriate funds.

This common wisdom is reflected by Presidential commitments to a "bi-partisan foreign policy" and by saying that "politics stops at the water's edge". It is reflected also by Congressional reluctance, at least in times of crisis, to criticize Presidential action. The President can and does play on feelings of patriotism and the need for unity. But unless the unity is genuinely there or the Presidential action quickly and demonstrably a success, he may pay a heavy political price for acting on his own. Vietnam and the dispatch of marines to the Dominican Republic in 1965 — in different degrees — serve to illustrate the point.

In general we have had an extremely successful bi-partisan foreign policy for the past quarter of a century and it has enjoyed, perhaps for that reason, a large measure of both Congressional and public support.

Today the agony of Vietnam has led the public and the Congress to question the relevance of that policy to the contemporary world and to raise questions which once seemed to have easy answers and which today are far more difficult to explain. In part these questions have been

---

1. S. Rep. No. 91-129, 91st Cong., 1st Sess. (1969).

raised as procedural and constitutional issues — by inquiry into the proper role of Congress.

One could argue that the role of Congress in its relationship with the Executive is not very important if there is general agreement on the policy which is being followed. Essentially procedural points can seldom be made effectively if they do not have a substantive objective. If students, for example, are wholly happy with the decisions of university administrators they are unlikely to spend time and energy trying to affect the decision-making process. And I believe the same is true with respect to foreign policy.

But a decision-making process should be examined for its capacity in times of crisis and difficulty as well as in times of relative agreement. And so I think this is a good time to examine and seek to understand the role of Congress in foreign policy.

The Constitution says relatively little about how foreign policy decisions should be made and foreign relations conducted. Even in the far calmer climate of this nation's infancy when — ironically — our foreign policy was "to steer clear of permanent alliances, with any portion of the foreign world" — the Founding Fathers appreciated the complexity of foreign affairs. They recognized that the voice of the United States in foreign matters was, of necessity, the voice of the Executive. Consistent with that basic necessity, they provided for the participation of Congress in a number of ways, direct and indirect. They did not seek a simple formula nor try to engrave the lines of authority comprehensively or clearly. Throughout our history the focus has always been upon the Presidency, and it is difficult to imagine how it could be otherwise. Jefferson put it succinctly: "The transaction of business with foreign nations is Executive altogether."

I think it is fair to say, as virtually every commentator has in fact said throughout our history, that under our Constitutional system the source of an effective foreign policy is Presidential power. His is the sole authority to communicate formally with foreign nations; to negotiate treaties; to command the armed forces of the United States. His is a responsibility born of the need for speed and decisiveness in an emergency. His is the responsibility for controlling and directing all the external aspects of the Nation's power. To him flow all of the vast intelligence and information connected with national security. The President, of necessity, has a pre-eminent responsibility in this field.

This was always the case. John Jay observed in THE FEDERALIST that the Presidency possesses great inherent strengths in the direction of foreign affairs: the unity of the office, its capacity for secrecy and speed, and its superior sources of information.

But, as Professor Corwin has said:

Despite all this, actual practice under the Constitution has shown that while the President is usually in a position to propose, the Senate and Congress are often in a technical position at least to dispose. The verdict of history, in short, is that the power to determine the substantive content of American foreign policy is a divided power, with the lion's share falling usually to the President, though by no means always.[2]

The Constitution left to the judgment and wisdom of the Executive and the Congress the task of working out the details of their relationships. Disagreements susceptible of decision by the Supreme Court have been rare. As a result, controversies over the line of demarcation in foreign affairs have been settled, in the end, by the instinct of the nation and its leaders for political responsibility.

In leaving the job of working out the details of this relationship to the judgment and wisdom of the Executive and Congress, the framers of the Constitution acted wisely. Certainly they did not eliminate dispute as to power or role; we have had that from the outset of our history. Nor did they eliminate the possibility that the Executive, acting unwisely, could plunge this country into disastrous wars, although that was a concern. Nor did they insure that the Congress could not frustrate the wisest and most productive foreign policy imaginable.

They did not do and could not have done any of these things. They could and did insure that neither the President nor the Congress could long do without the other in the conduct of foreign affairs. They did recognize the need for Presidential initiative to an extent that they did not contemplate it in domestic matters. In the context of the times such initiative was not a particularly important one. If Presidential initiative is far more important today, as it undoubtedly is, it has also evolved in the domestic arena in ways not contemplated in our early history.

We have experienced, therefore, not only a dramatic growth in United States involvement in world affairs, but also a growth of Executive initiative and leadership in all fields. Clearly these developments have made more difficult an application of the flexible Constitutional formula. But we would do well to remember that it has never been an easy formula to apply, even early in our history.

Members of Congress have frequently criticized acts of the Executive as exceeding his power when acting without the support of a Congressional vote. Early examples are President John Adams' use of troops in the Mediterranean, President Jefferson's Louisiana Purchase agreement, and President Monroe's announcement of his famous Doctrine. In 1846 President Polk sent American forces into the disputed territory between Corpus Christi and the Rio Grande River, an action which began the

---

2. E. CORWIN, THE PRESIDENT: OFFICE AND POWERS: 1787-1948; HISTORY AND ANALYSIS OF PRACTICE AND OPINION (1948).

Mexican War. Presidents Roosevelt, Taft and Wilson frequently used American armed forces without authorization by Congress in protection of U.S. lives and property in Latin America and the Caribbean. While Congress was not consulted in any formal way in advance, during that period of our history the acts were generally popular, and in many instances both houses of Congress gave retroactive approval to Presidential action.

It can be maintained, as the Senate Foreign Relations Committee currently does, that Franklin Roosevelt expanded Executive power in foreign affairs to an unprecedented degree. Acting on Presidential authority alone, he exchanged overage American destroyers for British bases in the Western Hemisphere, committed American forces to the defense of Greenland and Iceland, and authorized American naval vessels to escort convoys to Iceland provided at least one ship in each convoy flew the American or Icelandic flag. All of these actions were justified as an emergency use of Presidential power. But there can be little question that, despite President Roosevelt's belief in the wisdom and necessity of these acts, he took them on Executive authority alone because he did not believe that the ensuing Congressional debate, should he have put the matters to Congress, would have been consistent with our national interest. The political problem, of course, disappeared with the Japanese attack upon Pearl Harbor, though the Constitutional problem and precedent remained.

Throughout our history, as currently, Congressional concern has most often been focused on two exercises of Presidential authority which are particularly troublesome from both a political and Constitutional view. The first of these is the Presidential power to use the Armed Forces of the United States. The second is the power of the Executive to engage the United States in various kinds of "commitments" to foreign governments. Congress sees the first as related to its Constitutional power "to declare war" and the second as related primarily to the treaty power, but also to more general authority delegated to the Executive by statute. There is a wealth of conflicting historical precedent and Constitutional argument on both issues.

I doubt it is fruitful to rehearse legal arguments with respect to the Constitutional provisions in any detail. Clearly they do reflect the view that both the President and the Congress have a voice — the power over foreign policy is divided. But we cannot find the answers to an effective foreign policy in a recitation of specific Constitutional provisions "all of which," as Professor Corwin noted, "amounts to saying that the Constitution, considered only for its affirmative grants of power which are capable of affecting the issue, is an invitation to struggle for the privilege of directing American foreign policy."[3]

---

3. *Id.*

If it is true, as I have said, that neither can succeed in this struggle and that what is essential is cooperation between the President and the Congress, the problem is less a Constitutional issue than a political one. How, within the quite broad confines of the Constitution, can the political system be made to produce a workable foreign policy? And to what extent is this possible if there is a genuine division of view in the country as there seems to be today?

The accepted fact that it is the President who must speak for the country and the modern tradition of bi-partisanship in foreign policy only complicate the matter. On domestic problems the Executive can operate successfully on quite narrow Congressional margins if need be, and employ partisan politics to the extent that it proves helpful to secure legislative authority. But often in foreign affairs he feels correctly that the effectiveness of the policy he espouses depends on his ability to convince other nations that it will not significantly or abruptly change with a new Congress or even with a new President. We have been operating in the post-World War II world on the assumption that long-term relationships, whether military alliances or economic programs, are important. And so, understandably, have many other nations whose leaders have made significant political commitments in their countries and to their peoples on the assumption that the United States will, for example, maintain certain trade policies or levels of capital flow. Our ability to influence others often depends on their assessment of the constancy of our policy. This is a function of our size, our wealth, and our power in today's world. What we do, or what we fail to do, influences other nations whether we want to influence their decisions or not. As Prime Minister Trudeau of Canada recently remarked, "Being a next-door neighbor to the United States is like being in bed with an elephant."

Let us examine the power to use the armed forces of the United States. To resort to armed force, for any purpose, is clearly a major, and conceivably the ultimate decision, in terms of the exercise of governmental authority. More than any other act it requires, or ought to require, the maximum in terms of consensus. It should be supported by the Congress of the United States and whatever is necessary to insure the broadest kind of public support should be done. Clearly it was this sort of consideration which led the authors of the Constitution to temper the President's power as Commander-in-Chief with the power of Congress to declare war and to raise armies. The President was not empowered to plunge the United States into war without Congressional sanction.

It has long been recognized that even this seemingly clear principle has difficulties in application. At the time the Constitution was written the declaration of war itself was an important international act. War itself was regarded as an appropriate means of effecting national objectives. The declaration of war, as a political act, had important international significance. It affected, for example, the rights of neutrals vis-à-vis belligerents. Today all that has changed. War is no longer an accepted or acceptable act; the use of armed forces is, by international fiat, outlawed save in self-defense. The declaration of war, as such, no longer has international significance.

This interaction between accepted international doctrine, expressed in the U. N. Charter and sanctioned by the Congress of the United States, and the language of the Constitution, is troublesome. Viewed from the point-of-view of the separation of powers and the need for Congressional participation, the policies expressed by giving Congress the power to declare war remain valid. But viewed externally, as a national act, the declaration of war is itself no longer appropriate.

A further difficulty arises because even in terms of our own Constitutional doctrine, the Congressional power has always been subject to the exception that the President may employ the Armed Forces in self-defense against attack without the need for Congressional action. At least verbally this appears to have a relationship to Article 51 of the U. N. Charter which permits the use of Armed Forces in self-defense. And in an era in which U. S. forces are stationed in dozens of countries around the world — and which any use of force by anyone involves the possibility of large scale warfare — there is the danger that the power of Congress could be quickly emasculated.

The nature of both the world political system and the U. S. role in it, coupled with modern technology of warfare, has greatly complicated the problem of giving Congress a real voice in this most important of political acts, the engagement of U. S. forces. Any time the safety of U. S. troops stationed anywhere in the world is threatened there is a strong likelihood of a need for a quick response. Once engaged, it is often difficult, politically and militarily, to disengage.

Put differently, I doubt the President is likely to use force in a major way without the certainty of Congressional sanction, at least after the fact — when the prestige and emotions of the United States are already engaged and when the Congress, accordingly, is left little option. But in such an event the decision of Congress is not the same decision that the President made. He may have had choices as to the nature and magnitude of the response. The Congress may not, for it must make its decision in the context of a response already made. The facts have changed. Whatever one thinks of the Presidential decision involved, it is clear that the decision to use U. S. forces in Vietnam or the Dominican Republic was of a different type than the decision to withdraw them. In short, the President has a great capacity to put the Congress on the spot in circumstances in which it has little real choice but to back him. The Congress knows this, does not like it, and is floundering around in search of better solutions.

The problem of appropriate political process is further compounded by the system of alliances built up since World War II. If military alliances are to be effective, they must be credible; a certain amount of expectation as to prompt reaction needs to be built in. This is necessary to deter the enemy and necessary to keep ones allies. That is, after all, one important reason why so many U. S. troops are stationed abroad. While U. S. treaties formally reserve the right of the U. S. to determine for itself what is appropriate action, often with a reference to a decision made in accordance with its Constitutional processes, it is by no means clear that the time element will always be sufficient to permit Congressional action of a meaningful sort. That may or may not be the case. But to the extent either an ally or an enemy believes that the issue of U. S. involvement under appropriate circumstances could become a matter of prolonged political debate, the treaty is that much the less credible.

There is, in my judgment, no formal way of avoiding the kinds of problems that I have described. The President has great powers with respect to the use of the Armed Forces, and these powers have multiplied in the context of the U. S. position in the world today. But this does not mean that a President is likely to abuse those powers, or that he means to do so, or that he is not interested in the maximum of Congressional support and advice. While it is possible that he may do so, I believe that no President wishes to take action of such a serious nature without being confident that he has the support of Congress and the people for what he is doing. If there is an opportunity to seek such advice he will ordinarily, formally or informally, depending on circumstance, do so.

It may be a serious mistake for Congress to concentrate on the formalities of its role. In the world today the Congress is not well equipped to make many of the decisions which, however important, are pressed by time and circumstance. Presidential action with respect to the Cuban missile crisis presents a clear cut case where, despite the grave importance of the action contemplated, there was no adequate and secure mechanism for President Kennedy to consult with Congress. He did meet with Congressional leaders shortly before he announced his decision. This was a courtesy to the leadership, designed to secure their support in a time of crisis, but scarcely a suitable device for giving them a real role.

Let me turn to the other problem which bothers Congress, the problem of Executive commitments. From a legal and Constitutional viewpoint the Executive is scrupulously careful not to make binding commitments of the United States without either submitting these to the Senate for ratification as treaties, or acting within existing legislative authority. In this formal sense Congress has no legitimate complaint.

Yet it is true that diplomatic intercourse unavoidably creates expectations and thus affects decisions, even decisions not yet authorized or made. Sometimes, though 'rarely, a representative of the United States goes further than, in hindsight, he should have gone. If, for example, one is seeking to encourage a foreign government to reduce its defense budget and increase its expenditures on economic development, it is difficult to avoid encouraging a belief as to future U. S. action on which the reform depends. There is no legal prohibition on the Executive from promising a level of U. S. support subject, of course, to Congressional action authorizing and appropriating the necessary funds. Yet Congress is understandably irritated if this "commitment," however properly qualified, is then invoked as an argument in favor of the necessary authorization and appropriations.

The underlying problem, of course, is that Congress persists in treating necessarily long term programs as though they were not. It insists upon an annual review and declines to make a formal commitment to the long term. If this formal review were taken seriously in more than the formal sense I have indicated, it would be impossible to conduct a sensible foreign assistance program. Long term economic objectives cannot be accomplished on a hand-to-mouth basis.

In addition, Congress has the habit of dealing legislatively with specific problems. The fact that a number of different Congressional committees deal with different aspects of foreign policy complicates the job of the Executive. It is hard enough for the President to pull together the Executive Branch of government in consistent ways. It is even more difficult to get the Congress of the United States to appreciate that what one committee does may, in the field of foreign affairs, undo the efforts of another. Difficult and controversial pieces of legislation, such as that authorizing the AID Program, are riddled with prohibitions and requirements which are specific, ill-thought out, damaging to our overall objectives, and occasionally of dubious Constitutionality. Legislation affecting sugar quotas could be an important tool of foreign policy within a limited area, but almost never does the Congress pay the slightest attention to the recommendations of the Secretary of State. Sometimes such specific provisions end up in a piece of legislation as the result of misinformation, misunderstanding as to their consequences, and a touch of demagoguery. Legislation affecting our trade or economic assistance to countries doing business with North Vietnam, or with Cuba, are clumsy diplomacy. There are many examples of this kind of prohibition — prohibitions which can seriously affect other goals of the United States which the Congress, in a calmer mood, might well endorse.

This sort of ad hoc action by the Congress serves to aggravate relations between the Congress and the Executive with respect to foreign affairs. Professionals in the Department of State tend to see Congress as a necessary evil, a view annually documented for them by the more frustrating and less informed amendments to our foreign relations law. When these provisions, in their view, seriously handicap the conduct of foreign policy, there is an unavoidable tendency on their part to seek to minimize that impact. They tend to look for loopholes in or interpretations of the law which will permit them to avoid its most serious aspects. Congress, on the other hand, views this tendency as subverting its influence, and has no confidence that its voice will be heard and its views influential, unless it acts with the force of law — a force too rigid to deal with many subtleties in many situations.

In many respects I feel the problem of Congress and foreign policy is the product of misunderstanding. The Congress misunderstands its role — the points at which it could be effective and influential — and the Executive is little help. The result is too often a mutual distrust and disrespect. Perhaps the organization of Congress, its formal techniques of control, and the nature of foreign policy make this inevitable. But I hope that is not the case.

The role of Congress, the role which it can best play, is in helping to formulate and understand the broad outlines of our foreign policy. It cannot, and does not, deal well or effectively with details. If it feels that today the United States has too many commitments abroad, economic or military, and that our foreign policy is too comprehensive when it should be selective; if it believes that our military forces are overextended; then it should give some guidance to the President on where and how, in broad outline, our policy should be modified. Surely Congress can and should appreciate the fact that while stationing troops abroad may serve to deter military actions by others, it is also a source of potential involvement.

It should recognize and seek to assess potential gains against potential dangers at the time when that decision is appropriate, not after the die is effectively cast. Let me offer one concrete example. For the past eight years Secretaries McNamara and Clifford have testified at length as to the diplomatic and military assumptions which underlie our foreign policy. What they called a "posture statement" was and remains the bible of our involved foreign policy. It was the foundation of the Defense Department budget, and it laid out in broad terms our every diplomatic premise. It was also an annual invitation to the Congress to discuss and debate the fundamentals of our foreign policy. Yet it was virtually ignored by Congress.

These are difficult times in which to conduct our foreign policy, because there is much doubt and much debate. It will be the natural tendency of the Administration to seek to avoid such debate — a debate which in the present climate could seriously jeopardize legitimate goals. The Congress will, I suspect, use its specific powers to snipe away at some aspects of our foreign policy and seek a larger voice in its formulation. Such a situation could be dangerous. For it is clear that Congress can greatly handicap the President in the conduct of foreign policy and it is clear that the President needs the support of Congress.

I think a new Administration needs time to think through its problems and its long range objectives. I think when it has done so, it would be healthy for the country as a whole if these could be discussed, as candidly and frankly as security permits, with the Congress. And I would hope that in such discussions it will be possible for the country to secure for itself the same basic agreement that, by and large, it has enjoyed in the postwar period.

What the country needs at this time is a review and reassessment of fundamentals. Without it we will continue to be faced with doubts, with inconsistent laws, and with the dangers of Congressional-Executive confrontation. In such a situation both the President and the Congress will lose control. Neither can gain and the shrill voices of the right or the left will lead us on a crooked path.

Whether the President and the Congress can find accommodation I do not know. We can hope that current controversies will again be settled, as they have been in the past, by the instinct of the nation and its leaders for political responsibility.

The Appropriations Power as a Tool of Congressional Foreign Policy Making

GARRY J. WOOTERS

The commitment of American armed forces in Southeast Asia has recently caused intense controversy over the legitimacy of this involvement under domestic law.[1] The discussion centers on the respective roles of Congress and the President in the decision to employ the forces of the United States abroad. Most authorities agree that the role of the Congress has sharply diminished since the early years of our constitutional government.[2] For those who wish to see the Congress restored to its former position as a partner in the making of foreign and military policy, there appear to be two basic approaches. The first, essentially legalistic, attempts to determine the legality or constitutionality of particular actions of the President. The second approach, more practically oriented, accepts the past actions of the President as *fait accompli* and attempts to find methods by which the Congress can control future conduct of the Executive. The thrust of this Note is that the second approach is more constructive. The particular method to be examined is the appropriations power.

---

[1] Among the best of a number of recent works are Senate Comm. on Foreign Relations, National Commitments, S. Rep. No. 797, 90th Cong., 1st Sess. (1967) [hereinafter cited as National Commitments]; Faulkner, War in Vietnam; Is it Constitutional?, 56 Geo. L.J. 1123 (1968); Kurland, The Impotence of Reticence, 1968 Duke L.J. 619 (1968); Moore, The National Executive and the Use of the Armed Forces Abroad, 21 Nav. War College Rev. 28 (1969); Reveley, Presidential War-Making: Constitutional Prerogative or Usurpation?, 55 Va. L. Rev. 1243 (1969); Note, Congress, the President, and the Power to Commit Forces to Combat, 81 Harv. L. Rev. 1771 (1968).

The recent congressional debates over the war in Indochina have occasioned a number of excellent studies of the war powers of the President and Congress. See Indochina: The Constitutional Crisis, 116 Cong. Rec. S7117 (daily ed. May 13, 1970) [hereinafter cited as Yale Memo]. The basic research for this memorandum was done by students of the Yale Law School. The authors are Alexander Bickel, Elias Clark, Ramsey Clark, William T. Coleman, John Doar, John W. Douglas, George N. Lindsay, Burke Marshall, Louis F. Oberdorfer, Robert M. Pennoyer, Stephan J. Pollak, Paul C. Warmke, and Edwin M. Zimmerman. See also Legal Memorandum on the Amendment to End the War, 116 Cong. Rec. S7476 (daily ed. May 19, 1970) [hereinafter cited as Harv. Memo] (this memorandum was prepared by students of the Harvard Law School under the direction of the Harvard Law Review); Indochina: The Constitutional Crisis—Part II, 116 Cong. Rec. S7528 (daily ed. May 20, 1970) (this memorandum was read into the Congressional Record as a sequel to the Yale Memo, supra); The War in Southeast Asia: A Legal Position Paper, 116 Cong. Rec. S7824 (daily ed. May 26, 1970) (this paper was prepared by students of the Root-Tilden scholarship program at New York University); Symposium of Lawyers on Indochina, May 20, 1970, 116 Cong. Rec. S7967 (daily ed. May 28, 1970) [hereinafter cited as Lawyers Symposium] (the legal participants in the Symposium were Francis Plimpton, George Lindsay, Adrian DeWind, Robert McKay, Alexander Bickel, and Abram Chayes).

[2] "Our country has gone far toward the concentration in its national executive of unchecked power over foreign relations, particularly over the disposition and use of the armed forces." National Commitments, supra note 1, at 5. "The trauma of the Second World War and of the Cold War led to a third stage in which Congress—in penance for its policies during the twenties and thirties and fearful lest its interference harm national security—left the direction of foreign affairs largely to the President . . . ." Reveley, supra note 1, at 1263. "In the early part of the twentieth century, the executive began to exercise greater discretion in the use of American armed forces abroad. . . . Since 1945, the executive has regularly used military force abroad as a tool of diplomacy." Yale Memo, supra note 1, at S7118.

I. The Failure of the Legalistic Approach

The difficulty of delineating the proper roles of the Congress and the Executive with respect to the war-making powers is that the application of the Constitution in the present-day context is unclear. That document embodies several clauses that bear either directly or indirectly on the formulation of military and foreign policy. The authority given by these clauses is divided between the two branches. Congress has the power to declare war,[3] to grant letters of marque and reprisal,[4] to raise and support armies,[5] to provide and maintain a navy,[6] to make rules for the regulation of the land and naval forces,[7] to provide for the calling forth of the militia,[8] and to provide for organizing, arming, and disciplining the militia.[9] The Senate ratifies treaties.[10] The President holds the general executive power of the United States,[11] is the commander in chief of the army and navy,[12] and, with the consent of the Senate, makes treaties.[13] Other powers of either the President or Congress bear indirectly on the decision to employ force abroad. Of these, the appropriations power, vested in the Congress, is a principal example.[14]

The scholarly consensus is that the Framers of the Constitution intended that the allocation of powers between the legislative and executive branches be made along offensive-defensive lines.[15] Congress was intended to have the power to initiate hostilities, because such power was considered too great to be vested in a single man.[16] The President was to have limited defensive authority to react to a sudden attack threatening the sovereignty

---

3 U.S. Const. art. 1, § 8, cl. 11.

4 Id.

5 U.S. Const. art. 1, § 8, cl. 12.

6 U.S. Const. art. 1, § 8, cl. 13.

7 U.S. Const. art. 1, § 8, cl. 14.

8 U.S. Const. art. 1, § 8, cl. 15.

9 U.S. Const. art. 1, § 8, cl. 16.

10 U.S. Const. art. 2, § 2, cl. 2.

11 U.S. Const. art. 2, § 1, cl. 1.

12 U.S. Const. art. 2, § 2, cl. 1.

13 U.S. Const. art. 2, § 2, cl. 2.

14 U.S. Const. art. 1, § 9, cl. 7.

15 Support for this position may be drawn from the fact that earlier drafts of the Constitution gave Congress the power to "make" war. This was changed because it was feared that such language might prevent the President from defending against a sudden attack. Thus the word "declare" was substituted for "make." See generally Note, The War-Making Power: The Intentions of the Framers in the Light of Parliamentary History, 50 B.U.L. Rev. 5 (Special Issue 1970). See also National Commitments, supra note 1, at 8-9; Harv. Memo, supra note 1, at S7117; Lawyers Symposium, supra note 1, at S7967-68; Yale Memo, supra note 1, at S7117; Moore, supra note 1, at 29; Reveley, supra note 1, at 1281-83; Note, supra note 1, at 1773.

16 "Fear existed that if the President were given the right to wage war unilaterally, he might unwisely engage the country in ruinous conflict or use the existence of war to raise military forces with which to seize control of the country. Moreover, the Executive, like the Senate, was not directly elected, and thus lacked the moral authority to commit the entire country to so potentially devastating a course." Reveley, supra note 1, at 1284 n.138. See also Moore, supra note 1, at 29: "The Framers sought this restriction on Presidential power because of their fear of concentrated power in the President."

and integrity of the nation.[17] The rationale for giving the Executive the power to take unilateral action under certain limited circumstances appears to have been based on the physical realities of eighteenth century government. It was thought that Congress would only be in session for a short period each year, and if Congress were not in session when an attack occurred, it could not be assembled in time to direct the defense of the nation. In such circumstances it was necessary to give the President, as commander in chief, the duty to take the necessary measures for defense and then to go to the Congress as soon as possible.[18]

A persuasive case can be made that the intended balance of powers has been disturbed.[19] Most analysts see a trend of increasing executive domination over foreign and military policy making.[20] The reasons given for the expansion of presidential power are varied.[21] Many spring from the altered

---

[17] See note 15 supra and authorities cited therein.

[18] National Commitments, supra note 1, at 9. The Committee adds the interesting *caveat:* "Were the matter being considered now, in an age of long Congressional sessions, rapid transportation, and instantaneous communication, one may wonder whether it would be thought necessary to concede the executive any authority at all in this field." Id. Since the rationale for the power given to the President is the necessity for speed, it would seem axiomatic that he consult the Congress as soon as possible. See Reveley, supra note 1, at 1285. It has been argued that the need for speed is often exaggerated. "Perceiving, and sometimes exaggerating the need for prompt action, and lacking traditional guidelines for the making of decisions in an emergency, we [the Congress] have tended to think principally of what needed to be done and little, if at all, of the means of doing it." National Commitments, supra note 1, at 6. The same theme is sounded in Reveley, supra note 1, at 1294: "When speed is of the essence, the President can respond and then place the issue before Congress. It is questionable, however, that great speed is required in most decisions regarding the use of force."

[19] See generally National Commitments, supra note 1; Harv. Memo, supra note 1; Yale Memo, supra note 1; The War in Southeast Asia: A Legal Position Paper, 116 Cong. Rec. S7824 (daily ed. May 26, 1970).

[20] E.g., E. Corwin, The President: Office and Powers 1787-1948, at 318 (1948): "In the final result the constitutional practices of wartime have molded the Constitution to a greater or lesser extent for peacetime as well, and seem likely to do so still more pronouncedly under fresh conditions of crisis. For if we are to judge from the past, in each successive crisis the constitutional results of earlier crises reappear cumulatively and in magnified form." Many authorities find the trend accelerated since the Second World War. See, e.g., Harv. Memo, supra note 1, at S7478 ("the twentieth century, particularly during the crisis moments of the Cold War, saw increasing congressional acquiescence to broad presidential assertions of power"); Note, supra note 1, at 1790 ("though the history sketched above indicates a gradually shrinking interpretation of what is left to Congress of its power to declare 'war,' it is only during this century and particularly the last twenty years that the President has asserted powers over the military which, if taken at face value, all but reverse the original distribution between the Executive and Congress of the power to embark on war"). See also National Commitments, supra note 1, at 13; Reveley, supra note 1, at 1263, 1279.

[21] The Senate Foreign Relations Committee considered some of these reasons to be congressional unfamiliarity with the new role of the United States after the Second World War, insecurity in the face of executive expertise, and an historical guilt over the part it played in American unpreparedness for war. National Commitments, supra note 1, at 14.

Reveley, supra note 1, at 1265-70, lists the institutional advantages of the presidency, the Executive's ability to communicate directly with the people, the democratization of politics, far-sighted leadership by the Presidents, and the momentum of the burgeoning executive assumption of functions.

For a thorough discussion of the institutional problems of the Congress see Note,

security posture of the United States, especially since the end of the Second World War.[22] The concept of what is necessary for defense has changed drastically. The United States now has collective defense agreements with more than forty other nations,[23] indicating the possibility that it is no longer realistic to require that the President wait for an attack on the United States proper before he takes action.[24] The need for rapid action may be greater now than it was at the time the Constitution was drafted, although the ability to consult quickly with the Congress has also increased.[25] Modern defense decisions are more complex, and it can be argued that the Congress is no longer capable of playing a major role in the making of these decisions. The structural and informational advantages of the executive branch enable it to deal with these matters more efficiently and with greater security.[26] All these factors have contributed to expanded executive influence.

Many analysts do not find these arguments sufficiently persuasive to convince them to accept an altered and diminished role for the Congress in making the great decisions leading to war.[27] Though the nature of defense has changed, it is possible for Congress to play a more significant role in these areas than it has in past years.[28] The argument that the basic structure of the Government should not be altered out of convenience is compelling.[29] The failure of the legalistic approach is largely due to the

---

Historical and Structural Limitations on Congressional Abilities to Make Foreign Policy, 50 B.U.L. Rev. 51 (Special Issue 1970).

[22] "The increasing involvement of the United States in world affairs, the shift to an intensely competitive bipolar system, and the limitation of the lawful use of force to defense have greatly strengthened the hand of the Executive in the contest with Congress over the war power." Moore, supra note 1, at 29. See note 20 supra and authorities cited therein.

[23] See Moore, supra note 1, at 29; Reveley, supra note 1, at 1250 n.20.

[24] See discussion of the "collective security" theory of unilateral executive action, note 30 infra.

[25] See note 18 supra.

[26] E. Kolodziej, Congress and the Uncommon Defense 1945-1963, at 438-39 (1966). See generally Note, supra note 21.

[27] See especially the conclusions of the Senate Foreign Relations Committee, National Commitments, supra note 1, at 23-27.

[28] Id. A recurring suggestion is that while formal action by the Congress may not always be possible before the commitment of armed forces, the Legislature can be asked to ratify the action at the earliest possible time, and, where possible, congressional leaders could be consulted in advance. See, Moore, supra note 1, at 32; Note, supra note 1, at 1296-97 (suggesting that in the instances where the President must act without prior authorization he should *simultaneously* seek the approval of Congress); Reveley, supra note 1, at 1294-95.
There is some dispute as to how often the President has consulted with congressional leaders and how valuable the consultation has been. See Lawyers Symposium, supra note 1, at S7971-72. Mr. Chayes suggests that on most occasions Presidents have consulted with the congressional leadership before committing troops. Senators Fulbright and Kennedy took sharp issue with the value of these consultations, arguing that they were largely pro forma.

[29] Mr. Justice Cardozo's statement of the argument is eloquent:
Undoubtedly the conditions to which power is addressed are always to be considered when the exercise of power is challenged. Extraordinary conditions may call for extraordinary remedies. But the argument necessarily stops short of an attempt to justify action which lies outside the sphere of constitutional authority.

misguided belief that the problem can be resolved by making a clear, legal division of the war-making powers between the President and Congress. The point is that even if that division can be determined, the constitutional limits are not self-executing. Unless the executive branch can be persuaded that it has assumed unconstitutional powers, it will continue to act as it has in the past. Since there is at least minimal support for the constitutionality of increased presidential control, it is improbable that any President will be persuaded to accept a diminished role in foreign policy. The expansion of executive influence has been justified in the defensive terms suggested by the documents of the constitutional period.[30] With both sides claiming the support of the Constitution, arguments dealing with the legality of particular actions are likely to be unproductive, and the probability is strong that the federal courts, the usual arbitrator in a dispute between the other coordinate branches, will be unable, if not for constitutional reasons, at least for practical reasons, to resolve the conflict.[31] Where there can be no final decision that both the Congress and the President will accept, charges of illegality or unconstitutionality will only cause bitterness and diminish the prospects for a cooperative solution.

If, on the other hand, Congress had the ability to achieve its objectives by using a power clearly its alone, the Executive would be compelled to accede to its demands, unless it wished to effect a fundamental change in the notion of separation of powers.[32] Within constitutional limits, the branch with the

---

> Extraordinary conditions do not create or enlarge constitutional power. The Constitution established a national government with powers deemed to be adequate, as they have proved to be both in war and peace, but these powers of the national government are limited by the constitutional grants. Those who act under those grants are not at liberty to transcend the imposed limits because they believe that more or different power is necessary.

Schecter Poultry Corp. v. United States, 295 U.S. 495, 528-29 (1935).

[30] The Yale Memo, supra note 1, has divided the justifications for unilateral executive action into three basic classifications. Under the "self defense" theory, the President has the authority to defend the integrity of the nation from sudden attack. Id. at S7118. This justification is strongly supported by the constitutional documents. See note 15 supra. The problem has always been to determine the extent of the defensive authority. The battle was joined as early as the administration of President Jefferson. See Note, supra note 1, at 1779-80. But see Reveley, supra note 1, at 1287 n.148.

The legitimacy of the doctrine of "neutrality" is dependent on the conclusion that the American forces are taking no side in a conflict but are merely protecting the lives and property of citizens abroad. See Yale Memo, supra note 1, at S7118. The doctrine has little modern utility. Id. See also Note, supra note 1, at 1796-97. The doctrine rests on shaky theoretical ground, since the congressional power over letters of marque and reprisal suggests that the Framers intended Congress to have control over even limited use of force. See Reveley, supra note 1, at 1287-88.

The "collective defense" theory is currently the most important justification for executive use of armed forces. See Yale Memo, supra note 1, at S7118. It is also defensive in its justification, resting on the theory that senatorial ratification of a treaty providing that the security of the United States is linked with that of another nation indicates that the defense of that nation is necessary to protect the integrity of the United States. See the discussion of the effect of ratification of a treaty on the balance of power between Congress and the Executive at p. 42 infra.

[31] For a detailed treatment of the political question problem see generally Note, The Supreme Court as Arbitrator in the Conflict Between Presidential and Congressional War-Making Powers, 50 B.U.L. Rev. 78 (Special Issue 1970).

[32] Cf. Massachusetts v. Mellon, 262 U.S. 447, 488 (1923).

immediate power to effect its objectives will tend to expand its influence. Thus presidential power, justified under the grants of the Constitution, was expanded largely through the structural and informational advantages of the executive branch.[33] Congress may in the same manner use its most effective weapon, the appropriations power, to implement its grants of authority under the war powers.

Although analysis of the constitutional limits of power does not aid in the practical implementation of these limits, it is important to bear in mind that action by either branch must remain within the bounds of the constitutional framework, both with respect to the result to be accomplished and the means to be employed. Whatever the present state of respect for the law, the naked usurpation of functions committed to another branch of the Government will command little respect.[34] It is for this reason that this Note, while rejecting the *purely* legalistic approach, will discuss both the constitutional and practical problems involved in the exercise of the appropriations power to control the Executive in his conduct of military and foreign relations.

II. The Independent Nature of the Appropriations Power

There is no question that the appropriations power, if properly used, could be a powerful means of asserting pressure on the Executive.[35] No major military effort could be carried on by the President, certainly no conflict as large as that in Indochina, without extensive funding from the Congress.[36] The first inquiry must then be whether the appropriations power may legitimately be used by the Congress to formulate military and foreign policy. The analysis of legitimacy presents two distinct questions: (1) did the Framers intend that the "power of the purse" be used in this

---

[33] See note 21 supra.

[34] See Reveley, supra note 1, at 1278:

The ultimate restraint on the President, however, does not come from his own beliefs and abilities or from competing centers of power, but rather from the activities of the electorate, which continually expresses its views in various manifestations of public opinion, and periodically in federal elections. A President will fall from grace when his policies fail to meet popular needs and demands or when they involve him in activity which is widely viewed as illegitimate, because it transgresses popular conceptions of legality or morality. (citations omitted).

[35] The problem is not with the power, but with congressional reluctance to employ it. "Although control of the purse has been virtually a nonpower in the hands of postwar Congresses when funds were sought for the military, present reluctance to embark on major defense spending and criticism of the military establishment suggest that appropriations may emerge anew as a limiting factor. A few voices have been heard to suggest that funds supporting troops in the field be cut—traditionally, an unthinkable position." Reveley, supra note 1, at 1275 (citations omitted). On the reluctance of the Congress to employ the appropriations power see C. Rossiter, The American Presidency 51-52 (2d ed. 1960).

[36] See C. Rossiter, The American Presidency 54 (2d ed. 1960) ("no great policy, domestic or foreign, can be maintained effectively by a President without the approval of Congress in the form of laws and money"). Reveley, supra note 1, at 1274: "Thus virtually all presidential programs and ventures require implementing legislation and funding. Unlike parliamentary executives, the President has no ultimate weapons, such as dissolution or excommunication from party ranks, with which to beat reluctant legislators into submission."

manner, and, if so, (2) can congressional authorization or ratification of a particular policy bind the Congress to the financial support of that policy.

The answer to the first of these questions is clear from a reading of the Constitution and from an examination of the documents of those most intimately connected with its drafting. The grants of the war powers to the Congress are juxtaposed to references to the power of the purse. Thus, Congress raises and supports armies, but no appropriation for the military may be for a period longer than two years.[37] Congress *provides* and *maintains* the Navy.[38] In particular, the two-year limitation indicates that the Framers intended that the appropriations power be used to ensure civilian control over the military.[39] Jefferson expressed this relationship between the appropriations power and the presidential power in the strongest terms:[40]

> We have already given, in example, one effectual check to the dog of war, by transferring the power of letting him loose from the Executive to the Legislative body, from those who are to spend to those who are to pay.

The same view is supported in the Federalist Papers[41] and the letters of the delegates to the Constitutional Convention.[42] The intent of the Framers to provide for the control of military force through the appropriations power would appear to be settled.

The question of whether the Congress can bind itself through previous action to support a particular policy is only slightly more difficult. The taxing power is committed to Congress alone,[43] and no moneys from the Treasury may be spent except as authorized by law.[44] Thus, the appropriations power is plenary, and unless Congress is bound by a previous authorization or ratification of a particular policy, it could refuse to support a foreign military commitment.

The administration has pointed to three congressional actions as authorizing military participation in Southeast Asia:[45] passage of the Gulf of Tonkin

---

37 U.S. Const. art. 1, § 8.

38 Id.

39 See Lawyers Symposium, supra note 1, at S7968: "The Constitution establishes a situation in which both branches must be in agreement for the war to begin and continue. And that agreement must be a continuing agreement.

. . . The point is that Congress also is obligated to consider along with the appropriations legislation each year, whether it continues to concur in the action of the President." (remarks of Mr. Chayes). See generally E. Huzar, The Purse and the Sword 319 (1950); Note, The War-Making Powers: The Intentions of the Framers in the Light of Parliamentary History, 50 B.U.L. Rev. 5 (Special Issue 1970).

40 C. Warren, The Making of the Constitution 481 n.1 (1928).

41 The Federalist No. 26, in The Federalist and Other Constitutional Papers 140 (E. Scott ed. 1898) (A. Hamilton).

42 On June 6, 1787, Col. Marsh commented: "The purse and the sword ought never to get into the same hands, whether legislative or executive." 2 The Madison Papers 811 (1840).

43 U.S. Const. art. 1, § 8. The same provision gives Congress the duty to provide for the common defense.

44 Id.; U.S. Const. art. 1, § 9.

45 For a full exposition of the State Department's official justification for the

Resolution[46] and the congressional ratifications of the Southeast Asia Collective Defense Treaty[47] and the Charter of the United Nations.[48] It is necessary to examine these actions to determine if they have in any way restricted the ability of Congress to employ the appropriations power to alter the course of that involvement.

The effect of the Tonkin Resolution is unclear.[49] There was considerable disagreement at the time of its passage over the exact limits of the power it conferred on the President. While it was argued that the sweeping terms of the enactment made it the functional equivalent of a declaration of war, others disagreed that the Congress could give such a predated declaration.[50] Though some authorities feel that the scope of the authorization was sufficient to justify the present involvement of American forces in Vietnam,[51] the authorization could be repealed or nullified by subsequent action.[52] Even if the congressional action did constitute the *equivalent* of a declaration of war, it would have no effect on the appropriations power because that power remains unimpaired even in the face of a *formal* declaration of war.[53] This is the plain import of the two-year limitation on military appropriations. The Congress must examine its military appropriations at least once every two years to determine whether it continues to be in agreement with the Executive.[54] This conclusion is also compelled by the theory of representative government in which the recourse of the people is

---

American involvement in Vietnam see U.S. Dep't of State, The Legality of United States Participation in the Defense of Viet-Nam, 54 Dep't of State Bull. 474 (1966), reprinted in 75 Yale L.J. 1084 (1966).

[46] Vietnam Resolution, Pub. L. No. 88-408, § 1, 78 Stat. 384 (1964).

[47] Southeast Asia Collective Defense Treaty, Sept. 8, 1954, [1955] 1 U.S.T. 81, T.I.A.S. No. 3170.

[48] United Nations Participation Act of 1945, 22 U.S.C. §§ 287-287(e) (1964).

[49] "My judgment would be that the notorious vagueness of language and cloudiness of circumstances that surrounded that resolution, surrounded its passage, makes it virtually meaningless." Lawyers Symposium, supra note 1, at S7969 (remarks of Mr. Bickel); Note, supra note 1, at 1804-05.

[50] During the debates over the resolution the broadness of the language was objected to by Senator Morse, who described it as a "predated declaration of war." 110 Cong. Rec. 18,133 (1964). It was Senator Fulbright who attempted to allay the fears, saying the resolution was the best measure he could think of to prevent the enlargement of the war. Id. at 18,402-05. Although he conceded that he did not know the limits of the resolution he expressed confidence that it would allow the President to prevent further aggression. Under questioning by Senator Cooper he admitted that the resolution would allow the President to employ forces, which could lead to war. Id. at 18,409-10. The debates in the House showed a similar confusion, some representatives believing the resolution to be nothing more than a ratification of past actions, others fearing that it might be an abdication of the congressional power to declare war. Id. at 18,543-53.

[51] Note, supra note 1, at 1804.

[52] ". . . [W]hatever authorization might be implied by any stretch of the imagination from these resolutions or these actions in the past certainly could be withdrawn at any time or qualified at any time from the appropriations power or through the refusal to support the continued commitment of troops to those areas." Lawyers Symposium, supra note 1, at S7968 (remarks of Mr. McKay).

[53] See note 39 supra.

[54] U.S. Const. art. 1, § 9.

to the ballot. If the Congress could bind future sessions on a matter of such critical importance as the control over the military, the responsiveness of the Government to the electorate would be severely reduced.

The argument that the Congress is bound to finance executive action taken pursuant to a treaty is no more persuasive. Treaties are made by the President and ratified by a two-thirds vote of the Senate.[55] If the President and the Senate acting in concert could bind the Congress to support a war, a power vested by the Constitution in both houses of Congress, the war-declaring function could be circumvented.[56] If the Congress were further bound to appropriate moneys to carry out the provisions of a treaty, the appropriations power would be of little value indeed. It is well settled that a treaty ceases to be the supreme law of the land in the face of subsequent congressional action inconsistent with its terms.[57] That the appropriations power is unaffected by a previous treaty commitment is illustrated by the refusal of the Congress to appropriate funds to effectuate the provisions of the unpopular Jay Treaty.[58] In fact, the SEATO treaty provides that military aid may be given to member and protocol states in accordance with the constitutional procedures of the individual nations.[59] Such a provision indicates that this particular treaty cannot alter the internal balance between the congressional and the executive branches.

The conclusion is compelled that the ability of Congress to employ the appropriations power to influence the course of the war in Southeast Asia is appropriate, and unaffected by any previous action.

---

[55] U.S. Const. art. 2, § 2.

[56] This was the position taken by Madison with respect to the effect of treaties as reconstructed by E. Corwin, The President: Office and Powers 219-20, 463 n.21 (3d ed. 1948). Corwin states that the result is clear when a treaty and a subsequent statute conflict. The statute will prevail.

[57] Id. and materials cited therein.

[58] "Spokesmen for the administration, notably Hamilton, argued that in making treaties 'supreme law of the land' the Constitution converted the obligation of a treaty at international law into a *constitutional* obligation, and hence left Congress no discretion in such a situation. Madison and Gallitin answered that the very purpose of the Constitution in forbidding any money to be paid out of the Treasury except in consequence of 'an appropriation made by law' was to leave Congress a free agent in voting such appropriations. Although few if any treaty provisions have ever failed for lack of funds to carry them out, the latter view has in principle prevailed." Id. at 214 (citations omitted) (emphasis in original).

"There is no law that I know of that says that a treaty can override fundamental constitutional arrangements. There may be some changes that can be made by treaties or executive agreements in the relationship between the federal government and the states, but I don't know of any law that says a treaty can override basic constitutional arrangements." Lawyers Symposium, supra note 1, at S7970-71 (remarks of Mr. Bickel). A similar conclusion is reached in Note, supra note 1, at 1798-99.

[59] "[T]he Treaty shall be ratified and its provisions carried out by the Parties in accordance with their respective constitutional processes." Southeast Asia Collective Defense Treaty, Sept. 8, 1954, art. IX, para. 2, [1955], 1 U.S.T. 81, T.I.A.S. No. 3170.

III. Practical Problems with the Appropriations Process

Though use of the power of the purse to control the military is legitimate,[60] the practical implementation of this power may be difficult. The maximum amount of control would be achieved by detailing the uses to which appropriated money could be put. But the same factors that have contributed to the declining role of Congress in the conduct of foreign affairs[61] have made detailed control over military spending more difficult. Modern defense budgets are so large,[62] and the various projects and uses of defense moneys so numerous, that the Congress cannot consider each individual need in detail.[63] Modern weapons systems are so complex that the committees concerned with appropriations may not feel competent to dispute the claims of the executive departments that they are necessary for defense. The institutional and informational disadvantages of Congress may prevent them from assuming any broad role in the formulation of military policy until reforms are instituted.[64] These problems are compounded by the recognized need to allow the executive branch some latitude to meet changing needs and effect economies in the military sphere.[65] The result of these complications has been that Congress has evolved a number of devices to provide flexibility for the Executive in the use of defense funds. These same devices tend to prevent the Congress from exercising close control over defense spending.[66]

The executive branch may not spend moneys not properly appropriated by law.[67] In addition, appropriations may be used for only "the objects for which they are respectively made."[68] The general rule that appropriations be for a specific length of time would also effectively prevent the

---

[60] See discussion pp. 39-42 supra.

[61] See note 21 supra.

[62] The present defense budget is approximately $82 billion. The cost of the war in Indochina accounts for about $28 billion. The total cost of the war has been over $100 billion. The War in Southeast Asia: A Legal Position Paper, 116 Cong. Rec. S7824 (daily ed. May 26, 1970).

[63] "Congress cannot oversee in detail the immense and sprawling military establishment which presently directs the energies of almost four million civilian and military personnel and exercises varying controls over an additional five million non-governmental personnel engaged in defense contract work. Congress' appropriations power, in particular, is not put to the most effective use if it is solely directed toward specific control and management of Defense Department administration. These burdensome tasks are too heavy for any legislator, committee, or even the entire Congress to carry." E. Kolodziej, The Uncommon Defense and Congress 1945-1963, 439-40 (1966). See generally Note, supra note 21.

[64] See generally, Note, supra note 21.

[65] See E. Huzar, The Purse and the Sword 321 (1950).

[66] For a discussion of some of the incidents where the Executive has frustrated the appropriations power of Congress see Hollander, The President and Congress—Operational Control of the Armed Forces, 27 Mil. L. Rev. 49, 60-61 (1965). The incidents described are minor in nature, e.g., the funding of the Naval Academy after Congress had specifically refused to do so.

[67] U.S. Const. art. 1, § 9; 31 U.S.C. § 665(a) (1964).

[68] 31 U.S.C. § 628 (1964); cf. 31 U.S.C. § 638 (1964).

Executive from building a reserve for his own purposes.[69] However, the Congress frequently exercises its option to grant "no year" appropriations, making the funds appropriated available until spent.[70]

One device the Executive has occasionally used to frustrate Congress in the formulation of military and defense policy has been impoundment.[71] Using this technique the Executive may impound funds that Congress has appropriated for a particular project if the Executive considers it to be unwise, wasteful, or inexpedient. This technique has produced little conflict since authority to impound is specifically given to the Department of Defense in the Defense Department Appropriations Act of 1970.[72] Although impoundment may be used to prevent a particular program from being completed,[73] the President may not use the funds so impounded to create a reserve to use for his own purposes. Such a technique appears to be rejected by the Constitution and by statute.[74]

The ability to transfer money between departments and between projects within a department is one of the principal examples of executive flexibility.[75] In spite of the general provision that moneys may be used only for the purpose for which they were appropriated and for no other,[76]

[69] 31 U.S.C. § 718 (1964): "No specific or indefinite appropriation . . . in any regular appropriation Act shall be construed to be permanent or available continuously without reference to a fiscal year . . . unless it is made in terms expressly providing that it shall continue available beyond the fiscal year for which the Appropriations Act in which it is contained makes provision." See also Department of Defense Appropriations Act § 611, 83 Stat. 469 (1969); Chernak, Financial Control: Congress and the Executive, 17 Mil. L. Rev. 83, 94 (1966).

[70] Fisher, Funds Impounded by the President: The Constitutional Issue, 38 Geo. Wash. L. Rev. 124, 125 (1970); Department of Defense Appropriations Act, tit. IV, V, 83 Stat. 469 (1969); see 31 U.S.C.A. § 649(c) (Supp. 1970).

[71] Fisher, supra note 70, at 125-26. See generally E. Huzar, The Purse and the Sword 362-73 (1950).

[72] Department of Defense Appropriation Act of 1970 § 613(a), 83 Stat. 469 (1969). "During the current fiscal year, the President may exempt appropriations, funds, and contract authorizations available for military functions under the Department of Defense, from the provisions [31 U.S.C. § 665(c) (1964)] . . . whenever he considers such action to be necessary in the interest of national defense."

[73] The most recent example of a controversy between the Executive and Congress over impoundment of funds was over the development of the RS-70 manned bomber. The House Committee wished to compel the Department of Defense to develop the plane, and their version of the bill would have required the Department to spend not less than $491 million for the project. A compromise was reached and the final draft "authorized" that amount for the project but did not require it all to be spent. During the course of the debate, the committee report cited fifteen instances between 1949 and 1961 where the Executive had refused to spend funds appropriated by Congress for defense purposes. E. Kolodziej, The Uncommon Defense and Congress 1945-1963, at 412-17 (1966). For a discussion of the issues raised by impoundment discussed in the setting of the RS-70 dispute see Davis, Congressional Power to Require Defense Expenditures, 33 Ford. L. Rev. 39 (1964).

[74] "Thus an executive officer could not, on his own initiative, obligate appropriations and increase expenditures. In impounding funds, however, the President prevents rather than creates obligation, and reduces rather than increases expenditures." Fisher, supra note 70, at 130.

[75] For a discussion of the attitudes toward discretionary transfer authority in the Executive see E. Huzar, supra note 71, at 345-54.

[76] See note 68 supra.

transfer authority has been granted to the Department of Defense.[77] This condition is aggravated by the fact that certain apportionments or reapportionments may create the need for supplemental appropriations.[78] If the transfer statutes alone were involved, the restrictions imposed on such transfers could prevent the funding of any large scale projects not authorized by the Congress.[79] However, the availability of transfer authority becomes more significant when coupled with contract authority and emergency spending powers.[80] Congress, in recognition of the limitations on the budgeting process, has earmarked certain funds to be used in emergencies, or for needs that may arise when Congress is not in session.[81] An even more important factor in undermining congressional control over the military is the authority of the Executive to expand the size of the military and thereby create an unlimited obligation against the Government.[82]

There are undoubtedly many other devices that allow the executive departments generally, and the departments involved in defense and security specifically, to increase their control over the amount of funds available and the purposes for which those funds may be spent.[83] Detailed control over defense funding must wait until Congress reforms its budgeting techniques.[84] However, despite the ability of the Executive to frustrate congressional will in a number of ways,[85] it does not appear that any of these devices allows the President to carry on an armed conflict of substantial size without the approval of Congress.[86] Thus, the solution to the practical problems of appropriations for the military is for the Congress to attach

[77] 31 U.S.C. § 697 (1964). "Any appropriations to any department, agency, or corporation in the executive branch of the Government, for salaries and expenses, shall be available for the discharge of responsibilities, relating to the national defense, assigned to such department, agency, or corporation . . . and transfers may be made between appropriations or allocations within any such department, agency, or corporation as may be necessary to carry out this proviso . . . ." See Department of Defense Appropriation Act, tit. V, 83 Stat. 469 (1969); 31 U.S.C. § 717 (1964).

[78] 31 U.S.C. § 665(e)(1)(A)(B) (1964).

[79] Transfers may be made only from one authorized purpose to another. 31 U.S.C. § 697 (1964).

[80] For a discussion of the effects and nature of contingent and emergency funds see E. Huzar, The Purse and the Sword 339-45 (1950).

[81] Department of Defense Appropriation Act of 1970, tit. V., 83 Stat. 469 (1969) gives the Secretary of Defense contingency funds of $75,000,000 and $150,000,000 to be used for contingency needs.

[82] "Upon determination by the President that it is necessary to increase the number of military personnel for active duty beyond the number for which funds are provided in this Act, the Secretary of Defense is authorized to provide for the cost of such increased military personnel." Department of Defense Appropriations Act of 1970, § 613(c), Pub. L. No. 91-171, 83 Stat. 469 (1969). See also id. at §§ 620, 638 and 31 U.S.C. § 529(f) (1964).

[83] One of the other major problems is that funds may be "hidden" in other appropriations, creating reserves which may be shifted to other projects.

[84] An excellent discussion of the problems that the Congress faces in attempting to tighten control over the budgetary process with suggestions for reform may be found in E. Huzar, The Purse and the Sword 383-407 (1950). For a more general discussion of the needs of Congress, not directed particularly to the appropriations process, see generally P. Donham & R. Fahey, Congress Needs Help (1966); Note, supra note 21.

[85] See note 66 supra.

[86] See notes 35, 36, 62 supra.

particular prohibitions to budgetary measures. In this manner the Congress could specify those purposes it wished to prohibit when it felt it had the information and expertise to make a judgment. More detailed control could wait until reforms had been made. This approach would have the advantage of being most effective in influencing those policies requiring the greatest funding, since these cannot be accomplished through any of the methods of executive flexibility.

Unless the method of conditioning the appropriation is unconstitutional, Congress has a means of accomplishing major policy objectives in a precise and simple manner.

IV. Constitutional Difficulties—The Method of Appropriating

The major constitutional problem with conditional defense appropriations is that a particular restriction may impinge on the President's authority under either his general executive function or his power as commander in chief. This difficulty is part of the more general problem of separation of powers. That doctrine in its broadest terms provides:[87]

> The functions of the government under our system are apportioned. To the legislative department has been committed the duty of making laws, to the executive the duty of executing them. . . . The general rule is that neither may control, direct, or restrain the action of the other.

The problem is, of course, to define the proper roles of each branch. It would be possible for Congress, in formulating policy, to invade the general executive province by enacting particular kinds of restrictive legislation. In the same way, it is possible for the President, acting as commander in chief, to preclude Congress from exercising its legislative function.

It has been recognized by both the Executive and judiciary that Congress has the right to influence policy by conditioning appropriations bills to restrict the uses that may be made of the funds. Thus Theodore Roosevelt's Attorney General stated:[88]

> It is recognized that Congress may withhold appropriations as it chooses, and when making an appropriation may direct the purposes to which the appropriation may be devoted. It may also impose conditions with respect to the use of the appropriation. . . .

The courts also have recognized the general principle:[89]

> Congress in making appropriations has the power and authority not only to designate the purpose of the appropriations, but also the terms and conditions under which the executive department . . . may expend such appropriations. . . .
> The purpose of appropriations, the terms and conditions under

---

[87] Massachusetts v. Mellon, 262 U.S. 447, 488 (1923).
[88] 27 Op. Att'y Gen. 259 (1909).
[89] Spaulding v. Douglas Aircraft Co., Inc., 60 F. Supp. 985, 988 (S.D. Calif. 1945), aff'd, 154 F.2d 419 (9th Cir. 1946).

which said appropriation were made, is a matter solely in the hands of Congress and it is the plain and explicit duty of the executive branch of the government to comply with the same . . . .

Statements such as these would seem to leave unfettered the right of Congress to place whatever conditions it chooses on appropriations. Such broad generalizations are probably misleading. It is possible that Congress could write conditions or attach provisos to a bill that would invade the province of the Executive.

During the early years of the Eisenhower Administration, the Congress granted authority to the Department of Defense to transfer outside the department, work that had been performed for three or more years by department personnel. The authority was conditioned on obtaining the prior approval of both the House and Senate Armed Services Subcommittees.[90] In effect, the provision gave these committees a veto power over the transfers. Eisenhower's Attorney General was of the opinion that such a veto power vested in these committees was an unconstitutional invasion of the executive province. The decision to transfer work had traditionally been an executive function, which was now vested jointly in the Department of Defense and a part of the Congress with final authority in the legislative branch.[91]

If such a condition arguably violates the general division of functions between the executive and legislative branches, might not another type of condition violate the specific function of the President as commander in chief?

The answer must depend on the particular condition. Congress has adopted a number of restrictions on bills, including appropriations measures, that might have been thought to conflict with the authority of the commander in chief. During the administration of Theodore Roosevelt, Congress conditioned the appropriation for the Marine Corps on the requirement that the President maintain a ratio of 8 percent marines to navy enlisted men on battleships. The Bill was signed by Roosevelt and approved as constitutional by his Attorney General.[92] Even more striking was the provision of the Selective Training and Service Act of 1940 that no person inducted into the land forces of the United States under the provisions of the Act could be stationed outside of the Western Hemisphere or the territories and possessions of the United States.[93] The most recent

---

90 The Department of Defense Appropriations Act of 1956, ch. 488, 70 Stat. 455 (1956).
91 See Brownell, Separation of Powers: Executive and Legislative Branches, 60 Dick. L. Rev. 1 (1955).
92 27 Op. Att'y Gen. 259, 259-61 (1909).
93 Selective Training and Service Act of 1940, ch. 720, § 3(e), 54 Stat. 885, 886 (1940): "Persons inducted into the land forces of the United States under this Act shall not be employed beyond the limits of the Western Hemisphere except in the Territories and possessions of the United States, including the Philippine Islands." This provision was not repealed until after the beginning of the Second World War. See Lawyers Symposium, supra note 1, at S7969.

example of a condition limiting the authority of the President over the armed forces was the proviso to the Defense Appropriations Act of 1970 that no moneys appropriated by that or any other Act could be used to finance the introduction of ground combat troops into Laos or Thailand.[94] That Act was signed into law by President Nixon. It would seem that he did not consider it to be too serious an intrusion on his powers as commander in chief.

These acceptances of limitations by individual Presidents do not necessarily settle the validity of pending proposals to limit the authority of the President in Southeast Asia.[95] They do indicate that limitations similar in nature to those already accepted by past Presidents are at least within the twilight zone of overlap in powers between the Congress and the President that Mr. Justice Jackson described in *Youngstown Sheet & Tube Co. v. Sawyer*.[96] Justice Jackson postulated three zones of authority. In one, the authority is exclusively congressional and another is exclusively executive. The third is an area of overlap where action by either branch is legitimate in the absence of action by the other.[97] Within the twilight zone of overlap, however, once the Congress has acted, the President must carry out its wishes;[98] it is within the nature of the executive function that the President must execute laws unless they are unconstitutional.[99] Such an argument tips the balance in favor of the Congress in areas of conflict between the Executive and Congress.[100] Other authorities have suggested that the "necessary and proper" clause gives the Congress balance of power in these unclear areas once it has acted.[101]

Two pending bills serve to illustrate the technique of conditional appropriations.

---

[94] Pub. L. No. 91-171, 83 Stat. 469, § 643 (1969). See Harv. Memo, supra note 1, at S7479.

[95] The fact that one President did not consider a particular restriction as a usurpation of his power does not mean that another Chief Executive would have accepted it.

[96] 343 U.S. 579, 634 (1952) (concurring opinion).

[97] 343 U.S. at 637.

[98] See Indochina: The Constitutional Crisis, Part II, 116 Cong. Rec. S7528, S7529, 91st Cong., 1st Sess. (daily ed. May 20, 1970).

[99] Id.

[100] Id.

[101] Lawyers Symposium, supra note 1, at S7967-68. But see Reveley, supra note 1, at 1281: "In the third category, inherent powers, the President comes into his own. Whereas article II, section 1 vests in him the 'executive Power,' article I, section 1 vests in Congress only those 'legislative Powers *herein granted*.' Moreover, while the legislative article is quite tightly drawn, the executive article, in Corwin's words, 'is the most loosely drawn chapter of the Constitution.' Thus, the President can make a strong case that, as the holder of the executive power, he possesses residual authority to go beyond the enumerated powers to take whatever steps he deems necessary for the country's security. Congress, to the contrary, confronts a linguistic hurdle. Arguably, however, 'herein granted' is not an insurmountable barrier where foreign policy is involved." (emphasis in original).

Cooper-Church

The so-called Cooper-Church Amendment[102] is the most constitutionally sound of the present attempts to restrict military appropriations. It does not challenge the present conduct of the war by the President; rather it seeks to enforce the stated policy of the administration by withdrawing funds for the maintainance of ground forces in Cambodia after the date by which the President has said withdrawal will be completed.[103] It states a policy of the Congress rather than attempting to interfere with the tactical conduct of the war. In the sense that it prevents a reintroduction of troops into Cambodia under its terms, it is similar to the restrictions imposed by the Defense Appropriations Act of 1970.[104] President Nixon's major objection is that the Amendment will cause him to lose face since it will seem that the Congress does not trust him.[105] It would appear that this mistakes the motivation behind the proposal.[106] In any case, it goes to the wisdom of the measure and not the authority of Congress to enact it.

Hatfield-McGovern

The Hatfield-McGovern Bill[107] raises slightly more serious problems of constitutionality in that its intent is to require the President to alter, against his will, his conduct of the war in Indochina. The claim of intrusion becomes stronger if the President invokes his authority as commander in chief and determines that a withdrawal under the terms of the Bill cannot be safely executed. Nevertheless, the Bill is arguably a policy determination by the Congress that it is in the best interest of the United States to withdraw from the conflict. The withdrawal timetable is only a broad outline, and the time period set is arguably reasonable. This is precisely

---

[102] S. Amend. 620, 91st Cong., 2d Sess. (1970). The bill provides in relevant part:
  In order to avoid the involvement of the United States in a wider war in Indochina and expedite the withdrawal of American forces from Vietnam, it is hereby provided that, unless specifically authorized by law hereafter enacted, no funds authorized or appropriated pursuant to this Act or any other law may be expended for the purpose of:
  (1) retaining United States ground forces in Cambodia.
[103] N.Y. Times, June 4, 1970, at 18, col. 3 (text of President Nixon's message of June 3, 1970).
[104] See supra note 95 and accompanying text.
[105] President Nixon's letter to Senator Scott, N.Y. Times, June 6, 1970, at 5, col. 1.
[106] See the explanation by Senator Church of the purposes and motivation behind the proposal at 116 Cong. Rec. S7106 (daily ed. May 13, 1970).
[107] S. Amend. 609, 91st Cong., 2d Sess. (1970). This bill provides:
  Unless the Congress shall have declared war, no part of any funds appropriated pursuant to this Act or any other law shall be expended in Vietnam after December, 1970, for any purpose arising from military conflict; Provided that, funds may be expended as required for the safe and systematic withdrawal of all United States military personnel, the termination of United States military operations, the provision of assistance to South Vietnam in amounts and for purposes specifically authorized by the Congress, the exchange of prisoners, the arrangement of asylum for Vietnamese who might be physically endangered by the withdrawal of United States forces, and Further Provided, that the withdrawal of all United States military personnel shall be completed no later than June 30, 1971 . . . .

the type of determination that the Congress must be able to make if it is to have any role in the great decisions of war and peace. Under these circumstances, if such a measure is passed, the President must execute it to the best of his abilities.[108]

V. Conclusion

Congress has, in the appropriations process, a method through which to influence the conduct of American foreign affairs. By employing a selective approach, as illustrated by pending legislation concerning the conflicts in Indochina, it may choose particular issues over which it wishes to exert control, thus avoiding the problems of overtaxed facilities and limited competence over the broad range of policy-making decisions. As congressional confidence and capabilities grow, its role may be expanded proportionally.

If Congress wishes to exert a stronger influence in foreign policy, the process should begin soon. Since the trend toward executive control over the international commitments of the United States has accelerated in the past decade, any delay will make the task more difficult. Unless the legislative branch is willing to accept a profoundly altered role from that which the Framers intended, it must seek to retard and reverse that growing executive hegemony. At the same time, Congress must act with certainty and conviction, for any assertion of congressional influence over major policy making is likely to be met with determined opposition from the Executive. Should the Congress precipitate a crisis and compel, over presidential objection, a course of action that later proves to be "wrong," confidence in its abilities would be shaken to the point where executive power would expand without significant opposition.

Thus the Congress faces a difficult problem. Forceful action must be taken in the near future, and the action must prove ultimately to have been proper. The power of the purse can be successfully asserted, but Congress must supply the necessary will and wisdom.

---

[108] At least one respected constitutional law authority has stated unequivocally that both bills are constitutional. "So, I am as clear as I can be, I don't have any doubt under the sun that Congress, no matter what the legality and validity of presidential action now, has present power to make the foreign policy of the United States, as it sees fit to do, and to appropriate or not to appropriate money in pursuance of that policy, as it sees fit to do.

"I don't have any question, in other words, to be quite specific, on the constitutional foundation for either the Cooper-Church or the McGovern-Hatfield amendment." Lawyers Symposium, supra note 1, at S7971 (remarks of Mr. Bickel).

III. THE CONSTITUTIONAL DEBATE ON THE VIETNAM WAR

C. Matters of Judicial Prerogative

Viet-Nam in the
Courts of the United States:
"Political Questions"

LOUIS HENKIN

Since, as Tocqueville noticed long ago, "Scarcely any political question arises in the United States that is not resolved, sooner or later, into a judicial question," it comes as no surprise that the rending issues of the Viet-Nam war have knocked at judicial doors in the United States in various guises. But, invoking a defense which courts have developed since Tocqueville wrote, lower courts have largely rejected these issues under the doctrine that some political questions are "political questions" and are not justiciable.[1] And the Supreme Court of the United States (invoking yet another modern defense) has denied *certiorari* and refused to review the principal cases.

International lawyers, in particular, will regret the Supreme Court's abstention if only because there is crying need to shore up the constitutional underpinnings of the "political question" doctrine, and to redefine

---

[1] *E.g.*, Luftig *v.* McNamara, 373 F. 2d 664 (D.C. Cir., 1967), cert. denied, 387 U. S. 945 (1967); Mora *v.* McNamara, 387 F. 2d 862 (D.C. Cir., 1967), cert. denied, 389 U. S. 934 (1967). For other cases raising issues related to the Viet-Nam war, see United States *v.* Mitchell, 369 F. 2d 323 (2d Cir., 1966), cert. denied, 386 U. S. 972 (1967); Shiffman *v.* Selective Service Board, 391 U. S. 930 (1968); Zwicker *v.* Boll, 270 F. Supp. 131 (W.D. Wis., 1967), affirmed per curiam, 391 U. S. 353 (1968). The Court heard argument and upheld the conviction for "draft-card burning" in O'Brien *v.* United States, 391 U. S. 367 (1968).

its scope and content, particularly as it relates to issues of American foreign affairs.

Issues of foreign affairs have always been cited as prime examples—and a principal justification—of the "political question" doctrine: the Supreme Court gave them special mention when it last dealt with that doctrine in *Baker* v. *Carr*.[2] But in that case, as before, the Court did not tell us precisely what the doctrine is; as before, moreover, it seemed to be using "political question" to describe two very different kinds of questions, as to which the function of courts is and ought to be very different too.

Strictly the political question doctrine is narrow and precise. It is a principle of extraordinary judicial abstention. It applies especially—perhaps exclusively—to claims that the political branches have failed to live up to constitutional requirements or limitations. The Court says, in effect, that although generally judicial review of the actions of the political branches of government is fundamental to our system, there are some claims which the courts will not hear (and, of course, afford them no relief). In other words, the courts say, in substance: "It may be that, as the petitioner claims, the political branches have indeed violated the Constitution, but in this instance we are unable to consider that question and give the relief requested." So, for example, the Court has held that it will not hear claims that there has been a failure to carry out the requirement that "The United States shall guarantee to every State in this Union a Republican Form of Government" (Article IV, Sec. 4).[3] It would probably refuse to review a judgment of impeachment, since the Constitution provides that "The Senate shall have the sole Power to try all Impeachments." (Article 1, Sec. 3.)[4]

Unfortunately, the Court has often also described other questions as "political," but in those cases, I submit, it was using the phrase in a very different sense. The courts have said, for example, that their concern under the Constitution is only whether the political branches of government, Federal or State, have exceeded constitutional limitations: as long as they act within their constitutional powers, how they exercise that power, *e.g.*, the wisdom or unwisdom of what they do, is a "political" question which is not for the courts to consider. Such statements, I suggest, imply no special doctrine of judicial abstention; in that sense there are political questions in virtually every case, whenever the Court reads and applies the Constitution or an Act of Congress. In such cases the courts are saying only: "We have reviewed your constitutional claim and we find that the action complained of is within the powers granted by the Constitution. It violates no constitutional limitations on that power,

---

[2] 369 U. S. 186 (1962).

[3] Luther *v.* Borden, 7 How. 1 (U. S., 1849).

[4] Clearly the Court would not review impeachment proceedings on a simple writ of error. I doubt that the Court would consider even claims that a particular impeachment proceeding denied due process. In the latter case, of course, the Court would be abstaining on a basis closer to a pure political question. Compare note 12 below.

either because the Constitution imposes no relevant limitations, or because it is amply within the limits prescribed.''

In regard to foreign affairs, I believe, the Supreme Court has never found a true ''political question.'' All the cases usually cited (including those noted in *Baker* v. *Carr*) involve political questions, if at all, only in the second sense: the Constitution gave the President (or the Congress) the authority to act in the manner complained of; he having done so, the courts must give effect to that action. The courts, then, are not refraining from judging the action by constitutional standards; they judge, but find it not wanting.

Thus, for example, when the President (or the Congress) asserts American sovereignty, or denies the sovereignty of a foreign Power, to particular territory, the courts have felt bound by their action, because the powers in question are lodged by the Constitution in the President (or the Congress).[5] The Court will not decide to whom the territory in question belongs as a matter of international law, because that question is irrelevant. Under the Constitution the President (or the Congress) acting within his powers is not prevented from violating international law or other international obligations of the United States.

When the President decides to recognize or not to recognize a foreign government, the Court accepts that political act and is bound by it,[6] not from any special doctrine of judicial abstention but because the power to recognize or not to recognize is given by the Constitution to the President. Again, it refuses to consider whether under international law the foreign entity is or is not a state or a government, not because it feels compelled to abstain but because that question is irrelevant. Generally, domestic legal consequences flow not from the status of a foreign ''state'' or ''government'' in international law, but from recognition or non-recognition by the political branches.

When a foreign Power has violated a treaty with the United States, the appropriate response by the United States—whether it shall go to war, treat the treaty as broken and void, file a diplomatic protest, or do nothing —is a decision within the President's constitutional authority. If the President decides to condone a breach by a foreign government, the courts will continue to treat the agreement as an effective treaty.[7] They are not abstaining; they are giving effect to a valid exercise of power. (Put another way, breach by a foreign government may render a treaty voidable, and if the President decides not to void it, the courts will of course enforce the treaty.)

5 Foster & Elam v. Neilson, 2 Peters 253 (U. S., 1829); Williams v. Suffolk Insurance Co., 13 Peters 415 (U. S., 1839); Jones v. United States, 137 U. S. 202 (1890). Most of the cases noted here, and others, are discussed in a fine article by Professor Edwin Dickinson, ''The Law of Nations as National Law: 'Political Questions,' '' 104 U. Pa. Law Rev. 451 (1956), but he makes of them something more and somewhat different.

6 Rose v. Himely, 4 Cranch 241 (U. S., 1808); Gelston v. Hoyt, 3 Wheat. 246 (U. S., 1818); Guaranty Trust Co. v. United States, 304 U. S. 126 (1938).

7 Charlton v. Kelly, 229 U. S. 447 (1913).

When, by enacting legislation inconsistent with treaty obligations, Congress decides that the United States should violate the treaty, the Court applies the statute,[8] again, because Congress has acted within its constitutional powers; the Constitution does not forbid Congress to disregard international law.

In the much-confused area of sovereign immunity, too, what the Supreme Court has said in effect is, that while a court can decide the question of immunity as a matter of international law when the political branches do not indicate otherwise,[9] they have the power under the Constitution to "legislate" national policy on the question. When the President, then, decides that immunity should be granted or withheld, the courts are bound by such "legislation" as by any other,[10] even if his "law" is inconsistent with international law. (The act of state doctrine, too, we now know, is not a question of judicial abstention but rather one of legislation (whether by the President, the Congress, or the courts) of national policy that effect be given to foreign law in certain circumstances.) [11]

In none of these cases, I emphasize, did the Court say that the President or the Congress may have violated their constitutional powers but the courts are in no position to give relief. It is true that the courts sometimes spoke of the special political quality of foreign relations and the need for the nation to speak with one voice, but it did so, in effect, to explain the broad constitutional powers of the President or Congress.[12] In

[8] Whitney v. Robertson, 124 U. S. 190 (1888); Chinese Exclusion Case, 130 U. S. 581 (1889).

[9] Compare Ex parte Muir, 254 U. S. 522 (1921).

[10] Ex parte Peru, 318 U. S. 578 (1943); Republic of Mexico v. Hoffman, 324 U. S. 30 (1945).

[11] Compare Banco Nacional de Cuba v. Sabbatino, 376 U. S. 398 (1964); Bernstein v. Van Heyghen Frères, 163 F. 2d 246 (2d Cir., 1947), cert. denied, 332 U. S. 772 (1947), 210 F. 2d 375 (2d Cir., 1954); the Second Hickenlooper Amendment, 79 Stat. 653, 659, 22 U.S.C. §2370(e)(2) (Supp. I, 1965).

[12] The Court was not saying anything different in cases like Chicago and Southern Air Lines v. Waterman S.S. Corp., 333 U. S. 103, 112–114 (1948): "But even if courts could require full disclosure, the very nature of executive decisions as to foreign policy is political, not judicial. Such decisions are wholly confided by our Constitution to the political departments of the government, Executive and Legislative. They are delicate, complex, and involve large elements of prophecy. They are and should be undertaken only by those directly responsible to the people whose welfare they advance or peril. They are decisions of a kind for which the Judiciary has neither aptitude, facilities nor responsibility and which has long been held to belong in the domain of political power not subject to judicial intrusion or inquiry." See also United States v. Curtiss-Wright Export Corp., 299 U. S. 304, 319–321 (1936). In that case, the Court held that an action by the President pursuant to delegation by Congress was amply within their powers; it did not say that the constitutional validity of the action could not be examined.

Whether the Court would hear claims that in reaching such foreign decisions the President violated some general prohibition in the Constitution—e.g., that he denied due process of law—is a different question and one to which the Court has not addressed itself. Refusal to do so would be closer to what I call a strict "political question," although the doctrine might well contemplate abstention as to some constitutional claims, not others. Compare Gomillion v. Lightfoot, 364 U. S. 339 (1960).

no case did the Court *have* to use the phrase "political question": in no case was it abstaining from deciding an issue which could have led to a different result.

The cases arising out of the Viet-Nam war have raised two principal issues: One is whether the actions of the United States violated international law, in particular the treaty obligations assumed in the Kellogg-Briand Pact and the U.N. Charter. That issue, I have said, is political only in my second sense. The answer the courts have always given is that, although international law is law of the land to be applied by the courts, the Constitution does not prohibit the political branches, when acting within their delegated powers, to disregard treaties or other obligations of international law. The courts could and would decide that issue without using the words "political question."

But the Viet-Nam cases also raise a very different question: whether the President has exceeded his constitutional powers and infringed on the powers of Congress by engaging in war not declared or authorized by Congress. That question, of course, is political in a very deep sense, but so is every claim by a citizen that the President (or the Congress) has exceeded his powers to the petitioner's detriment. Without apparent hesitation the Court decided that President Truman exceeded his constitutional powers (and invaded those of Congress) when he seized the steel mills.[13] The question is whether there is some special reason why the courts are debarred from deciding, or have the discretion to refuse to decide, that the President exceeded his powers in Viet-Nam.

I do not purport to know the answer. I am satisfied that no case, surely none of the foreign affairs cases, has determined that issue. It may indeed turn on differences which have only been adumbrated, principally by professors. Professor Wechsler has suggested that the courts may abstain only when they must, when the Constitution as a matter of fair interpretation has rendered a question not judicially reviewable.[14] If so, the courts could refuse to decide this issue in regard to Viet-Nam only by finding that the language of the Constitution, or "the Constitution as a whole," or something else relevant to constitutional interpretation, denies the courts power to review claims that the President has exceeded his powers in the respects here relevant. Professor Bickel, on the other hand, sees in the doctrine "something greatly more flexible, something of prudence," a substantial measure of discretion to "sit out" some issues even if only because it is not "politic" for courts to consider them.[15] In be-

---

[13] Youngstown Sheet & Tube Co. *v.* Sawyer, 343 U. S. 579 (1952).

[14] Wechsler, "Toward Neutral Principles of Constitutional Law," 73 Harv. Law Rev. 1, 9 (1959).

[15] Bickel, "The Supreme Court, 1960 Term—Foreword: The Passive Virtues," 75 Harv. Law Rev. 40, 46 (1961). Later (at p. 75) he says: "Such is the basis of the political question doctrine: the court's sense of lack of capacity, compounded in unequal parts of the strangeness of the issue and the suspicion that it will have to yield more often and more substantially to expediency than to principle; the sheer momentousness of it, which unbalances judgment and prevents one from subsuming the normal calculations of probabilities; the anxiety not so much that judicial judgment will be

tween, perhaps (although probably closer to Professor Bickel), Mr. Justice
Frankfurter, the leading contemporary proponent of the political question
doctrine on the Supreme Court, has inveighed against "disregard of inherent limits in the effective exercise" of the Court's "judicial Power"
which "not only presages the futility of judicial intervention" but may
well impair "the Court's position" and "the Court's authority." [16]   (It
is not clear whether he is saying that in such cases the Constitution requires
the courts to abstain, or that they have discretion to do so, if only the
general discretion of an equity court to deny relief.)

It may be that the doctrine of political questions includes (or should
include) an obligation (or a right) of the courts to refuse to step into
major confrontations between President and Congress, especially to protect the Congressional domain when Congress itself is able but unwilling
to do it.[17]   It may be that courts should not consider issues of war and
peace, where a judicial decision adverse to the President could have grave
consequences for the national interest in its international relations, where
indeed the President might feel compelled to disregard the Court, to the
detriment of the Court and of the nation.   It may even be, indeed, that
there is or ought to be a doctrine that the courts will abstain from considering any challenge to the conduct of the foreign relations of the United
States.   But the Court has never yet told us so.

---

ignored, as that perhaps it should be, but won't; finally and in sum ("in a mature
democracy") the inner vulnerability of an institution which is electorally irresponsible
and has no earth to draw strength from."

16 See his dissent in Baker v. Carr, 369 U. S. 186, 266, 267 (1962).   Compare his
opinion in Colegrove v. Green, 328 U. S. 549 (1946).

17 It may even be that Viet-Nam can be readily transformed into my second, easy
kind of political question by holding there is no issue of usurpation by the President,
no conflict with Congress of any constitutional dimension, because Congress effectively
authorized, ratified or acquiesced in what the President has done.

The Justiciability of Challenges to the Use of Military Forces Abroad

JOHN NORTON MOORE

To his colleagues from abroad, the American lawyer seems to have an extraordinary preoccupation with the judicial process. Whether because of the major role of the Supreme Court in the American system, the strength of the common law tradition, or the dominance of the Langdell-Ames case method of instruction in American law schools, it is second nature for the American lawyer to turn to the courts for solution of major issues. It is not surprising, then, that the controversy surrounding the Vietnam War has given rise to a multitude of cases in American courts. These cases have arisen in a variety of contexts, including prosecution for refusal to be inducted,[1] prosecution for destroying Selective Service records or other acts of civil disobedience against the War,[2] suits by servicemen to prevent their being sent to Vietnam,[3] and taxpayer suits seeking injunctions

---

* This article is a revised version of a paper presented at a Regional Meeting of the American Society of International Law on "The Constitution and the Use of Military Force Abroad" at the University of Virginia, Feb. 28 — March 1, 1969. I am indebted to Professor Peter W. Low for his helpful suggestions on the earlier paper.

1. *See, e.g.,* Mitchell v. United States, 386 U.S. 972 (1967); Kemp v. United States, 415 F.2d 1185 (5th Cir. 1969); United States v. Owens, 415 F.2d 1308 (6th Cir. 1969); United States v. Sisson, 294 F. Supp. 511, 515, 520 (D. Mass. 1969), *prob. juris. noted,* 38 U.S.L.W. 3113 (U.S. Oct. 13, 1969); United States v. Gillette, 420 F.2d 298 (2d Cir. 1970).
2. *See, e.g.,* United States v. Rehfield, 416 F.2d 273 (9th Cir. 1969); United States v. Spock, 416 F.2d 165 (1st Cir. 1969). United States v. Berrigan, 283 F. Supp. 336 (D. Md. 1968), 417 F.2d 1002 (4th Cir. 1969), *appeal dismissed,* 38 U.S.L.W. (U.S. Feb. 24, 1970).
3. *See, e.g.,* Mora v. McNamara, 389 U.S. 934 (1967). Massachusetts recently passed an Act requiring the State Attorney General to bring suit to prevent servicemen from Massachusetts from being required:
   > [t]o serve outside the territorial limits of the United States in the conduct of armed hostilities not an emergency and not otherwise authorized in the powers granted to the President of the United States in Article 2, Section 2, of the Constitution of the United States designating the President as the Commander-in-Chief, unless such hostilities were initially authorized or subsequently ratified by a congressional declaration of war according to the constitutionally established procedures in Article 1, Section 8, of the Constitution of the United States.

   The Act, which was accompanied by much publicity, is intended to force Supreme Court consideration of the justiciability of the constitutional issues in the use of United States troops in the Vietnam War. Though it may achieve its objective of requiring the Court to fully consider the justiciability issue, the implication in the Act that the only congressional authorization of the use of armed forces abroad which is constitutionally permissible is a formal declaration of war, may make the Act unconstitutional. [1970] Mass. Acts Ch. 174.

to end American involvement.[4] Though the diversity of the contexts in which these cases arise assures a large number of legal issues, four major claims seem to run through most of these cases. They are, claims that American involvement has not been constitutionally authorized, that American participation is in violation· of international law, that the method of conducting hostilities violates international law, and that participation in the War will entail personal responsibility under the Nuremberg principles.[5] To date, these claims have been treated as nonjusticiable "political questions" by every domestic court which has considered them. And the Supreme Court, by refusing to grant certiorari to review them, has acquiesced in this judgment, albeit without reasons.[6]

During the past few years several articles have been written taking the courts to task for refusing to meet these issues on the merits.[7]

---

4. *See, e.g.*, Velvel v. Johnson, 287 F. Supp. 846 (D. Kan. 1968).
5. A fifth claim is that one who is conscientiously opposed to participation in a particular war may not constitutionally be conscripted for combat service in that war. In *United States v. Sisson*, 297 F. Supp. 902 (D. Mass. 1969), *prob. juris. noted*, 38 U.S.L.W. 311 (U.S. Oct. 13, 1969), Judge Wyzanski held that the free exercise of religious clause of the First Amendment and the due process clause of the Fifth Amendment constitutionally barred the conscription for combat service in Vietnam of one who was conscientiously opposed to the War. In doing so, Judge Wyzanski drew a distinction between declared and undeclared wars and foreign wars and wars in defense of the homeland.

> [T]his Court . . . assumes that a conscientious objector, religious or otherwise, may be conscripted for some kinds of service in peace or in war. This court further assumes that in time of declared war or in defense of the homeland against invasion, all persons may be conscripted even for combat service.

Id. at 908. Anticipating an appeal to the Supreme Court, Judge Wyzanski also based the decision on the conclusion that the distinction in the 1967 Selective Service Act between religious conscientious objectors and those objecting on other grounds violates the free exercise and establishment clauses of the First Amendment. Judge Wyzanski's holding has enormous significance for the constitutional law concerning conscientious objection, but seems to be confined in its impact to the operation of the selective service laws. The case is currently pending before the Supreme Court. For the Solicitor General's Memorandum to the Supreme Court in the *Sisson* case, see 8 INT'L LEG. MAT. 1248 (1969).

The jury nullification issue, argued by William Kunstler during the course of the panel on "The Use of Domestic Courts to Challenge Employment of Military Force Abroad," might be listed as a sixth claim. It arises, however, only in cases presented to a jury and is largely a dispute about the breadth of the judges charged to the jury. Among other problems, the Kunstler position raises serious questions about location of prescriptive competence in a democratic system and uniformity in the administration of justice. So far he has not persuasively answered either question. See Kunstler, *Jury Nullification in Conscience Cases*, 10 VA. J. INT'L L. 71 (1969).
6. See Mora v. McNamara, 389 U.S. 934 (1967) (in brief opinions Justices Stewart and Douglas dissented from the denial of certiorari); Mitchell v. United States, 386 U.S. 972 (1967) (in a brief opinion Mr. Justice Douglas dissented from the denial of certiorari).
7. *See* Schwartz & McCormack, *The Justiciability of Legal Objections to the American Military Effort in Vietnam*, 46 TEXAS L. REV. 1033 (1968); Velvel, *The*

Professor Warren Schwartz articulately presents this point of view when he says:

> In the Vietnam case the personal stakes could not be higher. The litigants are being directed to place their lives in jeopardy and perhaps even take the lives of others in a conflict they assert to be illegal and immoral.[8]
>
> If the judiciary, the organ of government most fundamentally committed to the vindication of constitutional principle, decides it cannot play its accustomed role in the Vietnam controversy, our basic institutional alternative to lawlessness is lost.[9]

While agreeing with Professor Schwartz and others who urge that the judiciary should fairly meet the challenge, I believe that they greatly oversimplify the difficulties in judicial decision on the merits of these major claims. First, they have focused largely on the constitutional rather than the International law claims and as a result have failed to adequately consider the full range of problems inherent in judicial decision of the Vietnam issues. Second, even on the constitutional issue, they have not adequately taken into account the reasons for judicial abstention stemming from the separation of powers and the nature of the judicial process. This is not to suggest that the opposite extreme, that there is no role for the judiciary in considering challenges to the use of military forces abroad, is correct, but only that the issues are a great deal more difficult than has yet been admitted by the proponents of either position. Similarly, to suggest that fundamental policies may sometimes favor abstention is not to suggest that courts should stand mute about their reasons for decision.

War in Viet Nam: Unconstitutional, Justiciable and Jurisdictionally Attackable, 16 KANSAS L. REV. 449 (1968). *See also* Henkin, *Viet-Nam in the Courts of the United States: "Political Questions",* 63 AM. J. INT'L L. 284 (1969); Forman, *The Nuremberg Trials and Conscientious Objection to War: Justiciability under United States Municipal Law,* 1969 PROC. AM. SOC'Y INT'L L. 157. The proceedings of the complete panel on "The Nuremberg Trials and Objection to Military Service in Viet-Nam," are also useful. *See id.* at 140-181.

8. Schwartz & McCormack, *supra* note 7, at 1045.
9. *Id.* at 1036. Professor Schwartz may overstate the case when he implies that challenges to the use of the armed forces abroad are the "accustomed role" of the judiciary. There is an abundance of sweeping judicial language, which probably overstates the case in the other direction, suggesting no role at all for the judiciary in this area. For example, Mr. Justice Jackson, writing for the Court in *Johnson v. Eisentrager,* 339 U.S. 763 (1950), said:
>   Certainly it is not the function of the Judiciary to entertain private litigation—even by a citizen—which challenges the legality, the wisdom, or the propriety of the Commander-in-Chief in sending our armed forces abroad or to any particular region. . . .
Id. at 789.

In a democratic society there are strong reasons for judicial candor in decision making.[10] And like all other judicial decisions, decisions to abstain from consideration of a claim on the merits should be supported by adequate reasons rather than simply invocation of the "political question" formula or denial of certiorari. Such reasons, if rooted in important policies, are every bit as principled as decision on the merits. Thus, to pose the issue of abstention as one of "unspoken ad hoc adjustments" versus principled decision making, as Professor Schwartz has done, is to miss the point.[11] Judge Wyzanski saw the point when in holding that a defendant in a prosecution for refusal to be inducted could not challenge the legality of the Vietnam War he wrote:

> It is not an act of abdication when a court says that political questions of this sort are not within its jurisdiction. It is a recognition that the tools with which a court can work, the data which it can fairly appraise, the conclusions which it can reach as a basis for entering judgments, have limits.[12]

There may also be room for Professor Bickel's judgment that the newness of some issues or the difficulty of foreseeing the limits of principle may justify some "expedient muddling through."[13] In fact, the decisions uniformly denying justiciability of challenges to the Vietnam War on what is at best sparse reasoning may be examples of this. Ultimately, however, if abstention is to be justifiable, it must be rooted in policies which command allegiance and which in their generality transcend any particular case. The real question must be what is the strength of any such policies in contexts such as Vietnam?

The Functions of Justiciability

Justiciability in its broadest sense refers to a range of policies for judicial abstention on the merits of a particular claim. These policies are inarticulately embodied in the doctrines of standing, ripeness, adversariness and political question. Though interrelated, they can most usefully be considered as abstention because of inadequate assurance of full adversary presentation of the issues, and abstention

---

10. While the author does not embrace all of the arguments of Professor Herbert Wechsler in his famous "neutral principle" article, Wechsler made an important point worth emphasizing when he stressed the need for candid judicial articulation of reasons for decision. Wechsler, *Toward Neutral Principles of Constitutional Law*, 73 Harv. L. Rev. 1, 20-22 (1959).
11. Schwartz & McCormack, *supra*, note 7, at 1053.
12. United States v. Sisson, 294 F. Supp. 511, 515 (D. Mass. 1968), *prob. juris. noted*, 38 U.S.L.W. 3113 (U.S. Oct. 13, 1969).
13. *See* A. Bickel, The Least Dangerous Branch (1962); Scharpf, *Judicial Review and the Political Question: A Functional Analysis*, 75 Yale L. J. 517, 534 (1966).

because of more fundamental and less easily removed considerations stemming from the separation of powers and the nature of the judicial process.[14]

Because of the great effect a major war has on all of us and the variety of contexts in which challenges to a war can be presented, it is safe to say that these lesser reasons for abstention, embodied in the doctrines of standing, ripeness and adversariness, will not be present in some if not in most cases seeking to challenge the use of armed forces abroad. In the middle of the heated Vietnam debate arguments for abstention based on the danger of inadequate adversary presentation seem strangely out of place. And if the challenge is presented in a prosecution for refusal to be sent to Vietnam such arguments seem positively grotesque. As such, these lesser reasons for abstention should not bar consideration of the merits in cases in which the litigants have a personal stake in the outcome.[15]

The more fundamental policies for abstention stemming from the separation of powers and the nature of the judicial process, however, cut across the range of contexts in which challenges to the War are made and raise persistent questions about the wisdom of judicial review of such challenges. These more fundamental policies for abstention are usually invoked by reference to the "political question" doctrine. The "political question" doctrine, however, subsumes two different but interrelated reasons for abstention.[16] The first is simply that the decision of a particular question has been constitutionally entrusted to another branch for decision. Or perhaps a better way to state the same thing is that the court has reviewed the contested action and found that it is within the constitutional competence of the deciding branch, whether Congress, the Executive or both. If the reasons for the judgment that the issue is constitutionally entrusted to another branch are persuasive, presumably such "abstention" would be noncontroversial. For such a decision is a decision on the merits as much as any constitutional judgment delimiting the separation of powers. The second reason for abstention is somewhat different. It is that even though the contested action may in fact violate constitutional principles, there are prudential reasons why the courts

---

14. See generally authorities cited note 13 supra.

15. This is not to suggest that these lesser reasons for abstention might not serve useful purposes in some contexts. For example, it may be that criminal prosecution for destruction of a draft card or for refusal to be inducted is not the proper place to consider challenges to the use of military forces abroad. Whether they are or not, however, relevance rather than the danger of inadequate adversary presentation would seem the real issue. Thus, the illegality of a particular war would not necessarily taint the entire Selective Service process (or the process of collection of federal revenues), and the illegality of an object of protest would not necessarily be a valid defense to prosecution for draft card burning. See United States v. Eberhardt, 417 F.2d 1009, 1012 (4th Cir. 1969). But see Sax, Civil Disobedience: The Law is Never Blind, SATURDAY REVIEW, Sept. 28, 1968, at 22.

16. See Henkin, supra note 7, at 285-86; Schwartz & McCormack, supra note 7, at 1041.

should not examine the constitutional claim. A short framework for analysis is not the place to debate the merits of the classical theory of judicial review championed by Professor Wechsler and challenged by Professor Bickel and others. Since it bears on this second reason for abstention, however, an outline of the skirmish is a useful starting point. Professor Wechsler has argued that the courts are constitutionally compelled to decide concrete controversies on the merits unless "the Constitution has committed the determination of the issue to another agency of government than the courts."[17] Professor Bickel, on the other hand, argues that courts may constitutionally abstain from decision on the merits for a number of systemic reasons which he refers to as "the passive virtues."[18] The considerable difficulty in reconciling Supreme Court cases with Professor Wechsler's test, and the difficulty in accepting his method of arriving at it by logical derivation from the supremacy clause and the judiciary article suggest that the merits of the prudential reasons given for abstention are a better guide for decision.

The most fruitful starting point for evaluating justiciability claims would seem to be the functional approach suggested by Professor Scharpf.[19] Under his approach the first task is to identify the systemic reasons for judicial abstention. Applying this approach, as well as maintaining the separate focus on both types of "political question" decisions, considerations relevant to the decision to abstain on challenges to the use of military forces abroad include:

1. Has the decision been constitutionally entrusted to the discretion of another branch of government?

2. Are there prudential or systemic considerations which suggest that it would be unwise for the judiciary to decide the issue on the merits?

    a. Will judicial consideration interfere with political resolution by another branch which has greater control of the problem and greater flexibility in solution?

    b. Are there "judicially discoverable and manageable standards for resolving" the issue?

    c. Does the court have sufficient access to information and is it suited for the problems of fact appraisal presented?

    d. Would judicial consideration interfere with a need for uniformity and consistency in foreign relations?

    e. Are there institutional checks in the system other than the courts which are capable of responding more sensitively to the challenge?

These considerations are suggested by analysis of the full range of

17. Wechsler, *supra* note 10, at 9.
18. *See* A. *Bickel, supra* note 13; Bickel, *Foreword: The Passive Virtues, Supreme Court, 1960 Term,* 75 HARV. L. REV. 40 (1961).
19. See Scharpf, *supra* note 13. at 566-97

"political question" cases, most recently the 1962 reapportionment case, *Baker v. Carr*,[20] as well as by the analysis of Professor Scharpf and some speculations of my own.

Though these two major questions subsumed under the "political question" doctrine provide a useful focus for analysis, in fact they seem inextricably related and the criteria for abstention on the second issue may well influence characterization on the first. Similarly, the answers to both questions are frequently interrelated with the merits of the claims presented. For example, if the answer to the constitutional claim is that military forces may not constitutionally be used abroad without a declaration of war, there would be no problem of judicially manageable standards. On the other hand, if the real constitutional issues are the extent of independent presidential authority to use force abroad and the limits of congressional delegation of authority to the President, there may well be a serious standards problem. To take another example, under existing precedents it is certainly clearer that the Congress and the President acting together may constitutionally disregard a valid treaty than that the President acting alone may do so. Characterization on the first issue, then, might possibly turn on the extent to which the contested action is congressional-executive action rather than simply executive action. Professor Schwartz refers to this feedback as "the dynamic relationship between construction and application of a governing standard."[21] This dynamic interrelation between the merits of the issue presented and the strength of the reasons for abstention suggests that answers in one context ought not be writ large as absolutes. It further suggests that analysis of the abstention question should be preceded by some awareness of the problems inherent in analysis on the merits.

If the reasons given above include most of the policies for judicial abstention, then the application of these policies to specific challenges to the use of armed forces abroad should suggest the wisdom of judicial abstention on each challenge. The four major challenges which seem to recur in a variety of contexts are: claims that the use of military forces abroad has not been constitutionally authorized, claims that the use of military forces in a particular war violates international law,

---

20. 369 U.S. 186, 217 (1962). *See generally* Scharpf, *supra* note 13.

21. Schwartz & McCormack, *supra* note 7, at 1043-44. Judge Wyzanski also noted this interrelation in his opinion in *United States v. Sisson:*

> The court has a procedural, as well as a substantive, problem. It must decide whether the question sought to be raised is in that category of political questions which are not within a court's jurisdiction and, if the issue falls within the court's jurisdiction, whether, as a matter of substance the defendant is right in his contention that the order is repugnant to the Constitution. Again, while those two aspects are technically separate, they are so close as often to overlap.

United States v. Sisson, 294 F. Supp. 511, 513 (D. Mass. 1968), *prob. juris. noted*, 38 U.S.L.W. 3113 (U.S. Oct. 13, 1969).

claims that the method of conducting hostilities violates international law, and claims that individual participation in a particular war would entail personal responsibility under the Nuremberg principles.[22] The next sections will examine the considerations for abstention with respect to each of these major claims. On each it will be useful to first briefly examine the nature of the controversy on the merits.

Claims that the use of military forces abroad has not been constitutionally authorized.

The controversy concerning the war power has raged at least since the clashes of Jefferson and Hamilton over the power of the President in the 1801 naval war against the Bashaw of Tripoli.[23] The three principal issues in the debate are: First, what independent authority does the President have to order the use of military forces abroad? Second, if congressional authorization is necessary, what form must it take? And third, may Congress delegate authority to use the armed forces abroad to the President, and if so, how broad a delegation is permissible?[24] The starting point of the debate is the Constitution, which gives Congress the power to declare war and which makes the President the Commander-in-Chief. A second major input is the nearly 200 years of constitutional experience in which successive Presidents and Congresses have interpreted these provisions. It is particularly relevant in this regard that during the present century there has been a strong tradition of substantial independent Executive authority to employ the armed forces abroad, highlighted by President Truman's use of a quarter of a million American troops in Korea. The extent to which this practice may have departed from the original constitutional scheme is hotly debated.

Applying the functional criteria previously set out, the first question is has the decision been constitutionally entrusted to the discretion of another branch of government? Professor Velvel answers this by making a distinction between the decision to use forces abroad which

---

22. *See* the discussion of other possible claims at note 5 *supra*.
23. For discussion on the merits of the war power controversy see Henkin, *Constitutional Issues in Foreign Policy*, 23 J. Int'l Affairs 210, 214-18 (1969); Kurland, *The Impotence of Reticence*, 1968 Duke L.J. 619; Moore, *The National Executive and the Use of the Armed Forces Abroad*, 21 Naval War College Rev. 28 (1969); Reveley, *Presidential War-Making: Constitutional Prerogative or Usurpation?* 55, Va. L. Rev. 1243 (1969); *supra* note 7; F. Wormuth, The Vietnam War: The President v. The Constitution (An Occasional Paper of the Center for the Study of Democratic Institutions, 1968); Note, *Congress, The President, and the Power to Commit Forces to Combat*, 81 Harv. L. Rev. 1771 (1969).
24. These issues are posed and discussed in Moore, *supra* note 23, at 30-35. A fourth and perhaps potentially more explosive set of issues is the extent to which Congress may limit or withdraw authority from the President to use the armed forces abroad. See *Fulbright Panel Votes to Repeal Tonkin Measure*, N.Y. Times, April 11, 1970, at 1, col. 5 (City ed.)

he characterizes as a "political question" and the decision as to which branch has the power to decide to commit forces abroad which he says is justiciable.

> [t]he question is not *whether* the nation is to fight a large war, but which branch of government has the *power to decide* if it is to fight such a war. The author would be the first to agree that *whether* this country is to fight is a political question; but which branch has the *power to decide whether to fight is a judicial question.*[25]

The difficulty with this seemingly attractive position is that the issue of who has the power to decide is not as unitary as Professor Velvel's characterization suggests. If the issue is the independent authority of the President to use force abroad and there has been no congressional participation in that decision, then a strong case can be made that the delineation of Executive authority is as much a judicial function as delineating the authority of Congress by declaring acts of Congress unconstitutional. That practice has been good law since *Marbury v. Madison.*[26] Moreover, the Court's negation of President Truman's asserted power to seize the steel mills in aid of the Korean war effort supports the Court's authority to be the final arbiter on questions of the constitutional authority of the President.[27] If the issue is the form of congressional authorization or the extent of the congressional power to delegate the war power to the President, however, it is not as clear that the Court should assert independent authority. Though such decisions are just as much decisions concerning the constitutional power of Congress, past precedent in the foreign affairs area suggests that the Court has left the form of authorization and the extent of delegation of the war power to the discretion of Congress. Thus, in the case of *Talbot v. Seeman,*[28] also authored by Chief Justice John Marshall, the Court did not feel that a formal declaration of war was required for congressional authorization of hostilities. More recently, the *Curtis-Wright*[29] case established a tradition of broad congressional power to delegate authority to the President in foreign affairs. In fact, even in domestic law where the power of the Executive is not as

---

25. Velvel, *supra* note 7, at 480. Professor Velvel must mean that the decision whether *Congress* or the *President* has the power to decide whether to fight is a judicial question. For if the Court decided that it had the power to decide whether to fight, the decision as to whether this country is to fight could hardly be termed a political question as he posits.

26. 5. U.S. (1 Cranch) 137 (1803).

27. Youngstown Sheet & Tube Co. v. Sawyer, 343 U.S. 579 (1952).

28. (The Amelia) 5 U.S. (1 Cranch) 1 (1801).

29. United States v. Curtiss-Wright Export Corp., 299 U.S. 304 (1936). One commentator interprets the *Curtiss-Wright* decision as withdrawing "virtually all constitutional limitation upon the scope of congressional delegation of power to the President to act in the area of international relations." Jones, *The President, Congress and Foreign Relations,* 29 Calif. L. Rev. 565, 575 (1941).

great, anti-delegation authority is largely defunct. If the constitutional requirement is congressional authorization of the commitment, it is a substantial extension to say that the process by which Congress chooses to provide that authorization and the degree of control which they exercise over it are matters for the courts. In the Vietnam context, however unsatisfactory the Tonkin Gulf Resolution is as a general practice,[30] it does establish congressional involvement and remove the constitutional issue from the category of simply ascertaining the limits of independent Executive authority. Decision on the merits in the Vietnam context, then, is inevitably tied up with the form of authorization and breadth of delegation issues both of which may have been constitutionally entrusted to Congress for decision.

The second question is are there prudential or systemic considerations which suggest that it would be unwise for the judiciary to decide the issue on the merits? Though not necessarily conclusive, at least three of the prudential criteria seem relevant to abstention on the constitutional claim. First, to challenge the constitutionality of the use of troops abroad while those troops are engaged in a major conflict may impair the ability of the President to negotiate a settlement or to otherwise disengage without total defeat. Even a declaratory judgment that a war is unconstitutional might strengthen the position of the opponent or cause him to hold out for greater concessions in negotiation, particularly in a war in which domestic public opinion may be an important factor. And if judicial decision sanctions refusal to be inducted for service in the war or has some other more concrete impact, this interference with the settlement process might be dramatic. Certainly it has the potential to be much more serious than Presidential inability to take over the steel mills during the Korean War. Since the courts do not have the kind of effective control of the total situation necessary for settlement of the war, they should be particularly sensitive to the impact which their decisions might have on the settlement efforts of other branches which do. Professor Schwartz has suggested as factors mitigating this risk that the government might win on the merits, that constitutional objection might be cured by subsequent congressional action, and that the courts could frame relief to minimize the impact.[31] Though these factors do mitigate the risks they do not take into account the psychological impact of declaring an on-going war unconstitutional or

---

30. Though in its historical context the Tonkin Gulf Resolution should be construed as a valid exercise of the congressional power to authorize the use of armed forces abroad, it is a sorry discharge of congressional responsibility. Moreover, the circumstances of its passage and the ambiguity of the congressional debates served to isolate the President and to increase the political cost of the War.

　　For discussion of the Tonkin Gulf Resolution and excerpts from the congressional debates see Moore & Underwood, *The Lawfulness of United States Assistance to the Republic of Vietnam*, 112 CONG. REC. 14943, 14,960-67, 14,983-89 (daily ed. July 14, 1966). See also Velvel, *supra* note 7, at 473-77.

31. *See* Schwartz & McCormack, *supra* note 7, at 1049-52.

of forcing a direct confrontation between Congress and the President during the course of a war.

Second, the constitutional issues raise major problems as to "judicially discoverable and manageable standards." If, of course, the Court was willing to say that absent a prior formal declaration of war the commitment of troops to combat abroad is unconstitutional, then the standards problem would not seem major. But the argument that a formal declaration of war is constitutionally required is the most extreme constitutional claim put forward.

The real issues seem to be the extent of independent Executive authority and the power of Congress to delegate its authority to the President. Either with or without congressional authorization, then, there is a serious standards problem. What is the test for independent Executive authority or an invalid delegation? Short of a no independent authority position, which seems unrealistic and policy defeating, there is no test as neat as the "one man one vote" of the reapportionment decisions. The dividing line which I have tentatively suggested for marking off Executive authority, "congressional authorization in all cases where regular combat units are committed to sustained hostilities,"[32] is still much less certain than this "one man one vote" standard. And what is a serious problem in the absence of congressional authorization is nearly insoluble in a Vietnam-type case where there is congressional involvement and the issue is the limits of the congressional power to exercise or delegate its authority. What standards comparable to "one man one vote" are discoverable on that issue? Must a time limitation be used, or an area limitation or a size of forces or weapons limitation? All of these factors and more may be critical for conflict management. This difficulty suggests the wisdom of entrusting the delegation issue to Congress.

Third, since these constitutional claims are intended to resolve a dispute about the relative role of Congress and the Executive and not to apply some constitutional prohibition limiting total governmental power to act, such as the Bill of Rights, if there are institutional checks other than judicial determination which each branch exercises on the other it is certainly relevant to the abstention decision. Although it would not be totally satisfactory in view of the demands to "support our boys" once a major commitment of troops abroad has been made, Congress could refuse to appropriate funds or to conscript the necessary troops, could censure the President as the House did President Polk for his Mexican War activities,[34] or could even institute impeachment proceedings against the President. And short of these checks, Congress can hold public hearings and mobilize public opinion in a manner which can have a major impact on Executive

32. *See* Moore, *supra* note 23, at 32. *See also* the more complete discussion of alternatives for drawing this line in Note, *Congress, The President, and the Power to Commit Forces to Combat, supra* note 23, at 1744-1803.
33. Reveley, *supra* note 23, at 1275.

discretion.[34] This existence of other institutional checks on the relationship between the political branches suggests that the judiciary should go slow in intervening in the processes of political adjustment between them. The felt necessities of the time and the interplay of the political branches may be a more reliable guide than overly neat apriori constitutional hypothesis.

Delay in decision until after the war would substantially ameliorate the first policy for abstention, that adverse decision might interfere with broader settlement. It would not, however, significantly negate the force of the second or third prudential policies for abstention.

Taken together, the answers to these first and second questions concerning abstention suggest that in a situation in which the armed forces abroad are committed pursuant to joint executive-congressional action, the courts should defer to the political interaction between Congress and the President rather than engage in a line drawing exercise for which there are no adequate constitutional guidelines. In a situation, however, in which the dominant issue is the extent of the independent Executive power to commit troops abroad, although there still may be significant costs from judicial action, it is not as clear that the courts should always abstain from decision. Vindication of the constitutional principle that major use of force ought to be acquiesced in by Congress may support some role for the Court in delineating Executive authority if it remains sensitive to the costs and difficulties of judicial involvement.

Claims that the use of the armed forces in a particular war violates international law.

Despite occasional sweeping judicial statements to the contrary, it is clear that not every decision affecting foreign relations requires abstention. One need not subscribe to the simplicities of either the monist or dualist theories of the relation between national and international law to recognize that "international law is part of our law."[35] Validly ratified treaties are, pursuant to the supremacy clause, part of the law of the land and in appropriate cases domestic courts may also apply customary international law. Moreover, for a nation vitally interested in strengthening international law, and in a system where there are too few viable international tribunals, it might be particularly useful to set an example by expanding the role of domestic courts in the creation and application of meaningful international standards. Professor Schwartz makes this point well:

> If the international legal system is to prevail over national conceptions with respect to the use of force, perhaps a person

---

34. The nationally televised hearings of the Senate Foreign Relations Committee on the Vietnam War are an example.
35. The Paquete Habana, 175 U.S. 677, 700 (1900).

should not be compelled to serve in support of a military effort contravening international standards.[36]

Despite strong tugs in this direction, there are persistent questions as to the suitability of domestic courts for such a role, at least in the absence of specific congressional authorization.

Applying the functional criteria for evaluation of abstention, the first question is has the decision been constitutionally entrusted to the discretion of another branch of government? Whatever the ought of this question, there is substantial authority for the proposition that decisions concerning foreign relations taken by the Congress or the president within their constitutional authority are valid whether or not in violation of international law. That is, within their constitutional sphere of action the political branches have the authority to violate international law if they so choose. In the *Chinese Exclusion Case*[37] a unanimous Supreme Court held that Congress may constitutionally override a valid treaty by later inconsistent enactments even though the nonapplication of the treaty would be a violation of international law. And of particular relevance to the waging aggressive war claim, Mr. Justice Field said in dictum:

> When once it is established that Congress possesses the power to pass an act, our province ends with its construction, and its application to cases as they are presented for determination. Congress has the power under the Constitution to declare war, and in two instances where the power has been exercised—in the war of 1812 against Great Britain, and in 1846 against Mexico—the propriety and wisdom and justice of its action were vehemently assailed by some of the ablest and best men in the country, but no one

---

36. Schwartz & McCormick, *supra* note 7, at 1040. Professor Wallace McClure has also been a strong supporter of the position that one ought not be compelled to serve in a war if that war is illegal under international law.

37. Chae Chan Ping v. United States, 130 U.S. 581 (1889). Just a year earlier, in Whitney v. Robertson, 124 U.S. 190 (1888), Mr. Justice Field said, in writing for a unanimous court:

> By the Constitution a treaty is placed on the same footing, and made of like obligation, with an act of legislation. Both are declared by that instrument to be the supreme law of the land and no superior efficacy is given to either over the other. When the two relate to the same subject, the courts will always endeavor to construe them so as to give effect to both, if that can be done without violating the language of either; but if the two are inconsistent, the one last in date will control the other, provided always the stipulation of the treaty on the subject is self-executing.

Id. at 194.

Arguably the subsequent executive-congressional exercise of the war power presents an even stronger case than other kinds of subsequent legislation.

See also Dickinson, *The Law of Nations as National Law; "Political Questions"*, 104 U. PA. L. REV. 451, 487-90 (1956). For an illustration from Great Britain, *see* Mortensen v. Peters, 14 Scots L.T.R. 227 (1906).

doubted the legality of the proceeding, and any imputation by this or any other court of the United States upon the motives of the members of Congress who in either case voted for the declaration, would have been justly the cause of animadversion.[38]

The principle of the *Chinese Exclusion Case* has been widely criticized, and it is true that it evolved in an earlier era when bilateral rather than multilateral treaties were the usual fare.[39] But any other decision would still raise substantial questions as to the source of the Court's constitutional authority to strike down joint actions of the political branches on the basis of international law. Moreover, although in some areas affecting foreign relations there may be a stronger constitutional case for the primacy of treaties or the courts may have primary competence, it is particularly questionable with respect to executive-congressional decisions to commit armed forces abroad.

The case of *Reid v. Covert*,[40] which established the preeminence of the Constitution over treaty obligations, also supports the authority of the political branches, when they are acting pursuant to their constitutional authority, to take domestically valid action even though in violation of international law. The Constitution makes the President the Commander-in-Chief and gives to Congress the power to declare war. In light of *Reid*, it is open to question whether these powers may be domestically limited by prior treaty obligations. Judge Northrop summarized these points in *United States v. Berrigan*[41] when he said:

> Whether the actions by the executive and the legislative branches in utilizing our armed forces are in accord with international law is a question which necessarily must be left to the elected representatives of the people and not to the judiciary. This is so even if the government's actions are contrary to valid treaties to which the government is a signatory. . . . The categorization of this defense as a "political question" is not an abdication of responsibility by the judiciary. Rather, it is a recognition that the responsibility is assumed by that level of government which under the Constitution and international law is authorized to commit the nation.[42]

---

38. Chae Chan Ping v. United States, *supra* note 37, at 603.
39. See the remarks of Professor Louis B. Sohn, 1969 PROC. AM. SOC'Y INT'L L. 180.
40. 354 U.S. 1 (1957). *Reid v. Covert* decided a very different issue involving the Bill of Rights jury trial guarantees. The argument which can be made on the basis of the *Reid* case, however, is that if the Constitution entrusts the war power to Congress and the President, that power cannot be constitutionally limited by agreement with a foreign nation.
41. 283 F. Supp. 336 (D. Md. 1968).
42. *Id.* at 342.

While it is clear from these decisions that Congress and the President acting together have constitutional authority to act even in violation of international law, the issue is not nearly so clear if the President, acting alone, violates a valid treaty approved by the Senate. The answer in that case lies somewhere in the poorly charted limits of Executive and Congressional authority in foreign relations issues. In any event, the focus must be on the constitutional authority of the President or Congress to take the action as well as on whether the action is in violation of international law. It is to be hoped (and urged) that Congress and the President will be sensitive to the importance of adherence to international law, but under the Constitution it is questionable whether the Court has authority to police the international law violations of the political branches when they are acting within their sphere of constitutional authority.

The second question is are there prudential or systemic considerations which suggest that it would be unwise for the judiciary to decide the international law issues on the merits? While they should not be taken as absolutes, at least four of the prudential criteria seem relevant to abstention on the international law claim.

First, there is a serious problem in ascertaining manageable standards for decision. Although the General Assembly has appointed a succession of Special Committees on the Question of Defining Aggression, the latest of which is still working on the question, there is still no agreed definition of aggression with which to implement the standards of the United Nations Charter or the Kellogg-Briand Pact.[43] Moreover, as is evidenced by the Vietnam War, since World War II the principal public order issue has become the control of intervention in internal conflict. The UN Charter is only poorly responsive to the problem of intervention and in the absence of a more adequate Charter framework there has been wide disagreement about the applicable nonintervention norms of customary international law.[44] As a result, if the issue is one of major use of force—and particularly intervention in internal conflict, as it is in the Vietnam War,[45] there is a severe standards problem. This problem is compounded on international law issues, because unlike the case with respect to domestic law a United States court cannot promulgate an international standard which will be definitive for any other nation. At most, the domestic formulation will simply be an input into the

---

43. *See generally* Report of the Special Committee on the Question of Defining Aggression, 24 U.N. GAOR, Supp. 20, U.N. Doc. A/7620 (1969); M. McDOUGAL & F. FELICIANO, LAW AND MINIMUM WORLD PUBLIC ORDER 143-160 (1961).

44. For an account of the Charter inadequacies in dealing with intervention and a review of the competing nonintervention norms see Moore, *The Control of Foreign Intervention in Internal Conflict*, 9 VA. J. INT'L L. 205 (1969).

45. For discussion on the merits of the legal issues in the Vietnam War see I & II THE VIETNAM WAR AND INTERNATIONAL LAW (R. Falk ed. 1968-69). Both volumes are sponsored by the "Civil War" Panel of the American Society of International Law.

much broader determination of international law by reference to state practice. The limited power of United States courts to clarify doubtful areas in international law means that domestic court jurisdiction could result in the United States following a restrictive view of international law without other nations feeling reciprocally bound. To some extent this problem is present with all applications by domestic courts of customary international law, and it can easily be overstated as a reason for abstention. Nevertheless, as the issues approach the most sensitive areas of national discretion, a lack of adequate international standards becomes a relevant consideration in deciding whether to exercise competence.

Second, and closely related to the first, judicial formulation of standards for decision in the most sensitive areas of national action may interfere with the ability of the political branches to formulate standards or to obtain international agreement on them. The decision on the desirability and content of a definition of aggression or whether the United States will follow the traditional or newer nonintervention norms are among the most sensitive issues of foreign relations. This problem of interference with the authority of the political branches and of uniformity and consistency in foreign relations is closely tied to the constitutional submission of foreign relations decisions to the political branches. If the political branches have by their actions taken a position in foreign relations, it is not clear that the courts have authority to override that action.

Thirdly, judicial determination by a domestic court during the course of conflict to the effect that a particular war violates international law may interfere with settlement by the political branches which are in the best position to terminate the conflict. Few major international conflicts are so one-sided that conformance with international law requires sacrifice of all of the objectives of either of the participants. Yet judicial declaration that a particular conflict is in violation of international law may contribute to the loss of even justifiable defensive objectives. Thus, if relief takes the form of a declaratory judgment it may have adverse psychological consequences on the goverment's negotiating position. And if it involves more effective sanctions, such as prohibition of induction, it might have a much more serious impact. Moreover, unlike the constitutional claims, the ameliorative devices which depend on subsequent congressional action would be unavailable. Another point relative to the settlement issue is that normally a domestic court has both parties to a dispute before it and may fashion relief fair to both. In adjudicating the legality of a war, however, the adversary is not subject to the jurisdiction of the court.

Fourth, a decision that a particular use of force is a violation of international law may require fact assessments which present particularly difficult problems for domestic courts. The assessment of the lawfulness of the Vietnam War, for example, involves fact determinations about the extent of military involvement of North Vietnam and the interrelation of Hanoi and the Viet Cong which a domestic court may be poorly equipped to handle.[46] Under some theories it might also involve questions of the statehood of North and South Vietnam or the validity of recognition of the Saigon government, which even in the nonwar context have been issues on which the courts have deferred to the Executive.[47] Moreover, adequate presentation of the government position might require disclosure of sensitive information compiled by the national intelligence agencies which would be prejudicial to future intelligence operations or settlement efforts.

Delay in decision until termination of hostilities would ameliorate the danger of interference with the settlement process, but the other three prudential considerations for abstention would still be largely operative.

The strength of these prudential considerations for abstention can be oversold and will certainly vary with the context. A court might feel in a particularly extreme context that the price of ignoring these prudential considerations is sufficiently offset by other considerations, particularly the importance of vindication of international law. The major issue which would still remain, however, would be the court's constitutional authority to declare the otherwise valid actions of the political branches invalid because in violation of international law. Existing precedents suggest that at least with respect to executive-congressional action such decisions have been constitutionally entrusted to Congress and the President.

Claims that the method of conducting hostilities violates international law.

Another international law claim, in addition to the claim that the use of the armed forces in a particular war violates international law, is that a particular method of conducting hostilities violates international law, that is, that the use of particular tactics or weapons systems or the treatment of civilians or prisoners of war violates international law. Since the United States is a party to most of the Hague and Geneva Conventions regulating the conduct of hostilities, many of these claims can be expected to have a specific treaty base. Though the awkwardness of demonstrating a "personal stake in the outcome" may make standing a more serious obstacle to claims in this category, one can imagine a number of contexts in which standing probably ought not bar consideration of the issues. For example, if a serviceman sought an injunction against widespread violations of the laws of war in a unit to which he had been assigned, or if a prisoner of

---

46. *See generally* Moore, *Law and Politics in the Vietnamese War: A Response to Professor Friedmann*, 61 AM. J. INT'L L. 1039 (1967).

47. *See generally* Moore, *The Role of the State Department in Judicial Proceedings*, 31 FORDHAM L. REV. 277 (1962), and authorities collected at 277 n. 8.

war sought protection under applicable treaties, both claimants would seem to have a very real personal stake in the outcome. Assuming the standing hurdle can be overcome, a case can be made for judicial activism in policing violations of the laws of war.

The first question concerning abstention, whether a decision has been constitutionally entrusted to another branch of government, would only be relevant in those contexts in which the Executive is alleged to have ordered a violation of a customary or treaty law obligation. In the absence of such an order, a treaty at least, represents an executive-congressional decision and if intended to be self-executing should be applied by the court. Many, if not most, of the violations of the laws of war probably fall into this category of unauthorized deviation from command directives and as such do not present a significant problem in judicially contradicting a constitutionally authorized decision-maker. The recent tragic events at Songmy are an example. Even when this first question is relevant, though, or when a clear command directive contradicts a prior treaty obligation, it is still not at all clear that a court should defer to the later Executive decision. Although the Constitution makes the President the Commander-in-Chief, it does not provide satisfactory guidance for the resolution of a clash between the Commander-in-Chief power and the treaty power. It is at least a reasonable resolution of such a clash that the treaty power would prevail and that departure from treaty or executive-congressional agreement standards would require Senate or Congressional participation. The uncertainties whether a particular treaty is meant to be self-executing and whether the power of the President as Commander-in-Chief can be limited by treaty may in particular cases somewhat qualify these tentative conclusions.

The second question, whether there are prudential or systemic considerations suggesting that it would be unwise for the judiciary to decide the issue on the merits, similarly turns up only weak reasons for abstention. In most contexts judicial policing of the laws of war would not have the severe impact on the conduct of the war which might accompany judicial consideration of participation claims. Even if the method of conducting hostilities were altered, the war effort could still proceed. In fact, there is good reason to believe that violations of the laws of war are usually counter-productive and that judicial intervention would more often than not better promote national goals. Certainly in view of the large number of applicable treaties to which the United States is a party, in most cases there would be no standards problem in policing violations of the laws of war. Similarly, though fact appraisal may be somewhat more difficult than in the usual domestic case, there do not seem to be any overwhelming obstacles either from the difficulty of fact appraisal or the need for uniformity and consistency in foreign relations. It might be urged, of course, that there are other institutions better suited to the role of policing violations of the laws of war, particularly self-policing by the military.

The argument proves too much, however, since the availability of other institutions is never by itself a wholly persuasive reason for abstention. Moreover, despite good faith efforts at self-policing, like all institutions the military has built in limitations which may hinder its own self-policing operations. For example, self-policing in the Vietnam War, though it seems to have been sincerely pursued, got off to a slow start and has certainly been inadequately implemented. In these circumstances a judicial boost to lagging policing efforts might have served both the national and the litigants', interests.

The wide variety of situations in which claims concerning the conduct of hostilities may arise precludes meaningful generalization in advance. Analysis of the functions served by judicial abstention, however, suggests that there are few fundamental obstacles to a more aggressive judicial role in policing violations of the laws of war.

Claims that individual participation in a particular war would entail personal responsibility under the Nuremberg principles.

One way in which the international law issues are sought to be presented in a variety of contexts challenging the use of armed forces abroad is by invocation of the Nuremberg principles. If the Nuremberg principles are invoked simply as one source of the international law obligations not to engage in aggressive war or not to violate the laws of war, such allegations raise the same justiciability problems as claims that the use of the armed forces in a particular war violates international law or claims that the method of conducting hostilities violates international law. If, however, the purpose in invoking the Nuremberg norms is to avoid personal liability, then different considerations are introduced. The 1945 Charter of the Nuremberg Tribunal, since codified by the International Law Commission, ascribes individual responsibility under international law for:

> (a) *Crimes against peace:* namely, planning, preparation, initiation or waging of a war of aggression, or a war in violation of international treaties, agreements or assurances. . . .
>
> (b) *War crimes:* namely, violations of the laws or customs of war. . . .
>
> (c) *Crimes against humanity:* namely, murder, extermination, enslavement, deportation, and other inhumane acts committed against any civilian population, before or during the war. . . . [48]

---

48. *Agreement for the Prosecution and Punishment of the Major War Criminals of the European Axis,* Aug. 8, 1945, 82 U.N.T.S. 279. *See generally* G. MUELLER & E. WISE, INTERNATIONAL CRIMINAL LAW 227-290 (1965).

For more detailed analysis of the justiciability of this third claim concerning allegations that participation in a particular war would be contrary to the Nuremberg principles see Forman, *supra* note 7.

At least acts in the category of "war crimes" are also substantially covered by the Uniform Code of Military Justice.[49] To the extent that an action would entail personal responsibility under the Nuremberg principles, the Uniform Code of Military Justice, or any other valid national or international standard, certainly the criminality of the action should be a valid defense to state compulsion to engage in it. The sense of justice boggles at the thought that a man may be legally compelled to perform an act entailing criminal liability.

The category of actions for which one may be held criminally accountable under the Nuremberg principles is much narrower, however, than is popularly supposed. Though the Nuremberg principles are not absolutely clear, the most widely shared interpretation of them is that no soldier is liable simply because he participates in an aggressive war.[50] To include participation as such would have hardly served the humanitarian objectives of Nuremberg, as hundreds of thousands of soldiers would have been subject to criminal liability when their only crime was to misperceive which side was the aggressor. Instead, for liability under the Nuremberg norms there must be personal participation in high level planning or in the commission of a war crime or crime against humanity such as the killing or torturing of prisoners of war. Benjamin Forman, the Assistant General Counsel for International Affairs of the Department of Defense, recently summarized this general Nuremberg law in a paper delivered at the 1969 annual meeting of the American Society of International Law:

> No Nuremberg norm makes it criminal to be a soldier or, as such, to carry on belligerent activities injurious to others in accordance with the laws and customs of war, even though the war be an aggressive war. The crime against peace can be committed only by those in a position to shape or influence the policy that initiates or continues it. . . .
>
> As to war crimes and crimes against humanity, liability is similarly individual. The individual must himself commit the substantive offense or conspire to do so.[51]

Perhaps the greatest barrier to invocation of the Nuremberg principles as a defense against personal accountability, then, is that

---

49. See Forman, *supra* note 7, at 161, D'Amato, Gould, & Woods, *War Crimes and Vietnam: The "Nuremberg Defense" and the Military Service Resister*, 57 CALIF. L. REV. 1055 (1969).

50. Claims that clearly identified belligerents are "war criminals" simply because combatants in a military apparatus engaged in aggressive war have not been accepted by the world community, including the International Military Tribunal at Nuremberg, and are clearly in contravention to accepted "standards of human rights for contexts of violence." See M. McDOUGAL & F. FELICIANO, *supra* note 40 at 528, 531-34, 541-42, 530-61.

51. Forman, *supra* note 7, at 163.

there may be no accountability. Certainly the typical soldier will not be participating in high level planning necessary for liability under the crimes against peace count. Unless a claimant alleges that he will be personally participating in violation of the laws of war or of crimes against humanity, then, invocation of the Nuremberg principles for the purpose of avoiding individual liability seems to be beside the point. And if his allegation is that he will be personally participating in war crimes or crimes against humanity constituting war crimes, it is implicit in Articles 90-92 of the Uniform Code of Military Justice [52] that the illegality of the order to participate in such actions is a valid defense to an action for noncompliance. In fact, the refusal of a soldier to participate in such acts which he should reasonably know are unlawful is not only permitted but required by domestic law.[53] Here too, then, depending on the timing and the specifics of the allegations, the invocation of the Nuremberg principles may be largely beside the point. Thus, it is clear that a soldier would have a valid defense to a charge that he refused to carry out an order to kill prisoners of war or unarmed civilians in his custody (but he would not need Nuremberg to prevail). In fact, as a large segment of the American public seems to have unfortunately ignored in the much publicized "Green Beret" and "Songmy" cases, the carrying out of such an order which the soldier should reasonably know is unlawful is a violation of both international and domestic law. As a result of this duty, it seems doubtful whether general allegations of the possibility of participating in war crimes could be raised as a defense to an order to report for induction.

It would seem that the existing defenses in domestic law and the areas of individual accountability under the Nuremberg principles are reasonably congruent, at least for the typical soldier. In contexts presenting severe pressure to participate in war crimes, however, this congruence may provide insufficient protection for the claimant. Thus, if a soldier is assigned to a force or unit which he alleges engages repeatedly in a practice which violates the laws of war, it seems reasonable to adjudicate this claim on the merits either in an action to block an assignment or obtain a transfer or in an action to obtain injunctive relief against the continuation of the illegal practices. The kinds of severe pressures an individual soldier would be subjected to in such a unit and the risk which he runs in disobeying an order at his peril should his judgment about its illegality be wrong strongly suggest that judicial intervention is proper in such a context. The examination of evidence in the *Levy* trial concerning allegations of widespread violations of the laws of war by the "Green Berets" supports this conclusion. It is also supported by the weakness of

---

52. 10 U.S.C. §§ 890-92 (1964). The illegality of an order is explicitly said to be a defense in the discussion of Articles 90-92 in MANUAL FOR COURTS-MARTIAL (1969), Exec. Order No. 11, 476,34, Fed. Reg. 10826-30 (1969). See also ARMY FIELD MANUAL FM 27-10, THE LAW OF LAND WARFARE 182-83 (1956); Forman, *supra* note 7, at 164.
53. *See* United States v. Kinder, 14 C.M.R. 742 (1954).

reasons for abstention when the claim is violation of the laws of war. To prevail, of course, a claimant must still prove his case.

Lack of accountability rather than any more fundamental "political question" would seem to be the principal bar to broad invocation of the Nuremberg principles on a theory of avoidance of personal liability. Moreover, in the absence of personal accountability or severe pressures to participate in illegal conduct, it is doubtful whether an individual litigant has the necessary "personal stake in the outcome of the controversy" to satisfy the standing test which the Supreme Court recently enunciated in *Flast v. Cohen*,[54] at least if the purpose of invoking the Nuremberg norms is to avoid personal accountability. And if the purpose of invoking the Nuremberg norms is to challenge the legality of the war itself, that is to avoid participation in an allegedly illegal war even though participation would not lead to personal accountability, then the more fundamental justiciability policies rather than standing would seem to be the principal bar. In most cases, of course, the two reasons for invoking the Nuremberg norms come mixed together. But whether the difficulty is thought of as relevance, standing, or justiciability, in all but a fairly narrow class of cases involving personal responsibility or a risk of severe pressure to conform to an unlawful practice constituting a war crime, the Nuremberg challenges to the use of military forces abroad will probably be unsuccessful.

Conclusion

The tradition of judicial review runs deep in the American system. It is not every issue, however, which is constitutionally entrusted to the judiciary or which is suitable for judicial action. To date no court has held a challenge to the commitment of military forces abroad justiciable.[55] The invocation in these cases of the "political question" formula without explanation of its justification or the denial of certiorari without reasons, however, is an unsatisfactory judicial response. Particularly when faced with challenges presented by

---

54. 392 U.S. 83, 99-101 (1968). Quoting *Baker v. Carr*, the Court sharply distinguished between standing and justiciability:

> The "gist of the question of standing" is whether the party seeking relief has "alleged such a personal stake in the outcome of the controversy as to assure that concrete adverseness which sharpens the presentation of issues upon which the court so largely depends for illumination of difficult constitutional questions." . . . In other words, when standing is placed in issue in a case, the question is whether the person whose standing is challenged is a proper party to request an adjudication of a particular issue and not whether the issue itself is justiciable. Thus, a party may have standing in a particular case, but the federal court may nevertheless decline to pass on the merits of the case because, for example, it presents a political question.

Id at 99-100.
55. But see the discussion of *United States v. Sisson, supra* note 5.

sincere individuals, some of whom are involuntarily serving in a war to which they object, courts have a duty to fully articulate reasons for their decision. Full articulation calls for identification of the functions served by "justiciability" and their application to the major claims challenging the use of the armed forces abroad. Such a functional analysis of the reasons for judicial abstention is likely to please neither the activists nor the strict constructionists. There are important systemic policies suggesting that for the most part the resolution of claims that a particular use of force abroad has not been constitutionally authorized or is in violation of international law should be left to the interplay of political forces. Nevertheless, the newness and range of the challenges to the use of military forces abroad suggest a lack of wisdom in dogmatic assertion that there is no role for judicial action on such challenges, particularly on challenges to initial commitments instituted solely on the authority of the President. Moreover, there may be considerable room for a more active judicial role in policing violations of the laws of war.[56] Whatever the ultimate resolution of these issues, their importance and complexity calls for full articulation of the reasons for decision.

---

56. See D'Amato, Gould & Woods, *supra* note 48.

Judicial Power,
the "Political Question Doctrine,"
and Foreign Relations

MICHAEL E. TIGAR*

The words "political question doctrine" are set off by inverted commas to denote my view that there is, properly speaking, no such thing. Rather, there is a cluster of disparate legal rules and principles any of which may, in a given case, dictate a result on the merits, lead to dismissal for want of article three[1] jurisdiction, prevent a party from airing an issue the favorable resolution of which might terminate the litigation in his favor, or authorize a federal court in its discretion and as a matter of prudence to decline jurisdiction to hear a case or decide an issue. A redefinition of the "political question doctrine" and isolation from it of other possible bases for refusal to decide constitutional issues are the burdens of the concluding sections of this article.

One conclusion of that analysis will be that the legality, in some accepted sense of the term, of American participation in an undeclared war in Indochina is susceptible of judicial resolution in a properly brought case. This conclusion is, I am sure, unsurprising: It has been reached by others.[2] I have been and remain unsatisfied, however, by the historical, logical and textual constitutional support thus far marshalled for such assertions. And I am disturbed by the way in which formulations of the "political question doctrine" by the Supreme Court[3] and by ardent and articulate adherents of the doctrine threaten to debase the currency of legal rules and norms as constraints upon American military action.

---

* Much appreciation is due Robert W. Zweben, a third-year student at the National Law Center, George Washington University, without whose research assistance, ideas, and valuable suggestions this article would not have come to be.

[1] U.S. CONST. art. III.

[2] See, e.g., Schwartz & McCormack, *The Justiciability of Legal Objections to the American Military Effort in Vietnam*, 46 TEX. L. REV. 1033 (1968); Hughes, *Civil Disobedience and the Political Question Doctrine*, 43 N.Y.U.L. REV. 1 (1968). Compare United States v. Sisson, 294 F. Supp. 511, 515, 520 (D. Mass. 1968); Scharpf, *Judicial Review and the Political Question: A Functional Analysis*, 75 YALE L.J. 517 (1966) [hereinafter cited as Scharpf].

[3] See, e.g., Baker v. Carr, 369 U.S. 186, 209-237 (1962); Powell v. McCormack, 395 U.S. 486, 517-49 (1969), *discussed in Comments on* Powell v. McCormack, 17 U.C.L.A. L. REV. 1 (1969). See also Colegrove v. Green, 328 U.S. 549 (1946) (opinion of Frankfurter, J.).

This article begins with a discussion of the limitations—constitutional, statutory and decisional—upon the power and duty of federal courts to decide cases and controversies. I conclude that, contrary to a view often expressed in recent years, the federal courts do not have an ambulatory and discretionary power to refuse decision of cases over which they have jurisdiction. In the second section of the article, I focus particularly upon the "political question doctrine" in historical perspective, and argue that it was at its origin and through the first century of its development a collection of legal rules grounded in constitutional principle and not at all a device for leaving litigants without an authoritative decision of questions involving the separation of powers. In the concluding section, I urge that the federal courts—in light of proper limitations on their power and in particular the doctrine of "political questions" —have the power, and in an appropriate case, the duty, to decide the constitutional and federal law issues posed by American military involvement abroad, in Indochina today and in any future conflict.

I. A CRITICAL ANALYSIS OF THEORIES OF JUDICIAL POWER

Alexander Bickel has written what is unmistakably the most studied and eloquent analysis of the political question doctrine in the decisional law of the Supreme Court, and has done so in the context of an impressive reformulation of the grounds upon which the Supreme Court may refuse to decide constitutional issues and cases.[4] Professors Wechsler[5] and Gunther[6] have each joined the issue, and Professor Scharpf,[7] in an article in *Yale Law Journal*, has sought to resolve the debate by shifting its ground.[8]

---

[4] A. BICKEL, THE LEAST DANGEROUS BRANCH (1962) [hereinafter cited as BICKEL], (especially Chapter 4, "The Passive Virtues").

[5] H. WECHSLER, PRINCIPLES, POLITICS AND FUNDAMENTAL LAW 3-48 (1961) [hereinafter cited as WECHSLER]; Wechsler, Book Review, 75 YALE L.J. 672 (1966).

[6] Gunther, *The Subtle Vices of the "Passive Virtues"—A Comment on Principle and Expediency in Judicial Review*, 64 COLUM. L. REV. 1 (1964) [hereinafter cited as Gunther].

[7] Scharpf, *supra* note 2.

[8] Bickel, in THE LEAST DANGEROUS BRANCH, focused upon the Supreme Court to the virtual exclusion of the lower federal courts in setting out the constitutional theory of which his discussions of the political question doctrine is constitutive. *See* BICKEL at 173. Indeed, Professor Wechsler has faulted this preoccupation, saying that "the conception of judicial review has never been regarded as a special doctrine governing the role of the Supreme Court, as distinguished from the lower courts in the judicial hierarchy; and the techniques for the avoidance of decision that Bickel so lucidly describes are addressed to the propriety of any judicial intervention, not merely to adjudication by the highest court." Wechsler, Book Review, 75 YALE L.J. 672, 675 (1966). I think Wechsler's criticism is unjustified. The Supreme Court is different from the lower federal courts, in ways which both indispensably support

The central thrust of Bickel's argument is that the Court ought in a number of situations—which Bickel describes suggestively but not exhaustively—refrain from deciding issues or cases brought to it. Among the devices available for "not doing"—to be employed when one agrees that a particular case should not be decided—is the "political question doctrine." There are, however, others, and Bickel refers to all these devices collectively as the "passive virtues."[9] These devices fall into two categories in Bickel's analysis: constitutional limits on the power of the Court and prudential limits self-imposed as rationales for declining to exercise jurisdiction which article three clearly gives. The constitutional limits inhere in the "cases" and "controversies" language of article three, with its requirements of adversity, constitutional standing,

---

and unavoidably cast doubt upon Bickel's hypothesis. We must, when considering limitations upon the "judicial power," prudential or constitutionally mandated, mark well that the Court sits not so much to safeguard the rights of litigants as to superintend the positive law of the American federal system. Certainly this is true for the years since the establishment of the discretion to deny certiorari, and thus avoid an adjudication on the merits, and is documented in the formal and informal law of granting or denial of the writ. Sup. Ct. R. 38, 39, 41, 28 U.S.C. §§ 1254-56 (1964); Bickel at 173; Wechsler, *supra* note 5, at 15; H. M. Hart & H. Wechsler, The Federal Courts and the Federal System 1394-1422 (1953) [hereinafter cited as Hart & Wechsler]. Even in the years which preceded the grant of this discretion in 1925, the Court was apart not merely because at the apex; since the time of Marshall, its overtly and designedly political role in shaping American institutions has distinguished it from lower courts. The Court is, after all, the only judicial institution mentioned in the Constitution. Its early and repeated clashes with co-ordinate branches and with the states are a part of every history schoolbook. For lawyers, Charles Warren's treatment remains the best. C. Warren, The Supreme Court in United States History (1947) [hereinafter cited as Warren]. *See also* A. Beveridge, The Life of John Marshall (1919). Much of the explanation for the Court's dominant position in shaping the philosophy of judicial power lies, no doubt, in the Justices' circuit trial court assignments, which persisted until 1869. 2 Warren at 501. The *Burr* case, some of the rulings in which caused President Jefferson acute anguish, was tried on circuit by Marshall. Marshall ruled that the President was amenable to service of process. United States v. Burr, 25 Cas. 30, 34 (No. 14,692d) (C.C.D. Va. 1807). *See* 8 J. Wigmore, Evidence § 2371, at 750-51 (McNaughton rev. ed. 1961). The *Habeas Corpus* Case, a direct (though in the end ineffectual) challenge to President Lincoln, was authored by Taney, sitting on circuit in Baltimore. See 2 Warren at 368-74. Justice Story's opinions on circuit were often designed as innovative. *See*, *e.g.*, Greene v. Darling, 10 Fed. Cas. 1144 (No. 5165) (C.C.D. R.I. 1828); Comment, *Automatic Extinction of Cross-Demands:* Compensatio *from Rome to California*, 53 Calif. L. Rev. 224, 251-52 (1965). *See generally* 1 Warren at 158-68.

Bickel does not, if I understand him, say that the lower courts should not use devices such as the political question doctrine to avoid adjudication on the merits. Rather, he focuses upon the Supreme Court because, since Marbury v. Madison, 5 U.S. (1 Cranch) 137 (1803), no constitutional pronouncement save the Court's is final and authoritative, and because the Court itself, rather than the "federal courts" generally, has stood at the center of controversies over the role of the judiciary in the federal system.

9 Bickel at 111.

and a dispute sufficiently ripe to be denominated a "case."[10] The prudential limits upon the exercise of power include species of standing[11] and ripeness,[12] as well as the discretionary power to deny

---

[10] *See* Ashwander v. TVA, 297 U.S. 288, 345-48 (1936) (Brandeis, J., concurring); Muskrat v. United States, 219 U.S. 346 (1911). The definition of the Court's proper role began in earnest with its refusal to give President Jefferson an advisory opinion on questions of foreign relations, see HART & WECHSLER, *supra* note 8, at 75-76, and with the Court's declination to administer a veterans' pension system, Hayburn's Case, 2 Dall. 409 (1792).

The "case and controversy" requirement is essentially a command that the federal courts limit themselves to deciding lawsuits in the adversary mold: there must be real, not feigned, adversity of interests; the parties must have a stake in the outcome of the controversy in which one stands to win or the other to lose something in consequence of the judgment; and the controversy must have reached a point in development that permits the parties to demonstrate how the legal rules for which each contends will work a harm upon the loser or confer a benefit upon the winner. It is easy to see that the "case and controversy" requirement carries with it a number of assumptions which more broadly underlie the "adversary system," with its supposition that the parties to a dispute will be motivated by self-interest to develop fully the factual and legal arguments behind their dispute. *See generally* C. WRIGHT, FEDERAL COURTS § 12 (1963).

[11] "Standing" is a term which gives lawyers, scholars and courts considerable difficulty. *See generally* Flast v. Cohen, 392 U.S. 83 (1968). Perhaps the confusion has been encouraged, if not engendered, by careless use of the term to refer to several quite distinct limitations upon the power and the willingness of federal courts to entertain claims of violation of federal rights. The varying and sometimes recondite uses of "standing" in the cases make analysis doubly difficult.

First, "standing" is sometimes used to refer to the procedural capacity of a litigant to sue or be sued. *See* A. EHRENZWEIG, CONFLICT OF LAWS §§ 11-24 (1959).

Second, "standing" is sometimes used to denote a limit upon the judicial power, and to refer generally to the requirement that litigants have a genuine and not a sham contrariety of interests, both qualitatively and quantitatively. Cases in which the requisite "qualitative" adversity was lacking include Muskrat v. United States, 219 U.S. 346 (1911), and FCC v. Sanders Bros. Radio Station, 309 U.S. 470 (1940). The question is double-edged in these cases: will the Court decline, on the basis of judicially-fashioned rules of restraint to take the case? (see *Muskrat*); and, on the other hand, may Congress bestow standing upon a class of litigants without falling afoul of the proscription on advisory opinions—stated affirmatively as the case or controversy requirement (see *Sanders Bros. Radio Station*). The "quantitative" dimension of standing was considered in Flast v. Cohen, 392 U.S. 83 (1968), in which the Court limited Frothingham v. Mellon, 262 U.S. 447 (1923). Frothingham had rejected a taxpayers' suit directed at a federal statute upon the ground that the interest of a taxpayer in the outcome of the litigation was but a comminute share of the interest of the community at large, and not sufficiently direct and immediate. *See also* Doremus v. Board of Educ., 342 U.S. 429 (1952).

A third use of the term "standing" has been in reference to questions essentially of ripeness. United States v. Storer Broadcasting Co., 351 U.S. 192 (1956), is such a case. There the FCC had adopted a rule stating that licenses for television broadcasting would not be granted if the applicant had a direct or indirect interest in more than five other stations. Storer, which had reached the limit under the rule, sued for a declaration that the rule was invalid. This Court concluded that Storer had "standing" to sue, resting its decision upon a perception of the statutory judicial review standard and a finding of present harm to Storer. 351 U.S. at 197-99. The Court recognized that "standing," in the sense it had used the term, carried along with it the notion of ripeness. Taking the question out of "standing" language, one could cast it as, "Should Storer have gone through the license-application process before coming to court?" This requirement may also be termed

certiorari or summarily dispose of an appeal.[13] Bickel also includes among the passive virtues some principles of substantive law—the "void for vagueness" doctrine[14] and the law of delegation of au-

---

one of "finality." *See* Joint Anti-Fascist Refugee Comm. v. McGrath, 341 U.S. 123, 154-56 (1951) (Frankfurter, J. concurring).

A fourth "standing" issue is that of "legal wrong," a term which appeared in section 10 of the old Administrative Procedure Act and which now appears in the judicial review provisions of recodified Title 5, 5 U.S.C. § 702 (Supp. IV 1969). *See* United States v. Storer Broadcasting Co., 351 U.S. 192, 198-99 (1956); Tennessee Elec. Power Co. v. TVA, 306 U.S. 118 (1939). The "standing" issue in "legal wrong" cases really goes to the merits of the claim being asserted, for "standing" is denied or upheld based upon whether the harm complained of is legally cognizable.

Fifth: Closely related to the fourth meaning but distinct from it, is the issue of "standing" raised when *B* seeks to complain of a violation of rights which are said to "belong" to *A*. Mr. Justice Frankfurter termed this the problem of "directness." Joint Anti-Fascist Refugee Comm. v. McGrath, 341 U.S. 123, 153-54 (1951). This fifth notion of standing has been an issue in search and seizure cases, most recently Alderman v. United States, 394 U.S. 165 (1969). In these cases, the Court has held that in a case, United States v. *A*, *A* cannot complain of the admission into evidence of items unlawfully seized from *B*.

All of the foregoing five definitions of "standing" may operate to limit judicial review of illegal searches and seizures, though obviously in different ways. For example, if the Court should decide that a criminal defendant may challenge the admission into evidence against him of *any and all* material seized in violation of the fourth amendment, it might limit the rule to post-indictment motions under FED. R. CIV. P. 41(e), and retain the traditional concept of standing for pre-indictment Rule 41(e) motions. The ground for such a distinction might rest upon principles of "standing" in the sense of "ripeness": a potential defendant, not yet indicted, might be held to be not close enough to being harmed by illegality which did not violate "his" right of privacy. The Court might not, that is, wish to decide the fourth amendment question until it had to. *See* Joint Anti-Fascist Refugee Comm. v. McGrath, 341 U.S. 123, 155 (1951) (Frankfurter, J. concurring).

Another application of the fifth definition of "standing" is Barrows v. Jackson, 346 U.S. 249 (1953). *See also* Pierce v. Society of Sisters, 268 U.S. 510 (1925); NAACP v. Button, 371 U.S. 415 (1963). Other "vicarious assertion" cases are collected and analyzed in Sedler, *Standing to Assert Constitutional Jus Tertii in the Supreme Court*, 71 YALE L.J. 599 (1962), and in the opinions of Justice Frankfurter in Joint Anti-Fascist Refugee Comm. v. McGrath, 341 U.S. 123, 149 (1951). *See also* the opinion of Mr. Justice Jackson which, while it does not extensively discuss legal theory, characteristically takes a workman-like and practical approach to the issues. 341 U.S. at 186-87. *Compare* the opinion of Mr. Justice Black, 341 U.S. at 142, *with* the opinion of Mr. Justice Douglas, 341 U.S. at 174.

[12] There are some lawsuits ripe enough to be cases and controversies, but as to which the Court may nonetheless decline jurisdiction, in order that the parties may have a chance to use nonjudicial means to settle the controversy or in order that the way in which the legal rules in issue will affect the litigants will become clearer. *See, e.g.*, Abbott Labs. v. Gardner, 387 U.S. 136 (1967); note 11 *supra*.

[13] The power summarily to dispose of an appeal is not the power to avoid an adjudication on the merits, at least technically. *Compare* WECHSLER, *supra* note 5, at 4-15, 47 and Gunther, *supra* note 6, at 10-13 *with* BICKEL at 71, 126, 174.

[14] *See* Note, *The Void for Vagueness Doctrine in the Supreme Court*, 109 U. PA. L. REV. 67 (1960). The doctrine is not a device for avoiding constitutional adjudication, of course, for it rests upon the proposition that statutes, to satisfy due process requirements, must provide an ascertainable standard for the conduct of those to whom they are addressed. Many modern applications of the doctrine are in the free speech field, where precision of regulation is necessary to ensure that statutes do not

thority.[15] These last are means of avoiding decision of constitutional issues, not of avoiding decision altogether.

The "political question doctrine," Bickel argues, is rooted both in the Constitution and in considerations of prudence. For its constitutional basis, Bickel accepts Professor Wechsler's formulation:

> I submit that in cases of the kind that I have mentioned, as in others that I do not pause to state, the only proper judgment that may lead to an abstention from decision is that the Constitution has committed the determination of the issue to another agency of government than the courts. Difficult as it may be to make that judgment wisely, whatever factors may be rightly weighed in situations where the answer is not clear, what is involved is in itself an act of constitutional interpretation, to be made and judged by standards that should govern the interpretive process generally. That, I submit, is *toto caelo* different from a broad discretion to abstain or intervene.[16]

But, Bickel argues, there is also a discretionary power, rooted in considerations not of constitutional command but of prudence, to refuse to decide "political questions" when they meet the following test:

> Such is the foundation, in both intellect and instinct, of the political-question doctrine: the Court's sense of lack of capacity, compounded in unequal parts of (a) the strangeness of the issue and its intractability to principled resolution; (b) the sheer momentousness of it, which tends to unbalance judicial judgment; (c) the anxiety, not so much that the judicial judgment will be ignored, as that perhaps it should but will not be; (d) finally ("in a mature democracy"), the inner vulnerability, the self-doubt of an institution which is electorally irresponsible and has no earth to draw strength from.[17]

---

tred upon protected rights. *See* NAACP v. Button, 371 U.S. 415 (1963); Aptheker v. Secretary of State, 378 U.S. 500, 516 (1964).

Bickel's justification for including the doctrine among the reasons for "not doing" is therefore difficult to understand. It has been applied in cases posing deep conflicts between branches and in federal-state cases of some moment. *See* United States v. Robel, 389 U.S. 258 (1967); Cox v. Louisiana, 379 U.S. 536 (1965); Comment, *The University and the Public: The Right of Access by Nonstudents to University Property*, 54 CALIF. L. REV. 132 (1966).

[15] "Delegation" cases are today among the most controversial on the docket. I do not, of course, refer to the old-style cases in which the Court flayed the Congress and Executive for abdication of responsibility and held delegations of power void for being standardless and overbroad. *See* L. JAFFE, JUDICIAL CONTROL OF ADMINISTRATIVE ACTION 41-72 (1965). Since Kent v. Dulles, 357 U.S. 116 (1958), in which the Court held the Secretary of State had no authority to deny passports based on the political affiliations, and Greene v. McElroy, 360 U.S. 474 (1959), in which the Court held that the Department of Defense lacked authority to deny security clearances without a hearing, the Court has asked "has the administrator been given the power he claims?" as a means of avoiding decision of serious constitutional questions. *See, e.g.*, Gutknecht v. United States, 396 U.S. 295 (1970); Schneider v. Smith, 390 U.S. 17 (1968); United States v. Robel, 389 U.S. 258, 269-82 (1967) (Brennan, J. concurring).

[16] WECHSLER, *supra* note 5, at 13-14.

[17] BICKEL at 184.

In order to evaluate Bickel's view of the political question doctrine, one must see it in the context of his lengthy discussion of the "passive virtues." Analysis of Bickel's theory also provides a framework within which to view competing views of the Court's constitutional jurisdiction.

It should be clear that in pursuit of his main theme—the value of devices for not deciding—Bickel has aggregated the most disparate sorts of legal rules and principles, and, as I shall argue, in a way which poses dangers to values which he, in common with many, regards as worthy of protection. I do not speak here of the difficulty in regarding summary dispositions of appeals as a means of not deciding; Professor Gunther has considered this question in detail.[18] Nor do I intend to comment in detail upon the confusion which may spring from including vagueness and delegation rationales as among the passive virtues.[19] Two propositions lie at the heart of Bickel's theory: first, that the Court as an institution is incapable of deciding certain kinds of issues and occupies a position in the constitutional system which counsels it to avoid decision of other issues; second, that the Court may permissibly take refuge in a series of justifications for not deciding which he enumerates and defends. As to the first point, I believe him to have idealized the concept of the frame of government to a level of abstraction leading to conclusions unsupported in the history of the Court and our lawlife. On the second, I think he has propounded a theory of judicial non-review which, if taken by the Court as the basis of its work, will isolate it still further from the forces which make its decisions responsive to democratic values and even from the arguments made by counsel for litigants at its bar.

A.   *The Court as a Counter-Majoritarian Institution*

The Court's role, for Bickel, is defined by its "counter-majoritarian" character, which he deduces from the Court's position in the constitutional scheme.[20] Justices are not popularly elected, they serve for life, are not expressly made responsible to anyone nor any principle save that of "good behavior,"[21] and were surely conceived of by the framers as inclined to check excesses generated by the popular will. The framers' intention is reflected in part in the constitutional basis for judicial review in the service of con-

---

18 *See* note 6 *supra.*
19 *See* notes 14 & 15 *supra.*
20 BICKEL at 16-23.
21 U.S. CONST. art. III, § 1. *See* Chandler v. Judicial Council of the Tenth Circuit, 382 U.S. 1003, 1004-06 (1966) (Black, J., dissenting).

stitutional principle.[22] But if we examine the Court in the performance of the judicial review function, we see that it is no more counter-majoritarian in the nature of things than the Congress and the President are majoritarian in the nature of things. The Court affirms and enforces many constitutional values which are not in the mold that permits it to be described as counter-majoritarian. Now, the "counter-majoritarian" aspect of its duty is no doubt important: free speech, free press, religious liberty, due process, among other values, have all at times been safeguarded by the Court against attack by institutions representing the majority of Americans then qualified to vote.[23] But it is also true that the Court, in tending constitutional principles, upholds values which make majoritarian institutions work, and which prevent them from being subverted and overthrown by the powerful forces which strive to harness state power to their interests. Surely majoritarian principles justify, if they were not the explicit rationale for, the white primary[24] and reapportionment[25] cases, and even a number of free speech cases, in which the free and open debate thought essential to the maintenance of democratic institutions has been safeguarded.[26] Majoritarian principles may even be advanced as plausible and intelligible justification for the representative-seating cases of *Bond v. Floyd*[27] and *Powell v. McCormack*.[28] Yet these cases are among those in which the Court has been criticized, and even by Professor Bickel,[29] for being too venturesome. Granted that in the reapportionment field the lack of judicially-manageable standards may be and has been advanced as a sufficient ground for judicial non-review, but Bickel at any rate has not chosen to take this ground save as subordinate to his main concern with the Court's institutional role.[30]

---

[22] *See* Wechsler, *supra* note 5, at 5-10, and the authorities he cites; HART & WECHSLER, *supra* note 8, at 312-40.

[23] This article is not concerned with whether the "majoritarian" institutions truly do, or ought to, reflect popular will. There is no claim that the country or its institutions are in any absolute sense responsive to the will of the people who are subject to them. *See* Tigar, Book Review, 78 YALE L.J. 892 (1969). A longer essay on this subject, "The Jurisprudence of Insurgency," will appear in the Fall of 1970 in a collection issued by Pantheon and edited by Professor Herman Schwartz.

[24] *E.g.*, Terry v. Adams, 345 U.S. 461 (1953); Smith v. Allwright, 321 U.S. 649 (1944).

[25] *E.g.*, Reynolds v. Sims, 377 U.S. 533 (1964).

[26] *See* New York Times v. Sullivan, 376 U.S. 254 (1964).

[27] 385 U.S. 116 (1966). *Bond* held that the Georgia legislature violated Bond's first amendment rights by refusing him a seat because of his beliefs and utterances.

[28] 395 U.S. 486 (1969). To underscore the point, *Powell* was brought into court by Powell himself and thirteen of his constituents, suing as class representatives under FED. R. CIV. P. 23.

[29] BICKEL at 189-97.

[30] *Id.*

Indeed, one may suggest that the principal difference between most of the judicial activism of the early 1930's and most of the activism of the Warren Court is in the latter Court's assertion of its widest powers of review in precisely those areas in which the democratic process needed the Court's protection in order to survive or come into existence. It is not therefore, permissible to label the court a "counter-majoritarian" institution if by this term is meant that the Court must inevitably uphold, or has usually upheld, antidemocratic principles.

Now it may be objected that I have missed the meaning of "counter-majoritarian," and that it has reference for Bickel not to the values in whose service a particular Court may be, but to the process of decision itself by a group of men who are not accountable in the same sense that legislators and Presidents are accountable. That is, the Court's power has only the Constitution to justify it, while legislators and the President can point to a popular mandate which gives them a legitimacy apart from the constitutional sanction given their powers. Of course, such an assertion would not be strictly accurate, for the nomination and confirmation process, as well as myriad subtle forces of which Professor Bickel is supremely aware, exert pressures from institutions which are, in the constitutional scheme of things, majoritarian.[31] But if Bickel's argument rests upon the premise that the Court is institutionally counter-majoritarian in the constitutional system, there is, in addition, both a formal and a logical objection to it. First, whatever the appellation is intended to denote, it has an undesirable connotative content for Bickel, and his argument is unclear as to whether political philosophy or the framers' intent—or maybe both—counsel the Court to restrain itself. And this is the formal objection: the connotation of "counter-majoritarian" as "in fact" undemocratic is clearly invoked to persuade us of Bickel's view, while the term denotes only the Court's institutional position in the constitutional system and is defended by reasoned argument only to this extent.

The logical objection is this: if the term "counter-majoritarian" refers only in a specific descriptive sense to the Court's institutional role in the separation of powers scheme, then the term has no normative content whatever. It simply tells us a fact about the

---

31 Whether or not Mr. Dooley was right in saying that the Supreme Court reads the election returns, pressure upon the Court from majoritarian institutions has taken and may take the form of proposals (successful and unsuccessful) that Congress limit the Court's jurisdiction, proposals such as FDR's "court-packing" plan, and refusals by responsible executive officials to enforce the Court's commands. *See* Wechsler, *The Courts and the Constitution*, 65 COLUM. L. REV. 1001 (1965); 1 WARREN, *supra* note 8, at 729-79; Kaplan, *Comment*, 64 COLUM. L. REV. 223 (1964).

Court, not analytically different from the fact that there are to be, under article one, two Senators from each State. We cannot deduce from this assertion anything about what the Court *should* do, or what the framers intended that it do. Any argument which attempts to lead from the assertion that the court is "counter-majoritarian" to the assertion that it should decide or refrain from deciding in particular ways must necessarily go beyond consideration of the institutional arrangement of the branches of government to make a normative judgment.

To put the matter differently, any admonitions that Professor Bickel, or Professor Wechsler, or I, may address to the Supreme Court are precatory, in the sense that the Court can decide any case that reaches it and read out a decision which announces any rule of law upon which the Justices decide. Our test for determining which admonitions are wisest, or truest, will customarily be whether they follow logically upon precedent as decided by the Court, whether they have a demonstrable constitutional footing in the text of the document as read in the informing light of history, or whether they follow from premises about democratic government which we state and gain assent to before taking the step of setting out our admonitions.

In sum, I wonder at the utility of the term "counter-majoritarian" as a touchstone for analysis of the Court's proper role. The term has the quality of vagueness and elusiveness which will not yield when one seeks to isolate from it identifiable elements of justification for Professor Bickel's argument. It is rooted in neither history, nor precedent, nor in the article three limitations on the judicial power. Insisted upon as a rationale for non-decision, the spectre of counter-majoritarianism may permit forces outside the Court to turn institutions majoritarian by design into institutions majoritarian in name only. If we are truly seekers after the democratic values conjured by the connotations of majoritarian, we do not need the passive virtues in quite all the splendor and with quite all the breadth in which Professor Bickel offers them. Rather, our precatory admonition to the Court must be an immensely more subtle one resting upon a concern that the power of review which is plainly there be limited in ways which attend the overriding interests of democratic control of institutional decisions and protection of individual liberty against majority or minority incursion. Some of the justifications for not deciding issues or cases will be, in the nature of legal principles, based upon considerations of practical wisdom, some upon textually-demonstrable constitutional rule, and others upon a concern for democratic values.

B. *Can One Be Virtuous Though Passive?*

But what of the virtues themselves, taken one at a time? Are they not reasonable? Certainly as principled bases of non-decision many of them are unexceptionable. What has worried many of Bickel's critics is the assertedly unprincipled way in which Bickel urges that virtue be practiced.

Bickel lists, as I have said, the justifications for not deciding cases or issues. Then there appears this paragraph:

> It follows that there are limits to the occasions on which these doctrines and devices may be used, limits that inhere in their intellectual content and intrinsic significance. Indeed, with the possible exception of what I have called ripeness of the issue, which is merely a catch-all label for a certain order of considerations relating to the merits, none of these techniques totally lacks content of its own, and none is thus always available at will. Even the device of certiorari has some intrinsic meaning and will not be readily usable on all occasions. This is doubly true of the other concepts I have dealt in. Yet one or another of them will generally be available, and there will often be room for choice among two or three, and room certainly for an election whether or not to resort to any. We have had steadily in view the process of election—the elements that enter into a decision to avoid a constitutional issue.[32]

This paragraph has been taken, and not without justification, as a clarion call for abandonment of principled bases of decision.[33] Analyzed by one anxious to find fault, Bickel seems to say that when a majority of the Court feels that it must not or cannot or should not decide a constitutional case, it will in most cases find some one of the passive virtues ready to hand. The practice of the most appropriate or most justifiable passive virtue will then solve the feeling of unease about deciding the hard case. The apparent willingness to permit the passive virtues to become *post hoc* justifications for refusal to decide has aroused Bickel's critics, both because principled decisions are generally to be preferred and because Bickel's implicit defense of cynicism contradicts his insistence elsewhere upon principle.[34]

To the extent that one shares Professor Wechsler's view of the Court's power to refrain from deciding federal constitutional questions, there is a further ground for criticism.[35] Wechsler's position is essentially this: the Constitution has made a choice of the

---

[32] BICKEL at 170.
[33] Gunther, *supra* note 6, at 10.
[34] *Id.* at 12-13.
[35] *See* note 5 *supra.*

limits on the Court's power not to decide. It has determined which hard questions the Court may legitimately duck, and has even provided indisputably and clearly for judicial review in the *Marbury v. Madison* sense. The checks upon this power, including those derived from congressional limitations of the Court's jurisdiction, mark also the limits within which the duty of judicial review must be performed.

Moreover, Bickel, it is shown above, premises much of his argument upon the assertedly "counter-majoritarian" character of the Court. One of the ways in which the Court is counter-majoritarian lies in its insulation from contemporaneous social goals and values hammered out in the democratic process. But a willingness —indeed eagerness—to decide cases upon grounds not stated militates against whatever responsibility may be built into the system by which the Court's members are appointed and live and work. The Court's decisions, or non-decisions, to the extent that they rest upon grounds not articulated, are insulated from public criticism and debate. This debate has an impact upon the Court to an uncertain, though undeniably important, extent.

Further, and particularly in constitutional cases, the Court's willingness to regard abstention from decision as a principle in itself without a clearly-articulated set of reasons for not deciding insulates it from arguments made at its bar by advocates for the persons and interests whose legal rights are in issue. That is, if the Court looks first to ill-defined considerations of appropriateness in deciding whether to decide, and then seizes upon the justification for not deciding which lies most readily at hand, it will become impossible for counsel to argue out in a rational way the reasons why not deciding is or is not appropriate. Arguments about the passive virtues, in certiorari petitions, jurisdictional statements, briefs and oral argument, will become sophistic in the sense that gave Sophists a bad name in Athens:[36] disputation will mask the subject of discussion rather than advance consideration of it.

It is important for the Court to be responsive to advocates at its bar, for with the increasing importance of institutional litigants —the Solicitor General,[37] the American Civil Liberties Union, the NAACP Legal Defense and Education Fund,[38] and so on—in the Court's constitutional caseload, advocates are more than ever rep-

---

[36] B. RUSSELL, A HISTORY OF WESTERN PHILOSOPHY 73-81 (1945).

[37] Werdegar, *The Solicitor General and Administrative Due Process: A Quarter Century of Advocacy*, 36 GEO. WASH. L. REV. 481 (1968).

[38] *See* the Court's acknowledgement of these groups in NAACP v. Button, 371 U.S. 415, 431 (1963). *See* Ginger, *Litigation as a Form of Political Action*, 9 WAYNE STATE L. REV. 453 (1963).

resentative of the public interests served or harmed by differing decisions on constitutional issues, and therefore objectively counter the forces which tend to isolate the Court from democratic values and goals. It will do nothing save nurture legal fictions[39] if decisional rationales, or rationales for avoiding constitutional decision, are transmuted into mere devices to be employed in the service of other values.

The Bickel cosmology of virtue also erodes, because it pays little attention to, the independent and quite important justifications for a number of the "passive virtues," other than the justification for all of them in the large that they promote passivity. The devices which Bickel collects under the name passive virtues have less in common than they have to distinguish themselves from one another, and it may certainly be argued that he does not carry the burden of persuading the reader that they should be regarded as relatively interchangeable.

A final point: Bickel overlooks the differing impact of a decision not to decide upon litigants in different postures: civil plaintiffs, civil defendants, criminal defendants, and habeas corpus petitioners, and by this means obscures the distinction between a decision on the merits and a procedural dismissal. This distinction has, as is argued below, at least as important a consequence as the "declaration of non-unconstitutionality" which Bickel argues persuasively accompanies the rejection of a constitutional claim on the merits.[40]

C. *Another View of the Judicial Power*

It is certainly true that constitutional crisis may be avoided through refusal by the Court to decide constitutional issues. But there are times past in which such a refusal would have carried disastrous consequences, or at least would have undermined the Court's ability to play the role which even Professor Bickel would agree that it must.[41] My reluctance to find a virtue in passivity is illustrated by my reaction to his suggestions that the Court should have ducked the constitutional issues in *Dred Scott* and taken so long in deciding the *Steel Seizure Case* that the parties could work

---

[39] Legal fictions have their uses, of course, in an open, common law system. They are often new legal rules travelling incognito. H. MAINE, ANCIENT LAW (1st ed. 1861).

[40] BICKEL at 130-31.

[41] Given some uncertainty over President Eisenhower's will to enforce judicial commands about integration, see Kaplan, *supra* note 31, at 223, the decision in Cooper v. Aaron, 385 U.S. 1 (1958), is surely such a case. So, too, were Cherokee Nation v. Georgia, 30 U.S. (5 Pet.) 1 (1831), and Marbury v. Madison, 5 U.S. (1 Cranch) 137 (1801). *See generally* 1 WARREN, *supra* note 8.

out a settlement. In both of those cases the appropriateness of the Court's action seems not open to doubt.

Dred Scott[42] arose when forces on either side were gathering for a showdown on the slavery issue. Politicians were choosing positions, orators were exhorting, John Brown was fighting in Kansas, and the conflict between the industrial and agrarian economies was taking the path which was to end in Civil War.[43] In the midst of the struggle, there was the view that the matter might somehow be smoothed over by a Supreme Court decision on slavery.[44] But in retrospect, one can, I think, see that the clash was all but inevitable, and that some basic dislocation of the constitutional structure established in 1789 was necessary to deal with the question of slavery and reallocate national commitments to establish the primacy of free labor. The Court's candid declaration in *Dred Scott* was a signal that if slavery was to be dealt with, it would have to be through the political departments of government, through the amending process, or failing that, in some more violent way. In *Dred Scott* the Court in effect declined an invitation to rewrite the constitutional compact by sanctioning the piecemeal destruction of Southern interests, and refused at the same time to take the unprincipled course of raising hopes that it would do so at some time in the future when the case became riper, or when some other condition was fulfilled that made the passive virtues less virtuous.

In the *Steel Seizure Case*,[45] the Court's intervention stands as proof that in some instances the Court can be sensitive to the problem of governmental illegality so swift to take its toll that only immediate and authoritative judicial action will do any good. Action which comes later is of no use: damages are not adequate (or not available against the sovereign), and an injunction to the responsible official not to do similar conduct in the future is unavailable if the plaintiff cannot show an immediate threat that the challenged conduct will be repeated. A refusal to decide in such a case, or a delay which obviates the need to decide, suggests to the alleged

---

42 Scott v. Sandford, 60 U.S. (19 How.) 393 (1857).

43 *See* W. WILLIAMS, THE CONTOURS OF AMERICAN HISTORY 284-300 (1961); B. DUNHAM, HEROES AND HERETICS 443-50 (1964); A TREASURY OF GREAT REPORTING 139-43 (L. Snyder ed. 1962).

44 2 WARREN, *supra* note 8, at 294-300, recounting Justice Grier's assurance to President Buchanan, which led the latter to predict in his inaugural address that the question of slavery was about to be "finally settled" by the Supreme Court, a reference to *Dred Scott*.

45 Youngstown Sheet & Tube Co. v. Sawyer, 343 U.S. 579 (1952). In these cases, President Truman had ordered the steel mills seized and run by federal troops, invoking a generalized "war power." The Court upheld the mill owners.

offender that the challenged exercise of power is worth the risk again since there is no practical restraint upon it.[46]

Granted that the power-wielder may disregard the Court's admonition in such a case as the *Steel Seizure Case*, but violation of an express judicial command may either provide an occasion for the political process to function by causing public censure of the official, or demonstrate that the political process is ineffective to redeem the constitutional promise of justice and must therefore be changed in fundamental ways.

Dred Scott and the *Steel Seizure Case* are merely examples which raise broad-gauge considerations about constitutional adjudication. What may we say are the relevant criteria in assessing, in general, the Court's obligation to decide a constitutional case?

To begin, I put aside any question about the propriety of constitutional judicial review. There is no need to redo that argument.[47] We come then to a number of identifiable limits on the power, or the duty, or both, to decide. First, there are a group of constitutional and statutory limitations framed with specific reference to the federal courts. The jurisdiction of federal courts is limited by article three to cases and controversies.[48] Thus, the Court must refuse to decide a constitutional issue or other federal question when the claimant lacks a stake in the outcome of the litigation, or the claim lacks maturity to the extent that a judicial opinion would not affect real as opposed to hypothetical and speculative interests. Too, the Court may determine that it has not been given the power to decide the issue—that the power resides elsewhere to formulate the judgment the claimant seeks.[49] There are, in addition, a host of other jurisdictional requirements, some finding express textual support in the constitution[50] and others enacted under the congressional authority over the "inferior federal courts" and over the appellate jurisdiction.[51] The plaintiff in any action bears some

---

[46] Bickel elsewhere shows his sensitivity to this problem in quoting Justice Jackson's warning of the result of validating the power asserted in the Japanese relocation cases. BICKEL at 131, *quoting* Korematsu v. United States, 323 U.S. 214, 242, 245-46 (1944) (dissenting opinion). *See generally* J. TEN BROEK, E. BARNHART & F. MATSON, PREJUDICE, WAR, AND THE CONSTITUTION (1954).

[47] *See* note 5 *supra*.

[48] *See* notes 10-12 *supra*.

[49] *See* text accompanying notes 95-99 *infra*.

[50] *E.g.*, the diversity jurisdiction, U.S. CONST. art. III, § 2. *See* Strawbridge v. Curtiss, 7 U.S. (3 Cranch) 267 (1806).

[51] *See* WECHSLER, *supra* note 5, at 14. The extent of Congress's power to limit the jurisdiction of the federal courts is discussed in HART & WECHSLER, *supra* note 8, at 312-40.

burden to show that factually and legally the prerequisites to jurisdiction are satisfied, and the court must at least go far enough to decide whether it has jurisdiction.[52]

The second source of limitation upon the Court's power lies in the law of remedies and the substantive law which the Court superintends.[53] To take one example, there are some instances in which equity denies an injunction because the matter is simply too complicated for the chancellor to administer.[54] As another instance, the Supreme Court has decided that in a criminal case styled *United States v. A*, *A* cannot complain of the admission into evidence against him of evidence obtained in an unlawful search of *B*, because the harm to *A* is not sufficiently direct or immediate for the remedial law to take notice of.[55] In each of these cases there is nothing in the constitution which forbids a federal court to act. The court could make a new or different rule about the injunctive power, and since it clearly has jurisdiction of the criminal case and *A* is clearly harmed by the governmental conduct in question, there is no constitutional inhibition upon the Court saying that he has "standing."[56]

A third limitation upon the Court's power is the canon of interpretation which counsels against deciding a constitutional issue when the claimant can get all the relief he wants on a nonconstitutional theory. Stated more broadly, the Court seeks the narrowest possible ground on which to decide.[57]

The fourth and final limitation upon the exercise of judicial power is the most controversial.[58] This limitation is the discretionary refusal to decide a case or issue of which the court has jurisdiction and which falls within the substantive and procedural mold of cases in which the law customarily or in the run of cases provides a remedy.[59] Refusal, for want of ripeness or for failure

---

[52] C. Wright, Federal Courts § 16 (1963).

[53] The sources of law which the Court administers are various: the Constitution; laws and treaties of the United States; customary international law, The Paquete Habana, 175 U.S. 677 (1900), Banco Nacional de Cuba v. Sabbatino, 376 U.S. 398 (1964); the admiralty law, Hess v. United States, 361 U.S. 314 (1960); and state law in diversity cases, Erie R.R. v. Tompkins, 304 U.S. 64 (1938). As to *Erie*, see text accompanying note 144 *infra*.

[54] 27 Am. Jur. 2d *Equity* § 106 (1966).

[55] *See* note 11 *supra*.

[56] *Id.*

[57] *See, e.g.*, Kent v. Dulles, 357 U.S. 116 (1958).

[58] The limitation is upon the "exercise" of power, not upon the power itself.

[59] One might include here such doctrines as that the Court will not consider the invalidity of a statute at the insistence of one who has availed himself of its benefits. Ashwander v. TVA, 297 U.S. 288, 345-48 (1936) (Brandeis, J., concurring), and the roundly criticized principle that the Court will not entertain a constitutional challenge

to exhaust administrative remedies, to hear a case, falls into this classification. This final class of discretionary grounds for non-decision is the one whose defensibility traditionalists regard as questionable at best, though for Professor Bickel it is essential to the maintenance of the Court's proper relationship with coordinate branches of government. I suggest, however, that such discretionary devices for decision-avoidance as (nonconstitutional) ripeness,[60] primary jurisdiction,[61] and some applications of the doctrine of exhaustion of administrative remedies,[62] are entirely defensible as a matter of both prudence and constitutional principle. Disagreement with this view rests, I think, upon an uncritical equation of the power to decide with the duty to decide.

It is one thing, after all, to say that every claimant asserting a federal right has, subject to the constitutionally-exercised power of the Congress over the jurisdiction of article three courts, the right to a federal judicial forum in which to litigate his claim on merits. It is quite another thing to say that whenever a litigant in such a posture presents a claim in a judicial forum that the court must then and there decide it. There is no principled objection that I can see to the Court, for reasons entirely aside from the restrictions on timing of litigation inherent in the general law of remedies, declaring that considerations of federalism or comity, or regard for a coordinate branch of government require that it not now decide the constitutional issue tendered by the claimant. So long as the effect of such a decision is only to require the claimant to exhaust other remedies, or to await a greater danger of harm to his federally-protected right, so long as it is clear that these doctrines are court-made means to serve principled purposes, and so long as it is understood that they may be discarded when other principles require it,[63] there is no retreat from the general principle

---

to a statute at the behest of one whose violation of the statute was covertly fraudulent. Dennis v. United States, 384 U.S. 855, 864-67 (1966).

[60] *See* note 12 *supra*.

[61] *See* L. JAFFE, JUDICIAL CONTROL OF ADMINISTRATIVE ACTION 121-51 (1965).

[62] *See generally* McKart v. United States, 395 U.S. 185 (1969). "Ripeness" denotes the degree of factual and legal development of the principles at stake in the action. "Exhaustion of administrative remedies" denotes a requirement that the litigant aggrieved by governmental action present his claim to some administrative body for determination; if he fails to do so, he may be denied a judicial remedy altogether since the administration avenue that he "ought" to have pursued may be closed. *McKart* contains a discussion of this principle. "Primary jurisdiction" denotes a decision about allocation of initial competences to decide.

[63] When constitutional liberties are at stake, the courts have been quick to cast aside ripeness, exhaustion and primary jurisdiction barriers to decision. *See, e.g.,* Wolff, v. Selective Serv. Local Bd. No. 16, 372 F.2d 817 (2d Cir. 1967); Dombrowski v. Pfister, 380 U.S. 479 (1965). Even the presence of a clearcut statutory interpretation issue may lead the Court to say that, for example, the "exhaustion" requirement should be dispensed with. McKart v. United States, 395 U.S. 185 (1969).

that a federal forum must be generally available for the decision of any federal claim.[64] Retreat from that principle, to iterate, must be sounded by the Congress under its article three powers, or by the Court upon a finding that article three does not reach the claimant's case. The refusal to decide based upon ripeness, or exhaustion, or primary jurisdiction is the deferral of decision, not the abdication of authority to decide. Deferral of decision may, of course, result in never having to decide, for the other forum may resolve the problem or the threatened harm never come to pass.

It should be noted as well that deferral of decision is not possible with respect to cases in all procedural postures. It is difficult to justify in a habeas corpus case, in which the petitioner asserts that he is detained in violation of the Constitution, laws and treaties of the United States, and the custodian must come forward and state the grounds for the detention. For a court to assert, in such a case, that while it has authority, under the Constitution and the statutory grant of habeas jurisdiction, to decide, it will in its discretion refuse to do so, leaving the petitioner in custody, appears justifiable upon no ground of constitutional principle or generally applicable precedent.[65] Similarly, when the claim of federal right is raised in defense of a criminal prosecution in which the impact of refusal is that the claimant is convicted, refusing to decide cannot be justified by resort to any generally applicable principle.[66] More of this in the concluding section.

II. What Is—And Is Not—A Political Question

I have sought thus far to outline a general view of the limitations upon the power and duty of federal courts to decide cases and controversies involving claims of federal right. This discussion provides an introduction to and framework within which to view the following discussion of the "political question" doctrine. The view taken here of the power and duty to decide is, I submit, borne out by a critical analysis of the political question cases decided prior to *Colegrove v. Green*,[67] the reapportionment case undercut by *Baker v. Carr*.[68] The principal defect in political question discus-

---

[64] *See generally* HART & WECHSLER, *supra* note 8, at 312-40. *Compare Ex parte* McCardle, 74 U.S. (7 Wall.) 506 (1868) *with Ex parte* Yerger, 75 U.S. (8 Wall.) 85 (1868). *See also* Oestereich v. Selective Serv. Local Bd. No. 11, 393 U.S. 233, 239 (1968) (Harlan, J., concurring).

[65] *See generally* R. SOKOL, FEDERAL HABEAS CORPUS 1-27, 308-40, 346-47 (1969). *See Ex parte* Yerger, 75 U.S. (8 Wall.) 85 (1869).

[66] *See* notes 172-75 *infra* and accompanying text.

[67] 328 U.S. 549 (1946).

[68] 369 U.S. 186 (1962).

sions in *Colegrove* and after, I shall argue, rests upon an insufficient attention to the detailed principled justifications for judicial refusals to decide issues and cases.

Indeed, the current discussions of the political question doctrine are characterized by either a level of generalization which approaches the meaningless, or a simple enumeration of the "political question cases" without an attempt to analyze their various rationales. The Wechsler formulation of the political question doctrine, quoted in section I of this article, terms a political question one which the Constitution requires to be decided by an organ of government other than the judiciary. This view does not intelligibly account for all the cases, though it comes closest of any current definition to having a foundation in constitutional principle. Bickel defines the political question doctrine, in the passage quoted in section I, in terms of the Court's sense of unease at straying into the decision of difficult and delicate questions involving the separation of powers and requiring "political" expertise or sensitivity to make an intelligent decision. Bickel's view is perhaps a direct descendant of Justice Frankfurter's dictum in *Colegrove v. Green* that "[c]ourts ought not to enter this political thicket."[69]

Another important contemporary statement is that of Justice Brennan in *Baker v. Carr*, a statement the more significant because it concluded with the holding that reapportionment of state legislatures is not a political question:

> It is apparent that several formulations which vary slightly according to the settings in which the questions arise, may describe a political question, although each has one or more elements which identify it as essentially a function of the separation of powers. Prominent on the surface of any case held to involve a political question is found a textually demonstrable constitutional commitment of the issue to a coordinate political department; or a lack of judicially discoverable and manageable standards for resolving it; or the impossibility of deciding without an initial policy determination of a kind clearly for nonjudicial discretion; or the impossibility of a court's undertaking independent resolution without expressing lack of the respect due coordinate branches of government; or an unusual need

---

[69] Colegrove v. Green, 328 U.S. 549, 556 (1946). To the extent that Frankfurter's *Colegrove* opinion held that the political question doctrine was one of federalism rather than of separation of the powers of the three constitutional limbs of government, his view was rejected in Baker v. Carr, 369 U.S. at 210. This rejection was proper, as the discussion below will show. Turning to Frankfurter's discussion of the political question cases in *Colegrove*, his short summary of a few leading cases, 328 U.S. at 556, describes the political question as foreclosing judicial inquiry into decisions committed finally to other branches. There is no hint that this determination is to rest on other than careful analysis of the constitutional provisions invoked as a barrier to decision. *See* text accompanying notes 78-114 *infra*.

for unquestioning adherence to a political decision already made; or the potentiality of embarrassment from multifarious pronouncements by various departments on one question.[70]

Justice Brennan also attacked the question from a different direction by enumerating the fields in which the doctrine had been applied: foreign relations,[71] status of Indian tribes,[72] dates of duration of hostilities,[73] validity of certain legislative acts,[74] and republican form of government cases.[75]

The Brennan formulation may at first sight seem the most reasonable, for it at least seeks to classify the cases in which nondecision is appropriate, and to enumerate in detail the elements of a decision not to decide. However, comfort drawn from the *Baker v. Carr* formulation is short-lived when one sees that presence of any element justifying non-decision, or the determination that a case is in a field in which non-decision is appropriate, is a necessary but not a sufficient condition precedent to refusing decision. The lengthy list of elements and "fields" of non-decision ultimately advances analysis no more than Bickel's or Justice Frankfurter's shorter, more suggestive definitions. One is still left with an ill-defined, discretionarily-applied "barrier" to decision.[76]

All of these definitions, it seems to me, rest upon a mistaken legal and historical premise. I say this not because of the simple fact that courts, having the power to decide whether they have the power to decide, are the arbiters of the limits upon this doctrine.[77] Rather, attention to the doctrine's history reveals that it is—in the full-blown terms in which Justices Brennan and Frankfurter and Professor Bickel set it out—a recent invention based upon a misreading or distortion of the early "political question" cases. Surely this failure to take account of its early definition and meaning is important in assessing whether the doctrine has any basis in article three, and surely the acute and repeatedly challenged sense of the proper spheres of the branches of government expressed by Marshall, Story, Taney and their contemporaries should have some

---

70 369 U.S. at 217.

71 *Id.* at 211-13.

72 *Id.* at 215-17.

73 *Id.* at 213-14.

74 *Id.* at 214-15.

75 *Id.* at 218-26.

76 *Id.* at 214: "the political question barrier falls away."

77 The "power" to decide, to which this article is addressed, might better be termed the "legal capacity" to decide, to distinguish this use of the term "power" from use of the term to signify "might." The Romans had a word for each concept of "power": *potentia* means "might," and *potestas* refers to "legal capacity" or "jurisdiction."

weight in assessing the prudential considerations said to support the maintenance and even expansion of the doctrine. That is, if it can be demonstrated that the political question doctrine has not historically had the role and meaning assigned to it by some justices and some scholars, then one will be left to argue whether there are any prudential or textual constitutional reasons for refusing to decide.

Turning to the early political question cases, we see that they fall into several groups, none involving discretionary refusals to decide, and only one involving a "barrier" to decision in the *Baker v. Carr* sense.

A. *Cases Assessing Generally-Addressed Commands by Co-ordinate Branches*

In *Williams v. Suffolk Ins. Co.*,[78] the plaintiff sued for loss of ship and cargo upon a marine insurance policy issued by the defendant. The defendant claimed that the master of the insured vessel had been negligent, in that he had persisted in taking seals off the Falkland Islands after a demand by the government of Buenos Aires, which claimed jurisdiction over the Falklands, that he refrain from doing so. The President of the United States had repeatedly asserted that the islands were open to vessels of all nations, including the United States, for hunting seals. The Court determined that it would not interfere with the executive's determination. The precise question framed by the circuit court and certified for determination was:

> Whether . . . it is competent for the Circuit Court in this cause, to inquire into and ascertain by other evidence [than that used by the executive in making its determination], the title of said government of Buenos Ayres to the sovereignty of said Falkland Islands; and if such evidence satisfies the Court, to decide against the doctrines and claims set up and supported by the American government . . . .[79]

The Court held that the decision as to which nation or government has sovereignty over an island or country is for the executive branch to make, given its power respecting foreign relations. "The action of the political branches of the government, in a matter that belongs to them, is conclusive."[80]

Ten years earlier, in *Foster v. Neilson*,[81] the plaintiff had sued on an 1804 Spanish land grant. The defendant disputed the title, claim-

---

[78] 38 U.S. (13 Pet.) 415 (1839).
[79] *Id.* at 417.
[80] *Id.* at 420.
[81] 27 U.S. (2 Pet.) 253 (1829).

ing that the territory in question had not been in the Spanish government's domain at the time of the grant. The Court held for the defendant, noting that the United States, through both the executive and legislative branches, had taken the position that all titles purportedly based upon grants like the plaintiff's were at least presumptively void. A commission had been established by the Congress to try out the question in individual cases. The Court upheld the executive and congressional determination.

The principle established in these cases, and others decided in the same period, was carried forward into this century in *Oetjen v. Central Leather Co.*[82] There the dispute was over the ownership of hides confiscated in Mexico by Pancho Villa, acting under a commission from the revolutionary government of General Carranza. The Court upheld the title of the party claiming through the Carranza government, upon the basis that that government had been recognized by the United States. Recognition of a foreign government by the executive branch, the Court held, binds the judicial branch. The legitimacy of the Carranza government having been established, the Court proceeded to uphold the taking of the hides (although it might have cut the inquiry short on this score merely by invoking the act of state doctrine).[83]

These cases, typical of many which speak of political questions in the context of foreign relations, invoke no barrier to decision of the lawsuit before the Court. The Court's decision is no more nor less than an assertion that the Constitution commits to the executive branch the power to recognize foreign governments, and to make a determination of the territorial limits of the sovereignty of the United States and other nations. The statement "this is a political question and the Court will not upset the Executive's determination" is no different analytically from the statement "this is a question arising under the commerce clause and the congressional enactment before us was within the power of Congress to pass." The Court, that is, decides that the President has acted within his powers in making a declaration, based upon the ascertainment of "legislative facts,"[84] and amounting to a "law or rule," in the sense of a "command" which "obliges generally to acts or

---

[82] 246 U.S. 297 (1918).

[83] *Id.* at 303-04. The Court in *Oetjen* spoke expressly of the "act of state" doctrine. *See also* Banco Nacional de Cuba v. Sabbatino, 376 U.S. 398 (1964). The "act of state" doctrine, a principle of federal law derived through analysis of the customary international law which the Court applies under the authority of The Paquete Habana, 175 U.S. 677 (1900), is a principle of recognition of transnational judgments or decrees.

[84] *See generally* 1 K. DAVIS, ADMINISTRATIVE LAW TREATISE §§ 7.02, 7.06 (1958).

forbearances of a class." The Court's decision in each of these cases determined that the law or rule in question was within the legal power of the person making it to make, then formulated an individually-addressed command based upon it. This individually-addressed command, which one might term "occasional or particular" in the sense that it "obliges to a specific act or forbearance, or to acts of forbearance which it determines specifically or individually,"[85] was embodied in the Court's judgment.

As another instance of the same principle, consider the *Chinese Exclusion Case*,[86] in which the Congress had passed a statute which arguably abrogated a treaty with the Emperor of China. The Court said that "[t]he question whether our government is justified in disregarding its engagements with another nation is not one for the determination of the courts,"[87] and its holding amounts to the assertion that the Congress has the constitutional power to abrogate treaties by the process of enacting subsequent legislation.

B. *Cases Involving an Application of the Parol Evidence Rule*

Another species of case is represented by *In re Baiz*,[88] in which the Court held that the petitioner was not entitled to diplomatic immunity from process. The Court said at the conclusion of its opinion:

> Regarding the matter in hand as, in its general nature, one of delicacy and importance, we have not thought it desirable to discuss the suggestions of counsel in relation to the remedy, but have preferred to examine into and pass upon the merits.
>
> We ought to add that while we have not cared to dispose of this case upon the mere absence of technical evidence, we do not assume to sit in judgment upon the decision of the executive in reference to the public character of a person claiming to be a foreign minister, and therefore have the right to accept the certificate of the State Department that a party is or is not a privileged person, and cannot properly be asked to proceed upon argumentative or collateral proof.[89]

Baiz deals with the diplomatic immunity provisions of law now codified at 22 U.S.C. §§ 252-53. These provisions have been often

---

85 The language is that of J. AUSTIN, THE PROVINCE OF JURISPRUDENCE DETERMINED 18-26 (Hart ed. 1954). Austin is here drawing a distinction between "individually-addressed" commands, which are issued (under the American constitutional system) to individuals or readily-identifiable groups by the judiciary or the executive branch, and generally applicable legal rules or principles which are a part of the legislative function. The orthodox distinction between "adjudication" and "rulemaking" in administrative procedure suggests the difference.

86 Chae Chan Ping v. United States, 130 U.S. 581 (1889).

87 *Id.* at 602.

88 135 U.S. 403 (1890).

89 *Id.* at 431-32.

construed, and it is usual to accept State Department certifications concerning the status of a person claiming immunity.[90] To the extent that these certifications are relied upon in the manner approved in *Baiz*, the Court is doing no more than fashioning and applying a rule of evidence. The Court holds only that the certificate of the State Department cannot generally be impeached with parol evidence. This holding rests in part upon "deference" to the executive branch, but also upon considerations of policy identical to those underlying similar parol evidence rules. For example, the verdict of a jury as rendered and recorded in open court is well-nigh conclusive and may not be impeached by parol except in unusual and limited circumstances.[91] The promotion of certainty and the honoring of reliances brought into being by the State Department's practice and, as well, independently justifiable, supports the *Baiz* rule.

In the same vein is *Field v. Clark*.[92] in which the Court refused to go behind the signatures of the Speaker of the House of Representatives and the President of the Senate on a bill, and to consider a claim that the bill as passed by the Congress differed from that enrolled and signed by the President and Speaker. The Court stated that it would reflect a lack of respect for a coequal department if it were not to "accept, as having passed Congress, all bills authenticated" in this manner.[93]

Field v. Clark and *In re Baiz*, though commonly called "political question" cases, do not. therefore. involve a refusal to decide. Moreover, the Court has recognized that deference and not surrender is involved in fashioning rules of evidence when political considerations are at stake. Most clearly in the law of privilege it has said "[j]udicial control over the evidence in a case cannot be abdicated to the caprice of executive officers."[94]

---

[90] The precedents are collected and discussed in Hellenic Lines, Ltd. v. Moore, 345 F.2d 978 (D.C. Cir. 1965). *See also* United States *ex rel*. Casanova v. Fitzpatrick, 214 F. Supp. 425 (S.D.N.Y. 1963). The "evidentiary" character of the certificate is illustrated by Banco de Espana v. Federal Reserve Bank, 28 F. Supp. 958, 972 (S.D.N.Y. 1939), *aff'd*, 114 F.2d 438 (2d Cir. 1940), holding that if the diplomat chooses not to invoke his immunity, for example to testify in a case, he may do so. The question whether the waiver was improper is between him and his government. The immunity, of course, belongs to the government in question, and may be waived by it. *Id*.

[91] 8 J. WIGMORE, EVIDENCE § 2348 (McNaughton rev. ed. 1961).

[92] 143 U.S. 649 (1892).

[93] *Id*. at 672.

[94] United States v. Reynolds, 345 U.S. 1 (1953). *See* 8 J. WIGMORE, EVIDENCE § 2379(g), at 808-10 (McNaughton rev. ed. 1961), noting that in England the decision as to whether the privilege for official information exists is for a political minister, while in this country the decision is the court's. Wigmore approves the

C. *Cases Involving the Constitutional Commitment to Other Agencies of Power to Issue Individually-Addressed Commands*

Another class of what might be termed "political question" cases are those involving a constitutionally-based commitment of the power to issue "occasional or particular" commands to another branch of government than the judiciary. The trial of impeachments by the Senate may be an example,[95] and in *Powell v. McCormack*[96] the respondents earnestly contended that determinations as to the seating of representatives were of such a nature. The issue has arisen in other contexts, however. The Congress is given the power to provide for the governance of the land and naval forces, which may involve giving courts martial and other agencies the power to issue binding commands directed to individuals. The flourishing growth of administrative tribunals vested with such power is similarly an exercise of congressional power which may, it has been argued, permit the Congress to foreclose the judiciary from interfering with agencies thus created. As to military tribunals, the claim of constitutional withdrawal from courts of the power to decide has been faced and resolved in favor of review on habeas corpus, and lately through the injunctive power.[97] And the Court has carefully limited the sphere within which courts martial, rather than article three courts, may issue commands at all.[98] Administrative agencies, even those whose determinations are made "final" by statute, find the Court superintending them with a hint that the Constitution compels judicial review.[99] The operation of "separation of powers" logic in such cases measures the deference given to the determinations of military and administrative bodies, and

---

American rule: "A court which abdicates its inherent function of determining the facts upon which the admissibility of evidence depends ·will furnish to bureaucratic officials too ample opportunities for abusing the privilege. . . . Both principle and policy demand that the determination of the privilege shall be for the court." *See also* Cambell v. Eastland, 307 F.2d 478 (5th Cir. 1962); Zimmerman v. Poindexter, 74 F. Supp. 933 (D. Hawaii 1947). Governmental claims of privilege are routinely overruled when the personal liberty of a litigant is in issue. *See* Alderman v. United States, 394 U.S. 165 (1969); Dennis v. United States, 384 U.S. 855 (1966); Roviaro v. United States, 353 U.S. 53 (1957); United States v. Coplon, 185 F.2d 629 (2d Cir. 1950); Zimmerman v. Poindexter, 74 F. Supp. 933 (D. Hawaii 1947).

95 U.S. CONST. art. I, § 3, cl. 6-7. Since the judgment in such a case would not extend to a restraint upon personal liberty, habeas corpus might not be available.

96 395 U.S. 486 (1969), *discussed in Comments on* Powell v. McCormack 17 U.C.L.A. L. REV. 1 (1969).

97 *See* United States *ex rel.* Creary v. Weeks, 259 U.S. 336 (1922); Comment, *Investigative Procedures in the Military: A Search for Absolutes*, 53 CALIF. L. REV. 878 (1965).

98 O'Callahan v. Parker, 395 U.S. 258 (1969).

99 Estep v. United States, 327 U.S. 114, 119-20 (1946). HART & WECHSLER, *supra* note 8, at 340, interpret *Estep* as saying that "jurisdiction always is jurisdiction only to decide constitutionally."

does not signify a general and discretionary invocation of a barrier to decision. Looking more broadly at the cases in which a constitutional basis is sought for the assertion that the final power to issue individually-addressed commands resides elsewhere than the judiciary, the determination of the constitutional issue thus tendered is made by the Court on a basis applicable not to a class of issues or problems, but on the basis of the legally-demonstrable competence of the non-judicial body. These cases may involve some of the same kinds of separation of powers considerations as do cases such as *Oetjen* or cases such as *Baiz*, but they involve the making of an entirely different sort of determination.

D. *The "Republican Form of Government" Cases: A Hybrid*

The "republican form of government" cases are difficult to explain, particularly in light of Justice Frankfurter's analysis of the guaranty clause in the reapportionment cases.[100] The text should be the starting point for analysis:

> The United States shall guarantee to every State in this Union a Republican Form of Government, and shall protect each of them against Invasion; and on Application of the Legislature, or of the Executive (when the Legislature cannot be convened) against domestic Violence.[101]

One ought, in analyzing the clause, to begin by inquiring what structures and practices of government are uniquely safeguarded by it.[102] Many attributes of the "republican form of government" are safeguarded by provisions of the Bill of Rights applicable to the states, among them the free speech and free press guarantee. The thirteenth, fourteenth and fifteenth amendments, and the Reconstruction legislation in aid of them, contain, as both the *Colegrove* majority and the *Baker v. Carr* majority would have agreed,[103] provisions which are designed to foster and extend republican institutions. When we consider the guaranty clause in isolation from other guarantees of rights bound up with republican institutions, therefore, we address a rather narrow class of cases.[104]

---

[100] Colegrove v. Green, 328 U.S. 549 (1946) (opinion of Frankfurter, J.); Baker v. Carr, 369 U.S. 186, 266 (1962). Frankfurter begins with the broad proposition that guaranty clause cases are nonjusticiable, and argues as well that cases involving "political" as distinct from "personal" rights are not justiciable. The former assertion is discussed in the text below. The latter assertion rests simply upon a judgment as to whether one who claims his vote has been "debased" has been harmed in a way which the law of remedies can notice.

[101] U.S. CONST. art. IV, § 4.

[102] *See* Baker v. Carr,.369 U.S. 186, 241-50 (1962) (Douglas, J., concurring).

[103] Frankfurter impliedly conceded in *Colegrove* that the "white primary" cases were rightly decided. 328 U.S. at 552.

[104] In addition to Justice Douglas's concurring opinion in *Baker*, cited in note 102 *supra, see, e.g.*, Bond v. Floyd, 385 U.S. 116 (1966).

Luther v. Borden[105] was a trespass case, the plaintiff claiming under the rebel government of Rhode Island, and the defendant claiming under the "established" or "charter" government. The plaintiff asserted that the charter government was not "republican" and that the rebels had de facto control of the subject property at the time the cause of action arose. The Court held the question not subject to judicial resolution, and upheld a dismissal of the plaintiff's suit. The Court's opinion rests upon its finding that Congress has the power to decide which government of a state to recognize, and that the "political" department had sole authority to determine whether the guaranty clause was appropriate to be invoked. There is some textual support for the latter assertion in the language of the clause, and the decisions are explicable as holding that the Constitution commits the decision—the issuance or nonissuance of an occasional or particular command—to another branch, at least insofar as the command is thought of as issued to a state or government as an entity. Of course, the command or decision, though so addressed, will almost surely have collateral consequences upon individuals in the state, and as to them will be a generally-addressed command.

True, the Court in *Baker v. Carr* sought to include "lack of criteria by which a court could determine which form of government was republican"[106] among the grounds of decision in *Luther*. There is no textual support in the *Luther* opinion for such an assertion, and "lack of criteria" is, in any event, only another way of saying that the interpretation of the guaranty clause would present a question of first impression.

Georgia v. Stanton,[107] an attempt to invoke the judicial power against reconstruction, failed also, the Court holding that the legislation in question amounted to a judgment that Georgia did not have a republican form of government and required intervention of federal authority to establish one.

None of the cases goes so far as to say that every question arising out of an executive or congressional assertion of power under the guaranty clause is beyond judicial review. If in the course of its action the Executive should imprison some recalcitrant state official, his right to sue in habeas corpus is not drawn into question by any interpretation of the guaranty clause.[108] And the "republi-

---

[105] 48 U.S. (7 How.) 1 (1849).

[106] 369 U.S. at 222. *Compare id.* at n.48.

[107] 73 U.S. (6 Wall.) 50 (1867).

[108] Although the Court yielded to the Congress in *Ex parte* McCardle, 74 U.S. (7 Wall.) 506 (1868), and held that it had validly been deprived of appellate jurisdiction in a habeas corpus case, in *Ex parte* Yerger, 75 U.S. (8 Wall.) 85 (1868) it did not. Indeed, the Court's earlier decision in *Ex parte* Milligan, 71 U.S. (4 Wall.)

can form of government" cases do not, as Justice Douglas has pointed out, foreclose even quite sweeping judicial review of the exercise of executive power when such exercise is claimed to threaten other rights guaranteed by the Federal Constitution, laws and treaties.[109]

There have not been enough "political question" cases under the guaranty clause to permit a conclusion broader than this: the clause uniquely governs a narrow class of cases and the decisions construing the clause hold it to establish both that the political department may issue certain sorts of individually-addressed and certain forms of generally-addressed commands. There is no judicial power to compel the issuance of the generally-addressed command, just as there is no such power to compel the issuance of any other sort of generally-addressed command.[110] And there is no reason to doubt that a decision to invoke the clause is reviewable, although one must concede that the matter is far from settled.

E. *Immunity of the President's Person*

Mississippi v. Johnson,[111] often termed a "political question" case,[112] held that President Andrew Johnson could not be sued. Though the case also involved a "guaranty clause issue," the President's immunity may perhaps be termed a "political question." To make this concession does not admit a generalized judicial power to abstain from deciding certain sorts of issues.

First, the President is not immune from *all* process of any sort, or at least there is quite respectable authority for saying so.[113]

---

2 (1866) affirms as well the Court's power in habeas corpus. *See* HART & WECHSLER *supra* note 8, at 292 n.1.

[109] *See* Justice Douglas's concurring opinion in *Baker*, 369 U.S. at 241-50; note 108 *supra*.

[110] That is, there is no power to compel the Congress to pass a law respecting interstate commerce, although it has power to do so. Had the Congress never legislated in this field, it is difficult to imagine a Court ordering it either to get busy and think about the problem or to pass some particular law at the behest of a particular plaintiff. While it is true that this notion of judicial power rests ultimately upon a hard-to-justify distinction between "misfeasance" and "nonfeasance," there is a sense in which our entire legal system rests upon such a notion. The notion that plaintiffs have the burden of proof, and the extensive case law defining and protecting the "status quo ante" the litigation, are expressive of this concept. *See* Cleary, *Presuming and Pleading: An Essay on Juristic Immaturity*, 12 STAN. L. REV. 5 (1959).

[111] 71 U.S. (4 Wall.) 475 (1866). It is surely not remarkable that a great deal of the political question law was made during and immediately after the Civil War, by a Court constituted as a pro-North institution.

[112] *See, e.g.*, Justice Frankfurter's *Colegrove* opinion, 328 U.S. at 556.

[113] *See* United States v. Burr, 25 F. Cas. 30, 34-35. (C.C.D. Va. 1807). Chief Justice Marshall demolished the claim of the President to a plenary immunity from process. Marshall indicated that the President may be liable to produce documents under subpoena, and to have his deposition taken, although his personal appearance at a trial might be excused due to the burdens of office.

Second, and more important, as to almost any question on which one might wish to sue the President there will generally be some subordinate official who can be reached.[114]

F. The "Modern" View of the Political Question Doctrine

In sum, the "political question doctrine" does not seem to be a doctrine at all, but a group of quite different legal rules and principles, each resting in part upon deference to the political branches of government. Such an assertion, however, while setting forth a characteristic of the political question cases, does not uniquely describe them. The idea of deference to coordinate branches is evident in a number of other contexts as well, such as in assessing the constitutionality of statutes. The general assertion that a political question is one which courts should not decide because they do not wish to enter the "political thicket" is, therefore, meaningless. Its invention, in the perhaps worthy service of integrating a disparate collection of precedent, has served in subsequent cases to becloud the issue which the Court must confront when deciding not to decide. It is no doubt healthy that the doctrine, in the broad form stated by Mr. Justice Frankfurter in *Colegrove v. Green*, has not found a majority willing to press it to the limits suggested by Frankfurter's definition. However, the notion has persisted, despite the results in *Baker v. Carr* and *Powell v. McCormack*, perhaps in part because of the vague and general "test" for political questions set out in those cases, that there is a means for the Court to avoid deciding any case or issue upon the basis of a broad, highly general, and almost entirely discretionary principle of nondecision. This view is of course subject to the same criticisms which may be made of Professor Bickel's apothesis of the passive virtues.

With the above discussion as background, one can see in particular why the Brennan formulation in *Baker v. Carr* represents an unsatisfactory effort to rationalize a collection of disparate precedent. Consider the various elements of the Brennan "test." The first of the stated grounds, "textually demonstrable constitutional commitment,"[115] is in accord with a group of the precedents, although the phrase uncritically lumps together commitments of power

---

[114] *E.g.*, the Attorney General when it is sought to reach some practice of his department, as in Kennedy v. Mendoza-Martinez, 372 U.S. 144 (1963); or the Secretary of State, as in Aptheker v. Secretary of State, 378 U.S. 500 (1964). In a related context, Justice Frankfurter remarked that to approve a legal theory under which no officer of government could be reached with process in a given case would be to approve a "fox-hunting theory of justice that ought to make Bentham's skeleton rattle." United States *ex rel.* Touhy v. Ragen, 340 U.S. 462, 473 (1951) (concurring opinion).

[115] 369 U.S. at 217.

to make individually-addressed and generally-addressed commands. The second, "lack of judicially discoverable and manageable standards,"[116] is not the mark of a political question, but appears to restate the principle of ripeness and the equity principle that the chancellor cannot intervene where the dispute will not permit the entry of a judicially-manageable mandatory decree. The "impossibility of deciding without an initial policy determination of a kind clearly for nonjudicial discretion"[117] rationale is meaningless except as a restatement of the doctrine of "exhaustion of administrative remedies" or ripeness, for it assumes the existence of a nonjudicial body with the power to decide initially and appears to require that that body's decision be obtained in the first instance. The only application of this rationale not analyzable in ripeness or exhaustion terms would be one in which there was no way for the litigant against whom the political question doctrine was invoked to obtain the required preliminary determination. In cases in which "political question" means that some coordinate branch has the power to issue generally-addressed commands, that department usually cannot be compelled to issue such a command. To take another illustration, the State Department, when its view as to recognition of a foreign government or some other question of policy is important, has at times been less than clear about its position.[118] There is no means to compel the Department to come up with a clearer answer, and the courts have solved this question by either trying to guess at the Department's position, or by going on to decide the matter independently, sometimes in clear recognition that waiting for the Department would be futile and a possible departure from the judicial obligation to decide.[119]

Such an instance of the "preliminary decision" rationale elides with the next *Baker* justification for the political question doctrine, "the impossibility of the court's undertaking independent resolution without expressing lack of the respect due coordinate branches of government."[120] Unless this rationalization is designed to express in another way the principle that some commands, general and particular, are left to the coordinate branches of government to be

---

116 *Id.*

117 *Id.*

118 *See* HART & WECHSLER, *supra* note 8, at 196-97, discussing some far-fetched judicial attempts to divine the State Department's intentions. Banco Nacional de Cuba v. Sabbatino, 376 U.S. 398, 420 (1964), & particularly note 19 and the accompanying text, discusses judicial deference to Executive Department determinations in the field of extranational recognition of judgments. *See also* the discussion in Hellenic Lines, Ltd. v. Moore, 345 F.2d 978 (D.C. Cir. 1965).

119 HART & WECHSLER, *supra* note 8, at 196-97.

120 369 U.S. at 217.

framed in final form, it has no support in the cases and provides no definable guide to decision. What conceivably can "lack of respect" mean, as a principle of decision, to a Court which decided *Marbury* or the *Steel Seizure Case*? The criterion "unusual need for adherence to a political decision already made,"[121] to the extent it reflects the cases, speaks to the question of commitment of a decision to another branch.

The final *Baker* test, "the potentiality of embarrassment from multifarious pronouncements by various departments on one question,"[122] has not been used in the older cases as an independent basis for invoking the political question doctrine, but as a spur to finding that the question in issue had been committed to another branch for decision in one of the senses described above. There have, indeed, been cases involving the most delicate questions of foreign relations in which executive action by officers acting within the scope of their duties has been condemned by the Court,[123] and the condemnation made the basis of an occasional or particular command that the damage done by the officers be redressed.[124]

It is appropriate, too, at this point, to note another stated justification for invoking the political question doctrine, first set out in an article by Professor Scharpf[125] and adopted by a distinguished district judge.[126] Scharpf states that "difficulties of access to information"[127] may provide a justification for not deciding. While it is true that "political question" cases, particularly those involving the guaranty clause and foreign relations, involve issues as to which fact-gathering is difficult, this does not at all justify invocation of a barrier to decision. A less drastic remedy will suffice. The difficulties which the adversary system has in reconstructing past events tend, as a review of the cases shows, to be resolved by familiar rules of evidence which fall generally into three categories: allocation of the burden of going forward,[128] allocation of the risk of nonpersuasion,[129] and parol evidence rules.[130] These rules may rest

---

[121] *Id.*

[122] *Id.*

[123] *See, e.g.,* Marbury v. Madison, 5 U.S. (1 Cranch) 137 (1803); The Paquete Habana, 175 U.S. 677 (1900).

[124] The Paquete Habana is an example.

[125] Scharpf, *supra* note 2.

[126] United States v. Sisson, 294 F. Supp. 511, 515, 520 (D. Mass. 1968)

[127] Scharpf, *supra* note 2, at 567.

[128] See the discussion in Alderman v. United States, 394 U.S. 165 (1969), of the defendant's burden of going forward and the government's burden of proof in a case involving unlawful electronic surveillance.

[129] In the field of conflicts of law involving a foreign law the American courts have persisted in applying the absurd rule that the foreign law must be pleaded and proved by the party relying upon it. *See* A. EHRENZWEIG, CONFLICT OF LAWS

in part as we have seen in the discussion of, for example, *In re Baiz*, upon considerations of deference to a "political branch" of government. They may also rest, as does the presumption of regularity[131]—the presumption that an official duty was lawfully performed—upon related reasons of extrinsic policy.[132] They also rest upon an assessment of the probabilities inherent in the situations to which they address themselves: the assumption that an official record is accurate, or that the officer who attests that a certain thing is so is acting within the scope of his authority.[133] But the application of these rules has always been tempered with the understanding that to the extent they are shortcuts to finding the truth in a majority of cases, they may be discarded when they are shown to impede that process.[134] To the extent that these rules reflect considerations of deference to political branches or reflect judgments about other matters of extrinsic policy, they give way in the face of countervailing considerations of individual legal right.

G. *Concluding General Observations*

The foregoing analysis seeks to demonstrate that neither a reading of the "political question" cases themselves, nor an earnest attempt to understand restatements of "political question" law, permits one to say that there is a coherent, single principle which permits or requires non-decision of an identifiable class of cases. We do see that "political question" cases rest in some measure upon

---

§ 127 (1962). Otherwise, the court may assume the foreign law to be the same as the domestic law. While this rule may be ridiculous, the notion that the difficulties of finding out what is the state of affairs in a foreign country (Scharpf's reason for applying the political question doctrine to foreign relations cases) should be resolved by allocating the burden of proof is not. *See* Walton v. Arabian-American Oil Co., 233 F.2d 541 (2d Cir. 1956), *cert. denied*, 352 U.S. 872 (1956).

[130] *See* notes 88-94 *supra* and accompanying text.

[131] The "presumption of regularity" crops up in many contexts to help the government show that official duty was lawfully performed. Selective service cases are filled with discussions of the presumption: *e.g.*, Greer v. United States, 378 F.2d 931, 933 (5th Cir. 1967). For a more general discussion, see my treatment of the problem in SEL. SERV. L. REP., Practice Manual ¶ 2404, at 1148 n.7.

[132] *See* Wigmore's discussion of the parol evidence rule relating to the verdict of a jury, 8 J. WIGMORE, EVIDENCE § 2348 (McNaughton rev. ed. 1961), and the more general discussion of the parol evidence rule in 9 J. WIGMORE, EVIDENCE §§ 2400-78 (3d ed. 1940).

[133] For an application of this assumption, see Fed. R. CIV. P. 44. For a more general discussion of the principle that an official record, taken as a whole, is proof that the things there recorded, and only those, took place, see 5 J. WIGMORE, EVIDENCE § 1633, at 519 (3d ed. 1940).

[134] United States v. Procter & Gamble Co., 174 F. Supp. 233, 237 (D.N.J. 1959): "[T]his presumption or [*sic*] regularity . . . is effective, like other presumptions of fact, only in the absence of evidence to the contrary."

deference to coordinate branches, but we see that other sorts of cases do also. We do not see in the law of political questions an authority to refuse to decide any given issue always, at all times, and by whomever raised. This assertion does not, of course, answer the problem entirely. That there is no general principle of non-decision which meets all the cases to which the wit of judges and ordinary men would seek to apply it does not tend inevitably to the conclusion that there are no cases, or no class of cases, in which non-decision is appropriate. The field of foreign relations is one in which the foregoing analysis may fruitfully be tested, not because such a test will finally determine the worth of the analysis, but because it is a political question arena of some importance.

III. American Military Involvement as a Political Question

None of the authority commonly cited by those who oppose a judicial consideration of American military involvement abroad suggests that there is *no* judicial power respecting foreign relations, or that the view of the United States government upon questions of international law is for the President finally to decide. Rather, the foreign relations-international law cases demonstrate that the judiciary will determine the sphere within which the Executive and the Congress, or the two of them jointly, have authority within the constitutional system, and will defer to competent exercises of that authority to issue both general and particular commands.

To be sure, there are judicial expressions of hesitancy about the power to decide foreign relations issues. Often quoted is a dictum in *Marbury v. Madison:*

> If some acts be examinable, and others not, there must be some rule of law to guide the court in the exercise of its jurisdiction.

> In some instances there may be difficulty in applying the rule to particular cases; but there cannot, it is believed, be much difficulty in laying down the rule.

> By the Constitution of the United States, the President is invested with certain important political powers, in the exercise of which he is to use his own discretion, and is accountable only to his country in his political character, and to his own conscience. To aid him in the performance of these duties, he is authorized to appoint certain officers, who act by his authority and in conformity with his orders.

> In such cases, their acts are his acts; and whatever opinion may be entertained of the manner in which executive discretion may be used, still there exists, and can exist, no power to control that discretion. The subjects are political. They respect the nation, not individual

rights, and being entrusted to the executive, the decision of the executive is conclusive. The application of this remark will be perceived by adverting to the act of congress for establishing the department of foreign affairs. This officer, as his duties were prescribed by that act, is to conform precisely to the will of the President. He is the mere organ by whom that will is communicated. The acts of such an officer, as an officer, can never be examinable by the courts.[135]

A close reading of this statement reveals that it does not purport to exclude all questions of foreign relations from judicial cognizance, but only certain functions of the Secretary of State. The evidentiary privilege for official information—the "executive privilege"[136]—reflects this concern, as do the parol evidence rule cases such as *In re Baiz*, and the deference paid to State Department declarations in other foreign relations contexts. It has been held, along this line, that a spy cannot sue for his wages on a contract to commit espionage;[137] not because the Court will refuse to decide such cases, but because a part of every such contract is an understanding that litigation upon it is at best a breach of good faith. By bringing his suit alleging the contract exists, the plaintiff pleads himself out of court. The President's power respecting foreign relations has also been invoked in cases upholding his power to make an occasional or particular command, even one with great economic consequences, as in the *Curtiss-Wright Export Case*.[138]

These isolated and celebrated cases give a distorted view of the role of the federal courts, particularly the Supreme Court, in fashioning and applying principles of international law in the sphere of American foreign relations. A closer analysis of the cases is required.

To begin, there is an arena in which the judiciary claims complete sway. When neither the Executive nor the Congress has acted, and when the Court finds no commitment of the power to decide in the first instance to either of these branches, it will apply rules of written and customary international law to the settlement of disputes between private persons.[139] These rules may be derived from treaties.[140] They may also be derived from customary interna-

---

[135] 5 U.S. (1 Cranch) 137, 165-66 (1803).

[136] The "executive privilege," "narrowly confined to cases involving the national security," Cambell v. Eastland, 307 F.2d 478 (5th Cir. 1962), is extensively discussed in 8 J. Wigmore, Evidence §§ 2367-79 (McNaughton rev. ed. 1961).

[137] Totten v. United States, 92 U.S. 105 (1875).

[138] United States v. Curtiss-Wright Export Corp., 299 U.S. 304 (1936), contains a sweeping statement of the President's power in the field of foreign relations which is not borne out by the cases and not necessary to the decision in that case.

[139] *See* Banco Nacional de Cuba v. Sabbatino, 376 U.S. 398 (1964).

[140] U.S. Const. art. III, § 2.

tional law.[141] The admiralty jurisdiction involves federal courts in the latter sort of lawmaking.[142] But even without express article three warrant, the Court has concluded that the federal judiciary is empowered to find and apply rules of customary international law in the same way that a common law court finds and applies municipal rules of decision.[143] While considerations of federalism have since *Erie R. R. v. Tompkins*[144] kept the federal courts away from such lawmaking with respect to municipal legal rules, its authority in the international sphere is undoubted. Indeed, the case which *Erie* overruled, *Swift v. Tyson*,[145] rested upon a theoretical foundation which brought that case within the ambit of federal courts' common law power upon the basis of considerations not unlike those whch motivate it in the international law field. *Swift* was a commercial law case, and Justice Story's opinion reflects the view that commercial law was, as it had been since the *praetor peregrinus* of Roman times and until a late date in English legal history, a species of *jus gentium* pertaining to the class of merchants without regard to nationality.[146]

Rules of international law may be applied by the Supreme Court with respect to certain transnational disputes in the formulation of rules concerning recognition of extranational judgments and decrees,[147] and in the formulation of choice of law rules in transnational controversies.[148]

The Court has also not retired from the field when the Executive or Congress claims that the formulation of a general or occasional command with respect to foreign relations is within its competence. It has reached and decided the merits, in the face of a "war power" claim, in the *Japanese Relocation Cases*,[149] and in

---

[141] The Paquete Habana, 175 U.S. 677 (1900).

[142] *See generally* Stolz, *Pleasure Boating and Admiralty: Erie at Sea*, 51 CALIF. L. REV. 661 (1963).

[143] The Paquete Habana, 175 U.S. 677 (1900).

[144] 304 U.S. 64 (1938).

[145] 41 U.S. (16 Pet.) 1 (1842).

[146] *See id.* at 19, for Justice Story's discussion of the international character of the commercial law. It was the reluctance of the common law courts to apply law merchant principles that led to the early expansion of the equity jurisdiction in England and the establishment of commercial courts to serve the class of merchants and traders. *See* T. PLUCKNETT, A CONCISE HISTORY OF THE COMMON LAW, 604-35 (2d ed. 1936). As to the Roman Law, *see* Comment, *Automatic Extinction of Cross-Demands: Compensatio from Rome to California*, 53 CALIF. L. REV. 224, 228 (1965).

[147] Banco Nacional de Cuba v. Sabbatino, 376 U.S. 398 (1964).

[148] *See* A. EHRENZWEIG, PRIVATE INTERNATIONAL LAW § 9 (1967).

[149] Korematsu v. United States, 323 U.S. 214 (1944); Hirabayashi v. United States, 320 U.S. 81 (1943).

the *Steel Seizure Case*,[150] to give two examples. The deference displayed in these cases is just that—deference, not surrender, a deference that is rooted in the notion of separate and equal branches of government and that precedes a decision on the merits as to whether the Constitution gives the Executive the power he claimed to have. Decisions that consider the dangers of the nation speaking with two voices in foreign affairs do not use the language of abdication but of decision that the scheme of separation of powers validates the claim that the Executive has the power to decide which he claims to have.[151]

Consider now the case of American involvement in Indochina. First, it is claimed by opponents of the war that the President has exceeded his constitutional authority in sending vast numbers of American troops to another country to fight without a congressional authorization for him to do so.[152] Interestingly, it is also claimed that the process of conscripting those troops is unlawful,[153] but no one has suggested that the courts do not have the power to decide this issue, or ought not, in the exercise of some presumed discretion, decide it; this though the impact of an adverse decision on the merits of the exercise by the President of his powers would be incalculable.

It is also claimed by opponents of the American involvement in Indochina that our participation involves violation of treaties to which the United States is a party, which define certain acts, whether committed by nations or by individuals, as crimes against international law.[154] Some of these treaties have been interpreted to consider in mitigation, but not in exoneration, that an individual was under orders to do the conduct denounced as criminal.[155]

Third, it is claimed that American participation in Indochina may involve this country in violation of rules of customary international law regulating the conduct of warfare.[156]

One may quickly see that litigation of these issues might pre-

---

[150] Youngstown Sheet & Tube Co. v. Sawyer, 343 U.S. 579 (1952), *discussed in* HART & WECHSLER, *supra* note 8, at 1200-12.

[151] *See* Banco Nacional de Cuba v. Sabbatino, 376 U.S. 398 (1964); Oetjen v. Central Leather Co., 246 U.S. 297 (1918); The Paquete Habana, 175 U.S. 677 (1900).

[152] *See* SEL. SERV. L. REP., Practice Manual ¶ 2329, at 1140 and authorities there cited.

[153] *See* Friedman, *Conscription and the Constitution: The Original Understanding*, 67 MICH. L. REV. 1493 (1969).

[154] *See generally* SEL. SERV. L. REP., Practice Manual ¶¶ 2326-33 at 1138-42. *See also* Mora v. McNamara, 389 U.S. 934 (1967); Mitchell v. United States, 386 U.S. 972 (1967) (Douglas, J., dissenting from denial of certiorari).

[155] *Id.*

[156] *Id.*

sent the following questions: whether government officials or those acting in concert with them are violating international law; whether the United States Government is violating such law; and whether the executive branch has trespassed upon some constitutional obligation which it owes to the people generally. These issues raise in turn procedural difficulties which might stand in the way of a court deciding the merits, as well as the question whether one of the particular political question principles may be invoked as a barrier to judicial decision.

Consider, first, the case of a civil plaintiff seeking a declaratory judgment and injunction against executive officers, and alleging each of the three general grounds mentioned above. While a suit against the President might be barred by doctrines peculiar to the Presidential office, suits against subordinate officers of government would not face the same difficulty. The first issues to be confronted would be those of constitutional standing, ripeness in the constitutional sense and the requisite adversity—the article three requirements. These are not issues peculiar to so-called "political" questions. A court might well decide that the plaintiff lacked standing with respect to his international law claims, both because such claims are arguably properly raised only by nations which are offended by unlawful behavior of other nations,[157] and because to the extent that individuals are affected, those individuals are Indochinese and not Americans. With respect to other international law claims, arising under the "individual responsibility" treaties, the court might well question the plaintiff's standing to sue in the sense that it did not appear that he is being asked to violate international law. The ripeness issue might be raised in the sense that the case lacked sufficient development of the factual and legal basis of the alleged harm to be a "case and controversy."

Again, the court might regard the case as inappropriate for decision upon some nonconstitutional ground, including nonconstitutional ripeness of the kind discussed above, or upon the basis that an injunction would tax the administrative powers of an equity court beyond their wonted limits. Were the plaintiff to overcome these hurdles, he would have the burden of going forward and the risk of non-persuasion and might find it difficult to meet a burden of establishing his case by the required quantum of evidence. There are justifications for insisting upon a heavy burden of proof. And since the executive decisions in question would in the typical injunction or declaratory judgment suit be challenged not as occasional or particular commands but as general decisions of policy,

---

[157] *See* L. Orfield & E. Re, International Law 177-79 (2d ed. 1965).

the deference due judgments about "legislative fact," would be among the considerations called into play by the Executive in defending the case. But, "what if?" What if the Court should find it necessary to find, if it were to inquire about the merits, that the war was somehow "illegal?" It seems to me at that point that the Court cannot upon any principle finding root in the constitutional system of rules evade its obligation to decide.

Cries of dissent from this view may be based upon several grounds. Some viewers of the Court would question the wisdom of the Court arrogating to itself such power, upon general principles similar to those invoked by Professor Bickel. But in considering such complaints, one ought to consider as well the enormous power which the Constitution commits to the executive branch with respect to military and foreign affairs matters, and ask what if any checks the framers could have intended to provide. Patrick Henry expressed concern on this score in the debates on ratification:

> If your American chief be a man of ambition and abilities, how easy is it for him to render himself absolute! The army is in his hands, and if he be a man of address, it will be attached to him, and it will be the subject of long meditation with him to seize the first auspicious moment to accomplish his design; and, sir, will the American spirit solely relieve you when this happens? I would rather infinitely—and I am sure most of this Convention are of the same opinion—have a King, Lords, and Commons, than a government so replete with such insupportable evils. If we make a King, we may prescribe the rules by which he shall rule his people, and interpose such checks as shall prevent him from infringing them; but the President, in the field, at the head of his army, can prescribe the terms on which he shall reign master, so far that it will puzzle any American ever to get his neck from under the galling yoke. I cannot with patience think of this idea. If ever he violates the laws, one of two things will happen: he shall come at the head of his army, to carry everything before him; or he will give bail, or do what Mr. Chief Justice will order him.[158]

There are also those who argue that the Court should not "become involved" because its decision might be disregarded.[159] Would not the judgment of the Court against the war be a confession, they urge, of its own inability to change the course of events to which its decision is addressed? Such worries seem to me ill-conceived, although upon a premise that may evoke dissent from some. Earlier in this article I discussed *Dred Scott*, and concluded that the Court, in deciding that case, fulfilled its duty to chart the limits upon the power of the constitutional compact, and therefore

---

158 *Quoted in* 1 DOCUMENTS OF AMERICAN HISTORY 147 (H. Commager ed. 1944).
159 Bickel so argues.

of the existing system of positive law, to accommodate the growing demand for abolition. There were those, of course, Justice Grier and President Buchanan among them, who believed that *Dred Scott* would set at rest the controversy about slavery. But that to one side, I would contend that *Dred Scott* is a classic case of the Court upholding what the existence of a written constitution necessarily implies: that agencies of government must when pressed give a reason for behaving as they do, and that when the agency of government which is the last resort of the victim of some alleged governmental misconduct has spoken in such terms, the populace is given a choice between abiding by the authoritative decision thus made, or of altering the frame of government to accommodate its demands.

This argument assumes that the Constitution assigns spheres of competence to departments of government and to the electorate. It assumes that the only one of these agencies with the conceded power to act upon the basis of no identifiable principle is the electorate. The alternative amounts, it seems to me, to an insistence upon absolutism. By absolutism, I do not mean the assertion within a particular ambit of the power to make discretionary decisions: such power may be saved from a claim that it is unlimited if the power-wielder recognizes or is made to recognize that his discretion extends only to particular matters committed to him by legal rules which he can identify, or that his discretion as to particular matters may be checked if he passes certain bounds even within that ambit.[160]

The notion that the Constitution establishes these spheres of competence is basic to the notion of a written constitution, representing as it does the crystalizing out of legal rules and principles upon the basis of the social conditions of 1787. This notion is also reflected in the case law of "political questions," which as we have

---

[160] Jaffe, *Standing to Secure Judicial Review: Public Actions*, 74 Harv. L. Rev. 1265, 1303 (1961), states that there are areas of public life which are rule-free, either because of a decision that the actor is better left without a rule to guide him, or that a rule is only one among a number of considerations. Surely what Professor Jaffe means is something like that set out in the sentence above: an area or discretion to make commands, subject to correction for abuse and subject to limitation to ensure the actor keeps within it. It seems to me that while Chicago & Southern Air Lines, Inc. v. Waterman S.S. Corp., 333 U.S. 103 (1948), holding that a Presidential international air route award is not subject to judicial review, is explicable as a case holding that the President is confided with power to make certain types of occasional or particular commands, it is not rightly decided. Better, it seems, to recognize that insofar as the President was exerting his power over foreign relations in his decision, his discretion is unreviewable. But if the foreign relations questions can be shown to be out of the case, then review seems proper.

seen is not unprincipled law but based upon a judicial determination of the powers of the departments of government.

The Court can evade the impact of this argument, it seems to me, only by deciding that the Executive is committed with the final authority to make decisions about war and peace which, at least as they take the form of general commands not addressed to a particular plaintiff—as in our declaratory judgment and injunction case—are not reviewable. This decision, which would follow one line of political question authority, would have some support, although meager, in principle, at least up to the point that the President, for example, said that he had the power to declare war and that Congress had no such power. The last case would be distinguishable as being too clear to permit argument that the President was not misreading the constitutional compact. But in all cases save this one, we would know the limits to which the rule of law will carry us in the conduct of war, and that is a judgment which the article three courts, if we assume away all the principled bases of non-decision discussed above, have the duty to make.

This duty arises from the words of article three itself, which speaks of "cases" and "controversies" within certain limits and raising certain kinds of issues. And if in a given case there be no statutory limit on the Court's jurisdiction, and if there be no demonstrable commitment of the decision to another branch, and if there be no more chance of postponing decision for another day upon some consideration of, say, ripeness, from whence derives the determination not to answer the legal question the plaintiff asks? I do not mean to foreclose the question whether the Constitution commits the decision in such a case to another branch, but only to suggest that the case law of the "political question" doctrine, and the concept of judicial review implicit in *Marbury,* requires that it be answered.

Let me suggest an argument that the decisions concerning the conduct of warfare are not the Executive's alone. The argument rests upon the acknowledged power of the Court to find and apply rules of international law and to probe into questions involving foreign relations when those questions involve considerations of private right. I also suggest that it will turn upon an assessment of the importance, in the constitutional scheme, of some check upon the executive's control of the military, and of the constitutional commitment to the Congress of the power to declare war. At this point, when deciding who should decide, rather than at the point of making up out of whole cloth discretionary principles of non-decision, must the weight of "separation of powers" arguments be measured. It it true that the Framers believed we should speak with one voice on these questions, no matter whose voice that turned out to be? Or is it more likely that the constitutional document is the more honored by the view that the successive consideration by all the councils of the nation should be available?[161] And if the seriousness of these questions has not led the Court to postpone, avoid, or defer decision upon some ground generally applicable to constitutional cases, then, taking it as given by this preliminary "decision to decide" that some concern of private right is inevitably involved, in which a decision one way will adversely affect an interest the law recognizes in the general run of cases, there is evidence that the Court was intended to have the power to delimit the sphere of executive discretion by imposing limits not only as to the matters on which he might decide, but as to the content of the decisions he might make within these bounds.[162] One would, that is, require some more explicit evidence than the document offers of a constitutional commitment of the power to decide in any way whatever before holding that the Court may not inquire into the propriety of executive action. Not only is such evidence lacking, but the cases in which the Court has reached and decided questions of foreign relations, even those involving the "war power," point in the opposite direction. Just as there is no "political question" doctrine in the broad, unprincipled sense urged by some, so there is no "war power" in the sense of a generalized grant of authority to the executive branch. The text of the Constitution, with its detailed description of the powers of the Congress over foreign and military affairs,[163] the Federalist papers, with their discussion of the principles back of this enumeration,[164] and the case law[165] militate against the claim that there is a "war power."

Consider now, as an alternative, the case not of a civil plaintiff, but of a criminal defendant or habeas corpus litigant. What of a selective service registrant who seeks to challenge the legality of the war in which he is conscripted to fight, who refuses induction and thereby makes himself subject to criminal prosecution? And what, in the same breath, of the soldier who refuses an order to get on a ship bound for a war the legality of which he challenges,

---

[161] See SEL. SERV. L. REP., Practice Manual ¶ 2329 at 1140.

[162] See generally WECHSLER, supra note 5, at 4-15; HART & WECHSLER, supra note 8, at 312-40.

[163] I refer here to the detailed breakdown in article one of the war-making and army-raising power given to Congress, and the relatively limited grant of authority to the Executive in article two.

[164] THE FEDERALIST Nos. 24-29 (A. Hamilton).

[165] See, e.g., Youngstown Sheet & Tube Co. v. Sawyer, 343 U.S. 579 (1952).

or who is prosecuted for failure to obey an order to shoot a civilian, and who seeks habeas corpus review of his court martial conviction?

Perhaps in some of these cases non-constitutional ripeness poses an issue whether there is a threat of imminent harm to the claimant. One might question in the case of the registrant whether the prospect of harm at the point of induction is real enough that he can litigate it in his criminal prosecution, or must await litigation over a more direct and immediate order to participate in unlawful activity.[166] And as to the international law rights of the Vietnamese nation and people, one must consider the conventional objection that the claimant cannot assert rights which do not "belong" to him.

But assume away these problems for the moment, and leave aside the obstacles discussed above to resolving the issue in favor of the claimant—burden of proof and so on. To refuse to decide the issue upon the ground that it is a "political question" would require hurdling a number of obstacles to non-decision, designedly placed in the path of courts in deciding cases where liberty is at stake. Two principal questions arise.

To begin, it is true that precedent committing to other agencies the determination of issues which may arise in such cases may be said to stand in the way of decision. The World War II judicial review cases, *Lockerty v. Phillips*[167] and *Yakus v. United States*,[168] are examples. But in these, the Court properly declined jurisdiction because Congress had merely limited the federal forums available to test the legality of executive determinations and to challenge the constitutionality of congressional enactments, and there arose no issue of depriving the litigant of a federal judicial hearing of his constitutional claims. Congress has not created such alternative means, and has not imposed such restrictions upon the cases of which we speak here. And in cases challenging the legality of American military involvement in criminal courts, the reasons for not deciding are even less cogent than in the civil case. That is, the courts cannot, save upon the most convincing demonstration of constitutional imperative, both lend their weight to denial of liberty and at the same moment deny the litigant whose liberty is imperiled the opportunity to litigate all legal issues which stand between him and his freedom. "Jurisdiction," as Professors Hart

---

166 *See* note 12 *supra* and accompanying text.
167 319 U.S. 182 (1943).
168 321 U.S. 414 (1944).

and Wechsler have said, "always is jurisdiction only to decide constitutionally."[169] And if that is so, there is no "discretion" to refuse to decide. That is, once it appears that a federal court has jurisdiction to decide a class of cases, the Constitution forbids foreclosing determination of the merits of such cases.[170]

Pushing in upon the decision about power to decide in a criminal case is the defendant's right to a judicial forum within which to litigate his federal claim.[171] Obtruding upon every habeas corpus case is the historic view that habeas corpus to test custody is the last refuge of liberty denied, and that the custodian must answer to a court as to what basis there is in law for the detention.[172] Does this assertion mean that the court must in a criminal or habeas corpus case, decide the legality of the international involvement which the defendant or petitioner has declined? Not necessarily. This question has arisen before, and it is surprising that courts have not moved easily from earlier analogous decisions into the discussion of review of American military activity. In *United States v. Coplon*,[173] *United States v. Andolschek*,[174] and *Alderman v. United States*,[175] the assertion was made that certain government documents should not be revealed to the defendant, though they were either essential in the preparation of the defense or contained proof of governmental wrongdoing which might, if explored in an adversary hearing, lead to suppression of certain evidence against the accused and perhaps dismissal of the charges. Rather than demand that the evidence be produced, the Court put the government to the option: disclose or dismiss. A similar option is put to the government in cases involving turnover of prior statements of government witnesses under the Jencks Act and, under the Federal Rules of Criminal Procedure, with respect to other failures to make discovery. If, therefore, the claim of presidential power, pressed earnestly in the cited cases, cannot serve to justify a limited exception to the force of the exclusionary rule, one has a difficult time justifying a limitation upon the duty of the Court to consider the legality of a detention by consideration of all the legal rules which are conceded to be operative under the Constitution, laws and treaties of the United States.

---

[169] *See* HART & WECHSLER, *supra* note 8, at 340.

[170] *See* United States v. Klein, 80 U.S. (13 Wall.) 128 (1872).

[171] *See* HART & WECHSLER, *supra* note 8, at 323-25. *See also* United States v. Klintock, 18 U.S. (5 Wheat.) 144 (1820).

[172] *See* notes 65, 108 *supra*.

[173] 185 F.2d 629 (2d Cir. 1950).

[174] 142 F.2d 503 (2d Cir. 1944).

[175] 394 U.S. 165 (1969).

This determination does not necessarily involve the Executive in litigating the validity of its claim to possess lawfully the power it exercises in conducting a war: it says only that so long as the Executive stays out of the federal courts, its "right to be let alone" is perhaps arguable, but when it comes into court it must be bound by the rules fashioned by the judiciary and the Congress for the protection of litigants' rights.

If there is a discretion not to decide, this is it: dismissal of a criminal case when the executive refuses to litigate the validity of its claim of power, and release from custody of a habeas petitioner when the executive resists inquiry into all the provisions of the "Constitution, laws and treaties," which the habeas corpus statute requires be inquired into when custody is challenged.

IV. CONCLUSION

The view of judicial review put forward here is surely not novel. Indeed, one hesitates to enter into a field so well plowed by others. It seems important, though, to combat the notion that non-rules should somehow be synthesized, developed and elaborated by a series of non-decisions leading to a non-law of justification for ignoring the principles of order crystallized out in 1787 and embodied in the Constitution. It seems worthwhile to say that the notion that non-law can be elaborated in this way is of fairly recent origin and not supported by previous authority.

The notion that the President and his advisors have a broad, sweeping and arbitrary power to enforce the laws, or conduct military affairs, in any way they see fit is gaining increasing currency. This notion is aided, abetted and eventually given credence by a generalized and undifferentiated "deference"—which amounts in reality to capitulation—to assertions of executive power. In reality, if one examines the case law and history of judicial review, deference has been a burden-shifting and burden-building device. The litigant with a claim against a coordinate branch must carry the argument, bear the risk of non-persuasion and be able to convince by an appropriate quantum of proof. These rules may also at times be phrased as rules of ripeness or exhaustion, requiring the factual and legal picture to be filled in with considerable detail before the Court commits itself. This is the form which deference may permissibly take. To refer to an absolute refusal to decide, grounded in no explicit constitutional command, as "deference," is to misdescribe what is in fact surrender.

It is all very well, in this connection, to speak of "the people" as the ultimate guardian of principle in such a case, and perhaps to so regard them is appropriate when justifying non-decision of broad-scale affirmative declaratory judgment or injunction suits addressed to large questions of national policy. But "the people"— this same undifferentiated mass—had historically, unmistakably and, at times, militantly insisted that when executive power immediately threatens personal liberty, a judicial remedy must be available.[176] This remedy need not, it has been thought, await the outcome of any election. Far from bespeaking a sensitive regard for a coordinate branch, therefore, judicial abdication in such cases contributes to the erosion of the formal structural guarantees which the Constitution codified. That these guarantees are eroding is evident from many events, and the reasons why have been commented upon. But for the Court to contribute to their erosion is, while understandable, not justifiable in terms of the principles of decision which are the Court's to keep.

---

[176] R. Sokol, Federal Habeas Corpus 3-18 (1969).

The Justiciability of Legal Objections to the American Military Effort in Vietnam

WARREN F. SCHWARTZ

WAYNE McCORMACK

Lawyers, legal scholars,[1] and government officials[2] have acrimoniously debated the legality of the American involvement in Vietnam[3] in a peculiar context in which "legality" is considered without regard to the process of adjudication and enforcement in which the issues may appropriately be decided.[4] The two principal legal objections[5] to

---

[1] References to the voluminous body of writing on the legal issues raised by military action in Vietnam are collected in R. HULL & J. NOVOGROD, LAW AND VIETNAM 193-206 (1967); Robertson, *The Debate Among International Lawyers About the Vietnam War,* 46 TEXAS L. REV. 898 n.1 (1968). Significant recent work includes C. CHAUMONT, A CRITICAL STUDY OF AMERICAN INTERVENTION IN VIETNAM (1968); Velvel, *The War in Vietnam: Unconstitutional, Justiciable and Jurisdictionally Attackable,* 16 KAN. L. REV. 449 (1968); Note, *Congress, the President, and the Power to Commit Forces to Combat,* 81 HARV. L. REV. 1771 (1968) [hereinafter cited as Harvard Note].

[2] Office of the Legal Adviser, U.S. Dep't of State, *The Legality of United States Participation in the Defense of Vietnam,* 54 DEP'T STATE BULL. 474 (1966), reprinted in 75 YALE L.J. 1085 (1966). *See also* note 49 *infra.*

[3] The Lawyers Committee on American Policy Towards Vietnam, composed of both international law scholars and practicing attorneys, makes the most comprehensive attack, finding violations of international, constitutional, and treaty law. *Memorandum of Law of Lawyers Committee on American Policy Towards Vietnam,* 112 CONG. REC. 2666 (1966). LAWYERS COMM. ON AMERICAN POLICY TOWARDS VIETNAM, VIETNAM AND INTERNATIONAL LAW (1967). In addition, scholars such as Richard Falk, William Standard, Quincy Wright, and Lawrence R. Velvel conclude that the present military involvement is illegal in material respects. Falk, *International Law and the United States Role in the Viet Nam War,* 75 YALE L.J. 1122 (1966); Standard, *United States Intervention in Vietnam Is Not Legal,* 52 A.B.A.J. 627 (1966); Wright, *Legal Aspects of the Viet-Nam Situation,* 60 AM. J. INT'L L. 750 (1966); Velvel, *supra* note 1. Professor Wolfgang Friedmann criticizes one article containing a defense of the legality of military action like that advanced as the official governmental justification as an expression of a basic view of international law which "does not permit it to be employed as a restraint on national action where the two clash." Friedmann, *Law and Politics in the Vietnamese War: A Comment,* 61 AM. J. INT'L L. 776, 778 (1967). The debate has occasionally taken on a rather personal tone. *See* Moore, *International Law and the United States Role in Viet Nam: A Reply,* 76 YALE L.J. 1051 (1967) (criticizing Falk, *supra*); Falk, *International Law and the United States Role in Viet Nam: A Response to Professor Moore,* 76 YALE L.J. 1095 (1967). Professor David Robertson has recently registered his distress over the quality of this debate, particularly with respect to the practice of both sides in mischaracterizing the other's position and in selective use of the available facts. Robertson, *supra* note 1. Some analysts have candidly admitted that they find it impossible to debate the subject dispassionately, because of "a certain sanity of the heart which may well accompany the sciences of international relations and law." C. CHAUMONT, *supra* note 1, at 5. There is a rejection of the "traditional emphasis on morally neutral research." Velvel, *supra* note 1, at 1. Whatever the motivation, the gravity of the charges and the seriousness with which they are pressed are what concern us here.

[4] Velvel, *supra* note 1, is the first treatment of the issues of justiciability in domestic litigation. The article considers the "declaration of war" objection and concludes that the issues posed are justiciable.

[5] Other claims of illegality which do not bear directly on the validity of the present effort have been asserted. The most serious of these is that the United States violated the Geneva Accords of 1954 by supporting the Diem regime in its refusal to engage in

America's Vietnam involvement are: (1) The United States has violated its treaty obligations and applicable norms of international law,[6] and (2) The President has exceeded his constitutional powers by committing American troops to a war in Vietnam without the requisite declaration of war by Congress.

The first asserted objection to the American involvement in Vietnam is based on the actions of the United States in (1) becoming a party to various nonaggression pacts,[7] (2) adopting and reaffirming these pacts and the principles embodied in them as controlling individual conduct as a matter of international law—even if an individual is acting under a contrary mandate of domestic law—by signing the Agreement of London governing the trial of Nazi war criminals,[8] and (3) becoming

consultation concerning, or to participate in, the elections designed to unify Vietnam contemplated by the Accords, and by providing military assistance to and entering into a military alliance with the Diem regime. *Compare, e.g.,* LAWYERS COMM. ON AMERICAN POLICY TOWARDS VIETNAM, VIETNAM AND INTERNATIONAL LAW 43-52 (1967) (urging violation) [hereinafter cited as LAWYERS COMM.] *with* McDougal, Moore & Underwood, *The Lawfulness of United States Assistance to the Republic of Vietnam,* 112 CONG. REC. 14,943, 14,956-60 (daily ed. July 14, 1966) (finding no violation and support for subsequent American military support of the South Vietnamese government) *and* R. HULL & J. NOVOGROD, *supra* note 1, at 37-51 (concluding that by reason of the ambiguity of the Accords, the uncertainty of permissible responses to alleged breaches by an opposing party, and the limited purpose of the Accords, they cannot "by themselves . . . be dispositive of the legal issues arising out of the Vietnam conflict." *Id.* at 50).

The Accords may be important, however, if they support the conclusion that Vietnam is to be viewed as a single country for purposes of determining the lawfulness of American military intervention. If the Accords created one independent nation, divided into two zones for the express purpose of facilitating elections for the entire country, it is urged that American intervention in a civil war is illegal. *E.g.,* Standard, *supra* note 3, at 630; *Memorandum of Law of Lawyers Committee on American Policy Towards Vietnam, supra* note 3, at 2669. Most observers have now come to the conclusion that the effect of the Geneva Accords, whatever their intent, was to establish two de facto states, at least for purposes of determining the right of the United States to assist South Vietnam in defending itself from an attack originating in North Vietnam. R. HULL & J. NOVOGROD, *supra* note 1, at 51. *See* Moore, *The Lawfulness of Military Assistance to the Republic of Viet-Nam,* 61 AM. J. INT'L L. 1, 3 (1967).

Objections have also been raised to the methods employed in conducting the war. The objections amount to charges of war crimes in the bombing of civilian populations, mistreatment of prisoners, use of illegal weapons, and pressing civilians into service. Brief for Appellant (accused) at 174-86, United States v. Levy, CM 416463 (B.O.R. No. 2 1968); CLERGY AND LAYMEN CONCERNED ABOUT VIETNAM, IN THE NAME OF AMERICA (1968).

[6] It is not necessary to treat separately the various allegations concerning international law, since the relevant principles may be derived from the treaty obligations of the United States, most significantly the United Nations Charter. If there were no such treaties, and international law based on common understanding and practice alone had to be applied, this might be a relevant factor in deciding which of the issues posed are "political questions."

[7] Pan-American Conference, 49 Stat. 3363 (1933), T.S. No. 906; Kellog-Briand Pact, 46 Stat. 2343 (1928), T.S. No. 796; Hague Conventions, 36 Stat. 2199 (1907), T.S. No. 536, 32 Stat. 1779 (1899), T.S. No. 392.

[8] Agreement of London, 59 Stat. 1544 (1945), E.A.S. No. 472; Judgment & Sentences of the International Military Tribunal at Nuremburg (Gov't Printing Office 1947), reprinted in 41 AM. J. INT'L L. 172 (1947) and 6 F.R.D. 69 (1946). The Agreement of London was an executive agreement signed by the President in his capacity as commander-in-chief of the armed forces to govern the trial of persons in occupied territories. It does not, therefore, directly control the future conduct of the United States or any of the persons subject

a party to the United Nations Charter.[9] The critics of American involvement in Vietnam urge that the principles derived from these agreements generally proscribe the use of force by the United States and limit this country's right of self-defense to responding proportionately to the use of massive external force against either the United States or an assisted country.[10]

The second asserted objection to the American involvement in Vietnam is based on the constitutional necessity for a congressional declaration of war before the President may engage forces in "war." This argument places heavy reliance on the constitutional history of the grant to Congress of the power "to declare war."[11] It is urged that constitutional history demonstrates that the express purpose of this provision was to prevent a commitment of American troops to a major confrontation with a foreign power by the President unless he has first obtained popular consent manifested in a congressional declaration.[12]

---

to its laws. Article 6 of the Charter of the International Tribunal, incorporated into the Agreement, provided in pertinent part:

> The following acts or any of them, are crimes coming within the jurisdiction of the Tribunal for which there shall be individual responsibility:
>
> (a) Crimes against peace: namely, planning, preparation, initiation or waging of a war of aggression, or a war in violation of international treaties, agreements or assurances . . . .

[9] 59 Stat. 1031 (1945), T.S. No. 993. Article 2(4) provides that: "All members shall refrain in their international relations from the threat or use of force against the territorial integrity or political independence of any state . . . ."

[10] Article 51 of the United Nations Charter provides authorization for the use of force by members of the United Nations. "Nothing in the present Charter shall impair the inherent right of individual or collective self-defense if an armed attack occurs against a Member of the United Nations, until the Security Council has taken the measures necessary to maintain international peace and security." The key word is "armed attack," which is read as indicated in the text by those asserting illegality. They claim that this meaning was contemplated and adopted in article 51 with the understanding that lesser types of aggression must be dealt with through the organs of the United Nations. LAWYERS COMM. 26-31. Those defending the legality of our involvement urge that with the advent of guerrilla wars, in which outside intervention takes the form of covert infiltration, the concept of "armed attack" must be read as permitting assistance to a country subject to aggression of this kind. The word "inherent" provides further complications. It can be read to allow the use of force even without an armed attack.

A second contention, which Professor Robertson may be right in labelling a makeweight, is that article 51 does not permit a member of the United Nations to assist a nonmember, leaving assistance to a nonmember proscribed by the general prohibition of article 2. See LAWYERS COMM. 36-41. But cf. Robertson, supra note 1, at 911.

[11] The original draft of the Constitution, consciously departing from English practice in which the right to wage war was lodged in the Crown, gave Congress the power to "make war." This was changed to "declare war"—in Madison's view so that the President could "repel sudden attacks." It is urged that, in view of this history, with all due regard to the present international security interests of the United States and the need for executive flexibility in using American forces in support of those interests, a military conflict like that in Vietnam is a "war" that the President cannot wage without the requisite congressional authorization. See LAWYERS COMM. 80; Harvard Note 1771, 1773.

[12] It has been urged also that there is some intermediate commitment of forces short of total war when a "declaration of war" is not necessary but when some form of congressional authorization may nevertheless be essential. A similar view is that the "declaration of war" contemplated by article I, § 8 need not be made in terms so long as the broad

We believe that these questions of the legality of the American commitment in Vietnam are worth asking and answering and that there is a priori much to be said for drawing them into our domestic legal process. This is to be preferred to a debate in which the participants can taste the heady wine of charging high government officials with lawlessness (or patriotically defending them against such charges), believing that no real harm will be done since no remedy against their lawlessness is available anyway.

Of course the desire for a judicial resolution of the legal issues presented by the Vietnam war is based on far more than the belief that institutional answers are likely to be better than academic ones formulated outside of the process of adjudication and enforcement. The intense opposition to the Vietnam conflict has manifested itself in a wide range of protest actions, many of them reflecting a profound despair with the adequacy of the judicial and legislative process to deal fairly with the merits of the legal and moral objections raised. If the judiciary, the organ of government most fundamentally committed to the vindication of constitutional principle, decides it cannot play its accustomed role in the Vietnam controversy, our basic institutional alternative to lawlessness is lost.

There are, of course, many good reasons why a court will not decide an issue tendered by a litigant. The threshold requirement of justiciability, a "case or controversy" with an appropriate litigant asserting a grievance to which the court may properly address itself, must be met. Beyond this, overriding considerations, usually subsumed under the "political question" doctrine, may compel abstention even though the issue is otherwise appropriate for judicial determination.

We will consider the justiciability of the legal objections to the American role in Vietnam within the context of a soldier relying on them to obtain an injunction against his forced participation in the fighting in Vietnam. We limit ourselves to this case because it is the most appropriate one for determination. For convenience we shall refer to this action as "the Vietnam case."[13]

One case like the one on which we will focus has arisen. In *Mora v. McNamara*[14] plaintiffs sought an injunction against enforcement of

---

consensual basis contemplated by the Constitution is assured by congressional concurrence in the action taken. Under either of these views, the question then becomes whether the Gulf of Tonkin resolution and subsequent appropriation bills satisfy the constitutional requirement. See McDougal, Moore & Underwood, *supra* note 5, at 14,960-67; R. HULL & J. NOVOGROD, *supra* note 1, at 169-87; Harvard Note 1798-1803; LAWYERS COMM. 79-82; Velvel, *supra* note 1, at 465-66, 472-79.

[13] *See* note 61 *infra.*

[14] 389 U.S. 934 (1967).

military orders directing them to report to a port of embarkation for shipment to Vietnam and a declaratory judgment that the American military effort in Vietnam is illegal. The court of appeals had affirmed a dismissal of the complaint primarily on the ground that the issues presented were "political questions."[15] Certiorari was denied, with Justices Douglas[16] and Stewart filing separate dissenting opinions. The Stewart dissent concluded that:

> These are large and deeply troubling questions. Whether the Court would ultimately reach them depends, of course, upon the resolution of serious preliminary issues of justiciability. We cannot make these problems go away simply by refusing to hear the case of three obscure Army privates. I intimate not even tentative views upon any of these matters, but I think the Court should squarely face them by granting certiorari and setting this case for oral argument.[17]

The purpose of this Article is to consider these "preliminary issues of justiciability."

I. STANDING

If the Vietnam case presents a "standing" issue,[18] it does so because the litigation does not fall within the classic mold of an objection to a statute raised when the program is applied to a litigant whose conduct is the subject of regulation. In the Vietnam case, the objection is not to military service but to the use of force for purposes asserted to be unlawful. Consequently, the litigant's grievance is not with government action improperly directed at him but rather with participation in a program unlawful at its source on grounds of equal applicability to all persons protected by the Constitution.

---

15 Luftig v. McNamara, 373 F.2d 664 (D.C. Cir. 1967), aff'g 252 F. Supp. 819 (D.D.C. 1966). The court also approved the district court's alternative holding that this was a suit against the United States without its consent. 252 F. Supp. at 821. This much-neglected doctrine, which would not in its most extended form apply to constitutional objections, could not provide an adequate ground for dismissal. See Velvel, supra note 1, at 447-48; Jones, Jurisdiction of the Federal Courts to Review the Character of Military Administrative Discharges, 57 COLUM. L. REV. 917, 952 (1957).

16 Justice Douglas earlier dissented from the denial of certiorari in Mitchell v. United States, 386 U.S. 972 (1967). His opinion emphasized the Agreement of London and the Nuremburg trials, indicating that serious questions existed about standing, the availability of the contention as a defense, and the merits of the alleged treaty violations. Id. at 973-74.

17 389 U.S. 934, 935 (1967).

18 Since the court of appeals decided the case on the absence of consent to sue and on "political question" grounds, the opinion could be read as implicitly sustaining plaintiffs' standing. Moreover, the memorandum in opposition submitted by the Solicitor General relied exclusively on these grounds and did not urge that plaintiffs lacked standing. In light of plaintiffs' subsequent court martial for refusal to obey an order to embark for Vietnam, the substantiality of the "standing" issue also appears somewhat doubtful. See note 61 infra.

Although the Court has frequently articulated the need for a concrete individual grievance,[19] it has also recognized the need to grant standing in cases, like the Vietnam case, in which it is simply not possible for any person to have a special grievance raising the legal objections that the Court wishes to consider.[20] Thus, when application of a particular governmental program consists of conferring benefits, as in the recent case of *Flast v. Cohen*,[21] involving federal aid to private religious schools, no appropriate concrete grievance can arise from a discreet application of the program, but nonetheless it may be subject to serious constitutional objections. In this type of case the Court's only alternative to insulating the program from attack is to allow standing to a plaintiff who may have an "inadequately concrete" grievance according to the traditional rubric of the standing doctrine. When confronted with this alternative in *Flast*, the Court opted to allow the taxpayers to sue.[22]

Similarly, in a case in which the objection is to the very existence of a general government program, any given case arising on application could be disposed of on the narrow ground of invalidity as applied. But standing to raise the general constitutional issue has been recognized in challenges to licensing schemes[23] and to overly broad statutes.[24] Again, in these cases the Court, faced with the fact that, of necessity, no particular plaintiff can lay any special claim to the general objection it wishes to adjudicate, has chosen not to immunize the government

---

19 *See, e.g.*, Tileston v. Ullman, 318 U.S. 44 (1943); Frothingham v. Mellon, 262 U.S. 447 (1923).

20 *See, e.g.*, Baker v. Carr, 369 U.S. 186 (1962); Barrows v. Jackson, 346 U.S. 249 (1953); Pierce v. Society of Sisters, 268 U.S. 510 (1925). *See generally Hearings on S. 2097 Before the Subcomm. on Constitutional Rights of the Comm. on the Judiciary*, 89th Cong., 2d Sess. (1966).

21 392 U.S. 83 (1968) *Flast* involved a challenge by a taxpayer to a government spending program that included grants to religious institutions. Application of the program could benefit only recipients, although the money expended was collected by means of taxation. It seems clear that the taxpayer's interest in effective enforcement of the first amendment is only negligibly, if at all, greater than that of any other resident. This is the rationale of Frothingham v. Mellon, 262 U.S. 447 (1923), which was not overruled by the Court. Since the first amendment was designed to protect nontaxpayers and noncitizens as well, the real question of standing is when a "public interest" can be vindicated by a private individual. *See* Jaffe, *The Citizen as Litigant in Public Actions: The Non-Hohfeldian or Ideological Plaintiff*, 116 U. PA. L. REV. 1033 (1968).

22 The Court in *Flast* distinguished Frothingham v. Mellon, 262 U.S. 441 (1923), on the untenable ground that an individual may have no standing to assert the proper allocation of power between the state and federal governments. The rationale that we attribute to the *Flast* case makes the two cases readily distinguishable. In *Frothingham*, the federal appropriations were to be used in approved state programs that would have direct and concrete effect on individual interests. *Id.* at 460. Challenges to congressional power in that case could be considered more suitably with reference to grievances arising from discreet application of the program.

23 *E.g.*, Times Film Corp. v. City of Chicago, 365 U.S. 43 (1961).

24 *E.g.*, Dombrowski v. Pfister, 380 U.S. 479 (1965).

program from attack, but rather has settled for a plaintiff with a substantial enough interest to assure serious litigation of the issues and simply decided for itself how broadly it wished to cast its decision.[25]

Moreover, there have been cases in which a more concrete grievance may arise upon application, but the Court chooses to pass on a general objection. Thus, attack on statutory schemes that have not yet been implemented or applied has been allowed when the additional concreteness will add nothing important and the Court wishes to pass promptly on the legality of the program.[26]

Clearly, in all these cases the Court has recognized that it cannot or it need not frame the issue that it wishes to decide by selecting a plaintiff with a special grievance precisely matching the questions that must be determined.

The soldiers seeking to avoid participation in the Vietnam war do satisfy the criteria functionally required to have standing. They surely meet the threshold requirement of a substantial enough interest to assure a serious presentation of the issues. Their interest in not having their lives put in jeopardy or being faced with the necessity of taking other lives is obviously more substantial than the interests of the *Flast* taxpayers in proper use of their contributions to the national revenues.

Moreover, there can be no more appropriate plaintiff to challenge the war,[27] since—discounting the possibility of suit by a Vietnamese— the most direct objects of the challenged activity cannot be before the Court. In this respect the Vietnam case is much like *Flast*. There, application consisted of conferring a benefit; here, the victims are not potential plaintiffs. Thus in both cases "application" will not yield a suitable plaintiff. Moreover, with respect to standing, the plaintiffs in the Vietnam case are in a much stronger position than the plaintiffs in cases such as *Flast* and *Baker v. Carr*. While, like the *Flast* and *Baker v. Carr* plaintiffs, they are in a sense attempting to vindicate an interest shared with every member of the public, they have suffered a very special and serious consequence of the challenged action.

It is also clear that these are the type of general objections which the Court has often heard in advance of enforcement on motion of a plaintiff with a substantial interest. This is so simply because the issues

---

[25] *See* Bickel, *Foreword: The Passive Virtues, Supreme Court, 1960 Term*, 75 HARV. L. REV. 40, 53 (1961).

[26] Adler v. Board of Educ., 342 U.S. 485 (1952); Carter v. Carter Coal Co., 298 U.S. 238 (1936); *see* Scharpf, *Judicial Review and the Political Question: A Functional Analysis*, 75 YALE L.J. 517, 530-33 (1966).

[27] *See* note 61 *infra*.

are themselves general, and from a functional point of view one plaintiff (assuming the minimum substantiality of interest) is as good as another since he is not really litigating his own special grievance anyway.

The so-called Nuremberg principles, embodied in the Agreement of London, provide further grounds for affording standing with respect to the objection based on treaties and international norms. Under these principles an individual may be held responsible for violations of international law even when his conduct is authorized by domestic law. If a person seeking to avoid service in Vietnam could be subject to individual responsibility under the Agreement of London,[28] he has an additional interest in obtaining a determination of these issues.[29] We realize that the risk of international sanctions, at the moment at least, is entirely theoretical. But even if a soldier is not subject to individual responsibility, the fundamental meaning of Nuremberg remains. If the international legal system is to prevail over national conceptions with respect to the use of force, perhaps a person should not be compelled to serve in support of a military effort contravening international standards. It should be emphasized that we invoke this principle only for the limited purpose of suggesting that our national position at Nuremberg is a factor favoring adjudication of claims that we are violating international norms on the assumption that they have been assimilated into our domestic legal system.

We have dealt with standing as a principled determination of the litigant's ability to raise the issues. We have concluded that there is nothing inhering in the proper functioning of the judicial process that precludes a court from addressing itself to the issues presented in the Vietnam case. Of course, there is a possibility that the court will use "standing" and other procedural grounds as vehicles of discretionary abstention actually based on practical political considerations. We will consider this possibility in the second phase of our discussion of "political questions."

---

28 The standard for imposing criminal responsibility is by no means clear but may require a participation at the policy level. The Tribunal's primary emphasis, however, was on the knowledge and intent of the individual. Wright, *The Law of the Nuremburg Trial*, 41 AM. J. INT'L L. 38, 67 (1947).

29 The effect of such a determination would depend on several subordinate issues. It is not clear, for example, whether a domestic judicial decision holding that the Vietnam involvement is not a "war of aggression" would be followed by an International Tribunal, at least to the extent of exonerating an individual, because the requisite "wilfulness" is removed. Or if a gradual withdrawal is directed, would the interim American fighting lose its character as a "war of aggression"?

II. POLITICAL QUESTIONS

The consequence of labelling an issue a "political question" is that the matter is left to the autonomous determination of the executive and legislative branches of government and presumably to the check of the popular will on those branches. Two related, but basically different, grounds for characterizing an issue as a "political question" have been advanced: (1) Is the substantive question one which, as a matter of principle, should be left to the unlimited discretion of the responsible branch? (for convenience we refer to this as "the constitutional political question"), and (2) Even if the issue is not of this character, should the court nevertheless stay its hand in this particular case because of practical political considerations warranting that neutral principles give way to political accommodation? The second pragmatic determination may be given effect not only by characterizing the issue as a "political question," but also by invoking doctrines of avoidance such as standing, ripeness, and so forth.

The relationship between these two aspects of a judicial decision to abstain is dynamic and complex. A court, uncertain whether it is prepared to characterize an issue as a constitutional political question, may, on "political" grounds in the second sense, try to avoid decision in the hope that the political process will resolve the issue and thus remove the necessity for making the more fundamental judgment. Conceivably, too, in resolving its doubts about whether an issue is a constitutional political question, a court may be influenced by practical political considerations similar to those underlying the avowedly practical political judgment in the second sense.

A. The Constitutional Political Question

In *Baker v. Carr*,[30] the Court described the basis of this aspect of the "political question" doctrine in these terms:

> Deciding whether a matter has in any measure been committed by the Constitution to another branch of government, or whether the action of that branch exceeds whatever authority has been committed, is itself a delicate exercise in constitutional interpretation, and is a responsibility of this Court as ultimate interpreter of the Constitution.

Although there is substantial disagreement whether this deter-

---

[30] 369 U.S. 186, 211 (1962).

mination is controlled exclusively by the Constitution[31] or allows a measure of discretion in marking out the proper role of the judiciary,[32] it is clear that "political question" is merely a label to be applied to an issue after the Court has made its decision that the issue must on principle be left to another branch for autonomous determination.

There is wide agreement that, with respect to the conduct of foreign affairs, courts should leave certain matters to the autonomous judgment of the executive, because those matters must be decided solely on the basis of an ad hoc determination of how the national interest will best be served.[33] Thus, for example, it has been decided that the State Department has the power to grant sovereign immunity without regard to uniform criteria in order to improve relations with a foreign government, and the Department's decision to grant immunity in any particular case is conclusive on the courts.[34] The judicial decision that the State Department power must be plenary is itself a principled resolution of legal issues in which the national interest in free use of the grant of sovereign immunity to further diplomatic objectives is assigned priority over the litigant's interest in obtaining a remedy.

The nature of this determination underscores the crucial difference between disposition of the Vietnam case on the ground of a constitutional political question and avoidance of the case for practical political reasons. To decide that a question is a constitutional political question requires a reasoned conclusion that it ought to be committed to the unfettered determination of a political branch. This decision is, in short, an acknowledged abstention on principle, not an adroit silent avoidance.

Several of the subordinate issues in the Vietnam controversy—such as the executive determinations about the nature of the parties

---

[31] Wechsler, *Toward Neutral Principles of Constitutional Law*, 73 HARV. L. REV. 1, 6 (1959).

[32] Bickel, *supra* note 25, at 51, 76.

[33] These cases are reviewed in Baker v. Carr, 369 U.S. 186, 211-14 (1962). Bickel describes them as "questions . . . held to be political pursuant to a decision on principle that there ought to be discretion free of principled values . . . ." Bickel, *supra* note 25, at 75. Wechsler refers to them as instances in which ". . . the Constitution has committed to another agency of government the autonomous determination of the issue raised . . . ." Wechsler, *supra* note 31, at 7-8. Wechsler refers *inter alia* to H. HART & H. WECHSLER, THE FEDERAL COURTS AND THE FEDERAL SYSTEM 194-95 (1953), in which cases like those referred to in *Baker v. Carr* are discussed with apparent approval.

[34] Chemical Natural Resources, Inc. v. Venezuela, 420 Pa. 134, 215 A.2d 864 (1966), reviews the applicable decisions and concludes that this is the meaning assigned the sovereign immunity doctrine by the Supreme Court. Consequently, the Department's suggestion is to be followed even though the Court believes that it conflicts with the announced policy in the famous Tate Letter, in 26 DEP'T STATE BULL. 984 (1952), that immunity will not be granted with respect to "commercial activities." *But see* RESTATEMENT OF FOREIGN RELATIONS § 72 (1965).

to the conflict, the gravity of the danger presented, and the necessity of taking immediate action—may be constitutional political questions. Resolution of these subordinate issues requires subtle assessments of priority, feasibility, and long-range national goals which perhaps on principle ought to be left to the autonomous judgment of the executive.[35]

Even if these executive determinations are given conclusive weight, the two basic questions in the Vietnam case pose issues that are not constitutional political questions. The claims that (1) the executive exceeded its powers when it undertook the present military involvement without a congressional declaration of war (or other adequate congressional authorization), and (2) that the use of unilateral force violates our treaty obligations, raise questions of the type that have been consistently regarded as justiciable. At least, questions of construction of the provisions of the Constitution and relevant treaties that are asserted to circumscribe the exercise of power by the President cannot be left to his autonomous determination. The Court has repeatedly addressed itself to questions of the proper allocation of power between Congress and the President[36] and the constitutional limits of the President's war powers.[37] The claim that the President has violated limitations on the use of force imposed by treaty would also appear to raise justiciable issues of power allocation under the rationale of those cases.

There is, however, a serious operational problem in defining the limits of the political question doctrine as applied to the two major issues. The difficulty arises from the dynamic relationship between construction and application of a governing standard.[38] The degree to which the normative standards formulated lend importance to subordinate issues of executive judgment will determine the extent to which the ultimate issues are "political" or "nonpolitical." More fac-

---

35 It is not clear that even these judgments will be given conclusive weight in cases touching directly on individual liberty. The World War II Japanese removal and internment cases involved similar executive determinations. The Court accorded great deference to the Executive's discretion but sustained the action only after finding reasonable factual support for the premises on which the exercise of discretion was based. *See* Korematsu v. United States, 323 U.S. 214, 218 (1944); Hirabayashi v. United States, 320 U.S. 81, 93-99 (1943).

36 *See, e.g.,* Youngstown Sheet & Tube Co. v. Sawyer, 343 U.S. 579 (1952); United States v. Belmont, 301 U.S. 324 (1937); The Pocket Veto Case, 279 U.S. 655 (1929); United States v. Guy W. Capps, Inc., 204 F.2d 655 (4th Cir. 1953), *aff'd on other grounds,* 348 U.S. 296 (1955). *See* Scharpf, *supra* note 26, at 542, 585.

37 *See, e.g.,* Youngstown Sheet & Tube Co. v. Sawyer, 343 U.S. 579 (1952); Korematsu v. United States, 323 U.S. 214 (1944); Ex parte Milligan, 71 U.S. (4 Wall.) 2 (1866); The Prize Cases, 67 U.S. (2 Black) 635 (1862); Mitchell v. Harmony, 54 U.S. (13 How.) 113 (1851).

38 The classic exposition of this problem is found in H. HART & A. SACKS, THE LEGAL PROCESS: BASIC PROBLEMS IN THE MAKING AND APPLICATION OF LAW 369-85 (Tentative ed. 1958).

tors, including most critically matters such as the assessment of the dangers presented, the appropriateness of measures taken to meet the dangers, and the priority of long-range foreign policy objectives may become relevant as one moves on a continuum of possible legal standards defining the breadth of presidential discretion. For example, if the Constitution were construed to permit executive commitment of forces in combat with a foreign power only when the executive can show an imminent threat to the physical security of the nation, then no judgment made by the executive with respect to our involvement in Vietnam would be relevant in determining the legality of the action taken and the issue could not be characterized to any degree as a "political question." If, however, the constitutional limitation is construed as vesting a broad discretion in the President to deploy forces to serve "the national interest," then the ultimate issue approaches a constitutional political question.

The objection to the executive action based on the United Nations Charter and earlier nonaggression pacts raises a similar range of issues depending on the construction of the "self-defense" exception to the general proscription of the use of force. Construction of the treaties may vary from a prohibition of assistance by force disproportionate to that provided by another country to the opposing indigenous faction, to a prohibition of assistance by force absent a massive attack across an international boundary, to a prohibition of all unilateral assistance by force to a nonmember of the United Nations. If the latter prohibition is adopted as controlling, the ultimate issue raises no constitutional political question. As more variables that must be contemporaneously assessed and acted upon by the executive are introduced into the normative standard, the ultimate issue approaches a constitutional political question.

Thus the resolution of the two ultimate issues in the Vietnam case requires a judicial choice from among normative standards posing different subordinate issues. Although certain of the subordinate issues may be constitutional political questions, the crucial point cannot be doubted: The choice of criteria to be included in the normative standard is a question for judicial disposition.

There is a further consideration strongly supporting the conclusion that the issues in the Vietnam case are not constitutional political questions. The doctrine has rarely been invoked in cases involving substantial impact on valued personal interests,[39] even in cases in which

---

[39] Scharpf, *supra* note 26, at 542; *see* Reid v. Covert, 354 U.S. 1 (1957). H. HART & H. WECHSLER, *supra* note 33, at 330-35, take violent exception to the cases holding that admis-

there have been substantial grounds for allowing plenary power to the executive.[40] In the Vietnam case the personal stakes could not be higher. The litigants are being directed to place their lives in jeopardy and perhaps even take the lives of others in a conflict they assert to be illegal and immoral.

Thus on the aspect of the "political question" doctrine that involves a principled decision to accord unfettered discretion to a political branch, we conclude that the Court must undertake the analysis we have indicated and thus mark out the proper bounds of decision. We believe, moreover, that this analysis yields the result that the two questions of power to which we have referred pose basic issues which are justiciable.

B. The Practical Decision To Abstain

The question that remains is the proper measure of the Court's discretion to abstain because of practical political considerations. In examining this question, two types of cases must be distinguished. In one the Court abstains because it concludes that in a tolerably short time (sometimes shortened by the goad provided by the Court in abstaining)[41] the political process may resolve the issue and thus make judicial disposition unnecessary. The second type of case is the more difficult one. Here the issue is not whether to abstain to allow the political process to achieve a solution, but rather whether to abstain because the result dictated by constitutional principle is at odds with political action that has deeply committed the nation and that commands widespread popular support.

There are fundamentally conflicting approaches to these problems. Under one view, of which Professor Wechsler is the best known advocate, the Court is under a constitutional obligation to decide the issue so long as "the law of remedies" tenders it as an essential element in a "case or controversy."[42] Under the opposing view, championed most prominently by Professor Bickel, there is no constitutional obligation to decide and a decision to abstain need not be "principled"

---

sion of aliens is a "political question" so that the due process clause is not applicable to the procedures provided by statute.

[40] See, e.g., Greene v. McElroy, 360 U.S. 474 (1959); Kent v. Dulles, 357 U.S. 116 (1958); Korematsu v. United States, 323 U.S. 214 (1944); United States ex rel. French v. Weeks, 259 U.S. 326 (1922). The Court has also heard claims in cases in which the same considerations would have militated for legislative plenary power. Afroyim v. Rusk, 387 U.S. 253 (1967); Kennedy v. Mendoza-Martinez, 372 U.S. 144 (1963).

[41] For Professor Bickel, the "with all deliberate speed" formula followed by denial of certiorari for a reasonable time while the states try to put their racial houses in order, typifies this approach. Bickel, supra note 25, at 50-51.

[42] Wechsler, supra note 31, at 6.

—as it would be if it were pursuant to the avowed doctrine that constitutes the "law of remedies"—but may rest on a practical judgment that it is better to leave the matter to the political branches—at least for the time being.[43]

(1) Abstention To Afford Further Opportunity
for a Political Solution

We believe that, under either view, abstention in the Vietnam case on the ground that further opportunity should be afforded for a political solution is not justified. We examined above the "law of remedies" and concluded that the Vietnam case is an appropriate vehicle for the resolution of these substantive issues.[44] We therefore need not comment further on this question.[45]

Bickel's practical political view of the matter contemplates that a court employ the full range of its techniques of avoidance—ripeness, standing, abstract questions, and the like and, in the case of the Supreme Court, most significantly, its discretion in granting certiorari[46] —whenever it is thought desirable to give "the electoral institutions their head."[47] The purpose of abstention in this conception is to allow more time so that the political process can yield a result that takes due account of applicable principle but assimilates that principle into a practical solution that can command widespread support.

---

[43] Bickel, *supra* note 25, at 51.

[44] A further word should perhaps be said about the requirement of "ripeness." In Professor Scharpf's functional analysis and in most of the cases applying the doctrine, the emphasis is on the concreteness which further implementation will provide. Scharpf, *supra* note 26, at 532; H. HART & H. WECHSLER, *supra* note 33, at 148. In the Vietnam case, as we have indicated, implementation does not aid in framing the issues. In these cases there is, of course, the further possibility that subsequent action, either in the course of implementation or by new legislation, will moot the issue. Professor Bickel focuses on this function of the doctrine. He cites the earlier refusal to review the Connecticut birth control statute in Poe v. Ullman, 367 U.S. 497 (1961), on the ground that the statute had not been enforced, as the classic example. Since the statute was a "dead letter," no real political pressure to test its validity in contemporary circumstances could be exerted. A. BICKEL, THE LEAST DANGEROUS BRANCH 147 (1962). By extension of the Bickel view, it could be urged that the consideration of the Vietnam issues in the political process has not fully matured and that, particularly when impact on the litigant is not certain (for example, in the case of a man ordered to report for induction), further time should be granted before the court intervenes. It is difficult to believe, however, that it could be seriously urged that the "ripeness" ground of avoidance should be applied with respect to a soldier under orders to report for transport to Vietnam.

[45] The "law of remedies" might dictate that these issues not be allowed as defenses in criminal prosecution for refusal to participate in or for obstruction of the Vietnam conflict. See n.61 *infra*.

[46] Cases before the Court on appeal are somewhat inconvenient. Apparently, dismissal "for the want of a substantial federal question" is to operate as the functional equivalent— although admittedly only by doing some disservice to its avowed meaning as a determination on the merits. See Bickel, *supra* note 25, at 126.

[47] *Id.* at 47-51.

Even under such an approach, abstention in the Vietnam case is not warranted. First, there is considerable doubt that the political process can effectively check the President in committing further forces (or certainly in maintaining present levels) when (1) the executive denies Congress any constitutionally mandated role in deciding whether forces will be sent to Vietnam,[48] and when (2) all the vast resources of patriotism and loyalty are at the disposal of the executive *after* he has committed "our boys" to combat.

There is, moreover, an even more fundamental reason why abstention on practical grounds to allow time for a political solution is not justified. It is claimed that the action that is under attack has circumvented the very political process that the framers of the Constitution intended as a check on the President's power to commit American forces to combat. Thus, unless it is established through the courts that Congress has an indispensable role to play, the political branch can never perform its intended function.

This situation, then, is much like the one in *Baker v. Carr*. There the decision in allocating power within the state was, as perhaps is the decision to commit troops to combat, political in the profoundest sense. But it became clear that despite the wide range of reasonable choice that might be open to state legislatures, apportionment was not being carried out under any rational standard but rather was being used simply to perpetuate the existing power structure. It thus became necessary for the Court to impose rationality in order to restore the very integrity of the political process.

Similarly, if, in the Vietnam case, the role of Congress is not once established, the political process will remain permanently impaired. It is about as unlikely that a President will, absent judicial intervention, dilute his power by acknowledging the authority of Congress to control the commitment of troops to combat as it was that the state legislators would have weakened their power base through reapportionment.[49] Thus, as in *Baker v. Carr*, since the political process is itself impaired by the challenged action, there is compelling practical need to restore the effectiveness of the responsible political branch.[50]

---

[48] *See* the statement of Mr. Katzenbach, appearing as an administration witness before the Senate Committee on Foreign Relations, quoted in Mora v. McNamara, 389 U.S. 934, 935-36 (1967).

[49] At least in theory a similar argument exists with respect to the objections based on the United Nations Charter. There, the unilateral action has deprived the Security Council of its international political role in authorizing the use of force. U.N. CHARTER art. 42.

[50] This seems an appropriate place for once more emphasizing that we take no position on the merits of the substantive issues raised.

In sum, then, abstention to afford further opportunity for a political solution is not justified.

(2)   The Practical Decision To Abstain Permanently

The decision to abstain permanently on practical grounds must be distinguished from the decision to abstain on "principle" which we discussed above. Although both have the effect of conferring plenary power, the reasons underlying the respective decisions are fundamentally different. It is true that when a court determines on principle to leave a matter to the unfettered discretion of another branch, the result finds further support in avoiding the practical consequences of a clash between the judiciary and the agency performing the function. *Baker v. Carr* articulates these factors as "the impossibility of a court's undertaking independent resolution without expressing lack of respect due coordinate branches of government; or an unusual need for unquestioning adherence to a political decision already made; or the potentiality of embarrassment from multifarious pronouncements by various departments on one question."[51]

However, as we have indicated, factors of this kind have not been held sufficient to warrant abstention when the issue presented is the basic allocation of power between Congress and the President or the limits of the President's power to act.[52] Moreover, when vital personal interests, such as those involved in the Vietnam controversy, have been at stake, the courts have likewise refused to characterize the issues as "political questions."[53] The Vietnam case falls within the class where the Court has "disregarded considerable functional doubts about its capacity to arrive at realistic and responsible decisions . . ." because it "finds the determination of such issues so central to its function that it is willing to pay a very high price in order to avoid a general delegation of this task to the political or military authorities . . . ."[54] And, of course, *Baker v. Carr*, in which the functional grounds for abstention were very compelling, confirms that the Court will not defer decision on these grounds when there is a real need to vindicate principles allocating power in our constitutional system or protecting the individual in the exercise of political rights.

---

[51] Baker v. Carr, 369 U.S. 186, 217 (1962).

[52] *See* nn.36-37 *supra.*

[53] *See* n.39 *supra.* Professor Scharpf, whose penetrating analysis has been a touchstone for much that is said in this article, describes these as the "normative limitations" on the issues that may be properly called "political questions." Scharpf, *supra* note 26, at 583. They are matters that are too important to be immunized from review or to allow one agency by its own fiat to allocate power to itself.

[54] *Id.* at 584.

It cannot be gainsaid, however, that the Court could abstain, even if a need for decision as strong as that present in earlier cases were present, on the straightforward ground that so unpopular a decision would jeopardize its position in the constitutional system. Here the difference in the Wechsler and Bickel attitudes to the proper bases for abstention manifest themselves—perhaps as critically in method as in result.

The Wechsler view rests on a notion of constitutional compulsion to decide if the "law of remedies" tenders the issue. There is, however, no plain textual command in the Constitution that a "law of remedies" cannot include a factor of institutional security—or essential stability in immunizing from attack actions by the President that have deeply committed the nation to a particular course. And, of course, consistent with the Wechsler view, these factors might conceivably be strong enough to warrant the conclusion that the matter has been committed by the Constitution to the "autonomous determination" of the executive.

What is essential, however, is that under the Wechsler view, these considerations would be put on the line as defensible doctrine. The same result could be reached, under the Bickel view, on practical grounds, by a combination of avoidance by the lower courts (standing, "political questions," ripeness) and denial of certiorari by the Supreme Court, which could thus avoid stating any ground for its abstention. Indeed this is one of the principal aims of the practical use of these devices contemplated by the Bickel view—decision is avoided unless principle can realistically be vindicated.[55]

We know of no controlling authority that requires us to take either view. What is really involved is one's basic conception of the role of law in society. We much prefer the Wechsler view. If people are going to be told to obey the law and go to Vietnam because they may be lawfully commanded to do so, then the directions they are required to honor should be based on reasons that are plainly stated and justified on principle. We regard this as our most significant conclusion. The Court should address itself to the issues we pose with the neutrality, reason, and dispassion that is supposed to mark the judicial process—and make it worthwhile to have courts.

For several reasons, such a decision need not in any event precipitate an intolerable clash with the executive and the popular support that the President's actions command.

---

[55] Bickel, *supra* note 25, at 47-51.

First of all, the Government may win. This is relevant not because the outcome should be anticipated and the issues held justiciable if the Government seems a safe winner. Rather, what must be appreciated is that if the Government prevails, the risks of confrontation will not materialize. If it loses, the decision represents a profound condemnation of governmental action in a case in which all the built-in preferences of the decisional process are at work to sustain the action. Obviously, and quite properly, the Court will construe both operative facts and governing provisions in light of present world realities and the urgent necessity for fast, decisive, and flexible executive action to cope with those realities. Contemporary judgment of the executive will either be accepted or subjected to extremely limited review.[56] Conflict between judiciary and executive will arise only if all these forces tending toward judicial restraint are overcome and the executive action held illegal.

The second factor mitigating the risks of ultimate conflict is that the objection based on the absence of a declaration of war, the one most clearly satisfying the other criteria for justiciability and perhaps presenting the most serious substantive issue, can be readily cured by subsequent congressional action.[57] This action might not have to be a declaration of war,[58] but would have to authorize the involvement in Vietnam in terms explicit enough to satisfy whatever rule the Court lays down. Only if Congress refuses this authorization will the fundamental confrontation occur. Of course, a decision on this question would not be an idle gesture, even if subsequent congressional action moots the particular issue. Congress would be forced to face the matter squarely, and in authorizing what has gone before, it might impose meaningful checks on further escalation by unilateral executive action. Moreover, for future cases, the essential role of Congress would be established.

There is still a third way that the risks of a confrontation might be mitigated. The Court could make a preliminary determination of justiciability, in the sense of sustaining the litigant's standing and rejecting any blanket refusal to decide on "political question" grounds. It could then order reargument indicating the issues in which it was principally interested. Conceivably, confronted with such a decision, the executive might press Congress for a more liberal conscientious

---

[56] The cases involving the internment of persons of Japanese ancestry took such an approach. *See* note 37 *supra*.

[57] The other objections could be cured by Security Council Action under article 42 of the United Nations Charter.

[58] *See* Harvard Note 1798-1805.

objector law[59] extending to people objecting on principle to the Vietnam conflict. Such a law would represent a species of accommodation between the desire to free people from service that they regard as improper participation in wrongful conduct and the desire to avoid a challenge to the legality of the conflict while it still continues. Illegality would admittedly remain untested unless those domestic interests suffering indirect injury from the consequences of the Vietnam effort were granted standing. But the reasons for intervening on behalf of people indirectly affected by the Vietnam conflict are certainly less compelling than those supporting the claims of people asked to participate directly in the conflict. Whether they are nonetheless sufficiently compelling is an issue that would have to be faced only if the cases brought by servicemen seeking to avoid participation in the Vietnam conflict were mooted by enactment of an extended conscientious objector law.[60]

The final method of mitigating an ultimate confrontation is by framing the relief afforded.[61] A determination of illegality need not

---

[59] *See* Hochstadt, *The Right to Exemption from Military Service of Conscientious Objector to a Particular War*, 3 HARV. CIV. LIB.-CIV. RIGHTS L. REV. 1 (1967).

[60] Velvel, *supra* note 1, at 503, reads *Flast* as supporting a taxpayers' suit testing the Vietnam involvement with respect to the "declaration of war" objection.

[61] Indeed, the primary reason for choosing the Mora-type civil plaintiff in the Vietnam case is to allow injunctive relief. The others that have arisen are all criminal prosecutions for failure to comply with legal obligations to participate in the military effort or for proscribed interference with that effort.

There have been several unsuccessful attempts to litigate various of these issues: (1) as a defense to prosecution for failure to report for induction or for civilian work in lieu of military service, United States v. Holmes, 387 F.2d 781 (7th Cir. 1967), cert. denied, 391 U.S. 936 (1968) (related question of draft without declaration of war); United States v. Hogans, 387 F.2d 359 (2d Cir. 1966); Mitchell v. United States, 369 F.2d 323 (2d Cir. 1966), cert. denied, 386 U.S. 972 (1967) (Douglas, J., dissenting); (2) as a defense to prosecution for burning draft cards on the related ground that a draft without declaration of war is unconstitutional, United States v. O'Brien, 391 U.S. 367 (1968) (Douglas, J., dissenting, would have considered the issues); (3) as a defense to counseling draft evasion, United States v. Coffin, Criminal No. 68-1-F (D. Mass., filed Jan. 5, 1968); (4) as a defense to prosecution for destroying draft records, United States v. Berrigan, 283 F. Supp. 336 (D. Md. 1968); (5) as a defense in court martial prosecution for refusal to obey an order to report to Vietnam, United States v. Johnson, 18 U.S.C.M.A. 246, 38 C.M.R. 44 (1967).

In addition, an officer has sought to avoid training combat pilots for service in Vietnam because of his moral objections to our military effort there. Noyd v. McNamara, 378 F.2d 538 (10th Cir. 1967), cert. denied, 389 U.S. 1022 (1967) (Douglas, J., dissenting). A subsequent court martial conviction of this officer for violating a direct order to train pilots for service in Vietnam is now pending on appeal. *See* Comment, *God, the Army, and Judicial Review: The In-Service Conscientious Objector*, 56 CALIF. L. REV. 379 (1968); Morse v. Boswell, N.Y. Times, Oct. 8, 1968, at 74, col. 4.

In these criminal cases, if the defense of illegality were entertained and sustained, then theoretically all persons similarly situated would immediately be freed of further legal obligation. If, however, injunctive relief were granted, account could be taken of the need for a gradual adjustment of governmental action to the requirements of law and the military effort brought to an end "with all deliberate speed." In the meantime, it is possible that no particular individual could avoid participation on the ground that the activity is illegal. The question whether to allow these defenses is, however, by no means an easy one.

require immediate total withdrawal of the American military presence. The Court has often recognized the need to let government officials adjust their conduct to the requirements of law "with all deliberate speed."[62] If indeed the American military involvement in Vietnam makes practical sense, then it ought to be possible to turn over the actual fighting to the South Vietnamese over a reasonable period of time. This is in any event the present avowed direction of American policy.

Again it must be appreciated that this factor of mitigation should not be judged in isolation. It would have to be invoked only after all the other methods of accommodation have failed. If it is therefore assumed that, after taking into account the vital need for broad discretion in the conduct of foreign affairs and giving due deference to the contemporary judgments of the responsible officials, the Court has held that the executive has committed American forces in violation of law and, as to the objection based on the absence of congressional authorization, Congress has refused to validate the executive action, then a result requiring planned long-range withdrawal of American forces appears much less extraordinary.

III. CONCLUSION

We conclude that the Vietnam case is an appropriate vehicle for deciding the legal issues raised. A reasoned delineation of the issues that may properly be characterized as "political questions" must be undertaken. We believe, moreover, that the claims of illegality pose issues concerning the basic power of the executive which are justiciable.

Undoubtedly, considerable, perhaps total, deference to the executive in formulating and implementing premises must be given so long as the range of considerations taken into account fall within the bounds of the executive discretion conferred by law. We cannot escape the

---

Although it is true, as we have indicated, that the injunction action is a better vehicle for decision, the litigants in these criminal cases do have a vital interest to vindicate. Moreover, at least insofar as the "declaration of war" objection is concerned, the possibility of subsequent congressional action supplying the requisite authority does considerably mitigate the practical consequences of a decision sustaining the defense. Finally, these cases have arisen after the failure of the courts to entertain the type of action which would permit a more flexible solution of the problem.

62 Bickel refers to this formula as establishing principles but allowing necessary accommodations of institutions—performing an educational as well as a legitimatizing role.
> Indeed, very often the court engages in a Socratic dialogue with the other institutions and with society as a whole concerning the necessity for this or that measure, for this or that compromise. Is not this the meaning of the deliberate-speed formula itself, which resembles poetry and resembles equity techniques of discretionary accommodation between principle and expediency . . . ?

Bickel, *supra* note 25, at 50.

conclusion, however, that if the executive action, measured by a substantive rule, fashioned in light of the urgent necessities confronting those entrusted with the exercise of the awesome power possessed by the United States, and applied with all of the deference properly afforded to the people who must make the contemporaneous decisions necessary to exercise this power, cannot be squared with the Constitution, then the Court must strike down the unlawful executive action.

What is really at stake is the viability of our constitutional system. Courts must assimilate into doctrine the painful accommodations between expediency and principle that are manifested in cases of great social significance, rather than depend on unspoken ad hoc adjustments. Otherwise, the claim that the rule of law (at least in cases that matter very much) is a rationalization of result rather than a reasoned basis of decision, and therefore entitled to little respect, must be honored. Recent events leave little doubt that there will be ample opportunity to entertain such claims.

IV. SPECIAL QUESTIONS OF INTERNATIONAL LAW

Legitimacy and Legal Rights of Revolutionary Movements with Special Reference to the Peoples' Revolutionary Government of South Viet Nam*

THOMAS M. FRANCK
NIGEL S. RODLEY

INSURGENT MOVEMENTS AND EXTERNAL ASSISTANCE

INTERNATIONAL law is, or tends to become, what states do in practice. In regard to movements for the overthrow of governments, the traditional policy has been a rationalistic one which attempted to maintain status quo regimes and to measure the rights and duties of revolutionary movements by the degree of their success in establishing themselves as the new status quo. Roughly speaking, there were three grades of revolutionary self-fulfillment. In ascending order these were: rebellion, insurrection and belligerency. While rebellions had few rights recognized in international legal practice, revolutionary belligerents at the other end of the spectrum were virtually accorded equal treatment in law with the regimes they were fighting to replace. To establish a state of belligerency certain minimal conditions must be met:

> [F]irst, there must exist within the State an armed conflict of a general (as distinguished from a purely local) character; secondly, the insurgents must occupy and administer a substantial portion of national territory; thirdly, they must conduct the hostilities in accordance with the rules of war and through organized armed forces acting under a responsible authority; fourthly, there must exist circumstances which make it necessary for outside States to define their attitude by means of recognition of belligerency. Recognition of belligerency is in essence a declaration ascertaining the existence of these conditions of fact.[1]

A classic example of a belligerent was the Confederate States of America during the American Civil War.[2] Rebellions, on the

* The authors gratefully acknowledge the assistance of Gary Flack, student, New York University School of Law.

1 H. Lauterpacht, Recognition in International Law 176 (1947).
2 W. Bishop, International Law 339 (2d ed. 1962).

other hand, are relatively localized uprisings which cannot reasonably be expected to overthrow the established authority. The Indian language riots and the East European rebellions against Soviet control like the one in Berlin in 1953 are considered in this class.[3] The Watts and Newark riots in the United States might now be added to the list. The third classification, insurgency, includes all movements that are more general than rebellion but less pervasive than belligerency.

These traditional legal classifications have always suffered from the general malaise of all international legal categories. With the absence of an impartial international judicial system of general recourse, each state applied the categories itself, infusing into the process enough self-interested, deliberate distortion to bring the categories into disrepute as mere polemic devices.[4] However, today this classification system also suffers from something much more serious—it no longer responds either to the needs of good order or to the emerging practice of the international community.

Two principal new factors fundamentally altering the circumstances and practice of civil wars since World War II were identified as long ago as 1963. At that time, long before the Viet Nam escalation, it was noted that civil wars, which had previously been at the periphery of hostile collective behavior, have largely replaced aggression between states as the principal outlet for the war urge.[5] Furthermore, civil wars are no longer merely conflicts between domestic forces within a state; instead they have become limited wars between outside powers, usually the superpowers, using domestic surrogates.[6]

There have, of course, always been civil wars and insurrections fed from abroad. The American Revolution owes its success in some measure to this time-honored practice. The struggle that

---

[3] See R. Falk, International Aspects of Civil Strife 198-99 (J. Rosenau ed. 1964).

[4] Winfield, speaking of Phillimore's treatise on intervention, thought a reader "might close the book with the impression that intervention may be anything from a speech of Lord Palmerston's in the House of Commons to the Partition of Poland." Winfield, The History of Intervention in International Law, 3 Brit. Y.B. Int'l L. 130 (1922-1923).

[5] "Violent encounter of major rivals in world affairs has always been primarily a matter of warfare *between* states; now suddenly it is participation in warfare *within* states." Falk, supra note 3, at 185.

[6] "This congeries of capability, risk, goal, and necessity places great emphasis upon the strategic manipulation of intrastate violence by groupings of nations contending for dominance in the world today. If empire once depended primarily upon the extent of colonial occupation, it now increasingly depends upon the capacity to influence the outcome of important internal wars." Id. at 189.

was waged against Spain by Latin-American insurgent regimes had the benevolent neutrality if not the open support of the United States.[7] Britain and Spain fought a "civil" war in Portugal after the death of King John VI in 1825. That war, as described by a commentator, had a quaintly familiar ring:

> Hostile inroads into the territory of Portugal were concerted in Spain, and executed with the connivance of the Spanish authorities, by Portuguese troops, belonging to the party of the Pretender, who had deserted into Spain, and were received and succored by the Spanish authorities on the frontiers. Under these circumstances, the British government received an application from the regency of Portugal, claiming, in virtue of the ancient treaties of alliance and friendship subsisting between the two crowns, the military aid of Great Britain against the hostile aggression of Spain. In acceding to that application, and sending a corps of British troops for the defence of Portugal, it was stated by the British minister that . . . . They went to Portugal in the discharge of a sacred obligation, contracted under ancient and modern treaties. When there, nothing would be done by them to enforce the establishment of the constitution; but they must take care that nothing was done by others to prevent it from being fairly carried into effect. . . . [I]nterference on behalf of Portugal was [Britain's] duty, unless they were prepared to abandon the principles of national faith and national honor.[8]

Germany did its bit for the Russian revolution by sending Lenin to Petrograd; and the Spanish civil war was fought as much between Russia and Germany as between the falangists and the loyalists. Moreover, in the past the great powers have not only intervened in civil wars to fight each other, but also to negotiate settlements in keeping with a mutually acceptable concept of the balance of power. The settlement of Belgian independence emerged from such a mixture of indigenous revolution, external armed intervention and great power negotiations.

Elements of present conditions are thus apparent in the past, but there is also an important difference. Since the advent of nuclear weapons, the externally assisted civil war, military coup and war of national liberation have become almost the only instruments for modifying the world balance of power. One of the superpowers enthusiastically embraces assisted, armed insurrection as an instrument of national policy while the other does so with a show of reluctant *noblesse oblige*. It appears we are all under the thrall of what has been termed "the universal vocation

---

[7] See G. Wilson, International Law 66-70 (1935). See also H. Wheaton, Elements of International Law § 67 (Wilson ed. 1936).

[8] Wheaton, supra note 7, § 68 at 91-95.

of the ideologies of our century."[9] The Soviet textbook on International Law published by the Academy of Sciences of the U.S.S.R. notes that "[w]ar is the continuation of policy by other means"—attributing this sentiment to Lenin.[10] To this it adds another theme attributed to Lenin: the dichotomy between just and unjust wars.

> A just war is a non-predatory, liberatory war. Its aim is the defence of a people against external attacks and attempts to enslave it. Just wars include defensive wars and wars of national liberation. All progressive mankind sympathises with such wars and supports those fighting for freedom and independence. . . .
>
> The wars against the peace-loving peoples of Korea, Viet Nam and Egypt, which aimed at the enslavement of the peoples, were aggressive and unjust. But the liberatory war of the Korean and Vietnamese peoples and the defensive war waged by the Egyptian people against the Anglo-French-Israeli aggressor were just in character.[11]

This constitutes a remarkable evolution in the practice of international relations since the nineteenth century when the status of belligerency was developed, not primarily to sanction aid to the forces of change but to permit other states to proclaim their neutrality.[12]

Any such previous reticence has now been discarded. "Thus," it has been pointed out, "the Afro-Asian and Communist states

---

[9] R. Aron, Peace and War 730 (1966).

[10] Y. Korovin, International Law 401 (an undated publication of the Academy of Science of the U.S.S.R., Institute of Law, Foreign Languages Publishing House, Moscow).

[11] Id. at 402-03.

[12] Lauterpacht, supra note 1, at 176-85. Compare The United Kingdom's Foreign Enlistment Act of 1819, 5 Geo. 3, c. 69 which sought to prevent British subjects from serving on either side in civil wars with 18 U.S.C. § 960 (1964) which makes it a crime in the United States to plan, organize or participate in an expedition against any state with which the United States is at peace. In the nineteenth century it was well established that a third state may in no way be involved in aiding insurgents, or even permitting activity within its territory by opponents of a recognized regime. See Emperor of Austria v. Day & Kossuth, [1861] 2 Giff. 628 (Ch.). Wheaton, supra note 7, § 125, at 166-68. When Austria, France, Prussia and Russia met at the Congress of Verona in 1822 to set events in motion which ultimately led to French intervention in revolutionary Spain, Lord Castlereagh, the British Foreign Secretary, strongly objected. He was convinced that the revolution did not afford

> a case of that direct and imminent danger to the safety and interests of other States, which might justify a forcible interference. . . . No proof had been produced to the British government of any design, on the part of Spain, to invade the territory of France; of any attempt to introduce disaffection among her soldiery; . . . and, so long as the struggles and disturbances of Spain should be confined within the circle of her own territory, they could not be admitted by the British government to afford any plea for foreign interference.

Id. § 66, at 80.

appear pledged to repudiate the norms of nonintervention as a general principle of restraint."[13] Under these circumstances it is only "the ultra-legalist who would paralyze our response to Communist patterns of aggression by a pedantic insistence upon asymmetrical adherence by the West to the restraints of law."[14] For example, if it is only permissible in law to aid a revolutionary movement after it has attained the de facto status of a belligerent, then aid to incipient rebellions and to insurgents is illegal. However, if one side claims a right, indeed, a duty to aid movements of national liberation even at the earliest stage of their inception, then both sides should and will feel free to engage in civil uprisings at the earlier stages. In fact this, it would seem, is exactly where practices have brought us. Since, as was noted, the three stages of revolution had largely become tools of self-serving polemics, their falling into disuse is no great loss. The practice which the Russians and Chinese have chosen and the United States, Britain and France have adopted is that each major power is free to extend help to forces within another sovereign state, regardless whether those forces are characterized as ethnic or linguistic rebels, freedom fighters, military officers planning a coup, or the recognized regime. The only limitation is that the degree of overtness or covertness with which the help is extended, as well as its quantity and sophistication, will prudently be related to how well the rebel movement is succeeding and is able to receive and use aid.

Since the traditional three categories of revolution have become irrelevant in practice and also in policy, there is no reason for their survival in law. The policy behind the three categories was to restrict external intervention in a civil war for as long as possible, at least until the rebel movement had firmly established itself in a large part of the national territory as a permanent fact of international life. This policy reflected the general preference of what has been called the Westphalia-type international system for the status quo.[15] However, much of the world no longer believes that the purpose of the international system is to serve as a mutual protection society for its actors. Thus in practice the system no longer inherently gives preferred protection to governments against those who seek to change the government by force. Today, being recognized or represented in

---

[13] Falk, supra note 3, at 189.
[14] Id. at 187.
[15] 1 R. Falk & C. Black, The Future of the International Legal Order—Trends and Patterns 32 (1969).

the General Assembly of the United Nations is not in the least tantamount to community protection. Nations recognize governments and vote for their accreditation with one hand while aiding their overthrow with the other. Since the practice and the political policy from which it springs is endemic, it is futile for the law to insist on branding it as "illegal." For example, in perhaps the least controversial instance, it has been widely accepted as consistent and even morally imperative for states to continue to recognize the Government of South Africa and to sit with its representatives in the General Assembly while openly voting and acting to hamper and overturn that regime.

In terms of practice and policy, it has always been accepted by the Communists that the liberation movement in South Viet Nam could be helped and encouraged by friendly outside powers. It is useless to state that this is illegal simply because the Viet Cong, or the National Liberation Front (NLF) or the Peoples' Revolutionary Government of South Viet Nam (PRG) are not, or at an earlier stage were not, legitimate belligerents. Any force anywhere may now receive help to the extent that help can reach them. Any state will aid an insurgent group whenever it gets the opportunity for a perfectly sensible reason—the belief that it will serve its self-interest. Therefore, there is no point in lawyers insisting that what was illegal in Frederick the Great's day is now illegal and ever will be illegal, world without end. Governments no longer share an overriding interest in protecting each other per se. Without that overriding mutual commitment to each other, the old law is dead.

The role of law in the international community today is not to alter the patterns of behavior of states. In a conflict between perceived national self-interest and international law it is almost invariably the latter which suffers. Rather, the function of international law is to stake out the minimal areas of mutually-perceived overlap in the self-interest of states and to try to minimize in specific cases idiosyncratic deviations from the mutually-established, normative patterns of conduct. Principal among the mutually-perceived overlaps of self-interest is the desire for survival in the nuclear era. Whenever a state's policy may reasonably be expected to lead to its destruction, that policy cannot be to its advantage, no matter how disadvantageous it may also be to its opponent. Thus all states, even the most powerful, share a common self-interest in avoiding "total kill" situations. It is in this area of nuclear confrontation that law may usefully play a role. Thus it is for law to regulate the emerging phenomenon of surrogate civil wars not in accordance with a tradition favoring the status quo, but with a view to ensuring the survival of mankind. Law can hope to do no more than prohibit those categories of external participation in civil conflict *which are mutually recognized by each party, in general if not in every circumstance, as the kind of practice which is likely to give rise to a nuclear war of total destruction.* This ultimate threat of nuclear catastrophe circumscribes the ambit of activity which can usefully be described as "illegal" in civil war situations. Lesser exigencies may arise which cause states to limit by agreement the scope of a civil war, or even to impose a settlement through the instrumentality of the superpowers or of regional or international organization. These are optional, ad hoc possibilities and they are privileges, not duties of the system.

The first duty or legal obligation limiting the right to intervene in civil conflict is geographical. The practice of the United States in the case of the Berlin, Hungarian, Polish and Czech crises has been mutually reciprocated by the Soviet Union in the Cuban missile and Dominican crises.[16] Both superpowers have in practice come to recognize that within the historical precincts of the other, they will not give aid or encouragement to rebel movements whether these be, as in Czechoslovakia, a government being ousted or, as in Poland or Hungary, a new faction struggling for control. Castro, it should be remembered, came to power with United States, not Soviet help. When the United States clamped down on his regime during the missile crisis, the Soviet Union backed away. As a result it is safe to assume that Castro's ultimate survival will depend not on Russia but on his own ability to rally Cubans against any future United States-supported efforts to overthrow his regime and to make an invasion by United States forces too costly for Washington to contemplate.

This reciprocal principle now evolving limits United States involvement in Eastern Europe and Soviet involvement in Central America and the Caribbean. It does so because both superpowers recognize the other as determined to risk nuclear war if necessary to preserve regional preeminence, and both are unwilling, as a matter of their own calculated self-interest, to challenge that credible determination. It might be that we are seeing in the Viet Nam war the rise of a similar area of preeminence for China as a new superpower. However, before coming to that

---

[16] For a study of this mutuality see Franck & Weisband, The Johnson-Brezhnev Doctrines: Verbal Behavior Analysis of Superpower Confrontation, 3 N.Y.U. Center for International Studies Policy Papers No. 2 (1970).

conclusion it is necessary to recall that China's credibility as an equal of the United States and Russia is still very much an infant future contingency, and that by far the preponderance of military support for North Viet Nam and the PRG is believed to come not from China but from Russia.[17]

Outside the areas of superpower preeminence are large parts of the world in which surrogate-type civil wars and insurrection are likely to continue as manifestations of United States-Soviet jockeying for power. Even in these areas, however, the overriding mutual desire for survival imposes limitations which might be regarded as legal. Both sides, for example, have resisted the temptation to effect a quick win by supplying nuclear weapons to the side they support. Both have consciously tried to refrain from themselves destroying the property or personnel of the other. The United States has not mined Haiphong harbor despite certain evident advantages to be gained thereby; it also has apologized for rare, accidental injury to Soviet ships and has avoided bombing areas where Russians are known to work and live. The Russians in North Viet Nam have wholly refrained from engaging directly in hostile military acts towards United States forces. Something of the pattern, in reverse, may be emerging in the Middle Eastern conflict.

The Viet Nam war is likely to be the beginning of a new norm governing and limiting, as a matter of perceived mutual interest, the participation of the major powers in surrogate civil wars. For some time the United States, Britain and France have continued to send troops into the gray areas not in their immediate regional sphere of interest in order to influence the outcome of civil insurrections. The British did it in East Africa to protect the Nyerere, Obote and Kenyatta regimes. They did it, too, in Jordan in 1958 and in the Congo in 1963. The United States sent troops to Lebanon and to Viet Nam. France has sent troops to Gabon and Chad. Russia, however, has never sent fighting personnel into a civil war situation outside its eastern European precincts. It has involved itself heavily in intra-state strategic contests, but has avoided involving its fighting forces. The Soviets' reasoning is neither moral nor legal, but highly practical and strategic: the costs are too high and the benefits too low. This unfavorable cost-benefit ratio has to do with such factors as overextended lines of communication and supply, as well as the inutility of fighting with conventional armed forces in an

---

[17] Interview with Robert Barnett, Deputy Assistant Secretary of State for Far Eastern and Pacific Affairs, in New York City, May 6, 1970.

alien culture and predominantly rural society where there are few capturable fixed targets such as large towns and industrial complexes that control the country as a whole.

Most recently, the United States Government itself appears to have begun to learn this lesson of self-interested abstention, although the incursion into Cambodia shows that the extent of the lesson's absorption remains in doubt. In the words of President Nixon:

> The United States will keep all its treaty commitments. We shall provide a shield if a nuclear power threatens the freedom of a nation allied with us, or of a nation whose survival we consider vital to our security and the security of the region as a whole. In cases involving other types of aggression we shall furnish military and economic assistance when requested and as appropriate. But we shall look to the nation directly threatened to assume the primary responsibility of providing the manpower for its defense.[18]

The effect of the Nixon doctrine is to attempt to equalize, tactically, the United States and the Soviet Union. Henceforth indigenous non-Communists must organize, overtly or covertly, in accordance with populist and strategic precepts that will be successful in their locality. If they can succeed in this with minimal United States training and support, they can expect more support up to, but not including the use of troops. If they need foreign troops to win a civil war, these will have to be obtained from a sympathetic and culturally and politically congenial neighboring small state. If victory can only be assured through the involvement of United States military forces, then it is likely that victory could not be ensured even with such involvement. United States forces might enter such a situation only if Soviet (or, perhaps, Chinese) troops were actively introduced in support of the other side.

It is probable that the emerging international law regarding external support for civil wars will embrace the following principles:

1. The traditional distinctions in law between rebellion, insurgency and belligerency will no longer decide the legality of external aid to either status quo or revolutionary forces.
2. Aid to any rebellious movement, to the extent that it cannot be prevented by the status quo regime, will be

---

[18] United States Foreign Policy for the 1970's, H.R. Doc. No. 91-258, 91st Cong., 2d Sess. (1970) (a report to the Congress by Richard Nixon, President of the United States).

legal. Third-party states will have no obligation of neutrality or non-intervention. The principle of non-intervention in internal conflicts will cease to be applicable except when one superpower intervenes within the other superpower's sphere of preeminence.

3. Within a sphere of superpower preeminence the other superpower and its allies may not aid any revolutionary movements with troops or material.

4. Outside the superpower spheres, neither superpower, in its legal right to support revolutionary or status quo forces, will engage its own troops in active combat.

5. Both superpowers will refrain from the direct or indirect use of force by their own forces or those of the faction they support against men and transport of the other superpower except to the extent that these are actually engaged in fighting contrary to rule 4.

One advantage of legitimating what is in any event happening—the general intervention of third states in civil wars—is that it permits international law to regulate the nature and scope of these interventions on the basis of reciprocal principles. In this sense international law, like law dealing with drug addiction, cannot hope to influence the situation so long as the law itself induces everyone to pretend that the problem does not exist. Of course, it would be fine if there were no problem; but since there is, the way to begin to influence its course is to remove the legal stigma and allow it to come to the surface. It is quite senseless that North Vietnamese in South Viet Nam or Cambodia should have to pretend that they do not exist or that Americans should have to pretend that the Viet Cong ·were all merely North Vietnamese in disguise to give legal cover for United States aid to Saigon. The decision to intervene or not to intervene should be allowed to be an open political choice which may, of course, be dependent to some extent on what the other side is doing or might do. But like any other aspect of limited warfare in the nuclear age, the form and extent of such intervention should be regulated by mutual, normative considerations of what constitutes tolerable levels of hostility.[19]

In summary, the greatest permissible level of external intervention in civil wars must be determined by international law—in this context international law being the mutually perceived self-

---

[19] The theory of tacit limitations on parties to an international conflict herein incorporated owes much to Thomas C. Schelling. See T. Schelling, **The Strategy of Conflict** (1960).

interest of those nations capable of destroying civilization if that level is surpassed. Under modern circumstances insistence on the illegality of all intervention is a futile and counterproductive enterprise.[20] However, the imposition of realistic limits on the way states intervene is not. At one time it had been hoped that a disinterested body, or a body in which disinterested parties held the balance of power, could devise and implement these safety levels. The United Nations Security Council, General Assembly and Secretary General each helped to bring such a possibility to world attention in the Congo Operation. However, it was firmly rejected first by the Russians, then by the Afro-Asians in the context of the Congo Operation and its expenses, next by Secretary General U Thant who is a strict constructionist and does not conceive of his office in the independent-activist sense of a Dag Hammerskjöld and, finally, by the United States itself which no longer takes the United Nations very seriously as an instrument of policy or law since its votes reflect neither real power nor real principles. If, therefore, normative limits to the level of external interventions in civil wars are to be set and maintained, it must be through the evolution of reciprocal patterns of interactions between the United States and the Soviet Union. There is some reason to hope that the shared desire to survive will lead to the development of this new kind of international law.[21]

II

Validity Accorded Acts of Insurgent Movements by Third Parties

In several other respects the traditional law governing civil war situations is insufficient to meet the demands of contemporary circumstances. Among the unresolved problems are: (1) the effect of diplomatic negotiations and agreements between revolutionary movements and third parties, and (2) the validity to be accorded decrees, etc. of revolutionary movements in the legal systems of third parties. International law treats both these problems as a part of the larger question of recognition. Recognition, however, is increasingly regarded as a "high political

---

[20] For example, the U.N. Charter, art. 2, para. 4, prohibits all military hostilities between states except under art. 51, by way of collective self-defense. Here, again, the absence of any disinterested court to define "self-defense" in specific instances, has made the prohibition meaningless. It is best abandoned. See Franck, Who Killed Article 2(4)? (manuscript for publication in Am. J. Int'l L., Oct. 1970).

[21] See Franck & Weisband, supra note 16.

act."[22] Some governments extend recognition to others as a reward for their good or friendly behavior. Others, such as Great Britain, tend to recognize a government on the basis of its "effectiveness" as demonstrated by continued control over the bulk of the population.[23] Either policy, however, remains a political one and practice is not consistent. The British have refused to recognize the Rhodesian revolutionary regime for valid political reasons even though its effective control is beyond doubt. Several African countries which ordinarily apply the effectiveness test recognize the wholly fictional severance by United Nations fiat of Namibia from South Africa.[24] So long as it is clear that recognition is a political act, however, these inconsistencies are perfectly unexceptionable. Difficulties begin when recognition is tortured into a legal doctrine as a matter subject to law. It is surely quite futile to argue about a "duty" on the part of Washington to recognize Peking. In the absence of an impartial tribunal deciding legal cases between Communist China and the United States by reference to genuine world law, the issue is moot. There can be no duty to recognize, and, indeed, no *law* pertaining to recognition so long as each state's exercise of its political discretion is not subject to review by an impartial tribunal. Therefore, recognition or absence of recognition has no meaning beyond an expression of political approval or disapproval except in those countries like Britain, where, as a matter of political preference, it is sometimes based upon a factual determination of effectiveness. The fact of recognition is sometimes, if not always, accepted by the courts. Whereas British nonrecognition is given great, if not controlling evidentiary weight by British courts in legal questions involving rights or

---

[22] The statement of Warren Austin, United States representative on the United Nations Security Council, on May 18, 1948 is the classic enunciation of this:

> I should regard it as highly improper for me to admit that any country on earth can question the sovereignty of the United States of America in the exercise of that high political act of recognition of the *de facto* status of a state. Moreover, I would not admit here, by implication or by direct answer, that there exists a tribunal of justice . . . that can pass upon the legality or the validity of that act of my country.

3 U.N. SCOR, No. 68, at 16 (1948).

[23] "A Government which enjoys the habitual obedience of the bulk of the population with a reasonable expectancy of permanence, can be said to represent the State in question and as such to be entitled to recognition." 1 L. Oppenheim, International Law 131 (8th ed. 1955).

[24] "[A] considerable number of Members of the United Nations [had] already agreed to recognize as valid the Travel and Identity Documents to be issued by the Council for Namibia." 7 U.N. Monthly Chronicle 3 (No. 3, Mar. 1970).

obligations deriving from the status of a revolutionary regime,[25] the courts of the United States regard executive nonrecognition as far less conclusive.[26]

Politically, a state can gain little or nothing by attaching legal consequences to the "high political act of recognition." To do so is more likely to bring the law into disrepute by making the courts appear subservient to politics and by encouraging fraudulent dealing, usually in matters only derivatively involving the unrecognized state. For example, the doctrine of *caveat emptor* is not a sensible sanction to apply against Americans trading in East German goods within the United States.[27] If the political policy is to hamper trade with East Germany, it should be pursued through import control and trade regulations, not by encouraging fraud, breach of contract or the voiding of testamentary dispositions.[28]

Furthermore, the attachment of legal consequences to the act of recognition may even defeat international political goals by preventing states from acting in their own political self-interest. The most notable instances of this occur in diplomacy. States which have a genuine, mutually perceived political interest

---

[25] Aksionairnoye Obschestvo Dlia Mechanicheskoyi Obrabotky Diereva (1) A.M. Luther (Co. for Mechanical Working A.M. Luther) v. James Sagor & Co., [1921] 1 K.B. 456 (C.A.); Carl Zeiss Stiftung v. Rayner & Keeler Ltd., [1965] 1 Ch. 596.

[26] See Bank of China v. Wells Fargo Bank & Union Trust Co., 104 F. Supp. 59 (N.D. Cal. 1952), modified on other grounds, 209 F.2d 467 (9th Cir. 1953) (conclusive); Bank of China v. Wells Fargo Bank & Union Trust Co., 92 F. Supp. 920 (N.D. Cal. 1952) (no decision reached); M. Salimoff & Co. v. Standard Oil Co., 262 N.Y. 220, 186 N.E. 679 (1933) (not conclusive); Upright v. Mercury Business Machs. Co., 13 App. Div. 2d 36, 213 N.Y.S.2d 417 (1st Dep't 1961) (not conclusive). See also Chief Justice Taft's opinion as sole arbitrator in the Tinoco Claims Arbitration (Great Britain v. Costa Rica) [Oct. 18, 1923], 18 Am. J. Int'l L. 147 (1924). Taft held:

> The non-recognition by other nations of a government claiming to be a national personality, is usually appropriate evidence that it has not attained the independence and control entitling it by international law to be classed as such. But when recognition *vel non* of a government is by such nations determined by inquiry, not into its *de facto* sovereignty and complete governmental control, but into its illegitimacy or irregularity of origin, their non-recognition loses something of evidential weight on the issue with which those applying the rules of international law are alone concerned. What is true of the non-recognition of the United States in its bearing upon the existence of a *de facto* government under Tinoco for thirty months is probably in a measure true of the non-recognition by her Allies in the European War. Such non-recognition for any reason, however, cannot outweigh the evidence disclosed by this record before me as to the *de facto* character of Tinoco's government, according to the standard set by international law.

Id. at 154.

[27] Upright v. Mercury Business Machs. Co., 13 App. Div. 2d 36, 213 N.Y.S.2d 417 (1st Dep't 1961).

[28] Kolovrat v. Oregon, 366 U.S. 187 (1961).

in negotiating with one another have difficulty in doing so because this might imply "constructive recognition" by one of the other, which in turn would have many undesired consequences by operation of law.

Of course, a situation such as this is absurd. International law, as a weak and humble servant of the international community, ought not to have unexpected consequences. If it were to be otherwise, the tail would wag the dog.[29] Surely it should be possible for regimes to speak to each other, to enter into certain limited negotiations, and even to maintain channels of continuous contact without any unintended results flowing from the *consequential operation* of a mythical force called international law which has nothing to do with the political matters at hand. To introduce a relationship between international law and political intercourse among regimes at various levels is to do violence to both law and politics.

Fortunately, today this is widely recognized. The Warsaw talks between the United States and the Peoples' Republic of China would be hampered if certain other events in the incipient relationship between the two governments were to follow not by mutual political choice but by operation of law.[30] Furthermore, it is not helpful to emphasize that the Arab States, by being in the United Nations with Israel, have inadvertently extended recognition in the form of a treaty relationship. Conversely, neither the Paris peace talks between the United States and the North Vietnamese nor the Sino-Canadian Wheat Agreements could have been achieved if nonrecognition had been given strict legal significance. The United Nations was faced with a similar problem during the Indonesian war of independence. The United Nations Charter refers such a "dispute" to the Security Council for resolution,[31] but the words of the Charter speak of "any dispute, the continuance of which is likely to endanger the maintenance of international peace."[32] The Netherlands took the position that any attempt by the United Nations to take up the

---

[29] It is not uncommon for the purely political acts of a state to have surprising legal consequences through the operation of international law. For two notable cases of an unwary state hoisting itself by its own petard see Case Concerning Sovereignty Over Certain Frontier Land (Belgium/Netherlands), [1959] I.C.J. 209; Case of the Legal Status of Eastern Greenland, [1933] P.C.I.J., ser. A/B, No. 53.

[30] See Lee, Treaty Relations of the Peoples' Republic of China: A Study of Compliance, 116 U. Pa. L. Rev. 244 (1967). However, the United States has avoided regarding the agreements as treaties or executive agreements. Id. at 260.

[31] U.N. Charter art. 34.

[32] Id. art. 33, para. 1. See Documentary Supplement infra.

matter would inevitably have the collateral effect of recognizing that the dispute was international, thereby accepting the rebel demands to be recognized as an independent state. Fortunately, the Security Council was able to divorce its search for a political solution from unwanted legal concomitants by declaring its political jurisdiction "without prejudice" to the legal rights and status of the parties.[33]

The law of international diplomatic relations and negotiations ought to operate very peripherally, in procedural ways (*e.g.*, accreditation, repository matters, etc.), to facilitate the negotiation of agreements between regimes. It certainly should not hamper negotiations either by demanding that the parties do things they do not want to do as a prerequisite to negotiation (*e.g.*, recognition), or by insisting that undesired ancillary consequences would flow from the act of negotiating (*e.g.*, recognition, again). The real role of law in diplomacy is to help in the principled application of an agreement after one has been reached by the political process. Therefore, diplomatic negotiations should be solely a matter of political discretion, whereas the disposition of legal cases in courts should be determined by law.

Surprisingly enough however, the validity of the acts of a revolutionary movement must be based on the same criterion in both the political and the legal sphere. Both in diplomatic negotiations and in the adjudication of rights arising out of the validity of acts having a connection with the authority or territory of the revolutionary movement, the test must be that of effectiveness. In the political instance, however, its application is fittingly discretionary. States may and do, but have no duty to, enter into negotiations, diplomatic intercourse and even written agreements with governments that are sufficiently in control of the subject-matter to be worth dealing with. The law simply does not stand in their way and treats the fruits of such diplomacy as legitimate. As for situations of adjudication in the courts of third parties, it has frequently been the practice to give legal effect to the decrees and acts of an effective government, recognized or not.[34] In civil war situations, moreover, effect can be given to the decrees and acts of a revolutionary regime insofar as they vest within the area of the regime's effective control.[35] This may be done by the device of splitting de facto from

---

[33] 2 U.N. SCOR 1617 (1947).

[34] See text accompanying notes 25-26 supra.

[35] Agricultural Cooperative Ass'n of Lithuania Lietukis v. The Denny, 127 F.2d 404 (3d Cir. 1942), rev'g 40 F. Supp. 92 (D.N.J. 1941); S.S. Aranatzazu Mendi, [1939] A.C. 256; Banco de Bilbao v. Sascha, [1938] 2 K.B. 176.

de jure recognition, or simply by treating recognition as a political fact of only evidentiary interest to the law. In the case of the PRG, of course, the evidence of their effective control of large areas of South Viet Nam is beyond doubt[36] and courts of law, as distinct from political organs, ought to consider the evidence to that effect,[37] whatever the circumstances of recognition or nonrecognition.

---

[36] According to one United States authority: "In certain areas the Viet Minh, and the N.L.F., controlled the lives of the people for nearly two years in something closely resembling a Communist state." D. Pike, Viet Cong: The Organization and Techniques of the National Liberation Front of South Vietnam 271 (1966).

[37] The political act of recognition by a very large number of states carries evidentiary weight for purposes of the legal determination of effectiveness. The PRG has permanent diplomatic representation in the following countries, in chronological order: Algeria, North Korea, Syria, German Democratic Republic, Poland, Rumania, Cuba, Yugoslavia, Congo (Brazzaville), Democratic Republic of Viet Nam (the status of the mission here is unclear), U.S.S.R., Czechoslovakia, Bulgaria, Hungary, Mongolia, China, Southern Yeman, U.A.R., Albania, Mauretania, Sudan, Mali, Iraq, Tanzania. Telephone call to New York Times Archives, May 18, 1970.

V. PROSPECTS FOR SETTLEMENT

The Viet Nam Negotiations

HENRY A. KISSINGER*

THE peace negotiations in Paris have been marked by the classic Vietnamese syndrome: optimism alternating with bewilderment; euphoria giving way to frustration. The halt to the bombing produced another wave of high hope. Yet it was followed almost immediately by the dispute with Saigon over its participation in the talks. The merits of this issue aside, we must realize that a civil war which has torn a society for twenty years and which has involved the great powers is unlikely to be settled in a single dramatic stroke. Even if there were mutual trust—a commodity not in excessive supply—the complexity of the issues and the difficulty of grasping their interrelationship would make for complicated negotiations. Throughout the war, criteria by which to measure progress have been hard to come by; this problem has continued during the negotiations. The dilemma is that almost any statement about Viet Nam is likely to be true; unfortunately, truth does not guarantee relevance.

The sequence of events that led to negotiations probably started with General Westmoreland's visit to Washington in November 1967. On that occasion, General Westmoreland told a Joint Session of Congress that the war was being won militarily. He outlined "indicators" of progress and stated that a limited withdrawal of American combat forces might be undertaken beginning late in 1968. On January 17, 1968, President Johnson, in his State of the Union address, emphasized that the pacification program—the extension of the control of Saigon into the countryside—was progressing satisfactorily. Sixty-seven percent of the population of South Viet Nam lived in relatively secure areas; the figure was expected to rise. A week later, the Tet offensive overthrew the assumptions of American strategy.

What had gone wrong? The basic problem has been conceptual:

* This article was written before Mr. Kissinger was appointed Assistant to the President for National Security Affairs and therefore should be understood as a statement of his personal views at that time and not as a statement of official U.S. Government policy.

the tendency to apply traditional maxims of both strategy and "nation-building" to a situation which they did not fit.

American military strategy followed the classic doctrine that victory depended on a combination of control of territory and attrition of the opponent. Therefore, the majority of the American forces was deployed along the frontiers of South Viet Nam to prevent enemy infiltration and in the Central Highlands where most of the North Vietnamese main-force units—those units organized along traditional military lines—were concentrated. The theory was that defeat of the main forces would cause the guerrillas to wither on the vine. Victory would depend on inflicting casualties substantially greater than those we suffered until Hanoi's losses became "unacceptable."

This strategy suffered from two disabilities: (a) the nature of guerrilla warfare; (b) the asymmetry in the definition of what constituted unacceptable losses. A guerrilla war differs from traditional military operation because its key prize is not control of territory but control of the population. This depends, in part, on psychological criteria, especially a sense of security. No positive program can succeed unless the population feels safe from terror or reprisal. Guerrillas rarely seek to hold real estate; their tactic is to use terror and intimidation to discourage coöperation with constituted authority.

The distribution of the population in Viet Nam makes this problem particularly acute. Over 90 percent of the population live in the coastal plain and the Mekong Delta; the Central Highlands and the frontiers, on the other hand, are essentially unpopulated. Eighty percent of American forces came to be concentrated in areas containing less than 4 percent of the population; the locale of military operations was geographically removed from that of the guerrilla conflict. As North Vietnamese theoretical writings never tired of pointing out, the United States could not hold territory and protect the population simultaneously. By opting for military victory through attrition, the American strategy produced what came to be the characteristic feature of the Vietnamese war: military successes that could not be translated into permanent political advantage. (Even the goal of stopping infiltration was very hard to implement in the trackless, nearly impenetrable jungles along the Cambodian and Laotian frontiers.)

As a result, the American conception of security came to have little in common with the experience of the Vietnamese villagers. American maps classified areas by three categories of control, neatly shown in various colors: Government, contested and Viet Cong. The formal criteria were complicated, and depended to an unusual extent on reports by officers whose short terms of duty (barely 12 months) made it next to impossible for them to grasp the intangibles and nuances which constitute the real elements of control in the Vietnamese countryside. In essence, the first category included all villages which contained some governmental authority; "contested" referred to areas slated to be entered by governmental cadres. The American notion of security was a reflection of Western administrative theory; control was assumed to be in the hands of one of the contestants more or less exclusively.

But the actual situation in Viet Nam was quite different; a realistic security map would have shown few areas of exclusive jurisdiction; the pervasive experience of the Vietnamese villager was the ubiquitousness of both sides. Saigon controlled much of the country in the daytime, in the sense that government troops could move anywhere if they went in sufficient force; the Viet Cong dominated a large part of the same population at night. For the villagers, the presence of Government during the day had to be weighed against its absence after dark, when Saigon's cadres almost invariably withdrew into the district or provincial capitals. If armed teams of administrators considered the villages unsafe at night, the villagers could hardly be expected to resist the guerrillas. Thus, the typical pattern in Viet Nam has been dual control, with the villagers complying with whatever force was dominant during a particular part of the day.

The political impact of this dual control was far from symmetrical, however. To be effective, the Government had to demonstrate a very great capacity to provide protection; probably well over 90 percent. The guerrillas' aim was largely negative: to prevent the consolidation of governmental authority. They did not need to destroy all governmental programs; indeed in some areas, they made no effort to interfere with them. They did have to demonstrate a capability to punish individuals who threw in their lot with Saigon. An occasional assassination or raid served to shake confidence for months afterwards.

The North Vietnamese and Viet Cong had another advantage which they used skillfully. American "victories" were empty unless they laid the basis for an eventual withdrawal. The North Vietnamese and Viet Cong, fighting in their own country, needed merely to keep in being forces sufficiently strong to dominate the population after the United States tired of the war. We fought a military war; our opponents fought a political one. We sought physical attrition; our opponents aimed for our psychological exhaustion. In the process, we lost sight of one of the cardinal maxims of guerrilla war: the guerrilla wins if he does not lose. The conventional army loses if it does not win. The North Vietnamese used their main forces the way a bullfighter uses his cape —to keep us lunging in areas of marginal political importance.

The strategy of attrition failed to reduce the guerrillas and was in difficulty even with respect to the North Vietnamese main forces. Since Hanoi made no attempt to hold any territory, and since the terrain of the Central Highlands cloaked North Vietnamese movements, it proved difficult to make the opposing forces fight except at places which they chose. Indeed, a considerable majority of engagements came to be initiated by the other side; this enabled Hanoi to regulate its casualties (and ours) at least within certain limits. The so-called "kill-ratios" of United States to North Vietnamese casualties became highly unreliable indicators. Even when the figures were accurate they were irrelevant, because the level of what was "unacceptable" to Americans fighting thousands of miles from home turned out to be much lower than that of Hanoi fighting on Vietnamese soil.

All this caused our military operations to have little relationship to our declared political objectives. Progress in establishing a political base was excruciatingly slow; our diplomacy and our strategy were conducted in isolation from each other. President Johnson had announced repeatedly that we would be ready to negotiate, unconditionally, at any moment, anywhere. This, in effect, left the timing of negotiations to the other side. But short of a complete collapse of the opponent, our military deployment was not well designed to support negotiations. For purposes of negotiating, we would have been better off with 100 percent control over 60 percent of the country than with 60 percent control of 100 percent of the country.

The effort to strengthen Saigon's political control faced other problems. To be effective, the so-called pacification program had to meet two conditions: (a) it had to provide security for the population; (b) it had to establish a political and institutional link between the villages and Saigon. Neither condition was ever met: impatience to show "progress" in the strategy of attrition caused us to give low priority to protection of the population; in any event, there was no concept as to how to bring about a political framework relating Saigon to the countryside. As a result, economic programs had to carry an excessive load. In Viet Nam—as in most developing countries—the overwhelming problem is not to *buttress* but to *develop* a political framework. Economic progress that undermines the existing patterns of obligation—which are generally personal or feudal—serves to accentuate the need for political institutions. One ironic aspect of the war in Viet Nam is that, while we profess an idealistic philosophy, our failures have been due to an excessive reliance on material factors. The communists, by contrast, holding to a materialistic interpretation, owe many of their successes to their ability to supply an answer to the question of the nature and foundation of political authority.

The Tet offensive brought to a head the compounded weaknesses—or, as the North Vietnamese say, the internal contradictions—of the American position. To be sure, from a strictly military point of view, Tet was an American victory. Viet Cong casualties were very high; in many provinces, the Viet Cong infrastructure of guerrillas and shadow administrators surfaced and could be severely mauled by American forces. But in a guerrilla war, purely military considerations are not decisive: psychological and political factors loom at least as large.

On that level the Tet offensive was a political defeat in the countryside for Saigon and the United States. Two claims had been pressed on the villages. The United States and Saigon had promised that they would be able to protect an ever larger number of villages. The Viet Cong had never made such a claim; they merely asserted that they were the real power and presence in the villages and they threatened retribution upon those who collaborated with Saigon or the United States.

As happened so often in the past, the Viet Cong made their claim stick. Some twenty provincial capitals were occupied. Though the Viet Cong held none (except Hué) for more than a few days, they were there long enough to execute hundreds of Vietnamese on the basis of previously prepared lists. The words "secure area" never had the same significance for Vietnamese civilians as for Americans, but, if the term had any meaning, it applied to the provincial and district capitals. This was precisely where the Tet offensive took its most severe toll. The Viet Cong had made a point which far transcended military considerations in importance: there are no secure areas for Vietnamese civilians. This has compounded the already great tendency of the Vietnamese population to await developments and not to commit itself irrevocably to the Saigon Government. The withdrawal of government troops from the countryside to protect the cities and the consequent increase in Viet Cong activity in the villages even in the daytime have served to strengthen this trend. One result of the Tet offensive was to delay—perhaps indefinitely—the consolidation of governmental authority, which in turn is the only meaningful definition of "victory" in guerrilla warfare.

For all these reasons, the Tet offensive marked the watershed of the American effort. Henceforth, no matter how effective our actions, the prevalent strategy could no longer achieve its objectives within a period or with force levels politically acceptable to the American people. This realization caused Washington, for the first time, to put a ceiling on the number of troops for Viet Nam. Denied the very large additional forces requested, the military command in Viet Nam felt obliged to begin a gradual change from its peripheral strategy to one concentrating on the protection of the populated areas. This made inevitable an eventual commitment to a political solution and marked the beginning of the quest for a negotiated settlement. Thus the stage was set for President Johnson's speech of March 31, which ushered in the current negotiations.

II. THE ENVIRONMENT OF NEGOTIATIONS

Of course, the popular picture that negotiations began in May is only partially correct. The United States and Hanoi have rarely been out of touch since the American commitment in Viet Nam started to escalate. Not all these contacts have been face to face. Some have been by means of public pronouncements. Between 1965 and 1968, the various parties publicly stated their positions in a variety of forums: Hanoi announced Four Points, the NLF put forth Five Points, Saigon advanced Seven Points and the United States—perhaps due to its larger bureaucracy—promulgated Fourteen.

These public pronouncements produced a fairly wide area of apparent agreement on some general principles: that the Geneva

Accords could form the basis of a settlement, that American forces would be withdrawn ultimately, that the reunification of Viet Nam should come about through direct negotiation between the Vietnamese, that (after a settlement) Viet Nam would not contain foreign bases. The United States has indicated that three of Hanoi's Four Points are acceptable.[1]

There is disagreement about the status of Hanoi's forces in the South; indeed, Hanoi has yet to admit that it has forces in the South—though it has prepared a "fall-back position" to the effect that North Vietnamese forces in the South cannot be considered "external." The role of the NLF is equally in dispute. Saigon rejects a separate political role for the NLF; the NLF considers Saigon a puppet régime. There is no agreement about the meaning of those propositions which sound alike or on how they are to be enforced.

In addition to negotiations by public pronouncements, there have been secret contacts which have been described in many books and articles.[2] It has been alleged that these contacts have failed because of a lack of imagination or a failure of coördination within our Government. (There have also been charges of deliberate sabotage.) A fair assessment of these criticisms will not be possible for many years. But it is clear that many critics vastly oversimplify the problem. Good will may not always have been present; but even were it to motivate all sides, rapid, dramatic results would be unlikely. For all parties face enormous difficulties. Indeed, the tendency of each side to overestimate the freedom of manœuvre of the other has almost certainly increased distrust. It has caused Hanoi to appear perversely obstinate to Washington and Washington to seem devious to Hanoi.

Both the Hanoi Government and the United States are limited in their freedom of action by the state of mind of the population of South Viet Nam which will ultimately determine the outcome of the conflict. The Vietnamese people have lived under foreign rule for approximately half of their history. They have maintained a remarkable cultural and social cohesion by being finely attuned to the realities of power. To survive, the Vietnamese have had

[1] These are: withdrawal of U.S. forces, the provision of the Geneva agreements calling for neutrality for North and South Viet Nam, and reunification on the basis of popular wishes. The United States has rejected the third point which implies that the internal arrangements for South Viet Nam should be settled on the basis of the NLF program—though the United States has agreed to consider the NLF program among others.

[2] See, for example, Kraslow and Loory, "The Secret Search for Peace in Vietnam." New York: Random House, 1968.

to learn to calculate—almost instinctively—the real balance of forces. If negotiations give the impression of being a camouflaged surrender, there will be nothing left to negotiate. Support for the side which seems to be losing will collapse. Thus, all the parties are aware—Hanoi explicitly, for it does not view war and negotiation as separate processes; we in a more complicated bureaucratic manner—that *the way* negotiations are carried out is almost as important as *what* is negotiated. The choreography of how one enters negotiations, what is settled first and in what manner is inseparable from the substance of the issues.

Wariness is thus imposed on the negotiators; a series of deadlocks is difficult to avoid. There are no "easy" issues, for each issue is symbolic and therefore in a way prejudges the final settlement. On its merits, the debate about the site of the conference—extending over a period of four weeks in April and May—was trivial. Judged intellectually, the four weeks were "wasted." But they did serve a useful function: they enabled the United States to let Saigon get used to the idea that there *would* be negotiations and to maintain that it retained control over events. It would not be surprising if Hanoi had a similar problem with the NLF.

The same problem was illustrated by the way the decision to stop the bombing was presented. Within twenty-four hours after announcement of the halt, both Hanoi and Saigon made statements of extraordinary bellicosity, which, taken literally, would have doomed the substantive talks about to begin. But their real purpose was to reassure each side's supporters in the South. Saigon especially has had a difficult problem. It has been pictured by many as perversely stubborn because of its haggling over the status of the NLF. However, to Saigon, the status of the NLF cannot be a procedural matter. For South Viet Nam it has been very nearly the central issue of the war. Washington must bear at least part of the responsibility for underestimating the depth and seriousness of this concern.

The situation confronted by Washington and Hanoi internationally is scarcely less complex. Much of the bitter debate in the United States about the war has been conducted in terms of 1961 and 1962. Unquestionably, the failure at that time to analyze adequately the geopolitical importance of Viet Nam contributed to the current dilemma. But the commitment of 500,000 Americans has settled the issue of the importance of Viet Nam. For what is involved now is confidence in American promises. However fashionable it is to ridicule the terms "credibility" or "prestige," they are not empty phrases; other nations can gear their actions to ours only if they can count on our steadiness. The collapse of the American effort in Viet Nam would not mollify many critics; most of them would simply add the charge of unreliability to the accusation of bad judgment. Those whose safety or national goals depend on American commitments could only be dismayed. In many parts of the world—the Middle East, Europe, Latin America, even Japan—stability depends on confidence in American promises. Unilateral withdrawal, or a settlement which unintentionally amounts to the same thing, could therefore lead to the erosion of restraints and to an even more dangerous international situation. No American policymaker can simply dismiss these dangers.

Hanoi's position is at least as complicated. Its concerns are not global; they are xenophobically Vietnamese (which includes, of course, hegemonial ambitions in Laos and Cambodia). But Hanoi is extraordinarily dependent on the international environment. It could not continue the war without foreign material assistance. It counts almost as heavily on the pressures of world public opinion. Any event that detracts from global preoccupations with the war in Viet Nam thus diminishes Hanoi's bargaining position. From this point of view, the Soviet invasion of Czechoslovakia was a major setback for Hanoi.

Hanoi's margin of survival is so narrow that precise calculation has become a way of life; caution is almost an obsession. Its bargaining position depends on a fine assessment of international factors—especially of the jungle of intra-communist relations. In order to retain its autonomy, Hanoi must manœuvre skillfully between Peking, Moscow and the NLF. Hanoi has no desire to become completely dependent on one of the communist giants. But, since they disagree violently, they reinforce Hanoi's already strong tendency toward obscurantist formulations. In short, Hanoi's freedom of manœuvre is severely limited.

The same is true of the Soviet Union, whose large-scale aid to Hanoi makes it a semi-participant in the war. Moscow must be torn by contradictory inclinations. A complete victory for Hanoi would tend to benefit Peking in the struggle for influence among the communist parties of the world; it would support the Chinese argument that intransigence toward the United States is, if not without risk, at least relatively manageable. But a defeat of Hanoi would demonstrate Soviet inability to protect "fraternal" communist countries against the United States. It would also weaken a potential barrier to Chinese influence in Southeast Asia and enable Peking to turn its full fury on Moscow. For a long time, Moscow has seemed paralyzed by conflicting considerations and bureaucratic inertia.

Events in Czechoslovakia have reduced Moscow's usefulness even further. We would compound the heavy costs of our pallid reaction to events in Czechoslovakia if our allies could blame it on a quid pro quo for Soviet assistance in extricating us from Southeast Asia. Washington therefore requires great delicacy in dealing with Moscow on the Viet Nam issue. It cannot be in the American interest to add fuel to the already widespread charge that the superpowers are sacrificing their allies to maintain spheres of influence.

This state of affairs would be enough to explain prolonged negotiations progressing through a series of apparent stalemates. In addition, a vast gulf in cultural and bureaucratic style between Hanoi and Washington complicates matters further. It would be difficult to imagine two societies less meant to understand each other than the Vietnamese and the American. History and culture combine to produce almost morbid suspiciousness on the part of the Vietnamese. Because survival has depended on a subtle skill in manipulating physically stronger foreigners, the Vietnamese style of communication is indirect and, by American standards, devious—qualities which avoid a total commitment and an overt test of strength. The fear of being made to look foolish seems to transcend most other considerations. Even if the United States accepted Hanoi's maximum program, the result might well be months of haggling while Hanoi looked for our "angle" and made sure that no other concessions were likely to be forthcoming.

These tendencies are magnified by communist ideology, which defines the United States as inherently hostile, and by Hanoi's experience in previous negotiations with the United States. It may well feel that the Geneva Conferences of 1954 and 1962 (over Laos) deprived it of part of its achievements on the battlefield.

All this produces the particular negotiating style of Hanoi: the careful planning, the subtle, indirect methods, the preference for opaque communications which keep open as many options as possible toward both foe and friend (the latter may seem equally important to Hanoi). North Viet Nam's diplomacy operates in cycles of reconnaissance and withdrawal to give an opportunity to assess the opponent's reaction. This is then followed by another diplomatic sortie to consolidate the achievements of the previous phase or to try another route. In this sense, many contacts with Hanoi which seemed "abortive" to us, probably served (from Hanoi's point of view) the function of defining the terrain. The methods of Hanoi's diplomacy are not very different from Viet Cong military strategy and sometimes appear just as impenetrable to us.

If this analysis is correct, few North Vietnamese moves are accidental; even the most obtuse communication is likely to serve a purpose. On the other hand, it is not a style which easily lends itself to the sort of analysis at which we excel: the pragmatic, legal dissection of individual cases. Where Hanoi makes a fetish of planning, Washington is allergic to it. We prefer to deal with cases as they arise, "on their merits." Pronouncements that the United States is ready to negotiate do not guarantee that a negotiating position exists or that the U.S. Government has articulated its objectives.

Until a conference comes to be scheduled, two groups in the American bureaucracy usually combine to thwart the elaboration of a negotiating position: those who oppose negotiations and those who favor them. The opponents generally equate negotiations with surrender; if they agree to discuss settlement terms at all, it is to define the conditions of the enemy's capitulation. Aware of this tendency and of the reluctance of the top echelon to expend capital on settling disputes which involve no immediate practical consequences, the advocates of negotiations coöperate in avoiding the issue. Moreover, delay serves their own purposes in that it enables them to reserve freedom of action for the conference room.

Pragmatism and bureaucracy thus combine to produce a diplomatic style marked by rigidity in advance of formal negotiations and excessive reliance on tactical considerations once negotiations start. In the preliminary phases, we generally lack a negotiating program; during the conference, bargaining considerations tend to shape internal discussions. In the process, we deprive ourselves of criteria by which to judge progress. The over-concern with tactics suppresses a feeling for nuance and for intangibles.

The incompatibility of the American and North Vietnamese styles of diplomacy produced, for a long time, a massive breakdown of communication—especially in the preliminary phases of negotiation. While Hanoi was feeling its way toward negotiations, it bent all its ingenuity to avoid clear-cut, formal commitments. Ambiguity permitted Hanoi to probe without giving away much in return; Hanoi has no peers in slicing the salami very thin. It wanted the context of events rather than a formal document to define its obligations, lest its relations with Peking or the NLF be compromised.

Washington was unequipped for this mode of communication. To a government which equates commitments with legally enforceable obligations, Hanoi's subtle changes of tense were literally incomprehensible. In a press conference in February 1968, President Johnson said, "As near as I am able to detect, Hanoi has not changed its course of conduct since the very first response it made. Sometimes they will change 'will' to 'would' or 'shall' to 'should,' or something of the kind. But the answer is all the same." A different kind of analysis might have inquired why Hanoi would open up a channel for a meaningless communication, especially in the light of a record of careful planning which made it extremely unlikely that a change of tense would be inadvertent.

Whatever the might-have-beens, Hanoi appeared to Washington as devious, deceitful and tricky. To Hanoi, Washington must have seemed, if not obtuse, then cannily purposeful. In any event, the deadlock produced by the difference in negotiating style concerned specific clauses less than the philosophical issue of the nature of an international "commitment" or the meaning of "trickery." This problem lay at the heart of the impasse over the bombing halt.

III. LESSONS OF THE BOMBING HALT

The bombing halt occupied the first six months of the Paris talks. The formal positions were relatively straightforward. The American view was contained in the so-called San Antonio formula which was put forth by President Johnson in September 1967: "The United States is willing to stop all aerial and naval bombardment of North Viet Nam when this will lead promptly to productive discussions. We, of course, assume that while discussions proceed, North Viet Nam would not take advantage of the bombing cessation or limitation." In its main outlines, the American position remained unchanged throughout the negotiations.

Hanoi's reaction was equally simple and stark. It scored the obvious debating point that it could guarantee useful but not "productive" talks since that depended also on the United States.[3] But in the main, Hanoi adamantly insisted that the bombing halt had to be "unconditional." It rejected all American proposals for reciprocity as put forward, for example, by Secretary Rusk: respect for the DMZ, no attack on South Vietnamese cities, reduction in the level of military operations.

Though this deadlock had many causes, surely a central problem was the difficulty each side had in articulating its real concern. Washington feared "trickery;" it believed that once stopped, the bombing would be politically difficult, if not impossible, to start again even in the face of considerable provocation. Too, it needed some assurance as to how the negotiations would proceed *after* a bombing halt. Washington was aware that a bombing halt which did not lead rapidly to substantive talks could not be sustained domestically.

The legalistic phrasing of these concerns obscured their real merit. If bombing were resumed under conditions of great public indignation, it would be much harder to exercise restraint in the choice of targets and much more difficult to stop again in order to test Hanoi's intentions. The frequently heard advice to "take risks for peace" is valid only if one is aware that the consequences of an imprudent risk are likely to be escalation rather than peace.

Hanoi, in turn, had a special reason for insisting on an unconditional end of the bombing. A government as subtle as Hanoi must have known that there are no "unconditional" acts in the relation of sovereign states, if only because sovereignty implies the right to reassess changing conditions unilaterally. But Hanoi has always placed great reliance on the pressures of world opinion; the "illegality" of U.S. bombing was therefore a potent political weapon. Reciprocity would jeopardize this claim; it would suggest that bombing might be justified in some circumstances. Hanoi did not want a formula under which the United States

[3] Article by Wilfred Burchett, *The New York Times*, October 21, 1967.

could resume bombing "legally" by charging violations of an understanding. Finally, Hanoi was eager to give the impression to its supporters in the South that it had induced us to stop "unconditionally" as a symbol of imminent victory. For the same reason, it was important to us that *both* sides in South Viet Nam believe there had been reciprocity.

As a result, six months were devoted to defining a quid pro quo which could be represented as unconditional. The issue of the bombing halt thus raised the question of the nature of an international commitment. What is the sanction for violation of an understanding? The United States, for a long time, conducted itself as if its principal safeguard was a formal, binding commitment by Hanoi to certain restraints. In fact, since no court exists to which the United States could take Hanoi, the American sanction was what the United States could do unilaterally should Hanoi "take advantage" of the bombing pause. Hanoi's fear of the consequences is a more certain protection against trickery than a formal commitment. Communicating what we meant by taking advantage turned out to be more important than eliciting a formal North Vietnamese response.

The final settlement of the problem seems to have been arrived at by this procedure. In his address announcing the bombing halt, President Johnson stressed that Hanoi is clear about our definition of "take advantage." Hanoi has not formally acknowledged these terms; it has, in fact, insisted that the bombing halt was unconditional. But Hanoi can have little doubt that the bombing halt would not survive if it disregarded the points publicly stated by Secretary Rusk and President Johnson.

If the negotiations about the bombing halt demonstrate that tacit bargaining may play a crucial role in an ultimate settlement, they also show the extraordinary danger of neglecting the political framework. Washington had insisted throughout the negotiations that Saigon participate in the substantive talks which were to follow a bombing halt. President Johnson, in his speech announcing the bombing halt, implied that Saigon's participation satisfied the requirement of the San Antonio formula for "productive talks." How we came to insist on a condition which was basically neither in our interest nor Saigon's cannot be determined until the records are available—if then. It should have been clear that the participation of Saigon was bound to raise the issues of the status of the NLF and the internal structure of

Viet Nam—issues which, as will be seen below, it is in every-body's interest to defer to as late a stage of the negotiations as possible.

Having made Saigon's participation a test case, we advanced the "your side, our side" formula. Under it, Saigon and the NLF are to participate in the conference. Each side can claim that it is composed of two delegations; its opponent is free to insist that it really deals with only one delegation. Thus the United States does not "recognize" the NLF and insists that Hanoi is its nego-tiating partner; Hanoi can take a similar view and maintain its refusal to deal formally with Saigon. It is difficult to disentangle from public sources whether Saigon ever agreed to this formula and whether it understood that our formula amounted to giving the NLF equal status.[4]

On the face of it, Saigon's reluctance to accept equal status with the NLF is comprehensible for it tends to affect all other issues, from ceasefire to internal structure. The merits of the dis-pute aside, the public rift between Saigon and Washington com-promised what had been achieved. To split Washington and Saigon had been a constant objective of Hanoi; if the Paris talks turn into an instrument to accomplish this, Hanoi will be tempted to use them for political warfare rather than for serious discus-sions.

Clearly, there is a point beyond which Saigon cannot be given a veto over negotiations. But equally, it is not preposterous for Saigon to insist on a major voice in decisions affecting its own country. And it cannot strengthen our position in Paris to *begin* the substantive discussions with a public row over the status of a government whose constitutionality we have insistently pressed on the world for the past two years. The impasse has demon-strated that to deal with issues on an ad hoc basis is too risky;

[4] Clashes with our allies in which both sides claim to have been deceived occur so frequently as to suggest structural causes (see Skybolt, the Non-Proliferation Treaty, now the bombing halt). What seems to be happening is the same bureaucratic deadlock internationally which was noted above within our Government. When an issue is fairly abstract—before there is a prospect for an agreement—our diplomats tend to present our view in a bland, relaxed fash-ion to the ally whose interests are involved but who is not present at the negotiations. The ally responds equally vaguely for three reasons: (a) he may be misled into believing that no decision is imminent and therefore sees no purpose in making an issue; (b) he is afraid that if he forces the issue the decision will go against him; (c) he hopes the problem will go away because agreement will prove impossible. When agreement seems imminent, American diplomats suddenly go into high gear to gain the acquiescence of the ally. He in turn feels tricked by the very intensity and suddenness of the pressure while we are outraged to learn of objections heretofore not made explicit. This almost guarantees that the ensuing con-troversy will take place under the most difficult conditions.

before we go much further in negotiations, we need an agreed concept of ultimate goals and how to achieve them.

IV. CEASEFIRE AND COALITION GOVERNMENT

Substantive negotiations confront the United States with a major conceptual problem: whether to proceed step by step, discussing each item "on its merits," or whether to begin by attempting to get agreement about some ultimate goals.

The difference is not trivial. If the negotiations proceed step by step through a formal agenda, the danger is great that the bombing halt will turn out to be an admission ticket to another deadlock. The issues are so interrelated that a partial settlement foreshadows the ultimate outcome and therefore contains all of its complexities. Mutual distrust and the absence of clarity as to final goals combine to produce an extraordinary incentive to submit all proposals to the most searching scrutiny and to erect hedges for failure or bad faith.

This is well illustrated by two schemes which public debate has identified as suitable topics for the next stage of negotiations: ceasefire and coalition government.

It has become axiomatic that a bombing halt would lead—almost automatically—to a ceasefire. However, negotiating a ceasefire may well be tantamount to establishing the preconditions of a political settlement. If there existed a front line with unchallenged control behind it, as in Korea, the solution would be traditional and relatively simple: the two sides could stop shooting at each other and the ceasefire line could follow the front line. But there are no front lines in Viet Nam; control is not territorial, it depends on who has forces in a given area and on the time of day. If a ceasefire permits the Government to move without challenge, day or night, it will amount to a Saigon victory. If Saigon is prevented from entering certain areas, it means in effect partition which, as in Laos, tends toward permanency. Unlike Laos, however, the pattern would be a crazy quilt, with enclaves of conflicting loyalties all over the country.

This would involve the following additional problems: (1) It would lead to an intense scramble to establish predominant control before the ceasefire went into effect. (2) It would make next to impossible the verification of any withdrawal of North Vietnamese forces that might be negotiated; the local authorities in areas of preponderant communist control would doubtless certify that no external forces were present and impede any effort at international inspection. (3) It would raise the problem of the applicability of a ceasefire to guerrilla activity in the non-communist part of the country; in other words, how to deal with the asymmetry between the actions of regular and of guerrilla forces. Regular forces operate on a scale which makes possible a relatively precise definition of what is permitted and what is proscribed; guerrilla forces, by contrast, can be effective through isolated acts of terror difficult to distinguish from normal criminal activity.

There would be many other problems: who collects taxes and how, who enforces the ceasefire and by what means. In other words, a tacit de facto ceasefire may prove more attainable than a negotiated one. By the same token, a formal ceasefire is likely to predetermine the ultimate settlement and tend toward partition. Ceasefire is thus not so much a step toward a final settlement as a form of it.

This is even more true of another staple of the Viet Nam debate: the notion of a coalition government. Of course, there are two meanings of the term: as a means of legitimizing partition, indeed as a disguise for continuing the civil war; or as a "true" coalition government attempting to govern the whole country. In the first case, a coalition government would be a façade with non-communist and communist ministries in effect governing their own parts of the country. This is what happened in Laos, where each party in the "coalition government" wound up with its own armed forces and its own territorial administration. The central government did not exercise any truly national functions. Each side carried on its own business—including civil war. But in Laos, each side controlled contiguous territory, not a series of enclaves as in South Viet Nam. Too, of all the ways to bring about partition, negotiations about a coalition government are the most dangerous because the mere participation of the United States in talking about it could change the political landscape of South Viet Nam.

Coalition government is perhaps the most emotionally charged issue in Viet Nam, where it tends to be identified with the second meaning: a joint Saigon-NLF administration of the entire country. There can be no American objection, of course, to direct negotiations between Saigon and the NLF. The issue is whether the United States should be party to an attempt to *impose* a coalition government. We must be clear that our involvement in such an effort may well destroy the existing political structure of South Viet Nam and thus lead to a communist takeover.

Some urge negotiations on a coalition government for precisely this reason: as a face-saving formula for arranging the communist political victory which they consider inevitable. But those who believe that the political evolution of South Viet Nam should not be foreclosed by an American decision must realize that the subject of a coalition government is the most thankless and tricky area for negotiation *by outsiders*.

The notion that a coalition government represents a "compromise" which will permit a new political evolution hardly does justice to Vietnamese conditions. Even the non-communist groups have demonstrated the difficulty Vietnamese have in compromising differences. It is beyond imagination that parties that have been murdering and betraying each other for 25 years could work together as a team giving joint instructions to the entire country. The image of a line of command extending from Saigon into the countryside is hardly true of the non-communist government in Saigon. It would be absurd in the case of a coalition government. Such a government would possess no authority other than that of each minister over the forces he controlled either through personal or party loyalty.

To take just one example of the difficulties: Communist ministers would be foolhardy in the extreme if they entered Saigon without bringing along sufficient military force for their protection. But the introduction of communist military forces into the chief bastion of governmental strength would change the balance of political forces in South Viet Nam. The danger of a coalition government is that it would decouple the non-communist elements from effective control over their armed forces and police, leaving them unable to defend themselves adequately.

In short, negotiations seeking to impose a coalition from the outside are likely to change markedly and irreversibly the political process in South Viet Nam—as Vietnamese who believe that a coalition government cannot work quickly choose sides. We would, in effect, be settling the war on an issue least amenable to outside influence, with respect to which we have the least grasp of conditions and the long-term implications of which are most problematical.

This is not to say that the United States should resist an outcome freely negotiated among the Vietnamese. It does suggest that any negotiation on this point by the United States is likely to lead either to an impasse or to the collapse of Saigon.

V. WHERE DO WE GO FROM HERE?

Paradoxical as it may seem, the best way to make progress where distrust is so deep and the issues so interrelated may be to seek agreement on ultimate goals first and to work back to the details to implement them.

This requires an analysis of the strengths and weaknesses of both sides. Hanoi's strength is that it is fighting among its own people in familiar territory, while the United States is fighting far away. As long as Hanoi can preserve some political assets in the South, it retains the prospect of an ultimately favorable political outcome. Not surprisingly, Hanoi has shown a superior grasp of the local situation and a greater capacity to design military operations for political ends. Hanoi relies on world opinion and American domestic pressures; it believes that the unpopularity of the war in Viet Nam will ultimately force an American withdrawal.

Hanoi's weaknesses are that superior planning can substitute for material resources only up to a point. Beyond it, differences of scale are bound to become significant and a continuation of the war will require a degree of foreign assistance which may threaten North Viet Nam's autonomy. This Hanoi has jealously safeguarded until now. A prolonged, even if ultimately victorious war might leave Viet Nam so exhausted as to jeopardize the purpose of decades of struggle.

Moreover, a country as sensitive to international currents as North Viet Nam cannot be reassured by recent developments. The Soviet invasion of Czechoslovakia removed Viet Nam as the principal concern of world opinion, at least for a while. Some countries heretofore critical of the United States remembered their own peril and their need for American protection; this served to reduce the intensity of public pressures on America. Hanoi's support of Moscow demonstrated the degree of Hanoi's dependence on the U.S.S.R.; it also may have been intended to forestall Soviet pressures on Hanoi to be more flexible by putting Moscow in Hanoi's debt. Whatever the reason, the vision of a Titoist Viet Nam suddenly seemed less plausible— all the more so as Moscow's justification for the invasion of

Czechoslovakia can provide a theoretical basis for an eventual Chinese move against North Viet Nam. Finally, the Soviet doctrine according to which Moscow has a right to intervene to protect socialist domestic structures made a Sino-Soviet war at least conceivable. For Moscow's accusations against Peking have been, if anything, even sharper than those against Prague. But in case of a Sino-Soviet conflict, Hanoi would be left high and dry. International crises threatening to overshadow Viet Nam in successive years—the Middle East in 1967; Central Europe in 1968—thus may have convinced Hanoi that time is not necessarily on its side.

American assets and liabilities are the reverse of these. No matter how irrelevant some of our political conceptions or how insensitive our strategy, we are so powerful that Hanoi is simply unable to defeat us militarily. By its own efforts, Hanoi cannot force the withdrawal of American forces from South Viet Nam. Indeed, a substantial improvement in the American military position seems to have taken place. As a result, we have achieved our minimum objective: Hanoi is unable to gain a military victory. Since it cannot force our withdrawal, it must negotiate about it. Unfortunately, our military strength has no political corollary; we have been unable so far to create a political structure that could survive military opposition from Hanoi after we withdraw.

The structure of the negotiation is thus quite different from Korea. There are no front lines with secure areas behind them. In Viet Nam, negotiations do not ratify a military status quo but create a new political reality. There are no unambiguous tests of relative political and military strength. The political situation for both sides is precarious—within Viet Nam for the United States, internationally for Hanoi. Thus it is probable that neither side can risk a negotiation so prolonged as that of Panmunjom a decade and a half ago. In such a situation, a favorable outcome depends on a clear definition of objectives. The limits of the American commitment can be expressed in two propositions: first, the United States cannot accept a military defeat, or a change in the political structure of South Viet Nam brought about by external military force; second, once North Vietnamese forces and pressures are removed, the United States has no obligation to maintain a government in Saigon by force.

American objectives should therefore be (1) to bring about

a staged withdrawal of external forces, North Vietnamese and American, (2) thereby to create a maximum incentive for the contending forces in South Viet Nam to work out a political agreement. The structure and content of such an agreement must be left to the South Vietnamese. It could take place formally on the national level. Or, it could occur locally on the provincial level where even now tacit accommodations are not unusual in many areas such as the Mekong Delta.

The details of a phased, mutual withdrawal are not decisive for our present purposes and, in any case, would have to be left to negotiations. It is possible, however, to list some principles: the withdrawal should be over a sufficiently long period so that a genuine indigenous political process has a chance to become established; the contending sides in South Viet Nam should commit themselves not to pursue their objectives by force while the withdrawal of external forces is going on; in so far as possible, the definition of what constitutes a suitable political process or structure should be left to the South Vietnamese, with the schedule for mutual withdrawal creating the time frame for an agreement.

The United States, then, should concentrate on the subject of the mutual withdrawal of external forces and avoid negotiating about the internal structure of South Viet Nam for as long as possible. The primary responsibility for negotiating the internal structure of South Viet Nam should be left for direct negotiations among the South Vietnamese. If we involve ourselves deeply in the issue of South Viet Nam's internal arrangements, we shall find ourselves in a morass of complexities subject to two major disadvantages. First, we will be the party in the negotiation least attuned to the subtleties of Vietnamese politics. Second, we are likely to wind up applying the greater part of our pressure against Saigon as the seeming obstacle to an accommodation. The result may be the complete demoralization of Saigon, profound domestic tensions within the United States and a prolonged stalemate or a resumption of the war.

Whatever the approach, the negotiating procedure becomes vital; indeed, it may well determine the outcome and the speed with which it is achieved.

Tying the bombing halt to Saigon's participation in the substantive discussions was probably unwise—all the more so as Hanoi seems to have been prepared to continue bilateral talks.

The participation of Saigon and the NLF raised issues about status that would have been better deferred; it made a discussion of the internal structure of South Viet Nam hard to avoid. Nevertheless, the principles sketched above, while now more difficult to implement, can still guide the negotiations. The tension between Washington and Saigon can even prove salutary if it forces both sides to learn that if they are to negotiate effectively they must confront the fundamental issues explicitly.

As these lines are being written, the formula for resolving the issue of Saigon's participation in the conference is not yet clear. But the general approach should be the same whatever the eventual compromise.

The best procedure would be to establish three forums. If the South Vietnamese finally appear in Paris—as is probable—the four-sided conference should be looked upon primarily as a plenary session to legitimize the work of two negotiating committees which need not be formally established and could even meet secretly: (a) between Hanoi and the United States, and (b) between Saigon and the NLF. Hanoi and Washington would discuss mutual troop withdrawal and related subjects such as guarantees for the neutrality of Laos and Cambodia. (The formula could be the implementation of the Geneva Accords which have been accepted in principle by both sides.) Saigon and the NLF would discuss the internal structure of South Viet Nam. The third forum would be an international conference to work out guarantees and safeguards for the agreements arrived at in the other committees, including international peacekeeping machinery.

If Saigon continues to refuse the "our side, your side" formula, the same procedure could be followed. The subcommittees would become principal forums and the four-sided plenary session could be eliminated. The international "guaranteeing conference" would not be affected.

To be sure, Saigon, for understandable reasons, has consistently refused to deal with the NLF as an international entity. But if Saigon understands its own interests, it will come to realize that the procedure outlined here involves a minimum and necessary concession. The three-tiered approach gives Saigon the greatest possible control over the issues that affect its own fate; direct negotiations between the United States and the NLF would be obviated. A sovereign government is free to talk to any group that represents an important domestic power base without thereby conferring sovereignty on it; it happens all the time in union negotiations or even in police work.

But why should Hanoi accept such an approach? The answer is that partly it has no choice; it cannot bring about a withdrawal of American forces by its own efforts, particularly if the United States adopts a less impatient strategy—one better geared to the protection of the population and sustainable with substantially reduced casualties. Hanoi may also believe that the NLF, being better organized and more determined, can win a political contest. (Of course, the prerequisite of a settlement is that both sides think they have a chance to win or at least to avoid losing.) Above all, Hanoi may not wish to give the United States a permanent voice in internal South Vietnamese affairs, as it will if the two-sided approach is followed. It may be reinforced in this attitude by the belief that a prolonged negotiation about coalition government may end no more satisfactorily from Hanoi's point of view than did the Geneva negotiations over Viet Nam in 1954 and Laos in 1962. As for the United States, if it brings about a removal of external forces and pressures, and if it gains a reasonable time for political consolidation, it will have done the maximum possible for an ally—short of permanent occupation.

To be sure, Hanoi cannot be asked to leave the NLF to the mercy of Saigon. While a coalition government is undesirable, a mixed commission to develop and supervise a political process to reintegrate the country—including free elections—could be useful. And there must be an international presence to enforce good faith. Similarly, we cannot be expected to rely on Hanoi's word that the removal of its forces and pressures from South Viet Nam is permanent. An international force would be required to supervise access routes. It should be reinforced by an electronic barrier to check movements.

A negotiating procedure and a definition of objectives cannot guarantee a settlement, of course. If Hanoi proves intransigent and the war goes on, we should seek to achieve as many of our objectives as possible unilaterally. We should adopt a strategy which reduces casualties and concentrates on protecting the population. We should continue to strengthen the Vietnamese army to permit a gradual withdrawal of some American forces, and we should encourage Saigon to broaden its base so that it is stronger for the political contest with the communists which sooner or later it must undertake.

No war in a century has aroused the passions of the conflict in Viet Nam. By turning Viet Nam into a symbol of deeper resentments, many groups have defeated the objective they profess to seek. However we got into Viet Nam, whatever the judgment of our actions, ending the war honorably is essential for the peace of the world. Any other solution may unloose forces that would complicate prospects of international order. A new Administration must be given the benefit of the doubt and a chance to move toward a peace which grants the people of Viet Nam what they have so long struggled to achieve: an opportunity to work out their own destiny in their own way.

The International Control Commission
Experience and the Role of an
Improved International Supervisory Body
in the Vietnamese Settlement

JOHN S. HANNON, JR.

I. Introduction

The Vietnam peace negotiations continue, amid rampant speculation as to the possible terms of a settlement of that tragic conflict. An issue equally as important as the substantive content of any settlement is the nature and scope of the "impartial" supervisory body which will undoubtedly be formed to oversee its implementation. Ambassador Harriman, in the very first meeting with the North Vietnamese in Paris, underscored the importance of such a supervisory body: ". . . one of our major tasks will be to devise more effective ways of supervising any agreement and insuring the fair and equitable investigation of complaints." He stressed the need for "strengthening" any international supervision, and the inadequacy of existing procedures.[1] If the Paris negotiations are to produce an effective supervisory body, a great deal must be learned from its predecessor, the International Control Commission for Vietnam,[2] or "ICC/Vietnam," which, since its formation as part of the Geneva Agreements of 1954, has attempted to perform the tasks of supervision and control in Vietnam.

While the ICC has served useful functions at times, most would agree with Chester Cooper that its experience would require "careful review and strengthening" if the United States and its allies are to have any faith in Communist compliance with the eventual settlement.[3] In contrast to the flood of analyses of various international supervisory missions serving under United Nations sponsorship, very

1. N.Y. Times, May 14, 1968, at 18, col. 5.
2. The 1954 Geneva Conference established separate supervisory commissions for Cambodia, Laos, and Vietnam. Originally entitled "International Commissions for Supervision and Control," popular usage over the years has shortened this to "ICC." Unless otherwise designated, future references to "ICC" in this paper refer solely to ICC/Vietnam. All three ICCs operated on a "troika" format, with representatives from Canada, Poland, and India, each with one vote.
3. According to Cooper, who was one of the U.S. officials responsible for working out the U.S. negotiating position, "Major changes in its [the International Control Commission's] terms of reference and its mode of operation must be worked out, together with provisions for increasing its strength and improving its mobility . . . ." Cooper, *The Complexities of Negotiation*, 46 FOREIGN AFFAIRS 454, 464 (1968).

little has ever been published on the ICC experience,[4] despite the magnitude of the conflict in Vietnam and the extreme difficulty of fashioning a settlement for Vietnam that would have any degree of permanence. If the hopes of the international community for lasting peace in Southeast Asia are ever to be realized, the formulators of a new supervisory body for Vietnam must take into account the disastrous experiences of the ICC/Vietnam. Despite some inadequacy of source material,[5] this article attempts to provide a basic analysis of these ICC difficulties.

Even apart from its relation to the absorbing issue of a potential Vietnam settlement, analysis of ICC operations is vital because, in the words of Canada's Paul Martin, the ICC/Vietnam ". . . in many ways represents the severest test to which international peace-keeping has been put." [6] In contrast to most of the United Nations' supervisory entities,[7] the ICC operated in an area of major concern be-

---

4. The most illuminating study of the ICC/Vietnam is David Wainhouse's INTERNATIONAL PEACE OBSERVATION at 489-501 and 517-25 (1966). The only study specifically focused on the ICC experience is an unpublished M.A. thesis by a Canadian Army officer, Edmond Blais, *The International Commission for Supervision and Control in Indo-China* (Georgetown University, 1959). The Canadian view on the ICC is admirably presented by Paul Martin, Secretary of State for External Affairs, in CANADA AND THE QUEST FOR PEACE, ch. 2 (1967) and by John W. Holmes, Canada's observer at the 1954 Geneva Conference and subsequently responsible for Canada's policymaking with regard to the ICC: J. Holmes, *Political and Philosophical Aspects of U.N. Security Forces*, in PEACE-KEEPING: EXPERIENCE AND EVALUATION (THE OSLO PAPERS) 81 (P. Frydenberg, ed. 1964); J. Holmes, *Techniques of Peacekeeping in Asia*, in CHINA AND THE PEACE OF ASIA 231 (A. Buchan ed. 1965).

5. Since the ICC failed to generate an acceptable level of publicity for its operations, the analyst has recourse only to its eleven regular reports. *See* the First through Eleventh *Interim Reports of the International Commission for Supervision and Control in Vietnam* and the *1962 Special Report to the Co-Chairmen of the Geneva Conference on Indo-China:* First and Second Reports, CMD. NO. 9461 (1955); Third Report, CMD. NO. 9499 (1955); Fourth Report, CMD. NO. 9654 (1955); Fifth Report, CMD. NO. 9706 (1956); Sixth Report, CMND. NO. 0031 (1957); Seventh Report, CMND. NO. 0335 (1957); Eighth Report, CMND. NO. 0509 (1958); Ninth Report, CMND. NO. 0726 (1959); Tenth Report, CMND. NO. 1040 (1960); Eleventh Report, CMND. NO. 1551 (1961); 1962 Special Report, CMND. NO. 1755 (1962); [hereinafter cited as First Rept., Second Rept., etc.]. Since the reports come directly from the entity under analysis, some adjustment must be made for the possibility the ICC has filtered out some of its own errors and omissions. The British Papers by Command, in which the ICC Reports were published, compound the difficulty (and indicate possible lack of public interest in ICC activities) by omitting many of the Appendices. But despite these difficulties, the ICC Reports furnish an adequate summary of the ICC's major difficulties.

6. P. MARTIN, CANADA AND THE QUEST FOR PEACE 35 (1967).

7. Since activation of U.N. peace observation missions has heretofore required the consent of the United States and the "negative" consent of the Soviet Union (either by abstention in the Security Council or by not marshalling opposition in the General Assembly), the United Nations has been

tween the power blocs. Moreover, its tasks were as extensive as any supervisory body has handled—supervision of an armistice agreement after eight years of bloody warfare (1946-54) ; an extensive regroupment of armed forces totalling hundreds of thousands; transfer of large segments of territory and facilities between the combatants; a guarantee of freedom from reprisals covering thirty million people; a transfer of population from North to South totalling nearly one million persons; an exchange of over 75,000 prisoners of war; and a ban on the introduction of military personnel and equipment throughout both zones of Vietnam.

II. The Basic Principles of International Peace-Supervision

According to David Wainhouse, the "official usage" now recognizes a distinction between "peace-keeping" and "peace observation." [8] "Peace-keeping" is "a form of collective action by which a considerable military force is used to bring about a cessation of hostilities. The classic example of this (and likely to remain the only major example) was in Korea in 1951-53, after the U.N. Security Council (during the absence of the USSR delegation) voted to use "U.N. forces" to repel the North Korean aggression. In direct contrast, "peace observation" involves international action to prevent or terminate hostilities by means short of the threat or use of naked force. The numbers of men involved in peace observation is much lower than in peace-keeping, and peace observers are limited to use of force only in cases of self-defense. While the line between peace-keeping and peace observation can become very thin, most of the U. N. operations have been primarily in the latter category: Suez (UNEF), Lebanon (UNOGIL), Kashmir (UNMOGIP), West New Guinea (UNTEA), Yemen (UNYOM), and Cyprus (UNFICYP). The Congo operation tended to blur the distinction: here the number of U.N. personnel was much larger (around 20,000), and force was ultimately employed to secure freedom of movement. At any rate, any supervisory body issuing forth from a Vietnam settlement would probably be more of the peace observation variety, bearing arms primarily for self-defense purposes, and tasked with the duty of supervision of the acts of the parties in as impartial a manner as possible in the Vietnam context.

Such peace observation missions are dispatched most commonly in areas of great tension where hostilities are imminent or already underway. Suez in 1956, the Congo in 1960, Cyprus in 1964 are examples of peace observation missions interposed in hopes of cooling down hostile parties. But peace observation is merely the beginning

---

unable to act where delegations from both great powers are present and in disagreement—the usual situation in areas of major cold war concern.

8. D. Wainhouse, International Peace Observation 2 (1966) [hereinafter Wainhouse].

of the process of arranging a settlement of the underlying dispute; conciliation, mediation, judicial settlement, or some other process must accompany it. In the Inter-American system of peace observation, the additional task of mediation is performed by the peace observation mission itself.[9] Such responsibility is not the usual case, however. Thus, for instance, in Yemen and in Cyprus the United Nations appointed other mediators; and in Cyprus the Secretary General emphasized that the peace observation mission and the mediation effort ". . . are separate and distinct undertakings and shall be kept so." [10] Still, peace observation missions have been used to supervise the implementation of agreements already arrived at by the parties. This was the case with the ICCs as also with the U.N. missions in Yemen and West New Guinea and would probably be so with any future supervisory body for Vietnam.

The purpose of a peace observation mission is to provide a "moral presence," a form of deterrence to further violations by the parties.[11] Its task is to focus world attention on the conduct of the parties and to furnish as accurate and as impartial a record of the parties' activities as possible. When it detects violations, its role is to bring the parties together and induce them to settle the matter. Responsibility for the actual implementation of the settlement remains with the parties to that settlement.[12]

Where the parties fail to agree following certain violations, the peace observation mission has two "sanctions." The first is to give the matter as much publicity as possible throughout the world, to bring to bear whatever pressure world public opinion is able to exert. The effectiveness of this course is debatable.[13] Second, and far more

---

9. *Id.* at 559.

10. *Id.* at 459.

11. A. Cox, Prospects for Peacekeeping 4-6 (1967); R. Russell, United Nations Experience With Military Forces: Political and Legal Aspects 5 (Brookings Inst. Staff Paper, 1964); Wainhouse, *supra* note 8, at 549.

12. P. Martin, *supra* note 6, at 44 (with specific reference to the ICC/Vietnam).

13. This is neither the time nor place to discuss the effect of world public opinion on international relations. General E. L. M. Burns, the Commander of UNEF, saw little effect in the peace observation arena:

> It is sometimes urged that bringing serious breaches . . . before the Security Council served a useful purpose, in that 'World Public Opinion' was informed of the facts of the case, and would consequently be a sort of moral sanction against the aggressor. I regret to say that this idea never seemed to work out.

Wainhouse, at 564, citing E.L.M. Burns, Between Arab and Israeli 280 (1963). World public opinion remains the *only* sanction available to peace observation missions beyond direct pressure against the parties either by the mission itself, with its limited resources, or by the organization or countries which first established that mission. The fact that such missions continue to be formed argues that the sanctions currently available have at least a minimum acceptability. Wainhouse appears to accept this analy-

important, the mission can relay the facts back to the organization which established it—the United Nations, or in this case, the members of the Geneva Conference. The individual governments represented in this organization can then exert pressure on the recalcitrant parties. The effectiveness of the peace observation mission is thus directly dependent upon the backing it receives from outside itself. Where an international agreement is breached and the parties remain recalcitrant, the peace observation mission has not automatically failed; for if it has found the facts and reported them with accuracy and impartiality, it has done its job. Either those who established the mission have failed to come to its aid and to pressure the parties to observe the terms of the agreement, or the desire of one or both of the parties to circumvent the agreement has been too strong for the amount of pressure applied from outside.[14] A mixture of both factors sealed the fate of the ICC/Vietnam.

The tasks of such peace observation missions have been infinitely varied, but a pattern of more common tasks has been identified in the excellent study by David Wainhouse and associates: [15]

A. Quasi-military Tasks—
    1. Supervision of the cease-fire;
    2. Establishment of demarcation lines;
    3. Establishment of demilitarized and defensive zones; [16]
    4. Regroupment of forces;
    5. Bans on introducing fresh troops/arms and establishing military bases;
    6. Exchange of prisoners of war and civilian internees.[17]

---

sis, and argues that to maximize the effect of public opinion, citations of violations by the parties should be phrased in specific terms and adequately publicized in hopes of making the situation uncomfortable for the general officer in whose jurisdiction the violation occurred. WAINHOUSE, at 564-65. The United States apparently believes in the usefulness of publicity in the peace observation context, for in 1961 Secretary of State Dean Rusk, in discussing the administration's proposals for improvements in the ICC/-Laos, stated "There should be some effective method of informing governments and the world at large about a finding by the control body that the conditions of peace and neutrality [of Laos], as defined, have been violated." Rusk, *United States Outlines Program to Insure Genuine Neutrality for Laos*, 44 DEP'T STATE BULL. 844, 847 (1961).

14. Committee on Peacekeeping Operations, White House Conference on International Cooperation, *Remarks*, in BLUEPRINT FOR PEACE 65, 67 (1966). Committee members included Andrew Cordier, Frank Altschul, Donald G. Brennan, Clark Eichelberger, Ernest Gross, Joseph E. Johnson, Sol Linowitz, Francis O. Wilcox, and Ruth E. Russell.

15. WAINHOUSE, at 558-80.

16. A demilitarized zone is one in which no military personnel, equipment, or installations are authorized; a defensive zone may include military personnel, equipment, and installations, but only up to a designated level. WAINHOUSE, at 562.

17. Civilian internees include any civilians who were detained by a combatant; often these include political opponents and former government officials.

B. Quasi-political Tasks—
  1. Political reporting;
  2. Radio monitoring;
  3. Exchange of civilian populations;
  4. Transfer of territory;
  5. Guarantee of democratic freedoms;
  6. Supervision of elections;
  7. Observation of neutrality provisions.

The remarkable fact about the ICC/Vietnam was that, whereas most peace observation missions under United Nations auspices were delegated a fairly narrow range of tasks, the ICC/Vietnam received a very broad mandate.[18] It was to supervise all of the quasi-military tasks listed above except supervision of the cease-fire, as well as all of the quasi-political tasks except political reporting and radio monitoring.[19] Since the personnel of all three ICCs (Vietnam, Laos and Cambodia) taken together numbered less than one thousand men in the 1954-55 period, the ICC/Vietnam's assignment was indeed one of herculean dimensions. But none of its assigned tasks exceeded the above pattern; and, with the exception of supervision of elections,[20] the "terms of reference" of the ICC (the enumeration of its tasks, as listed in the Agreement on the Cessation of Hostilities in Vietnam) were clear, and adequately detailed. The ICC's problems arose elsewhere.

III. RESPONSIBILITY FOR IMPLEMENTING THE GENEVA AGREEMENTS

A. *The ICC*

The composition of the ICC—representatives of Canada, India and Poland—was settled less than forty-eight hours before the end of the Geneva Conference.[21] The ICC members accordingly had no voice

---

18. Agreement on the Cessation of Hostilities in Vietnam, July 20, 1954, in Senate Comm. on Foreign Relations, 89th Cong., 2d Sess., BACKGROUND INFORMATION RELATING TO SOUTHEAST ASIA AND VIETNAM 36-48 (2d rev. ed.) Comm. Print 1966 [hereinafter cited as BACKGROUND INFORMATION].
19. The ICC was not required to issue any reports at stated intervals, political, economic or military. Its only reporting responsibility was in event of violations of the Geneva Agreements. Radio monitoring is usually conducted only when the Commission has access to only part of its area of responsibility, as in Korea, where the Neutral Nations Supervisory Commission was often barred from North Korea. WAINHOUSE, at 573.
20. The task of supervising elections in Vietnam was listed not in the Agreement on the Cessation of Hostilities but rather in the Final Declaration of the Geneva Conference [see BACKGROUND INFORMATION at 67], where no amplifying instructions were given. Since the political situation had altered drastically by July, 1956, the elections were never held, and the issue of the type of ICC personnel to be used, the nature of their duties, and similar problems never arose.
21. The composition of the supervisory body had been a major issue throughout the Geneva Conference. The deadlock was broken by a concession from the Communist side on July 18, within 48 hours of the July 20 deadline

whatever in the decisions on the scope of the ICC's responsibilities and powers.[22] When the invitations were extended, Canada initially expressed some doubts, but accepted within the week with no further questioning.[23] The ICC was charged with "control and supervision" of the "proper execution" of the Agreement on the Cessation of Hostilities in Vietnam by the parties (France, the Vietminh) (Art. 34), to include "control, observation, inspection and investigation" (Art. 36). Several tasks were stressed with particularity: control of the movement of the armed forces of the parties; supervision of the demarcation lines between re-grouping areas and the demilitarized zone; control of the exchange of prisoners of war and civilian internees; and supervision of the provisions regarding introduction of armed forces, arms, munitions, and other types of war materiel (Art. 36). Not listed in Article 36 but soon to become of major importance were ICC supervision of freedom from reprisals and the dual guarantee of democratic liberties (Art. 14(c)) and freedom of movement (during the first 300 days) (Art. 14(d)). The ICC was empowered to conduct investigations, either on its own initiative or on request of the Joint Commission of the Parties (Art. 37), and to inform the parties of measures necessary to settle incidents (Art. 39). ICC recommendations were to be adopted by majority vote (Art. 41), except on amendments or additions to the Armistice Agreement and on violations which "might lead to a resumption of hostilities" (refusal of a party to effect the movements specified in the regroupment plan; violations by the armed forces of one party of the regrouping zones, territorial waters or airspaces of the other), where unanimity was required (Art. 42). The ICC was to inform the members of the Ge-

---

imposed by French Premier Mendes-France, who had promised to resign if no agreement had been reached by then. While both Canada and India had "observers" at this phase of the Conference, they had not engaged in the deliberations on the supervisory body, and the hour was now too late.

22. This has unfortunate ramifications, in that the countries which furnish peace observation mission personnel might well feel greater responsibility if they had participated in framing the supervisory body's terms of reference. During the 1953 Korean armistice negotiations, the United States submitted a draft of the final agreements to Switzerland, which eventually supplied one of the four delegations to the Neutral Nations Supervisory Commission. The Swiss passed a number of suggestions back to the United States, but it was too late for any of these to be incorporated. Unfortunately some of the suggestions dealt with problems that assumed major significance in short order after the NNSC began its operations. Freymond, *Supervising Agreements: The Korean Experience*, 37 FOREIGN AFFAIRS 496, 502 (1959).

23. At first Canada demanded assurances that the ICC would have a "reasonable chance" to perform its tasks, and deferred its acceptance until full information could be made available. N.Y. Times, July 23, 1954, at 1, col. 2. But within a week, conscious of the "serious consequences" which would follow any rejection (it had taken over two months of stormy negotiations to produce the Canada-India-Poland formula), Canada accepted the invitation without further public comment. N.Y. Times, July 29, 1954, at 2, col. 7.

neva Conference in all cases where ICC activities were being hindered or where one of the parties refused to implement one of its recommendations (Art. 43). The Commanders of the Forces of the parties were to afford the ICC full protection and all possible assistance and cooperation (Art. 25) and to ensure that persons under their commands who violated any of the Agreement's provisions were suitably punished (Art. 22).

B. *The Parties*

Responsibility for the execution of the Agreement was placed squarely on the parties (Art. 28) and their successors (Art. 27). To facilitate execution of provisions requiring joint action, the parties were to establish a Joint Commission (Art. 30), composed of an equal number of representatives from each of the two parties (Art. 31), with the President of each delegation holding the rank of General (Art. 32). The Joint Commission would ensure execution of a simultaneous and general cease-fire, regroupment of armed forces, and observance of the demarcation lines between the regrouping zones and of the demilitarized sectors. It would ensure liaison between the parties on preparing and carrying out plans for the execution of these provisions, and endeavor to solve any disputed questions (Art. 33). The Joint Commission's duties with respect to observance of the demarcation lines between regrouping zones and in the demilitarized sectors (Arts. 3, 6, 7, 8, 9) were particularly far-reaching. It was to be notified in advance of the introduction of war materiel, arms, and munitions (Art. 17(e)), and of military personnel (Art. 16(f)), into Vietnam; and it could request the ICC to conduct investigations (Art. 37). The Commanders of the Forces of the Parties were to afford full protection and all possible assistance and cooperation to the Joint Commission (Art. 25).

IV. Early ICC Operations: The "Honeymoon" Phase

The ICC was given broad latitude in fashioning its internal structure; since only its troika composition posed major difficulties, and this had been specified in the Armistice Agreement, little need be said about this internal organization.[24] The Indian representative functioned both as ICC Chairman and as *ex officio* Secretary General, giving him an overview of the entire ICC operation and fairly broad powers. The ICC used three Committees (Operations, Administration and Freedoms),[25] each with a troika structure. Later a Legal Com-

---

24. The ICC organizational system is described in detail in First Rept. at 7-12.
25. The Operations Committee was composed of military advisers from each of the three countries, and dealt with military and logistical matters. The Freedom Committee utilized political advisers from each of the countries, and supervised the guaranties of democratic freedoms and the right to move to the other zone (within the first 300 days). The Administrative Committee, similarly troika in structure, handled accommodations, transportation, and the usual sea of paper work. First Rept. at 8-9.

mittee was appointed. India by agreement furnished most of the personnel for the Secretariat, which included Administration, Operations and Petitions sections,[26] plus a Public Relations Unit (which failed to gain widespread publicity for ICC reports on the subsequent violations).

The Armistice Agreement designated seven fixed teams for each of the northern and southern zones of Vietnam, specifying their locations. The ICC referred to the fixed teams as the "eyes and ears" of the Commission. Mobile teams were also used as needed for special investigations. Each of these teams required two officers from each of the three delegations, plus a liaison officer and an interpreter from each of the parties, and possibly also communications or Secretariat personnel. In short, the mobile teams were questionably "mobile."

The first ICC personnel arrived in Vietnam on August 11, 1954, nearly three weeks after the Armistice Agreement had been signed. Despite the troika format, the numbers of personnel dispatched by the three countries were quite varied; taking together the personnel of the three ICCs (Cambodia, Laos, Vietnam), there were in the early days 160 Canadians, 300 Poles, and 500 Indians. The large Indian complement was attributable to its responsibility for staffing the Secretariat, while the Polish delegation was larger by far than the Canadian, in the words of one observer, because the Poles brought their "political commissars" along.[27] Since each delegation had only one vote in the ICC meetings, the disparity in numbers made no difference at the highest level.

Analysis of the early days of ICC operations shows that the degree of implementation of the Geneva Agreements followed the desires of the parties. The provisions which the parties sincerely desired to implement, those of a military nature (cease-fire, regroupment), were carried out with a minimum of intransigence. Implementation of the provisions of a more political nature (ban on reprisals, guarantee of democratic liberties, freedom of movement to the other zone), in which the parties were far less willing to cooperate, required extensive prodding from the ICC, and in many instances resulted only in flagrant violation and fruitless investigation. But during these early days, the ICC remained relatively optimistic and very flexible, adapting its resources with considerable ingenuity to meet the needs of the situation.

26. The Administration section handled personnel, logistics, and liaison matters; Operations dealt with the ICC's mobile and fixed investigation teams; and Petitions administered the collection of complaints from Vietnamese nationals as to violations of the armistice guaranties and channeled them to the proper authorities for investigation and further action, as necessary. First Rept. at 8.
27. E. Blais, *supra* note 4.

A. *Military Provisions*

The ICC stressed the responsibility of the parties for execution of the Armistice Agreements (Art. 28) and the vital importance of the Joint Commission for joint planning and the settlement of disputes.[28]

1. *Cease-Fire.* Article 10 charged the military commanders with ordering and enforcing the cease-fire. The dates and times for execution were specified for each of three zones of Vietnam (Northern, Central, Southern). Since the last of these dates was August 11, the day on which the first ICC personnel arrived in Vietnam, the ICC was unable to supervise this phase; but, realizing the difficulties in assembling such an *ad hoc* supervisory body, the Geneva Conference members had not charged the ICC with any responsibilities regarding the cease-fire. Fortunately both parties were anxious to implement the cease-fire, and all deadlines were met, with only minor incidents.[29]

2. *Regroupment.* Articles 1 and 15 provided for regroupment of the opposing forces in mutually exclusive "provisional assembly areas" within 15 days and ultimate withdrawal to the north or south of the demilitarized zone within 300 days. The initial regroupment was concluded within the fifteen-day period, but again without ICC supervision since its personnel had not arrived until a few days later.[30] During the 300-day period for final withdrawal into the two zones, the ICC was required to supervise the demarcation lines between regroupment areas as well as the demilitarized zone. None of the fourteen fixed teams was designated specifically for these locations, and the ICC's mobile teams were all busy with other tasks (supervising prisoner exchanges, investigating the massive number of complaints received on reprisals and violations of democratic freedoms, and the like).[31] Thus the ICC's only major contribution to the entire cease-fire and regroupment phase was its arranging for the Joint Commission to plan the ultimate withdrawals,[32] which were completed in advance of the 300-day deadline without incident,[33] due to the parties' mutual desire to have an end to the fighting. Given the guerrilla warfare context and the jumbled military situation at the time of cease-fire, with pockets of Vietminh and French forces interspersed throughout the length and breadth of Vietnam, this was no mean accomplishment.

The presence of peace observation teams in the field in the first days after a cease-fire is highly desirable. In the confused state of affairs, where tempers have not yet cooled and reprisals are most likely, where some military units may not have received adequate

---

28. First Rept. at 11.
29. First Rept. at 12-14.
30. First Rept. at 14.
31. First Rept. at 13.
32. First Rept. at 14,17.
33. WAINHOUSE, at 520.

notice of the armistice or may have chosen to disregard it, peace observation forces have a very positive role to play. Since the interest of the international community in a final settlement still runs high at this point, prompt and impartial reporting by the observers may well generate strong and effective pressure on the parties from many quarters if violations do occur. Secondly, if the observers are to be in position at cease-fire, advance notice to the countries which may be asked to supply units is a vital consideration. Preparedness for peace observation missions has advanced but little since 1954 (Canada and the Scandinavian countries are the shining exceptions [34]), and the rambling impromptu approach sadly remains the general rule. Advance notice is, of course, excruciatingly difficult where the negotiations cut across the major power blocs and the composition of the supervisory body poses a major issue. But given the conditions of the current war, with the intense bitterness between the combatants, the attempt must be made. Similar considerations indicate the desirability of far higher numbers of peace observation personnel during the first few months, when their tasks are most numerous and complex. The ICC was woefully understaffed to effectively carry on its assigned tasks during those first months.

3. *Exchange of Prisoners of War and Civilian Internees.* Although Article 21 required liberation of all prisoners of war and civilian internees within thirty days after the cease-fire, the ICC arrived in Vietnam with but ten days remaining, only to discover that no exchanges had been made due to procedural disputes. Control of these exchanges was one of the major ICC tasks (Art. 36), and the ICC proved more useful here, speedily arranging a compromise under which the French then released 65,477 persons and received 11,706 from the Vietminh, with ICC mobile teams supervising the exchanges.[35]

The residual cases were to pose insuperable difficulties, however. The ICC's Second Report viewed the attitude of the parties regarding these exchanges as "not as cooperative" as envisaged in the Armistice Agreement.[36] The ICC's Fourth Report listed "status unknown" on seventy-one per cent of the 30,373 French claims and twenty per cent of the 13,615 Vietminh claims.[37] Wainhouse views discrepancies as inevitable, due to faulty calculation, escape and prior release of some prisoners, desertions/defections, and the nature of guerrilla warfare, with its malnutrition and disease. But he regards ICC operations in this area as a qualified success.[38] With the number of cases which lingered on through subsequent reports and then quietly dropped from

---

34. *See, e.g.,* Haekkerup, *Scandinavia's Peace-Keeping Forces for U.N.,* 42 FOREIGN AFFAIRS 675 (1963).
35. First Rept. at 17,18.
36. Second Rept. at 46.
37. Fourth Rept. at 29.
38. WAINHOUSE, at 572.

sight, nagging doubts remain about the effectiveness of the procedures employed.

Subsequent arrangements for prisoner exchanges should provide for repatriation as soon as possible, with strong requirements of cooperation from the parties, and personal questioning of any prisoners who allegedly refuse repatriation. The utmost of pressure must be exerted to clear up residual cases rapidly, with full access by the observers to the records of the parties and to any areas suspected of concealing prisoners or internees. Sufficient numbers of observers must be provided in order to make the necessary investigations rapidly. Any cases of mistreatment of prisoners or internees should be grounds for some form of sanction against the offending party.

B. *Transfer of Civil Administration and Public Property*

The division of Vietnam involved the transfer of large segments of territory and valuable facilities. Articles 14 and 15 contain extensive provisions for ensuring a smooth transition. The parties were to coordinate their activities to ensure no break in the transfer of responsibilities (Art. 14(b)), and to permit no destruction or sabotage of public property or injury to the life and property of the civilian population (Art. 15(d)). Time limits were specified for all transfers (Art. 15(f)(2)), and the Joint Commission and ICC were to ensure that steps be taken to safeguard the forces in the course of withdrawal and transfer (Art. 15(e)).

While the Joint Commission was able to conduct the withdrawal of military personnel and the transfer of civil administration with little ICC activity, its inability to function smoothly on the transfer of public property and essential public services required the ICC to intervene in essentially all of the arrangements.[39] The ICC performed this function extremely well, in perhaps its finest hour, coordinating the activities of the parties, arranging meetings, issuing detailed "suggestions," and providing fixed and mobile teams to supervise every detail of the actual transfer.

In the transfer of Hanoi, the ICC set up discussions between the parties, and urged them to make plans similar to those involved in the successful military exchanges. It arranged for the parties to prepare inventories of stock and equipment of public offices and utilities, under ICC mobile team supervision. The essential services in Hanoi (water, electricity, transport) were all operated by private French concerns which refused to continue operating the services despite DRV (Democratic Republic of Vietnam) entreaties and promises. The ICC discussed the problem with the parties, proposed terms to ensure no break in these services, and arranged for the early arrival and training of DRV personnel to effect the switch-over without interruption.[40] The ICC then provided five mobile teams and super-

---

39. First Rept. at 14-16; Second Rept. at 46.
40. First Rept. at 14-16.

—2

vised the military transfer of Hanoi, sector by sector, without incident.[41] Similar ICC operations were performed in the transfer of Haiphong, with the ICC providing detailed suggestions to the parties on the orderly transfer of public services, examining inventory lists, and deciding which property could be removed by the French.[42] While the turn-over of civil administration in parts of Central and Southern Vietnam did not always proceed without a break in continuity, the ICC continued to stress the need for the parties to plan and coordinate the exchanges, pointing out the successful Hanoi example.[43] In the end, the ICC could proudly report adherence to the time limits while transferring these public properties and essential services "intact and in running order in all areas." [44] This was indeed a type of mission the ICC was well-suited to perform.

C. *Political Provisions*

The Agreement contained two extremely short provisions which quickly became major difficulties. Article 14(c) required both parties to refrain from reprisals or discrimination against any persons or organizations on account of their activities during hostilities, and guaranteed democratic liberties. Article 14(d) required the parties to permit and to *assist* any civilians who desired to move to the other zone during the first 300 days. The ICC arranged for widespread publicity of the provisions of Articles 14(c) and 14(d) through press releases and requests to the parties for extensive publicity campaigns.[45] It exerted strong pressure against the DRV to reform its clumsy, slow, complex procedures on the administrative processing of persons desiring to move south,[46] and eventually issued detailed recommendations on improved procedures.[47] It sent out mobile teams to investigate complaints (almost half the mobile teams dispatched by the ICC in the early years were to investigate complaints under these two articles) ; and in some instances it was able to report the obtaining of relief or the closing of the case as unwarranted.

Yet by its Fourth Report the ICC could only bemoan the delay and obstruction from both DRV and French zones on both Articles 14(c) and 14(d), contrasting this with the full cooperation received from both High Commands on purely military matters.[48] Typical of this obstruction was the DRV's submission of 320,000 complaints of violation of Article 14(d) from "friends and relations" of those who had moved to the South, alleging forced evacuation and requesting ICC

---

41. First Rept. at 15.
42. Second Rept. at 51-52.
43. First Rept. at 28.
44. Fourth Rept. at 6.
45. First Rept. at 21.
46. First Rept. at 23.
47. Second Rept. at 47, 52-54.
48. Fourth Rept. at 15-16.

assistance in returning these people to the DRV. ICC mobile teams contacted 25,000 of the 121,000 persons in refugee camps in the South, and reported no foundation to this incredible number of complaints.[49] The ICC soon reported that both sides used "religious, social and local influences" to pressure the population on its choices under Article 14(d), and that both sides made 14(d) allegations more to get the ICC to condemn the other side than out of any solicitude for the individuals concerned.[50] The ICC listed many instances where DRV authorities proved unable or unwilling to control crowds hostile to ICC teams attempting to conduct 14(d) investigations. The crowds often manhandled or dragged away witnesses, and at the least caused considerable delay.[51] The Canadian representative felt that the atmosphere of "suspicion, fear and rumor" in the DRV inhibited freedom of choice under Article 14(d) and found good reason to believe the DRV officials took special measures to prevent the full discovery of facts by ICC teams. Soldiers, political cadres and local militia were frequently stationed in the houses of Roman Catholics, with orders to prevent them from leaving their houses to speak to the teams; while other persons were called away to meetings organized to coincide with the arrival of ICC teams.[52] He also stated that, despite the parties' responsibility for implementation of Article 14(d), the ICC during this period was forced to devote a "major portion" of its time and energy to processing 14(d) investigations.[53] And, as discussed *infra* in Section VI(e), most analysts agree that large numbers of reprisals and denials of democratic freedom occurred in both zones. The ICC experience was far from satisfactory in the Article 14(c) and 14(d) areas.

V. Deadlock in Southeast Asia, 1956

A. *The Problem*

Any remnants of the "honeymoon phase" disappeared in 1955 and early 1956, when serious doubts were raised about the future effectiveness of the ICC and indeed of the entire settlement envisioned by the Geneva Agreements of 1954. In the process, the most critical defects of the settlement and of the ICC arrangement came to light.

While the Agreement on the Cessation of Hostilities in Vietnam contained a "successor clause" (Art. 27) purporting to bind the successors of either party to enforce those Agreements, only the Vietminh and France actually signed the document. The problem of the status of the State of Vietnam (the Diem government) as a successor to France was to assume major proportions and eventually result

---

49. Fourth Rept. at 11-12.
50. Fourth Rept. at 12-13.
51. Fourth Rept., App. V.
52. Fourth Rept. at 19-20.
53. Fourth Rept. at 23.

in total deadlock in 1956.[54] In 1954 the Diem government had been in an extremely weak "control position," and was ignored by the French in working out a settlement with the Vietminh. Although the State of Vietnam refused to accede to the Geneva Agreements and reserved "full freedom of action," France was expected to remain in control of the southern zone, and some observers predicted the collapse of the Diem government despite the French presence. But in late 1954 the State of Vietnam began to receive ever-increasing support from the United States, and was able to demand and obtain full withdrawal of the French forces by April, 1956, two months before the elections specified in the Final Declaration of the Geneva Conference and designed to unify Vietnam.[55]

This caused enormous difficulties for the ICC. While Diem, who proclaimed his government the "Republic of Vietnam" (RVN) in October, 1955,[56] offered full protection and "practical cooperation" to the ICC, the RVN would not formally accept legal responsibility for implementing the remaining provisions of the Geneva Agreements, claiming it had not signed them and was not bound by them. The ICC countered that it could not operate effectively under a freely revocable "practical understanding," and that the Diem government's independent attitude placed the ICC mission in "serious jeopardy." The ICC had been established by the Geneva Agreements, drew its authority from this source, and had "no other sanction." [57]

Together with the effectiveness of the ICC and its duration, the entire settlement reached at Geneva in 1954 was thrown into question by the RVN position. While the viability of the provision for all-Vietnam elections in 1956 remains a hotly-disputed issue,[58] the ICC clearly expected its operations to cease in 1956 with supervision of these elections. Due to the refusal of Diem even to enter into the consultations designed to plan the actual conduct of those elections, much less the elections themselves, the ICC remorsefully saw itself ". . . faced with the prospect of continuing its activities inde-

54. For the entire narrative of events, see Hannon, *A Political Settlement for Vietnam: The 1954 Geneva Conference and Its Current Implications*, 8 VA. J. INT'L L. 4 (1967), from which most of the material for section V is taken.
55. Final Declaration of the Geneva Conference, July 21, 1954, §§ 6 and 7, in BACKGROUND INFORMATION at 67.
56. Diem had staged a referendum in October, 1955, between himself and former Emperor Bao Dai. The voters were given ballots with the pictures of the two candidates on them; 98.2 per cent of the voters managed to deposit the correct picture in the ballot box. Diem then proclaimed the establishment of the Republic of Vietnam, with himself as its President. G. KAHIN & J. LEWIS, THE UNITED STATES IN VIET NAM 71-72 (1967). The DRV protested this action as a violation of the Geneva Agreement provisions calling for elections to unify the country nine months later.
57. Fourth Rept. at 16-18.
58. The author has elsewhere contended that elections *were* an integral part of the Geneva bargain. *See* Hannon, *supra* note 54, especially at 48-54.

finitely . . ." [59] in a powerless status due to the RVN's refusal to accept legal responsibility.

B. *Absence of Consultative Machinery*

While the entire political situation in Southeast Asia was thus thrown into question, the ICC itself had few resources with which to respond. Article 41 of the Armistice Agreement did empower the ICC to formulate recommendations on amendments and additions to the Agreement "to ensure a more effective execution;" but the ICC does not appear to have taken major initiatives under this provision, which seems to be more "gap-filling" in nature than a mandate to *enforce* the Armistice Agreement or even to re-negotiate the political balance across cold-war lines once the settlement had gone awry. In the words of Canada's Paul Martin,

> . . . [T]he Commission was not envisaged as an enforcement agency: it had not been given the terms of reference, the authority, or the resources to impose its will on the parties, and was expected to leave the actual task of keeping the peace to those directly involved, to act in such a way as to encourage observance of the Cease-Fire Agreement, and to keep the members of the 1954 conference informed of results. The deterioration of the situation in Viet Nam had complex origins, and although the weaknesses of the supervisory process no doubt contributed to the eventual breakdown, there were other important factors arising out of the nature of the 1954 settlement itself, the policies and objectives of the two Viet Nams, and the atmosphere created by the policies of the major world powers.[60]

While the ICC/Laos did become deeply involved in political negotiations between the parties and recommended a settlement which was actually accepted and carried out (for a short period of time),[61] the ICC/Vietnam's strenuous efforts to get the DRV and RVN working together in the Joint Commission, dealing with military problems, came to naught. Given the rigid positions of the two sides, it is hard to find major fault with the ICC's activities in this regard.

Unfortunately, neither of the classic "sanctions" normally available to peace observation missions were available to the ICC. Two years had passed since the war ended in Indo-China, world attention was now focused on other problems, and recourse to world public opinion as a means of pressuring the recalcitrant parties proved unavailing. And unlike missions under United Nations auspices, which always have recourse to the establishing organization for new instruc-

---

59. Fourth Rept. at 17.
60. P. MARTIN, *supra* note 6, at 45-46.
61. Holmes, *Techniques of Peacekeeping in Asia,* in CHINA AND THE PEACE OF ASIA 231, 247-48 (A. Buchan ed. 1965).

tions and support if and when the situation changes,[62] the Geneva Conference totally failed to provide the peace observation mission with such consultative machinery. Thus, the ICC was not capable of pressuring the parties either to conform to the underlying agreement or to negotiate a new agreement, or of reinterpreting the mission of the peace observation body to conform to the changed situation. As David Wainhouse summarized the major defect of the Geneva Agreements from the ICC standpoint,

> . . . [T]he Geneva Conference of 1954 created an international peace-observation instrumentality without providing it with . . . the constant guidance and the backstopping such an operation requires and would have had if the Indo-China problem had been brought under the United Nations. It is a wonder that the ICC functioned at all . . . .[63]

At the time the Geneva Agreements were promulgated, they did appear to provide for such permanent consultative machinery. The seven countries at the Geneva Conference who adhered to the Final Declaration (both the United States and the State of Vietnam issued reservations) agreed to "consult one another" on questions forwarded by the ICC and "to study such measures as may prove necessary to ensure that the agreements . . . are respected" (Art. 13). But while measures may have been "studied" once the Agreements came into jeopardy in 1955-56, no joint action was ever taken. Perhaps the ultimate sanction was the possibility of reconvening the Geneva Conference. The DRV in early 1956 demanded this and solicited lukewarm support from the USSR and Communist China.[64] But the Conference has never been reconvened to deal with Vietnam.[65]

---

62. A situation comparable to the Vietnam situation of 1956, though by no means of the same complexity or magnitude, is that of the United Nations Observation Mission in Yemen. This entity was formed to "observe, certify, and report" on the implementation of a disengagement agreement between Saudi Arabia, which had been furnishing arms and supplies to Yemeni royalists, and the U.A.R., which had dispatched troops to Yemen to support the regime of Abdullah Sallal, the opponent of the royalists. The agreement was simply not observed by the parties: the Sallal regime proved so shaky that it would fall if all the Egyptian troops were withdrawn, and Saudi Arabia continued to supply arms to the royalists. The U.N. Secretary-General thereupon appointed a well-respected diplomat as his Special Representative to Yemen and as head of the observer mission. The diplomat, Pier Spinelli, was welcomed by all the parties, and was able to at least attempt conciliation. Thus the observer mission was thereby transformed from military to political in orientation, evidencing a degree of support and flexibility totally lacking to the ICC. When the conciliation effort failed, the entire observer mission was withdrawn, rather than allowing it to linger on as the ICC/Vietnam was to do. WAINHOUSE, at 421-35.

63. WAINHOUSE, at 499.

64. DOCUMENTS RELATING TO BRITISH INVOLVEMENT IN THE INDO-CHINA CONFLICT 1945-65, CMND. No. 2834, at 117-119 (1966).

65. The Geneva Conference was of course reconvened, with additional mem-

The only remaining entity to which the ICC could turn was the Co-Chairmen of the Geneva Conference, Great Britain and the Soviet Union. The Co-Chairmen are not even mentioned in the Geneva Agreements, and at the close of the Conference they had agreed only to perform minor functions incidental to winding-up the affairs of the Conference.[66] The ICC was to report violations to the *members* of the Conference, not to the Co-Chairmen. But when the other arrangements proved unworkable, the Co-Chairmen, for reasons of "practical convenience," agreed to distribute the ICC reports and bring the views of the ICC before the other members. The Co-Chairmen stressed the belief that this implied no further obligations than those assumed by the other members of the Conference;[67] but in actual practice they had indeed assumed a larger share of the responsibility for implementation of the Agreements, as their fruitless efforts to improve the Vietnam situation have demonstrated.

The continuing responsibilities portioned out in the Geneva Agreements on Laos in 1954 were quite comparable to those for Vietnam. After the 1962 Geneva Conference on Laos, the Co-Chairmen were explicitly given the duty of supervising the observance of the Agreements.[68] This had been interpreted as an explicit recognition of the "operational gulf" which previously existed between the respective ICCs and the members of the 1954 Geneva Conference,[69] and once again highlights a most serious defect.

C. *Lack of an Adequate Solution*

Since the Co-Chairmen were the only remaining authority to which the ICC could appeal in its dilemma, it asked the Co-Chairmen to give urgent consideration to both issues: the legal responsibility of the Republic of Vietnam under the Armistice Agreements, and the failure to progress toward elections. Further, it asked them to prescribe the necessary measures to resolve this deadlock.[70] The famous May 8, 1956 response of the Co-Chairmen was quite weak and furnished little assistance to the ICC. While they "strongly urged" both the RVN and the DRV to implement the Agreements, they merely requested that both sides "transmit their views" on the time required for holding consultations and proceeding with elections. France was

---

bers, to deal with the problems of Laos in 1962. But this came only after a Kennedy-Khrushchev agreement in Vienna in 1961.

66. The Co-Chairmen were to resolve the matter of finances for the Geneva Conference, and to issue the invitations to Canada, India and Poland to participate in the ICC. WAINHOUSE, at 495.

67. Fourth Rept. at 2.

68. Protocol to the Declaration on the Neutrality of Laos, Art. 8, 47 DEP'T STATE BULL. 261, 262 (1962): "The Co-Chairmen shall exercise supervision over the observance of this Protocol and the Declaration on the Neutrality of Laos. The Co-Chairmen will keep the members of the Conference constantly informed and when appropriate will consult with them."

69. WAINHOUSE, at 499.

70. Fourth Rept. at 16-18.

asked to use its "good offices" to settle the dispute (which is rather comical since Diem had insisted that the French get out of the South and the French withdrawal was now complete).[71]

This response left the ICC in a quandary from which it has never recovered. The Co-Chairmen asked it to "persevere" and yet had done nothing to resolve the underlying dispute or even to improve the co-operation to be expected from the parties. With the absolutely incompatible positions taken by the RVN and the DRV and the extreme difficulty of finding another solution which both major power blocs could accept, perhaps no other response was possible in 1956. But the duration of the ICC's mission thereby became open-ended, while its powers remained wholly inadequate for it to maintain peaceful conditions in Vietnam in and of itself. In the ensuing years, the Co-Chairmen have continued to discuss ICC problems with the other Geneva Conference members, but have offered few suggestions and no solutions. While subsequent ICC Reports continued to express the "utmost confidence" in the Co-Chairmen and to request that "urgent consideration" be given to its problems, little improvement was forthcoming. The first major acts of terrorism began in the RVN in a matter of months.

VI. Major ICC Problem Areas Since 1956

In the years since 1956, both the RVN and the DRV have persisted in their own interpretations of the Geneva Agreements, refused to implement many specific ICC recommendations, and proved quite adept at devising methods of curtailing ICC operations. With its "troika" composition, the ICC developed its own internal difficulties. Financial problems caused a cutback of about forty-five per cent in ICC personnel and facilities in 1960.[72] The combination of factors forced the ICC into the position of maintaining little more than a "presence" in Vietnam, a form of potential as yet untapped.[73] The following sections discuss some of the major ICC difficulties and offer some recommendations.

A. *The Joint Commission*

As discussed in section III(b) *supra,* the Joint Commission of representatives of the parties was assigned important tasks. From 1954 to 1956, composed of French and DRV representatives, it performed these functions well, resolving disputes and executing the military provisions with some prodding from the ICC. But as the RVN began to take over responsibilities in the South, its independent attitude caused the Joint Commission to function less satisfactorily; and after the French forces were withdrawn in April, 1956, the Joint

---

71. Sixth Rept. at 31.
72. Eleventh Rept. at 5.
73. In the 1962 Special Report, the ICC spoke of a "serious deterioration" in the situation: both RVN and DRV were now refusing access to the few

Commission did not function at all.[74] The Co-Chairmen saw the Joint Commission as an "essential part of the machinery" [75] and both they and the ICC made many unsuccessful attempts over the years to revive it. All foundered on the refusal of the RVN to participate on an equal basis with the DRV.[76] The demise of the Joint Commission removed from the ICC its primary means of dispute-resolution—bringing the two sides together to discuss their problems and seek solutions, with the ICC making various recommendations. It also solidified the atmosphere of total distrust between North and South. Since the Joint Commission had been given particular responsibility for the demilitarized zone (Arts. 3, 6, 7, 8, 9), its inactivity after 1956 was to have dire consequences for that area.

The failure of the RVN to assume the responsibility for implementing the Agreements, as symbolized by the failure of the Joint Commission, underscores the absolute necessity of negotiating a settlement which clearly binds all parties who may ever be in a position to destroy a settlement unacceptable to them. The RVN, the National Liberation Front, the DRV, and any other groups which might eventually attain a meaningful power position must be brought directly into the settlement process. No delegation should be ignored, and negotiations should result in a settlement which clearly articulates the responsibilities of all parties and which has gained common assent.

B. *The ICC's "Troika" Composition*

In attempting to analyze the problem of the "troika" composition of the ICC, with its Canadian, Indian, and Polish representatives, it is vital to examine the ICC's predecessor in the divided-country arena, the Neutral Nations Supervisory Commission in Korea (NNSC).[77] The NNSC was designed to conduct investigations con-

---

mobile teams the ICC even attempted to send out, leading to a "near-breakdown." WAINHOUSE, at 524. It seemed curiously symbolic of the reduced state of the ICC that at the height of the Tet Offensive of early 1968, some of the heaviest fighting in Saigon occurred in the vicinity of the ICC compound.

74. Sixth Rept. at 9,25.
75. Sixth Rept. at 9-10.
76. The Co-Chairmen's message to France on May 8, 1956, asked France to discuss the problem with the RVN and reach an agreement facilitating the work of the ICC and the Joint Commission. Sixth Rept. at 9. An arrangement was worked out, under which the RVN government accredited a liaison mission to the ICC, but no mention was made of RVN relations with the Joint Commission. France agreed only to establish a "French Mission to the Central Joint Commission," claiming the Co-Chairmen had implied that France had no further responsibilities. Seventh Rept. at 21-22. Since the RVN thereafter refused to participate in the Joint Commission under any circumstances (Ninth Rept. at 17), France withdrew even this "token mission" in mid-1958. Eighth Rept. at 6. The ICC continued to protest the situation, but to no avail.
77. The discussion of the NNSC comes from WAINHOUSE, at 342-57. *See also* Freymond, *supra* note 22, which has some excellent recommendations at 502-03.

cerning the agreements to cease the introduction of military personnel and equipment into North and South Korea. Its leadership was composed of four senior officers, two nominated by the U.N. Command (from Switzerland and Sweden), two by the North Koreans and Communist Chinese (from Poland and Czechoslovakia).

The NNSC was to establish five fixed teams in major seaports in the North, and five in the South, holding 10 additional teams in reserve. It soon became evident that entries and exits of military personnel and equipment in North Korea were taking place outside these five ports, but the ten mobile teams could not even begin an investigation unless a majority of the four officers voted affirmatively, and somehow the vote often came out tied. Even when a NNSC team did get to a railroad station in North Korea, after giving the two hours' advance notice required by the North Koreans, the Czech and Polish members of the team refused to board a train if the station master asserted there was no military cargo on board. During the first month of NNSC operations, the Swiss and Swedish members began claiming that the Poles and Czechs simply were not neutral. The NNSC was reduced to a token presence in June, 1956, just three years after the Korean Armistice Agreement was signed, but has lingered on ever after, just as the ICC.

As the 1954 Geneva Conference began to discuss Vietnam, the Communist negotiators demanded that the supervisory body there also be composed of representatives from Poland and Czechoslavakia, plus India and "one or two other Asian states." Obviously they again sought an absolute veto power. Anthony Eden of Great Britain refused to accept two communist states after the Korean experience, and wanted the five Colombo nations (India, Ceylon, Pakistan, Indonesia and Burma) to handle the supervision, since they were both Asian *and* neutral. The Communists rejected this, and the two sides engaged in endless recriminations and argumentation over whether communist representatives could be neutral. Finally Chou En-lai proposed the ICC "troika" formula less than 48 hours before Mendes-France's deadline for reaching a final settlement.[78] Unanimity was required on amendments and additions to the Armistice Agreement and on questions of violations which "might lead to a resumption of hostilities." While the latter provision might seem very broad in scope, it was by no means all-inclusive, and at least some limit was placed on possible interpretations by listing specific instances: refusals to effect the movements called for in the regroupment plan, and violations of the regrouping zones/territorial waters/air space of the other party. On all other matters, ICC recommendations needed only a majority vote.[79] The ICC troika and its voting provisions were clearly an improvement over the Korean experience.

---

78. WAINHOUSE, at 490-91.
79. Agreement on the Cessation of Hostilities in Vietnam, July 20, 1954, Arts. 41 & 42, in BACKGROUND INFORMATION at 47.

The Agreements themselves contained no specific illumination on whether the Poles and Canadians were to be explicit spokesmen for the Communists and the Western countries; and the Canadians, imbued with the broader goals of international peace observation, have steadfastly maintained that objectivity has been their guideline [80] (query whether the Poles would accept this assertion). The voting record of Poland in the ICC leaves little doubt as to its interpretation of its responsibilities.[81] In practice, even the Canadians admit that the partisan position of the Poles made it "essential for the Canadians to see that the case of the non-Communists got a hearing." [82]

John Holmes of Canada, ever the realist, asserts that the troika formula cannot be roundly condemned since it accurately reflected the actual situation of the parties both in Southeast Asia and at the bargaining table and allowed at least some maneuvering. While stalemate remained the rule, not the exception, the Indian representative often wielded a decisive influence, either by inducing compromise, by choosing sides or by remaining neutral. Holmes points to numerous occasions where Canadian-Indian decisions produced some action, "on procedural matters at least." Finally, he argues that a blanket policy of majority ICC rule would be futile unless it represented a position which both sides were prepared to accept (which of course is manifestly *not* the case in a 2-1 troika vote).[83]

But even granting all these points, the troika formula remains a most unsatisfactory method of decision-making, far removed from the type of neutral, impartial peace observation so earnestly sought by Dag Hammarskjold. First, each delegate represents his own government, and has to look to it for at least some policy guidance. This places a "middleman" between the delegate and the peace observation mission, and causes substantial delays as well. Secondly, where two of the three delegates are viewed as advocates, an enormous burden rests on the third member, whose government is thus placed squarely between the two major power blocs and is made to bear the heavy load of responsibility for every decision, with all its foreign policy and balance-of-power implications. To require "one Asian neutral" to perform this service year-in, year-out, in the torrent of emotions stirred up by the Vietnam problem, is simply asking too much.[84] And action on "procedural matters" alone is only a halting

---

80. P. MARTIN, *supra* note 6, at 50; Holmes, *supra* note 61, at 239; Blais, *supra* note 4, at 142-44.
81. A Canadian Army officer asserts that the Polish ICC delegation was "unhindered by moral responsibility and well-schooled in the act of the double negative," and accuses it of covert liaison with Communist elements in Vietnam, furnishing advance warning of ICC operations to avoid any unseemly situations. Blais, *supra* note 4, at 142-44.
82. Holmes, *supra* note 61, at 239.
83. *Id.*
84. *See* P. MARTIN, *supra* note 6, at 49-51.

first step toward a neutral body which calls both procedural and substantive matters "as it sees them" and then takes action.

The constant bickering in the ICC over the proper interpretation and even over the actual facts, with frequent two-to-one splits and "dissenting opinions" in the reports, is not an ideal peace observation model. The end of the line came in the last regular ICC report, where the Canadian and Indian delegates finally rebuked the Polish delegate publicly by reminding him of the ICC's responsibility for conducting all investigations "without attempting to prejudge the merits of the case." [85] Finally, when either three or even six military officers must be dispatched to conduct even the simplest investigation, the troika becomes inordinately wasteful of the meager resources available to peace observation missions. It is small wonder that most Western observers longingly look beyond the troika structure to that of the United Nations peace observation missions. But since this is to form an important part of the concluding recommendations, it is not further developed here.

C. *Finances*

The financing of peace observation missions has been a very grave problem, one which nearly brought the United Nations to a standstill in 1963. The ICC experience proved no exception, and over the years it has been a problem third only to the inadequacy of consultative machinery and the ICC's troika composition. The provision in the Armistice Agreement seems simple and straightforward: "The costs involved in the operations of . . . the International Commission and its Inspection Teams shall be shared equally between the two parties" (Art. 26). But the arrangement worked out by the ICC representatives during their initial meeting in New Delhi and adopted in early 1956 by the Co-Chairmen was somewhat different:

1. Pay and allowances of delegation personnel—supervisory powers;
2. Common pool expenses (food, lodging, medical services and transport to and from home country of delegation personnel) —contributing powers (China, France, UK and USSR, in equal shares) ;
3. Local expenses (scheduled transport, board, etc.)—parties to Geneva Agreements (Democratic Republic of Vietnam and France, in equal shares).[86]

In December, 1956, a few months after the French military forces had been withdrawn from Vietnam, France refused to bear further ICC expenses and even claimed a refund. Eventually India accepted the responsibilities abdicated by France.[87] Once the ICC's mission

---

85. Eleventh Rept. at 23.
86. WAINHOUSE, at 494.
87. *Id.*

was extended for an indefinite duration, the ICC's staff and facilities were reduced considerably to effect basic economies.[88] But by 1961 the ICC was still forced to report a "deteriorating position" due to lack of adequate funds;[89] and by mid-1964 it was reported in Saigon that India had wearied of advancing funds for the ICC and "in the future would not be inclined to pass the begging bowl again."[90]

Careful attention must be paid to the financing arrangements for any future peace observation mission, to ensure that adequate funds remain available to maintain the supervisory body in the numerical strength required to perform its mission effectively. Since a far greater number of personnel than that of the ICC would be most desirable, especially in the first months after the cease-fire, so that fixed and mobile teams will be available in strength to conduct investigations and maintain a supervisory capacity throughout Vietnam and not just in a few centers, the United States must guard against pressures to "save money" at the expense of effective supervision. Although Congress will undoubtedly be reluctant to fund more than the country's "fair share," this will be mandatory if the funds can be raised no other way. The U.N. Congo operation, with 18,000 personnel in the field, cost about $110 million a year. When compared to the daily expense of sustaining combat operations in Vietnam at the 1965-68 level of intensity, even that price would seem eminently reasonable if it contributed to a lasting settlement.

The costs of supervision will most likely be borne in large part by the parties to the settlement, possibly assisted to some minor extent by other countries interested in a lasting settlement. It remains most important that none of the parties gain an immediate stranglehold over the operations of the supervisory body merely by refusing to pay its share exactly when due. Nor is nonpayment an unlikely prospect. Communist China has been constantly in arrears on its 17.6 per cent share of the costs of the ICC/Laos as specified in the 1962 Agreements, and the DRV has not even paid its 1.5 per cent of those costs. While the 1962 Agreements made some provision for such contingencies by "allowing" for voluntary contributions by other parties in excess of their stated shares, all governments are understandably reluctant to assume such a role. There is thus a need for some type of prearranged payment system, either by paying a lump sum into

---

88. In April, 1957, the ICC discontinued its own coastal courier air service and reduced its communications staff significantly. While the ICC realized that the commercial substitutes would not be as efficient, it "remained satisfied" the change-over would not be detrimental. Seventh Rept. at 6. On July 20, 1960, the Co-Chairmen told the ICC that the general situation in Southeast Asia proved "beyond doubt" the need for the further "valuable services" of the ICC, but went on to recommend reductions in personnel to achieve economies. The ICC concurred, and eventually arranged a 45 per cent reduction in expenditures as compared to the 1955-57 period. Eleventh Rept. at 5.

89. Eleventh Rept. at 27.

90. WAINHOUSE, at 497.

a common treasury to cover that party's share of the expenses as projected over the duration of the mission, at least as initially planned (if a relatively short-run operation, as with the expected two-year duration of the ICC/Vietnam), or by having the parties pay their shares a year in advance. If a party fails to pay at the specified time, the other parties then have a lengthy period to exert pressure or search out other sources before "the shoe begins to pinch." Since those countries furnishing personnel to the supervisory body are often sending their very best men, as well as paying their salaries, they should not be expected to assume further financial obligations.

D. *ICC Freedom of Movement/Access*

For complete effectiveness, peace observation missions should have full freedom of movement and access to all installations, persons, documents and other necessary information, as well as the facilities to utilize this authority. While this has unfortunately been the exception in peace observation activities to date,[91] the Armistice Agreement appeared to extend to the ICC all the necessary authority and facilities:

> . . . [T]hey shall have the right to move freely and shall receive from the local civil and military authorities all facilities they may require for the fulfillment of their tasks (provision of personnel, placing at their disposal documents needed for supervision, summoning witnesses necessary for holding enquiries, ensuring the security and freedom of movement of the inspection teams, etc.) . . . . . They shall have at their disposal such modern means of transport, observation and communication as they may require. (Art. 35).

This was supported by providing for suitable punishment of violators belonging to the military forces of either side (Art. 22). But the actual experience of the ICC was far less satisfactory, as both sides found innumerable ways of flaunting these provisions. While this caused a serious reduction in ICC operations and effectiveness across the board, it had especially serious repercussions on the ICC's ability to supervise the ban on the introduction of fresh troops, military personnel, arms, and munitions into either zone of Vietnam (Arts. 16-20).

First, both sides occasionally used the "straight-arm approach" by openly refusing to furnish ICC teams with necessary documents (aircraft and ship cargo manifests, harbor registers, airport tower registers and legal dossiers on convicted persons) or by barring ICC access to military and civilian installations as well as to complainants, witnesses, and prisoners. Both sides were guilty of such conduct on innumerable occasions, and specific instances of these flagrant violations of Article 35 often persisted through several subsequent ICC

---

91. *Id.* at 563.

reports without any improvement in the situation.[92] The absence of pressure on the parties from some form of permanent consultative machinery to which the ICC could turn for support took a heavy toll here. Certainly the letters from the Co-Chairmen to the parties, "deploring" their attitudes in this regard, provided only a modicum of assistance.

Beyond this rather heavy-handed approach, both sides eventually developed more subtle tactics for withholding access from the ICC.

1. *Transportation.* The parties were to furnish the ICC with such "modern means of transport" as they required. This unfortunately conformed to the general norm; for peace observation missions have seldom maintained self-sufficiency as to transport and have generally relied on the parties or used commercial facilities.[93] While the ICC acquired its own jeeps, and did obtain several liaison aircraft and helicopters, in the main it was totally dependent on the parties for air and sea transport. "Unavailability of transport" soon became a major excuse, manipulated by both sides for lengthy periods lasting

---

92. The ICC reports are literally awash with violations of Article 35. A few examples will suffice:

DRV. On January 25, 1956, an ICC mobile team was withdrawn at DRV insistence from its position on the DRV—Communist China border at Phuc Hoa, where it had been controlling the entry of military equipment from China. The DRV claimed a mobile team could not be kept in position for more than a month without becoming a fixed team, and Article 35 provided only for seven fixed teams within the DRV, all at other designated locations. Despite ICC protests that the armistice agreements said nothing about the length of time a mobile team could be kept in one location, the ICC never did prevail, and ever after had to cover this area on a most random basis by using a mobile team dispatched from elsewhere. Sixth Rept. at 19; Seventh Rept. at 13; Eighth Rept. at 13; Tenth Rept. at 15.

RVN. A comparable illustration on the RVN side was the refusal to grant ICC teams access to the military sections of Saigon airport. Incoming foreign aircraft often taxied directly to this area; since cargo manifests were also denied the team, these flights avoided ICC supervision altogether. Again this situation persisted through several reports. Fifth Rept. at 12; Sixth Rept. at 23; Seventh Rept. at 16; Eighth Rept. at 12; Ninth Rept. at 14. In 1962, as the RVN military effort began to expand, the ICC's situation broke down completely as to supervising the ban on introduction of military personnel and war materiel; thereafter the ICC was persistently denied access to vital installations, and could only report a "steady and continuous arrival of war materiel" without being able even to estimate its quantity and nature. 1962 Special Report at 8.

DRV/RVN. The ICC had difficulties with both sides on obtaining concurrence to the reconnaissance of airfields, with many, many refusals. At one point the RVN concurred on only one of nine such requests. Seventh Rept. at 14. The RVN denied access to harbor registers and airport control tower registers. Eighth Rept. at 12; Tenth Rept. at 20. At one point the RVN met all ICC requests for reconnaissance of airfields and offshore islands with demands for an equal number of ICC reconnaissance missions in the DRV; the ICC rejected any such concept of "parity" and eventually prevailed on the point, after considerable delay (Sixth Rept. at 20), only to have the same claim crop up again later (Tenth Rept. at 16).

93. WAINHOUSE, at 589.

through several ICC reports,[94] to prevent ICC inspection of vast areas of the two zones. Since ICC visits were quite sporadic even when transport was available (in one area of the DRV the ICC requested permission to perform a reconnaissance of a particular road some fifteen or more months after its prior visit, and even then the DRV stalled for months),[95] the situation became quite absurd.

2. *Notice.* A protocol signed by the original parties required the ICC to give thirty minutes' notice of intended fixed team operations and two hours' notice of mobile team operations.[96] By the fifth ICC report, the RVN was demanding twenty-four to forty-eight hours notice of any ICC team operations, claiming this was necessary for "security reasons." [97] The DRV also occasionally demanded extended advance notice.[98] These unwarranted demands by both sides dragged on through several ICC reports, causing great delay in ICC activities and obviously giving the party concerned ample advance warning to ensure local conditions were "just right" for an ICC visit.

3. *Security.* The military commanders of both sides were required to give "full protection" to the ICC personnel (Art. 25), and this was reinforced in the freedom of movement provisions (Art. 35). Yet ICC personnel were beaten and some were killed, and personal property was occasionally damaged or destroyed.[99] In the early days of the armistice, the DRV demonstrated a significant capability for turning out an "angry crowd" of villagers to interrupt ICC investigations, often causing inordinate delay. The RVN used "security precautions" as its reason for requiring twenty-four to forty-eight hours of advance notice of ICC operations. Often the assertion by local authorities or a liaison officer of inability to provide security to an ICC team caused the unsuccessful termination of that mission, even though conditions in the region did not appear dangerous.

4. *Liaison Officers.* ICC investigation teams were furnished with a liaison officer by each side. These are traditional adjuncts to peace

---

94. *See, e.g.,* Sixth Rept. at 25-26 (difficulty in obtaining air and sea transport from DRV; DRV refuses to allow a French naval vessel to enter its waters to offload 4 boats for ICC; 3 teams unable to conduct investigations); Seventh Rept. at 14-15 (still no boats for 2 ICC teams in DRV, reconnaissance of DRV offshore islands therefore not completed; RVN has failed to provide boats for 5 ICC teams for over 9 months); Eighth Rept. at 13 (still no boat for 1 ICC team in DRV, or for the 5 teams in RVN; no air transport for 1 team in RVN); Ninth Rept. at 15 (no improvement in sea transport situation since (8)); Tenth Rept. at 21 (still no improvement since (8)); Eleventh Rept. at 21 (still no improvement since (8)); Eleventh Rept. at 27 (road vehicles of ICC wearing out, now many breakdowns).

95. Eleventh Rept. at 16.

96. Sixth Rept. at 22.

97. Fifth Rept. at 14.

98. *See, e.g.,* Fourth Rept. at 32.

99. The most notorious example of violence against ICC personnel was the demonstration in Saigon on July 20, 19[5]5, the first anniversary of the

observation teams, ensuring day-to-day contact with the party concerned, facilitating housing/food/transport/communications, and in particular familiarizing the observers with local conditions and introducing them to local civilian and military authorities.[100] Evidently the ICC teams could not proceed without the liaison officers from both parties, and they became fertile sources of obstruction and delay. The absence or intransigence of either liaison officer brought an ICC team's operations to a standstill.[101]

The various methods of obstruction and delay caused a serious diminution in the effectiveness of the ICC. Yet the problem was not in the text of the Armistice Agreement, for all these actions by the parties were guarded against in express language. The basic failure was the absence of any supporting body to which the ICC could turn for diplomatic pressure and other forms of action once the parties began these obstructions. Supervisory bodies clearly should not have to fight their way to freedom of movement, as in the U.N. Congo operation.[102]

Beyond this, any future settlement must ensure that full freedom of movement and access are specifically granted to the peace observation mission, and the consultative body must ensure that this occurs in actual practice. This should include the possibility of aerial reconnaissance by the observers. The U.N. Kashmir experience has

---

signing of the armistice agreement. The personal papers, clothing, equipment and even the automobiles of ICC personnel were destroyed by the demonstrators. The Diem government failed to summon the necessary protection for the ICC. WAINHOUSE, at 521. At least two ICC personnel were killed much later in the RVN. Seventh Rept. at 6. Some demonstrations in the DRV have involved violence to ICC teams. *See, e.g.*, Third Rept. at 11.

100. WAINHOUSE, at 583.
101. The liaison officers discovered innumerable reasons for refusing to proceed. See the extensive list of examples in Fourth Rept., App. V. The 1962 report charged both DRV and RVN with using such excuses as (1) the liaison officer is sick and without replacement; (2) he is simply "unavailable;" (3) he has referred the matter up the chain of command and is awaiting instructions. 1962 Special Rept., Annexure 1, at 12-20. Eventually both DRV and RVN liaison officers began to construe restrictively the written instructions an ICC team had received from headquarters, and to refuse to allow the team to go beyond their interpretations of its mission. Sixth Rept. at 26. For some time a "furious" argument over the French-RVN demand that liaison officers wear civilian clothes when crossing a demarcation line into the other zone brought ICC team activity to a halt. Fifth Rept. at 14.
102. During 1961 and 1962, the Katangese Gendarmerie conducted a program of harassment, kidnapping, and even murder of U.N. personnel. Part of the campaign included the setting up of roadblocks, denial of access to airports, and even direct military attacks on the U.N. personnel. After a considerable period of provocation, the U.N. forces fought back and defeated the gendarmerie. ONUC based its action on its basic agreement with the central government, which guaranteed freedom of movement throughout the Congo. Urquhart, *United Nations Peace Forces and the Changing United Nations*, 17 INT'L ORG. 338, 348 (1963).

demonstrated that classified military information, as would be obtained by such reconnaissance, can be kept in strictest confidence where it discloses no violations of the agreement.[103] The ICC experience argues persuasively in favor of providing the peace observers with their own sources of transportation. The requirements for notice to the parties of investigation team movements, and for concurrence by that party, should be held to a minimum or totally eliminated. While the parties should be held to stringent requirements of ensuring the security of the observers, the peace observation mission should also be allowed to furnish its own security forces. Such units, placed under clear and limited instructions on the use of force, could accompany investigation teams and prevent the intolerable delays and excuses foisted on the ICC by the parties in the name of "security." Investigation teams should be empowered to conduct operations despite the absence of a liaison officer, and these officers should in no event be allowed to interpret the authority of the team. Failure by the parties to comply with any of the express provisions on movement and access should be immediately designated a violation and referred to that party for corrective action during a short time period. If the action is not taken by that deadline, it should be immediately referred to the consultative body, which should meet promptly and provide corrective action.

E. *Article 14(c)*

Reference was made in section IV(c) *supra* to the ICC's extreme difficulty in supervising the Article 14(c) guarantees of democratic liberties and freedom from reprisals. These difficulties continued and even increased after 1956. Common varieties of complaints included arrest, detention, murder, massacre, and mass "concentration" of families of former resistance workers (grouping them together in camps). The ICC conducted investigations and forwarded the complaints and results to the authorities, stressing the Article 22 requirement of punishment of personnel who violate Article 14(c). Where the offenders were not within the civil or military administration, the ICC demanded punishment under the laws of the zone concerned.[104] The ICC then attempted to follow up the action taken by the authorities, listing some instances of reduction in rank, issuance of reprimands, or even trials of offenders.[105] But the reports of corrective action, when compared to the number of complaints received and to the incredible number of reprisals listed by various scholars,[106] seem pitifully few in number.

---

103. WAINHOUSE, at 552.
104. Fourth Rept. at 10.
105. Fourth Rept., App. V, at 37-41.
106. Professors Kahin and Lewis cite a RVN Ministry of Information document listing a total of 48,250 communists and political sympathizers who were jailed during the 1954-60 period. They claim these statistics were

The ICC's difficulties were heightened by the attitude of the parties. The Joint Commission had never established the Committee on Freedoms the ICC had requested, and the ICC had been forced to spend "a large amount of time and energy" conducting investigations and trying to get the parties to carry out their obligations. Due to low manpower levels, there were also substantial areas of Vietnam where the ICC had been unable to conduct investigations and simply "couldn't say" that there had been no violations.[107] Once the French had withdrawn, the Diem government refused any cooperation with the ICC on these matters.[108] Although the number of complaints grew as Diem's repressive measures increased, some complaints being of a "very serious nature," the ICC could not even dispatch investigation teams due to the RVN attitude.[109] At the same time, the ICC received no further complaints from residents of the DRV, who were now living "in the shadow of the Communists." [110] The ICC continued to express grave concern over the continued failures of both RVN and DRV to cooperate, but eventually sank to little more than forwarding complaints to the other side.[111]

John Holmes, who had considerable experience with ICC problems as a policy-maker for Canada, scores the impracticability of the 1954 Armistice provision requiring the ICC, with its very limited number of personnel, to act as an *ombudsman* in a context of extended and extremely bitter civil war. At the same time, as Holmes readily admits,[112] a provision banning reprisals seems absolutely mandatory in any future settlement. Vietnamese have again been set off against Vietnamese in prolonged and savage warfare. The NLF's policy statement of late 1967 threatens to punish the "die-hard agents" of the Americans in no less than three of its fourteen points.[113] At the start of any cease-fire, all sides should be required to proclaim a general amnesty. The peace observation mission should be large enough to maintain substantial numbers of investigation teams in the field, and not merely dispatch teams as complaints are received, as was the

---

low, and cite Philippe Devillers, the noted French journalist, as estimating 50,000 were in jail by 1956. The notorious history of Diem's Law 10/59 and its campaign stands as another instance of RVN repression. G. KAHIN & J. LEWIS, *supra* note 56, at 100-101. Somehow Professors Kahin and Lewis fail to discuss comparable statistics dealing with the DRV. William Bundy lists a Bernard B. Fall estimate that in 1955-56 some 50,000 political opponents were killed in the DRV. B. Fall, cited in Address by William P. Bundy, Asst. Secretary of State for East Asian and Pacific Affairs, to the National Student Association, Aug. 15, 1967, Dep't State Publ. 8295, East Asian & Pac. Ser. 166, at 5.

107. Fourth Rept. at 9.
108. Fifth Rept. at 8.
109. Sixth Rept. at 13.
110. Holmes, *supra* note 61, at 245.
111. Eighth Rept. at 7-8; Ninth Rept. at 9.
112. Holmes, *supra* note 61, at 245.
113. N.Y. Times, Dec. 15, 1967, at 16, cols. 2, 5, and 8.

ICC practice. These teams should have express powers of access to all prisons, military installations, and any other suspected detention centers, and the right to interview any and all detainees and inspect all records. In view of the 320,000 bogus complaints filed by the DRV in 1954-55 claiming Article 14(d) violations by the French and the Diem government, it may be unreasonable to require the teams to investigate every single complaint, from any source whatever. At the same time, in view of the DRV's methods of discouraging complaints regarding its own activities, those complaints which do reach the observers should be treated with some respect. A reasonable medium must be sought, perhaps involving some type of penalty for the filing of groundless complaints. The observers should be armed and accompanied by the supervisory body's own security forces. In view of the U.N. Congo force's unhappy experiences with stringent self-defense—only instructions on use of force, whereby they had to stand aside even where atrocities were committed in their presence,[114] serious consideration should be given to a clean break with peace observation precedents by allowing resort to force to prevent such atrocities, where practicable. Naturally very precise limiting instructions would be required, and use of force by the peace observation mission should be subject to a careful impartial review. But given the tense situation in Vietnam, this possibility of employing "preventive force" seems necessary. Finally, the action taken by the parties to punish violations must be carefully followed up by the observers; and where no action is taken, immediate recourse must be had to the permanent consultative body for further action. The parties might become more interested in ensuring observance of these guaranties if payment of a fine or an indemnity was required for every violation reported by the observers, or a certain number of votes were subtracted from that side's tally for each violation (if elections were part of the settlement), or some similar sanction were provided.

VII. Undeveloped ICC Potential

Since the major United States intervention of 1965 there have been several as yet unsuccessful efforts to use the ICC's potential as a positive means of reducing the gravity of the Vietnam conflict. Both Canada's 1966 attempt to promote peace negotiations through the ICC and the United States' 1968 attempt to strengthen the ICC to investigate violations of the Cambodian border were defeated at the diplomatic level. The United States' May, 1968 proposal to re-demilitarize the "demilitarized" zone under reinvigorated ICC supervision remains a distinct possibility, but only a possibility, thus far.

---

114. Bloomfield, *Headquarters-Field Relations: Some Notes on the Beginning and End of ONUC*, 17 Int'l Org. 377 (1963).

A. *Efforts to Arrange Peace Negotiations Through the ICC*

In early 1966, Canada's Secretary of State for External Affairs, Paul Martin, expressed hope for the possibility of using the ICC to promote peace negotiations for Vietnam. He asserted that the ICC countries had a long close association with the problem of Vietnam and were the only group of countries with ready access to both sides.[115] Martin discussed the possibilities with U.N. Secretary General U Thant, Ambassador Arthur Goldberg, and Secretary of State Dean Rusk, with very encouraging response.[116] Of the other ICC members, it was assumed that Poland would bow to whatever position the USSR developed, and that India's support for the Canadian initiative would consequently be necessary to produce a "salutary effect" on the USSR.[117] But within two weeks Canada's Special Envoy Chester Ronning returned from a visit to Hanoi with the belief that neither India nor Poland considered the time ripe for negotiations;[118] and within a month Indira Gandhi admitted an unwillingness for India to take the lead on the Martin proposal due to its border dispute with Communist China.[119] Reportedly India was willing to participate in the effort, but felt all three ICC members must first reach agreement.[120] Since Poland then rejected any such use of the ICC,[121] the Canadian initiative came to naught.

B. *ICC Participation in the Cambodia Border Issue*

The 1968 effort by the United States to strengthen the ICC/Cambodia to enable it to supervise the border with Vietnam was not the first attempt to allot to the ICC a role on Cambodian border violations. The 1954 Agreements had tasked ICC/Cambodia with such supervision,[122] but after joint ICC/Cambodia—ICC/Vietnam efforts to do so had been blocked by the RVN's uncooperative attitude, the ICCs played an essentially passive role.[123] The United States itself

---

115. Dai, *Canada's Role in the International Commission for Supervision and Control in Viet Nam*, 4 CAN. Y.B. INT'L L. 161, 174 (1966).
116. N.Y. Times, Feb. 19, 1966, at 1, col. 7, and at 4, col. 2. (U Thant); *id.*, Feb. 22, 1966, at 2, col. 8 (Rusk); *id.*, Mar. 29, 1966, at 5, col. 1 (Goldberg).
117. *Id.*, Feb. 19, 1966, at 4, cols. 3-4.
118. *Id.*, Mar. 17, 1966, at 8, col. 3.
119. *Id.*, Apr. 2, 1966, at 6, col. 3.
120. Dai, *supra* note 115, at 175.
121. *Id.*
122. Under the Agreement on the Cessation of Hostilities in Cambodia, July 20, 1954, (BACKGROUND INFORMATION at 50) the ICC/Cambodia was to "see that the frontiers are respected" and control the introduction of military personnel and equipment along the frontiers (Art. 13). These provisions were subject to a unanimous vote within the ICC as to violations of the frontiers by foreign military forces (Art. 21).
123. The government of Cambodia began forwarding complaints of such violations to ICC/Cambodia in early 1957. These were forwarded to ICC/-Vietnam and thence to the RVN government, expressing hopes that direct negotiations between RVN and Cambodia would produce an amicable set-

made a fruitless effort in May, 1967 to get the ICC/Cambodia to resume active supervision of the border, with an offer of helicopters and other equipment.

The U.S. felt that three ICC mobile teams with the increased mobility plus independent authority to conduct investigations would bring considerable improvement in the Cambodian border situation. Western diplomats blamed the USSR, Poland, and "to some degree" India for stalling that 1967 effort.[124]

The 1968 effort began in early January, when the United States appealed to India as Chairman of the ICC to take the lead in strengthening the ICC to investigate border incidents, and again offered helicopters and other equipment.[125] Canada was reported strongly in favor of an increased role, but while India was sympathetic,[126] it saw little chance of increasing ICC activity unless Poland also consented.[127] While India deliberated, the U.S. special mission to Cambodia under Chester Bowles obtained Sihanouk's support for an increased ICC role.[128] Shortly thereafter, the USSR asserted that any increase in the ICC role could occur only after both unanimous consent by the three ICC countries plus that of *all* the Geneva Conference members. The United States countered that a simple majority vote of the ICC would suffice.[129] After a tangled series of procedural wranglings over who could accept what from whom, India finally announced that the ICC could not accept equipment from the United States since it was not a "party" to the 1954 Geneva Agreements which established the ICC.[130] The ICC role on complaints of Cambodian border violations remains passive.

It is difficult to accept this reasoning as the actual basis for India's decision. While the 1954 Agreements say nothing about the possibility of receiving equipment from countries which were not "parties" to the Geneva Agreements, it is equally devoid of provisions regarding offers of equipment from the five non-signatories (UK, USSR, Communist China, Laos, Cambodia) which supported the decisions

---

tlement. Seventh Rept. at 5; Eighth Rept. at 5. Meanwhile an *ad hoc* committee of ICC/Cambodia investigated one of these complaints and reported a violation by the RVN. Ninth Rept. at 5. The RVN government then denied the competence of the ICCs to consider Cambodian border issues and rejected the conclusion of the one *ad hoc* investigation. Tenth Rept. at 5. Thereafter the ICCs merely passed complaints and RVN denials back and forth and conducted no further investigations. Eleventh Rept. at 5.

124. N.Y. Times, Dec. 12, 1967, at 1, col. 1.
125. *Id.*, Jan. 2, 1968, at 2, col. 4.
126. *Id.*, Dec. 31, 1967, at 2, col. 3.
127. *Id.*, Jan. 2, 1968, at 2, col. 4.
128. On January 4, Sihanouk had complained that Poland, backed by the USSR, was paralyzing ICC efforts to check reports of intrusion by foreign troops. *Id.*, Jan. 5, 1968, at 2, cols. 7-8. Sihanouk then reached agreement with the Bowles mission on strengthening ICC/Cambodia to police the border. *Id*, Jan. 11, 1968, at 1, col. 8.
129. *Id.*, Jan. 13, 1968, at 1, col. 8 and at 3, col. 1.
130. *Id.*, Feb. 7, 1968, at 11, col. 1.

at Geneva. The requirement that the parties furnish the ICCs with adequate transportation and other facilities was no doubt intended merely to ensure the ICCs would be able to function properly. Given the torturous problems of financing such missions, it is difficult to imagine that the 1954 Geneva Conference would have raised the slightest objection if some of the equipment could be obtained without cost from other sources.

The 1966 effort to seek negotiations through the ICC and the 1968 effort to increase the ICC's role in supervision of the Cambodian border share several common characteristics. Both would appear well within the scope of operations allotted to the ICC in the various 1954 Agreements. From the very start, Canada favored both operations, while the Soviet Union opposed them and Poland followed the Soviet approach. India was initially interested in both operations, but refused to commit itself. After an interval of over a month in each case, India finally stressed the need for unanimity within the ICC. Since Poland and Canada were at opposite ends of the spectrum on both issues, the ICC therefore declined to act.

Both of these initiatives offered some hope of reducing the major threat to world public order posed by the Vietnam war. It is easy to criticize the Soviet Union for its opposition. It is equally easy to criticize Poland, which never demonstrated even the remotest trace of an independent, carefully-reasoned position as should be demanded of a member of a supposedly impartial peace observation body. And India's timidity seems most unbecoming of a country which historically has viewed itself as the great "peacekeeper". But such criticism of India overlooks its inordinately delicate position as the neutral member of a troika. Here, as elsewhere in the ICC experience, India was forced to play the "swing man" role between diametrically opposed positions. And it was clearer here that the polar positions were occupied not by Poland and Canada, but rather by the USSR and the United States, each of which unleashed tremendous pressure on India to vote its own way. A news dispatch at the height of the 1968 "debate" over the ICC role in Cambodia described the situation with painful accuracy, characterizing India as "torn between the conflicting positions of the United States and the Soviet Union." [131] Not even "one Asian neutral" of India's stature should be expected to continually resolve major disputes between the two super powers.

C. *Current Proposals to "Re-demilitarize" the "Demilitarized Zone"*

The very first substantive proposal advanced by the United States at the Paris negotiations in May, 1968, was that the "demilitarized zone" between the RVN and the DRV, the scene of considerable military activity since the war broadened in 1965, now be made into a genuine buffer zone by pulling apart the forces there. The United States felt this would cause considerable improvement in one of the

131. *Id.*, Jan. 20, 1968, at 3, cols. 3-4.

most volatile areas of the conflict, and also serve as an important test case of the good faith of the parties to the negotiations.[132]

While the ICC was not mentioned in the U.S. proposal, its supervision of the demilitarized zone was one of the four tasks strongly emphasized in Article 36 of the 1954 Armistice Agreements. Presumably the ICC could play an important role in any such re-demilitarization, for even with its limitations it could provide the most useful check of the "good faith" of the parties in complying with such an arrangement, and its conclusions could be taken by simply majority vote. While the North Vietnamese promptly insisted that none of their forces were located in the zone at present (contrary to U.S. intelligence reports) and that the United States alone had destroyed the demilitarized status of the zone,[133] this did not seem to imply a final rejection. Scanning the long list of measures which the two sides could take to de-escalate the conflict, the re-demilitarization of the zone offers one of the easiest, clearest, and most hopeful possibilities. The zone is not particularly large; the pull-backs could be monitored and certified far more easily than in many other areas of Vietnam; and the DRV's forces and its logistics chain already have practically free access to the RVN through Cambodia and do not need to station men and equipment in the zone even to continue their current level of military operations in the South. Thus the re-demilitarization of the zone offers considerable promise, and should be watched for in future months (or years).

VIII. Improving the ICC Machinery—The 1962 Geneva Conference on Laos

The ICC/Laos formed by the 1954 Geneva Agreements was very similar to the ICC/Vietnam in its powers and duties, its composition and facilities. It proved reasonably successful in supervising the implementation of the Agreement on the Cessation of Hostilities in Laos, and actually withdrew from Laos on July 19, 1958.[134] When conditions worsened there in 1961, the Co-Chairmen of the 1954 Conference reconvened the ICC/Laos,[135] and the necessity of improving its powers and facilities to supervise the Laotian settlement negotiated at Geneva in 1962 became a central issue of that 1962 Conference. The initial positions taken by the Communist and Western negotiators and the compromises reached have important bearing on the characteristics of any future peace observation mission for Vietnam, for they show the extent of Western dissatisfaction with the 1954 ICC

---

132. For the United States DMZ proposals and their reasoning, see *id.*, May 14, 1968, at 18, col. 5; *id.*, May 16, 1968, at 16, col. 2; *id.*, May 20, 1968, at 1, col. 6.
133. *Id.*, May 16, 1968, at 16, col. 4.
134. *See* the discussion in Wainhouse, at 501-03.
135. *Hearings on S. 1627 Before the Subcomm. on the Far East and the Pacific of the House Comm. on Foreign Affairs*, 88th Cong., 1st Sess., at 3 (1963).

formula and give at least some indication of the progress in negotiating positions since 1954. The 1962 ICC/Laos alterations also have special significance for the United States, as Secretary of State Dean Rusk had indicated in advance of the negotiations just what alterations the U.S. would seek in the ICC formula.[136] Thus the initial bargaining positions of Communist and Western negotiators at the 1962 Geneva Conference,[137] and the compromise ICC formula as promulgated in the Protocol to the Declaration on the Neutrality of Laos,[138] merit examination.

The most important addition to the Agreements was the establishment of a specific consultative body, by naming the Co-Chairmen of the Conference, again Great Britain and the Soviet Union, to "exercise supervision over the observance of this Protocol and the Declaration on the Neutrality of Laos." The ICC was then tasked with immediately reporting to the Co-Chairmen any violations, all significant steps taken under the Protocol, plus "any other important information which may assist the Co-Chairmen in carrying out their functions," which of course now included express supervision of the implementation of the Agreements. This system came much closer to the ideal peace observation mission "chain of command;" if the acts of the parties bring the degree of implementation of the underlying agreements into question, and the parties refuse to make necessary adjustments, the peace observation mission relays the details to a consultative body, which can then meet and take action.

The other tasks of the revised ICC/Laos were quite similar to the "quasi-military" tasks of the ICC/Vietnam: supervision of the cease-fire, the withdrawal of foreign troops, and the ban on the introduction of troops/armaments/war materiel into Laos. It is notable that the 1962 Agreements on Laos contained no political provisions requiring ICC supervision (ban on reprisals, guarantee of democratic liberties, etc.).

A considerable attempt was made by the Western conference members to overcome the severe handicaps of the troika system. Secretary Rusk, in his 1961 "bargaining list," urged that the ICC take all decisions by majority vote, with the right to file majority and minority reports, so that the ICC might ". . . not be paralyzed by a veto." This was adopted as the initial Western position at Geneva, with the Soviet Union insisting that all decisions except those on procedural matters must be taken by a unanimous vote. Under the compromise solution (Art. 14), a unanimous vote would be required for conclusions on major questions sent to the Co-Chairmen, on all ICC recommenda-

---

136. *See* Rusk, *United States Outlines Program to Insure Genuine Neutrality for Laos*, 44 DEP'T STATE BULL. 844, 847 (1961).
137. The bargaining positions are taken from Czyzak and Salans, *The International Conference on the Settlement of the Laotian Question and the Geneva Agreements of 1962*, 57 AM. J. INT'L L. 300, 310-14 (1963).
138. Protocol to the Declaration on the Neutrality of Laos, Arts. 8-19, 47 DEP'T STATE BULL. 261, 262-63 (1962).

tions, and on ICC conclusions relating both to violations of the provisions on the withdrawal of foreign troops from Laos and to the ban on the introduction of foreign troops, armaments, and war materiel. A simple majority vote suffices for all other questions, including those on procedural matters and on the important decision to initiate and carry out investigations.

It is difficult to conclude that this voting formula is an improvement on that of the ICC/Vietnam, formed eight years before (1954). Whereas ICC/Laos recommendations must be taken by unanimous vote, those of ICC/Vietnam are taken by majority vote unless dealing with amendments/additions to the basic Agreements or with the vague provision on violations which might lead to resumption of hostilities. ICC/Laos must also reach a unanimous decision on violations of the only significant provisions it was to supervise: the withdrawal of foreign troops and the ban on introduction of foreign troops/armaments/military equipment. While a majority vote dispatches an investigation team, unanimity is required to reach any conclusion as to a violation and to make recommendations based on its findings. On controversial issues, the Indian representative has been changed from the "swing man" into the man whose vote determines which side's position becomes the majority or minority report of a non-decision or non-recommendation. The information compiled by the peace observation mission is still relayed to the consultative body (the Co-Chairmen)—a very important function. But the ICC/Laos has lost considerable flexibility in dealing with the parties on a lower level in Southeast Asia, since it is now unable to adopt a recommendation with which to pressure those parties if the Pole and the Canadian are on opposite sides of an issue. The Article 14 language that ICC members "will work harmoniously and in cooperation with each other" poorly disguises the enormous potential for disunity and stalemate ensconced in these voting provisions.

The 1961 Rusk proposals demanded "full access to all parts of the country" for the ICC. The France-United States initial draft at Geneva in 1962 followed this, insisting on "free and unrestricted access" to all parts of Laos and cataloging many of the problem areas previously encountered on access to documents, military installations, and the like.[139] The Soviet draft does not even mention access—the ICC would, in agreement with the Laotian government, "set up suitable groups" for the sole purpose of supervising and controlling the withdrawals. The final provision (Art. 16) is nearly as vague: "The points to which the Commission and its inspection teams go for the

---

139. The France-United States draft provided the ICC with "full freedom to inspect, at any time, all aerodromes, installations or establishments and all units, organizations and activities which are or might be of a military nature;" "access to aircraft and shipping registers, to manifests and other relevant documents;" and "all authority for investigation, inspection and verification necessary for the performance of their duties." Czyzak & Salans, *supra* note 137, at 313.

purposes of investigation and their length of stay at those points shall be determined in relation to the requirements of the particular investigation." State Department attorneys have stated that this provision is intended to insure freedom of access to any point in Laos in the course of an investigation, with the duration to be as long as necessary.[140] But the express language of the provision is not that clear, since it does not state who will make the determination as to the necessities of that particular investigation. If the parties are allowed to interpret ICC requirements, the access problem once again assumes major dimensions. Indeed, within a year after the Protocol was signed, access to the Communist-held areas of Laos was once again being denied to ICC investigation teams, and the Co-Chairmen were unable to resolve this impasse.[141]

The initial France-United States draft also stated that the absence of the representative from one of the ICC member countries would not prevent the ICC itself or one of its investigating teams from carrying on its activities. The Soviet draft made no mention of this problem, and its negotiators won the day, for the final agreement (again Art. 16) places a positive duty on each of the ICC countries to ensure continual representation but makes no provision for any measures which could be taken in the absence of a representative. In May, 1963, the Polish delegate intentionally withdrew from the ICC deliberations, claiming the ICC had dispatched teams to the Plain of Jars without the concurrence of the Communist member of the Laotian coalition government. The Co-Chairmen themselves split on the Polish interpretation and were unable to take action.[142] Clearly a troika peace observation entity coupled with a Co-Chairmanship is not an ideal means of maintaining the peace.

Beginning with the Rusk proposals of 1961, the West sought transportation and communication facilities which would be under the sole control of the ICC, and here at least it was successful. Article 17 furnishes the ICC with the transportation and communication necessary to properly perform its duties. While these facilities can be leased from the Laotian government, they must remain under the administrative control of the Commission.

The 1962 Agreements made fairly clear arrangements for financial obligations (Art. 18). The ICC countries would each pay the salaries and allowances of their own nationals serving on the ICC. The Laotian government would provide accommodations and other "appropriate" local services. All other capital or running expenses would be taken from a fund amassed by contributions as follows: (1) Communist China, France, USSR, United Kingdom, United States—17.6 per cent

---

140. *Id.*
141. Wainhouse, at 510-11.
142. *Id.* And the ICC/Laos has not filed any reports during 1967 and 1968, due to the refusal of the Polish delegate to sign certain types of reports. N.Y. Times, Feb. 7, 1968, at 1, col. 8.

each; (2) Burma, Cambodia, DRV, Laos, RVN, Thailand—1.5 per cent each. In actual practice, Communist China and the DRV have not adequately met their obligations.

As to the actual functioning of the "renovated" ICC/Laos, the State Department in 1963 termed its activities a qualified success.[143] But the ICC/Laos had its difficulties, both internal and external, as mirrored by the walkout of the Polish representative in 1963, the denial of access to Communist-held territory, and the inability of the Co-Chairmen to decide on a common ICC policy. A more serious effect on the maintenance of peace in Laos has been caused by the inability of the political aspects of the 1962 settlement to withstand the test of time. The situation worsened over the next few years, as the coalition government never functioned very effectively and the outside powers once again began pursuing independent policies on Laos. Even the very finest peace observation machinery (and certainly the 1962 ICC/Laos is not that) cannot hold together a settlement which the parties find unacceptable, at least where the outside powers are equally at odds and do not rally in support of the peace observation mission.

On the whole, the 1962 ICC/Laos did not embody very many of the initial Western proposals for improvements, nor very many of the suggestions contained in this article. The troika provisions became more onerous than ever, the access requirements were not improved, the absence of the Polish member caused major difficulties, and the absence of concurrence among the parties remained a problem. Although the ICC now had adequate transport, it could not use it to investigate in Communist-held areas. A consultative body was established, but with a composition of just two members it was itself highly susceptible to deadlock. The 1962 ICC/Laos, just as the 1954 ICC/Vietnam, remained a symbol of the stalemated nature of the big-power confrontation.

IX. Conclusion—A Role for the United Nations in the Vietnam Settlement

There are many reasons why a peace observation mission will be a vital part of any future settlement on Vietnam. First, the parties want it so. Ambassador Harriman called for the "strengthening" of international supervision at the very first session of the Paris negotiations, and predicted the effort would form one of the major tasks of the negotiations.[144] The present conflict has been intense and bitter, and the parties will want a check on the "good faith" of the other side during the implementation of any settlement. Second, the inter-

---

143. *See* the statements of State Department officials, including the Assistant Secretary of State for Far Eastern Affairs, in Hearings on S. 1627, *supra* note 135.
144. N.Y. Times, May 14, 1968, at 18, col. 5.

national community similarly wants such a check, in the interests of world peace. Finally, an improved supervisory body could provide major assistance in the actual implementation of the settlement, bringing the parties together in Vietnam at a lower level to plan out the tasks laid down in the general agreement and to resolve any disputes, pressuring the parties to conform to the agreements, and providing observers to ensure a smooth transition to peacetime activity. If the settlement contains a ban on reprisals, provision for elections, transfer of persons or territory, or guarantees of neutrality, properly qualified supervisory personnel have essential roles to play in seeing these provisions are properly implemented. The necessity for a supervisory body in Vietnam's future makes it all the more essential that the mistakes of the ICC experience not be repeated, if any other arrangement can be negotiated.

The powers, duties, and facilities of that supervisory body must be carefully worked out during the negotiation process and described clearly in its terms of reference.[145] While there is enormous pressure to reach an early settlement and cease-fire, this simply must not come at the expense of a clearly articulated settlement in which the expectations of all the parties coincide.

The supervisory body for Vietnam should operate under the auspices of the United Nations. All who have analyzed the ICC experience have either openly endorsed this or have looked longingly at various strengths of U.N. peace observation facilities which are simply unavailable to *ad hoc* entities like the ICC.[146] A comparison tells why: a permanent consultative body readily available for guidance

---

145. *See* WAINHOUSE, at 550-51; Freymond, *supra* note 22, at 502.

146. Major Edmond Blais strongly urged United Nations sponsorship. He felt the ICC lacked the required authority to implement its decisions, and that the Co-Chairmen had generated little support for the ICC. By contrast, the United Nations had means of formulating specific solutions and of providing direction to the peace observation mission in the field, and provided the recourse to public opinion that was "completely lacking" to *ad hoc* entities. Blais, *supra* note 4, at 147. David Wainhouse asserts that the United Nations could have given the ICC the backstopping, support and guidance it so sorely lacked. WAINHOUSE, at 499. Paul Martin, whose country (Canada) has had the most extensive experience with international peace observation, concludes his review of Canada's ICC experience with the statement that ". . . the United Nations is the most suitable international instrument to keep the peace," since it is more likely to provide a fair hearing than any other entity. P. MARTIN, *supra* note 6, at 31. John Holmes finds the absence of United Nations' logistics facilities a "great disadvantage" for the ICC, since it was critically dependent on the parties themselves. He also finds a disadvantage to the ICC since the ICC members were representatives of states and not "impartial agents" like the U.N. Secretary General. Holmes felt the governments of these three states thereby played a more active role in ICC affairs than when states merely turn over certain personnel to a U.N. operation. But Holmes does find some flexibility in the ICC, since it did not operate "under the constant attention of a politically sensitive Assembly." Holmes, *supra* note 61, at 241-42.

and support or at least for discussions spelling out the positions of the power blocs (U.N.) versus an entity continued by happenstance which merely publishes the reports and fails to agree on common policy or provide effective support (the Co-Chairmen); peace observation personnel with at least a basic level of impartiality and loyalty to a single international entity (U.N.) versus personnel who are merely representatives of governments, which provide the actual policy guidance (ICC); a world-wide communications and logistics system (U.N.) versus a crucial dependence on the parties (ICC); a forum which receives world-wide attention and maintains an extensive publications and information service (U.N.) versus a small public relations committee unable to obtain space in the world press (ICC); a permanent Secretariat capable of providing essential services rapidly once the mission is formed (U.N.) versus an *ad hoc* approach to all services (ICC). The ICCs in Indo-China, together with the NNSC in Korea, have been the only major peace observation missions since World War Two which have not operated under the United Nations or a regional organization. The experience has been so totally negative that it should not be foisted upon Vietnam again if a lasting settlement is truly desired.

While United Nations peace observation techniques are demonstrably imperfect,[147] they contrast most favorably with those of the ICC. The United Nations has a vast amount of experience in the conduct of peace observation missions, and has shown a considerable capability for developing the type of innovations necessary to overcome the inevitable problems which arise in the course of these missions.[148] In addition, the facilities of the U.N. Secretariat—which can rapidly provide a newly-formed mission with such necessary services as administration, financial procedures, legal/political counsel, public information, logistics, and communications — far outstrip those available to any type of non-affiliated, *ad hoc* peace observation entity.[149]

Moreover, the United Nations, with its extensive world membership, would have vastly superior resources from which to draw the highly specialized personnel which ideally should form the peace observation mission. Too often in the past, peace observation missions have been the exclusive preserve of the professional military, and the terms of reference of these missions have rarely itemized require-

147. The worst example is the Congo operation. *See* the discussion of ONUC in R. RUSSELL, *supra* note 11, at 86-126. For example, there was one period when U.N. Headquarters under Secretary General Hammarskjold insisted on an extremely narrow privilege to use force in the Congo by ONUC forces, while those in the field were "contemptuous" of the Secretary General's legality and had developed their own policy. *Id.* at 116-17.
148. WAINHOUSE, at 220, 542.
149. *Summary Study of the Experience Derived from the Establishment and Operation of the Force: report of the Secretary General*, (9 Oct. 1958) 13 U.N. GAOR, Annexes, Agenda Item No. 65, at 8, 13, U.N. Doc. A/3943.

ments for specific types of professional or technical personnel. Although the Final Declaration of the 1954 Geneva Agreements contained a provision for all-Vietnam elections, there was no provision for the judges, political scientists, public administration specialists, and others who, together with military observers, would be indispensable to adequate supervision of those elections. Drawing on the extremely successful experience of its predecessor, the League of Nations, in providing both judges and military observers from many countries to supervise the Saar plebiscite of 1935,[150] the United Nations could properly staff the supervision of any elections specified in the Vietnam settlement. The United Nations could also supply elements of national police forces, trained in surveillance and investigation, to control the flow of arms or military personnel to Vietnam and to conduct investigations concerning reprisals and other suspected violations of a fairly wide range.[151] There is no reason to believe the professional military are more capable of handling such specialized matters, and due to the small numbers of highly trained national police capable of such international service, they would necessarily have to be drawn from a fairly wide range of countries. The United Nations operation in the Congo, with its political, military, and technical specialists all operating in a single organizational structure, serves as a most illuminating precedent.[152] With the vital importance of a Vietnam settlement for the maintenance of world order, the United Nations could also search out more readily an eminent, internationally respected statesman to lead the peace observation mission during the crucial early stages of the settlement, and ensure that *all* personnel were of the highest caliber.

United Nations participation in the Vietnam settlement should be approved by the Security Council. The Security Council has the primary responsibility under the U.N. Charter for the maintenance of international peace and security; and, despite an initial flurry of peace observation activity by the General Assembly following the "Uniting for Peace" resolution, by and large the U.N. peace observation missions have been initiated by the Security Council.[153] Both the United

---

150. The League of Nations provided some twenty experienced judges, drawn from Italy, Switzerland, Sweden, Ireland, Norway, and Spain. The military personnel included 1500 from Great Britain, 1300 from Italy, 250 from the Netherlands, and 250 from Sweden. The plebiscite, to determine whether the Saar would remain a part of France as arranged in the Treaty of Versailles or be returned to Germany, was conducted without serious disorder. Germany won. WAINHOUSE, at 20-29.

151. *See* A. Cox, *supra* note 11, at 99-100; Address by Prime Minister Lester Pearson (Canada), Carleton University, Press Release of May 7, 1964, in R. RUSSELL, *supra* note 11, at 157, 160.

152. R. RUSSELL, *supra* note 11, at 91-92.

153. Paul Martin indicates that interventions by the General Assembly in peace observation mission activity have been the exception and will not happen again if the Security Council acts responsibly. P. MARTIN, *supra* note 6, at 30. *See also* WAINHOUSE, at 540, 548.

States [154] and the Soviet Union [155] appear to favor Security Council supervision of peace observation missions, and this would furnish an excellent opportunity for them to work together in pursuit of the highly elusive detente so often speculated about in recent times. The peace observation mission should be organized by the Secretary-General, who has extensive experience in such matters and can use the services of a U.N. Secretariat with long years of experience in organizing and administering such missions.

Naturally, when the Vietnam war is viewed in context, United Nations participation in a Vietnam settlement faces major obstacles. But since the settlement would actually be negotiated outside the United Nations, many of these obstacles would fall away, and the others do not appear totally unsurmountable. For instance, although Secretary General U Thant has rejected any meaningful role for the United Nations in the Vietnam conflict because some of the main parties are not U.N. members,[156] here the settlement would be negotiated with the full active participation of certain non-members, and would have been reached only through the consent of the major combatants. Similarly, although Vietnam involves a direct confrontation between the major power blocs, and the Hammarskjold theory of "preventive diplomacy" [157] would appear to bar U.N. participation, the conflict would already have been resolved prior to any action by the Security Council, and a Security Council deadlock would be most unlikely. Similarly, the fairly recent tendency of the United States to avoid use of the United Nations for dealing with major international issues and to act unilaterally instead, due to the changing character of the voting membership,[158] would have no bearing here where the major issue—the nature of the settlement—has already been resolved.

Lest the parties to the settlement feel the United Nations would remove the implementation of that settlement from their direct control, the standard procedure if and when problems arise is for the peace observation mission to bring the *parties* together to work out a com-

---

154. The Committee on Peacekeeping Operations organized by President Johnson to participate in the White House Conference on International Cooperation had a membership with considerable experience in peace observation (for its specific membership, see *supra* note 14). It found unanimous agreement that the Security Council has primary responsibility for such matters. Committee on Peacekeeping Operations, *supra* note 14, at 66.

155. The Soviet Union issued detailed memorandums in 1964 and 1967 strongly supporting the primary role of the Security Council in peace observation operations. Their content is discussed in A. Cox, *supra* note 11, at 35-41.

156. L. MILLER, WORLD ORDER AND LOCAL DISORDER 195 (1967).

157. Hammarskjold felt the U.N. could not effectively influence problems which were clearly the subject of a conflict between the power blocs, for then the Security Council would be deadlocked by a veto and the Secretary-General could not act short of risking the impairment of his position and powers. Hammarskjold, *The Positive Role of the United Nations in a Split World*, 7 U.N. REVIEW No. 4 at 24 (1960).

158. A. Cox, *supra* note 11, at 22-23.

promise. This practice was followed by the ICC.[159] Moreover, if the parties then remain deadlocked, the Security Council can only *recommend* certain measures, it cannot force them on those parties.[160] And the U.N. experience in Yemen has shown that the current Secretary-General is quite capable of remaining within a mandate entrusted to him by the parties to an international agreement which calls for U.N. supervision.[161] Finally, all parties could appoint "representatives" to meet regularly with the Secretary-General to discuss problems concerning the peace observation mission. This could be done without raising any questions of implied membership in the United Nations. But U.N. "membership" need not be such an all-encompassing difficulty. If the Vietnam settlement provides for separate North and South Vietnams for any appreciable period of time, both could and should be presented to the U.N. Security Council for membership. Contrary to the cases of the other divided countries, Korea and Germany, the extensive maneuverings at the United Nations in 1957-58 over membership for the Republic of Vietnam [162] hold some promise for the present, for the Soviet Union there argued that *both* the Republic of Vietnam and the Democratic Republic of Vietnam were separate and independent states and *both* should be admitted together.[163] Since the Security Council determines membership questions and since the Security Council would deal with the peace observation mission for Vietnam, the acceptance by the Security Council of the observation mission might well provide an introduction to U.N. membership for these two entities. If elections were eventually to be held to determine Vietnam's future, the U.N. representation could be readjusted at that time.

The troika formula has proven quite unsatisfactory. As a final possibility, rather than again resorting to troika machinery, personnel from Communist countries should be asked to participate in a peace observation mission under United Nations control. At the worst, a relatively small number of totally partial Communist peace observers in a U.N. mission would not be able to wreak the havoc caused by the Communist representative in a troika, for the head of the U.N. mission would presumably forward generally impartial reports from other observers throughout Vietnam, and he could still make recommendations to the parties and pressure them to conform to the gen-

---

159. N.Y. Times, Oct. 20, 1954, at 12, col. 3.
160. R. RUSSELL, *supra* note 11, at 140.
161. The terms of reference for the U.N. Yemen mission (UNYOM) required it merely to "observe, certify and report" on the implementation of an agreement between the U.A.R. and Saudi Arabia. The U.N. Commander insisted the mission could not be effective even in this limited task without dispatching teams on investigations. The Secretary-General interpreted his mandate very narrowly and rejected such activity. The U.N. Commander then resigned. WAINHOUSE, at 427-28.
162. *See* Moore & Underwood, *The Lawfulness of United States Assistance to the Republic of Viet Nam,* 5 DUQUESNE L. REV. 235, 263-67 (1967).
163. *Id.* at 265.

—3

eral interpretation of the settlement. At the best, participation by reasonably impartial Communist personnel might set a very exciting precedent in the tattered annals of international organizations. If the Vietnam settlement is one which *both* major power blocs genuinely desire to implement, there is little reason why the Communist personnel should not be reasonably impartial. U.N. Secretariat officials from Czechoslovakia, Hungary, and Bulgaria participated in the U.N. peace observation mission in Cyprus and performed their tasks without incident.[164] Yugoslavia has been a strong and effective participant in several U.N. missions.[165] Certainly any Communist personnel who participated in a Vietnam mission would be conscious of the precedent, and, since the Soviet Union has been urging U.N. use of East European personnel, it would well understand the consequences of bias and prejudice in the first test case of these personnel.[166] Finally, as John Holmes states, participation by Communist personnel in U.N. peace observation missions would be ". . . primarily a reflection of rather than a cause of changing great power relations."[167]

There has been considerable speculation that the United States might seek a peace observation mission which includes personnel from the neutral nations of Asia. The proposals made by the United States at the first session in Paris included the following:

> We believe the nations of Asia—which have a crucial interest in the peace and stability of the region—should be associated with the monitoring of the agreements at which we may arrive.[168]

There has been no subsequent explanation of the precise manner in which the nations of Asia would be "associated with" the supervisory process. Most likely the concept is viewed as a cross between the troika and United Nations participation: three or four Asian neutral nations, each with one vote in the supervisory entity. There is an immediate practical difficulty, in that it would be extremely difficult to find three or four Asian nations, regardless how "neutral" they supposedly are, which would be fully acceptable to both sides. The United Nations, on the other hand, could draw on a vastly larger number of nations, at least some of which actually *are* neutral on the Vietnam issue. And a peace observation mission formed around several Asian nations would be yet another *ad hoc*, nonaffiliated entity in a context where the only other two (the NNSC, the ICC) have been failures. Due to its *ad hoc* nature, it would lack many features common to United Nations operations, including two of extreme importance.

---

164. A. Cox, *supra* note 11, at 43.
165. *Id.* at 44.
166. *Id.*
167. Holmes, *Political and Philosophical Aspects of U.N. Security Forces*, in PEACE-KEEPING: EXPERIENCE AND EVALUATION (THE OSLO PAPERS) 81, 92 (P. Frydenberg, ed. 1964).
168. W. Averell Harriman, in N.Y. Times, May 14, 1968, at 18, col. 5.

First, it would have no permanent consultative body which it could petition for guidance or support *unless* the parties to the settlement establish some sort of entity. If the parties merely agree to consult one another, or express willingness to re-convene the conference which negotiated the settlement in the first place, the situation is precariously close to that of the ICC. Second, it would not have the extensive services organization available to a U.N. peace observation mission, for communications, logistics, administration, public information, finance, and so forth. Such a supervisory body of Asian neutrals should be a concept to which the United States negotiators could retreat only if and when the United Nations route proves quite impossible.

The supervision of a negotiated settlement to the Vietnam war will require a peace observation mission which is greatly expanded in comparison to the unfortunate ICC, both in personnel and in powers and facilities. A troika formula should be avoided and a genuinely impartial composition sought, under United Nations sponsorship if at all possible. The peace observation mission must have access to some type of permanent consultative body for guidance and support. A specific forum must be established in which the parties to the settlement can plan together and resolve any disputes during the implementation of that settlement. The peace observation mission's personnel should be professionally qualified for the types of tasks they are to perform. It should have adequate resources for communications, transport, logistics and the like, and not be dependent on the parties. The mission should have full access to installations, persons, and documents necessary to perform its task, and should maintain its own security forces. It must have the powers necessary to act as a stabilizing factor, capable of preventing reprisals. And it must be adequately financed. But the most important means of ensuring the "effectiveness" of the peace observation mission rests in a carefully negotiated, clearly articulated settlement of the Vietnam conflict, in which all necessary parties are bound and also are genuinely desirous of implementing the specific provisions of that settlement.

The Neutralization of South Vietnam: Pros and Cons*

CYRIL E. BLACK
ORAN R. YOUNG

I.

Among the proposals that have been made in the course of the debate on possible settlements of the conflict in South Vietnam, neutralization has been prominently mentioned but never adequately discussed.[1] What would be its advantages to the various parties to this dispute, and what problems does it present?

The neutralization of a state is achieved by means of a formal agreement between the neutralized state and guarantor states. Under such an agreement, the neutralized state is bound to refrain from entering into alliances or collective security agreements with other states, from permitting the conduct of military operations by other states on its territory, and from admitting onto its territory armaments or other war materials except those required for its own defense. The neutralized state also agrees to defend its independence and territorial integrity in case it is attacked by other states.

The guaranteeing states, for their part, agree to recognize the independence and territorial integrity of the neutralized state, to defend it in case it is attacked, and to refrain from committing military or political acts that might impair its neutrality. Such an agreement may also include provisions for joint action by the neutralized state and the guarantor states to establish international machinery to supervise the agreement and to support its effectiveness in other ways.

It is important to make the distinction (since it has led to a good deal of misunderstanding) between neutralization on the one hand and neutrality, neutralism, and other forms of nonalignment. The purpose of

---

*This essay was written in September-October 1968. Consequently, it reflects the political issues in the forefront of the debate over Vietnam at that time. No effort has been made to revise the essay in the light of intervening occurrences.

1 This essay represents an application to the specific problems of South Vietnam of the more general considerations presented in Cyril E. Black, Richard A. Falk, Klaus Knorr, and Oran R. Young, *Neutralization and World Politics* (Princeton: Princeton University Press, 1968); and in the study by the same authors on "Neutralization in Southeast Asia: Problems and Prospects," prepared at the request of the Committee on Foreign Relations, United States Senate (Washington, D.C., October 10, 1966).

neutralization is to remove from international controversy states that are objects of conflict, and to guarantee their territorial integrity and self-determination. The central point is that neutralization is not a unilateral action, but is an agreement reached jointly by the neutralized state and the guarantor states. The resulting status is generally referred to as permanent, or perpetual, neutrality because it is valid in times of peace as well as in times of war.

Neutrality, by contrast, is a unilateral policy of abstaining from participation in an ongoing war between other states. It is a unilateral policy that involves no guarantees by other states. The United States, for example, pursued a policy of neutrality between 1937 and 1941, in the sense that it sought to avoid participation on either side of the European conflicts of those years. Neutralism and other forms of non-alignment are even vaguer terms, which refer to policies of refraining from participation in alliance systems in times of peace. Sweden, Yugoslavia, India, and Cambodia, among others, pursue neutralist policies in the sense that they refuse to align themselves with any of the existing alliance systems. These are purely national policies, which have no standing in international law and do not affect the policies of other states.

The principal neutralized states today (i.e., states enjoying a status of permanent neutrality) are Switzerland, Austria, and Laos. The profound differences in the situations in which these three states find themselves reflect the diversity of cases to which neutralization is applicable. The problem of adding a state such as South Vietnam to this select list is not one of following one or another of these models precisely, but rather of drawing imaginatively on the historical experience with neutralization to devise a form of agreement suited to the conditions prevailing with respect to South Vietnam.

II.

Even when the major participants in a conflict favor neutralization in principle, efforts to negotiate the details of a neutralization agreement are apt to be hampered by diplomatic ambiguities and rigidities. Neutralization for any state can be negotiated only when diverse perceptions and expectations converge favorably. Moreover, the war in Vietnam has now become irrevocably, though often intangibly, linked with other important international problems. Any settlement, therefore, will have great symbolic significance for other international relationships. Because of this, Vietnam cannot simply be set apart from the remainder of international relations and a neutralization arrangement negotiated on this basis.

Against this background, we can distinguish several preconditions for the neutralization of South Vietnam. Since no participant would gain a clear-cut victory in the short run under the terms of a neutralization arrangement, a stalemate in the hostilities together with a continued determination on the part of the major participants to avoid defeat would appear to be necessary. In fact, it is the dilemma posed by these twin conditions that makes neutralization seem like an interesting alternative. If we think of stalemate in broad rather than narrow terms, however, there is good reason to suppose that these conditions are now beginning to operate. The mounting of the costs to all parties that remain trapped in the stalemate considerably increases the attractiveness of intermediate solutions such as neutralization.

Another condition for the negotiation of a neutralization agreement is the existence of an international political environment allowing for flexibility in negotiations. The occurrence of the Berlin crisis in 1961, for example, delayed the negotiations over Laos for a number of months. And the Soviet invasion of Czechoslovakia in August 1968, has similarly added to the international climate elements that increase the difficulties of negotiating a settlement for the Vietnam conflict. Nevertheless, the international negotiating environment does not now appear to preclude the possibility of agreeing on a neutralization arrangement for South Vietnam. In particular, there is reason to believe that the United States and North Vietnam are both becoming more anxious to find an acceptable way to end the war as the costs of prosecuting it further mount steadily. While the exact timing of efforts to agree on neutralization and the negotiating tactics that could be employed to accomplish this end would certainly be highly sensitive to ups and downs in international relations, therefore, the present international climate does not appear to make neutralization impossible.

Some of the rigidities and impediments involved in the actual negotiation of a neutralization arrangement for South Vietnam can doubtless be circumvented by tactical initiatives relating to issues that have acquired great symbolic significance, such as the suspension of the bombing of North Vietnam. The importance of tactical initiatives of this kind, however, is often overemphasized. While they can be important in allowing negotiations to proceed, they are unlikely to alter the basic interests among the parties to the conflict. There is a popular tendency to discuss initiatives of this kind as though they were ends in themselves rather than tactical devices through which to help bring about the achievement of a settlement for the main issues.

III.

While the mere negotiation of a neutralization agreement may have important consequences in itself, much of the significance of neutralization as a device for managing power in international relations derives from the extent to which arrangements of this kind can be maintained over time. The maintenance of neutralization would not be an all-or-nothing issue, and it is possible to conceive of a variety of intermediate outcomes between perfect maintenance and outright failure. The contemporary case of Laos illustrates the extent to which the specific terms of a neutralization arrangement can be violated without completely diminishing the overall significance of the arrangement as a device for managing power in the international arena.

In general, the following factors are likely to determine the extent to which a neutralization agreement is maintained: the international political environment; the internal political, economic, and social viability of the neutralized state; and problems arising from ambiguous political boundaries, such as the periodic migration of peoples across official frontiers, and the relative ease of covert intervention on the part of outside states. If the involved outside powers are resolved to support neutralization it may prove successful even when the neutralized state is experiencing considerable civil strife. A fully viable neutralized state, such as Switzerland, can maintain its status of permanent neutrality successfully even when conflicts among the guarantor states reach the point of overt hostilities. The difficulties associated with problems of boundaries, on the other hand, are apt to be especially severe when one or both of the conditions stated above do not obtain.

It is clear that maintenance would be one of the critical problems in any attempt to neutralize South Vietnam. At a minimum, the two major intervening states, the United States and North Vietnam, would have to refrain from large-scale interventions in South Vietnam in the future. They could refrain on the basis either of reciprocal deterrence or of some more explicit agreement, but it clearly is a critical problem of neutralization. In addition, though neutralization imposes no formal limitations on the fundamental nature of the government of a neutralized state, that government should at least be able and willing to maintain its obligations under a neutralization arrangement.

A fundamental question that would be asked by Americans as well as by South Vietnamese is whether the North Vietnamese can be trusted not to intervene in the politics of a neutralized South Vietnam. They have violated the "Declaration on the Neutrality of Laos," of which North Vietnam is a signatory and guarantor, and they have shown equally little respect for the self-neutralization of Cambodia. For similar reasons, the North Vietnamese would certainly ask questions about the trustworthiness of American policy. Perhaps the best answer to these problems of trust is that neutralization might be agreed to under conditions that do not depend on trust alone. For example, if the United States continues to maintain significant forces within striking distance of both North and South Vietnam, in Thailand and elsewhere, it would retain a certain control over the situation. There is also the possibility that the United States might provide substantial postwar aid to North Vietnam as well as to South Vietnam. Some forms of neutralization would also be possible if both the United States and North Vietnam sought to reduce their involvement in South Vietnam gradually over a fairly long period of time, eyeing each other suspiciously all the while.

In addition, the maintenance of neutralization for South Vietnam would probably necessitate the development of control machinery of substantial proportions, even though this requirement would add materially to the difficulty of negotiating such an arrangement.

In the first place, observation and supervision would almost certainly be necessary. Though machinery of the type set up for Laos might prove adequate, renewed attention should probably be given to the more extensive proposals set forth by France and the United States at Geneva in 1961.[2] In addition, it is possible to establish formal enforcement machinery. Such machinery could range all the way from specific arrangements for consultation among the guarantor powers to the establishment of an international force to be stationed in South Vietnam for a considerable period. In general, however, extensive enforcement machinery would raise serious problems of negotiation since it would require detailed arrangements for recruitment, financing, and control.

There is of course a wide range of specific formats for control machinery. Observation and supervision arrangements can be based on national contingents, established within the framework of the United

---

[2] The texts of the "Declaration on the Neutrality of Laos," the French proposals presented by Jean Chauvel, and the American proposals presented by W. Averell Harriman can be found in *Neutralization and World Politics*, pp. 169-190.

Nations, or tied to a special control regime as in the case of Laos. Enforcement procedures can range from the establishment of a large international force to be stationed on the ground in South Vietnam, to informal agreements on the part of the leading guarantor states to honor their commitments under the terms of a neutralization arrangement. There are no control procedures likely to prove efficacious, however, without at least tacit agreements involving reciprocal deterrence among the principal outside powers and leading to at least minimal "rules of the game" to limit the scope of civil strife within the neutralized state.

IV.

Permanent neutrality accompanied by international guarantees would not in itself constitute a settlement of the conflict in South Vietnam. It would be only one of several components of such a solution. Another component would be specific arrangements for the cessation of hostilities, which would have to be negotiated as a separate issue, whatever form an ultimate solution might take. A third component to a settlement would be composition of a postwar government in South Vietnam, and the procedures of its selection. These components are interrelated to the extent that agreement on each depends to some extent on the other two, but each involves relationships among essentially different sets of interests.

The pros and cons of neutralization must be evaluated not only on their own merits but also in terms of alternative bases for a settlement. Of the available alternatives, only two appear at present to be out of the question: the unconditional surrender and withdrawal of either North Vietnam or the United States. Between these extremes there is a considerable range of possibilities.

One possibility would involve the withdrawal of both American and North Vietnamese forces from South Vietnam, leaving the latter with a sovereign and independent government the composition of which would be adapted to reflect the realities of the situation obtaining at the end of the conflict. The workability of such a settlement would depend, among other things, on whether the contending political forces within South Vietnam could reach some sort of accommodation. The entire conflict has its origin in the attempt of the National Liberation Front to overthrow the government of South Vietnam. It is by no means certain that the latter, in the absence of American forces, would be sufficiently strong to govern either without the NLF or with it.

The other possible alternative would involve the continued presence of sizable American forces in South Vietnam for an indefinite period. The North Vietnamese forces might be withdrawn from the field, in which case the situation might resemble that in South Korea, but more likely than not a substantial number of them would remain. This solution would depend in part on the stability of the relationship between the reduced American and North Vietnamese forces. It would depend also in substantial part on the willingness of the American public to continue supporting a major commitment in South Vietnam over a long period of time. The present cost of $30 billion and 10,000 American lives a year has come to be regarded by many as too high a price for the benefits that it purchases. What would be a tolerable level of costs over a long period of growing needs for the investment of resources at home?

It is in comparison with alternatives such as these that the results of neutralizing South Vietnam must be evaluated. The principal gain for South Vietnam associated with permanent neutrality under international guarantee (regardless of the composition of its government) would be the increased prospect of self-determination and territorial integrity under conditions in which hostilities would cease and foreign military forces would be withdrawn. The price for this gain would be the presence of international control machinery as well as the limitations on the sovereignty of South Vietnam implied in the obligations to refrain from entering into alliances and security agreements and to provide for defense in case of outside attack. In a regional perspective, the neutralization of South Vietnam would tend to reduce, or at least contain, the traditional friction between Vietnam and Thailand. To this extent neutralization would have a stabilizing effect on the politics of Southeast Asia. It is more difficult, however, to predict the impact on the expansionist tendencies that North Vietnam has displayed in Laos and Cambodia. Would North Vietnam find its original interest in unifying all the former provinces of French Indochina too costly in political terms, or would the forces withdrawn from South Vietnam become more readily available for use against other neighbors?

It is equally difficult to evaluate the possible effects of the neutralization of South Vietnam on the major powers. Whatever level of conflict might continue in South Vietnam after a settlement, at the very least the withdrawal of American and North Vietnamese forces would tend to reduce international tensions. This was the effect of the neutralization of Laos, even though the actual level of conflict in that country has not been greatly reduced. To the extent that the Soviet Union and China might also be guarantors of a neutralization agreement, their role in Southeast Asia could be correspondingly reduced. If, as seems more likely, the United States and North Vietnam were the only guarantors of the agreement, the policies of the Soviet Union and China in these regions might not be greatly affected. Even if the only international result of neutralization were the cessation of hostilities between the United States and North Vietnam, this would still be a major achievement. The war has had international consequences that have been disproportionate to its strategic significance, and the cessation of hostilities would have correspondingly beneficial effects.

V.

Who would favor the neutralization of South Vietnam and why? This is a highly complex question.

In international terms, neutralization would mean that there would be no clear-cut winner of the Vietnam conflict in the short run. Among other things, therefore, neutralization would tend to produce some degree of isolation of the outcome of the Vietnam conflict from the broader environment of international relations and it would soften the impact of any demonstration effects that might result from the settlement of the Vietnam War. Though these consequences could be expected to be distasteful to ideologically inclined elites in all parts of the world, they would appeal strongly to leaders in all those states concerned with the mounting costs of the conflict and willing to settle for any outcome whose immediate negative consequences were small even though the settlement did not result in large gains.

In local terms, neutralization would mean both that the ultimate fate of South Vietnam would not be settled immediately and that certain ground rules (e.g., no appeals for outside intervention) would be imposed on the continuation of conflict in the area. Civil strife could continue but only on the basis of indigenous resources. Similarly, eventual political unification with North Vietnam would be possible on the basis of an agreement freely arrived at by the two governments. Indeed, neutralization itself might be limited to a specified period, such as twenty years. Since in all likelihood neither the Saigon government nor the NLF would have achieved a clear-cut victory at the time neutralization was agreed to, and since the eventual government of South Vietnam might well differ substantially from the present composition of either of these parties, it seems clear that the more extreme elements within both these groups would strenuously resist a settlement involving neutralization. The less extreme elements, on the other hand, might well find neutralization quite attractive. Such an arrangement would not turn any party into a clear-cut loser; it would allow all factions an opportunity to gain positions of influence in the eventual governing arrangements for South Vietnam, and it would permit the initiation of many badly needed projects presently shelved because of the large costs of the war. The probability of the local parties' supporting such an arrangement would be particularly great if the principal outside parties encouraged such an outcome through the exercise of direct pressure coupled with promises of economic aid after the war was ended. •

In assessing the specific pros and cons of neutralization, it seems useful to divide the parties into three groups: the principal intervenors (the United States and North Vietnam), the major local parties (the Saigon government and the NLF), and major outside powers with interests in the conflict (the Soviet Union and China). At present, the positions of the United States and North Vietnam appear to be becoming increasingly evenly balanced. The more extreme elements in both countries tend to view the conflict in ideological terms, to think that the outcome of the conflict will have far-reaching repercussions for the positions of their countries in international relations, and to retain hopes for a decisive victory in Vietnam. Yet, for both sides, the economic, political, and human costs of the war are mounting steadily; involvement in the conflict prevents the initiation of other important projects, and the underlying symmetry of the actual hostilities makes long-term stalemate increasingly probable. Under the circumstances, there is reason to believe that the reciprocal pressures for a negotiated settlement are now growing substantially. And the specific possibility of neutralization is attractive in this connection since neither side would lose decisively and since it would still be possible for each side to hope for a more favorable outcome eventually.

The situation with respect to the local parties is more sensitive, since the conflict may at any time become an issue of survival for both the Saigon government and the NLF. The possibility that under neutralization local struggles for political influence could continue in South Vietnam might make it possible for both sides to accept such an arrangement. But it is to be expected that each of the local parties will be highly suspicious of any change in the conflict that might favor one side or the other and that might increase the ultimate control of the outside powers over the situation. Despite the fact that neutralization might hold considerable attractions for some of the factions within the local parties, therefore, it is to be expected that acceptance on their part would depend to a considerable extent on the exercise of political pressure by the United States and North Vietnam as well as on the concomitant attractions of the prospect of postwar economic aid.

The reactions of the Soviet Union and China to the possibility of neutralizing South Vietnam seem likely to differ extensively. The Soviet Union has strong incentives to favor an end at least to the international aspects of the war in Vietnam: the dangers of escalation that might draw the Soviet Union in deeper; the economic costs of supporting the war; the resultant opportunity costs affecting domestic projects; and the political liabilities of the conflict in the struggle for international political influence. Powerful elements within the Soviet Union appear to be acutely conscious of these problems. Nevertheless, developments in recent months, centering on the invasion of Czechoslovakia and its repercussions, have apparently increased the influence of Soviet factions who have different priorities and who might well desire a continuation of the Vietnam conflict. At present, therefore, the Soviet Union seems to be so internally divided on the issue of Vietnam as to be unable to play a leading role in the search for a settlement. China, on the other hand, would appear to be considerably less divided on the issue but most unlikely to support a settlement involving the neutralization of South Vietnam. Because the dominant factions in China appear to be interested in testing fully the Maoist doctrine of wars of national liberation, in keeping American resources and policy bogged down in an unresolved war in Vietnam, and ultimately in increasing Chinese influence over North Vietnam, it is reasonable to expect them to favor the continuation of the war on an indecisive basis. Moreover, except in the unlikely event of American invasion, the costs to China of its continuation are minimal. Under the circumstances, it is to be expected that China would oppose a settlement involving neutralization and that the Soviet Union would, at best, find it difficult at this time to become a guarantor state for a neutralization arrangement. These factors by no means obviate the possibilities of neutralizing South Vietnam as part of an overall settlement for the conflict. They do emphasize the point, however, that the United States and North Vietnam would have to play the critical roles both in negotiating such an arrangement and in guaranteeing it after its establishment.

VI.

The pros and cons of a settlement involving the neutralization of South Vietnam must be evaluated in terms not only of the circumstances bearing immediately on that country and its neighbors, but also of the role of neutralization more generally as an acceptable means of managing power in situations of international conflict.

It must be recognized that, although the neutralization of states by international guarantee has a history that goes back to 1815, it has not yet been firmly established in international practice. The historical experience with neutralization may be seen in two phases. The first emerged at the time of the peace settlement in 1815, when the permanent neutrality of Switzerland was guaranteed by Austria, France, Great Britain, Prussia, and Russia. Switzerland had in fact established a unilateral policy of neutrality for over a century before the peace of Europe was disturbed by the French Revolution, and the arrangement of 1815 was in effect a return to this policy on the basis of a multilateral guarantee.

The neutralization of Belgium in 1839 and of Luxembourg in 1867 followed the Swiss model in important respects and was under the guarantee of the same five powers. What these three cases had in common was a strategic position with respect to the major powers that made it important to remove them as a potential source of dispute and possibly of war. At the same time there was a significant difference to the extent that Belgium and Luxembourg accepted neutralization rather unwillingly as a price of independence from the Netherlands, whereas Switzerland was not only willing but eager to have its traditional policy of neutrality reaffirmed. There were also other cases of neutralization of a more ephemeral character in the nineteenth century.

A second phase began in 1955 with the neutralization of Austria. This case differs from its predecessors in that there was no formal guarantee by the major powers that signed the Austrian State Treaty—France, the Soviet Union, the United Kingdom, and the United States. Instead, Austria undertook in a separate agreement with the Soviet Union to accept the obligation to practice permanent neutrality of the type maintained by Switzerland in return for the acceptance by the Soviet Union of the State Treaty—and with it the termination of the four-power occupation of Austria. The actual neutralization of Austria took the form of a Federal Constitutional Statute, adopted after the signature of the State Treaty, under the terms of which the Austrian parliament established a policy of permanent neutrality. The Austrian status of permanent neutrality was subsequently recognized by the four powers, and by many other states as well, but it was not formally guaranteed by any of them.

Yet another pattern is represented by the case of Laos, which was neutralized under the terms of a declaration signed at Geneva in 1962 by thirteen countries. The guarantors include the People's Republic of China, France, the Soviet Union, the United Kingdom, and the United States, and the declaration itself is a detailed document drafted with considerable care.

No two of these five major historical cases of neutralization are exactly the same, and they reflect the fact that no established pattern for the details of neutralization has emerged in the course of the 154 years since the first of these agreements was concluded in 1815. It should also be recognized that each of these cases has significant short-comings. The maintenance of Swiss neutrality has depended more on the determination and military potential of the Swiss themselves than on outside guarantees. Belgium and Luxembourg, for their part, were both overrun in 1914, and their status as permanent neutrals was terminated by the Treaty of Versailles in 1919. Austria was reluctant in 1955 to accept a status of permanent neutrality—although it has since come to appreciate the advantages this status confers upon it—and the unusual pattern of self-neutralization and of the international recognition upon which it rests does not represent a precedent that any other country is likely to follow. In the case of Laos, civil strife and significant intervention by other states have continued since 1962 despite the presence of an international commission.

This is not the sort of record that would lead a state to accept today a status of permanent neutrality without grave misgivings, were it not for the fact that these five cases also exemplify a major achievement: in each case, countries that had been or were likely to become objects of dispute among major states have ceased to be sources of international conflict. Switzerland has now sustained its neutrality long enough to justify the term "permanent." The neutrality of Belgium and Luxembourg survived several major European crises, and was terminated only in the course of the greatest international conflict that Europe had ever known and in which many other international institutions also succumbed. The neutrality arrangements for Austria and Laos have been established too recently to permit one to draw major conclusions. One can at least say, however, that Austrian neutrality seems to be firmly established, and that the major powers have not again come into overt conflict over Laos.

What recommends a status of permanent neutrality for a settlement in South Vietnam is not that it is a method of handling a situation of conflict that has never failed in the past, but rather that it has certain characteristic strengths that seem peculiarly applicable to the situation. Neutralization offers a framework for settlement that would tend to minimize the impact of the Vietnam conflict on the international political environment, while enhancing the prospect of self-determination and territorial integrity for South Vietnam. At the same time, it would be flexible enough to accommodate considerable political change within South Vietnam itself. The method should not be to follow any past model of neutralization exactly, but rather to draw imaginatively on past experience with neutralization and with peace-keeping procedures, in order to devise an agreement especially suited to the conditions prevailing in Vietnam.

VI. WORLD ORDER PERSPECTIVES

What We Should Learn from Vietnam

RICHARD A. FALK

THE FUTURE of American policy in Asia will be shaped by the ways in which our leaders interpret the Vietnam experience of the last ten years. At present, three principal interpretations of America's long involvement in the Vietnam war are contending for dominant influence. The "lesson of Vietnam," as public officials understand it, will probably be a shifting composite of these three views. All three of them assume in differing degree that the United States should use its military strength to defeat and discourage revolutionary movements in Asian countries and to contain Chinese power.

I find this unfortunate, for each of the most common interpretations is so fundamentally misguided as to preclude enlightened changes in U.S. policy toward Asia in the seventies. I believe a fourth line of interpretation of American involvement in Vietnam, absent from the debate in Washington, provides a better basis for comprehending the past and planning for the future.

Three Interpretations

We still do not know how the Vietnam war will finally end, and thus we cannot know whether the outcome of the war will be generally understood as an American victory, a stalemate or compromise, an NLF victory, or indeed if there will be any consensus at all. It is already clear that the NLF and North Vietnam have scored an extraordinary success against overwhelming odds, although at a very high cost to themselves in blood and destruction. But it remains impossible to tell whether the war will eventually end because the Saigon regime collapses, because domestic dissent in America causes a rapid and total U.S. withdrawal, or, conversely, because the U.S. launches some desperate kind of re-escalation, or even because a negotiated compromise is worked out in Paris at some point. Future American policy in Asia will depend heavily on how the final outcome in Vietnam is actually perceived by policy-makers. At this point, however, it seems fair to suppose an inconclusive ending to the war with enough ambiguity to support a number of differing interpretations on who won and who lost what. We can also suppose that regardless of the outcome, a consensus will emerge around the conclusion that American involvement in Vietnam was too costly to serve as a model for future U.S. foreign policy.

Despite these imponderables, three different interpretations dominate the Vietnam debate at the present time: that the war has been

Position 1: A qualified success;
Position 2: A failure of proportion;
Position 3: A qualified failure of tactics.

Position 1—that the war has been a qualified success—is the view of most professional military men and the American Right. They see American involvement in Vietnam as a proper exercise of military power, but feel that our effort has been compromised by Presidential insistence on pursuing limited ends by limited means. They criticize Washington for seeking "settlement" rather than "victory," and join the Left in condemning President Johnson for his failure to declare war on North Vietnam. They argue that our armed forces have had to fight the war with one hand tied behind their backs, pointing to the refusal to authorize bombing the dikes in North Vietnam, restrictions on targets in Hanoi and Haiphong, and the failure to impose a blockade on shipping to North Vietnam.

Even though victory has not been sought by all means at our disposal, this view does not regard the Vietnam war as a failure. In a characteristic statement, Colonel William C. Moore of Bolling Air Force Base, writing in the *Air University Review*, argues: "there is reason to believe that Ho Chi Minh would never have initiated action in Vietnam had he vaguely suspected that U.S. determination would escalate the war to its current magnitude. There is also reason to believe that this lesson has not been lost on other would-be aggressors." Such an interpretation of the lesson of Vietnam relies on two assumptions: first, that the Vietnam war was similar to the Korean war in which the United States may also have shrunk back from the complete execution of its mission, but in which it at least displayed a willingness to defend a non-Communist country against attack by a Communist aggressor. Position 1 sees the Vietnam war as a war of conquest by one country against another, the NLF as a mere agent of Hanoi whose role is to pretend that the war is a civil war and thereby discourage an effective response. In short, Position 1 accepts fully the view presented during the Johnson Presidency by Dean Rusk and Walt Rostow. The implication for the future is that the United States is not about to be fooled into treating Communist-led insurgencies any differently from outright Communist aggression against a friendly state.

The second assumption of Colonel Moore's assessment has an even greater implication for the future because it views Vietnam as demonstrating that deterrence works in a counterinsurgency setting as well as it has worked in the nuclear setting. In Colonel Moore's words: "This willingness to escalate is the key to deterring future aggressions at the lower end of the spectrum of war. This, I think, is why history will be kind to President Johnson and Secretary of State Rusk, because if we continue to stand firm in Vietnam as they advocate, then the world will have made incalculable progress toward eliminating war as the curse of mankind."[1] Thus, the key to the future is American willingness to escalate the conflict to high levels of destructivity—so high, in fact, that no prudent revolutionary would ever initiate a war if confronted by such a prospect. Position 1 is critical of Johnson's war diplomacy only insofar as it failed to carry the logic of escalation to higher levels on the battlefield and at home.

This interpretation also claims that the American decision to fight in Vietnam gained time for other anti-Communist regimes in Asia to build up their capacities for internal security and national defense, assuming that the American effort in Vietnam created a shield that held back the flow of revolutionary forces across the continent of Asia. More extravagant exponents of this line of interpretation even contend, on the most slender evidence, that the Indonesian generals would not have reacted so boldly and successfully to the Communist bid for power in Djakarta in October 1965 had not the American presence in Vietnam stiffened their resolve.

Advocates of Position 1 tend to admire the Dominican intervention of 1965, where massive force was used and results quickly achieved with little loss of life. The domestic furor over the Dominican intervention disappeared quickly, mainly as a consequence of its success and brevity. Sophisticated adherents to Position 1 admire the Soviet intervention of August 1968 in Czechoslovakia for similar reasons. This model of overwhelming capability (rather than the slow escalation of capability as in Vietnam) is likely to influence the doctrine and future proposals of those who favor interventionary diplomacy.

The second position—that the war is a failure of proportion—is widely held by American liberals. They feel that the Vietnam war was

[1] Colonel William C. Moore, "History, Vietnam, and the Concept of Deterrence," *Air University Review*, xx (Sept.-Oct. 1969) 58-63.

a mistake from the moment President Johnson decided in 1965 to bomb North Vietnam and to introduce large numbers of American ground combat forces. Position 2 also, by and large, rejects the notion that the war was caused by the aggression of one state against another, but views Vietnam instead as an international civil war in which both sides have received considerable outside support. One of the most revealing formulations of this position is found in Townsend Hoopes' book, *The Limits of Intervention*. Mr. Hoopes, who served in the Pentagon from January 1965 to February 1969, first as Deputy Assistant Secretary of Defense for International Security Affairs and then as Under Secretary of the Air Force, explains the failure of Vietnam as the result of a loss of a sense of proportion by decision-makers at the top. He builds a convincing insider's case that Johnson and his principal advisers were locked into a rigidly doctrinaire view of the war and hence were unable to moderate their objectives to conform with the costs in blood, dollars, and domestic cohesion. Writing of the situation prevailing in Washington late in 1967, just a few months before Johnson's withdrawal speech of March 31, 1968, Hoopes says: "The incredible disparity between the outpouring of national blood and treasure and the intrinsic U.S. interests at stake in Vietnam was by this time widely understood and deplored at levels just below the top of the government. But the President and the tight group of advisers around him gave no sign of having achieved a sense of proportion." Such a view of the lesson of Vietnam had no quarrel with our initial objective to defend Saigon and defeat the NLF, but urged that our effort to do so be abandoned if it could not be made to succeed within a reasonable time and at a reasonable cost. Many members of government during the Kennedy period who originally supported America's role in Vietnam later came to hold similar views, concluding either that the war was weakening our ability to uphold more significant interests in Europe and the Middle East, or that the disproportionate costs of the Vietnam war deprived the country of energies and resources that were desperately needed to solve domestic problems.

Former Ambassador Edwin Reischauer, respected among liberals, has carried this kind of analysis to a more general level of interpretation: "The 'central lesson' of Vietnam—at least as the American public perceives it—is already quite obvious . . . the limited ability of the United States to control at a reasonable cost the course of events in a nationally aroused less developed nation. . . . I believe," Reischauer adds, "that we are moving away from the application to Asia of the 'balance of power' and 'power vacuum' concepts of the cold war, and in the process we no doubt will greatly downgrade our strategic interest in most of the less developed world."[2] According to Reischauer, the means used in Vietnam were disproportionate to the end pursued, and, in general, a country like the United States cannot effectively use its military power to control the outcome of Vietnam-type struggles.

David Mozingo takes this argument one step further, recognizing the need for a perspective on Asia that is suited to the special historical and political conditions prevailing there, a perspective that might even suggest the end of a rigid policy of containment of China. "Since the Korean war," he argues, "United States policy in Asia has been modeled after the containment doctrine so successfully applied in Europe after 1947. . . . Washington has seen the problem of Chinese power in Asia in much the same light as that posed by Soviet power in Europe and has behaved as if both threats could be contained by basically the same kind of responses. In Asia," Mozingo continues, "the containment doctrine has been applied in an area where a nation-state system is only beginning to emerge amidst unpredictable upheavals of a kind that characterized Europe three centuries earlier. . . . The kinds of American technical and economic power that could help restore the historic vitality of the European system would seem at best to have only partial relevance to the Asian situation."[3] Such a view of the Vietnam experience supports a policy that emphasizes a more specific, less abstract appreciation of how to relate American economic, military, and political power to a series of particular struggles for control going on in various Asian countries.

Among the lessons drawn from Vietnam is the futility of aiding a foreign regime that lacks the capacity to govern its society and the conclusion that certain types of intervention, if carried too far, help produce results that are the opposite of the goals of the intervenor. The American failure in Vietnam is partly laid to ignorance about Vietnamese realities and partly to exaggerated confidence in the ability of massive military intervention to fulfill political objectives. This is essentially the view of Stanley Hoffmann.[4] Again, as with Hoopes, the search is for an effective foreign policy, combined with a sense of proportion

[2] Richard N. Pfeffer (ed.), *No More Vietnams?* (New York: Harper & Row, 1968), pp. 267-68.

[3] David P. Mozingo, *The United States in Asia: Evolution and Containment* (New York: Council on Religion and International Affairs, 1967), pp. 7-8.

[4] See esp. Hoffmann in Pfeffer (ed.) *op.cit.*, pp. 193-203.

and an awareness of the inherent limits imposed on American policy. But, like Colonel Moore's interpretation, this liberal critique does not repudiate American objectives in Vietnam. The main lesson for the future, according to Professor Samuel Huntington, who served as head of Hubert Humphrey's Vietnam task force during the 1968 Presidential campaign, is to keep Vietnam-type involvements in the future "reasonably limited, discreet, and covert."[5]

The third, and now dominant interpretation of the Vietnam war—that it is a qualified failure of tactics—is the one favored by President Nixon and such important foreign policy advisers as Henry Kissinger, William Rogers, and Melvin Laird. The Nixon doctrine, announced at Guam on July 25, 1969, is an explicit effort to avoid repeating the mistakes of Vietnam, as these leaders understand them, without altering the basic mission of American policy in Asia. The Nixon Administration is critical of the Vietnam effort to the extent that it believes the same ends could have been achieved at lesser cost in American blood and treasure, and, as a result, with less strain on American society. In his November 3, 1969 address on Vietnam, President Nixon explained the Nixon doctrine as embodying "three principles as guidelines for future American policy toward Asia": "First, the United States will keep all of its treaty commitments. Secondly, we shall provide a shield if a nuclear power threatens the freedom of a nation allied with us or of a nation whose survival we consider vital to our security. Third, in cases involving other types of aggression, we shall furnish military and economic assistance when requested in accordance with our treaty commitments. But we shall look to the nation directly threatened to assume the primary responsibility of providing the manpower for its defense." The "central thesis" of the doctrine, according to the President, is ". . . that the United States will participate in the defense and development of allies and friends, but that America cannot—and will not—conceive *all* the plans, design *all* the programs, execute *all* the decisions and undertake *all* the defense of the free nations of the world. We will help where it makes a real difference and is considered in our interest." (p. 19)

Thus, the Nixon doctrine backs a step away from the world order absolutism of Johnsonian diplomacy and instead advocates specific assessments of each potential interventionary situation in terms of its strategic importance to the United States and the ability of America to

5 *Ibid.*, p. 255.

control the outcome. It is difficult, however, to extract much sense of concrete policy from the rhetoric of the State of the World message to Congress last February 18: "The fostering of self-reliance is the new purpose and direction of American involvement in Asia."

In practical terms, such a position seems midway between those of Colonel Moore and Mr. Hoopes: uphold *all* treaty commitments, give *all* allied regimes our help and advice, but get fully involved in a direct military way only when vital interests are at stake and when the military instrument can be used effectively, which means successfully, quickly and without losing too many American lives. "Vietnamization," as one expression of the Nixon doctrine, leaves the main burden of ground combat to Saigon's armed forces, without any reduction in logistic support, B-52 air strikes and long-distance artillery support. Ambassador Ellsworth Bunker is reported to have said that the policy of Vietnamization involves only changing the color of the bodies. Another expression of the Nixon doctrine seems to be an escalation of American involvement in Laos, increasing our covert role in training and financing government forces and staging saturation bombing raids on contested areas, thereby causing a new flow of refugees and seeking to deprive the Pathet Lao of its rural population base.

A Critique

These three positions identify the present boundaries of serious political debate in the United States. It is likely that the early seventies will witness a struggle for ascendancy between the advocates of the liberal view (Position 2) and the advocates of the Nixon doctrine (Position 3). Extending the doctrine of deterrence to counterinsurgency situations (Position 1) could gain support if the political forces behind George Wallace or Barry Goldwater gained greater influence as "a third force" in American politics or significantly increased their already strong influence within the Agnew-Mitchell wing of the Nixon Administration.

Position 1 accepts "victory" as the proper goal of the American involvement in Vietnam and regards the means used as appropriate to the end of defeating the insurgency in South Vietnam, whether that insurgency is viewed as a species of civil war or as an agency of North Vietnamese aggression. In contrast, Position 2 shifted away from victory as a goal and moved toward the advocacy of some kind of mutual withdrawal of foreign forces and toward some effort to reach a settlement by non-military means once it became evident that the means required for the more ambitious goal were so costly in lives, dollars, and domestic support. Position 3 specifies the goal of the involvement as obtaining conditions of self-determination for South Vietnam and its present governing regime, a position that seems to imply an outcome of the war that is close to total victory; however, there is a certain ambiguity as to whether the real goals are not more modest than the proclaimed goals. In any event, Position 3 regards the means used to have been unnecessarily costly, given the goals of the involvement, and accepts, at least in theory, the desirability of a nonmilitary outcome through a negotiated settlement of the war.

Position 1 seems to interpret Vietnam as a qualified success and to favor, if anything, a less constrained military effort in the future to defeat any Communist-led insurgencies that may erupt on the Asian mainland in the 1970's. As with strategic doctrine, the deterrence of insurgent challenges rests on the possession of a credible capability and on a willingness to respond with overwhelming military force to any relevant challenge.

Position 2, which is much less tied to an overall doctrine, views the post-Kennedy phases of the Vietnam involvement as a clear mistake and argues for a much greater emphasis on nonmilitary responses to insurgent challenges. This position also seeks to limit overt intervention to situations in which its impact can be swift and effective. Position 2, therefore, depends on having a fairly secure regime in power in the country that is the scene of the struggle. It also emphasizes keeping a sense of proportion throughout such an involvement, either by way of a ceiling on the magnitude of the commitment or by way of a willingness to liquidate an unsuccessful commitment.

Position 3 is midway between the first two positions in tone and apparent emphasis. It develops a more globalist strategy, emphasizing that the U.S. has far-flung treaty relations with Asian countries and that it is important to our overall preeminence in world affairs and the continuing need to resist Communist pressures that these commitments be honored. The merits of the particular case are thus tied to a global strategy, but there is an effort to shift more of the burdens of response to the local government. What this means in those cases where the government cannot meet these burdens, as was surely the case in Vietnam all along, is very unclear. What happens under Position 3 when self-reliance fails? The prevailing response to this question may well determine the central line of American foreign policy in Asia throughout the 1970's.

Both Positions 2 and 3 look toward Japan as a more active partner in the development of a common Asian policy. President Nixon's decision to return Okinawa to Japan by 1972 arises out of this hope for sharing the geopolitical burdens of the region with Japan in the mid- and late seventies.

What is most surprising about these three positions is the extent to which they accept the premise of an American counterrevolutionary posture toward political conflict in Asia. To be clear, however, this espousal of counterrevolutionary doctrine is applicable only in situations that appear to be revolutionary. Where there is no formidable radical challenge on the domestic scene, as in India or Japan, the American preference is clearly for moderate democracy, indeed the kind of political orientation that the United States imposed upon Japan during the military occupation after World War II. However, where an Asian society is beset by struggle between a rightist incumbent regime and a leftist insurgent challenger, then American policy throws its support, sometimes strongly, to the counterrevolutionary side. As a result, there has been virtually no disposition to question the American decision to support the repressive and reactionary Saigon regime provided that support could have led to victory in Vietnam at a reasonable cost. In fact, the last four American presidents have been in agreement on the political wisdom of the decision to help Saigon prevail in its effort to create a strong anti-Communist state in South Vietnam, thereby defying both the military results of the first Indochina war and the explicit provisions on the reunification of Vietnam embodied in the Geneva Accords of 1954. Positions 1 and 3 share an acceptance, although to varying degrees, of the basic postulates of "the domino theory." Position 2 is least inclined to endorse the image of falling dominoes, and some of its adherents (such as Donald Zagoria in *China in Crisis*) indeed argue that the prospects for Communism need to be assessed on a country-by-country basis, and the success or failure of Communism in Vietnam or Laos will not necessarily have much impact upon the prospect for revolution in other Asian countries.

McGeorge Bundy, a belated convert to Position 2 (after an earlier allegiance to the moderate form of Position 1), gave up on the war because its burden was too great on American society. Nevertheless, he took pains to reaffirm the wisdom of the original undertaking: "I remind you also, if you stand on the other side, that my argument against escalation and against an indefinite continuation of our present course has been based not on moral outrage or political hostility to the objective, but rather on the simple and practical ground that escalation will not work and that a continuation of our present course is unacceptable."[6] Arthur Schlesinger, Jr., has said: "The tragedy of Vietnam is the tragedy of the overextension and misapplication of valid principles. The original insights of collective security and liberal evangelism were generous and wise."[7] Actually, adherents of Position 2, while sharply dissenting from the Vietnam policies of both Johnson and Nixon, still maintain the spirit of an earlier statement by McGeorge Bundy, made at a time when he was rallying support for Johnson's air war against North Vietnam: "There are wild men in the wings, but on the main stage even the argument on Vietnam turns on tactics, not fundamentals."[8]

Unfortunately, from my perspective, these so-called wild men still remain in the wings, if anything, further removed than ever from the center of the political stage, for positions 1, 2, and 3 all affirm the continuing wisdom of two American objectives in Asia: first, to prevent Chinese expansion, if necessary by military means, and second, to prevent any anti-Communist regime, however repressive, reactionary, or isolated from popular support, from being toppled by internal revolutionary forces, whether or not abetted by outside help.

The Excluded Fourth Position

There is another interpretation which has been largely excluded from the public dialogue thus far. It repudiates our present objectives in Vietnam on political and moral grounds. It holds, *first*, there is no reason to believe that China has expansive military aims in Asia; *second*, even if China were militarily expansive, it would not be desirable or necessary for the United States to defend China's victims; and *third*, there is neither occasion nor justification for aiding repressive governments merely because they follow anti-Communist policies. I favor this fourth position for several good reasons. There is no evidence that China needs containing by an American military presence in Asia. Of course, countries in the shadow of a dominant state tend to fall under

[6] McGeorge Bundy, "De Pauw Address" in Falk (ed.), *The Vietnam War and International Law*, 2 (1969).

[7] Arthur Schlesinger, Jr., "Vietnam and the End of the Age of Superpowers," *Harper's Magazine* (March 1969), 41-49.

[8] McGeorge Bundy, "The End of Either/Or," *Foreign Affairs*, xlv, 189-201.

the influence of that state whenever it is effectively governed. This process is universal and has deep historical roots in Asia. But there are important countervailing forces.

First, China is preoccupied with its own domestic politics and with principal foreign struggles against the Soviet Union and Formosa. Second, many of the countries surrounding China have struggled at great sacrifice to achieve independence, and their search for domestic autonomy is much stronger than any common ideological sentiment that might tempt Asian Communist regimes to subordinate their independence to Peking. Third, China's foreign policy may often have been crude and ill-conceived, but it has rarely exhibited any intention to rely on military force to expand its influence beyond its boundaries; its uses of force against India, Tibet, and the Soviet Union have been to support its claims to disputed territory, and its entry into the Korean war seemed motivated mainly by a reasonable concern about danger to its industrial heartland.

The evidence thus suggests that the American effort to contain China in Asia is a determination to contend with a paper tiger.

More significantly, the multifaceted conflicts in Asia cannot be comprehended in abstract or ideological terms. Asia is undergoing a two-phase revolution that began as a struggle against colonialism during World War II and will continue for at least another decade. The first phase represented the struggle to reacquire national control over the apparatus of government by defeating foreign rule. This struggle is largely completed. In most parts of Asia the colonial system has collapsed and foreigners have been removed from power. But in several Asian countries, including South Vietnam, the native groups allied with the colonial system have clung to political power, stifling social progress and economic reform. Thailand, although never formally a colony, continues to be governed by a traditional elite that is ill-inclined to initiate the reforms needed to build a society devoted to the welfare of its population as a whole.

After formal independence is won, the second phase of Asian national revolutions involves continuing struggle against the residues of the colonial system, including the more informal patterns of domination that result from American donations of military equipment, foreign aid, and political and economic advice. Most governments in Asia today are composed of conservative forces that hold onto their positions of power and privilege with the aid of such donations and advice, usually at the expense of their own people. Therefore, the second phase of the revolutionary struggle involves wresting political control from traditional ruling classes and instituting a mass-based program of land reform, education, public hygiene, and economic development. In most of Asia, aside from India, the United States is allied with regimes that are trying to hold back this second surge of the revolutionary impulse that has swept across the Third World to crush the colonial system.

Position 4 accepts this analysis of political conflict in Asia and would adjust American policy accordingly. First of all, it seeks accommodation with China through a flexible compromise of outstanding issues, including the future of Formosa. What is implied here is the removal of the American military presence from the area, especially the withdrawal of the Seventh Fleet and the elimination of our military bases on Formosa. Such a course would leave the outcome of the Chinese civil war, which has not yet been fully resolved, to the contending forces on both sides. It would encourage the possibility of negotiations between Peking and Taipei as to the governance of Formosa, perhaps allowing for semi-autonomous status within the Chinese People's Republic, with guarantees of a measure of economic and political independence for the island.

An American accommodation with China would help the United States handle an increasingly competitive economic relationship with Japan in the 1970's and give Washington more bargaining power in relation to the Soviet Union. More importantly, accommodation with China could make it possible to proceed more rapidly with arms control and disarmament, to denuclearize world politics, and to resist pressures to proliferate weapons of mass destruction to additional countries.

Position 4 favors as well a total abandonment of America's counter-revolutionary foreign policy. This would mean renouncing all treaty relations with governments that are repressing their own populations and holding back the forces of self-determination. Clearly such a revision of policy would require the renunciation of American treaty obligations to promote the security of the regimes now governing South Vietnam, Cambodia, Laos, South Korea, Formosa, Thailand, and the Philippines. The only commitment that should be reaffirmed is our obligation under the U.N. Charter to resist overt military aggression of the Korea-type. Position 4 would imply an end to large-scale military assistance and covert interference in the affairs of Asian countries. Civil strife is likely to occur in several Asian countries and dislodge present governments, but to the extent that it tends to reflect the true balance of political forces within these national societies, it would be beneficial for the welfare of the population and for the stability of each country and the region. At present, several regimes are being maintained in power only through a combination of domestic oppression and American support.

There seems virtually no prospect for the adoption, or even the discussion, of Position 4 during the 1970's unless major shifts in American political life occur. Only extraordinary domestic pressure, fueled perhaps by economic troubles at home and foreign policy setbacks abroad are likely to produce a change of leadership and a change of world outlook in America.

Yet in historic retrospect, it is important to appreciate that Position 4 once was close to being our foreign policy. Its rejection by today's American leaders is not an inevitable outcome of U.S. policy in Asia after World War II. Franklin Roosevelt was opposed to restoring the French colonial administration in Indochina at the end of the war. If Indochina had been allowed to become independent after the Japanese left, Ho Chi Minh would clearly have emerged as the leader of a united Vietnam, and perhaps of a united Indochina. In his initial Proclamation of Independence of September 25, 1945, Ho Chi Minh explicitly referred to the French and American Revolutions as the main sources of inspiration for the Vietnamese struggle for national independence. The Communist response was not altogether enthusiastic—the Soviet Union initially withheld recognition from Ho Chi Minh's Republic of Vietnam, and in 1947, Maurice Thorez, the Communist Vice-Premier of France, actually countersigned the order for French military action against the newly proclaimed Republic. As O. E. Clubb points out: "In 1945 and 1946 the Ho Chi Minh government looked mainly to the United States and Nationalist China for foreign political support."[9] In the period since World War II anticolonialism probably would have been a better guideline for American foreign policy in Asia than anti-Communism. And even now it would make better sense. It would work better because it accords more closely with historic trends in Asia, with the dynamics of national self-determination in most non-Communist Asian countries, and because it flows more naturally out of America's own best heritage and proudest tradition.

[9] O. Edmund Clubb, Jr., *The United States and the Sino-Soviet Bloc in Southeast Asia* (Washington: The Brookings Institution, 1962), p. 15.

Controlling Local Conflicts[1]

ELLIOT L. RICHARDSON

It is a privilege to be asked to participate in this extraordinary symposium.

Distinguished Soviet and American citizens are today mingling in this hall and exchanging views in a public forum, a fact which in itself contributes to a more positive relationship between our two countries.

Privately organized meetings such as this add a valuable dimension to official contact. I congratulate all involved on this initiative and hope that your discussions will be fruitful and will lead to other such meetings, with the next round perhaps taking place in the Soviet Union.

My remarks today were composed with an eye both to the unique nature of this audience and the title of your convocation. I seek to focus your concern on the grave hazards to world peace which arise when local conflicts threaten to escalate to the point of confrontation between the Soviet Union and the United States. Neither of our two countries—no country, indeed—can afford to underestimate these hazards.

There are many questions on which the United States and the Soviet Union disagree. We are likely to continue to disagree. There is nothing to be gained by pretending that this is not the case. Despite these differences we also have areas of common interest. I should like to concentrate today on how we can maximize one of those areas of common interest: how we can most effectively insulate ourselves against the escalation of local conflicts. Whatever strengthens and promotes this common interest will also serve the cause of peace. To this end I would like to suggest three simultaneous and complementary forms of action.

The first involves acknowledging and developing what I shall refer to as "spheres of restraint"; the second calls for encouraging regional self-policing and the development of regional institutions and capabilities; and the third requires strengthening United Nations mechanisms so that they can more effectively cope with local conflicts.

As I look at the world situation that now seems to be emerging, I see an uneasy equilibrium at the center in which the crucial element is the

---

[1] Address made before the Second National Convocation on the Challenge of Building Peace sponsored by the Fund for Peace at New York, N.Y., on April 29, 1970 (press release 133).

U.S.-U.S.S.R. bilateral strategic relationship. In recent years we have both come to recognize the need to give this strategic relationship greater stability.

Significant headway has already been made. Agreements on a partial test ban treaty, the banning of nuclear weapons from Antarctica and from outer space, and the Nuclear Nonproliferation Treaty have been followed by a draft treaty barring weapons of mass destruction from the seabed. The strategic arms limitation talks now underway in Vienna have even greater potential for stabilizing our strategic relationship. Extremely sensitive and complex matters touching upon the vital security of each side are at stake. But if solutions continue to be pursued in the same serious manner in which the talks have begun, we are confident that ways can be found to limit the dangers and costs of the strategic arms race.

Beyond this central strategic equilibrium and destined, I believe, to become increasingly important are complex new configurations of power involving other countries and, in some cases, new regional groupings. In some areas of the world the power of the United States is involved in the local balance; in some areas Soviet power is involved; in other regions we are both involved, directly or indirectly.

Certain regions where both of us are now deeply involved are so important to the central configuration of power that accommodations will require a careful process of negotiation on outstanding issues. Central Europe, for which the NATO ministerial meeting recently proposed mutual and balanced force reductions, is the outstanding example.

Development of "Spheres of Restraint"

In other areas, however, where neither of us is now so heavily committed, progress can be made toward reducing the danger of expanded local conflict by deliberately limiting our involvement. This does not require that we agree on the origin and merits of the conflict in question nor that we forgo all interest in the area. What is required is that we do agree, either tacitly or explicitly, to refrain from any action, direct or indirect, which might disturb its internal equilibrium.

Since the world of the 1970's is not likely to be a placid one, this will not be an easy task. Experience has shown that the process of modernization is inevitably accompanied by convulsion and dislocation. Turmoil and turbulence are thus unfortunately likely to continue to accompany rapid social change in large parts of the world. Peaceful development—economic or political—is a process that has thus far eluded much of mankind.

The temptations, the impatience, and the anger which will be stirred by continuing eruptions and violence in developing areas emphasize the need for major-power abstention. The development of spheres of restraint will require that both major powers recognize that their long-term interests are not furthered by attempts to gain short-term—and often fleeting—advantage.

Each side has its own views as to what constitute current examples of such attempts. I believe, for instance, that the Soviet Union should realize that any immediate gains it might make by attempting to take advantage of the troubled Middle East situation are far outweighed by the danger of stirring up a wider conflict. When in such an area one of us—in this case the U.S.S.R.—involves itself militarily, it is inevitable that the other will take notice and react.

We in the United States, meanwhile, must come to terms with the fact that violent upheaval, however repugnant to our preference for orderly and peaceful change, is going to continue to occur. We must realize that in most such situations U.S. power is neither a desirable nor an effective prescription.

In addition to realizing that we have neither a moral right nor a duty to intervene in every local quarrel, both the United States and the U.S.S.R. must also recognize that our power to deal with such disputes is sharply circumscribed by the new confidence and strength of many of the smaller nations. In many cases, to be sure, our participation—together with such leverage as we can usefully exercise—can help the parties find an acceptable formula for a settlement. This is what we are seeking to do in our discussions on the Middle East. But such efforts should not lead us to believe that an imposed solution, even where we can agree on its basic elements, is a lasting solution. Where persuasion fails, coercion is not an acceptable option.

These perceptions are reflected in the way the Nixon administration is attempting to remold U.S. foreign policy. They can be seen in the more precise manner in which we are now setting the limits of our obligations. As President Nixon has put it, ". . . we have commitments because we are involved. Our interests must shape our commitments, rather than the other way around."[2] Accordingly, we are being more

---

[2] For text of President Nixon's foreign policy report to the Congress on Feb. 18, see *Department of State Bulletin* (March 9, 1970).

exact in the delineation of those U.S. interests which, when threatened, must call forth a response.

We hope that the Soviet Union is also undertaking a new look at its own real interests around the world to see whether they, too, might not, to advantage, be defined more narrowly. To the extent it does so, the development of spheres of restraint will become an easier task.

But even if both of us successfully pursue a course faithful to a recognition of spheres of restraint, this may not, in itself, be sufficient to insulate local conflicts and to prevent the risk of escalation. A second form of action, therefore, will also be important; that is, encouraging regional efforts to develop institutions for coping with local problems and disputes.

Encouragement of Regional Initiatives

The Charter of the United Nations, in articles 33 and 52, clearly envisages regional efforts which can contribute to the preservation of peace. These aspects of the charter should be given increasing attention, especially by the developing countries.

While experience to date does not suggest that major successes will soon be achieved in this way, the record is not without promise. From the dispute between Costa Rica and Nicaragua two decades ago to the more recent conflict between El Salvador and Honduras, the Organization of American States has demonstrated a useful capacity for peacemaking. The Organization of African Unity has also scored some success in mediating disputes—as in those between Ethiopia and Somalia and between Morocco and Algeria, both in 1964. Nor should one discount the efforts made by the OAU in other instances where, although success was not achieved, some restraint was encouraged and useful experience gained.

In Asia, too, regional organizations are beginning to develop. These, as President Nixon observed in his report to the Congress on foreign policy, can be bulwarks of peace. We look forward to their undertaking such a role in the future, and even now we hope that the nations of the area can help resolve the conflict in Southeast Asia, for certainly they have a paramount interest in seeing this accomplished.

It will be especially important, however, to guard against expecting too much too quickly from the emergent regional consciousness in various parts of the world. The necessary concentration of regional power and the formation of institutions for regional action will take time.

Early failures or false starts should not lead us to abandon the encouragement of truly regional initiatives.

Strengthening U.N. Peacekeeping Mechanisms

Since regional action to maintain local stability or control local conflicts will not, in many cases, be adequate, a third form of action is also necessary: U.S.-Soviet cooperation in United Nations efforts to contain and, if possible, settle local conflicts. If this is to be accomplished, the United Nations role in the prevention, isolation, and resolution of local conflicts will have to be revitalized.

The U.N., now in its 25th anniversary year, has done well in fostering economic development, scientific interchange, and in the area of human rights. It must now be strengthened and enabled to do the job its charter envisions in the maintenance of peace. The central questions here are when and how peacekeeping can most effectively be brought into play and how the United States and the Soviet Union can best join with others to make it work.

It is time to break through the 6-year-old impasse on peacekeeping procedures and peacekeeping machinery. An effective and reliable new set of ground rules must be developed, one which allows for a quick response in emergencies. United Nations action must take account of the interests of all, be impartial in intent and application, and call forth the cooperation of the contending parties as well as of those nations on whom the U.N. must depend for manpower and funds. Procedures should also be politically responsive, efficient in administration, and adaptable to rapidly evolving events.

Among the key points on which the United States believes progress should be made are: the uses of "voluntary" peacekeeping, more precision and realism toward the balance of responsibilities between the Security Council and the Secretary General, firmer arrangements for ensuring the availability of personnel and facilities, widening the area of recruitment of peacekeepers, and more reliable and equitable sharing of costs.

I am glad to be able to take note today of the fact that the United States and the Soviet Union have already been discussing some of these matters both in informal meetings and in the negotiations of a United Nations working group in an attempt to work out guidelines for future international action. Although differences of approach exist between us with respect both to interpretation of the charter and to practical mechanics, these need not stand in the way of uncovering sufficient common ground to afford a practical basis for certain U.N. peacekeeping operations. The responsibility for action, in any case, lies with the entire international community, not with the United States and the Soviet Union alone. The middle powers in particular must continue to play a key role in energizing and activating peacekeeping efforts.

When referring to peacekeeping I do not speak of it as applying only to actions taken after conflict is perilously close or has broken out. If the international community is to be insulated against the potential impact of local conflicts, efforts must be started at an early stage; quarrels and disputes cannot be ignored until the peace has been ruptured.

The U.N. Charter does not, after all, contemplate that the U.N. should be the last resort in efforts to preserve the peace. Articles 14, 33, and 36 of the charter lay the basis for timely action by the General Assembly and the Security Council to recommend appropriate procedures or methods of adjustment of international disputes. It is a sad commentary on recent trends that these articles have largely fallen into disuse, and some of the blame must surely be borne by the United States and the Soviet Union.

Article 99 is also relevant to this discussion. Under this provision the Secretary General may bring to the attention of the Security Council any matter which in his opinion may threaten the maintenance of international peace and security. In assigning the responsibility to the Secretary General, the charter thus provides, in effect, for an early warning system. The responsibility for action resides elsewhere, but realistic and imaginative efforts are now called for to bring this potentially significant role of the Secretary General more fully into play.

If the full potential of the Secretary General's role has been neglected, the same can also be said of the Security Council. In September of last year, Foreign Minister Gromyko called attention to the power of the Security Council to consider general as well as specific problems affecting the maintenance of peace.

The Government of Finland, which has been especially interested in such proposals, has suggested making the Security Council more of a center for world consultations by holding regular meetings at the Foreign Minister level. The United States hopes that some agreed way can be found to pursue this possibility. Also worth exploring is a recent Brazilian proposal to set up small informal subcommittees of the Security Council to examine the fundamental issues in specific disputes and to provide good offices for peaceful settlement of disputes.

Revival of the moribund International Court of Justice would also help to strengthen the mechanisms designed to settle disputes peacefully. Secretary Rogers last Saturday proposed several ways to enhance the role of the Court, which does not now have a single pending case before it.

The Secretary suggested that greater use be made of the chambers of the Court; that the chambers meet outside The Hague; that regional chambers be established, particularly in the developing world; and that regional organizations be given access to the Court. Noting that the major problem is the failure of states to submit disputes to the Court, Secretary Rogers underlined the intention of the United States to make more use of the Court in its own international disputes. He encouraged other states to do the same, adding: "Mankind eventually must become wise enough to settle disputes in peace and justice under law."

The approaches I have outlined—the creation of spheres of restraint, the encouragement of regional institutions, and the strengthening of international peacekeeping machinery—will not by themselves, it is true, bring us to this goal. Neither will they guarantee our safe passage to a securely ordered world free of the shadow of thermonuclear war. They are, however, steps on the way, steps we can take now.

If we succeed in these, we shall have the chance to take other, longer steps. If we do not succeed in these, we may never have that chance.

The Causes of Peace and Conditions of War

WILLIAM T. R. FOX

WHAT KEEPS wars going and what finally makes them stop? How can wars be made to end? Astonishingly little has been written in direct answer to these questions.[1] In this introductory article to a symposium on how wars end, the special case of thermonuclear central war is not separately treated. For many and perhaps most purposes, however, the general problem of war termination and the special problem of ending a two-way thermonuclear war may require separate analysis, if only because history has to be invented and alternative scenarios written to breathe life into and to test speculations about a class of events for which there are no historical examples.

The protracted, large-scale, limited wars of the post-colonial second half of the twentieth century are wars which have stayed limited, but they have also stayed wars. They, too, are without exact historical parallel; for the escalation of limited war did not, prior to the Korean and Vietnam wars, raise the spectre of thermonuclear Armageddon. Nevertheless, these wars are in important respects like those of pre-atomic times. Understanding how these earlier wars ended (or dragged on) is essential to a study of how the Korea or Vietnam type of war can be made to end. Inevitably in the 1970's, where thermonuclear war is not specified, statements about war termination will be read in terms of their relevance to understanding and controlling the course of events in protracted conflicts such as those in Korea and Vietnam. Only limited wars are likely to be protracted wars, and only in protracted war is "termination" identified as an urgent problem.

Military and diplomatic historians have described in the most meticulous detail how particular wars have run their course and particular peace settlements have been reached, and President Nixon has been getting all kinds of public and private advice on how to end the particular war from which the United States has been seeking in 1970 to extricate itself. The general analyses of international relations schol-

---

[1] See, however, *Journal of Peace Research* 4 (1969), Special Issue on Peace Research in History, guest editor, Berenice A. Carroll (Oslo, Norway: Universitetsforlaget, 1969); and Herman Kahn, William Pfaff, and Edmund Stillman, "War Termination Issues and Concepts" (Croton-on-Hudson, N.Y.: Hudson Institute, 1968). The Hudson Institute study, done under United States Air Force contract HI-921/3-RR, deals almost exclusively with the termination of nuclear war.

ars are far oftener concerned, however, with explaining how peace is lost than in explaining how it can be won back again.[2] They are also far richer, except in the field of international law, in their prescriptions for preventing and deterring war than in their prescriptions for limiting, de-escalating, and terminating war once started—except insofar as winning incidentally involves terminating. Clausewitz emphasized the political control of violence, but not every strategist who came after him reflected his emphasis. Had writers on strategy done so, war termination in protracted limited war would have been a less neglected topic.

Unlike Clausewitz, the idolaters of war as an ennobling human activity, the advocates of war à l'outrance, and the exemplars of a strategy of "victory"—the code word for the full achievement of announced war aims by fighting, rather than by some combination of fighting and diplomacy, no matter what the cost and however extreme (or moderate) the war aims—have been supremely uninterested in how to wind down and finally stop wars. To all of them, political limitations on the use of violence to contain, de-escalate, and end fighting are likely to appear meddlesome. The disciples of Jomini, Foch, and MacArthur expect peace to be imposed, not negotiated. In the United States, at least, "no political meddling" with the military commander in the completion of his appointed military task is a shibboleth almost as powerful as "civilian control."

In the dawn of the thermonuclear era of world politics, the students of apocalyptic war were not concerned with how apocalyptic wars end and very little concerned with any other kind of war at all. As Thomas C. Schelling has pointed out, the common view was that thermonuclear war could not be "brought" to an end; it was like a string of firecrackers which must go off in turn, once one is ignited.[3] The absolute weapon seemed to make absolute war obsolete; and the interesting problem seemed at first to be only how to make sure that possessors of thermonuclear weapons were all equally deterred. By 1970, fortunately, strategic theorists had spelled out the inadequacies of the "string of firecrackers" approach to thermonuclear war.[4] Slowing down, limiting,

---

[2] The outstanding work on the causes of war and conditions of peace remains Quincy Wright, *A Study of War*, 2 vols. (Chicago: University of Chicago Press, 1942); 2nd ed., 1 vol., with "A Commentary on War Since 1942" added (University of Chicago Press, 1965).

[3] Thomas C. Schelling, *Arms and Influence* (New Haven, Conn.: Yale University Press, 1966), pp. 20-21.

[4] Most notably, Herman Kahn, beginning with *On Thermonuclear War* (Princeton, N.J.: Princeton University Press, 1960). The most explicit rejection of the "string of firecrackers"

and halting the thermonuclear exchange has become a major intellectual concern of writers on strategy. The "hot line," the doctrine of flexible response, and the development of "no cities" strategies are evidence of a will on all sides to assert as effective political control over thermonuclear violence as over lesser forms of violence.

Nuclear weapons have not been fired in anger since Hiroshima and Nagasaki. The same "missing rungs in the ladder of escalation" which have kept a quarter-century of sub-nuclear violence stabilized at sub-nuclear levels seem also to have been missing rungs in the ladder of conflict resolution. As the major actor in two of the longest, bloodiest, and most cruelly frustrating of these limited wars, the United States stands in greatest need of a doctrine for asserting effective political control over large-scale sub-nuclear war and its termination.

Winding Down Limited Wars

Viewing war as a disease to be stamped out, a "public health" way of viewing war, is an essential research orientation but one which seems to divert attention away from viewing large-scale limited war as a kind of infection which the infected patients need to have controlled and cleared up promptly. To change the metaphor, viewing war as an interval between periods of diplomacy, or as an interruption in the normal and continuous procedures of conflict resolution among sovereign states, seems to discourage work in any systematic and theoretical way on how force and diplomacy may be used together to achieve early war termination on a basis that rationally balances costs and benefits at each step as the war is wound down.

Students of international conflict resolution often find it uncongenial to think of war as a "normal" procedure in any systematic classification of conflict resolution procedures.[5] War does indeed reflect a failure of diplomacy and third-party settlement, but in this era of limited war it is not a statistically rare phenomenon. Even in the *Journal of Conflict Resolution*, which has done much to bring the analytical skills of economists and social psychologists to bear on the unsolved problems of political scientists and historians, attention to the specific problems of making wars end is slight.

This is not to say that any less effort ought to be devoted to the Kant-

---

view of nuclear war has been by the advocates of a "flexible response" strategy. See William W. Kaufmann, *The McNamara Strategy* (New York: Harper & Row, 1964).

[5] War is not one of the procedures discussed by Julius Stone in *International Encyclopedia of the Social Sciences*, s.v. "International Conflict Resolution."

ian quest for lasting peace, but only that more effort should be applied to the Clausewitzian quest for political control of violence after, as well as before, a war has started. Academic international relations scholarship has in some previous periods of national crisis followed rather than led events; only *after* the country had been almost split apart by the protraction of the Vietnam war and the apparent failure of coercive diplomacy, was war termination identified as a subject of great theoretical interest and urgent practical concern.[6] Some scholars may have felt that work on how to make large-scale limited war end on an "acceptable" basis (however "acceptable" may be defined) somehow would confer legitimacy on and involve collaboration with the system that produced large-scale limited wars. The goal of "no more Koreas and no more Vietnams" would, if this reasoning were carried on to its logical conclusion, be compromised should research on war termination point the way to mitigating the anguish of a war-weary United States.

The Traditional American Approach

Old-fashioned aspirations for "victory" and new-fashioned visions of curing the world of the war disease are not the only causes for the neglect of war termination studies. A third inhibitor to studying "the causes of peace" is the traditional American approach to war. The country, it is commonly believed, does not deliberately embark on large-scale war; it only enters "foreign" wars when some great aggressor attacks it or seems on the point of so overreaching himself that he must be stopped before he upsets the whole international political order in a major theater of world political conflict. While this major theater before 1945 could only be Europe and this traditional approach is today recognized on all sides as inapplicable to thermonuclear war, and indeed to any kind of war in Europe, it seems to be enjoying a second incarnation in Asia in large-scale limited war.[7]

The United States has not prepared for the present era's large-scale, limited, protracted Asian wars, any more than it prepared to fight in

---

[6] The author specifically includes himself in the academic group whose theoretical interest in how wars end emerged only after the Vietnam war had come to dwarf the Korean war in terms of American experience with protracted large-scale limited war.

[7] With its central role in the military arrangements of NATO and large forces in Europe a quarter-century after the end of World War II, the United States approach to European and North Atlantic security problems is far from what is here described as the traditional American approach. In the Korean and Vietnam wars the United States departed from another long-standing tradition, to avoid involvement in large-scale ground fighting on the Asian mainland.

Europe's large-scale, unlimited, protracted wars earlier in the twentieth century. But then and now, however, the applicable tradition, in Henry Stimson's words, is to apply "one's whole, undiluted strength" to winning back the peace that the enemy has broken. Large-scale mobilization after a war has begun, rather than large-scale preparedness in anticipation of fighting that war, means that war protraction rather than early war termination is the first military objective. Only then can time be gained to avoid early defeat and bring the nation's whole, undiluted strength to bear so as to assure ultimate victory. Each large-scale protracted war is, in this view, seen as a unique event. One does not negotiate with the enemy as an equal, but undertakes a crusade to clear away every obstacle to a fresh start for a new and improved international system. "The strategy of inundation," to use Eisenhower's phrase in his *Crusade for Europe,* and the goal of "unconditional surrender," Franklin Roosevelt's Casablanca Conference formula, may have been appropriate for Ulysses S. Grant in the American Civil War, for Roosevelt in the war against Hitler as the embodiment of absolute evil, and for other true crusades. It offers little guidance in the conduct of large-scale, sub-nuclear, protracted, "postcolonial" war.

The Boer War may in fact provide an historical experience more relevant to the American problems in Korea and Vietnam than the American Civil War or the two World Wars of this century. A major power could find no way to prevent hostilities against a tiny opponent from dragging on.[8] From the Peace of Vereeniging, which in 1902 ended the fighting in South Africa but brought no immediate reconciliation, the defeated General Smuts thought he learned that in a peace of reconciliation the terms ought to be established before the enemy is finally defeated and perforce compelled to accept whatever amalgam of magnanimity, vindictiveness, and wisdom the victor chooses to impose. Sir Keith Hancock's judgment is that Smuts believed that the Boer War lasted a year longer than any British interest required. Fifteen years later, as Britain's most trusted Empire soldier-statesman, he almost refused to sign the Treaty of Versailles because of his strong views as to the futility of a vindictive, dictated peace.[9] A "Wilson peace," as opposed to a "Lloyd George-Clemenceau peace,"

8 See James Eayrs' essay on "Force and Impotence" in his *Fate and Will in Foreign Policy* (Toronto: CBC Publications, 1967), especially pp. 70-75.

9 For a brief account of Smuts' views as to the outcome of the Boer War and World War I, see W. K. Hancock's essay "From War to Peace" in his *Four Studies of War and Peace in This Century* (Cambridge: At the University Press, 1961), pp. 33-58.

would, in his view, have been more likely to emerge from pre-armistice negotiations than from dictation to the prostrate vanquished enemy. It might also have emerged earlier.

The United States has, of course, proclaimed in the Korean and Vietnam wars no goals so sweeping as "unconditional surrender."[10] On the other hand, United States tactics for enticing the enemy to the bargaining table have been notably unsuccessful in both wars. Even after seventeen years there is only an uneasy armistice along the Thirty-eighth Parallel; and unsuccessful as was the effort to bomb Hanoi to the conference table, efforts to lure Hanoi into meaningful negotiations in Paris have hardly been more successful since American bombing of the North was curtailed in 1968.

The Power of the Small Belligerent

Unless one side chooses simply to abandon the field or unconditionally surrenders, it takes two to end a war. It is not, however, in the limiting cases of unilateral withdrawal and unconditional surrender that the problem of war termination poses an intellectual challenge. As Finland's Winter War with the Soviet Union in 1939-40 showed, the side whose war aims in a local war require only that the enemy not finally defeat it, is a formidable opponent even to a major power. It is especially formidable, as the Vietnam war shows, if that major power's government is for domestic or world political reasons anxious to limit, wind down, and stop the fighting. The small-power belligerent, determined to outwait its major-power opponent questing for de-escalation and peace, may make a peace of reconciliation almost as hard to achieve as any other kind of peace. In such asymmetrical, protracted colonial and postcolonial wars, the local belligerent must take care only not to make such "outrageous" demands or adopt such horrifying tactics as to rebuild the major power's home front support for carrying on the war. He can charge a high price just for letting the major power disengage.

The case of "pure withdrawal" may indeed be as hard to envision as Paul Kecskemeti found "pure surrender" to be when he studied war termination in World War II.[11] Just as the obviously vanquished still

[10] General MacArthur's disastrous march to the Yalu in late October, 1950, suggested that he, for one, never quite got the word. See Dean Acheson, *Present at the Creation* (New York: Norton, 1969), chs. 47 and 48.

[11] Paul Kecskemeti, *Strategic Surrender* (Stanford, Calif.: Stanford University Press, 1958). A furor was stirred up by Senator Styles Bridges' ludicrous charge that this book, a research study by the government-supported RAND Corporation, was a prescription for

has some spoiling capability, and therefore bargaining capacity, until the shooting has stopped, the surrender formalities are completed, the weapons of the defeated gathered up, so the local enemy in asymmetrical war can charge a high and negotiable price to a major power bent on withdrawal. Troops have to be protected while other troops are being withdrawn, and at least minimum provision made for the future of the local allies. There may in fact be no such thing as unilateral termination by a simple act of withdrawal. The most rigorous critics of continued American military involvement in Southeast Asia may indeed find as great a challenge in research on how wars end as those who would demand more of Hanoi as the price of termination. In any case, one must negotiate with an enemy who is still fighting.

We have attributed the theoretical and doctrinal vacuum as to how wars end to three quite separate causes: (1) the dominant "public health" view of the war disease by most peace researchers, (2) insufficient attention by military strategists to the problem of the rational political control of violence during war, and (3) a specific American war tradition, such that the makers of American military policy seem almost to have a trained incapacity for avoiding stalemate in protracted, large-scale, limited war. In discussing this last subject we have already embarked on a consideration of what keeps one kind of war from ending. Let us turn to consider the more general problem.

What keeps a war going? If the two sides have incompatible, unrealized, minimum war objectives and additional human and material resources which they are willing to allocate to the war, the answer is obvious. Until there is some change in the goals, expectations, and calculations of at least one of the belligerents, the fighting goes on; and not all changes lead toward peace. A large tactical success may open the way to inflating war objectives, and thus postpone rather than hasten the day when terms of settlement will be offered which the enemy might reasonably be expected to accept.[12] I have argued else-

---

United States surrender. Evidently, for men of the Bridges persuasion, even the contemplation of a war outcome in which there is deviation by the victorious United States from the single acceptable goal of unconditional surrender violates some deeply embedded taboos.

12 Morton H. Halperin, *Limited War in the Nuclear Age* (New York: John Wiley, 1963), p. 32, makes this point and the additional point that there is also "pressure on the losing side to expand the war in order to reverse the battlefield decision. . . ."

The brilliantly successful Inchon landing in September, 1950, which led to the almost total destruction of the 400,000-man North Korean army operating south of the Thirty-eighth Parallel, would be a classic example of a government's decision to inflate its war

where that the United States has in fact after such tactical successes "snatched unlimited stalemate from the jaws of limited victory" in both the Korean and Vietnam wars, i.e., discovered a negative solution to the problem of war termination.[13]

Let us posit a situation which might "rationally" call for one side to make a "turn toward peace." The United States, for example, found itself in a far different situation in Southeast Asia in early 1967 than in the dark days of early 1965. Sukarno was gone, Communist China was caught in the throes of "cultural revolution," and American arms had stabilized the military situation in South Vietnam. Yet it was another whole year before the great American peace overture of March, 1968 —a year in which the loss of American lives reached a level which could not be sustained in limited war, in which urban riots convulsed the nation, and in which inflation raced out of control.

Factors of Policy Paralysis

What are some of the factors that predispose toward policy paralysis, even when "total victory" as a war aim is vigorously eschewed? Mobilization patterns and war strategies take time to achieve results, and the war-makers may judge that the military policies selected have not yet been fully translated into bargaining capacity at a peace table. The statesman-politician may be led by his senior military advisers to conclude the time is not ripe for terminating the war on terms that realize fully on the military investment already made.

Even when there has been ample time to demonstrate the final ineffectiveness or unacceptable cost of a given strategy, a kind of technological *hubris* may particularly bedevil the American policy maker. In large-scale limited war, there are, by definition, as yet unmobilized resources (otherwise the war would be unlimited); but it is the hope

---

objective in the aftermath of a battlefield success if General MacArthur's decision to march to the Yalu had in fact reflected Truman Administration policy. As Dean Acheson's memoirs (*loc. cit.*) show, however, even MacArthur's Washington critics, the men responsible for maintaining political controls over American fighting in Korea, were actively canvassing the prospects for expanding the war aims to include a united, independent, and democratic Korea.

[13] William T. R. Fox, "Next Steps in Vietnam Policy," privately circulated in 1967; published in *Social Progress* (March-April, 1968), pp. 34-42. On the other hand, Secretary of State Dean Rusk seemed to belong to the "no compromise of declared war objectives" school when he testified in 1966 that "I would be misleading you if I told you that I thought that I know where, when, and how this matter will be resolved" (quoted in Eayrs, *op.cit.*, p. 22). From his vantage point it appeared to be the other side's decisions that stalemated the Vietnam conflict.

of better rather than simply more products of American defense industry that may delay reconsideration of an ineffective strategy or scaling down unattainable or unacceptably costly goals. There are always better weapons in the pipeline than on the battlefield, and better ones on the drawing boards than in production. What an irony it will be if the brilliant American advances in helicopter technology demonstrated in ground fighting in Vietnam seem in retrospect to have delayed by two or three years the discovery of policies which would terminate an unwinnable war!

Policy paralysis may result from what Lewin and Miller have described in intrapersonal conflict terms as the "approach-avoidance" conflict.[14] Here the jackass is not immobilized by being pulled in opposite directions by two equally sweet-smelling bales of hay. His problem is more difficult: a skunk sits on his hay and the closer the jackass moves to both, the greater his anguish. It is perhaps not too far-fetched to develop by analogy a model of intranational conflict. The sweet smell of disengagement and peace and the evil smell of unrealized war aims (in which tens of thousands of lives and billions of dollars may have been invested) work at cross purposes. Unless one smell definitely prevails over the other, capacity to make clear policy is paralyzed. In our American governmental system, with its separation of powers, the turn in policy in 1967-68 was delayed because one part of the government smelled the new-mown hay of deescalation and peace while another smelled mainly the malodorous musk of military failure. One need not summon up the image of an anthropomorphic, monster superpower on the edge of a nervous breakdown for the analogy of approach-avoidance to have relevance. In an atmosphere of polarized immoderation—with one group calling for early termination by victory, whatever the escalation necessary, however great the cost, and however evil the by-product in domestic and world political consequences; and a second group calling for early termination, whatever the sacrifice of war aims necessary, however humiliating the frustration and failure, and however disastrous the events which follow abandonment of the struggle—resolute pursuit of some middle way may command wholly insufficient domestic political support; it matters not how rational the in-between, moderate policy may appear in cost-benefit terms. Paradoxically, the more urgent the demands for termination by groups with diametrically opposed programs for termi-

---

14 See Kenneth Boulding, *Conflict and Defense* (New York: Harper Torchbooks, 1962), ch. 5, for a discussion of "approach-avoidance" in terms relevant to interpersonal conflict.

nation, the less may be the chance of a policy commanding sufficient domestic support which would in fact end the war.

Let us now assume, however, that, one way or another, one belligerent does take a great turn toward peace—as, for example, the United States did in President Johnson's speech of March 31, 1968. On that day the President announced the sharp curtailment of bombing of North Vietnam and his own abdication from the seat of power as an earnest of the seriousness of his peace move.[15] In the typical case, one side decides before the other does to search for ways of limiting, winding down, and stopping the war, even at some cost to its original war aims. When we ask, "Why does a war go on when one side wants to quit?" we are really asking why the first side to decide to seek peace, on what it considers to be very moderate terms, may have very great difficulty in bringing the other side to a similar point of view.

We have already described what happened in one difficult case, that of a major power's faraway small-power opponent, which in Raymond Aron's terms was content simply "not to lose" and in no particular hurry to accommodate a peace-seeking major-power opponent. A more general answer to the question of why war goes on when one side wants to make peace is that its "moderate" conditions are not moderate enough to satisfy the minimum war objectives of an opponent with resources to carry on the struggle. "No peace just yet" is a typical response to peace overtures by an opponent who believes it can get better terms later on.

Hitler's Spectacular Failure

The most spectacular failure of a war termination effort in the history of modern war, that of Hitler's Germany in the summer of 1940, is instructive as to another aspect of the problem of why wars go on when one side is ready to stop. With the occupation of Denmark, Norway, Holland, and Belgium, and the collapse of the entire French military effort, Hitler's force stood astride the whole of Western Europe facing a beleaguered Britain. Hitler could not, however, translate an unimaginably vast military success into any kind of political settlement with Britain, because he had a totally insoluble credibility prob-

---

[15] It is intriguing, though fruitless, to speculate how much of the effectiveness of this bold move toward early war termination was lost by the successive assassinations of Dr. Martin Luther King and Robert Kennedy. These two tragedies left the United States portrayed before the world as incapable of managing violence at home and therefore unfit to wield it abroad. It is at least arguable that without the two assassinations, Hanoi would have felt the pressure of world opinion to make a reciprocating gesture of de-escalation.

lem. Too many times, in too few years, too recently, he had made light-ning moves of his military forces—into the Rhineland, into Austria, and into Czechoslovakia—and won reluctant acquiescence to succes-sive *faits accomplis* by asserting in each case that he had no further demands in Europe. Given the circumstances, the British government could see little point, no matter how bleak its military prospects, in accommodating to the self-designated victor's demand for peace. The pitcher had gone to the well one too many times, and it failed Hitler on its most crucial trip.

To say what makes war go on is also to say a good deal about what makes it stop, for one has specified conditions whose absence presuma-bly would make for peace. Not all these conditions whose absence makes for peace are equally manipulable in what we have called the typical war-termination situation, in which one side has embarked on an earnest search for a way out of war and the other has not yet re-ciprocated. The causes of peace are multiple,[16] and some of them are largely beyond the control of the combatants on either side.

There are, for example, inherent limitations on the uses to which a major power can put its enormous apparatus of coercion; and ultimate recognition of these limits may lead to moderate war aims and peace. In a struggle with a lesser power, the major power has the material possibility of "out-escalating" its enemy; but, as we have already noted, there are missing rungs in the ladder of escalation (and particularly in war with an enemy who is perceived as a surrogate for another major power). Wholly apart from this, escalation works both ways. As Michael Howard has reminded us, Clausewitz favored requiring the smallest possible sacrifices of the enemy, so that the enemy would not fight harder by virtue of feeling that with escalated destruction in prospect, there is more to lose.[17] At a different level of constraint, the great power potential of large, advanced, industrial states in these last decades of the twentieth century may be associated with popular atti-tudes which call for sharply increased allocation for social services and higher wages, and for the rigorous assertion of domestic priorities over

---

[16] See Halperin, *op.cit.*, p. 32n., who emphasizes that action to end (or not to end) a local, limited war may be based on a calculation of interests in other theaters of world political competition far removed from the particular local war in question.

[17] Michael Howard, "War as an Instrument of Policy," in H. Butterfield and M. Wight, eds., *Diplomatic Investigations* (Cambridge, Mass.: Harvard University Press, 1966), pp. 196-198. Professor Howard contrasts Clausewitz' teachings about the political control of vio-lence, and the least possible use of it, with General MacArthur's views as set forth in the Senate Hearings in 1951 after MacArthur's recall.

the competing demands of the armed services in support of the nation's foreign policies.[18] Thus, pressures build up continuously against
sustained, large-scale limited war for any goal less urgent than national
survival.

In a thermonuclear war there is the mutual interest of belligerents
in preserving each other's cities, in not destroying the enemy government (which alone has the means to bring unspent armed forces under
control), and in having assured, instantaneous, two-way communication in the war crisis as well as in peace.[19] All are indications of the
poverty of a military capability disproportionate to any known political goal but deterrence, and thus all are constraints making for early
war termination.

"Sledgehammer and Walnut"

In limited war, "the duel between sledgehammer and walnut," to use
James Eayrs' felicitous phrase, more and more favors the walnut.[20]
Local intelligence is likely to be superior to major-power intelligence,
and the major power's limited war is likely to be a minor power's unlimited war, especially in the post-imperial age. Furthermore in protracted limited war there are many bystanders—in the world at large
and among skeptics on the major power's home front—ready to judge
and disposed to judge critically. To make matters worse for the major
power, the bystanders will hold the sledgehammer to a higher standard of accountability than the walnut.

Finally, one pressure for early termination should operate in every
kind of war except, perhaps, one such as that in Nigeria, in which the
prospective losers can look forward only to annihilation or total conquest. This is a belligerent's need to commence bargaining while he
still controls significant military assets. A threat to break off negotiations as a way of insuring better terms for agreeing to stop fighting can
then be made credible.

In the First and Second World Wars, protracted military stalemate
led to ever higher levels of military mobilization. After three years of
fighting an apparently interminable war on the Flanders front in
World War I, a young British officer in one of R. H. Mottram's stories
observed: "This war depends on turning a crank. The side that goes

---

[18] In this, the United Kingdom may be leading the way. See the suggestive review article
by Harold and Margaret Sprout, "The Dilemma of Rising Demands and Insufficient Resources," *World Politics* 22, no. 4 (July, 1968).

[19] Halperin, *op.cit.*, p. 101.   [20] Eayrs, *op.cit.*, p. 72.

on turning it efficiently the longer will win."[21] Until one side stopped cranking, however, the wars went on. In asymmetrical, protracted, sub-nuclear post-colonial war—limited for the major power but unlimited for its opponent—the case appears to be different. Stability in the local military balance—stalemate is another name for stability—may in large-scale limited war be the situation most conducive to war termination, whether by negotiation or by letting the war fade away. Such stability may give the smaller power confidence that it can negotiate with an enemy it still mistrusts without risking the survival of the regime. It may bring down casualties for the major power to levels that ease the domestic pressures for "instant" peace, and so, by demonstrating that it too can wait, weaken the small-power opponent's incentives for delaying tactics.

It thus appears in the case of limited war that for the turn toward negotiated peace to lead to peace, enough force must still be applied to keep the military situation stable. Political control over the use of that force must be carefully exercised, however, to insure that the force not be used in ways which destroy the credibility of the peace overture.

Least-cost, highest-return, earliest-termination strategies call for a continuing calculus. On any reasonable estimate, sacrifices still to be endured must not appear disproportionate to gains still to be realized. This triple objective also calls for an open negotiating stance. Only the least possible may be required of the opponent if one is determined to attract him to the bargaining table.

We have posited "early war termination" as only one of the three goals to be sought by the active peace-seeker. Significant trade-offs therefore may exist between earlier termination, fuller realization of other military policy objectives, and lower levels of sacrifice. Suppose, however, that the enemy's readiness to negotiate peace is closely related to his estimate as to how urgent is the need for an early peace on the part of the side making the peace overture. The lowered level of sacrifice which relieves domestic pressures for peace at any price, or victory at any cost, may then be optimum for making the enemy believe that the peace-seeking power can afford to wait and that there is accordingly no point to making it wait. Both early termination and achievement of other policy objectives associated with the war thus may possibly follow from a low-cost strategy.

The peace-seeker may have a problem of communication. He will

21 *Spanish Farm Trilogy* (New York: Dial Press, 1927), p. 517.

have no trouble making sure that a message is transmitted, even though war involves suspension of diplomatic relations. There are always third parties through which messages can be sent. The problem is partly one of having a peace overture message understood correctly and partly one of framing the message so that it generates a series of back-and-forth messages that cumulatively move toward the desired war termination. As for the misunderstanding, attitudes of mistrust may harden in a struggle which lasts many years. Hanoi, for example, seems to have felt cheated by the aftermath of the 1954 Geneva settlement and may suspect trickery in the Paris negotiations.[22] As for generating effective interchange, the side not yet ready for peace may also be anxious not to legitimate any moderation of its war aims by bargaining in public. "Bench mark" proposals based on some alleged status quo ante or other[23] have the double advantage of apparent precision and apparent legitimacy. They may be marginally easier to accept than otherwise equally rational proposals.

The open negotiating stance and the constant economizing policy calculus thus require a full cataloguing of every element in the prewar status. The bargain finally struck can then, so far as possible, be made up of elements which are both "understood" and "legitimate." Peace, when it finally comes, can then both revive trust and save face.

Protracted Peacemaking

To write of "peace when it finally comes" implies that, at least in a protracted war, when the momentum of violence has been built up and supporting attitudes have hardened, peacemaking will be protracted too. The six-year negotiation to end the Thirty Years' War is a classic illustration. The recipient of a peace overture, we have said, is likely to view it as a trick, to win world opinion or relax the opponent's vigilance and will to fight; or he will see it as evidence of weakness, in which case the probability of getting better terms later may seem very good. Willingness to persist in the face of rebuffs must therefore be an element of an open negotiating stance.

Another element is a great deal of awareness of the "Oriental bazaar" quality of the early stages of public bargaining over the terms of peace. Scorn and accusations of bad faith are par for the course of the peace-seeker. This must indeed be so, for bargaining capability is

---

[22] Robert F. Randle, *Geneva, 1954: The Settlement of the Indo-Chinese War* (Princeton, N.J.: Princeton University Press, 1969), pp. 359-61, 426-27, 551-52, 559, 567-68.

[23] Schelling, *op.cit.*, p. 141.

enhanced if the public response is sufficiently hostile in tone to keep open an option to return to the battlefield for additional evidence as to which side may realistically insist on what. A minor power engaged in an unlimited war against a major power fighting a limited war may be especially reluctant to allow its people's hopes for an early peace to be aroused and to risk a letdown in morale if the peace hopes are dashed.

Let us assume, however, that behind the barrage of unfriendly public discourse and in spite of persistent mistrust, the two sides have moved closer to each other in terms of scaled-down minimum peace terms and realistic shared estimates of the two sides' military prospects in the future fighting, if it occurs. This would mean that they have digested the "election returns" from the fighting fronts and come to understand the extent to which the other side has moderated its war objectives. Early termination has become a shared goal, and some de-escalation has occurred on both sides. The incompatibility of the two sides' minimum war objectives is less pronounced. The door to peace is at least slightly ajar and may at any moment be opened swiftly. The international community, if only because its members fear the spread of the infection of the war disease, may encourage the two sides to get on with the peacemaking.

It still takes two to make peace, and the central question in the typical problem of war termination remains how one side can maximize the chance that its peace overtures will elicit a favorable response from the other side. In the spasm of a thermonuclear exchange there is no reason to doubt that both sides will be eager for prompt termination. Failure in prewar strategic planning to develop absolutely foolproof and destruction-proof command and control systems (to assure continuous political control even over nuclear violence) and to explore a range of alternatives to a fully automatic string-of-firecrackers program of nuclear destruction would, however, cripple political and diplomatic efforts to stop the war. The same may indeed be said of NATO planning for a contingency in Europe in which the possibility of resort to nuclear sanctions is inherent.[24]

24 On the need for war-ending and war-delaying strategies in Europe to assure time "to unravel misunderstanding" and further to narrow the range of circumstances in which the North Atlantic allies might feel compelled to invoke nuclear sanctions, see the forthcoming volume reporting on ACDA-sponsored research on arms control and European security systems by Warner R. Schilling and his colleagues in the Institute of War and Peace Studies at Columbia University, to be published by the University Press at the end of 1970. Existing strategies seem to depend for their deterrent effectiveness on the presumed autom-

For the rest, which means for large-scale limited war, assuming that the peace-seeking side is doing well all the little things that will help bring the other to the peace table (or help let the war fade away), the main choice seems to be that posed by Jan Christian Smuts in the Boer War and again as the battlefields fell silent in 1918. Is the peace of reconciliation best assured by being magnanimous only after one or both sides have fought to utter military exhaustion, or is a healing peace more promptly and effectively achieved by making it before either side's efforts are fully spent? Lord Milner in 1902 and Lloyd George in 1918 do not seem to have been much interested in a peace of reconciliation, either before or after victory. Woodrow Wilson, like General Smuts, was very much interested in such a peace. His Fourteen Points suggest that, like Smuts, Wilson believed that magnanimity and moderation before the fighting had completely ended made for both an earlier and a better ending of war. There is nothing in 1970 to suggest that Smuts and Wilson were wrong then, or would be wrong today, if they held similar views about the large-scale limited wars of the present post-colonial era.

---

aticity of a nuclear response to a non-nuclear attack which cannot be effectively countered by non-nuclear military means. The problem does not arise in the case of the large-scale unambiguous nuclear first strike, unlikely in any event but extremely unlikely in the European theater alone; here one must presume an automatic Western nuclear response. It arises in the ambiguous situations in which inadequate conventional military power denies time for thorough explorations of misunderstanding and miscalculation and hence of alternatives to the use of tactical nuclear weapons.

VII. DOCUMENTARY APPENDICES

President Nixon's Address to the Nation on "Military Action in Cambodia," April 30, 1970

Following is a transcript of President Nixon's televised address last night as recorded by The New York Times:

Good evening my fellow Americans.

Ten days ago in my report to the nation on Vietnam I announced a decision to withdraw an additional 150,000 Americans from Vietnam over the next year. I said then that I was making that decision despite our concern over increased enemy activity in Laos, in Cambodia and in South Vietnam.

And at that time I warned that if I concluded that increased enemy activity in any of these areas endangered the lives of Americans remaining in Vietnam, I would not hesitate to take strong and effective measures to deal with that situation.

Despite that warning, North Vietnam has increased its military aggression in all these areas, and particularly in Cambodia.

After full consultation with the National Security Council, Ambassador Bunker, General Abrams and my other advisers, I have concluded that the actions of the enemy in the last 10 days clearly endanger the lives of Americans who are in Vietnam now and would constitute an unacceptable risk to those who will be there after withdrawal of another 150,000.

To protect our men who are in Vietnam, and to guarantee the continued success of our withdrawal and Vietnamization program, I have concluded that the time has come for action.

Tonight, I shall describe the actions of the enemy, the actions I have ordered to deal with that situation, and the reasons for my decision.

Neutral Since 1945

Cambodia—a small country of seven million people—has been a neutral nation since the Geneva Agreement of 1954, an agreement, incidentally, which was signed by the government of North Vietnam.

American policy since then has been to scrupulously respect the neutrality of the Cambodian people. We have maintained a skeleton diplomatic session of fewer than 15 in Cambodia's capital, and that only since last August.

For the previous four years, from 1965 to 1969 we did not have any diplomatic mission whatever in Cambodia, and for the past five years we have provided no military assistance whatever and no economic assistance to Cambodia.

North Vietnam, however, has not respected that neutrality. For the past five years, as indicated on this map, as you see here, North Vietnam has occupied military sanctuaries all along the Cambodian frontier with South Vietnam. Some of these extend up to 20 miles into Cambodia.

The sanctuaries are in red, and as you note they are on both sides of the border.

They are used for hit-and-run attacks on American and South Vietnamese forces in South Vietnam. These Communist-occupied territories contain major base camps, training sites, logistics facilities, weapons and ammunition factories, airstrips and prisoner of war compounds.

And for five years neither the United States nor South Vietnam has moved against these enemy sanctuaries because we did not wish to violate the territory of a neutral nation.

Even after the Vietnamese Communists began to expand these sanctuaries four weeks ago, we counseled patience to our South Vietnamese allies and imposed restraints on our own commanders.

In contrast to our policy the enemy in the past two weeks has stepped up his guerrilla actions and he is concentrating his main force in these sanctuaries that you see in this map, where they are building up the large massive attacks on our forces and those of South Vietnam.

North Vietnam in the last two weeks has stripped away all pretence of respecting the sovereignty or the neutrality of Cambodia. Thousands of their soldiers are invading the country from the sanctuaries. They are encircling the capital of Pnompenh. Coming from these sanctuaries as you see here, they had moved into Cambodia and are encircling the capital.

Cambodian Call for Help

Cambodia, as a result of this, has sent out a call to the United States, to a number of other nations, for assistance. Because if this enemy effort succeeds, Cambodia would become a vast enemy staging area and a springboard for attacks on South Vietnam along 600 miles of frontier: a refuge where enemy troops could return from combat without fear of retaliation.

North Vietnamese men and supplies could then be poured into that country, jeopardizing not only the lives of our men but the people of South Vietnam as well.

Now confronted with this situation we had three options:

First, we can do nothing. Now, the ultimate result of that course of action is clear. Unless we indulge in wishful thinking, the lives of Americans remaining in Vietnam after our next withdrawal of 150,000 would be gravely threatened.

Let us go to the map again.

Here is South Vietnam. Here is North Vietnam. North Vietnam already occupies this part of Laos. If North Vietnam also occupied this whole band in Cambodia or the entire country, it would mean that South Vietnam was completely outflanked and the forces of Americans in this area as well as the South Vietnamese would be in an untenable military position.

Aid Won't Be Effective

Our second choice is to provide massive military assistance to Cambodia itself and, unfortunately, while we deeply sympathize with the plight of seven million Cambodians whose country has been invaded, massive amounts of military assistance could not be rapidly and effectively utilized by this small Cambodian Army against the immediate trap.

With other nations we shall do our best to provide the small arms and other equipment which the Cambodian Army of 40,000 needs and can use for its defense.

But the aid we will provide will be limited for the purpose of enabling Cambodia to defend its neutrality and not for the purpose of making it an active belligerent on one side or the other.

Our third choice is to go to the heart of the trouble.

And that means cleaning out major North Vietnamese- and Vietcong-occupied territories, these sanctuaries which serve as bases for attacks on both Cambodia and American and South Vietnamese forces in South Vietnam.

Some of these, incidentally are as close to Saigon as Baltimore is to Washington. This one, for example, is called the Parrot's Beak—it's only 33 miles from Saigon.

Now faced with these three options, this is the decision I have made. In cooperation with the armed forces of South Vietnam, attacks are being launched this week to clean out major enemy sanctuaries on the Cambodian-Vietnam border. A major responsibility for the ground operation is being assumed by South Vietnamese forces.

For example, the attacks in several areas, including the Parrot's Beak, that I referred to a moment ago, are exclusively South Vietnamese ground operations, under South Vietnamese command, with the United States providing air and logistical support.

There is one area, however, immediately above the parrot's beak where I have concluded that a combined American and South Vietnamese operation is necessary.

'Action Is Essential'

Tonight, American and South Vietnamese units will attack the headquarters for the entire Communist military operation in South Vietnam. This key control center has been occupied by the North Vietnamese and Vietcong for five years in blatant violation of Cambodia's neutrality.

This is not an invasion of Cambodia. The areas in which these attacks will be launched are completely occupied and controlled by North Vietnamese forces.

Our purpose is not to occupy the areas. Once enemy forces are driven out of these sanctuaries and once their military supplies are destroyed, we will withdraw.

These actions are in no way directed to security interests of any nation. Any government that chooses to use these actions as a pretext for harming relations with the United States will be doing so on its own responsibility and on its own initiative and we will draw the appropriate conclusions.

And now, let me give you the reasons for my decision.

A majority of the American people, a majority of you listening to me are for the withdrawal of our forces from Vietnam. The action I have taken tonight is indispensable for the continuing success of that withdrawal program.

A majority of the American people want to end this war rather than to have it drag on interminably.

The action I have taken tonight will serve that purpose.

A majority of the American people want to keep the casualties of our brave men in Vietnam at an absolute minimum.

The action I take tonight is essential if we are to accomplish that goal.

We take this action not for the purpose of expanding the war into Cambodia but for the purpose of ending the war in Vietnam, and winning the just peace we all desire.

We have made and will continue to make every possible effort to end this war through negotiation at the conference table rather than through more fighting in the battlefield.

Let's look again at the record.

We stopped the bombing of North Vietnam. We have cut air operations by over 20 per cent. We've announced the withdrawal of over 250,000 of our men. We've offered to withdraw all of our men if they will withdraw theirs. We've offered to negotiate all issues with only one condition: and that is that the future of South Vietnam be determined, not by North Vietnam, and not by the United States, but by the people of South Vietnam themselves.

Attacks Cited

The answer of the enemy has been intransigeance at the conference table, belligerence at Hanoi, massive military aggression in Laos and Cambodia and stepped-up attacks in South Vietnam designed to increase American casualties.

This attitude has become intolerable.

We will not react to this threat to American lives merely by plaintive diplomatic protests.

If we did, credibility of the United States would be destroyed in every area of the world where only the power of the United States deters aggression.

Tonight, I again warn the North Vietnamese that if they continue to escalate the fighting when the United States is withdrawing its forces, I shall meet my responsibility as commander and chief of our armed forces to take the action I consider necessary to defend the security of our American men.

The action I have announced tonight puts the leaders of North Vietnam on notice that we will be patient in working for peace. We will be conciliatory at the conference table, but we will not be humiliated. We will not be defeated.

We will not allow American men by the thousands to be killed by an enemy from privileged sanctuary.

The time came long ago to end this war through peaceful negotiations. We stand ready for those negotiations. We've made major efforts many of which must remain secret.

Peace Offers Cited

I say tonight all the offers and approaches made previously remain on the conference table whenever Hanoi is ready to negotiate seriously.

But if the enemy response to our most conciliatory offers for peaceful negotiation continues to be to increase its attacks and humiliate and defeat us, we shall react accordingly.

My fellow Americans, we live in an age of anarchy, both abroad and at home. We see mindless attacks on all the great institutions which have been created by free civilizations in the last 500 years. Even here in the United States, great universities are being systematically destroyed.

Small nations all over the world find themselves under attack from within and from without. If when the chips are down the world's most powerful nation—the United States of America—acts like a pitiful, helpless giant, the forces of totalitarianism and anarchy will threaten free nations and free institutions throughout the world.

It is not our power but our will and character that is being tested tonight.

Challenge to U.S.

The question all Americans must ask and answer tonight is this:

Does the richest and strongest nation in the history of the world have the character to meet a direct challenge by a group which rejects every effort to win a just peace, ignores our warning, tramples on solemn agreements, violates the neutrality of an unarmed people and uses our prisoners as hostages?

If we fail to meet this challenge all other nations will be on notice that despite its overwhelming power the United States when a real crisis comes will be found wanting.

During my campaign for the Presidency, I pledged to bring Americans home from Vietnam. They are coming home. I promised to end this war. I shall keep that promise. I promised to win a just peace. I shall keep that promise.

We shall avoid a wider war, but we are also determined to put an end to this war.

In this room, Woodrow Wilson made the great decision which led to victory in World War I.

Franklin Roosevelt made the decisions which led to our victory in World War II.

Dwight D. Eisenhower made decisions which ended the war in Korea and avoided war in the Middle East.

Mentions Kennedy Decision

John F. Kennedy in his finest hour made the great decision which removed Soviet nuclear missiles from Cuba and the western hemisphere.

I have noted that there's been a great deal of discussion with regard to this decision I have made. And I should point out that I do not contend that it is in the same magnitude as these decisions that I have just mentioned.

But between those decisions and this decision, there is a difference that is very fundamental. In those decisions the American people were not assailed by counsels of doubt and defeat from some of the most widely known opinion leaders of the nation.

I have noted, for example, that a Republican Senator has said that this action I have taken means that my party has lost all chance of winning the November elections, and others are saying today that this move against enemy sanctuaries will make me a one-term President.

Easy Path 'Tempting'

No one is more aware than I am of the political consequences of the action I've taken. It is tempting to take the easy political path, to blame this war on previous Administrations, and to bring all of our men home immediately—regardless of the consequences, even though that would mean defeat for the United States; to desert 18 million South Vietnamese people who have put their trust in us; to expose them to the same slaughter and savagery which the leaders of North Vietnam inflicted on hundreds of thousands of North Vietnamese who chose freedom when the Communists took over North Vietnam in 1954.

To get peace at any price now, even though I know that a peace of humiliation for the United States would lead to a bigger war or surrender later.

I have rejected all political considerations in making this decision. Whether my party gains in November is nothing compared to the lives of 400,000 brave Americans fighting for our country and for the cause of peace and freedom in Vietnam.

'One-Term President'

Whether I may be a one-term President is insignificant compared to whether by our failure to act in this crisis the United States proves itself to be unworthy to lead the forces of freedom in this critical period in world history.

I would rather be a one-term president and do what I believe was right than to be a two-term President at the cost of seeing America become a second-rate power and to see this nation accept the first defeat in its proud 190-year history.

I realize in this war there are honest, deep differences in this country about whether we should have become involved, that there are differences to how the war should have been conducted.

But the decision I announce tonight transcends those differences, for the lives of American men are involved. The opportunity for a 150,000 Americans to come home in the next 12 months is involved. The future of 18-million people in South Vietnam and 7-million people in Cambodia is involved, the possibility of winning a just peace in Vietnam and in the Pacific is at stake.

It is customary to conclude a speech from the White House by asking support for the President of the United States.

Tonight, I depart from that precedent. What I ask is far more important. I ask for your support for our brave men fighting tonight halfway around the world, not for territory, not for glory but so that their younger brothers and their sons and your sons can have a chance to grow up in a world of peace and freedom, and justice.

Thank you, and good night.

Ambassador Charles Yost's
Letter of May 5, 1970 to the
United Nations Security Council

I HAVE the honour to refer to the letters of 7 and 27 February 1965 from the Permanent Representative of the United States of America to the President of the Security Council concerning the aggression against the Republic of Viet-Nam and to inform you of the following acts of armed aggression by forces of North Viet-Nam based in Cambodia which have required appropriate measures of collective self-defence by the armed forces of the Republic of Viet-Nam and the United States of America.

For five years North Viet-Nam has maintained base areas in Cambodia against the expressed wishes of the Cambodian Government. These bases have been used in violation of Cambodian neutrality as supply points and base areas for military operations against the Republic of Viet-Nam. In recent weeks North Viet-Namese forces have rapidly expanded the perimeters of these base areas and expelled the Cambodian Government presence from the areas. The North Viet-Namese forces have moved quickly to link the bases along the border with South Viet-Nam into one continuous chain as well as to push the bases deeper into Cambodia. Concurrently, North Viet-Nam has stepped up guerrilla actions into South Viet-Nam and is concentrating its main forces in these base areas in preparation for further massive attacks into South Viet-Nam.

These military actions against the Republic of Viet-Nam and its armed forces and the armed forces of the United States require appropriate defensive measures. In his address to the American people on 30 April President Nixon stated:

"... if this enemy effort succeeds, Cambodia would become a vast enemy staging area and a springboard for attacks on South Viet-Nam along 600 miles of frontier: a refuge where enemy troops could return from combat without fear of retaliation.

"North Viet-Namese men and supplies could then be poured into that country, jeopardizing not only the lives of our men but the people of South Viet-Nam as well."

The measures of collective self-defence being taken by United States and South Viet-Namese forces are restricted in extent, purpose and time. They are confined to the border areas over which the Cambodian Government has ceased to exercise any effective control and which has been completely occupied by North Viet-Namese and Viet Cong forces. Their purpose is to destroy the stocks and communications equipment that are being used in aggression against the Republic of Viet-Nam. When that purpose is accomplished, our forces and those of the Republic of Viet-Nam will promptly withdraw. These measures are limited and proportionate to the aggressive military operations of the North Viet-Namese forces and the threat they pose.

The United States wishes to reiterate its continued respect for the sovereignty, independence, neutrality and territorial integrity of Cambodia. Our purpose in taking these defensive measures was stated by President Nixon, in his address of 30 April, as follows:

> "We take this action not for the purpose of expanding the war in Cambodia but for the purpose of ending the war in Viet-Nam and winning the just peace we all desire.
>
> "We have made and will continue to make every possible effort to end this war through negotiation at the conference table rather than through more fighting in the battlefield."

I would request that my letter be circulated to the members of the Security Council.

Accept, etc.

(Signed) Charles W. YOST

A Report on the Conclusion of
the Cambodian Operation
Statement of President Nixon,
June 30, 1970[1]

Together with the South Vietnamese, the armed forces of the United States have just completed successfully the destruction of enemy base areas along the Cambodian-South Viet-Nam frontier. All American troops have withdrawn from Cambodia on the schedule announced at the start of the operation.

The allied sweeps into the North Vietnamese and Viet Cong base areas along the Cambodian-South Vietnamese border:

—will save American and allied lives in the future;

—will assure that the withdrawal of American troops from South Viet-Nam can proceed on schedule;

—will enable our program of Vietnamization to continue on its current timetable;

—should enhance the prospects for a just peace.

At this time, it is important to review the background for the decision, the results of the operation, their larger meaning in terms of the conflict in Indochina—and to look down the road to the future.

It is vital to understand at the outset that Hanoi left the United States no reasonable option but to move militarily against the Cambodian base areas. The purpose and significance of our operations against the Cambodian sanctuaries can only be understood against the backdrop of what we are seeking to accomplish in Viet-Nam— and the threat that the Communist bases in Cambodia posed to our objectives. Nor can that military action of the last 2 months be divorced from its cause—the threat posed by the constant expansion of North Vietnamese aggression throughout Indochina.

A Record of Restraint

America's purpose in Viet-Nam and Indochina remains what it has been—a peace in which the peoples of the region can devote themselves to development of their own societies, a peace in which all the peoples of Southeast Asia can determine their own political future without outside interference.

<hr>

[1] Issued at San Clemente, Calif., on June 30 (White House press release).

When this administration took office, the authorized strength of American troops in South Viet-Nam was 549,500—the high-water mark of American military presence in Southeast Asia. The United States had been negotiating at Paris for 10 months, but nothing had been agreed upon other than the shape of the bargaining table. No comprehensive allied peace proposal existed. There was no approved plan to reduce America's involvement in the war—in the absence of a negotiated settlement.

Since January of 1969, we have taken steps on all fronts to move toward peace. Along with the Government of South Viet-Nam, we have put forward a number of concrete and reasonable proposals to promote genuine negotiations. These proposals were first outlined by me 13 months ago, on May 14, 1969, and by President Thieu on July 11, 1969.[2] Through both public and private channels, our proposals have been repeated and amplified many times since.

These proposals are designed to secure the removal of all foreign military forces from South Viet-Nam and to establish conditions in which all political forces can compete freely and fairly in the future of the country. Our principal goal has been to enable the people of South Viet-Nam to determine their future free of outside interference.

To indicate our good faith, to improve the climate for negotiations, we changed the orders to our commanders in South Viet-Nam. This has helped to reduce casualties. We have cut tactical air operations in South Viet-Nam by more than 20 percent. We initiated a troop withdrawal program which, during the course of next spring, will bring American troop strength 265,000 men below the level authorized when this administration took office.

These are not the actions of a government pursuing a military solution. They are the decisions of a government seeking a just peace at the conference table.

But Hanoi has ignored our unilateral gestures and rejected every offer of serious negotiations. Instead it has insisted that—as a precondition to talks—we pledge unconditionally to withdraw all American forces from South Viet-Nam and to overthrow the elected government.

These proposals are not a basis for negotiation; they are a demand for surrender. For the United States to accept these conditions would make the negotiations meaningless. Acceptance of such conditions would assure in advance Communist domination of South Viet-Nam.

With Hanoi's intransigence on the negotiating front, this administration was faced with essentially three options.

2 For background, see BULLETIN of June 2, 1969, p. 457, and July 28, 1969, p. 61.

We could have continued the maximum existing level of American involvement in Viet-Nam. But this was incompatible with the Nixon doctrine of increasing responsibilities for the Asian countries; and it was unacceptable to the American people.

We could have begun the immediate withdrawal of all our forces. We rejected this course of capitulation which would have only won temporary respite at the price of graver crises later. We also rejected that course as both incompatible with America's commitments and tradition, and disastrous in terms of its long-range consequences for peace in the Pacific and peace in the world.

We selected instead a third option—that of gradually shifting the total combat burden to the South Vietnamese.

Since the beginning of this administration 17 months ago, it has been our policy to train and equip the South Vietnamese to take over the burden of their own defense from American troops. Even in the absence of progress at the peace table in Paris, and despite continued enemy pressures in South Viet-Nam, this policy of "Vietnamization" has permitted us to carry out repeated withdrawals of American troops.

As our policy has been tested, more and more Americans have been brought home. By June of 1969, we could announce the pullout of 25,000 American troops. They came home. In September of 1969, we announced the withdrawal of an additional 35,000 American troops. They came home.

In December of 1969, we announced the withdrawal of 50,000 more American troops. They were home by spring of this year. On April 20, I announced the forthcoming withdrawal of an additional 150,000 Americans to be completed during next spring—50,000 of them will be home or on their way home by the 15th of October.

A Policy in Transition

This transfer of primary responsibility for self-defense from American forces to Asian forces reflects our approach to foreign policy. Increasingly, the United States will look to the countries of the region to assume the primary responsibility for their own security—while America moves gradually from a leading to a supporting role.

To be successful this policy requires the striking of a careful balance—whether in South Viet-Nam or elsewhere in Asia. While the growing strength of our allies, and the growing measure of their regional cooperation, allows for a reduction in American presence—they could not survive a sudden and precipitous American withdrawal from our responsibilities. This would lead to a collapse of local strength in the transition period between the old era of principal U.S. involvement to the new era of partnership and emphasis on local and regional cooperation.

Doing too much for an allied people can delay their political maturity, promote a sense of dependency, and diminish that nation's incentive to stand on its own feet. But doing too little for an ally can induce a sense of despair, endanger their right of self-determination, and invite their defeat when confronted by an aggressor.

As we have proceeded with Vietnamization it has been with these principles in mind.

Looking at American policy in Viet-Nam these 17 months, this administration—in the generosity of its negotiating offers, in the limitations on its military actions, and in the consistency of its troop withdrawals—has written a record of restraint. The response from the enemy over those same 17 months has been intransigence in Paris, belligerence from Hanoi, and escalation of the war throughout Indochina.

Enemy attacks in Viet-Nam increased during April.

This past winter Hanoi launched a major offensive against the legitimate government of Laos which they themselves had helped to establish under the 1962 Geneva accords. For years, in violation of those accords, North Vietnamese troops have occupied Laotian territory and used its eastern regions as a highway for the export of aggression into South Viet-Nam.

In March and April of this year, Communist troops used their long-held bases in Cambodia to move against the Government of Cambodia in a way which increased the long-term threat to allied forces in South Viet-Nam as well as to the future of our Vietnamization and withdrawal programs. These new violations, too, took place against a backdrop of years of Communist disregard of the neutrality and territorial integrity of Cambodia—guaranteed in the 1954 Geneva agreements to which Hanoi was a signatory.

Background of the April 30 Decision

In assessing the April 30 decision to move against the North Vietnamese and Viet Cong sanctuaries in Cambodia, four basic facts must be remembered.

It was North Viet-Nam—not we—which brought the Viet-Nam war into Cambodia.

For 5 years, North Viet-Nam has used Cambodian territory as a sanctuary from which to attack allied forced in South Viet-Nam. For 5 years, American and allied forces—to preserve the concept of Cambodian neutrality and to confine the conflict in Southeast Asia—refrained from moving against those sanctuaries.

It was the presence of North Vietnamese troops on Cambodian soil that contributed to the downfall of Prince Sihanouk. It was the indignation of the Cambodian people against the presence of Vietnamese Communists in their country that led to riots in Phnom Penh which contributed to Prince Sihanouk's ouster—an ouster that surprised no nation more than the United States. At the end of Sihanouk's rule, the United States was making efforts to improve relations with his government and the Prince was taking steps against the Communist invaders on his national soil.

It was the government appointed by Prince Sihanouk and ratified by the Cambodian National Assembly—not a group of usurpers—which overthrew him with the approval of the National Assembly. The United States had neither connection with, nor knowledge of, these events.

It was the major expansion of enemy activity in Cambodia that ultimately caused allied troops to end 5 years of restraint and attack the Communist base areas.

The historical record is plain.

Viet Cong and North Vietnamese troops have operated in eastern Cambodia for years. The primary objective of these Communist forces has been the support of Hanoi's aggression against South Viet-Nam. Just as it has violated the 1962 Geneva accords on Laos, North Viet-Nam has consistently ignored its pledge, in signing the 1954 Geneva accords, to respect Cambodian neutrality and territorial integrity.

In a May 1967 Phnom Penh radio broadcast, Prince Sihanouk's following remarks were reported to the Cambodian people:

> I must tell you that the Vietnamese communists and the Viet Cong negotiated with us three or four times but that absolutely nothing comes out of the negotiations . . . After I expelled the French and after the French troops left Cambodia, Viet Minh remained in our country in order to conquer it. How can we have confidence in the Viet Minh? . . . If we side with the Viet Minh we will lose our independence.

Late in 1969, Prince Sihanouk ordered Cambodia's underequipped and weak armed forces to exercise some measure of control over North Vietnamese and Viet Cong Communist forces occupying Cambodian territory.

At the same time, the Communist forces were actively preparing in their base areas for new combat in South Viet-Nam. These areas—on the Cambodian side of the Viet-Nam-Cambodian border—have for years served as supply depots and base camps for enemy troops infiltrated through Laos into South Viet-Nam. They have also served as sanctuaries for North Vietnamese and Viet Cong headquarters elements and for combat troops to rest, refit, and resupply on their return from South Viet-Nam.

Our screening of more than 6 tons of documents captured in the Cambodian operations has provided conclusive proof of Communist reliance on Cambodia as a logistic and infiltration corridor and as a secure area from which Communist designs on Viet-Nam as well as in Cambodia itself could be carried out.

On January 6, 1970, Prince Sihanouk departed on vacation in France. His Prime Minister, Lon Nol, and Deputy Prime Minister, Sirik Matak, were left in charge. In early March, with Sihanouk still in power, there were public demonstrations, first in the eastern provinces of Cambodia and later in Phnom Penh, against flagrant North Vietnamese violation of Cambodia's territorial integrity.

On March 13, Prince Sihanouk left Paris for Moscow and Peking, avowedly to seek Soviet and Chinese assistance in persuading the Vietnamese Communists to reduce the presence of North Vietnamese and Viet Cong forces in Cambodia.

Then, on March 18, the Cambodian National Assembly by unanimous vote declared that Prince Sihanouk was no longer Chief of State. Cheng Heng was retained as Acting Chief of State. Lon Nol and Sirik Matak kept their positions. Reasons for Sihanouk's ouster included growing objections to his mishandling of the economy and to his bypassing of the Cabinet and National Assembly; but resentment over North Viet-Nam's flagrant misuse of Cambodian territory certainly contributed. Sihanouk arrived in Peking the same day and met with the Peking leadership as well as with the North Vietnamese Prime Minister, who had hastened to Peking to greet him. Thereafter Sihanouk has increasingly identified himself with the Communist cause in Indochina.

This Government had no advance warning of the ouster of Sihanouk, with whom we had been attempting to improve relations. Our initial response was to seek to preserve the status quo with regard to Cambodia and to try to prevent an expansion of Communist influence. The immunity of the Cambodian sanctuaries had been a serious military handicap for us for many years. But we had refrained from moving against them in order to contain the conflict. We recognized both the problems facing Sihanouk and the fact that he had exercised some measure of control over Communist activities, through regulation of the flow of rice and military supplies into the sanctuaries from coastal ports. We considered that a neutral Cambodia outweighed the military benefits of a move against the base areas.

This is why diplomatically our first reaction to Sihanouk's overthrow was to encourage some form of accommodation in Cambodia. We spoke in this sense to interested governments. And we made clear through many channels that we had no intention of exploiting the Cambodian upheaval for our own ends.

These attempts ran afoul of Hanoi's designs. North Viet-Nam and the Viet Cong withdrew their representation from Phnom Penh. North Vietnamese and Viet Cong forces began to expand their base areas along the border.

By April 3, they were beginning to launch attacks against Cambodian forces in Svay Rieng Province. Later these attacks were extended to other outposts in eastern Cambodia, forcing Cambodian troops to evacuate border positions in the Parrot's Beak area by April 10. Communist attacks were also directed against Mekong River traffic.

By April 16, the North Vietnamese and Viet Cong troops began to launch isolated attacks deep into Cambodia including an attack on the capital of Takeo Province south of Phnom Penh.

Despite escalating Communist activity in Cambodia, we continued to exercise restraint. Though the implications of the Communist actions for our efforts in Viet-Nam were becoming increasingly ominous, Communist intentions in Cambodia were still not absolutely clear. The military moves by the North Vietnamese and Viet Cong in Cambodia could still be interpreted as temporary actions to secure their base camps in light of the uncertainties following Sihanouk's removal.

When I made my April 20 speech announcing the withdrawal of 150,000 troops over the next year, I knew that we might be at a crossroads in Cambodia.[3] I nevertheless made the announcement because it would leave no doubt about our intention to deescalate the conflict.

I also used the occasion to restate very forthcoming political principles for a negotiated peace. At the same time I described the pattern of North Vietnamese aggression in Indochina and acknowledged that my withdrawal decision involved some risks when viewed against this

[3] For text, see BULLETIN of May 11, 1970, p. 601.

enemy escalation. I therefore reiterated my determination to take strong and effective measures if increased enemy action in Laos, Cambodia, or South Viet-Nam jeopardized the security of our remaining forces in Viet-Nam.

Within days of my April 20 speech, Communist intentions became painfully and unamibiguously clear. In the face of our restraint and our warnings, the North Vietnamese continued to expand their territorial control, threatening to link up their base areas. From a series of isolated enclaves, the base areas were rapidly becoming a solid band of self-sustaining territory stretching from Laos to the sea from which any pretense of Cambodian sovereignty was rapidly being excluded.

—On April 20, North Vietnamese forces temporarily captured Saang, only 18 miles south of Phnom Penh.

—On April 22, Communist forces assaulted the town of Snuol east of Phnom Penh.

—On April 23, they attacked the town of Mimot and an important bridge linking the town of Snuol and the capital of Kratie Province on Route 13.

—On April 24, they moved on the resort city of Kep.

—On April 26, they attacked some ships on the Mekong and occupied the town of Angtassom, a few miles west of Takeo.

—They then attacked the city of Chhlong, on the Mekong River north of Phnom Penh, and the port city of Kampot.

—During this same period, they cut almost every major road leading south and east out of Phnom Penh.

The prospect suddenly loomed of Cambodia's becoming virtually one large base area for attack anywhere into South Viet-Nam along the 600 miles of the Cambodian frontier. The enemy in Cambodia would have enjoyed complete freedom of action to move forces and supplies rapidly across the entire length of South Viet-Nam's flank to attack our forces in South Viet-Nam with impunity from well-stocked sanctuaries along the border.

We thus faced a rapidly changing military situation from that which existed on April 20.

The possibility of a grave new threat to our troops in South Viet-Nam was rapidly becoming an actuality.

This pattern of Communist action prior to our decision of April 30 makes it clear the enemy was intent both on expanding and strengthening its military position along the Cambodian border and overthrowing the Cambodian Government. The plans were laid, the orders issued, and already being implemented by Communist forces.

Not only the clear evidence of Communist actions—but supporting data screened from more than 6 tons of subsequently captured Communist documents—leaves no doubt that the Communists' move against the Cambodian Government preceded the U.S. action against the base areas.

Three Options

On April 30, before announcing our response, I outlined the three basic choices we had in the face of the expanding Communist threat.[4]

First, we could do nothing. This would have eroded an important restraint on the loss of American lives. It would have run the risk of Cambodia's becoming one vast enemy staging area, a springboard for attacks on South Viet-Nam without fear of retaliation. The dangers of having done nothing would not have fully materialized for several months, and this Government might have been commended for exercising restraint. But, as withdrawals proceeded, our paralysis would have seriously jeopardized our forces in Viet-Nam and would have led to longer lists of American casualties. The United States could not accept the consequences of inaction in the face of this enemy escalation. The American men remaining in South Viet-Nam after our withdrawal of 150,000 would have been in severe jeopardy.

Our second choice was to provide massive assistance to Cambodia. This was an unrealistic alternative. The small Cambodian army of 30,000 could not effectively utilize any massive transfusion of military assistance against the immediate enemy threat. We also did not wish to get drawn into the permanent direct defense of Cambodia. This would have been inconsistent with the basic premises of our foreign policy.

After intensive consultations with my top advisers, I chose the third course. With the South Vietnamese we launched joint attacks against the base areas so long occupied by Communist forces.

Our military objectives were to capture or destroy the arms, ammunition, and supplies that had been built up in those sanctuaries over a period of years and to disrupt the enemy's communication network. At the least this would frustrate the impact of any Communist success

[4] For President Nixon's address to the Nation on Apr. 30, see BULLETIN of May 18, 1970, p. 617.

in linking up their base areas if it did not prevent this development altogether.

I concluded that, regardless of the success of Communist assaults on the Cambodian Government, the destruction of the enemy's sanctuaries would:

—remove a grave potential threat to our remaining men in South Viet-Nam, and so reduce future American casualties.

—give added assurance of the continuance of our troop withdrawal program.

—ensure the timetable for our Vietnamization program.

—increase the chances of shortening the war in South Viet-Nam.

—enhance the prospects of a negotiated peace.

—emphasize to the enemy whether in Southeast Asia or elsewhere that the word of the United States—whether given in a promise or a warning—was still good.

The Military Operations

Ten major operations were launched against a dozen of the most significant base areas with 32,000 American troops and 48,000 South Viet-Namese participating at various times. As of today, all Americans, including logistics personnel and advisers, have withdrawn, as have a majority of the South Vietnamese forces.

Our military response to the enemy's escalation was measured in every respect. It was a limited operation for a limited period of time with limited objectives.

We have scrupulously observed the 21-mile limit on penetration of our ground combat forces into Cambodian territory. These self-imposed time and geographic restrictions may have cost us some military advantages, but we knew that we could achieve our primary objectives within these restraints. And these restraints underscored the limited nature of our purpose to the American people.

My June 3 interim report pointed up the success of these operations and the massive amounts of supplies we were seizing and destroying.[5] We have since added substantially to these totals. A full inventory is attached as an appendix to the report. Here are some highlights.

According to latest estimates from the field, we have captured:

—22,892 individual weapons—enough to equip about 74 full-strength North Vietnamese infantry battalions—and 2,509 big crew-

[5] For President Nixon's address to the Nation on June 3, see BULLETIN of June 22, 1970, p. 761.

served weapons—enough to equip about 25 full-strength North Vietnamese infantry battalions;

—More than 15 million rounds of ammunition, or about what the enemy has fired in South Viet-Nam during the past year;

—14 million pounds of rice, enough to feed all the enemy combat battalions estimated to be in South Viet-Nam for about 4 months;

—143,000 rockets, mortars, and recoilless-rifle rounds, used against cities and bases. Based on recent experience, the number of mortars, large rockets, and recoilless-rifle rounds is equivalent to what the enemy shoots in about 14 months in South Viet-Nam;

—Over 199,552 antiaircraft rounds, 5,482 mines, 62,022 grenades, and 83,000 pounds of explosives, including 1,002 satchel charges;

—Over 435 vehicles, and destroyed over 11,688 bunkers and other military structures.

And while our objective has been supplies rather than personnel, the enemy has also taken a heavy manpower loss—11,349 men killed and about 2,328 captured and detainees.

These are impressive statistics. But what is the deeper meaning of the piles of enemy supplies and the rubble of enemy installations?

We have eliminated an immediate threat to our forces and to the security of South Viet-Nam—and produced the prospect of fewer American casualties in the future.

We have inflicted extensive casualties and very heavy losses in material on the enemy—losses which can now be replaced only from the North during a monsoon season and in the face of counteraction by South Vietnamese ground and U.S. air forces.

We have ended the concept of Cambodian sanctuaries, immune from attack, upon which the enemy military had relied for 5 years.

We have dislocated supply lines and disrupted Hanoi's strategy in the Saigon area and the Mekong Delta. The enemy capacity to mount a major offensive in this vital populated region of the South has been greatly diminished.

We have effectively cut off the enemy from resupply by the sea. In 1969, well over half of the munitions being delivered to the North Vietnamese and Viet Cong in Cambodia came by sea.

We have, for the time being, separated the Communist main-force units—regular troops organized in formal units similar to conventional armies—from the guerrillas in the southern part of Viet-Nam. This should provide a boost to pacification efforts.

We have guaranteed the continuance of our troop withdrawal pro-

SIGNIFICANT ENEMY LOSSES IN CAMBODIA[1]

I.	*Ammunition*[2]	
	Machine Rounds	4,067,177
	Rifle Rounds	10,694,990
	Total Small Arms (Machinegun and Rifle Rounds)	14,762,167
	Antiaircraft Rounds	199,552
	Mortar Rounds	68,539
	Large Rocket Rounds	2,123
	Small Rocket Rounds	43,160
	Recoilless-Rifle Rounds	29,185
	Grenades	62,022
	Mines	5,482
II.	*Weapons*	
	Individual	22,892
	Crew-served	2,509
III.	*Food*	
	Rice (lbs.)	14,046,000
	Man-Months of Rice	309,012
	Total Food (lbs.)	14,518,000
IV.	*Faciliites*	
	Bunkers / Structures destroyed	11,688
V.	*Transportation*	
	Vehicles	435
	Boats	167
VI.	*Examples of Other Equipment*	
	Radios	248
	Generators	49
	Total Communications Equipment (lbs.)	58,600
	Miscellaneous Explosives (lbs.)	83,000
	(including 1,002 satchel charges)	
	Medical Supplies (lbs.)	110,800
	Documents (lbs.)	12,400
VII.	*Personnel*	
	Enemy Killed in Action	11,349
	POW's (includes detainees)	2,328

[1] As of June 29, 1970, based on latest available data from the field—subject to change.

[2] Figures do not include 70 tons of assorted ammunition.

gram. On June 3, I reaffirmed that 150,000 more Americans would return home within a year and announced that 50,000 would leave Viet-Nam by October 15.

We have bought time for the South Vietnamese to strengthen themselves against the enemy.

We have witnessed visible proof of the success of Vietnamization as the South Vietnamese performed with skill and valor and competence far beyond the expectation of our commanders or American advisers.

The morale and self-confidence of the Army of South Viet-Nam is higher than ever before.

These then are the major accomplishments of the operations against the Cambodian base areas. Americans can take pride in the leadership of General Abrams [Gen. Creighton W. Abrams, Commander, U.S. Military Assistance Command, Viet-Nam] and in the competence and dedication of our forces.

There is another way to view the success of these operations. What if we had chosen the first option—and done nothing?

The enemy sanctuaries by now would have been expanded and strengthened. The thousands of troops he lost, in killed or captured, would be available to attack American positions and with the enormous resources that we captured or destroyed still in his hands.

Our Vietnamization program would be in serious jeopardy; our withdrawals of troops could only have been carried out in the face of serious threat to our remaining troops in Viet-Nam.

We would have confronted an adversary emboldened by our timidity, an adversary who had ignored repeated warnings.

The war would be a good deal further from over than it is today.

Had we stood by and let the enemy act with impunity in Cambodia —we would be facing a truly bleak situation.

The allied operations have greatly reduced these risks and enhanced the prospects for the future. However, many difficulties remain and some setbacks are inevitable. We still face substantial problems, but the Cambodian operations will enable us to pursue our goals with greater confidence.

When the decision to go into Cambodia was announced on April 30, we anticipated broad disagreement and dissent within the society. Given the divisions on this issue among the American people, it could not have been otherwise.

But the majority of the Americans supported that decision—and now that the Cambodian operation is over, I believe there is a wide measure of understanding of the necessity for it.

Although there remains disagreement about its long-term significance, about the cost to our society of having taken this action—there can be little disagreement now over the immediate military success that has been achieved. With American ground operations in Cambodia ended, we shall move forward with our plan to end the war in Viet-Nam and to secure the just peace on which all Americans are united.

The Future

Now that our ground forces and our logistic and advisory personnel have all been withdrawn, what will be our future policy for Cambodia?

The following will be the guidelines of our policy in Cambodia:

1. There will be no U.S. ground personnel in Cambodia except for the regular staff of our Embassy in Phnom Penh.

2. There will be no U.S. advisers with Cambodian units.

3. We will conduct—with the approval of the Cambodian Government—air interdiction missions against the enemy efforts to move supplies and personnel through Cambodia toward South Viet-Nam and to reestablish base areas relevant to the war in Viet-Nam. We do this to protect our forces in South Viet-Nam.

4. We will turn over material captured in the base areas in Cambodia to the Cambodian Government to help it defend its neutrality and independence.

5. We will provide military assistance to the Cambodian Government in the form of small arms and relatively unsophisticated equipment in types and quantities suitable for their army. To date we have supplied about $5 million of these items, principally in the form of small arms, mortars, trucks, aircraft parts, communications equipment, and medical supplies.

6. We will encourage other countries of the region to give diplomatic support to the independence and neutrality of Cambodia. We welcome the efforts of the Djakarta group of countries[6] to mobilize world opinion and encourage Asian cooperation to this end.

7. We will encourage and support the efforts of third countries who wish to furnish Cambodia with troops or material. We applaud the efforts of Asian nations to help Cambodia preserve its neutrality and independence.

I will let the Asian governments speak for themselves concerning their future policies. I am confident that two basic principles will govern the actions of those nations helping Cambodia:

—They will be at the request of, and in close concert with, the Cambodian Government.

—They will not be at the expense of those nations' own defense—

6 Australia, Indonesia, Japan, Korea, Laos, Malaysia, New Zealand, the Philippines, Singapore, South Viet-Nam, Thailand. [Footnote in original.]

indeed they will contribute to their security, which they see bound up with events in Cambodia.

The South Vietnamese plan to help. Of all the countries of Southeast Asia, South Viet-Nam has most at stake in Cambodia. A North Vietnamese takeover would, of course, have profound consequences for its security. At the same time, the leaders of South Viet-Nam recognize that the primary focus of their attention must be on the security of their own country. President Thieu has reflected these convictions in his major radio and TV address of June 27. Our understanding of Saigon's intentions is as follows:

1. South Vietnamese forces remain ready to prevent reestablishment of base areas along South Viet-Nam's frontier.

2. South Vietnamese forces will remain ready to assist in the evacuation of Vietnamese civilians and to respond selectively to appeals from the Cambodian Government should North Vietnamese aggression make this necessary.

3. Most of these operations will be launched from within South Viet-Nam. There will be no U.S. air or logistics support. There will not be U.S. advisers on these operations.

4. The great majority of South Vietnamese forces are to leave Cambodia.

5. The primary objective of the South Vietnamese remains Vietnamization within their country. Whatever actions are taken in Cambodia will be consistent with this objective.

In this June 27 speech President Thieu emphasized that his government will concentrate on efforts within South Viet-Nam. He pledged that his country will always respect the territory, borders, independence, and neutrality of Cambodia and will not interfere in its internal politics. His government does not advocate stationing troops permanently in Cambodia or sending the South Vietnamese army to fight the war for the Cambodian army.

Under the foreign policy guidelines first outlined at Guam a year ago, I stressed that a threatened country should first make maximum efforts in its own self-defense. The Cambodian people and soldiers are doing that against the superior force of the North Vietnamese and Viet Cong invaders. The majority of the Cambodian people support the present government against the foreign intruders. Cambodian troops have remained loyal and have stood up well in the face of great pressures from a better armed and experienced foe.

Secondly, our policy stresses there should be regional cooperation where a country is not strong enough to defend herself. Cambodia's neighbors are providing that cooperation by joining with her in a collective effort. Each of them is a target of Communist aggression; each has a stake in Cambodia's neutrality and independence.

Third, the United States will assist such self-help and regional actions where our participation can make a difference. Over the long term, we expect the countries of Asia to provide increasingly for their own defense. However, we are now in a transitional phase when nations are shouldering greater responsibilities but when U.S. involvement, while declining, still plays an important role.

In this interim period, we must offset our lower direct involvement with increased military and economic assistance. To meet our foreign policy obligations while reducing our presence will require a redirection—both quantitatively and qualitatively—in our assistance programs.

Prince Sihanouk wrote in December 1969 about the Communist threat to his country and the balance presented by American forces in Southeast Asia. In a generally anti-American article in the official Cambodian government party newspaper, he stated:

> On the diplomatic and political plane, the fact that the U.S. remains in our region and does not yet leave it allows us maneuverings. . . . to assure on the one hand our more than honorable presence in the concert of nations. . . . this presence (and this is an irony of fate for the anti-imperialists that we are) is an essential condition for the "respect," the "friendship" and even for the aid of our socialist "friends." When the U.S. has left these regions, it is certain that the Cambodia of the Sangkum will be the objective of the shellings of the heavy Communist guns: unfriendliness, subversion, aggressions, infiltrations and even occupations.

The Search for Peace

In our search for a lasting peace in Southeast Asia, we are applying the three basic principles of our foreign policy which are set forth in the foreign policy report to Congress last February:[7] partnership, strength, and willingness to negotiate.

—The partnership of our Vietnamization program and of our support for regional defense efforts.

—The strength of our action against the Communist bases in Cambodia and the steadfastness of the American people to see the war through to an honorable conclusion.

[7] The complete text of the report appears in the BULLETIN of Mar. 9, 1970.

—The willingness to negotiate expressed in our generous proposals for a settlement and in our flexibility once Hanoi agrees to serious negotiations.

All three elements are needed to bring peace in Southeast Asia. The willingness to negotiate will prove empty unless buttressed by the willingness to stand by just demands. Otherwise negotiations will be a subterfuge for capitulation. This would only bring a false and transitory peace abroad and recrimination at home.

While we search for genuine negotiation we must continue to demonstrate resolution both abroad and at home and we must support the common defense efforts of threatened Asian nations.

To the leaders in Hanoi, I say the time has come to negotiate. There is nothing to be gained in waiting. There is never an ideal moment when both sides are in perfect equilibrium.

The lesson of the last 2 months has reinforced the lessons of the last 2 years—the time has come to negotiate a just peace.

In Cambodia, the futility of expanded aggression has been demonstrated. By its actions in Cambodia, North Viet-Nam and the Viet Cong provoked the destruction of their sanctuaries and helped to weld together the independent states of Southeast Asia in a collective defense effort, which will receive American support.

The other side cannot impose its will through military means. We have no intention of imposing ours. We have not raised the terms for a settlement as a result of our recent military successes. We will not lower our minimum terms in response to enemy pressure. Our objective remains a negotiated peace with justice for both sides and which gives the people of South Viet-Nam the opportunity to shape their own future.

With major efforts the North Vietnamese can perhaps rebuild or readjust Cambodian supply areas over a period of months. They can pursue their war against South Viet-Nam and her neighbors. But what end would a new round of conflict serve? There is no military solution to this conflict. Sooner or later, peace must come. It can come now, through a negotiated settlement that is fair to both sides and humiliates neither. Or it can come months or years from now, with both sides having paid the further price of protracted struggle.

We would hope that Hanoi would ponder seriously its choice, considering both the promise of an honorable peace and the costs of continued war.

We repeat: All our previous proposals, public and private, remain on the conference table to be explored, including the principles of a just political settlement that I outlined on April 20.

We search for a political solution that reflects the will of the South Vietnamese people and allows them to determine their future without outside interference.

We recognize that a fair political solution should reflect the existing relationship of political forces.

We pledge to abide by the outcome of the political process agreed upon by the South Vietnamese.

For our part, we shall renew our efforts to bring about genuine negotiations both in Paris and for all of Indochina. As I said in my address last September to the United Nations General Assembly:

"The people of Viet-Nam, North and South alike, have demonstrated heroism enough to last a century . . . The people of Viet-Nam, North and South, have endured an unspeakable weight of suffering for a generation. And they deserve a better future."

We call on Hanoi to join us at long last in bringing about that better future.

The Nuremberg Principles

THE General Assembly of the United Nations unanimously affirmed the principles of international law recognized in the Charter of the Nuremberg Tribunal on December 11, 1946. The principles were formulated by the International Law Commission, a United Nations organ of legal experts from all legal systems charged, among other things, with promoting codification of international law.

Principles of International Law Recognized in the Charter of the Nuremberg Tribunal and in the Judgment of the Tribunal

As formulated by the International Law Commission, June-July 1950.

Principle I

Any person who commits an act which constitutes a crime under international law is responsible therefor and liable to punishment.

Principle II

The fact that internal law does not impose a penalty for an act which constitutes a crime under international law does not relieve the person who committed the act from responsibility under international law.

Principle III

The fact that a person who committed an act which constitutes a crime under international law acted as Head of State or responsible government official does not relieve him from responsibility under international law.

Principle IV

The fact that a person acted pursuant to order of his Government or of a superior does not relieve him from responsibility under international law, provided a moral choice was in fact possible to him.

Principle V

Any person charged with a crime under international law has the right to a fair trial on the facts and law.

Principle VI

The crimes hereinafter set out are punishable as crimes under international law:

a. Crimes against peace:

(i) Planning, preparation, initiation or waging of a war of aggression or a war in violation of international treaties, agreements or assurances;

(ii) Participation in a common plan or conspiracy for the accomplishment of any of the acts mentioned under (i).

b. War crimes:

Violations of the laws or customs of war which include, but are not limited to, murder, ill-treatment or deportation to slave-labour or for any other purpose of civilian population of or in occupied territory, murder or ill-treatment of prisoners of war or persons on the seas, killing of hostages, plunder of public or private property, wanton destruction of cities, towns, or villages, or devastation not justified by military necessity.

c. Crimes against humanity:

Murder, extermination, enslavement, deportation and other inhuman acts done against any civilian population, or persecutions on political, racial or religious grounds, when such acts are done or such persecutions are carried on in execution of or in connexion with any crime against peace or any war crime.

Principle VII

Complicity in the commission of a crime against peace, a war crime, or a crime against humanity as set forth in Principle VI is a crime under international law.

Geneva Convention Relative to the
Treatment of Prisoners of War, 1949

ARTICLE 85

Prisoners of war prosecuted under the laws of the Detaining Power for acts committed prior to capture shall retain, even if convicted, the benefits of the present Convention.

ARTICLE 102

A prisoner of war can be validly sentenced only if the sentence has been pronounced by the same courts according to the same procedure as in the case of members of the armed forces of the Detaining Power, and if, furthermore, the provisions of the present Chapter have been observed.

North Vietnam's Reservation to Article 85

"The Democratic Republic of Vietnam declares that prisoners of war prosecuted and convicted for war crimes or for crimes against humanity, in accordance with principles laid down by the Nuremberg Court of Justice, shall not benefit from the present Convention, as specified in Article 85."

501. RESPONSIBILITY FOR ACTS OF SUBORDINATES

In some cases, military commanders may be responsible for war crimes committed by subordinate members of the armed forces, or other persons subject to their control. Thus, for instance, when troops commit massacres and atrocities against the civilian population of occupied territory or against prisoners of war, the responsibility may rest not only with the actual perpetrators but also with the commander. Such a responsibility arises directly when the acts in question have been committed in pursuance of an order of the commander concerned. The commander is also responsible if he has actual knowledge, or should have knowledge, through reports received by him or through other means, that troops or other persons subject to his control are about to commit or have committed a war crime and he fails to take the necessary and reasonable steps to insure compliance with the law of war or to punish violators thereof.

509. DEFENSE OF SUPERIOR ORDERS

a. The fact that the law of war has been violated pursuant to an order of a superior authority, whether military or civil, does not deprive the act in question of its character of a war crime, nor does it constitute a defense in the trial of an accused individual, unless he did not know and could not reasonably have been expected to know that the act ordered was unlawful. In all cases where the order is held not to constitute a defense to an allegation of war crime, the fact that the individual was acting pursuant to orders may be considered in mitigation of punishment.

b. In considering the question whether a superior order constitutes a valid defense, the court shall take into consideration the fact that obedience to lawful military orders is the duty of every member of the armed forces; that the latter cannot be expected, in conditions of war discipline, to weigh scrupulously the legal merits of the orders received; that certain rules of warfare may be controversial; or that an act otherwise amounting to a war crime may be done in obedience to orders conceived as a measure of reprisal. At the same time it must be borne in mind that members of the armed forces are bound to obey only lawful orders (*e.g., UCMJ, Art. 92*).

Peace Proposals of the Provisional
Revolutionary Government of South Vietnam:
May 1969 Ten Point Program;
September 1970 Eight Point Program

Principles and Main Content of an Overall Solution to the
South Viet Nam Problem to Help Restore Peace In Viet Nam

(expounded by Mr. Tran Buu Kiem, Chief of the Delegation of the South Viet Nam National Front for Liberation, at the 16th Plenary Session of the Paris Conference on Viet Nam, May 8, 1969)

"Proceeding from a desire to reach a political solution with a view to ending the U.S. imperialist's war of aggression in South Viet Nam and helping restore peace in Viet Nam ;

On the basis of the guarantee of the fundamental national rights of the Vietnamese people ;

Proceeding from the fundamental principles of the 1954 Geneva Agreements on Viet Nam and the actual situation in Viet Nam ;

On the basis of the Political Programme and the 5-point position of the South Viet Nam National Front for Liberation, which keep with the 4-point stand of the Government of the Democratic Republic of Viet Nam ;

The South Viet Nam National Front for Liberation sets forth the principles and main content of an overall solution to the South Viet Nam problem to help restore peace in Viet Nam as follows :

1 — To respect the Vietnamese people's fundamental national rights, i.e. independence, sovereignty, unity and territorial integrity, as recognized by the 1954 Geneva Agreements on Viet Nam.

2 — The U.S. Government must withdraw from South Viet Nam all U.S. troops, military personnel, arms and war matériel, and all troops, military personnel, arms and war materiel of the other foreign countries of the U.S. camp without posing any condition whatsoever ; liquidate all U.S. military bases in South Viet Nam ; renounce all encroachments on the sovereignty, territory and security of South Viet Nam and the Democratic Republic of Viet Nam.

3 — The Vietnamese people's right to fight for the defence of their Fatherland is the sacred, inalienable right to self-defence of all peo-

ples. *The question of the Vietnamese armed forces in South Viet Nam shall be resolved by the Vietnamese parties among themselves.*

4 — *The people of South Viet Nam settle themselves their own affairs without foreign interference. They decide themselves the political regime of South Viet Nam through free and democratic general elections. Through free and democratic general elections, a Constituent Assembly will be set up, a Constitution worked out, and a coalition Government of South Viet Nam installed, reflecting national concord and the broad union of all social strata.*

5 — *During the period intervening between the restoration of peace and the holding of general elections, neither party shall impose its political regime on the people of South Viet Nam.*

The political forces representing the various social strata and political tendencies in South Viet Nam, that stand for peace, independence and neutrality, including those persons who, for political reasons, have to live abroad, will enter into talks to set up a provisional coalition government based on the principle of equality, democracy and mutual respect with a view to achieving a peaceful, independent, democratic and neutral South Viet Nam.

The provisional coalition government is to have the following tasks:

a) *To implement the agreements to be concluded on the withdrawal of the troops of the United States and the other foreign countries of the American camp, etc.*

b) *To achieve national concord, and a broad union of all social strata, political forces, nationalities, religious communities, and all persons, no matter what their political beliefs and their past may be, provided they stand for peace, independence and neutrality.*

c) *To achieve broad democratic freedoms - freedom of speech, freedom of the press, freedom of gathering, freedom of belief, freedom to form political parties and organizations, freedom to demonstrate, etc. ; to set free those persons jailed on political grounds ; to prohibit all acts of terror, reprisal and discrimination against people having collaborated with either side, and who are now in the country or abroad, as provided for in the 1954 Geneva Agreements on Viet Nam.*

d) *To heal the war wounds, to restore and develop the economy, to restore the normal life of the people, and to improve the living conditions of the labouring people.*

e) *To hold free and democratic general elections in the whole of South Viet Nam with a view to achieving the South Viet Nam people's right to self-determination, in accordance with the content of point 4 mentioned above.*

6 — *South Viet Nam will carry out a foreign policy of peace and neutrality :*

To carry out a policy of good neighbourly relations with the Kingdom of Cambodia on the basis of respect for her independence, sovereignty, neutrality and territorial integrity within her present borders ; to carry out a policy of good neighbourly relations with the Kingdom of Laos on the basis of respect for the 1962 Geneva Agreements on Laos.

To establish diplomatic, economic and cultural relations with all countries, irrespective of political and social regime, including the United States, in accordance with the five principles of peaceful coexistence : mutual respect for the independence, sovereignty and territorial integrity, non-aggression, non-interference in the internal affairs, equality and mutual benefit, peaceful coexistence ; to accept economic and technical aid with no political conditions attached from any country.

7 — *The reunification of Viet Nam will be achieved step by step, by peaceful means, through discussions and agreement between the two zones, without foreign interference.*

Pending the peaceful reunification of Viet Nam, the two zones reestablish normal relations in all fields on the basis of mutual respect.

The military demarcation line between the two zones at the 17th parallel, as provides for by the 1954 Geneva Agreements, is only of a provisional character and does not constitute in any way a political or territorial boundary. The two zones reach agreement on the statute of the Demilitarized Zone, and work out modalities for movements across the provisional military demarcation line.

8 — *As provided for in the 1954 Geneva Agreements on Viet Nam, pending the peaceful reunification of Viet Nam, the two zones North and South of Viet Nam undertake to refrain from joining any military alliance with foreign countries, not to allow any foreign country to maintain military bases, troops and military personnel on their respective soil, and not to recognize the protection of any country or military alliance or bloc.*

9 — *To resolve the aftermath of the war :*

a) *The parties will negotiate the release of the armymen captured in war.*

b) *The U.S. Government must bear full responsibility for the losses and devastations it has caused to the Vietnamese people in both zones.*

10 — *The parties shall reach agreement on an international supervision about the withdrawal from South Viet Nam of the troops, military personnel, arms and war materiel of the United States and the other foreign countries of the American camp.*

The principles and content of the overall solution expounded above form an integrated whole. On the basis of these principles and content, the parties shall reach understanding to the effect of concluding agreements on the above-mentional questions with a view to ending the war in South Viet Nam, and contributing to restore peace in Viet Nam."

Peace Initiative

(Statement by Mme Nguyen thi Binh, Minister for Foreign Affairs and Chief of the Delegation of the Provisional Revolutionary Government of the Republic of South Viet Nam, at the 84th Plenary Session of the Paris Conference on Viet Nam, September 16, 1970)

"To respond to the deep desire for peace of broad sectors of the people in South Viet Nam, in the United States and in the world, on the instructions of the Provisional Revolutionary Government of the Republic of South Viet Nam, I would like to further elaborate on a number of points in the 10-point Overall Solution as follows:

1 — The U.S. Government must put an end to its war of aggression in Viet Nam, stop the policy of "Vietnamization" of the war, totally withdraw from South Viet Nam troops, military personnel, weapons, and war materials of the United States as well as troops, military personnel, weapons, and war materials of the other foreign countries in the U.S. camp, without posing any condition whatsoever, and dismantle all U.S. military bases in South Viet Nam.

In case the U.S. Government declares it will withdraw from South Viet Nam all its troops and those of the other foreign countries in the U.S. camp by June 30, 1971, the People's Liberation Armed Forces will refrain from attacking the withdrawing troops of the United States and those of the other foreign countries in the U.S. camp ; and the parties will engage at once in discussions on :

— the question of ensuring safety for the total withdrawal from South Viet Nam of U.S. troops and those of the other foreign countries in the U.S. camp.

— the question of releasing captured militarymen.

2 — The question of Vietnamese armed forces in South Viet Nam shall be resolved by the Vietnamese parties among themselves.

3 — The warlike and fascist Thieu-Ky-Khiem administration, an instrument of the U.S. policy of aggression, are frantically opposing peace, striving to call for the intensification and expansion of the war, and for the prolongation of the U.S. military occupation of South Viet Nam, and are enriching themselves with the blood of the people. They are serving the U.S. imperialist aggressors who massacre their compatriots and devastate their country. They have stepped up the "pacification" campaigns to terrorize the people and hold them in the vice of their regime, set up a barbarous system of jails of the type of "tiger cages" in Con Dao and established a police regime of the utmost cruelty in South Viet Nam. They carry out ferocious repression against those who stand for peace, independence, neutrality and democracy, regardless of their social stock, political tendencies and religions ; they repress those who are not of their clan. They increase forcible press-ganging and endeavour to plunder the property of the South Viet Nam people so as to serve the U.S. policy of "Vietnamization" of the war. The restoration of genuine peace in South Viet Nam necessitates the formation in Saigon of an administration without Thieu, Ky, and Khiem, an administration which stands for peace, independence, neutrality, which improves the people's living conditions, which ensures democratic liberties such as freedom of speech, freedom of press, freedom of assembly, freedom of belief, etc., and releases those who have been jailed for political reasons, and dissolves concentration camps so that the inmates therein may return to and live in their native places. The Provisional Revolutionary Government of the Republic of South Viet Nam is prepared to enter into talks with such an administration on a political settlement of the South Viet Nam problem so as to put an end to the war and restore peace in Viet Nam.

4 — The South Viet Nam people will decide themselves the political regime of South Viet Nam through really free and democratic general elections, elect a national assembly, work out a Constitution of a national and democratic character, and set up a government reflecting the entire people's aspirations and will for peace, independence, neutrality, democracy and national concord.

The general elections must be held in a really free and democratic way. The modalities of the elections must guarantee genuine freedom and equality during the electoral campaigns and vote proceedings to all citizens, irrespective of their political tendencies, including those who are living abroad. No party shall usurp for itself the right to organize general elections and lay down their modalities. The general elections organized by the U.S. puppet administration in Saigon at the bayonets of the U.S. occupying troops cannot be free and democratic.

A provisional government of broad coalition is indispensable for the organization of really free and democratic general elections and also for ensuring the right to self-determination of the South Viet Nam people during the transitory period between the restoration of peace and the holding of general elections.

5 — The provisional coalition government will include three components :

— Persons of the Provisional Revolutionary Government of the Republic of South Viet Nam.

— Persons of the Saigon Administration, really standing for peace, independence, neutrality, and democracy.

— Persons of various political and religious forces and tendencies standing for peace, independence, neutrality and democracy including those who, for political reasons, have to live abroad.

The provisional coalition government will implement the agreements reached by the parties.

The provisional coalition government will carry out a policy of national concord, ensure the democratic freedoms of the people, prohibit all acts of terror, reprisal, and discrimination against those who have collaborated with either side, stabilize and improve the living conditions of the people and organize general elections to form a coalition government.

The provisional coalition government will pursue a foreign policy of peace and neutrality, practise a policy of good neighbourhood with the Kingdom of Laos and the Kingdom of Cambodia, respect the sovereignty, independence, neutrality, and territorial integrity of these two countries ; it will establish diplomatic relations with all countries regardless of their political regime, including the United States, in accordance with the five principles of peaceful coexistence.

6 — Viet Nam is one, the Vietnamese people is one. The reunification of Viet Nam will be achieved step by step, by peaceful means, on the basis of discussions and agreements between the two zones, without coercion or annexion from either side, without foreign interference. The time for reunification as well as all questions relating to the reunification will be discussed and agreed upon by both zones. Pend-

ing the peaceful reunification of the country, the two zones will re-establish normal relations in all fields on the basis of equality and mutual respect, and will respect each other's political regime, internal and external policies.

7 — The parties will decide together measures aimed at ensuring the respect and the correct implementation of the provisions agreed upon.

8 — After the agreement on and signing of accords aimed at putting an end to the war and restoring peace in Viet Nam, the parties will implement the modalities that will have been laid down for a cease-fire in South Viet Nam.

To attain a peaceful settlement of the Viet Nam problem, the Provisional Revolutionary Government of the Republic of South Viet Nam declares its readiness to get henceforth in touch with the forces or persons of various political tendencies and religions in the country and abroad, including members of the present Saigon Administration, except Thieu, Ky and Khiem."

President Nixon's Address to the Nation on "A New Peace Initiative for All Indochina," October 7, 1970[1]

Good evening, my fellow Americans. Tonight I would like to talk to you about a major new initiative for peace.

When I authorized operations against the enemy sanctuaries in Cambodia last April, I also directed that an intensive effort be launched to develop new approaches for peace in Indochina.

In Ireland on Sunday, I met with the chiefs of our delegation to the Paris talks. This meeting marked the culmination of a Government-wide effort begun last spring on the negotiation front. After considering the recommendations of all my principal advisers, I am tonight announcing new proposals for peace in Indochina.

This new peace initiative has been discussed with the Governments of South Viet-Nam, Laos, and Cambodia. All support it. It has been made possible in large part by the remarkable success of the Vietnamization program over the past 18 months. Tonight I want to tell you what these proposals are and what they mean.

First, I propose that all armed forces throughout Indochina cease firing their weapons and remain in the positions they now hold. This would be a "cease-fire-in-place." It would not in itself be an end to the conflict, but it would accomplish one goal all of us have been working toward: an end to the killing.

I do not minimize the difficulty of maintaining a cease-fire in a guerrilla war where there are no front lines. But an unconventional war may require an unconventional truce; our side is ready to stand still and cease firing.

I ask that this proposal for a cease-fire-in-place be the subject for immediate negotiation. And my hope is that it will break the logjam in all the negotiations.

This cease-fire proposal is put forth without preconditions. The general principles that should apply are these:

A cease-fire must be effectively supervised by international observers, as well as by the parties themselves. Without effective supervision a cease-fire runs the constant risk of breaking down. All concerned

1 Made to the Nation on television and radio on Oct. 7 (White House press release).

must be confident that the cease-fire will be maintained and that any local breaches of it will be quickly and fairly repaired.

A cease-fire should not be the means by which either side builds up its strength by an increase in outside combat forces in any of the nations of Indochina.

And a cease-fire should cause all kinds of warfare to stop. This covers the full range of actions that have typified this war, including bombing and acts of terror.

A cease-fire should encompass not only the fighting in Viet-Nam but in all of Indochina. Conflicts in this region are closely related. The United States has never sought to widen the war. What we do seek is to widen the peace.

Finally, a cease-fire should be part of a general move to end the war in Indochina.

A cease-fire-in-place would undoubtedly create a host of problems in its maintenance. But it has always been easier to make war than to make a truce. To build an honorable peace, we must accept the challenge of long and difficult negotiations.

By agreeing to stop the shooting, we can set the stage for agreements on other matters.

A second point of the new initiative for peace is this:

I propose an Indochina peace conference. At the Paris talks today, we are talking about Viet-Nam. But North Vietnamese troops are not only infiltrating, crossing borders, and establishing bases in South Viet-Nam—they are carrying on their aggression in Laos and Cambodia as well.

An international conference is needed to deal with the conflict in all three states of Indochina. The war in Indochina has been proved to be of one piece; it cannot be cured by treating only one of its areas of outbreak.

The essential elements of the Geneva accords of 1954 and 1962 remain valid as a basis for settlement of problems between states in the Indochina area. We shall accept the results of agreements reached between these states.

While we pursue the convening of an Indochina peace conference, we will continue the negotiations in Paris. Our proposal for a larger conference can be discussed there as well as through other diplomatic channels.

The Paris talks will remain our primary forum for reaching a negotiated settlement, until such time as a broader international conference produces serious negotiations.

The third part of our peace initiative has to do with the United States forces in South Viet-Nam.

In the past 20 months, I have reduced our troop ceilings in South Viet-Nam by 165,000 men. During the spring of next year, these withdrawals will have totaled more than 260,000 men—about one-half the number that were in South Viet-Nam when I took office.

As the American combat role and presence have decreased, American casualties have also decreased. Our casualties since the completion of the Cambodian operation were the lowest for a comparable period in the last 4½ years.

We are ready now to negotiate an agreed timetable for complete withdrawals as part of an overall settlement.

We are prepared to withdraw all our forces as part of a settlement based on the principles I spelled out previously and the proposals I am making tonight.

Fourth, I ask the other side to join us in a search for a political settlement that truly meets the aspirations of all South Vietnamese.

Three principles govern our approach:

—We seek a political solution that reflects the will of the South Vietnamese people.

—A fair political solution should reflect the existing relationship of political forces in South Viet-Nam.

—And we will abide by the outcome of the political process agreed upon.

Let there be no mistake about one essential point: The other side is not merely objecting to a few personalities in the South Vietnamese Government. They want to dismantle the organized non-Communist parties and insure the takeover by their party. They demand the right to exclude whomever they wish from government.

This patently unreasonable demand is totally unacceptable.

As my proposals today indicate, we are prepared to be flexible on many matters. But we stand firm for the right of all the South Vietnamese people to determine for themselves the kind of government they want.

We have no intention of seeking any settlement at the conference table other than one which fairly meets the reasonable concerns of both sides. We know that when the conflict ends, the other side will still be there. And the only kind of settlement that will endure is one that both sides have an interest in preserving.

Finally, I propose the immediate and unconditional release of all prisoners of war held by both sides.

War and imprisonment should be over for all these prisoners. They and their families have already suffered too much.

I propose that all prisoners of war, without exception, without condition, be released now to return to the place of their choice.

And I propose that all journalists and other innocent civilian victims of the conflict be released immediately as well.

The immediate release of all prisoners of war would be a simple act of humanity.

But it could be even more. It could serve to establish good faith, the intent to make progress, and thus improve the prospects for negotiation.

We are prepared to discuss specific procedures to complete the speedy release of all prisoners.

The five proposals that I have made tonight can open the door to an enduring peace in Indochina.

Ambassador Bruce will present these proposals formally to the other side in Paris tomorrow. He will be joined in that presentation by Ambassador Lam representing South Viet-Nam.

Let us consider for a moment what the acceptance of these proposals would mean.

Since the end of World War II, there has always been a war going on somewhere in the world. The guns have never stopped firing. By achieving a cease-fire in Indochina, and by holding firmly to the cease-fire in the Middle East, we could hear the welcome sound of peace throughout the world for the first time in a generation.

We could have some reason to hope that we had reached the beginning of the end of war in this century. We might then be on the threshold of a generation of peace.

The proposals I have made tonight are designed to end the fighting throughout Indochina and to end the impasse in negotiations in Paris. Nobody has anything to gain by delay and only lives to lose.

There are many nations involved in the fighting in Indochina. Tonight, all those nations, except one, announce their readiness to agree to a cease-fire. The time has come for the Government of North Viet-

Nam to join its neighbors in a proposal to quit making war and to start making peace.

As you know, I have just returned from a trip which took me to Italy, Spain, Yugoslavia, England, and Ireland.[2]

Hundreds of thousands of people cheered me as I drove through the cities of those countries. They were not cheering for me as an individual. They were cheering for the country I was proud to represent—the United States of America. For millions of people in the free world, the nonaligned world, and the Communist world, America is the land of freedom, of opportunity, of progress.

I believe there is another reason they welcomed me so warmly in every country I visited, despite their wide differences in political systems and national backgrounds.

In my talks with leaders all over the world, I find that there are those who may not agree with all of our policies. But no world leader to whom I have talked fears that the United States will use its great power to dominate another country or to destroy its independence. We can be proud that this is the cornerstone of America's foreign policy.

There is no goal to which this nation is more dedicated, and to which I am more dedicated, than to build a new structure of peace in the world where every nation, including North Viet-Nam as well as South Viet-Nam, can be free and independent with no fear of foreign aggression or foreign domination.

I believe every American deeply believes in his heart that the proudest legacy the United States can leave during this period when we are the strongest nation of the world is that our power was used to defend freedom, not to destroy it; to preserve the peace, not to break the peace.

It is in that spirit that I make this proposal for a just peace in Viet-Nam and in Indochina.

I ask that the leaders in Hanoi respond to this proposal in the same spirit. Let us give our children what we have not had in this century: a chance to enjoy a generation of peace.

Thank you. Good night.

[2] Documentation related to President Nixon's trip to Europe Sept. 27-Oct. 5 will be printed in a later issue of the BULLETIN.

The National Commitments Resolution
Senate Resolution 85,
91st Congress, 1st Session,
Adopted June 25, 1969

Whereas accurate definition of the term "national commitment" in recent years has become obscured: Now, therefore, be it

Resolved, That (1) a national commitment for the purpose of this resolution means the use of the Armed Forces of the United States on foreign territory, or a promise to assist a foreign country, government, or people by the use of the Armed Forces or financial resources of the United States, either immediately or upon the happening of certain events, and (2) it is the sense of the Senate that a national commitment by the United States results only from affirmative action taken by the executive and legislative branches of the United States Government by means of a treaty, statute, or concurrent resolution of both Houses of Congress specifically providing for such commitment.

Amendment to the Foreign Military Sales Act
(Cooper-Church Amendment)

Limitations on United States involvement in Cambodia.

In concert with the declared objectives of the President of the United States to avoid the involvement of the United States in Cambodia after July 1, 1970, and to expedite the withdrawal of American forces from Cambodia, it is hereby provided that unless specifically authorized by law hereafter enacted, no funds authorized or appropriated pursuant to this act or any other law may be expended after July 1, 1970, for the purposes of—

(1) Retaining United States forces in Cambodia;

(2) Paying the compensation or allowances of, or otherwise supporting, directly or indirectly, any United States personnel in Cambodia who furnish military instruction to Cambodian forces or engage in any combat activity in support of Cambodian forces;

(3) Entering into or carrying out any contract or agreement to provide any contract or agreement to provide military instruction in Cambodia, or to provide persons to engage in any combat activity in support of Cambodian forces; or

(4) Conducting any combat activity in the air above Cambodia in direct support of Cambodian forces.

Nothing contained in this section shall be deemed to impugn the constitutional power of the President as Commander in Chief, including the exercise of that constitutional power which may be necessary to protect the lives of United States armed forces wherever deployed. Nothing contained in this section shall be deemed to impugn the constitutional powers of Congress including the power to declare war and to make rules for the Government and regulation of the armed forces of the United States.

Official Statements about the "Understanding" of the United States Government with Respect to Termination of the Bombardment of North Vietnam

EXCERPTS: PRESIDENT NIXON'S NEWS CONFERENCE OF DECEMBER 10, 1970

Won't you be seated, please. Miss Thomas has the first question tonight.

1. U.S. Policy on Vietnam

Q. Mr. President, a question about Vietnam. Our recent air strikes have raised speculation that our policy of not bombing North Vietnam may be undergoing a subtle change. What is our policy? Also, despite the objection by the Saigon Government and the Vietcong, do you plan to propose a unilateral cease-fire from Christmas through Tet in a bid for peace?

A. Let me answer the second part of the question first. We are prepared to have cease-fires on a limited basis over the holiday seasons.

As you know, the North Vietnamese have turned down any extended cease-fire over the holiday seasons out of hand.

We, of course, could not have any extended cease-fire unilaterally, because that would be very dangerous for our forces. If it's a brief cease-fire, we will do it. If it's extended, we will not.

With regard to the second part of your question, the bombing of North Vietnam: You may recall that, a few weeks ago, there was bombing of installations in North Vietnam, after the North Vietnamese had fired on some of our unarmed reconnaissance planes.

Now, there's been, I note, some speculation in the press and also some charges from North Vietnam that there is no understanding that reconnaissance planes are to fly over North Vietnam since the bombing halt was announced.

I want to be very sure that that understanding is clear. First, President Johnson said there was such an understanding at the time of the bombing halt. Secretary Clifford did. And Ambassador Vance did.

But if there is any misunderstanding, I want to indicate the understanding of this President with regard to the flying of reconnaissance planes over North Vietnam.

I must insist that there be continued reconnaissance over North Vietnam because, as we are withdrawing our forces, I have to see whether or not there's any chance of a strike against those forces that remain. And we have to watch for the build-up.

If our planes are fired upon, I will not only order that they return the fire, but I will order that the missile site be destroyed and that the military complex around that site which supports it also be destroyed by bombing.

That is my understanding.

Beyond that, there is another understanding with regard to the bombing of North Vietnam which at a number of these press conferences, and in my speech on Nov. 3, and in four televised speeches to the nation last year, I have stated. I restate it again tonight.

At a time that we are withdrawing from North Vietnam—from South Vietnam—it is vitally important that the President of the United States, as Commander in Chief, take the action that is necessary to protect our remaining forces, because the number of our ground combat forces is going down very, very steadily.

Now, if, as a result of my conclusion that the North Vietnamese by their infiltration threaten our remaining forces—if they thereby develop a capacity and proceed possibly to use that capacity to increase the level of fighting in South Vietnam—then I will order the bombing of military sites in North Vietnam, the passes that lead from North Vietnam into South Vietnam, the military complexes and the military supply lines.

That will be the reaction I shall take. I trust that that is not necessary, but let there be no misunderstanding with regard to this President's understanding about either reconnaissance flights or about a step-up of the activities.

. . .

6. Progress in Peace Talks

Q. Mr. President, does what you said a while ago about bombing of North Vietnam, and indications we've had from other officials of probably more raids to try to free American prisoners—does all that mean that you have abandoned hope for the Paris peace talks to reach a negotiated settlement?

A. Not at all. We're continuing those talks. As you note today, Ambassador Bruce made an offer, which refined the offer we had made earlier of a complete exchange of all prisoners of war. He offered to exchange, upon the part of both the United States and South Vietnam, 8,200 North Vietnamese that we have prisoner for approximately 800 Americans and other allied prisoners that they had. That's a 10-to-1 ratio, but we're willing to do that.

Their failure to accept that offer will pinpoint something that is pretty generally getting known around the world, and that is that this nation is an international outlaw, that it does not adhere to the rules of international conduct. But we are going to continue the negotiations as long as they are willing to negotiate and as long as there's some hope to make progress in the prisoner issue, or on a cease-fire and an earlier end to the war than the Vietnamization process will inevitably bring.

EXCERPTS: STATEMENT BY XUAN THUY, CHIEF OF THE DELEGATION OF THE GOVERNMENT OF THE DEMOCRATIC REPUBLIC OF VIETNAM, AT THE 95TH PLENARY SESSION OF THE PARIS CONFERENCE ON VIETNAM, DECEMBER 17, 1970

. . . The statements regarding the Viet Nam problem made by President Nixon in his press conference on December 10, 1970 constitute a U.S. new escalation of threats of using violence against the Democratic Republic of Viet Nam. The U.S. authorities, particularly Mr. M. Laird, have repeatedly resorted in the past to impetuous menaces, but this time Mr. Nixon, the U.S. President himself, has done so in most bellicist and brazen statements.

Since his fallacious allegations about the so-called "understanding" could not stand up to the truth that there had been no "understanding" whatsoever, Mr. Nixon had to gratuitously affirm that that was "his own understanding." Then what was his understanding? *He gave himself the right to extend the war to North.Viet Nam at any moment, under the pretext of protecting American reconnaissance aircraft and American forces in South Viet Nam.*

Mr. Nixon cynically said that the United States "would continue to carry out air reconnaissance over North Viet Nam" and if U.S. aircraft are fired upon, he "will not only order that they return the fire, but he will order that the missile site be destroyed and that the military complex around that site be destroyed and that the military complex around that site which supports it also be destroyed by bombing."

Mr. Nixon also enlarged his "understanding" to the extent of saying: "If, as a result of my conclusion that the North Vietnamese, by their infiltration, threaten our remaing forces, if they thereby develop a capacity and proceed possibly to use that capacity to increase the level of fighting in South Viet Nam, then I will order the bombing of military sites in North Viet Nam, the passes that lead from North Viet Nam into South Viet Nam, the military complexes, the military supply lines," etc. . .

We severely condemn and totally reject Mr. Nixon's talks about war and aggression. We are convinced that the Vietnamese people will appropriately riposte in case the sovereignty and security of the D.R.V.N. are encroached upon. . . .

EXCERPTS: NEWS CONFERENCE OF SECRETARY OF STATE WILLIAM P. ROGERS, DECEMBER 23, 1970

Q. The Communist negotiators in Paris this morning, in listing their price for accepting the cease-fire and really beginning the talks, said that we must end U.S. reconnaissance flights over North Vietnam—promise to withdraw by mid-1971—but they omitted their usual reference to getting rid of the Saigon Government. Do you see any significance in this omission?

A. At the moment we do not. I have just finished talking with our negotiators in Paris, and they feel that the proposals that were made by the other side are essentially the same proposals that they have made previously.

Q. For about two years we've heard a great deal about the understanding made with Hanoi in Paris. The terms we heard were that Hanoi had to accept Saigon into the talks and to refrain from shelling the cities of South Vietnam and refrain from abusing the demilitarized zone between North and South Vietnam if we were to sustain the bombing halt. At his last news conference the President said we would resume the bombing if the enemy developed and used the capacity to increase the fighting generally in the South. Now, is the President changing or expanding or abandoning the understanding?

A. In answer to the last part of your question, and without referring to the premise, let me say that what the President said at his press conference is not a new policy. He has said on every occasion in which he addressed the public that as our Vietnamization program proceeded, as American troops are being replaced by the troops of South Vietnam, that if the enemy mounted an offensive or took other action which jeopardized the lives or safety of American forces that he would take the action that he considered necessary to protect them.

Now, he said in his press conference: Lest there be any misunderstanding on the part of the North Vietnamese, let me say what I will do in the event American forces as they withdraw are put in jeopardy.

He said that he would take necessary action, including the bombing of military sites, military bases, supply lines and passes, to protect the lives of Americans who are withdrawing from South Vietnam. He said also that he hoped that wouldn't be necessary.

Now, he didn't say that was any part of the understanding. Obviously, it couldn't be part of the understanding. At the time the understanding was reached, there wasn't any Vietnamization program. Americans were not being withdrawn from South Vietnam. So it's quite a different situation.

And what he said, very clearly—and I'm sure that the other side got the message—is that there should be no misunderstanding that we were under any restrictions or inhibitions in the process of our troop replacement—that we would take whatever steps were necessary, that he thought were necessary, to protect American lives and safety.

Now, I think also it should be said that we have a great deal of discussion in this country about the understanding; and I think it's a perfectly proper subject for discussion. But, in a sense, it's somewhat academic because the other side constantly says we never had any understanding. General Giap said it yesterday. He said the idea of the understanding is a fabrication. Well, if there's no understanding, then there are no restrictions.

Impact of the Bombing

Q. How effective was the bombing in North Vietnam from 1965 to '68, in your estimate, and what would it accomplish if it were resumed —that it did not accomplish last time?

A. I think that it's a simplification to suggest that the comments that I have just made or that the comments the President made were analogous to those that you have referred to. He was not talking about bombing as it was done before. He was talking about what to do, that he would do whatever was necessary to protect American lives, American men; and I don't think that he was saying that we are thinking about renewing regular bombings the way they were conducted before. He is saying that we are going to maintain our options to protect American men.

Q. Regardless of the public position taken by the North Vietnamese, in advance of the bombing halt in the fall of 1968 was there discussion with the North Vietnamese about reconnaissance flights? And is it the position of this Government that there was an understanding governing such flights?

A. Yes. Now, the semantics sometimes get involved because people are apt to suggest that the words "understanding" and "agreement" are synonymous. Not necessarily. An understanding can be a method of operating, and neither side promises anything but it is understood this is how they will conduct themselves.

Now, I think it's quite clear that there has been an understanding and that generally it's been observed. There have been violations, in fact, there were violations over the weekend.

But generally, though, it's quite clear that there was an understanding, and it included the elements that we referred to: no violation of the DMZ, no rocketing of cities, and that our reconnaissance planes would continue to fly over North Vietnam.

Johnson Stand Recalled

Now let me read this:

"At the time of the 1968 bombing halt, the United States agreed to 'stop all air, naval and artillery bombardment and all other acts involving the use of force against North Vietnam.' The United States specifically rejected a formula proposed by the North Vietnamese calling for us to stop all 'acts of war.' This formula was rejected in order to permit the continuation of reconnaisance flights. This took place well in advance of the actual bombing halt.

"In summarizing the understanding at a meeting of his advisers on Oct. 29, 1968, President Johnson stated, 'Both Hanoi and Moscow are clear that we shall continue reconnaissance of North Vietnam. That is why we agreed to stop only acts of force and not acts of war.'

"We informed the North Vietnamese as early as Nov. 14, that, if the firing against our reconnaissance aircraft were to continue, we would have to take the necessary actions to defend our planes and protect our pilots.

"The then Defense Secretary Clifford told the press on Nov. 24, 'In the Paris conversations that we have had for all these many months, it was made very clear to the representatives of North Vietnam that we would continue to maintain reconnaissance.'

"On Jan. 9, 1969, Messrs. Harriman and Vance expressed gratification to Soviet representatives Zorin and Oberemko, in Paris, that North Vietnam had not been firing on our reconnaissance aircraft. And there was no challenge to this contention on the part of Messrs. Harriman and Vance.

"So that the actions of the North Vietnamese following the bombing halt showed, we believe, that they understood what was expected of them. Violation of the DMZ and shelling of the cities decreased very substantially and the vast majority of our reconnaissance flights—and we have flown many since the bombing halt—have not been fired upon."

So I say in answer to your question: Yes, we think there was an understanding; yes, we think the evidence is convincing on that point.

. . .

Q. After the President's press conference, Secretary of Defense Laird gave a press conference in which he seemed to indicate that another part of his [Vietnam] understanding was genuine negotiations at Paris. Is the bombing halt predicated on some sort of negotiations?

A. No, I don't think so. I think the statement the President made in his press conference obviously reflects the policy of this Administration. Now, I read very carefully what the Secretary of Defense said in his press conference, and I didn't interpret it the way some of you did.

He read from a statement that was made by a former defense official, and in that, that statement did convey the thought that one of the conditions of the bombing halt was the continuation of good-faith negotiations in Paris, but that's not the premise on which we are operating.

The President's position is that, as Commander in Chief of the Armed Forces, he feels responsible to protect American lives; and as our forces withdraw from South Vietnam, if the North Vietnamese take action which he thinks is going to jeopardize the lives and safety of those men, he will take action that he thinks is appropriate.

Q. On the Middle East, when you say that the United States is prepared to play a role in peace-making or peace preservation out there, do you include the possibility of U.S. participation physically with troops in an international peace-keeping force of some kind?

A. We have not formed any conclusions on that subject. There have been some speculations that we might be willing to consider a joint Soviet-United States peace-keeping force, just involving the two nations. That concept, with just the two of us involved, would be totally impractical, and we have never given any thought to it.

Now, we have not excluded the possibility that the United States might play a peace-keeping role if it was accepted by the parties themselves, and that it was not a substitute for agreement, but it would be an added assurance that the agreement would be observed. And if it could be done under the auspicies of the Security Council of the United Nations.

I don't want to leave the impression that this is a policy that we have formulated. I just say we have not excluded that possibility.

EXCERPTS: INTERVIEW OF FOUR CORRESPONDENTS WITH PRESIDENT NIXON AT THE WHITE HOUSE, JANUARY 4, 1971

. . .

MR. CHANCELLOR: Mr President, let me ask you a question about Vietnam, as though nobody was going to ask you tonight.

MR. NIXON: I didn't expect that.

MR. CHANCELLOR: I—last month you sent a number of bombers into North Vietnam, and we were told that they bombed missile sites and antiaircraft installations because the North Vietnamese had fired on an American reconnaissance plane.

But then a few days later, sir, we learned that apparently that opportunity was used to make very heavy bombing raids on supply lines and the Mugia Pass and in the passes from North Vietnam into Laos.

Now, I'm confused. Because of all the talk about the understanding with North Vietnam, with the new criteria on the bombing, you seem to have put on, and the fact that what many people got out of this one series of raids was that we quite enlarged the reasons for our going north to bomb.

MR. NIXON: Mr. Chancellor, I have no desire to resume the bombing of North Vietnam. We do not want to go back to the bombing of the strategic targets in North Vietnam, and we do not want, even, to bomb military targets unless it becomes necessary to do so and, this is the key point, to protect American forces.

Now, with regard to the understanding, let's see what it is. First, there was an understanding. President Johnson said so. Dean Rusk said so. Clark Clifford said so. Mr. Harriman said so. There was an understanding that after the bombing halt, that unarmed reconnaissance planes could fly over North Vietnam with impunity.

We had to insist on that because otherwise we would have no intelligence with regard to what they were planning on an attack. So when they fire on those planes, I've given instructions that we will take out the SAM site or whatever it is that has fired upon them. We will continue to do so. And if they say there is no understanding in that respect, then there are no restraints whatever on us. And so we must have that in mind.

Now the other understanding is one that I have laid down. It is a new one. It is a new one which goes along with our Vietnamization program and our withdrawal program.

End of Combat Role Foreseen

I pointed out a moment ago what has happened in Vietnam—the fact that our casualties are a third of what they were two years ago, the fact that we have 265,000 out of Vietnam now and that we now can see the end of the American combat role in Vietnam. We can see that coming.

We must realize, however, as Secretary Rogers pointed out in his news conference at the State Department a few days ago, that in May of this year, most American combat forces—ground combat forces—will have been withdrawn from Vietnam. But there will still be 280,000 there left to withdraw.

Now the President of the United States as Commander in Chief owes a responsibility to those men to see that they are not subjected to an overwhelming attack from the North. That's why we must continue reconnaissance, And that is why, also, if the enemy at a time we are trying to de-escalate, at a time we are withdrawing, starts to build up its infiltration, starts moving troops and supplies through the Mugia Pass and the other passes, then I as Commander in Chief will have to order bombing strikes on those key areas.

That was one of the reasons for this strike. And it will be done again if they continue to threaten our remaining forces in Vietnam. But only on those military targets, and only if necessary.

MR. CHANCELLOR: Does it bother you, sir, that this was not made as clear then as you have made it now?

MR. NIXON: Oh, it's been made clear only since we began our withdrawal program. You see, this is a new policy.

MR. CHANCELLOR: Pardon me, sir, I meant in just a month ago, in December when the first announcement came out.

MR. NIXON: Well, I made it clear not just a month ago but in November. You may recall that on Nov. 3—I made my speech on Nov. 3—I warned the North Vietnamese then that if at a time we were withdrawing they stepped up their infiltration and threatened our remaining forces that I would retaliate.

I have said that on eight different occasions, on national television and national radio. I have said it also in other messages to them that have gotten to them very loud and very clear. So there's no question about the understanding, and that was why we did this.

MR. SMITH: You talked about the situation through May of '71. I hate to ask a hypothetical question but people do ask them.

MR. NIXON: Everybody else does.

MR. SMITH: And one of your own military advisers put it to me, not to get an answer from me because I don't know, just to tell me what was on his mind. Suppose, say, in 1972, our role is virtually eliminated, we're passive, we have few troops there, then the North Vietnamese attack and begin to come into control of the country. What is our policy then? Do we stand aside?

MR. NIXON: Well, Mr. Smith, our Vietnamization policy has been very carefully drawn up, and we are withdrawing in a measured way on the basis that the South Vietnamese will be able to defend themselves as we withdraw. And, it's working. For example, did you realize, I'm sure you do because I think it was reported on your network, all of our naval forces now—combat forces—have been removed. The South Vietnamese Navy has taken over. And so it will be in these other areas.

When the time comes in 1972 that you speak of, it is possible, of course, that at that time North Vietnam might launch an attack. But I am convinced that at that time, based on the training program of the South Vietnamese, based on the watershed that occurred when they jelled and became a fighting, confident unit after the Cambodian intervention, I am convinced that they will be able to hold their own and defend themselves in 1972.

Now that doesn't answer your hypothetical question, but I'm simply not going to borrow trouble by saying that I expect them to fail. I don't think they will.

Civil War Panel

RICHARD J. BARNET, Director, Institute for Policy Studies; author of *Who Wants Disarmament?*

THOMAS EHRLICH, Associate Professor of Law, Stanford Law School

RICHARD A. FALK, Milbank Professor of International Law and Practice, Princeton University

TOM J. FARER, Assistant Professor of Law, Columbia University

WOLFGANG FRIEDMANN, *Chairman*, Civil War Panel; Professor of Law, Columbia University; author of *The Changing Structure of International Law*

G. W. HAIGHT, Member of New York Bar

ELIOT D. HAWKINS, Member of New York Bar

BRUNSON MacCHESNEY, Professor of Law, Northwestern University; former President of the American Society of International Law

MYRES S. McDOUGAL, Sterling Professor of Law, Yale University; former President of the American Society of International Law; co-author of *Law and Minimum World Public Order*

JOHN NORTON MOORE, Professor of Law and Director of the Graduate Program, University of Virginia School of Law

STEPHEN SCHWEBEL, Executive Director of the American Society of International Law and Professor of International Law at the School of Advanced International Studies, The Johns Hopkins University; former Assistant Legal Adviser of the Department of State

JOHN R. STEVENSON, Legal Adviser, United States Department of State; former President of the American Society of International Law

HOWARD J. TAUBENFELD, Professor of Law, Southern Methodist University; co-author of *Controls for Outer Space*

BURNS H. WESTON, Associate Professor of Law, University of Iowa

Contributors

GERALD J. ADLER, Professor of Law, University of California at Davis

GEORGE H. ALDRICH, Deputy Legal Adviser, Department of State

WILLIAM SPRAGUE BARNES, Professor, Fletcher School of Law and Diplomacy

JOHN C. BENDER, Assistant Director of the Center for International Studies, New York University; Member of the New York Bar

CYRIL E. BLACK, Director of the Center of International Studies and Duke Professor of Russian History, Princeton University

ROBERT H. BORK, Professor of Law, Yale University

ANTHONY A. D'AMATO, Assistant Professor of Law, Northwestern University

RICHARD A. FALK, Milbank Professor of International Law and Practice, Princeton University

BENJAMIN FORMAN, Assistant General Counsel (International Affairs), Department of Defense

WILLIAM T. R. FOX, Director of the Institute of War and Peace Studies and James T. Shotwell Professor of International Relations, Columbia University

THOMAS M. FRANCK, Director of the Center for International Studies and Professor of Law, New York University

JOHN H. E. FRIED, Professor of Political Science, City University of New York

WOLFGANG FRIEDMANN, Professor of Law, Columbia University

ERIC F. GOLDMAN, Rollins Professor of History, Princeton University; former Special Consultant to the President, 1963-1966

HARVEY L. GOULD, J. D., 1969, Northwestern University

JOHN S. HANNON, JR., Member of the Virginia Bar

JOHN LAWRENCE HARGROVE, Director of Studies, American Society of International Law

LOUIS HENKIN, Hamilton Fish Professor of International Law and Diplomacy, Columbia University

NICHOLAS DEB. KATZENBACH, Vice-President and General Counsel of I.B.M. Corporation; former United States Attorney General and Under-Secretary of State

HENRY A. KISSINGER, Assistant to the President for National Security Affairs

JEAN LACOUTURE, *Le Monde*

WAYNE MCCORMACK, Associate Editor, *Texas Law Review*

JOHN NORTON MOORE, Professor of Law and Director of the Graduate Program, University of Virginia School of Law

WILLIAM V. O'BRIEN, Director of the Institute of International Polity, Georgetown University

JORDAN J. PAUST, Captain, JAGC, U.S. Army; Instructor of International and Comparative Law, Judge Advocate General's School, Charlottesville, Virginia

WILLIAM H. REHNQUIST, Assistant Attorney General, Office of Legal Counsel, United States Department of Justice

W. TAYLOR REVELEY, III, LL.B., University of Virginia, 1968

ELLIOT L. RICHARDSON, Secretary of Health, Education, and Welfare and former Deputy Secretary of State

NIGEL S. RODLEY, Visiting Lecturer, New School for Social Research

WILLIAM D. ROGERS, Partner, Arnold and Porter Law Firm, Washington, D.C.

ALFRED P. RUBIN, Associate Professor of Law, University of Oregon

JOSEPH L. SAX, Professor of Law, University of Michigan

WARREN F. SCHWARTZ, Professor of Law, University of Texas

JOHN R. STEVENSON, Legal Adviser, United States Department of State

TELFORD TAYLOR, Professor of Law, Columbia Law School

MICHAEL E. TIGAR, Visiting Fellow, Center for the Study of Democratic Institutions, summer 1971; counsel, Kennedy and Rhine, San Francisco, California; Member of the District of Columbia Bar

LARRY D. WOODS, Associate Director of Law Reform, Atlanta Legal Aid Society, Inc.

BEVERLY WOODWARD, political philosopher and author

GARRY J. WOOTERS, student, Boston University Law School

QUINCY WRIGHT, late Professor of Law Emeritus, University of Chicago

ORAN R. YOUNG, Professor of Politics, Princeton University

Permissions*

JEAN LACOUTURE, "From the Vietnam War to an Indochina War." Reprinted by permission of the author and publisher from *Foreign Affairs*, Vol. 48, 1970, pp. 617-628. Copyright held by the Council on Foreign Relations, Inc., New York.

JOHN R. STEVENSON, "United States Military Action in Cambodia: Questions of International Law." Reprinted by permission of the author from *Department of State Bulletin*, June 22, 1970, pp. 765-770.

RICHARD A. FALK, "The Cambodian Operation and International Law." Reprinted by permission of the author and publisher from *American Journal of International Law*, Vol. 65, 1971, pp. 1-25.

JOHN NORTON MOORE, "Legal Dimensions of the Decision to Intercede in Cambodia." Reprinted by permission of the author and publisher from *American Journal of International Law*, Vol. 65, 1971, pp. 38-75.

GEORGE H. ALDRICH, "Comments on the Articles on the Legality of the United States Action in Cambodia." Reprinted by permission of the author and publisher from *American Journal of International Law*, Vol. 65, 1971, pp. 76-77.

WOLFGANG FRIEDMANN, "Comments on the Articles of the Legality of the United States Action in Cambodia." Reprinted by permission of the author and publisher from *American Journal of International Law*, Vol. 65, 1971, pp. 77-79.

JOHN LAWRENCE HARGROVE, "Comments on the Articles on the Legality of the United States Action in Cambodia." Reprinted by permission of the author and publisher from *American Journal of International Law*, Vol. 65, 1971, pp. 81-83.

JOHN H. E. FRIED, "United States Military Intervention in Cambodia in the Light of International Law." Reprinted by permission of the author.

JOHN C. BENDER, "Self-Defense and Cambodia: A Critical Appraisal." Reprinted by permission of the author and publisher from *Boston University Law Review*, Vol. 50, 1970, pp. 130-139.

* Permissions are listed to correspond to the sequence of the materials included in this volume.

printed by permission of the author and publisher from *Proceedings of the American Society of International Law, 1969*, Washington, D.C., pp. 157-164.

ANTHONY A. D'AMATO, HARVEY L. GOULD, and LARRY D. WOODS, "War Crimes and Vietnam: The Nuremberg Defense and the Military Service Resister." Reprinted by permission of the authors and Fred B. Rothman & Co. from *California Law Review*, Vol. 57, 1969, pp. 1055-1110.

JOSEPH SAX, "Conscience and Anarchy: The Prosecution of War Resisters." Reprinted by permission of the author and the publisher from *Yale Review*, Vol. LVII, 4, Summer 1968, pp. 481-494.

BEVERLY WOODWARD, "Nuremberg Law and U.S. Courts." Reprinted by permission of the author from *Dissent*, March-April 1969, pp. 128-136.

ERIC F. GOLDMAN, "The President, the People, and the Power to Make War." Reprinted by permission of the author and publisher from *American Heritage*, Vol. 21, 1970, pp. 28-35.

QUINCY WRIGHT, "The Power of the Executive to Use Military Forces Abroad." Reprinted by the kind permission of the Editors from the *Virginia Journal of International Law*, Vol. 10, 1969, pp. 43-57.

W. TAYLOR REVELEY, III, "Presidential War-Making: Constitutional Prerogative or Usurpation?" Reprinted by permission of the author and Fred B. Rothman & Co. from *Virginia Law Review*, Vol. 55, 1969, pp. 1243-1305.

NICHOLAS DEB. KATZENBACH, "Congress and Foreign Policy." Reprinted by permission of the author and publisher from *Cornell International Law Journal*, Vol. 3, 1970, pp. 33-43.

GARRY J. WOOTERS, "The Appropriations Power As a Tool of Congressional Foreign Policy Making." Reprinted by permission of the author and publisher from *Boston University Law Review*, Vol. 50, Special Issue 1970, pp. 34-50.

LOUIS HENKIN, "Viet-Nam in the Courts of the United States: 'Political Questions.'" Reprinted by permission of the author and publisher from *American Journal of International Law*, Vol. 63, 1969, pp. 284-289.

JOHN NORTON MOORE, "The Justiciability of Challenges to the Use of Military Forces Abroad." Reprinted by permission of the author and editors from the *Virginia Journal of International Law*, Vol. 10, 1969, pp. 85-107.

MICHAEL E. TIGAR, "Judicial Power, the 'Political Question' Doctrine, and Foreign Relations." Reprinted by permission of the author and publisher from *UCLA Law Review*, Vol. 17, 1970, pp. 1135-1179.

WARREN F. SCHWARTZ and WAYNE McCORMACK, "The Justiciability of Legal Objections to the American Military Effort in Vietnam." Reprinted by permission of the author and Fred B. Rothman & Co. from *Texas Law Review*, Vol. 46, 1968, pp. 1033-1053.

THOMAS M. FRANCK and NIGEL S. RODLEY, "Legitimacy and Legal Rights of Revolutionary Movements with Special Reference to the Peoples' Revolutionary Government of South Viet Nam." Reprinted by permission of the author and publisher from *New York University Law Review*, Vol. 45, 1970, pp. 679-694.

HENRY A. KISSINGER, "The Vietnam Negotiations." Reprinted by permission of the author and publisher from *Foreign Affairs*, Vol. 47, 1969, pp. 211-234. Copyright held by the Council on Foreign Relations, Inc., New York.

JOHN S. HANNON, JR., "The International Control Commission Experience and the Role of an Improved International Supervisory Body in the Vietnam Settlement." Reprinted by permission of the author and publisher from *Virginia Journal of International Law*, Vol. 9, 1968, pp. 20-65.

RICHARD A. FALK, "What We Should Learn from Vietnam." Reprinted by permission of the author and publisher from *Foreign Policy*, Winter 1970-71, pp. 98-144, copyright 1970 by National Affairs, Inc.

ELLIOT L. RICHARDSON, "Controlling Local Conflicts." Reprinted by permission from *Department of State Bulletin*, Vol. 62, 1970, pp. 628-631.

WILLIAM T. R. FOX, "The Causes of Peace and Conditions of War." Reprinted by permission of the author and the American Academy of Political and Social Science from *Annals*, Vol. 392, 1970, pp. 2-13.

Index

ABM system, 589
Abrams, Gen. Creighton, 395, 865, 887
abstention, by foreign powers, 730-31;
  permanent, 714-18; political solution
  and, 712-14; Supreme Court decision
  on, 711-12
Acheson, Dean, 150n, 181, 852n, 854n
Adams, John, 165, 171, 469, 598
Adams, John Quincy, 492
Adler, Gerald J., 281-326
Adler, Mortimer, 292
Afroyim v. Rusk, 711n
Agence France-Press, 70
aggression, Communist patterns of, 727;
  defined, 404; "lesson" of, 828; U.S.
  deterrence of, 141
Aggression and World Order (Stone), 73
"aggressor," identification of, 43; unfair
  trials of, 212
Agnew, Spiro T., 47, 48n, 833
Agreement of London, *see* London
  Agreement
Aguinaldo, Emilio, 391
AID (Agency for International
  Development) program, 595, 603
air raids, on cities, 222, 435-36; morale
  and, 320-22. *See also* bombing
Air University Review, 828
air war, Vietnam, 13, 23, 173, 328-30,
  436-37, 499, 915-16; *see also* bombing;
  bombing halt
Alderman v. United States, 684, 696
Aldrich, George H., 96-97, 148
Algerian Republic, 121
Algerian War (1957), 51, 77-78, 118, 121
Alstoetter, Josef, 416n
Altmark case, 29, 72n, 122
Altschul, Frank, 769n
American Bar Association, 344
American Civil Liberties Union, 665
American foreign policy, *see* foreign policy;
  United States
American Friends Service Committee, 389
American Journal of International Law, 27n
American Revolution, 314, 724-25
American Society of International Law, 3
amnesty, for conscientious objectors, 345
Anna Maria incident, 72n
Annam, Vietnam, 10
antipersonnel bombs, 442-43
Appleman, John Alan, 194, 239, 422n
appropriations power, Constitutional
  difficulties in, 618-22; foreign policy
  and, 606-22; independent nature of,
  611-15; practical problems in, 615-18
Arab-Israeli War, 49, 78, 122, 224, 507
Arab League, 75n

Arens, Richard, 66n
armed aggression, 498
armed attack, imminence of, 49; as test in
  Cambodia incursion, 99n; UN Charter
  and, 701n
armed force, first recourse to, 210-11;
  foreign policy and, 523-24; international
  law and, 642-47; as last resort, 523-24;
  legality of, 210-13; support of by
  Congress, 612; and UN Charter, 30, 601;
  U.S. use of, 523-24, 600-01, 631-53
Armistice Agreement (1954), 789-93, 799;
  and International Control Commission,
  772-74
Armour, Ambassador, 157-58
army discipline, hostages and, 253
Army Field Manual, 110, 116, 204, 221
  333-34, 370n, 374n, 412, 416, 483, 896;
  and Law of Land Warfare, 28-29; war
  crimes and, 334-35
Army Field Manual of 1863, 313
Aron, Raymond, 118n, 726n, 856
arsenic sprays, 448
Asia, counterrevolutionary posture in, 835;
  future U.S. policy in, 832; national
  revolutions in, 837; political conflict
  in, 836-39; regional organizations in,
  843-44; rightist-leftist struggle in,
  835; self-reliance policy in, 832-35.
  See also Southeast Asia
atomic bombing, of Hiroshima and
  Nagasaki, 420, 484, 849. *See also* nuclear
  war
Atoppeu, South Vietnam, 15
attrition, vs. guerrilla war, 744
Austin, J., 676n
Austin, Warren, 734n
Austria, neutrality of, 812, 822

bacteriological warfare, 220, 225, 410,
  443n
Bagehot, Walter, 544, 545n
Baiz case, 676-77, 679, 685, 687, 689
Baker, J., 287n, 294n, 306n, 310n, 315n,
  317n, 319n, 324n
Baker v. Carr, 404n, 461, 578n, 626-27, 630n,
  637, 652n, 654n, 671-72, 679-80, 682, 684,
  701n, 705, 707-08, 713-14
balance of power, foreign policy and, 528
balance of terror, world order and, 56, 211,
  729, 848, 858
Ball, M., 150n
Bao Dai, Emperor, 151, 779n
Barbary Wars, 178, 536, 565n, 569n
Barclay, T., 296n, 308n, 314n, 318n
Barnes, William Sprague, 148-60
Barnett, Robert, 730

soldier, court-martialing of for civilian attacks, 379; as "criminal," 405

Solf, W., 363

Son My massacre, 3-4, 327-45, 436n, 455, 651; court-martial following, 380-82, 387, 393-94, 396; "covering up" of, 387, 393; disclosures of, 380-81; events of, 336-37; evidence at, 328-30, 425-26; personal responsibility in, 330-35, 337, 395; reaction to, 328; 379-80; "war-is-hell" stand in, 341

Son Ngoc Minh, 11

Sørenson, M., 107n

Souphanouvong, Prince, 11, 15, 18

Southeast Asia, Communist expansion in, 499-500; deadlock in (1956), 778-83; lasting peace in, 706; peace program in, 890-91; U.S. withdrawal from, 24

Southeast Asia Collective Defense Treaty, 613. See also SEATO

Southeast Asia Resolution, 84-85, 87, 89-90, 92, 94

Southeast Asia Treaty Organization, see SEATO; Asia

South Korea, attack on, 49; defense of, 45. See also Korean War

South Vietnam, activities incident to defense of, 69-75; Cambodian invasions and, 888-89; Civilians Convention and, 366-70; crop destruction in, 317, 447; defoliants used in, 389, 447; early role of, 788-95; "international character" of conflict in, 348; killing of civilians in, 4, 311-12, 327-45; lawfulness of activities in Cambodia, 69-81; legitimacy and legal rights in, 723-38; and Lon Nol government, Cambodia, 63; military justice code in, 355-56; My Lai incident in, 346-58; neutralization of, 811-23; peace talks and, 747-48, 755; permanent neutrality for, 816; political change in, 760; Provisional Government in, 54; "retaliation" against, 13; revolutionary movements in, 723-38; sovereignty of, 335; "threat" to, in self-defense argument, 143-45; torture of prisoners in, 428, 431-32; U.S. bombing of, 311-12; U.S. personnel in, 391. See also Saigon government; Son My massacre; Vietnam; Vietnam War

Souvanna Phouma, see Phouma, Souvanna

Soviet Union, China and, 760, 837-38; Communist expansion and, 506-07; confrontation with U.S., 840-41; and Czechoslovakia invasion, 36, 53, 98, 749-50, 759, 813, 829; in Eastern Europe, 20; in Finland war, 852; Ho Chi Minh and, 839; and Hungarian invasion, 36; hypothetical air strike by, 78n; international law textbook from, 726;

just war defined by, 726; and peacekeeping machinery, 844-45; neutral South Vietnam and, 818; and Nixon Administration, 842; "nonintervention" policy of, 730-31; and North Vietnam, 730, 750, 759; "spheres of restraint" and, 841-43

Spaight, J., 284n, 303n, 316n

Spanier, J., 575n

Spanish-American War, 492, 502, 518, 539n

Speer, Albert, 240, 414-15

"spheres of restraint," Soviet Union and, 841-43

Spinelli, Pier, 781n

Spock, Benjamin, 463, 465

Sprout, Harold, 858n

Sprout, Margaret, 858n

Standard, William, 699n

Stanleyville operations, Congo, 49

Starke, J. G., 109

starvation, war targets and, 317-19

State Department (U.S.), Congress and, 603-04; recognition of foreign government by, 683; sovereign immunity and, 708

status quo, Westphalia-type system for, 727

Steel Seizure case, 460, 555, 666-68, 684, 689

steel strike, armed force and, 514

Stevenson, Adlai, 34n, 51

Stevenson, John R., 23-33, 35, 39, 43, 49n, 51n, 61n, 71n, 99b, 176n, 177

Stewart, Potter, 207

Stillman, Edmund, 847n

Stimson, Henry L., 107n, 851

Stone, Harlan Fiske, 332, 451n

Stone, Julius, 45n, 66n, 73n, 75n, 117n, 247, 849n

Story, Joseph, 688

Streicher, Julius, 240, 414-15

Styer, Lt. Gen. Wilhelm D., 264-80, 396

Suez crisis (1956), 40, 49, 482, 767

Sukarno, Achmed, 854

superior orders, in war crimes trials, 201-02, 208-09, 382-93, 452-53

Supreme Court, U.S., 164-65, 172; abstention from Vietnam decision by, 665, 711-14; as counter-majoritarian institution, 660-63; foreign affairs and, 626; foreign power and, 627; international law and, 226, 402-03, 519, 690-91; judicial power of, 630; law of war and, 410; on military court-martials, 356; mitigation factor and, 717-18; Nuremberg norms and, 652; "packing" plan for, 662n; permanent abstention from Vietnam case by, 714-18; "political question" doctrine and, 626-27, 656, 675-76; on prejudicial publicity, 380-81; President and, 509, 555, 662; role of, 631; in Sabbatino case, 204; on Selective Service